Documents to Accompany

America's History

Volume 2: Since 1865

SIXTH EDITION
Henretta Brody Dumenil

DOCUMENTS TO ACCOMPANY

America's History

Volume 2: Since 1865

Kevin J. Fernlund
University of Missouri—St. Louis

Bedford / St. Martin's
Boston • New York

Cover art: Expansive View of Newly Built Houses Jammed Side-by-side, Divided by a Never-ending Street Clogged with Moving Vans Unloading Families' Possessions on Moving Day. © J. R. Eyerman. Getty Images/Time & Life Pictures; Levittown, PA; Detailed Map. © State Museum of Pennsylvania, Pennsylvania Historical and Museum Commission, and The Historical Society of Washington, DC.

Copyright © 2008 by Bedford/St. Martin's

All rights reserved. No part of this book may be reproduced, stored in a retrieval system, or transmitted in any form or by any means, electronic, mechanical, photocopying, recording, or otherwise, except as may be expressly permitted by the applicable copyright statutes or in writing by the Publisher.

Manufactured in the United States of America.

2 1 0 9
l k j i h

For information, write: Bedford/St. Martin's, 75 Arlington Street, Boston, MA 02116 (617-399-4000)

ISBN-10: 0-312-45441-4
ISBN-13: 978-0-312-45441-8

Preface

Volume 2 of *Documents to Accompany America's History*, Sixth Edition, brings together almost two hundred primary source documents to enrich the study of *America's History*, Sixth Edition. It is our goal that this reader will enhance the educational experience of both students and instructors by adding breadth and depth to many facets of American history that deserve a closer look. In addition to key speeches, laws, contemporary accounts, letters, oral histories, autobiographies, and other written documents, the collection includes political cartoons, statistical tables, and figures that shed light on all aspects of political, social, and cultural history.

Following the chapter organization of *America's History*, Sixth Edition, the documents in each chapter of this reader are grouped into three or four sets corresponding to the main headings of the textbook chapter. Each set begins with an introduction that places that group's documents within their wider historical context. The individual documents follow, each with its own headnote and questions, allowing instructors the flexibility to focus on an individual document or explore a particular section in depth. The wide array of readings enriches a student's learning experience, offering interesting comparisons and contrasts to specific features in the textbook itself. Many of the document sets also present pieces with opposing views meant to stimulate debate in the university classroom. The document set concludes with Questions for Further Thought designed to help students recognize connections among the documents and realize how the documents illustrate or exemplify larger themes.

Upon concluding the preparation of this volume, I would like to take this opportunity to acknowledge the editors of prior editions of the reader; to offer a special note of thanks to one of my graduate students, Elizabeth Pickard, for her assistance; to thank the students in my course "The Curriculum and Methods for Teaching History and the Social Studies" (fall 2005) for their questions and insights; to thank the librarians and staff at the St. Louis Mercantile Library (University of Missouri–St. Louis) and the McFarlin Library (University of Tulsa) for their help. And I would above all like to express my appreciation for the support my wife, Sharon Corn Fernlund, has given to me.

Kevin J. Fernlund

Contents

Preface ... v

CHAPTER 15
Reconstruction, 1865–1877 ... 1

Presidential Reconstruction ... 1
- 15-1 Andrew Johnson, Plan of Reconstruction (1865) ... 2
- 15-2 Carl Schurz, Report on Conditions in the South (1865) ... 3
- 15-3 Philip A. Bell, Reconstruction (1865) ... 7
- 15-4 The Mississippi Black Codes (1865) ... 8
- 15-5 The Civil Rights Act of 1866 ... 10

Radical Reconstruction ... 12
- 15-6 Thaddeus Stevens, Black Suffrage and Land Redistribution (1867) ... 12
- 15-7 The Fourteenth Amendment and Woman Suffrage (1873, 1875) ... 14
- 15-8 Richard H. Cain, An Advocate of Federal Aid for Land Purchase (1868) ... 17

The Undoing of Reconstruction ... 19
- 15-9 Thomas Nast, The Rise and Fall of Northern Support for Reconstruction (1868, 1874) ... 20
- 15-10 President Grant Refuses to Aid Republicans in Mississippi (1875) ... 22
- 15-11 The Slaughterhouse Cases (1873) ... 24
- 15-12 Susan Myrick Interviews Ex-Slave Catherine Beale (1929) ... 27

PART FOUR
A Maturing Industrial Society, 1877–1914

CHAPTER 16
The American West ... 29

The Great Plains ... 29
- 16-1 Custer's Last Stand, *Helena Daily Herald* (July 4, 1876) ... 30
- 16-2 Helen Hunt Jackson, *A Century of Dishonor* (1881) ... 31
- 16-3 The Dawes Severalty Act (1887) ... 33
- 16-4 Buffalo Bird Woman, Beginning a Garden (1917) ... 34
- 16-5 Howard Ruede, Letter from a Kansas Homesteader (1878) ... 37

16-6	John Wesley Powell, Report on the Lands of the Arid Region (1878)	38
16-7	William E. Smythe, On Irrigation (1905)	40

The Far West — 43

16-8	On Chinese Immigration (1876, 1882)	44
16-9	The White Caps, *Nuestra Plataforma:* Hispanics Protest Anglo Encroachment in New Mexico (1890)	45
16-10	Charles Fletcher Lummis, *The Land of Poco Tiempo* (1893)	46
16-11	Mormon Renunciation of Polygamy, Woodruff Manifesto (1890)	48
16-12	John Muir, A Perilous Night on Shasta's Summit (1888)	49

CHAPTER 17
Capital and Labor in the Age of Enterprise, 1877–1900 — 53

Industrial Capitalism Triumphant — 53

17-1	Justin Smith Morrill, On the Origin of the Land-Grant College Act (c. 1874)	53
17-2	Henry George, *Progress and Poverty* (1879)	55
17-3	Andrew Carnegie, The Gospel of Wealth (1889)	57

The World of Work — 60

17-4	On Child Labor (1877)	61
17-5	Lillie B. Chase Wyman, Studies of Factory Life: Among the Women (1888)	62
17-6	Anonymous (A Black Domestic), More Slavery at the South (c. 1912)	63
17-7	Frederick Winslow Taylor, *Principles of Scientific Management* (1911)	65

The Labor Movement — 68

17-8	On Agrarian Discontent, 1887	68
17-9	Terrence V. Powderly, The Army of Unemployed (1887)	69
17-10	Eugene V. Debs, How I Became a Socialist (1902)	71
17-11	Testimony Before the U.S. Strike Commission on the Pullman Strike (1894)	73

CHAPTER 18
The Industrial City: Building It, Living in It — 77

Urbanization — 77

18-1	Frederick Law Olmsted, Calvert Vaux, Central Park (1858)	77
18-2	Julian Ralph, Colorado and Its Capital (1893)	80
18-3	Louis H. Sullivan, The Tall Office Building Artistically Considered (1896)	83

Upper Class/Middle Class — 85

18-4	Thorstein Veblen, Conspicuous Consumption (1899)	86
18-5	Catharine E. Beecher, The Christian Family (1869)	88
18-6	Theodore Dreiser, *Sister Carrie* (1900)	90

City Life — 93

18-7	Jacob Riis, *How the Other Half Lives* (1890)	93
18-8	The Immigrant Experience: Letters Home (1901–1903)	96
18-9	Giuseppe Giacosa, A Visitor in Chicago (1892)	98
18-10	Josiah Strong, The Dangers of Cities (1886)	100

CHAPTER 19
Politics in the Age of Enterprise, 1877–1896 — 103

The Politics of the Status Quo, 1877–1893 — 103

19-1	James Bryce, *The American Commonwealth* (1888)	103
19-2	William Graham Sumner, The Forgotten Man (1883)	107

Politics and the People — 110

- 19-3 Republican and Democratic State Platforms on the Bennett English-Language School Law (Wisconsin, 1890) and the Liquor Question (Iowa, 1889) — 110
- 19-4 Frances E. Willard, Woman and Temperance (1876) — 112
- 19-5 Elizabeth Cady Stanton, The Solitude of Self (1892) — 115

Race and Politics in the New South — 117

- 19-6 The 1890 Mississippi Constitution — 118
- 19-7 Ida B. Wells, Lynching at the Curve (1892) — 119
- 19-8 Booker T. Washington, Atlanta Exposition Address (1895) — 120
- 19-9 W. E. B. Du Bois, Of Mr. Booker T. Washington and Others (1903) — 122

The Crisis of American Politics: The 1890s — 126

- 19-10 Democrat and Republican National Platforms on the Currency, the Tariff, and Federal Elections (1892) — 127
- 19-11 People's (Populist) Party National Platform (1892) — 130
- 19-12 Henry Demarest Lloyd, *Wealth Against Commonwealth* (1894) — 132
- 19-13 William Jennings Bryan, Cross of Gold Speech (1896) — 134
- 19-14 Henry Adams, On Politics in the 1890s (1918) — 137

CHAPTER 20
The Progressive Era — 139

The Course of Reform — 139

- 20-1 John Dewey, My Pedagogic Creed (1897) — 139
- 20-2 Walter Rauschenbusch, The Church and the Social Movement (1907) — 141
- 20-3 Lincoln Steffens, Tweed Days in St. Louis (1902) — 143
- 20-4 Jane Addams, *Twenty Years at Hull-House* (1910) — 144
- 20-5 Margaret Sanger, *The Case for Birth Control* (1917) — 146
- 20-6 Progressivism and Compulsory Sterilization (1907) — 149
- 20-7 Robert M. La Follette, Autobiography (1913) — 149

Progressivism and National Politics — 152

- 20-8 Theodore Roosevelt, The Struggle for Social Justice (1912) — 152
- 20-9 Woodrow Wilson, The New Freedom (1912) — 154
- 20-10 Louis D. Brandeis, Shall We Abandon the Policy of Competition? (1912) — 156
- 20-11 Hetch Hetchy Debate, Sweeping Back the Flood (1909) — 158

CHAPTER 21
An Emerging World Power, 1877–1914 — 161

The Roots of Expansion — 161

- 21-1 James G. Blaine, The American System (1881) — 161
- 21-2 Alfred Thayer Mahan, *The Influence of Sea Power upon History* (1890) — 163
- 21-3 Frederick Jackson Turner, The Significance of the Frontier in American History (1893) — 165

An American Empire — 167

- 21-4 Albert J. Beveridge, The March of the Flag (1898) — 168
- 21-5 William James, The Philippines Tangle (1899) — 170

Onto the World Stage — 173

- 21-6 William McKinley, On Prayer and the Philippines (1899) — 174
- 21-7 R. C. Bowman, Cartoon on the Philippines and Cuba (1901) — 175
- 21-8 John Hay, Open Door Notes (1899, 1900) — 176
- 21-9 Mark Twain, To the Person Sitting in Darkness (1901) — 177
- 21-10 Theodore Roosevelt, The Roosevelt Corollary to the Monroe Doctrine (1904, 1905) — 180

PART FIVE
The Modern State and Society, 1914–1945

CHAPTER 22
War and the American State, 1914–1920 — 183
Great War, 1914–1918 — 183
- 22-1 Don't Rock the Boat (1915) — 184
- 22-2 Zimmermann Telegram (1917) — 185
- 22-3 Woodrow Wilson, War Message to Congress (1917) — 185
- 22-4 Robert M. La Follette, Antiwar Speech (1917) — 188
- 22-5 Hervey Allen, German Dugouts (1918) — 192
- 22-6 Posters from the Anti-Venereal Disease Campaign (1917–1918) — 194

War on the Home Front — 195
- 22-7 Bernard M. Baruch, The War Industries Board (1917–1918) — 195
- 22-8 Marcus L. Hansen, The Home Front: The Young Women's Christian Association (1920) — 197
- 22-9 Wartime Propaganda Poster (c. 1917) — 199
- 22-10 George Creel, The Home Front: The Four Minute Men (1920) — 200
- 22-11 Help Us to Help (1917) — 202

An Unsettled Peace, 1919–1920 — 203
- 22-12 Woodrow Wilson, Fourteen Points (1918) — 203
- 22-13 Treaty of Versailles, Select Articles (1919) — 205
- 22-14 Henry Cabot Lodge, Speech Before the Senate (1919) — 207
- 22-15 Woodrow Wilson, Speech in Indianapolis, Indiana (1919) — 209
- 22-16 Report on the Chicago Race Riot (1919) — 210
- 22-17 W. E. B. Du Bois, Returning Soldiers (1919) — 213

CHAPTER 23
Modern Times, 1920–1932 — 215
The Business-Government Partnership of the 1920s — 215
- 23-1 Herbert Hoover, American Individualism (1922) — 215
- 23-2 Andrew W. Mellon, Fundamental Principles of Taxation (1924) — 218

A New National Culture — 220
- 23-3 Bruce Barton, *The Man Nobody Knows* (1925) — 221
- 23-4 Advertisement for Listerine (1923) — 222
- 23-5 Robert S. Lynd, Helen Merrell Lynd, Remaking Leisure in Middletown (1929) — 222

Redefining American Identity — 226
- 23-6 The Ku Klux Klan (1924) — 227
- 23-7 William Jennings Bryan, Clarence Darrow, Transcript of the Scopes Trial (1925) — 229
- 23-8 H. L. Mencken, Introduction to Friedrich W. Nietzche's *The Antichrist* (1918) — 233
- 23-9 Charles A. Lindbergh, Preparing to Fly (1927) — 236
- 23-10 Cabinet Meeting—If Al Were President (1928) — 238
- 23-11 Marcus Garvey, Editorial in *Negro World* (1924) — 239

The Onset of the Great Depression, 1929–1932 — 242
- 23-12 Herbert Hoover's Plan (1931) — 242
- 23-13 John T. McCutcheon, A Wise Economist Asks a Question (1931) — 246
- 23-14 Mirra Komarovsky, Mr. Patterson (1940) — 247
- 23-15 Meridel Le Sueur, Women on the Breadlines (1932) — 248
- 23-16 Richard Wright, Communism in the 1930s — 251

CHAPTER 24

Redefining Liberalism: The New Deal, 1933–1939 — 255

The New Deal Takes Over, 1933–1935 — 255

- 24-1   Franklin D. Roosevelt, First Inaugural Address (1933) — 255
- 24-2   Rexford G. Tugwell, Design for Government (1933) — 258
- 24-3   *Business Week* Editorial (1933) — 259
- 24-4   Franklin D. Roosevelt, Criticism of a U.S. Supreme Court Decision (1935) — 260
- 24-5   Huey P. Long, The Long Plan (1933) — 262

The Second New Deal, 1935–1938 — 263

- 24-6   Harlan F. Stone, Dissenting Opinion, *United States v. Butler* (1936) — 263
- 24-7   Republican and Democratic National Platforms (1936) — 264
- 24-8   Norman Thomas, What Was the New Deal? (1936) — 266
- 24-9   The Federal Antilynching Bills (1938) — 268

The New Deal's Impact on Society — 270

- 24-10 Eleanor Roosevelt, The State's Responsibility for Fair Working Conditions (1933) — 270
- 24-11 Mary Heaton Vorse, The Sit-Down Strike at General Motors (1937) — 271
- 24-12 Lorena Hickok, Field Report on Arizona to Harry L. Hopkins (1934) — 273
- 24-13 Paul B. Sears, *Deserts on the March* (1937) — 276

CHAPTER 25

The World at War, 1939–1945 — 279

The Road to War — 279

- 25-1   Gerald P. Nye, The Profits of War and Preparedness (1934) — 280
- 25-2   C. D. Batchelor, The Reluctance to Go to War (1936) — 282
- 25-3   Franklin D. Roosevelt, Fireside Chat on the Great Arsenal of Democracy (1940) — 283
- 25-4   Franklin D. Roosevelt, Four Freedoms Speech (1941) — 285

Organizing for Victory — 287

- 25-5   Billion-Dollar Watchdog (1943) — 287
- 25-6   Norma Yerger Queen, Women Working at the Home Front (1944) — 290
- 25-7   Mother, When Will You Stay Home Again? (1944) — 291
- 25-8   Wartime Posters: The Japanese and Venereal Disease as Enemies (c. 1944) — 293

Life on the Home Front — 294

- 25-9   Remembering the War Years on the Home Front (1984) — 294
- 25-10 Executive Order 9066 to Prescribe Military Areas (1942) — 296

Fighting and Winning the War — 297

- 25-11 Ernie Pyle, Street Fighting (1944) — 298
- 25-12 William McConahey, Dorothy Wahlstrom, Remembering the Holocaust (1945) — 302
- 25-13 Albert Einstein, Letter to President Roosevelt (1939) — 304
- 25-14 Henry L. Stimson, The Decision to Use the Atomic Bomb (1945) — 305

PART SIX
The Age of Cold War Liberalism, 1945–1980

CHAPTER 26

Cold War America, 1945–1960 — 311

The Cold War — 311

- 26-1   Nikolai Novikov, Telegram: A Soviet View of U.S. Foreign Policy (1946) — 311
- 26-2   George F. Kennan, Containment Policy (1947) — 316

26-3	Arthur Vandenberg, On NATO (1949)	319
26-4	NSC-68 (1950)	320

The Truman Era — 327

26-5	Lyndon B. Johnson, The American West: America's Answer to Russia (1950)	328
26-6	Joseph R. McCarthy, Communists in the U.S. Government (1950)	331
26-7	Civil Rights and the National Party Platforms (1948)	333
26-8	*Brown v. Board of Education of Topeka* (1954)	335
26-9	The Southern Manifesto (1956)	338
26-10	Rosa Parks, Describing My Arrest (1955)	339

Modern Republicanism — 340

26-11	Nikita Khrushchev, Peaceful Coexistence (1956)	340
26-12	John Foster Dulles, Cold War Foreign Policy (1958)	343
26-13	Dwight D. Eisenhower, Farewell Address (1961)	345

CHAPTER 27
The Age of Affluence, 1945–1960

Economic Powerhouse — 349

27-1	George M. Humphrey, The Interstate Highway System (1955)	349
27-2	Herbert Block, "Let's See, Now—Where Can We Raise More Taxes?" (1953)	350
27-3	Help Wanted—Women (1957)	352

The Affluent Society — 354

27-4	Green Acres (1950)	354
27-5	Neil Morgan, The Footloose Migration (1961)	356

The Other America — 358

27-6	Carey McWilliams, *North from Mexico* (1949)	358
27-7	Herbert Gans, Boston's West Enders (1962)	361
27-8	What Does Chicago's Renewal Program Mean? (1963)	362
27-9	Michael Harrington, *The Other America* (1962)	363

CHAPTER 28
The Liberal Consensus: Flaming Out, 1960–1968

John F. Kennedy and the Politics of Expectation — 367

28-1	Theodore H. White, The Television Debates (1960)	367
28-2	John F. Kennedy, Inaugural Address (1961)	371
28-3	Students for a Democratic Society, The Port Huron Statement (1962)	372

Lyndon B. Johnson and the Great Society — 374

28-4	Barry Goldwater, Acceptance Speech at the Republican National Convention (1964)	374
28-5	Lyndon B. Johnson, Address at the University of Michigan (1964)	377
28-6	The Wilderness Act (1964)	379

Into the Quagmire, 1960–1968 — 380

28-7	The Gulf of Tonkin Resolution (1964)	380
28-8	Lyndon B. Johnson, Peace Without Conquest (1965)	381
28-9	Philip Caputo, The Splendid Little War (1965)	383

Coming Apart — 385

28-10	Malcolm X and Yusef Iman, Black Nationalism (1964)	386
28-11	Inés Hernández, Para Teresa	388
28-12	DRUMS Committee of the Menominee, The Consequences of Termination for the Menominee of Wisconsin (1971)	389
28-13	National Organization for Women, Statement of Purpose (1966)	391

1968: A Year of Shocks — 393
- 28-14 Edward Abbey, *Desert Solitaire: A Season in the Wilderness* (1968) — 393
- 28-15 Daniel Patrick Moynihan, Memorandum on Benign Neglect (1970) — 396

CHAPTER 29
The 1970s: Toward a Conservative America — 399

The Nixon Years — 399
- 29-1 Dan Rather's Conversation with President Nixon (1972) — 400
- 29-2 Richard Nixon, Vietnamization and the Nixon Doctrine (1969) — 405
- 29-3 Richard Nixon, The Invasion of Cambodia (1970) — 407
- 29-4 Watergate: Taped White House Conversations (1972) — 408

Battling for Civil Rights: The Second Stage — 410
- 29-5 Gloria Steinem, Statement in Support of the Equal Rights Amendment (1970) — 411
- 29-6 Phyllis Schlafly, *The Power of the Positive Woman* (1977) — 413

Lean Years — 415
- 29-7 Gallup Polls, National Problems, 1950–1999 — 415
- 29-8 Rachel Carson, And No Birds Sing (1962) — 417
- 29-9 William Serrin, *Homestead* (1970s) — 420

Politics in the Wake of Watergate — 423
- 29-10 Jimmy Carter, The National Crisis of Confidence (1979) — 424
- 29-11 Ronald Reagan, Acceptance Speech, National Republican Convention (1980) — 425

PART SEVEN
Entering a New Era: Conservatism, Globalization, Terrorism, 1980–2006

CHAPTER 30
The Reagan Revolution and the End of the Cold War, 1980–2001 — 429

The Rise of Conservatism — 429
- 30-1 Ronald Reagan, Remarks at the Annual Convention of the National Association of Evangelicals (1983) — 429
- 30-2 Creationism, the Public Schools, and the First Amendment, *Edwards v. Aguillard* (1987) — 434

The Reagan Presidency, 1981–1989 — 436
- 30-3 Donald T. Regan, For the Record (1988) — 437

Defeating Communism and Creating a New World Order — 439
- 30-4 Francis Fukuyama, The End of History (1989) — 440
- 30-5 George H. W. Bush, Iraqi Aggression in Kuwait (1990) — 444
- 30-6 David Maraniss, University Students Reflect on the Gulf War (1991) — 445
- 30-7 Samuel P. Huntington, The Clash of Civilizations? (1993) — 446

The Clinton Presidency, 1993–2001 — 452
- 30-8 *Contract with America* (1994) — 452
- 30-9 Bill Clinton, State of the Union Address (1996) — 454

CHAPTER 31
A Dynamic Economy, A Divided People, 1980–2000 — 457

America in a Global Economy and Society — 457
- 31-1 George Gilder, *Wealth and Poverty* (1981) — 457
- 31-2 Jonathan Kozol, *Rachel and Her Children* (1988) — 459
- 31-3 Bill Clinton, On World Trade Talks in Seattle (1999) — 461

New Technology — 464
- 31-4   Bill Gates, Friction-Free Capitalism (1995) — 464

Culture Wars — 466
- 31-5   Don't Ask, Don't Tell (1993) — 466
- 31-6   Proposition 187 (1994) — 468
- 31-7   U.S. Census Bureau, On Women-Owned Businesses (1996) — 470

CHAPTER 32
Into the Twenty-First Century — 473

The Advent of George W. Bush — 473
- 32-1   *Bush v. Gore* (2000) — 474
- 32-2   Stephen Goldsmith, What Compassionate Conservatism Is—and Is Not (2000) — 475

American Hegemony Challenged — 478
- 32-3   Bush on Iraq (2002) — 479
- 32-4   U.S. National Security Strategy (2002) — 483

Unfinished Business — 485
- 32-5   Report on Catastrophic Hurricane Evacuation Plan Evaluation (2006) — 486

Documents to Accompany

America's History

Volume 2: Since 1865

CHAPTER FIFTEEN

Reconstruction
1865–1877

Presidential Reconstruction

Planning for Reconstruction began to take shape in December 1863, when President Lincoln laid out his ideas in a presidential proclamation. His pronouncement opened a debate that became the central issue in American politics for more than a decade. The power struggle that followed led to a collision between the executive and legislative branches of government, the displacement of presidential Reconstruction by congressional Reconstruction, and the first impeachment of a president of the United States.

Reconstruction involved fundamental questions. To begin with, who had the primary responsibility for Reconstruction—the president or Congress? Believing that rebuilding the Union was simply a matter of suppressing "rebels" under presidential war powers, Lincoln's successor, Andrew Johnson, took the early initiative, establishing provisional governments that were supposed to purge secessionists from southern leadership, repudiate secession and Confederate debts, and recognize the end of slavery (Document 15-1). Beyond these measures Johnson was unwilling to go: a former southern slaveholder himself, he had no sympathy for blacks; in addition, as a southern Democrat he was firmly devoted to states' rights. Although Johnson was satisfied with these measures, northerners were hearing increasingly alarming reports that white southerners were refusing to recognize their defeat; engaging in brutal reprisals against blacks, northern whites, and southern Unionists; and enacting "Black Codes" that appeared to be backdoor attempts to restore slavery (Documents 15-2, 15-3, and 15-4). A rising tide of northern outrage pushed the Republican-dominated Congress toward the views of the Republicans' radical wing; in 1866, over the violent opposition of President Johnson, Congress undertook an unprecedented extension of federal power. With the Civil Rights Act of 1866 (Document 15-5) and the Fourteenth Amendment, Congress declared for the first time that federal citizenship was not restricted by race and guaranteed all citizens the "equal protection of the laws," even if it required federal intervention into the affairs of a state. The outcome of the Civil War was beginning to force fundamental changes in the constitutional character of the American political system, with profound consequences for subsequent American history.

15-1 Plan of Reconstruction (1865)

Andrew Johnson

As the Civil War came to an end, Lincoln's successor, Andrew Johnson, moved quickly to implement his plan for Reconstruction, which differed little from Lincoln's plan (see text pp. 458–459). Johnson acted largely on his own, without much consultation with Congress. In particular, he ignored Congress's demand for a harsher policy toward the former Confederate states.

On May 29, 1865, President Johnson set forth his plan in two presidential proclamations. In the first he promised amnesty to all rebels who would swear an oath of future loyalty, except for certain high-ranking officials and officers of the Confederacy, who had to petition for a presidential pardon.

In the second proclamation, which appears below, Johnson announced the creation of a provisional government for North Carolina. After appointing William W. Holden, a North Carolina Unionist who had opposed secession, as the provisional governor, Johnson described the means by which that state could be restored to the Union. Johnson intended this plan to serve as a model for the other seceded states, hoping that all could be restored before Congress reconvened in December.

Johnson's approach to Reconstruction was very different from that proposed by the Wade-Davis Bill (see text p. 458), which stipulated that more than 50 percent of the voters who were qualified in 1860 in each southern state had to be able to prove their past loyalty and swear future loyalty to the Union. Johnson and Congress also differed about allowing former Confederate leaders to participate in Reconstruction and in government. Presidents Lincoln and Johnson envisioned temporary disqualification; Congress favored permanent exclusion.

Source: James D. Richardson, ed., *A Compilation of the Messages and Papers of the Presidents* (Washington, DC: U.S. Government Printing Office, 1896–1899), 6:312–313.

Whereas the fourth section of the fourth article of the Constitution of the United States declares that the United States shall guarantee to every State in the Union a republican form of government and shall protect each of them against invasion and domestic violence; and

Whereas the President of the United States is by the Constitution made Commander in Chief of the Army and Navy, as well as chief civil executive officer of the United States, and is bound by solemn oath faithfully to execute the office of President of the United States and to take care that the laws be faithfully executed; and

Whereas the rebellion which has been waged by a portion of the people of the United States against the properly constituted authorities of the Government . . . and

Whereas it becomes necessary and proper to carry out and enforce the obligations of the United States to the people of North Carolina in securing them in the enjoyment of a republican form of government:

Now, therefore, in obedience to the high and solemn duties imposed upon me by the Constitution of the United States and for the purpose of enabling the loyal people of said State to organize a State government whereby justice may be established, domestic tranquillity insured, and loyal citizens protected in all their rights of life, liberty, and property, I, Andrew Johnson, President of the United States and Commander in Chief of the Army and Navy of the United States, do hereby appoint William W. Holden provisional governor of the State of North Carolina, whose duty it shall be, at the earliest practicable period, to prescribe such rules and regulations as may be necessary and proper for convening a convention composed of delegates to be chosen by that portion of the people of said State who are loyal to the United States, and no others, for the purpose of altering or amending the constitution thereof, and with authority to exercise within the limits of said State all the powers necessary and proper to enable such loyal people of the State of North Carolina to restore said State to its constitutional relations to the Federal Government and to present such a republican form of State government as will entitle the State to the guaranty of the United States therefor and its people to protection by the United States against invasion, insurrection, and domestic violence: *Provided*, That in any election that may be hereafter held for choosing delegates to any State convention as aforesaid no person shall be qualified as an elector or shall be eligible as a member of such convention unless he shall have previously taken and subscribed the oath of amnesty as set forth in the President's proclamation of May 29, A.D. 1865, and is a voter qualified as prescribed by the constitution and laws of the State of North Carolina in force immediately before the 20th day of May, A.D. 1861, the date of the so-called ordinance of secession; and the said convention, when convened, or the legislature that may be thereafter assembled, will prescribe the qualification of electors and the eligibility of persons to hold office under the constitution and laws of the State — a power the people of the several States composing the Federal Union have rightfully exercised from the origin of the Government to the present time.

And I do hereby direct —

. . . That the military commander of the department and all officers and persons in the military and naval service aid and assist the said provisional governor in carrying into effect this proclamation; and they are enjoined to abstain from in any way hindering, impeding, or discouraging the loyal people from the organization of a State government as herein authorized.

Questions

1. According to President Johnson, what was his authority for this proclamation? Who was to be in charge of the process?
2. What steps did Johnson prescribe for restoring civil government in North Carolina?
3. Under Johnson's plan, would freedmen be able to vote? (*Hint:* See the section starting "*Provided.*")

15-2 Report on Conditions in the South (1865)

Carl Schurz

By December 1865, when Congress was gathering in Washington for a new session, Johnson had declared that all the Confederate states but Texas had met his requirements for restoration. Newly elected senators and congressmen from the former Confederacy had arrived to take seats in Congress.

Johnson's efforts to restore the South stalled. Congress exercised its constitutional authority to deny seats to delegations from the South and launched an investigation into conditions there. In response to a Senate resolution requesting "information in relation to the States of the Union lately in rebellion," Johnson painted a rosy picture: "In 'that portion of the Union lately in rebellion' the aspect of affairs is more promising than, in view of all the circumstances, could well have been expected. The people throughout the entire south evince a laudable desire to renew their allegiance to the government, and to repair the devastations of war by a prompt and cheerful return to peaceful pursuits. An abiding faith is entertained that their actions will conform to their professions, and that, in acknowledging the supremacy of the Constitution and the laws of the United States, their loyalty will be unreservedly given to the government, whose leniency they cannot fail to appreciate, and whose fostering care will soon restore them to a condition of prosperity. It is true, that in some of the States the demoralizing effects of war are to be seen in occasional disorders, but these are local in character, not frequent in occurrence, and are rapidly disappearing as the authority of civil law is extended and sustained."

Johnson's message to the Senate was accompanied by a report from Major General Carl Schurz. Among the subjects on which Schurz reported were whether southern whites had accepted defeat and emancipation, and whether ex-slaves and southern Unionists were safe in the South and were receiving fair treatment. Schurz's report was apparently largely ignored by President Johnson, who had assigned him to make the report but was not happy with what he said.

Schurz went to considerable lengths to get an accurate reading of attitudes in the South. He tried to get a representative sample of people to interview in his three-month tour of portions of South Carolina, Georgia, Alabama, Mississippi, and Louisiana and gathered documentary evidence as well as interviews. Then he tried to analyze his findings carefully and make recommendations on the basis of those findings. Clearly, he believed that Reconstruction in the South involved more than the restoration of civil government.

Source: U.S. Congress, Senate, 39th Cong., 1st sess., 1865, Ex. Doc. No. 2, 1–5, 8, 36–39, 41–44.

SIR: ... You informed me that your "policy of reconstruction" was merely experimental, and that you would change it if the experiment did not lead to satisfactory results. To aid you in forming your conclusions upon this point I understood to be the object of my mission, ...

CONDITION OF THINGS IMMEDIATELY AFTER THE CLOSE OF THE WAR

In the development of the popular spirit in the south since the close of the war two well-marked periods can be distinguished. The first commences with the sudden collapse of the confederacy and the dispersion of its armies, and the second with the first proclamation indicating the "reconstruction policy" of the government.... When the news of Lee's and Johnston's surrenders burst upon the southern country the general consternation was extreme. People held their breath, indulging in the wildest apprehensions as to what was now to come.... Prominent Unionists told me that persons who for four years had scorned to recognize them on the street approached them with smiling faces and both hands extended. Men of standing in the political world expressed serious doubts as to whether the rebel States would ever again occupy their position as States in the Union, or be governed as conquered provinces. The public mind was so despondent that if readmission at some future time under whatever conditions had been promised, it would then have been looked upon as a favor. The most uncompromising rebels prepared for leaving the country. The masses remained in a state of fearful expectancy....

Such was, according to the accounts I received, the character of that first period. The worst apprehensions were gradually relieved as day after day went by without bringing the disasters and inflictions which had been vaguely anticipated, until at last the appearance of the North Carolina proclamation substituted new hopes for them. The development of this second period I was called upon to observe on the spot, and it forms the main subject of this report.

RETURNING LOYALTY

... [T]he white people at large being, under certain conditions, charged with taking the preliminaries of "reconstruction" into their hands, the success of the experiment depends upon the spirit and attitude of those who either attached themselves to the secession cause from the beginning, or, entertaining originally opposite views, at least followed its fortunes from the time that their States had declared their separation from the Union....

I may group the southern people into four classes, each of which exercises an influence upon the development of things in that section:

1. Those who, although having yielded submission to the national government only when obliged to do so, have a clear perception of the irreversible changes produced by the war, and honestly endeavor to accommodate themselves to the new order of things. Many of them are not free from traditional prejudice but open to conviction, and may be expected to act in good faith whatever they do. This class is composed, in its majority, of persons of mature age—planters, merchants, and professional men; some of them are active in the reconstruction movement, but boldness and energy are, with a few individual exceptions, not among their distinguishing qualities.

2. Those whose principal object is to have the States without delay restored to their position and influence in the Union and the people of the States to the absolute control of their home concerns. They are ready, in order to attain that object, to make any ostensible concession that will not prevent them from arranging things to suit their taste as soon as that object is attained. This class comprises a considerable number, probably a large majority, of the professional politicians who are extremely active in the reconstruction movement. They are loud in their praise of the President's reconstruction policy, and clamorous for the withdrawal of the federal troops and the abolition of the Freedmen's Bureau.

3. The incorrigibles, who still indulge in the swagger which was so customary before and during the war, and still hope for a time when the southern confederacy will achieve its independence. This class consists mostly of young men, and comprises the loiterers of the towns and the idlers of the country. They persecute Union men and negroes whenever they can do so with impunity, insist clamorously upon their "rights," and are extremely impatient of the presence of the federal soldiers. A good many of them have taken the oaths of allegiance and amnesty, and associated themselves with the second class in their political operations. This element is by no means unimportant; it is strong in numbers, deals in brave talk, addresses itself directly and incessantly to the passions and prejudices of the masses, and commands the admiration of the women.

4. The multitude of people who have no definite ideas about the circumstances under which they live and about the course they have to follow; whose intellects are weak, but whose prejudices and impulses are strong, and who are apt to be carried along by those who know how to appeal to the latter....

FEELING TOWARDS THE SOLDIERS AND THE PEOPLE OF THE NORTH

... [U]pon the whole, the soldier of the Union is still looked upon as a stranger, an intruder—as the "Yankee," "the enemy."...

It is by no means surprising that prejudices and resentments, which for years were so assiduously cultivated and so violently inflamed, should not have been turned into affection by a defeat; nor are they likely to disappear as long as the southern people continue to brood over their losses and misfortunes. They will gradually subside when those who entertain them cut resolutely loose from the past and embark in a career of new activity on a common field with those whom they have so long considered their enemies.... [A]s long as these feelings exist in their present strength, they will hinder the growth of that reliable kind of loyalty which springs from the heart and clings to the country in good and evil fortune.

SITUATION OF UNIONISTS

... It struck me soon after my arrival in the south that the known Unionists—I mean those who during the war had been to a certain extent identified with the national cause—were not in communion with the leading social and political circles; and the further my observations extended the clearer it became to me that their existence in the south was of a rather precarious nature.... Even Governor [William L.] Sharkey, in the course of a conversation I had with him in the presence of Major General Osterhaus, admitted that, if our troops were then withdrawn, the lives of northern men in Mississippi would not be safe.... [General Osterhaus said]: "There is no doubt whatever that the state of affairs would be intolerable for all Union men, all recent immigrants from the north, and all negroes, the moment the protection of the United States troops were withdrawn."...

NEGRO INSURRECTIONS AND ANARCHY

... [I do] not deem a negro insurrection probable as long as the freedmen were assured of the direct protection of the national government. Whenever they are in trouble, they raise their eyes up to that power, and although they may suffer, yet, as long as that power is visibly present, they continue to hope. But when State authority in the south is fully restored, the federal forces withdrawn, and the Freedmen's Bureau abolished, the colored man will find himself turned over to the mercies of those whom he does not trust. If then an attempt is made to strip him again of those rights which he justly thought he possessed, he will be apt to feel that he can hope for no redress unless he procure it himself. If ever the negro is capable of rising, he will rise then....

There is probably at the present moment no country in the civilized world which contains such an accumulation of anarchical elements as the south. The strife of the antagonistic tendencies here described is aggravated by the passions inflamed and the general impoverishment brought about by a long and exhaustive war, and the south will have to suffer the evils of anarchical disorder until means are found to effect a final settlement of the labor question in accordance with the logic of the great revolution.

THE TRUE PROBLEM—DIFFICULTIES AND REMEDIES

In seeking remedies for such disorders, we ought to keep in view, above all, the nature of the problem which is to be solved. As to what is commonly termed "reconstruction," it is not only the political machinery of the States and their constitutional relations to the general government, but the whole organism of southern society that must be reconstructed, or rather constructed anew, so as to bring it in harmony with the rest of American society. The difficulties of this task are not to be considered overcome when the people of the south take the oath of allegiance and elect governors and legislatures and members of Congress, and militia captains. That this would be done had become certain as soon as the surrenders of the southern armies had made further resistance impossible, and nothing in the world was left, even to the most uncompromising rebel, but to submit or to emigrate. It was also natural that they should avail themselves of every chance offered them to resume control of their home affairs and to regain their influence in the Union. But this can hardly be called the first step towards the solution of the true problem, and it is a fair question to ask, whether the hasty gratification of their desire to resume such control would not create new embarrassments.

The true nature of the difficulties of the situation is this: The general government of the republic has, by proclaiming the emancipation of the slaves, commenced a great social revolution in the south, but has, as yet, not completed it. Only the negative part of it is accomplished. The slaves are emancipated in point of form, but free labor has not yet been put in the place of slavery in point of fact. And now, in the midst of this critical period of transition, the power which originated the revolution is expected to turn over its whole future development to another power which from the beginning was hostile to it and has never yet entered into its spirit, leaving the class in whose favor it was made completely without power to protect itself and to take an influential part in that development. The history of the world will be searched in vain for a proceeding similar to this which did not lead either to a rapid and violent reaction, or to the most serious trouble and civil disorder. It cannot be said that the conduct of the southern people since the close of the war has exhibited such extraordinary wisdom and self-abnegation as to make them an exception to the rule.

In my despatches from the south I repeatedly expressed the opinion that the people were not yet in a frame of mind to legislate calmly and understandingly upon the subject of free negro labor. And this I reported to be the opinion of some of our most prominent military commanders and other observing men. It is, indeed, difficult to imagine circumstances more unfavorable for the development of a calm and unprejudiced public opinion than those under which the southern people are at present laboring. The war has not only defeated their political aspirations, but it has broken up their whole social organization....

In which direction will these people be most apt to turn their eyes? Leaving the prejudice of race out of the question, from early youth they have been acquainted with but one system of labor, and with that one system they have been in the habit of identifying all their interests. They know of no way to help themselves but the one they are accustomed to....

It is certain that every success of free negro labor will augment the number of its friends, and disarm some of the prejudices and assumptions of its opponents. I am convinced one good harvest made by unadulterated free labor in the south would have a far better effect than all the oaths that have been taken, and all the ordinances that have as yet been passed by southern conventions. But how can such a result be attained? The facts enumerated in this report, as well as the news we receive from the south from day to day, must make it evident to every unbiased observer that unadulterated free labor cannot be had at present, unless the national government holds its protective and controlling hand over it.... One reason why the southern people are so slow in accommodating themselves to the new order of things is, that they confidently expect soon to be permitted to regulate matters according to their own notions. Every concession made to them by the government has been taken as an encouragement to persevere in this hope, and, unfortunately for them, this hope is nourished by influences from other parts of the country. Hence their anxiety to have their State governments restored *at once*, to have the troops withdrawn, and the Freedmen's Bureau abolished, although a good many discerning men know well that, in view of the lawless spirit still prevailing, it would be far better for them to have the general order of society firmly maintained by the federal power until things have arrived at a final settlement. Had, from the beginning, the conviction been forced upon them that the adulteration of the new order of things by the admixture of elements belonging to the system of slavery would under no circumstances be permitted, a much larger number would have launched their energies into the new channel, and, seeing that they could do "no better," faithfully co-operated with the government. It is hope which fixes them in their perverse notions. That hope nourished or fully gratified, they will persevere in the same direction. That hope destroyed, a great many will, by the force of necessity, at once accommodate themselves to the logic of the change. If, therefore, the national government firmly and unequivocally announces its policy not to give up the control of the free-labor reform until it is finally accomplished, the progress of that reform will undoubtedly be far more rapid and far less difficult than it will be if the attitude of the government is such as to permit contrary hopes to be indulged in....

IMMIGRATION [AND CAPITAL]

[The south would benefit] from immigration of northern people and Europeans.... The south needs capital. But capital is notoriously timid and averse to risk.... Capitalists will be apt to consider — and they are by no means wrong in doing so — that no safe investments can be made in the south as long as southern society is liable to be convulsed by anarchical disorders. No greater encouragement can, therefore, be given to capital to transfer itself to the south than the assurance that the government will continue to control the development of the new social system in the late rebel States until such dangers are averted by a final settlement of things upon a thorough free-labor basis.

How long the national government should continue that control depends upon contingencies. It ought to cease as soon as its objects are attained; and its objects will be attained sooner and with less difficulty if nobody is permitted to indulge in the delusion that it will cease *before* they are attained. This is one of the cases in which a determined policy can accomplish much, while a half-way policy is liable to spoil things already accomplished....

NEGRO SUFFRAGE

It would seem that the interference of the national authority in the home concerns of the southern States would be rendered less necessary, and the whole problem of political and social reconstruction be much simplified, if, while the masses lately arrayed against the government are permitted to vote, the large majority of those who were always loyal, and are naturally anxious to see the free labor problem successfully solved, were not excluded from all influence upon legislation. In all questions concerning the Union, the national debt, and the future social organization of the south, the feelings of the colored man are naturally in sympathy with the views and aims of the national government. While the southern white fought against the Union, the negro did all he could to aid it; while the southern white sees in the national government his conqueror, the negro sees in it his protector; while the white owes to the national debt his defeat, the negro owes to it his deliverance; while the white considers himself robbed and ruined by the emancipation of the slaves, the negro finds in it the assurance of future prosperity and happiness. In all the important issues the negro would be led by natural impulse to forward the ends of the government, and by making his influence, as part of the voting body, tell upon the legislation of the States, render the interference of the national authority less necessary.

As the most difficult of the pending questions are intimately connected with the status of the negro in southern society, it is obvious that a correct solution can be more easily obtained if he has a voice in the matter. In the right to vote he would find the best permanent protection against oppressive class-legislation, as well as against individual persecution. The relations between the white and black races, even if improved by the gradual wearing off of the present animosities, are likely to remain long under the troubling influence of prejudice. It is a notorious fact that the rights of a man of some political power are far less exposed to violation than those of one who is, in matters of public interest, completely subject to the will of others....

In discussing the matter of negro suffrage I deemed it my duty to confine myself strictly to the practical aspects of the subject. I have, therefore, not touched its moral merits nor discussed the question whether the national government is competent to enlarge the elective franchise in the States lately in rebellion by its own act; I deem it proper, however, to offer a few remarks on the assertion frequently put forth, that the franchise is likely to be extended to the colored man by the voluntary action of the southern whites themselves. My observation leads me to a contrary opinion. Aside from a very few enlightened men, I found but one class of people in favor of the enfranchisement of the blacks: it was the class of Unionists who found themselves politically ostracised and looked upon the enfranchisement of the loyal negroes as the salvation of the whole loyal element. But their numbers and influence are sadly insufficient to secure such a result. The masses are strongly opposed to colored suffrage; anybody that dares to advocate it is stigmatized as a dangerous fanatic; nor do I deem it probable that in the ordinary course of things prejudices will wear off to such an extent as to make it a popular measure. . . .

DEPORTATION OF THE FREEDMEN

. . . [T]he true problem remains, not how to remove the colored man from his present field of labor, but how to make him, where he is, a true freeman and an intelligent and useful citizen. The means are simple: protection by the government until his political and social status enables him to protect himself, offering to his legitimate ambition the stimulant of a perfectly fair chance in life, and granting to him the rights which in every just organization of society are coupled with corresponding duties.

CONCLUSION

I may sum up all I have said in a few words. If nothing were necessary but to restore the machinery of government in the States lately in rebellion in point of form, the movements made to that end by the people of the south might be considered satisfactory. But if it is required that the southern people should also accommodate themselves to the results of the war in point of spirit, those movements fall far short of what must be insisted upon.

Questions

1. Why did Schurz recommend keeping the Freedmen's Bureau and the army in the South? How did that differ from what Johnson wanted?
2. Why did Schurz suggest that it might be wise to give African Americans in the South the vote?
3. What did Schurz say about the Unionists in the South? About the emergence of a free labor system?

15-3 Reconstruction (1865)

Philip A. Bell

President Andrew Johnson's plan of reconstruction (see Document 15-1) was justly criticized by those who had anticipated far-reaching changes in the South after the Civil War, and none was more vocal in expressing his disgruntlement than Philip A. Bell. A leading African American journalist and abolitionist prior to the war, Bell founded *The Elevator* in 1865 to champion the rights of southern blacks. That emboldened ex-Confederates had resumed control of Johnson's state governments and enacted Black Codes (see Document 15-4) that aimed to reduce the newly freed population to plantation laborers under a system of quasi-slavery was simply unacceptable to Bell. In his September 15, 1865, *Elevator* editorial, Bell posed what was arguably the fundamental question pertaining to the status of the ex-Confederate states and, in no uncertain terms, articulated the Radical Republicans' opposition to the president's plan.

Source: Excerpt from *The Black Abolitionist Papers*, ed. C. Peter Ripley, et al. (Chapel Hill: University of North Carolina Press, 1992), 5:369–370. Used by permission of the publisher.

This is the most important subject which now engages the attention of the American people, for on it depends the future welfare of the nation, and the destinies of a race but partially redeemed from bondage. It is a question which absorbs the minds of all reflecting men, and all energies, all thoughts are now directed to that point. Not only in America, but in Europe, also, does this subject attract marked attention, as it involves other momentous subjects of civil, political, and philanthropic importance, as well as the theory of republican or representative government.

The whole subject seems to revolve itself into this: Have the rebel States ever lost or renounced their position as members of the Union? If they have not, as President Johnson avers, why threat them as territories or subjugated provinces by appointing officers which it is the prerogative of the State to elect? Why prescribe rules and regulations for their government, when they have their own State Constitution? All that is required, according to this theory, is for them to resume their former functions, acknowledge the supremacy of the General Government, and take their position again as States of the Union. They can establish slavery, for until the Constitutional Amendments are confirmed, Congress cannot prohibit slavery by virtue of the Proclamation, for the necessity which called for that is passed, and the States return to the "Union as it was and the Constitution as it is."

We must confess we were somewhat inclined to President Johnson's theory, but we cannot reconcile the idea of an appointing power for States which are members of the Union—integral portions thereof. We have seen the fallacy of that theory which the practice of the President contradicts, and are now convinced that the rebel States have no rights which the Government is bound to respect.

If the theory of the President is correct, he has overstepped the bounds of his authority by appointing Provisional Governors over sovereign States which had their fundamental laws intact, and had power to elect their own Governors. If he has that power, he should exercise it to its fullest extent—first, by appointing *all* the officers of State government, and, secondly, by appointing men of sound Union sentiments, not endeavor to coax and conciliate the rebels by appointing men of known secession proclivities, some of whom have taken an active part in the rebellion.

Again—it must be obvious to all that by allowing the rebel States to return to the Union without purgation, is but sowing seed for future difficulties.

We now come to the most important point, and to which Government has paid no attention whatever—the suffrage question. In his various proclamations, the President has declared what classes are not entitled to citizenship, but he has apparently lost sight of the negro population, which will ever be a disturbing element as long as they are an oppressed race. They form a large proportion of the Southern States, and will become as necessary to the Government in the future as they have been in the past, if they are treated like men and have the rights of citizens. But in their present anomalous position as freedmen, not freemen, they can render the Government no aid political, and in case of another outbreak, they would not render military service to a government which has once broken faith with them.

Considerable speculation is raised on qualifications for voters. We were never very democratic in our political opinions; we care not for universal suffrage—what we want is equal suffrage; and in reconstructing the States we only desire "Equality before the Law." The difficulty on this point is to make the qualifications such as to take in the most worthy and intelligent, and exclude the vicious and ignorant. No human judgment, nor laws framed by fallible man, could do that—hence we must expect, under any qualification, some who are worthy and capable would be excluded, and others the reverse, admitted. Still we will be content with any law which bears equally on all.

Questions

1. What was the basis of Bell's claim that the "rebel States have no rights which the [federal] Government is bound to respect"? What did he see as the principal shortcoming of the Johnson plan?

2. Given the southern defense of secession as a "constitutional" right (see Documents 13-7, 14-1, and 14-2), was Bell justified in his assertions about Reconstruction and the powers of the federal government?

3. Compare Bell's views on Reconstruction with those of Charles Sumner (Document 13-11) and Thaddeus Stevens (Document 15-6). Were they identical? Did they share the same priorities?

15-4 The Mississippi Black Codes (1865)

As Carl Schurz reported, after the Civil War whites in the South sought a system of race relations in which African Americans would be clearly subordinate to whites and would constitute a readily accessible and controllable workforce (see text p. 461).

Immediately after the Civil War southern whites wrote or revised vagrancy laws and the old slave codes as a means of establishing the system of race relations they wanted. Following is one of their most famous attempts to codify race relations, the Black Codes passed by the Mississippi legislature.

The Mississippi codes gave blacks rights they had not had before and clearly acknowledged that chattel slavery had ended. The codes recognized the right of African Americans to own property, though not in incorporated towns or cities. (Before the Civil War there were black property owners in Mississippi and even a few black slaveholders, but their legal standing was not clear.) The 1865 codes also recognized marriages among blacks as legal.

Not all the southern states passed comprehensive Black Codes, and some codes were much less stringent than those of Mississippi. South Carolina's codes differed in that they restricted blacks to buying property in cities or towns.

The creators of the codes drew their ideas from the world in which they lived. Slavery had just ended very abruptly, and the ravages of war were ever present. The men who drafted these codes used the old slave codes from the South, vagrancy laws from the North and the South, laws for former slaves in the British West Indies, and antebellum laws for free blacks. They were also aware that most northern states had laws that discriminated against African Americans and that very few northern states allowed African Americans to vote.

Most of these codes and similar measures were declared void by the Union army officials who were stationed in the former Confederate states. Subsequently, during Reconstruction, the rights of African Americans were greatly expanded (see text pp. 464–472).

Source: Laws of Mississippi, 1865, pp. 82ff.

1. CIVIL RIGHTS OF FREEDMEN IN MISSISSIPPI

... That all freedmen, free negroes, and mulattoes may sue and be sued ... may acquire personal property ... and may dispose of the same in the same manner and to the same extent that white persons may: [but no] freedman, free negro, or mulatto ... [shall] rent or lease any lands or tenements except in incorporated cities or towns, in which places the corporate authorities shall control the same....

All freedmen, free negroes, or mulattoes who do now and have herebefore lived and cohabited together as husband and wife shall be taken and held in law as legally married, and the issue shall be taken and held as legitimate for all purposes; that it shall not be lawful for any freedman, free negro, or mulatto to intermarry with any white person; nor for any white person to intermarry with any freedman, free negro, or mulatto; and any person who shall so intermarry, shall be deemed guilty of felony, and on conviction thereof shall be confined in the State penitentiary for life; and those shall be deemed freedmen, free negroes, and mulattoes who are of pure negro blood, and those descended from a negro to the third generation, inclusive, though one ancestor in each generation may have been a white person....

[F]reedmen, free negroes, and mulattoes are now by law competent witnesses ... in civil cases [and in criminal cases where they are the victims]....

All contracts for labor made with freedmen, free negroes, and mulattoes for a longer period than one month shall be in writing, and in duplicate ... and said contracts shall be taken and held as entire contracts, and if the laborer shall quit the service of the employer before the expiration of his term of service, without good cause, he shall forfeit his wages for that year up to the time of quitting.

... Every civil officer shall, and every person may, arrest and carry back to his or her legal employer any freedman, free negro, or mulatto who shall have quit the service of his or her employer before the expiration of his or her term of service without good cause; and said officer and person shall be entitled to receive for arresting and carrying back every deserting employee aforesaid the sum of five dollars....

... If any person shall persuade or attempt to persuade, entice, or cause any freedman, free negro, or mulatto to desert from the legal employment of any person before the expiration of his or her term of service, or shall knowingly employ any such deserting freedman, free negro, or mulatto, or shall knowingly give or sell to any such deserting freedman, free negro, or mulatto, any food, raiment, or other thing, he or she shall be guilty of a misdemeanor....

2. MISSISSIPPI APPRENTICE LAW

... It shall be the duty of all sheriffs, justices of the peace, and other civil officers of the several counties in this State, to report to the probate courts of their respective counties semi-annually, at the January and July terms of said courts, all freedmen, free negroes, and mulattoes, under the age of eighteen, in their respective counties, beats or districts, who are orphans, or whose parent or parents have not the means or who refuse to provide for and support said minors; ... the clerk of said court to apprentice said minors to some competent and suitable person, on such terms as the court may direct, having a particular care to the interest of said minor: *Provided,* that the former owner of said minors shall have the preference when, in the opinion of the court, he or she shall be a suitable person for that purpose....

... In the management and control of said apprentice, said master or mistress shall have the power to inflict such moderate corporal chastisement as a father or guardian is allowed to inflict on his or her child or ward at common law: *Provided,* that in no case shall cruel or inhuman punishment be inflicted....

3. MISSISSIPPI VAGRANT LAW

... That all rogues and vagabonds, idle and dissipated persons, beggars, jugglers, or persons practicing unlawful games or plays, runaways, common drunkards, common nightwalkers, pilferers, lewd, wanton, or lascivious persons, in speech or behavior, common railers and brawlers, persons who neglect their calling or employment, misspend what they earn, or do not provide for the support of themselves or their families, or dependents, and all other idle and disorderly persons, including all who neglect all lawful business, habitually misspend their time by frequenting houses of ill-fame, gaming-houses, or tippling shops, shall be deemed and considered vagrants, under the provisions of this act, and upon conviction thereof shall be fined not exceeding one hundred dollars . . . and be imprisoned at the discretion of the court, not exceeding ten days.

. . . All freedmen, free negroes and mulattoes in this State, over the age of eighteen years, found on the second Monday in January, 1866, or thereafter, with no lawful employment or business, or found unlawfully assembling themselves together, either in the day or night time, and all white persons so assembling themselves with freedmen, free negroes or mulattoes, or usually associating with freedmen, free negroes or mulattoes, on terms of equality, or living in adultery or fornication with a freed woman, free negro or mulatto, shall be deemed vagrants, and on conviction thereof shall be fined in a sum not exceeding, in the case of a freedman, free negro or mulatto, fifty dollars, and a white man two hundred dollars, and imprisoned at the discretion of the court, the free negro not exceeding ten days, and the white man not exceeding six months. . . .

4. PENAL LAWS OF MISSISSIPPI

. . . That no freedman, free negro or mulatto, not in the military service of the United States government, and not licensed so to do by the board of police of his or her county, shall keep or carry fire-arms of any kind, or any ammunition, dirk or bowie knife. . . .

. . . Any freedman, free negro, or mulatto committing riots, routs, affrays, trespasses, malicious mischief, cruel treatment to animals, seditious speeches, insulting gestures, language, or acts, or assaults on any person, disturbance of the peace, exercising the function of a minister of the Gospel without a license from some regularly organized church, vending spirituous or intoxicating liquors, or committing any other misdemeanor, the punishment of which is not specifically provided for by law, shall, upon conviction thereof in the county court, be fined not less than ten dollars, and not more than one hundred dollars, and may be imprisoned at the discretion of the court, not exceeding thirty days. . . .

. . . If any freedman, free negro, or mulatto, convicted of any of the misdemeanors provided against in this act, shall fail or refuse for the space of five days, after conviction, to pay the fine and costs imposed, such person shall be hired out by the sheriff or other officer, at public outcry, to any white person who will pay said fine and all costs, and take said convict for the shortest time.

Questions

1. What was the intent of these laws?
2. Who was charged with enforcing them? ("Every civil officer shall, and every person may, arrest and carry back to his or her legal employer . . .") Who was considered a "person"? Who was not a "person"?
3. How were vagrants defined? Were these laws based on the assumption that the only vagrants were African Americans? What restrictions were placed on the freedom of expression of African Americans? What restrictions were placed on their freedom of association? On whites in Mississippi?

15-5 The Civil Rights Act of 1866

When Congress reconvened in December 1865, it blocked President Johnson's attempts to restore the South quickly. It extended the life of the Freedmen's Bureau over the president's veto and passed another landmark law, the Civil Rights Act of 1866, again over the president's veto (see text p. 465). This act made African Americans citizens and countered the 1857 *Dred Scott* decision, in which the Supreme Court had declared that no African American who was descended from a slave was or could ever be a citizen (Document 13-12).

Doubts about the constitutionality and permanence of the Civil Rights Act of 1866 prompted Congress to pass the Fourteenth Amendment (see text pp. 465–466). Ratified in 1868, this amendment for the first time constitutionally defined citizenship and some of the basic rights of citizenship; it also embraced the Republican program for Reconstruction.

Source: U.S. Statutes at Large, 14 (1868?), 27ff.

An Act to protect all Persons in the United States in their Civil Rights, and furnish the Means of their Vindication.

Be it enacted, That all persons born in the United States and not subject to any foreign power, excluding Indians not taxed, are hereby declared to be citizens of the United States; and such citizens, of every race and color, without regard to any previous condition of slavery or involuntary servitude, except as a punishment for crime whereof the party shall have been duly convicted, shall have the same right, in every State and Territory in the United States, to make and enforce contracts, to sue, be parties, and give evidence, to inherit, purchase, lease, sell, hold, and convey real and personal property, and to full and equal benefit of all laws and proceedings for the security of person and property, as is enjoyed by white citizens, and shall be subject to like punishment, pains, and penalties, and to none other, any law, statute, ordinance, regulation, or custom, to the contrary notwithstanding.

SEC. 2. *And be it further enacted*, That any person who, under color of any law, statute, ordinance, regulation, or custom, shall subject, or cause to be subjected, any inhabitant of any State or Territory to the deprivation of any right secured or protected by this act, or to different punishment, pains, or penalties on account of such person having at any time been held in a condition of slavery or involuntary servitude, except as a punishment for crime whereof the party shall have been duly convicted, or by reason of his color or race, than is prescribed for the punishment of white persons, shall be deemed guilty of a misdemeanor, and, on conviction, shall be punished by fine not exceeding one thousand dollars, or imprisonment not exceeding one year, or both, in the discretion of the court.

SEC. 3. *And be it further enacted*, That the district courts of the United States, . . . shall have, exclusively of the courts of the several States, cognizance of all crimes and offences committed against the provisions of this act, and also, concurrently with the circuit courts of the United States, of all causes, civil and criminal, affecting persons who are denied or cannot enforce in the courts or judicial tribunals of the State or locality where they may be any of the rights secured to them by the first section of this act. . . .

SEC. 4. *And be it further enacted*, That the district attorneys, marshals, and deputy marshals of the United States, the commissioners appointed by the circuit and territorial courts of the United States, with powers of arresting, imprisoning, or bailing offenders against the laws of the United States, the officers and agents of the Freedmen's Bureau, and every other officer who may be specially empowered by the President of the United States, shall be, and they are hereby, specially authorized and required, at the expense of the United States, to institute proceedings against all and every person who shall violate the provisions of this act, and cause him or them to be arrested and imprisoned, or bailed, as the case may be, for trial before such court of the United States or territorial court as by this act has cognizance of the offence. . . .

SEC. 8. *And be it further enacted*, That whenever the President of the United States shall have reason to believe that offences have been or are likely to be committed against the provisions of this act within any judicial district, it shall be lawful for him, in his discretion, to direct the judge, marshal, and district attorney of such district to attend at such place within the district, and for such time as he may designate, for the purpose of the more speedy arrest and trial of persons charged with a violation of this act; and it shall be the duty of every judge or other officer, when any such requisition shall be received by him, to attend at the place and for the time therein designated.

SEC. 9. *And be it further enacted*, That it shall be lawful for the President of the United States, or such person as he may empower for that purpose, to employ such part of the land or naval forces of the United States, or of the militia, as shall be necessary to prevent the violation and enforce the due execution of this act.

SEC. 10. *And be it further enacted*, That upon all questions of law arising in any cause under the provisions of this act a final appeal may be taken to the Supreme Court of the United States.

Questions

1. What was the intent of the Civil Rights Act?

2. Who was responsible for enforcing this law, and what powers might they use? Was it necessary to wait until the law was violated before officers of the law could act?

3. According to the Fourteenth Amendment, who is a citizen of the United States? What rights does the amendment say citizens have? What does "equal protection of the laws" mean?

Questions for Further Thought

1. Compare President Johnson's description of conditions in the South (Document 15-1) with that of General Schurz (Document 15-2). Which do you find to be more accurate? Why?
2. Schurz reported that if Reconstruction meant that the social order of the former Confederate states had to be "constructed anew," then Johnson's program (Document 15-1) was a failure. Based on your reading of the Mississippi Black Codes (Document 15-4), to what extent was Shurz correct in his assessment?
3. Compare the Mississippi Black Codes (Document 15-4) with the Civil Rights Act of 1866 (Document 15-5). Why do you think Congress believed that it had to pass the Civil Rights Act and then adopt the Fourteenth Amendment?

Radical Reconstruction

When only Tennessee ratified the Fourteenth Amendment (and was readmitted to the Union), congressional Republicans, strengthened by their victories in the 1866 congressional elections, passed the Reconstruction Acts. These laws forced unreconstructed former Confederate states to meet Republican conditions for readmission, including granting African American men the vote. While these measures were called radical by their detractors (and this phase of Reconstruction referred to as "radical Reconstruction"), these measures actually fell far short of what some in Congress desired (Document 15-6). They fell even further short of the hopes of women's rights advocates that the vote might be extended to them as well as blacks—a frustration that seriously split the movement, but led ultimately to the creation of a new, and eventually successful, woman suffrage movement (Document 15-7).

During Reconstruction African Americans obtained a number of civil and political rights, most especially in the realm of politics. While no former Confederate state was controlled by blacks, a large group of African American politicians surged into prominence, seeking to use government power to help constituents who previously had not even been regarded as citizens (Document 15-8). While many of these new political rights were lost in the years following Reconstruction, other gains, especially in social and economic realms, were more enduring. At the insistence of the freed slaves, planters dismantled much of the old slave regime, replacing gang labor and the old slave quarters with a new system of individual plots worked by families for shares of the crops. Black marriages were formalized, and African Americans gained control over their family lives. They pursued education, built new institutions such as the black church, and began to acquire property. While white racism and white landlord power raised enormous barriers to black advancement, through the years increasing (though still small) numbers of African Americans became property holders.

15-6 Black Suffrage and Land Redistribution (1867)

Thaddeus Stevens

The Radical Republicans, including Congressman Thaddeus Stevens of Pennsylvania, believed that besides the vote, freedmen would need an economic basis for controlling their lives (see text p. 466). Below are excerpts from the remarks of Thaddeus Stevens and from a bill in which he proposed to alter the South drastically.

Source: Congressional Globe, 3 January 1867, 252; 19 March 1867, 203.

ON BLACK SUFFRAGE

Unless the rebel States, before admission, should be made republican in spirit, and placed under the guardianship of loyal men, all our blood and treasure will have been spent in vain. I waive now the question of punishment which, if we are wise, will still be inflicted by moderate confiscations.... Impartial suffrage, both in electing the delegates and ratifying their proceedings, is now the fixed rule. There is more reason why colored voters should be admitted in the rebel States than in the Territories. In the States they form the great mass of the loyal men. Possibly with their aid loyal governments may be established in most of those States. Without it all are sure to be ruled by traitors; and loyal men, black and white, will be oppressed, exiled, or murdered. There are several good reasons for the passage of this bill. In the first place, it is just. I am now confining my argument to negro suffrage in the rebel States. Have not loyal blacks quite as good a right to choose rulers and make laws as rebel whites? In the second place, it is a necessity in order to protect the loyal white men in the seceded States. The white Union men are in a great minority in each of those States. With them the blacks would act in a body; and it is believed that in each of said States, except one, the two united would form a majority, control the States, and protect themselves. Now they are the victims of daily murder....

Another good reason is, it would insure the ascendency of the Union party.... I believe ... that on the continued ascendency of that party depends the safety of this great nation. If impartial suffrage is excluded in the rebel States, then every one of them is sure to send a solid rebel representative delegation to Congress, and cast a solid rebel electoral vote. They, with their kindred Copperheads of the North, would always elect the President and control Congress. While slavery sat upon her defiant throne, and insulted and intimidated the trembling North, the South frequently divided on questions of policy between Whigs and Democrats, and gave victory alternately to the sections. Now, you must divide them between loyalists, without regard to color, and disloyalists, or you will be the perpetual vassals of the free-trade, irritated, revengeful South.... I am for negro suffrage in every rebel State. If it be just, it should not be denied; if it be necessary, it should be adopted; if it be a punishment to traitors, they deserve it.

BILL ON LAND REDISTRIBUTION

Whereas it is due to justice, as an example to future times, that some proper punishment should be inflicted on the people who constituted the "confederate States of America," both because they, declaring an unjust war against the United States for the purpose of destroying republican liberty and permanently establishing slavery, as well as for the cruel and barbarous manner in which they conducted said war, in violation of all the laws of civilized warfare, and also to compel them to make some compensation for the damages and expenditures caused by said war: Therefore,

Be it enacted by the Senate and House of Representatives of the United States of America in Congress assembled, That all the public lands belonging to the ten States that formed the government of the so-called "confederate States of America" shall be forfeited by said States and become forthwith vested in the United States....

That out of the lands thus seized and confiscated the slaves who have been liberated by the operations of the war and the amendment to the Constitution or otherwise, who resided in said "confederate States" on the 4th day of March, A.D. 1861, or since, shall have distributed to them as follows, namely: to each male person who is the head of a family, forty acres; to each adult male, whether the head of a family or not, forty acres; to each widow who is the head of a family, forty acres — to be held by them in fee-simple, but to be inalienable for the next ten years after they become seized thereof....

That out of the balance of the property thus seized and confiscated there shall be raised, in the manner hereinafter provided, a sum equal to fifty dollars, for each homestead, to be applied by the trustees hereinafter mentioned toward the erection of buildings on the said homesteads for the use of said slaves; and the further sum of $500,000,000, which shall be appropriated as follows, to wit: $200,000,000 shall be invested in United States six per cent securities; and the interest thereof shall be semi-annually added to the pensions allowed by law to pensioners who have become so by reason of the late war; $300,000,000, or so much thereof as may be needed, shall be appropriated to pay damages done to loyal citizens by the civil or military operations of the government lately called the "confederate States of America."...

That in order that just discrimination may be made, the property of no one shall be seized whose whole estate on the 4th day of March, A.D. 1865, was not worth more than $5,000, to be valued by the said commission, unless he shall have voluntarily become an officer or employé in the military or civil service of the "confederate States of America," or in the civil or military service of some one of said States.

Questions

1. On what grounds did Stevens justify granting African American men the vote?
2. What did Stevens want to do with land confiscated in the South?
3. Why do you think Congress rejected Stevens's land confiscation and redistribution proposal? Do you think that if Congress had adopted the proposal, it would have made a difference in the history of the South or the United States? Why or why not?

15-7 The Fourteenth Amendment and Woman Suffrage (1873, 1875)

As noted in the text, not only did the Fourteenth and Fifteenth Amendments ignore the demands of the women's rights movement for equal access to the ballot box, but the Fourteenth Amendment introduced the word *male* for the first time into the U.S. Constitution. Nonetheless, many suffragists continued to believe that the newly formalized and broadened definition of American citizenship established by the Fourteenth Amendment could be used to gain women the vote through a judicial ruling. In 1872 a number of suffragists, including Susan B. Anthony, voted in the presidential election; Anthony was indicted and brought to trial, providing her the opportunity she sought to make her case (Document 15-7a). Anthony was blocked from making her appeal, but another suffragist, Virginia Minor of Missouri, sued the official who blocked her from the ballot box and saw her case reach the Supreme Court. The Court's decision (Document 15-7b), handed down in 1875, effectively ended all hopes that gender relations as well as race relations had been "reconstructed" by the Fourteenth Amendment, and strengthened the movement for a constitutional woman suffrage amendment. Furthermore, by effectively separating the right to vote from fundamental citizenship rights, the Court also helped set the stage for the later movement to use "color-blind" laws to disfranchise African Americans.

Sources: From Ruth Barnes Moynihan, Cynthia Russett, and Laurie Crumpacker, eds., *Second to None: A Documentary History of American Women* (Lincoln: University of Nebraska Press, 1993), 2:16–19. Used by permission of the University of Nebraska Press. This selection first appeared in *The Life and Work of Susan B. Anthony*, vol. 3 (Indianapolis: Bowen-Merrill, 1898).

(a) I Stand Before You Under Indictment (1873)

Friends and Fellow-Citizens:—I stand before you under indictment for the alleged crime of having voted at the last presidential election, without having a lawful right to vote. It shall be my work this evening to prove to you that in thus doing, I not only committed no crime, but instead simply exercised my citizen's right, guaranteed to me and all United States citizens by the National Constitution beyond the power of any State to deny.

Our democratic-republican government is based on the idea of the natural right of every individual member thereof to a voice and a vote in making and executing the laws. We assert the province of government to be to secure the people in the enjoyment of their inalienable rights. We throw to the winds the old dogma that government can give rights. No one denies that before governments were organized each individual possessed the right to protect his own life, liberty and property. When 100 or 1,000,000 people enter into a free government, they do not barter away their natural rights; they simply pledge themselves to protect each other in the enjoyment of them through prescribed judicial and legislative tribunals. They agree to abandon the methods of brute force in the adjustment of their differences and adopt those of civilization. Nor can you find a word in any of the grand documents left us by the fathers which assumes for government the power to create or to confer rights. The Declaration of Independence, the United States Constitution, the constitutions of the several States and the organic laws of the Territories, all alike propose to *protect* the people in the exercise of their God-given rights. Not one of them pretends to bestow rights.

> All men are created equal, and endowed by their Creator with certain inalienable rights. Among these are life, liberty and the pursuit of happiness. To secure these, governments are instituted among men, deriving their just powers from the consent of the governed.

Here is no shadow of government authority over rights, or exclusion of any class from their full and equal enjoyment. Here is pronounced the right of all men, and "consequently," as the Quaker preacher said, "of all women," to a voice in the government. And here, in this first paragraph of the Declaration, is the assertion of the natural right of all to the ballot; for how can "the consent of the governed" be given, if the right to vote be denied? Again:

> Whenever any form of government becomes destructive of these ends, it is the right of the people to alter or abolish it, and to institute a new government, laying its foundations on such principles, and organizing its powers in such form, as to them shall seem most likely to effect their safety and happiness.

Surely the right of the whole people to vote is here clearly implied; for however destructive to their happiness this government might become, a disfranchised class could neither alter nor abolish it, nor institute a new one, except by the old brute force method of insurrection and rebellion. One-half of the people of this nation today are utterly powerless to blot from the statute books an unjust law, or to write there a new and just one. The women, dissatisfied as they are with this form of government, that enforces taxation without representation—that compels them to obey laws to which they never have given their consent—that imprisons and hangs them without a trial by a jury of their peers—that robs them, in marriage, of the custody of their own persons, wages and children—are this half of the people who are left wholly at the mercy of the other half, in direct violation of the spirit and letter of the declarations of the framers of this government, every one of which was based on the immutable principle of equal rights to all. By these declarations, kings, popes, priests, aristocrats, all were alike dethroned and placed on a common level, politically, with the lowliest born subject or serf. By them, too, men, as such, were deprived of their divine right to rule and placed on a political level with women. By the practice of these declarations all class and caste distinctions would be abolished, and slave, serf, plebeian, wife, woman, all alike rise from their subject position to the broader platform of equality.

The preamble of the Federal Constitution says:

We, the people of the United States, in order to form a more perfect union, establish justice, insure domestic tranquillity, provide for the common defence, promote the general welfare and secure the blessings of liberty to ourselves and our posterity, do ordain and establish this Constitution for the United States of America.

It was we, the people, not we, the white male citizens, nor we, the male citizens; but we, the whole people, who formed this Union. We formed it not to give the blessings of liberty but to secure them; not to the half of ourselves and the half of our posterity, but to the whole people—women as well as men. It is downright mockery to talk to women of their enjoyment of the blessings of liberty while they are denied the only means of securing them provided by this democratic-republican government—the ballot....

For any State to make sex a qualification, which must ever result in the disfranchisement of one entire half of the people, is to pass a bill of attainder, an ex post facto law, and is therefore a violation of the supreme law of the land. By it the blessings of liberty are forever withheld from women and their female posterity. For them, this government has no just powers derived from the consent of the governed. For them this government is not a democracy; it is not a republic. It is the most odious aristocracy ever established on the face of the globe. An oligarchy of wealth, where the rich govern the poor; an oligarchy of learning, where the educated govern the ignorant; or even an oligarchy of race, where the Saxon rules the African, might be endured; but this oligarchy of sex which makes father, brothers, husband, sons, the oligarchs over the mother and sisters, the wife and daughters of every household; which ordains all men sovereigns, all women subjects—carries discord and rebellion into every home of the nation.... The moment you deprive a person of his right to a voice in the government, you degrade him from the status of a citizen of the republic to that of a subject. It matters very little to him whether his monarch be an individual tyrant, as is the Czar of Russia, or a 15,000,000 headed monster, as here in the United States; he is a powerless subject, serf or slave; not in any sense a free and independent citizen....

Though the words persons, people, inhabitants, electors, citizens, are all used indiscriminately in the national and State constitutions, there was always a conflict of opinion, prior to the war, as to whether they were synonymous terms, but whatever room there was for doubt, under the old regime, the adoption of the Fourteenth Amendment settled that question forever in its first sentence:

All persons born or naturalized in the United States, and subject to the jurisdiction thereof, are citizens of the United States, and of the State wherein they reside.

The second settles the equal status of all citizens:

No State shall make or enforce any law which shall abridge the privileges or immunities of citizens of the United States; nor shall any State deprive any person of life, liberty or property without due process of law, or deny to any person within its jurisdiction the equal protection of the laws.

The only question left to be settled now is: Are women persons? I scarcely believe any of our opponents will have the hardihood to say they are not. Being persons, then, women are citizens, and no State has a right to make any new law, or to enforce any old law, which shall abridge their privileges or immunities. Hence, every discrimination against women in the constitutions and laws of the several States is today null and void, precisely as is every one against negroes.

Is the right to vote one of the privileges or immunities of citizens? I think the disfranchised ex-rebels and ex-State prisoners all will agree that it is not only one of them, but the one without which all the others are nothing. Seek first the kingdom of the ballot and all things else shall be added, is the political injunction....

If once we establish the false principle that United States citizenship does not carry with it the right to vote in every State in this Union, there is no end to the petty tricks and cunning devices which will be attempted to exclude one and another class of citizens from the right of suffrage. It will not always be the men combining to disfranchise all women; native born men combining to abridge the rights of all naturalized citizens, as in Rhode Island. It will not always be the rich and educated who may combine to cut off the poor and ignorant; but we may live to see the hardworking, uncultivated day laborers, foreign and native born, learning the power of the ballot and their vast majority of numbers, combine and amend State constitutions so as to disfranchise the Vanderbilts, the Stewarts, the Conklings and the Fentons. It is a poor rule that won't work more ways than one. Establish this precedent, admit the State's right to deny suffrage, and there is no limit to the confusion, discord, and disruption that may await us. There is and can be but one safe principle of government—equal rights to all. Discrimination against any class on account of color, race, nativity, sex, property, culture, can but embitter and disaffect that class, and thereby endanger the safety of the whole people. Clearly, then, the national government not only must define the rights of citizens, but must stretch out its powerful hand and protect them in every State of this Union.

(b) *Minor v. Happersett* (1875)

MR. CHIEF JUSTICE MORRISON R. WAITE DELIVERED THE OPINION OF THE COURT:

The question is presented in this case, whether, since the adoption of the fourteenth amendment, a woman, who is a citizen of the United States and of the State of Missouri, is a voter in that State, notwithstanding the provision of the constitution and laws of the State, which confine the right of suffrage to men alone. . . . The argument is, that as a woman, born or naturalized in the United States and subject to the jurisdiction thereof, is a citizen of the United States and of the State in which she resides, she has the right of suffrage as one of the privileges and immunities of her citizenship, which the State cannot by its laws or constitution abridge.

There is no doubt that women may be citizens. They are persons, and by the fourteenth amendment "all persons born or naturalized in the United States and subject to the jurisdiction thereof" are expressly declared to be "citizens of the United States and of the State wherein they reside." But, in our opinion, it did not need this amendment to give them that position . . . sex has never been made one of the elements of citizenship in the United States. In this respect men have never had an advantage over women. The same laws precisely apply to both. The fourteenth amendment did not affect the citizenship of women any more than it did of men . . . Mrs. Minor . . . has always been a citizen from her birth, and entitled to all the privileges and immunities of citizenship.

If the right of suffrage is one of the necessary privileges of a citizen of the United States, then the constitution and laws of Missouri confining it to men are in violation of the Constitution of the United States, as amended, and consequently void. The direction question is, therefore, presented whether all citizens are necessarily voters.

The Constitution does not define the privileges and immunities of citizens. For that definition we must look elsewhere. In this case we need not determine what they are, but only whether suffrage is necessarily one of them.

It certainly is nowhere made so in express terms. The United States has no voters in the States of its own creation. The elective officers of the United States are all elected directly or indirectly by state voters. . . . [I]t cannot for a moment be doubted that if it had been intended to make all citizens of the United States voters, the framers of the Constitution would not have left it to implication. . . .

It is true that the United States guarantees to every State a republican form of government. . . . No particular government is designated as republican, neither is the exact form to be guaranteed, in any manner especially designated. . . . When the Constitution was adopted . . . all the citizens of the States were not invested with the right of suffrage. In all, save perhaps New Jersey, this right was only bestowed upon men and not upon all of them. . . . Under these circumstances it is certainly now too late to contend that a government is not republican, within the meaning of this guaranty in the Constitution, because women are not made voters. . . . If suffrage was intended to be included within its obligations, language better adapted to express that intent would most certainly have been employed. . . .

. . . For nearly ninety years the people have acted upon the idea that the Constitution, when it conferred citizenship, did not necessarily confer the right of suffrage. If uniform practice long continued can settle the construction of so important an instrument as the Constitution of the United States confessedly is, most certainly it has been done here. Our province is to decide what the law is, not to declare what it should be.

We have given this case the careful consideration its importance demands. If the law is wrong, it ought to be changed; but the power for that is not with us. . . . No argument as to woman's need of suffrage can be considered. We can only act upon her rights as they exist.

Questions

1. What case did Anthony make for treating voting as an "inalienable right"?
2. What did Anthony see as the consequence of denying that the right to vote is intrinsic to citizenship? Is her view prophetic?
3. Compare the reasoning of Anthony and of Chief Justice Waite on the question of whether the right to vote is one of the "privileges and immunities" of citizenship. What sorts of evidence do they cite?

15-8 An Advocate of Federal Aid for Land Purchase (1868)

Richard H. Cain

With the enactment of the Reconstruction Act of 1867, the cast of political leadership in the South dramatically changed. One good example of the new men rising to prominence was Richard H. Cain (1825–1887). Born in Virginia of African American and Cherokee parents, Cain was raised in Ohio, attending Wilberforce University and becoming a minister in the African Methodist Episcopal (A.M.E.) Church. After spending the Civil War as pastor of a Brooklyn church, he went south in 1865 as a missionary; reorganizing the Emmanuel A.M.E. Church of Charleston, South Carolina, Cain built it into the largest A.M.E. congregation in the state and used it as a political base. He was a delegate to the South Carolina constitutional convention of 1868; served as a state senator from 1868 to 1870; unsuccessfully sought the Republican nomination for lieutenant governor in 1872; and served in the U.S. House of Representatives from 1873 to 1875 and again from 1877 to 1879. Cain left South Carolina in 1880 and spent the remainder of his life as a bishop and college president in the A.M.E. Church.

Like many successful African American preachers, Cain was an astute businessman, eager to lend his services to build up the black community. Like many other black politicians, he saw the issue of land for the freedmen as paramount. An early advocate of redistribution of confiscated lands à la Thaddeus Stevens (Document 15-6), at the constitutional convention Cain advocated petitioning the federal government to appropriate $1 million to finance land purchases by the freedmen. When his proposal was attacked by C. P. Leslie, a white Republican delegate, Cain defended it with the following remarks.

Source: Proceedings of the Constitutional Convention of South Carolina (Charleston: Denny and Perry, 1868), 378–382.

. . . Mr. CAIN. I offer this resolution with good intentions. I believe there is need of immediate relief to the poor people of the State. I know from my experience among the people, there is pressing need of some measures to meet the wants of the utterly destitute. The gentleman says it will only take money out of the Treasury. Well that is the intention. I do not expect to get it anywhere else. I expect to get the money, if at all, through the Treasury of the United States, or some other department. It certainly must come out of the Government. I believe such an appropriation would remove a great many of the difficulties now in the State and do a vast amount of good to poor people. It may be that we will not get it, but that will not debar us from asking. It is our privilege and right. Other Conventions have asked from Congress appropriations. Georgia and other States have sent in their petitions. One has asked for $30,000,000 to be appropriated to the Southern States. I do not see any inconsistency in the proposition presented by myself.

Mr. C. P. LESLIE. Suppose I should button up my coat and march up to your house and ask you for money or provisions, when you had none to give, what would you think of me?

Mr. CAIN. You would do perfectly right to run the chance of getting something to eat. This is a measure of relief to those thousands of freed people who now have no lands of their own. I believe the possession of lands and homesteads is one of the best means by which a people is made industrious, honest and advantageous to the State. I believe it is a fact well known, that over three hundred thousand men, women and children are homeless, landless. The abolition of slavery has thrown these people upon their own resources. How are they to live? I know the philosopher of the New York *Tribune* says, "root hog or die;" but in the meantime we ought to have some place to root. My proposition is simply to give the hog some place to root. I believe if the proposition is sent to Congress, it will certainly receive the attention of our friends. I believe the whole country is desirous to see that this State shall return to the Union in peace and quiet, and that every inhabitant of the State shall be made industrious and profitable to the State. I am opposed to this Bureau system. I want a system adopted that will do away with the Bureau, but I cannot see how it can be done unless the people have homes. As long as people are working on shares and contracts, and at the end of every year are in debt, so long will they and the country suffer. But give them a chance to buy lands, and they become steady, industrious men. That is the reason I desire to bring this money here and to assist them to buy lands. It will be the means of encouraging them to industry if the petition be granted by Congress. It will be the means of meeting one of the great wants of the present among the poor. It will lay the foundation for the future prosperity of the country as no other measure will at this time, because it will bring about a reconciliation in the minds of thousands of these helpless people, which nothing else can. This measure, if carried out, will bring capital to the State and stimulate the poor to renewed efforts in life, such as they never had before. Such a measure will give to the landholders relief from their embarrassments financially, and enable them to get fair compensation for their lands. It will relieve the Government of the responsibility of taking care of the thousands who now are fed at the Commissaries and fostered in laziness. I have gone through the country and on every side I was besieged with questions: How are we to get homesteads, to get lands? I desire to devise some plan, or adopt some measure by which we can dissipate one of the arguments used against us, that the African race will not work. I do not believe the black man hates work any more than the white man does. Give these men a place to work, and I will guarantee before one year passes, there will be no necessity for the Freedman's Bureau, or any measure aside from those measures which a people may make in protecting themselves.

But a people without homes become wanderers. If they possess lands they have an interest in the soil, in the State, in its commerce, its agriculture, and in everything pertaining to the wealth and welfare of the State. If these people had homes along the lines of railroads, and the lands were divided and sold in small farms, I will guarantee our railroads will make fifty times as much money, banking systems will be advanced by virtue of the settlement of the people throughout the whole State. We want these large tracts of land cut up. The land is productive, and there is nothing to prevent the greatest and highest prosperity. What we need is a system of small farms. Every farmer owning his own land will feel he is in possession of something. It will have a tendency to settle the minds of the people in the State and settle many difficulties. In the rural districts now there is constant discontent, constant misapprehension between the parties, a constant disregard for each other. One man won't make an engagement to work, because he fears if he makes a contract this year, he will be cheated again as he thinks he was last year. We have had petitions from planters asking the Convention to disabuse the minds of the freedmen of the thought that this Convention has any lands at its disposal, but I do desire this Convention to do something at least to relieve the wants of these poor suffering people. I believe this measure, if adopted and sent to Congress, will indicate to the people that this Convention does desire they shall possess homes and have relief.

Some of my friends say that the sum is too small, and ask why I do not make it more. I made it a million, because I thought there would be more probability of getting one million than five. It might be put into the hands of the Bureau, and I am willing to trust the Bureau. . . .

I do not desire to have a foot of land in this State confiscated. I want every man to stand upon his own character. I want these lands purchased by the government, and the people afforded an opportunity to buy from the government. I believe every man ought to carve out for himself a character and position in this life. I believe every man ought to be made to work by some means or other, and if he does not, he must go down. I believe if the same amount of money that has been employed by the Bureau in feeding lazy, worthless men and women, had been expended in purchasing lands, we would to-day have no need of the Bureau. Millions upon millions have been expended, and it is still going on *ad infinitum*. I propose to let the poor people buy these lands, the government to be paid back in five years time. It is one of the great cries of the enemies of reconstruction, that Congress has constantly fostered laziness. I want to have the satisfaction of showing that the freedmen are as capable and willing to work as any men on the face of the earth. This measure will save the State untold expenses. I believe there are hundreds of persons in the jail and penitentiary cracking rock to-day who have all the instincts of honesty, and who, had they an opportunity of making a living, would never have been found in such a place. I think if Congress will accede to our request, we shall be benefited beyond measure, and save the State from taking charge of paupers, made such by not having the means to earn a living for themselves.

I can look to a part of my constituency, men in this hall, mechanics, plasterers, carpenters, engineers, men capable of doing all kind of work, now idle because they cannot find any work in the city. Poverty stares them in the face, and their children are in want. They go to the cotton houses, but can find no labor. They are men whose honesty and integrity has never been called in question. They are suffering in consequence of the poverty-stricken condition of the city and State. I believe the best measure is to open a field where they can labor, where they can take the hoe and the axe, cut down the forest, and make the whole land blossom as the Garden of Eden, and prosperity pervade the whole land.

Now, the report of Major General Howard gives a surplus of over seven millions in the Freedman's Bureau last year. Out of that seven millions I propose we ask Congress to make an appropriation of one million, which will be properly distributed and then leave several millions in that Department, my friend from Barnwell notwithstanding.

I think there could be no better measure for this Convention to urge upon Congress. If that body should listen to our appeal, I have no doubt we shall be benefited. This measure of relief, it seems to me, would come swiftly. It is a swift messenger that comes in a week's time after it is passed; so that in the month of February or March the people may be enabled to go to planting and raising crops for the ensuing year. One gentleman says it will take six months or a year, but I hope, with the assistance of the Government, we could accomplish it in less time.

Mr. C. P. LESLIE. Did you ever see the Government do anything quick?

Mr. R. H. CAIN. They make taxes come quick. If this measure is carried out, the results will be that we will see all along our lines of railroad and State roads little farms, log cabins filled with happy families, and thousands of families coming on the railroads with their products. There will also spring up depots for the reception of cotton, corn and all other cereals. Prosperity will return to the State, by virtue of the people being happy, bound to the Government by a tie that cannot be broken. The taxes, that are so heavy now that men are compelled to sell their horses, will be lightened. I want to see the State alive, to hear the hum of the spindle and the mills! I want to see cattle and horses, and fowls, and everything that makes up a happy home and family. I want to see the people shout with joy and gladness. There shall then be no antagonism between white men and black men, but we shall all realize the end of our being, and realize that we are all made to dwell upon the earth in peace and happiness. The white man and the black man may then work in harmony, and secure prosperity to all coming generations.

Questions

1. What arguments did Cain make in favor of his proposal? To what present policies, especially of the Freedmen's Bureau, did he object?
2. In certain respects, Cain's proposal can be characterized as *conservative*. How? Would you agree, or not?
3. How would you characterize Cain's intentions toward the *whites* of South Carolina?

Questions for Further Thought

1. Compare Cain's argument on land reform (Document 15-8) to that of Thaddeus Stevens (Document 15-6). To what degree did Cain, like Stevens, see land redistribution as a means of punishing "rebels"? What did each man see as the proper role of the federal government in "reconstructing" the South?
2. Susan B. Anthony's argument (Document 15-7a) rested on an analogy between the status of women in the pre-Reconstruction United States and the status of African Americans. How well did that analogy work?
3. In view of the preceding documents, just how "radical" would you say radical Reconstruction really was? Bear in mind the meaning of the word *radical*—to desire change not on the surface of society, but *at its roots*.

The Undoing of Reconstruction

Northern support for Reconstruction was never reliable. Because most white northerners feared that President Johnson's program threatened to undo the Union victory and place Confederates back in the saddle (Document 15-9a), they preferred the program of congressional Republicans. However, they were at best only slightly more liberal in their racial views than were southerners, and over time northerners were increasingly receptive to southern white arguments that blacks were not to be trusted to govern (Document 15-9b).

Most southern whites, of course, opposed congressional Reconstruction from the outset, though the vehemence of the opposition fluctuated. The animosity of southern whites toward Reconstruction, Republicans, and African Americans intensified when elections were contested or when sensitive issues were placed before the public. The Ku Klux Klan was especially active during such times, despite legislation passed against it.

The final undoing of Reconstruction came in the mid-1870s. A serious economic crisis struck the nation in 1873, plunging it into depression. New, economic issues, such as unemployment, labor conflict, and monetary policy, increasingly took precedence over the aging agenda of the sectional conflict, while northern lack of sympathy for blacks became increasingly important in shaping federal policy toward the South (Document 15-10). At the same time, southern whites got bolder, organizing paramilitary organizations to carry elections by whatever means were necessary. In such states as Mississippi and South Carolina, the end of Reconstruction resulted not so much from an election as from a white counterrevolution.

15-9 The Rise and Fall of Northern Support for Reconstruction (1868, 1874)

Thomas Nast

Evidence of broad northern support for the Republican program could be found in many places other than the ballot box. Illustrations from *Harper's Weekly,* such as the one in the text (p. 477) and the one here from 1868 titled "This Is a White Man's Government," reflected popular attitudes in the North in the 1860s. However, northern support for Reconstruction began to erode as early as 1868 and was exhausted by 1874 (see text pp. 478–479), the year the *Harper's Weekly* illustration presented here appeared. Both cartoons are by Thomas Nast.

The first cartoon satirizes the Democratic Party in 1868, with its platform rejecting the Congressional Reconstruction Acts as "unconstitutional, null, and void." Nathan

(A) *Thomas Nast, "This Is a White Man's Government" (1868)*

Bedford Forrest—the Confederate general who became the first grand wizard of the Ku Klux Klan—is represented in the center, while to his right stands an Irish immigrant, depicted (as was common in Nast cartoons) as a barbaric hoodlum. The third figure (to Forrest's left) is the Democratic candidate for president in 1868, Governor Horatio Seymour—depicted here as the prosperous associate of New York financiers. This unholy alliance unites in what to Nast were the characteristic Democratic Party activities of racial oppression and treason, illustrated by scenes from the New York draft riots (see Document 14-9) and the postwar South, and by their trampling on the prostrate form of a black Union soldier.

The second cartoon shows a sharp shift in opinion on the part of both Nast and his audience. The cartoon illustrates a derisive news account of the black-majority

(B) *Thomas Nast, "Colored Rule in a Reconstructed State" (1874)*

South Carolina House of Representatives, reprinted from the white conservative *Charleston News*. In 1868 the views of the *News* would have been dismissed as "disloyal" by Nast's employer, *Harper's Weekly*; by 1874 the magazine was allowing those views a respectful hearing, and its famous cartoonist was giving them his stamp of approval. Why?

Sources: Thomas Nast, "This Is a White Man's Government," *Harper's Weekly*, 5 September 1868; Thomas Nast, "Colored Rule in a Reconstructed State," *Harper's Weekly*, 14 March 1874. Art courtesy of the Research Libraries, New York Public Library.

Questions

1. Note the picture of African Americans presented here and in the illustration on text page 477. Contrast that with the portrayal of government by southern whites.
2. Compare the portrayal of African Americans in the last illustration with that in the earlier illustrations.
3. What do you think accounts for the change?

15-10 President Grant Refuses to Aid Republicans in Mississippi (1875)

As one of three southern states with a black-majority population, one whose black voters were well organized, Mississippi should logically have remained secure for the Republicans. However, in the state election year of 1875, white Democrats launched a campaign of systematic violent intimidation of black and Republican voters. Against the massive mobilization of white "Rifle Clubs," the government of Governor Adelbert Ames was helpless, and in September Ames sent President Grant a desperate plea for federal troops. Grant and his attorney general, Edwards Pierrepont, turned down Ames's request; Pierrepont's letter to Ames of September 14, quoting Grant, was subsequently released to the press (Document 15-10a). Thanks to a catastrophic decline in Republican votes and blatant ballot-box stuffing, Democrats "redeemed" the state in a landslide. One of the few survivors of the Democratic onslaught, African American congressman John R. Lynch, wrote some years later of a postelection encounter with President Grant, who explained to him the political considerations behind his abandonment of Mississippi Republicans (Document 15-10b).

Sources: New York Times, 17 September 1875, 1; John Roy Lynch, *The Facts of Reconstruction* (New York: Neale Publishing Co., 1913), 150–153.

(a) Pierrepont's Letter of Refusal

DEPARTMENT OF JUSTICE, WASHINGTON, SEPT. 14, 1875.

To Gov. Ames, Jackson, Miss.:

This hour I have had dispatches from the President. I can best convey to you his ideas by extracts from his dispatch: "The whole public are tired out with these annual Autumnal outbreaks in the South, and the great majority are ready now to condemn any interference on the part of the Government. I heartily wish that peace and good order may be restored without issuing the proclamation; but if it is not the proclamation must be issued, and if it is I shall instruct the commander of the forces to have *no child's play*. If there is a necessity for military interference, there is justice in such interference as shall deter evil-doers. . . . I would suggest the sending of a dispatch (or better, a private messenger,) to Gov. Ames, urging him to strengthen his own position by exhausting his own resources in restoring order before he receives Government aid. He might accept the assistance offered by the citizens of Jackson and elsewhere. . . .

Gov. Ames and his advisors can be made perfectly secure. As many of the troops in Mississippi as he deems necessary may be sent to Jackson. If he is betrayed by those who offer assistance, he will be in a position to defeat their ends and punish them."

You see by this the mind of the President, with which I and every member of the Cabinet who has been consulted are in full accord. You see the difficulties—you see the responsibilities which you assume. We cannot understand why you do not strengthen yourself in the way the President suggests, nor do we see why you do not call the Legislature together, and obtain from them whatever powers, money, and arms you need. The Constitution is explicit that the Executive of the State can call upon the President for aid in suppressing "domestic violence" only "when the Legislature cannot be convened," and the law expressly says: "In case of an insurrection in any State against the Government thereof, it shall be lawful for the President, on application of the Legislature of such State, or of the Executive, when the Legislature cannot be convened, to call," &c. It is the plain meaning of the Constitution and laws when taken together that the Executive of the State may call upon the President for military aid to quell "domestic violence" only in case of an insurrection in any State against the Government thereof when the Legislature cannot be called together. You make no suggestions even that there is any insurrection against the Government of the State, or that the Legislature would not support you in any measures you might propose to preserve the public order. I suggest that you take all lawful means and all needed measures to preserve the peace by the forces in your own State, and let the country see that the citizens of Mississippi, who are largely favorable to good order, and who are largely Republican, have the courage and the manhood to fight for their rights and to destroy the bloody ruffians who murder the innocent and inoffending freedmen. Everything is in readiness. Be careful to bring yourself strictly within the Constitution and the laws, and if there is such resistance to your State authorities as you cannot, by all the means at your command, suppress, the President will swiftly aid you in crushing those lawless traitors to human rights.

Telegraph me on receipt of this, and state explicitly what you need. Very respectfully yours,
EDWARDS PIERREPONT, Attorney General.

(b) Grant's Subsequent Explanation

... I then informed the President that there was another matter about which I desired to have a short talk with him, that was the recent election in Mississippi. After calling his attention to the sanguinary struggle through which we had passed, and the great disadvantages under which we labored, I reminded him of the fact that the Governor, when he saw that he could not put down without the assistance of the National Administration what was practically an insurrection against the State Government, made application for assistance in the manner and form prescribed by the Constitution, with the confident belief that it would be forthcoming. But in this we were, for some reason, seriously disappointed and sadly surprised. The reason for this action, or rather non-action, was still an unexplained mystery to us. For my own satisfaction and information I should be pleased to have the President enlighten me on the subject.

The President said that he was glad I had asked him the question, and that he would take pleasure in giving me a frank reply. He said he had sent Governor Ames' requisition to the War Department with his approval and with instructions to have the necessary assistance furnished without delay. He had also given instructions to the Attorney-General to use the marshals and the machinery of the Federal judiciary as far as possible in coöperation with the War Department in an effort to maintain order and to bring about a condition which would insure a peaceable and fair election. But before the orders were put into execution a committee of prominent Republicans from Ohio had called on him. (Ohio was then an October State,—that is, her elections took place in October instead of November.) An important election was then pending in that State. This committee, the President stated, protested against having the requisition of Governor Ames honored. The committee, the President said, informed him in a most emphatic way that if the requisition of Governor Ames were honored, the Democrats would not only carry Mississippi,—a State which would be lost to the Republicans in any event,—but that Democratic success in Ohio would be an assured fact. If the requisition were not honored it would make no change in the result in Mississippi, but that Ohio would be saved to the Republicans. The President assured me that it was with great reluctance that he yielded,—against his own judgment and sense of official duty,—to the arguments of this committee, and directed the withdrawal of the orders which had been given the Secretary of War and the Attorney-General in that matter.

This statement, I confess, surprised me very much.

"Can it be possible," I asked, "that there is such a prevailing sentiment in any State in the North, East or West as renders it necessary for a Republican President to virtually give his sanction to what is equivalent to a suspension of the Constitution and laws of the land to insure Republican success in such a State? I cannot believe this to be true, the opinion of the Republican committee from Ohio to the contrary notwithstanding. What surprises me more, Mr. President, is that you yielded and granted this remarkable request. That is not like you. It is the first time I have ever known you to show the white feather. Instead of granting the request of that committee, you should have rebuked the men,—told them that it is your duty as chief magistrate of the country to enforce the Constitution and laws of the land, and to protect American citizens in the exercise and enjoyment of their rights, let the consequences be what they may; and that if by doing this Ohio should be lost to the Republicans it ought to be lost. In other words, no victory is worth having if it is to be brought about upon such conditions as those,—if it is to be purchased at such a fearful cost as was paid in this case."

"Yes," said the President, "I admit that you are right. I should not have yielded. I believed at the time that I was making a grave mistake. But as presented, it was duty on one side, and party obligation on the other. Between the two I hesitated, but finally yielded to what was believed to be party obligation. If a mistake was made, it was one of the head and not of the heart. That my heart was right and my intentions good, no one who knows me will question. If I had believed that any effort on my part would have saved Mississippi I would have made it, even if I had been convinced that it would have resulted in the loss of Ohio to the Republicans. But I was satisfied then, as I am now, that Mississippi could not have been saved to the party in any event and I wanted to avoid the responsibility of the loss of Ohio, in addition. This was the turning-point in the case...."

Questions

1. Do you think that Grant was correct in his argument against federal intervention? Was there really nothing that the federal government and the national Republican Party could have done to "save" Mississippi?

2. Had Governor Ames convened the Mississippi legislature to deal with "the bloody ruffians," how successful do you think he would have been?

3. What does Grant's decision illuminate about how Republicans, and many people in the North, had come to view the South and the progress of Reconstruction—especially in the Deep South—by the mid-1870s?

15-11 The Slaughterhouse Cases (1873)

The failure of Reconstruction might be traced to several causes: the readiness of southerners to engage in acts of violence and intimidation (Document 15-2); the unwillingness of the federal government to repel these actions and to intervene on behalf of freed blacks (Document 15-10); the fragmentation of the Republican Party; and the onset of economic depression, which deflected national attention away from the "old" problems of sectionalism and civil rights. But no less important were the actions of the U.S. Supreme Court. Beginning in the 1870s, the Court issued a series of crucial decisions that weakened the Fourteenth Amendment, limiting the legal basis for federal intervention in the South. The decision in the slaughterhouse cases, 1873, was the first and most important of these. In 1869 the Louisiana legislature granted the Crescent City Slaughterhouse Company a monopoly over the butchering business in New Orleans. Butchers not included in the monopoly filed suit, claiming that the monopoly deprived them of their property without due process and violated their rights as citizens under the Fourteenth Amendment. In a 5-to-4 majority decision, the Court ruled against the butchers, all of whom were white, by finding that they had no standing under the provisions of the amendment, whose "main purpose was to establish the citizenship of the negro." It then proceeded to define precisely what rights were protected by the Fourteenth Amendment.

Source: The Butchers' Benevolent Association of New Orleans v. The Crescent City Live-Stock Landing and Slaughter-House Company, 83 U.S. 36 (1873).

Mr. Justice Miller, now April 14th, 1873, delivered the opinion of the court.

The plaintiffs . . . allege that the statute is a violation of the Constitution of the United States in these several particulars:

That it creates an involuntary servitude forbidden by the thirteenth article of amendment;

That it abridges the privileges and immunities of citizens of the United States;

That it denies to the plaintiffs the equal protection of the laws; and,

That it deprives them of their property without due process of law; contrary to the provisions of the first section of the fourteenth article of amendment.

This court is thus called upon for the first time to give construction to these articles.

We do not conceal from ourselves the great responsibility which this duty devolves upon us. No questions so far-reaching and pervading in their consequences, so profoundly interesting to the people of this country, and so important in their bearing upon the relations of the United States, and of the several States to each other and to the citizens of the States and of the United States, have been before this court during the official life of any of its present members....

The first section of the fourteenth article, to which our attention is more specially invited, opens with a definition of citizenship—not only citizenship of the United States, but citizenship of the States. No such definition was previously found in the Constitution, nor had any attempt been made to define it by act of Congress. It had been the occasion of much discussion in the courts, by the executive departments, and in the public journals. It had been said by eminent judges that no man was a citizen of the United States, except as he was a citizen of one of the States composing the Union. Those, therefore, who had been born and resided always in the District of Columbia or in the Territories, though within the United States, were not citizens. Whether this proposition was sound or not had never been judicially decided. But it had been held by this court, in the celebrated Dred Scott case, only a few years before the outbreak of the civil war, that a man of African descent, whether a slave or not, was not and could not be a citizen of a State or of the United States. This decision, while it met the condemnation of some of the ablest statesmen and constitutional lawyers of the country, had never been overruled; and if it was to be accepted as a constitutional limitation of the right of citizenship, then all the negro race who had recently been made freemen, were still, not only not citizens, but were incapable of becoming so by anything short of an amendment to the Constitution.

To remove this difficulty primarily, and to establish a clear and comprehensive definition of citizenship which should declare what should constitute citizenship of the United States, and also citizenship of a State, the first clause of the first section was framed.

"All persons born or naturalized in the United States, and subject to the jurisdiction thereof, are citizens of the United States and of the State wherein they reside."

The first observation we have to make on this clause is, that it puts at rest both the questions which we stated to have been the subject of differences of opinion. It declares that persons may be citizens of the United States without regard to their citizenship of a particular State, and it overturns the Dred Scott decision by making *all persons* born within the United States and subject to its jurisdiction citizens of the United States. That its main purpose was to establish the citizenship of the negro can admit of no doubt. The phase, "subject to its jurisdiction" was intended to exclude from its operation children of ministers, consuls, and citizens or subjects of foreign States born within the United States.

The next observation is more important in view of the arguments of counsel in the present case. It is, that the distinction between citizenship of the United States and citizenship of a State is clearly recognized and established. Not only may a man be a citizen of the United States without being a citizen of a State, but an important element is necessary to convert the former into the latter. He must reside within the State to make him a citizen of it, but it is only necessary that he should be born or naturalized in the United States to be a citizen of the Union.

It is quite clear, then, that there is a citizenship of the United States, and a citizenship of a State, which are distinct from each other, and which depend upon different characteristics or circumstances in the individual.

We think this distinction and its explicit recognition in this amendment of great weight in this argument, because the next paragraph of this same section, which is the one mainly relied on by the plaintiffs in error, speaks only of privileges and immunities of citizens of the United States, and does not speak of those of citizens of the several States. The argument, however, in favor of the plaintiffs rests wholly on the assumption that the citizenship is the same, and the privileges and immunities guaranteed by the clause are the same.

The language is, "No State shall make or enforce any law which shall abridge the privileges or immunities of citizens of *the United States*." It is a little remarkable, if this clause was intended as a protection to the citizen of a State against the legislative power of his own State, that the word citizen of the State should be left out when it is so carefully used, and used in contradistinction to citizens of the United States, in the very sentence which precedes it. It is too clear for argument that the change in phraseology was adopted understandingly and with a purpose.

Of the privileges and immunities of the citizen of the United States, and of the privileges and immunities of the citizen of the State, and what they respectively are, we will presently consider; but we wish to state here that it is only the former which are placed by this clause under the protection of the Federal Constitution, and that the latter, whatever they may be, are not intended to have any additional protection by this paragraph of the amendment.

If, then, there is a difference between the privileges and immunities belonging to a citizen of the United States as such, and those belonging to the citizen of the State as such, the latter must rest for their security and protection where they have heretofore rested; for they are not embraced by this paragraph of the amendment....

The constitutional provision there alluded to did not create those rights, which it called privileges and immunities of citizens of the States. It threw around them in that clause no security for the citizen of the State in which they were claimed or exercised. Nor did it profess to control the power of the State governments over the rights of its own citizens.

Its sole purpose was to declare to the several States, that whatever those rights, as you grant or establish them to your own citizens, or as you limit or qualify, or impose restrictions on their exercise, the same, neither more nor less, shall be the measure of the rights of citizens of other States within your jurisdiction.

It would be the vainest show of learning to attempt to prove by citations of authority, that up to the adoption of the recent amendments, no claim or pretence was set up that those rights depended on the Federal government for their existence or protection, beyond the very few express limitations which the Federal Constitution imposed upon the States — such, for instance, as the prohibition against ex post facto laws, bills of attainder, and laws impairing the obligation of contracts. But with the exception of these and a few other restrictions, the entire domain of the privileges and immunities of citizens of the States, as above defined, lay within the constitutional and legislative power of the States, and without that of the Federal government. Was it the purpose of the fourteenth amendment, by the simple declaration that no State should make or enforce any law which shall abridge the privileges and immunities of *citizens of the United States*, to transfer the security and protection of all the civil rights which we have mentioned, from the States to the Federal government? And where it is declared that Congress shall have the power to enforce that article, was it intended to bring within the power of Congress the entire domain of civil rights heretofore belonging exclusively to the States? . . .

We are convinced that no such results were intended by the Congress which proposed these amendments, nor by the legislatures of the States which ratified them.

Having shown that the privileges and immunities relied on in the argument are those which belong to citizens of the States as such, and that they are left to the State governments for security and protection, and not by this article placed under the special care of the Federal government, we may hold ourselves excused from defining the privileges and immunities of citizens of the United States which no State can abridge, until some case involving those privileges may make it necessary to do so.

But lest it should be said that no such privileges and immunities are to be found if those we have been considering are excluded, we venture to suggest some which owe their existence to the Federal government, its National character, its Constitution, or its laws.

One of these is well described in the case of *Crandall* v. *Nevada*. It is said to be the right of the citizen of this great country, protected by implied guarantees of its Constitution, "to come to the seat of government to assert any claim he may have upon that government, to transact any business he may have with it, to seek its protection, to share its offices, to engage in administering its functions. He has the right of free access to its seaports, through which all operations of foreign commerce are conducted, to the subtreasuries, land offices, and courts of justice in the several States." . . .

Another privilege of a citizen of the United States is to demand the care and protection of the Federal government over his life, liberty, and property when on the high seas or within the jurisdiction of a foreign government. Of this there can be no doubt, nor that the right depends upon his character as a citizen of the United States. The right to peaceably assemble and petition for redress of grievances, the privilege of the writ of *habeas corpus*, are rights of the citizen guaranteed by the Federal Constitution. The right to use the navigable waters of the United States, however they may penetrate the territory of the several States, all rights secured to our citizens by treaties with foreign nations, are dependent upon citizenship of the United States, and not citizenship of a State. One of these privileges is conferred by the very article under consideration. It is that a citizen of the United States can, of his own volition, become a citizen of any State of the Union by a *bonâ fide* residence therein, with the same rights as other citizens of that State. To these may be added the rights secured by the thirteenth and fifteenth articles of amendment, and by the other clause of the fourteenth, next to be considered.

But it is useless to pursue this branch of the inquiry, since we are of opinion that the rights claimed by these plaintiffs in error, if they have any existence, are not privileges and immunities of citizens of the United States within the meaning of the clause of the fourteenth amendment under consideration.

Questions

1. On what basis did the Court rule that the Fourteenth Amendment distinguishes between state and federal citizenship?

2. What sort of rights qualified as the rights of federal citizens? What sort of rights qualified as rights of state citizens? Which set of rights would be more important in the everyday lives of most Americans?

3. Following the reasoning of the Court, to whom were blacks supposed to appeal in cases involving violations of their civil and political rights? Why might this not be in their best interest?

15-12 Susan Myrick Interviews Ex-Slave Catherine Beale (1929)

By the 1890s, as the bitterness of the Civil War was giving way to romantic myths about the Lost Cause and a reconciliationist literature was obligingly promoting the Southern "Redeemers" version of the "evils" of Reconstruction, a distorted image of plantation life began to take hold in the popular imagination. In this absurdly mawkish rendering of life in the Old South, kind masters and faithful slaves united to create an idyllic world. That world had disappeared with the defeat of the Confederacy, its promoters suggested, but not altogether. Survivors were still around, including former slaves. Partly out of a misdirected sense of nostalgia, then, but also in pursuit of human interest stories, newspapers and magazines between 1890 and 1940 featured interviews with former slaves. Often conducted with great skill by professional journalists, these interviews have since constituted a valuable source of information for historians seeking to complement white eyewitness accounts with those derived from the slaves themselves. The following interview first appeared in the Macon (Georgia) *Telegraph*, February 10, 1929.

Source: Excerpt from *Slave Testimony: Two Centuries of Letters, Speeches, Interviews, and Autobiographies*, ed. John W. Blasingame (Baton Rouge: Louisiana State University Press, 1977), 574–578. Used by permission of the publisher.

Aunt Catherine speaks in a high, rather shrill voice which paradoxically enough is soft. Except when she tries to walk, this voice is the main indication of her years, though her hair is snowy white and that is a pretty good sign of age in one of her race, for the Negro is not apt to grow gray, as is the white person. Her face is remarkably free from wrinkles and her mind is clear. She does not use the ordinary Negro dialect which is commonly found in old Negroes in general, speaks with pretty good English, occasionally relapsing into careless speech, but in the main only dropping her R's and G's as the average Southerner. . . .

"Do you remember about being sold as a slave?"

"Yessum, me an' my sister was brought from Virginia and sold here when I was eleven an' Miss Leila was one year old. I remember living with my mother and papa and my sister with a Mistuh Goode in Virginia. We belonged to them, they had a heap er Niggers. Mistuh Goode had a wife named Miss Annie and a sister named Miss Kate. Ole Master, he died an after he was buried a few weeks, Miss Kate took me and my sister out on the back steps and tol' us we would have to be sold. She said she hated it because she had to sell us and take us away from our mother and family but there wasn't any money an' they had to have some from some place and they had decided to sell us.

"She took us to Richmond an' sold us to a slave buyer an' he brought us to Macon. There was a whole drove of Niggers; the slave buyer brought us in droves like horses an' cows. . . .

There was in her patient old voice no hint of animosity toward the slave driver or the world in general for her hardships. She was merely reciting facts as she recalled them, with as impersonal [a] manner as if the people had been some others and she were not concerned at all with the affair.

"Do you remember being put on the block and sold when you arrived in Macon?" I shuddered a little at the words, thinking (even though I am Southern for many generations and my father was a Confederate soldier), how horrible it seemed that human beings had been bought and sold as cattle and horses, and wondering if it could be true that I was actually talking to one, seemingly so gentle and peaceful now, who had undergone this ordeal.

"Yessum, I was sold to Mistuh Joe Blackshear from Twiggs an' I lived with them most all the rest of my life. He was living at Oak Ridge then, close to what they called Fitzpatrick, when he bought me, but he moved to a place about two miles from Bullard Station."

"Do you remember much about the War? You must have been old enough to recall it?"

"Yessum, I was grown woman befo's I ever heard tell of the war. I didn't know much about it then. I know Mr. Tom Blackshear, he went to the Wah an' he got shot. But out on the plantation, we didn't know nothing about what was going on."

"But when Sherman's army came through, didn't they burn things and drive off horses and cows?" I insisted.

"No'm they didn't do no burnin' nor nothing like that at our house. You know where Ol' Marion wuz?"

I nodded, for I recalled hearing that Marion was at one time the county seat of Twiggs and that it was in what is now Pulaski county and not very far from Hawkinsville.

"Wellum, they dont a heap of burnin' over there an' er heap of damage, I hear em say. But they didn't hurt nuthin' at our place."

"Did they tell you were free?"

"Yessum, but we didn't know no difference. We stayed on with Ole Marster. Old Mistis was good to us an' we didn't have no where to go if we had er left. Ole Marster was sort er crabbed but he wasn't never mean an' there wasn't no slaves whipped on that place. I hear tell that fokes that had overseers, they would whup the niggers. But there aint no scar on me. All my bones is whole! I aint never been drove to work, I jest went myself. I never was treated mean. I can set up nights and think and I say to myself, 'Thank God! Thankee Jesus! I had a good life!'"

"Did you come to Macon with the Blackshears, Aunt Catherine?"

"Yessum, I lived with them most all my life. Old Marster's oldest son Dr. James Emmett Blackshear, he was a medicine doctor, he come to Macon. Old Mistis had six children. Albert come first an then James Emmett an I think the next one was Henry and then Tom and William[,] Miss Leila come in there some where, I forgot which one she was next to. Mr. Tom he come to Macon and took pictures here for a long time."

Many of Macon's oldest inhabitants will recall T. B. Blackshear, who was a photographer here for many years, with a studio at No. 13 Cotton avenue. . . .

"Who else did you work for in Macon?"

"I worked for Mrs. Cabiness a long time, I went there when Miss Emmie wasn't no moren so high (she raised her hand to indicate a girl of ten or eleven years and went on) I helped raise Mr. Emory Cabiness, he called me Mammy and I sho loved that chile. Many's the time I been down to the school ter git him an it would be raining an he would say, 'Here, Mammy, you take the umbrella, I can run fast and not get wet.'" . . .

"Aunt Catherine, can you remember anything about the plantation in Virginia, what games you played and how you worked and what you did? . . .

"No'm, I don't remember nuthin about games. We never did play none. We had taskes to do. We had little patches of cotton then an' the[re] wasn't no gins like the[re] was after the Wah, and we had to work in the field in the day an' at night we had to pick out the seed fo' we went to bed. An' we had to clean the wool, we had to pick the burrs an' sticks out so it would be clean an' could be carded an' spun an' wove. We had to spin our own thread then an' make our own cloth too. We had the geeses to drive in the barn an' pick."

She sighed a little at the recollection and said, "Them feather mattresses was the nicest! Not like these things fokes sleep on now!

Questions

1. Before using any bit of information as evidence, historians must answer questions pertaining to the reliability of the source from whence it came and the circumstances under which it was generated. How reliable is the information conveyed by Catherine Beale? Is the fact that the interview was conducted nearly sixty-five years after her emancipation significant?

2. What can you say about Susan Myrick, the interviewer? Do her editorial comments reveal anything about her? What was her family background? Is Myrick's background relevant in determining the reliability of the information she got from Catherine Beale?

3. Catherine Beale moved to Macon as a slave and was still living there at the time of the interview. Many of the descendants of her former master were also living in Macon. How might this circumstance have affected the answers she gave to Susan Myrick, the reporter for the *Telegraph*?

Questions for Further Thought

1. Compare and contrast northern and southern views of blacks (Documents 15-9a, 15-9b, and 15-12. How were they the same? How were they different? What impact did the northern view of blacks have on the progress of Reconstruction?

2. If the Republican Party had pressed ahead with Reconstruction, do you think that it could have achieved its goals?

3. According to the Supreme Court's decision in the slaughterhouse cases (Document 15-11), did the president have the authority to intervene in Mississippi (Document 15-10)? Does this justify his failure to intervene? Explain.

PART FOUR *A Maturing Industrial Society, 1877–1914*

CHAPTER SIXTEEN

The American West

The Great Plains

According to historian Walter Prescott Webb, the Great Plains environment possessed three distinguishing characteristics: (1) it was comparatively flat; (2) it was treeless; and (3) it was a "region where rainfall is insufficient for the ordinary intensive agriculture common to lands of a humid climate." Nevertheless, in the years following the Civil War, large numbers of ranchers, farmers, and miners poured onto the Great Plains. They rapidly transformed the Plains environment by replacing the native buffalo and wildlife with cattle and livestock, by plowing up the native grasses to plant wheat and other crops, and by mining for gold in the Black Hills. At the same time, the original inhabitants were forced off their lands and onto reservations. To be sure, native peoples put up an armed and heroic resistance. One of the most famous of these instances was the Battle of the Little Bighorn River on June 25, 1876, otherwise known as "Custer's Last Stand" (Document 16-1). However, by 1890 these patriots were vanquished by the vastly superior military force that the U.S. government sent against them.

As America industrialized, built great cities, attracted millions of immigrants, and became a world power, a new generation of pioneer farmers tried to settle the Great Plains. It was incredibly hard and heartbreaking work. Some succeeded; others failed. The Plains environment posed unusually tough new challenges for the region's farmers. The solution, which took decades to work out, was complex and involved new technologies, new farming techniques, irrigation, new laws and public policies, as well as numerous other adjustments, including abandoning certain lands altogether, and ultimately, and critically, generous government subsidies. But in the 1870s and 1880s, farmers like Howard Ruede (Document 16-5) were very much on their own. And their collective experience eventually produced such widespread agrarian discontent that it gave rise to a remarkable third-party movement known as the Populist Party. In a sense, this story of success and failure has repeated itself again and again, most dramatically during the Dust Bowl years, but also in more recent times. Indeed, along the western and more arid half of the grasslands, population continues to shift and decline, leading some contemporary commentators to wonder whether settlement here on the western plains had not, after all, been a huge and costly mistake.

In Document 16-1, the *Helena Daily Herald* reports the sensational story of George Custer's controversial attack on a large Indian encampment in Montana Territory and the annihilation of the men in his detachment. Helen Hunt Jackson criticizes the failure of the U.S. government to keep its promises to Native Americans (Document 16-2). In 1887,

Congress tried to deal with the plight of Native Americans through the Dawes Severalty Act (Document 16-3). In Document 16-4, Buffalo Bird Woman looks back on a way of life prior to her removal to the reservation. In Document 16-5, Howard Ruede, a young Kansas homesteader, in a letter home to Pennsylvania, describes a typical week on the frontier. John Wesley Powell reports (Document 16-6) to Congress on the arid character of the American West. And William E. Smythe expounds on the "miracle of irrigation" in Document 16-7.

16-1 Custer's Last Stand, *Helena Daily Herald* (July 4, 1876)

In July 1876, the United States was proudly celebrating its centennial as a capitalistic, democratic, and Christian nation, one which had fought to preserve the union, abolish slavery, and open the West to the settlement of free men and women. The nation was in a high mood and success and progress were its watchwords. Thus, the American public was shocked and angered at the news of a U.S. military defeat by Native American tribes out on the high plains. In hindsight, the decision of George Armstrong Custer, a commanding officer in the Seventh Cavalry who had distinguished himself during the Civil War, to attack a village of 6,000 to 7,000 people, including many experienced warriors, in the valley of the Little Bighorn, seems rash and foolhardy. Outnumbered, Custer and his men were quickly surrounded and annihilated. Two hundred sixty-three of the 7th Cavalrymen were killed; 350 survived. It was a great victory for the Plains Indians, a bright spot on what was otherwise a long road of loss and decline. Ever since that June day under the Montana sun, Custer's "Last Stand" has been the subject of controversy. At times, the dashing blond-haired Custer has been portrayed as a tragic hero; at other times, as vainglorious and blinded by his own ambitions. How Native Americans have been portrayed has also sharply changed with the times. Andrew Fisk, the editor of the *Helena Daily Herald*, a Montana newspaper, reported Custer's defeat in emotionally charged language late on July 4th. He then flashed the news to the rest of the nation.

Source: Colonel W. A. Graham, *The Custer Myth: A Source Book of Custeriana* (New York: Bonanza Books, 1953), 350–351.

HELENA DAILY HERALD
EXTRA

July 4, 1876

A TERRIBLE FIGHT

Gen. Custer and his Nephew

KILLED

The Seventh Cavalry cut to pieces

The Whole Number Killed 315

---

*From our Special Correspondent
Mr. W. H. Norton*

Stillwater, M. T.,
July 2nd, 1876.

Muggins Taylor, scout for Gen. Gibbons, got here last night, direct from Little Horn River with telegraphic despatches. General Custer found the Indian camp of about two thousand lodges on the Little Horn, and immediately attacked the camp. Custer took five companies and charged the thickest portion of the camp.

Nothing is Known of the Operation

of this detachment, only as they trace it by the dead. Major Reno commanded the other seven companies and attacked the lower portion of the camp. The Indians poured in a murderous fire from all directions. Besides the greater portion fought on horseback. Custer, his two brothers, a nephew and a brother-in-law were

All Killed

and not one of his detachment escaped, 207 men were buried in one place and the killed are estimated at 300 with only 31 wounded. The Indians surrounded Reno's command and held them one day in the hills

Cut Off from Water

until Gibbons's command came in sight, when they broke camp in the night and left.

The Seventh Fought Like Tigers

and were overcome by mere brute force. The Indian loss cannot be estimated, as they bore off and cached most of their killed. The remnant of the Seventh Cavalry and Gibbon's command are returning to the mouth of the Little Horn, where the steamboat lies. The Indians got all the arms of the killed soldiers. There were seventeen commissioned officers killed.

The Whole Custer Family

died at the head of their column. The exact loss is not known as both Adjutants and the Sergeant Major were killed. The Indian camp was from three to four miles along and was twenty miles up the Little Horn from its mouth. The Indians actually pulled men off their horses in some instances. I give this as Taylor told me, as he was over the field after the battle.

The above is confirmed by other letters which say Custer met a fearful disaster.

The next day, the *Herald* followed its July fourth Extra with a short editorial which read:

HELENA DAILY HERALD

Wednesday, July 5, 1876

EDITORIAL

The news received last evening of the defeat of Custer and the massacre of his entire command, fell upon the festivities of the day with a gloom that could not be shaken off. There is only too much reason to believe that the facts given in the extras of last evening are literally true. The parties from whom the facts were received are too well known to leave a reasonable doubt.

Questions

1. What underlying assumptions and values are made explicit here about U.S. and Native American fighting men?
2. What effect was the story intended to have on readers?

16-2 *A Century of Dishonor* (1881)

Helen Hunt Jackson

Born in Amherst, Massachusetts, Helen Hunt Jackson (1830–1885) was raised in the New England moral climate that nurtured the abolitionist and woman suffrage movements of the mid-nineteenth century. However, this childhood friend of Emily Dickinson showed no interest in reform causes until her second marriage and her move to Colorado in 1875. Ironically, it was during a trip to Boston in 1879 that Jackson heard the Ponca chief Standing Bear speak on the plight of the Plains Indians.

The incident served as a conversion experience, and Jackson began making herself an expert on the history of relations between the government and Native Americans. Within two years she published *A Century of Dishonor*. Not all readers were pleased with Jackson's condemnation of the government for its mistreatment of Native Americans. Because the book was "written in good English" by an author "intensely in earnest," Theodore Roosevelt feared that it was "capable of doing great harm."

Source: Excerpt from Helen Hunt Jackson, *A Century of Dishonor* (New York: Harper and Brothers, 1881; reprint, New York: Harper and Row, 1965), 338–342.

In 1869 President Grant appointed a commission of nine men, representing the influence and philanthropy of six leading States, to visit the different Indian reservations, and to "examine all matters appertaining to Indian affairs."

In the report of this commission are such paragraphs as the following: "To assert that 'the Indian will not work' is as true as it would be to say that the white man will not work.

"Why should the Indian be expected to plant corn, fence lands, build houses, or do anything but get food from day to day, when experience has taught him that the product of his labor will be seized by the white man to-morrow? The most industrious white man would become a drone under similar circumstances. Nevertheless, many of the Indians" (the commissioners might more forcibly have said 130,000 of the

Indians) "are already at work, and furnish ample refutation of the assertion that 'the Indian will not work.' There is no escape from the inexorable logic of facts.

"The history of the Government connections with the Indians is a shameful record of broken treaties and unfulfilled promises. The history of the border white man's connection with the Indians is a sickening record of murder, outrage, robbery, and wrongs committed by the former, as the rule, and occasional savage outbreaks and unspeakably barbarous deeds of retaliation by the latter, as the exception.

"Taught by the Government that they had rights entitled to respect, when those rights have been assailed by the rapacity of the white man, the arm which should have been raised to protect them has ever been ready to sustain the aggressor.

"The testimony of some of the highest military officers of the United States is on record to the effect that, in our Indian wars, almost without exception, the first aggressions have been made by the white man; and the assertion is supported by every civilian of reputation who has studied the subject. In addition to the class of robbers and outlaws who find impunity in their nefarious pursuits on the frontiers, there is a large class of professedly reputable men who use every means in their power to bring on Indian wars for the sake of the profit to be realized from the presence of troops and the expenditure of Government funds in their midst. They proclaim death to the Indians at all times in words and publications, making no distinction between the innocent and the guilty. They irate the lowest class of men to the perpetration of the darkest deeds against their victims, and as judges and jurymen shield them from the justice due to their crimes. Every crime committed by a white man against an Indian is concealed or palliated. Every offence committed by an Indian against a white man is borne on the wings of the post or the telegraph to the remotest corner of the land, clothed with all the horrors which the reality or imagination can throw around it. Against such influences as these the people of the United States need to be warned."

To assume that it would be easy, or by any one sudden stroke of legislative policy possible, to undo the mischief and hurt of the long past, set the Indian policy of the country right for the future, and make the Indians at once safe and happy, is the blunder of a hasty and uninformed judgment. The notion which seems to be growing more prevalent, that simply to make all Indians at once citizens of the United States would be a sovereign and instantaneous panacea for all their ills and all the Government's perplexities, is a very inconsiderate one. To administer complete citizenship of a sudden, all round, to all Indians, barbarous and civilized alike, would be as grotesque a blunder as to dose them all round with any one medicine, irrespective of the symptoms and needs of their diseases. It would kill more than it would cure. Nevertheless, it is true, as was well stated by one of the superintendents of Indian Affairs in 1857, that, "so long as they are not citizens of the United States, their rights of property must remain insecure against invasion. The doors of the federal tribunals being barred against them while wards and dependents, they can only partially exercise the rights of free government, or give to those who make, execute, and construe the few laws they are allowed to enact, dignity sufficient to make them respectable. While they continue individually to gather the crumbs that fall from the table of the United States, idleness, improvidence, and indebtedness will be the rule, and industry, thrift, and freedom from debt the exception. The utter absence of individual title to particular lands deprives every one among them of the chief incentive to labor and exertion—the very mainspring on which the prosperity of a people depends."

All judicious plans and measures for their safety and salvation must embody provisions for their becoming citizens as fast as they are fit, and must protect them till then in every right and particular in which our laws protect other "persons" who are not citizens.

There is a disposition in a certain class of minds to be impatient with any protestation against wrong which is unaccompanied or unprepared with a quick and exact scheme of remedy. This is illogical. When pioneers in a new country find a tract of poisonous and swampy wilderness to be reclaimed, they do not withhold their hands from fire and axe till they see clearly which way roads should run, where good water will spring, and what crops will best grow on the redeemed land. They first clear the swamp. So with this poisonous and baffling part of the domain of our national affairs—let us first "clear the swamp."

However great perplexity and difficulty there may be in the details of any and every plan possible for doing at this late day anything like justice to the Indian, however hard it may be for good statesmen and good men to agree upon the things that ought to be done, there certainly is, or ought to be, no perplexity whatever, no difficulty whatever, in agreeing upon certain things that ought not to be done, and which must cease to be done before the first steps can be taken toward righting the wrongs, curing the ills, and wiping out the disgrace to us of the present condition of our Indians.

Cheating, robbing, breaking promises—these three are clearly things which must cease to be done. One more thing, also, and that is the refusal of the protection of the law to the Indian's rights of property, "of life, liberty, and the pursuit of happiness."

When these four things have ceased to be done, time, statesmanship, philanthropy, and Christianity can slowly and surely do the rest. Till these four things have ceased to be done, statesmanship and philanthropy alike must work in vain, and even Christianity can reap but small harvest.

Questions

1. Why didn't official reports that were critical of U.S. government policy toward Native Americans have a greater effect on the American public?

2. What was the importance of granting citizenship to Native Americans? What problems with granting citizenship does Jackson see?
3. What was Jackson's prescription for improved relations with Native Americans?

16-3 The Dawes Severalty Act (1887)

Congress responded to Helen Hunt Jackson and other critics of its Native American policy with the Dawes Severalty Act of 1887. The act attempted to "mainstream" Indians into American society: reservations were to be abolished, and Native Americans were to be given land. The act accomplished little beyond reducing the amount of land under Native American control, and the reservation policy was revived in the 1930s.

Source: United States, *Statutes at Large*, 24:388 ff.

Be it enacted by the Senate and House of Representatives of the United States of America in Congress assembled, That in all cases where any tribe or band of Indians has been, or shall hereafter be, located upon any reservation created for their use, either by treaty stipulation or by virtue of an act of Congress or executive order setting apart the same for their use, the President of the United States be, and he hereby is, authorized, whenever in his opinion any reservation or any part thereof of such Indians is advantageous for agricultural and grazing purposes, to cause said reservation, or any part thereof, to be surveyed, or resurveyed if necessary, and to allot the lands in said reservation in severalty to any Indian located thereon in quantities as follows:

To each head of a family, one-quarter of a section;

To each single person over eighteen years of age, one-eighth of a section;

To each orphan child under eighteen years of age, one-eighth of a section; and

To each other single person under eighteen years now living, or who may be born prior to the date of the order of the President directing an allotment of the lands embraced in any reservation, one-sixteenth of a section: *Provided*, That in case there is not sufficient land in any of said reservations to allot lands to each individual of the classes above named in quantities as above provided, the lands embraced in such reservation or reservations shall be allotted to each individual of each of said classes pro rata in accordance with the provisions of this act: *And provided further*, That where the treaty or act of Congress setting apart such reservation provides for the allotment of lands in severalty in quantities in excess of those herein provided, the President, in making allotments upon such reservation, shall allot the lands to each individual Indian belonging thereon in quantity as specified in such treaty or act: *And provided further*, That when the lands allotted are only valuable for grazing purposes, an additional allotment of such grazing lands, in quantities as above provided, shall be made to each individual. . . .

And provided further, That at any time after lands have been allotted to all the Indians of any tribe as herein provided, or sooner if in the opinion of the President it shall be for the best interests of said tribe, it shall be lawful for the Secretary of the Interior to negotiate with such Indian tribe for the purchase and release by said tribe, in conformity with the treaty or statute under which such reservation is held, of such portions of its reservation not allotted as such tribe shall, from time to time, consent to sell, on such terms and conditions as shall be considered just and equitable between the United States and said tribe of Indians, which purchase shall not be complete until ratified by Congress, and the form and manner of executing such release shall also be prescribed by Congress: *Provided however*, That all lands adapted to agriculture, with or without irrigation so sold or released to the United States by any Indian tribe shall be held by the United States for the sole purpose of securing homes to actual settlers and shall be disposed of by the United States to actual and bona fide settlers only in tracts not exceeding one hundred and sixty acres to any one person, on such terms as Congress shall prescribe, subject to grants which Congress may make in aid of education: *And provided further*, That no patents shall issue therefor except to the person so taking the same as and for a homestead, or his heirs, and after the expiration of five years occupancy thereof as such homestead; and any conveyance of said lands so taken as a homestead, or any contract touching the same, or lien thereon, created prior to the date of such patent, shall be null and void. And the sums agreed to be paid by the United States as purchase money for any portion of any such reservation shall be held in the Treasury of the United States for the sole use of the tribe or tribes of Indians; to whom such reservations belonged; and the same, with interest thereon at three per cent per annum, shall be at all times subject to appropriation by Congress for the education and civilization of such tribe or tribes of Indians or the members thereof. . . . And hereafter in the employment of Indian police, or any other employees in the public service among any of the Indian tribes or bands affected by this act, and where Indians can perform the duties required, those Indians who have availed themselves of the provisions of this act and become citizens of the United States shall be preferred.

SEC. 6. That upon the completion of said allotments and the patenting of the lands to said allottees, each and every member of the respective bands or tribes of Indians to whom allotments have been made shall have the benefit of and be subject to the laws, both civil and criminal, of the State or Territory in which they may reside; and no Territory shall pass or enforce any law denying any such Indian within its jurisdiction the equal protection of the law. And every Indian born within the territorial limits of the United States to whom allotments shall have been made under the provisions of this act, or under any law or treaty, and every Indian born within the territorial limits of the United States who has voluntarily taken up, within said limits, his residence separate and apart from any tribe of Indians therein, and has adopted the habits of civilized life, is hereby declared to be a citizen of the United States, and is entitled to all the rights, privileges, and immunities of such citizens, whether said Indian has been or not, by birth or otherwise, a member of any tribe of Indians within the territorial limits of the United States without in any manner impairing or otherwise affecting the right of any such Indian to tribal or other property.

Questions

1. What was the stated purpose of this act?
2. Why did Congress offer citizenship to Native Americans?
3. To what extent was the Dawes Act coercive?

16-4 Beginning a Garden (1917)

Buffalo Bird Woman

Buffalo Bird Woman (Max'diwiac) was born in 1839 in the Hidatsa village of Sakakawea, situated on the Knife River in what is today western North Dakota. The Hidatsas, along with the Mandans and the Arikaras, developed a successful agricultural village in the middle Missouri basin that dated back centuries before Anglos arrived on the Great Plains. By the nineteenth century, however, this ancient way of life was endangered by an inexorably expanding American civilization. In 1912, long after being removed to the Fort Berthold Indian Reservation in North Dakota, Buffalo Bird Woman, at the age of seventy-three, was sought out by Gilbert L. Wilson, an anthropologist and student of "primitive agriculture." Wilson chose to interview her because, according to his sources, she was "a conservative and sighs for the good old times," had "quick intelligence and a memory that is marvelous," and knew "more about old ways of raising corn and squashes than any one else" on the reservation.

Source: Gilbert L. Wilson, "Beginning a Garden" from *Buffalo Bird Woman's Garden: Agriculture of the Hidatsa Indians* (1917; St. Paul: Minnesota Historical Society Press, 1987), 9–15. Copyright © 1987 by the Minnesota Historical Society. Reprinted by permission of the Minnesota Historical Society Press.

TURTLE

My great-grandmother, as white men count their kin, was named Ata'kic, or Soft-white Corn. She adopted a daughter, Mata'tic, or Turtle. Some years after, a daughter was born to Ata'kic, whom she named Otter.

Turtle and Otter both married. Turtle had a daughter named Ica'wikec, or Corn Sucker;[1] and Otter had three daughters, Want-to-be-a-woman, Red Blossom, and Strikes-many-women, all younger than Corn Sucker.

The smallpox year at Five Villages left Otter's family with no male members to support them. Turtle and her daughter were then living in Otter's lodge; and Otter's daughters, as Indian custom bade, called Corn Sucker their elder sister.

It was a custom of the Hidatsas, that if the eldest sister of a household married, her younger sisters were also given to her husband, as they came of marriageable age. Left without male kin by the smallpox, my grandmother's family was hard put to it to get meat; and Turtle gladly gave her daughter to my father, Small Ankle, whom she knew to be a good hunter. Otter's daughters, reckoned as Corn Sucker's sisters, were

---
[1] Corn sucker, i.e., the extra shoot or stem that often springs up from the base of the maize plant. [*Wilson's note.*]

given to Small Ankle as they grew up; the eldest, Want-to-be-a-woman, was my mother.

When I was four years old, my tribe and the Mandans came to Like-a-fishhook bend. They came in the spring and camped in tepees, or skin tents. By Butterfly's winter count, I know they began building earth lodges the next winter. I was too young to remember much of this.

Two years after we came to Like-a-fishhook bend, smallpox again visited my tribe; and my mother, Want-to-be-a-woman, and Corn Sucker, died of it. Red Blossom and Strikes-many-women survived, whom I now called my mothers. Otter and old Turtle lived with us; I was taught to call them my grandmothers.

CLEARING FIELDS

Soon after they came to Like-a-fishhook bend, the families of my tribe began to clear fields, for gardens, like those they had at Five Villages. Rich black soil was to be found in the timbered bottom lands of the Missouri. Most of the work of clearing was done by the women.

In old times we Hidatsas never made our gardens on the untimbered, prairie land, because the soil there is too hard and dry. In the bottom lands by the Missouri, the soil is soft and easy to work.

My mothers and my two grandmothers worked at clearing our family's garden. It lay east of the village at a place where many other families were clearing fields.

I was too small to note very much at first. But I remember that my father set boundary marks—whether wooden stakes or little mounds of earth or stones, I do not now remember—at the corners of the field we claimed. My mothers and my two grandmothers began at one end of this field and worked forward. All had heavy iron hoes, except Turtle, who used an old fashioned wooden digging stick.

With their hoes, my mothers cut the long grass that covered much of the field, and bore it off the line, to be burned. With the same implements, they next dug and softened the soil in places for the corn hills, which were laid off in rows. These hills they planted. Then all summer they worked with their hoes, clearing and breaking the ground between the hills.

Trees and bushes I know must have been cut off with iron axes; but I remember little of this, because I was only four years old when the clearing was begun.

I have heard that in very old times, when clearing a new field, my people first dug the corn hills with digging sticks; and afterwards, like my mothers, worked between the hills, with bone hoes. My father told me this.

Whether stone axes were used in old times to cut the trees and undergrowths, I do not know. I think fields were never then laid out on ground that had large trees on it.

DISPUTE AND ITS SETTLEMENT

About two years after the first ground was broken in our field, a dispute I remember, arose between my mothers and two of their neighbors, Lone Woman and Goes-to-next-timber.

These two women were clearing fields adjoining that of my mothers; the three fields met at a corner. I have said that my father, to set up claim to his field, had placed marks, one of them in the corner at which met the fields of Lone Woman and Goes-to-next-timber; but while my mothers were busy clearing and digging up the other end of their field, their two neighbors invaded this marked-off corner; Lone Woman had even dug up a small part before she was discovered.

However, when they were shown the mark my father had placed, the two women yielded and accepted payment for any rights they might have.

It was our Indian rule to keep our fields very sacred. We did not like to quarrel about our garden lands. One's title to a field once set up, no one every thought of disputing it; for if one were selfish and quarrelsome, and tried to seize land belonging to another, we thought some evil would come upon him, as that some one of his family would die. There is a story of a black bear who got into a pit that was not his own, and had his mind taken away from him for doing so!

TURTLE BREAKING SOIL

Lone Woman and Goes-to-next-timber having withdrawn, my grandmother, Turtle, volunteered to break the soil of the corner that had been in dispute. She was an industrious woman. Often, when my mothers were busy in the earth lodge, she would go out to work in the garden, taking me with her for company. I was six years old then, I think, quite too little to help her any, but I liked to watch my grandmother work.

With her digging stick, she dug up a little round place in the center of the corner; and circling around this from day to day, she gradually enlarged the dug-up space. The point of her digging stick she forced into the soft earth to a depth equal to the length of my hand, and pried up the soil. The clods she struck smartly with her digging stick, sometimes with one end, sometimes with the other. Roots of coarse grass, weeds, small brush and the like, she took in her hand and shook, or struck them against the ground, to knock off the loose earth clinging to them; she then cast them into a little pile to dry.

In this way she accumulated little piles, scattered rather irregularly over the dug-up ground, averaging, perhaps, four feet, one from the other. In a few days these little piles had dried; and Turtle gathered them up into a heap, about four feet high, and burned them, sometimes within the cleared ground, sometimes a little way outside.

In the corner that had been in dispute, and in other parts of the field, my grandmother worked all summer. I do not remember how big our garden was at the end of her summer's work, nor how many piles of roots she burned; but I remember distinctly how she put the roots of weeds and grass and brush into little piles to dry, which she then gathered into heaps and burned. She did not attempt to burn over the whole ground, only the heaps.

Afterwards, we increased our garden from year to year until it was as large as we needed. I remember seeing my grandmother digging along the edges of the garden with her digging stick, to enlarge the field and make the edges even and straight.

I remember also, that as Turtle dug up a little space, she would wait until the next season to plant it. Thus, additional ground dug up in the summer or fall would be planted by her the next spring.

There were two or three elm trees in the garden; these my grandmother left standing.

It must not be supposed that upon Turtle fell all the work of clearing land to enlarge our garden; but she liked to have me with her when she worked, and I remember best what I saw her do. As I was a little girl then, I have forgotten much that she did; but this that I have told, I remember distinctly.

TURTLE'S PRIMITIVE TOOLS

In breaking ground for our garden, Turtle always used an ash digging stick; and when hoeing time came, she hoed the corn with a bone hoe. Digging sticks are still used in my tribe for digging wild turnips; but even in my grandmother's lifetime, digging sticks and bone hoes, as garden tools, had all but given place to iron hoes and axes.

My grandmother was one of the last women of my tribe to cling to these old fashioned implements. Two other women, I remember, owned bone hoes when I was a little girl; but Turtle, I think, was the very last one in the tribe who actually worked in her garden with one.

This hoe my grandmother kept in the lodge, under her bed; and when any of the children of the household tried to get it out to look at it, she would cry, "Let that hoe alone; you will break it!"

BEGINNING A FIELD IN LATER TIMES

As I grew up, I learned to work in the garden, as every Hidatsa woman was expected to learn; but iron axes and hoes, bought of the traders, were now used by everybody, and the work of clearing and breaking a new field was less difficult than it had been in our grandfathers' times. A family had also greater freedom in choosing where they should have their garden, since with iron axes they could more easily cut down any small trees and bushes that might be on the land. However, to avoid having to cut down big trees, a rather open place was usually chosen.

A family, then, having chosen a place for a field, cleared off the ground as much as they could, cutting down small trees and bushes in such way that the trees fell all in one direction. Some of the timber that was fit might be taken home for firewood; the rest was let lie to dry until spring, when it was fired. The object of felling the trees in one direction was to make them cover the ground as much as possible, since firing them softened the soil and left it loose and mellow for planting. We sought always to burn over all the ground, if we could.

Before firing, the family carefully raked off the dry grass and leaves from the edge of the field, and cut down any brush wood. This was done that the fire might not spread to the surrounding timber, nor out on the prairie. Prairie fires and forest fires are even yet not unknown on our reservation.

Planting season having come, the women of the household planted the field in corn. The hills were in rows, and about four feet or a little less apart. They were rather irregularly placed the first year. It was easy to make a hill in the ashes where a brush heap had been fired, or in soil that was free of roots and stumps; but there were many stumps in the field, left over from the previous summer's clearing. If the planter found a stump stood where a hill should be, she placed the hill on this side the stump or beyond it, no matter how close this brought the hill to the next in the row. Thus, the corn hills did not stand at even distances in the row the first year; but the rows were always kept even and straight.

While the corn was coming up, the women worked at clearing out the roots and smaller stumps between the hills; but a stump of any considerable size was left to rot, especially if it stood midway between two corn hills, where it did not interfere with their cultivation.

My mothers and I used to labor in a similar way to enlarge our fields. With our iron hoes we made hills along the edge of the field and planted corn; then, as we had opportunity, we worked with our hoes between the corn hills to loosen up the soil.

Although our tribe now had iron axes and hoes from the traders, they still used their native made rakes. These were of wood or of the antler of a black-tailed deer. It was with such rakes that the edges of a newly opened field were cleaned of leaves for the firing of the brush, in the spring.

TREES IN THE GARDEN

Trees were not left standing in the garden, except perhaps one to shade the watchers' stage. If a tree stood in the field, it shaded the corn; and that on the north side of the tree never grew up strong, and the stalks would be yellow.

Cottonwood trees were apt to grow up in the field, unless the young shoots were plucked up as they appeared.

OUR WEST FIELD

The field which Turtle helped to clear, lay, I have said, east of the village. I was about nineteen years old, I think, when my mothers determined to clear ground for a second field, west of the village.

There were five of us who undertook the work, my father, my two mothers, Red Blossom and Strikes-many-women, my sister, Cold Medicine, and myself. We began in the fall, after harvesting the corn from our east garden, so that we had leisure for the work; we had been too busy to begin earlier in the season.

We chose a place down in the bottoms, overgrown with willows; and with our axes we cut the willows close to the ground, letting them lie as they fell.

I do not know how many days we worked; but we stopped when we had cleared a field of about seventy-five by one hundred yards, perhaps. In our east, or yellow corn field, we counted nine rows of corn to one *na'xu*; and I remember that when we came to plant our new field, it had nine *na'xu*.

BURNING OVER THE FIELD

The next spring my father, his two wives, my sister and I went out and burned the felled willows and brush which the spring sun had dried. We did not burn them every day; only when the weather was fine. We would go out after breakfast, burn until tired of the work, and come home.

We sought to burn over the whole field, for we knew that this left a good, loose soil. We did not pile the willows in heaps, but loosened them from the ground or scattered them loosely but evenly over the soil. In some places the ground was quite bare of willows; but we collected dry grass and weeds and dead willows, and strewed them over these bare places, so that the fire would run over the whole area of the field.

It took us about four days to burn over the field.

It was well known in my tribe that burning over new ground left the soil soft and easy to work, and for this reason we thought it a wise thing to do.

Questions

1. Compare the Hidatsas' knowledge of agriculture to that of the white settlers (see text pp. 495–498).
2. How did moving to a reservation change Buffalo Bird Woman's way of life?
3. What does Buffalo Bird Woman's gardening say about the Hidatsa culture's relationship with nature?

16-5 Letter from a Kansas Homesteader (1878)

Howard Ruede

In March 1877, at the age of twenty-three, Howard Ruede of Bethlehem, Pennsylvania, arrived in Osborne County, located in central western Kansas. Ruede, a printer by trade, eventually settled on a site near Kill Creek, a tributary of the South Solomon River, fifteen miles southwest of Osborne. Ruede's letters to his family in Pennsylvania capture the precariousness of daily life on the new frontier. Not everyone who tried would make it. Between 1888 and 1892, half the population in western Kansas would call it quits, painting "In God We Trusted, in Kansas We Busted!" on the sides of their retreating covered wagons.

Source: From *Sod-House Days: Letters from a Kansas Homesteader, 1877–1878*, ed. John Ise (1937; Cooper Square Publishers, 1966), 212–215. Copyright © 1937 by Columbia University Press. Reprinted with the permission of the publisher.

Sunday, February 24, 1878

At the Dugout, Kill Creek, Kansas

I reckon I'll have to give a history of last week, as it was a very interesting one for me. On Monday we turned out about 5:30, and by 6 I was on the road to Osborne. The suddenness of my departure was caused by a conversation I had with Hoot in reference to having the use of his team for a couple of days to haul hay for a shed in which to put my team when I brought it from Schweitzer's. He said if I'd get the oxen I might put them behind his straw stack till I had a shelter for them, and might water them at his well until I had a well dug. So I concluded that as I could have the use of his team for only one day, I had better take up his offer and do my own hauling. I had just crossed my east line when I met August Fritsche on his way to mill. Requested him to bring my grist. He said he did not know me. Told him who I was, and he said he would bring it as far as Sam Hoot's. I could not make him understand where my dugout was. Walked to Harry Humphrey's five miles from town, and rode with him the rest of the way. Arrived in Osborne about 9:30 and went to see Watson & Gillette, who had a wagon for sale. The price was $40. That was $10 more than I had. Then to Herzog's to see what Charley wants for his wagon. He was not home, but I got my dinner by waiting for him. He wanted $50 so that was no go. Back to W. & G.'s to see if they would not come down. But they would not. Next tried Ed Humphrey. He would sell for $30. As that was the highest figure I could go, I went to see the vehicle. Found the tongue was broken, as well as the hind bolster, and the box was not much account. I closed the bargain because I could hear of no other wagon for sale. Then went to Sears. John wanted something to read, so I took him the Phantom Ship. When I came near the house I saw Mrs. S. looking out the window and saw she did not recognize me, as I was shaved clean. Knocked at the door, and walked in and bid her "Good evening." Then she knew who I was, and we had a good laugh at her for not recognizing me at once. Had supper and then went to Schweitzer's. Talked awhile and then paid him for the oxen—$60. Turned in about 10. Next morning after breakfast Wally went out and yoked the oxen for me, and I started for town. When I got there Ed Humphrey had the wagon at the blacksmith shop, getting it repaired, and wanted to back out of the bargain. I had heard of another wagon for sale for $15 so I borrowed one of Ed's horses and rode about 4 miles from town to see the owner and the wagon but could find neither. I wanted to get a wagon offered to me for $15 or $20, so I could back Ed down on his price, but he saved me the trouble. I did not let him off very easy. Priced all the wagons I could hear or think of, but could not get a satisfactory price. At last I came across C. G. Paris and asked him whether he knew of a wagon for sale. He replied that he had one. How much? $35. Make it $30 and I'll take it. He argued about ten minutes with me, saying he'd take $30 and never ask me for the other V. Told him I did not do business on that line; that I had $30 to pay for a wagon, and I wanted a receipt in full, that I would not go in debt for even $5. Could apparently make no impression on him, so I went up town and bought a chain, and started for home without a wagon. I had not got out of town before he called me back, saying he'd take $30. So I tied the oxen, paid him and got a receipt. Then I again started for home. Got to the river, and after a little trouble succeeded in riding across on ox-back. After poking along for 2½ hours, I arrived at Paris' house. The wagon was not there, and I lost an hour getting it. Did not get home till 9:45, and found Pa and Geo. in bed. Tied the cattle to the wagon and threw them a bunch of hay, and then went in to have some supper (I had eaten nothing since breakfast) and read your letter and one from Ad. Turned in at 11. Wednesday was rainy. Didn't haul anything, but tied the oxen at Hoot's straw stack, and stayed indoors all day. Thursday was clear, so I borrowed Hoot's hay rack and Pa and I went for a load. Put on as much as we thought the oxen could pull and started for home. Had gone half a mile when we got stuck in a prairie dog hole, and had to get help to pull out. Threw off part of the hay and got as far as Fritsche's where, in going up a rise, the oxen suddenly geed off and upset hay, wagon and everything. Took them off from the wagon and fixed up things again, and finally got home with about half the hay we started with. Since then we have hauled hay on the wagon box and it goes much better. We pile it up pretty high and tie it on. There are two or three more loads to haul, and by the time it is all up we will have a pretty good stable. The cattle mind me pretty well now, and I am getting used to walking two miles an hour alongside the wagon. Today we all went over to Hoot's to meeting. Was at Graybill's to dinner. Mrs. Graybill offered to do our washing if I would furnish the tub and rubbing board (so I furnished the articles) and half the soap. That will let Pa off from washing. Bub was down town yesterday and bought a curry comb, so now we can get the dirt out of the oxen's hides. I have something less than a dollar, and Pa has a whole dollar in cash, but we are happy anyhow. I'll have to trust to Providence to put work in my way to raise about $20 to buy a breaking plow, hoe, fork and rake, and timber for the new sod addition we intend to put to the ranch. I had those 6 bushels of wheat ground; the miller takes off 1/6 for toll, so that from 5 bushels of wheat I got nearly 200 lbs. of flour. From about $4 worth of wheat I got about $6 worth of flour. That grist panned out better than any I have yet sent to mill. I am the Kill Creek correspondent of the Farmer, and am on the D. H. list of that journal.

Questions

1. What were some of the daily challenges that Ruede and other frontier farmers faced?
2. How has farming on the Great Plains changed since 1878?
3. What issues do Great Plains farmers today share with Ruede?

16-6 Report on the Lands of the Arid Region (1878)

John Wesley Powell

In 1869, John Wesley Powell was the first person to travel the length of the Grand Canyon by boating down the mighty Colorado River. He was a government scientist as well as an explorer and became an expert on the lands and native peoples of the American West. As a result of his research, Powell concluded that there were two Americas, one humid and one arid. The dividing line between the wet and dry halves of America was the one hundredth meridian. Powell succinctly explained to Congress the significance of this fact of geography: "To a great extent, the redemption of all these lands will require extensive and comprehensive plans, for the execution of which aggregated capital or cooperative labor will be necessary. Here, individual farmers, being poor men, cannot undertake the task."

Source: Excerpt from "The Physical Characteristics of the Region" in *Report on the Lands of the Arid Region of the United States, with a More Detailed Account of the Lands of Utah*, ed. Wallace Stegner (1875; Cambridge, MA: Belknap Press of Harvard University Press, 1962), 11–14. Reprinted with permission of Brandt & Brandt Literary Agents on behalf of the Wallace Stegner Estate.

PHYSICAL CHARACTERISTICS OF THE ARID REGION

The eastern portion of the United States is supplied with abundant rainfall for agricultural purposes, receiving the necessary amount from the evaporation of the Atlantic Ocean and the Gulf of Mexico; but westward the amount of aqueous precipitation diminishes in a general way until at last a region is reached where the climate is so arid that agriculture is not successful without irrigation. This Arid Region begins about midway in the Great Plains and extends across the Rocky Mountains to the Pacific Ocean. But on the northwest coast there is a region of greater precipitation, embracing western Washington and Oregon and the northwest corner of California. The winds impinging on this region are freighted with moisture derived from the great Pacific currents; and where this waterladen atmosphere strikes the western coast in full force, the precipitation is excessive, reaching a maximum north of the Columbia River of 80 inches annually. But the rainfall rapidly decreases from the Pacific Ocean eastward to the summit of the Cascade Mountains. It will be convenient to designate this humid area as the Lower Columbia Region. Rain gauge records have not been made to such an extent as to enable us to define its eastern and southern boundaries, but as they are chiefly along high mountains, definite boundary lines are unimportant in the consideration of agricultural resources and the questions relating thereto. In like manner on the east the rain gauge records, though more full, do not give all the facts necessary to a thorough discussion of the subject; yet the records are such as to indicate approximately the boundary between the Arid Region, where irrigation is necessary to agriculture, and the Humid Region, where the lands receive enough moisture from the clouds for the maturing of crops. Experience teaches that it is not wise to depend upon rainfall where the amount is less than 20 inches annually, if this amount is somewhat evenly distributed throughout the year; but if the rainfall is unevenly distributed, so that "rainy seasons" are produced, the question whether agriculture is possible without irrigation depends upon the time of the "rainy season" and the amount of its rainfall. Any unequal distribution of rain through the year, though the inequality be so slight as not to produce "rainy seasons," affects agriculture either favorably or unfavorably. If the spring and summer precipitation exceeds that of the fall and winter, a smaller amount of annual rain may be sufficient; but if the rainfall during the season of growing crops is less than the average of the same length of time during the remainder of the year, a greater amount of annual precipitation is necessary. In some localities in the western portion of the United States this unequal distribution of rainfall through the seasons affects agriculture favorably, and this is true immediately west of the northern portion of the line of 20 inches of rainfall, which extends along the plains from our northern to our southern boundary.

The isohyetal or mean annual rainfall line of 20 inches, as indicated on the rain chart accompanying this report, begins on the southern boundary of the United States, about 60 miles west of Brownsville, on the Rio Grande del Norte, and intersects the northern boundary about 50 miles east of Pembina. Between these two points the line is very irregular, but in middle latitudes makes a general curve to the westward. On the southern portion of the line the rainfall is somewhat evenly distributed through the seasons, but along the northern portion the rainfall of spring and summer is greater than that of fall and winter, and hence the boundary of what has been called the Arid Region runs farther to the west. Again, there is another modifying condition, namely, that of temperature. Where the temperature is greater, more rainfall is needed; where the temperature is less, agriculture is successful with a smaller amount of precipitation. But geographically this temperature is dependent upon two conditions—altitude and latitude. Along the northern portion of the line latitude is an important factor, and the line of possible agriculture without irrigation is carried still farther westward. This conclusion, based upon the consideration of rainfall and latitude, accords with the experience of the farmers of the region, for it is a well known fact that agriculture without irrigation is successfully carried on in the valley of the Red River of the North, and also in the southeastern portion of Dakota Territory. A much more extended series of rain-gauge records than we now have is necessary before this line constituting the eastern boundary of the Arid Region can be well defined. It is doubtless more or less meandering in its course throughout its whole extent from south to north, being affected by local conditions of rainfall, as well as by the general conditions above mentioned; but in a general way it may be represented by the one hundredth meridian, in some places passing to the east, in others to the west, but in the main to the east.

The limit of successful agriculture without irrigation has been set at 20 inches, that the extent of the Arid Region should by no means be exaggerated; but at 20 inches agriculture will not be uniformly successful from season to season. Many droughts will occur; many seasons in a long series will be fruitless; and it may be doubted whether, on the whole, agriculture will prove remunerative. On this point it is impossible to speak with certainty. A larger experience than the history of agriculture in the western portion of the United States affords is necessary to a final determination of the question.

In fact, a broad belt separates the Arid Region of the west from the Humid Region of the east. Extending from the one hundredth meridian eastward to about the isohyetal line of 28 inches, the district of country thus embraced will be subject more or less to disastrous droughts, the frequency of which will diminish from west to east. For convenience let this be called the Sub-humid Region. Its western boundary is the line already defined as running irregularly along the one hundredth meridian. Its eastern boundary passes west of the isohyetal line of 28 inches of rainfall in Minnesota, running approximately parallel to the western boundary line above described. Nearly one-tenth of the whole area of the United States, exclusive of Alaska, is embraced in this Sub-humid Region. In the western portion disastrous droughts will be frequent; in the eastern portion infrequent. In the western portion agriculturists will early resort to irrigation to secure immunity from such disasters, and this event will be hastened because irrigation when properly conducted is a perennial source of fertilization, and is even remunerative for this purpose alone; and for the same reason the inhabitants of the eastern part will gradually develop irrigating methods. It may be confidently expected that at a time not far distant irrigation will be practiced to a greater or less extent throughout this Sub-humid Region. Its settlement presents problems differing materially from those pertaining to the region to the westward. Irrigation is not immediately necessary, and hence agriculture does not immediately depend upon capital. The region may be settled and its agricultural capacities more or less developed, and the question of the construction of irrigating canals may be a matter of time and convenience. For many reasons, much of the sub-humid belt is attractive to settlers: it is almost destitute of forests, and for this reason is more readily subdued, as the land is ready for the plow. But because of the lack of forests the country is more dependent upon railroads for the transportation of building and fencing materials and for fuel. To a large extent it is a region where timber may be successfully cultivated. As the rainfall is on a general average nearly sufficient for continuous successful agriculture, the amount of water to be supplied by irrigating canals will be comparatively small, so that its streams can serve proportionally larger areas than the streams of the Arid Region. In its first settlement the people will be favored by having lands easily subdued, but they will have to content against a lack of timber. Eventually this will be a region of great agricultural wealth, as in general the soils are good. From our northern to our southern boundary no swamp lands are found, except to some slight extent in the northeastern portion, and it has no excessively hilly or mountainous districts. It is a beautiful prairie country throughout, lacking somewhat in rainfall; but this want can be easily supplied by utilizing the living streams; and, further, these streams will afford fertilizing materials of great value.

Questions

1. What insights does Powell's article offer on western farming? How did it predict the failure of many individual farmers who moved to the West toward the end of the nineteenth century?
2. In what ways did Powell predict that the settlement of the western frontier would differ from the earlier settlement of the eastern frontiers?

16-7 On Irrigation (1905)

William E. Smythe

William Ellsworth Smythe was born in 1861 in Massachusetts, where his father was a wealthy shoe manufacturer. The young Smythe left home to move to Kearny, Nebraska, and, in 1889, became a newspaper editor at the *Omaha Bee*. Watching both the land and the livelihoods drawn from the land wither away in a severe drought, Smythe became an ardent convert to irrigation as the solution to agriculture in the arid West. Typical of newspaper men of this period, Smythe was more of a booster, almost a utopian, than a person of reason and facts. Unlike Powell, there was more romance than science in his vision of the West. Still, both men were committed to the older ideals of Jeffersonian democracy and believed that with intelligent modification, U.S. institutions could be made to thrive in this newest, if driest, region of the nation.

Source: William E. Smythe, *The Conquest of Arid America* (1899; Seattle: University of Washington Press, 1969), pp. 41–48.

THE beauty of Damascus is the theme of poets. Speaking of this ancient capital an anonymous writer remarks that "the cause of its importance as a city in all the ages is easily seen as you approach it from the south. Miles before you see the mosques of the modern city the fountains of a copious and perennial stream spring from among the rocks and brushwood at the base of the Anti-Lebanon, creating a wide area about them, rich with prolific vegetation." He continues:

"There are the 'streams of Lebanon,' which are poetically spoken of in the Songs of Solomon, and the 'rivers of Damascus,' which Naaman, not unnaturally, preferred to all the 'waters of Israel.' This stream, with its many branches, is the inestimable treasure of Damascus. While the desert is a fortification round Damascus, the river, where the habitations of men must always have been gathered, as along the Nile, is its life.

"The city, which is situated in a wilderness of gardens of flowers and fruits, has rushing through its streets the limpid and refreshing current; nearly every dwelling has its fountain, and at night the lights are seen flashing on the waters that dash along from their mountain home. As you first view the city from one of the overhanging ridges you are prepared to excuse the Mohammedans for calling it the earthly paradise. Around the marble minarets, the glittering domes, and the white buildings, shining with ivory softness, a maze of bloom and fruitage—where olive and pomegranate, orange and apricot, plum and walnut, mingle their varied tints of green—is presented to the sight, in striking contrast to the miles of barren desert over which you have just ridden."

This is the miracle of irrigation in the Syrian desert. It is no more miraculous in that far-eastern country than in our own West. Nor is Damascus more beautiful than Denver, Salt Lake City, or than any one of a score of modern towns in California. But because Damascus is ancient and historic, and looks down on mankind from the biblical past, it possesses a degree of interest with which it is difficult to invest much better and more important places of our own country and our own time. It is well, then, to remember that not only the beauty of Damascus, but the glories of the Garden of Eden itself, were products of irrigation. "A river went out of Eden to water the Garden," says the Bible story.

No consideration of the subject can be appreciative when it starts with the narrow view that irrigation is merely an adjunct to agriculture. It is a social and industrial factor, in a much broader sense. It not only makes it possible for a civilization to rise and flourish in the midst of desolate wastes; it shapes and colors that civilization after its own peculiar design. It is not merely the life-blood of the field, but the source of institutions. These wider and more subtle influences are difficult to define in abstract terms, but we may trace them clearly through the history of various communities which have grown up in conformity with these conditions.

The essence of the industrial life which springs from irrigation is its democracy. The first great law which irrigation lays down is this: There shall be no monopoly of land. This edict it enforces by the remorseless operation of its own economy. Canals must be built before water can be conducted upon the land. This entails expense, either of money or of labor. What is expensive cannot be had for naught. Where water is the foundation of prosperity it becomes a precious thing, to be neither cheaply acquired nor wantonly wasted. Like a city's provisions in a siege, it is a thing to be carefully husbanded, to be fairly distributed according to men's needs, to be wisely expanded by those who receive it. For these reasons men cannot acquire as much irrigated land, even from the public domain, as they could acquire where irrigation was unnecessary. It is not only more difficult to acquire in large bodies, but yet more difficult to retain. A large farm under irrigation is a misfortune; a great farm, a calamity. Only the small farm pays. But this small farm blesses its proprietor with industrial independence and crowns him with social equality. That is democracy.

Industrial independence is, in simplest terms, the guarantee of subsistence from one's own labors. It is the ability to earn a living under conditions which admit of the smallest possible element of doubt with the least possible dependence upon others. Irrigation fully satisfies this definition.

The canal is an insurance policy against loss of crops by drought, while aridity is a substantial guarantee against injury by flood. Of all the advantages of irrigation, this is the most obvious. Scarcely less so, however, is its compelling power in the matter of production. Probably there is no spot of land in the United States where the average crop raised by dependence upon rainfall might not be doubled by intelligent irrigation. The rich soils of the arid region produce from four to ten times as largely with irrigation as the soil of the humid region without it. As the measure of value is not area, but productive capacity, twenty acres in the Far West should equal one hundred acres elsewhere. Such is the actual fact.

A little further on we shall see that not merely the quantity of crops, but their quality as well, responds to the influence of irrigation. We shall see how this art favors the production of the wide diversity of products required for a generous living. Certainly, abundance, variety—all this upon an area so small as to be within the control of a single family through its own labor—are the elements which compose industrial independence under irrigation. The conditions which prevail where irrigation is not necessary—large farms, hired labor, a strong tendency to the single crop—are here reversed. Intensive cultivation and diversified production are inseparably related to irrigation. These constitute a system of industry the fruit of which is a class of small landed proprietors resting upon a foundation of economic independence.

This is the miracle of irrigation on its industrial side.

As a factor in the social life of the civilization it creates, irrigation is no less influential and beneficent. Compared with the familiar conditions of country life which we have known in the East and central West, the change which irrigation brings amounts to a revolution. The bane of rural life is its loneliness. Even food, shelter, and provision for old age do not furnish protection against social discontent where the conditions deny the advantages which flow from human association. Better a servant in the town than a proprietor in the country!—such has been the verdict of recent generations who have grown up on the farm and left it to seek satisfaction for their social instincts in the life of the town. The starvation of the soul is almost as real as the starvation of the body.

Irrigation compels the adoption of the small-farm unit. This is the germ of new social possibilities, and we shall see to what extent they have already been realized as we proceed. During the first and second eras of colonization in this country the favorite size for a farm was about four hundred acres, of which from a fourth to a half was gradually cleared and the rest retained in woodland. The Mississippi Valley was settled mostly in quarter-sections, containing one hundred and sixty acres each. The productive capacity of land is so largely increased by irrigation, and the amount which one family can cultivate by its own labor consequently so much reduced, that the small-farm unit is a practical necessity in the arid region.

Where settlement has been carried out upon the most enlightened lines irrigated farms range from five to twenty acres upon the average, rarely exceeding forty acres at the maximum. It is perfectly obvious, of course, that a twenty-acre unit means that neighbors will be eight times as numerous as in a country settled up in quarter-sections—that where farms are ten acres in size neighbors will be multiplied by sixteen. Thus in its most elementary aspect the society of the arid region differs materially from that of a country of large farms. Eight or sixteen families upon a quarter-section are much better than no neighbors at all, but irrigation goes further than this in revolutionizing the social side of rural life.

A very-small-farm unit makes it possible for those who till the soil to live in the town. The farm village, or home centre, is a well-established feature of life in Arid America, and a feature which is destined to enjoy wide and rapid extension. Each four or five thousand acres of cultivated land will sustain a thrifty and beautiful hamlet, where all the people may live close together and enjoy most of the social and educational advantages within the reach of the best eastern town. Their children will have kindergartens as well as schools, and public libraries and reading-rooms as well as churches. The farm village, lighted by electricity, furnished with domestic water through pipes, served with free postal delivery, and supplied with its own daily newspapers at morning and evening, has already been realized in Arid America. The great cities of the western valleys will not be cities in the old sense, but a long series of beautiful villages, connected by lines of electric motors, which will move their products and people from place to place. In this scene of intensely cultivated land, rich with its bloom and fruitage, with its spires and roofs, and with its carpets of green and gold stretching away to the mountains, it will be difficult for the beholder to say where the town ends and the country begins.

This is the miracle of irrigation upon its social side.

Irrigation is the foundation of truly scientific agriculture. Tilling the soil by dependence upon rainfall is, by comparison, like a stage-coach to the railroad, like the tallow dip to the electric light. The perfect conditions for scientific agriculture would be presented by a place where it never rained, but where a system of irrigation furnished a never-failing water supply which could be adjusted to the varying needs of different planets. It is difficult for those who have been in the habit of thinking of irrigation as merely a substitute for rain to grasp the truth that precisely the contrary is the case. Rain is the poor dependence of those who cannot obtain the advantages of irrigation. The western farmer who has learned to irrigate thinks it would be quite as illogical for him to leave the watering of his potato-patch to the caprice of the clouds as for the housewife to defer her wash-day until she could catch rain-water in her tubs.

The supreme advantage of irrigation consists not more in the fact that it assures moisture regardless of the weather than in the fact that it makes it possible to apply that moisture just when and just where it is needed. For instance, on some cloudless day the strawberry-patch looks thirsty and cries for water through the unmistakable language of its leaves. In the Atlantic States it probably would not rain that day, such is the perversity of nature, but if it did it would rain alike on the just and unjust—on the strawberries, which would be benefited by it, and on the sugar-beets, which crave only the uninterrupted sunshine that they may pack their tiny cells with saccharine matter. In the arid region there is practically no rain during the growing season. Thus the scientific farmer sends the water from his canal through the little furrows which divide the lines of strawberry plants, but permits the water to go singing past his field of beets.

Plants and trees require moisture as well as sunshine and soil, and for three reasons: first, that the tiny roots may extract the chemical qualities from the soil; then, that there may be sap and juice; finally, that there may be moisture to evaporate or transpire from the leaves. But while all plant-life requires moisture, all kinds of it do not require the same amount, nor do they desire to receive it at the same time and in the same manner. Just as the skilful teacher studies the individualities of fifty different boys, endeavoring to discover how he may most wisely vary his methods to obtain the best results from each, so the scientific farmer studies his fifty different plants or trees and adjusts his artificial "rainfall" in the way which will produce the highest outcome. With the aid of colleges, experimental farms, and county institutes, wonderful progress has been made along these lines in recent years. This progress will continue until the agriculture and horticulture practised on the little farms of Arid America shall match the marvellous results won by research and inventive genius in every other field of human endeavor.

This is the miracle of irrigation upon its scientific side.

Questions

1. For Smythe, irrigation was a technology that would revolutionize life in the West. Explain.
2. What was the connection, for Smythe, between irrigation and democracy?

Questions for Further Thought

1. Compare and contrast the attitudes toward Native Americans found in Documents 16-1 and 16-2.
2. In what ways was settlement of the arid West going to be different from the settlement of America's humid frontiers?

The Far West

The Rockies, the Sonoran and Mojave Deserts, the Columbia and Colorado Plateaus, the Ilano Estacado, the Great Basin, the Rio Grande Valley, the Sierra Nevada and the Cascades, and the Pacific Slope—these formed the Far West. In this vast and varied region, Anglos (white Americans) interacted not only with Native Americans but also with Hispanics whose ancestors had settled parts of the region centuries before. Anglos also encountered Chinese immigrants. Although Anglos and the Chinese came to the Far West for the same reasons—to find opportunity or, better, strike it rich—race relations between the two, with few exceptions, were marked by the same kind of hostility and prejudice that characterized the Jim Crow South. Indeed, at the same time the legal edifice of segregation was being erected across the former Confederate states, Congress responded to white nativist fear and anger in California and elsewhere by moving to stop the flow of Chinese immigrants into the country. Just as there was a movement in the West to ensure white supremacy through exclusion, reservations, and other means of social control, there was also a determined effort to eliminate significant cultural differences within the Anglo community as well. Utah was refused statehood until the Church of Jesus Christ of Latter-day Saints (the LDS or Mormon Church), a powerful religious force in Utah and the surrounding area, renounced the practice of plural marriage (Document 16-11). Other westerners, such as John Muir, were moved by the incredible beauty and variety of the West, which opened up entirely new scientific and artistic vistas to the older cultural centers back east and which would help define a new western culture that would over time become every bit as vibrant as its eastern counterpart.

Document 16-8a spells out the positions of the national political parties on Chinese immigration. Document 16-8b reveals Congress's subsequent action relative to the immigration of Chinese laborers. Document 16-9 is the political platform of Las Gorras Blancas or the "White Caps." In Document 16-10, Charles Fletcher Lummis helped lead the way in appreciating that the existing cultures in the region, namely the old Hispanic civilization of California and the Southwest, offered the basis for inventing a new, alternative American culture. Document 16-11 is the Woodruff Manifesto (1890). Document 16-12 is a selection from one of John Muir's influential nature writings.

16-8 On Chinese Immigration (1876, 1882)

In 1874 and 1875, President Grant criticized aspects of Chinese immigration in his State of the Union Addresses, emphasizing the involuntary nature of contract immigration and the importation of women for "shameful purposes." Both major political parties addressed the issue of Chinese ("Mongolian") immigration in their national platforms for 1876.

Immigration has always made Americans uneasy, in part because of a fear that newcomers would not be assimilated. Chinese immigrants provoked extreme anxiety on the West Coast with their different language, customs, and dress. Congress responded to the pleas of nativists by passing the Chinese Exclusion Act in 1882 (see text p. 511).

The revision in 1880 of the Burlingame Treaty paved the way for the enactment of this law, which suspended the immigration of Chinese laborers for ten years. Representatives from the East and Midwest supported the measure by 112–37, those from the West and South by 89–0. The law was subsequently renewed and tightened.

Sources: Donald Bruce Johnson, comp., *National Party Platforms*, 2 vols. (rev. ed., Urbana: University of Illinois Press, 1978), 1:1840–1956, 50, 54. United States, *Statutes at Large*, 22:58 ff.

(a) Republican and Democratic National Platforms on Chinese Immigration (1876)

REPUBLICAN	DEMOCRATIC
11. It is the immediate duty of Congress fully to investigate the effects of the immigration and importation of Mongolians on the moral and material interests of the country.	Reform is necessary to correct the omissions of a Republican Congress and the errors of our treaties and our diplomacy, which . . . [have] exposed our brethren of the Pacific coast to the incursions of a race not sprung from the same great parent stock, and in fact now by law denied citizenship through naturalization as being unaccustomed to the traditions of a progressive civilization, one exercised in liberty under equal laws; and we denounce the policy which . . . tolerates the revival of the coolie-trade in Mongolian women for immoral purposes, and Mongolian men held to perform servile labor contracts, and demand such modification of the treaty with the Chinese Empire, or such legislation within constitutional limitations, as shall prevent further importation or immigration of the Mongolian race.

(b) The Chinese Exclusion Act (1882)

Whereas, in the opinion of the Government of the United States the coming of Chinese laborers to this country endangers the good order of certain localities within the territory thereof: Therefore,

Be it enacted by the Senate and House of Representatives of the United States of America in Congress assembled, That from and after the expiration of ninety days next after the passage of this act, and until the expiration of ten years next after the passage of this act, the coming of Chinese laborers to the United States be, and the same is hereby, suspended; and during such suspension it shall not be lawful for any Chinese laborer to come, or, having so come after the expiration of said ninety days, to remain within the United States. . . .

SEC. 4. That for the purpose of properly identifying Chinese laborers who were in the United States on the seventeenth day of November, eighteen hundred and eighty, or who shall have come into the same before the expiration of ninety days next after the passage of this act, and in order to furnish them with the proper evidence of their right to go from and come to the United States of their free will and accord, as provided by the treaty between the United States and China dated November seventeenth, eighteen hundred and eighty, the collector of customs of the district from which any such Chinese laborer shall depart from the United States shall, in person or by deputy, go on board each vessel having on board any such Chinese laborer and cleared or about to sail from his district for a foreign port, and on such vessel make a list of all such Chinese laborers, which shall be entered in registry-books to be kept for that purpose, in which shall be stated the name, age, occupation, last place of residence, physical marks or peculiarities, and all facts necessary for the identification of each of such Chinese laborers, which books shall be safely kept in the custom-house; and every such Chinese laborer so departing from the United States shall be entitled to, and shall receive, free of any charge or cost upon application therefor, from the collector or his deputy, at the time such list is taken, a certificate, signed by the collector or his deputy and attested by his seal of office, in such form as the Secretary of the Treasury shall prescribe, which certificate shall contain a statement of the name, age, occupation, last place of residence, personal description, and facts of identification of the Chinese laborer to whom the certificate is issued, corresponding with the said list and registry in all particulars. . . .

SEC. 14. That hereafter no State court or court of the United States shall admit Chinese to citizenship; and all laws in conflict with this act are hereby repealed.

Questions

1. Why might the Democrats have been more outspoken than the Republicans in the parties' 1876 platforms regarding Chinese immigration?
2. How did Sections 4 and 14 of the Chinese Exclusion Act affect Chinese immigrants?

16-9 *Nuestra Platforma*: Hispanics Protest Anglo Encroachment in New Mexico (1890)

The White Caps

With the Treaty of Guadalupe Hidalgo (1848), which concluded the U.S. war with Mexico, Hispanics who were living in California, Arizona, New Mexico, and Texas suddenly found themselves foreigners in their native land: the Mexican North became the American Southwest by right of U.S. conquest. Not surprisingly, the process of political incorporation, which took decades to complete, created racial tensions as well as class and economic conflicts. One such conflict erupted in San Miguel County in the territory of New Mexico when Anglo interests in the 1880s tried to enclose the communal lands of Hispanic villagers. Taking matters into their own hands, angry local residents, known as Las Gorras Blancas, or "the White Caps," resisted these encroachments by cutting the Anglos' newly strung barbed wire and committing other acts of destruction. The White Caps also put their grievances in writing and on the night of March 11, 1890, posted copies of "Our Platform" throughout the town of Las Vegas.

Source: From *Foreigners in Their Native Land: Historical Roots of the Mexican Americans*, ed. David J. Weber (Albuquerque: University of New Mexico, 1973), 234–236. Copyright © 1973 by The University of New Mexico Press. Reprinted by permission of The University of New Mexico Press.

NUESTRA PLATFORMA—

Our purpose is to protect the rights and interests of the people in general and especially those of the helpless classes.

We want the Las Vegas Grant settled to the benefit of all concerned, and this we hold is the entire community within the Grant.

We want no "land grabbers" or obstructionists of any sort to interfere. We will watch them.

We are not down on lawyers as a class, but the usual knavery and unfair treatment of the people must be stopped.

Our judiciary hereafter must understand that we will sustain it only when "Justice" is its watchword.

We are down on race issues, and will watch race agitators.

We favor irrigation enterprises, but will fight any scheme that tends to monopolize the supply of water sources to the detriment of residents living on lands watered by the same streams.

The people are suffering from the effects of partisan "bossism" and these bosses had better quietly hold their peace. The people have been persecuted and hauled about in every which way to satisfy their caprices.

We must have a free ballot and fair court and the will of the Majority shall be respected.

We have no grudge against any person in particular, but we are the enemies of bulldozers and tyrants.

If the old system should continue, death would be a relief to our suffering. And for our rights our lives are the least we can pledge.

If the fact that we are law-abiding citizens is questioned, come out to our houses and see the hunger and desolation we are suffering; and "this" is the result of the deceitful and corrupt methods of "bossism."

The White Caps 1,500 Strong and Gaining Daily

Questions

1. If you were to reduce this platform to one or two slogans, what would they be? Do the White Caps' demands seem reasonable?
2. Referring to the text (p. 510), what ultimately became of New Mexico's peasants (or *campesinos*)?
3. What connections can be made between the experiences of the White Caps and Native Americans in the new "American" West?

16-10 *The Land of Poco Tiempo* (1893)

Charles Fletcher Lummis

Charles F. Lummis (1859–1928) was born in Lynn, Massachusetts, and studied at Harvard University. He moved to Chillicothe, Ohio, and worked as a reporter for the *Scioto Gazette*. In 1884, he walked, or "tramped," his way from Cincinnati, Ohio, to Los Angeles, California, a sojourn that took 143 days. Lummis rediscovered the Spanish heritage and Native American cultures of California and the American Southwest and made a career of popularizing the peoples and land in this part of the country, thereby helping to establish this region as a place set apart from the rest of the nation. His book, *The Land of Poco Tiempo*, focused on New Mexico, which he called the home of "Pretty Soon."

Source: Excerpt from Charles F. Lummis, *The Land of Poco Tiempo* (1893; New York: Charles Scribner's Sons, 1913), 3–12.

SUN, silence, and adobe—that is New Mexico in three words. If a fourth were to be added, it need be only to clinch the three. It is the Great American Mystery—The National Rip Van Winkle—the United States which is *not* United States. Here is the land of *poco tiempo*—the home of "Pretty Soon." Why hurry with the hurrying world? The "Pretty Soon" of New Spain is better than the "Now! Now!" of the haggard States. The opiate sun soothes to rest, the adobe is made to lean against, the hush of day-long noon would not be broken. Let us not hasten—*mañana* will do. Better still, *pasado mañana*.

New Mexico is the anomaly of the Republic. It is a century older in European civilization than the rest, and several centuries older still in a happier semi-civilization of its own. It had its little walled cities of stone before Columbus had grandparents-to-be; and it has them yet. The most incredible pioneering the world has ever seen overran it with the zeal of a prairie-fire three hundred and fifty years ago; and the embers of that unparalleled blaze of exploration are not quite dead to-day. The most superhuman marches, the most awful privations, the most devoted heroism, the most unsleeping vigilance wrested this bare, brown land to the world; and having wrested it, went to sleep. The winning was the wakefullest in history—the after-nap eternal. It never has wakened—one does not know that it ever can. Nature herself does little but sleep, here. A few semi-bustling American towns wart the Territorial map. It is pockmarked with cattle-ranches and mines, where Experience has wielded his costly birch over millionaire pupils from the East and from abroad. But the virus never reached the blood — the pits are only skin-deep. The Saxon excrescences are already asleep too. The cowboy is a broken idol. He no longer "shoots up the town," nor riddles heels reluctant for the dance. His day is done; and so is that of the argonaut. They both are with us, but their lids are heavy. And around them is New Spain again, dreamy as ever after their rude but short-lived nudging. The sheep — which feed New Mexico — doze again on the mesas, no longer routed by their long-horned foes; and where sheep are, is rest. The brown or gray adobe hamlets of the descendants of those fiery souls who wreaked here a commonwealth before the Saxon fairly knew there was a New World; the strange terraced towns of the aboriginal pioneers who out-Spaniarded the Spaniards by unknown centuries; the scant leaven of incongruous American brick — all are under the spell. And the abrupt mountains, the echoing, rock-walled cañons, the sunburnt mesas, the streams bankrupt by their own shylock sands, the gaunt, brown, treeless plains, the ardent sky, all harmonize with unearthly unanimity.

"Picturesque" is a tame word for it. It is a picture, a romance, a dream, all in one. It is our one corner that is the sun's very own. Here he has had his way, and no discrepancy mars his work. It is a land of quaint, swart faces, of Oriental dress and unspelled speech; a land where distance is lost, and the eye is a liar; a land of ineffable lights and sudden shadows; of polytheism and superstition, where the rattlesnake is a demigod, and the cigarette a means of grace, and where Christians mangle and crucify themselves — the heart of Africa beating against the ribs of the Rockies.

There are three typical races in New Mexico now — for it would be wrong to include the ten per cent. "American" interpolation as a type. With them I have here nothing to do. They are potential, but not picturesque. Besides them and around them are the real autochthones [aboriginal inhabitants], a quaint ethnologic trio. First, the nine thousand Pueblo Indians — peaceful, fixed, house-dwelling and home-loving tillers of the soil; good Catholics in the churches they have built with a patience infinite as that of the Pyramids; good pagans everywhere else. Then the ten thousand Navajo Indians — whose other ten thousand is in Arizona — sullen, nomad, horse-loving, horse-stealing, horse-living vagrants of the saddle; pagans first, last, and all the time, and inventors of the mother-in-law joke gray centuries before the civilized world awoke to it. Last of all, the Mexicans; in-bred and isolation-shrunken descendants of the Castilian world-finders; living almost as much against the house as in it; ignorant as slaves, and more courteous than kings; poor as Lazarus, and more hospitable than Crœsus; Catholics from A to Izzard, except when they take occasion to be Penitentes — and even then fighting to bring their matted scourges and bloody crosses into the church which bars its door to them. The Navajos have neither houses nor towns; the Pueblos have nineteen compact little "cities;" and the Mexicans several hundred villages, a part of which are shared by the invader. The few towns of undiluted gringo hardly count in summing up the Territory of three hundred by four hundred miles.

If New Mexico lacks the concentration of natural picturesqueness to be found elsewhere, it makes up in universality. There are almost no waterfalls, and not a river worthy of the name. Cañons are rare, and inferior to those of Colorado and the farther Southwest. The mountains are largely skyward miles of savage rock; and forests are far between. But every landscape is characteristic, and even beautiful — with a weird, unearthly beauty, treacherous as the flowers of its cacti. Most of New Mexico, most of the year, is an indescribable harmony in browns and grays, over which the enchanted light of its blue skies casts an eternal spell. Its very rocks are unique — only Arizona shares those astounding freaks of form and color carved by the scant rains and more liberal winds of immemorial centuries, and towering across the bare land like the milestones of forgotten giants. The line of huge buttes of blood-red sandstone which stretches from Mt. San Mateo to the Little Colorado, including the "Navajo Church" and a thousand minor wonders, is typically New Mexican. The Navajo Reservation — which lies part in this Territory and part in Arizona — is remarkably picturesque throughout, with its broad plains hemmed by giant mesas split with wild cañons. So are the regions about Jemez, Cochití, Taos, Santa Fé, Acoma, and a few others.

The most unique pictures in New Mexico are to be found among its unique Pueblos. Their quaint terraced architecture is the most remarkable on the continent; and there is none more picturesque in the world. It remains intact only in the remoter pueblos — those along the Rio Grande have been largely Mexicanized into one-storied tameness. Laguna, on the Atlantic & Pacific Railroad, has some three-story terraced houses still. Acoma, on its dizzy island-cliff, twenty miles southwest, is all three-storied; and Taos, in its lovely, lonely valley far to the north, is two great pyramid-tenements of six stories.

And the Pueblos — they are picturesque anywhere and always, but particularly in their dances, races, and other ceremonials. These are Indians who are neither poor nor naked; Indians who feed themselves, and ask no favors of Washington; Indians who have been at peace for two centuries, and fixed residents for perhaps a millennium; Indians who were farmers and irrigators and six-story-house builders before a New World had been beaten through the thick skull of the Old; Indians who do not make pack-beasts of their squaws — and who have not "squaws," save in the vocabulary of less-bred barbarians. They had nearly a hundred republics in America centuries before *the* American Republic was conceived; and they have maintained their ancient democracy through all the ages, unshamed by the corruption of a voter, the blot of a defalcation or malfeasance in office. They are, under the solemn pledge of our Government in the treaty of Guadelupe Hidalgo, citizens; and are the most flagrantly wronged in our country. Their numerous sacred dances are by far the most picturesque sights in America, and the least viewed by Americans, who never found anything more striking abroad. The mythology of Greece and Rome is less than theirs in complicated comprehensiveness, and they are a more interesting ethnologic study than the tribes of inner Africa, and less known of by their white countrymen. . . .

A Pueblo Clotho Spinning in the Sun

Life is the least vital feature of New Mexico. The present is a husk—the past was a romance and a glory. The Saxon invasion which came with the railroad has reacted almost to syncope. It is in little hope of revivification until the settlement of land titles shall be effected, and a national shame of forty years effaced. The native, stirred to unwonted perspiration by the one-time advent of the prodigal *peso*, has dropped back to ease with dignity—dignity in rags, mayhap, but always dignity. To the old ways he has not wholly returned—just to the old joy of living, the broad content of sitting and remembering that one has lungs for this ozone and eyes for this day-dream. I would not be understood that it is idleness. There is work; but such unfatal work! The *paisano* has learned to live even while he works—wherein he is more wise than we, who slave away youth (which is life) in chasing that which we are past enjoyment of when we overtake it. He tills his fields and tends his herds; but there is no unseemly haste, no self-tripping race for wealth. *Lo que puede*—that which can be—is enough. It needs not to plough deep, nor to dun the land with fertilizers. The land has taken it easy, too, and after three centuries of uncrowded fruition appears not exhausted, but restful and conservative. Why urge it? There will be enough! The river's roily pulse circulates in ten thousand *acequias*, and gives drink to the thirsty fields, cupped with their little irrigating-beds. Its sediment is fertilizer sufficient. So shall the brown bean, the quenchless chile, the corn and the wheat, fill the store-room—and what need of more?

Questions

1. In his discussion of New Mexico, Lummis used the term *picturesque*. What did he mean by the term and how did he use it here?
2. Lummis discussed New Mexico as a land of three races or cultures. What were they?
3. While Lummis admired New Mexico, discuss how he also used New Mexico as foil to criticize mainstream U.S. culture.

16-11 Mormon Renunciation of Polygamy, Woodruff Manifesto (1890)

Many Americans were drawn West by the prospect of adventure, opportunity, the chance to start over, or to build a new and better kind of life. Other Americans were forced West by pressures at home. The removal of the Five Civilized Tribes to Indian Territory—what became present-day Oklahoma—was one case in point. The exodus of the Mormons out of Nauvoo, Illinois, in 1846 for the sanctuary of the Great Basin the following year was another. National concerns over polygamy, block voting, and theocracy, however, kept Utah a territory for five decades until Wilford Woodruff, the president of the LDS Church, finally renounced the practice of plural marriage on September 24, 1890. The territory was subsequently admitted to the Union in 1896.

Source: Gustive O. Larson, *The Americanization of Utah for Statehood* (San Marino: The Huntington Library, 1971), 263–264.

To Whom It May Concern:

Press dispatches having been sent for political purposes from Salt Lake City, which have been widely published, to the effect that the Utah Commission, in their recent report to the Secretary of Interior, allege that plural marriages are still being solemnized, and that forty or more such marriages have been contracted in Utah since last June or during the past year; also that in public discourses the leaders of the Church have taught, encouraged and urged the continuance of the practice of polygamy—

I, therefore, as President of the Church of Jesus Christ of Latter-day Saints, do hereby, in the most solemn manner, declare that these charges are false. We are not teaching polygamy or plural marriage, nor permitting any person to enter into its practice, and I deny that forty or any other number of pleural marriages have, during that period, been solemnized in our Temples or in any other place in the Territory.

One case has been reported, in which the parties alleged that the marriage was performed in the Endowment House, in Salt Lake City, in the spring of 1889. . . . In consequence of this alleged occurrence the Endowment House was, by my instruction, taken down without delay.

Inasmuch as laws have been enacted by Congress forbidding plural marriages, which laws have been pronounced constitutional by the Court of the last resort, I hereby declare, my intention to submit to those laws, and to use my influence with the members of the Church over which I preside to have them do likewise. . . .

And now I publicly declare that my advice to the Latter-day Saints is to refrain from contracting any marriage forbidden by the laws of the land.

Wilford Woodruff
President of the Church of Jesus
Christ of Latter-day Saints.

Questions

1. What prompted Woodruff to make this proclamation?
2. To what authority did Woodruff defer?

16-12 A Perilous Night on Shasta's Summit (1888)

John Muir

A son of the Wisconsin frontier, John Muir came to California in 1868, where he soon fell in love with the Sierra Nevada, which he called the "range of light." Muir would later devote his life to protecting these mountains from exploitation so that future generations might enjoy them. To this end, he helped organize the Sierra Club in 1892 and was an early leader in the wilderness preservation movement, which would become a significant political force in the twentieth century. Muir's nature writing was distinguished by an intensity that bordered on religious enthusiasm. In 1875 he climbed Mount Shasta, a towering volcanic peak that was located in northern California and sacred to the Klamath and Modoc tribes. On the night of April 28, 1875, Muir had the good "fortune," as he put it, of getting caught in a blizzard atop Mount Shasta, thus experiencing nature firsthand in all of its terrible beauty.

Source: Excerpt from "A Perilous Night on Shasta's Summit" in *Steep Trails*, ed. William Frederic Badé (1888; Boston: Houghton Mifflin, 1918), 67–81. Reprinted by permission of the Houghton Mifflin Company.

On the 28th of April [1875] I led a party up the mountain for the purpose of making a survey of the summit with reference to the location of the Geodetic monument. On the 30th, accompanied by Jerome Fay, I made another ascent to make some barometrical observations, the day intervening between the two ascents being devoted to establishing a camp on the extreme edge of the timber-line. Here, on our red trachyte bed, we obtained two hours of shallow sleep broken for occasional glimpses of the keen, starry night. At two o'clock we rose, breakfasted on a warmed tin-cupful of coffee and a piece of frozen venison broiled on the coals, and started for the summit. Up to this time there was nothing in sight that betokened the approach of a storm; but on gaining the summit, we saw toward Lassen's Butte hundreds of square miles of white cumuli boiling dreamily in the sunshine far beneath us, and causing no alarm.

The slight weariness of the ascent was soon rested away, and our glorious morning in the sky promised nothing but enjoyment. At 9 A.M. the dry thermometer stood at 34° in the shade and rose steadily until at 1 P.M. it stood at 50°, probably influenced somewhat by radiation from the sun-warmed cliffs. A common bumble-bee, not at all benumbed, zigzagged vigorously about our heads for a few moments, as if unconscious of the fact that the nearest honey flower was a mile beneath him.

In the mean time clouds were growing down in Shasta Valley—massive swelling cumuli, displaying delicious tones of purple and gray in the hollows of their sun-beaten bosses. Extending gradually southward around on both sides of Shasta, these at length united with the older field towards Lassen's Butte, thus encircling Mount Shasta in one continuous cloud-zone. Rhett and Kalmath Lakes were eclipsed beneath clouds scarcely less brilliant than their own silvery disks. The Modoc Lava Beds, many a snow-laden peak far north in Oregon, the Scott and Trinity and Siskiyou Mountains, the peaks of the Sierra, the blue Coast Range, Shasta Valley, the dark forests filling the valley of the Sacramento, all in turn were obscured or buried, leaving the lofty cone on which we stood solitary in the sunshine between two skies— a sky of spotless blue above, a sky of glittering cloud beneath. The creative sun shone glorious on the vast expanse of cloudland; hill and dale, mountain and valley springing into existence responsive to his rays and steadily developing in beauty and individuality. One huge mountain-cone of cloud, corresponding to Mount Shasta in these newborn cloud-ranges, rose close alongside with a visible motion, its firm, polished bosses seeming so near and substantial that we almost fancied we might leap down upon them from where we stood and make our way to the lowlands. No hint was given, by anything in their appearance, of the fleeting character of these most sublime and beautiful cloud mountains. On the contrary they impressed one as being lasting additions to the landscape.

The weather of the springtime and summer, throughout the Sierra in general, is usually varied by slight local rains and dustings of snow, most of which are obviously far too joyous and life-giving to be regarded as storms—single clouds growing in the sunny sky, ripening in an hour, showering the heated landscape, and passing away like a thought, leaving no visible bodily remains to stain the sky. Snow-storms of the same gentle kind abound among the high peaks, but in spring they not unfrequently attain larger proportions, assuming a violence and energy of expression scarcely surpassed by those bred in the depths of winter. Such was the storm now gathering about us.

It began to declare itself shortly after noon, suggesting to us the idea of at once seeking our safe camp in the timber and abandoning the purpose of making an observation of the barometer at 3 P.M.,—two having already been made, at 9 A.M. and 12 M., while simultaneous observations were made at Strawberry Valley. Jerome peered at short intervals over the ridge, contemplating the rising clouds with anxious gestures in the rough wind, and at length declared that if we did not make a speedy escape we should be compelled to pass the rest of the day and night on the summit. But anxiety to complete my observations stifled my own instinctive promptings to retreat, and held me to my work. No inexperienced person was depending on me, and I told Jerome that we two mountaineers should be able to make our way down through any storm likely to fall.

Presently thin, fibrous films of cloud began to blow directly over the summit from north to south, drawn out in long fairy webs like carded wool, forming and dissolving as if by magic. The wind twisted them into ringlets and whirled them in a succession of graceful convolutions like the outside sprays of Yosemite Falls in flood-time; then, sailing out into the thin azure over the precipitous brink of the ridge they were drifted together like wreaths of foam on a river. These higher and finer cloud fabrics were evidently produced by the chilling of the air from its own expansion caused by the upward deflection of the wind against the slopes of the mountain. They steadily increased on the north rim of the cone, forming at length a thick, opaque, ill-defined embankment from the icy meshes of which snow-flowers began to fall, alternating with hail. The sky speedily darkened, and just as I had completed my last observation and boxed my instruments ready for the descent, the storm began in serious earnest. At first the cliffs were beaten with hail, every stone of which, as far as I could see, was regular in form, six-sided pyramids with rounded base, rich and sumptuous-looking, and fashioned with loving care, yet seemingly thrown away on those desolate crags down which they went rolling, falling, sliding in a network of curious streams.

After we had forced our way down the ridge and past the group of hissing fumaroles, the storm became inconceivably violent. The thermometer fell 22° in a few minutes, and soon dropped below zero. The hail gave place to snow, and darkness came on like night. The wind, rising to the highest pitch of violence, boomed and surged amid the desolate crags; lightning-flashes in quick succession cut the gloomy darkness; and the thunders, the most tremendously loud and appalling I ever heard, made an almost continuous roar, stroke following stroke in quick, passionate succession, as though the mountain were being rent to its foundations and the fires of the old volcano were breaking forth again.

Could we at once have begun to descend the snow-slopes leading to the timber, we might have made good our escape, however dark and wild the storm. As it was, we had first to make our way along a dangerous ridge nearly a mile and a half long, flanked in many places by steep ice-slopes at the head of the Whitney Glacier on one side and by shattered precipices on the other. Apprehensive of this coming darkness, I had taken the precaution, when the storm began, to make the most dangerous points clear to my mind, and to mark their relations with reference to the direction of the wind. When, therefore, the darkness came on, and the bewildering drift, I felt confident that we could force our way through it with no other guidance. After passing the "Hot Springs" I halted in the lee of a lava-block to let Jerome, who had fallen a little behind, come up. Here he opened a council in which, under circumstances sufficiently exciting but without evincing any bewilderment, he maintained, in opposition to my views, that it was impossible to proceed. He firmly refused to make the venture to find the camp, while I, aware of the dangers that would necessarily attend our efforts, and conscious of being the cause of his present peril, decided not to leave him.

Our discussions ended, Jerome made a dash from the shelter of the lava-block and began forcing his way back against the wind to the "Hot Springs," wavering and struggling to resist being carried away, as if he were fording a rapid stream. After waiting and watching in vain for some flaw in the storm that might be urged as a new argument in favor of attempting the descent, I was compelled to follow. "Here," said Jerome, as we shivered in the midst of the hissing, sputtering fumaroles, "we shall be safe from frost." "Yes," said I, "we can lie in this mud and steam and sludge, warm at least on one side; but how can we protect our lungs from the acid gases, and how, after our clothing is saturated, shall we be able to reach camp without freezing, even after the storm is over? We shall have to wait for sunshine, and when will it come?"

The tempered area to which we had committed ourselves extended over about one fourth of an acre; but it was only about an eighth of an inch in thickness, for the scalding gas-jets were shorn off close to the ground by the oversweeping flood of frosty wind. And how lavishly the snow fell only mountaineers may know. The crisp crystal flowers seemed to touch one another and fairly to thicken the tremendous blast that carried them. This was the bloom-time, the summer of the cloud, and never before have I seen even a mountain cloud flowering so profusely.

When the bloom of the Shasta chaparral is falling, the ground is sometimes covered for hundreds of square miles to a depth of half an inch. But the bloom of this fertile snow-cloud grew and matured and fell to a depth of two feet in a few hours. Some crystals landed with their rays almost perfect, but most of them were worn and broken by striking against one another, or by rolling on the ground. The touch of these snow-flowers in calm weather is infinitely gentle — glinting, swaying, settling silently in the dry mountain air, or massed in flakes soft and downy. To lie out alone in the mountains of a still night and be touched by the first of these small silent messengers from the sky is a memorable experience, and the fineness of that touch none will forget. But the storm-blast laden with crisp, sharp snow seems to crush and bruise and stupefy with its multitude of stings, and compels the bravest to turn and flee.

The snow fell without abatement until an hour or two after what seemed to be the natural darkness of the night. Up to the time the storm first broke on the summit its development was remarkably gentle. There was a deliberate growth of clouds, a weaving of translucent tissue above, then the roar of the wind and the thunder, and the darkening flight of snow. Its subsidence was not less sudden. The clouds broke and vanished, not a crystal was left in the sky, and the stars shone out with pure and tranquil radiance.

During the storm we lay on our backs so as to present as little surface as possible to the wind, and to let the drift pass over us. The mealy snow sifted into the folds of our clothing and in many places reached the skin. We were glad at first to see the snow packing about us, hoping it would deaden the force of the wind, but it soon froze into a stiff, crusty heap as the temperature fell, rather augmenting our novel misery.

When the heat became unendurable, on some spot where steam was escaping through the sludge, we tried to stop it with snow and mud, or shifted a little at a time by shoving with our heels; for to stand in blank exposure to the fearful wind in our frozen-and-broiled condition seemed certain death. The acrid incrustations sublimed from the escaping gases frequently gave way, opening new vents to scald us; and, fearing that if at any time the wind should fall, carbonic acid, which often formed a considerable portion of the gaseous exhalations of volcanoes, might collect in sufficient quantities to cause sleep and death, I warned Jerome against forgetting himself for a single moment, even should his sufferings admit of such a thing.

Accordingly, when during the long, dreary watches of the night we roused from a state of half-consciousness, we called each other by name in a frightened, startled way, each fearing the other might be benumbed or dead. The ordinary sensations of cold give but a faint conception of that which comes on after hard climbing with want of food and sleep in such exposure as this. Life is then seen to be a fire, that now smoulders, now brightens, and may be easily quenched. The weary hours wore away like dim half-forgotten years, so long and eventful they seemed, though we did nothing but suffer. Still the pain was not always of that bitter, intense kind that precludes thought and takes away all capacity for enjoyment. A sort of dreamy stupor came on at times in which we fancied we saw dry, resinous logs suitable for campfires, just as after going days without food men fancy they see bread.

Frozen, blistered, famished, benumbed, our bodies seemed lost to us at times — all dead but the eyes. For the duller and fainter we became the clearer was our vision, though only in momentary glimpses. Then, after the sky cleared, we gazed at the stars, blessed immortals of light, shining with marvelous brightness with long lance rays, near-looking and new-looking, as if never seen before. Again they would look familiar and remind us of stargazing at home. Oftentimes imagination coming into play would present charming pictures of the warm zone below, mingled with others near and far. Then the bitter wind and the drift would break the blissful vision and dreary pains cover us like clouds. "Are you suffering much?" Jerome would inquire with pitiful faintness. "Yes," I would say, striving to keep my voice brave, "frozen and burned; but never mind,

Jerome, the night will wear away at last, and to-morrow we go a-Maying, and what campfires we will make, and what sunbaths we will take!"

The frost grew more and more intense, and we became icy and covered over with a crust of frozen snow, as if we had lain cast away in the drift all winter. In about thirteen hours — every hour like a year — day began to dawn, but it was long ere the summit's rocks were touched by the sun. No clouds were visible from where we lay, yet the morning was dull and blue, and bitterly frosty; and hour after hour passed by while we eagerly watched the pale light stealing down the ridge to the hollow where we lay. But there was not a trace of that warm, flushing sunrise splendor we so long had hoped for.

As the time drew near to make an effort to reach camp, we became concerned to know what strength was left us, and whether or no we could walk; for we had lain flat all this time without once rising to our feet. Mountaineers, however, always find in themselves a reserve of power after great exhaustion. It is a kind of second life, available only in emergencies like this; and, having proved its existence, I had no great fear that either of us would fail, though one of my arms was already benumbed and hung powerless.

At length, after the temperature was somewhat mitigated on this memorable first of May, we arose and began to struggle homeward. Our frozen trousers could scarcely be made to bend at the knee, and we waded the snow with difficulty. The summit ridge was fortunately wind-swept and nearly bare, so we were not compelled to lift our feet high, and on reaching the long home slopes laden with loose snow we made rapid progress, sliding and shuffling and pitching headlong, our feebleness accelerating rather than diminishing our speed. When we had descended some three thousand feet the sunshine warmed our backs and we began to revive. At 10 A.M. we reached the timber and were safe.

Half an hour later we heard Sisson shouting down among the firs, coming with horses to take us to the hotel. After breaking a trail through the snow as far as possible he had tied his animals and walked up. We had been so long without food that we cared but little about eating, but we eagerly drank the coffee he prepared for us. Our feet were frozen, and thawing them was painful, and had to be done very slowly by keeping them buried in soft snow for several hours, which avoided permanent damage. Five thousand feet below the summit we found only three inches of new snow, and at the base of the mountain only a slight shower of rain had fallen, showing how local our storm had been, notwithstanding its terrific fury. Our feet were wrapped in sacking, and we were soon mounted and on our way down into the thick sunshine — "God's Country," as Sisson calls the Chaparral Zone. In two hours' ride the last snow-bank was left behind. Violets appeared along the edges of the trail, and the chaparral was coming into bloom, with young lilies and larkspurs about the open places in rich profusion. How beautiful seemed the golden sunbeams streaming through the woods between the warm brown boles of the cedars and pines! All my friends among the birds and plants seemed like *old* friends, and we felt like speaking to every one of them as we passed, as if we had been a long time away in some far, strange country.

In the afternoon we reached Strawberry Valley and fell asleep. Next morning we seemed to have risen from the dead. My bedroom was flooded with sunshine, and from the window I saw the great white Shasta cone clad in forests and clouds and bearing them loftily in the sky. Everything seemed full and radiant with the freshness and beauty and enthusiasm of youth. Sisson's children came in with flowers and covered my bed, and the storm on the mountain-top vanished like a dream.

Questions

1. How do you think Muir would have defined *wilderness*?
2. What insights into the origins of America's national parks does Muir's writing provide?

Questions for Further Thought

1. Compare and contrast the experiences of Native Americans, Chinese Americans, and Hispanic Americans in the American West with those of African Americans in the American South.

2. The American West invited John Wesley Powell's call for cooperation (Document 16-6), Charles Fletcher Lummis's romanticization of Hispanic culture (Document 16-10), and John Muir's intensely personal, physical response (Document 16-12). How does each point of view contribute to your understanding of this unique and distinctive region of the country?

CHAPTER SEVENTEEN

Capital and Labor in the Age of Enterprise
1877–1900

Industrial Capitalism Triumphant

Late-nineteenth-century America underwent a remarkable economic transformation. Many manufacturers still worked agricultural products into *consumer goods*—footwear, textiles, furniture, paper, and the like—to be purchased by individuals. But other manufacturers, increasingly important, produced iron and steel and related equipment: locomotives, rolling stock, and rails for railroads; machinery for factories, mines, and oil fields; and various forms for construction. These *capital goods*, purchased by businesses, added to economic growth. By century's end, the United States stood as the world's ranking industrial nation.

Steel and railroads defined the new economic order. The former were essential to a broad range of private enterprises and public undertakings; the latter were crucial to cheap, reliable overland transportation and the creation of a national economy. In the process of developing an integrated national economy, railroads standardized both track gauge (width) and time (dividing the nation into four time zones).

Economic growth brought with it declining prices, increasing real incomes, and widening economic inequality. The period also witnessed recurring economic depressions, especially those of 1873 and 1893, and social conflict arose out of hard times and labor-management confrontations.

Contemporary participants and observers reflected on the transformation of America's economy and society—some to change (Justin Smith Morrill in Document 17-1), some to question (Henry George in Document 17-2), and some to celebrate (Andrew Carnegie in Document 17-3).

17-1 On the Origin of the Land-Grant College Act (c. 1874)

Justin Smith Morrill

A Vermonter and son of a blacksmith, Justin Smith Morrill (1810–1898) was a Congressman best known for legislation that bears his name, the Morrill Act, which was signed into law by Abraham Lincoln on July 2, 1862. Although Morrill himself did not enjoy the benefits of a university education, the act was to provide the sons of farmers and workers of limited means with access to a national system of land-grant colleges, but one controlled and administered entirely at the state level. The measure was to be paid for with proceeds from the sale of public lands (each state was entitled to 30,000 acres for each member of its Congressional delegation). The act helped to expand and democratize higher education and was one of a number of important factors in the rapid modernization of the U.S. economy in the last quarter of the nineteenth century. The following document is from Morrill's 1874 recollection of the origin and purpose of this landmark legislation.

Source: Excerpt from William B. Parker, "The Land-Grant College Acts," in *The Life and Public Services of Justin Smith Morrill* (1924; Boston: Houghton Mifflin Company, 1971), Ch. 11, 262–263. Printed with permission of the publisher.

The idea of obtaining a land grant for the foundation of colleges I think I had formed as early as 1856. I remember to have broached the subject to Hon. William Hebard, the former member of Congress from the 2d District, and he observed that such a measure would be all very well, but that of course I could not expect it to pass. Where I obtained the first hint of such a measure, I am wholly unable to say. Such institutions had already been established in other countries and were supported by their governments, but they were confined exclusively to agriculture, and this for our people, with all their industrial aptitudes and ingenious inventions, appeared to me unnecessarily limited. If the purpose was not suggested by the well-known fact of the existence of Agricultural Schools in Europe it was supported by this fact and especially by constant reflections upon the following points, viz.:

First, that the public lands of most value were being rapidly dissipated by donations to merely local and private objects, where one State alone might be benefited at the expense of the property of the Union.

Second, that the very cheapness of our public lands, and the facility of purchase and transfer, tended to a system of bad-farming or strip and waste of the soil, by encouraging short occupancy and a speedy search for new homes, entailing upon the first and older settlements a rapid deterioration of the soil, which would not be likely to be arrested except by more thorough and scientific knowledge of agriculture and by a higher education of those who were devoted to its pursuit.

Third, being myself the son of a hard-handed blacksmith, the most truly honest man I ever knew, who felt his own deprivation of schools (never having spent but six weeks inside of a schoolhouse), I could not overlook mechanics in any measure intended to aid the industrial classes in the procurement of an education that might exalt their usefulness.

Fourth, that most of the existing collegiate institutions and their feeders were based upon the classic plan of teaching those only destined to pursue the so-called learned professions, leaving farmers and mechanics and all those who must win their bread by labor, to the haphazard of being self-taught or not scientifically taught at all, and restricting the number of those who might be supposed to be qualified to fill places of higher consideration in private or public employments to the limited number of the graduates of the literary institutions. The thoroughly educated, being most sure to educate their sons, appeared to be perpetuating a monopoly of education inconsistent with the welfare and complete prosperity of American institutions.

Fifth, that it was apparent, while some localities were possessed of abundant instrumentalities for education, both common and higher, many of the States were deficient and likely so to remain unless aided by the common fund of the proceeds of the public lands, which were held for this purpose more than any other.

Upon these points and some others I had meditated long and had delved in more or less statistical information, convincing to myself but not the most attractive for a public speech, as I have often found such data, indispensable as it is to the basis of most of our legislative measures, less welcome than even very cheap rhetoric interesting to few and entertaining to none. Discreet legislators cannot get on without reliable facts.

Questions

1. What was the "classic plan of teaching" and how was the Morrill Act to democratize higher education?
2. What is the land-grant institution(s) in your state?

17-2 *Progress and Poverty* (1879)

Henry George

Born to a poor family in Philadelphia, Henry George (1839–1897) moved to California in 1857. He found work as a journalist in the young and rapidly growing city of San Francisco. George observed that although California and the rest of the nation were entering an age of unprecedented wealth, poverty persisted, and social inequality was widening dramatically. To lessen these problems, George proposed that land values, or economic rent, should be taxed and the revenues returned to the public. Moreover, George believed that a "single tax" on land value would eliminate the need for all other taxes and therefore would actually be a boon to capital and labor. George's argument, laid out in his book *Progress and Poverty*, made him famous, and he went on to become a major reform figure in the United States and Great Britain.

Source: Henry George, "Of the Effect upon Individuals and Classes" from *Progress and Poverty: An Inquiry into the Cause of Industrial Depressions and of Increase of Want with Increase of Wealth: The Remedy* (1879; Garden City, NY: Doubleday, Page, 1926), 445–451.

When it is first proposed to put all taxes upon the value of land, and thus confiscate rent, all land holders are likely to take the alarm, and there will not be wanting appeals to the fears of small farm and homestead owners, who will be told that this is a proposition to rob them of their hard-earned property. But a moment's reflection will show that this proposition should commend itself to all whose interests as land holders do not largely exceed their interests as laborers or capitalists, or both. And further consideration will show that though the large land holders may lose relatively, yet even in their case there will be an absolute gain. For, the increase in production will be so great that labor and capital will gain very much more than will be lost to private land ownership, while in these gains, and in the greater ones involved in a more healthy social condition, the whole community, including the land owners themselves, will share.

In a preceding chapter I have gone over the question of what is due to the present land holders, and have shown that they have no claim to compensation. But there is still another ground on which we may dismiss all idea of compensation. They will not really be injured.

It is manifest, of course, that the change I propose will greatly benefit all those who live by wages, whether of hand or of head — laborers, operatives, mechanics, clerks, professional men of all sorts. It is manifest, also, that it will benefit all those who live partly by wages and partly by the earnings of their capital — storekeepers, merchants, manufacturers, employing or undertaking producers and exchangers of all sorts — from the peddler or drayman to the railroad or steamship owner — and it is likewise manifest that it will increase the incomes of those whose incomes are drawn from the earnings of capital, or from investments other than in lands, save perhaps the holders of government bonds or other securities bearing fixed rates of interest, which will probably depreciate in selling value, owing to the rise in the general rate of interest, though the income from them will remain the same.

Take, now, the case of the homestead owner — the mechanic, storekeeper, or professional man who has secured himself a house and lot, where he lives, and which he contemplates with satisfaction as a place from which his family cannot be ejected in case of his death. He will not be injured; on the contrary, he will be the gainer. The selling value of his lot will diminish — theoretically it will entirely disappear. But its usefulnes to him will not disappear. It will serve his purpose as well as ever. While, as the value of all other lots will diminish or disappear in the same ratio, he retains the same security of always having a lot that he had before. That is to say, he is a loser only as the man who has bought himself a pair of boots may be said to be a loser by a subsequent fall in the price of boots. His boots will be just as useful to him, and the next pair of boots he can get cheaper. So, to the homestead owner, his lot will be as useful, and should he look forward to getting a larger lot, or having his children, as they grow up, get homesteads of their own, he will, even in the matter of lots, be the gainer. And in the present, other things considered, he will be much the gainer. For though he will have more taxes to pay upon his land, he will be released from taxes upon his house and improvements, upon his furniture and personal property, upon all that he and his family eat, drink, and wear, while his earnings will be largely increased by the rise of wages, the constant employment, and the increased briskness of trade. His only loss will be, if he wants to sell his lot without getting another, and this will be a small loss compared with the great gain.

And so with the farmer. I speak not now of the farmers who never touch the handles of a plow, who cultivate thousands of acres and enjoy incomes like those of the rich Southern planters before the war; but of the working farmers who constitute such a large class in the United States — men who own small farms, which they cultivate with the aid of their boys, and perhaps some hired help, and who in Europe would be called peasant proprietors. Paradoxical as it may appear to these men until they understand the full bearings of the proposition, of all classes above that of the mere laborer they have most to gain by placing all taxes upon the value of land. That they do not now get as good a living as their hard work ought to give them, they generally feel, though they may not be able to trace the cause. The fact is that taxation, as now levied, falls on them with peculiar severity. They are taxed on all their improvements—houses, barns, fences, crops, stock. The personal property which they have cannot be as readily concealed or undervalued as can the more valuable kinds which are concentrated in the cities. They are not only taxed on personal property and improvements, which the owners of unused land escape, but their land is generally taxed at a higher rate than land held on speculation, simply because it is improved. But further than this, all taxes imposed on commodities, and especially the taxes which, like our protective duties, are imposed with a view of raising the prices of commodities, fall on the farmer without mitigation. For in a country like the United States, which exports agricultural produce, the farmer cannot be protected. Whoever gains, he must lose. Some years ago the Free Trade League of New York published a broadside containing cuts of various articles of necessity marked with the duties imposed by the tariff, and which read something in this wise: "The farmer rises in the morning and draws on his pantaloons taxed 40 per cent. and his boots taxed 30 per cent., striking a light with a match taxed 200 per cent.," and so on, following him through the day and through life, until, killed by taxation, he is lowered into the grave with a rope taxed 45 per cent. This is but a graphic illustration of the manner in which such taxes ultimately fall. The farmer would be a great gainer by the substitution of a single tax upon the value of land for all these taxes, for the taxation of land values would fall with greatest weight, not upon the agricultural districts, where land values are comparatively small, but upon the towns and cities where land values are high; whereas taxes upon personal property and improvements fall as heavily in the country as in the city. And in sparsely settled districts there would be hardly any taxes at all for the farmer to pay. For taxes, being levied upon the value of the bare land, would fall as heavily upon unimproved as upon improved land. Acre for acre, the improved and cultivated farm, with its buildings, fences, orchard, crops, and stock could be taxed no more than unused land of equal quality. The result would be that speculative values would be kept down, and that cultivated and improved farms would have no taxes to pay until the country around them had been well settled. In fact, paradoxical as it may at first seem to them, the effect of putting all taxation upon the value of land would be to relieve the harder working farmers of all taxation.

But the great gain of the working farmer can be seen only when the effect upon the distribution of population is considered. The destruction of speculative land values would tend to diffuse population where it is too dense and to concentrate it where it is too sparse; to substitute for the tenement house, homes surrounded by gardens, and fully to settle agricultural districts before people were driven far from neighbors to look for land. The people of the cities would thus get more of the pure air and sunshine of the country, the people of the country more of the economies and social life of the city. If, as is doubtless the case, the application of machinery tends to large fields, agricultural population will assume the primitive form and cluster in villages. The life of the average farmer is now unnecessarily dreary. He is not only compelled to work early and late, but he is cut off by the sparseness of population from the conveniences, the amusements, the educational facilities, and the social and intellectual opportunities that come with the closer contact of man with man. He would be far better off in all these respects, and his labor would be far more productive, if he and those around him held no more land than they wanted to use.* While his children, as they grew up, would neither be so impelled to seek the excitement of a city nor would they be driven so far away to seek farms of their own. Their means of living would be in their own hands, and at home.

In short, the working farmer is both a laborer and a capitalist, as well as a land owner, and it is by his labor and capital that his living is made. His loss would be nominal; his gain would be real and great.

In varying degrees is this true of all land holders. Many land holders are laborers of one sort or another. And it would be hard to find a land owner not a laborer, who is not also a capitalist—while the general rule is, that the larger the land owner the greater the capitalist. So true is this that in common thought the characters are confounded. Thus to put all taxes on the value of land, while it would be largely to reduce all great fortunes, would in no case leave the rich man penniless. The Duke of Westminster, who owns a considerable part of the site of London, is probably the richest land owner in the world. To take all his ground rents by taxation would largely reduce his enormous income, but would still leave him his buildings and all the income from them, and doubtless much personal property in various other shapes. He would still have all he could by any possibility enjoy, and a much better state of society in which to enjoy it.

So would the Astors of New York remain very rich. And so, I think, it will be seen throughout—this measure would make no one poorer but such as could be made a great deal poorer without being really hurt. It would cut down great fortunes, but it would impoverish no one.

Wealth would not only be enormously increased; it would be equally distributed. I do not mean that each indi-

---

*Besides the enormous increase in the productive power of labor which would result from the better distribution of population there would be also a similar economy in the productive power of land. The concentration of population in cities fed by the exhaustive cultivation of large, sparsely populated areas, results in a literal draining into the sea of the elements of fertility. How enormous this waste is may be seen from the calculations that have been made as to the sewage of our cities, and its practical result is to be seen in the diminishing productiveness of agriculture in large sections. In a great part of the United States we are steadily exhausting our lands.

vidual would get the same amount of wealth. That would not be equal distribution, so long as different individuals have different powers and different desires. But I mean that wealth would be distributed in accordance with the degree in which the industry, skill, knowledge, or prudence of each contributed to the common stock. The great cause which concentrates wealth in the hands of those who do not produce, and takes it from the hands of those who do, would be gone. The inequalities that continued to exist would be those of nature, not the artificial inequalities produced by the denial of natural law. The non-producer would no longer roll in luxury while the producer got but the barest necessities of animal existence.

The monopoly of the land gone, there need be no fear of large fortunes. For then the riches of any individual must consist of wealth, properly so-called—of wealth, which is the product of labor, and which constantly tends to dissipation, for national debts, I imagine, would not long survive the abolition of the system from which they spring. All fear of great fortunes might be dismissed, for when every one gets what he fairly earns, no one can get more than he fairly earns. How many men are there who fairly earn a million dollars?

Questions

1. According to George's plan, on what basis or terms would new wealth be created?
2. What economic developments of the late nineteenth century influenced George's proposal?
3. How would George's "remedy" affect the laborer, the farmer, and the wealthy capitalist?

17-3 The Gospel of Wealth (1889)

Andrew Carnegie

Andrew Carnegie (1835–1919) was unusual among America's business leaders in that he was an immigrant of humble origins. Carnegie was a firm believer in the "law of competition," and although he recognized that "the law may be hard for the individual," he nevertheless believed that "it is best for the race, because it ensures the survival of the fittest in every department." However, like Henry George (Document 17-2), Carnegie was deeply concerned about the growing divide in America between the rich and the poor. As one of the country's great creators of wealth, Carnegie did not question the underlying economic system that concentrated wealth in the hands of the few, but he argued that the wealthy had a duty to properly administer their money to "produce the most beneficial results for the community."

Source: Excerpt from Andrew Carnegie, "The Gospel of Wealth," in *The Gospel of Wealth and Other Timely Essays* (1889; New York: Century Co., 1901), 7–19.

We start, then, with a condition of affairs under which the best interests of the race are promoted, but which inevitably gives wealth to the few. Thus far, accepting conditions as they exist, the situation can be surveyed and pronounced good. The question then arises,—and if the foregoing be correct, it is the only question with which we have to deal,—What is the proper mode of administering wealth after the laws upon which civilization is founded have thrown it into the hands of the few? And it is of this great question that I believe I offer the true solution. It will be understood that fortunes are here spoken of, not moderate sums saved by many years of effort, the returns from which are required for the comfortable maintenance and education of families. This is not wealth, but only competence, which it should be the aim of all to acquire, and which it is for the best interests of society should be acquired.

There are but three modes in which surplus wealth can be disposed of. It can be left to the families of the decedents; or it can be bequeathed for public purposes; or, finally, it can be administered by its possessors during their lives. Under the first and second modes most of the wealth of the world that has reached the few has hitherto been applied. Let us in turn consider each of these modes. The first is the most injudicious. In monarchical countries, the estates and the greatest portion of the wealth are left to the first son, that the vanity of the parent may be gratified by the thought that his name and title are to descend unimpaired to succeeding generations. The condition of this class in Europe to-day teaches the failure of such hopes or ambitions. The successors have become impoverished through their follies, or from the fall in the value of land. Even in Great Britain the strict law of entail has been found inadequate to maintain an hereditary class. Its soil is rapidly passing into the hands of the stranger. Under republican institutions the division of property among the children is much fairer; but the question which forces itself upon thoughtful men in all lands is, Why should men leave great fortunes to their children? If this is done from affection, is it not misguided affection? Observation teaches that, generally speaking, it is not well for the children that they should be so burdened. Neither is it well for the State. Beyond providing for the wife and daughters moderate sources of income, and very moderate allowances indeed, if any, for the sons, men may well hesitate; for it is no longer questionable that great sums bequeathed often work more for the injury than for the good of the recipients. Wise men will soon conclude that, for the best interests of the members of their families, and of the State, such bequests are an improper use of their means.

It is not suggested that men who have failed to educate their sons to earn a livelihood shall cast them adrift in poverty. If any man has seen fit to rear his sons with a view to their living idle lives, or, what is highly commendable, has instilled in them the sentiment that they are in a position to labor for public ends without reference to pecuniary considerations, then, of course, the duty of the parent is to see that such are provided for in moderation. There are instances of millionaires' sons unspoiled by wealth, who, being rich, still perform great services to the community. Such are the very salt of the earth, as valuable as, unfortunately, they are rare. It is not the exception, however, but the rule, that men must regard; and, looking at the usual result of enormous sums conferred upon legatees, the thoughtful man must shortly say, "I would as soon leave to my son a curse as the almighty dollar," and admit to himself that it is not the welfare of the children, but family pride, which inspires these legacies.

As to the second mode, that of leaving wealth at death for public uses, it may be said that this is only a means for the disposal of wealth, provided a man is content to wait until he is dead before he becomes of much good in the world. Knowledge of the results of legacies bequeathed is not calculated to inspire the brightest hopes of much posthumous good being accomplished by them. The cases are not few in which the real object sought by the testator is not attained, nor are they few in which his real wishes are thwarted. In many cases the bequests are so used as to become only monuments of his folly. It is well to remember that it requires the exercise of not less ability than that which acquires it, to use wealth so as to be really beneficial to the community. Besides this, it may fairly be said that no man is to be extolled for doing what he cannot help doing, nor is he to be thanked by the community to which he only leaves wealth at death. Men who leave vast sums in this way may fairly be thought men who would not have left it at all had they been able to take it with them. The memories of such cannot be held in grateful remembrance, for there is no grace in their gifts. It is not to be wondered at that such bequests seem so generally to lack the blessing.

The growing disposition to tax more and more heavily large estates left at death is a cheering indication of the growth of a salutary change in public opinion. The State of Pennsylvania now takes—subject to some exceptions—one tenth of the property left by its citizens. The budget presented in the British Parliament the other day proposes to increase the death duties; and, most significant of all, the new tax is to be a graduated one. Of all forms of taxation this seems the wisest. Men who continue hoarding great sums all their lives, the proper use of which for public ends would work good to the community from which it chiefly came, should be made to feel that the community, in the form of the State, cannot thus be deprived of its proper share. By taxing estates heavily at death the State marks its condemnation of the selfish millionaire's unworthy life.

It is desirable that nations should go much further in this direction. Indeed, it is difficult to set bounds to the share of a rich man's estate which should go at his death to the public through the agency of the State, and by all means such taxes should be graduated, beginning at nothing upon moderate sums to dependants, and increasing rapidly as the amounts swell, until of the millionaire's hoard, as of Shylock's, at least

The other half
Comes to the privy coffer of the State.

This policy would work powerfully to induce the rich man to attend to the administration of wealth during his life, which is the end that society should always have in view, as being by far the most fruitful for the people. Nor need it be feared that this policy would sap the root of enterprise and render men less anxious to accumulate, for, to the class whose ambition it is to leave great fortunes and be talked about after their death, it will attract even more attention, and, indeed, be a somewhat nobler ambition, to have enormous sums paid over to the State from their fortunes.

There remains, then, only one mode of using great fortunes; but in this we have the true antidote for the temporary unequal distribution of wealth, the reconciliation of the rich and the poor—a reign of harmony, another ideal, differing, indeed, from that of the Communist in requiring only the further evolution of existing conditions, not the total overthrow of our civilization. It is founded upon the present most intense Individualism, and the race is prepared to put it in practice by degrees whenever it pleases. Under its sway we shall have an ideal State, in which the surplus wealth of the few will become, in the best sense, the property of the many, because administered for the common good; and this wealth, passing through the hands of the few, can be made a much more potent force for the elevation of our race than if distributed in small sums to the people themselves. Even the poorest can be made to see this, and to agree that great sums gathered by some of their fellow-citizens and spent for public purposes, from which the masses reap the principal benefit, are more valuable to them than if scattered among themselves in trifling amounts through the course of many years....

Poor and restricted are our opportunities in this life, narrow our horizon, our best work most imperfect; but rich men should be thankful for one inestimable boon. They have it in their power during their lives to busy themselves in organizing benefactions from which the masses of their fellows will derive lasting advantage, and thus dignify their own lives. The highest life is probably to be reached, not by such imitation of the life of Christ as Count Tolstoi gives us, but, while animated by Christ's spirit, by recognizing the changed conditions of this age, and adopting modes of expressing this spirit suitable to the changed conditions under which we live, still laboring for the good of our fellows, which was the essence of his life and teaching, but laboring in a different manner.

This, then, is held to be the duty of the man of wealth: To set an example of modest, unostentatious living, shunning display or extravagance; to provide moderately for the legitimate wants of those dependent upon him; and, after doing so, to consider all surplus revenues which come to him simply as trust funds, which he is called upon to administer, and strictly bound as a matter of duty to administer in the manner which, in his judgment, is best calculated to produce the most beneficial results for the community—the man of wealth thus becoming the mere trustee and agent for his poorer brethren, bringing to their service his superior wisdom, experience, and ability to administer, doing for them better than they would or could do for themselves.

We are met here with the difficulty of determining what are moderate sums to leave to members of the family; what is modest, unostentatious living; what is the test of extravagance. There must be different standards for different conditions. The answer is that it is as impossible to name exact amounts or actions as it is to define good manners, good taste, or the rules of propriety; but, nevertheless, these are verities, well known, although indefinable. Public sentiment is quick to know and to feel what offends these. So in the case of wealth. The rule in regard to good taste in the dress of men or women applies here. Whatever makes one conspicuous offends the canon. If any family be chiefly known for display, for extravagance in home, table, or equipage, for enormous sums ostentatiously spent in any form upon itself—if these be its chief distinctions, we have no difficulty in estimating its nature or culture. So likewise in regard to the use or abuse of its surplus wealth, or to generous, free-handed coöperation in good public uses, or to unabated efforts to accumulate and hoard to the last, or whether they administer or bequeath. The verdict rests with the best and most enlightened public sentiment. The community will surely judge, and its judgments will not often be wrong.

The best uses to which surplus wealth can be put have already been indicated. Those who would administer wisely must, indeed, be wise; for one of the serious obstacles to the improvement of our race is indiscriminate charity. It were better for mankind that the millions of the rich were thrown into the sea than so spent as to encourage the slothful, the drunken, the unworthy. Of every thousand dollars spent in so-called charity to-day, it is probable that nine hundred and fifty dollars is unwisely spent—so spent, indeed, as to produce the very evils which it hopes to mitigate or cure. A well-known writer of philosophic books admitted the other day that he had given a quarter of a dollar to a man who approached him as he was coming to visit the house of his friend. He knew nothing of the habits of this beggar, knew not the use that would be made of this money, although he had every reason to suspect that it would be spent improperly. This man professed to be a disciple of Herbert Spencer; yet the quarter-dollar given that night will probably work more injury than all the money will do good which its thoughtless donor will ever be able to give in true charity. He only gratified his own feelings, saved himself from annoyance—and this was probably one of the most selfish and very worst actions of his life, for in all respects he is most worthy.

In bestowing charity, the main consideration should be to help those who will help themselves; to provide part of the means by which those who desire to improve may do so; to give those who desire to rise the aids by which they may rise; to assist, but rarely or never to do all. Neither the individual nor the race is improved by almsgiving. Those worthy of assistance, except in rare cases, seldom require assistance. The really valuable men of the race never do, except in case of accident or sudden change. Every one has, of course, cases of individuals brought to his own knowledge where temporary assistance can do genuine good, and these he will not overlook. But the amount which can be wisely given by the individual for individuals is necessarily limited by his lack of knowledge of the circumstances connected with each. He is the only true reformer who is as careful and as anxious not to aid the unworthy as he is to aid the worthy, and, perhaps, even more so, for in almsgiving more injury is probably done by rewarding vice than by relieving virtue.

The rich man is thus almost restricted to following the examples of Peter Cooper, Enoch Pratt of Baltimore, Mr. Pratt of Brooklyn, Senator Stanford, and others, who know that the best means of benefiting the community is to place within its reach the ladders upon which the aspiring can rise—free libraries, parks, and means of recreation, by which men are helped in body and mind; works of art, certain to give pleasure and improve the public taste; and public institutions of various kinds, which will improve the general condition of the people; in this manner returning their surplus wealth to the mass of their fellows in the forms best calculated to do them lasting good.

Thus is the problem of rich and poor to be solved. The laws of accumulation will be left free, the laws of distribution free. Individualism will continue, but the millionaire will be but a trustee for the poor, intrusted for a season with a great part of the increased wealth of the community, but administering it for the community far better than it could or would have done for itself. The best minds will thus have reached a stage in the development of the race in which it is clearly seen that there is no mode of disposing of surplus wealth creditable to thoughtful and earnest men into whose hands it flows, save by using it year by year for the general good. This day already dawns. Men may die without incurring the pity of their fellows, still sharers in great business enterprises from which their capital cannot be or has not been withdrawn, and which is left chiefly at death for public uses; yet the day is not far distant when the man who dies leaving behind him millions of available wealth, which was free for him to administer during life, will pass away "unwept, unhonored, and unsung," no matter to what uses he leaves the dross which he cannot take with him. Of such as these the public verdict will then be: "The man who dies thus rich dies disgraced."

Such, in my opinion, is the true gospel concerning wealth, obedience to which is destined some day to solve the problem of the rich and the poor, and to bring "Peace on earth, among men good will."

Questions

1. According to Carnegie, how should the wealth of the rich be redistributed to the poor?
2. What distinction did Carnegie make between philanthropy—that is, his gospel of wealth—and the charity that he saw practiced?
3. What are some of the lasting contributions that Carnegie made to American society?

Questions for Further Thought

1. Morrill, George, and Carnegie were all concerned about the future of democracy in a changing society. Explain.
2. What are the main points of disagreement between George and Carnegie?
3. What do you find most persuasive in George's argument? In Carnegie's?

The World of Work

"Free labor" ideology, which extolled the ability of men to rise from being wage-earning laborers to craftsmen or landowning farmers, was important to the early Republican Party. But from mid-century on, "the world of work" was becoming increasingly stratified; entrepreneurs did indeed employ wage earners, but relatively few of these laborers would become independent farmers or craftsmen. In addition to men, children and women were employed in the new mines and factories.

Indeed, women were an important element in the growing labor force. In 1900 they constituted about 25 percent of all workers, with about one-third each in industry, domestic service, and some white-collar fields. Before the end of the nineteenth century, few married white women—but a considerable number of married African American women—worked outside the home. However, as northern industrial states began to prohibit child labor and limit the working hours of adolescents, thereby reducing the incomes of working-class families, more married women felt the need to take jobs outside of the home.

Document 17-4 is an account of child labor in Pennsylvania. Documents 17-5 and 17-6 illuminate aspects of the lives and labors of women in very different settings. Meanwhile, Frederick Winslow Taylor (Document 17-7), who had trained as an engineer, was gaining on-the-job experience that would make him the high priest of "scientific management" in industry (see text p. 538).

17-4 On Child Labor (1877)

The U.S. transition to an industrial economy was a painful one for many who were involved. Children were initially exploited, and sometimes exposed to very dangerous working conditions. The practice shocked contemporary observers, however, and child labor was eventually proscribed by law. The following selection is from a correspondent for the *Labor Standard* (May 17, 1877) who described the breaker room in the Hickory Colliery, near St. Clair in Pennsylvania's coal country.

Source: Anthony Bimba, *The Molly Maguires* (New York: International Publishers, 1932), 30–32. Reprinted with permission of the publisher.

In these works 300 men and boys are employed; and when I went through the buildings and through the mine I saw them all. Among all these 300, although I was with them for hours, I did not hear a laugh or even see a smile.

In a little room in this big, black shed—a room not twenty feet square—where a broken stove, red-hot, tries vainly to warm the cold air that comes in through the open window, forty boys are picking their lives away. The floor of the room is an inclined plane, and a stream of coal pours constantly in from some unseen place above, crosses the room, and pours out again into some unseen place below. Rough board seats stretch across the room, five or six rows of them, very low and very dirty, and on these the boys sit, and separate the slate from the coal as it runs down the inclined plane. It is a painful sight to see the men going so silently and gloomily about their work, but it is a thousand times worse to see these boys. They work here, in this little black hole, all day and every day, trying to keep cool in summer, trying to keep warm in winter, picking away among the black coals, bending over till their little spines are curved, never saying a word all the live-long day.

I stood and watched these boys for a long time, without being seen by them, for their backs are turned toward the entrance door and the coal makes such a racket that they cannot hear anything a foot from their ears. They were muffled up in old coats and old shawls and old scarfs, and ragged mittens to keep their hands from freezing, and as they sat and picked and picked, gathering little heaps of blackened slate by their sides, they looked more like so many black dwarfs than like a party of fresh young boys. The air was cold enough and the work was lively enough to paint any boy's cheeks in rosy colors; but if there was a red cheek in the room it was well hidden under the coating of black dust that covered everything. These little fellows go to work in this cold, dreary room at seven o'clock in the morning and work till it is too dark to see any longer. For this they get from $1 to $3 a week. One result of their work is the clean, free coal, that burns away to ashes in the grate; another result I found in a little miners' graveyard, beside a pretty little church, where more than every other stone bears the name of some little fellow under fifteen years of age.

The boys are all sizes and ages, from little fellows scarce big enough to be wearing pantaloons up to youths of fifteen and sixteen. After they reach this age they go to work in the mine, for there they can make more money. Not three boys in all this roomful could read or write. Shut in from everything that is pleasant, with no chance to learn, with no knowledge of what is going on about them, with nothing to do but work, grinding their little lives away in this dusty room, they are no more than the wire screens that separate the great lumps of coal from the small. They have no games; when their day's work is done they are too tired for that. They know nothing but the difference between slate and coal.

The smallest of the boys do not get more than $1 a week, and from this the pay goes up to $2 and $3. Some of them live several miles from the colliery, and are carried to the mine every morning in the cars and back again every night, the company charging them ten cents for each trip and deducting the fares from their wages at the end of the month. Sometimes, after the boys have got to the mine, they find that some accident has stopped the work; then they have nothing to do for the day and get no pay. In this way, I am told, it is no unusual thing for a boy to find, at the end of the month, that his indebtedness to the company for railroad fares is some dollars more than the company's indebtedness to him for labor; so that he has worked all the month for a few dollars less than nothing.

Question

1. The correspondent seemed to invite consideration of broader moral and social concerns. What were they?

17-5 Studies of Factory Life: Among the Women (1888)

Lillie B. Chase Wyman

Lillie B. Chase Wyman wrote her article on factory workers in Rhode Island in response to a statement that it was "very much needed . . . for rich men to find out how poor men live." Poor women and children needed a voice, too, as this excerpt makes clear.

Source: Lillie B. Chase Wyman, "Studies of Factory Life: Among the Women," *Atlantic Monthly* 62 (September 1888), 320–321.

Two years ago, a ten-hour law was enacted in Rhode Island. Philanthropists and workmen urged the passage of the bill. They were concerned about the health of the workwomen, the undermining of whose strength involved not only suffering, but the weakness of the next generation. The manufacturers, so far as they took any action, opposed the law. Some of them were sure their business would be ruined, if it went on to the statute book. Others were merely afraid that financial disasters would be the result. The women themselves were not consulted, and, according to the fashion of the republic, had no part nor lot in deciding their own destiny. Various sorts of men, workmen, manufacturers, and legislators deliberated together about woman's flesh and blood, considered her maternal capacities and her muscular strength, and compared them with the exactions of business and of machinery. She stood and waited — or rather she worked and waited — their decision that sixty hours a week in a factory was enough for her and for her little children. The bill passed, and there was no financial collapse.

There is a young girl working in a thread factory in the State who was much pleased to have some more leisure time. She was taking a Chautauqua course of reading with her mother. She lives some distance from the mill, and so does not go home to dinner. Under the new arrangement she had an hour's recess at noon. She carried her book as well as her lunch, and employed the extra moments in reading. She was anxious to obtain a complete copy of the Iliad, having read some portions of it in the prescribed course, which made her desire to know the whole poem. She read translations of some of the Greek plays, and was glad to have the opportunity to borrow a version of the Electra of Sophocles; and when she returned it, she said she liked it better than any of the others she had read. This girl is, however, unique in my experience. She is a Protestant, of English parentage. From childhood on she has shown an earnest nature. She always tried to do what seemed right to her, or what might help some one else. It was a terrible cross to her to be obliged to leave school when she was about fourteen, and go into the mill, but she did it; and her character shows its fine fibre now, in that she does her duty simply, trying constantly to improve herself, but not trying to get into any place which she is not fitted to fill thoroughly. She is not a sham lady nor a sham worker because she has a desire for something besides spindles and a taste for something other than clothes. She dresses simply, and is very willing to use her Saturday half-holidays visiting in behalf of the Associated Charities.

Homely but pathetic was the rejoicing of a hard-worked Irish widow over the ten-hour law. She had been the mother of thirteen or fourteen children, but most of them died; and last of all, her husband, a handsome man, whom she seemed to consider a being quite superior to herself, died, after a protracted illness. He did the housework long after he could not do other labor, so that she might be the chief wage-earner of the family. After his death, she said: "I fretted a deal for him, — I couldn't help it. I know he had been sick a long time, but you miss a person just the same if they have been sick; an' he was such a clean man about the house, an' kept it so neat when he was able to be about."

In a worldly way she manages very well without him. She and a grown girl and two young lads work in the mill. Two younger children profess to guard the house, and sometimes go to school. The daughter takes books occasionally from the village library, and she has read *The Scarlet Letter* and even the *Blithedale Romance*. She said she liked these stories about as well as she did Marion Harland's novels. The mother found the ten-hour law a great help. "Why," said she, "the extra quarter of an hour at noon gives me time to mix my bread; an' then when I comes home at night, at six o'clock, it is ready to put in the pans, an' I can do that while Katie sets the table; an' after supper, an' the dishes are washed, I can bake; an' then I am through, an' ready to go to bed, mebbe afore it's quite nine o'clock. Oh, it's splendid, the best thing as ever 'appened. I used to be up till 'way into the night, bakin', after my day's work in the mill was done."

She probably was glad of the Saturday half-holiday, because it gave her a good chance to do her washing. Holidays, to women like her, mean little but the time to do some different kind of work from that by which they earn their living. Her boy rejoiced in healthy fashion. "Saturdays," says he, "when you are let out at one o'clock, you don't feel as if you'd been at work at all."

Questions

1. What might an advocate of woman suffrage have made of Wyman's account?
2. What significance did the people that Wyman interviewed attach to the state's ten-hour law?

17-6 More Slavery at the South (c. 1912)

**Anonymous
(A Black Domestic)**

As the textbook notes, more than one-fourth of the nonfarm workforce in 1900 consisted of women, most of whom worked out of necessity. Outside of teaching, social work, and nursing, women did not expect to enjoy a professional career (or equal pay), and a majority worked in factories or as domestics. This reading details the work of an African American woman. Although caring for white children gave her a degree of social status, she found her life "just as bad as, if not worse than, it was during the days of slavery."

Source: Anonymous (A Negro Nurse), "More Slavery at the South," *The Independent* 72 (January 25, 1912), 196–200, in W. Elliot Brownlee and Mary M. Brownlee, *Women in the American Economy: A Documentary History, 1675 to 1929* (New Haven, CT: Yale University Press, 1976), 244–249.

I am a negro woman, and I was born and reared in the South. I am now past forty years of age and am the mother of three children. My husband died nearly fifteen years ago, after we had been married about five years. For more than thirty years—or since I was ten years old—I have been a servant in one capacity or another in white families in a thriving Southern city, which has at present a population of more than 50,000. In my early years I was at first what might be called a "house-girl," or better, a "house-boy." I used to answer the doorbell, sweep the yard, go on errands, and do odd jobs. Later on I became a chambermaid.... Still later I was graduated into a cook, in which position I served at different times for nearly eight years in all. During the last ten years I have been a nurse. I have worked for only four different families during all these thirty years. But, belonging to the servant class, which is the majority class among my race at the South, and associating only with servants, I have been able to become intimately acquainted not only with the lives of hundreds of household servants, but also with the lives of their employers. I can, therefore, speak with authority on the so-called servant question; and what I say is said out of an experience which covers many years.

To begin with, then, I should say that more than two-thirds of the negroes of the town where I live are menial servants of one kind or another, and besides that more than two-thirds of the negro women here, whether married or single, are compelled to work for a living,—as nurses, cooks, washerwomen, chambermaids, seamstresses, hucksters [peddlers], janitresses, and the like. I will say, also, that the condition of this vast host of poor colored people is just as bad as, if not worse than, it was during the days of slavery. Though today we are enjoying nominal freedom, we are literally slaves. And, not to generalize, I will give you a sketch of the work I have to do—and I'm only one of many.

I frequently work from fourteen to sixteen hours a day. I am compelled by my contract, which is oral only, to sleep in the house. I am allowed to go home to my own children, the oldest of whom is a girl of 18 years, only once in two weeks, every other Sunday afternoon—even then I'm not permitted to stay all night. I not only have to nurse a little white child, now eleven months old, but I have to act as playmate or "handy-andy," not say governess, to three other children in the home, the oldest of whom is only nine years of age. I wash and dress the baby two or three times each day; I give it its meals, mainly from a bottle; I have to put it to bed each night; and, in addition, I have to get up and attend to its every call between midnight and morning. If the baby falls to sleep during the day, as it has been trained to do every day about eleven o'clock, I am not permitted to rest. It's "Mammy, do this," or "Mammy, do that," or "Mammy, do the other," from my mistress, all the time. So it is not strange to see "Mammy" watering the lawn in front with the garden hose, sweeping the sidewalk, mopping the porch and halls, dusting around the house, helping the cook, or darning stockings. Not only so, but I have to put the other three children to bed each night as well as the baby, and I have to wash them and dress them each morning. I don't know what it is to go to church; I don't know what it is to go to a lecture or entertainment or anything of the kind; I live a treadmill life; and I see my own children only when they happen to see me on the streets when I am out with the children, or when my children come to the "yard" to see me, which isn't often, because my white folks don't like to see their servants' children hanging around their premises. You might as well say that I'm on duty all the time—from sunrise to sunrise, every day in the week. I am the slave, body and soul, of this family. And what do I get for this work—this lifetime bondage? The pitiful sum of ten dollars a month! And what am I expected to do with these ten dollars? With this money I'm expected to pay my house rent, which is four dollars per month, for a little house of two rooms, just big enough to turn round in; and I'm expected, also to feed and clothe myself and three children. For two years my oldest child, it is true, has helped a little toward our support by taking in a little washing at home. She does the washing and ironing of two white families, with a total of five persons; one of these families pays her $1.00 per week, and the other 75 cents per week, and my daughter has to furnish her own soap and starch and wood. For six months my youngest child, a girl about thirteen years old, has been nursing, and she receives $1.50 per week but has no night work. When I think of the low rate of wages we poor colored people receive, and when I hear so much said about our unreliability, our untrustworthiness, and even our vices, I recall the story of the private soldier in a certain army who, once upon a time, being upbraided by the commanding officer because the heels of his shoes were not polished, is said to have replied: "Captain, do you expect all the virtues for $13 per month?"

Of course, nothing is being done to increase our wages, and the way things are going at present it would seem that nothing could be done to cause an increase in wages. We have no labor unions or organizations of any kind that could demand for us a uniform scale of wages for cooks, washerwomen, nurses, and the like; and, for another thing, if some negroes did here and there refuse to work for seven and eight and ten dollars a month, there would be hundreds of other negroes right on the spot ready to take their places and do the same work, or more, for the low wages that had been refused. So that, the truth is, we have to work for little or nothing or become vagrants! And that, of course, in this State would mean that we would be arrested, tried, and despatched to the "State Farm," where we would surely have to work for nothing or be beaten with many stripes!

Nor does this low rate of pay tend to make us efficient servants. The most that can be said of us negro household servants in the South—and I speak as one of them—is that we are to the extent of our ability willing and faithful slaves. We do not cook according to scientific principles because we do not know anything about scientific principles. Most of our cooking is done by guesswork or by memory. We cook well when our "hand" is in, as we say, and when anything about the dinner goes wrong, we simply say, "I lost my hand today!" We don't know anything about scientific food for babies, nor anything about what science says must be done for infants at certain periods of their growth or when certain symptoms of disease appear; but somehow we "raise" more of the children than we kill, and, for the most part, they are lusty chaps—all of them. But the point is, we do not go to cooking-schools nor to nurse-training schools, and so it cannot be expected that we should make as efficient servants without such training as we should make were such training provided. And yet with our cooking and nursing, such as it is, the white folks seem to be satisfied—perfectly satisfied. I sometimes wonder if this satisfaction is the outgrowth of the knowledge that more highly trained servants would be able to demand better pay! . . .

Another thing—it's a small indignity, it may be, but an indignity just the same. No white person, not even the little children just learning to talk, no white person at the South ever thinks of addressing any negro man or woman as Mr., or Mrs., or Miss. The women are called, "Cook," or "Nurse," or "Mammy," or "Mary Jane," or "Lou," or "Dilcey," as the case might be, and the men are called "Bob," or "Boy," or "Old Man," or "Uncle Bill," or "Pate." In many cases our white employers refer to us, and in our presence, too, as their "niggers." No matter what they call us—no matter what they teach their children to call us—we must tamely submit, and answer when we are called; we must enter no protest; if we did object, we should be driven out without the least ceremony, and, in applying for work at other places, we should find it very hard to procure another situation. In almost every case, when our intending employers would be looking up our record, the information would be given by telephone or otherwise that we were "impudent," "saucy," "dishonest," and "generally unreliable." In our town we have no such thing as an employment agency or intelligence bureau, and, therefore, when we want work, we have to get out on the street and go from place to place, always with hat in hand, hunting for it. . . .

You hear a good deal nowadays about the "service pan." The "service pan" is the general term applied to "left-over" food, which in many a Southern home is freely placed at the disposal of the cook, or, whether so placed or not, it is usually disposed of by the cook. In my town, I know, and I guess in many other towns also, every night when the cook starts for her home she takes with her a pan or a plate of cold victuals. The same thing is true on Sunday afternoon after dinner—and most cooks have nearly every Sunday afternoon off. Well, I'll be frank with you, if it were not for the service pan, I don't know what the majority of our Southern colored families would do. The service pan is the mainstay in many a home. Good cooks in the South receive on an average $8 per month. Porters, butlers, coachmen, janitors, "office boys" and the like, receive on an average $16 per month. Few and far between are the colored men in the South who receive $1 or more per day. Some mechanics do; as, for example, carpenters, brick masons, wheelwrights, blacksmiths, and the like. The vast majority of negroes in my town are serving in menial capacities in homes, stores and offices. Now taking it for granted, for the sake of illustration, that the husband receives $16 per month and the wife $8. That would be $24 between the two. The chances are that they will have anywhere from five to thirteen children between them. Now, how far will $24 go toward housing and feeding and clothing ten or twelve persons for thirty days? And, I tell you, with all of us poor people the service pan is a great institution; it is a great help to us, as we wag along the weary way of life. And then most of the white folks expect their cooks to avail themselves of these perquisites; they allow it; they expect it. I do not deny that the cooks find opportunity to hide away at times, along with the cold "grub," a little sugar, a little flour, a little meal, or a little piece of soap; but I indignantly deny that we are thieves. We don't steal; we just "take" things—they are a part of the oral contract, expressed or implied. We understand it, and most of the white folks understand it. Others may denounce the service pan, and say that it is used only to support idle negroes, but many a time, when I was a cook, and had the responsibility of rearing my three children upon my lone shoulders, many a time I have had occasion to bless the Lord for the service pan!

Questions

1. How did domestic work humiliate women like the narrator?
2. What was the paradox that the narrator experienced in working for white families?
3. What was the service pan? What was its significance to African American workers?

17-7 *Principles of Scientific Management* (1911)

Frederick Winslow Taylor

Frederick Winslow Taylor (1856–1915) combined an American love of machines with a passion for improving production systems. Taylor believed so deeply in the ideal of efficiency that he designed his own tennis racquet and golf putter. Trained as an engineer, he began to implement his notion of "scientific management" in the 1890s. Taylor argued that productivity could be improved through better-designed machines and work habits as well as a pay formula based on piecework. This selection is taken from his *Principles of Scientific Management*, published in 1911.

There were skeptics, and in 1912 Taylor went before a special committee of the U.S. House of Representatives to defend what he called "this great mental revolution." However, critics persisted in charging that scientific management dehumanized work by emphasizing machines and productivity.

Source: From Frederick Winslow Taylor, *Scientific Management* (New York: Harper and Brothers, 1947; reprint, Westport, CT: Greenwood Press, 1972), 58–67.

To return now to our pig-iron handlers at the Bethlehem Steel Company. If Schmidt had been allowed to attack the pile of 47 tons of pig iron without the guidance or direction of a man who understood the art, or science, of handling pig iron, in his desire to earn his high wages he would probably have tired himself out by 11 or 12 o'clock in the day. He would have kept so steadily at work that his muscles would not have the proper periods of rest absolutely needed for recuperation, and he would have been completely exhausted early in the day. By having a man, however, who understood this law, stand over him and direct his work, day after day, until he acquired the habit of resting at proper intervals, he was able to work at an even gait all day long without unduly tiring himself.

Now one of the very first requirements for a man who is fit to handle pig iron as a regular occupation is that he shall be so stupid and so phlegmatic that he more nearly resembles in his mental make-up the ox than any other type. The man who is mentally alert and intelligent is for this very reason entirely unsuited to what would, for him, be the grinding monotony of work of this character. Therefore the workman who is best suited to handling pig iron is unable to understand the real science of doing this class of work. He is so stupid that the word "percentage" has no meaning to him, and he must consequently be trained by a man more intelligent than himself into the habit of working in accordance with the laws of this science before he can be successful.

The writer trusts that it is now clear that even in the case of the most elementary form of labor that is known, there is a science, and that when the man best suited to this class of work has been carefully selected, when the science of doing the work has been developed, and when the carefully selected man has been trained to work in accordance with this science, the results obtained must of necessity be overwhelmingly greater than those which are possible under the plan of "initiative and incentive."

Let us, however, again turn to the case of these pig-iron handlers, and see whether, under the ordinary type of management, it would not have been possible to obtain practically the same results.

The writer has put the problem before many good managers, and asked them whether, under premium work, piece work, or any of the ordinary plans of management, they would be likely even to approximate 47 tons per man per day, and not a man has suggested that an output of over 18 to 25 tons could be attained by any of the ordinary expedients. It will be remembered that the Bethlehem men were loading only 12½ tons per man.

To go into the matter in more detail, however: As to the scientific selection of the men, it is a fact that in this gang of 75 pig-iron handlers only about one man in eight was physically capable of handling 47½ tons per day. With the very best of intentions, the other seven out of eight men were physically unable to work at this pace. Now the one man in eight who was able to do this work was in no sense superior to the other men who were working on the gang. He merely happened to be a man of the type of the ox,—no rare specimen of humanity, difficult to find and therefore very highly prized. On the contrary, he was a man so stupid that he was unfitted to do most kinds of laboring work, even. The selection of the man, then, does not involve finding some extraordinary individual, but merely picking out from among very ordinary men the few who are especially suited to this type of work. Although in this particular gang only one man in eight was suited to doing the work, we had not the slightest difficulty in getting all the men who were needed—some of them from inside of the works and others from the neighboring country—who were exactly suited to the job.

Under the management of "initiative and incentive" the attitude of the management is that of "putting the work up to the workmen." What likelihood would there be, then, under the old type of management, of these men properly selecting themselves for pig-iron handling? Would they be likely to get rid of seven men out of eight from their own gang and retain only the eighth man? No! And no expedient could be devised which would make these men properly select themselves. Even if they fully realized the necessity of doing so in order to obtain high wages (and they are not sufficiently intelligent properly to grasp this necessity), the fact that their friends or their brothers who were working right alongside of them would temporarily be thrown out of a job because they were not suited to this kind of work would entirely prevent them from properly selecting themselves, that is, from removing the seven out of eight men on the gang who were unsuited to pig-iron handling.

As to the possibility, under the old type of management, of inducing these pig-iron handlers (after they had been properly selected) to work in accordance with the science of doing heavy laboring, namely, having proper scientifically determined periods of rest in close sequence to periods of work. As has been indicated before, the essential idea of the ordinary types of management is that each workman has become more skilled in his own trade than it is possible for any one in the management to be, and that, therefore, the details of how the work shall best be done must be left to him. The idea, then, of taking one man after another and training him under a competent teacher into new working habits until he continually and habitually works in accordance with scientific laws, which have been developed by some one else, is directly antagonistic to the old idea that each workman can best regulate his own way of doing the work. And besides this, the man suited to handling pig iron is too stupid properly to train himself. Thus it will be seen that with the ordinary types of management the development of scientific knowledge to replace rule of thumb, the scientific selection of the men, and inducing the men to work in accordance with these scientific principles are entirely out of the question. And this because the philosophy of the old management puts the entire responsibility upon the workmen, while the philosophy of the new places a great part of it upon the management.

With most readers great sympathy will be aroused because seven out of eight of these pig-iron handlers were thrown out of a job. This sympathy is entirely wasted, because almost all of them were immediately given other jobs with the Bethlehem Steel Company. And indeed it should be understood that the removal of these men from pig-iron handling, for which they were unfit, was really a kindness to themselves, because it was the first step toward finding them work for which they were peculiarly fitted, and at which, after receiving proper training, they could permanently and legitimately earn higher wages.

Although the reader may be convinced that there is a certain science back of the handling of pig iron, still it is more than likely that he is still skeptical as to the existence of a science for doing other kinds of laboring. One of the important objects of this paper is to convince its readers that every single act of every workman can be reduced to a science. With the hope of fully convincing the reader of this fact, therefore, the writer proposes to give several more simple illustrations from among the thousands which are at hand.

For example, the average man would question whether there is much of any science in the work of shoveling. Yet there is but little doubt, if any intelligent reader of this paper were deliberately to set out to find what may be called the foundation of the science of shoveling, that with perhaps 15 to 20 hours of thought and analysis he would be almost sure to have arrived at the essence of this science. On the other hand, so completely are the rule-of-thumb ideas still dominant that the writer has never met a single shovel contractor to whom it had ever even occurred that there was such a thing as the science of shoveling. This science is so elementary as to be almost self-evident.

For a first class shoveler there is a given shovel load at which he will do his biggest day's work. What is this shovel load? Will a first-class man do more work per day with a shovel load of 5 pounds, 10 pounds, 15 pounds, 20, 25, 30, or 40 pounds? Now this is a question which can be answered only through carefully made experiments. By first selecting two or three first-class shovelers, and paying them extra wages for doing trustworthy work, and then gradually varying the shovel load and having all the conditions accompanying the work carefully observed for several weeks by men who were used to experimenting, it was found that a first-class man would do his biggest day's work with a shovel load of about 21 pounds. For instance, that this man would shovel a larger tonnage per day with a 21-pound load than with a 24-pound load or than with an 18-pound load on his shovel. It is, of course, evident that no shoveler can always take a load of exactly 21 pounds on his shovel, but nevertheless, although his load may vary 3 or 4 pounds one way or the other, either below or above the 21 pounds, he will do his biggest day's work when his average for the day is about 21 pounds.

The writer does not wish it to be understood that this is the whole of the art or science of shoveling. There are many other elements, which together go to make up this science. But he wishes to indicate the important effect which this one piece of scientific knowledge has upon the work of shoveling.

At the works of the Bethlehem Steel Company, for example, as a result of this law, instead of allowing each shoveler to select and own his own shovel, it became necessary to provide some 8 to 10 different kinds of shovels, etc., each one appropriate to handling a given type of material; not only so as to enable the men to handle an average load of 21 pounds, but also to adapt the shovel to several other requirements which become perfectly evident when this work is studied as a science. A large shovel tool room was built, in which were stored not only shovels but carefully designed and standardized labor implements of all kinds, such as picks, crowbars, etc. This made it possible to issue to each workman a shovel which would hold a load of 21 pounds of whatever class of material they were to handle: a small shovel for ore, say, or a large one for ashes. Iron ore is one of the heavy materials which are handled in a works of this kind, and rice coal, owing to the fact that it is so slippery on the shovel, is one of the lightest materials. And it found on studying the rule-of-thumb plan at the Bethlehem Steel Company, where each shoveler owned his own shovel, that he would frequently go from shoveling ore, with a load of about 30 pounds per shovel, to handling rice coal, with a load on the same shovel of less than 4 pounds. In the one case, he was so overloaded that it was impossible for him to do a full day's work, and in the other case he was so ridiculously underloaded that it was manifestly impossible to even approximate a day's work.

Briefly to illustrate some of the other elements which go to make up the science of shoveling, thousands of stop-watch observations were made to study just how quickly a laborer, provided in each case with the proper type of shovel, can push his shovel into the pile of materials and then draw it out properly loaded. These observations were made first when pushing the shovel into the body of the pile. Next when shoveling on a dirt bottom, that is, at the outside edge of the pile, and next with a wooden bottom, and finally with an iron bottom. Again a similar accurate time study was made of the time required to swing the shovel backward and then throw the load for a given horizontal distance, accompanied by a given height. This time study was made for various combinations of distance and height. With data of this sort before him, coupled with the law of endurance described in the case of the pig-iron handlers, it is evident that the man who is directing shovelers can first teach them the exact methods which should be employed.

Questions

1. In what ways did Taylor exhibit a bias against workers? How did he cloak that bias in a mantle of objective science?
2. Who was likely to benefit from and who was likely to be hurt by scientific management?

Questions for Further Thought

1. What were the contradictions posed by child labor to a society that otherwise cherished free enterprise?
2. Compare and contrast the lives, on the job and off, of the Rhode Island factory workers described by Lillie B. Chase Wyman (Document 17-5) and the anonymous African American domestic (Document 17-6).
3. What do the accounts of female workers' lives (Documents 17-5 and 17-6) reveal about the lives of their children?
4. Frederick Winslow Taylor (Document 17-7) appeared to sense that Americans deferred to the power of "science." Why might they have done so? In what ways would scientific management discourage innovation on the work floor?

The Labor Movement

When Thomas B. McGuire, a wagon driver, told a Senate committee in 1883 that he had once hoped to "become something of a capitalist eventually," he gave plaintive voice to an aspiration of many working-class Americans (see text p. 540). McGuire had found it impossible to succeed as an independent cabdriver. Economic change had reduced opportunities among those who viewed themselves as the heirs of the self-employed of an earlier America.

Labor unrest grew on the farm and in the factory during the 1870s and 1880s (Document 17-8), and the Knights of Labor were the initial beneficiary. Under the leadership of Terence V. Powderly, the Knights were an urban version of the Grange, combining the social activities with group action (Document 17-9). Beset by various problems, however, the group was in fatal decline by the 1890s. In its place, the American Federation of Labor (AFL), which brought together "pure and simple" trade unions, emerged as the nation's preeminent labor organization. Meanwhile, some workers turned to more radical movements, including socialism or anarchism; the latter was a factor in the Haymarket Square riot in Chicago during 1886 (see text p. 543).

Trade unionism accepted capitalism; socialism did not. The defeat of the American Railway Union in the strike and boycott against the Pullman Palace Car Company helped turn the union's leader, Eugene V. Debs, into a socialist (Document 17-10). Document 17-11 provides insight into management's position leading to the Pullman crisis.

17-8 On Agrarian Discontent (1887)

The transformation of the American economy was dramatic, as was who did and who did not benefit from these sweeping changes. *The Progressive Farmer*, a Raleigh, North Carolina, farm journal, analyzed the situation for its readers with clarity, frankness, and a sense of discontent in its April 28, 1887, issue.

Source: Excerpt from *Progressive Farmer* (Raleigh), April 28, 1887, in *The Populist Revolt: A History of the Farmers' Alliance and the People's Party* by John D. Hicks (1931; Lincoln: University of Nebraska Press, 1961), 54.

There is something radically wrong in our industrial system. There is a screw loose. The wheels have dropped out of balance. The railroads have never been so prosperous, and yet agriculture languishes. The banks have never done a better or more profitable business, and yet agriculture languishes. Manufacturing enterprises never made more money or were in a more flourishing condition, and yet agriculture languishes. Towns and cities flourish and "boom" and grow and "boom," and yet agriculture languishes. Salaries and fees were never so temptingly high and desirable, and yet agriculture languishes.

Questions

1. In terms of the analysis here, what would have made the industrial system right again?
2. Compare this document with Document 17-9. Implied in both is the assumption that farmers and workers have a moral claim or hold a key place that other participants in the economy do not have. Explain.

17-9 The Army of Unemployed (1887)

Terence V. Powderly

The growth of the factory system left the working class unsettled. Periodically, as with the Haymarket Square riot and the Pullman boycott, discontent led to violence. But overall, workers were more concerned with finding a way to protect their interests.

The Knights of Labor, founded in 1869, offered some promise in that regard. The group's use of ritual and ceremony cloaked it in nineteenth-century respectability: the Knights could claim that they were little different from the Masons. The Knights were not a union in the modern sense; they focused on education rather than organization. Although membership reached 700,000 by 1885, the Knights did not win any significant victories.

In the following selection, Terence V. Powderly, the Knights' Grand Master Workman, struggles to offer a solution to the labor problems of the 1880s.

Source: From George E. McNeill, ed., *The Labor Movement: The Problem of Today* (Boston: A. M. Bridgeman, and New York: M. W. Hazen, 1887; reprint, New York: Augustus M. Kelley, 1971), 577–584.

The Cincinnati riots, that occurred less than one year ago, were not brought about through the agitation of the labor-leader. If the demand for "the removal of unjust technicalities, delays and discriminations in the administration of justice," had been listened to when first made by the Knights of Labor, Cincinnati would have been spared sorrow and disgrace, and her "prominent citizens" would not have had to lead a mob, in order to open the eyes of the country to the manner in which her courts were throttled, and virtue and truth were trampled upon in her temples of justice. That the army of the discontented is gathering fresh recruits day by day, is true; and if this army should become so large, that, driven to desperation, it should one day arise in its wrath, and grapple with its real or fancied enemy, the responsibility for that act must fall upon the heads of those who could have averted the blow, but who turned a deaf ear to the supplication of suffering humanity, and gave the screw of oppression an extra turn, because they had the power. Workingmen's organizations are doing all they can to avert the blow; but if that day dawns upon us, it will be chargeable directly to men who taunt others with unequal earnings, and distort the truth, as was done in an interview recently had with Mr. William H. Vanderbilt: —

> One of the troubles in this country, just now, is the relation of wages to the cost of production. A skilled workman, in almost every branch of business, gets every day money enough to buy a barrel of flour. I don't refer to ordinary laborers, but to men skilled at their trades. The man who makes the article receives as much wages, in many instances, as the article is worth when it is finished. This is not exactly fair, in my opinion, and must be adjusted. Until wages bear a truer relation to production, there can be no real prosperity in the country.

I have seen no denial of the above, and take it for granted that it is a correct report. Mr. Vanderbilt starts out well enough; but he is in error when he says that "a skilled workman, in almost every branch of business, gets money enough every day to buy a barrel of flour." I know of no business in the United States, in which a skilled mechanic, working regularly at his trade day by day, gets money enough for his day's labor to buy a barrel of flour. That they earn the price of a barrel of flour, I do not deny; but that they get it, is not true. It may be that Mr. Vanderbilt refers to superintendents, foremen or contractors; for they are the only ones that receive such wages. The average wages paid to the skilled mechanic will not exceed $2.50 a day. I know of but few branches of business in which men can command that price. The wages of skilled mechanics are on the decline, while the price of flour remains unchanged, from $5.75 to $8.50 a barrel. If Mr. Vanderbilt will demonstrate how one can purchase a six-dollar barrel of flour for two dollars and a half, he will have solved a very difficult problem for the workingman....

It may be said that many of the employees of the manufacturing establishments are minors, and consequently cannot perform as great an amount of labor as a corresponding number of adults. That argument might have had some weight years ago, but now it is fruitless. The age and strength of the workman are no longer regarded as factors in the field of production; it is the skill of the operator in managing a labor-saving machine that is held to be the most essential. It is true that a child can operate a machine as successfully as a man, and that muscle is no longer a requisite in accomplishing results. It is also true that less time is required to perform a given amount of labor than heretofore. This being the case, the plea for shorter hours is not unreasonable. Benjamin Franklin said, one hundred years ago, that "if the workers of the world would labor but four hours each day, they could produce enough in that length of time to supply the wants of mankind." While it is true that the means of supplying the wants of man have increased as if by magic, yet man has acquired no new wants; he is merely enabled to gratify his needs more fully. If it were true in Franklin's time that four hours of toil each day would prove sufficient to minister to the necessities of the world's inhabitants, the argument certainly has lost none of its force since then. At that time, it took the sailing-vessel three months to cross the ocean; the stage-coach made its thirty or forty miles a day; the electric wire was not dreamed of; and the letter that traveled but little faster than the stage-coach was the quickest medium of communication.

It required six days' labor at the hands of the machinist, with hammer, chisel and file to perfect a certain piece of machinery at the beginning of this century. The machinist of the present day can finish a better job in six hours, with the aid of a labor-saving machine. In a yarn-mill in Philadelphia, the proprietor says that improved machinery has caused a displacement of fifty per cent. of the former employees within five years, and that one person, with the aid of improved machinery, can perform the work that it took upward of one hundred carders and spinners to do with the tools and implements in use at the beginning of this century. In Massachusetts, it has been estimated that 318,768 men, women and children do, with improved machinery, the work that it would require 1,912,468 men to perform, if improved machinery were not in use. To insure safety on a passenger-train, it is no longer necessary to have a brakeman at each end of the car; the automatic air-brake does the work, while one brakeman can shout, "All right here!" for the whole train. The employee that has had a limb cut off in a collision, must beg for bread or turn the crank of a hand-organ, and gather his pennies under the legend, "Please assist a poor soldier, who lost his leg at Gettysburg." He is no longer stationed, flag in hand, at the switch; the automatic lever directs the course of the train, and renders the one-legged switchman unnecessary. It is said that the iron-moulder recently invented is capable of performing as much labor as three skilled workmen; while the following dispatch to a Philadelphia paper, from Mahanoy City, shows what is being done in the mines.—

> For the past three years the reduction in wages has been systematic and steady. When one of the officials of one of the great companies was interviewed on the matter, he replied that the advance in labor-saving machinery had lightened the labor of the men. A miner at one of the Reading collieries says that some months ago he expended a large sum for a patent drill, which enabled him to do five times the usual amount of work. He was employed in driving a gangway, the price paid being $10 a yard; but at the end of the week, when the officials saw the amount of work he had done, the rate was reduced to $4.50 a yard. . . .

A great many remedies are recommended for the ills that I speak of. Let me deal with what seems to be the most unimportant,—the reduction of the hours of labor to eight a day. Men, women and children are working from ten to eighteen hours a day, and two million men have nothing to do. If four men, following a given occupation, at which they work ten hours a day, would rest from their labors two hours each day, the two hours taken from the labor of each, if added together, would give the tramp that stands looking on, an opportunity of stepping into a position at eight hours a day. It is said that a vast majority of those who are idle would not work, if they had work to do. That statement is untrue; but let us admit that five hundred thousand of the two million idle men would not work, and we still have a million and a half who are anxious and willing to work. If but six million of the seventeen million producers will abstain from working ten, fifteen, and eighteen hours a day, and work but eight, the one million and a half of idle men that are willing to work, can again take their places in the ranks of the world's producers. Need it be said, that a million and a half of new hats will be needed; that a corresponding number of pairs of shoes, suits of clothing, and a hundred other things will be required; that the wants of these men and their families will be supplied; that shelves will be emptied of their goods, and that the money expended will again go into circulation. It would entail hardship on some branches of business, to require men employed in them to work eight hours a day. Miners and those working by contract could not very well adopt the eight-hour plan, without lengthening their hours of labor. Before giving the matter a second thought, many of these men look upon the eight-hour agitation as of no consequence to them. If a mechanic is thrown out of employment, and cannot find anything to do at his trade, he turns toward the first place where an opportunity for work is presented. If he is re-enforced by two million idle men, the number that apply at the mouth of the mine, or seek to secure contracts at lower figures, becomes quite large; and the miner and contract-man grumble, because so many men are crowding in upon them in quest of work. Every new applicant for work in the mine makes it possible for the boss to let his contract to a lower bidder; therefore, it is clearly to the interest of the miner to assist in reducing the hours of labor in the shop, mill and factory, to the end that the idle millions may be gathered in from the streets to self-sustaining positions.

The eight-hour system, to be of value to the masses, must be put in operation all over the country; for the manufacturers of one State cannot successfully compete with those of other States, if they run their establishments but eight hours, while others operate theirs ten or twelve hours a day. The movement should be national, and should have the hearty co-operation of all men. . . .

When the President of the United States issued his Thanksgiving proclamation, in 1884, there were millions of men and women in want of bread, notwithstanding "the abundant harvests and continued prosperity which God hath vouchsafed to this nation;" and the cry, not of thanksgiving, went up from millions of farmers, of "Too much wheat!" Doubting as to the exact meaning of the Creator in growing so much wheat, they invoked the aid of such institutions as the Chicago Board of Trade, in the hope of thwarting the will of God, by cornering wheat. These men invoked blessings on their Thanksgiving dinners, and thanked God for the turkey, while they hoarded the wheat away from those who asked for bread.

Give men shorter hours in which to labor, and you give them more time to study, and learn why bread is so scarce, while wheat is so plenty. You give them more time in which to learn that millions of acres of American soil are controlled by alien landlords, that have no interest in America but to draw a revenue from it. You give them time to learn that America belongs to Americans, native and naturalized, and that the landlord who drives his tenant from the Old World must not be permitted to exact tribute from him when he settles in our country.

Questions

1. How does Powderly's use of the term *mechanic* suggest that the Knights were a backward-looking movement?
2. What did Powderly suggest as a remedy for the workers' situation?
3. How did Powderly characterize businessmen?

17-10 How I Became a Socialist (1902)

Eugene V. Debs

For some people, the goals of organized labor were too limited. Even if the AFL won some victories, the economy would remain firmly under the control of a capitalist elite. Rather than accept that prospect, some workers turned to socialism.

The movement had a deep if limited appeal. Socialism promised to address inequality in industrial America by giving workers—the great majority of the population—control over the economy and the government. This was not Jeffersonian or Jacksonian democracy, and socialism remained a marginal idea as long as it appeared to be a Marxist import from Europe.

Eugene V. Debs (1855–1926) helped make socialism respectable, even mainstream, in the first decades of the twentieth century (see text pp. 544–547). Debs came from a middle-class family in Terre Haute, Indiana, and at one time had been a conventional Democrat and trade unionist. In this essay, Debs explains the reasons for his change of philosophy. The "anarchists" he mentions were the four Chicago labor figures who were hanged for their role in the Haymarket Square riot of 1886 (see text p. 543).

Source: Eugene V. Debs, "How I Became a Socialist," *The Comrade* (April 1902).

As I have some doubt about the readers of *The Comrade* having any curiosity as to "how I became a socialist" it may be in order to say that the subject is the editor's, not my own; and that what is here offered is at his bidding—my only concern being that he shall not have cause to wish that I had remained what I was instead of becoming a socialist.

On the evening of February 27, 1875, the local lodge of the Brotherhood of Locomotive Firemen was organized at Terre Haute, Indiana, by Joshua A. Leach, then grand master, and I was admitted as a charter member and at once chosen secretary. "Old Josh Leach," as he was affectionately called, a typical locomotive fireman of his day, was the founder of the brotherhood, and I was instantly attracted by his rugged honesty, simple manner and homely speech. How well I remember feeling his large, rough hand on my shoulder, the kindly eye of an elder brother searching my own as he gently said: "My boy, you're a little young, but I believe you're in earnest and will make your mark in the brotherhood." Of course, I assured him that I would do my best. What he really thought at the time flattered my boyish vanity not a little when I heard of it. He was attending a meeting at St. Louis some months later, and in the course of his remarks said: "I put a tow-headed boy in the brotherhood at Terre Haute not long ago, and some day he will be at the head of it."...

My first step was thus taken in organized labor and a new influence fired my ambition and changed the whole current of my career. I was filled with enthusiasm and my blood fairly leaped in my veins. Day and night I worked for the brotherhood. To see its watchfires glow and observe the increase of its sturdy members were the sunshine and shower of my life. To attend the "meeting" was my supreme joy, and for ten years I was not once absent when the faithful assembled.

At the convention held in Buffalo in 1878 I was chosen associate editor of the magazine, and in 1880 I became grand secretary and treasurer. With all the fire of youth I entered upon the crusade which seemed to fairly glitter with possibilities. For eighteen hours at a stretch I was glued to my desk reeling off the answers to my many correspondents. Day and night were one. Sleep was time wasted and often, when all oblivious of her presence in the still small hours my mother's hand turned off the light, I went to bed under protest. Oh, what days! And what quenchless zeal and consuming vanity!...

My grip was always packed; and I was darting in all directions. To tramp through a railroad yard in the rain, snow or sleet half the night, or till daybreak, to be ordered out of the roundhouse for being an "agitator," or put off a train, sometimes passenger, more often freight, while attempting to deadhead over the division, were all in the program, and served to whet the appetite to conquer. One night in midwinter at Elmira, New York, a conductor on the Erie kindly dropped me off in a snowbank, and as I clambered to the top I ran into the arms of a policeman, who heard my story and on the spot became my friend.

I rode on the engines over mountain and plain, slept in the cabooses and bunks, and was fed from their pails by the swarthy stokers who still nestle close to my heart, and will until it is cold and still.

Through all these years I was nourished at Fountain Proletaire. I drank deeply of its waters and every particle of my tissue became saturated with the spirit of the working class. I had fired an engine and been stung by the exposure and hardship of the rail. I was with the boys in their weary watches, at the broken engine's side and often helped to bear their bruised and bleeding bodies back to wife and child again. How could I but feel the burden of their wrongs? How could the seed of agitation fail to take deep root in my heart?

And so I was spurred on in the work of organizing, not the firemen merely, but the brakemen, switchmen, telegraphers, shopmen, trackhands, all of them in fact, and as I had now become known as an organizer, the calls came from all sides and there are but few trades I have not helped to organize and less still in whose strikes I have not at some time had a hand.

In 1894 the American Railway Union was organized and a braver body of men never fought the battle of the working class.

Up to this time I had heard but little of socialism, knew practically nothing about the movement, and what little I did know was not calculated to impress me in its favor. I was bent on thorough and complete organization of the railroad men and ultimately the whole working class, and all my time and energy were given to that end. My supreme conviction was that if they were only organized in every branch of the service and all acted together in concert they could redress their wrongs and regulate the conditions of their employment. The stockholders of the corporation acted as one, why not the men? It was such a plain proposition—simply to follow the example set before their eyes by their masters—surely they could not fail to see it, act as one, and solve the problem.

It is useless to say that I had yet to learn the working of the capitalist system, the resources of its masters and the weakness of its slaves. Indeed, no shadow of a "system" fell athwart my pathway; no thought of ending wage misery marred my plans. I was too deeply absorbed in perfecting wage servitude and making it a "thing of beauty and a joy forever."

It all seems very strange to me now, taking a backward look, that my vision was so focalized on a single objective point that I utterly failed to see what now appears as clear as the noonday sun—so clear that I marvel that any workingman, however dull, uncomprehending, can resist it.

But perhaps it was better so. I was to be baptized in socialism in the road of conflict and I thank the gods for reserving to this fitful occasion the fiat, "Let there be light!"—the light that streams in steady radiance upon the broad way to the socialist republic.

The skirmish lines of the A.R.U. were well advanced. A series of small battles was fought and won without the loss of a man. A number of concessions was made by the corporations rather than risk an encounter. Then came the fight on the Great Northern, short, sharp, and decisive. The victory was complete—the only railroad strike of magnitude ever won by an organization in America.

Next followed the final shock—the Pullman strike—and the American Railway Union again won, clear and complete. The combined corporations were paralyzed and helpless. At this juncture there was delivered, from wholly unexpected quarters, a swift succession of blows that blinded me for an instant and then opened wide my eyes—and in the gleam of every bayonet and the flash of every rifle *the class struggle was revealed*. This was my first practical lesson in socialism, though wholly unaware that it was called by that name.

An army of detectives, thugs and murderers was equipped with badge and beer and bludgeon and turned loose; old hulks of cars were fired; the alarm bells tolled; the people were terrified; the most startling rumors were set afloat; the press volleyed and thundered, and over all the wires sped the news that Chicago's white throat was in the clutch of a red mob; injunctions flew thick and fast, arrests followed, and our office and headquarters, the heart of the strike, was sacked, torn out and nailed up by the "lawful" authorities of the federal government; and when in company with my loyal comrades I found myself in Cook County Jail at Chicago, with the whole press screaming conspiracy, treason and murder, and by some fateful coincidence I was given the cell occupied just previous to his execution by the assassin of Mayor Carter Harrison, Sr., overlooking the spot, a few feet distant, where the anarchists were hanged a few years before, I had another exceedingly practical and impressive lesson in socialism.

Acting upon the advice of friends we sought to employ John Harlan, son of the Supreme Justice, to assist in our defense—a defense memorable to me chiefly because of the skill and fidelity of our lawyers, among whom were the brilliant Clarence Darrow and the venerable Judge Lyman Trumbull, author of the thirteenth amendment to the Constitution, abolishing slavery in the United States.

Mr. Harlan wanted to think of the matter overnight; and the next morning gravely informed us that he could not afford to be identified with the case, "for," said he, "you will be tried upon the same theory as were the anarchists, with probably the same result." That day, I remember, the jailer, by way of consolation, I suppose, showed us the bloodstained rope used at the last execution and explained in minutest detail, as he exhibited the gruesome relic, just how the monstrous crime of lawful murder is committed.

But the tempest gradually subsided and with it the bloodthirstiness of the press and "public sentiment." We were not sentenced to the gallows, nor even to the penitentiary—though put on trial for conspiracy—for reasons that will make another story.

The Chicago jail sentences were followed by six months at Woodstock and it was here that socialism gradually laid hold of me in its own irresistible fashion. Books and pamphlets and letters from socialists came by every mail and I began to read and think and dissect the anatomy of the system in which workingmen, however organized, could be shattered and battered and splintered at a single stroke....

It was at this time, when the first glimmerings of socialism were beginning to penetrate, that Victor L. Berger—and I have loved him ever since—came to Woodstock, as if a providential instrument, and delivered the first impassioned message of socialism I had ever heard—the very first to set the "wires humming in my system." As a souvenir of that visit there is in my library a volume of *Capital*, by Karl Marx, inscribed with the compliments of Victor L. Berger, which I cherish as a token of priceless value.

The American Railway Union was defeated but not conquered—overwhelmed but not destroyed. It lives and pulsates in the socialist movement, and its defeat but blazed the way to economic freedom and hastened the dawn of human brotherhood.

Questions

1. What makes Debs's story persuasive?
2. To what extent was Debs a romantic?
3. How did the Pullman boycott affect Debs's thinking?

17-11 Testimony Before the U.S. Strike Commission on the Pullman Strike (1894)

Andrew Carnegie's practice regarding labor unions differed from his rhetoric, as was revealed during the Homestead strike (1892), but rhetoric and policy were as one at the Pullman Palace Car Company, prompting a strike and boycott that created a national crisis two years later (see text pp. 544–545).

In this document, Thomas H. Wickes, second vice president of the Pullman Palace Car Company, responded to the questions of John D. Kernan, a member of the U.S. Strike Commission. That body was formed under the terms of the Arbitration Act of 1888, which provided for voluntary arbitration and temporary investigatory commissions (comprising the U.S. commissioner of labor and two presidential appointees) in labor-management disputes involving interstate railways. President Grover Cleveland initiated the commission investigation of 1894 at the request of labor. The commission conducted hearings during August and September and reported to the president that November.

Source: U.S. Strike Commission, *Report on the Chicago Strike of June–July, 1894.* . . . Senate. Executive Document No. 7, 53rd Congress, 3rd Session (Washington, DC: U.S. Government Printing Office, 1895), 621–622.

---

222 (Commissioner KERNAN). Has the company had any policy with reference to labor unions among its help?—Ans. No; we have never objected to unions except in one instance. I presume that there are quite a number of unions in our shops now.

223 (Commissioner KERNAN). What are they?—Ans. I couldn't tell you, but I have heard of some of them. I suppose the cabinetmakers have a union, and I suppose the car builders have a union, and the carvers and the painters and other classes of men. We do not inquire into that at all.

224 (Commissioner KERNAN). That is, unions among themselves in the works?—Ans. Members of the craft, belonging to other unions; that is, the cabinet union might have its headquarters in Chicago and our men would be members of it; but we did not object to anything of that kind.

225 (Commissioner KERNAN). The only objection you ever made was to the American Railway Union, wasn't it?—Ans. Yes, sir.

226 (Commissioner KERNAN). What is the basis of your objection to that union?—Ans. Our objection to that was that we would not treat with our men as members of the American Railway Union, and we would not treat with them as members of any union. We treat with them as individuals and as men.

227 (Commissioner KERNAN). That is, each man as an individual, do you mean that?—Ans. Yes, sir.

228 (Commissioner KERNAN). Don't you think, Mr. Wickes, that would give the corporation a very great advantage over those men if it could take them up one at a time and discuss the question with him. With the ability that you have got, for instance, where do you think the man would stand in such a discussion?—Ans. The man has got probably more ability than I have.

229 (Commissioner KERNAN). You think that it would be fair to your men for each one of them to come before you and take up the question of his grievances and attempt to maintain his end of the discussion, do you?—Ans. I think so, yes. If he is not able to do that that is his misfortune.

230 (Commissioner KERNAN). Don't you think that the fact that you represent a vast concentration of capital, and are selected for that because of your ability to represent it, entitles him if he pleases to unite with all of the men of his craft and select the ablest one they have got to represent the cause?—Ans. As a union?

231 (Commissioner KERNAN). As a union.—Ans. They have the right; yes, sir. We have the right to say whether we will receive them or not.

232 (Commissioner KERNAN). Do you think you have any right to refuse to recognize that right in treating with the men?—Ans. Yes, sir; if we chose to.

233 (Commissioner KERNAN). If you chose to. Is it your policy to do that?—Ans. Yes, sir.

234 (Commissioner KERNAN). Then you think that you have the right to refuse to recognize a union of the men designed for the purpose of presenting, through the ablest of their members, to your company the grievances which all complain of or which any complain of?—Ans. That is the policy of the company; yes, sir. If we were to receive these men as representatives of the unions they could probably force us to pay any wages which they saw fit, and get the Pullman company in the same shape that some of the railroads are by making concessions which ought not to be made.

235 (Commissioner KERNAN). Don't you think that the opposite policy, to wit, that all your dealings with the men, as individuals, in case you were one who sought to abuse your power, might enable you to pay to the men, on the other hand, just what you saw fit?—Ans. Well, of course a man in an official position, if he is arbitrary and unfair, could work a great deal of injustice to the men; no doubt about that. But then it is a man's privilege to go to work somewhere else.

236 (Commissioner KERNAN). Don't you recognize as to many men, after they had become settled in a place at work of that kind, that really that privilege does not amount to much?—Ans. We find that the best men usually come to the front; the best of our men don't give us any trouble with unions or anything else. It is only the inferior men—that is, the least competent—that give us the trouble as a general thing.

237 (Commissioner KERNAN). As a rule, then, the least competent men make the most trouble, do they?—Ans. Yes, sir; if these gentlemen allow themselves to be led by the incompetent men that is their misfortune.

Question

1. What light do the exchanges between Kernan and Wickes shed on labor-management relations at Pullman? Does any particular question-and-answer exchange strike you as especially illuminating?

Questions for Further Thought

1. What did American farmers and workers seem to want from the new industrial system?

2. Drawing on Documents 17-3, 17-7, 17-11, and the text, come to an understanding of businessmen's reading of "capital and labor in the age of enterprise."

3. Drawing on Documents 17-5, 17-6, 17-9, 17-10, and the text, come to an understanding of workers' reading of "capital and labor in the age of enterprise."

CHAPTER EIGHTEEN

The Industrial City: Building It, Living in It

Urbanization

As the United States moved west across the continent, new cities sprang up on sites where only a few years before the buffalo had literally roamed and the antelope played. Even cities with origins dating back to the early colonial era remained relatively undeveloped until well into the nineteenth century. As of the late 1850s, the land in Manhattan's center, for example, while hardly wild was still in rough condition. After a good deal of political wrangling and litigation, land in this area was set aside for a park, which was not in itself so unusual. What was unusual was the brilliant, innovative, and winning plan, "Greensward" (Document 18-1), that Frederick Law Olmsted and Calvert Vaux entered into a design contest in 1858. In Document 18-2, Julian Ralph, a journalist writing for *Harper's New Monthly Magazine*, describes for eastern readers fin-desiècle Denver, a city that in a single generation had passed from a mining camp to a sprawling urban oasis set amidst the western wilderness. But even as American cities in the West and elsewhere in the country during the second half of the nineteenth century expanded horizontally, builders took advantage of the new technology made possible by the Industrial Revolution to expand cities vertically as well. Moreover, the dramatic appearance of the tall office building and later the "skyscraper" called for a new and revolutionary aesthetic, as famed architect Louis H. Sullivan explains in Document 18-3.

18-1 Central Park (1858)

Frederick Law Olmsted, Calvert Vaux

Frederick Law Olmsted was born in 1822 in Hartford, Connecticut, to a well-to-do family and studied agricultural science at Yale. Calvert Vaux was born in England and became a citizen in 1856, by which time he had proven his talents in art and design. In New York City, the two men worked together on the proposal, "Greensward," for Manhattan's Central Park, which they presented in 1858 and which won the competition. The design served as the basis for what would become one of the most famous parks in the world, and demonstrated that American cities could be something far more than mere places to make money. One of the design's innovative features was the four sunken transverse roads at 65th, 79th, 85th, and 97th Streets. The transverse thoroughfares were to facilitate city traffic and, at the same time, serve to preserve the park's natural aesthetic, since this busy flow was to run below eye-level.

Source: Excerpt, "The Greensward Plan: 1858," in *The Papers of Frederick Law Olmsted, v. 3: Creating Central Park*, ed. Charles E. Beveridge and David Schuyler (Baltimore: Johns Hopkins University Press, 1983), 119–122.

Description of a Plan for the Improvement of the Central Park "GREENSWARD."

REPORT.

TOPOGRAPHICAL SUGGESTIONS

A general survey of the ground allotted to the park, taken with a view to arrive at the leading characteristics which present themselves, as all-important to be considered in adapting the actual situation to its purpose, shows us, in the first place, that it is very distinctly divided into two tolerably equal portions, which, for convenience sake, may be called the upper and lower parks.

THE UPPER PARK

The horizon lines of the upper park are bold and sweeping and the slopes have great breadth in almost every aspect in which they may be contemplated. As this character is the highest ideal that can be aimed at for a park under any circumstances, and as it is in most decided contrast to the confined and formal lines of the city, it is desirable to interfere with it, by cross-roads and other constructions, as little as possible. Formal planting and architectural effects, unless on a very grand scale, must be avoided; and as nearly all the ground between the Reservoir and 106th Street (west of the Boston road) is seen in connection, from any point within itself, a unity of character should be studiously preserved in all the gardening details.

THE LOWER PARK

The lower park is far more heterogeneous in its character, and will require a much more varied treatment. The most important feature in its landscape, is the long rocky and wooded hill-side lying immediately south of the Reservoir. Inasmuch as beyond this point there do not appear to be any leading natural characteristics of similar consequence in the scenery, it will be important to draw as much attention as possible to this hill-side, to afford facilities for rest and leisurely contemplation upon the rising ground opposite, and to render the lateral boundaries of the park in its vicinity as inconspicuous as possible. The central and western portion of the lower park is an irregular table-land; the eastern is composed of a series of graceful undulations, suggesting lawn or gardenesque treatment. In the extreme south we find some flat alluvial meadow; but the general character of the ground is rugged and there are several bold, rocky bluffs, that help to give individuality to this part of the composition.

Such being the general suggestions that our survey has afforded, it becomes necessary to consider how the requirements of the Commissioners, as given in their instructions, may be met with the least sacrifice of the characteristic excellencies of the ground.

PRELIMINARY CONSIDERATIONS

Up to this time, in planning public works for the city of New York, in no instance has adequate allowance been made for its increasing population and business; not even in the case of the Croton Aqueduct, otherwise so well considered. The City-Hall, the best architectural work in the State, and built to last for centuries, does not at this time afford facilities for one-third the business for which it was intended. The present Post-Office, expensively fitted up some ten years ago, no longer answers its purpose, and a new one of twice its capacity is imperatively demanded. The Custom-House expressly designed for permanence and constructed to that end at enormous expense less than twenty years ago, is not half large enough to accommodate the present commerce of the city.

The explanation of this apparently bad calculation is mainly given with the fact, that at every census since that of 1800, the city's rate of increase has been found to be over-running the rate previously established.

A wise forecast of the future gave the proposed park the name of Central. Our present chief magistrate, who can himself remember market-gardens below Canal street, and a post-and-rail fence on the north side of City-Hall park, warned his coadjutors, in his inaugural message, to expect a great and rapid movement of population toward the parts of the island adjoining the Central Park. A year hence, five city railroads will bring passengers as far up as the park, if not beyond it. Recent movements to transfer the steamboat-landings and railroad stations, although as yet unsuccessful, indicate changes we are soon to expect.

The 17,000 lots withdrawn from use for building purposes in the park itself, will greatly accelerate the occupation of the adjoining land. Only twenty years ago Union Square was "out of town;" twenty years hence, the town will have enclosed the Central Park. Let us consider, therefore, what will at that time be satisfactory, for it is then that the design will have to be really judged. No longer an open suburb, our ground will have around it a continuous high wall of brick, stone, and marble. The adjoining shores will be lined with commercial docks and warehouses; steamboat and ferry landings, railroad stations, hotels, theatres, factories, will be on all sides of it and before it: all [of] which our park must be made to fit.

The demolition of Columbia College, and the removal of the cloistral elms which so long enshadowed it; the pertinacious demand for a division of Trinity churchyard; the numerous instances in which our old graveyards have actually been broken up; the indirect concession of the most important space in the City-Hall park for the purposes of a thoroughfare and the further contraction it is now likely to suffer; together with the constant enormous expenditure of the city, and sacrifices of the citizens, in the straightening and widening of streets, are all familiar facts, that teach us a lesson of the most pressing importance in our present duty. To its application we give the first place in our planning.

THE TRANSVERSE ROADS

Our instructions call for four transverse roads. *Each* of these will be the single line of communication between one side of the town and the other, for a distance equal to that between Chambers street and Canal street. If we suppose but one crossing of Broadway to be possible in this interval, we shall realize what these transverse roads are destined to become. Inevitably they will be crowded thoroughfares, having nothing in common with the park proper, but every thing at variance with those agreeable sentiments which we should wish the park to inspire. It will not be possible to enforce the ordinary police regulations of public parks upon them. They must be constantly open to all the legitimate traffic of the city, to coal carts and butchers' carts, dust carts and dung carts; engine companies will use them, those on one side [of] the park rushing their machines across it, with frantic zeal at every alarm from the other; ladies and invalids will need special police escort for crossing them, as they do in lower Broadway. Eight times in a single circuit of the park will they oblige a pleasure drive or stroll to encounter a turbid stream of coarse traffic, constantly moving at right angles to the line of the park itself.

The transverse roads will also have to be kept open, while the park proper will be useless for any good purpose after dusk; for experience has shown that even in London, with its admirable police arrangements, the public cannot be secured safe transit through large open spaces of ground after nightfall.

FOREIGN EXAMPLES

These public thoroughfares will then require to be well lighted at the sides, and, to restrain marauders pursued by the police from escaping into the obscurity of the park, strong fences or walls, six or eight feet high, will be necessary. One such street passes through the Regent's Park of London, at the Zoological Gardens. It has the objection that the fence, with its necessary gates at every crossing of the park drives, roads or paths, is not only a great inconvenience, but a disagreeable object in the landscape.

To avoid a similar disfigurement, an important street, crossing across the garden of the Tuileries [in Paris], is closed by gates at night, forcing all who would otherwise use it, to go a long distance to the right or left.

The form and position of the Central Park are peculiar in respect to this difficulty, and such that precedent in dealing with it is rather to be sought in the long and narrow Boulevards of some of the old Continental cities of Europe, than in the broad parks with which, from its area in acres, we are most naturally led to compare it. The Boulevards referred to are, however, generally used only as promenades, not as drives or places of ceremony. In frequent instances, in order not to interrupt the alleys, the streets crossing them are made in the form of causeways, and carried over on high arches. This, of course, prevents all landscape gardening, since it puts an abrupt limit to the view. Some expedient is needed for the Central Park, by which the convenience of the arrangement may be retained, while the objection is as far as possible avoided.

THE PRESENT DESIGN

In the plan herewith offered to the Commission, each of the transverse roads is intended to be sunk so far below the general surface, that the park drives may, at every necessary point of intersection, be carried entirely over it, without any obvious elevation or divergence from their most attractive routes. The banks on each side will be walled up to the height of about seven feet, thus forming the protective barrier required by police considerations; and a little judicious planting on the tops or slopes of the banks above these walls will in most cases entirely conceal both the roads and the vehicles moving in them, from the view of those walking or driving in the park.

If the position which has just been taken with regard to the necessity for permanently open transverse thoroughfares is found to be correct, it follows necessarily that the 700 acres allowed to the new park must, in the first instance, be subdivided definitely, although it is to be hoped to some extent invisibly, into five separate and distinct sections, only connected here and there by roads crossing them; and if the plan of making these thoroughfares by sunken roads is approved, they will, as it appears to us from the nature of the ground, have to be laid down somewhat on the lines indicated on the plan. If so, the problem to be solved is narrowed in its dimensions, and the efforts of the landscape gardener can be no longer directed to arranging a design that shall agreeably use up the space of 700 acres allotted, but [instead] to making some plan that shall have unity of effect as a whole, and yet avoid all collision in its detailed features with the intersecting lines thus suggested. It is on this basis that the present plan has, in the first instance, been founded. If the sunken transverse roads were omitted, the design would not be less complete in character, but it is, on the other hand, so laid out that the transverse thoroughfares do not interfere inaterially with its general or detailed effect.

Questions

1. What was Olmsted and Vaux's basic criticism of New York City's previous urban planning?
2. How did the proposed transverse thoroughfares address the problems that Olmsted and Vaux found with parks in Europe?

18-2 Colorado and Its Capital (1893)

Julian Ralph

Americans experienced enormous social, cultural, economic, political, technological, and scientific changes in the second half of the nineteenth century. As America modernized and became a world power, perhaps no change was more dramatic than the rise of the city. And nowhere was the process of urbanization exposed in sharper relief than in the relatively underdeveloped American West. Julian Ralph visited Denver, Colorado, in 1893 and gave his readers a tour of this new civilization at the foot of the Rocky Mountains.

Source: Julian Ralph, "Colorado and Its Capital," *Harper's New Monthly Magazine* (May 1893), 935–943.

Denver's peculiarity and strength lie in its being all alone in the heart of a vast region between the Canadian border and the Gulf of Mexico; but it has been brought suddenly near to us. Not all the fast railway riding is done in the East in these days. The far Western steeds of steel are picking up their heels in grand fashion for those who enjoy fast riding. On a palace-car train of the Union Pacific Railroad between Omaha and Denver the regular time is nearly fifty miles an hour, and the long run is made in one night, between supper and breakfast. Denver is only fifty-three hours of riding-time from New York as I write—twenty-five hours from New York to Chicago, and twenty-eight hours from Chicago to Denver.

I am going to ask the reader to spend Saturday and Sunday in Denver with me. Instead of dryly cataloguing what is there, we will see it for ourselves. I had supposed it to be a mountain city, so much does an Eastern man hear of its elevation, its mountain resorts, and its mountain air. It surprised me to discover that it was a city of the plains. There is nothing in the appearance of the plains to lead one to suppose that they tilt up like a toboggan slide, as they do, or that Denver is a mile above sea-level, as it is. But a part of its enormous good fortune is that although it is a plains city, it has the mountains for near neighbors—a long peaked and scalloped line of purple or pink or blue or snow-clad green, according to when they are viewed. . . .

. . . Every Western city has its own patent map, usually designed to show that it is in the centre of creation, but Denver's map is more truthful, and merely locates it in the middle of the country west of the Mississippi. It shows the States east of that river without a single railroad, while a perfect labyrinth of railroads crisscross the West in frantic efforts to get to Denver. . . .

In all other respects the patent Denver map is reliable. It shows that this city of 135,000 souls stands all alone, without a real rival, in a vast rich region. It is 1000 miles from Chicago, 400 from Salt Lake City, 600 from Kansas City, and the same distance from the Missouri River. If you drew a circle of 1000 miles diameter, with Denver in its centre, you would discover no real competitor; but the people have adopted what they call their "thousand-mile theory," which is that Chicago is 1000 miles from New York, and Denver is 1000 miles from Chicago, and San Francisco is 1000 miles from Denver, so that, as any one can see, if great cities are put at that distance apart, as it seems, then these are to be the four great ones of America.

Denver is a beautiful city—a parlor city with cabinet finish—and it is so new that it looks as if it had been made to order, and was just ready for delivery. How the people lived five years ago, or what they have done with the houses of that period, does not appear, but at present everything—business blocks, churches, clubs, dwellings, street cars, the park—all look brand-new, like the young trees. The first citizen you talk to says: "You notice there are no old people on the streets here. There aren't any in the city. We have no use for old folks here." So, then, the people also are new. It is very wonderful and peculiar. . . . The first things that impress you in the city are the neatness and width of the streets, and the number of young trees that ornament them most invitingly. The next thing is the remarkable character of the big business buildings. It is not that they are bigger and better than those of New York and Chicago—comparisons of that sort are nonsensical—but they are massive and beautiful, and they possess an elegance without and a roominess and lightness within that distinguish them as superior to the show buildings of most of the cities of the country. The hotels are even more remarkable, from the one down by the impressive big depot, which is the best-equipped third-class hotel in the country, to the Brown's Palace and the Métropole, both of steel and stone, which are just as good as men know how to make hotels.

The residence districts are of a piece with the rest. Along the tree-lined streets are some of the very prettiest villas it is any man's lot to see at this time. They are not palaces, but they are very tasteful, stylish, cozy, and pretty homes, all built of brick or stone, in a great variety of pleasing colors and materials, and with a proud showing of towers, turrets, conservatories, bay-windows, gables, and all else that goes to mark this period, when men build after widely differing plans to compliment their own taste and the skill of originating draughtsmen. The town spreads over an enormous territory, as compared with the space a city of its size should take up, but we must learn that modern methods of quick transit are so cheap that they are being adopted everywhere, and wherever they are used the cities are spreading out. Denver has cable and electric cars, but it is the electric roads that are the city-spreaders. They whiz along so fast that men do not hesitate to build their homes five or six miles from their stores and offices, where they can get garden and elbow room. We are going to see all our cities shoot out in this way. It promotes beauty in residence districts, and pride in the hearts of those who own the pretty homes. It carries the good health that comes with fresh air. But it entails a great new expense upon modern city government, for the streets and the mains and sewers and police and fire systems all have to be extended to keep pace with the electric flight of the people, who, in turn, must stand the taxes. Not that they are high in Denver, or in those other electric-car-peppered capitals, Minneapolis and St. Paul, but they are higher than they would be if the people were crowded into smaller spaces. In Denver the government has spared itself and the people one source of anxiety by ordering that, no matter where the houses reach to, it shall be a fire-proof city. The fire lines follow the extension, and every house must be of brick or stone. . . .

We shall see that on its worst side the city is Western, and that its moral side is Eastern. It will be interesting to see how one side dominates the other, and both keep along together. But in the mean time what is most peculiar is the indifference with which the populace regards murder among those gamblers and desperadoes who are a feature of every new country, and who are found in Denver, though, I suspect, the ladies and children never see them, so well separated are the decent and the vicious quarters. It is said that not very long ago it was the tacit agreement of the people that it was not worth while to put the county to the cost or bother of seriously pursuing, prosecuting, and hanging or imprisoning a thug who murdered another thug. It was argued that there was one bad man less, and that if the murderer was at large another one would kill him. The axiom that "only bad men are the victims of bad men" obtained there, as it did in Cheyenne and Deadwood, and does in Butte. To-day a murder in a dive or gambling-hell excites little comment and no sensation in Denver, and I could distinctly see a trace of the old spirit in the speech of the reputable men when I talked to them of the one crime of the sort that took place while I was there.

The night side of the town is principally corralled, as they say; that is, its disorderly houses are all on one street. There is another mining-town characteristic—wide-open gambling. The "hells" are mainly abovestairs, over saloons. The vice is not flaunted as it is in certain other cities; but once in the gaming-places, the visitor sees them to be like those my readers became acquainted with in Butte, Montana—great open places, like the board-rooms in our stock exchanges, lined with gambling lay-outs. They are crowded on this Saturday night with rough men in careless dress or in the apparel of laborers. These are railroad employés, workers from the nearest mines, laborers, clerks—every sort of men who earn their money hard, and think to make more out of it by letting it go easily. Roulette, red and black, and faro are the games. . . .

Queer characters illustrate queer stories in these places, just as they do in the mining regions, but with the difference that all the stories of luck in the mines are cast with characters who are either rich or "broke," while in the hells they seem never to be in luck when you happen on them. They were flush yesterday, and will be to-morrow—if you will "stake" them with something to gamble with. The man who once had a bank of his own and the one who broke the biggest bank in Leadville were mere ordinary *dramatis personœ* when I looked in, but the towering giant of the place was the man who at twenty-six years of age had killed twenty-six men, all so justly, however, that he never stood trial for one episode. This is part of the "local color" in any picture of Denver; but, on the other hand, the best of that color is, as I have hinted, of the tone of lovely firesides, elegance, wealth, and refinement.

From the gaming to the fruit fair, that happens to be in progress, we are eager to go. The fruit or orchard exhibition was an unlooked-for consummation in so new a State. It was a sight of the dawn of the fruit industry where the best orchards were not five years old. . . .

It was interesting to read the progress of Denver in the remarks of those who were presented to me during that visit to the fruit show. One gentleman was interested in the electric-light plant, and said that it is so powerful that during a recent decoration of the streets in honor of a convention that was held there, no less than 22,000 incandescent and four 5000 candle-power search-lights were used in the display. In few cities in the world, he said, is this light so generally and so lavishly used. He added that few of the dwellings, except in the poorest quarter, are without telephones.

A public official volunteered the information that since 1870 the percentage of increase of population has been greater in Denver than in any other city of the land, it being something more than 2000 per cent. A bevy of smiling young women was pointed out as representative art students; for there is a Denver Art League which has sixty members, and aims to maintain classes in oil and watercolor work and sculpture.... A merchant spoke of the Chamber of Commerce, to the enterprise and kindness of which, and especially of the secretary, I was afterward indebted. I learned that this watchful organization of promoters of the commercial welfare of the city maintains a fine free library, containing a collection of books that now numbers 20,000 volumes, and is constantly increasing. No less than 77,000 volumes were read in the homes of its patrons last year. The reading-room is kept open on all the days of the year, and the city government has passed an ordinance appropriating $500 a month, from the fines imposed by the police magistrates, for the benefit of this valuable institution. Another new acquaintance urged me to see the public schools of the city. The high-school building cost $325,000, and is the second most costly and complete one in existence. Many of the ward or district schools cost a fifth, and some cost more than a fifth, of that large sum. I could not then nor there farther insist upon the opinions that have engendered the only criticisms that have passed between myself in these papers and the new West which I am describing. The report of the Denver Board of Education is before me, and if I read it aright, it declares that the common-school system embraces a course of twelve years of study, eight in the common schools and four in the high-school. Drawing, music, physical culture, and German are mentioned as among the studies in the grammar grades, while the wide gamut between algebra and Greek, with military training for the boys, comprises the high-school course. The 700 high-school pupils are said to be of the average age of seventeen years. I reiterate that this is education for the well-to-do at the expense of the poor. If Denver is like any other town of my acquaintance, the poor cannot release their children from toil during twelve years after they are of an age to be sent to school. The disparity between the sum of 9500 in the common schools and the sum of 700 in the high-school makes it appear that Denver is no exception to the rule.... However, the spirit in which Denver maintains and elaborates her school system is beyond all criticism; it is, indeed, creditable and wonderful. If we do not agree about the result, I can at least testify to the impression I received — that the whole people are honestly and enthusiastically proud of their schools, and that of their elaborate kind they are among the best in the country....

... Others in the crowds were workers in the cotton factory; in a knitting-mill that has been removed there from the East; in the three large establishments where preserves, fruit pickles, and sauces are made; in the making of fire-brick, drain-pipe, jugs, jars, churns, and other coarse pottery; in the manufacture of the best mining machinery in the world, whole outfits of which have been shipped to China and South Africa, to say nothing of Mexico and our own mining regions, which are all supplied from Denver. Other operatives work upon the hoisting machinery and pumping machines, of which the Denver patterns are celebrated. Still others in the streets work at the stock-yards, where there are two large packing companies, and where nearly 200,000 hogs, cattle, and sheep were slaughtered last year. A mill for the manufacture of news paper has been in operation for a year, and now (October, '92) three other paper-mills are about to be erected, the aim being to make book and letter paper, Manilas, coarse wrapping-paper, and flooring and roofing papers, as well as to produce the pulp used in these manufactures.

The three smelting-works employ nearly 400 men, and handled 400,000 tons of ore, producing $24,500,000 in gold, silver, lead, and copper, last year. In addition to the twenty foundries and machine shops of whose work I have spoken, there are thirty other iron-working establishments, making tin and sheet-iron work and wire-work. In another year a barbed-wire factory and a wire and nail making plant will be in operation. There are sixty brick-making firms. Leather-workers are numerous, but all the leather is imported; there is no tannery there. Paint and white-lead making are large industries; there are six breweries; and eight firms engage in wood-working and the making of building material. In a sentence, this busy metropolis is manufacturing for the vast territory around it, with 339 manufacturing establishments, employing 9000 operatives, and producing $46,000,000 worth of goods.

The Chamber of Commerce advertises the need of woollen mills, stocking factories, tanneries, boot and shoe factories, glue factories, and potteries, but declares that Denver will give no subsidies to get them. "The natural advantages of the centre of a region as large as the German Empire, without a rival for 600 miles in any direction, combined with cheap fuel, fine climate, abundant supply of intelligent labor at reasonable prices, unutilized local raw materials, a good and ever-growing local market, protected against Eastern competition by from 1000 to 2000 miles of railroad haul — these are the inducements that Denver offers to new manufacturing plants."

And now we will fancy it is Sunday in Denver. The worshippers are coming out of the churches. But in the streets rush the cable cars with their week-day clanging of bells. On the car roofs are the signs, "To Elitch's Gardens," where, according to the papers next day, there are "music and dancing and bangle-bedizened women." Other cars rush toward the City Park, where the State Capital Band is to play. "Oho!" thought the critical Eastern visitors; "we are in the presence of the usual American Sunday, with the gin-mills and the gambling-places all wide open." Not so. So far as I could see, not a bar-room was open. The shades were up, and the desolate interiors were in plain view from the streets. The gambling-saloons were tight shut. No one loitered near them. Here, then, had reappeared the Sunday of the Atlantic coast, for the local ordinances are enforced, and require the closing of the saloons and "hells" from Saturday midnight until Monday morning.

Except for the cling-clang of the street cars, an Eastern-Sunday hush was upon the town. Just as we see them in New

York, country couples, strangers there, walked arm in arm in the business quarter, looking in the shop windows; German families, children and all, in stiff Sunday best, streamed along in queues behind the fathers; idle young men with large cigars leaned against the corners and the corner lamp-posts, and the business streets were nine-tenths dead. Thousands gathered in the park, just as they do on such a Sunday in New York. Beyond that the silence and stagnation of Sunday were on the town. In the Denver Club the prosperous men loafed about, and looked in at the great round table in the private dining-room with thoughts of the grand dinners it had borne. In the pretty homes were many circles wherein the West was discussed just as it is in New York, with sharp words for its gambling, its pistol-carrying, and its generally noisy Sundays. It was strange to hear in the West such talk of the West. It was easy to see the source of the influence that brought about that quiet day of worship. Yet in the same homes, in the same circles, was heard the most fulsome lauding of Denver and Colorado—praise that seemed to lift those altitudinous places even nearer to the clouds. With only the happiest memories and kindest wishes, then, adieu to Denver.

Questions

1. How was Denver similar to its older urban counterparts in the East?
2. In what ways was Denver a distinctly western city?
3. Who might have been Ralph's target audience? Why would they be interested in learning about Denver, Colorado?

18-3 The Tall Office Building Artistically Considered (1896)

Louis H. Sullivan

Louis H. Sullivan (1856–1924), famous for his motto "form follows function," was one of America's great architects. He worked out of Chicago and was one of the first architects to identify and address the design problems that were posed by the modern office building. Sullivan's rational solutions helped prepare a new aesthetic that would be embodied by the skyscrapers that came to dominate America's great cities. These impressive structures epitomized America's ability to meet challenges, such as limited space in cities, with innovative solutions, and became powerful symbols of the nation's progress and place in the world.

Source: Louis H. Sullivan, "The Tall Office Building," *Lippincott's Magazine* 57 (March 1896), 403–409.

The architects of this land and generation are now brought face to face with something new under the sun—namely, that evolution and integration of social conditions, that special grouping of them, that results in a demand for the erection of tall office buildings.

It is not my purpose to discuss the social conditions; I accept them as the fact, and say at once that the design of the tall office building must be recognized and confronted at the outset as a problem to be solved—a vital problem, pressing for a true solution.

Let us state the conditions in the plainest manner. Briefly, they are these: offices are necessary for the transaction of business; the invention and perfection of the high-speed elevators make vertical travel, that was once tedious and painful, now easy and comfortable; development of steel manufacture has shown the way to safe, rigid, economical constructions rising to a great height; continued growth of population in the great cities, consequent congestion of centers and rise in value of ground, stimulate an increase in number of stories; these successfully piled one upon another, react on ground values—and so on, by action and reaction, interaction and inter-reaction. Thus has come about that form of lofty construction called the "modern office building." It has come in answer to a call, for in it a new grouping of social conditions has found a habitation and a name.

Up to this point all in evidence is materialistic, an exhibition of force, of resolution, of brains in the keen sense of the word. It is the joint product of the speculator, the engineer, the builder.

Problem: How shall we impart to this sterile pile, this crude, harsh, brutal agglomeration, this stark, staring exclamation of eternal strife, the graciousness of those higher forms of sensibility and culture that rest on the lower and fiercer passions? How shall we proclaim from the dizzy height of this strange, weird, modern housetop the peaceful evangel of sentiment, of beauty, the cult of a higher life?

This is the problem; and we must seek the solution of it in a process analogous to its own evolution—indeed, a continuation of it—namely, by proceeding step by step from general to special aspects, from coarser to finer considerations.

It is my belief that it is of the very essence of every problem that it contains and suggests its own solution. This I believe to be natural law. Let us examine, then, carefully the elements, let us search out this contained suggestion, this essence of the problem.

The practical conditions are, broadly speaking, these:

Wanted—1st, a story below-ground, containing boilers, engines of various sorts, etc.—in short, the plant for power, heating, lighting, etc. 2nd, a ground floor, so called, devoted to stores, banks, or other establishments requiring large area, ample spacing, ample light, and great freedom of access. 3rd, a second story readily accessible by stairways—this space usually in large subdivisions, with corresponding liberality in structural spacing and expanse of glass and breadth of external openings. 4th, above this an indefinite number of stories of offices piled tier upon tier, one tier just like another tier, one office just like all the other offices—an office being similar to a cell in a honeycomb, merely a compartment, nothing more. 5th, and last, at the top of this pile is placed a space or story that, as related to the life and usefulness of the structure, is purely physiological in its nature—namely, the attic. In this the circulatory system completes itself and makes its grand turn, ascending and descending. The space is filled with tanks, pipes, valves, sheaves, and mechanical etcetera that supplement and complement the force-originating plant hidden belowground in the cellar. Finally, or at the beginning rather, there must be on the ground floor a main aperture or entrance common to all the occupants or patrons of the building.

This tabulation is, in the main, characteristic of every tall office building in the country. As to the necessary arrangements for light courts, these are not germane to the problem, and as will become soon evident, I trust need not be considered here. These things, and such others as the arrangement of elevators, for example, have to do strictly with the economics of the building, and I assume them to have been fully considered and disposed of to the satisfaction of purely utilitarian and pecuniary demands. Only in rare instances does the plan or floor arrangement of the tall office building take on an aesthetic value, and this usually when the lighting court is external or becomes an internal feature of great importance.

As I am here seeking not for an individual or special solution, but for a true normal type, the attention must be confined to those conditions that, in the main, are constant in all tall office buildings, and every mere incidental and accidental variation eliminated from the consideration, as harmful to the clearness of the main inquiry.

The practical horizontal and vertical division or office unit is naturally based on a room of comfortable area and height, and the size of this standard office room as naturally predetermines the standard structural unit, and, approximately, the size of window openings. In turn, these purely arbitrary units of structure form in an equally natural way the true basis of the artistic development of the exterior. Of course the structural spacings and openings in the first or mercantile story are required to be the largest of all; those in the second or quasi-mercantile story are of a somewhat similar nature. The spacings and openings in the attic are of no importance whatsoever (the windows have no actual value), for light may be taken from the top, and no recognition of a cellular division is necessary in the structural spacing.

Hence it follows inevitably, and in the simplest possible way, that if we follow our natural instincts without thought of books, rules, precedents, or any such educational impedimenta to a spontaneous and "sensible" result, we will in the following manner design the exterior of our tall office building—to wit:

Beginning with the first story, we give this a main entrance that attracts the eye to its location, and the remainder of the story we treat in a more or less liberal, expansive, sumptuous way—a way based exactly on the practical necessities, but expressed with a sentiment of largeness and freedom. The second story we treat in a similar way, but usually with milder pretension. Above this, throughout the indefinite number of typical office tiers, we take our cue from the individual cell, which requires a window with its separating pier, its sill and lintel, and we, without more ado, make them look all alike because they are all alike. This brings us to the attic, which, having no division into office-cells, and no special requirement for lighting, gives us the power to show by means of its broad expanse of wall, and its dominating weight and character, that which is the fact—namely, that the series of office tiers has come definitely to an end.

This may perhaps seem a bald result and a heartless, pessimistic way of stating it, but even so we certainly have advanced a most characteristic stage beyond the imagined sinister building of the speculator-engineer-builder combination. For the hand of the architect is now definitely felt in the decisive position at once taken, and the suggestion of a thoroughly sound, logical, coherent expression of the conditions is becoming apparent.

When I say the hand of the architect, I do not mean necessarily the accomplished and trained architect. I mean only a man with a strong, natural liking for buildings, and a disposition to shape them in what seems to his unaffected nature a direct and simple way. He will probably tread an innocent path from his problem to its solution, and therein he will show an enviable gift of logic. If he have some gift for form in detail, some feeling for form purely and simply as form, some love for that, his result in addition to its simple straightforward naturalness and completeness in general statement, will have something of the charm of sentiment.

However, thus far the results are only partial and tentative at best; relatively true, they are but superficial. We are doubtless right in our instinct but we must seek a fuller justification, a finer sanction, for it.

I assume now that in the study of our problem we have passed through the various stages of inquiry, as follows: 1st, the social basis of the demand for tall office buildings; 2nd, its literal material satisfaction; 3rd, the elevation of the question from considerations of literal planning, construction, and equipment, to the plane of elementary architecture as a direct outgrowth of sound, sensible building; 4th, the question again elevated from an elementary architecture to the beginnings of true architectural expression, through the addition of a certain quality and quantity of sentiment.

But our building may have all these in a considerable degree and yet be far from that adequate solution of the problem I am attempting to define. We must now heed the imperative voice of emotion.

It demands of us, what is the chief characteristic of the tall office building? And at once we answer, it is lofty. This loftiness is to the artist-nature its thrilling aspect. It is the very open organ-tone in its appeal. It must be in turn the dominant chord in his expression of it, the true excitant of his imagination. It must be tall, every inch of it tall. The force and power of altitude must be in it, the glory and pride of exaltation must be in it. It must be every inch a proud and soaring thing, rising in sheer exultation that from bottom to top it is a unit without a single dissenting line—that it is the new, the unexpected, the eloquent peroration of most bald, most sinister, most forbidding conditions.

The man who designs in this spirit and with the sense of responsibility to the generation he lives in must be no coward, no denier, no bookworm, no dilettante. He must live of his life and for his life in the fullest, most consummate sense. He must realize at once and with the grasp of inspiration that the problem of the tall office building is one of the most stupendous, one of the most magnificent opportunities that the Lord of Nature in His beneficence has ever offered to the proud spirit of man.

That this has not been perceived—indeed, has been flatly denied—is an exhibition of human perversity that must give us pause.

Questions

1. Sullivan stated that the tall modern office building had "come in answer to a call." Based on the text (pp. 552–555) and Sullivan's article, what social and economic changes made skyscrapers necessary? What technological advances made them possible?
2. Besides technology and planning, what else was necessary for creating such a "lofty construction" as the skyscraper?
3. How does Sullivan's piece underscore the tremendous changes that were taking place in America at the turn of the century?

Questions for Further Thought

1. Compare Documents 18-1 and 18-3. What aesthetic considerations did America's cities inspire?
2. In late-nineteenth-century America, newer as well as older cities expanded horizontally and vertically. Explain.
3. Based on both the text and Ralph's account of Denver, what were the principal advantages and attractions that cities had to offer Americans of the period?

Upper Class/Middle Class

"To clear, cultivate and transform the huge uninhabited continent which is their domain, the Americans need the everyday support of an energetic passion; that passion can only be the love of wealth," Alexis de Tocqueville wrote. That same passion carried over into urban life.

The wealthy were the most obvious beneficiaries of urbanism, although daily newspapers gave millions the vicarious thrill of reading about the Astors and the Vanderbilts.

Some members of the elite collected art, others collected European nobility (as in-laws), and nearly every rich person seemed to build a lavish mansion or summer home. However, not all millionaires spent their money exclusively on themselves. John Rockefeller and Andrew Carnegie, among others, took seriously the Christian obligation of stewardship. Rockefeller financed the University of Chicago, and Carnegie took a particular interest in funding public libraries.

The Industrial Revolution produced wealth for more than the fortunate few. The manufacturing economy also created a sizable, largely urban middle class (see text pp. 558–566). Its members fought to reform the cities and, when that failed, began to move to the suburbs. With husbands out of the house, middle-class housewives took charge of family and household matters (see text pp. 561–562). In the process, they grew interested in political issues and women's rights. The middle class also provided an audience for both high and popular culture.

The following selections give a sense of the emotional and intellectual ferment of American cities. In Document 18-4, social critic Thorstein Veblen argues that "conspicuous consumption" by the wealthy had a definite purpose. Catharine Beecher (Document 18-5) offers her view on how women might create the ideal middle-class household. Theodore Dreiser's *Sister Carrie* (Document 18-6) succeeds both as fiction and as social history.

18-4 Conspicuous Consumption (1899)

Thorstein Veblen

Thorstein Veblen (1857–1929) published *The Theory of the Leisure Class* in 1899. Veblen's thesis centered on the idea of conspicuous consumption. In his view, the purchases and interests of the wealthy were intended to demonstrate their superiority. The theory proved more popular than its author. Something of an iconoclast, Veblen failed to capitalize on the critical success of his work. He held a series of teaching jobs before his death.

Source: From Thorstein Veblen, *The Theory of the Leisure Class: An Economic Study of Institutions* (1899; reprint, New York: Modern Library, 1934), 73–75, 140–143.

During the earlier stages of economic development, consumption of goods without stint, especially consumption of the better grades of goods—ideally all consumption in excess of the subsistence minimum,—pertains normally to the leisure class. This restriction tends to disappear, at least formally, after the later peaceable stage has been reached, with private ownership of goods and an industrial system based on wage labour or on the petty household economy. But during the earlier quasi-peaceable stage, when so many of the traditions through which the institution of a leisure class has affected the economic life of later times were taking form and consistency, this principle has had the force of a conventional law. It has served as the norm to which consumption has tended to conform, and any appreciable departure from it is to be regarded as an aberrant form, sure to be eliminated sooner or later in the further course of development.

The quasi-peaceable gentleman of leisure, then, not only consumes of the staff of life beyond the minimum required for subsistence and physical efficiency, but his consumption also undergoes a specialisation as regards the quality of the goods consumed. He consumes freely and of the best, in food, drink, narcotics, shelter, services, ornaments, apparel, weapons and accoutrements, amusements, amulets, and idols or divinities. In the process of gradual amelioration which takes place in the articles of his consumption, the motive principle and the proximate aim of innovation is no doubt the higher efficiency of the improved and more elaborate products for personal comfort and wellbeing. But that does not remain the sole purpose of their consumption. The canon of reputability is at hand and seizes upon such innovations as are, according to its standard, fit to survive. Since the consumption of these more excellent goods is an evidence of wealth, it becomes honorific; and conversely, the failure to consume in due quantity and quality becomes a mark of inferiority and demerit.

This growth of punctilious discrimination as to qualitative excellence in eating, drinking, etc., presently affects not only the manner of life, but also the training and intellectual activity of the gentleman of leisure. He is no longer simply the successful, aggressive male,—the man of strength, resource, and intrepidity. In order to avoid stultification he must also cultivate his tastes, for it now becomes incumbent on him to discriminate with some nicety between the noble and the ignoble in consumable goods. He becomes a connoisseur in creditable viands of various degrees of merit, in manly beverages and trinkets, in seemly apparel and architecture, in weapons, games, dancers, and the narcotics. This cultivation of the æsthetic faculty requires time and application, and the demands made upon the gentleman in this direction therefore tend to change his life of leisure into a more or less arduous application to the business of learning how to live a life of ostensible leisure in a becoming way. Closely related to the requirement that the gentleman must consume freely and of the right kind of goods, there is the requirement that he must know how to consume them in a seemly manner. His life of leisure must be conducted in due form. Hence arise good manners in the way pointed out in an earlier chapter. High-bred manners and ways of living are items of conformity to the norm of conspicuous leisure and conspicuous consumption.

Conspicuous consumption of valuable goods is a means of reputability to the gentleman of leisure. As wealth accumulates on his hands, his own unaided effort will not avail to sufficiently put his opulence in evidence by this method. The aid of friends and competitors is therefore brought in by resorting to the giving of valuable presents and expensive feasts and entertainments. Presents and feasts had probably another origin than that of naïve ostentation, but they acquired their utility for this purpose very early, and they have retained that character to the present; so that their utility in this respect has now long been the substantial ground on which these usages rest. Costly entertainments, such as the potlatch or the ball, are peculiarly adapted to serve this end. The competitor with whom the entertainer wishes to institute a comparison is, by this method, made to serve as a means to the end. He consumes vicariously for his host at the same time that he is a witness to the consumption of that excess of good things which his host is unable to dispose of single-handed, and he is also made to witness his host's facility in etiquette. . . .

In the case of those domestic animals which are honorific and are reputed beautiful, there is a subsidiary basis of merit that should be spoken of. Apart from the birds which belong in the honorific class of domestic animals, and which owe their place in this class to their non-lucrative character alone, the animals which merit particular attention are cats, dogs, and fast horses. The cat is less reputable than the other two just named, because she is less wasteful; she may even serve a useful end. At the same time the cat's temperament does not fit her for the honorific purpose. She lives with man on terms of equality, knows nothing of that relation of status which is the ancient basis of all distinctions of worth, honour, and repute, and she does not lend herself with facility to an invidious comparison between her owner and his neighbours. The exception to this last rule occurs in the case of such scarce and fanciful products as the Angora cat, which have some slight honorific value on the ground of expensiveness, and have, therefore, some special claim to beauty on pecuniary grounds.

The dog has advantages in the way of uselessness as well as in special gifts of temperament. He is often spoken of, in an eminent sense, as the friend of man, and his intelligence and fidelity are praised. The meaning of this is that the dog is man's servant and that he has the gift of an unquestioning subservience and a slave's quickness in guessing his master's mood. Coupled with these traits, which fit him well for the relation of status—and which must for the present purpose be set down as serviceable traits—the dog has some characteristics which are of a more equivocal æsthetic value. He is the filthiest of the domestic animals in his person and the nastiest in his habits. For this he makes up in a servile, fawning attitude towards his master, and a readiness to inflict damage and discomfort on all else. The dog, then, commends himself to our favour by affording play to our propensity for mastery, and as he is also an item of expense, and commonly serves no industrial purpose, he holds a well-assured place in men's regard as a thing of good repute. The dog is at the same time associated in our imaginations with the chase—a meritorious employment and an expression of the honourable predatory impulse.

Standing on this vantage ground, whatever beauty of form and motion and whatever commendable mental traits he may possess are conventionally acknowledged and magnified. And even those varieties of the dog which have been bred into grotesque deformity by the dog-fancier are in good faith accounted beautiful by many. These varieties of dogs—and the like is true of other fancy-bred animals—are rated and graded in æsthetic value somewhat in proportion to the degree of grotesqueness and instability of the particular fashion which the deformity takes in the given case. For the purpose in hand, this differential utility on the ground of grotesqueness and instability of structure is reducible to terms of a great scarcity and consequent expense. The commercial value of canine monstrosities, such as the prevailing styles of pet dogs both for men's and women's use, rests on their high cost of production, and their value to their owners lies chiefly in their utility as items of conspicuous consumption. Indirectly, through reflection upon their honorific expensiveness, a social worth is imputed to them; and so, by an easy substitution of words and ideas, they come to be admired and reputed beautiful. Since any attention bestowed upon these animals is in no sense gainful or useful, it is also reputable; and since the habit of giving them attention is consequently not deprecated, it may grow into an habitual attachment of great tenacity and of a most benevolent character. So that in the affection bestowed on pet animals the canon of expensiveness is present more or less remotely as a norm which guides and shapes the sentiment and the selection of its object. The like is true, as will be noticed presently, with respect to affection for persons also; although the manner in which the norm acts in that case is somewhat different.

The case of the fast horse is much like that of the dog. He is on the whole expensive, or wasteful and useless—for the industrial purpose. What productive use he may possess, in the way of enhancing the well-being of the community or making the way of life easier for men, takes the form of exhibitions of force and facility of motion that gratify the popular æsthetic sense. This is of course a substantial serviceability. The horse is not endowed with the spiritual aptitude for servile dependence in the same measure as the dog; but he ministers effectually to his master's impulse to convert the "animate" forces of the environment to his own use and discretion and so express his own dominating individuality through them. The fast horse is at least potentially a race-horse, of high or low degree; and it is as such that he is peculiarly serviceable to his owner. The utility of the fast horse lies largely in his efficiency as a means of emulation; it gratifies the owner's sense of aggression and dominance to have his own horse outstrip his neighbour's. This use being not lucrative, but on the whole pretty consistently wasteful, and quite conspicuously so, it is honorific, and therefore gives the fast horse a strong presumptive position of reputability. Beyond this, the race horse proper has also a similarly non-industrial but honorific use as a gambling instrument.

Questions

1. How does conspicuous consumption work?
2. Where do dogs and racehorses fit into Veblen's thesis?
3. Was Veblen's theory applicable only to the rich in the nineteenth century?

18-5 The Christian Family (1869)

Catharine E. Beecher

Like her sister, Harriet Beecher Stowe, the author of *Uncle Tom's Cabin*, Catharine E. Beecher (1800–1878) hoped to reach a wide audience through her writings. *The American Woman's Home* was subtitled in part "a guide to the formation and maintenance of economical, healthful, beautiful and Christian homes" (see text p. 561) and was dedicated "to THE WOMEN OF AMERICA, in whose hands rest the real destinies of the republic, as moulded by the early training and preserved amid the maturer influences of home." Beecher's more famous sister was listed as a coauthor to increase the book's popularity; Catharine did most of the writing.

Source: From Catharine E. Beecher and Harriet Beecher Stowe, *The American Woman's Home: or, Principles of Domestic Science* (J. B. Ford, 1869; reprint, Watkins Glen, NY: Library of Victorian Culture, American Life Foundation, 1979), 17–22.

It is the aim of this volume to elevate the honor and the remuneration of all employments that sustain the many difficult and varied duties of the family state, and thus to render each department of woman's profession as much desired and respected as are the most honored professions of men.

What, then, is the end designed by the family state which Jesus Christ came into this world to secure?

It is to provide for the training of our race to the highest possible intelligence, virtue, and happiness, by means of the self-sacrificing labors of the wise and good, and this with chief reference to a future immortal existence.

The distinctive feature of the family is self-sacrificing labor of the stronger and wiser members to raise the weaker and more ignorant to equal advantages. The father undergoes toil and self-denial to provide a home, and then the mother becomes a self-sacrificing laborer to train its inmates. The useless, troublesome infant is served in the humblest offices; while both parents unite in training it to an equality with themselves in every advantage. Soon the older children become helpers to raise the younger to a level with their own. When any are sick, those who are well become self-sacrificing ministers. When the parents are old and useless, the children become their self-sacrificing servants.

Thus the discipline of the family state is one of daily self-devotion of the stronger and wiser to elevate and support the weaker members. Nothing could be more contrary to its first principles than for the older and more capable children to combine to secure to themselves the highest advantages, enforcing the drudgeries on the younger, at the sacrifice of their equal culture.

Jesus Christ came to teach the fatherhood of God and consequent brotherhood of man. He came as the "first-born

Son" of God and the Elder Brother of man, to teach by example the self-sacrifice by which the great family of man is to be raised to equality of advantages as children of God. For this end, he "humbled himself" from the highest to the lowest place. He chose for his birthplace the most despised village; for his parents the lowest in rank; for his trade, to labor with his hands as a carpenter, being "subject to his parents" thirty years. And, what is very significant, his trade was that which prepares the family home, as if he would teach that the great duty of man is labor — to provide for and train weak and ignorant creatures. Jesus Christ worked with his hands nearly thirty years, and preached less than three. And he taught that his kingdom is exactly opposite to that of the world, where all are striving for the highest positions. "Whoso will be great shall be your minister, and whoso will be chiefest shall be servant of all."

The family state then, is the aptest earthly illustration of the heavenly kingdom, and in it woman is its chief minister. Her great mission is self-denial, in training its members to self-sacrificing labors for the ignorant and weak: if not her own children, then the neglected children of her Father in heaven. She is to rear all under her care to lay up treasures, not on earth, but in heaven. All the pleasures of this life end here; but those who train immortal minds are to reap the fruit of their labor through eternal ages.

To man is appointed the out-door labor — to till the earth, dig the mines, toil in the foundries, traverse the ocean, transport merchandise, labor in manufactories, construct houses, conduct civil, municipal, and state affairs, and all the heavy work, which, most of the day, excludes him from the comforts of a home. But the great stimulus to all these toils, implanted in the heart of every true man, is the desire for a home of his own, and the hopes of paternity. Every man who truly lives for immortality responds to the beatitude, "Children are a heritage from the Lord: blessed is the man that hath his quiver full of them!" The more a father and mother live under the influence of that "immortality which Christ hath brought to light," the more is the blessedness of rearing a family understood and appreciated. Every child trained aright is to dwell forever in exalted bliss with those that gave it life and trained it for heaven.

The blessed privileges of the family state are not confined to those who rear children of their own. Any woman who can earn a livelihood, as every woman should be trained to do, can take a properly qualified female associate, and institute a family of her own, receiving to its heavenly influences the orphan, the sick, the homeless, and the sinful, and by motherly devotion train them to follow the self-denying example of Christ, in educating his earthly children for true happiness in this life and for his eternal home.

And such is the blessedness of aiding to sustain a truly Christian home, that no one comes so near the pattern of the All-perfect One as those who might hold what men call a higher place, and yet humble themselves to the lowest in order to aid in training the young, "not as men-pleasers, but as servants to Christ, with good-will doing service as to the Lord, and not to men." Such are preparing for high places in the kingdom of heaven. "Whosoever will be chiefest among you, let him be your servant."

It is often the case that the true humility of Christ is not understood. It was not in having a low opinion of his own character and claims, but it was in taking a low place in order to raise others to a higher. The worldling seeks to raise himself and family to an equality with others, or, if possible, a superiority to them. The true follower of Christ comes down in order to elevate others.

The maxims and institutions of this world have ever been antagonistic to the teachings and example of Jesus Christ. Men toil for wealth, honor, and power, not as means for raising others to an equality with themselves, but mainly for earthly, selfish advantages. Although the experience of this life shows that children brought up to labor have the fairest chance for a virtuous and prosperous life, and for hope of future eternal blessedness, yet it is the aim of most parents who can do so, to lay up wealth that their children need not labor with the hands as Christ did. And although exhorted by our Lord not to lay up treasure on earth, but rather the imperishable riches which are gained in toiling to train the ignorant and reform the sinful, as yet a large portion of the professed followers of Christ, like his first disciples, are "slow of heart to believe."

Not less have the sacred ministries of the family state been undervalued and warred upon in other directions; for example, the Romish Church has made celibacy a prime virtue, and given its highest honors to those who forsake the family state as ordained by God. Thus came great communities of monks and nuns, shut out from the love and labors of a Christian home; thus, also, came the monkish systems of education, collecting the young in great establishments away from the watch and care of parents, and the healthful and self-sacrificing labors of a home. Thus both religion and education have conspired to degrade the family state.

Still more have civil laws and social customs been opposed to the principles of Jesus Christ. It has ever been assumed that the learned, the rich, and the powerful are not to labor with the hands, as Christ did, and as Paul did when he would "not eat any man's bread for naught, but wrought with labor, not because we have not power" [to live without handwork,] "but to make ourselves an example." (2 Thess. 3.)

Instead of this, manual labor has been made dishonorable and unrefined by being forced on the ignorant and poor. Especially has the most important of all hand-labor, that which sustains the family, been thus disgraced; so that to nurse young children, and provide the food of a family by labor, is deemed the lowest of all positions in honor and profit, and the last resort of poverty. And so our Lord, who himself took the form of a servant, teaches, "How hardly shall they that have riches enter the kingdom of heaven!" — that kingdom in which all are toiling to raise the weak, ignorant, and sinful to such equality with themselves as the children of a loving family enjoy. One mode in which riches have led to antagonism with the true end of the family state is in the style of living, by which the hand-labor, most important to health, comfort, and beauty, is confined to the most ignorant and neglected members of society, without any effort being made to raise them to equal advantages with the wise and cultivated.

And, the higher civilization has advanced, the more have children been trained to feel that to labor, as did Christ and Paul, is disgraceful, and to be made the portion of a degraded class. Children of the rich grow up with the feeling that servants are to work for them, and they themselves are not to work. To the minds of most children and servants, "to be a lady," is almost synonymous with "to be waited on, and do no work." It is the earnest desire of the authors of this volume to make plain the falsity of this growing popular feeling, and to show how much happier and more efficient family life will become when it is strengthened, sustained, and adorned by family work.

Questions

1. To what extent did Beecher offer a conventional view of women?
2. In what way did she broaden or modernize women's role in society?
3. What prejudice did she reveal?

18-6 *Sister Carrie* (1900)

Theodore Dreiser

In 1900, Theodore Dreiser (1871–1945) published *Sister Carrie*, the story of a small-town Wisconsin girl. Carrie Meeber leaves Columbia City for a factory job in Chicago. She hates the work and eventually becomes a successful (though unhappy) actress in New York. This story of an independent woman—and one who lived out of wedlock with men—shocked its turn-of-the-century audience. Worried that the public would reject such a non-Victorian work, the publisher printed only a thousand copies of *Sister Carrie* and virtually ignored it. The book finally received greater acceptance when it was reissued in 1912.

Source: Theodore Dreiser, *Sister Carrie* (New York: Doubleday, Page, 1900; reprint, New York: Bantam Books, 1958), 28–33.

It was with weak knees and a slight catch in her breathing that she came up to the great shoe company at Adams and Fifth Avenue and entered the elevator. When she stepped out on the fourth floor there was no one at hand, only great aisles of boxes piled to the ceiling. She stood, very much frightened, awaiting some one.

Presently Mr. Brown came up. He did not seem to recognise her.

"What is it you want?" he inquired.

Carrie's heart sank.

"You said I should come this morning to see about work—"

"Oh," he interrupted. "Um—yes. What is your name?"

"Carrie Meeber."

"Yes," said he. "You come with me."

He led the way through dark, box-lined aisles which had the smell of new shoes, until they came to an iron door which opened into the factory proper. There was a large, low-ceiled room, with clacking, rattling machines at which men in white shirt sleeves and blue gingham aprons were working. She followed him diffidently through the clattering automatons, keeping her eyes straight before her, and flushing slightly. They crossed to a far corner and took an elevator to the sixth floor. Out of the array of machines and benches, Mr. Brown signalled a foreman.

"This is the girl," he said, and turning to Carrie[,] "You go with him." He then returned, and Carrie followed her new superior to a little desk in a corner, which he used as a kind of official centre.

"You've never worked at anything like this before, have you?" he questioned, rather sternly.

"No, sir," she answered.

He seemed rather annoyed at having to bother with such help, but put down her name and then led her across to where a line of girls occupied stools in front of clacking machines. On the shoulder of one of the girls who was punching eye-holes in one piece of the upper, by the aid of the machine, he put his hand.

"You," he said, "show this girl how to do what you're doing. When you get through, come to me."

The girl so addressed rose promptly and gave Carrie her place.

"It isn't hard to do," she said, bending over. "You just take this so, fasten it with this clamp, and start the machine."

She suited action to word, fastened the piece of leather, which was eventually to form the right half of the upper of a man's shoe, by little adjustable clamps, and pushed a small steel rod at the side of the machine. The latter jumped to the task of punching, with sharp, snapping clicks, cutting circular bits of leather out of the side of the upper, leaving the holes which were to hold the laces. After observing a few times, the girl let her work at it alone. Seeing that it was fairly well done, she went away.

The pieces of leather came from the girl at the machine to her right, and were passed to the girl at her left. Carrie saw at once that an average speed was necessary or the work would pile up on her and all those below would be delayed. She had no time to look about, and bent anxiously to her task. The girls at her left and right realised her predicament and feelings, and, in a way, tried to aid her, as much as they dared, by working slower.

At this task she laboured incessantly for some time, finding relief from her own nervous fears and imaginings in the humdrum, mechanical movement of the machine. She felt, as the minutes passed, that the room was not very light. It had a thick odour of fresh leather, but that did not worry her. She felt the eyes of the other help upon her, and troubled lest she was not working fast enough.

Once, when she was fumbling at the little clamp, having made a slight error in setting in the leather, a great hand appeared before her eyes and fastened the clamp for her. It was the foreman. Her heart thumped so that she could scarcely see to go on.

"Start your machine," he said, "start your machine. Don't keep the line waiting."

This recovered her sufficiently and she went excitedly on, hardly breathing until the shadow moved away from behind her. Then she heaved a great breath.

As the morning wore on the room became hotter. She felt the need of a breath of fresh air and a drink of water but did not venture to stir. The stool she sat on was without a back or foot-rest, and she began to feel uncomfortable. She found, after a time, that her back was beginning to ache. She twisted and turned from one position to another slightly different, but it did not ease her for long. She was beginning to weary.

"Stand up, why don't you?" said the girl at her right, without any form of introduction. "They won't care."

Carrie looked at her gratefully. "I guess I will," she said.

She stood up from her stool and worked that way for a while, but it was a more difficult position. Her neck and shoulders ached in bending over.

The spirit of the place impressed itself on her in a rough way. She did not venture to look around, but above the clack of the machine she could hear an occasional remark. She could also note a thing or two out of the side of her eye.

"Did you see Harry last night?" said the girl at her left, addressing her neighbour.

"No."

"You ought to have seen the tie he had on. Gee, but he was a mark."

"S-s-t," said the other girl, bending over her work. The first, silenced, instantly assumed a solemn face. The foreman passed slowly along, eyeing each worker distinctly. The moment he was gone, the conversation was resumed again.

"Say," began the girl at her left, "what jeh think he said?"

"I don't know."

"He said he saw us with Eddie Harris at Martin's last night."

"No!" They both giggled.

A youth with tan-coloured hair, that needed clipping very badly, came shuffling along between the machines, bearing a basket of leather findings under his left arm, and pressed against his stomach. When near Carrie, he stretched out his right hand and gripped one girl under the arm.

"Aw, let me go," she exclaimed angrily. "Duffer."

He only grinned broadly in return.

"Rubber!" he called back as she looked after him. There was nothing of the gallant in him.

Carrie at last could scarcely sit still. Her legs began to tire and she wanted to get up and stretch. Would noon never come? It seemed as if she had worked an entire day. She was not hungry at all, but weak, and her eyes were tired, straining at the one point where the eye-punch came down. The girl at the right noticed her squirmings and felt sorry for her. She was concentrating herself too thoroughly—what she did really required less mental and physical strain. There was nothing to be done, however. The halves of the uppers came piling steadily down. Her hands began to ache at the wrists and then in the fingers, and towards the last she seemed one mass of dull, complaining muscles, fixed in an eternal position and performing a single mechanical movement which became more and more distasteful, until at last it was absolutely nauseating. When she was wondering whether the strain would ever cease, a dull-sounding bell clanged somewhere down an elevator shaft, and the end came. In an instant there was a buzz of action and conversation. All the girls instantly left their stools and hurried away; in an adjoining room, men passed through, coming from some department which opened on the right. The whirling wheels began to sing in a steadily modifying key, until at last they died away in a low buzz. There was an audible stillness, in which the common voice sounded strange.

Carrie got up and sought her lunch box. She was stiff, a little dizzy, and very thirsty. On the way to the small space portioned off by wood, where all the wraps and lunches were kept, she encountered the foreman, who stared at her hard.

"Well," he said, "did you get along all right?"

"I think so," she replied, very respectfully.

"Um," he replied, for want of something better, and walked on.

Under better material conditions, this kind of work would not have been so bad, but the new socialism which involves pleasant working conditions for employees had not then taken hold upon manufacturing companies.

The place smelled of the oil of the machines and the new leather—a combination which, added to the stale odours of the building, was not pleasant even in cold weather. The floor, though regularly swept every evening, presented a littered surface. Not the slightest provision had been made for the comfort of the employees, the idea being that something was gained by giving them as little and making the work as hard and unremunerative as possible. What we know of foot-rests, swivel-back chairs, dining-rooms for the girls, clean aprons and curling irons supplied free, and a decent cloak room, were unthought of. The washrooms were disagreeable, crude, if not foul places, and the whole atmosphere was sordid.

Carrie looked about her, after she had drunk a tinful of water from a bucket in one corner, for a place to sit and eat. The other girls had ranged themselves about the windows or the work-benches of those of the men who had gone out. She saw no place which did not hold a couple or a group of girls, and being too timid to think of introducing herself, she sought out her machine and, seated upon her stool, opened her lunch on her lap. There she sat listening to the chatter and comment about her. It was, for the most part, silly and graced by the current slang. Several of the men in the room exchanged compliments with the girls at long range.

"Say, Kitty," called one to a girl who was doing a waltz step in a few feet of space near one of the windows, "are you going to the ball with me?"

"Look out, Kitty," called another, "you'll jar your back hair."

"Go on, Rubber," was her only comment.

As Carrie listened to this and much more of similar familiar badinage among the men and girls, she instinctively withdrew into herself. She was not used to this type, and felt that there was something hard and low about it all. She feared that the young boys about would address such remarks to her—boys who . . . seemed uncouth and ridiculous. She made the average feminine distinction between clothes, putting worth, goodness, and distinction in a dress suit, and leaving all the unlovely qualities and those beneath notice in overalls and jumper.

She was glad when the short half hour was over and the wheels began to whirr again. Though wearied, she would be inconspicuous. This illusion ended when another young man passed along the aisle and poked her indifferently in the ribs with his thumb. She turned about, indignation leaping to her eyes, but he had gone on and only once turned to grin. She found it difficult to conquer an inclination to cry.

The girl next to her noticed her state of mind. "Don't you mind," she said. "He's too fresh."

Carrie said nothing, but bent over her work. She felt as though she could hardly endure such a life. Her idea of work had been so entirely different. All during the long afternoon she thought of the city outside and its imposing show, crowds, and fine buildings. Columbia City and the better side of her home life came back. By three o'clock she was sure it must be six, and by four it seemed as if they had forgotten to note the hour and were letting all work overtime. The foreman became a true ogre, prowling constantly about, keeping her tied down to her miserable task. What she heard of the conversation about her only made her feel sure that she did not want to make friends with any of these. When six o'clock came she hurried eagerly away, her arms aching and her limbs stiff from sitting in one position.

As she passed out along the hall after getting her hat, a young machine hand, attracted by her looks, made bold to jest with her.

"Say, Maggie," he called, "if you wait, I'll walk with you."

It was thrown so straight in her direction that she knew who was meant, but never turned to look.

In the crowded elevator, another dusty, toil-stained youth tried to make an impression on her by leering in her face.

One young man, waiting on the walk outside for the appearance of another, grinned at her as she passed.

"Ain't going my way, are you?" he called jocosely.

Carrie turned her face to the west with a subdued heart. As she turned the corner, she saw through the great shiny window the small desk at which she had applied. There were the crowds, hurrying with the same buzz and energy-yielding enthusiasm. She felt a slight relief, but it was only at her escape. She felt ashamed in the face of better dressed girls who went by. She felt as though she should be better served, and her heart revolted.

Questions

1. According to Dreiser, why did so many women work in such difficult conditions?
2. What did the banter between workers accomplish?
3. How does *Sister Carrie* succeed as social history in ways that a factory-inspection report from that era could not?

Questions for Further Thought

1. Compare the ways in which Catharine Beecher (Document 18-5) and Theodore Dreiser (Document 18-6) portray American women. Is one portrait more realistic than the other? Why or why not?

2. Thorstein Veblen (Document 18-4) thought he could expose the vanity and purposeful extravagance of the rich. The term *conspicuous consumption* has become part of our vocabulary, but our fascination with the rich and famous has not abated. Why?

3. Which is a more important gauge of American society in 1900, that Theodore Dreiser could publish *Sister Carrie* (Document 18-6) or that his publisher abandoned the novel in fear of protests? Why?

City Life

Unlike most Europeans, who tend to think of themselves as part of a national community, Americans have always celebrated their individuality. Rugged frontierism became a powerful myth, but city life did not make for individualism. Success in business was a product of chain of command and interdependence. Even going from one end of a city to the other meant depending on strangers such as streetcar conductors and bridge tenders, and directions could come in Polish, Yiddish, or Italian. To their credit, Americans adapted, some more quickly than others.

For Mark Twain, New York was "too large," an inconvenience; for immigrants, it was dangerously crowded. The journalist Jacob Riis, a Danish immigrant, noted that New York's Thirteenth Ward had a population density of 274,432 people *per square mile* in 1890. In that setting, diseases like smallpox, diphtheria, cholera, typhoid fever, typhus, and tuberculosis became all too familiar to the residents.

When extensive urban suffering made it obvious by the turn of the century that change was necessary, the urban middle class formed numerous reform groups for public health, decent housing, and better schools and playgrounds. Some reformers argued the cause of good government, whereas others demanded change in the name of Christianity. However, large segments of the urban population were not interested in reform. Their needs were satisfied by machine politics (see text pp. 568–572), with perhaps some public entertainment on the side (see text pp. 574–577, and "Voices from Abroad: José Martí, Coney Island, 1881," text p. 575).

Document 18-7 is an excerpt from Jacob Riis's *How the Other Half Lives* (1890). The letters that make up Document 18-8 show how a Polish family dealt with the uncertainties of the immigration experience. The Italian visitor Giuseppe Giacosa (Document 18-9) provides an eyewitness account of an industrial city and one of its by-products—smoke. Finally, the Reverend Josiah Strong (Document 18-10) expresses his fears of city life and its effect on the older order of things.

18-7 *How the Other Half Lives* (1890)

Jacob Riis

Born in Denmark in 1849, Jacob A. Riis immigrated in 1870 to the United States. After personally struggling to make it in his new home, New York City, he worked as a police reporter for the *Tribune*. Riis reported on the harsh conditions immigrants, like himself, had to face and combined reporting with photography to communicate what life was really like for those struggling to claim a place in the United States, especially those forced into New York's squalid tenements. The result was *How the Other Half Lives*, published in 1890. Riis found immigrant housing an issue begging to be taken up by the progressive-minded reformers who, by the next decade, would come to influence the nation's politics. The following is a chapter from Riis's famous book discussing the history of the tenement house and the shocking living conditions he found there.

Source: Jacob A. Riis, "Genesis of the Tenement," in *How the Other Half Lives: Studies Among the Tenements of New York* (New York: Dover Publications, 1971), 4–11, excluding photographs.

THE first tenement New York knew bore the mark of Cain from its birth, though a generation passed before the writing was deciphered. It was the "rear house," infamous ever after in our city's history. There had been tenant-houses before, but they were not built for the purpose. Nothing would probably have shocked their original owners more than the idea of their harboring a promiscuous crowd; for they were the decorous homes of the old Knickerbockers, the proud aristocracy of Manhattan in the early days.

It was the stir and bustle of trade, together with the tremendous immigration that followed upon the war of 1812, that dislodged them. In thirty-five years the city of less than a hundred thousand came to harbor half a million souls, for whom homes had to be found. Within the memory of men not yet in their prime, Washington had moved from his house on Cherry Hill as too far out of town to be easily reached. Now the old residents followed his example; but they moved in a different direction and for a different reason. Their comfortable dwellings in the once fashionable streets along the East River front fell into the hands of real-estate agents and boarding-house keepers; and here, says the report to the Legislature of 1857, when the evils engendered had excited just alarm, "in its beginning, the tenant-house became a real blessing to that class of industrious poor whose small earnings limited their expenses, and whose employment in workshops, stores, or about the warehouses and thoroughfares, render a near residence of much importance." Not for long, however. As business increased, and the city grew with rapid strides, the necessities of the poor became the opportunity of their wealthier neighbors, and the stamp was set upon the old houses, suddenly become valuable, which the best thought and effort of a later age have vainly struggled to efface. Their "*large* rooms were partitioned into *several smaller ones*, without regard to light or ventilation, the rate of rent being lower in proportion to space or height from the street; and they soon became filled from cellar to garret with a class of tenantry living from hand to mouth, loose in morals, improvident in habits, degraded, and squalid as beggary itself." It was thus the dark bedroom, prolific of untold depravities, came into the world. It was destined to survive the old houses. In their new rôle, says the old report, eloquent in its indignant denunciation of "evils more destructive than wars," "they were not intended to last. Rents were fixed high enough to cover damage and abuse from this class, from whom nothing was expected, and the most was made of them while they lasted. Neatness, order, cleanliness, were never dreamed of in connection with the tenant-house system, as it spread its localities from year to year; while reckless slovenliness, discontent, privation, and ignorance were left to work out their invariable results, until the entire premises reached the level of tenant-house dilapidation, containing, but sheltering not, the miserable hordes that crowded beneath mouldering, water-rotted roofs or burrowed among the rats of clammy cellars." Yet so illogical is human greed that, at a later day, when called to account, "the proprietors frequently urged the filthy habits of the tenants as an excuse for the condition of their property, utterly losing sight of the fact that it was the tolerance of those habits which was the real evil, and that for this they themselves were alone responsible."

Still the pressure of the crowds did not abate, and in the old garden where the stolid Dutch burgher grew his tulips or early cabbages a rear house was built, generally of wood, two stories high at first. Presently it was carried up another story, and another. Where two families had lived ten moved in. The front house followed suit, if the brick walls were strong enough. The question was not always asked, judging from complaints made by a contemporary witness, that the old buildings were "often carried up to a great height without regard to the strength of the foundation walls." It was rent the owner was after; nothing was said in the contract about either the safety or the comfort of the tenants. The garden gate no longer swung on its rusty hinges. The shell-paved walk had become an alley; what the rear house had left of the garden, a "court." Plenty such are yet to be found in the Fourth Ward, with here and there one of the original rear tenements.

Worse was to follow. It was "soon perceived by estate owners and agents of property that a greater percentage of profits could be realized by the conversion of houses and blocks into barracks, and dividing their space into smaller proportions capable of containing human life within four walls. . . . Blocks were rented of real estate owners, or 'purchased on time,' or taken in charge at a percentage, and held for under-letting." With the appearance of the middleman, wholly irresponsible, and utterly reckless and unrestrained, began the era of tenement building which turned out such blocks as Gotham Court, where, in one cholera epidemic that scarcely touched the clean wards, the tenants died at the rate of one hundred and ninety-five to the thousand of population; which forced the general mortality of the city up from 1 in 41.83 in 1815, to 1 in 27.33 in 1855, a year of unusual freedom from epidemic disease, and which wrung from the early organizers of the Health Department this wail: "There are numerous examples of tenement-houses in which are lodged several hundred people that have a *pro rata* allotment of ground area scarcely equal to two square yards upon the city lot, court-yards and all included." The tenement-house population had swelled to half a million souls by that time, and on the East Side, in what is still the most densely populated district in all the world, China not excluded, it was packed at the rate of 290,000 to the square mile, a state of affairs wholly unexampled. The utmost cupidity of other lands and other days had never contrived to herd much more than half that number within the same space. The greatest crowding of Old London was at the rate of 175,816. Swine roamed the streets and gutters as their principal scavengers.[1] The death of a child in a tenement was registered at the Bureau of Vital Statistics as "plainly due to suffocation in the foul air of an unventilated apartment," and the Senators, who had come down from Albany to find out what was the matter with New York, reported that "there are annually cut off from the population by disease and death enough human beings to people a city, and enough human labor to sustain it." And yet experts had testified that, as compared with uptown, rents were from twenty-five to thirty per cent. higher in the worst slums of the lower wards, with such accommodations as were enjoyed, for instance, by a "family with boarders" in Cedar Street, who fed hogs in the cellar that contained eight or ten loads of manure; or "one room 12 × 12 with five families living in it, comprising twenty persons of both sexes and all ages, with only two beds, without partition, screen, chair, or table." The rate of rent has been successfully maintained to the present day, though the hog at least has been eliminated.

Lest anybody flatter himself with the notion that these were evils of a day that is happily past and may safely be forgotten, let me mention here three very recent instances of tenement-house life that came under my notice. One was the burning of a rear house in Mott Street, from appearances one of the original tenant-houses that made their owners rich. The fire made homeless ten families, who had paid an average of $5 a month for their mean little cubbyholes. The owner himself told me that it was *fully* insured for $800, though it brought him in $600 a year rent. He evidently considered himself especially entitled to be pitied for losing such valuable property. Another was the case of a hard-working family of man and wife, young people from the old country, who took poison together in a Crosby Street tenement because they were "tired." There was no other explanation, and none was needed when I stood in the room in which they had lived. It was in the attic with sloping ceiling and a single window so far out on the roof that it seemed not to belong to the place at all. With scarcely room enough to turn around in they had been compelled to pay five dollars and a half a month in advance. There were four such rooms in that attic, and together they brought in as much as many a handsome little cottage in a pleasant part of Brooklyn. The third instance was that of a colored family of husband, wife, and baby in a wretched rear rookery in West Third Street. Their rent was eight dollars and a half for a single room on the top-story, so small that I was unable to get a photograph of it even by placing the camera outside the open door. Three short steps across either way would have measured its full extent.

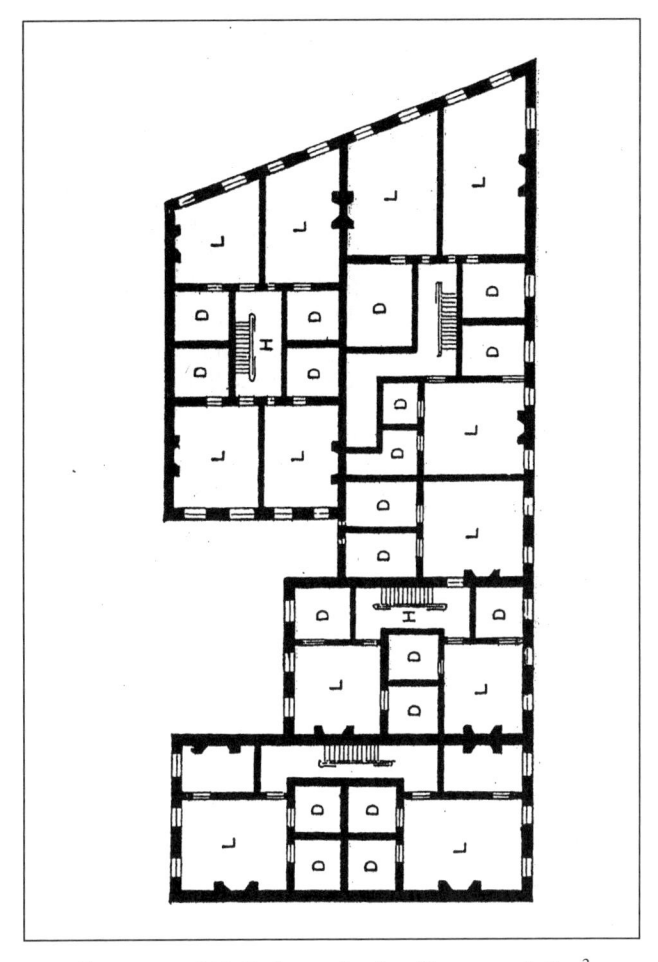

Tenement of 1863, for twelve families on each flat.[2]
D, DARK. L, LIGHT. H, HALLS.

---

[1] It was not until the winter of 1867 that owners of swine were prohibited by ordinance from letting them run at large in the built-up portions of the city.

[2] This "unventilated and fever-breeding structure" the year after it was built was picked out by the Council of Hygiene, then just organized, and presented to the Citizens' Association of New York as a specimen "multiple domicile" in a desirable street, with the following comment: "Here are twelve living-rooms and twenty-one bedrooms, and only six of the latter have any provision or possibility for the admission of light and air, excepting through the family sitting- and living-room; being utterly dark, close, and unventilated. The living-rooms are but 10 × 12 feet; the bedrooms 6½ × 7 feet."

There was just one excuse for the early tenement-house builders, and their successors may plead it with nearly as good right for what it is worth. "Such," says an official report, "is the lack of houseroom in the city that any kind of tenement can be immediately crowded with lodgers, if there is space offered." Thousands were living in cellars. There were three hundred underground lodging-houses in the city when the Health Department was organized. Some fifteen years before that the old Baptist Church in Mulberry Street, just off Chatham Street, had been sold, and the rear half of the frame structure had been converted into tenements that with their swarming population became the scandal even of that reckless age. The wretched pile harbored no less than forty families, and the annual rate of deaths to the population was officially stated to be 75 in 1,000. These tenements were an extreme type of very many, for the big barracks had by this time spread east and west and far up the island into the sparsely settled wards. Whether or not the title was clear to the land upon which they were built was of less account than that the rents were collected. If there were damages to pay, the tenant had to foot them. Cases were "very frequent when property was in litigation, and two or three different parties were collecting rents." Of course under such circumstances "no repairs were ever made."

The climax had been reached. The situation was summed up by the Society for the Improvement of the Condition of the Poor in these words: "Crazy old buildings, crowded rear tenements in filthy yards, dark, damp basements, leaking garrets, shops, outhouses, and stables[3] converted into dwellings, though scarcely fit to shelter brutes, are habitations of thousands of our fellow-beings in this wealthy, Christian city." "The city," says its historian, Mrs. Martha Lamb, commenting on the era of aqueduct building between 1835 and 1845, "was a general asylum for vagrants." Young vagabonds, the natural offspring of such "home" conditions, overran the streets. Juvenile crime increased fearfully year by year. The Children's Aid Society and kindred philanthropic organizations were yet unborn, but in the city directory was to be found the address of the "American Society for the Promotion of Education in Africa."

---

[3] "A lot 50 × 60, contained twenty stables, rented for dwellings at $15 a year each; cost of the whole $600."

Questions

1. What were some of the "evils" of tenement-house life that Riis reported?
2. Do you think there was a sensational aspect to his writing?

18-8 The Immigrant Experience: Letters Home (1901–1903)

The American city could be a forbidding place for newcomers. To gauge the extent of immigrants' experiences, sociologists William I. Thomas (1863–1947) and Florian Znaniecki (1882–1958) undertook a massive research project that led to the publication of *The Polish Peasant in Europe and America* (1918). Their work focused on letters exchanged between immigrants in the United States and their families and friends in the old country. Thomas and Znaniecki hoped to demonstrate how city life overwhelmed rural immigrants and led to their "social disorganization."

Source: Letters from Konstanty and Antoni Butkowski to their parents, December 6, 1901–April 21, 1903, in William I. Thomas and Florian Znaniecki, *The Polish Peasant in Europe and America*, 2nd ed. (New York: Knopf, 1927; reprint, New York: Dover, 1958), 782–789.

SOUTH CHICAGO, December 6, 1901

DEAR PARENTS: I send you my lowest bow, as to a father and mother, and I greet you and my brothers with these words: "Praised be Jesus Christus," and I hope in God that you will answer me, "For centuries of centuries. Amen."

And now I wish you, dearest parents, and you also, dearest brother, to meet the Christmas eve and merry holidays in good health and happiness. May God help you in your intentions. Be merry, all of you together. [Health and success; letter received.] I could not answer you at once, for you know that when one comes from work he has no wish to occupy himself with writing [particularly] as I work always at night. . . . I sent you money, 100 roubles, on November 30. I could not send more now, for you know that winter is coming and I must buy clothes. I inform you that Marta has no work yet. She will get work after the holidays, and it may happen that she will marry.... I inform you about Jasiek, my brother, that he wrote me a letter from Prussia asking me to take him to America, but he is still too young. Inform me about Antoni, how his health is, for in the spring I will bring him to me. I will send him a ship-ticket, if God grants me health. [Greetings for family and relatives.]

[KONSTANTY BUTKOWSKI]

February 17, 1902

DEAREST PARENTS: ... I inform you that I have sent a ship-ticket for Antoni.... Expect to receive it soon.... And remember, Antoni, don't show your papers to anybody, except in places where you must show them.... And if you receive the ticket soon, don't wait, but come at once. And if you receive it a week or so before Easter, then don't leave until after the holidays. But after the holidays don't wait; come at once.... And send me a telegram from the Castle Garden. You won't pay much and I shall know and will go to the railway-station. Take 15 roubles with you, it will be enough, and change them at once for Prussian money. As to the clothes, take the worst which you have, some three old shirts, that you may have a change on the water. And when you come across the water happily, then throw away all these rags. Bring nothing with you except what you have upon yourself. And don't bring any good shoes either, but everything the worst. As to living, take some dry bread and much sugar, and about half a quart of spirits, and some dry meat. You may take some onions, but don't take any cheese.... And be careful in every place about money. Don't talk to any girls on the water.... Learn in Bzory when Wojtek will come, for he comes to the same place where I am, so you would have a companion. And about Jan Plonka, if he wants to come, he is not to complain about [reproach] me for in America there are neither Sundays nor holidays; he must go and work. I inform [him] that I shall receive him as my brother. If he wishes he may come....

[KONSTANTY BUTKOWSKI]

June 13 [1902]

DEAREST PARENTS: ... Konstanty works in the same factory as before and earns $2 a day. I have yet no work, but don't be anxious about me, dear parents ... for I came to a brother and uncle, not to strangers. If our Lord God gives me health, I shall work enough in America. [News about friends and relatives.] Now I inform you, dear parents, about Wladyslawa Butkowska [cousin]. She lives near us, we see each other every day. She is a doctor's servant. And this doctor has left his wife in Chicago and came [sic] to South Chicago. She cooks for him, and she is alone in his house, so people talk about her, that she does not behave well. He pays her $5 a week. I don't know whether it is true or not, but people talk thus because he has left his wife....

[ANTONI BUTKOWSKI]

November 11 [1902]

DEAREST PARENTS:... Now I inform you about Antoni, that he is working in Chicago; it costs 15 cents to go to him. He is boarding, as well as Marta, with acquaintances, with Malewski. He has an easy and clean work, but he earns only enough to live, for he is unable to do heavy work. I see them almost every evening. I go to them. And Marta works in a tailor-shop, but she refuses to listen to me, else she would have been married long ago. So I inform you that I loved her as my own sister, but now I won't talk to her any more, for she refuses to listen. Family remains family only in the first time after coming from home, and later they forget and don't wish any more to acknowledge the familial relations; the American meat inflates them.

I have nothing more to write, except that we are all in good health. Moreover, I declare about your letters, give them to somebody else to write, for neither wise nor fool can read such writing. If such writers are to write you may as well not send letters, for I won't read them, only I will throw them into the fire, for I cannot understand. I beg you, describe to me about our country, how things are going on there. And please don't be angry with me for this which I shall write. I write you that it is hard to live alone, so please find some girl for me, but an orderly [honest] one, for in America there is not even one single orderly girl....

KONSTANTY BUTKOWSKI

December 21 [1902]

I, your son, Konstanty Butkowski, inform you, dear parents, about my health.... I thank you kindly for your letter, for it was happy. As to the girl, although I don't know her, my companion, who knows her, says that she is stately and pretty. I believe him, as well as you, my parents. For although I don't know her, I ask you, my dear parents, and as you will write me so it will be well. Shall I send her a ship-ticket, or how else shall I do? Ask Mr. and Mrs. Sadowski [her parents], what they will say. And I beg you, dear parents, give them my address and let them write a letter to me, then I shall know with certainty. And write me, please, about her age and about everything which concerns her. I don't need to enumerate; you know yourselves, dear parents. For to send a ship-ticket it is not the same as to send a letter which costs a nickel; what is done cannot be undone. So I beg you once more, as my loving parents, go into this matter and do it well, that there may be no cheating.... I shall wait for your letter with great impatience, that I may know what to do....

KONSTANTY BUTKOWSKI

Please inform me, which one is to come, whether the older or the younger one, whether Aleksandra or Stanislawa. Inform me exactly.

CHICAGO, December 31, 1902

DEAR PARENTS: ... If Konstanty wrote you to send him a girl answer him that he may send a ship-ticket either to the one from Popów or to the one from Grajewo. Let the one come which is smarter, for he does not know either of them, so send the one which pleases you better. For in America it is so: Let her only know how to prepare for the table, and be beautiful. For in America there is no need of a girl who knows how to spin and to weave. If she knows how to sew, it is well. For if he does not marry he will never make a fortune and will never have anything; he wastes his work and has nothing. And if he marries he will sooner put something aside. For he won't come back any more. In America it is so: Whoever does not intend to return to his country, it is best for him to marry young; then he will sooner have something, for a bachelor in America will never have anything, unless he is particularly self-controlled. [Greetings, wishes, etc.]

ANTONI BUTKOWSKI

SOUTH CHICAGO, April 21, 1903

Now I, Antoni, your son, my dearest parents, and my uncle and the whole family, we inform you that your son Konstanty is no longer alive. He was killed in the foundry [steel-mills]. Now I inform you, dear parents, that he was insured in an association for $1,000. His funeral will cost $300. And the rest which remains, we have the right to receive this money. So now I beg you, dear parents, send an authorization and his birth-certificate to my uncle, Piotr Z., for I am still a minor and cannot appear in an American lawsuit. When he joined his association he insured himself for $1,000 . . . and made a will in your favor, dear parents. But you cannot get it unless you send an authorization to our uncle, for the lawsuit will be here, and it would be difficult for you to get the money [while remaining] in our country, while we shall get it soon and we will send it to you, dear parents. So now, when you receive this letter, send us the papers soon. Only don't listen to stupid people, but ask wise people. . . .

Now I inform you, dear parents, that strange people will write to you letters. Answer each letter, and answer thus, that you commit everything to Piotr Z. For they will try to deceive you, asking to send the authorization to them. But don't listen to anybody . . . only listen to me, as your son; then you will receive money paid for your son and my brother. [Repeats the advice; wishes from the whole family.]

Now I beg you, dear parents, don't grieve. For he is no more, and you won't raise him, and I cannot either. For if you had looked at him, I think your heart would have burst open with sorrow [he was so mutilated]. But in this letter I won't describe anything, how it was with him. It killed him on April 20. In the next letter I shall describe to you everything about the funeral. . . . Well, it is God's will; God has wished thus, and has done it. Only I beg you, dear parents, give for a holy mass, for the sake of his soul. And he will be buried beautifully, on April 22.

[ANTONI BUTKOWSKI]

Questions

1. What were the everyday concerns of Konstanty and his brother Antoni?
2. How did the relationship between Konstanty and his parents change over time? How did his letters show this?
3. Does the correspondence reveal more than the sociologists intended? If so, what?

18-9 A Visitor in Chicago (1892)

Giuseppe Giacosa

Rudyard Kipling said of Chicago, "Having seen it, I urgently desire never to see it again. It is inhabited by savages." Kipling might have added that the residents were smoke-eating savages, at that. Coal, used for residential heating and industrial power, led to what now would be recognized as a serious air pollution problem. Giuseppe Giacosa (1847–1906) encountered that problem during a visit from Italy in 1892.

Source: From *Nuova Antologia* (March 1893), 16–28, trans. L. B. Davis, in *As Others See Chicago: Impressions of Visitors, 1673–1933*, ed. Bessie Louise Pierce, 276–278. Copyright © 1933 by the University of Chicago Press. Reprinted by permission of the University of Chicago Press.

I had two different impressions of Chicago, one sensual and immediate, which comes from seeing persons and things. The other, intellectual and gradual, born from intelligence, induction and comparisons. To the eye, the city appears abominable. . . . I would not want to live there for anything in the world. I think that whoever ignores it is not entirely acquainted with our century and of what is its ultimate expression.

During my stay of one week, I did not see in Chicago anything but darkness: smoke, clouds, dirt and an extraordinary number of sad and grieved persons. Certain remote quarters are the exception, in which there breathes from little houses and tiny gardens a tranquil air of rustic habitation where a curious architecture with diverting and immature whims makes a pleasant appearance, where the houses seem to be toys for the use of the hilarious people who live there in complete repose, eating candy, swinging in their faithful little rocking chairs, and contemplating oleographs.[1]

But with the exception of these rare cases, the rich metropolis gave me a sense of oppression so grave that I still doubt whether, beyond their factories, there exist celestial spaces. Was it a storm-cloud? I cannot say, because the covered sky spreads a light equal and diffused, which makes no shade; while here, depending on the time of day, a few thick shadows line the houses. And I can not even say that a ghost of the sun shines, because the appearance of things close up makes me always uncertain and confused. I am inclined to believe that that spacious plain, *café au lait* in colour, which stretches along the edge of the city, which appears to the eye three hundred paces wide, and which disappears in gray space, might be the lake; but I could not press close to it with security. Certainly the ships plow through a dense atmosphere rather than a watery plain.

I recall one morning when I happened to be on a high railroad viaduct. From it the city seemed to smolder a vast unyielding conflagration, so much was it wrapped in smoke.... Perhaps, in Chicago, I was influenced by bad weather, by which incentive I do not affirm how things may be, but that I saw them thus, and hence was born the ill-tempered, pouting expression which I read on almost every face. It made me feel, in noting it, how I interpose in such a crowd; a few might show a little courtesy, I do not mean with hats off, but by a nod or glance of recognition. They all were running about desperately. In New York there are more people than in Chicago, and none idle; nevertheless I observe on their streets our same quick friendliness. Here, it seems to me, all might be lost, as I, without company in the formidable tumult. Or if two persons should discourse together, their speech would be in a whining tone, low and nasal, without the least variance of accent.... They say that all Americans have nasal voices. That does not seem to me true of New Yorkers, or only slightly; but it could be said of Chicagoans that their voices come out of their nostrils, and that articulation is made in the pharynx. It is a positive fact that a great many noses in Chicago are in a continuous pathological condition. I have seen in many shop windows certain apparatus for covering the nose, a kind of nasal protector, or false nostrils—but without intent to deceive. I did not see any in operation, however; October, as it seems, still yields to the most delicate the use of the natural nose, but the kingdom of the artificial must be nearby, and I cannot forgive myself for having missed seeing it.

Furthermore, the mass of factories is overpowering without being imposing. That immense building, the Auditorium, where there is a hotel for more than 1,000 guests, an abundance of seats and writing desks of every kind, a conservatory of music, and on the sixth or seventh floor, I don't recall which, a theatre seating 8,000 persons; is this not marvelous to think upon? Its vastness lacks ostentation; it is a vastness of the whole, ostentation means a coordination of parts. All the immense factories of Chicago have low, squatty doors and suffocating stories which the menacing building crushes ridiculously. The two floors of the Tolomei Palace at Siena would be, in Chicago, divided into eight compartments. Certain important houses of twenty stories do not measure one and half voltas, the height of the Stozzi Palace. Surely they take care to mask the frequency of compartments by means of openings which reach from the first floor to the fourth, but to see this from the street, in the height of a single window, three men seated at three writing desks, people and furniture almost suspended in the air, and leaning against a transparent wall, gives one a feeling of irritating unrest....

The dominant characteristic of the exterior life of Chicago is violence. Everything leads you to extreme expressions: dimensions, movements, noises, rumors, window displays, spectacles, ostentation, misery, activity, and alcoholic degradation.

---

[1] An oleograph is a chromolithograph printed with oil paint on canvas in imitation of an oil painting. [*Original note.*]

Questions

1. Giacosa, familiar with historic Italian cities, might have had preconceived notions about what a city should be. Did he betray any prejudices in describing Chicago?

2. What sources of pollution do you imagine that Giacosa encountered?

3. Why might many Americans of the period have celebrated the smokiness of their cities?

18-10 The Dangers of Cities (1886)

Josiah Strong

Americans accepted the city, among other reasons, because it generated prosperity. By the second half of the nineteenth century, a large urban middle class was confident in its success but worried about the future of city life. The Reverend Josiah Strong (1847–1916), a Congregational pastor, addressed some of those concerns in *Our Country*, first published in 1886. Strong did not want to sit by as nature ran its course in the American city, as social Darwinists recommended. However, Strong's call to action reflected the prejudices of his day.

Source: From *Our Country: Its Possible Future and Its Present Crisis* (1886; reprint, ed. Jurgen Herbst, Cambridge, MA: The Belknap Press of Harvard University Press, 1963), 171–174, 176, 183–185. Copyright © 1963 by the President and Fellows of Harvard College; copyright © renewed 1991. Reprinted by permission of the publisher.

The city is the nerve center of our civilization. It is also the storm center. The fact, therefore, that it is growing much more rapidly than the whole population is full of significance....

The city has become a serious menace to our civilization, because in it, excepting Mormonism, each of the dangers we have discussed is enhanced, and all are focalized. It has a peculiar attraction for the immigrant. Our fifty principal cities in 1880 contained 39.3 per cent of our entire German population, and 45.8 per cent of the Irish. Our ten larger cities at that time contained only nine per cent of the entire population, but 23 per cent of the foreign. While a little less than one-third of the population of the United States was foreign by birth or parentage, sixty-two per cent of the population of Cincinnati was foreign, eighty-three per cent of Cleveland, sixty-three per cent of Boston, eighty per cent of New York, and ninety-one per cent of Chicago. A census of Massachusetts, taken in 1885, showed that in 65 towns and cities of the state 65.1 per cent of the population was foreign by birth or parentage.

Because our cities are so largely foreign, Romanism finds in them its chief strength.

For the same reason the saloon, together with the intemperance and the liquor power which it represents, is multiplied in the city. East of the Mississippi there was, in 1880, one saloon to every 438 of the population; in Boston, one to every 329; in Cleveland, one to every 192; in Chicago, one to every 179; in New York, one to every 171; in Cincinnati, one to every 124. Of course the demoralizing and pauperizing power of the saloons and their debauching influence in politics increase with their numerical strength.

It is the city where wealth is massed; and here are the tangible evidences of it piled many stories high. Here the sway of Mammon is widest, and his worship the most constant and eager. Here are luxuries gathered—everything that dazzles the eye, or tempts the appetite; here is the most extravagant expenditure. Here, also, is the *congestion* of wealth the severest. Dives and Lazarus are brought face to face; here, in sharp contrast, are the *ennui* of surfeit and the desperation of starvation. The rich are richer, and the poor are poorer, in the city than elsewhere; and, as a rule, the greater the city, the greater are the riches of the rich and the poverty of the poor. Not only does the proportion of the poor increase with the growth of the city, but their condition becomes more wretched. The poor of a city of 8,000 inhabitants are well off compared with many in New York; and there are hardly such depths of woe, such utter and heart-wringing wretchedness in New York as in London....

Socialism centers in the city, and the materials of its growth are multiplied with the growth of the city. Here is heaped the social dynamite; here roughs, gamblers, thieves, robbers, lawless and desperate men of all sorts, congregate; men who are ready on any pretext to raise riots for the purpose of destruction and plunder; here gather foreigners and wage-workers who are especially susceptible to social arguments; here skepticism and irreligion abound; here inequality is the greatest and most obvious, and the contrast between opulence and penury the most striking; here is suffering the sorest. As the greatest wickedness in the world is to be found not among the cannibals of some far-off coast, but in Christian lands where the light of truth is diffused and rejected, so the utmost depth of wretchedness exists not among savages who have few wants, but in great cities, where, in the presence of plenty and of every luxury men starve. Let a man become the owner of a home, and he is much less susceptible to socialistic propagandism. But real estate is so high in the city that it is almost impossible for a wage-worker to become a householder....

1. In gathering up the results of the foregoing discussion of these several perils, it should be remarked that to preserve republican institutions requires a *higher average* intelligence and virtue among large populations than among small. The government of 5,000,000 people was a

simple thing compared with the government of 50,000,000; and the government of 50,000,000 is a simple thing compared with that of 500,000,000. There are many men who can conduct a small business successfully, who are utterly incapable of managing large interests. In the latter there are multiplied relations whose harmony must be preserved. A mistake is farther reaching. It has, as it were, a longer leverage. This is equally true of the business of government. The man of only average ability and intelligence discharges creditably the duties of mayor in his little town; but he would fail utterly at the head of the state or the nation. If the people are to govern, they must grow more intelligent as the population and the complications of government increase. And a higher morality is even more essential. As civilization increases, as society becomes more complex, as labor-saving machinery is multiplied and the division of labor becomes more minute, the individual becomes more fractional and dependent. Every savage possesses all the knowledge of the tribe. Throw him upon his own resources, and he is self-sufficient. A civilized man in like circumstances would perish. The savage is independent. Civilize him, and he becomes dependent; the more civilized, the more dependent. And, as men become more dependent on each other, they should be able to rely more implicitly on each other. More complicated and multiplied relations require a more delicate conscience and a stronger sense of justice. And any failure in character or conduct under such conditions is farther reaching and more disastrous in its results.

Is our progress in morals and intelligence at all comparable to the growth of population? The nation's illiteracy has not been discussed, because it is not one of the perils which peculiarly threaten the West; but any one who would calculate our political horoscope must allow it great influence in connection with the baleful stars which are in the ascendant. But the danger which arises from the corruption of popular morals is much greater. The republics of Greece and Rome, and if I mistake not, all the republics that have ever lived and died, were more intelligent at the end than at the beginning; but growing intelligence could not compensate decaying morals. What, then, is our moral progress? Are popular morals as sound as they were twenty years ago? There is, perhaps, no better index of general morality than Sabbath observance; and everybody knows there has been a great increase of Sabbath desecration in twenty years. We have seen that we are now using as a beverage 29 per cent more of alcohol per caput [per head] than we were fifty years ago. Says Dr. S. W. Dike: "It is safe to say that divorce has been doubled, in proportion to marriages or population, in most of the Northern States within thirty years. Present figures indicate a still greater increase." And President Woolsey,[1]

speaking of the United States, said in 1883: "On the whole, there can be little, if any, question that the ratio of divorces to marriages or to population exceeds that of any country in the Christian world." While the population increased thirty per cent from 1870 to 1880, the number of criminals in the United States increased 82.33 per cent. It looks very much as if existing tendencies were in the direction of the deadline of vice. Excepting Mormonism, all the perils which have been discussed seem to be increasing more rapidly than the population. *Are popular morals likely to improve under their increasing influence?*

2. The fundamental idea of popular government is the distribution of power. It has been the struggle of liberty for ages to wrest power from the hands of one or the few, and lodge it in the hands of the many. We have seen, in the foregoing discussion, that centralized power is rapidly growing. The "boss" makes his bargain, and sells his ten thousand or fifty thousand voters as if they were so many cattle. Centralized wealth is centralized power; and the capitalist and corporation find many ways to control votes. The liquor power controls thousands of votes in every considerable city. The president of the Mormon Church casts, say, sixty thousand votes. The Jesuits, it is said, are all under the command of one man in Washington. The Roman Catholic vote is more or less perfectly controlled by the priests. That means that the Pope can dictate some hundreds of thousands of votes in the United States. Is there anything unrepublican in all this? And we must remember that, if present tendencies continue, these figures will be greatly multiplied in the future. And not only is this immense power lodged in the hand of one man, which in itself is perilous, but it is wielded without the slightest reference to any policy or principle of government, solely in the interests of a church or a business, or for personal ends.

The result of a national election may depend on a single state; the vote of that state may depend on a single city; the vote of that city may depend on a "boss," or a capitalist, or a corporation; or the election may be decided, and the policy of the government may be reversed, by the socialist, or liquor, or Roman Catholic or immigrant vote.

It matters not by what name we call the man who wields this centralized power—whether king, czar, pope, president, capitalist, or boss. Just so far as it is absolute and irresponsible, it is dangerous.

3. These several dangerous elements are singularly netted together, and serve to strengthen each other. It is not necessary to prove that any *one* of them is likely to destroy our national life, in order to show that it is imperiled. A man may die of wounds no one of which is fatal. No sober-minded man can look fairly at the facts, and doubt that *together* these perils constitute an array which will seriously endanger our free institutions, if the tendencies which have been pointed out continue; and especially is this true in view of the fact that these perils peculiarly confront the West, where our defense is weakest.

---

[1] Theodore Dwight Woolsey (1801–1889) was the president of Yale College from 1846 to 1871.

Questions

1. What problems did Strong associate with immigrants and "the liquor power"?
2. Why did he fear the growth of socialism in the cities?
3. How did Strong stereotype Mormon and Catholic voters? Why did he assume that Protestant voters would act differently?

Question for Further Thought

1. Julian Ralph's description of Denver (Document 18-2) was largely positive. But on what points would Ralph's views concur with those found in Strong's sermon (Document 18-10)?

CHAPTER NINETEEN

Politics in the Age of Enterprise
1877–1896

The Politics of the Status Quo, 1877–1893

"The Undoing of Reconstruction" (see text pp. 476–481) involved not only the defeat of Republican governments in the former Confederate states but also a retreat from the activism of the federal and state governments, North as well as South, that had characterized the Republican Party during the Civil War and the early postwar years. The economic depression that followed the Panic of 1873 led businessmen to oppose public spending, borrowing, and taxes; hard times contributed to the Democrats' recapture of the House of Representatives in 1874. This midterm victory of the Democrats, who held a narrower view of government than the Republicans, ushered in a period of generally divided government in Washington, D.C. From the late 1870s into the 1890s, national politics remained intensely partisan and highly competitive, but it no longer involved sustained debate over national issues of fundamental importance (see text pp. 584–589).

James Bryce, a Briton, offered the most celebrated reading of American politics during the late nineteenth century: *The American Commonwealth* (Document 19-1). The relative inactivity of national government during much of this period reflected in part the pervasiveness of "the ideology of individualism" (see text pp. 587–588), the most famous social Darwinist exponent of which was William Graham Sumner (Document 19-2).

19-1 *The American Commonwealth* (1888)

James Bryce

James Bryce (1838–1922), a Scot, taught law at Oxford University in England and sat in the House of Commons and later (as Viscount Bryce of Dechmont) in the House of Lords. When he wrote *The American Commonwealth*, he had traveled in the United States three times for a total of nine months. A number of like-minded Americans assisted in writing the book and in publishing later revisions. Bryce served as British ambassador to the United States between 1906 and 1913.

Source: James Bryce, *The American Commonwealth*, 2 vols. (London and New York: Macmillan, 1888); rev. ed., with an introduction by Gary L. McDowell, 2 vols. (Indianapolis: Liberty Fund, 1995), 2:731–740.

THE POLITICIANS

Institutions are said to form men, but it is no less true that men give to institutions their colour and tendency. It profits little to know the legal rules and methods and observances of government, unless one also knows something of the human beings who tend and direct this machinery, and who, by the spirit in which they work it, may render it the potent instrument of good or evil to the people. These men are the politicians.

What is one to include under this term? In England it usually denotes those who are actively occupied in administering or legislating, or discussing administration and legislation. That is to say, it includes ministers of the Crown, members of Parliament (though some in the House of Commons and the majority in the House of Lords care little about politics), a few leading journalists, and a small number of miscellaneous persons, writers, lecturers, organizers, agitators, who occupy themselves with trying to influence the public. Sometimes the term is given a wider sweep, being taken to include all who labour for their political party in the constituencies, as, e.g., the chairmen and secretaries of local party associations, and the more active committeemen of the same bodies. The former, whom we may call the inner-circle men, are professional politicians in this sense, and in this sense only, that politics is the main though seldom the sole business of their lives. But at present extremely few of them make anything by it in the way of money. A handful hope to get some post; a somewhat larger number find that a seat in Parliament enables them to push their financial undertakings or make them at least more conspicuous in the commercial world. But the gaining of a livelihood does not come into the view of the great majority at all. The other class, who may be called the outer circle, are not professionals in any sense, being primarily occupied with their own avocations; and none of them, except here and there an organizing secretary, or registration, agent, and here and there a paid lecturer, makes any profit out of the work. . . .

To see why things are different in the United States, why the inner circle is much larger both absolutely and relatively to the outer circle than in Europe, let us go back a little and ask what are the conditions which develop a political class. The point has so important a bearing on the characteristics of American politicians that I do not fear to dwell somewhat fully upon it.

In self-governing communities of the simpler kind—for one may leave absolute monarchies and feudal monarchies on one side—the common affairs are everybody's business and nobody's special business. Some few men by their personal qualities get a larger share of authority, and are repeatedly chosen to be archons, or generals, or consuls, or burgomasters, or landammans, but even these rarely give their whole time to the state, and make little or nothing in money out of it. This was the condition of the Greek republics, of early Rome, of the cities of mediæval Germany and Italy, of the cantons of Switzerland till very recent times.

When in a large country public affairs become more engrossing to those who are occupied in them, when the sphere of government widens, when administration is more complex and more closely interlaced with the industrial interests of the community and of the world at large, so that there is more to be known and to be considered, the business of a nation falls into the hands of the men eminent by rank, wealth, and ability, who form a sort of governing class, largely hereditary. The higher civil administration of the state is in their hands; they fill the chief council or legislative chamber and conduct its debates. They have residences in the capital, and though they receive salaries when actually filling an office, and have opportunities for enriching themselves, the majority possess independent means, and pursue politics for the sake of fame, power, or excitement. Those few who have not independent means can follow their business or profession in the capital, or can frequently visit the place where their business is carried on. This was the condition of Rome under the later republic, and of England and France till quite lately—indeed it is largely the case in England still—as well as of Prussia and Sweden.

Let us see what are the conditions of the United States.

There is a relatively small leisured class of persons engaged in no occupation and of wealth sufficient to leave them free for public affairs. So far as such persons are to be found in the country, for some are to be sought abroad, they are to be found in a few great cities.

There is no class with a sort of hereditary prescriptive right to public office, no great families whose names are known to the people, and who, bound together by class sympathy and ties of relationship, help one another by keeping offices in the hands of their own members.

The country is a very large one, and has its political capital in a city without trade, without manufactures, without professional careers. Even the seats of state governments are often placed in comparatively small towns. Hence a man cannot carry on his gainful occupation at the same time that he attends to "inner-circle" politics.

Members of Congress and of state legislatures are invariably chosen from the places where they reside. Hence a person belonging to the leisured class of a great city cannot get into the House of Representatives or the legislature of his state except as member for a district of his own city.

The shortness of terms of office, and the large number of offices filled by election, make elections very frequent. All these elections, with trifling exceptions, are fought on party lines, and the result of a minor one for some petty local office, such as county treasurer, affects one for a more important post, e.g., that of member of Congress. Hence constant vigilance, constant exertions on the spot, are needed. The list of voters must be incessantly looked after, newly admitted or newly settled citizens enrolled, the active local men frequently consulted and kept in good humour, meetings arranged for, tickets (i.e., lists of candidates) for all vacant offices agreed upon. One election is no sooner over than another approaches and has to be provided for, as the English sporting man reckons his year by "events," and thinks of Newmarket after Ascot, and of Goodwood after Newmarket.

Now what do these conditions amount to? To this—a great deal of hard and dull election and other local political work to be done. Few men of leisure to do it, and still fewer men of leisure likely to care for it. Nobody able to do it in addition to his regular business or profession. Little motive for anybody, whether leisured or not, to do the humbler and local parts of it (i.e., so much as concerns the minor elections), the parts which bring neither fame nor power.

If the work is to be done at all, some inducement, other than fame or power, must clearly be found. Why not, someone will say, the sense of public duty? I will speak of public duty presently; meantime let it suffice to remark that to rely on public duty as the main motive power in politics is to assume a commonwealth of angels. Men such as we know them must have some other inducement. Even in the Christian church there are other than spiritual motives to lead its pastors to spiritual work; nor do all poets write because they seek to express the passion of their souls. In America we discover a palpable inducement to undertake the dull and toilsome work of election politics. It is the inducement of places in the public service. To make them attractive they must be paid. They are paid, nearly all of them, memberships of Congress and other federal places, state places (including memberships of state legislatures), city and county places. Here then—and to some extent even in humbler forms, such as the getting of small contracts or even employment as labourers—is the inducement, the remuneration for political work performed in the way of organizing and electioneering. Now add that besides the paid administrative and legislative places which a democracy bestows by election, judicial places are also in most of the states elective, and held for terms of years only; and add further, that the holders of nearly all those administrative places, federal, state, and municipal, which are not held for a fixed term, are liable to be dismissed, as indeed many still are so liable and are in practice dismissed, whenever power changes from one party to another, so that those who belong to the party out of office have a direct chance of office when their party comes in. The inducement to undertake political work we have been searching for is at once seen to be adequate, and only too adequate. The men needed for the work are certain to appear because remuneration is provided. Politics has now become a gainful profession, like advocacy, stockbroking, the dry goods trade, or the getting up of companies. People go into it to live by it, primarily for the sake of the salaries attached to the places they count on getting, secondarily in view of the opportunities it affords of making incidental and sometimes illegitimate gains. Every person in a high administrative post, whether federal, state, or municipal, and, above all, every member of Congress, has opportunities of rendering services to wealthy individuals and companies for which they are willing to pay secretly in money or in money's worth. The better officials and legislators—they are the great majority, except in large cities—resist the temptation. The worst succumb to it, and the prospect of these illicit profits renders a political career distinctly more attractive to an unscrupulous man.

We find therefore that in America all the conditions exist for producing a class of men specially devoted to political work and making a livelihood by it. It is work much of which cannot be done in combination with any other kind of regular work, whether professional or commercial. Even if the man who unites wealth and leisure to high intellectual attainments were a frequent figure in America, he would not take to this work; he would rather be a philanthropist or cultivate arts and letters. It is work which, steadily pursued by an active man, offers an income. Hence a large number of persons are drawn into it, and make it the business of their life; and the fact that they are there as professionals has tended to keep amateurs out of it.

There are, however, two qualifications which must be added to this statement of the facts, and which it is best to add at once. One is that the mere pleasure of politics counts for something. Many people in America as well as in England undertake even the commonplace work of local canvassing and organizing for the sake of a little excitement, a little of the agreeable sense of self-importance, or from that fondness for doing something in association with others which makes a man become secretary to a cricket club or treasurer of a fund raised by subscription for some purpose he may not really care for. And the second qualification is that pecuniary motives operate with less force in rural districts than in cities, because in the former the income obtainable by public office is too small to induce men to work long in the hope of getting it. Let it therefore be understood that what is said in this chapter refers primarily to cities, and of course also to persons aiming at the higher federal and state offices; and that I do not mean to deny that there is plenty of work done by amateurs as well as by professionals.

Having thus seen what are the causes which produce professional politicians, we may return to inquire how large this class is, compared with the corresponding class in the free countries of Europe, whom we have called the inner circle.

In America the inner circle, that is to say, the persons who make political work the chief business of life, for the time being, includes:

Firstly. All members of both houses of Congress.
Secondly. All federal officeholders except the judges, who are irremovable, and who have sometimes taken no prominent part in politics.
Thirdly. A large part of the members of state legislatures. How large a part, it is impossible to determine, for it varies greatly from state to state.... But the line between a professional and nonprofessional politician is too indefinite to make any satisfactory estimate possible.
Fourthly. Nearly all state officeholders, excluding all judges in a very few states, and many of the judges in the rest.
Fifthly. Nearly all holders of paid offices in the greater and in many of the smaller cities, and many holders of paid offices in the counties. There are, however, great differences in this respect between different states, the New England states and the newer states of the Northwest, as well as some Southern states,

choosing many of their county officials from men who are not regularly employed on politics, although members of the dominant party.

Sixthly. A large number of people who hold no office but want to get one, or perhaps even who desire work under a municipality. This category includes, of course, many of the "workers" of the party which does not command the majority for the time being, in state and municipal affairs, and which has not, through the president, the patronage of federal posts. It also includes many expectants belonging to the party for the time being dominant, who are earning their future places by serving the party in the meantime.

All the above may fairly be called professional or inner-circle politicians, but of their number I can form no estimate, save that it must be counted by hundreds of thousands, inasmuch as it practically includes nearly all state and local and most federal officeholders as well as most expectants of public office.

It must be remembered that the "work" of politics means in America the business of winning nominations (of which more anon) and elections, and that this work is incomparably heavier and more complex than in England, because:

(1) The voters are a larger proportion of the population; (2) the government is more complex (federal, state, and local) and the places filled by election are therefore far more numerous; (3) elections come at shorter intervals; (4) the machinery of nominating candidates is far more complete and intricate; (5) the methods of fighting elections require more technical knowledge and skill; (6) ordinary private citizens do less election work, seeing that they are busier than in England, and the professionals exist to do it for them.

I have observed that there are also plenty of men engaged in some trade or profession who interest themselves in politics and work for their party without any definite hope of office or other pecuniary aim. They correspond to what we have called the outer-circle politicians of Europe. It is hard to draw a line between the two classes, because they shade off into one another, there being many farmers or lawyers or saloonkeepers, for instance, who, while pursuing their regular calling, bear a hand in politics, and look to be some time or other rewarded for doing so. When this expectation becomes a considerable part of the motive for exertion, such an one may fairly be called a professional, at least for the time being, for although he has other means of livelihood, he is apt to be impregnated with the habits and sentiments of the professional class.

The proportion between outer-circle and inner-circle men is in the United States a sort of ozonometer by which the purity and healthiness of the political atmosphere may be tested. Looking at the North only, for I have no tolerable data as to the South, and excluding congressmen, the proportion of men who exert themselves in politics without pecuniary motive is largest in New England, in the country parts of New York, in northern Ohio, and the Northwestern states, while the professional politicians most abound in the great cities — New York, Philadelphia, Brooklyn, Boston, Baltimore, Buffalo, Cincinnati, Louisville, Chicago, St. Louis, New Orleans, San Francisco. This is because these cities have the largest masses of ignorant voters, and also because their municipal governments, handling large revenues, offer the largest facilities for illicit gains.

I shall presently return to the outer-circle men. Meantime let us examine the professionals somewhat more closely; and begin with those of the humbler type, whose eye is fixed on a municipal or other local office, and seldom ranges so high as a seat in Congress.

As there are weeds that follow human dwellings, so this species thrives best in cities, and even in the most crowded parts of cities. It is known to the Americans as the "ward politician," because the city ward is the chief sphere of its activity, and the ward meeting the first scene of its exploits. A statesman of this type usually begins as a saloon- or barkeeper, an occupation which enables him to form a large circle of acquaintances, especially among the "loafer" class who have votes but no reason for using them one way more than another, and whose interest in political issues is therefore as limited as their stock of political knowledge. But he may have started as a lawyer of the lowest kind, or lodginghouse keeper, or have taken to politics after failure in storekeeping. The education of this class is only that of the elementary schools. If they have come after boyhood from Europe, it is not even that. They have of course no comprehension of political questions or zeal for political principles; politics mean to them merely a scramble for places or jobs. They are usually vulgar, sometimes brutal, not so often criminal, or at least the associates of criminals. It is they who move about the populous quarters of the great cities, form groups through whom they can reach and control the ignorant voter, pack meetings with their creatures.

Their methods and their triumphs must be reserved for a later chapter. Those of them who are Irish, an appreciable though diminishing proportion in a few cities, have seldom Irish patriotism to redeem the mercenary quality of their politics. They are too strictly practical for that, being regardful of the wrongs of Ireland only so far as these furnish capital to be used with Irish voters. Their most conspicuous virtues are shrewdness, a sort of rough good-fellowship with one another, and loyalty to their chiefs, from whom they expect promotion in the ranks of the service. The plant thrives in the soil of any party, but its growth is more vigorous in whichever party is for the time dominant in a given city.

English critics, taking their cue from American pessimists, have often described these men as specimens of the whole class of politicians. This is misleading. The men are bad enough both as an actual force and as a symptom. But they are confined to a few great cities, those eleven or twelve I have already mentioned; it is their achievements there, and particularly in New York, where the mass of ignorant immigrants is largest, that have made them famous.

In the smaller cities, and in the country generally, the minor politicians are mostly native Americans, less ignorant and more respectable than these last-mentioned street vultures. The barkeeping element is represented among them, but the bulk are petty lawyers, officials, federal as well as state and county, and people who for want of a better occupation have turned office seekers, with a fair sprinkling of storekeepers, farmers, and newspaper men. The great majority have some regular avocation, so that they are by no means wholly professionals. Law is of course the business which best fits in with politics. They are only a little below the level of the class to which they belong, which is what would be called in England the lower middle, or in France the *petite bourgeoisie*, and they often suppose themselves to be fighting for Republican or Democratic principles, even though in fact concerned chiefly with place hunting. It is not so much positive moral defects that are to be charged on them as a slightly sordid and selfish view of politics and a laxity in the use of electioneering methods.

These two classes do the local work and dirty work of politics. They are the rank and file. Above them stand the officers in the political army, the party managers, including the members of Congress and chief men in the state legislatures, and the editors of influential newspapers. Some of these have pushed their way up from the humbler ranks. Others are men of superior ability and education, often college graduates, lawyers who have had practice, less frequently merchants or manufacturers who have slipped into politics from business. There are all sorts among them, creatures clean and unclean, as in the sheet of St. Peter's vision, but that one may say of politicians in all countries. What characterizes them as compared with the corresponding class in Europe is that their whole time is more frequently given to political work, that most of them draw an income from politics and the rest hope to do so, that they come more largely from the poorer and less cultivated than from the higher ranks of society, and that they include but few men who have pursued any of those economical, social, or constitutional studies which form the basis of politics and legislation, although many are proficients in the arts of popular oratory, of electioneering, and of party management.

Questions

1. What was Bryce's view of politics in the United States?
2. How did Bryce's familiarity with politics in Great Britain influence his view of politics in the United States?
3. How did Bryce see politics in America's larger cities? What factors did Bryce deem significant to understanding city politics?

19-2 The Forgotten Man (1883)

William Graham Sumner

Social Darwinism invoked science to argue that society should not go out of its way to help the poor or to check the abuses of the robber barons. Its proponents tried to apply Charles Darwin's theory of natural selection not just to plants and animals but to society (see text pp. 587–588). The most prominent American social Darwinist was Yale professor William Graham Sumner (1840–1910), who warned, "If we do not like the survival of the fittest, we have only one possible alternative, and that is the survival of the unfittest."

Source: William Graham Sumner, "The Forgotten Man," an address to the Brooklyn Historical Society in 1883, in *The Forgotten Man and Other Essays*, ed. Albert Galloway Keller (New Haven, CT: Yale University Press, 1919).

Now you know that "the poor and the weak" are continually put forward as objects of public interest and public obligation. In the appeals which are made, the terms "the poor" and "the weak" are used as if they were terms of exact definition. Except the pauper, that is to say, the man who cannot earn his living or pay his way, there is no possible definition of a poor man. Except a man who is incapacitated by vice or by physical infirmity, there is no definition of a weak man.

The paupers and the physically incapacitated are an inevitable charge on society. About them no more need be said. But the weak who constantly arouse the pity of humanitarians and philanthropists are the shiftless, the imprudent, the negligent, the impractical, and the inefficient, or they are the idle, the intemperate, the extravagant, and the vicious. Now the troubles of these persons are constantly forced upon public attention, as if they and their interests deserved especial consideration, and a great portion of all organized and unorganized effort for the common welfare consists in attempts to relieve these classes of people. I do not wish to be understood now as saying that nothing ought to be done for these people by those who are stronger and wiser. That is not my point. What I want to do is to point out the thing which is overlooked and the error which is made in all these charitable efforts. The notion is accepted as if it were not open to any question that if you help the inefficient and vicious you may gain something for society or you may not, but that you lose nothing. This is a complete mistake. Whatever capital you divert to the support of a shiftless and good-for-nothing person is so much diverted from some other employment, and that means from somebody else. I would spend any conceivable amount of zeal and eloquence if I possessed it to try to make people grasp this idea. Capital is force. If it goes one way it cannot go another. If you give a loaf to a pauper you cannot give the same loaf to a laborer. Now this other man who would have got it but for the charitable sentiment which bestowed it on a worthless member of society is the Forgotten Man. The philanthropists and humanitarians have their minds all full of the wretched and miserable whose case appeals to compassion, attacks the sympathies, takes possession of the imagination, and excites the emotions. They push on towards the quickest and easiest remedies and they forget the real victim.

Now who is the Forgotten Man? He is the simple, honest laborer, ready to earn his living by productive work. We pass him by because he is independent, self-supporting, and asks no favors. He does not appeal to the emotions or excite the sentiments. He only wants to make a contract and fulfill it, with respect on both sides and favor on neither side. He must get his living out of the capital of the country. The larger the capital is, the better living he can get. Every particle of capital which is wasted on the vicious, the idle, and the shiftless is so much taken from the capital available to reward the independent and productive laborer. But we stand with our backs to the independent and productive laborer all the time. We do not remember him because he makes no clamor; but I appeal to you whether he is not the man who ought to be remembered first of all, and whether, on any sound social theory, we ought not to protect him against the burdens of the good-for-nothing. In these last years I have read hundreds of articles and heard scores of sermons and speeches which were really glorifications of the good-for-nothing, as if these were the charge of society, recommended by right reason to its care and protection. We are addressed all the time as if those who are respectable were to blame because some are not so, and as if there were an obligation on the part of those who have done their duty towards those who have not done their duty. Every man is bound to take care of himself and his family and to do his share in the work of society. It is totally false that one who has done so is bound to bear the care and charge of those who are wretched because they have not done so. The silly popular notion is that the beggars live at the expense of the rich, but the truth is that those who eat and produce not, live at the expense of those who labor and produce. The next time that you are tempted to subscribe a dollar to a charity, I do not tell you not to do it, because after you have fairly considered the matter, you may think it right to do it, but I ask you to stop and remember the Forgotten Man and understand that if you put your dollar in the savings bank it will go to swell the capital of the country which is available for division amongst those who, while they earn it, will reproduce it with increase.

Let us now go on to another class of cases. There are a great many schemes brought forward for "improving the condition of the working classes." I have shown already that a free man cannot take a favor. One who takes a favor or submits to patronage demeans himself. He falls under obligation. He cannot be free and he cannot assert a station of equality with the man who confers the favor on him. The only exception is where there are exceptional bonds of affection or friendship, that is, where the sentimental relation supersedes the free relation. Therefore, in a country which is a free democracy, all propositions to do something for the working classes have an air of patronage and superiority which is impertinent and out of place. No one can do anything for anybody else unless he has a surplus of energy to dispose of after taking care of himself. In the United States, the working classes, technically so called, are the strongest classes. It is they who have a surplus to dispose of if anybody has. Why should anybody else offer to take care of them or to serve them? They can get whatever they think worth having and, at any rate, if they are free men in a free state, it is ignominious and unbecoming to introduce fashions of patronage and favoritism here. A man who, by superior education and experience of business, is in a position to advise a struggling man of the wages class, is certainly held to do so and will, I believe, always be willing and glad to do so; but this sort of activity lies in the range of private and personal relations.

I now, however, desire to direct attention to the public, general, and impersonal schemes, and I point out the fact that, if you undertake to lift anybody, you must have a fulcrum or point of resistance. All the elevation you give to one must be gained by an equivalent depression on someone else. The question of gain to society depends upon the balance of the account, as regards the position of the persons who undergo the respective operations. But nearly all the schemes for "improving the condition of the working man" involve an elevation of some working men at the expense of other working men. When you expend capital or labor to elevate some persons who come within the sphere of your influence, you interfere in the conditions of competition. The advantage of some is won by an equivalent loss of others. The difference is not brought about by the energy and effort of the persons themselves. If it were, there would be nothing to be said about it, for we constantly see people surpass others in the rivalry of life and carry off the prizes which the others must do without. In the cases I am discussing, the difference is brought about by an interference which must be partial, arbitrary, accidental, controlled by favoritism and personal preference. I do not say, in this case, either, that we ought to do no work of this kind. On the contrary, I believe that the arguments for it quite outweigh, in many cases, the arguments against it. What I desire, again, is to bring out the forgotten element which we always need to remember in order to make a wise decision as to any scheme of this kind. I want to call to mind the Forgotten Man, because, in this case also, if we recall him and go to look for him, we shall find him patiently and perseveringly, manfully and independently struggling against adverse circumstances without complaining or begging. If, then, we are led to heed the groaning and complaining of others and to take measures for helping these others, we shall, before we know it, push down this man who is trying to help himself.

Let us take another class of cases. So far we have said nothing about the abuse of legislation. We all seem to be under the delusion that the rich pay the taxes. Taxes are not thrown upon the consumers with any such directness and completeness as is sometimes assumed; but that, in ordinary states of the market, taxes on houses fall, for the most part, on the tenants and that taxes on commodities fall, for the most part, on the consumers, is beyond question. Now the state and municipality go to great expense to support policemen and sheriffs and judicial officers, to protect people against themselves, that is, against the results of their own folly, vice, and recklessness. Who pays for it? Undoubtedly the people who have not been guilty of folly, vice, or recklessness. Out of nothing comes nothing. We cannot collect taxes from people who produce nothing and save nothing. The people who have something to tax must be those who have produced and saved.

When you see a drunkard in the gutter, you are disgusted, but you pity him. When a policeman comes and picks him up you are satisfied. You say that "society" has interfered to save the drunkard from perishing. Society is a fine word, and it saves us the trouble of thinking to say that society acts. The truth is that the policeman is paid by somebody, and when we talk about society we forget who it is that pays. It is the Forgotten Man again. It is the industrious workman going home from a hard day's work, whom you pass without noticing, who is mulcted of a percentage of his day's earnings to hire a policeman to save the drunkard from himself. All the public expenditure to prevent vice has the same effect. Vice is its own curse. If we let nature alone, she cures vice by the most frightful penalties. It may shock you to hear me say it, but when you get over the shock, it will do you good to think of it: a drunkard in the gutter is just where he ought to be. Nature is working away at him to get him out of the way, just as she sets up her processes of dissolution to remove whatever is a failure in its line. Gambling and less mentionable vices all cure themselves by the ruin and dissolution of their victims. Nine-tenths of our measures for preventing vice are really protective towards it, because they ward off the penalty. "Ward off," I say, and that is the usual way of looking at it; but is the penalty really annihilated? By no means. It is turned into police and court expenses and spread over those who have resisted vice. It is the Forgotten Man again who has been subjected to the penalty while our minds were full of the drunkards, spendthrifts, gamblers, and other victims of dissipation. Who is, then, the Forgotten Man? He is the clean, quiet, virtuous, domestic citizen, who pays his debts and his taxes and is never heard of out of his little circle. Yet who is there in the society of a civilized state who deserves to be remembered and considered by the legislator and statesman before this man?

Another class of cases is closely connected with this last. There is an apparently invincible prejudice in people's minds in favor of state regulation. All experience is against state regulation and in favor of liberty. The freer the civil institutions are, the more weak or mischievous state regulation is. The Prussian bureaucracy can do a score of things for the citizen which no governmental organ in the United States can do; and, conversely, if we want to be taken care of as Prussians and Frenchmen are, we must give up something of our personal liberty.

Questions

1. Why did Sumner oppose all attempts to help the weak?
2. To what extent was Sumner a true friend of the "Forgotten Man," especially if that man found himself unemployed in the Panic of 1893?
3. What would be the ultimate cost to a society that allowed nature to eliminate vice through people's destruction, as Sumner proposes?

Question for Further Thought

1. How did James Bryce and William Graham Sumner contribute to the late-nineteenth-century view that government should play a limited role?

Politics and the People

However unimaginative and limited national government appeared during the late nineteenth century, politics engaged not only party leaders and workers but also the citizenry. The rank and file frequently attended political gatherings and, of greater significance, regularly voted in impressively large numbers. The political parties' coalitions were primarily based on cultural identities—religious, ethnic, racial, and regional—rather than on economic class or occupation. Once formed, political party identifications proved to be enduring, even across generational lines. Thus voters who became disaffected with their party in particular situations were more likely to abstain on election day than to vote for the opposing party (see text pp. 589–594).

Late-nineteenth-century partisan political culture was aggressively masculine—in political offices and party conventions and on election day, when men voted in male surroundings such as barbershops and cigar stores. Women were permitted to vote in government elections in four states, three of which were admitted to the Union during the 1890s. Women did vote in school board and tax-related elections in some states. In one religiously divisive Boston School Board election, an outpouring of female voters testified to the motivational power of Protestant-Catholic conflict among women as well as men. During the period, women worked to create a political culture of their own—some claiming political rights for women as for all citizens and others arguing in terms of advancing causes of concern to women (see text pp. 594–595).

A series of documents illuminates political issues central to politics from the 1870s into the 1890s. Document 19-3 reports the Republican and Democratic platforms on English-language schooling and on alcohol prohibition in Wisconsin and Iowa. Documents 19-4 and 19-5 highlight the arguments for woman suffrage, another contentious issue of the day.

19-3 Republican and Democratic State Platforms on the Bennett English-Language School Law (Wisconsin, 1890) and the Liquor Question (Iowa, 1889)

Unlike political campaigns marked by Protestant-Catholic conflict, which usually worked to the Republicans' advantage by costing the Democrats Protestant support, other cultural controversies threatened the Republicans. Thus state laws in Wisconsin and Illinois that required public and private schools (Protestant, especially Lutheran, as well as Catholic) to employ English as the language of instruction angered German Americans, contributing to unusual Democratic gubernatorial and presidential election victories in both states between 1890 and 1892. Campaigns involving the liquor question also threatened the Republicans. If they took a prohibitionist position, they risked losing German supporters to the Democrats; if they moved too far from that position, they risked losing prohibitionist adherents to the Prohibition Party. In Iowa, the issue contributed to Democratic gubernatorial election victories in 1889 and 1891, the party's first there since 1850 (see text pp. 594–595).

Source: The Tribune Almanac and Political Register (New York: Tribune Association, 1890, 1891): *1890*, 21–22; *1891*, 84–86.

(a) Wisconsin (1890)

REPUBLICAN

THE SCHOOL QUESTION

The Republican party, in convention assembled, declares its devotion to the common school as the chief factor in the education of the people, and pledges itself to support, strengthen and defend it.

It recognizes as valuable auxiliaries in the work of popular education the private and parochial schools supported without aid from public funds, and disclaims absolutely any purpose whatever to interfere in any manner with such schools, either as to their terms, government or branches to be taught therein.

We affirm the right and duty of the State to enact laws that will guarantee all children sufficient instruction in the legal language of the State to enable them to read and write the same. We believe that the compulsory education law passed by the last Legislature is wise and humane in all its essential purposes, and we are opposed to its repeal,[1] but at the same time we assert that the parent or guardian has the right to select the time of the year and the place, whether public or private, and wherever situated, in which his child or ward shall receive instruction, and we pledge ourselves to modify the existing law so that it shall conform to the foregoing declarations.

We are unalterably opposed to any union of Church and State, and will resist any attempt upon the part of either to invade the domain of the other. We repudiate as a gross misrepresentation of our purposes the suggestion, come whence it may, that we will in any manner invade the domain of conscience, trample upon parental rights or religious liberty. Our only purpose in respect to the educational policy of the State is to secure to all children within its borders at the earliest practicable age proper equipment for the discharge of the ordinary duties of citizenship, and to this end, alike important to the State, to the children and to the parents of the children, we invite the co-operation and aid of all broad-minded and patriotic people. . . .

DEMOCRATIC

DENUNCIATION OF THE REPUBLICAN PARTY

We, the Democrats of Wisconsin, in convention assembled, declare our continued opposition to all forms of paternalism and centralization. The Republican party is the exponent of these dangerous principles. . . .

THE SCHOOL QUESTION

We oppose any division or diversion of public school funds to sectarian uses. The Democratic party created the public school system of this State, and will always jealously guard and maintain it. The Bennett law is a local manifestation of the settled Republican policy of paternalism.

Favoring laws providing for the compulsory attendance at school of all children, we believe that the school law in force prior to the passage of the Bennett law guaranteed to all children of the State opportunity for education, and in this essential feature was stronger than the Bennett law. The underlying principle of the Bennett law is needless interference with parental rights and liberty of conscience, and the provisions for its enforcement place the accused at the mercy of the School Directors and deny his right to trial by jury and according to the law of the land. To mask this tyrannical invasion of individual and constitutional rights the shallow plea of defence of the English language is advanced.

The history of this State, largely peopled with foreign citizens, demonstrates the fact that natural causes and the necessity of the situation are advancing the growth of the English language to the greatest possible extent. We therefore denounce the law as unnecessary, unwise, unconstitutional, un-American, and undemocratic, and demand its repeal. . . .

---

[1] The act of April 18, 1890 (popularly known as the Bennett law), requires that every child between seven and fourteen years shall attend some public or private day school in the city, town or district in which the child resides, for a period not less than twelve weeks nor more than twenty-four weeks in each year, the periods to be fixed and announced by the respective school boards. Penalties are provided. Section 5 provides that "No school shall be regarded as a school under this act, unless there shall be taught therein, as part of the elementary education of children, reading, writing, arithmetic and United States history in the English language." [*Original note.*]

(b) Iowa (1889)

REPUBLICAN	DEMOCRATIC
. . . That we reaffirm the past utterances of the Republican party of Iowa upon prohibition, which has become the settled policy of the State and upon which there should be no backward step. We stand for the complete enforcement of the law.	. . . In the interest of true temperance we demand the passage of a carefully guarded license tax law which shall provide for the issuance of licenses in towns, townships and municipal corporations of the State by vote of the people of such corporations, and which shall provide that for each license an annual tax of $500 be paid into the county treasury, and such further tax as the town, township or municipal corporation shall prescribe, the proceeds thereof to go to the use of such municipalities. We also arraign the Republican party for changing the pharmacy laws of the State, by which a great hardship and gross indignity has been imposed on honorable pharmacists and upon all the people requiring liquor for the actual necessities of medicine. . . .

Questions

1. What was the thrust of the Wisconsin Republicans' argument in favor of the Bennett English-Language School Law?
2. What was the thrust of the Wisconsin Democrats' argument against the law?
3. What was the meaning of the Iowa Democrats' advocacy of "true temperance"? How does their position differ from that of the Republicans?

19-4 Woman and Temperance (1876)

Frances E. Willard

The reform movements of the nineteenth century brought women out of the home and into the larger community. Abolition and temperance touched on politics, which in turn led to the call for suffrage and women's right to shape responses to the issues that affected them (see text pp. 594–595). Frances E. Willard (1839–1898), a founder of the Woman's Christian Temperance Union, emerged as a leader of the suffrage movement. The following selection is excerpted from Willard's first major temperance speech, delivered in 1876. Willard likens the alcohol interests to Chimborazo, the highest peak in Ecuador.

Source: Frances E. Willard, "Woman and Temperance," a speech delivered in 1876, in Frances E. Willard, *Woman and Temperance or, The Work and Workers of the Woman's Christian Temperance Union* (1883; reprint, New York: Arno Press, 1972), 452–457.

The rum power looms like a Chimborazo among the mountains of difficulty over which our native land must climb to reach the future of our dreams. The problem of the rum power's overthrow may well engage our thoughts as women and as patriots. To-night I ask you to consider it in the light of a truth which Frederick Douglass has embodied in these words: "We can in the long run trust all the knowledge in the community to take care of all the ignorance of the community, and all of its virtue to take care of all of its vice." The difficulty in the application of this principle lies in the fact that vice is always in the active, virtue often in the passive. Vice is aggressive. It deals swift, sure blows, delights in keen-edged weapons, and prefers a hand-to-hand conflict, while virtue instinctively fights its unsavory antagonist at arm's length; its great guns are unwieldy and slow to swing into range.

Vice is the tiger, with keen eyes, alert ears, and cat-like tread, while virtue is the slow-paced, complacent, easygoing elephant, whose greatest danger lies in its ponderous weight and consciousness of power. So the great question narrows down to one of two(?) methods. It is not, when we look carefully into the conditions of the problem, How shall we develop more virtue in the community to offset the tropical growth of vice by which we find ourselves environed? but rather, How the tremendous force we have may best be brought to bear, how we may unlimber the huge cannon now pointing into vacancy, and direct their full charge at short range upon our nimble, wily, vigilant foe?

As bearing upon a consideration of that question, I lay down this proposition: All pure and Christian sentiment concerning any line of conduct which vitally affects humanity will, sooner or later, crystallize into law. But the keystone of law can only be firm and secure when it is held in place by the arch of that keystone, which is public sentiment. . . .

There is a class whose instinct of self-preservation must forever be opposed to a stimulant which nerves, with dangerous strength, arms already so much stronger than their own, and so maddens the brain God meant to guide those arms, that they strike down the wives men love, and the little children for whom, when sober, they would die. The wife, largely dependent for the support of herself and little ones upon the brain which strong drink paralyzes, the arm it masters, and the skill it renders futile, will, in the nature of the case, prove herself unfriendly to the actual or potential source of so much misery. But besides this primal instinct of self-preservation, we have, in the same class of which I speak, another far more high and sacred—I mean the instinct of a mother's love, a wife's devotion, a sister's faithfulness, a daughter's loyalty. And now I ask you to consider earnestly the fact that none of these blessed rays of light and power from woman's heart, are as yet brought to bear upon the rum-shop at the focus of power. They are, I know, the sweet and pleasant sunshine of our homes; they are the beams which light the larger home of social life and send their gentle radiance out even into the great and busy world. But I know, and as the knowledge has grown clearer, my heart was thrilled with gratitude and hope too deep for words, that in a republic all these now divergent beams of light can, through that magic lens, that powerful sun-glass which we name the ballot, be made to converge upon the rum-shop in a blaze of light that shall reveal its full abominations, and a white flame of heat which, . . . shall burn this cancerous excrescence from America's fair form. Yes, for there is nothing in the universe so sure, so strong, as love; and love shall do all this—the love of maid for sweetheart, wife for husband, of a sister for her brother, of a mother for her son. And I call upon you who are here to-day, good men and brave—you who have welcomed us to other fields in the great fight of the angel against the dragon in society—I call upon you thus to match force with force, to set over against the liquor-dealer's avarice our instinct of self-preservation; and to match the drinker's love of liquor with our love of him! When you can centre all this power in that small bit of paper which falls

"As silently as snow-flakes fall upon the sod,
But executes a freeman's will as lightnings do the will of God,"

the rum power will be as much doomed as was the slave power when you gave the ballot to the slaves.

In our argument it has been claimed that by the changeless instincts of her nature and through the most sacred relationships of which that nature has been rendered capable, God has indicated woman, who is the born conservator of home, to be the Nemesis of home's arch enemy, King Alcohol. And further, that in a republic, this power of hers may be most effectively exercised by giving her a voice in the decision by which the rum-shop door shall be opened or closed beside her home.

This position is strongly supported by evidence. About the year 1850 petitions were extensively circulated in Cincinnati (later the fiercest battle ground of the woman's crusade), asking that the liquor traffic be put under the ban of law. Bishop Simpson—one of the noblest and most discerning minds of his century—was deeply interested in this movement. It was decided to ask for the names of women as well as those of men, and it was found that the former signed the petition more readily and in much larger numbers than the latter. Another fact was ascertained which rebuts the hackneyed assertion that women of the lower class will not be on the temperance side in this great war. For it was found—as might, indeed, have been most reasonably predicted—that the ignorant, the poor (many of them wives, mothers, and daughters of intemperate men), were among the most eager to sign the petition.

MANY A HAND WAS TAKEN FROM THE WASH-TUB

to hold the pencil and affix the signature of women of this class, and many another, which could only make the sign of the cross, did that with tears, and a hearty "God bless you." "That was a wonderful lesson to me," said the good Bishop, and he has always believed since then that God will give our enemy into our hands by giving to us an ally still more powerful, woman with the ballot against rum-shops in our land. It has been said so often that the very frequency of reiteration has in some minds induced belief that women of the better class will never consent to declare themselves at the polls. But tens of thousands from the most tenderly-sheltered homes have gone day after day to the saloons, and have spent hour after hour upon their sanded floors, and in their reeking air—places in which not the worst politician would dare to locate the ballot box of freemen—though they but stay a moment at the window, slip in their votes, and go their way.

Nothing worse can ever happen to women at the polls than has been endured by the hour on the part of conservative women of the churches in this land, as they, in scores of towns, have plead with rough, half-drunken men to vote the temperance tickets they have handed them, and which, with vastly more of propriety and fitness they might have dropped into the box themselves. They could have done this in a moment, and returned to their homes, instead of spending the whole day in the often futile endeavor to beg from men like these the votes which should preserve their homes from the whisky serpent's breath for one uncertain year. I spent last May in Ohio, traveling constantly, and seeking on every side to learn the views of the noble women of the

Crusade. They put their opinions in words like these: "We believe that as God led us into this work by way of the saloons,

HE WILL LEAD US OUT BY WAY OF THE BALLOT.

We have never prayed more earnestly over the one than we will over the other. One was the Wilderness, the other is the Promised Land."

A Presbyterian lady, rigidly conservative, said: "For my part, I never wanted to vote until our gentlemen passed a prohibition ordinance so as to get us to stop visiting saloons, and a month later repealed it and chose a saloon-keeper for mayor."

Said a grand-daughter of Jonathan Edwards, a woman with no toleration toward the Suffrage Movement, a woman crowned with the glory of gray hairs — a central figure in her native town —

AND AS SHE SPOKE THE COURAGE AND FAITH OF THE PURITANS THRILLED HER VOICE —

"If, with the ballot in our hands, we can, as I firmly believe, put down this awful traffic, I am ready to lead the women of my town to the polls, as I have often led them to the rum shops."

We must not forget that for every woman who joins the Temperance Unions now springing up all through the land, there are at least a score who sympathize but do not join. Home influence and cares prevent them, ignorance of our aims and methods, lack of consecration to Christian work — a thousand reasons, sufficient in their estimation, though not in ours, hold them away from us. And yet they have this Temperance cause warmly at heart; the logic of events has shown them that there is but one side on which a woman may safely stand in this great battle, and on that side they would indubitably range themselves in the quick, decisive battle of election day, nor would they give their voice a second time in favor of the man who had once betrayed his pledge to enforce the most stringent law for the protection of their homes. There are many noble women, too, who, though they do not think as do the Temperance Unions about the deep things of religion, and are not as yet decided in their total abstinence sentiments, nor ready for the blessed work of prayer, are nevertheless decided in their views of Woman Suffrage, and ready to vote a Temperance ticket side by side with us. And there are the drunkard's wife and daughters, who from very shame will not come with us, or who dare not, yet who could freely vote with us upon this question; for the folded ballot tells no tales.

Among other cumulative proofs in this argument from experience, let us consider, briefly, the attitude of the Catholic Church toward the Temperance Reform. It is friendly, at least. Father Matthew's spirit lives to-day in many a faithful parish priest. In our procession on the Centennial Fourth of July, the banners of Catholic Total Abstinence Societies were often the only reminders that the Republic has any temperance people within its borders, as they were the only offset to brewers' wagons and distillers' casks, while among the monuments of our cause, by which this memorable year is signalized, their fountain in Fairmount Park — standing in the midst of eighty drinking places licensed by our Government — is chief. Catholic women would vote with Protestant women upon this issue for the protection of their homes.

Again, among the sixty thousand churches of America, with their eight million members, two-thirds are women. Thus, only one-third of this trustworthy and thoughtful class has any voice in the laws by which, between the church and the public school, the rum shop nestles in this Christian land. Surely all this must change before the Government shall be upon His shoulders "Who shall one day reign King of nations as He now reigns King of saints."

Furthermore, four-fifths of the teachers in this land are women, whose thoughtful judgment, expressed with the authority of which I speak, would greatly help forward the victory of our cause. And, finally, by those who fear the effect of the foreign element in our country, let it be remembered that we have sixty native for every one woman who is foreign born, for it is men who emigrate in largest number to our shores.

When all these facts (and many more that might be added) are marshaled into line, how illogical it seems for good men to harangue us as they do about our "duty to educate public sentiment to the level of better law," and their exhortations to American mothers to "train their sons to vote aright." As said Mrs. Governor Wallace, of Indiana — until the Crusade an opponent of the franchise — "What a bitter sarcasm you utter, gentlemen, to us who have the public sentiment of which you speak, all burning in our hearts, and yet are not permitted to turn it to account."

Let us, then, each one of us, offer our earnest prayer to God, and speak our honest word to man in favor of this added weapon in woman's hands, remembering that every petition in the ear of God, and every utterance in the ears of men, swells the dimensions of that resistless tide of influence which shall yet float within our reach all that we ask or need. Dear Christian women who have crusaded in the rum shops, I urge that you begin crusading in halls of legislation, in primary meetings, and the offices of excise commissioners. Roll in your petitions, burnish your arguments, multiply your prayers. Go to the voters in your town — procure the official list and see them one by one — and get them pledged to a local ordinance requiring the votes of men and women before a license can be issued to open rum-shop doors beside your homes; go to the Legislature with the same; remember this may be just as really Christian work as praying in saloons was in those other glorious days. Let us not limit God, whose modes of operation are so infinitely varied in nature and in grace. I believe in the correlation of spiritual forces, and that the heat which melted hearts to tenderness in the Crusade is soon to be the light which shall reveal our opportunity and duty as the Republic's daughters.

Questions

1. Why did Willard invoke the name of the abolitionist Frederick Douglass in her speech on temperance?
2. To what extent was her argument based on a kind of political feminism?
3. How did Catholics, usually viewed as unsympathetic to the temperance movement, fare with Willard as compared with their treatment by her contemporaries?

19-5 The Solitude of Self (1892)

Elizabeth Cady Stanton

Elizabeth Cady Stanton (1815–1902) became involved in the antislavery and women's rights causes as early as 1840. With Lucretia Mott, Stanton led in the calling of the Seneca Falls Women's Rights Convention in 1848; she drafted the Declaration of Sentiments adopted there. During Reconstruction, Stanton and Susan B. Anthony opposed subordinating woman suffrage to the cause of winning the vote for black men. She subsequently campaigned for a woman suffrage amendment to the Constitution and, still later, stressed the need for federal action in behalf of universal suffrage, which would protect the vote of blacks, increasingly threatened in southern states, and extend the vote to women (see text p. 469). Stanton delivered her speech on "The Solitude of Self" at a meeting of the National American Woman Suffrage Association (NAWSA), at which she stepped down as the group's president.

Source: Elizabeth Cady Stanton, "The Solitude of Self," in *The Woman's Column* (January 1892), 2–3, excerpted in Ellen Carol DuBois, ed., *The Elizabeth Cady Stanton–Susan B. Anthony Reader: Correspondence, Writings, Speeches*, rev. ed. (Boston: Northeastern University Press, 1992), 246–254.

The point I wish plainly to bring before you on this occasion is the individuality of each human soul; our Protestant idea, the right of individual conscience and judgement; our republican idea, individual citizenship. In discussing the rights of woman, we are to consider, first, what belongs to her as an individual, in a world of her own, the arbiter of her own destiny, an imaginary Robinson Crusoe, with her woman, Friday, on a solitary island. Her rights under such circumstances are to use all her faculties for her own safety and happiness.

Secondly, if we consider her as a citizen, as a member of a great nation, she must have the same rights as all other members, according to the fundamental principles of our Government.

Thirdly, viewed as a woman, an equal factor in civilization, her rights and duties are still the same—individual happiness and development.

Fourthly, it is only the incidental relations of life, such as mother, wife, sister, daughter, which may involve some special duties and training. . . .

The strongest reason for giving woman all the opportunities for higher education, for the full development of her faculties, her forces of mind and body; for giving her the most enlarged freedom of thought and action; a complete emancipation from all forms of bondage, of custom, dependence, superstition; from all the crippling influences of fear—is the solitude and personal responsibility of her own individual life. The strongest reason why we ask for woman a voice in the government under which she lives; in the religion she is asked to believe; equality in social life, where she is the chief factor; a place in the trades and professions, where she may earn her bread, is because of her birthright to self-sovereignty; because, as an individual, she must rely on herself. No matter how much women prefer to lean, to be protected and supported, nor how much men desire to have them do so, they must make the voyage of life alone, and for safety in an emergency, they must know something of the laws of navigation. To guide our own craft, we must be captain, pilot, engineer; with chart and compass to stand at the wheel; to watch the winds and waves, and know when to take in the sail, and to read the signs in the firmament over all. It matters not whether the solitary voyager is man or woman; nature, having endowed them equally, leaves them to their own skill and judgment in the hour of danger, and, if not equal to the occasion, alike they perish.

To appreciate the importance of fitting every human soul for independent action, think for a moment of the immeasurable solitude of self. We come into the world alone, unlike all who have gone before us, we leave it alone, under circumstances peculiar to ourselves. No mortal ever has been, no mortal ever will be like the soul just launched on the sea of life. There can never again be just such a combination of prenatal influences; never again just such environments as make up the infancy, youth and manhood of this one. Nature never repeats herself, and the possibilities of one human soul will never be found in another. No one has ever found two blades of ribbon grass alike, and no one will ever find two human beings alike. Seeing, then, what must be the infinite diversity in human character, we can in a measure appreciate the loss to a nation when any large class of the people is uneducated and unrepresented in the government.

We ask for the complete development of every individual, first, for his own benefit and happiness. In fitting out an army, we give each soldier his own knapsack, arms, powder, his blanket, cup, knife, fork and spoon. We provide alike for all their individual necessities; then each man bears his own burden.

Again, we ask complete individual development for the general good; for the consensus of the competent on the whole round of human interests, on all questions of national life; and here each man must bear his share of the general burden. It is sad to see how soon friendless children are left to bear their own burdens, before they can analyze their feelings; before they can even tell their joys and sorrows, they are thrown on their own resources. The great lesson that nature seems to teach us at all ages is self-dependence, self-protection, self-support. . . .

We ask no sympathy from others in the anxiety and agony of a broken friendship or shattered love. When death sunders our nearest ties, alone we sit in the shadow of our affliction. Alike amid the greatest triumphs and darkest tragedies of life, we walk alone. On the divine heights of human attainment, eulogized and worshipped as a hero or saint, we stand alone. In ignorance, poverty and vice, as a pauper or criminal, alone we starve or steal; alone we suffer the sneers and rebuffs of our fellows; alone we are hunted and hounded through dark courts and alleys, in by-ways and high-ways; alone we stand in the judgment seat; alone in the prison cell we lament our crimes and misfortunes; alone we expiate them on the gallows. In hours like these we realize the awful solitude of individual life, its pains, its penalties, its responsibilities; hours in which the youngest and most helpless are thrown on their own resources for guidance and consolation. Seeing, then, that life must ever be a march and a battle, that each soldier must be equipped for his own protection, it is the height of cruelty to rob the individual of a single natural right.

To throw obstacles in the way of a complete education is like putting out the eyes; to deny the rights of property is like cutting off the hands. To refuse political equality is to rob the ostracized of all self-respect; of credit in the market place; of recompense in the world of work, of a voice in choosing those who make and administer the law, a choice in the jury before whom they are tried, and in the judge who decides their punishment. [Think of] . . . woman's position! Robbed of her natural rights, handicapped by law and custom at every turn, yet compelled to fight her own battles, and in the emergencies of life to fall back on herself for protection. . . .

. . . An uneducated woman trained to dependence, with no resources in herself, must make a failure of any position in life. But society says women do not need a knowledge of the world, the liberal training that experience in public life must give, all the advantages of collegiate education; but when for the lack of all this, the woman's happiness is wrecked, alone she bears her humiliation; and the solitude of the weak and the ignorant is indeed pitiable. In the wild chase for the prizes of life, they are ground to powder.

In age, when the pleasures of youth are passed, children grown up, married and gone, the hurry and bustle of life in a measure over, when the hands are weary of active service, when the old arm chair and the fireside are the chosen resorts, then men and women alike must fall back on their own resources. . . . If, from a life-long participation in public affairs, a woman feels responsible for the laws regulating our system of education, the discipline of our jails and prisons, the sanitary condition of our private homes, public buildings and thoroughfares, an interest in commerce, finance, our foreign relations, in any or all these questions, her solitude will at least be respectable, and she will not be driven to gossip or scandal for entertainment.

The chief reason for opening to every soul the doors to the whole round of human duties and pleasures is the individual development thus attained, the resources thus provided under all circumstances to mitigate the solitude that at times must come to everyone.

Inasmuch, then, as woman shares equally the joys and sorrows of time and eternity, is it not the height of presumption in man to propose to represent her at the ballot box and the throne of grace, to do her voting in the state, her praying in the church, and to assume the position of high priest at the family altar?

Nothing strengthens the judgment and quickens the conscience like individual responsibility. Nothing adds such dignity to character as the recognition of one's self-sovereignty; the right to an equal place, everywhere conceded—a place earned by personal merit, not an artificial attainment by inheritance, wealth, family and position. Conceding, then, that the responsibilities of life rest equally on man and woman, that their destiny is the same, they need the same preparation for time and eternity. The talk of sheltering woman from the fierce storms of life is the sheerest mockery, for they beat on her from every point of the compass, just as they do on man, and with more fatal results, for he has been trained to protect himself, to resist, and to conquer. Such are the facts in human experience, the responsibilities of individual sovereignty. Rich and poor, intelligent and ignorant, wise and foolish, virtuous and vicious, man and woman; it is ever the same, each soul must depend wholly on itself. . . .

Women are already the equals of men in the whole realm of thought, in art, science, literature and government. . . . The poetry and novels of the century are theirs, and they have touched the keynote of reform, in religion, politics and social life. They fill the editor's and professor's chair, plead at the bar of justice, walk the wards of the hospital, speak from the pulpit and the platform. Such is the type of womanhood that an enlightened public sentiment welcomes to-day, and such the triumph of the facts of life over the false theories of the past.

Is it, then, consistent to hold the developed woman of this day within the same narrow political limits as the dame with the spinning wheel and knitting needle occupied in the past? No, no! Machinery has taken the labors of woman as well as man on its tireless shoulders; the loom and the spinning wheel are but dreams of the past; the pen, the brush, the easel, the chisel, have taken their places, while the hopes and ambitions of women are essentially change....

And yet, there is a solitude which each and every one of us has always carried with him, more inaccessible than the ice-cold mountains, more profound than the midnight sea; the solitude of self. Our inner being which we call ourself, no eye nor touch of man or angel has ever pierced. It is more hidden than the caves of the gnome; the sacred adytum of the oracle; the hidden chamber of Eleusinian mystery, for to it only omniscience is permitted to enter.

Such is individual life. Who, I ask you, can take, dare take on himself the rights, the duties, the responsibilities of another human soul?

Questions

1. What is the significance of the title of Stanton's address?
2. What were her arguments in favor of women's rights, including the right to vote?

Questions for Further Thought

1. Compare and contrast the views of Frances Willard and William Graham Sumner relative to society's proper response to the damages of alcohol.
2. Did the ideology of individualism (see text pp. 587–588) make anti-Catholicism inevitable, or were other important factors present?
3. How might Willard have reacted to the Prohibition planks of the Republican and Democratic platforms in Iowa (Document 19-3)?

Race and Politics in the New South

For a number of years after the end of Reconstruction in 1877, southern race relations and politics retained some measure of fluidity. Even though blacks were still subordinated and segregation was widespread, not until the late 1880s and especially the 1890s did de jure segregation, segregation in law, become the rule. Meanwhile, through the 1880s, the Republicans managed to remain competitive in a few former Confederate states and a number of congressional districts. It was this surviving competitiveness, and the closeness of the national political balance, that prompted congressional Republicans to seek a federal elections law in 1890 to protect southern supporters and the GOP from Democratic fraud. African Americans, though badly weakened by the collapse of Republican state governments as Reconstruction waned, still won a few victories within largely black districts. Independents (such as Virginia's Readjusters) challenged the Democrats during the 1880s, likewise the Populists during the 1890s, both sometimes with success, especially where they gained biracial support and cooperated with the Republicans (see text pp. 595–599).

At best, though, the Democrats' opponents were only temporarily successful. Within Congress, the Democrats sidetracked the federal elections bill. Within the southern states, they employed whatever means necessary to defeat their foes. To maintain dominance without fraud, intimidation, and violence, which might have revived support for a federal elections law, the Democrats drafted state constitutions and laws to restrict the suffrage, especially of African Americans and poor, ill-educated whites, thereby breaking the backs of the Republicans and the Populists (see text pp. 597–599).

Document 19-6 presents the suffrage provisions of the Mississippi State Constitution of 1890. Violence, lynchings, and riots played a role in the imposition of the drastic racial order. Lynchings of African Americans numbered one hundred or more per year in all but two years (1891 and 1901), reaching a peak in 1892. Document 19-7 reports a triple lynching in Tennessee. For the reactions to these developments by two African American leaders, Booker T. Washington and W. E. B. Du Bois, see Documents 19-8 and 19-9.

19-6 The 1890 Mississippi Constitution

Long before George Orwell conceived of doublespeak, there was the 1890 Mississippi Constitution. It had the veneer of a liberal document, complete with a lengthy bill of rights, but the text also included a section that detailed how voting rights could be denied (see text pp. 597–598). Such disfranchisement schemes persisted in the South into the 1960s.

Source: Francis N. Thorpe, ed., *The Federal and State Constitutions . . . of the United States* (Washington, DC: U.S. Government Printing Office, 1909), 4:2120–2121.

We, the people of Mississippi, in Convention assembled, grateful to Almighty God, and invoking His blessing on our work, do ordain and establish this Constitution. . . .

ARTICLE 12. FRANCHISE

SEC. 240. All elections by the people shall be by ballot.

SEC. 241. Every male inhabitant of this State, except idiots, insane persons and Indians not taxed, who is a citizen of the United States, twenty-one years old and upwards, who has resided in this State two years, and one year in the election district, or in the incorporated city or town, in which he offers to vote, and who is duly registered as provided in this article, and who has never been convicted of bribery, burglary, theft, arson, obtaining money or goods under false pretenses, perjury, forgery, imbezzlement or bigamy, and who has paid, on or before the first day of February of the year in which he shall offer to vote, all taxes which may have been legally required of him, and which he has had an opportunity of paying according to law, for the two preceding years, and who shall produce to the officers holding the election satisfactory evidence that he has paid said taxes, is declared to be a qualified elector; but any minister of the gospel in charge of an organized church shall be entitled to vote after six months residence in the election district, if otherwise qualified.

SEC. 242. The legislature shall provide by law for the registration of all persons entitled to vote at any election, and all persons offering to register shall take the following oath or affirmation: "I ——— ———, do solemnly swear (or affirm) that I am twenty-one years old, (or I will be before the next election in this county) and that I will have resided in this State two years, and ——— election district of ——— county one year next preceding the ensuing election [or if it be stated in the oath that the person proposing to register is a minister of the gospel in charge of an organized church, then it will be sufficient to aver therein, two years residence in the State and six months in said election district], and am now in good faith a resident of the same, and that I am not disqualified from voting by reason of having been convicted of any crime named in the constitution of this State as a disqualification to be an elector; that I will truly answer all questions propounded to me concerning my antecedents so far as they relate to my right to vote, and also as to my residence before my citizenship in this district; that I will faithfully support the constitution of the United States and of the State of Mississippi, and will bear true faith and allegiance to the same. So help me God." In registering voters in cities and towns, not wholly in one election district, the name of such city or town may be substituted in the oath for the election district. Any willful and corrupt false statement in said affidavit, or in answer to any material question propounded as herein authorized, shall be perjury.

SEC. 243. A uniform poll tax of two dollars, to be used in aid of the common schools, and for no other purpose, is hereby imposed on every male inhabitant of this State between the ages of twenty-one and sixty years, except persons who are deaf and dumb or blind, or who are maimed by loss of hand or foot; said tax to be a lien only upon taxable property. The board of supervisors of any county may, for the purpose of aiding the common schools in that county, increase the poll tax in said county, but in no case shall the entire poll tax exceed in any one year three dollars on each poll. No criminal proceedings shall be allowed to enforce the collection of the poll tax.

Sec. 244. On and after the first day of January, A.D., 1892, every elector shall, in addition to the foregoing qualifications, be able to read any section of the constitution of this State; or he shall be able to understand the same when read to him, or give a reasonable interpretation thereof. A new registration shall be made before the next ensuing election after January the first, A.D., 1892.

Questions

1. What methods of disfranchisement did this constitution allow?
2. What purpose was served by Section 244 of Article 12?

19-7 Lynching at the Curve (1892)

Ida B. Wells

Violence was not an abstract concept for an African American like Ida B. Wells, who was born a slave in 1862. She worked as a teacher before becoming the part owner of a Memphis newspaper in 1889 (see text pp. 598–599). The lynching that Wells describes here persuaded her to leave Memphis. Wells eventually settled in Chicago, where she took part in suffrage and other reform activities until her death in 1931.

Source: Excerpted from *Crusade for Justice: The Autobiography of Ida B. Wells*, ed. Alfreda M. Duster, 47–51. Copyright 1970 by the University of Chicago Press. Reprinted by permission of the University of Chicago Press.

While I was thus carrying on the work of my newspaper, happy in the thought that our influence was helpful and that I was doing the work I loved and had proved that I could make a living out of it, there came the lynching in Memphis which changed the whole course of my life. I was on one of my trips away from home. I was busily engaged in Natchez when word came of the lynching of three men in Memphis. It came just as I had demonstrated that I could make a living by my newspaper and need never tie myself down to school teaching.

Thomas Moss, Calvin McDowell, and Henry Stewart owned and operated a grocery story in a thickly populated suburb. Moss was a letter carrier and could only be at the store at night. Everybody in town knew and loved Tommie. An exemplary young man, he was married and the father of one little girl, Maurine, whose godmother I was. He and his wife Betty were the best friends I had in town. And he believed, with me, that we should defend the cause of right and fight wrong wherever we saw it.

He delivered mail at the office of the *Free Speech*, and whatever Tommie knew in the way of news we got first. He owned his little home, and having saved his money he went into the grocery business with the same ambition that a young white man would have had. He was the president of the company. His partners ran the business in the daytime.

They had located their grocery in the district known as the "Curve" because the streetcar line curved sharply at that point. There was already a grocery owned and operated by a white man who hitherto had had a monopoly on the trade of this thickly populated colored suburb. Thomas's grocery changed all that, and he and his associates were made to feel that they were not welcome by the white grocer. The district being mostly colored and many of the residents belonging either to Thomas's church or to his lodge, he was not worried by the white grocer's hostility.

One day some colored and white boys quarreled over a game of marbles and the colored boys got the better of the fight which followed. The father of the white boys whipped the victorious colored boy, whose father and friends pitched in to avenge the grown white man's flogging of a colored boy. The colored men won the fight, whereupon the white father and grocery keeper swore out a warrant for the arrest of the colored victors. Of course the colored grocery keepers had been drawn into the dispute. But the case was dismissed with nominal fines. Then the challenge was issued that the vanquished whites were coming on Saturday night to clean out the People's Grocery Company.

Knowing this, the owners of the company consulted a lawyer and were told that as they were outside the city limits and beyond police protection, they would be justified in protecting themselves if attacked. Accordingly the grocery company armed several men and stationed them in the rear of the store on that fatal Saturday night, not to attack but to repel a threatened attack. And Saturday night was the time when men of both races congregated in their respective groceries.

About ten o'clock that night, when Thomas was posting his books for the week and Calvin McDowell and his clerk were waiting on customers preparatory to closing, shots rang out in the back room of the store. The men stationed there had seen several white men stealing through the rear door and fired on them without a moment's pause. Three of these men were wounded, and others fled and gave the alarm.

Sunday morning's paper came out with lurid headlines telling how officers of the law had been wounded while in the discharge of their duties, hunting up criminals whom they had been told were harbored in the People's Grocery Company, this being "a low dive in which drinking and gambling were carried on: a resort of thieves and thugs." So ran the description in the leading white journals of Memphis of this successful effort of decent black men to carry on a legitimate business. The same newspaper told of the arrest and jailing of the proprietor of the store and many of the colored people. They predicted that it would go hard with the ringleaders if these "officers" should die. The tale of how the peaceful homes of that suburb were raided on that quiet Sunday morning by police pretending to be looking for others who were implicated in what the papers had called a conspiracy, has been often told. Over a hundred colored men were dragged from their homes and put in jail on suspicion.

All day long on that fateful Sunday white men were permitted in the jail to look over the imprisoned black men. Frenzied descriptions and hearsays were detailed in the papers, which fed the fires of sensationalism. Groups of white men gathered on the street corners and meeting places to discuss the awful crime of Negroes shooting white men.

There had been no lynchings in Memphis since the Civil War, but the colored people felt that anything might happen during the excitement. Many of them were in business there.

Several times they had elected a member of their race to represent them in the legislature in Nashville. And a Negro, Lymus Wallace, had been elected several times as a member of the city council and we had had representation on the school board several times. Mr. Fred Savage was then our representative on the board of education.

The manhood which these Negroes represented went to the county jail and kept watch Sunday night. This they did also on Monday night, guarding the jail to see that nothing happened to the colored men during this time of race prejudice, while it was thought that the wounded white men would die. On Tuesday following, the newspapers which had fanned the flame of race prejudice announced that the wounded men were out of danger and would recover. The colored men who had guarded the jail for two nights felt that the crisis was past and that they need not guard the jail the third night.

While they slept a body of picked men was admitted to the jail, which was a modern Bastille. This mob took out of their cells Thomas Moss, Calvin McDowell, and Henry Stewart, the three officials of the People's Grocery Company. They were loaded on a switch engine of the railroad which ran back of the jail, carried a mile north of the city limits, and horribly shot to death. One of the morning papers held back its edition in order to supply its readers with the details of that lynching.

From its columns was gleaned the above information, together with details which told that "It is said that Tom Moss begged for his life for the sake of his wife and child and his unborn baby"; that when asked if he had anything to say, told them to "tell my people to go West—there is no justice for them here"; that Calvin McDowell got hold of one of the guns of the lynchers and because they could not loosen his grip a shot was fired into his closed fist. When the three bodies were found, the fingers of McDowell's right hand had been shot to pieces and his eyes were gouged out. This proved that the one who wrote that news report was either an eyewitness or got the facts from someone who was.

Questions

1. How and why did the lynching take place?
2. Why would public officials allow a lynching, which by its very nature represents a challenge to authority?
3. For the supporters of Jim Crow in Memphis, the lynching served one purpose. How did it affect the black community?

19-8 Atlanta Exposition Address (1895)

Booker T. Washington

During his lifetime, Booker T. Washington (1856–1915) was hailed as an African American hero: he was a former slave who went on to found the Tuskegee Institute (see text pp. 624–626). His accommodationist approach did not win support for long.

Washington's reputation suffered after his death, especially during the civil rights movement of the 1960s, when he was criticized as an apologist for segregation. More recently, however, some black leaders have revived his concept of self-help. Both ideas — segregation and group autonomy — appear in Washington's Atlanta Exposition Address of 1895.

Source: Booker T. Washington, *Up from Slavery: An Autobiography* (1900; reprint, Williamstown, MA: Corner House, 1978), 218–225.

Mr. President and Gentlemen of the Board of Directors and Citizens.

One-third of the population of the South is of the Negro race. No enterprise seeking the material, civil, or moral welfare of this section can disregard this element of our population and reach the highest success. I but convey to you, Mr. President and Directors, the sentiment of the masses of my race when I say that in no way have the value and manhood of the American Negro been more fittingly and generously recognized than by the managers of this magnificent Exposition at every stage of its progress. It is a recognition that will do more to cement the friendship of the two races than any occurrence since the dawn of our freedom.

Not only this, but the opportunity here afforded will awaken among us a new era of industrial progress. Ignorant and inexperienced, it is not strange that in the first years of our new life we began at the top instead of at the bottom; that a seat in Congress or the state legislature was more sought than real estate or industrial skill; that the political convention of stump speaking had more attractions than starting a dairy farm or truck garden.

A ship lost at sea for many days suddenly sighted a friendly vessel. From the mast of the unfortunate vessel was seen a signal, "Water, water; we die of thirst!" The answer from the friendly vessel at once came back, "Cast down your bucket where you are." A second time the signal, "Water, water; send us water!" ran up from the distressed vessel, and was answered, "Cast down your bucket where you are." The captain of the distressed vessel, at last heeding the injunction, cast down his bucket, and it came up full of fresh, sparkling water from the mouth of the Amazon River. To those of my race who depend on bettering their condition in a foreign land or who underestimate the importance of cultivating friendly relations with the Southern white man, who is their next-door neighbour, I would say: "Cast down your bucket where you are" — cast it down in making friends in every manly way of the people of all races by whom we are surrounded.

Cast it down in agriculture, mechanics, in commerce, in domestic service, and in the professions. And in this connection it is well to bear in mind that whatever other sins the South may be called to bear, when it comes to business, pure and simple, it is in the South that the Negro is given a man's chance in the commercial world, and in nothing is this Exposition more eloquent than in emphasizing this chance. Our greatest danger is that in the great leap of slavery to freedom we may overlook the fact that the masses of us are to live by the productions of our hands, and fail to keep in mind that we shall prosper in proportion as we learn to dignify and glorify common labour and put brains and skill into the common occupations of life; shall prosper in proportion as we learn to draw the line between the superficial and the substantial, the ornamental gewgaws of life and the useful. No race can prosper till it learns that there is as much dignity in tilling a field as in writing a poem. It is at the bottom of life we must begin, and not at the top. Nor should we permit our grievances to overshadow our opportunities.

To those of the white race who look to the incoming of those of foreign birth and strange tongue and habits for the prosperity of the South, were I permitted I would repeat what I say to my own race, "Cast down your bucket where you are." Cast it down among the eight millions of Negroes whose habits you know, whose fidelity and love you have tested in days when to have proved treacherous meant the ruin of your firesides. Cast down your bucket among these people who have, without strikes and labour wars, tilled your fields, cleared your forests, builded your railroads and cities, and brought forth treasures from the bowels of the earth, and helped make possible this magnificent representation of the progress of the South. Casting down your bucket among my people, helping and encouraging them as you are doing on these grounds, and to education of head, hand, and heart, you will find that they will buy your surplus land, make blossom the waste places in your fields, and run your factories. While doing this, you can be sure in the future, as in the past, that you and your families will be surrounded by the most patient, faithful, law-abiding, and unresentful people that the world has seen. As we have proved our loyalty to you in the past, in nursing your children, watching by the sick-bed of your mothers and fathers, and often following them with tear-dimmed eyes to their graves, so in the future, in our humble way, we shall stand by you with a devotion that no foreigner can approach, ready to lay down our lives, if need be, in defence of yours, interlacing our industrial, commercial, civil, and religious life with yours in a way that shall make the interests of both races one. In all things that are purely social we can be as separate as the fingers, yet one as the hand in all things essential to mutual progress.

There is no defence or security for any of us except in the highest intelligence and development of all. If anywhere there are efforts tending to curtail the fullest growth of the Negro, let these efforts be turned into stimulating, encouraging, and making him the most useful and intelligent citizen. Effort or means so invested will pay a thousand per cent. interest. These efforts will be twice blessed—"blessing him that gives and him that takes."

There is no escape through law of man or God from the inevitable:—

The laws of changeless justice bind
   Oppressor with oppressed;
And close as sin and suffering joined
   We march to fate abreast.

Nearly sixteen millions of hands will aid you in pulling the load upward, or they will pull against you the load downward. We shall constitute one-third and more of the ignorance and crime of the South, or one-third its intelligence and progress; we shall contribute one-third to the business and industrial prosperity of the South, or we shall prove a veritable body of death, stagnating, depressing, retarding every effort to advance the body politic.

Gentlemen of the Exposition, as we present to you our humble effort at an exhibition of our progress, you must not expect overmuch. Starting thirty years ago with ownership here and there in a few quilts and pumpkins and chickens (gathered from miscellaneous sources), remember the path that has led from these to the inventions and production of agricultural implements, buggies, steam-engines, newspapers, books, statuary, carving, paintings, the management of drug-stores and banks, has not been trodden without contact with thorns and thistles. While we take pride in what we exhibit as a result of our independent efforts, we do not for a moment forget that our part in this exhibition would fall far short of your expectations but for the constant help that has come to our educational life, not only from the Southern states, but especially from Northern philanthropists, who have made their gifts a constant stream of blessing and encouragement.

The wisest among my race understand that the agitation of questions of social equality is the extremest folly, and that progress in the enjoyment of all the privileges that will come to us must be the result of severe and constant struggle rather than of artificial forcing. No race that has anything to contribute to the markets of the world is long in any degree ostracized. It is important and right that all privileges of the law be ours, but it is vastly more important that we be prepared for the exercises of these privileges. The opportunity to earn a dollar in a factory just now is worth infinitely more than the opportunity to spend a dollar in an opera-house.

In conclusion, may I repeat that nothing in thirty years has given us more hope and encouragement, and drawn us so near to you of the white race, as this opportunity offered by the Exposition; and here bending, as it were, over the altar that represents the results of the struggles of your race and mine, both starting practically empty-handed three decades ago, I pledge that in your effort to work out the great and intricate problem which God had laid at the doors of the South, you shall have at all times the patient, sympathetic help of my race; only let this be constantly in mind, that, while from representations in these buildings of the product of field, of forest, of mine, of factory, letters, and art, much good will come, yet far above and beyond material benefits will be that higher good, that, let us pray God, will come, in a blotting out of sectional differences and racial animosities and suspicions, in a determination to administer absolute justice, in a willing obedience among all classes to the mandates of law. This, this, coupled with our material prosperity, will bring into our beloved South a new heaven and a new earth.

Questions

1. What was Washington's message to blacks? to whites?
2. Why did Washington mention immigrants?
3. What did he mean in saying, "In all things that are purely social we can be as separate as the fingers, yet one as the hand in all things essential to mutual progress"?

19-9 Of Mr. Booker T. Washington and Others (1903)

W. E. B. Du Bois

Unlike Booker T. Washington, W. E. B. Du Bois never experienced slavery. Du Bois was born in Great Barrington, Massachusetts, in 1868 and was educated at Fisk and Harvard, where he earned a Ph.D. As the selection here indicates, Du Bois could not accept Washington's toleration of segregation (see text p. 625). His call for social equality led him to participate in the founding of the NAACP. Du Bois spent his last years in Ghana, where he died in 1963. Du Bois's critique of Washington appears in *The Souls of Black Folk*, first published in 1903.

Source: From W. E. B. Du Bois, *The Souls of Black Folk* (A. C. McClurg, 1903; reprint, New York: Penguin, 1989), 36–50.

Easily the most striking thing in the history of the American Negro since 1876 is the ascendancy of Mr. Booker T. Washington. It began at the time when war memories and ideals were rapidly passing; a day of astonishing commercial development was dawning; a sense of doubt and hesitation overtook the freedmen's sons,—then it was that his leading began. Mr. Washington came, with a simple definite programme, at the psychological moment when the nation was a little ashamed of having bestowed so much sentiment on Negroes, and was concentrating its energies on Dollars. His programme of industrial education, conciliation of the South, and submission and silence as to civil and political rights, was not wholly original; the Free Negroes from 1830 up to wartime had striven to build industrial schools, and the American Missionary Association had from the first taught various trades; and Price and others had sought a way of honorable alliance with the best of the Southerners. But Mr. Washington first indissolubly linked these things; he put enthusiasm, unlimited energy, and perfect faith into this programme, and changed it from a by-path into a veritable Way of Life. And the tale of the methods by which he did this is a fascinating study of human life.

It startled the nation to hear a Negro advocating such a programme after many decades of bitter complaint; it startled and won the applause of the South, it interested and won the admiration of the North; and after a confused murmur of protest, it silenced if it did not convert the Negroes themselves.

To gain the sympathy and coöperation of the various elements comprising the white South was Mr. Washington's first task; and this, at the time Tuskegee was founded, seemed, for a black man, well-nigh impossible. And yet ten years later it was done in the word spoken at Atlanta: "In all things purely social we can be as separate as the five fingers, and yet one as the hand in all things essential to mutual progress." This "Atlanta Compromise" is by all odds the most notable thing in Mr. Washington's career. The South interpreted it in different ways: The radicals received it as a complete surrender of the demand for civil and political equality; the conservatives, as a generously conceived working basis for mutual understanding. So both approved it, and to-day its author is certainly the most distinguished Southerner since Jefferson Davis, and the one with the largest personal following.

Next to this achievement comes Mr. Washington's work in gaining place and consideration in the North. Others less shrewd and tactful had formerly essayed to sit on these two stools and had fallen between them; but as Mr. Washington knew the heart of the South from birth and training, so by singular insight he intuitively grasped the spirit of the age which was dominating the North. And so thoroughly did he learn the speech and thought of triumphant commercialism, and the ideals of material prosperity, that the picture of a lone black boy poring over a French grammar amid the weeds and dirt of a neglected home soon seemed to him the acme of absurdities. One wonders what Socrates and St. Francis of Assisi would say to this.

And yet this very singleness of vision and thorough oneness with his age is a mark of the successful man. It is as though Nature must needs make men narrow in order to give them force. So Mr. Washington's cult has gained unquestioning followers, his work has wonderfully prospered, his friends are legion, and his enemies are confounded. To-day he stands as the one recognized spokesman of his ten million fellows, and one of the most notable figures in a nation of seventy millions. One hesitates, therefore, to criticise a life which, beginning with so little, has done so much. And yet the time is come when one may speak in all sincerity and utter courtesy of the mistakes and shortcomings of Mr. Washington's career, as well as of his triumphs, without being thought captious or envious, and without forgetting that it is easier to do ill than well in the world.

The criticism that has hitherto met Mr. Washington has not always been of this broad character. In the South especially has he had to walk warily to avoid the harshest judgments,— and naturally so, for he is dealing with the one subject of deepest sensitiveness to that section. Twice—once when at the Chicago celebration of the Spanish-American War he alluded to the color-prejudice that is "eating away the vitals of the South," and once when he dined with President Roosevelt— has the resulting Southern criticism been violent enough to threaten seriously his popularity. In the North the feeling has several times forced itself into words, that Mr. Washington's counsels of submission overlooked certain elements of true manhood, and that his educational programme was unnecessarily narrow. Usually, however, such criticism has not found open expression, although, too, the spiritual sons of the Abolitionists have not been prepared to acknowledge that the schools founded before Tuskegee, by men of broad ideals and self-sacrificing spirit, were wholly failures or worthy of ridicule. While, then, criticism has not failed to follow Mr. Washington, yet the prevailing public opinion of the land has been but too willing to deliver the solution of a wearisome problem into his hands, and say, "If that is all you and your race ask, take it."

Among his own people, however, Mr. Washington has encountered the strongest and most lasting opposition, amounting at times to bitterness, and even to-day continuing strong and insistent even though largely silenced in outward expression by the public opinion of the nation. Some of this opposition is, of course, mere envy; the disappointment of displaced demagogues and the spite of narrow minds. But aside from this, there is among educated and thoughtful colored men in all parts of the land a feeling of deep regret, sorrow, and apprehension at the wide currency and ascendancy which some of Mr. Washington's theories have gained. These same men admire his sincerity of purpose, and are willing to forgive much to honest endeavor which is doing something worth the doing. They coöperate with Mr. Washington as far as they conscientiously can; and, indeed, it is no ordinary tribute to this man's tact and power that, steering as he must between so many diverse interests and opinions, he so largely retains the respect of all.

But the hushing of the criticism of honest opponents is a dangerous thing. It leads some of the best of the critics to unfortunate silence and paralysis of effort, and others to burst into speech so passionately and intemperately as to lose listeners. Honest and earnest criticism from those whose interests are most nearly touched,—criticism of writers by readers, of government by those governed, of leaders by those led,—this is the soul of democracy and the safeguard of modern society. If the best of the American Negroes receive by outer pressure a leader whom they had not recognized before, manifestly there is here a certain palpable gain. Yet there is also irreparable loss,—a loss of that peculiarly valuable education which a group receives when by search and criticism it finds and commissions its own leaders. The way in which this is done is at once the most elementary and the nicest problem of social growth. History is but the record of such group-leadership; and yet how infinitely changeful is its type and character! And of all types and kinds, what can be more instructive than the leadership of a group within a group?—that curious double movement where real progress may be negative and actual advance be relative retrogression. All this is the social student's inspiration and despair. . . .

Mr. Washington represents in Negro thought the old attitude of adjustment and submission; but adjustment at such a peculiar time as to make his programme unique. This is an age of unusual economic development, and Mr Washington's programme naturally takes an economic cast, becoming a gospel of Work and Money to such an extent as apparently almost completely to overshadow the higher aims of life. Moreover, this is an age when the more advanced races are coming in closer contact with the less developed races, and the race-feeling is therefore intensified; and Mr. Washington's programme practically accepts the alleged inferiority of the Negro races. Again, in our own land, the reaction from the sentiment of war time has given impetus to race-prejudice against Negroes, and Mr. Washington withdraws many of the high demands of Negroes as men and American citizens. In other periods of intensified prejudice all the Negro's tendency to self-assertion has been called forth; at this period a policy of submission is advocated. In the history of nearly all other races and peoples the doctrine preached at such crises has been that manly self-respect is worth more than lands and houses, and that a people who voluntarily surrender such respect, or cease striving for it, are not worth civilizing.

In answer to this, it has been claimed that the Negro can survive only through submission. Mr. Washington distinctly asks that black people give up, at least for the present, three things,—

First, political power,

Second, insistence on civil rights,

Third, higher education of Negro youth,—

and concentrate all their energies on industrial education, the accumulation of wealth, and the conciliation of the South. This policy has been courageously and insistently advocated for over fifteen years, and has been triumphant for perhaps ten years. As a result of this tender of the palm-branch, what has been the return? In these years there have occurred:

1. The disfranchisement of the Negro.

2. The legal creation of a distinct status of civil inferiority for the Negro.

3. The steady withdrawal of aid from institutions for the higher training of the Negro.

These movements are not, to be sure, direct results of Mr. Washington's teachings; but his propaganda has, without a shadow of doubt, helped their speedier accomplishment. The question then comes: Is it possible, and probable, that nine millions of men can make effective progress in economic lines if they are deprived of political rights, made a servile caste, and allowed only the most meagre chance for developing their exceptional men? If history and reason give any distinct answer to these questions, it is an emphatic *No*. And Mr. Washington thus faces the triple paradox of his career:

1. He is striving nobly to make Negro artisans business men and property-owners; but it is utterly impossible, under modern competitive methods, for workingmen and property-owners to defend their rights and exist without the right of suffrage.

2. He insists on thrift and self-respect, but at the same time counsels a silent submission to civic inferiority such as is bound to sap the manhood of any race in the long run.

3. He advocates common-school and industrial training, and depreciates institutions of higher learning; but neither the Negro common-schools, nor Tuskegee itself, could remain open a day were it not for teachers trained in Negro colleges, or trained by their graduates.

This triple paradox in Mr. Washington's position is the object of criticism by two classes of colored Americans. One class is spiritually descended from Toussaint the Savior, through Gabriel, Vesey, and Turner, and they represent the attitude of revolt and revenge; they hate the white South blindly and distrust the white race generally, and so far as they agree on definite action, think that the Negro's only hope lies in emigration beyond the borders of the United States. And yet, by the irony of fate, nothing has more effectually made this programme seem hopeless than the recent course of the United States toward weaker and darker peoples in the West Indies, Hawaii, and the Philippines,—for where in the world may we go and be safe from lying and brute force?

The other class of Negroes who cannot agree with Mr. Washington has hitherto said little aloud. They deprecate the sight of scattered counsels, of internal disagreement; and especially they dislike making their just criticism of a useful and earnest man an excuse for a general discharge of venom from small-minded opponents. Nevertheless, the questions involved are so fundamental and serious that it is difficult to see how men like the Grimkes, Kelly Miller, J. W. E. Bowen, and other representatives of this group, can much longer be silent. Such men feel in conscience bound to ask of this nation three things:

1. The right to vote.
2. Civic equality.
3. The education of youth according to ability.

They acknowledge Mr. Washington's invaluable service in counselling patience and courtesy in such demands; they do not ask that ignorant black men vote when ignorant whites are debarred, or that any reasonable restrictions in the suffrage should not be applied; they know that the low social level of the mass of the race is responsible for much discrimination against it, but they also know, and the nation knows, that relentless color-prejudice is more often a cause than a result of the Negro's degradation; they seek the abatement of this relic of barbarism, and not its systematic encouragement and pampering by all agencies of social power from the Associated Press to the Church of Christ. They advocate, with Mr. Washington, a broad system of Negro common schools supplemented by thorough industrial training; but they are surprised that a man of Mr. Washington's insight cannot see that no such educational system ever has rested or can rest on any other basis than that of the well-equipped college and university, and they insist that there is a demand for a few such institutions throughout the South to train the best of the Negro youth as teachers, professional men, and leaders.

This group of men honor Mr. Washington for his attitude of conciliation toward the white South; they accept the "Atlanta Compromise" in its broadest interpretation; they recognize, with him, many signs of promise, many men of high purpose and fair judgment, in this section; they know that no easy task has been laid upon a region already tottering under heavy burdens. But, nevertheless, they insist that the way to truth and right lies in straightforward honesty, not in indiscriminate flattery; in praising those of the South who do well and criticising uncompromisingly those who do ill; in taking advantage of the opportunities at hand and urging their fellows to do the same, but at the same time in remembering that only a firm adherence to their higher ideals and aspirations will ever keep those ideals within the realm of possibility. They do not expect that the free right to vote, to enjoy civic rights, and to be educated, will come in a moment; they do not expect to see the bias and prejudices of years disappear at the blast of a trumpet; but they are absolutely certain that the way for a people to gain their reasonable rights is not by voluntarily throwing them away and insisting that they do not want them; that the way for a people to gain respect is not by continually belittling and ridiculing themselves; that, on the contrary, Negroes must insist continually, in season and out of season, that voting is necessary to modern manhood, that color discrimination is barbarism, and that black boys need education as well as white boys.

In failing thus to state plainly and unequivocally the legitimate demands of their people, even at the cost of opposing an honored leader, the thinking classes of American Negroes would shirk a heavy responsibility,—a responsibility to themselves, a responsibility to the struggling masses, a responsibility to the darker races of men whose future depends so largely on this American experiment, but especially a responsibility to this nation,—this common Fatherland. It is wrong to aid and abet a national crime simply because it is unpopular not to do so. The growing spirit of kindliness and reconciliation between the North and South after the frightful differences of a generation ago ought to be a source of deep congratulation to all, and especially to those whose mistreatment caused the war; but if that reconciliation is to be marked by the industrial slavery and civic death of those same black men, with permanent legislation into a position of inferiority, then those black men, if they are really men, are called upon by every consideration of patriotism and loyalty to oppose such a course by all civilized methods, even though such opposition involves disagreement with Mr. Booker T. Washington. We have no right to sit silently by while the inevitable seeds are sown for a harvest of disaster to our children, black and white....

The South ought to be led, by candid and honest criticism, to assert her better self and do her full duty to the race she has cruelly wronged and is still wronging. The North—her co-partner in guilt—cannot salve her conscience by plastering it with gold. We cannot settle this problem by diplomacy and suaveness, by "policy" alone. If worse come to worst, can the moral fibre of this country survive the slow throttling and murder of nine millions of men?

The black men of America have a duty to perform, a duty stern and delicate,—a forward movement to oppose a part of the work of their greatest leader. So far as Mr. Washington preaches Thrift, Patience, and Industrial Training for the masses, we must hold up his hands and strive with him, rejoicing in his honors and glorying in the strength of this Joshua called of God and of man to lead the headless host. But so far as Mr. Washington apologizes for injustice, North or South, does not rightly value the privilege and duty of voting, belittles the emasculating effects of caste distinctions, and opposes the higher training and ambition of our brighter minds,—so far as he, the South, or the Nation, does this,—we must unceasingly and firmly oppose them. By every civilized and peaceful method we must strive for the rights which the world accords to men, clinging unwaveringly to those great words which the sons of the Fathers would fain forget: "We hold these truths to be self-evident: That all men are created equal; that they are endowed by their Creator with certain unalienable rights; that among these are life, liberty, and the pursuit of happiness."

Questions

1. Which aspects of Washington's philosophy did Du Bois criticize?
2. Who did Du Bois expect to lead in the criticism of Washington?
3. What role did Du Bois envision for blacks in American society?
4. In this essay, does Du Bois appear to have considered himself an American or an African American? Why would that matter in regard to his view of Washington?

Questions for Further Thought

1. Which philosophy was better suited to the Jim Crow world of Mississippi: Booker T. Washington's (Document 19-8) or W. E. B. Du Bois's (Document 19-9)? Why?
2. How did the Mississippi Constitution (Document 19-6) encourage the kind of violence described by Ida B. Wells in Document 19-7?
3. How did Du Bois explain Washington's success? What criticisms of Washington did Du Bois voice?
4. Which aspects of Washington's speech have enjoyed a resurgence in popularity among African Americans? Why?

The Crisis of American Politics: The 1890s

From time to time, American politics enters periods of crisis, during which "politics as usual" gives way to intense controversy over issues of national significance. Thus deepening sectional conflict during the 1850s gave birth to the Republican Party, which went on to win the presidency in 1860, with momentous consequences. Similarly, during the 1890s, issues arising out of economic hard times further defined politics, again to the advantage of the GOP.

Storm signals were already apparent when Grover Cleveland, a Democrat, became president in March 1893. The previous year had witnessed a classic labor-management clash at Homestead, Pennsylvania, while agrarian discontent in the South and West had led to the creation of the national People's (Populist) Party. Then, in 1893, business failures led to a panic, following which the nation slid into a serious economic depression, adding urban unrest to rural protest (see text pp. 599–607).

Against this backdrop, President Cleveland sought to stem the decline of treasury gold reserves by ending monthly government purchases of silver under the Sherman Silver Purchase Act. He succeeded in doing so in 1893, but he alienated western and southern inflationists in the process. Next, Congress enacted the Wilson-Gorman Tariff Act of 1894, which superseded the McKinley Tariff, disappointing ardent tariff reformers (including the president) but enabling the Republicans to excoriate the Democrats for failing to appreciate the need for tariff protection, especially during hard times. The Republicans went on to score widespread victories in the midterm elections that year. During 1895 and 1896, southern and western Democrats came to dominate their party, which at its 1896 national convention declared itself for free silver, refused to endorse the administration of President Cleveland, and nominated William Jennings Bryan for president. Many Gold Democrats deserted the party. Despite their own Silverite defections, the Republicans, defending gold as the nation's monetary standard, defeated the Free-Silver Democrats and their Populist allies in the climactic presidential election of 1896 (see text pp. 605–607).

Document 19-10 includes both the Democratic and Republican National Platforms on the currency, the tariff, and federal elections (1892). Document 19-11 is the 1892 national platform of the People's Party. Document 19-12 is an excerpt from Henry Demarest Lloyd's *Wealth against Commonwealth* (1894). William Jennings Bryan's "Cross of Gold" speech, which electrified the Democratic National Convention of 1896, appears in Document 19-13. The final document is a relevant section from Henry Adams's autobiography, *The Education of Henry Adams* (1918).

19-10 Democratic and Republican National Platforms on the Currency, the Tariff, and Federal Elections (1892)

By the standards of the time, political conflict was sharp between 1888 and 1892 (see text pp. 584–587). Republican successes in 1888 gave the party control of the presidency and both houses of Congress, an unusual development during the period, enabling the GOP to seek enactment of an ambitious agenda to achieve the party's major goals. In 1890, the Republicans won passage of the Sherman Silver Purchase Act to mollify western inflationists without embracing free silver, which was opposed in the East, and the McKinley Tariff Act, proof of the party's continued commitment to the protective tariff. However, they failed to secure enactment of the Lodge Federal Elections Bill, demonized by the Democrats as "the Force Bill." The bill proposed federal judicial supervision of federal elections on the petition of one hundred voters within a congressional district or city of twenty thousand, a measure aimed at curbing Democratic election fraud in the South and urban North. Meanwhile, the Democrats scored widespread gains in the midterm elections of 1890, recapturing the House of Representatives, and mounting discontent in the South and West, especially among farmers, led eventually to the creation of a national People's (Populist) Party during 1892.

In their national platforms of 1892, the Democrats and the Republicans dealt with the monetary, tariff, and federal election issues; they also referred to cultural issues prominent in state politics. (For the 1892 national platform of the People's Party, see Document 19-11).

Source: Donald Bruce Johnson, comp., *National Party Platforms*, rev. ed., 2 vols. (Urbana: University of Illinois Press, 1978), 1:*1840–1956*, 86–89, 93–95.

Party Platforms of 1892

DEMOCRATIC

... [W]e solemnly declare that the need of a return to these fundamental principles of free popular government, based on home rule and individual liberty, was never more urgent than now, when the tendency to centralize all power at the Federal capital has become a menace to the reserved rights of the States that strikes at the very roots of our Government under the Constitution as framed by the fathers of the Republic.

We warn the people of our common country, jealous for the preservation of their free institutions, that the policy of Federal control of elections, to which the Republican party has committed itself, is fraught with the gravest dangers, scarcely less momentous than would result from a revolution practically establishing monarchy on the ruins of the Republic. It strikes at the North as well as at the South, and injures the colored citizen even more than the white; it means a horde of deputy marshals at every polling place, armed with Federal power; returning boards appointed and controlled by Federal authority, the outrage of the electoral rights of the people in the several States, the subjugation of the colored people to the control of the party in power, and the reviving of race antagonisms, now happily abated, of the utmost peril to the safety and happiness of all; a measure deliberately and justly described by a leading Republican Senator as "the most infamous bill that ever crossed the threshold of the Senate." Such a policy, if sanctioned by law, would mean the dominance of a self-perpetuating oligarchy of office-holders, and the party first intrusted with its machinery could be dislodged from power only by an appeal to the reserved right of the people to resist oppression, which is inherent in all self-governing communities. Two years ago this revolutionary policy was emphatically condemned by the people at the polls, but in contempt of that verdict the Republican party has defiantly declared in its latest authoritative utterance that its success in the coming elections will mean the enactment of the Force Bill and the usurpation of despotic control over elections in all the States.

Believing that the preservation of Republican government in the United States is dependent upon the defeat of this policy of legalized force and fraud, we invite the support of all citizens who desire to see the Constitution maintained in its integrity with the laws pursuant thereto, which have given our country a hundred years of unexampled prosperity; and we pledge the Democratic party, if it be intrusted with power, not only to the defeat of the Force Bill, but also to relentless opposition to the Republican policy of profligate expenditure, which, in the short space of two years, has squandered an enormous surplus and emptied an overflowing Treasury, after piling new burdens of taxation upon the already overtaxed labor of the country.

We denounce Republican protection as a fraud, a robbery of the great majority of the American people for the benefit of the few. We declare it to be a fundamental principle of the Democratic party that the Federal Government has no constitutional power to impose and collect tariff duties, except for the purpose of revenue only, and we demand that the collection of such taxes shall be limited to the necessities of the Government when honestly and economically administered.

We denounce the McKinley tariff law enacted by the Fifty-first Congress as the culminating atrocity of class legislation; we indorse the efforts made by the Democrats of the present Congress to modify its most oppressive features in the direction of free raw materials and cheaper manufactured goods that enter into general consumption; and we promise its repeal as one of the beneficent results that will follow the action of the people in intrusting power to the Democratic party. Since the McKinley tariff went into operation there have been ten reductions of the wages of the laboring man to one increase. We deny that there has been any increase of prosperity to the country since that tariff went into operation, and we point to the fullness and distress, the wage reductions and strikes in the iron trade, as the best possible evidence that no such prosperity has resulted from the McKinley Act.

We call the attention of thoughtful Americans to the fact that, after thirty years of restrictive taxes against the importation of foreign wealth, in exchange for our agricultural surplus, the homes and farms of the country have become burdened with a real estate mortgage debt of over $2,500,000,000, exclusive of all other forms of indebtedness; that in one of the chief agricultural States of the West there appears a real estate mortgage debt averaging $165 per capita of the total population, and that similar conditions and tendencies are shown to exist in other agricultural-exporting States. We denounce a policy which fosters no industry so much as it does that of the Sheriff.

Trade interchange, on the basis of reciprocal advantages to the countries participating, is a time-honored doctrine of the Democratic faith, but we denounce the sham reciprocity which juggles with the people's desire for enlarged foreign markets and freer exchanges by pretending to establish closer trade relations for a country whose articles of export are almost exclusively agricultural products with other countries that are also agricultural, while erecting a custom-house barrier of prohibitive tariff taxes against the richest countries of the world, that stand ready to take our entire surplus of products, and to exchange therefor commodities which are necessaries and comforts of life among our own people....

We denounce the Republican legislation known as the Sherman Act of 1890 as a cowardly make-shift, fraught with possibilities of danger in the future, which should make all of its supporters, as well as its author, anxious for its speedy repeal. We hold to the use of both gold and silver as the standard money of the country, and to the coinage of both gold and silver without discriminating against either metal or charge for mintage, but the dollar unit of coinage of both metals must be of equal intrinsic and exchangeable value, or be adjusted through international agreement or by such safeguards of legislation as shall insure the maintenance of the parity of the two metals and the equal power of every dollar at all times in the markets and in the payment of debts; and we demand that all paper currency shall be kept at par with and redeemable in such coin. We insist upon this policy as especially necessary for the protection of the farmers and laboring classes, the first and most defenseless victims of unstable money and a fluctuating currency....

Popular education being the only safe basis of popular suffrage, we recommend to the several States most liberal appropriations for the public schools. Free common schools are the nursery of good government, and they have always received the fostering care of the Democratic party, which favors every means of increasing intelligence. Freedom of education, being an essential of civil and religious liberty, as well as a necessity for the development of intelligence, must not be interfered with under any pretext whatever. We are opposed to State interference with parental rights and rights of conscience in the education of children as an infringement of the fundamental Democratic doctrine that the largest individual liberty consistent with the rights of others insures the highest type of American citizenship and the best government. . . .

We are opposed to all sumptuary laws,[1] as an interference with the individual rights of the citizen. . . .

REPUBLICAN

. . . We reaffirm the American doctrine of protection. We call attention to its growth abroad. We maintain that the prosperous condition of our country is largely due to the wise revenue legislation of the Republican congress.

We believe that all articles which cannot be produced in the United States, except luxuries, should be admitted free of duty, and that on all imports coming into competition with the products of American labor, there should be levied duties equal to the difference between wages abroad and at home. We assert that the prices of manufactured articles of general consumption have been reduced under the operations of the tariff act of 1890. . . .

We point to the success of the Republican policy of reciprocity,[2] under which our export trade has vastly increased and new and enlarged markets have been opened for the products of our farms and workshops. We remind the people of the bitter opposition of the Democratic party to this practical business measure, and claim that, executed by a Republican administration, our present laws will eventually give us control of the trade of the world.

The American people, from tradition and interest, favor bi-metallism, and the Republican party demands the use of both gold and silver as standard money, with such restrictions and under such provisions, to be determined by legislation, as will secure the maintenance of the parity of values of the two metals so that the purchasing and debt-paying power of the dollar, whether of silver, gold, or paper, shall be at all times equal. The interests of the producers of the country, its farmers and its workingmen, demand that every dollar, paper or coin, issued by the government, shall be as good as any other.

We commend the wise and patriotic steps already taken by our government to secure an international conference, to adopt such measures as will insure a parity of value between gold and silver for use as money throughout the world.

We demand that every citizen of the United States shall be allowed to cast one free and unrestricted ballot in all public elections, and that such ballot shall be counted and returned as cast; that such laws shall be enacted and enforced as will secure to every citizen, be he rich or poor, native or foreign-born, white or black, this sovereign right, guaranteed by the Constitution. The free and honest popular ballot, the just and equal representation of all the people, as well as their just and equal protection under the laws, are the foundation of our Republican institutions, and the party will never relax its efforts until the integrity of the ballot and the purity of elections shall be fully guaranteed and protected in every State.

SOUTHERN OUTRAGES

We denounce the continued inhuman outrages perpetrated upon American citizens for political reasons in certain Southern States of the Union. . . .

The ultimate reliance of free popular government is the intelligence of the people, and the maintenance of freedom among men. We therefore declare anew our devotion to liberty of thought and conscience, of speech and press, and approve all agencies and instrumentalities which contribute to the education of the children of the land, but while insisting upon the fullest measure of religious liberty, we are opposed to any union of Church and State. . . .

INTEMPERANCE

We sympathize with all wise and legitimate efforts to lessen and prevent the evils of intemperance and promote morality.

---

[1] Sumptuary laws regulated personal behavior on moral grounds—for example, Prohibition.
[2] Reciprocity, introduced in 1890, allowed for the tariff-free importation of specified products from Western Hemisphere nations in return for their admitting American exports on the same terms.

Questions

1. What major differences between the Democratic and Republican platform positions can you identify?
2. A platform states the party's positions on the issues and also employs language about the party and its opponents that is designed to elicit emotional responses from supporters. Do these platforms contain terms and characterizations that strike you?
3. Do the parties' state and national platforms (Documents 19-3 and 19-10) resemble each other in significant ways?

19-11 People's (Populist) Party National Platform (1892)

Responding to the worsening economic situation and building on earlier organizational and political experience (the Patrons of Husbandry or Grange, the farmers' alliances), agrarians and other protesters, already active on the state level, formed a national party, framed a national platform, and ran a national ticket in 1892 (see text pp. 599–607 and Map on p. 602).

As the text notes (pp. 602–604), women played roles in the farmers' alliances and in the Populist Party that were closed to them in the two major parties. Mary Elizabeth Lease was one such woman, Luna Kellie another. Kellie served as secretary of the Nebraska Alliance and edited and wrote for an Alliance newspaper there.

Source: Donald Bruce Johnson, comp., *National Party Platforms*, rev. ed., 2 vols. (Urbana: University of Illinois Press, 1978), 1:*1840–1956*, 89–91.

Assembled upon the 116th anniversary of the Declaration of Independence, the People's Party of America in their first national convention, invoking upon their action the blessing of Almighty God, put forth in the name and on behalf of the people of this country, the following preamble and declaration of principles:

PREAMBLE

The conditions which surround us best justify our co-operation; we meet in the midst of a nation brought to the verge of moral, political, and material ruin. Corruption dominates the ballot-box, the Legislatures, the Congress, and touches even the ermine of the bench. The people are demoralized; most of the States have been compelled to isolate the voters at the polling places to prevent universal intimidation and bribery. The newspapers are largely subsidized or muzzled, public opinion silenced, business prostrated, homes covered with mortgages, labor impoverished, and the land concentrating in the hands of capitalists. The urban workmen are denied the right to organize for self-protection; imported pauperized labor beats down their wages, a hireling standing army, unrecognized by our laws, is established to shoot them down, and they are rapidly degenerating into European conditions. The fruits of the toil of millions are boldly stolen to build up colossal fortunes for a few, unprecedented in the history of mankind; and the possessors of these, in turn despise the Republic and endanger liberty. From the same prolific womb of governmental injustice we breed the two great classes—tramps and millionaires.

The national power to create money is appropriated to enrich bond-holders; a vast public debt payable in legal tender currency has been funded into gold-bearing bonds, thereby adding millions to the burdens of the people.

Silver, which has been accepted as coin since the dawn of history, has been demonetized to add to the purchasing power of gold by decreasing the value of all forms of property as well as human labor, and the supply of currency is purposely abridged to fatten usurers, bankrupt enterprise, and enslave industry. A vast conspiracy against mankind has been organized on two continents, and it is rapidly taking possession of the world. If not met and overthrown at once, it forebodes terrible social convulsions, the destruction of civilization, or the establishment of an absolute despotism.

We have witnessed for more than a quarter of a century the struggles of the two great political parties for power and plunder, while grievous wrongs have been inflicted upon the suffering people. We charge that the controlling influence dominating both these parties have permitted the existing dreadful conditions to develop without serious effort to prevent or restrain them. Neither do they now promise us any substantial reform. They have agreed together to ignore, in the coming campaign, every issue but one. They propose to drown the outcries of a plundered people with the uproar of a sham battle over the tariff, so that capitalists, corporations, national banks, rings, trusts, watered stock, the demonetization of silver and the oppressions of the usurers may all be lost sight of. They propose to sacrifice our homes, lives, and children on the altar of mammon; to destroy the multitude in order to secure corruption funds from the millionaires.

Assembled on the anniversary of the birthday of the nation, and filled with the spirit of the grand general and chief who established our independence, we seek to restore the government of the Republic to the hands of "the plain people," with which class it originated. We assert our purposes to be identical with the purposes of the National Constitution, to form a more perfect union and establish justice, insure domestic tranquillity, provide for the common defense, promote the general welfare, and secure the blessings of liberty for ourselves and our posterity.

We declare that this Republic can only endure as a free government while built upon the love of the whole people for each other and for the nation; that it cannot be pinned together by bayonets; that the civil war is over and that every passion and resentment which grew out of it must die with it, and that we must be in fact, as we are in name, one united brotherhood of freemen.

Our country finds itself confronted by conditions for which there is no precedent in the history of the world; our annual agricultural productions amount to billions of dollars in value, which must, within a few weeks or months be exchanged for billions of dollars' worth of commodities consumed in their production; the existing currency supply is wholly inadequate to make this exchange; the results are falling prices, the formation of combines and rings, the impoverishment of the producing class. We pledge ourselves that, if given power, we will labor to correct these evils by wise and reasonable legislation, in accordance with the terms of our platform.

We believe that the power of government—in other words, of the people—should be expanded (as in the case of the postal service) as rapidly and as far as the good sense of an intelligent people and the teachings of experience shall justify, to the end that oppression, injustice and poverty, shall eventually cease in the land.

While our sympathies as a party of reform are naturally upon the side of every proposition which will tend to make men intelligent, virtuous and temperate, we nevertheless regard these questions, important as they are, as secondary to the great issues now pressing for solution, and upon which not only our individual prosperity, but the very existence of free institutions depend; and we ask all men to first help us to determine whether we are to have a republic to administer, before we differ as to the conditions upon which it is to be administered, believing that the forces of reform this day organized will never cease to move forward, until every wrong is remedied, and equal rights and equal privileges securely established for all the men and women of this country.

PLATFORM

We declare, therefore,

First—That the union of the labor forces of the United States this day consummated shall be permanent and perpetual; may its spirit enter into all hearts for the salvation of the Republic and the uplifting of mankind.

Second—Wealth belongs to him who creates it, and every dollar taken from industry without an equivalent is robbery. "If any will not work, neither shall he eat." The interests of rural and civic labor are the same; their enemies are identical.

Third—We believe that the time has come when the railroad corporations will either own the people or the people must own the railroads, and should the government enter upon the work of owning and managing all railroads, we should favor an amendment to the Constitution by which all persons engaged in the government service shall be placed under a civil service regulation of the most rigid character, so as to prevent the increase of the power of the national administration by the use of such additional government employees.

Finance—We demand a national currency, safe, sound, and flexible, issued by the general government only, a full legal tender for all debts, public and private, and that without the use of banking corporations, a just, equitable and efficient means of distribution direct to the people, at a tax not to exceed 2 per cent per annum, to be provided as set forth by the sub-treasury plan of the Farmers' Alliance, or a better system; also by payments in discharge of its obligations for public improvements.

1. We demand free and unlimited coinage of silver and gold at the present legal ratio of 16 to 1.

2. We demand that the amount of circulating medium be speedily increased to not less than $50 per capita.

3. We demand a graduated income tax.

4. We believe that the money of the country should be kept as much as possible in the hands of the people, and hence we demand that all State and national revenues shall be limited to the necessary expenses of the government, economically and honestly administered.

5. We demand that postal savings banks be established by the government for the safe deposit of the earnings of the people and to facilitate exchange.

Transportation—Transportation being a means of exchange and a public necessity, the government should own and operate the railroads in the interest of the people. The telegraph and telephone, like the post office system, being a necessity for the transmission of news, should be owned and operated by the government in the interest of the people.

Land—The land, including all the natural sources of wealth, is the heritage of the people, and should not be monopolized for speculative purposes, and alien ownership of land should be prohibited. All land now held by railroads and other corporations in excess of their actual needs, and all lands now owned by aliens, should be reclaimed by the government and held for actual settlers only.

Questions

1. What are the main points of the preamble to the Populists' platform?
2. What are the key planks of the platform? Which depart most from major party positions of the time (1892)?
3. Referring to the text, appropriate "American Voices," and the documents in Chapters 16–19, explain the place that was held by the Populists in late-nineteenth-century protest and reform politics.

19-12 *Wealth Against Commonwealth* (1894)

Henry Demarest Lloyd

Henry Demarest Lloyd (1847–1903), an influential journalist and reformer, was a vocal critic of monopoly and big business. As Lloyd bitingly put it: "What we call Monopoly is Business at the end of its journey. The concentration of wealth, the wiping out of the middle classes, are other names for it." In *Wealth Against Commonwealth*, Lloyd provided a devastating critique of big business and transformed the images of its leaders from captains of industry to robber barons.

Source: Henry Demarest Lloyd, *Wealth Against Commonwealth* (New York: Harper and Brothers Publishers, 1894), 1–7.

Nature is rich; but everywhere man, the heir of nature, is poor. Never in this happy country or elsewhere—except in the Land of Miracle, where "they did all eat and were filled"—has there been enough of anything for the people. Never since time began have all the sons and daughters of men been all warm, and all filled, and all shod and roofed. Never yet have all the virgins, wise or foolish, been able to fill their lamps with oil.

The world, enriched by thousands of generations of toilers and thinkers, has reached a fertility which can give every human being a plenty undreamed of even in the Utopias. But between this plenty ripening on the boughs of our civilization and the people hungering for it step the "cornerers," the syndicates, trusts, combinations, with the cry of "over-production"—too much of everything. Holding back the riches of earth, sea, and sky from their fellows who famish and freeze in the dark, they declare to them that there is too much light and warmth and food. They assert the right, for their private profit, to regulate the consumption by the people of the necessaries of life, and to control production, not by the needs of humanity, but by the desires of a few for dividends. The coal syndicate thinks there is too much coal. There is too much iron, too much lumber, too much flour—for this or that syndicate.

The majority have never been able to buy enough of anything; but this minority have too much of everything to sell.

Liberty produces wealth, and wealth destroys liberty. "The splendid empire of Charles V.," says Motley, "was erected upon the grave of liberty." Our bignesses, cities, factories, monopolies, fortunes, which are our empires, are the obesities of an age gluttonous beyond its powers of digestion. Mankind are crowding upon each other in the centres, and struggling to keep each other out of the feast set by the new sciences and the new fellowships. Our size has got beyond both our science and our conscience. The vision of the railroad stockholder is not far-sighted enough to see into the office of the General Manager; the people cannot reach across even a ward of a city to rule their rulers; Captains of Industry "do not know" whether the men in the ranks are dying from lack of food and shelter; we cannot clean our cities nor our politics; the locomotive has more man-power than all the ballot-boxes, and mill-wheels wear out the hearts of workers unable to keep up beating time to their whirl. If mankind had gone on pursuing the ideals of the fighter, the time would necessarily have come when there would have been only a few, then only one, and then none left. This is what we are witnessing in the world of livelihoods. Our ideals of livelihood are ideals of mutual deglutition. We are rapidly reaching the stage where in each province only a few are left; that is the key to our times. Beyond the deep is another deep. This era is but a passing phase in the evolution of industrial Cæsars, and these Cæsars will be of a new type—corporate Cæsars.

For those who like the perpetual motion of a debate in which neither of the disputants is looking at the same side of the shield, there are infinite satisfactions in the current controversy as to whether there is any such thing as "monopoly." "There are none," says one side. "They are legion," says the other. "The idea that there can be such a thing is absurd," says one, who with half a dozen associates controls the source, the price, the quality, the quantity of nine-tenths of a great necessary of life. But "There will soon be a trust for every production, and a master to fix the price for every necessity of life," said the Senator who framed the United States Anti-Trust Law. This difference as to facts is due to a difference in the definitions through which the facts are regarded. Those who say "there are none" hold with the Attorney-General of the United States and the decision he quotes from the highest Federal court which has yet passed on this question[1] that no one has a monopoly unless there is a "disability" or "restriction" imposed by law on all who would compete. A syndicate that had succeeded in bottling for sale all the air of the earth would not have a monopoly in this view, unless there were on the statute-books a law forbidding every one else from selling air. No others could get air to sell; the people could not get air to breathe, but there would be no monopoly because there is no "legal restriction" on breathing or selling the atmosphere.

---

[1] Annual Report Attorney-General of the United States, 1893. [*Lloyd's note.*]

Excepting in the manufacture of postage-stamps, gold dollars, and a few other such cases of a "legal restriction," there are no monopolies according to this definition. It excludes the whole body of facts which the people include in their definition, and dismisses a great public question by a mere play on words. The other side of the shield was described by Judge Barrett, of the Supreme Court of New York. A monopoly he declared to be "any combination the tendency of which is to prevent competition in its broad and general sense, and to control and thus at will enhance prices to the detriment of the public. . . . Nor need it be permanent or complete. It is enough that it may be even temporarily and partially successful. The question in the end is, Does it inevitably tend to public injury?"[2]

Those who insist that "there are none" are the fortunate ones who came up to the shield on its golden side. But common usage agrees with the language of Judge Barrett, because it exactly fits a fact which presses on common people heavily, and will grow heavier before its grows lighter.

The committee of Congress investigating trusts in 1889 did not report any list of these combinations to control markets, "for the reason that new ones are constantly forming, and that old ones are constantly extending their relations so as to cover new branches of the business and invade new territories."

It is true that such a list, like a dictionary, would begin to be wrong the moment it began to appear. But though only an instantaneous photograph of the whirlwind, it would give an idea, to be gained in no other way, of a movement shadowing two hemispheres. In an incredible number of the necessaries and luxuries of life, from meat to tombstones, some inner circle of the "fittest" has sought, and very often obtained, the sweet power which Judge Barrett found the sugar trust had: It "can close every refinery at will, close some and open others, limit the purchases of raw material (thus jeopardizing, and in a considerable degree controlling, its production), artificially limit the production of refined sugar, enhance the price to enrich themselves and their associates at the public expense, and depress the price when necessary to crush out and impoverish a foolhardy rival."

Corners are "acute" attacks of that which combinations exhibit as chronic. First a corner, then a pool, then a trust, has often been the genesis. The last stage, when the trust throws off the forms of combination and returns to the simpler dress of corporations, is already well along. Some of the "sympathetical co-operations" on record have no doubt ceased to exist. But that they should have been attempted is one of the signs of the time, and these attempts are repeated again and again until success is reached.

The line of development is from local to national, and from national to international. The amount of capital changes continually with the recrystallizations in progress.

Not less than five hundred million dollars is in the coal combination, which our evidence shows to have flourished twenty-two years; that in oil has nearly if not quite two hundred millions; and the other combinations in which its members are leaders foot up hundreds of millions more. Hundreds of millions of dollars are united in the railroads and elevators of the Northwest against the wheat-growers. In cattle and meat there are not less than one hundred millions; in whiskey, thirty-five millions; and in beer a great deal more than that; in sugar, seventy-five millions; in leather, over a hundred millions; in gas, hundreds of millions. At this writing a union is being negotiated of all the piano-makers in the United States, to have a capital of fifty millions. Quite beyond ordinary comprehension is the magnitude of the syndicates, if there is more than one, which are going from city to city, consolidating all the gas-works, electric-lighting companies, street-railways in each into single properties, and consolidating these into vast estates for central corporations of capitalists, controlling from metropolitan offices the transportation of the people of scores of cities. Such a syndicate negotiating in December, 1892, for the control of the street-railways of Brooklyn, was said by the New York *Times*, "on absolute authority, to have subscribed $23,000,000 towards that end, before a single move had been made or a price set on a single share of stock." It was in the same hands as those busy later in gathering together the coal-mines of Nova Scotia and putting them under American control. There are in round numbers ten thousand millions of dollars claiming dividends and interest in the railroads of the United States. Every year they are more closely pooled. The public saw them marshalled, as by one hand, in the maintenance of the high passenger rates to the World's Fair in the summer of 1893.

Many thousands of millions of dollars are represented in these centralizations. It is a vast sum, and yet is but a minority of our wealth.

Laws against these combinations have been passed by Congress and by many of the States. There have been prosecutions under them by the State and Federal governments. The laws and the lawsuits have alike been futile.

In a few cases names and form of organization have been changed, in consequence of legal pursuit. The whiskey, sugar, and oil trusts had to hang out new signs. But the thing itself, the will and the power to control markets, livelihoods, and liberties, and the toleration of this by the public—this remains unimpaired; in truth, facilitated by the greater secrecy and compactness which have been the only results of the appeal to law.

The Attorney-General of the national government gives a large part of his annual report for 1893 to showing "what small basis there is for the popular impression" "that the aim and effect of this statute" (the Anti-Trust Law) "are to prohibit and prevent those aggregations of capital which are so common at the present day, and which sometimes are on so large a scale as to practically control all the branches of an extensive industry." This executive says of the action of the "co-ordinate" Legislature: "It would not be useful, even if it

---

[2] People of the State of New York *vs.* The North River Sugar Refining Company. Supreme Court of New York—at Circuit (January 9, 1889). New York Senate Trusts, 1889, p. 278. [*Lloyd's note.*]

were possible, to ascertain the precise purposes of the framers of the statute." He is the officer charged with the duty of directing the prosecutions to enforce the law; but he declares that since, among other reasons, "all ownership of property is a monopoly, . . . any literal application of the provisions of the statute is out of the question." Nothing has been accomplished by all these appeals to the legislatures and the courts, except to prove that the evil lies deeper than any public sentiment or public intelligence yet existent, and is stronger than any public power yet at call.

What we call Monopoly is Business at the end of its journey. The concentration of wealth, the wiping out of the middle classes, are other names for it. To get it is, in the world of affairs, the chief end of man.

There are no solitary truths, Goethe says, and monopoly—as the greatest business fact of our civilization, which gives to business what other ages gave to war and religion—is our greatest social, political, and moral fact.

The men and women who do the work of the world have the right to the floor. Everywhere they are rising to "a point of information." They want to know how our labor and the gifts of nature are being ordered by those whom our ideals and consent have made Captains of Industry over us; how it is that we, who profess the religion of the Golden Rule and the political economy of service for service, come to divide our produce into incalculable power and pleasure for a few, and partial existence for the many who are the fountains of these powers and pleasures.

Questions

1. According to Lloyd, what prevented the riches of the American economy from reaching society's poorest members?
2. Compare Lloyd's attack on monopolies with the People's (Populist) Party National Platform (Document 19-11). In what ways do they overlap?
3. Lloyd mentioned the 1890 Anti-Trust Law, which made trusts illegal. Why did this legislation fail to limit the power of monopolies and trusts?

19-13 Cross of Gold Speech (1896)

William Jennings Bryan

A former two-term congressman and unsuccessful senatorial aspirant from Nebraska, the youthful William Jennings Bryan (1860–1925) made his debut as a prime player on the national political stage at the contentious Democratic National Convention of 1896. He delivered his "Cross of Gold" speech during the debate over the platform, then went on to win the party's presidential nomination on the fifth roll-call ballot. Bryan also became the nominee of the People's Party and the National Silver Party. He went down to defeat in the presidential election that November. He later lost presidential elections in 1900 and 1908.

The Mr. Carlisle to whom Bryan refers in the speech is John G. Carlisle, a representative from Kentucky in 1878 who had taken an inflationist position.

Source: William Jennings Bryan, *The First Battle: A Story of the Campaign of 1896* (Chicago: W. B. Conkey, 1896), 199–206.

Mr. Chairman and Gentlemen of the Convention: I would be presumptuous, indeed, to present myself against the distinguished gentlemen to whom you have listened if this were a mere measuring of abilities; but this is not a contest between persons. The humblest citizen in all the land, when clad in the armor of a righteous cause, is stronger than all the hosts of error. I come to speak to you in defense of a cause as holy as the cause of liberty—the cause of humanity.

When this debate is concluded, a motion will be made to lay upon the table the resolution offered in commendation of the administration. We object to bringing this question down to the level of persons. The individual is but an atom; he is born, he acts, he dies; but principles are eternal; and this has been a contest over a principle.

Never before in the history of this country has there been witnessed such a contest as that through which we have just passed. Never before in the history of American politics has a great issue been fought out as this issue has been, by the voters of a great party. On the fourth of March, 1895, a few Democrats, most of them members of Congress, issued an address to the Democrats of the nation, asserting that the money question was the paramount issue of the hour; declaring that a majority of the Democratic party had the right to control the action of the party on this paramount issue; and concluding with the request that the believers in the free coinage of silver in the Democratic party should organize, take charge of, and control the policy of the Democratic party. Three months later, at Memphis, an organization was perfected, and the silver Democrats went forth openly and courageously proclaiming their belief, and declaring that, if successful, they would crystallize into a platform the declaration which they had made. Then began the conflict. With a zeal approaching the zeal which inspired the crusaders ... our silver Democrats went forth from victory unto victory until they are now assembled, not to discuss, not to debate, but to enter up the judgment already rendered by the plain people of this country. In this contest brother has been arrayed against brother, father against son. The warmest ties of love, acquaintance and association have been disregarded; old leaders have been cast aside when they have refused to give expression to the sentiments of those whom they would lead, and new leaders have sprung up to give direction to this cause of truth. Thus has the contest been waged, and we have assembled here under as binding and solemn instructions as were ever imposed upon representatives of the people....

When you (turning to the gold delegates) come before us and tell us that we are about to disturb your business interests, we reply that you have disturbed our business interests by your course.

We say to you that you have made the definition of a business man too limited in its application. The man who is employed for wages is as much a business man as his employer; the attorney in a country town is as much a business man as the corporation counsel in a great metropolis; the merchant at the cross-roads store is as much a business man as the merchant of New York; the farmer who goes forth in the morning and toils all day — who begins in the spring and toils all summer — and who by the application of brain and muscle to the natural resources of the country creates wealth, is as much a business man as the man who goes upon the board of trade and bets upon the price of grain; the miners who go down a thousand feet into the earth, or climb two thousand feet upon the cliffs, and bring forth from their hiding places the precious metals to be poured into the channels of trade are as much business men as the few financial magnates who, in a back room, corner the money of the world. We come to speak for this broader class of business men.

Ah, my friends, we say not one word against those who live upon the Atlantic coast, but the hardy pioneers who have braved all the dangers of the wilderness, who have made the desert to blossom as the rose — the pioneers out there (pointing to the West), who rear their children near to Nature's heart, where they can mingle their voices with the voices of the birds — out there where they have erected schoolhouses for the education of their young, churches where they praise their Creator, and cemeteries where rest the ashes of their dead — these people, we say, are as deserving of the consideration of our party as any people in this country. It is for these that we speak. We do not come as aggressors. Our war is not a war of conquest; we are fighting in the defense of our homes, our families, and posterity. We have petitioned, and our petitions have been scorned; we have entreated, and our entreaties have been disregarded; we have begged, and they have mocked when our calamity came. We beg no longer; we entreat no more; we petition no more. We defy them.

The gentleman from Wisconsin has said that he fears a Robespierre. My friends, in this land of the free you need not fear that a tyrant will spring up from among the people. What we need is an Andrew Jackson to stand, as Jackson stood, against the encroachments of organized wealth.

They tell us that this platform was made to catch votes. We reply to them that changing conditions make new issues; that the principles upon which Democracy rests are as everlasting as the hills, but that they must be applied to new conditions as they arise. Conditions have arisen, and we are here to meet those conditions. They tell us that the income tax ought not to be brought in here; that it is a new idea. They criticise us for our criticism of the Supreme Court of the United States. My friends, we have not criticised; we have simply called attention to what you already know. If you want criticisms, read the dissenting opinions of the court. There you will find criticisms. They say that we passed an unconstitutional law; we deny it. The income tax law was not unconstitutional when it was passed; it was not unconstitutional when it went before the Supreme Court for the first time; it did not become unconstitutional until one of the judges changed his mind, and we cannot be expected to know when a judge will change his mind. The income tax is just. It simply intends to put the burdens of government justly upon the backs of the people. I am in favor of an income tax. When I find a man who is not willing to bear his share of the burdens of the government which protects him, I find a man who is unworthy to enjoy the blessings of a government like ours.

They say that we are opposing national bank currency; it is true.... We say in our platform that we believe that the right to coin and issue money is a function of government. We believe it. We believe that it is a part of sovereignty, and can no more with safety be delegated to private individuals than we could afford to delegate to private individuals the power to make penal statutes or levy taxes. Mr. [Thomas] Jefferson, who was once regarded as good Democratic authority, seems to have differed in opinion from the gentleman who has addressed us on the part of the minority. Those who are opposed to this proposition tell us that the issue of paper money is a function of the bank, and that the Government ought to go out of the banking business. I stand with Jefferson rather than with them, and tell them, as he did, that the issue of money is a function of government, and that the banks ought to go out of the governing business.

They complain about the plank which declares against life tenure in office. They have tried to strain it to mean that which it does not mean. What we oppose by that plank is the life tenure which is being built up in Washington, and which excludes from participation in official benefits the humbler members of society.

Let me call your attention to two or three important things. The gentleman from New York says that he will propose an amendment to the platform providing that the proposed change in our monetary system shall not affect contracts already made. Let me remind you that there is no intention of affecting those contracts which according to present laws are made payable in gold; but if he means to say that we cannot change our monetary system without protecting those who have loaned money before the change was made, I desire to ask him where, in law or in morals, he can find justification for not protecting the debtors when the act of 1873 [dropping silver as a medium of exchange] was passed, if he now insists that we must protect the creditors.

He says he will also propose an amendment which will provide for the suspension of free coinage if we fail to maintain the parity within a year. We reply that when we advocate a policy which we believe will be successful, we are not compelled to raise a doubt as to our own sincerity by suggesting what we shall do if we fail. I ask him, if he would apply his logic to us, why he does not apply it to himself. He says he wants this country to try to secure an international agreement. Why does he not tell us what he is going to do if he fails to secure an international agreement? There is more reason for him to do that than there is for us to provide against the failure to maintain the parity. Our opponents have tried for twenty years to secure an international agreement, and those are waiting for it most patiently who do not want it at all.

And now, my friends, let me come to the paramount issue. If they ask us why it is that we say more on the money question than we say upon the tariff question, I reply that, if protection has slain its thousands, the gold standard has slain its tens of thousands. If they ask us why we do not employ in our platform all the things that we believe in, we reply that when we have restored the money of the Constitution all other necessary reforms will be possible; but that until this is done there is no other reform that can be accomplished.

Why is it that within three months such a change has come over the country? Three months ago, when it was confidently asserted that those who believe in the gold standard would frame our platform and nominate our candidates, even the advocates of the gold standard did not think that we could elect a president. And they had good reason for their doubt, because there is scarcely a State here today asking for the gold standard which is not in the absolute control of the Republican party. But note the change. Mr. McKinley was nominated at St. Louis upon a platform which declared for the maintenance of the gold standard until it can be changed into bimetallism by international agreement. Mr. McKinley was the most popular man among the Republicans, and three months ago everybody in the Republican party prophesied his election. How is today? Why, the man who was once pleased to think that he looked like Napoleon—that man shudders today when he remembers that he was nominated on the anniversary of the battle of Waterloo. Not only that, but as he listens he can hear with ever-increasing distinctness the sound of the waves as they beat upon the lonely shores of St. Helena.

Why this change? Ah, my friends, is not the reason for the change evident to any one who will look at the matter? No private character, however pure, no personal popularity, however great, can protect from the avenging wrath of an indignant people a man who will declare that he is in favor of fastening the gold standard upon this country, or who is willing to surrender the right of self-government and place the legislative control of our affairs in the hands of foreign potentates and powers.

We go forth confident that we shall win. Why? Because upon the paramount issue of this campaign there is not a spot of ground upon which the enemy will dare to challenge battle. If they tell us that the gold standard is a good thing, we shall point to their platform and tell them that their platform pledges the party to get rid of the gold standard and substitute bimetallism. If the gold standard is a good thing, why try to get rid of it? I call your attention to the fact that some of the very people who are in this convention today and who tell us that we ought to declare in favor of international bimetallism—thereby declaring that the gold standard is wrong and the principle of bimetallism is better—these very people four months ago were open and avowed advocates of the gold standard, and were then telling us that we could not legislate two metals together, even with the aid of all the world. If the gold standard is a good thing, we ought to declare in favor of its retention and not in favor of abandoning it; and if the gold standard is a bad thing why should we wait until other nations are willing to help us to let go? Here is the line of battle, and we care not upon which issue they force the fight; we are prepared to meet them on either issue or on both. If they tell us that the gold standard is the standard of civilization, we reply to them that this, the most enlightened of all the nations of the earth, has never declared for a gold standard and that both the great parties this year are declaring against it. If the gold standard is the standard of civilization, why, my friends, should we not have it? If they come to meet us on that issue we can present the history of our nation. More than that; we can tell them that they will search the pages of history in vain to find a single instance where the common people of any land have ever declared themselves in favor of the gold standard. They can find where the holders of fixed investments have declared for a gold standard, but not where the masses have.

Mr. Carlisle said in 1878 that this was a struggle between "the idle holders of idle capital" and "the struggling masses, who produce the wealth and pay the taxes of the country;" and, my friends, the question we are to decide is: Upon which side will the Democratic party fight; upon the side of "the idle holders of idle capital" or upon the side of "the struggling masses?" That is the question which the party must answer first, and then it must be answered by each individual hereafter. The sympathies of the Democratic party, as shown by the platform, are on the side of the struggling masses who have ever been the foundation of the Democratic party. There are two ideas of government. There are those who believe that, if you will only legislate to make the well-to-do prosperous, their prosperity will leak through on those below. The Democratic idea, however, has been that if you legislate to make the masses prosperous, their prosperity will find its way up through every class which rests upon them.

You come to us and tell us that the great cities are in favor of the gold standard; we reply that the great cities rest upon our broad and fertile prairies. Burn down your cities and leave our farms, and your cities will spring up again as if by magic; but destroy our farms and the grass will grow in the streets of every city in the country.

My friends, we declare that this nation is able to legislate for its own people on every question, without waiting for the aid or consent of any other nation on earth; and upon that issue we expect to carry every State in the Union. . . . It is the issue of 1776 over again. Our ancestors, when but three millions in number, had the courage to declare their political independence of every other nation; shall we, their descendants, when we have grown to seventy millions, declare that we are less independent than our forefathers? No, my friends, that will never be the verdict of our people. Therefore, we care not upon what lines the battle is fought. If they say bimetallism is good, but that we cannot have it until other nations help us, we reply that, instead of having a gold standard because England has, we will restore bimetallism, and then let England have bimetallism because the United States has it. If they dare to come out in the open field and defend the gold standard as a good thing, we will fight them to the uttermost. Having behind us the producing masses of this nation and the world, supported by the commercial interests, the laboring interests, and the toilers everywhere, we will answer their demand for a gold standard by saying to them: You shall not press down upon the brow of labor this crown of thorns, you shall not crucify mankind upon a cross of gold.

Questions

1. What reforms did Bryan propose in this speech?
2. Cite some powerful examples of Bryan's use of imagery.
3. How might that imagery have alienated the urban residents whose votes Bryan needed to be elected president?

19-14 On Politics in the 1890s (1918)

Henry Adams

Henry Adams was born in 1838 to one of the most prominent and distinguished families in the United States. Henry's great-grandfather was John Adams, the noted American patriot and the second president of the United States. Henry's grandfather was John Quincy Adams, who was also a U.S. president. Beyond this impressive pedigree, Adams was accomplished in his own right. *The Education of Henry Adams* is one of the most important American autobiographies, a select list that includes the autobiographies of Benjamin Franklin and Malcolm X. Adams was a member of America's elite and he possessed very strong views on American life and politics. The following passage is his evaluation of the significance of national politics in the last decade of the nineteenth century.

Source: Excerpt from "Chicago," in *The Education of Henry Adams: An Autobiography*, by Henry Adams (1918; Cambridge, MA: Riverside Press, 1946), 344–345.

The matter was settled at last by the people. For a hundred years, between 1793 and 1893, the American people had hesitated, vacillated, swayed forward and back, between two forces, one simply industrial, the other capitalistic, centralizing, and mechanical. In 1893, the issue came on the single gold standard, and the majority at last declared itself, once for all, in favor of the capitalistic system with all its necessary machinery. All one's friends, all one's best citizens, reformers, churches, colleges, educated classes, had joined the banks to force submission to capitalism; a submission long foreseen by the mere law of mass. Of all forms of society or government, this was the one he liked least, but his likes or dislikes were as antiquated as the rebel doctrine of State rights. A capitalistic system had been adopted, and if it were to be run at all, it must be run by capital and by capitalistic methods; for nothing could surpass the nonsensity of trying to run so complex and so concentrated a machine by Southern and Western farmers in grotesque alliance with city day-laborers, as had been tried in 1800 and 1828, and had failed even under simple conditions.

Questions

1. According to Henry Adams what, rather than who, prevailed in the political struggles of the 1890s? Explain.
2. What do you think Henry Adams would have thought of William Jennings Bryan's "Cross of Gold" speech? (Document 19-13).

Questions for Further Thought

1. Compare and contrast politics between 1889 and 1892 with politics between 1893 and 1896. The politics of which period more closely resembled the politics of the dozen or so years before 1889?
2. Relate the "Cross of Gold" speech (Document 19-13) to the People's (Populist) Party National Platform of 1892 (Document 19-11) and to earlier farmer and labor protests (see text and documents, Chapters 16–18).
3. To Adams, what was the larger significance of the political turmoil of the 1890s?

CHAPTER TWENTY

The Progressive Era

The Course of Reform

The industrialization and urbanization of the United States improved the quality of life for millions and created vast new opportunities. At the same time, numerous problems accompanied the country's modernization, such as monopoly, political and business corruption, and social injustice. With the vast new concentrations of wealth that occurred in the oil, steel, and other industries, a new and powerful elite emerged. To many observers, democracy itself seemed at risk. In response, a stunning array of calls for reform arose at the local, state, and national levels of government. Some problems defied solution, but many more were tackled with enormous energy and intelligence and with a strong belief in education, expertise, and efficiency.

In Document 20-1, John Dewey offers a rapidly changing nation a progressive vision of education. Walter Rauschenbusch, who had ministered in a New York City slum neighborhood, preaches a new Social Gospel (Document 20-2). Muckraker Lincoln Steffens covers corruption in the country's big cities, including St. Louis (Document 20-3). The term *muckraker* comes from John Bunyan's *The Pilgrim's Progress* (1678) and was applied by Theodore Roosevelt to reporters who raked or stirred up the country's muck. In Document 20-4, Jane Addams reports on life at Hull-House in Chicago. Margaret Sanger, who spearheaded a birth control movement, makes her case in Document 20-5. Document 20-6 is Indiana's pioneering compulsory sterilization law. Governor Robert M. La Follette of Wisconsin deals with political reform in Document 20-7.

20-1 My Pedagogic Creed (1897)

John Dewey

John Dewey (1859–1952), born and raised in Vermont, was a prolific writer. He made original contributions to philosophy, education, and many other subjects, including democracy. Dewey was particularly drawn to the problems of the individual in a society that was being dramatically reshaped by industrial and urban forces. He believed that educational theory and practice had to be changed if the nation's schools were to fulfill their role in a changing democratic society. Dewey's vision of progressive education, which includes such ideas as "learning by doing," has been influential, if controversial.

Source: From *John Dewey: The Early Works, 1882–1898* (Carbondale: Southern Illinois University Press, 1972), 5:*1895–1898,* 84–86. Reproduced by permission of the publisher.

I believe that all education proceeds by the participation of the individual in the social consciousness of the race. This process begins unconsciously almost at birth, and is continually shaping the individual's powers, saturating his consciousness, forming his habits, training his ideas, and arousing his feelings and emotions. Through this unconscious education the individual gradually comes to share in the intellectual and moral resources which humanity has succeeded in getting together. He becomes an inheritor of the funded capital of civilization. The most formal and technical education in the world cannot safely depart from this general process. It can only organize it; or differentiate it in some particular direction.

I believe that the only true education comes through the stimulation of the child's powers by the demands of the social situations in which he finds himself. Through these demands he is stimulated to act as a member of a unity, to emerge from his original narrowness of action and feeling and to conceive of himself from the standpoint of the welfare of the group to which he belongs. Through the responses which others make to his own activities he comes to know what these mean in social terms. The value which they have is reflected back into them. For instance, through the response which is made to the child's instinctive babblings the child comes to know what those babblings mean; they are transformed into articulate language and thus the child is introduced into the consolidated wealth of ideas and emotions which are now summed up in language.

I believe that this educational process has two sides—one psychological and one sociological; and that neither can be subordinated to the other or neglected without evil results following. Of these two sides, the psychological is the basis. The child's own instincts and powers furnish the material and give the starting point for all education. Save as the efforts of the educator connect with some activity which the child is carrying on of his own initiative independent of the educator, education becomes reduced to a pressure from without. It may, indeed, give certain external results but cannot truly be called educative. Without insight into the psychological structure and activities of the individual, the educative process will, therefore, be haphazard and arbitrary. If it chances to coincide with the child's activity it will get a leverage; if it does not, it will result in friction, or disintegration, or arrest of the child nature.

I believe that knowledge of social conditions, of the present state of civilization, is necessary in order properly to interpret the child's powers. The child has his own instincts and tendencies, but we do not know what these mean until we can translate them into their social equivalents. We must be able to carry them back into a social past and see them as the inheritance of previous race activities. We must also be able to project them into the future to see what their outcome and end will be. In the illustration just used, it is the ability to see in the child's babblings the promise and potency of a future social intercourse and conversation which enables one to deal in the proper way with that instinct.

I believe that the psychological and social sides are organically related and that education cannot be regarded as a compromise between the two, or a superimposition of one upon the other. We are told that the psychological definition of education is barren and formal—that it gives us only the idea of a development of all the mental powers without giving us any idea of the use to which these powers are put. On the other hand, it is urged that the social definition of education, as getting adjusted to civilization, makes of it a forced and external process, and results in subordinating the freedom of the individual to a preconceived social and political status.

I believe each of these objections is true when urged against one side isolated from the other. In order to know what a power really is we must know what its end, use, or function is; and this we cannot know save as we conceive of the individual as active in social relationships. But, on the other hand, the only possible adjustment which we can give to the child under existing conditions, is that which arises through putting him in complete possession of all his powers. With the advent of democracy and modern industrial conditions, it is impossible to foretell definitely just what civilization will be twenty years from now. Hence it is impossible to prepare the child for any precise set of conditions. To prepare him for the future life means to give him command of himself; it means so to train him that he will have the full and ready use of all his capacities; that his eye and ear and hand may be tools ready to command, that his judgment may be capable of grasping the conditions under which it has to work, and the executive forces be trained to act economically and efficiently. It is impossible to reach this sort of adjustment save as constant regard is had to the individual's own powers, tastes, and interests—say, that is, as education is continually converted into psychological terms.

In sum, I believe that the individual who is to be educated is a social individual and that society is an organic union of individuals. If we eliminate the social factor from the child we are left only with an abstraction; if we eliminate the individual factor from society, we are left only with an inert and lifeless mass. Education, therefore, must begin with a psychological insight into the child's capacities, interests, and habits. It must be controlled at every point by reference to these same considerations. These powers, interests, and habits must be continually interpreted—we must know what they mean. They must be translated into terms of their social equivalents—into terms of what they are capable of in the way of social service.

Questions

1. To Dewey, what was education?
2. What, according to Dewey, was a school?
3. What was "progressive" about Dewey's creed?

20-2 The Church and the Social Movement (1907)

Walter Rauschenbusch

While serving as the pastor of a Baptist Church in New York's Hell's Kitchen, Walter Rauschenbusch learned firsthand that the poor could not be satisfied merely by exhortations to faith. Rauschenbusch set out to apply the teachings of the Gospels to contemporary urban life. His writings on the Social Gospel, like the following selection from *Christianity and the Social Crisis* (1907), were those of a Christian socialist.

Source: Walter Rauschenbusch, *Christianity and the Social Crisis* (New York: Macmillan, 1907), 304–305, 328–331.

Other organizations may conceivably be indifferent when confronted with the chronic or acute poverty of our cities. The Christian Church cannot. The very name of "Christian" would turn into an indictment if it did not concern itself in the situation in some way.

One answer to the challenge of the Christian spirit has been the organization of institutional church work. A church perhaps organizes a day-nursery or kindergarten; a playground for the children; a meeting-place for young people, or educational facilities for those who are ambitious. It tries to do for people who are living under abnormal conditions what these people under normal conditions ought to do for themselves. This saving helpfulness toward the poor must be distinguished sharply from the money-making efforts of some churches called institutional, which simply run a continuous sacred variety performance.

Confront the Church of Christ with a homeless, playless, joyless, proletarian population, and that is the kind of work to which some Christian spirits will inevitably feel impelled. All honor to me! But it puts a terrible burden on the Church. Institutional work is hard work and costly work. It requires a large plant and an expensive staff. It puts such a strain on the organizing ability and the sympathies of the workers that few can stand it long. The Church by the voluntary gifts and labors of a few here tries to furnish what the entire coöperative community ought to furnish.

Few churches have the resources and leadership to undertake institutional work on a large scale, but most churches in large cities have some institutional features, and all pastors who are at all willing to do it, have institutional work thrust on them. They have to care for the poor. Those of us who passed through the last great industrial depression will never forget the procession of men out of work, out of clothes, out of shoes, and out of hope. They wore down our threshold, and they wore away our hearts. This is the stake of the churches in modern poverty. They are buried at times under a stream of human wreckage. They are turned aside constantly from their more spiritual functions to "serve tables." They have a right, therefore, to inquire who is unloading this burden of poverty and suffering upon them by underpaying, exhausting, and maiming the people. The good Samaritan did not go after the robbers with a shot-gun, but looked after the wounded and helpless man by the wayside. But if hundreds of good Samaritans travelling the same road should find thousands of bruised men groaning to them, they would not be such very good Samaritans if they did not organize a vigilance committee to stop the manufacturing of wounded men. If they did not, presumably the asses who had to lug the wounded to the tavern would have the wisdom to inquire into the causes of their extra work. . . .

In its struggle the working class becomes keenly conscious of the obstacles put in its way by the great institutions of society, the courts, the press, or the Church. It demands not only impartiality, but the kind of sympathy which will condone its mistakes and discern the justice of its cause in spite of the excesses of its followers. When our sympathies are enlisted, we develop a vast faculty for making excuses. If two dogs fight, our own dog is rarely the aggressor. Stealing peaches is a boyish prank when our boy does it, but petty larceny when that dratted boy of our neighbor does it. If the other political party grafts, it is a flagrant shame; if our own party does it, we regret it politely or deny the fact. If Germany annexes a part of Africa, it is brutal aggression; if England does it, she "fulfils her mission of civilization." If the business interests exclude the competition of foreign merchants by a protective tariff, it is a grand national policy; if the trades-unions try to exclude the competition of non-union labor, it is a denial of the right to work and an outrage.

The working class likes to get that kind of sympathy which will take a favorable view of its efforts and its mistakes, and a comprehension of the wrongs under which it suffers. Instead of that the pulpit of late has given its most vigorous interest to the wrongs of those whom militant labor regards as traitors to its cause. It has been more concerned with the fact that some individuals were barred from a job by the unions, than with the fact that the entire wage-working class is debarred from the land, from the tools of production, and from their fair share in the proceeds of production.

It cannot well be denied that there is an increasing alienation between the working class and the churches. That alienation is most complete wherever our industrial development has advanced farthest and has created a distinct class of wage-workers. Several causes have contributed. Many have dropped away because they cannot afford to take their share in the expensive maintenance of a church in a large city. Others because the tone, the spirit, the point of view in the churches, is that of another social class. The commercial and professional classes dominate the spiritual atmosphere in the large city churches. As the workingmen grow more class-conscious, they come to regard the business men as their antagonists and the possessing classes as exploiters who live on their labor, and they resent it when persons belonging to these classes address them with the tone of moral superiority. When ministers handle the labor question, they often seem to the working class partial against them even when the ministers think they are most impartial. Foreign workingmen bring with them the long-standing distrust for the clergy and the Church as tools of oppression which they have learned abroad, and they perpetuate that attitude here. The churches of America suffer for the sins of the churches abroad. The "scientific socialism" imported from older countries through its literature and its advocates is saturated with materialistic philosophy and is apt to create dislike and antagonism for the ideas and institutions of religion.

Thus in spite of the favorable equipment of the Church in America there is imminent danger that the working people will pass from indifference to hostility, from religious enthusiasm to anti-religious bitterness. That would be one of the most unspeakable calamities that could come upon the Church. If we would only take warning by the fate of the churches in Europe, we might avert the desolation that threatens us. We may well be glad that in nearly every city there are a few ministers who are known as the outspoken friends of labor. Their fellow-ministers may regard them as radicals, lacking in balance, and very likely they are; but in the present situation they are among the most valuable servants of the Church. The workingmen see that there is at least a minority in the Church that champions their cause, and that fact helps to keep their judgment in hopeful suspense about the Church at large. Men who are just as one-sided in favor of capitalism pass as sane and conservative men. If the capitalist class have their court-chaplains, it is only fair that the army of labor should have its army-chaplains who administer the consolations of religion to militant labor.

Thus the Church has a tremendous stake in the social crisis. It may try to maintain an attitude of neutrality, but neither side will permit it. If it is quiescent, it thereby throws its influence on the side of things as they are, and the class which aspires to a fitter place in the organization of society will feel the great spiritual force of the Church as a dead weight against it. If it loses the loyalty and trust of the working class, it loses the very class in which it originated, to which its founders belonged, and which has lifted it to power. If it becomes a religion of the upper classes, it condemns itself to a slow and comfortable death. Protestantism from the outset entered into an intimate alliance with the intelligence and wealth of the city population. As the cities grew in importance since the Reformation, as commerce overshadowed agriculture, and as the business class crowded the feudal aristocracy out of its leading position since the French Revolution, Protestantism throve with the class which had espoused it. It lifted its class, and its class lifted it.

Questions

1. In Rauschenbusch's opinion, why were churches supposed to help the poor?
2. What consequences did Rauschenbusch fear if churches failed to act?
3. Would (and should) the First Amendment have interfered with Rauschenbusch's call for an activist faith? Why or why not?

20-3 Tweed Days in St. Louis (1902)

Lincoln Steffens

Lincoln Steffens (1866–1936), born and educated in California, was a pioneer in muckraking and became famous for his searing accounts of municipal corruption. Steffens provided his readers with an informed, if sensational, look into how cities were really governed, and he epitomized the reform-minded journalism that was popular in the Progressive Era. Steffens's urban subjects included St. Louis, Minneapolis, Pittsburgh, New York, Philadelphia, and Chicago. These pieces, which appeared in *McClure's* magazine, were collected in *The Shame of the Cities* (1904). Here Steffens exposes the "shame" of St. Louis, which he likens to that of New York City. "Tweed," which appears in the title, refers to New York's Tweed Ring, the notoriously corrupt political machine that was led by William Marcy Tweed and controlled the city.

Source: Lincoln Steffens, *The Shame of the Cities* (New York: McClure, Phillips & Co., 1904), 29–36.

St. Louis, the fourth city in size in the United States, is making two announcements to the world: one that it is the worst-governed city in the land; the other that it wishes all men to come there (for the World's Fair) and see it. It isn't our worst-governed city; Philadelphia is that. But St. Louis is worth examining while we have it inside out. . . .

The corruption of St. Louis came from the top. The best citizens—the merchants and big financiers—used to rule the town, and they ruled it well. They set out to outstrip Chicago. The commercial and industrial war between these two cities was at one time a picturesque and dramatic spectacle such as is witnessed only in our country. Business men were not mere merchants and the politicians were not mere grafters; the two kinds of citizens got together and wielded the power of banks, railroads, factories, the prestige of the city, and the spirit of its citizens to gain business and population. And it was a close race. Chicago, having the start, always led, but St. Louis had pluck, intelligence, and tremendous energy. It pressed Chicago hard. It excelled in a sense of civic beauty and good government; and there are those who think yet it might have won. But a change occurred. Public spirit became private spirit, public enterprise became private greed.

Along about 1890, public franchises and privileges were sought, not only for legitimate profit and common convenience, but for loot. Taking but slight and always selfish interest in the public councils, the big men misused politics. The riff-raff, catching the smell of corruption, rushed into the Municipal Assembly, drove out the remaining respectable men, and sold the city—its streets, its wharves, its markets, and all that it had—to the now greedy business men and bribers. In other words, when the leading men began to devour their own city, the herd rushed into the trough and fed also.

So gradually has this occurred that these same citizens hardly realize it. Go to St. Louis and you will find the habit of civic pride in them; they still boast. The visitor is told of the wealth of the residents, of the financial strength of the banks, and of the growing importance of the industries, yet he sees poorly paved, refuse-burdened streets, and dusty or mud-covered alleys; he passes a ramshackle fire-trap crowded with the sick, and learns that it is the City Hospital; he enters the "Four Courts," and his nostrils are greeted by the odor of formaldehyde used as a disinfectant, and insect powder spread to destroy vermin; he calls at the new City Hall, and finds half the entrance boarded with pine planks to cover up the unfinished interior. Finally, he turns a tap in the hotel, to see liquid mud flow into wash-basin or bath-tub.

The St. Louis charter vests legislative power of great scope in a Municipal Assembly, which is composed of a council and a House of Delegates. Here is a description of the latter by one of Mr. Folk's grand juries:

"We have had before us many of those who have been, and most of those who are now, members of the House of Delegates. We found a number of these utterly illiterate and lacking in ordinary intelligence, unable to give a better reason for favoring or opposing a measure than a desire to act with the majority. In some, no trace of mentality or morality could be found; in others, a low order of training appeared, united with base cunning, groveling instincts, and sordid desires. Unqualified to respond to the ordinary requirements of life, they are utterly incapable of comprehending the significance of an ordinance, and are incapacitated, both by nature and training, to be the makers of laws. The choosing of such men to be legislators makes a travesty of justice, sets a premium on incompetency, and deliberately poisons the very source of the law."

These creatures were well organized. They had a "combine"—a legislative institution—which the grand jury described as follows:

"Our investigation, covering more or less fully a period of ten years, shows that, with few exceptions, no ordinance has been passed wherein valuable privileges or franchises are granted until those interested have paid the legislators the money demanded for action in the particular case. Combines in both branches of the Municipal Assembly are formed by members sufficient in number to control legislation. To one member of this combine is delegated the authority to act for the combine, and to receive and to distribute to each member the money agreed upon as the price of his vote in support of, or opposition to, a pending measure. So long has this practice existed that such members have come to regard the receipt of money for action on pending measures as a legitimate perquisite of a legislator."

One legislator consulted a lawyer with the intention of suing a firm to recover an unpaid balance on a fee for the grant of a switch-way. Such difficulties rarely occurred, however. In order to insure a regular and indisputable revenue, the combine of each house drew up a schedule of bribery prices for all possible sorts of grants, just such a list as commercial traveler takes out on the road with him. There was a price for a grain elevator, a price for a short switch; side tracks were charged for by the linear foot, but at rates which varied according to the nature of the ground taken; a street improvement cost so much; wharf space was classified and precisely rated. As there was a scale for favorable legislation, so there was one for defeating bills. It made a difference in the price if there was opposition, and it made a difference whether the privilege asked was legitimate or not. But nothing was passed free of charge. Many of the legislators were saloon-keepers—it was in St. Louis that a practical joker nearly emptied the House of Delegates by tipping a boy to rush into a session and call out, "Mister, your saloon is on fire,"—but even the saloon-keepers of a neighborhood had to pay to keep in their inconvenient locality a market which public interest would have moved.

From the Assembly, bribery spread into other departments. Men empowered to issue peddlers' licenses and permits to citizens who wished to erect awnings or use a portion of the sidewalk for storage purposes charged an amount in excess of the prices stipulated by law, and pocketed the difference. The city's money was loaned at interest, and the interest was converted into private bank accounts. City carriages were used by the wives and children of city officials. Supplies for public institutions found their way to private tables; one itemized account for food furnished the poorhouse included California jellies, imported cheeses, and French wines! A member of the Assembly caused the incorporation of a grocery company, with his sons and daughters the ostensible stockholders, and succeeded in having his bid for city supplies accepted although the figures were in excess of his competitors'. In return for the favor thus shown, he indorsed a measure to award the contract for city printing to another member, and these two voted aye on a bill granting to a third the exclusive right to furnish city dispensaries with drugs.

Men ran into debt to the extent of thousands of dollars for the sake of election to either branch of the Assembly. One night, on a street car going to the City Hall, a new member remarked that the nickel he handed the conductor was his last. The next day he deposited $5,000 in a savings bank. A member of the House of Delegates admitted to the Grand Jury that his dividends from the combine netted $25,000 in one year; a Councilman stated that he was paid $50,000 for his vote on a single measure.

Bribery was a joke. A newspaper reporter overheard this conversation one evening in the corridor of the City Hall:

"Ah there, my boodler!" said Mr. Delegate.

"Say there, my grafter!" replied Mr. Councilman. "Can you lend me a hundred for a day or two?"

"Not at present. But I can spare it if the Z—— bill goes through to-night. Meet me at F——'s later."

"All right, my jailbird; I'll be there."

Questions

1. What role did muckrakers like Steffens play in bringing about political reform?
2. How do the tone and coverage of Julian Ralph's 1893 article on Denver (Document 18-2) differ from Steffens's 1902 piece on St. Louis?

20-4 *Twenty Years at Hull-House* (1910)

Jane Addams

The text makes clear that settlement houses not only did "modest good" in poor neighborhoods but also gave meaning to the lives of those who served in them, providing these settlement-house workers with an understanding of both social reform and the class, ethnic, and political realities of city life (see text pp. 614–615). In this selection, Jane Addams (1860–1935), of Hull-House in Chicago, recounts part of her education in social work.

Source: Jane Addams, *Twenty Years at Hull-House: With Autobiographical Notes* (Phillips, 1910; reprint, New York: New American Library, n.d.), 200–204.

One of the striking features of our neighborhood twenty years ago, and one to which we never became reconciled, was the presence of huge wooden garbage boxes fastened to the street pavement in which the undisturbed refuse accumulated day by day. The system of garbage collecting was inadequate throughout the city but it became the greatest menace in a ward such as ours, where the normal amount of waste was much increased by the decayed fruit and vegetables discarded by the Italian and Greek fruit peddlers, and by the residuum left over from the piles of filthy rags which were fished out of the city dumps and brought to the homes of the rag pickers for further sorting and washing.

The children of our neighborhood twenty years ago played their games in and around these huge garbage boxes. They were the first objects that the toddling child learned to climb; their bulk afforded a barricade and their contents provided missiles in all the battles of the older boys; and finally they became the seats upon which absorbed lovers held enchanted converse. We are obliged to remember that all children eat everything which they find and that odors have a curious and intimate power of entwining themselves into our tenderest memories, before even the residents of Hull-House can understand their own early enthusiasm for the removal of these boxes and the establishment of a better system of refuse collection.

It is easy for even the most conscientious citizen of Chicago to forget the foul smells of the stockyards and the garbage dumps, when he is living so far from them that he is only occasionally made conscious of their existence, but the residents of a Settlement are perforce constantly surrounded by them. During our first three years on Halsted Street, we had established a small incinerator at Hull-House and we had many times reported the untoward conditions of the ward to the city hall. We had also arranged many talks for the immigrants, pointing out that although a woman may sweep her own doorway in her native village and allow the refuse to innocently decay in the open air and sunshine, in a crowded city quarter, if the garbage is not properly collected and destroyed, a tenement-house mother may see her children sicken and die, and that the immigrants must therefore not only keep their own houses clean, but must also help the authorities to keep the city clean.

Possibly our efforts slightly modified the worst conditions, but they still remained intolerable, and the fourth summer the situation became for me absolutely desperate when I realized in a moment of panic that my delicate little nephew for whom I was guardian could not be with me at Hull-House at all unless the sickening odors were reduced. I may well be ashamed that other delicate children who were torn from their families, not into boarding school but into eternity, had not long before driven me into effective action. Under the direction of the first man who came as a resident to Hull-House we began a systematic investigation of the city system of garbage collection, both as to its efficiency in other wards and its possible connection with the death rate in the various wards of the city.

The Hull-House Woman's Club had been organized the year before by the resident kindergartner who had first inaugurated a mothers' meeting. The members came together, however, in quite a new way that summer when we discussed with them the high death rate so persistent in our ward. After several club meetings devoted to the subject, despite the fact that the death rate rose highest in the congested foreign colonies and not in the streets in which most of the Irish American club women lived, twelve of their number undertook in connection with the residents, to carefully investigate the condition of the alleys. During August and September the substantiated reports of violations of the law sent in from Hull-House to the health department were one thousand and thirty-seven. For the club woman who had finished a long day's work of washing or ironing followed by the cooking of a hot supper, it would have been much easier to sit on her doorstep during a summer evening than to go up and down ill-kept alleys and get into trouble with her neighbors over the condition of their garbage boxes. It required both civic enterprise and moral conviction to be willing to do this three evenings a week during the hottest and most uncomfortable months of the year. Nevertheless, a certain number of women persisted, as did the residents, and three city inspectors in succession were transferred from the ward because of unsatisfactory services. Still the death rate remained high and the condition seemed little improved throughout the next winter. In sheer desperation, the following spring when the city contracts were awarded for the removal of garbage, with the backing of two well-known business men, I put in a bid for the garbage removal of the nineteenth ward. My paper was thrown out on a technicality but the incident induced the mayor to appoint me the garbage inspector of the ward.

The salary was a thousand dollars a year, and the loss of that political "plum" made a great stir among the politicians. The position was no sinecure whether regarded from the point of view of getting up at six in the morning to see that the men were early at work; or of following the loaded wagons, uneasily dropping their contents at intervals, to their dreary destination at the dump; or of insisting that the contractor must increase the number of his wagons from nine to thirteen and from thirteen to seventeen, although he assured me that he lost money on every one and that the former inspector had let him off with seven; or of taking careless landlords into court because they would not provide the proper garbage receptacles; or of arresting the tenant who tried to make the garbage wagons carry away the contents of his stable.

With the two or three residents who nobly stood by, we set up six of those doleful incinerators which are supposed to burn garbage with the fuel collected in the alley itself. The one factory in town which could utilize old tin cans was a window weight factory, and we deluged that with ten times as many tin cans as it could use — much less would pay for. We made desperate attempts to have the dead animals removed by the contractor who was paid most liberally by the city for that purpose but who, we slowly discovered, always made the police ambulances do the work, delivering the carcasses upon freight cars for shipment to a soap factory in Indiana where they were sold for a good price although the contractor himself was the largest stockholder in the concern. Perhaps our greatest achievement was the discovery of a pavement eighteen inches under the surface in a narrow street, although after it was found we triumphantly discovered a record of its existence in the city archives. The Italians living on the street were much interested but displayed little astonishment, perhaps because they were accustomed to see buried cities exhumed. This pavement became the *casus belli* [cause of war] between myself and the street commissioner when I insisted that its restoration belonged to him, after I had removed the first eight inches of garbage. The matter was finally settled by the mayor himself, who permitted me to drive him to the entrance of the street in what the children called my "garbage phaëton" and who took my side of the controversy.

Questions

1. How was garbage collected in Chicago?
2. Why were conditions bad in the neighborhood around Hull-House?
3. What did Addams accomplish as a garbage inspector?

20-5 *The Case for Birth Control* (1917)

Margaret Sanger

Margaret Sanger (1883–1966), born to a free-thinking Irish father and a religious Irish American Catholic mother, championed the cause of birth control in the United States. She encountered opposition not only from traditionalists but also from progressives like Theodore Roosevelt who were fearful of "race suicide" among "the better element," even as "the lower classes" grew in numbers (see text pp. 627–632). Since 1873, the federal "Comstock law" had proscribed as "obscene" the mailing of birth control devices and information; state laws also provided obstacles to the birth control movement.

Source: Margaret Sanger, *The Case for Birth Control* (New York: Modern Art, 1917), 5–7, 8–11, in Elliott J. Gorn, Randy Roberts, and Terry D. Bilhartz, eds., *Constructing the American Past: A Source Book of a People's History* (New York: HarperCollins, 1991), 2:205–210.

(*The following is the case for birth control, as I found it during my fourteen years' experience as a trained nurse in New York City and vicinity. It appeared as a special article in "Physical Culture," April 1917, and has been delivered by me as a lecture throughout the United States. It is a brief summary of facts and conditions, as they exist in this country.*)

For centuries woman has gone forth with man to till the fields, to feed and clothe the nations. She has sacrificed her life to populate the earth. She has overdone her labors. She now steps forth and demands that women shall cease producing in ignorance. To do this she must have knowledge to control birth. This is the first immediate step she must take toward the goal of her freedom.

Those who are opposed to this are simply those who do not know. Any one who like myself has worked among the people and found on one hand an ever-increasing population with its ever-increasing misery, poverty and ignorance, and on the other hand a stationary or decreasing population with its increasing wealth and higher standards of living, greater freedom, joy and happiness, cannot doubt that birth control is the livest issue of the day and one on which depends the future welfare of the race.

Before I attempt to refute the arguments against birth control, I should like to tell you something of the conditions I met with as a trained nurse and of the experience that convinced me of its necessity and led me to jeopardize my liberty in order to place this information in the hands of the women who need it.

My first clear impression of life was that large families and poverty went hand in hand. I was born and brought up in a glass factory town in the western part of New York State. I was one of eleven children — so I had some personal experience of the struggles and hardships a large family endures.

When I was seventeen years old my mother died from overwork and the strain of too frequent childbearing. I was left to care for the younger children and share the burdens of all. When I was old enough I entered a hospital to take up the profession of nursing.

In the hospital I found that seventy-five percent of the diseases of men and women are the result of ignorance of their sex functions. I found that every department of life was open to investigation and discussion except that shaded valley of sex. The explorer, scientist, inventor, may go forth in their various fields for investigation and return to lay the fruits of their discoveries at the feet of society. But woe to him who dares explore that forbidden realm of sex. No matter how pure the motive, no matter what miseries he sought to remove, slanders, persecutions and jail await him who dares bear the light of knowledge into that cave of darkness.

So great was the ignorance of the women and girls I met concerning their own bodies that I decided to specialize in woman's diseases and took up gynecological and obstetrical nursing.

A few years of this work brought me to a shocking discovery—that knowledge of the methods of controlling birth was accessible to the women of wealth while the working women were deliberately kept in ignorance of this knowledge!

I found that the women of the working class were as anxious to obtain this knowledge as their sisters of wealth, but that they were told that there are laws on the statute books against imparting it to them. And the medical profession was most religious in obeying these laws when the patient was a poor woman.

I found that the women of the working class had emphatic views on the crime of bringing children into the world to die of hunger. They would rather risk their lives through abortion than give birth to little ones they could not feed and care for.

For the laws against imparting this knowledge force these women into the hands of the filthiest midwives and the quack abortionists—unless they bear unwanted children—with the consequence that the deaths from abortions are almost wholly among the working-class women.

No other country in the world has so large a number of abortions nor so large a number of deaths of women resulting therefrom as the United States of America. Our law makers close their virtuous eyes. A most conservative estimate is that there are 250,000 abortions performed in this country every year.

How often have I stood at the bedside of a woman in childbirth and seen the tears flowing in gladness and heard the sigh of "Thank God" when told that her child was born dead! What can man know of the fear and dread of unwanted pregnancy? What can man know of the agony of carrying beneath one's heart a little life which tells the mother every instant that it cannot survive? Even were it born alive the chances are that it would perish within a year.

Do you know that three hundred thousand babies under one year of age die in the United States every year from poverty and neglect, while six hundred thousand parents remain in ignorance of how to prevent three hundred thousand more babies from coming into the world the next year to die of poverty and neglect?

I found from records concerning women of the underworld that eighty-five percent of them come from parents averaging nine living children. And that fifty percent of these are mentally defective.

We know, too, that among mentally defective parents the birth rate is four times as great as that of the normal parent. Is this not cause for alarm? Is it not time for our physicians, social workers and scientists to face this array of facts and stop quibbling about woman's morality? I say this because it is these same people who raise objection to birth control on the ground that it *may* cause women to be immoral.

Solicitude for woman's morals has ever been the cloak Authority has worn in its age-long conspiracy to keep women in bondage. . . .

Is woman's health not to be considered? Is she to remain a producing machine? Is she to have time to think, to study, to care for herself? Man cannot travel to his goal alone. And until woman has knowledge to control birth she cannot get the time to think and develop. Until she has the time to think, neither the suffrage question nor the social question nor the labor question will interest her, and she will remain the drudge that she is and her husband the slave that he is just as long as they continue to supply the market with cheap labor.

Let me ask you: Has the State any more right to ravish a woman against her will by keeping her in ignorance than a man has through brute force? Has the State a better right to decide when she shall bear offspring?

Picture a woman with five or six little ones living on the average working man's wage of ten dollars a week. The mother is broken in health and spirit, a worn out shadow of the woman she once was. Where is the man or woman who would reproach me for trying to put into this woman's hands knowledge that will save her from giving birth to any more babies doomed to certain poverty and misery and perhaps to disease and death?

Am I to be classed as immoral because I advocate small families for the working class while Mr. Roosevelt can go up and down the length of the land shouting and urging these women to have large families and is neither arrested nor molested but considered by all society as highly moral?

But I ask you which is the more moral—to urge this class of women to have only those children she desires and can care for, or to delude her into breeding thoughtlessly. Which is America's definition of morality?

You will agree with me that a woman should be free.

Yet no adult woman who is ignorant of the means to prevent conception can call herself free.

No woman can call herself free who cannot choose the time to be a mother or not as she sees fit. This should be woman's first demand.

Our present laws force women into one of two ways: Celibacy, with its nervous results, or abortion. All modern physicians testify that both these conditions are harmful; that celibacy is the cause of many nervous complaints, while abortion is a disgrace to a civilized community. Physicians claim that early marriage with knowledge to control birth would do away with both. For this would enable two young people to live and work together until such time as they could care for a family. I found that young people desire early marriage, and would marry early were it not for the dread of a large family to support. Why will not society countenance and advance this idea? Because it is still afraid of the untried and the unknown.

I saw that fortunes were being spent in establishing baby nurseries, where new babies are brought and cared for while the mothers toil in sweatshops during the day. I saw that society with its well-intentioned palliatives was in this respect like the quack, who cures a cancer by burning off the top while the deadly disease continues to spread underneath. I never felt this more strongly than I did three years ago, after the death of the patient in my last nursing case.

This patient was the wife of a struggling working man—the mother of three children—who was suffering from the results of a self-attempted abortion. I found her in a very serious condition, and for three weeks both the attending physician and myself labored night and day to bring her out of the Valley of the Shadow of Death. We finally succeeded in restoring her to her family.

I remember well the day I was leaving. The physician, too, was making his last call. As the doctor put out his hand to say "Good-bye," I saw the patient had something to say to him, but was shy and timid about saying it. I started to leave the room, but she called me back and said:

"Please don't go. How can both of you leave me without telling me what I can do to avoid another illness such as I have just passed through?"

I was interested to hear what the answer of the physician would be, and I went back and sat down beside her in expectation of hearing a sympathetic reply. To my amazement, he answered her with a joking sneer. We came away.

Three months later, I was aroused from my sleep one midnight. A telephone call from the husband of the same woman requested me to come immediately as she was dangerously ill. I arrived to find her beyond relief. Another conception had forced her into the hands of a cheap abortionist, and she died at four o'clock the same morning, leaving behind her three small children and a frantic husband.

I returned home as the sun was coming over the roofs of the Human Bee-Hive, and I realized how futile my efforts and my work had been. I, too, like the philanthropists and social workers, had been dealing with the symptoms rather than the disease. I threw my nursing bag into the corner and announced to my family that I would never take another case until I had made it possible for working women in America to have knowledge of birth control.

I found, to my utter surprise, that there was very little scientific information on the question available in America. Although nearly every country in Europe had this knowledge, we were the only civilized people in the world whose postal laws forbade it.

The tyranny of the censorship of the post office is the greatest menace to liberty in the United States to-day. The post office was never intended to be a moral or ethical institution. It was intended to be mechanically efficient; certainly not to pass upon the opinions in the matter it conveys. If we concede this power to this institution, which is only a public service, we might just as well give to the streetcar companies and railroads the right to refuse to carry passengers whose ideas they do not like.

I will not take up the story of the publication of "The Woman Rebel." You know how I began to publish it, how it was confiscated and suppressed by the post office authorities, how I was indicted and arrested for bringing it out, and how the case was postponed time and time again and finally dismissed by Judge Clayton in the Federal Court.

These, and many more obstacles and difficulties were put in the path of this philosophy and this work to suppress it if possible and discredit it in any case.

My work has been to arouse interest in the subject of birth control in America, and in this, I feel that I have been successful. The work now before us is to crystallize and to organize this interest into action, not only for the repeal of the laws but for the establishment of free clinics in every large center of population in the country where scientific, individual information may be given every adult person who comes to ask it. . . .

The free clinic is the solution for our problem. It will enable women to help themselves, and will have much to do with disposing of this soul-crushing charity which is at best a mere temporary relief.

Woman must be protected from incessant childbearing before she can actively participate in the social life. She must triumph over Nature's and Man's laws which have kept her in bondage. Just as man has triumphed over Nature by the use of electricity, shipbuilding, bridges, etc., so must woman triumph over the laws which have made her a childbearing machine.

Questions

1. What was Sanger's position regarding marriage? regarding abortion? regarding celibacy?
2. What, according to Sanger, would knowledge and the practice of birth control offer women?
3. What does the excerpt reveal about Sanger's attitudes toward social classes?

20-6 Progressivism and Compulsory Sterilization (1907)

Progressive Era debates over immigration and birth control included frequent references to the threat to American society posed by "inferior" people or groups. Eugenics, which sought to improve human heredity by selective breeding, influenced the policy of states regarding categories of people deemed hereditarily unfit to reproduce—for example, by prohibiting them from marrying or by sterilizing such men and women in state facilities, thus reducing the risks to society of their release. Indiana enacted the first such law in 1907 (reproduced in this selection); over the next thirty years, a number of other states followed suit.

In *Buck v. Bell* (1927), the U.S. Supreme Court upheld, 8–1, the constitutionality of Virginia's compulsory sterilization law, viewing it as protective of individuals and society, analogous to the compulsory vaccination of children in public schools, even though others were not required to undergo vaccination. Of Carrie Buck, allegedly feeble-minded, the child of a feeble-minded mother, and the mother of a feeble-minded child, Justice Oliver Wendell Holmes Jr. declared that rather than "waiting to execute degenerate offspring . . . or to let them starve for their imbecility, society can prevent those who are manifestly unfit from continuing their kind. . . . Three generations of imbeciles are enough."

Source: Laws of the State of Indiana, 1907, 377–378.

PREAMBLE

Whereas, Heredity plays a most important part in the transmission of crime, idiocy and imbecility;

PENAL INSTITUTIONS—SURGICAL OPERATIONS

Therefore, *Be it enacted by the general assembly of the State of Indiana*, That on and after the passage of this act it shall be compulsory for each and every institution in the state, entrusted with the care of confirmed criminals, idiots, rapists and imbeciles, to appoint upon its staff, in addition to the regular institutional physician, two (2) skilled surgeons of recognized ability, whose duty it shall be, in conjunction with the chief physician of the institution, to examine the mental and physical condition of such inmates as are recommended by the institutional physician and board of managers. If, in the judgment of this committee of experts and the board of managers, procreation is inadvisable and there is no probability of improvement of the mental condition of the inmate, it shall be lawful for the surgeons to perform such operation for the prevention of procreation as shall be decided safest and most effective. But this operation shall not be performed except in cases that have been pronounced unimprovable: *Provided*, That in no case shall the consultation fee be more than three ($3.00) dollars to each expert, to be paid out of the funds appropriated for the maintenance of such institution.

Questions

1. What assumption was made in the statute's preamble?
2. Which types of inmates were considered to be eligible for sterilization?
3. Did the screening process respect an inmate's human rights?
4. Besides procreation, what did the legislation seem to be intended to control?

20-7 Autobiography (1913)

Robert M. La Follette

Although he spent some thirty years in public office, Robert M. La Follette (1855–1925) was anything but a professional politician in the conventional sense. As a Wisconsin congressman, governor, and senator, La Follette left no doubt that he stood on the side of reform. His emphasis on social reform and expert administration during his governorship

(1901–1905) became known nationally as the Wisconsin Idea. In this excerpt from his autobiography, La Follette recalls his attempts to pass legislation involving direct primary elections and railroad taxation. Although both measures were defeated in the 1901 legislative session, La Follette ultimately succeeded in having them passed.

Source: Robert M. La Follette, *La Follette's Autobiography: A Personal Narrative of Political Experiences* (Madison, WI: Robert M. La Follette, 1913; reprint, Madison: University of Wisconsin Press, 1960), 105–108, 111.

All the governors before me, so far as I know, had sent in their messages to the legislature to be mumbled over by a reading clerk. I knew that I could make a very much stronger impression with my recommendations if I could present my message in person to the legislature in joint session. I felt that it would invest the whole matter with a new seriousness and dignity that would not only affect the legislators themselves, but react upon the public mind. This I did: and in consequence awakened a wide interest in my recommendations throughout the state.

The predominant notes in the message were direct primaries and railroad taxation—one political and one economic reform.

The railroads at that time paid taxes in the form of a license fee upon their gross earnings. The report of the Tax Commission showed that while real property in Wisconsin paid 1.19 per cent. of its market value in taxes, the railroads paid only .53 per cent. of their market value (based on the average value of stocks and bonds) or less than one half the rate paid by farmers, manufacturers, home owners and others. Upon this showing we contended that the railroads were not bearing their fair share of the burdens of the state. The Tax Commission suggested two measures of reform. One of their bills provided for a simple increase in the license tax, the other provided for a physical valuation of the railroads and a wholly new system of taxation upon an ad valorem basis, measures which I had earnestly advocated in my campaign speeches, and recommended in my message. I regarded this latter as the more scientific method of taxation. The Commission stated that while they had so framed the bills as to err on the side of injustice to the people rather than to the railroads, the passage of either of them would mean an increase of taxes paid by railroads and other public service corporations of more than three quarters of a million dollars annually.

No sooner had the taxation and direct primary bills been introduced than the lobby gathered in Madison in full force. Lobbyists had been there before, but never in such numbers or with such an organization. I never saw anything like it. The railroads, threatened with the taxation bills, and the bosses, threatened by the direct primary, evidently regarded it as the death struggle. Not only were the regular lobbyists in attendance but they made a practice during the entire winter of bringing in delegations of more or less influential men from all parts of the state, some of whom often remained two or three weeks and brought every sort of pressure to bear on the members of the legislature. The whole fight was centred upon me personally. They thought that if they could crush me, that would stop the movement. How little they understood! Even if they had succeeded in eliminating me, the movement, which is fundamental, would still have swept on! They sought to build up in the minds of the people the fear that the executive was controlling the legislative branch of the government. They deliberately organized a campaign of abuse and misrepresentation. Their stories were minutely detailed and spread about among the hotels and on railroad trains. They said that I had completely lost my head. They endeavored to give me a reputation for discourtesy and browbeating; stories were told of my shameless treatment of members, of my backing them up against the wall of the executive office, shaking my fist in their faces and warning them if they did not pass our bills I would use all my power to crush them. In so far as anything was said in disparagement of the administration members of the legislature it was that they were sycophants who took their orders every morning from the executive office. The newspapers, controlled by the machine interests, began to print these abusive statements and sent them broadcast. At first we took no notice of their campaign of misrepresentation, but it grew and grew until it got on the nerves of all of us. It came to be a common thing to have one after another of my friends drop in and say: "Governor, is it true that you have had a row with ——? Is it true that you ordered —— out of the executive office?"

It seems incredible, as I look back upon it now, that it could be humanly possible to create such an atmosphere of distrust. We felt that we were fighting something in the dark all the while; there was nothing we could get hold of.

In spite of it all, however, we drove straight ahead. After the bills prepared by the Tax Commission were in, the primary election bill was drafted and redrafted and introduced by E. Ray Stevens of Madison, one of the ablest men ever in public life in Wisconsin, and now a judge of the circuit court of the state. The committee having it in charge at once began a series of open meetings, and the lobby brought to Madison people from every part of the state to attend the hearings and to protest. Extended speeches were made against it, and these were promptly printed and sent broadcast. The most preposterous arguments were advanced. They argued that the proposed law was unconstitutional because it interfered with the "right of the people to assemble!" They tried to rouse the country people by arguing that it favored the cities; they said that city people could get out more readily to primaries than country people. It did not seem to occur to them that practically every argument they made against the direct primary applied far more strongly to the old caucus and convention system.

But we fought as vigorously as they, and presently it began to appear that we might get some of our measures through. It evidently made an impression on the lobby. One night, after the legislature had been in session about two months, Emanuel Phillipp came to my office. He moved his chair up close to mine.

"Now, look here," he said, "you want to pass the primary election bill, don't you? I will help you put it through."

"Phillipp," I said, "there is no use in you and me trying to mislead each other. I understand and you understand that the senate is organized against both the direct primary and taxation bills. You know that better than I do."

"Well," he said, "now look here. This railroad taxation matter—wouldn't you be willing to let that go if you could get your primary bill through? What good will it do you, anyhow, to increase railroad taxation? We can meet that all right just by raising rates or by changing a classification here and there. No one will know it and we can take back every cent of increased taxes in rates from the people."

"Phillipp," I said, "you have just driven in and clinched the argument for regulating your rates. And that is the next thing we are going to do. No," I said, "these pledges are straight promises."

"But," he argued, "if you can get this primary election bill through you will have done a great thing. And I will pass it for you, if you will let up on railroad taxation."

"Just how will you pass it?" I asked.

"How will I pass it?" he repeated. "How will I pass it? Why, I'll take those fellows over to a room in the Park Hotel, close the door and stand them up against the wall. And I'll say to them, 'You vote for the primary election bill!' And they'll vote for it, because I own them, they're mine!" And this was Phillipp's last interview with me. . . .

When we continued to make progress in spite of all this opposition the lobby made another move against us. It brought to bear all the great influence of the federal office-holders who were especially disturbed over the possible effect of a direct primary upon their control of the state. United States District Attorney Wheeler, an appointee of Spooner, and the United States District Attorney of the Eastern District, an appointee of Quarles, were much on the ground; so were United States Marshal Monahan and Collector of Internal Revenue Fink.

Finally, before the vote on the direct primary was taken in the senate, Senator Spooner, who rarely came to Wisconsin while Congress was in session, appeared in Madison. He was there only a few days, but he was visited by members of the senate, and we felt his influence strongly against us.

All the efforts of the lobby, combined with the opposition of the newspapers and the federal office-holders, was not without its effect upon our forces. Every moment from the time the senate convened down to the final vote on the railroad taxation bills they were weakening us, wearing us down, getting some men one way, some another, until finally before the close of the session they had not only the senate but a majority of the Republicans in the assembly. It was a pathetic and tragic thing to see honest men falling before these insidious forces. For many of them it meant plain ruin from which they never afterward recovered.

In order to make very clear the methods employed I shall here relate in detail the stories of several of the cases which came directly under my own observation. I shall withhold the real names of the Senators and Assemblymen concerned, because many of them were the victims of forces and temptations far greater than they could resist. If I could also give the names of the men really responsible for the corruption, bribery and debauchery—the men higher up, the men behind the lobbyists—I would do it without hesitation.

Questions

1. How did La Follette signal that he was different from previous governors?
2. What were the elements of his railroad tax proposal?
3. According to La Follette, how did the opposition counterattack?

Questions for Further Thought

1. How did the views of Morrill (Document 17-1) and Dewey (Document 20-1) on education agree? How did they differ?
2. What intellectual and moral traits did Jane Addams (Document 20-4), Margaret Sanger (Document 20-5), and Robert M. La Follette (Document 20-7) share?
3. What were the strengths and weaknesses of the reformers of the Progressive Era?

Progressivism and National Politics

Politics in the Progressive Era never lacked excitement. Tom Johnson, the mayor of Cleveland from 1901 to 1909, used circus tents to house his political rallies; an advocate of the single tax (on real estate, especially land held for speculation) and municipal ownership of public utilities, Johnson raced from rally to rally in his car, the Red Devil. Wisconsin governor and U.S. senator Robert La Follette was so combative that he earned the nickname Fighting Bob. And then there was Theodore Roosevelt.

Roosevelt drove conservative Republicans to despair. "Don't any of you realize there's only one life between this madman and the White House?" Republican boss Mark Hanna asked after Roosevelt's nomination as vice president in 1900. Hanna's fears were realized when President William McKinley was assassinated in 1901. Roosevelt virtually redefined the presidency and, in so doing, modernized the office. His progressivism drew heavily on the ideas of Alexander Hamilton and the leadership qualities of Abraham Lincoln. Roosevelt believed that government should foster social and economic progress, as outlined in Hamilton's "Report on Manufactures" (1791). In this view, government was best run by men who could demonstrate a combination of energy and wisdom, as Lincoln had during the Civil War and as Teddy Roosevelt thought he would do in the first decade of the new century. As president, Roosevelt put his ideas to work in his Square Deal with legislation aimed at the conservation of natural resources, railroad regulation, and consumer protection (see text pp. 627–633).

In keeping with his reputation as a trust-buster, Roosevelt thought that a modern economy could thrive under a system of regulation, not laissez-faire competition. That belief, coupled with a commitment to social justice, formed the basis of Roosevelt's New Nationalism in 1912. Woodrow Wilson disagreed with Roosevelt's theories, offering in their place an updated version of Jacksonian democracy (see text pp. 633–638). "What this country needs above all else," Wilson said during the 1912 presidential campaign, "is a body of laws which will look after the men who are on the make rather than the men who are already made." The Democrat and his New Freedom triumphed, but in his presidency Wilson borrowed much from the New Nationalism.

Document 20-8 offers a taste of Roosevelt's third-party rhetoric. In Document 20-9, Woodrow Wilson promises a New Freedom for the American people in a campaign speech. Progressive lawyer Louis Brandeis's faith in competition, as shown in Document 20-10, greatly influenced Woodrow Wilson. Document 20-11 is a prodevelopment editorial cartoon from the *San Francisco Call*.

20-8 The Struggle for Social Justice (1912)

Theodore Roosevelt

When Theodore Roosevelt (1858–1919) left the White House in 1908 and went on safari in Africa, a wag commented, "I hope some lion will do his duty." Roosevelt returned home safely only to be disappointed by the conservative politics of his successor, William Howard Taft (see text pp. 632–633). Roosevelt challenged Taft for the Republican presidential nomination in 1912 and, when that failed, formed his own Progressive Party. During the campaign, Roosevelt often spoke about issues of social justice.

Source: Theodore Roosevelt, *Progressive Principles: Selections from Addresses Made during the Presidential Campaign of 1912*, ed. Elmer H. Youngman (New York: Progressive National Service, 1913), 199–207.

Lincoln made his fight on the two great fundamental issues of the right of the people to rule themselves, and not to be ruled by any mere part of the people, and of the vital need that this rule of the people should be exercised for social and industrial justice in a spirit of broad charity and kindliness to all, but with stern insistence that privilege should be eliminated from our industrial life and should be shorn of its power in our political life.

In describing his actions I am using the words which we use at the present day; but they exactly and precisely set forth his position fifty years ago. This position is ours at the present day.

The very rich men whom we mean when we speak of Wall Street have at this crisis shown that they are not loyal to the cause of human rights, human justice, human liberty. The rich man who is a good citizen first of all and a rich man only next, stands on a level with all other good citizens, and the rich man of this type is with us in this contest just as other good citizens, who happen to be wage-workers or retail traders or professional men, are with us. But the rich man who trusts in his riches, the rich man who feels that his wealth entitles him to more than his share of political, social and industrial power, is naturally against us. So likewise the men of little faith, the timid men who fear the people and do not dare trust them, the men who at the bottom of their hearts disbelieve in our whole principle of democratic governmental rule, are also against us. . . .

The representatives of privilege, the men who stand for the special interests and against the rule of the plain people and who distrust the people, care very little for party names.

They oppose us who stand for the cause of progress and of justice. They were accurately described by Lincoln . . . when he said that there had been nothing in politics since the Revolution so congenial to their nature as the position taken by his opponents.

The same thing is true now. Those people are against me because they are against the cause I represent.

These men against whom we stand include the men who desire to exploit the people for their own purposes and to profit financially by the wicked alliance between crooked business and crooked politics. Of course, they include also a large number of worthy and respectable men, who have no improper purpose to serve but who either do not see far into the future, or who are misled as to the facts of the case. Finally, they include those who at this moment represent what Lincoln described as the "old exclusive silk-stocking Whigs — nearly all the Whigs of the nice exclusive sort." . . .

The boss system is based on and thrives by injustice. Wherever you get the boss, wherever you get a Legislature controlled by mercenary politicians, there you will always find that privilege flourishes; there you will always find the great special interests striking hands with the crooked politicians and helping them plunder the people in the interest of both wings of the corrupt alliance.

It is to the interest of every honest man, and perhaps most especially to the interest of the honest big business man, that this alliance shall be broken up, and that we shall have a genuine rule of the people in a spirit of honesty and fair play toward all.

There is far more in this contest than is involved in the momentary victory of any man or any faction.

We are now fighting one phase of the eternal struggle for right and for justice. . . .

As far as we are concerned, the battle is just begun, and we shall go on with it to the end. We hail as our brothers all who contend in any way for the great cause of human rights, for the realization in measurable degree of the doctrines of the brotherhood of man.

We do not for a moment believe that any system of laws, no matter how good, or that any governmental action, can ever take the place of the individual character of the average man and the average woman, which must always in the last analysis be the chief factor in that man's or that woman's success.

But we insist that without just laws and just governmental action the high standard of character of the average American will not suffice to get all that as a Nation we are entitled to.

We must, through the law, make conditions of life more fair, make equality of opportunity more real. We must strive for industrial as well as political democracy.

Every man who fights for the protection of children from excessive toil, for the protection of women from working in factories for too long hours, for the protection, in short, of the workingman and his family so that he may live decently and bring up his children honorably and well — every man who works for any such cause is our fellow worker and we hail him as such.

Remember, that when we work to make this country a better place to live in for those who have been harshly treated by fate, we are also at the same time making it a better place to live in for those who have been well treated by fate.

The great representatives and beneficiaries of privilege, nineteen-twentieths of whom are opposing us with intense animosity, are acting with the utmost short-sightedness from the standpoint of the welfare of their children and their children's children.

We who stand for justice wish to make this country a better place to live in for the man who actually toils, for the wage-worker, for the farmer, for the small business man; and in so striving, we are really defending the cause of the children of those beneficiaries of privilege against what would be fatal action by their fathers. . . .

None of us can really prosper permanently if there are masses among us who are debased and degraded.

The sons of the millionaires will find this a very poor country to live in if men and women who make up the bulk of our ordinary citizenship do not have conditions so shaped that they can lead self-respecting lives on a basis which will permit them to retain their own sense of dignity, to treat their children aright, and to take their part in the life of the community as good citizens.

Exactly as each of us in his private life must stand up for his own rights and yet must respect the rights of others and acknowledge in practical fashion that he is indeed his brother's keeper, so all of us taken collectively, the people as a whole, must feel our obligation to work by governmental action, and in all other ways possible, to make the conditions better for those who are unfairly pressed down in the fierce competition of modern industrial life.

I ask justice for those who in actual life meet with most injustice—and I ask this not only for their sakes but for our own sakes, for the sake of the children and the children's children who are to come after us.

The children of all of us will pay in the future if we do not do justice in the present.

This country will not be a good place for any of us to live in if we do not strive with zeal and efficiency to make it a reasonably good place for all of us to live in.

Nor can our object be obtained save through the genuine control of the people themselves. The people must rule or gradually they will lose all power of being good citizens. The people must control their own destinies or the power of such control will atrophy.

Our cause is the cause of the plain people. It is the cause of social and industrial justice to be achieved by the plain people through the resolute and conscientious use of all the machinery, public and private, State and National, governmental and individual, which is at their command.

This is a great fight in which we are engaged, for it is a fight for human rights, and we who are making it are really making it for every good citizen of this Republic, no matter to what party he may belong.

Questions

1. By Roosevelt's standards, what constitutes a moral rich man?
2. Why did Roosevelt invoke Abraham Lincoln in this speech?
3. How did Roosevelt define social justice?

20-9 The New Freedom (1912)

Woodrow Wilson

By 1912, it had been twenty years since the Democratic Party had won a presidential election. Voters were presented with no less than three parties backing progressive reform: Roosevelt's Progressive (or Bull Moose) Party, Eugene V. Debs's Socialist Party, and Woodrow Wilson's Democratic Party. In the end, the Democrats won with a campaign in which Wilson called for a "new freedom" from monopoly and its attendant evils. What follows is the text from a campaign speech Wilson delivered on October 3, 1912, that elucidates his progressive platform.

Source: From Arthur S. Link, ed., *The Papers of Woodrow Wilson* (Princeton, NJ: Princeton University Press, 1978), 25:322–327. Reprinted by permission of the publisher.

I want you particularly to notice that there are only two parties in the present campaign, or rather that there is one party and two fragments of another party. Because it is not Democrats that have gone over into the new party, it is almost exclusively Republicans. And what we are facing, therefore, is two segments of a great disrupted party, and those two segments are made up in this way. You know that on the one hand are those who call themselves the regular Republicans, and those on the other hand who try to arrogate to themselves entirely the name of Progressives. But what I want you to realize is that these Progressives have not drawn to themselves the old force, the old insurgent force, of the Republican party. . . .

You have therefore this extraordinary spectacle of the two branches of the Republican party, both of them led by men equally responsible for the very conditions which we are seeking to alter. And the reason that some of the insurgent Republicans are not following Mr. Roosevelt, the reason that men like Mr. La Follette, for example, are not following Mr. Roosevelt, is that they have already tested Mr. Roosevelt when he was President and have found that he was not willing to cooperate with them along any line that would be efficient in the checking of the evils of which we complain. So that the leader of the very movement which is proposed for our emancipation is a man who has been tried in this very matter and not found either willing or competent to accomplish the objects that we now seek.

In order to confirm my view of the matter, you have only to read Mr. La Follette's autobiography, and I advise every man who can lay his hands on a copy of the *American Review* to read that extraordinary narrative. There, in detail, it is told how Mr. La Follette and others like him carried proposals to the then President, Mr. Roosevelt, which would have made this campaign inconceivable. And after he had, following his first generous impulse, consented to cooperate with them, he subsequently drew back and refused to cooperate with them, under what influences I do not care to conjecture, because it is not my duty and it would be very distasteful to me to call in question the motives of these gentlemen. That is not my object or my desire. My object is merely to point out the fact that the very conditions we are trying to remedy were built up under these two gentlemen who are the opponents of the Democratic party. Therefore, to my mind it is a choice between Tweedledum and Tweedledee to choose between the leader of one branch of the Republican party and the leader of the other branch of the Republican party, because what the whole country knows to be true, these gentlemen deny.

The whole country knows that special privilege has sprung up in this land. The whole country knows, except these gentlemen, that it has been due chiefly to the protective tariff. These gentlemen deny that special privilege has been caused by the administration of the protective tariff. They deny what all the rest of the country has become convinced is true. And after they have denied the responsibility of the tariff policy for special privilege, they turn about to those creatures of special privilege which we call the trusts—those organizations which have created monopoly and created the high cost of living in this country—and deny that the tariff created them. Not only that, but deny that it is possible to reverse the process by which that monopoly was created, because in the very platform of the third party (if I had thought there would be light enough to read it to you, I would have brought it and read it), in the very platform of the third party, it is not said that they intend to correct the conditions of monopoly, but merely that they intend to assuage them, to render them less severe, to legalize and moderate the processes of monopoly. So that the two things we are fighting against, namely, excessive tariffs and almost universal monopoly, are the very things that these two branches of the Republican party both decline to combat. They do not so much as propose to lay the knife at any one of the roots of the difficulties under which we now labor. On the contrary, they intend to accept these evils and stagger along under the burden of excessive tariffs and intolerable monopolies as best they can through administrative commissions. I say, therefore, that it is inconceivable that the people of the United States, whose instinct is against special privilege and whose deepest convictions are against monopoly, should turn to either of these parties for relief when these parties do not so much as pretend to offer them relief.

It is this circumstance that puts me in a very sober mood. It is this process which makes me feel that great bodies of men of this sort have come together, not in order to whoop it up for a party, not in order to merely look at a candidate, but to show there is a great uprising in this country against intolerable conditions which only the Democratic party proposes to attack and to alter. Only the Democratic party is ready to attack and alter these things. Do you see any breach anywhere in the Democratic ranks? Don't you know that wherever you live men are coming as volunteers, recruits into the ranks of the Democrats? Don't you know that everywhere that you turn men are taking it for granted that the country must follow this party or else wander for another four years in the wilderness?

There are some noble people, there are some people of very high principle, who believe that they can turn in other quarters for relief, but they do so simply because there is one of these parties that blows beautiful bubbles for them to see float in the air of oratory, men who paint iridescent dreams of uplifted humanity, men who speak of going to the rescue of the helpless, men who speak of checking the oppression of those who are overburdened, men who paint the picture of the redemption of mankind and don't admit who they are, who are preaching this doctrine. They are the men whom we have seen and tested, and their conversion is after the time when they possessed the power to do these things and refused to do them.

Is humanity burdened now for the first time? Are men in need of succor now who were not in need of succor ten years ago? Are men now in need of protection by the government who did not need protection when these gentlemen exercised the tremendous power of the office of President? Is it not true that when Theodore Roosevelt was President of the United States the people of the United States were willing to follow him wherever he led? And where did he lead them? When did he turn in the direction of this great uplift of humanity? How long was the vision delayed? How impossible was it for him to see it when his arm was strong to come to the succor of the weak! And now he has seen it, when he wishes to regain their confidence, which by his failure to act he had forfeited!

And so I say it is not as if novices had come before us. It is not as if men had come before us who had seen these things all their lives and waited, waited in vain for an opportunity to do them. For we know the men we are dealing with, and we know that there are men in this third party who are following that leader notwithstanding the fact that they do not believe in him. They simply want a third party because they do not yet find themselves ready to trust the Democratic party and yet are unwilling to trust the regulars among the Republican party. So that they are hoping that something my happen, even under a leader whom they do not have full confidence in, that will enable mankind to find an opportunity to cast its masses against the gates of opportunity and at least burst them open by the great rush of their gathering multitudes. They do not look for guidance.

They merely hope for the consummation of their united power in a blind effort to escape something that they fear and dread.

Ah, gentlemen, shall they go under such shepherds? Shall they go deliberately so shepherded? Shall mankind follow those who could have succored them and did not?

Now, on the other hand, what can we say in all honesty and truth of the Democratic party? Why, gentlemen, the Democratic party was preaching these doctrines and offering you leaders to carry them out before these gentlemen ever admitted that anything was wrong or had any dream of the hopes of humanity. We didn't wait until the year 1912 to discover that the plain people in America had nothing to say about their government. We have been telling you that for half a generation and more. We have been warning you of the very things that have come to pass, in season and out of season. We have kept a straight course. We have never turned our faces for one moment from the faith that was in us—the faith in the common people of this great commonwealth, this great body of commonwealths, this great nation. And now what is happening? Why, with renewed hope, with renewed confidence, with renewed ardor of conviction, under leaders chosen after the freest fashion that our politics have ever witnessed—chosen freely at Baltimore, chosen yesterday freely for perhaps the first time within our recollection in the Empire State of New York—untrammeled leaders, leaders who have no obligations except to those who have trusted and believed in them, are now asked to lead the Democratic party along those paths of conviction which these other gentlemen have so recently found, which they have found only now that they see that these are the paths perhaps to a renewal of their power.

I would not speak, I would not say, one word of bitterness, but I do utter my profound protest against the idea that it is possible to do these things through the instrumentality of new converts. I say that those who are rooted and grounded in this faith, those who have been willing to stay out in the cold as minorities through half a generation, are men tried to the bottom of all that is in them. Their stuff is tried out in the furnace, and they are now ready to serve you, and they are ready as an absolutely united team. Where will you find any disinclination to take the signals from the leader? Where will you find any clefts in the Democratic ranks? Is it not true that this solid phalanx, with its banners now cast to the wind, is marching with a tread that shakes the earth to take possession of the government for the people of the United States? This is what heartens the men who are in this fight. This is what quickens their pulses. This is what makes everything worthwhile that has to be done in the honest conduct of a frank campaign.

For our object, as well call you to witness, throughout this campaign is to discuss not persons, but issues. We are not interested in persons. I tell you frankly, I am not interested even in the person who is the Democratic candidate for President. I am sorry for him. I am sorry for him because I believe he is going to be elected, and I believe that there will rest upon him the duty of carrying out these fundamental tasks. And there will be no greater burden in our generation than to organize the forces of liberty in our time in order to make conquest of a new freedom for America. It will be no child's play, but I believe that it will be possible. Because a man is not as big as his belief in himself. He is as big as the number of persons who believe in him. He is as big as the force that is back of him. He is as big as the convictions that move him. He is as big as the trust that is reposed in him by the people of the country. And with that trust, with that confidence, with that impulse of conviction and hope, I believe that the task is possible, and I believe that the achievement is at hand.

Questions

1. What two things did Wilson say that he was prepared to fight against? Why did this message resonate with the American people?
2. What political point did Wilson try to make by calling Taft and Roosevelt "Tweedledum" and "Tweedledee"?
3. What are the similarities and differences between Roosevelt's speech (Document 20-8) and Wilson's (Document 20-9)?

20-10 Shall We Abandon the Policy of Competition? (1912)

Louis D. Brandeis

Born in Virginia and raised in the South, Woodrow Wilson came naturally to a Democratic ideology that stressed the virtues of the common people and the free market (see text pp. 633–635). Both ideas thrived below the Mason-Dixon Line. Those beliefs were reinforced by Louis D. Brandeis (1856–1941), a famous lawyer and reformer who served as a Wilson campaign advisor. Brandeis authored his defense of competition in 1912.

Brandeis's comment on the "crimes of trade-union leaders" refers to a 1911 bombing of the offices of the *Los Angeles Times* that left twenty dead. Two labor activists, brothers James and John McNamara, were convicted for their roles in the explosion.

Source: From Osmond K. Fraenkel, ed., *The Curse of Bigness: Miscellaneous Papers* (1935), 104–108. Copyright 1935 by Louis D. Brandeis; renewed © 1962 by Susan Brandeis Gilbert and Elizabeth Brandeis Raushenbush. Used by permission of Viking Penguin, a division of Penguin Books USA Inc.

Shall we abandon as obsolete the long-cherished policy of competition, and accept in its place the long-detested policy of monopoly? The issue is not (as it is usually stated by advocates of monopoly), "Shall we have unrestricted competition or regulated monopoly?" It is, "Shall we have regulated competition or regulated monopoly?"

Regulation is essential to the preservation and development of competition, just as it is necessary to the preservation and best development of liberty. We have long curbed physically the strong, to protect those physically weaker. More recently we have extended such prohibitions to business. We have restricted theoretical freedom of contract by factory laws. The liberty of the merchant and manufacturer to lie in trade, expressed in the fine phrase of *caveat emptor* [let the buyer beware], is yielding to the better conceptions of business ethics, before pure-food laws and postal-fraud prosecutions. Similarly, the right to competition must be limited in order to preserve it. For excesses of competition lead to monopoly, as excesses of liberty lead to absolutism. The extremes meet.

The issue, therefore, is: Regulated competition *versus* regulated monopoly. The policy of regulated competition is distinctly a constructive policy. It is the policy of development as distinguished from the destructive policy of private monopoly.

It is asserted that to persist in the disintegration of existing unlawful trusts is to pursue a policy of destruction. No statement could be more misleading. Progress demands that we remove the obstacles in the path of progress; and private monopoly is the most serious obstacle.

One has heard of late the phrases: "You can't make people compete by law." "Artificial competition is undesirable."

These are truisms, but their implication is false. The suggestion is not that traders be compelled to compete, but that they be prevented from killing competition. Equally misleading is the phrase, "Natural monopolies should not be interfered with." There are no natural monopolies today in the industrial world. The Oil Trust and the Steel Trust have been referred to as natural monopolies, but they are both most unnatural. The Oil Trust acquired its control of the market by conduct which involved flagrant violations of law. Without the aid of criminal rebating, of bribery and corruption, the Standard Oil would never have acquired the vast wealth and power which enabled it to destroy its small competitors by price-cutting and similar practices.

The Steel Trust acquired control not through greater efficiency, but by buying up existing plants and ore supplies at fabulous prices. It is believed that not a single industrial monopoly exists today which is the result of natural growth. Competition has been suppressed either by ruthless practices or by an improper use of inordinate wealth and power....

The only argument that has been seriously advanced in favor of private monopoly is that competition involves waste, while the monopoly prevents waste and leads to efficiency. This argument is essentially unsound. The wastes of competition are negligible. The economies of monopoly are superficial and delusive. The efficiency of monopoly is at the best temporary.

Undoubtedly competition involves waste. What human activity does not? The wastes of democracy are among the greatest obvious wastes, but we have compensations in democracy which far outweigh that waste and make it more efficient than absolutism. So it is with competition. The waste is relatively insignificant. There are wastes of competition which do not develop, but kill. These the law can and should eliminate, by regulating competition.

It is true that the unit in business may be too small to be efficient. It is also true that the unit may be too large to be efficient, and this is no uncommon incident of monopoly.

Whenever trusts have developed efficiency, their fruits have been absorbed almost wholly by the trusts themselves. From such efficiency as they have developed, the community has gained substantially nothing.

The proposed Government commission to fix prices would not greatly relieve the evils attendant upon monopoly. It might reduce a trust's profits, but it would fail to reduce the trust's prices; because the limitation of the monopoly's profits would, by lessening this incentive, surely reduce the monopoly's efficiency.

To secure successful management of any private business, reward must be proportionate to success. The establishment of any rule fixing a maximum return on capital would, by placing a limit upon the fruits of achievement, tend to lessen efficiency.

No selling price for monopoly products could be set constitutionally at a point lower than that which would allow a reasonable return on capital. And in the absence of comparative data from any competing businesses producing the same article at less cost, it would be virtually impossible to determine that the cost should be lower.

The success of the Interstate Commerce Commission has been invoked as an argument in favor of licensing and regulating monopoly.

But the Interstate Commerce Commission has been effective principally in preventing rate increases and in stopping discrimination. In those instances where the Commission has reduced rates (as distinguished from preventing increases) the Commission rested its decisions largely on the ground that existing rates amount to discriminations against particular places or articles, or the lower rates were justified by a comparison with other rates of the same or other companies. Price-fixing of that nature applied to industrial thrusts would afford little protection to the public.

In the second place, there is a radical difference between attempts to fix rates for transportation and similar public services, and fixing prices in industrial businesses. Problems of transportation, while varying infinitely in detail, are largely the same throughout the whole country, and they are largely the same yesterday, today, and tomorrow. In industry we have, instead of uniformity, infinite variety; instead of stability, constant change.

In the third place, the problems of the Interstate Commerce Commission, relatively simple as they are, already far exceed the capacity of that or any single board. Think of the infinite questions which would come before an industrial commission seeking to fix rates, and the suffering of the community from the inability of that body promptly and efficiently to dispose of them.

Every business requires for its business health the *memento mori* [reminder of mortality] of competition from without. It requires likewise a certain competition from within, which can exist only where the ownership and management, on the one hand, and the employees, on the other, shall each be alert, hopeful, self-respecting, and free to work out for themselves the best conceivable conditions.

The successful, the powerful trusts, have created conditions absolutely inconsistent with these—America's—industrial and social needs. It may be true that as a legal proposition mere size is not a crime, but mere size may become an industrial and social menace, because it frequently creates as against possible competitors and as against the employees conditions of such gross inequality, as to imperil the welfare of the employees and of the industry.

In the midst of our indignation over the unpardonable crimes of trade-union leaders, disclosed at Los Angeles, would not our statesmen and thinkers seek to ascertain the underlying cause of this widespread, deliberate outburst of crimes of violence? What was it that led men like the McNamaras to believe really that the only recourse they had for improving the condition of the wage-earner was to use dynamite against property and life?

Certainly it was not individual depravity. Was it not because they, and men like them, believed that the wage-earner, acting singly, or collectively, is not strong enough to secure substantial justice? Is there not a causal connection between the development of these huge indomitable trusts and the horrible crimes now under investigation? Are not these irresistible trusts important contributing causes of these crimes—these unintelligent expressions of despairing social unrest? Is it not irony to speak of the equality of opportunity, in a country cursed with their bigness?

The right of labor to organize and to deal collectively with its employers should not be curtailed.

There is not the slightest danger that labor will assume control of industry. It has become exceedingly difficult for the unions to maintain themselves because of the constant inflow of foreign labor and the great number of non-union men. This maintains a state of competition, which, did it exist in the industrial and financial business of the country, would make unnecessary any change in existing laws.

The only right claimed by the labor unions is that of collective bargaining, and this right employers also should have and exercise. It would be perfectly proper for independent competing employers to form employers' organizations, and to deal with the labor unions upon exactly the same footing as is the case with unions—that is, collectively.

Nothing has been done to improve the conditions under which men labor, that has not increased their efficiency. Shorter hours often lead to greater production; and there is economy in high wages.

Questions

1. How did Brandeis counter the argument that some monopolies are inevitable or natural?
2. Why did he support competition instead of monopoly?
3. What were his views on organized labor?

20-11 Hetch Hetchy Debate, Sweeping Back the Flood (1909)

The price of progress has always been high. Thousands of America's most beautiful places were sacrificed in the name of economic development. Many argued that in exchange, the United States became one of the most powerful and advanced nations and enjoyed a

"Sweeping Back the Flood." Together with all the city's newspapers, the San Francisco Call *was a persistent advocate of the Hetch Hetchy water supply and attacked any group that opposed this use. (Bancroft Library, University of California, Berkeley.)*

standard of living that was the envy of the world. By the end of the nineteenth century, however, an organized opposition developed that tried to preserve some of the last best and visually arresting places. A battle royal broke out in California between those who wanted to preserve the Hetch Hetchy Valley, situated near San Francisco and likened in beauty to Yosemite Valley, and those who wanted to dam the Tuolumne River and turn the valley into a reservoir for San Francisco. The debate was lively and had national significance. One of the most ardent defenders of the valley and America's vanishing beauty was John Muir (compare Document 16-12) and the environmental organization he had helped to found, the Sierra Club. The valley was finally dammed.

Source: Holway R. Jones, *John Muir and the Sierra Club: The Battle for Yosemite* (San Francisco: Sierra Club, 1965), 183.

Questions

1. What does the cartoon suggest about the power of progress and those who would oppose it?

2. How is John Muir dressed? Apart from the politics, what does this depiction say about early-twentieth-century attitudes about gender?

Questions for Further Thought

1. What would Jane Addams (Document 20-4) have found appealing in Theodore Roosevelt's speech on social justice (Document 20-8)?

2. Draw distinctions between the political philosophies of Theodore Roosevelt and Woodrow Wilson.

CHAPTER TWENTY-ONE

An Emerging World Power
1877–1914

The Roots of Expansion

Many aspects of nineteenth-century American foreign policy were isolationist. Between 1814 and 1898, the United States avoided war with European nations, and American secretaries of state heeded George Washington's warning against entangling alliances. However, an active foreign policy did exist: the Louisiana and Alaska purchases, relations with Mexico, and the status of Native American tribes were important issues.

By the 1890s, a far more ambitious American foreign policy was evolving. The change reflected the status of the United States as an emerging economic power. By the turn of the century, American factory, oil, and steel products were competing for a share of the world market. The republic whose citizens had once made clothes at home was selling sewing machines worldwide. The republic that under Thomas Jefferson had all but abandoned its navy had begun an ambitious naval buildup by the century's end.

However, economic strength brought its own set of problems. Americans soon discovered that the modern world did not respond well to the counsel of eighteenth-century leaders, especially if the United States wanted to be a world power. Stepping onto the world stage meant answering a series of difficult questions: How was a democracy to act as a world power? What was the proper mix of self-interest and principle in foreign policy? Should the United States control overseas possessions, and what if the native peoples resisted? Both the American public and its leaders struggled over the answers in relation to Latin America, the Philippines, Cuba, Puerto Rico, and Hawaii.

James G. Blaine envisions an American empire in Document 21-1. Alfred Thayer Mahan's treatise on sea power (Document 21-2) challenges the assumptions of a society long suspicious of the military. Document 21-3 is an excerpt from Frederick Jackson Turner's famous frontier thesis.

21-1 The American System (1881)

James G. Blaine

James G. Blaine (1830–1893) was a highly respected politician and statesman. He represented Maine in Congress and was involved in many of the leading issues of his day, including Reconstruction and church-state separation. He served as secretary of state in the cabinets of President James Garfield (who was assassinated) and Garfield's successor, President Chester Arthur. Below is a letter Blaine, as secretary of state, wrote on December 1, 1881, to James M. Comly, the minister to Hawaii, in which he outlines his broad views on America's growth and expansion.

Source: Excerpt of letter from James G. Blaine to James M. Comly, in *Readings in American Foreign Policy*, eds. Robert A. Goldwin et al. (New York: Oxford University Press, 1959), 71–74.

... I have had recent occasion to set forth the vitally integral importance of our Pacific possessions, in a circular letter addressed on the 24th of June last to our representatives in Europe, touching the necessary guarantees of the proposed Panama Canal as a purely American waterway to be treated as part of our own coast line. The extension of commercial empire westward from those states is no less vitally important to their development than is their communication with the Eastern coast by the Isthmian channel. And when we survey the stupendous progress made by the western coast during the thirty years of its national life as a part of our dominion, its enormous increase of population, its vast resources of agriculture and mines, and its boundless enterprise, it is not easy to set a limit to its commercial activity or forsee a check to its maritime supremacy in the waters of the Orient, so long as those waters afford, as now, a free and neutral scope for our peaceful trade.

In thirty years the United States has acquired a legitimately dominant influence in the North Pacific, which it can never consent to see decreased by the intrusion therein of any element of influence hostile to its own. The situation of the Hawaiian Islands, giving them the strategic control of the North Pacific, brings their possession within the range of questions of purely American policy, as much so as that of the Isthmus itself. Hence the necessity, as recognized in our existing treaty relations, of drawing the ties of intimate relationship between us and the Hawaiian Islands so as to make them practically a part of the American system without derogation of their absolute independence. The reciprocity treaty of 1875 has made of Hawaii the sugar-raising field of the Pacific slope and gives to our manufacturers therein the same freedom as in California and Oregon. ...

The policy of this country with regard to the Pacific is the natural complement to its Atlantic policy. The history of our European relations for fifty years shows the jealous concern with which the United States has guarded its control of the coast from foreign interference, and this without extension of territorial possession beyond the main land. It has always been its aim to preserve the friendly neutrality of the adjacent states and insular possessions. Its attitude toward Cuba is in point. That rich island, the key to the Gulf of Mexico, and the field for our most extended trade in the Western Hemisphere is, though in the hands of Spain, a part of the American commercial system. Our relations, present and prospective, toward Cuba, have never been more ably set forth than in the remarkable note addressed by my predecessor, Mr. Secretary Everett, to the ministers of Great Britain and France in Washington, on the 1st of December, 1852, in rejection of the suggested tripartite alliance to forever determine the neutrality of the Spanish Antilles. In response to the proposal that the United States, Great Britain, and France, should severally and collectively agree to forbid the acquisition of control over Cuba, by any or all of them, Mr. Everett showed that, without forcing or even coveting possession of the island, its condition was essentially an American question; that the renunciation forever by this government of contingent interest therein would be far broader than the like renunciation by Great Britain or France; that if ever ceasing to be Spanish, Cuba must necessarily become American, and not fall under any other European domination, and that the ceaseless movement of segregation of American interests from European control and unification in a broader American sphere of independent life could not and should not be checked by any arbitrary agreement.

Nearly thirty years have demonstrated the wisdom of the attitude then maintained by Mr. Everett and have made indispensable its continuance and its extension to all parts of the American Atlantic system where a disturbance of the existing status might be attempted in the interest of foreign powers. The present attitude of this government toward any European project for the control of an isthmian route is but the logical sequence of the resistance made in 1852 to the attempted pressure of an active foreign influence in the West Indies.

Hawaii, although much farther from the Californian coast than is Cuba from the Floridian peninsula, holds in the western sea much the same position as Cuba in the Atlantic. It is the key to the maritime dominion of the Pacific states, as Cuba is the key to the Gulf trade. The material possession of Hawaii is not desired by the United States any more than was that of Cuba. But under no circumstances can the United States permit any change in the territorial control of either which would cut it adrift from the American system, whereto they both indispensably belong.

In this aspect of the question, it is readily seen with what concern this government must view any tendency toward introducing into Hawaii new social elements, destructive of its necessarily American character. The steady diminution of the native population of the islands, amounting to some ten per cent. between 1872 and 1878, and still continuing, is doubtless a cause of great alarm to the government of the kingdom, and it is no wonder that a solution should be sought with eagerness in any seemingly practicable quarter. The problem, however, is not to be met by a substitution of Mongolian supremacy for native control—as seems at first sight possible through the rapid increase in Chinese immigration to the islands. Neither is a wholesale introduction of the coolie element, professedly Anglo-Indian, likely to afford any more satisfactory outcome to the difficulty. The Hawaiian Islands cannot be joined to the Asiatic system. If they drift from their independent station it must be toward assimilation and identification with the American system, to which they belong by the operation of natural laws, and must belong by the operation of political necessity....

In this line of action the United States does its simple duty both to Hawaii and itself; and it cannot permit such obvious neglect of national interest as would be involved by silent acquiescence in any movement looking to a lessening of those American ties and the substitution of alien and hostile interests. It firmly believes that the position of the Hawaiian Islands as the key to the dominion of the American Pacific demands their neutrality, to which end it will earnestly co-operate with the native government. And if, through any cause, the maintenance of such a position of neutrality should be found by Hawaii to be impracticable, this government would then unhesitatingly meet the altered situation by seeking an avowedly American solution for the grave issues presented.

Questions

1. Blaine refered to an American system in the Atlantic and the Pacific. What did he mean by system?
2. According to Blaine, why are the positions of the Hawaiian Islands and of Cuba significant to U.S. foreign policy?

21-2 *The Influence of Sea Power upon History* (1890)

Alfred Thayer Mahan

Except in times of war, Americans have never favored the establishment of a large, standing military force. The navy, for example, was greatly expanded during the Civil War, only to deteriorate over the next twenty-five years. To naval officer Alfred Thayer Mahan (1840–1914), the situation had to be reversed if the United States was to become a true world power. Mahan's *The Influence of Sea Power upon History, 1660–1783* appeared in 1890 and had an enormous influence on U.S. foreign policy (see text pp. 646–648). Before the end of the decade, the U.S. Navy had modernized to the point where it easily defeated its Spanish counterpart.

Source: Alfred Thayer Mahan, *The Influence of Sea Power upon History, 1660–1783* (Boston: Little, Brown, 1890), 83–89.

As the practical object of this inquiry is to draw from the lessons of history inferences applicable to one's own country and service, it is proper now to ask how far the conditions of the United States involve serious danger, and call for action on the part of the government, in order to build again her sea power. It will not be too much to say that the action of the government since the Civil War, and up to this day, has been effectively directed solely to what has been called the first link in the chain which makes sea power. Internal development, great production, with the accompanying aim and boast of self-sufficingness, such has been the object, such to some extent the result. In this the government has faithfully reflected the bent of the controlling elements of the country, though it is not always easy to feel that such controlling elements are truly representative, even in a free country. However that may be, there is no doubt that, besides having no colonies, the intermediate link of a peaceful shipping, and the interests involved in it, are now likewise lacking. In short, the United States has only one link of the three.

The circumstances of naval war have changed so much within the last hundred years, that it may be doubted whether such disastrous effects on the one hand, or such brilliant prosperity on the other, as were seen in the wars between England and France, could now recur. In her secure and haughty sway of the seas England imposed a yoke on neutrals which will never again be borne; and the principle that the flag covers the goods is forever secured. The commerce of a belligerent can therefore now be safely carried on in neutral ships, except when contraband of war or to blockaded ports; and as regards the latter, it is also certain that there will be no more paper blockades. Putting aside therefore the question of defending her seaports from capture or contribution, as to which there is practical unanimity in theory and entire indifference in practice, what need has the United States of sea power? Her commerce is even now carried on by others; why should her people desire that which, if possessed, must be defended at great cost? So far as this question is economical, it is outside the scope of this work; but conditions which may entail suffering and loss on the country by war are directly pertinent to it. Granting therefore that the foreign trade of the United States, going and coming, is on board ships which an enemy cannot touch except when bound to a blockaded port, what will constitute an efficient blockade? The present definition is, that it is such as to constitute a manifest danger to a vessel seeking to enter or leave the port. This is evidently very elastic. Many can remember that during the Civil War, after a night attack on the United States fleet off Charleston, the Confederates next morning sent out a steamer with some foreign consuls on board, who so far satisfied themselves that no blockading vessel was in sight that they issued a declaration to that effect. On the strength of this declaration some Southern authorities claimed that the blockade was technically broken, and could not be technically re-established without a new notification. Is it necessary, to constitute a real danger to blockade runners, that the blockading fleet should be in sight? Half a dozen fast steamers, cruising twenty miles off-shore between the New Jersey and Long Island coast, would be a very real danger to ships seeking to go in or out by the principal entrance to New York; and similar positions might effectively blockade Boston, the Delaware, and the Chesapeake. The main body of the blockading fleet, prepared not only to capture merchant-ships but to resist military attempts to break the blockade, need not be within sight, nor in a position known to the shore. The bulk of Nelson's fleet was fifty miles from Cadiz two days before Trafalgar, with a small detachment watching close to the harbor. The allied fleet began to get under way at 7 A.M., and Nelson, even under the conditions of those days, knew it by 9.30. The English fleet at that distance was a very real danger to its enemy. It seems possible, in these days of submarine telegraphs, that the blockading forces in-shore and off-shore, and from one port to another, might be in telegraphic communication with one another along the whole coast of the United States, readily giving mutual support; and if, by some fortunate military combination, one detachment were attacked in force, it could warn the others and retreat upon them. Granting that such a blockade off one port were broken on one day, by fairly driving away the ships maintaining it, the notification of its being re-established could be cabled all over the world the next. To avoid such blockades there must be a military force afloat that will at all times so endanger a blockading fleet that it can by no means keep its place. Then neutral ships, except those laden with contraband of war, can come and go freely, and maintain the commercial relations of the country with the world outside.

It may be urged that, with the extensive sea-coast of the United States, a blockade of the whole line cannot be effectively kept up. No one will more readily concede this than officers who remember how the blockade of the Southern coast alone was maintained. But in the present condition of the navy, and, it may be added, with any additions not exceeding those so far proposed by the government, the attempt to blockade Boston, New York, the Delaware, the Chesapeake, and the Mississippi, in other words, the great centres of export and import, would not entail upon one of the large maritime nations efforts greater than have been made before. England has at the same time blockaded Brest, the Biscay coast, Toulon, and Cadiz, when there were powerful squadrons lying within the harbors. It is true that commerce in neutral ships can then enter other ports of the United States than those named; but what a dislocation of the carrying traffic of the country, what failure of supplies at times, what inadequate means of transport by rail or water, of dockage, of lighterage, of warehousing, will be involved in such an enforced change of the ports of entry! Will there be no money loss, no suffering, consequent upon this? And when with much pain and expense these evils have been partially remedied, the enemy may be led to stop the new inlets as he did the old. The people of the United States will certainly not starve, but they may suffer grievously. As for supplies which are contraband of war, is there not reason to fear that the United States is not now able to go alone if an emergency should arise?

The question is eminently one in which the influence of the government should make itself felt, to build up for the nation a navy which, if not capable of reaching distant countries, shall at least be able to keep clear the chief approaches to its own. The eyes of the country have for a quarter of a century been turned from the sea; the results of such a policy and of its opposite will be shown in the instance of France and of England. Without asserting a narrow parallelism between the case of the United States and either of these, it may safely be said that it is essential to the welfare of the whole country that the conditions of trade and commerce should remain, as far as possible, unaffected by an external war. In order to do this, the enemy must be kept not only out of our ports, but far away from our coasts.[1]

---

[1] The word "defence" in war involves two ideas, which for the sake of precision in thought should be kept separated in the mind. There is defence pure and simple, which strengthens itself and awaits attack. This may be called passive defence. On the other hand, there is a view of defence which asserts that safety for one's self, the real object of defensive preparation, is best secured by attacking the enemy. In the matter of sea-coast defence, the former method is exemplified by stationary fortifications, submarine mines, and generally all immobile works destined simply to stop an enemy if he tries to enter. The second method comprises all those means and weapons which do not wait for attack, but go to meet the enemy's fleet, whether it be but for a few miles, or whether to his own shores. Such a defence may seem to be really offensive war, but it is not; it becomes offensive only when its object of attack is changed from the enemy's fleet to the enemy's country. England defended her own coasts and colonies by stationing her fleets off the French ports, to fight the French fleet if it came out. The United States in the Civil War stationed her fleets off the Southern ports, not because she feared for her own, but to break down the Confederacy by isolation from the rest of the world, and ultimately by attacking the ports. The methods were the same; but the purpose in one case was defensive, in the other offensive.

The confusion of the two ideas leads to much unnecessary wrangling as to the proper sphere of army and navy in coast-defence. Passive defences belong to the army; everything that moves in the water to the navy, which has the prerogative of the offensive defence. If seamen are used to garrison forts, they become part of the land forces, as surely as troops, when embarked as part of the complement, become part of the sea forces. [*Mahan's note.*]

Can this navy be had without restoring the merchant shipping? It is doubtful. History has proved that such a purely military sea power can be built up by a despot, as was done by Louis XIV; but though so fair seeming, experience showed that his navy was like a growth which having no root soon withers away. But in a representative government any military expenditure must have a strongly represented interest behind it, convinced of its necessity. Such an interest in sea power does not exist, cannot exist here without action by the government. How such a merchant shipping should be built up, whether by subsidies or by free trade, by constant administration of tonics or by free movement in the open air, is not a military but an economical question. Even had the United States a great national shipping, it may be doubted whether a sufficient navy would follow; the distance which separates her from other great powers, in one way a protection, is also a snare. The motive, if any there be, which will give the United States a navy, is probably now quickening in the Central American Isthmus. Let us hope it will not come to the birth too late.

Here concludes the general discussion of the principal elements which affect, favorably or unfavorably, the growth of sea power in nations. The aim has been, first to consider those elements in their natural tendency for or against, and then to illustrate by particular examples and by the experience of the past. Such discussions, while undoubtedly embracing a wider field, yet fall mainly within the province of strategy, as distinguished from tactics. The considerations and principles which enter into them belong to the unchangeable, or unchanging, order of things, remaining the same, in cause and effect, from age to age. They belong, as it were, to the Order of Nature, of whose stability so much is heard in our day; whereas tactics, using as its instruments the weapons made by man, shares in the change and progress of the race from generation to generation. From time to time the superstructure of tactics has to be altered or wholly torn down; but the old foundations of strategy so far remain, as though laid upon a rock. There will next be examined the general history of Europe and America, with particular reference to the effect exercised upon that history, and upon the welfare of the people, by sea power in its broad sense. From time to time, as occasion offers, the aim will be to recall and reinforce the general teaching, already elicited, by particular illustrations. The general tenor of the study will therefore be strategical, in that broad definition of naval strategy which has before been quoted and accepted: "Naval strategy has for its end to found, support, and increase, as well in peace as in war, the sea power of a country." In the matter of particular battles, while freely admitting that the change of details has made obsolete much of their teaching, the attempt will be made to point out where the application or neglect of true general principles has produced decisive effects; and, other things being equal, those actions will be preferred which, from their association with the names of the most distinguished officers, may be presumed to show how far just tactical ideas obtained in a particular age or a particular service. It will also be desirable, where analogies between ancient and modern weapons appear on the surface, to derive such probable lessons as they offer, without laying undue stress upon the points of resemblance. Finally, it must be remembered that, among all changes, the nature of man remains much the same; the personal equation, though uncertain in quantity and quality in the particular instance, is sure always to be found.

Questions

1. According to Mahan, how could an enemy cripple American trade and commerce?
2. Why did he see this country's geographic isolation from other powerful nations as both a strength and a weakness?
3. In general, what was Mahan's view of history?

21-3 The Significance of the Frontier in American History (1893)

Frederick Jackson Turner

Frederick Jackson Turner (1861–1932), a young historian from the University of Wisconsin, presented a paper at the July 12, 1893, meeting of the American Historical Association in Chicago that would eventually change the way America conceived of its growing imperial power. He argued that the 1890 closing of the domestic frontier marked the end of a "great historic movement." With prophetic words, Turner went on to declare, "He would be a rash prophet who should assert that the expansive character of American life has now entirely ceased. Movement has been the dominant fact, and, unless this training has no effect upon a people, the American energy will continually demand a wider field for its exercise."

Source: Frederick Jackson Turner, *The Frontier in American History* (1893; New York: Holt, Rinehart, and Winston, 1947).

In a recent bulletin of the Superintendent of the Census for 1890 appear these significant words: "Up to and including 1880 the country had a frontier of settlement, but at present the unsettled area has been so broken into by isolated bodies of settlement that there can hardly be said to be a frontier line. In the discussion of its extent, its westward movement, etc., it can not, therefore, any longer have a place in the census reports." This brief official statement marks the closing of a great historic movement. Up to our own day American history has been in a large degree the history of the colonization of the Great West. The existence of an area of free land, its continuous recession, and the advance of American settlement westward, explain American development.

Behind institutions, behind constitutional forms and modifications, lie the vital forces that call these organs into life and shape them to meet changing conditions. The peculiarity of American institutions is, the fact that they have been compelled to adapt themselves to the changes of an expanding people—to the changes involved in crossing a continent, in winning a wilderness, and in developing at each area of this progress out of the primitive economic and political conditions of the frontier into the complexity of city life. Said Calhoun in 1817, "We are great, and rapidly—I was about to say fearfully—growing!" So saying, he touched the distinguishing feature of American life. All peoples show development; the germ theory of politics has been sufficiently emphasized. In the case of most nations, however, the development has occurred in a limited area; and if the nation has expanded, it has met other growing peoples whom it has conquered. But in the case of the United States we have a different phenomenon. Limiting our attention to the Atlantic coast, we have the familiar phenomenon of the evolution of institutions in a limited area, such as the rise of representative government; the differentiation of simple colonial governments into complex organs; the progress from primitive industrial society, without division of labor, up to manufacturing civilization. But we have in addition to this a recurrence of the process of evolution in each western area reached in the process of expansion. Thus American development has exhibited not merely advance along a single line, but a return to primitive conditions on a continually advancing frontier line, and a new development for that area. American social development has been continually beginning over again on the frontier. This perennial rebirth, this fluidity of American life, this expansion westward with its new opportunities, its continuous touch with the simplicity of primitive society, furnish the forces dominating American character. The true point of view in the history of this nation is not the Atlantic coast, it is the Great West. Even the slavery struggle, which is made so exclusive an object of attention by writers like Professor von Holst, occupies its important place in American history because of its relation to westward expansion.

In this advance, the frontier is the outer edge of the wave—the meeting point between savagery and civilization. Much has been written about the frontier from the point of view of border warfare and the chase, but as a field for the serious study of the economist and the historian it has been neglected.

The American frontier is sharply distinguished from the European frontier—a fortified boundary line running through dense populations. The most significant thing about the American frontier is, that it lies at the hither edge of free land. In the census reports it is treated as the margin of that settlement which has a density of two or more to the square mile. . . .

The Atlantic frontier was compounded of fisherman, fur-trader, miner, cattle-raiser, and farmer. Excepting the fisherman, each type of industry was on the march toward the West, impelled by an irresistible attraction. Each passed in successive waves across the continent. Stand at Cumberland Gap and watch the procession of civilization, marching single file—the buffalo following the trail to the salt springs, the Indian, the fur-trader and hunter, the cattle-raiser, the pioneer farmer—and the frontier has passed by. Stand at South Pass in the Rockies a century later and see the same procession with wider intervals between. The unequal rate of advance compels us to distinguish the frontier into the trader's frontier, the rancher's frontier, or the miner's frontier, and the farmer's frontier. When the mines and the cow pens were still near the fall line the traders' pack trains were tinkling across the Alleghanies, and the French on the Great Lakes were fortifying their posts, alarmed by the British trader's birch canoe. When the trappers scaled the Rockies, the farmer was still near the mouth of the Missouri. . . .

From the conditions of frontier life came intellectual traits of profound importance. The works of travelers along each frontier from colonial days onward describe certain common traits, and these traits have, while softening down, still persisted as survivals in the place of their origin, even when a higher social organization succeeded. The result is that to the frontier the American intellect owes its striking characteristics. That coarseness and strength combined with acuteness and inquisitiveness; that practical, inventive turn of mind, quick to find expedients;

that masterful grasp of material things, lacking in the artistic but powerful to effect great ends; that restless, nervous energy; that dominant individualism, working for good and for evil, and withal that buoyancy and exuberance which comes with freedom — these are traits of the frontier, or traits called out elsewhere because of the existence of the frontier. Since the days when the fleet of Columbus sailed into the waters of the New World, America has been another name for opportunity, and the people of the United States have taken their tone from the incessant expansion which has not only been open but has even been forced upon them. He would be a rash prophet who should assert that the expansive character of American life has now entirely ceased. Movement has been its dominant fact, and, unless this training has no effect upon a people, the American energy will continually demand a wider field for its exercise. But never again will such gifts of free land offer themselves. For a moment, at the frontier, the bonds of custom are broken and unrestraint is triumphant. There is not *tabula rasa*. The stubborn American environment is there with its imperious summons to accept its conditions; the inherited ways of doing things are also there; and yet, in spite of environment, and in spite of custom, each frontier did indeed furnish a new field of opportunity, a gate of escape from the bondage of the past; and freshness, and confidence, and scorn of older society, impatience of its restraints and its ideas, and indifference to its lessons, have accompanied the frontier. What the Mediterranean Sea was to the Greeks, breaking the bond of custom, offering new experiences, calling out new institutions and activities, that, and more, the ever retreating frontier has been to the United States directly, and to the nations of Europe more remotely. And now, four centuries from the discovery of America, at the end of a hundred years of life under the Constitution, the frontier has gone, and with its going has closed the first period of American history.

Questions

1. How did Turner define *frontier*?
2. According to Turner, how did the frontier define the American identity?
3. How could Turner's thesis be used to explain the development of an American "empire" abroad?

Questions for Further Thought

1. In what respects do Blaine's views on an American system, Mahan's treatise on sea power, and Turner's frontier thesis complement each other?
2. How do Mahan and Turner's views of history differ?

An American Empire

As a nation born fighting to free itself from the British empire, the United States has been troubled by imperial aspirations ever since. Advocates of a U.S. empire maintained that imperial prominence was America's Manifest Destiny (Document 21-4). Anti-imperialists argued that America's greatness was in its resistance of the temptation to rule over others — that empire and democracy were fundamentally at odds with each other. Less than a decade after Alfred Thayer Mahan's work on the influence of sea power (Document 21-2) and Frederick Jackson Turner's observation of the closing of the frontier (Document 21-3), the United States had annexed the Hawaiian Islands and gone to war with Spain. In the process, the United States had acquired overseas territory and was confronted with divisive and complex problems. In the Philippines, the United States began its rule in 1899 by attempting to crush a national independence movement that was led by Emilio Aguinaldo. U.S. suppression turned into a bloody and vicious guerrilla war that did not exhaust itself until 1902, horrifying Americans who had initially conceived of U.S. imperialism as a way to spread democratic values (Document 21-5).

21-4 The March of the Flag (1898)

Albert J. Beveridge

Albert J. Beveridge (1862–1927), a politician and historian, gave his famous campaign speech, "The March of the Flag," at Tomlinson Hall in Indianapolis on September 16, 1898. A Republican, he went on to serve Indiana in the U.S. Senate from 1899 to 1911, proving that the strong emotional appeal of imperialism made for good politics.

Source: Excerpt from Albert J. Beveridge, "The March of the Flag," in *The Meaning of the Times and Other Speeches* (Indianapolis: Bobbs-Merrill Company, 1908), 47–57. Copyright © 1908 by the Bobbs-Merrill Company.

It is a noble land that God has given us; a land that can feed and clothe the world; a land whose coastlines would inclose half the countries of Europe; a land set like a sentinel between the two imperial oceans of the globe, a greater England with a nobler destiny.

It is a mighty people that He has planted on this soil; a people sprung from the most masterful blood of history; a people perpetually revitalized by the virile, man-producing working-folk of all the earth; a people imperial by virtue of their power, by right of their institutions, by authority of their Heaven-directed purposes—the propagandists and not the misers of liberty.

It is a glorious history our God has bestowed upon His chosen people; a history heroic with faith in our mission and our future; a history of statesmen who flung the boundaries of the Republic out into unexplored lands and savage wilderness; a history of soldiers who carried the flag across blazing deserts and through the ranks of hostile mountains, even to the gates of sunset; a history of a multiplying people who overran a continent in half a century; a history of prophets who saw the consequences of evils inherited from the past and of martyrs who died to save us from them; a history divinely logical, in the process of whose tremendous reasoning we find ourselves to-day.

Therefore, in this campaign, the question is larger than a party question. It is an American question. It is a world question. Shall the American people continue their march toward the commercial supremacy of the world? Shall free institutions broaden their blessed reign as the children of liberty wax in strength, until the empire of our principles is established over the hearts of all mankind?

Have we no mission to perform, no duty to discharge to our fellow-man? Has God endowed us with gifts beyond our deserts and marked us as the people of His peculiar favor, merely to rot in our own selfishness, as men and nations must, who take cowardice for their companion and self for their deity—as China has, as India has, as Egypt has?

Shall we be as the man who had one talent and hid it, or as he who had ten talents and used them until they grew to riches? And shall we reap the reward that waits on our discharge of our high duty; shall we occupy new markets for what our farmers raise, our factories make, our merchants sell—aye, and, please God, new markets for what our ships shall carry?

Hawaii is ours; Porto Rico is to be ours; at the prayer of her people Cuba finally will be ours; in the islands of the East, even to the gates of Asia, coaling stations are to be ours at the very least; the flag of a liberal government is to float over the Philippines, and may it be the banner that Taylor unfurled in Texas and Fremont carried to the coast.

The Opposition tells us that we ought not to govern a people without their consent. I answer, The rule of liberty that all just government derives its authority from the consent of the governed, applies only to those who are capable of self-government. We govern the Indians without their consent, we govern our territories without their consent, we govern our children without their consent. How do they know that our government would be without their consent? Would not the people of the Philippines prefer the just, humane, civilizing government of this Republic to the savage, bloody rule of pillage and extortion from which we have rescued them?

And, regardless of this formula of words made only for enlightened, self-governing people, do we owe no duty to the world? Shall we turn these peoples back to the reeking hands from which we have taken them? Shall we abandon them, with Germany, England, Japan, hungering for them? Shall we save them from those nations, to give them a self-rule of tragedy?

They ask us how we shall govern these new possessions. I answer: Out of local conditions and the necessities of the case methods of government will grow. If England can govern foreign lands, so can America. If Germany can govern foreign lands, so can America. If they can supervise protectorates, so can America. Why is it more difficult to administer Hawaii than New Mexico or California? Both had a savage and an alien population; both were more remote from the seat of government when they came under our dominion than the Philippines are to-day.

Will you say by your vote that American ability to govern has decayed; that a century's experience in self-rule has failed of a result? Will you affirm by your vote that you are an infidel to American power and practical sense? Or will you say that ours is the blood of government; ours the heart of dominion; ours the brain and genius of administration? Will you remember that we do but what our fathers did—we but pitch the tents of liberty farther westward, farther southward—we only continue the march of the flag?

The march of the flag! In 1789 the flag of the Republic waved over 4,000,000 souls in thirteen states, and their savage territory which stretched to the Mississippi, to Canada, to the Floridas. The timid minds of that day said that no new territory was needed, and, for the hour, they were right. But Jefferson, through whose intellect the centuries marched; Jefferson, who dreamed of Cuba as an American state; Jefferson, the first Imperialist of the Republic—Jefferson acquired that imperial territory which swept from the Mississippi to the mountains, from Texas to the British possessions, and the march of the flag began!

The infidels to the gospel of liberty raved, but the flag swept on! The title to that noble land out of which Oregon, Washington, Idaho and Montana have been carved was uncertain; Jefferson, strict constructionist of constitutional power though he was, obeyed the Anglo-Saxon impulse within him, whose watchword then and whose watchword throughout the world to-day is, "Forward!": another empire was added to the Republic, and the march of the flag went on!

Those who deny the power of free institutions to expand urged every argument, and more, that we hear, to-day; but the people's judgment approved the command of their blood, and the march of the flag went on!

A screen of land from New Orleans to Florida shut us from the Gulf, and over this and the Everglade Peninsula waved the saffron flag of Spain; Andrew Jackson seized both, the American people stood at his back, and, under Monroe, the Floridas came under the dominion of the Republic, and the march of the flag went on! The Cassandras prophesied every prophecy of despair we hear, to-day, but the march of the flag went on!

Then Texas responded to the bugle calls of liberty, and the march of the flag went on! And, at last, we waged war with Mexico, and the flag swept over the southwest, over peerless California, past the Gate of Gold to Oregon on the north, and from ocean to ocean its folds of glory blazed.

And, now, obeying the same voice that Jefferson heard and obeyed, that Jackson heard and obeyed, that Monroe heard and obeyed, that Seward heard and obeyed, that Grant heard and obeyed, that Harrison heard and obeyed, our President to-day plants the flag over the islands of the seas, outposts of commerce, citadels of national security, and the march of the flag goes on!

Distance and oceans are no arguments. The fact that all the territory our fathers bought and seized is contiguous, is no argument. In 1819 Florida was farther from New York than Porto Rico is from Chicago to-day; Texas, farther from Washington in 1845 than Hawaii is from Boston in 1898; California, more inaccessible in 1847 than the Philippines are now. Gibraltar is farther from London than Havana is from Washington; Melbourne is farther from Liverpool than Manila is from San Francisco.

The ocean does not separate us from lands of our duty and desire—the oceans join us, rivers never to be dredged, canals never to be repaired. Steam joins us; electricity joins us—the very elements are in league with our destiny. Cuba not contiguous! Porto Rico not contiguous! Hawaii and the Philippines not contiguous! The oceans make them contiguous. And our navy will make them contiguous.

But the Opposition is right—there is a difference. We did not need the western Mississippi Valley when we acquired it, nor Florida, nor Texas, nor California, nor the royal provinces of the far northwest. We had no emigrants to people this imperial wilderness, no money to develop it, even no highways to cover it. No trade awaited us in its savage fastnesses. Our productions were not greater than our trade. There was not one reason for the land-lust of our statesmen from Jefferson to Grant, other than the prophet and the Saxon within them. But, to-day, we are raising more than we can consume, making more than we can use. Therefore we must find new markets for our produce.

And so, while we did not need the territory taken during the past century at the time it was acquired, we do need what we have taken in 1898, and we need it now. The resources and the commerce of these immensely rich dominions will be increased as much as American energy is greater than Spanish sloth. In Cuba, alone, there are 15,000,000 acres of forest unacquainted with the ax, exhaustless mines of iron, priceless deposits of manganese, millions of dollars' worth of which we must buy, to-day, from the Black Sea districts. There are millions of acres yet unexplored.

The resources of Porto Rico have only been trifled with. The riches of the Philippines have hardly been touched by the finger-tips of modern methods. And they produce what we consume, and consume what we produce—the very predestination of reciprocity—a reciprocity "not made with hands, eternal in the heavens." They sell hemp, sugar, cocoanuts, fruits of the tropics, timber of price like mahogany; they buy flour, clothing, tools, implements, machinery and all that we can raise and make. Their trade will be ours in time. Do you indorse that policy with your vote?

Cuba is as large as Pennsylvania, and is the richest spot on the globe. Hawaii is as large as New Jersey; Porto Rico half as large as Hawaii; the Philippines larger than all New England, New York, New Jersey and Delaware combined. Together they are larger than the British Isles, larger than France, larger than Germany, larger than Japan.

If any man tells you that trade depends on cheapness and not on government influence, ask him why England does not abandon South Africa, Egypt, India. Why does France seize South China, Germany the vast region whose port is Kaouchou?

Our trade with Porto Rico, Hawaii and the Philippines must be as free as between the states of the Union, because they are American territory, while every other nation on earth must pay our tariff before they can compete with us. Until Cuba shall ask for annexation, our trade with her will, at the very least, be like the preferential trade of Canada with England. That, and the excellence of our goods and products; that, and the convenience of traffic; that, and the kinship of interests and destiny, will give the monopoly of these markets to the American people.

The commercial supremacy of the Republic means that this Nation is to be the sovereign factor in the peace of the world. For the conflicts of the future are to be conflicts of trade—struggles for markets—commercial wars for existence. And the golden rule of peace is impregnability of position and invincibility of preparedness. So, we see England, the greatest strategist of history, plant her flag and her cannon on Gibraltar, at Quebec, in the Bermudas, at Vancouver, everywhere.

So Hawaii furnishes us a naval base in the heart of the Pacific; the Ladrones another, a voyage further on; Manila another, at the gates of Asia—Asia, to the trade of whose hundreds of millions American merchants, manufacturers, farmers, have as good right as those of Germany or France or Russia or England; Asia, whose commerce with the United Kingdom alone amounts to hundreds of millions of dollars every year; Asia, to whom Germany looks to take her surplus products; Asia, whose doors must not be shut against American trade. Within five decades the bulk of Oriental commerce will be ours.

No wonder that, in the shadows of coming events so great, free-silver is already a memory. The current of history has swept past that episode. Men understand, to-day, that the greatest commerce of the world must be conducted with the steadiest standard of value and most convenient medium of exchange human ingenuity can devise. Time, that unerring reasoner, has settled the silver question. The American people are tired of talking about money—they want to make it. Why should the farmer get a half-measure dollar of money any more that he should give a half-measure bushel of grain? . . .

There are so many real things to be done—canals to be dug, railways to be laid, forests to be felled, cities to be builded, fields to be tilled, markets to be won, ships to be launched, peoples to be saved, civilization to be proclaimed and the flag of liberty flung to the eager air of every sea. Is this an hour to waste upon triflers with nature's laws? Is this a season to give our destiny over to word-mongers and prosperity-wreckers? No! It is an hour to remember our duty to our homes. It is a moment to realize the opportunities fate has opened to us. And so it is an hour for us to stand by the Government.

Wonderfully has God guided us. Yonder at Bunker Hill and Yorktown His providence was above us. At New Orleans and on ensanguined seas His hand sustained us. Abraham Lincoln was His minister and His was the altar of freedom the Nation's soldiers set up on a hundred battle-fields. His power directed Dewey in the East and delivered the Spanish fleet into our hands, as He delivered the elder Armada into the hands of our English sires two centuries ago. The American people can not use a dishonest medium of exchange; it is ours to set the world its example of right and honor. We can not fly from our world duties; it is ours to execute the purpose of a fate that has driven us to be greater than our small intentions. We can not retreat from any soil where Providence has unfurled our banner; it is ours to save that soil for liberty and civilization.

Questions

1. What arguments did Beveridge make for the creation of an American empire? How did he invoke morality and religion to strengthen his case?
2. How did Beveridge answer critics who argued that the United States should not govern others without their consent?
3. What parts of Beveridge's speech are offensive to most modern ears? Why and how did the speech appeal to American audiences at the end of the nineteenth century?

21-5 The Philippines Tangle (1899)

William James

The anti-imperialists could count among their ranks some of the leading Americans of the day, including Mark Twain, William Graham Sumner, Jane Addams, Grover Cleveland, Benjamin Harrison, William Jennings Bryan, Carl Schurz, Samuel Gompers, Andrew Carnegie, William Dean Howells, and philosopher William James (1842–1910). William James's essay, "The Philippines Tangle," appeared on March 1,

1899, in the *Boston Evening Transcript.* The Anti-Imperialist League, which gave a formal voice to the opponents of U.S. overseas expansion, had been founded in Boston the previous summer.

Source: From *The Works of William James: Essays, Comments, and Reviews,* Frederick Burkhardt, general editor, and Fredson Bowers, textual editor (Cambridge: Harvard University Press, 1987), 154–158. Copyright © 1987 by the President and Fellows of Harvard College. Reprinted by permission of the publisher.

An observer who should judge solely by the sort of evidence which the newspapers present might easily suppose that the American people felt little concern about the performances of our Government in the Philippine Islands, and were practically indifferent to their moral aspects. The cannon of our gunboats at Manila and the ratification of the treaty have sent even the most vehement anti-imperialist journals temporarily to cover, and the bugbear of copperheadism has reduced the freest tongues for a while to silence. The excitement of battle, this time as always, has produced its cowing and disorganizing effect upon the opposition.

But it would be dangerous for the Administration to trust to these impressions. I will not say that I have been amazed, for I fully expected it; but I have been cheered and encouraged at the almost unanimous dismay and horror which I find individuals express in private conversation over the turn which things are taking. "A national infamy" is the comment on the case which I hear most commonly uttered. The fires of indignation are momentarily "banked," but they are anything but "out." They seem merely to be awaiting the properly concerted and organized signal to burst forth with far more vehemence than ever, as imperialism and the idol of a national destiny, based on martial excitement and mere "bigness," keep revealing their corrupting inwardness more and more unmistakably. The process of education has been too short for the older American nature not to feel the shock. We gave the fighting instinct and the passion of mastery their outing; we let them have the day to themselves, and temporarily committed our fortunes to their leading last spring, because we thought that, being harnessed in a cause which promised to be that of freedom, the results were fairly safe, and we could resume our permanent ideals and character when the fighting fit was done. We now see how we reckoned without our host. We see by the vividest of examples what an absolute savage and pirate the passion of military conquest always is, and how the only safeguard against the crimes to which it will infallibly drag the nation that gives way to it is to keep it chained for ever, is never to let it get its start. In the European nations it is kept chained by a greater mutual fear than they have ever before felt for one another. Here it should have been kept chained by a native wisdom nourished assiduously for a century on opposite ideals. And we can appreciate now that wisdom in those of us who, with our national Executive at their head, worked so desperately to keep it chained last spring.

But since then, Executive and all, we have been swept away by the overmastering flood. And now what it has swept us into is an adventure that in sober seriousness and definite English speech must be described as literally piratical. Our treatment of the Aguinaldo movement at Manila and at Iloilo is piracy positive and absolute, and the American people appear as pirates pure and simple, as day by day the real facts of the situation are coming to the light.

What was only vaguely apprehended is now clear with a definiteness that is startling indeed. Here was a people towards whom we felt no ill-will, against whom we had not even a slanderous rumor to bring; a people for whose tenacious struggle against their Spanish oppressors we have for years past spoken (so far as we spoke of them at all) with nothing but admiration and sympathy. Here was a leader who, as the Spanish lies about him, on which we were fed so long, drop off, and as the truth gets more and more known, appears as an exceptionally fine specimen of the patriot and national hero; not only daring, but honest; not only a fighter, but a governor and organizer of extraordinary power. Here were the precious beginnings of an indigenous national life, with which, if we had any responsibilities to these islands at all, it was our first duty to have squared ourselves. Aguinaldo's movement was, and evidently deserved to be, an ideal popular movement, which as far as it had had time to exist was showing itself "fit" to survive and likely to become a healthy piece of national self-development. It was all we had to build on, at any rate, so far — if we had any desire not to succeed to the Spaniards' inheritance of native execration.

And what did our Administration do? So far as the facts have leaked out, it issued instructions to the commanders on the ground simply to freeze Aguinaldo out, as a dangerous rival with whom all compromising entanglement was sedulously to be avoided by the great Yankee business concern. We were not to "recognize" him, we were to deny him all account of our intentions; and in general to refuse any account of our intentions to anybody, except to declare in abstract terms their "benevolence," until the inhabitants, without a pledge of any sort from us, should turn over their country into our hands. Our President's bouffe-proclamation was the only thing vouchsafed: "We are here for your own good; therefore unconditionally surrender to our tender mercies, or we'll blow you into kingdom come."

Our own people meanwhile were vaguely uneasy, for the inhuman callousness and insult shown at Paris and

Washington to the officially delegated mouthpieces of the wants and claims of the Filipinos seemed simply abominable from any moral point of view. But there must be reasons of state, we assumed, and good ones. Aguinaldo is evidently a pure adventurer "on the make," a blackmailer, sure in the end to betray our confidence, or our Government wouldn't treat him so, for our President is essentially methodistical and moral. Mr. McKinley must be in an intolerably perplexing situation, and we must not criticise him too soon. We assumed this, I say, though all the while there was a horribly suspicious look about the performance. On its face it reeked of the infernal adroitness of the great department store, which has reached perfect expertness in the art of killing silently and with no public squealing or commotion the neighboring small concern.

But that small concern, Aguinaldo, apparently not having the proper American business education, and being uninstructed on the irresistible character of our Republican party combine, neither offered to sell out nor to give up. So the Administration had to show its hand without disguise. It did so at last. We are now openly engaged in crushing out the sacredest thing in this great human world—the attempt of a people long enslaved to attain to the possession of itself, to organize its laws and government, to be free to follow its internal destinies according to its own ideals. War, said Moltke, aims at destruction, and at nothing else. And splendidly are we carrying out war's ideal. We are destroying the lives of these islanders by the thousand, their villages and their cities; for surely it is we who are solely responsible for all the incidental burnings that our operations entail. But these destructions are the smallest part of our sins. We are destroying down to the root every germ of a healthy national life in these unfortunate people, and we are surely helping to destroy for one generation at least their faith in God and man. No life shall you have, we say, except as a gift from our philanthropy after your unconditional submission to our will. So as they seem to be "slow pay" in the matter of submission, our yellow journals have abundant time in which to raise new monuments of capitals to the victories of Old Glory, and in which to extol the unrestrainable eagerness of our brave soldiers to rush into battles that remind them so much of rabbit hunts on Western plains.

It is horrible, simply horrible. Surely there cannot be many born and bred Americans who, when they look at the bare fact of what we are doing, the fact taken all by itself, do not feel this, and do not blush with burning shame at the unspeakable meanness and ignominy of the trick?

Why, then, do we go on? First, the war fever; and then the pride which always refuses to back down when under fire. But these are passions that interfere with the reasonable settlement of any affair; and in this affair we have to deal with a factor altogether peculiar with our belief, namely, in a national destiny which must be "big" at any cost, and which for some inscrutable reason it has become infamous for us to disbelieve in or refuse. We are to be missionaries of civilization, and to bear the white man's burden, painful as it often is. We must sow our ideals, plant our order, impose our God. The individual lives are nothing. Our duty and our destiny call, and civilization must go on.

Could there be a more damning indictment of that whole bloated idol termed "modern civilization" than this amounts to? Civilization is, then, the big, hollow, resounding, corrupting, sophisticating, confusing torrent of mere brutal momentum and irrationality that brings forth fruits like this! It is safe to say that one Christian missionary, whether primitive, Protestant or Catholic, of the original missionary type, one Buddhist or Mohammedan of a genuine saintly sort, one ethical reformer or philanthropist, or one disciple of Tolstoi would do more real good in these islands than our whole army and navy can possibly effect with our whole civilization at their back. He could build up realities, in however small a degree; we can only destroy the inner realities and indeed destroy in a year more of them than a generation can make good.

It is by their moral fruits exclusively that these benighted brown people, "half-devil and half-child" as they are, are condemned to judge a civilization. Ours is already execrated by them forever for its hideous fruits.

Shall it not in so far forth be execrated by ourselves? Shall the unsophisticated verdict upon its hideousness which the plain moral sense pronounces avail nothing to stem the torrent of mere empty "bigness" in our destiny, before which it is said we must all knock under, swallowing our higher sentiments with a gulp? The issue is perfectly plain at last. We are cold-bloodedly, wantonly and abominably destroying the soul of a people who never did us an atom of harm in their lives. It is bald, brutal piracy, impossible to dish up any longer in the cold pot-grease of President McKinley's cant at the recent Boston banquet—surely as shamefully evasive a speech, considering the right of the public to know definite facts, as can often have fallen even from a professional politician's lips. The worst of our imperialists is that they do not themselves know where sincerity ends and insincerity begins. Their state of consciousness is so new, so mixed of primitively human passions and, in political circles, of calculations that are anything but primitively human; so at variance, moreover, with their former mental habits; and so empty of definite data and contents; that they face various ways at once, and their portraits should be taken with a squint. One reads the President's speech with a strange feeling—as if the very words were squinting on the page.

The impotence of the private individual, with imperialism under full headway as it is, is deplorable indeed. But every American has a voice or a pen, and may use it. So, impelled by my own sense of duty, I write these present words. One by one we shall creep from cover, and the opposition will organize itself. If the Filipinos hold out long enough, there is a good chance (the canting game being already pretty well played out, and the piracy having to show itself henceforward naked) of the older American beliefs and sentiments coming to their rights again, and of the Administration being terrified into a conciliatory policy towards the native government.

The programme for the opposition should, it seems to me, be radical. The infamy and iniquity of a war of conquest must stop. A "protectorate," of course, if they will have it, though after this they would probably rather welcome any European Power; and as regards the inner state of the island, freedom, "fit" or "unfit," that is, home rule without humbugging phrases, and whatever anarchy may go with it until the Filipinos learn from each other, not from us, how to govern themselves. Mr. Adam's programme—which anyone may have by writing to Mr. Erving Winslow, Anti-Imperialist League, Washington, D.C.—seems to contain the only hopeful key to the situation. Until the opposition newspapers seriously begin, and the mass meetings are held, let every American who still wishes his country to possess its ancient soul—soul a thousand times more dear than ever, now that it seems in danger of perdition—do what little he can in the way of open speech and writing, and above all let him give his representatives and senators in Washington a positive piece of his mind.

Questions

1. How did James turn social Darwinism's "survival of the fittest" argument (see text pp. 587–588) upside down?
2. What actions did James accuse the United States of committing in the Philippines?

Questions for Further Thought

1. Compare and contrast the emotional tone of Albert J. Beveridge's speech (Document 21-4) with that of William James's essay (Document 21-5).
2. What similarities can you detect between Frederick Jackson Turner's "The Significance of the Frontier in American History" (Document 21-3) and Albert J. Beveridge's "The March of the Flag" (Document 21-4)?

Onto the World Stage

American foreign policy focused on two areas—the Caribbean and the Pacific. Beginning in the 1890s, European nations exhibited what the United States feared was an imperial interest in the Caribbean. For example, in 1895 Great Britain pressed a border claim for British Guiana against Venezuela. Grover Cleveland responded by invoking the Monroe Doctrine (see text p. 647).

Seven years after the Venezuela crisis, Venezuela defaulted on some loans. Great Britain, Germany, and Italy then sent a naval force that fired on Venezuelan military installations. This time Theodore Roosevelt mounted a diplomatic counteroffensive with the so-called Roosevelt Corollary to the Monroe Doctrine. Roosevelt warned that governmental incompetence by Caribbean nations would "force the United States, however reluctantly, in flagrant cases . . . of wrong doing or impotence, to the exercise of an international police power."

Although Europe heeded the warning, the United States was only partially successful as the dominant Caribbean power. Policymakers found that it was easier to build the Panama Canal (see text pp. 659–661) than to avoid invoking the Roosevelt Corollary. By 1917, American troops had landed at various times in Cuba, the Dominican Republic, Haiti, Mexico, and Nicaragua. Although the intent was to create order out of chaos, the policy resulted in anti-Americanism throughout the region.

In Asia, the United States spent two years putting down the insurrection of Philippine nationalists; these military operations cost some 4,300 American lives and as many as 300,000 Filipino lives. Once pacified, the islands were supposed to serve as a springboard for American business interests in China. However, China proved to be a difficult market to enter. Europeans were long established there, and in 1900 the Chinese attempted to end all foreign domination. Although the Boxer Rebellion (see text pp. 662–664) failed, it allowed Secretary of State John Hay to insist that all the powers recognize the independence of China, along with the legitimacy of American interests there.

In an interview with a group of church men (Document 21-6), President McKinley explains his prayerful decision to acquire the Philippine Islands for the United States. Document 21-7 offers a cartoonist's view of Cuban and Filipino conduct and American policy. John Hay's Open Door Notes are reprinted in Document 21-8. In Document 21-9, Mark Twain looks at the American empire from the other side. Document 21-10 is Roosevelt's Corollary to the Monroe Doctrine.

21-6 On Prayer and the Philippines (1899)

William McKinley

If the Gilded Age in American history began in 1865 with the assassination of President Lincoln, it ended in 1901 with the assassination of President William McKinley. In between these two bloody bookends, the United States had been transformed into a modern nation and world power. The U.S. experiment in imperialism under President McKinley stirred up a great deal of controversy at the time and the results appear mixed at best in retrospect. The Philippines initially proved difficult to pacify. Defending the islands was a major military problem and indeed they were later lost to the Japanese empire during World War II. Only after great sacrifice, difficulties, and expense were they brought back under U.S. control. Finally, a year after Japan's surrender, the United States granted the Philippines its independence in 1946. In this document, McKinley explains the context, rationale, and inspiration for this troubled imperialist adventure.

Source: Excerpt from "The Peace Negotiations," in *William McKinley*, by Charles S. Olcott (Boston: Houghton Mifflin Company, 1916), 2:108–111.

On the very day when the President wrote this letter, the Commissioners sent a long telegram expressing their individual views, and asking explicit instructions.

This was answered on the 26th:—

"The information which has come to the President since your departure convinces him that the acceptance of the cession of Luzon alone, leaving the rest of the islands subject to Spanish rule, or to be the subject of future contention, cannot be justified on political, commercial, or humanitarian grounds. The cession must be of the whole archipelago or none. The latter is wholly inadmissible, and the former must therefore be required. The President reaches this conclusion after most thorough consideration of the whole subject, and is deeply sensible of the grave responsibilities it will impose, believing that this course will entail less trouble than any other, and besides will best subserve the interests of the people involved, for whose welfare we cannot escape responsibility."

How the President came to this decision was told in a well-authenticated interview at the White House, November 21, 1899. He was receiving a committee representing the General Missionary Committee of the Methodist Episcopal Church, then in session in Washington.... After the visitors had presented a resolution of thanks to the President for his courtesy to the convention and listened to an appropriate response, they turned to leave, when the President said, earnestly:—

"Hold a moment longer! Not quite yet, gentlemen! Before you go I would like to say just a word about the Philippine business. I have been criticized a good deal about the Philippines, but don't deserve it. The truth is I didn't want the Philippines, and when they came to us, as a gift from the gods, I did not know what to do with them. When the Spanish War broke out, Dewey was at Hongkong, and I ordered him to go to Manila and to capture or destroy the Spanish fleet, and he had to; because, if defeated, he had no place to refit on that side of the globe, and if the Dons were victorious, they would likely cross the Pacific and ravage our Oregon and California coasts. And so he had to destroy the Spanish fleet, and did it! But that was as far as I thought then.

"When next I realized that the Philippines had dropped into our laps I confess I did not know what to do with them. I sought counsel from all sides—Democrats as well as Republicans—but got little help. I thought first we would take only Manila; then Luzon; then other islands, perhaps, also. I walked the floor of the White House night after night until midnight; and I am not ashamed to tell you, gentlemen, that I went down on my knees and prayed Almighty God for light and guidance more than one night. And one night late it came to me this way—I don't know how it was, but it came: (1) That we could not give them back to Spain—that would be cowardly and dishonorable; (2) that we could not turn them over to France or Germany—our commercial rivals in the Orient—that would be bad business and discreditable; (3) that we could not leave them to themselves—they were unfit for self-government—and they would soon have anarchy and misrule over there worse than Spain's was; and (4) that there was nothing left for us to do but to take them all, and to educate the Filipinos, and uplift and civilize and Christianize them, and by God's grace do the very best we could by them, as our fellow-men for whom Christ also died. And then I went to bed, and went to sleep, and slept soundly, and the next morning I sent for the chief engineer of the War Department (our map-maker), and I told him to put the Philippines on the map of the United States [pointing to a large map on the wall of his office], and there they are, and there they will stay while I am President!"

The Spanish Commissioners were slow to admit the altruistic motives of the United States and professed to be greatly shocked at the proposition to take the Philippines.

Questions

1. What assumptions did McKinley make about the peoples of the Philippines?
2. How did he portray the intentions of the United States?

21-7   Cartoon on the Philippines and Cuba (1901)

R. C. Bowman

R. C. Bowman, a cartoonist for the *Minneapolis Tribune*, here relates American policy toward the Philippines and Cuba to the conduct of Filipinos and Cubans.

Source: *Minneapolis Tribune* (1901), reprinted by permission in John J. Johnson, *Latin America in Caricature* (Austin and London: University of Texas Press, 1980), 209.

THE PHILIPPINES. "What yer got?"
CUBA. "Pie."
THE PHILIPPINES. "Where'd yer git it?"
CUBA. "Mah Uncle Sam gin it to me; any maybe ef you was half way decent he' gin you some."

Questions

1. How does the cartoonist's depiction of Cuba and the Philippines use racial stereotyping?
2. What importance do you attach to the gender, age, and clothing that Bowman selected for the characters in his cartoon?

21-8 Open Door Notes (1899, 1900)

John Hay

Unwilling to make a military commitment to China, the United States pressed its interests through diplomacy. The following notes from Secretary of State John Hay (1838–1905) made up the open-door policy, which remained in force until the triumph of Mao Ze-dong (Mao Tse-tung) and the Chinese Communist Party in 1949. Hay's first communication is to Andrew D. White, the American ambassador to Germany. His second is a telegram sent to the American embassies and missions in all the countries that wanted to trade with China.

Source: John Hay to Andrew D. White, September 6, 1899, and John Hay's circular letter to the powers cooperating in China, July 3, 1900, in Henry Steele Commager and Milton Cantor, eds., *Documents of American History*, 10th ed. (Englewood Cliffs, NJ: Prentice Hall, 1988), 2:9–11.

JOHN HAY TO ANDREW D. WHITE

Department of State, Washington, September 6, 1899
At the time when the Government of the United States was informed by that of Germany that it had leased from His Majesty the Emperor of China the port of Kiao-chao and the adjacent territory in the province of Shantung, assurance were given to the ambassador of the United States at Berlin by the Imperial German minister for foreign affairs that the rights and privileges insured by treaties with China to citizens of the United States would not thereby suffer or be in anywise impaired within the area over which Germany had thus obtained control.

More recently, however, the British Government recognized by a formal agreement with Germany the exclusive right of the latter country to enjoy in said leased area and the contiguous "sphere of influence or interest" certain privileges, more especially those relating to railroads and mining enterprises; but as the exact nature and extent of the rights thus recognized have not been clearly defined, it is possible that serious conflicts of interest may at any time arise not only between British and German subjects within said area, but that the interests of our citizens may also be jeopardized thereby.

Earnestly desirous to remove any cause of irritation and to insure at the same time to the commerce of all nations in China the undoubted benefits which should accrue from a formal recognition by the various powers claiming "spheres of interest" that they shall enjoy perfect equality of treatment for their commerce and navigation within such "spheres," the Government of the United States would be pleased to see His German Majesty's Government give formal assurance, and lend its cooperation in securing like assurances from the other interested powers, that each, within its respective sphere of whatever influence—

First. Will in no way interfere with any treaty port or any vested interest within any so-called "sphere of interest" or leased territory it may have in China.

Second. That the Chinese treaty tariff of the time being shall apply to all merchandise landed or shipped to all such ports as are within said "sphere of interest" (unless they be "free ports"), no matter to what nationality it may belong, and that duties so leviable shall be collected by the Chinese Government.

Third. That it will levy no higher harbor dues on vessels of another nationality frequenting any port in such "sphere" than shall be levied on vessels of its own nationality, and no higher railroad charges over lines built, controlled, or operated within its "sphere" on merchandise belonging to citizens or subjects of other nationality transported through such "sphere" than shall be levied on similar merchandise belonging to its own nationals transported over equal distances.

The liberal policy pursued by His Imperial German Majesty in declaring Kiao-chao a free port and in aiding the Chinese Government in the establishment there of a customhouse are so clearly in line with the proposition which this Government is anxious to see recognized that it entertains the strongest hope that Germany will give its acceptance and hearty support.

The recent ukase of His Majesty the Emperor of Russia declaring the port of Ta-lien-wan open during the whole of the lease under which it is held from China to the merchant ships of all nations, coupled with the categorical assurances made to this Government by His Imperial Majesty's representative at this capital at the same time and since repeated to me by the present Russian ambassador, seem to insure the support of the Emperor to the proposed measure. Our ambassador at the Court of St. Petersburg has in consequence, been instructed to submit it to the Russian Government and to request their early consideration of it. A copy of my instruction on the subject to Mr. Tower[1] is herewith inclosed for your confidential information.

The commercial interests of Great Britain and Japan will be so clearly served by the desired declaration of intentions, and the views of the Governments of these countries as to the desirability of the adopting of measures insuring the benefits of equality of treatment of all foreign trade throughout China are so similar to those entertained by the United States, that their acceptance of the propositions herein outlined and their cooperation in advocating their adoption by the other powers can be confidently expected. I enclosed herewith copy of the instruction which I have sent to Mr. Choate[2] on the subject.

In view of the present favorable conditions, you are instructed to submit the above considerations to His Imperial German Majesty's Minister for Foreign Affairs, and to request his early consideration of the subject.

---

[1] *Charlemagne Tower* (1848–1923) was the ambassador to Russia from 1899 to 1902.
[2] *Joseph H. Choate* (1832–1917), an attorney and diplomat, was ambassador to Great Britain from 1899 to 1905.

CIRCULAR TELEGRAM TO THE POWERS COOPERATING IN CHINA

Department of State, Washington, July 3, 1900
In this critical posture of affairs in China it is deemed appropriate to define the attitude of the United States as far as present circumstances permit this to be done. We adhere to the policy initiated by us in 1857 of peace with the Chinese nation, of furtherance of lawful commerce, and of protection of lives and property of our citizens by all means guaranteed under extraterritorial treaty rights and by the law of nations. If wrong be done to our citizens we propose to hold the responsible authors to the uttermost accountability. We regard the condition at Pekin as one of virtual anarchy, whereby power and responsibility are practically devolved upon the local provincial authorities. So long as they are not in overt collusion with rebellion and use their power to protect foreign life and property, we regard them as representing the Chinese people, with whom we seek to remain in peace and friendship. The purpose of the President is, as it has been heretofore, to act concurrently with the other powers; first, in opening up communication with Pekin and rescuing the American officials, missionaries, and other Americans who are in danger; secondly, in affording all possible protection everywhere in China to American life and property; thirdly, in guarding and protecting all legitimate American interests; and fourthly, in aiding to prevent a spread of the disorders to the other provinces of the Empire and a recurrence of such disasters. It is of course too early to forecast the means of attaining this last result; but the policy of the Government of the United States is to seek a solution which may bring about permanent safety and peace to China, preserve Chinese territorial and administrative entity, protect all rights guaranteed to friendly powers by treaty and international law, and safeguard for the world the principle of equal and impartial trade with all parts of the Chinese Empire.

Questions

1. What was the purpose of Hay's first Open Door note?
2. In what ways does his second note differ from the first?
3. Taken together, what do the notes say about the American attitude toward China?

21-9   To the Person Sitting in Darkness (1901)

Mark Twain

Although Secretary of State John Hay called the fight with Spain "a splendid little war," not everyone viewed it that way. A group of prominent Americans who opposed the acquisition of colonies founded the American Anti-Imperialist League. Among their number was famed author Mark Twain (1835–1910). He ostensibly addressed part of the following essay to "the person sitting in darkness"—that is, to a person in an undeveloped country.

Twain refers to Joseph Chamberlain, who as colonial secretary for the British government refused to consider South African independence. Chamberlain's policies helped cause the Boer War, which was being fought when Twain wrote this essay. The Mr. Croker to whom Twain refers later in the essay is Richard Croker, notorious "boss" of Tammany Hall, New York City's corrupt Democratic machine.

Source: Excerpted from Mark Twain, "To the Person Sitting in Darkness" (1901), in *Mark Twain: Collected Tales, Sketches, Speeches, and Essays, 1891–1910* (New York: Library of America, 1992), 465–473.

And by and by comes America, and our Master of the Game plays it badly—plays it as Mr. Chamberlain was playing it in South Africa. It was a mistake to do that; also, it was one which was quite unlooked for in a Master who was playing it so well in Cuba. In Cuba, he was playing the usual and regular *American* game, and it was winning, for there is no way to beat it. The Master, contemplating Cuba, said: "Here is an oppressed and friendless little nation which is willing to fight to be free; we go partners, and put up the strength of seventy million sympathizers and the resources of the United States: play!" Nothing but Europe combined could call that hand: and Europe cannot combine on anything. There, in Cuba, he was following our great tradition in a way which made us very proud of him, and proud of the deep dissatisfaction which his play was provoking in continental Europe. Moved by a high inspiration, he threw out those stirring words which proclaimed that forcible annexation would be "criminal aggression"; and in that utterance fired another "shot heard round the world." The memory of that fine saying will be outlived by the remembrance of no act of his but one—that he forgot it within the twelvemonth, and its honorable gospel along with it.

For, presently, came the Philippine temptation. It was strong; it was too strong, and he made that bad mistake: he played the European game, the Chamberlain game. It was a pity; it was a great pity, that error; that one grievous error, that irrevocable error. For it was the very place and time to play the American game again. And at no cost. Rich winnings to be gathered in, too; rich and permanent; indestructible; a fortune transmissible forever to the children of the flag. Not land, not money, not dominion—no, something worth many times more than that dross: our share, the spectacle of a nation of long harrassed and persecuted slaves set free through our influence; our posterity's share, the golden memory of that fair deed. The game was in our hands. If it had been played according to the American rules, Dewey would have sailed away from Manila as soon as he had destroyed the Spanish fleet—after putting up a sign on shore guaranteeing foreign property and life against damage by the Filipinos, and warning the Powers that interference with the emancipated patriots would be regarded as an act unfriendly to the United States. The Powers cannot combine, in even a bad cause, and the sign would not have been molested.

Dewey could have gone about his affairs elsewhere, and left the competent Filipino army to starve out the little Spanish garrison and send it home, and the Filipino citizens to set up the form of government they might prefer, and deal with the friars and their doubtful acquisitions according to Filipino ideas of fairness and justice—ideas which have since been tested and found to be as high an order as any that prevail in Europe or America.

But we played the Chamberlain game, and lost the chance to add another Cuba and another honorable deed to our good record.

The more we examine the mistake, the more clearly we perceive that it is going to be bad for the Business. The Person Sitting in Darkness is almost sure to say: "There is something curious about this—curious and unaccountable. There must be two Americans; one that sets the captive free, and one that takes a once-captive's new freedom away from him, and picks a quarrel with him with nothing to found it on; then kills him to get his land."

The truth is, the Person Sitting in Darkness *is* saying things like that; and for the sake of the Business we must persuade him to look at the Philippine matter in another and healthier way. We must arrange his opinions for him. I believe it can be done; for Mr. Chamberlain has arranged England's opinion of the South African matter, and done it most cleverly and successfully. He presented the facts—some of the facts—and showed those confiding people what the facts meant. He did it statistically, which is a good way. He used the formula: "Twice 2 are 14, and 2 from 9 leaves 35." Figures are effective; figures will convince the elect.

Now, my plan is a still bolder one than Mr. Chamberlain's, though apparently a copy of it. Let us be franker than Mr. Chamberlain; let us audaciously present the whole of the facts, shirking none, then explain them according to Mr. Chamberlain's formula. This daring truthfulness will astonish and dazzle the Person Sitting in the Darkness, and he will take the Explanation down before his mental vision has had time to get back into focus. Let us say to him:

"Our case is simple. On the 1st of May, Dewey destroyed the Spanish fleet. This left the Archipelago in the hands of its proper and rightful owners, the Filipino nation. Their army numbered 30,000 men, and they were competent to whip out or starve out the little Spanish garrison; then the people could set up a government of their own devising. Our traditions required that Dewey should now set up his warning sign, and go away. But the Master of the Game happened to think of another plan—the European plan. He acted upon it. This was, to send out an army—ostensibly to help the native patriots put the finishing touch upon their long and plucky struggle for independence, but really to take their land away from them and keep it. That is, in the interest of Progress and

Civilization. The plan developed, stage by stage, and quite satisfactorily. We entered into a military alliance with the trusting Filipinos, and they hemmed in Manila on the land side, and by their valuable help the place, with its garrison of 8,000 or 10,000 Spaniards, was captured—a thing which we could not have accomplished unaided at that time. We got their help by—by ingenuity. We knew they were fighting for their independence, and that they had been at it for two years. We knew they supposed that we also were fighting in their worthy cause—just as we had helped the Cubans fight for Cuban independence—and we allowed them to go on thinking so. *Until Manila was ours and we could get along without them.* Then we showed our hand. Of course, they were surprised—that was natural; surprised and disappointed; disappointed and grieved. To them it looked un-American; uncharacteristic; foreign to our established traditions. And this was natural, too; for we were only playing the American Game in public—in private it was the European. It was neatly done, very neatly, and it bewildered them. They could not understand it; for we had been so friendly—so affectionate, even—with those simple-minded patriots! We, our own selves, had brought back out of exile their leader, their hero, their hope, their Washington—Aguinaldo; brought him in a warship, in high honor, under the sacred shelter and hospitality of the flag; brought him back and restored him to his people, and got their moving and eloquent gratitude for it. Yes, we had been so friendly to them, and had heartened them up in so many ways! We had lent them guns and ammunition; advised with them; exchanged pleasant courtesies with them; placed our sick and wounded in their kindly care; intrusted our Spanish prisoners to their humane and honest hands; fought shoulder to shoulder with them against "the common enemy" (our own phrase); praised their mercifulness, praised their fine and honorable conduct; borrowed their trenches, borrowed strong positions which they had previously captured from the Spaniards; petted them, lied to them—officially proclaiming that our land and naval forces came to give them their freedom and displace the bad Spanish Government—fooled them, used them until we needed them no longer; then derided the sucked orange and threw it away. We kept the positions which we had beguiled them of; by and by, we moved a force forward and overlapped patriot ground—a clever thought, for we needed trouble, and this would produce it. A Filipino soldier, crossing the ground, where no one had a right to forbid him, was shot by our sentry. The badgered patriots resented this with arms, without waiting to know whether Aguinaldo, who was absent, would approve or not. Aguinaldo did not approve; but that availed nothing. What we wanted, in the interest of Progress and Civilization, was the Archipelago, unencumbered by patriots struggling for independence; and War was what we needed. We clinched our opportunity. It is Mr. Chamberlain's case over again—at least in its motive and intention; and we played the game as adroitly as he played it himself."

At this point in our frank statement of fact to the Person Sitting in Darkness, we should throw in a little trade taffy about the Blessings of Civilization—for a change and for the refreshment of his spirit—then go on with our tale:

We and the patriots having captured Manila, Spain's ownership of the Archipelago and her sovereignty over it were at an end—obliterated—annihilated—not a rag or shred of either remaining behind. It was then that we conceived the divinely humorous idea of *buying* both of these specters from Spain! [It is quite safe to confess this to the Person Sitting in Darkness, since neither he nor any other sane person will believe it.] In buying those ghosts for twenty millions, we also contracted to take care of the friars and their accumulations. [I think we also agreed to propagate leprosy and smallpox, but as to this there is doubt. But it is not important; persons afflicted with the friars do not mind other diseases.]

"With our Treaty ratified, Manila subdued, and our Ghosts secured, we had no further use for Aguinaldo and the owners of the Archipelago. We forced a war, and we have been hunting America's guest and ally through the woods and swamps ever since."

At this point in the tale, it will be well to boast a little of our war work and our heroisms in the field, so as to make our performance look as fine as England's in South Africa; but I believe it will not be best to emphasize this too much. We must be cautious. Of course, we must read the war telegrams to the Person, in order to keep up our frankness; but we can throw an air of humorousness over them, and that will modify their grim eloquence a little, and their rather indiscret [*sic*] exhibitions of gory exultation. Before reading to him the following display heads of the dispatches of November 18, 1900, it will be well to practice on them in private first, so as to get the right tang of lightness and gayety into them:

"ADMINISTRATION WEARY OF PROTRACTED HOSTILITIES!"

"REAL WAR AHEAD FOR FILIPINO REBELS"[1]

"WILL SHOW NO MERCY!" . . .

Of course, we must not venture to ignore our General MacArthur's reports—oh, why do they keep on printing those embarrassing things?—we must drop them trippingly from the tongue and take the chances:

During the last ten months our losses have been 268 killed and 750 wounded; Filipino loss, *three thousand two hundred and twenty-seven killed*, and 694 wounded.

We must stand ready to grab the Person Sitting in Darkness, for he will swoon away at this confession, saying: "Good God! those 'niggers' spare their wounded, and the Americans massacre theirs!"

---

[1] "Rebels!" Mumble that funny word—don't let the Person catch it distinctly.—M. T. [*Twain's note.*]

We must bring him to, and coax him and coddle him, and assure him that the ways of Providence are best, and that it would not become us to find fault with them; and then, to show him that we are only imitators, not originators, we must read the following passage from the letter of an American soldier lad in the Philippines to his mother, published in *Public Opinion*, of Decorah, Iowa, describing the finish of a victorious battle:

"WE NEVER LEFT ONE ALIVE. IF ONE WAS WOUNDED, WE WOULD RUN OUR BAYONETS THROUGH HIM."

Having now laid all the historical facts before the Person Sitting in Darkness, we should bring him to again, and explain them to him. We should say to him:

"They look doubtful, but in reality they are not. There have been lies; yes, but they were told in a good cause. We have been treacherous; but that was only in order that real good might come out of apparent evil. True, we have crushed a deceived and confiding people; we have turned against the weak and the friendless who trusted us; we have stamped out a just and intelligent and well-ordered republic; we have stabbed an ally in the back and slapped the face of a guest; we have bought a Shadow from an enemy that hadn't it to sell; we have robbed a trusting friend of his land and his liberty; we have invited our clean young men to shoulder a discredited musket and do bandits' work under a flag which bandits have been accustomed to fear, not to follow; we have debauched America's honor and blackened her face before the world; but each detail was for the best. We know this. The Head of every State and Sovereignty in Christendom and 90 per cent. of every legislative body in Christendom, including our Congress and our fifty state legislatures, are members not only of the church, but also of the Blessings-of-Civilization Trust. This world-girdling accumulation of trained morals, high principles, and justice cannot do an unright thing, an unfair thing, an ungenerous thing, an unclean thing. It knows what it is about. Give yourself no uneasiness; it is all right."

Now then, that will convince the Person. You will see. It will restore the Business. Also, it will elect the Master of the Game to the vacant place in the Trinity of our national gods; and there on their high thrones the Three will sit, age after age, in the people's sight, each bearing the Emblem of his service: Washington, the Sword of the Liberator; Lincoln, the Slave's Broken Chains; the Master, the Chains Repaired.

It will give the Business a splendid new start. You will see.

Everything is prosperous, now; everything is just as we should wish it. We have got the Archipelago, and we shall never give it up. Also, we have every reason to hope that we shall have an opportunity before very long to slip out of our congressional contract with Cuba and give her something better in the place of it. It is a rich country, and many of us are already beginning to see that the contract was a sentimental mistake. But now—right now—is the best time to do some profitable rehabilitating work—work that will set us up and make us comfortable, and discourage gossip. We cannot conceal from ourselves that, privately, we are a little troubled about our uniform. It is one of our prides; it is acquainted with honor; it is familiar with great deeds and noble; we love it, we revere it; and so this errand it is on makes us uneasy. And our flag—another pride of ours, our chiefest! We have worshipped it so; and when we have seen it in far lands—glimpsing it unexpectedly in that strange sky, waving its welcome and benediction to us—we have caught our breaths, and uncovered our heads, and couldn't speak, for a moment, for the thought of what it was to us and the great ideals it stood for. Indeed, we *must* do something about these things; it is easily managed. We can have a special one—our states do it: we can have just our usual flag, with the white stripes painted black and the stars replaced by the skull and crossbones.

And we do not need that Civil Commission out there. Having no powers, it has to invent them, and that kind of work cannot be effectively done by just anybody; an expert is required. Mr. Croker can be spared. We do not want the United States represented there, but only the Game.

By help of these suggested amendments, Progress and Civilization in that country can have a boom, and it will take in the Persons who are Sitting in Darkness, and we can resume Business at the old stand.

Questions

1. How did Twain say he would argue the cause of empire?
2. What was his real purpose in recounting recent events?
3. Why was Twain cynical?

21-10 The Roosevelt Corollary to the Monroe Doctrine (1904, 1905)

Theodore Roosevelt

After advising that it was wisdom to "speak softly and carry a big stick," President Theodore Roosevelt proceeded to speak and act as policeman of the Western Hemisphere, at least in areas of strategic importance to the United States—the Caribbean, Central America, and the northernmost nations of South America. The following excerpt offers his corollary to the Monroe Doctrine, which Roosevelt proclaimed in successive annual messages to Congress.

Source: Theodore Roosevelt, fourth annual message to Congress, December 6, 1904, and fifth annual message to Congress, December 5, 1905, in James D. Richardson, ed., *A Compilation of the Messages and Papers of the Presidents* (Washington, DC: U.S. Goverment Printing Office, n.d.), 10:831–832; 14:6944 ff.

ROOSEVELT'S ANNUAL MESSAGE TO CONGRESS, DECEMBER 6, 1904

... It is not true that the United States feels any land hunger or entertains any project as regards the other nations of the Western Hemisphere save such as are for their welfare. All that this country desires is to see the neighboring countries stable, orderly, and prosperous. Any country whose people conduct themselves well can count upon our hearty friendship. If a nation shows that it knows how to act with reasonable efficiency and decency in social and political matters, if it keeps order and pays its obligations, it need fear no interference from the United States. Chronic wrong doing, or an impotence which results in a general loosening of the ties of civilized society, may in America, as elsewhere, ultimately require intervention by some civilized nation, and in the Western Hemisphere the adherence of the United States to the Monroe Doctrine may force the United States, however reluctantly, in flagrant cases of such wrong doing or impotence, to the exercise of an international police power. If every country washed by the Caribbean Sea would show the progress in stable and just civilization which with the aid of the Platt amendment Cuba has shown since our troops left the island, and which so many of the republics in both Americas are constantly and brilliantly showing, all question of interference by this Nation with their affairs would be at an end. Our interests and those of our southern neighbors are in reality identical. They have great natural riches, and if within their borders the reign of law and justice obtains, prosperity is sure to come to them. While they thus obey the primary laws of civilized society they may rest assured that they will be treated by us in a spirit of cordial and helpful sympathy. We would interfere with them only in the last resort, and then only if it became evident that their inability or unwillingness to do justice at home and abroad had violated the rights of the United States or had invited foreign aggression to the detriment of the entire body of American nations. It is a mere truism to say that every nation ... which desires to maintain its freedom, its independence, must ultimately realize that the right of such independence can not be separated from the responsibility of making good use of it.

ROOSEVELT'S ANNUAL MESSAGE TO CONGRESS, DECEMBER 5, 1905

... It must be understood that under no circumstances will the United States use the Monroe Doctrine as a cloak for territorial aggression. We desire peace with all the world, but perhaps most of all with the other peoples of the American Continent.

There are, of course, limits to the wrongs which any self-respecting nation can endure. It is always possible that wrong actions toward this Nation, or toward citizens of this Nation, in some State unable to keep order among its own people, unable to secure justice from outsiders, and unwilling to do justice to those outsiders who treat it well, may result in our having to take action to protect our rights; but such action will not be taken with a view to territorial aggression, and it will be taken at all only with extreme reluctance and when it has become evident that every other resource has been exhausted.

Moreover, we must make it evident that we do not intend to permit the Monroe Doctrine to be used by any nation on this Continent as a shield to protect it from the consequences of its own misdeeds against foreign nations. If a republic to the south of us commits a tort against a foreign nation, such as an outrage against a citizen of that nation, then the Monroe Doctrine does not force us to interfere to prevent punishment of the tort, save to see that the punishment does not assume the form of territorial occupation.... The case is more difficult when it refers to a contractual obligation. Our own Government has always refused to enforce such contractual obligations on behalf of its citizens by an appeal to arms. It is much to be wished that all foreign governments would take the same view. But they do not; and in consequence we are liable at any time to be brought face to face with disagreeable alternatives. On the one hand, this country would certainly decline to go to war to prevent a foreign government from collecting a just debt; on the other hand, it is very inadvisable to permit any foreign power to take possession, even temporarily, of the custom houses of an American Republic in order to enforce the payment of its obligations; for such temporary occupation might turn into a permanent occupation. The only escape from these alternatives may at any time be that we must ourselves undertake to bring about some arrangement by which so much as possible of a just obligation shall be paid. It is far better that this country should put through such an arrangement, rather than allow any foreign country to undertake it. To do so insures the defaulting republic from having to pay debt of an improper character under duress, while it also insures honest creditors of the republic from being passed by in the interest of dishonest or grasping creditors. Moreover, for the United States to take such a position offers the only possible way of insuring us against a clash with some foreign power. The position is, therefore, in the interest of peace as well as in the interest of justice. It is of benefit to our people; it is of benefit to foreign peoples; and most of all it is really of benefit to the people of the country concerned.

Questions

1. Under what circumstances did Roosevelt propose to intervene in the affairs of Caribbean nations? Why would he abstain from intervention?
2. What was Roosevelt's view of Caribbean nations? Of the United States in relation to those nations?
3. What kind of precedent was involved in this proclamation of "an international police power"?

Questions for Further Thought

1. Drawing on the text and the documents for Chapter 21, reflect on the role of race in U.S. foreign affairs.
2. In what ways could John Hay's Open Door notes (Document 21-8) and the Roosevelt Corollary (Document 21-10) have antagonized the very people they ostensibly sought to protect? How might such feelings reveal themselves?
3. A number of factors, among them economic and strategic considerations and the presence or absence of other regional and outside powers, influence a nation's foreign policy. What factors influenced American foreign policy in the Far East? in the Caribbean?

PART FIVE   *The Modern State and Society, 1914–1945*

CHAPTER TWENTY-TWO

War and the American State
1914–1920

Great War, 1914–1918

When the Great War began in August 1914, both the Allies and the Central Powers expected victory within a matter of weeks. No one anticipated a war that would last four years and take 14.5 million lives.

In the Napoleonic Wars a century before, opposing armies had fired at one another with muskets across an open field. In 1914, the tactics remained largely the same, but the weapons had changed profoundly. With the use of machine guns and high-powered rifles, frontal assaults caused ruinous casualties. Combat on the Western Front quickly evolved into trench warfare. Opposing armies again faced one another, but this time it was from the confines of a 25,000-mile network of trenches protected by barbed wire, running across Belgium and France. Periodically, an army would mount an offensive, with soldiers pouring into the disputed no-man's land in an attempt to break through the enemy's lines. Casualties in a single battle often numbered in the hundreds of thousands on each side. Poison gas and artillery barrages added to the horror of a soldier's existence.

The war did not directly affect the United States at first, as President Woodrow Wilson tried to maintain a policy of neutrality. Although cultural ties and aggressive British propaganda generated sympathy for the Allies, such support was not universal. German Americans tended to support the old country, and Irish Americans were cool to the English, who appeared to be more interested in liberating Belgium than in freeing Ireland. Leading progressives, socialists, and pacifists all argued against war, and Henry Ford financed the voyage of a "peace ship," the passengers on which hoped to negotiate an end to the conflict. But circumstances conspired against Wilson. Even as the British navy swept the German merchant marine from the Atlantic, American trade with the Allies grew.

The Germans attempted to neutralize this trade advantage through U-boat, or submarine, warfare, and American lives were lost in unannounced attacks, such as that on the *Lusitania*. On different occasions in 1915 and 1916, President Wilson forced the Germans to abandon unrestricted submarine warfare, but in January 1917, Germany resumed its attacks. A month later, Americans learned that Germany had offered Mexico a chance to recover Texas, New Mexico, and Arizona if—in the event of war between the United States and Germany—Mexico declared war on the United States. In April, Congress voted for war.

Document 22-1 is an editorial cartoon entitled "Don't Rock the Boat." Document 22-2 is the Zimmermann Telegram, which strengthened the call for war. Document 22-3 is Woodrow Wilson's April 2, 1917, war message to Congress. Document 22-4 is drawn from a speech of Senator Robert M. La Follette opposing the declaration of war. Document 22-5 describes combat on the Western Front. Document 22-6 reproduces propaganda aimed at protecting servicemen from venereal disease.

22-1 Don't Rock the Boat (1915)

Maintaining neutrality was a difficult challenge for the Wilson administration, given the German use of submarines to try to negate the advantage the British enjoyed with their surface navy. Submarines, or U-boats, made good military sense but their use came at a great political cost to the Germans, because submarine warfare struck many as uncivilized, even cowardly, especially when targets included passenger liners, such as the *Lusitania*. In today's terms, the "collateral damage" was considered too high. In 1915, with the sinking of the *Lusitania*, Woodrow Wilson started taking a harder stand against Germany. William Jennings Bryan (1860–1925), the "Great Commoner," and three-time presidential nominee of the Democratic Party, served in Wilson's cabinet as secretary of state. However, he took issue with Wilson's growing partiality, and, out of principle, resigned from his office—a rare act for a high official in the U.S. government.

Source: Cartoon, "Don't Rock the Boat," from *The New York World*. Reprinted in *Bryan: The Great Commoner*, by J. C. Long (New York: D. Appleton & Company, 1928), 341. Reprinted with permission by Butler library, Columbia University, New York City.

Questions

1. What does this cartoon suggest about the relationship of patriotism and principle?
2. What is the proper role of a member of the president's cabinet, according to the editorial cartoonist?

22-2 The Zimmermann Telegram (1917)

Arthur Zimmermann

Arthur Zimmermann, the German foreign minister, proposed an alliance between Germany and Mexico to Mexican president Venustiano Carranza. The proposal was dispatched by telegram on January 19, 1917, but was intercepted, deciphered, and then made public on March 1, 1917. News of Zimmermann's offer angered U.S. citizens, especially those in states that bordered Mexico, and Wilson cited the proposed alliance in his war message to Congress as evidence that imperial Germany wanted to "stir up enemies against us at our very doors."

Source: Barbara W. Tuchman, *The Zimmermann Telegram* (1958; New York: Ballantine Books, 1966), 146.

We intend to begin unrestricted submarine warfare on the first of February. We shall endeavor in spite of this to keep the United States neutral. In the event of this not succeeding, we make Mexico a proposal of alliance on the following basis: make war together, make peace together, generous financial support, and an understanding on our part that Mexico is to reconquer the lost territory in Texas, New Mexico, and Arizona. The settlement in detail is left to you.

You will inform the President [of Mexico] of the above most secretly as soon as the outbreak of war with the United States is certain and add the suggestion that he should, on his own initiative, invite Japan to immediate adherence and at the same time mediate between Japan and ourselves.

Please call the President's attention to the fact that the unrestricted employment of our submarines now offers the prospect of compelling England to make peace within a few months. Acknowledge receipt.

Zimmermann

Questions

1. What was to be the basis of a German-Mexican alliance?
2. What historical grievance were the Germans trying to exploit?

22-3 War Message to Congress (1917)

Woodrow Wilson

Running on the slogan "He Kept Us out of War," Woodrow Wilson defeated the Republican challenger, Charles Evans Hughes, in the November 1916 presidential election. However, spurred by a sequence of events (see text pp. 677–678), Wilson started his second term by reluctantly reversing his campaign position. On April 2, 1917, he called the newly elected Congress into a special session and asked for a declaration of war. With a Senate vote of 82–6 and a House vote of 373–50, Congress complied.

Source: *The Messages and Papers of Woodrow Wilson* (New York: Review of Reviews Corporation, 1924), 1:372–383.

Gentlemen of the Congress:

I have called the Congress into extraordinary session because there are serious, very serious, choices of policy to be made, and made immediately, which it was neither right nor constitutionally permissible that I should assume the responsibility of making.

On the third of February last I officially laid before you the extraordinary announcement of the Imperial German Government that on and after the first day of February it was its purpose to put aside all restraints of law or of humanity and use its submarines to sink every vessel that sought to approach either the ports of Great Britain and Ireland or the western coasts of Europe or any of the ports controlled by the enemies of Germany within the Mediterranean. That had seemed to be the object of the German submarine warfare earlier in the war, but since April of last year the Imperial Government had somewhat restrained the commanders of its undersea craft in conformity with its promise then given to us that passenger boats should not be sunk and that due warning would be given to all other vessels which its submarines might seek to destroy, when no resistance was offered or escape attempted, and care taken that their crews were given at least a fair chance to save their lives in their open boats. The precautions taken were meagre and haphazard enough, as was proved in distressing instance after instance in the progress of the cruel and unmanly business, but a certain degree of restraint was observed. The new policy has swept every restriction aside. Vessels of every kind, whatever their flag, their character, their cargo, their destination, their errand, have been ruthlessly sent to the bottom without warning and without thought of help or mercy for those on board, the vessels of friendly neutrals along with those of belligerents. Even hospital ships and ships carrying relief to the sorely bereaved and stricken people of Belgium, though the latter were provided with safe conduct through the proscribed areas by the German Government itself and were distinguished by unmistakable marks of identity, have been sunk with the same reckless lack of compassion or of principle.

I was for a little while unable to believe that such things would in fact be done by any government that had hitherto subscribed to the humane practices of civilized nations. International law had its origin in the attempt to set up some law which would be respected and observed upon the seas, where no nation had right of dominion and where lay the free highways of the world. By painful stage after stage has that law been built up, with meagre enough results, indeed, after all was accomplished that could be accomplished, but always with a clear view, at least, of what the heart and conscience of mankind demanded. This minimum of right the German Government has swept aside under the plea of retaliation and necessity and because it had no weapons which it could use at sea except these which it is impossible to employ as it is employing them without throwing to the winds all scruples of humanity or of respect for the understandings that were supposed to underlie the intercourse of the world. I am not now thinking of the loss of property involved, immense and serious as that is, but only of the wanton and wholesale destruction of the lives of non-combatants, men, women, and children, engaged in pursuits which have always, even in the darkest periods of modern history, been deemed innocent and legitimate. Property can be paid for; the lives of peaceful and innocent people cannot be. The present German submarine warfare against commerce is a warfare against mankind.

It is a war against all nations. American ships have been sunk, American lives taken, in ways which it has stirred us very deeply to learn of, but the ships and people of other neutral and friendly nations have been sunk and overwhelmed in the waters in the same way. There has been no discrimination. The challenge is to all mankind. Each nation must decide for itself how it will meet it. The choice we make for ourselves must be made with a moderation of counsel and a temperateness of judgment befitting our character and our motives as a nation. We must put excited feeling away. Our motive will not be revenge or the victorious assertion of the physical might of the nation, but only the vindication of right, of human right, of which we are only a single champion.

When I addressed the Congress on the twenty-sixth of February last I thought that it would suffice to assert our neutral rights with arms, our right to use the seas against unlawful interference, our right to keep our people safe against unlawful violence. But armed neutrality, it now appears, is impracticable. Because submarines are in effect outlaws when used as the German submarines have been used against merchant shipping, it is impossible to defend ships against their attacks as the law of nations has assumed that merchantmen would defend themselves against privateers or cruisers, visible craft giving chase upon the open sea. It is common prudence in such circumstances, grim necessity indeed, to endeavour to destroy them before they have shown their own intention. They must be dealt with upon sight, if dealt with at all. The German Government denies the right of neutrals to use arms at all within the areas of the sea which it has proscribed, even in the defense of rights which no modern publicist has ever before questioned their right to defend. The intimation is conveyed that the armed guards which we have placed on our merchant ships will be treated as beyond the pale of law and subject to be dealt with as pirates would be. Armed neutrality is ineffectual enough at best; in such circumstances and in the face of such pretensions it is worse than ineffectual; it is likely only to produce what it was meant to prevent; it is practically certain to draw us into the war without either the rights or the effectiveness of belligerents. There is one choice we cannot make, we are incapable of making: we will not choose the path of submission and suffer the most sacred rights of our nation and our people to be ignored or violated. The wrongs against which we now array ourselves are no common wrongs: they cut to the very roots of human life.

With a profound sense of the solemn and even tragical character of the step I am taking and of the grave responsibilities which it involves, but in unhesitating obedience to what I deem my constitutional duty, I advise that the Congress declare the recent course of the Imperial German Government to be in fact nothing less than war against the government and people of the United States; that it formally accept the status of belligerent which has thus been thrust upon it; and that it take immediate steps not only to put the country in a more thorough state of defense but also to exert all its power and employ all its resources to bring the Government of the German Empire to terms and end the war.

What this will involve is clear. It will involve the utmost practicable cooperation in counsel and action with the governments now at war with Germany, and, as incident to that, the extension to those governments of the most liberal financial credits, in order that our resources may so far as possible be added to theirs. It will involve the organization and mobilization of all the material resources of the country to supply the materials of war and serve the incidental needs of the nation in the most abundant and yet the most economical and efficient way possible. It will involve the immediate full equipment of the navy in all respects but particularly in supplying it with the best means of dealing with the enemy's submarines. It will involve the immediate addition to the armed forces of the United States already provided for by law in case of war at least five hundred thousand men, who should, in my opinion, be chosen upon the principle of universal liability to service, and also the authorization of subsequent additional increments of equal force so soon as they may be needed and can be handled in training. It will involve also, of course, the granting of adequate credits to the Government, sustained, I hope, so far as they can equitably be sustained by the present generation, by well conceived taxation.

I say sustained so far as may be equitable by taxation because it seems to me that it would be most unwise to base the credits which will now be necessary entirely on money borrowed. It is our duty, I most respectfully urge, to protect our people so far as we may against the very serious hardships and evils which would be likely to arise out of the inflation which would be produced by vast loans.

In carrying out the measures by which these things are to be accomplished we should keep constantly in mind the wisdom of interfering as little as possible in our own preparation and in the equipment of our own military forces with the duty,—for it will be a very practical duty,—of supplying the nations already at war with Germany with the materials which they can obtain only from us or by our assistance. They are in the field and we should help them in every way to be effective there.

I shall take the liberty of suggesting, through the several executive departments of the Government, for the consideration of your committees, measures for the accomplishment of the several objects I have mentioned. I hope that it will be your pleasure to deal with them as having been framed after very careful thought by the branch of the Government upon which the responsibility of conducting the war and safeguarding the nation will most directly fall.

While we do these things, these deeply momentous things, let us be very clear, and make very clear to all the world what our motives and our objects are. My own thought has not been driven from its habitual and normal course by the unhappy events of the last two months, and I do not believe that the thought of the nation has been altered or clouded by them. I have exactly the same things in mind now that I had in mind when I addressed the Senate on the twenty-second of January last; the same that I had in mind when I addressed the Congress on the third of February and on the twenty-sixth of February. Our object now, as then, is to vindicate the principles of peace and justice in the life of the world as against selfish and autocratic power and to set up amongst the really free and self-governed peoples of the world such a concert of purpose and of action as will henceforth ensure the observance of those principles. Neutrality is no longer feasible or desirable where the peace of the world is involved and the freedom of its peoples, and the menace to that peace and freedom lies in the existence of autocratic governments backed by organized force which is controlled wholly by their will, not by the will of their people. We have seen the last of neutrality in such circumstances. We are at the beginning of an age in which it will be insisted that the same standards of conduct and responsibility for wrong done shall be observed among nations and their governments that are observed among the individual citizens of civilized states.

We have no quarrel with the German people. We have no feeling towards them but one of sympathy and friendship. It was not upon their impulse that their government acted in entering this war. It was not with their previous knowledge or approval. It was a war determined upon as wars used to be determined upon in the old, unhappy days when peoples were nowhere consulted by their rulers and wars were provoked and waged in the interest of dynasties or of little groups of ambitious men who were accustomed to use their fellow men as pawns and tools. Self-governed nations do not fill their neighbour states with spies or set the course of intrigue to bring about some critical posture of affairs which will give them an opportunity to strike and make conquest. Such designs can be successfully worked out only under cover and where no one has the right to ask questions. Cunningly contrived plans of deception or aggression, carried, it may be, from generation to generation, can be worked out and kept from the light only within the privacy of courts or behind the carefully guarded confidences of a narrow and privileged class. They are happily impossible where public opinion commands and insists upon full information concerning all the nation's affairs.

A steadfast concert for peace can never be maintained except by a partnership of democratic nations. No autocratic government could be trusted to keep faith within it or observe its covenants. It must be a league of honour, a partnership of opinion. Intrigue would eat its vitals away; the plottings of inner circles who could plan what they would and render account to no one would be a corruption seated at its very heart. Only free peoples can hold their purpose and their honour steady to a common end and prefer the interests of mankind to any narrow interest of their own....

We are accepting this challenge of hostile purpose because we know that in such a government, following such methods, we can never have a friend; and that in the presence of its organized power, always lying in wait to accomplish we know not what purpose, there can be no assured security for the democratic governments of the world. We are now about to accept gauge of battle with this natural foe to liberty and shall, if necessary, spend the whole force of the nation to check and nullify its pretensions and its power. We are glad, now that we see the facts with no veil of false pretence about them, to fight thus for the ultimate peace of the world and for the liberation of its peoples, the German peoples included: for the rights of nations great and small and the privilege of men everywhere to choose their way of life and of obedience. The world must be made safe for democracy. Its peace must be planted upon the tested foundations of political liberty. We have no selfish ends to serve. We desire no conquest, no dominion. We seek no indemnities for ourselves, no material compensation for the sacrifices we shall freely make. We are but one of the champions of the rights of mankind. We shall be satisfied when those rights have been made as secure as the faith and the freedom of nations can make them....

I have said nothing of the governments allied with the Imperial Government of Germany because they have not made war upon us or challenged us to defend our right and our honour. The Austro-Hungarian Government has, indeed, avowed its unqualified endorsement and acceptance of the reckless and lawless submarine warfare adopted now without disguise by the Imperial German Government, and it has therefore not been possible for this Government to receive Count Tarnowski, the Ambassador recently accredited to this Government by the Imperial and Royal Government of Austria-Hungary; but that Government has not actually engaged in warfare against citizens of the United States on the seas, and I take the liberty, for the present at least, of postponing a discussion of our relations with the authorities at Vienna. We enter this war only where we are clearly forced into it because there are no other means of defending our rights....

It is a distressing and oppressive duty, Gentlemen of the Congress, which I have performed in thus addressing you. There are, it may be, many months of fiery trial and sacrifice ahead of us. It is a fearful thing to lead this great peaceful people into war, into the most terrible and disastrous of all wars, civilization itself seeming to be in the balance. But the right is more precious than peace, and we shall fight for the things which we have always carried nearest our hearts, for democracy, for the right of those who submit to authority to have a voice in their own governments, for the rights and liberties of small nations, for a universal dominion of right by such a concert of free peoples as shall bring peace and safety to all nations and make the world itself at last free. To such a task we can dedicate our lives and our fortunes, everything that we are and everything that we have, with the pride of those who know that the day has come when America is privileged to spend her blood and her might for the principles that gave her birth and happiness and the peace which she has treasured. God helping her, she can do no other.

Questions

1. Outline Wilson's case against Germany.
2. How did Wilson frame the United States' involvement in the conflict? According to Wilson, what were Americans to fight for?
3. In what ways does this speech foreshadow Wilson's Fourteen Points and his support for the League of Nations (see text pp. 694–698)?

22-4 Anti-War Speech (1917)

Robert M. La Follette

In declaring America's war aims to be idealistic, not selfish, President Woodrow Wilson sought to distinguish between Germany's leaders and the German people, "with whom we have no quarrel," for whom we feel only "sympathy and friendship" (Document 22-3). Among the six senators and fifty representatives who would have nothing of Wilson's case for war, none was more sharply critical than Senator Robert M. La Follette (1855–1925).

In the following speech, given on April 4, La Follette rebuts the president point by point (see text p. 697).

Source: Congressional Record, Senate, 65th Congress, 1st Session (April 4, 1917), 227–229, 233, 234.

In his message of April 2 the President says:

> I was for a little while unable to believe that such things [referring to German submarine methods of warfare] would in fact be done by any Government that had heretofore subscribed to the humane practices of civilized nations. International law had its origin in the attempt to set up some law which would be respected and observed upon the sea, where no nation had right of dominion and where lay the free highways of the world. By painful stage after stage has that law been built up with meager enough results indeed, after all was accomplished that could be accomplished, but always with a clear view at least of what the heart and conscience of mankind demanded.

The recognition by the President that Germany had always heretofore subscribed to the humane practices of civilized nations is a most important statement. Does it not suggest a question as to why it is that Germany has departed from those practices in the present war? What the President had so admirably stated about international law and the painful stage by which it has been builded up is absolutely true. But in this connection would it not be well to say also that it was England, not Germany, who refused to obey the declaration of London, which represented the most humane ideas and was the best statement of the rules of international law as applied to naval warfare? Keep that in mind. Would it not have been fair to say, and to keep in mind, that Germany offered to abide by those principles and England refused; that in response to our request Germany offered to cease absolutely from the use of submarines in what we characterized an unlawful manner if England would cease from equally palpable and cruel violations of international law in her conduct of naval warfare?

The President in his message of April 2 says:

> The present German warfare against commerce is a warfare against mankind. It is a war against all nations.

Again referring to Germany's warfare he says:

> There has been no discrimination. The challenge is to all mankind.

Is it not a little peculiar that if Germany's warfare is against all nations the United States is the only nation that regards it necessary to declare war on that account? If it is true, as the President says, that "there has been no discrimination," that Germany has treated every neutral as she has treated us, is it not peculiar that no other of the great nations of the earth seem to regard Germany's conduct in this war as a cause for entering into it? Are we the only nation jealous of our rights? Are we the only nation insisting upon the protection of our citizens? Does not the strict neutrality maintained on the part of all the other nations of the earth suggest that possibly there is a reason for their action, and that that reason is that Germany's conduct under the circumstances does not merit from any nation which is determined to preserve its neutrality a declaration of war?

Norway, Sweden, the Netherlands, Switzerland, Denmark, Spain, and all the great Republics of South America are quite as interested in this subject as we are, and yet they have refused to join with us in a combination against Germany. I venture to suggest also that the nations named, and probably others, have a somewhat better right to be heard than we, for by refusing to sell war-material and munitions to any of the belligerents they have placed themselves in a position where the suspicion which attaches to us of a desire for war profits can not attach to them.

On August 4, 1914, the Republic of Brazil declared the exportation of war material from Brazilian ports to any of these powers at war to be strictly forbidden, whether such exports be under the Brazilian flag or that of any other country.

In that connection I note the following dispatch from Buenos Aires, appearing in the Washington papers of yesterday:

> President Wilson's war address was received here with interest, but no particular enthusiasm. . . . Government officials and politicians have adopted a cold shoulder toward the United States policy—an attitude apparently based on apprehension lest South American interests suffer.

The newspaper Razon's view was illustrative of this. "Does not the United States consider this an opportune time to consolidate the imperialistic policy everywhere north of Panama?" it said.

This is the question that neutral nations the world over are asking. Are we seizing upon this war to consolidate and extend an imperialistic policy? We complain also because Mexico has turned the cold shoulder to us, and are wont to look for sinister reasons for her attitude. Is it any wonder that she should also turn the cold shoulder when she sees us unite with Great Britain, an empire founded upon her conquests and subjugation of weaker nations? There is no doubt that the sympathy of Norway, Sweden, and other countries close to the scene of war is already with Germany. It is apparent that they view with alarm the entrance into the European struggle of the stranger from across the sea. It is suggested by some that our entrance into the war will shorten it. It is my firm belief, based upon such information as I have, that our entrance into the war will not only prolong it, but that it will vastly extend its area by drawing in other nations.

In his message of April 2, the President said:

> We have no quarrel with the German people—it was not upon their impulse that their Government acted in entering this war; it was not with their previous knowledge or approval.

Again he says:

> We are, let me say again, sincere friends of the German people and shall desire nothing so much as the early reestablishment of intimate relations of mutual advantage between us.

At least, the German people, then, are not outlaws. What is the thing the President asks us to do to these German people of whom he speaks so highly and whose sincere friend he declares us to be?

Here is what he declares we shall do in this war. We shall undertake, he says—

> The utmost practicable cooperation in council and action with the Governments now at war with Germany, and as an incident to that, the extension to those Governments of the most liberal financial credits in order that our resources may, so far as possible, be added to theirs.

"Practicable cooperation!" Practicable cooperation with England and her allies in starving to death the old men and women, the children, the sick and the maimed of Germany. The thing we are asked to do is the thing I have stated. It is idle to talk of a war upon a government only. We are leagued in this war, or it is the President's proposition that we shall be so leagued, with the hereditary enemies of Germany. Any war with Germany, or any other country for that matter, would be bad enough, but there are not words strong enough to voice my protest against the proposed combination with the entente allies. When we cooperate with those Governments we indorse their methods, we indorse the violations of international law by Great Britain, we indorse the shameful methods of warfare against which we have again and again protested in this war; we indorse her purpose to wreak upon the German people the animosities which for years her people have been taught to cherish against Germany; finally when the end comes, whatever it may be, we find ourselves in cooperation with our ally, Great Britain, and if we can not resist now the pressure she is exerting to carry us into the war, how can we hope to resist, then, the thousandfold greater pressure she will exert to bend us to her purposes and compel compliance with her demands?

We do not know what they are. We do not know what is in the minds of those who have made the compact, but we are to subscribe to it. We are irrevocably, by our votes here, to marry ourselves to a nondivorceable proposition veiled from us now. Once enlisted, once in the copartnership, we will be carried through with the purposes, whatever they may be, of which we now know nothing.

Sir, if we are to enter upon this war in the manner the President demands, let us throw pretense to the winds, let us be honest, let us admit that this is a ruthless war against not only Germany's army and her navy but against her civilian population as well, and frankly state that the purpose of Germany's hereditary European enemies has become our purpose. . . .

Just a word of comment more upon one of the points in the President's address. He says that this is a war "for the things which we have always carried nearest to our hearts—for democracy, for the right of those who submit to authority to have a voice in their own government." In many places throughout the address is this exalted sentiment given expression.

It is a sentiment peculiarly calculated to appeal to American hearts and, when accompanied by acts consistent with it, is certain to receive our support; but in this same connection, and strangely enough, the President says that we have become convinced that the German Government as it now exists—"Prussian autocracy" he calls it—can never again maintain friendly relations with us. His expression is that "Prussian autocracy was not and could never be our friend," and repeatedly throughout the address the suggestion is made that if the German people would overturn their Government it would probably be the way to peace. So true is this that the dispatches from London all hailed the message of the President as sounding the death knell of Germany's Government.

But the President proposes alliance with Great Britain, which, however liberty-loving its people, is a hereditary monarchy, with a hereditary ruler, with a hereditary House of Lords, with a hereditary landed system, with a limited and restricted suffrage for one class and a multiplied suffrage power for another, and with grinding industrial conditions for all the wageworkers. The President has not suggested that we make our support of Great Britain conditional to her granting home rule to Ireland, or Egypt, or India. We rejoice in the establishment of a democracy in Russia, but it will hardly be contended that if Russia was still an autocratic Government, we would not be asked to enter this alliance with her just the same. Italy and the lesser powers of Europe, Japan in the Orient; in fact, all of the countries with whom we are to enter into alliance, except France and newly revolutionized Russia, are still of the old order—and it will be generally conceded that no one of them has done as much for its people in the solution of municipal problems and in securing social and industrial reforms as Germany.

Is it not a remarkable democracy which leagues itself with allies already far overmatching in strength the German nation and holds out to such beleaguered nation the hope of peace only at the price of giving up their Government? I am not talking now of the merits or demerits of any government, but I am speaking of a profession of democracy that is linked in action with the most brutal and domineering use of autocratic power. Are the people of this country being so well represented in this war movement that we need to go abroad to give other people control of their governments? Will the President and the supporters of this war bill submit it to a vote of the people before the declaration of war goes into effect? Until we are willing to do that, it illy becomes us to offer as an excuse for our entry into the war the unsupported claim that this war was forced upon the German people by their Government "without their previous knowledge or approval."...

With Germany likewise our relations were friendly. Many hundreds of thousands of the subjects of Germany had emigrated to this country, and they and their descendants had shown themselves to be in every way most worthy and desirable citizens. The great Civil War which saved the Union was successful largely through the services rendered by Germans, both as officers and as men serving in the ranks. B. A. Gould, in a work dealing with some of the phases of the Civil War, and prepared soon after its close, among other things, presented a table of the relative number of foreign-born soldiers in the Union Army. I quote from that table as follows:

```
English ................................45,508
Canadian ..............................52,532
Irish ..................................144,221
German ...............................187,858
All other foreign born ...................48,410
```

Later and more careful investigation of the statistics show that there were in reality 216,000 native Germans in the Union Army, and, besides this, more than 300,000 Union soldiers who were born of German parents.

More than one-half a million of the men who carried the musket to keep this Government of ours undivided upon the map of the world were men who are now having their patriotism and loyalty to this country questioned, with secret-service men dogging their footsteps.

Who does not remember, among the most gallant and distinguished officers in the Union Army, Schurz, Sigel, Rosecrans, and scores of others? It is well to recall also that when President Lincoln issued his call for volunteers they volunteered much more largely from the German-settled States of the Middle West than from the war-mad States of the East. Is history to repeat itself?

The German people, either in this country or in the fatherland, need no tribute from me or from anyone else. In whatever land they have lived they have left a record of courage, loyalty, honesty, and high ideals second to no people which have ever inhabited this earth since the dawn of history. If the German people are less likely to be swept off their feet in the present crisis than some other nationalities, it is due to two facts. In the first place, they have a livelier appreciation of what war means than has the average American, and, in the second place, German speaking and reading people have had an opportunity to get both sides of the present controversy, which no one could possibly have, who has depended for his information solely on papers printed in English and English publications.

I have said that with the causes of the present war we have nothing to do. That is true. We certainly are not responsible for it. It originated from causes beyond the sphere of our influence and outside the realm of our responsibility. It is not inadmissible, however, to say that no responsible narrator of the events which have led up to this greatest of all wars has failed to hold that the Government of each country engaged in it is at fault for it. For my own part, I believe that this war, like nearly all others, originated in the selfish ambition and cruel greed of a comparatively few men in each Government who saw in war an opportunity for profit and power for themselves, and who were wholly indifferent to the awful suffering they knew that war would bring to the masses. The German people had been taught to believe that sooner or later war was inevitable with England and France and probably Russia allied against her. It is unfortunately true that there was much in the secret diplomacy of the years immediately preceding the breaking out of the war in 1914 to afford foundation for such belief. The secret treaty between France and England for the partition of Morocco, while making a public treaty with Germany, the terms of which were diametrically opposite to those of the secret treaty, did much to arouse the suspicion and hostility of the German people toward both France and England....

At this point, sir, I say, with all deference but with the absolute certainty of conviction, that the present administration made a fatal mistake, and if war comes to this country with Germany for the present causes it will be due wholly to that mistake. The present administration has assumed and acted upon the policy that it could enforce to the very letter of the law the principles of international law against one belligerent and relax them as to the other. That thing no nation can do without losing its character as a neutral nation and without losing the rights that go with strict and absolute neutrality....

Jefferson asserted that we could not permit one warring nation to curtail our neutral rights if we were not ready to allow her enemy the same privileges, and that any other course entailed the sacrifice of our neutrality.

That is the sensible, that is the logical position. No neutrality could ever have commanded respect if it was not based on that equitable and just proposition; and we from early in the war threw our neutrality to the winds by permitting England to make a mockery of it to her advantage against her chief enemy. Then we expect to say to that enemy, "You have got to respect my rights as a neutral." What is the answer? I say Germany has been patient with us. Standing strictly on her rights, her answer would be, "Maintain your neutrality; treat these other Governments warring against me as you treat me if you want your neutral rights respected."

Questions

1. What do you consider to be the strongest and weakest points of La Follette's argument against President Wilson's war message?
2. Why did La Follette and the president refer to the German people in positive terms? Might they have done so for somewhat different reasons?

22-5 German Dugouts (1918)

Hervey Allen

Poet and novelist Hervey Allen (1888–1949) joined the National Guard after his graduation from the University of Pittsburgh in 1915. Before going to France, Allen served with the expeditionary force that pursued Pancho Villa in Mexico (see text pp. 664–666). The following excerpt from Allen's wartime diary, *Toward the Flame*, offers a firsthand account of soldiering on the Western Front (see text pp. 674–679).

Source: Excerpted from *Toward the Flame: A War Diary* (1934), 112–119. Copyright 1926, 1934 by Hervey Allen. Copyright 1954, 1962, by Ann Andrews Allen. Reprinted by permission of Henry Holt and Co., Inc.

I awoke to hear the pleasant clinking of mess pans. The rain had stopped, but the forest was still dripping, and the mud was deep and peculiarly slippery. The captain and I crawled out, both about the same time, and made our way to the kitchen where a savory mess was being dished out, smoking hot gobs of bread and canned sweet potato, a favorite and frequent delicacy at the front. Paul and some of the other French soldiers were helping. By this time the men were happy again. A little rest and something to eat were doing wonders. The captain and I were not much behind the rest of the company as trenchermen, although I avoided eating much meat at the front.

We were issued beef in immense quantities, sometimes having to bury a whole quarter of it. It became tainted very easily, where of course there was no possible means of refrigeration. This meat ration came wrapped in burlap, generally reasonably fresh; but once open, it had to be carried around in the ration carts, and unless quickly cooked, it spoiled very rapidly, especially in those summer days along the Marne when the sun was hot.

Another thing which hastened the destruction of perishable food was the immense amount of decay all along the front. All those rotten woods were filled with dead horses, dead men, the refuse, excrement and the garbage of armies. The ground must have been literally alive with pus and decay germs. Scratch your hand, cut yourself in shaving, or get a little abrasion on your foot, and almost anything could happen. Bichloride tablets were invaluable; I always threw one into my canvas basin for good luck.

During the meal, Lieutenant Scott, who had been assistant division gas officer for a while, but who had now returned to the company, joined us, and mentioned that he was making all arrangements for a new gas alarm, having found some empty brass shells used for that purpose "over there"— and he pointed to a cape of trees that ran out from a wood-island into the surrounding fields.

That part of the world consisted of a great level plateau, prairie-like fields interspersed with woods, the "bois" of the French maps, like islands of all sizes and shapes. We were then camped in one of these wood "islands," and across "there," where the lieutenant had pointed, was another "island" in which were the remnants of a German battery. The captain and I strolled across after dinner, letting the warm sun dry us off.

The guns were still in their pits, as "Fritz" had left very suddenly here. The guns pointed their noses up at a high angle like hounds baying the moon, but they were silent now. The wood was full of little dugouts, walks, and houses. The Germans had evidently stayed here a long time. Out in the field were a large number of big shell craters in a line, *one, two, three* . . . where our 220's had evidently been ranging on the battery. They had come quite near, within fifty yards or so.

Along the edge of these thickets were a number of graves. I was greatly impressed by them. The crosses were well carved out of new wood, and the grave mounds carefully spaded. Here were wreaths of wax flowers, evidently sent from home, and a board giving the epitaph of the deceased, with his rank and honors: "He was a good Christian and fell in France fighting for the Fatherland, *Hier ruht in Gott* [Here he rests in God]." Verily, these seemed to be the same Goths and Vandals who left their graves even in Egypt; unchanged since the days of Rome, and still fighting her civilization, the woods-people against the Latins. Only the illuminating literary curiosity of a Tacitus was lacking to make the inward state of man visible by the delineation of the images of outer things.

We entered some of the dugouts, small, mound-like structures with straw inside. Some of the officers' were larger. There was a little beer garden in the middle of the wood with a chapel and a wreathed cross near by, white stones and twisting "rustic" paths. The railings and booths along these paths were made from roots and branches cleverly bent and woven, and sometimes carved. It reminded me of American "porch furniture" of a certain type. All quite German. Cast-off boots, shell-timers, one or two coats, and shrapnel-bitten helmets lay about with round Boche [an insulting nickname for "German"] hats, "the little round button on top." Picture post-cards and magazines, pistol holsters, and one or two broken rifles completed this cartoon of invasion.

All the litter of material thus left behind was useless. I noticed the pictures of some fat, and rather jolly-looking German girls, and piles of a vast quantity of shells. We looked around thoroughly, but were very wary of traps. I remember making up my mind to make for one of these dugouts in case we were shelled. One always kept a weather eye open.

About all this stuff there was at that time the dire taint of danger. Somehow everything German gave one the creeps. It was connected so intimately with all that was unpleasant, and associated so inevitably with organized fear, that one scarce regarded its owners as men. It seemed *then* as if we were fighting some strange, ruthless, insect-beings from another planet; that we had stumbled upon their nests after smoking them out. One had the same feeling as when waking up at night and realizing that there are rats under the bed.

The captain and I walked along the edge of the wood, encountering our French contingent on the way. They were "at home" in an old German dugout, happily squatted around several small fires, preparing their meal as *they* liked it. After a good deal of difficulty, they had prevailed on our mess sergeant to issue them their rations in bulk so that they could do their own cooking. Such little differences of customs are in reality most profound. Our physical habits were more like the Germans'!

The non-commissioned gas officer picked us up here. He was carrying back the big brass shell for a gas alarm. It gave forth a mellow musical note when touched with a bar of iron or a bayonet. The Germans had used this one themselves for that purpose, so it already had the holes and wire for suspending it. . . .

We moved before it was light, which is very early in summer time in France. The dim columns of men coming out of the woods, the lines of carts and kitchens assembling in the early, gray dawn, all without a light, and generally pretty silently, was always impressive.

In a few minutes we were headed back in the direction from which we had come. There was a full moon, or one nearly so, hanging low in the west. As I jolted along, on legs that seemed more like stilts than limbs with knees, the heavy equipment sagged at every step, and seemed to clink one's teeth together weakly. At last the weariness and the jangle took on a fagged rhythm that for me fell into the comfort of rhyme.

We were beginning to be pretty tired by now and even here needed relief. One no longer got up in the morning full of energy. Hunger, dirt, and strain were telling, and we felt more or less "all in" that day in particular. One was consciously weak.

Nevertheless the country was beautiful; the full moon just sinking in the west looked across the smoking, misty valleys at the rising sun. There was a gorgeous bloody-gold color in the sky, and the woods and fields sparkled deliciously green, looking at a little distance fresh and untouched. But that was only a distant appearance, for this was the country over which two days before the Americans had driven the Germans from one machine gun nest to another, and on from crest to crest. A nearer approach showed the snapped tree-trunks, the tossed branches and shell-pitted ground, and at one halt that we made, Nick called me down a little slope to see something.

There was a small spring in a draw beside the road, where two Germans were lying. One was a big, brawny fellow with a brown beard, and the other a mere lad. He looked to be about 14 or 15 with a pathetically childish chin, but he carried potatomasher bombs.[1] They had evidently stopped here to try to fill their canteens, probably both desperate with thirst, when they were overtaken by our men. The young boy must have sheltered himself behind the man while the latter held our fellows back a little. There was a scorched place up the side of the ravine where a hand grenade had exploded, but the big German had been surrounded, and killed by the bayonet right through his chest. His hands were still clutching at the place where the steel had gone through. He was one of the few I ever saw who had been killed by the bayonet. The boy was lying just behind him. His back appeared to have been broken, probably by a blow with the butt of a rifle, and he was contorted into a kind of arch, only his feet and shoulders resting on the ground. It was he who had probably thrown the grenade that had exploded near by. The little spring had evidently been visited by the wounded, as there were blood and first-aid wrappings about. I refused to have the company water tank filled there.

---

[1] *Potatomasher bombs* were German hand grenades, so named for their mallet-like shape. Allied hand grenades were baseball-shaped with notched indentations so that they scattered fragments; they became known as "pineapples."

194 CHAPTER 22 War and the American State, 1914–1920

Questions

1. Describe conditions at the front.
2. How did Allen regard the enemy?
3. What did he find at the small spring? What does that scene indicate about the unpredictability of combat?

22-6 Posters from the Anti–Venereal Disease Campaign (1917–1918)

As the text points out, the war intensified progressive campaigns against venereal disease and alcohol (see text pp. 691–692). Homosexuals in cosmopolitan seaports, as well as prostitutes in various settings, were of particular concern to authorities. Various means were employed by government and private agencies to ensure that America's citizen army was "fit to fight" and "the cleanest army in the world." Among the efforts were these propagandistic posters of the Social Hygiene Division of the Army Educational Commission.

Source: Posters, the American Social Hygiene Association Papers, Social Welfare History Archives Center, University of Minnesota, Minneapolis, reproduced by permission in Allan M. Brandt, *No Magic Bullet: A Social History of Venereal Disease in the United States*, expanded ed. (New York: Oxford University Press, 1987), 110 ff.

Questions

1. Compare and contrast the representation of women in the two posters.
2. How might these posters be considered products of the Progressive Era?

Posters from the U.S. Army's Anti–Venereal Disease Campaign (1917–1918)

Questions for Further Thought

1. Both Woodrow Wilson (Document 22-3) and Robert M. La Follette (Document 22-4) drew on American traditions and ideals to make their respective cases for and against participating in the Great War. What were some of these ideals, and how did these writers use them to build their contrasting arguments?

2. Compare and contrast the rhetoric of Albert J. Beveridge's "The March of the Flag" speech (Document 21-4) with Woodrow Wilson's war message (Document 22-3).

War on the Home Front

The war transformed American society, at least for its duration, and government grew in response to the demands of a worldwide conflict. Major agencies were created to channel the activities of government officials, civilian and military, and the business, agriculture, and labor sectors. Among these agencies were the War Industries Board, which coordinated the wartime mobilization of industry; the National War Labor Board; the Food Administration; the Fuel Administration; and the Railroad War Board (see text pp. 683–685). Business was the best organized of the private-interest groups, but the labor movement benefited from wartime prosperity and from favorable decisions of the War Labor Board relative to union organization, working hours, overtime pay, and equal pay for women. The wartime labor shortage increased opportunities for African Americans, Mexican Americans, and women (see text pp. 685–691).

Enthusiasm for the war was widespread, but opposition was considerable: feelings both ways frequently ran high. Propaganda sought to mobilize support for and marginalize opposition to the war. Under the circumstances, civil liberties became an early casualty of the war: federal, state, and local authorities and private groups suppressed dissent, legally, extra legally, and sometimes illegally (by violence) (see text pp. 692–694).

Document 22-7 excerpts the report of Bernard M. Baruch, chairman of the War Industries Board, on the board's activities. Document 22-8 deals with the wartime contributions of an established women's organization, the Young Women's Christian Association. Document 22-9 illustrates anti-German propaganda. Document 22-10 is from George Creel's history of the Committee on Public Information. In Document 22-11, thirty-one African American editors state the case for African American support for the war.

22-7 The War Industries Board (1917–1918)

Bernard M. Baruch

Central to the management of industry during wartime was the War Industries Board (see text pp. 684–685). Bernard M. Baruch (1870–1965), who became chairman of the WIB in 1918, here reports on its activities and suggests a peacetime role for such an organization based on wartime experience.

Source: Bernard M. Baruch, *American Industry in the War: A Report of the War Industries Board* (Washington, D.C.: U.S. Government Printing Office, 1921), 65–67, 69, 100; excerpted in Donald O. Dewey, ed., *Union and Liberty: A Documentary History of American Constitutionalism* (New York: McGraw-Hill, 1969), 220.

... Curtailment plans were carried out not by agreement among the concerns of an industry but by agreement between the industry as a group, on the one hand, and the Government, on the other. Many new trade practices were inaugurated in the same way. In many instances curtailment was the negative result of positive action in some other direction. This problem has already been considered at some length in the chapter on priorities. The plans and results of the Board's activities in carrying forward the conservation program are explained at some length in Part II of this book, in connection with the work of the various commodity sections dealing with the particular industries affected. Reference, by way of illustration, to some of these will be of general interest.

The conservation schedules for makers of men's and youth's clothing limited the length of sack coats and the length and sweep of overcoats, reduced the size of samples, and restricted each manufacturer to not more than 10 models of suits per season, resulting in a saving of 12 to 15 per cent in yardage. The number of trunks carried by traveling salesmen of dry goods houses underwent an average reduction of 44 per cent. The schedule for the women's garment industry was calculated as capable of saving 20 to 25 per cent in yardage.

The standardization of colors together with certain restrictions in styles of sweaters and analogous knitted articles released 33 per cent of the wool ordinarily used in that industry. A schedule providing that hosiery, underwear, and other knit goods, with certain small exceptions, should be packed for shipment in paper covered bales instead of pasteboard boxes resulted in a large saving in shipping space, while at the same time it released pasteboard to be used as a substitute for tin plate in the manufacture of containers for articles for which tin plate had been forbidden. It was estimated that this schedule would have effected an annual saving of 17,312 carloads of freight space, 141,000,000 cartons, and nearly a half million wooden packing cases....

The manufacturers of automobile tires agreed to a reduction from 287 styles and sizes of tires to 32, with a further reduction to 9 within two years. This had a tendency to release a large amount of rubber and capital tied up in stocks everywhere. A schedule was issued also to the rubber clothing and the rubber footwear industries, the former eliminating 272 styles and types and agreeing to bale their product instead of shipping it in cartons. Even bathing caps were restricted to one style and one color for each manufacturer.

Savings in the agricultural implement industry are among the most important effected. Implement manufacturers were able to simplify manufacturing operations and reduce their stocks of raw materials; manufacturers, dealers, and jobbers found it possible to do business with smaller stocks of finished products; the steel mills saved, because every variation in size or shape had required a different set of rolls, and so on. Schedules were issued to manufacturers of portable grain elevators, plows and tillage implements, grain drills and seeders, harvesters, mowers, hay rakes, ensilage machinery, spring-tooth harrows, farm wagons and trucks, land rollers and pulverizers, and cream separators. The number of sizes and types of steel plows was reduced from 312 to 76; planters and drills from 784 to 29; disk harrows from 589 to 38; buggy wheels from 232 to 4; spring-wagon wheels from 32 to 4; buggy axles from over 100 to 1; buggy springs from over 120 to 1; spring wagons from over 25 to 2; buggy shafts from 36 to 1; buggy bodies from over 20 to 1 style, two widths; spring-wagon bodies from 6 to 2....

The experience of the Conservation Division has clearly demonstrated that there are many practices in American industry which cost the ultimate consumers in the aggregate enormous sums without enriching the producers. These are often due to competitive demands, real or assumed. Many salesmen, in order to please the whims of particular customers, will insist upon the manufacture of new styles or new shapes of articles, requiring increased expense to the manufacturers and increased expense to both wholesalers and retailers in carrying more lines of stock; these in turn causing increased expense in maintaining salesmen and providing them with samples as well as in advertising. The consumer, the general public, is no better served by the satisfaction of these unreasonable demands, but the public ultimately pays the bill. We may well draw from this war experience a lesson to be applied to peace, by providing some simple machinery for eliminating wasteful trade practices which increase prices without in the remotest degree contributing to the well-being of the people. There is enough natural wealth in this country, and there is enough labor and technical skill for converting that wealth into objects of human satisfaction to provide abundantly for the elemental comforts of every person in the land. The problem before our Nation to-day is to bring about such adjustments of the industrial processes as lead toward that long-sought condition of life....

The question, then, is what kind of Government organization can be devised to safeguard the public interest while these associations are preserved to carry on the good work of which they are capable. The country will quite properly demand the vigorous enforcement of all proper measures for the suppression of unfair competition and unreasonable restraint of trade. But this essentially negative policy of curbing vicious practices should, in the public interest, be supplemented by a positive program, and to this end the experience of the War Industries Board points to the desirability of investing some Government agency, perhaps the Department of Commerce or the Federal Trade Commission, with constructive as well as inquisitorial powers—an agency whose duty it should be to encourage, under strict Government supervision, such cooperation and coordination in industry as should tend to increase production, eliminate waste, conserve natural resources, improve the quality of products, promote efficiency in operation, and thus reduce costs to the ultimate consumer.

Such a plan should provide a way of approaching industry, or rather of inviting industry to approach the Government, in a friendly spirit, with a view to help and not to hinder. The purpose contemplated is not that the Government should undertake any such far-reaching control over industry as was practiced during the war emergency by the War Industries Board; but that the experiences of the war should be capitalized; its heritage of dangerous practices should be fully realized that they might be avoided; and its heritage of wholesome and useful practices should be accepted and studied with a view to adapting them to the problems of peace. It is recommended that such practices of cooperation and coordination in industry as have been found to be clearly of public benefit should be stimulated and encouraged by a Government agency, which at the same time would be clothed with the power and charged with the responsibility of standing watch against and preventing abuses.

Questions

1. What most strikes you about the wartime operations of the War Industries Board, as described by Baruch?
2. What lessons for postwar America did Baruch see in the operations of the WIB?

22-8 The Home Front: The Young Women's Christian Association (1920)

Marcus L. Hansen

Not only were women able to take jobs in industry and government during wartime, but many (especially women from the middle class) also assumed leadership roles in women's organizations, which became increasingly involved in supporting the war effort on the home front (as this document reveals) and overseas.

Source: Excerpted from Marcus L. Hansen, "The Campaign of the Young Women's Christian Association," in *Welfare Campaigns in Iowa* (Iowa City: State Historical Society of Iowa, 1920), 100–103, 105–106, 108, 111–112.

In the recent struggle there were many active participants who did not shoulder a rifle. A year after the declaration of a state of war a million and a half men were in military service: at that time a million and a half women were engaged in the manufacture of war materials: and as the number in the one class increased, the other force expanded correspondingly. Most of these women were living a life just as novel, just as separated from their previous existence as were the soldiers: and the woman worker was as prone to homesickness and loneliness as was the recruit in the camp. If he needed welfare work and the people furnished it, should she not also be remembered?

The inspector general of the Iowa militia had reported in 1901, on the presence of women in the militia camps, that they were "a nuisance, underfoot, and a detriment to the good work and benefits expected of camp." But, whether a nuisance or not, women were bound to come to the places where the soldiers were—to enjoy a family picnic, to visit the sick in the hospital, or to say a final good-bye before the departure over-seas. Cast alone into a city of barracks, the mother, the sister, or the friend was just as bewildered as was the recruit on his first visit to the neighboring city. If the War Camp Community Service provided for him, should not someone think of her?

Welfare work among soldiers had as one object the preservation of their efficiency by removing the incentives to immorality. But who would guide past temptation in the vicinity of the military camp the girl now suddenly brought into contact with thousands of fighting men?

It was to the Young Women's Christian Association that the welfare of the industrial workers, the women in the camps, and the girls in the cantonment cities was entrusted. The Women's Branch of the Industrial Service Section of the Ordnance Department invited the Association to supervise the recreational activities in these industries. Upon the request of a camp commander the Association was ready to construct a Hostess House for the convenience of women visitors, and safeguards were thrown around the girls by the organization of Patriotic Leagues—an outgrowth of work which had already been done under the Social Morality Committee of this society.

The Young Women's Christian Association was not without experience in tasks of this nature. For fifty years there had existed local groups of young women, some associated with the International Board of Women's and Young Women's Christian Associations and some with the American committee. In December, 1906, a National Board of the Young Women's Christian Association was created by these local groups, and by the constitution adopted in 1909 general supervision over all the work was delegated to this board which consisted of fifty-six members and fifteen auxiliary members. The country was divided into eleven fields, each of which was represented on the National Board by one delegate. The North Central Field included Iowa, Minnesota, Nebraska, North Dakota, and South Dakota, and had its headquarters at Minneapolis, Minnesota. Each field had an executive secretary who was aided by industrial, extension, county, student, and office secretaries.

Following the precedent of the Young Men's Christian Association, the women organized a special War Work Council to which was delegated all activities which arose in connection with the war. The first problem was the financing of these various tasks, and it was with this subject that the War Work Council dealt at their first meeting held in New York City on June 7, 1917. It was there resolved that the country should be appealed to for $1,000,000 of which $50,000 would be expended in work abroad.

Although an active campaign was started to obtain $1,000,000, it did not remain the goal. So great was the demand for hostess houses, so insistent the appeal from abroad, that on October 9th decision was made to place the sum at $4,000,000 of which $1,000,000 would be expended in France and Russia....

How a rural county was organized is illustrated in a report written by Miss Caroline W. Daniels of Independence. "On Nov. 20, 1917, District Y. W. workers from Dubuque called a meeting in the High School Auditorium to organize Buchanan Co. About two dozen women were present. Miss Doris Campbell was chosen Sec-Treas. and I chairman. That afternoon Miss Campbell and I in her car began a tour of the newspaper offices of the county and that evening we had an organization meeting of prospective war leaders for Independence, the county seat. With the consent of the Red Cross officers we used their organization as a fulcrum throughout the county outside the Co. seat. Our method was to drive to every Red Cross group of workers; get permission to explain the need to them while they worked; arrange for some one of their number to take charge of a canvass in their town or township, or region; tell them of their share of the sum asked for from the county (basing this on population); and depart. The same method was used with any other groups we could get access to: —clubs, societies, etc. These groups received us with good will, and took our request as one of the war necessities that must be met, however weary and already over worked they felt. These visits were supplemented by letters, literature, posters, newspaper notices, announcements by townships of returns, etc., etc."

In the cities where there was a local branch of the Association the task was left to this organization. Accordingly, Dubuque was omitted from the plans made by the chairman of that district. The organization of Burlington became the center of the campaign in that city and its members were active workers in many Iowa cities. The scheme of the local campaigns was practically the same as that used by the men in their efforts—that is, competitive teams organized on military lines. Women served as captains, lieutenants, and privates; and at Fort Dodge they acted as "four minute men" presenting the merits of their cause in the theaters. In other places, however, women did not bear the entire responsibility. Sioux City had as its campaign manager, John O. Knutson, president of the Rotary Club; and on the executive and advisory committees appeared both men and women. Likewise, though the captains of the eighteen soliciting teams were women, many men served in the ranks....

Just as the high school boys were an effective factor in the raising of the fund of the Young Men's Christian Association, so the high school girls contributed to the success of the women's endeavor. Indeed, at Fort Dodge the system was much the same. High school girls were organized on military lines, with a major and two captains. Each captain chose a lieutenant and a corporal from each class. A meeting was held at which time pledge cards, stating the willingness of the girls to give fifty cents a month for ten months, were passed out with instructions to take them home and have them countersigned by their parents. When the cards were returned it was found that $635 had been pledged. More than forty girls of the East High School in Waterloo pledged five dollars each toward the cause. In Washington the high school girls conducted the local campaign and received pledges of more than eight hundred dollars....

Besides apathy and indifference there were in this campaign distinct objections to be overcome. Such was the "dancing girls story." A special article in a Chicago Sunday paper stated that the Young Women's Christian Association planned to bring several hundred girls to Camp Lewis, Washington, and pay them fifteen dollars weekly to dance with the soldiers of the cantonment who were to pay fifteen cents for each dance. In varying forms this story was widely copied and caused some people to hesitate in their giving, although it was immediately declared by campaign officials to be "absolutely false in every detail."

Even in remote rural districts rumors arose. The nature of the reports against which workers had to contend is illustrated by an incident occurring in one Iowa community. After considerable trouble a chairman was found for a township; but "later it was reported to us," states the narrative of the county chairman, "that she changed her mind and telephoned all around the neighborhood warning the women to have nothing to do with the movement as she had discovered (?) that it was all a scheme to collect money for building houses of ill fame for the soldiers of Camp Dodge!!! We bombarded her with publicity material, but got no returns from that township. In less virulent form we ran into this notion a number of times. The work for Red Cross nurses made instant appeal everywhere; but 'Hostess Houses' were either suspected or openly disapproved of. Work to keep safe young girls who flocked to Des Moines met with much criticism from country women who thought 'mothers should look after their own girls' 'that was what they were doing.'"

Questions

1. With which other voluntary organizations did the Young Women's Christian Association interact during wartime? What light does this coordination shed on voluntary organizations? What were the effects of the war on these organizations?
2. What does the document reveal about concerns regarding morals under wartime conditions?

22-9 Wartime Propaganda Poster (c. 1917)

Posters propagandized the war for a number of purposes, both specific and general—to encourage the purchase of government bonds during Liberty loans, increase enlistment in the armed forces, ensure compliance with various wartime programs, such as food conservation, and above all create support for the war (see text pp. 692–694).

Source: Historical Pictures / Stock Montage, Inc.

Poster from the U.S. Treasury Department's War Bond Program (c. 1917)

Questions

1. In what traditional ways does the poster portray gender roles?
2. What else strikes you about the poster?

22-10 The Home Front: The Four Minute Men (1920)

George Creel

Washington fought the propaganda war through the Committee on Public Information, which was headed by journalist George Creel (1876–1953). As described in the textbook (pp. 692–694), the CPI used speakers, movies, posters, and pamphlets to spread its message. This excerpt on the "four minute men" comes from Creel's history of the CPI, *How We Advertised America*.

Source: George Creel, *How We Advertised America: The First Telling of the Amazing Story of the Committee on Public Information That Carried the Gospel of Americanism to Every Corner of the Globe* (New York: Harper and Bros., 1920), 84–88, 90–92.

There was nothing more time-wasting than the flood of people that poured into Washington during the war, each burdened with some wonderful suggestions that could be imparted only to an executive head. Even so, all of them had to be seen, for not only was it their right as citizens, but it was equally the case that the idea might have real value. Many of our best suggestions came from the most unlikely sources.

In the very first hours of the Committee, when we were still penned in the navy library, fighting for breath, a handsome, rosy-cheeked youth burst through the crowd and caught my lapel in a death-grip. His name was Donald Ryerson. He confessed to Chicago as his home, and the plan that he presented was the organization of volunteer speakers for the purpose of making patriotic talks in motion-picture theaters. He had tried out the scheme in Chicago, and the success of the venture had catapulted him on the train to Washington and to me.

Being driven to the breaking-point has certain compensations, after all. It forces one to think quickly and confines thought largely to the positive values of a suggestion rather than future difficulties. Had I had the time to weigh the proposition from every angle, it may be that I would have decided against it, for it was delicate and dangerous business to turn loose on the country an army of speakers impossible of exact control and yet vested in large degree with the authority of the government. In ten minutes we had decided upon a national organization to be called the "Four Minute Men," and Mr. Ryerson rushed out with my appointment as its director.

When the armistice brought activities to a conclusion the Four Minute Men numbered 75,000 speakers, more than 7,555,190 speeches had been made, and a fair estimate of audiences makes it certain that a total of 134,454,514 people had been addressed. Notwithstanding the nature of the work, the infinite chances of blunder and bungle, this unique and effective agency functioned from first to last with only one voice ever raised to attack its faith and efficiency. As this voice was that of Senator Sherman of Illinois, this attack is justly to be set down as part of the general praise.

The form of presentation decided upon was a glass slide to be thrown on the theater-curtain, and worded as follows:

4 MINUTE MEN 4
(Copyright, 1917. Trade-mark.)

....
(Insert name of speaker)

will speak four minutes on a subject
of national importance. He speaks
under the authority of
THE COMMITTEE ON PUBLIC INFORMATION
GEORGE CREEL, Chairman
Washington, D.C.

A more difficult decision was as to the preparation of the matter to be sent out to speakers. We did not want stereotyped oratory, and yet it was imperative to guard against the dangers of unrestraint. It was finally agreed that regular bulletins should be issued, each containing a budget of material covering every phase of the question to be discussed, and also including two or three illustrative four-minute speeches. Mr. Waldo P. Warren of Chicago was chosen to write the first bulletin, and when he was called away his duties fell upon E. T. Gundlach, also of Chicago, the patriotic head of an advertising agency. These bulletins, however, prepared in close and continued consultation with the proper officials of each government department responsible for them, were also gone over carefully by Professor Ford and his scholars.

The idea, from the very first, had the sweep of a prairie fire. Speakers volunteered by the thousand in every state, the owners of the motion-picture houses, after a first natural hesitancy, gave exclusive privileges to the organization, and the various government departments fairly clamored for the services of the Four Minute Men. The following list of bulletins will show the wide range of topics:

Topic	Period
Universal Service by Selective Draft	May 12–21, 1917
First Liberty Loan	May 22-June 15, 1917
Red Cross	June 18–25, 1917
Organization	
Food Conservation	July 1–14, 1917
Why We Are Fighting	July 23-Aug. 5, 1917
The Nation in Arms	Aug. 6–26, 1917
The Importance of Speed	Aug. 19–26, 1917
What Our Enemy Really Is	Aug. 27-Sept. 23, 1917
Unmasking German Propaganda	Aug. 27-Sept. 23, 1917 (supplementary topic)
Onward to Victory	Sept. 24-Oct. 27, 1917
Second Liberty Loan	Oct. 8–28, 1917
Food Pledge	Oct. 29-Nov. 4, 1917
Maintaining Morals and Morale	Nov. 12–25, 1917
Carrying the Message	Nov. 26-Dec. 22, 1917
War Savings Stamps	Jan. 2–19, 1918
The Shipbuilder	Jan. 28-Feb. 9, 1918
Eyes for the Navy	Feb. 11–16, 1918
The Danger to Democracy	Feb. 18-Mar. 10, 1918
Lincoln's Gettysburg Address	Feb. 12, 1918
The Income Tax	Mar. 11–16, 1918
Farm and Garden	Mar. 25–30, 1918
President Wilson's Letter to Theaters	Mar. 31-Apr. 5, 1918
Third Liberty Loan	Apr. 6-May 4, 1918
Organization	(Republished Apr. 23, 1918)
Second Red Cross Campaign	May 13–25, 1918
Danger to America	May 27-June 12, 1918
Second War Savings Campaign	June 24–28, 1918
The Meaning of America	June 29-July 27, 1918
Mobilizing America's Man Power	July 29-Aug. 17, 1918
Where Did You Get Your Facts?	Aug. 26-Sept. 7, 1918
Certificates to Theater Members	Sept. 9–14, 1918
Register	Sept. 5–12, 1918
Four Minute Singing	For general use
Fourth Liberty Loan	Sept. 28-Oct. 19, 1918
Food Program for 1919	Changed to Dec. 1–7; finally cancelled
Fire Prevention	Oct. 27-Nov. 2, 1918
United War Work Campaign	Nov. 3–18, 1918
Red Cross Home Service	Dec. 7, 1918
What Have We Won?	Dec. 8–14, 1918
Red Cross Christmas Roll Call	Dec. 15–23, 1918
A Tribute to the Allies	Dec. 24, 1918

Almost from the first the organization has the projectile force of a French "75," [a French artillery piece] and it was increasingly the case that government department heads turned to the Four Minute Men when they wished to arouse the nation swiftly and effectively. At a time when the Third Liberty Loan was lagging, President Wilson bought a fifty-dollar bond and challenged the men and women of the nation to "match" it. The Treasury Department asked the Committee to broadcast the message, and paid for the telegrams that went out to the state and county chairmen. Within a few days fifty thousand Four Minute Men were delivering the challenge to the people of every community in the United States, and the loan took a leap that carried it over the top. General Crowder followed the same plan in his registration campaign, putting up the money for the telegrams that went to the state and county chairmen, and like Secretary McAdoo, he obtained the same swift service and instant results. . . .

National arrangements were made to have Four Minute Men appear at the meetings of lodges, fraternal organizations, and labor unions, and this work progressed swiftly. In most cases these speakers were selected from the membership of the organizations to whom they spoke.

Under the authority of state lecturers of granges, four minute messages, based upon the official bulletins, were given also at all meetings of the granges in many states. The work was next extended to reach the lumber-camps of the country, some five hundred organizations being formed in such communities. Indian reservations were also taken in, and furnished some of the largest and most enthusiastic audiences.

The New York branch organized a church department to present four-minute speeches in churches, synagogues, and Sunday-schools. The idea spread from city to city, from state to state, and proved of particular value in rural communities. Some of the states, acting under authority from headquarters, organized women's divisions to bring the messages of the government to audiences at matinée performances in the motion-picture theaters, and to the members of women's clubs and other similar organizations.

College Four Minute Men were organized, under instructors acting as chairmen, to study the regular Four Minute Men bulletins, and practise speaking upon the subjects thereof, each student being required to deliver at least one four-minute speech to the student body during the semester, in addition to securing satisfactory credits, in order to qualify as a Four Minute Man. This work was organized in 153 colleges. . . .

The Junior Four Minute Men was an expansion that proved to be almost as important as the original idea, for the youngsters of the country rallied with a whoop, and, what was more to the point, gave results as well as enthusiasm. Like so many other activities of the Committee, the Junior movement was more accidental than planned. At the request of the state of Minnesota the Washington office prepared a special War Savings Stamps bulletin. Results were so instant and remarkable that the idea had to be carried to other states, more than a million and a half copies of the bulletin being distributed to school-children during the campaign. Out of it all came the Junior Four Minute Men as a vital and integral part of the Committee on Public Information.

It was our cautious fear, at first, that regular school-work might be interrupted, but it soon developed that the idea had real educational value, helping teachers in their task instead of hindering. The general plan was for the teacher to explain the subject, using the bulletin as a text-book, and the children then wrote their speeches and submitted them to the teacher or principal. The best were selected and delivered as speeches or were read. In a few cases extemporaneous talks were given.

Details of the contests were left largely to the discretion of the teachers. In small schools there was generally one contest for the whole school. In schools of more than five or six classes it was usual to have separate contests for the higher and lower classes, and sometimes for each grade. There were many different ways of conducting these contests. Sometimes they were considered as a regular part of the school-work and were held in the class-room with no outsiders present, but more often they were made special events, the entire school, together with parents and other visitors, being present. Both boys and girls were eligible and the winners were given an official certificate from the government, commissioning them as four-minute speakers upon the specified topic of the contest. . . .

Questions

1. How did the "four minute men" program work?
2. Where was the potential for abuse in this program?
3. What significance do you see in the title of Creel's book?

22-11 Help Us to Help (1917)

The Crisis, a monthly magazine of the National Association for the Advancement of Colored People, edited by Dr. W. E. B. Du Bois, supported the war effort, as was revealed in Du Bois's editorials and in the publication of "Help Us to Help." Du Bois and the NAACP also sought support for the nondiscriminatory treatment of African American military personnel.

Source: "Help Us to Help," *The Crisis*, 16 (August 1918): 163–164.

From the petition of thirty-one Negro editors unanimously adopted at their meeting in Washington:

We American Negroes wish to affirm, first of all, our unalterable belief that the defeat of the German government and what it today represents is of paramount importance to the welfare of the world in general and to our people in particular.

We deem it hardly necessary, in view of the untarnished record of Negro Americans, to reaffirm our loyalty to Our Country and our readiness to make every sacrifice to win this war. We wish to use our every endeavor to keep all of these 12,000,000 people at the highest pitch, not simply of passive loyalty, but of active, enthusiastic and self-sacrificing participation in the war.

We are not unmindful of the recognition of our American citizenship in the draft, of the appointment of colored officers, of the designation of colored advisors to the Government departments and of other indications of a broadened public opinion; nevertheless, we believe today that justifiable grievances of the colored people are producing not disloyalty, but an amount of unrest and bitterness which even the best efforts of their leaders may not be always able to guide, unless they can have the active and sympathetic cooperation of the National and State governments. German propaganda among us is powerless, but the apparent indifference of our own Government may be dangerous.

The American Negro does not expect to have the whole Negro problem settled immediately; he is not seeking to hold-up a striving country and a distracted world by pushing irrelevant personal grievances as a price of loyalty; he is not disposed to catalogue, in this tremendous crisis, all his complaints and disabilities; he is more than willing to do his full share in helping to win the war for democracy and he expects his full share of the fruits thereof;—but he is to-day compelled to ask for that minimum of consideration which will enable him to be an efficient fighter for victory, namely:

(1) Better conditions of public travel.

(2) The acceptance of help where help is needed regardless of the color of the helper.

(3) The immediate suppression of lynching.

All these things are matters, not simply of justice, but of National and group efficiency; they are actions designed to still the natural unrest and apprehension among one-eighth of our citizens so as to enable them wholeheartedly and unselfishly to throw their every ounce of effort into this mighty and righteous war.

Questions

1. What is your assessment of this petition of thirty-one African American editors?
2. Drawing on the text (especially pp. 685–691) and this petition, compare and contrast the wartime strategy of the NAACP with that of the woman suffrage organizations.

Questions for Further Thought

1. Drawing on the text and documents from Chapters 20 and 22, make the case for or against this statement: the wartime period in America can be viewed as an extension of the Progressive Era.
2. Compare and contrast the depiction of women in the posters in Documents 22-6 and 22-9.

An Unsettled Peace, 1919–1920

One need only refer to the Reconstruction period after the Civil War (Chapter 15) to establish that America's major wars have sometimes been followed by intense conflict. The period of crisis after the Great War was brief, characterized by a range of conflicts that together made for two years of "unsettled peace" (see text pp. 698–701).

The terms of the peace proved politically divisive, as the U.S. Senate refused—on two votes late in 1919 and on a final roll call early the next year—to ratify the Treaty of Versailles, which would have involved the United States in the League of Nations. Meanwhile, nativism and racialism flourished, and wartime repression of dissent carried over into the postwar Red Scare, which provided the backdrop for bitter labor-management strife during the shift from a wartime economy to a peacetime economy.

Document 22-12 contains the heart of President Woodrow Wilson's "Fourteen Points" speech dealing with war aims in January 1918. Document 22-13 reproduces select articles from the Treaty of Versailles. In Documents 22-14 and 22-15, Senator Henry Cabot Lodge and President Wilson state their differing positions on the League of Nations (see Article 10 of the Treaty of Versailles in Document 22-13). Document 22-16 reports on the postwar race riot in Chicago, and Dr. W. E. B. Du Bois writes on "Returning Soldiers" in Document 22-17.

22-12 Fourteen Points (1918)

Woodrow Wilson

President Wilson (1856–1924) set out his Fourteen Points as the basis for a lasting peace in an address before Congress on January 8, 1918 (see text pp. 694–698). The timing of his speech reflected his concern that V. I. Lenin's Bolsheviks, who had seized power in Russia late in the previous year, were propagandizing a revolutionary ending of the war even as they were negotiating with the Germans to extricate Russia from that war, however harsh Germany's terms. Such a peace would free German forces to concentrate on the Western Front. Addressing war-weary Europe, Wilson sought to deal with the Bolsheviks, rally the Allies, and appeal to elements within the Central Powers.

Source: Woodrow Wilson, address to Congress, January 8, 1918; reprinted in *Papers of Woodrow Wilson*, ed. Arthur S. Link et al. (Princeton, NJ: Princeton University Press, 1984), 45:536–538. Reprinted by permission of the publisher.

I. Open covenants of peace, openly arrived at, after which there shall be no private international understandings of any kind but diplomacy shall proceed always frankly and in the public view.

II. Absolute freedom of navigation upon the seas, outside territorial waters, alike in peace and in war, except as the seas may be closed in whole or in part by international action for the enforcement of international covenants.

III. The removal, so far as possible, of all economic barriers and the establishment of an equality of trade conditions among all the nations consenting to the peace and associating themselves for its maintenance.

IV. Adequate guarantees given and taken that national armaments will be reduced to the lowest point consistent with domestic safety.

V. A free, open-minded, and absolutely impartial adjustment of all colonial claims, based upon a strict observance of the principle that in determining all such questions of sovereignty the interests of the populations concerned must have equal weight with the equitable claims of the government whose title is to be determined.

VI. The evacuation of all Russian territory and such a settlement of all questions affecting Russia as will secure the best and freest cooperation of the other nations of the world in obtaining for her an unhampered and unembarrassed opportunity for the independent determination of her own political development and national policy and assure her of a sincere welcome into the society of free nations under institutions of her own choosing; and, more than a welcome, assistance also of every kind that she may need and may herself desire. The treatment accorded Russia by her sister nations in the months to come will be the acid test of their good will, of their comprehension of her needs as distinguished from their own interests, and of their intelligent and unselfish sympathy.

VII. Belgium, the whole world will agree, must be evacuated and restored, without any attempt to limit the sovereignty which she enjoys in common with all other free nations. No other single act will serve as this will serve to restore confidence among the nations in the laws which they have themselves set and determined for the government of their relations with one another. Without this healing act the whole structure and validity of international laws is forever impaired.

VIII. All French territory should be freed and the invaded portions restored, and the wrong done to France by Prussia in 1871 in the matter of Alsace-Lorraine, which has unsettled the peace of the world for nearly fifty years, should be righted, in order that peace may once more be made secure in the interest of all.

IX. A readjustment of the frontiers of Italy should be effected along clearly recognizable lines of nationality.

X. The peoples of Austria-Hungary, whose place among the nations we wish to see safeguarded and assured, should be accorded the freest opportunity of autonomous development.

XI. Rumania, Serbia, and Montenegro should be evacuated; occupied territories restored; Serbia accorded free and secure access to the sea; and the relations of the several Balkan states to one another determined by friendly counsel along historically established lines of allegiance and nationality; and international guarantees of the political and economic independence and territorial integrity of the several Balkan states should be entered into.

XII. The Turkish portions of the present Ottoman Empire should be assured a secure sovereignty, but the other nationalities which are now under Turkish rule should be assured an undoubted security of life and an absolutely unmolested opportunity of autonomous development, and the Dardanelles should be permanently opened as a free passage to the ships and commerce of all nations under international guarantees.

XIII. An independent Polish state should be erected which should include the territories inhabited by indisputably Polish populations, which should be assured a free and secure access to the sea, and whose political and economic independence and territorial integrity should be guaranteed by international covenant.

XIV. A general association of nations must be formed under specific covenants for the purpose of affording mutual guarantees of political independence and territorial integrity to great and small states alike.

Questions

1. Which of the Fourteen Points concern specific nations or peoples? What guiding principle did Wilson advocate in determining their futures?

2. Of points I through V, which do you think was most important? Why?
3. What was the immediate importance of point VI and the symbolic importance of point VII?

22-13 Treaty of Versailles, Select Articles (1919)

The Allies were willing to base peace negotiations with Germany on President Woodrow Wilson's Fourteen Points (Document 22-12), but British, French, and Italian leaders did not view the future of Europe and the world through Wilson's eyes. Thus, the Treaty of Versailles reflects the American president's view but also bears the stamp of the European heads of state. Wilson referred to Article 10 as the "heart" of the Covenant of the League of Nations and to Article 11 as his "favorite article in the treaty."

Source: Treaty of Peace between the Allied and Associated Powers and Germany, Signed at Versailles, June 28, 1919, in *The Treaties of Peace, 1919–1923* (New York: Carnegie Endowment for International Peace, 1924), 1:14, 32, 47, 59, 62, 83, 95, 100, 101, 111, 123.

Part I. The Covenant of the League of Nations . . .

ARTICLE 10

The Members of the League undertake to respect and preserve as against external aggression the territorial integrity and existing political independence of all Members of the League. In case of any such aggression or in case of any threat or danger of such aggression the Council shall advise upon the means by which this obligation shall be fulfilled.

ARTICLE 11

Any war or threat of war, whether immediately affecting any of the Members of the League or not, is hereby declared a matter of concern to the whole League, and the League shall take any action that may be deemed wise and effectual to safeguard the peace of nations. In case any such emergency should arise the Secretary General shall on the request of any Member of the League forthwith summon a meeting of the Council.

It is also declared to be the friendly right of each Member of the League to bring to the attention of the Assembly or of the Council any circumstance whatever affecting international relations which threatens to disturb international peace or the good understanding between nations upon which peace depends. . . .

Part III. Boundaries of Germany . . .

SECTION III. LEFT BANK OF THE RHINE

ARTICLE 42

Germany is forbidden to maintain or construct any fortifications either on the left bank of the Rhine or on the right bank to the west of a line drawn 50 kilometres to the East of the Rhine.

ARTICLE 43

In the area defined above the maintenance and the assembly of armed forces, either permanently or temporarily, and military manœuvres of any kind, as well as the upkeep of all permanent works for mobilization, are in the same way forbidden.

ARTICLE 44

In case Germany violates in any manner whatever the provisions of Articles 42 and 43, she shall be regarded as committing a hostile act against the Powers signatory of the present Treaty and as calculated to disturb the peace of the world. . . .

SECTION V. ALSACE-LORRAINE . . .

ARTICLE 51

The territories which were ceded to Germany in accordance with the Preliminaries of Peace signed at Versailles on February 26, 1871, and the Treaty of Frankfort of May 10, 1871, are restored to French sovereignty as from the date of the Armistice of November 11, 1918.

The provisions of the Treaties establishing the delimitation of the frontiers before 1871 shall be restored.

ARTICLE 52

The German Government shall hand over without delay to the French Government all archives, registers, plans, titles and documents of every kind concerning the civil, military, financial, judicial or other administrations of the territories restored to French sovereignty. If any of these documents, archives, registers, titles or plans have been misplaced, they will be restored by the German Government on the demand of the French Government....

SECTION VII. CZECHO-SLOVAK STATE

ARTICLE 81

Germany, in conformity with the action already taken by the Allied and Associated Powers, recognises the complete independence of the Czecho-Slovak State which will include the autonomous territory of the Ruthenians to the south of the Carpathians. Germany hereby recognises the frontiers of this State as determined by the Principal Allied and Associated Powers and the other interested States....

SECTION VIII. POLAND

ARTICLE 87

Germany, in conformity with the action already taken by the Allied and Associated Powers, recognises the complete independence of Poland....

SECTION XIV. RUSSIA AND RUSSIAN STATES

ARTICLE 116

Germany acknowledges and agrees to respect as permanent and inalienable the independence of all the territories which were part of the former Russian Empire on August 1, 1914.

In accordance with the provisions of Article 259 of Part IX (Financial Clauses) and Article 292 of Part X (Economic Clauses) Germany accepts definitely the abrogation of the Brest-Litovsk Treaties and of all other treaties, conventions, and agreements entered into by her with the Maximalist Government in Russia.

The Allied and Associated Powers formally reserve the rights of Russia to obtain from Germany restitution and reparation based on the principles of the present Treaty....

Part V. Military, Naval and Air Clauses...

SECTION I. MILITARY CLAUSES

CHAPTER I. EFFECTIVES AND CADRES OF THE GERMAN ARMY

ARTICLE 159

The German military forces shall be demobilised and reduced as prescribed hereinafter.

ARTICLE 160

(I) By a date which must not be later than March 31, 1920, the German Army must not comprise more than seven divisions of infantry and three divisions of cavalry.

After that date the total number of effectives in the Army of the States constituting Germany must not exceed one hundred thousand men, including officers and establishments of depots. The Army shall be devoted exclusively to the maintenance of order within the territory and to the control of the frontiers....

CHAPTER III. RECRUITING AND MILITARY TRAINING

ARTICLE 173

Universal compulsory military service shall be abolished in Germany.

The German Army may only be constituted and recruited by means of voluntary enlistment....

ARTICLE 177

Educational establishments, the universities, societies of discharged soldiers, shooting or touring clubs and, generally speaking, associations of every description, whatever be the age of their members, must not occupy themselves with any military matters.

In particular they will be forbidden to instruct or exercise their members or to allow them to be instructed or exercised, in the profession or use of arms.

These societies, associations, educational establishments and universities must have no connection with the Ministries of War or any other military authority....

SECTION III. AIR CLAUSES

ARTICLE 198

The armed forces of Germany must not include any military or naval air forces....

Part VIII. Reparation

SECTION I. GENERAL PROVISIONS

ARTICLE 231

The Allied and Associated Governments affirm and Germany accepts the responsibility of Germany and her allies for causing all the loss and damage to which the Allied and Associated Governments and their nationals have been subjected as a consequence of the war imposed upon them by the aggression of Germany and her allies.

ARTICLE 232

The Allied and Associated Governments recognise that the resources of Germany are not adequate, after taking into account permanent diminutions of such resources which will result from other provisions of the present Treaty, to make complete reparation for all such loss and damage.

The Allied and Associated Governments, however, require, and Germany undertakes, that she will make compensation for all damage done to the civilian population of the Allied and Associated Powers and to their property during the period of the belligerency of each as an Allied or Associated Power against Germany by such aggression by land, by sea and from the air, and in general all damage as defined in Annex I hereto.

Questions

1. Compare and contrast Wilson's Fourteen Points (Document 22-12) with the terms of this peace treaty.
2. How did the treaty represent a compromise between Wilson and the European Allied leaders?

22-14 Speech Before the Senate (1919)

Henry Cabot Lodge

Senator Henry Cabot Lodge (1850–1924) spoke after the drafting of the League Covenant ("constitution") and before President Wilson rejoined the Versailles Conference. He addressed an outgoing Senate still in Democratic hands.

When the Senate elected in 1918 convened later in 1919 to deal with the treaty, Republican control (49–47) of the body enabled Lodge to become majority leader and chair of the foreign-relations committee.

Source: Henry Cabot Lodge, Speech to the U.S. Senate, February 28, 1919, in Henry Cabot Lodge, *The Senate and the League of Nations* (New York: Charles Scribner's Sons, 1925), 227–233.

Mr. President, all people, men and women alike, who are capable of connected thought abhor war and desire nothing so much as to make secure the future peace of the world. Everybody hates war. Everyone longs to make it impossible. We ought to lay aside once and for all the unfounded and really evil suggestion that because men differ as to the best method of securing the world's peace in the future, anyone is against permanent peace, if it can be obtained, among all the nations of mankind. . . . We all earnestly desire to advance toward the preservation of the world's peace, and difference in method makes no distinction in purpose. It is almost needless to say that the question now before us is so momentous that it transcends all party lines. . . . No question has ever confronted the United States Senate which equals in importance that which is involved in the league of nations intended to secure the future peace of the world. There should be no undue haste in considering it. My one desire is that not only the Senate, which is charged with responsibility, but that the press and the people of the country should investigate every proposal with the utmost thoroughness and weigh them all carefully before they make up their minds. If there is any proposition or any plan which will not bear, which will not court the most thorough and most public discussion, that fact makes it an object of suspicion at the very outset. . . .

In the first place, the terms of the league—the agreements which we make,—must be so plain and so explicit that no man can misunderstand them. . . . The Senate can take no action upon it, but it lies open before us for criticism and discussion. What is said in the Senate ought to be placed before the peace conference and published in Paris, so that the foreign Governments may be informed as to the various views expressed here.

In this draft prepared for a constitution of a league of nations, which is now before the world, there is hardly a clause about the interpretation of which men do not already differ. As it stands there is serious danger that the very nations which sign the constitution of the league will quarrel about the meaning of the various articles before a twelve-month has passed. It seems to have been very hastily drafted, and the result is crudeness and looseness of expression, unintentional, I hope. There are certainly many doubtful passages and open questions obvious in the articles which can not be settled by individual inference, but which must be made so clear and so distinct that we may all understand the exact meaning of the instrument to which we are asked to set our hands. The language of these articles does not appear to me to have the precision and unmistakable character which a constitution, a treaty, or a law ought to present. The language only too frequently is not the language of laws or statutes. The article concerning mandatories, for example, contains an argument and a statement of existing conditions. Arguments and historical facts have no place in a statute or a treaty. Statutory and legal language must assert and command, not argue and describe. I press this point because there is nothing so vital to the peace of the world as the sanctity of treaties. The suggestion that we can safely sign because we can always violate or abrogate is fatal not only to any league but to peace itself. You can not found world peace upon the cynical "scrap of paper" doctrine so dear to Germany. To whatever instrument the United States sets its hand it must carry out the provisions of that instrument to the last jot and tittle, and observe it absolutely both in letter and in spirit. If this is not done the instrument will become a source of controversy instead of agreement, of dissension instead of harmony. This is all the more essential because it is evident, although not expressly stated, that this league is intended to be indissoluble, for there is no provision for its termination or for the withdrawal of any signatory. We are left to infer that any nation withdrawing from the league exposes itself to penalties and probably to war. Therefore, before we ratify, the terms and language in which the terms are stated must be exact and as precise, as free from any possibility of conflicting interpretations, as it is possible to make them.

The explanation or interpretation of any of these doubtful passages is not sufficient if made by one man, whether that man be the President of the United States, or a Senator, or anyone else. These questions and doubts must be answered and removed by the instrument itself.

It is to be remembered that if there is any dispute about the terms of this constitution there is no court provided that I can find to pass upon differences of opinion as to the terms of the constitution itself. There is no court to fulfill the function which our Supreme Court fulfills. There is provision for tribunals to decide questions submitted for arbitration, but there is no authority to decide differing interpretations as to the terms of the instrument itself.

What I have just said indicates the vast importance of the form and the manner in which the agreements which we are to sign shall be stated. I now come to questions of substance, which seem to me to demand the most careful thought of the entire American people, and particularly of those charged with the responsibility of ratification. We abandon entirely by the proposed constitution the policy laid down by Washington in his Farewell Address and the Monroe doctrine. It is worse than idle, it is not honest, to evade or deny this fact, and every fairminded supporter of this draft plan for a league admits it. I know that some of the ardent advocates of the plan submitted to us regard any suggestion of the importance of the Washington policy as foolish and irrelevant. Perhaps it is. Perhaps the time has come when the policies of Washington should be abandoned; but if we are to cast them aside I think that at least it should be done respectfully and with a sense of gratitude to the great man who formulated them. For nearly a century and a quarter the policies laid down in the Farewell Address have been followed and adhered to by the Government of the United States and by the American people. I doubt if any purely political declaration has ever been observed by any people for so long a time. The principles of the Farewell Address in regard to our foreign relations have been sustained and acted upon by the American people down to the present moment. Washington declared against permanent alliances. He did not close the door on temporary alliances. He did not close the door on temporary alliances for particular purposes. Our entry in the great war just closed was entirely in accord with and violated in no respect the policy laid down by Washington. When we went to war with Germany we made no treaties with the nations engaged in the war against the German Government. The President was so careful in this direction that he did not permit himself ever to refer to the nations by whose side we fought as "allies," but always as "nations associated with us in the war." The attitude recommended by Washington was scrupulously maintained even under the pressure of the great conflict. Now, in the twinkling of an eye, while passion and emotion reign, the Washington policy is to be entirely laid aside and we are to enter upon a permanent and indissoluble alliance. That which we refuse to do in war we are to do in peace, deliberately, coolly, and with no war exigency. Let us not overlook the profound gravity of this step.

Washington was not only a very great man but he was also a very wise man. He looked far into the future and he never omitted human nature from his calculations. He knew well that human nature had not changed fundamentally since mankind had a history. Moreover, he was destitute of any personal ambitions to a degree never equaled by any other very great man known to us. In all the vital questions with which he dealt it was not merely that he thought of his country first and never thought of himself at all. He was so great a man that the fact that this country had produced him was enough of itself to justify the Revolution and our existence as a Nation. Do not think that I overstate this in the fondness of patriotism and with the partiality of one of his countrymen. The opinion I have expressed is the opinion of the world. . . .

That was the opinion of mankind then, and it is the opinion of mankind to-day, when his statue has been erected in Paris and is about to be erected in London. If we throw aside the political testament of such a man, which has been of living force down to the present instant, because altered circumstances demand it, it is a subject for deep regret and not for rejoicing. . . .

But if we put aside forever the Washington policy in regard to our foreign relations we must always remember that it carries with it the corollary known as the Monroe doctrine. Under the terms of this league draft reported by the committee to the peace conference the Monroe doctrine disappears. It has been our cherished guide and guard for nearly a century. The Monroe doctrine is based on the principle of self-preservation. To say that it is a question of protecting the boundaries, the political integrity, or the American States, is not to state the Monroe doctrine. . . . The real essence of that doctrine is that American questions shall be settled by Americans alone; that the Americas shall be separated from Europe and from the interference of Europe in purely American questions. That is the vital principle of the doctrine.

I have seen it said that the Monroe doctrine is preserved under article 10 [calling for a collective security agreement among League members]; that we do not abandon the Monroe doctrine, we merely extend it to all the world. How anyone can say this passes my comprehension. The Monroe doctrine exists solely for the protection of the American Hemisphere, and to that hemisphere it was limited. If you extend it to all the world, it ceases to exist, because it rests on nothing but the differentiation of the American Hemisphere from the rest of the world. Under this draft of the constitution of the league of nations, American questions and European questions and Asian and African questions are all alike put within the control and jurisdiction of the league. Europe will have the right to take part in the settlement of all American questions, and we, of course, shall have the right to share in the settlement of all questions in Europe and Asia and Africa. Europe and Asia are to take part in policing the American continent and the Panama Canal, and in return we are to have, by way of compensation, the right to police the Balkans and Asia Minor when we are asked to do so. Perhaps the time has come when it is necessary to do this, but it is a very grave step, and I wish now merely to point out that the American people ought never to abandon the Washington policy and the Monroe doctrine without being perfectly certain that they earnestly wish to do so. Standing always firmly by these great policies, we have thriven and prospered and have done more to preserve the world's peace than any nation, league, or alliance which ever existed. For this reason I ask the press and the public and, of course, the Senate to consider well the gravity of this proposition before it takes the heavy responsibility of finally casting aside these policies which we have adhered to for a century and more and under which we have greatly served the cause of peace both at home and abroad.

Questions

1. What aspect of the draft of the constitution for the League of Nations disturbed Lodge?
2. Why did he mention George Washington and other founders?
3. What was the supposed threat to the Monroe Doctrine?

22-15 Speech in Indianapolis, Indiana (1919)

Woodrow Wilson

President Wilson, at a disadvantage in the Senate battleground, sought to mobilize public support for the peace treaty by embarking on a major speaking tour during September 1919. He spoke in Indianapolis early in this effort, which ended when his health broke down toward the end of the month.

Source: From Thomas G. Paterson and Dennis Merrill, eds., *Major Problems in American Foreign Relations: Since 1914*, 4th ed. (Lexington, MA: D. C. Heath, 1995), 2:40–42.

You have heard a great deal about Article X of the Covenant of the League of Nations. Article X speaks the conscience of the world. Article X is the article which goes to the heart of this whole bad business, for that article says that the members of this League—and that is intended to be all the great nations of the world—engage to respect and to preserve against all external aggression the territorial integrity and political independence of the nations concerned. That promise is necessary in order to prevent this sort of war from recurring, and we are absolutely discredited if we fought this war and then neglect the essential safeguard against it.

You have heard it said, my fellow citizens, that we are robbed of some degree of our sovereign independence of choice by articles of that sort. Every man who makes a choice to respect the rights of his neighbors deprives himself of absolute sovereignty, but he does it by promising never to do wrong, and I cannot, for one, see anything that robs me of any inherent right that I ought to retain when I promise that I will do right.

We engage in the first sentence of Article X to respect and preserve from external aggression the territorial integrity and the existing political independence, not only of the other member states, but of all states. And if any member of the League of Nations disregards that promise, then what happens? The Council of the League advises what should be done to enforce the respect for that Covenant on the part of the nation attempting to violate it, and there is no compulsion upon us to take that advice except the compulsion of our good conscience and judgment. So that it is perfectly evident that if, in the judgment of the people of the United States, the Council adjudged wrong and that this was not an occasion for the use of force, there would be no necessity on the part of the Congress of the United States to vote the use of force. But there could be no advice of the Council on any such subject without a unanimous vote, and the unanimous vote would include our own, and if we accepted the advice we would be accepting our own advice. . . . There is in that Covenant not one note of surrender of the independent judgment of the government of the United States, but an expression of it, because that independent judgment would have to join with the judgment of the rest.

But when is that judgment going to be expressed, my fellow citizens? Only after it is evident that every other resource has failed, and I want to call your attention to the central machinery of the League of Nations. If any member of that League, or any nation not a member, refuses to submit the question at issue either to arbitration or to discussion by the Council, there ensues automatically by the engagements of this Covenant an absolute economic boycott. There will be no trade with that nation by any member of the League. There will be no interchange of communication by post or telegraph. There will be no travel to or from that nation. Its borders will be closed. No citizen or any other state will be allowed to enter it, and no one of its citizens will be allowed to leave it. It will be hermetically sealed by the united action of the most powerful nations in the world. And if this economic boycott bears with unequal weight, the members of the League agree to support one another and to relieve one another in any exceptional disadvantages that may arise out of it.

And I want you to realize that this war was won not only by the armies of the world, but it was won by economic means as well. Without the economic means, the war would have been much longer continued. What happened was that Germany was shut off from the economic resources of the rest of the globe, and she could not stand it. A nation that is boycotted is a nation that is in sight of surrender. Apply this economic, peaceful, silent, deadly remedy, and there will be no need for force. It is a terrible remedy. It does not cost a life outside the nation boycotted, but it brings a pressure upon that nation which, in my judgment, no modern nation could resist. . . .

I therefore want to call your attention, if you will turn to it when you go home, to Article XI, following Article X, of the Covenant of the League of Nations. That Article XI, let me say, is the favorite article in the treaty, so far as I am concerned. It says that every matter which is likely to affect the peace of the world is everybody's business, and that it shall be the friendly right of any nation to call attention in the League to anything that is likely to affect the peace of the world or the good understanding between nations, upon which the peace of the world depends, whether that matter immediately concerns the nation drawing attention to it or not. . . .

There is not an oppressed people in the world which cannot henceforth get a hearing at that forum, and you know, my fellow citizens, what a hearing will mean if the cause of those people is just. The one thing which those who have reason to dread, have most reason to dread, is publicity and discussion, because if you are challenged to give a reason why you are doing a wrong then it has to be an exceedingly good reason, and if you give a bad reason you confess judgment, and the opinion of mankind goes against you.

Questions

1. What case did Wilson make for Article 10 of the League Covenant?
2. Why did Wilson view Article 11 so positively?
3. What role did Wilson foresee for "absolute economic boycott[s]"? How apt is his analogy between such a boycott and the blockade of 1914 to 1918?

22-16 Report on the Chicago Race Riot (1919)

Wartime and immediate postwar developments affecting African Americans (increased black migration and heightened black expectations due to their military service in the war) intensified racial fears and anger among whites (see text pp. 698–699). Lynchings increased, especially in the South; riots broke out in the North, the most serious of which occurred in East Saint Louis (1917) and Chicago (1919). The Chicago riot report excerpted here was published three years after the episode.

Source: Excerpted from *The Negro in Chicago: A Study of Race Relations and a Race Riot in 1919* (1922; New York: Arno Press and New York Times, 1968), 17–21. Copyright © 1922 by the University of Chicago Press. Reprinted by permission.

... Racial outbreaks are often characterized by hangings, burnings, and mutilations, and frequently the cause given for them is a reported Negro attack upon a white woman. None of these features appeared in the Chicago riot. An attempted hanging was reported by a white detective but was unsubstantiated. A report that Joseph Lovings, one of the Negroes killed in the riot, was burned, was heralded abroad and even carried to the United States Senate, but it was false. The coroner's physicians found no burns on his body.

Reports of assaults upon women were at no time mentioned or even hinted at as a cause of the Chicago riot, but after the disorder started reports of such crimes were published in the white and Negro press, but they had no foundation in fact.

Of the ten women wounded in the Chicago riot, seven were white, two were Negroes, and the race of one is unknown. All but one of these ten injuries appears to have been accidental. The exception was the case of Roxy Pratt, a Negro woman who, with her brother, was chased down Wells Street from Forty-seventh by gangsters and was seriously wounded by a bullet. No cases of direct attacks upon white women by Negro men were reported.

The Commission has the record of numerous instances, principally during the first twenty-four hours, where individuals of opposing races met, knives or guns were drawn, and injury was inflicted without the element of mob stimulus.

On Monday mobs operated in sudden, excited assaults, and attacks on street cars provided outstanding cases, five persons being killed and many injured. Nicholas Kleinmark, a white assailant, was stabbed to death by a Negro named Scott, acting in self-defense. Negroes killed were Henry Goodman at Thirtieth and Union streets; John Mills, on Forty-seventy Street near Union; Louis Taylor at Root Street and Wentworth Avenue; and B. F. Hardy at Forty-sixth Street and Cottage Grove Avenue. All died from beatings.

Crowds armed themselves with stones, bricks, and baseball bats and scanned passing street cars for Negroes. Finding them, trolleys were pulled off wires and entrance to the cars forced. Negroes were dragged from under car seats and beaten. Once off the car the chase began. If possible, the vanguard of the mob caught the fleeing Negroes and beat them with clubs. If the Negro outran the pursuers, stones and bricks brought him down. Sometimes the chase led through back yards and over fences, but it was always short.

Another type of race warfare was the automobile raids carried on by young men crowded in cars, speeding across the dead line at Wentworth Avenue and the "Black Belt," and firing at random. Crowded colored districts, with people sitting on front steps and in open windows, were subjected to this menace. Strangely enough, only one person was killed in these raids, Henry Baker, Negro.

Automobile raids were reported wherever colored people had established themselves, in the "Black Belt," both on the main business streets and in the residence sections, and in the small community near Ada and Loomis streets in the vicinity of Ogden Park.

These raids began Monday night, continued spasmodically all day Tuesday, and were again prevalent that night. In spite of the long period, reports of motorcycle policemen show no white raiders arrested. One suspected raiding automobile was caught on State Street Tuesday night, after collision with a patrol wagon. One of the occupants, a white man, had on his person the badge and identification card of a policeman assigned to the Twenty-fourth Precinct. No case was worked up against him, and the other men in the machine were not heard of again in connection with the raid.

Most of the police motorcycle squad was assigned to the Stanton Avenue station, which was used as police headquarters in the "Black Belt." Several automobile loads of Negroes were arrested, and firearms were found either upon their persons or in the automobile.

In only two cases were Negroes aggressively rioting found outside of the "Black Belt." One of these was the case of the saloon-keeper already mentioned, and the other was that of a deputy sheriff, who, with a party of other men, said they were on the way to the Stock Yards to rescue some beleaguered members of their race. It is reported that they wounded five white people en route. Sheriff Peters said he understood that the deputy sheriff was attacked by white mobs and fired to clear the crowd. He was not convicted.

"Sniping" was a form of retaliation by Negroes which grew out of the automobile raids. These raiding automobiles were fired upon from yards, porches, and windows throughout the "Black Belt." One of the most serious cases reported was at Thirty-first and State Streets, where Negroes barricaded the streets with rubbish boxes. Motorcycle Policeman Cheney rammed through and was hit by a bullet. His companion officer following was knocked from his machine and the machine punctured with bullets.

After the wounding of Policeman Cheney and Sergeant Murray, of the Sixth Precinct, policemen made a thorough search of all Negro homes near the scene of the "sniping." Thirty-four Negroes were arrested. Of these, ten were discharged, ten were found not guilty, one was given one day in jail, one was given five days in jail, one was fined and put on probation, two were fined $10 and costs, one was fined $25; six were given thirty days each in the House of Correction, and one, who admitted firing twice but said he was firing at one of the automobiles, was sentenced to six months in the House of Correction. His case was taken to the appellate court.

Concerted retaliatory race action showed itself in the Italian district around Taylor and Loomis streets when rumor said that a little Italian girl had been killed or wounded by a shot fired by a Negro. Joseph Lovings, an innocent Negro, came upon the excited crowd of Italians. There was a short chase through back yards. Finally Lovings was dragged from his hiding-place in a basement and brutally murdered by the crowd. The coroner reported fourteen bullet wounds on his body, eight still having bullets in them; also various stab wounds, contusions of the head, and fractures of the skull. Rumor made the tale more hideous, saying that Lovings was burned after gasoline had been poured over the dead body. This was not true.

This same massing of race against race was shown in a similar clash between Italians and Negroes on the North Side. The results here, however, were not serious. It was reported in this last case that immediately after the fracas the Negroes and Italians were again on good terms. This was not true in the neighborhood of the Lovings outrage. Miss Jane Addams, of Hull-House, which is near the scene of Lovings' death, testified before the Commission that before the riot the Italians held no particular animosity toward Negroes, for those in the neighborhood were mostly from South Italy and accustomed to the dark-skinned races, but that they were developing antipathy. In the September following the riot, she said the neighborhood was still full of wild stories so stereotyped in character that they appeared to indicate propaganda spread for a purpose.

The gang which operated in the "Loop"[1] was composed partly of soldiers and sailors in uniform; they were boys of from seventeen to twenty-two, out for a "rough" time and using race prejudice as a shield for robbery. At times this crowd numbered 100. Its depredations began shortly after 2:00 A.M. Tuesday. The La Salle Street railroad station was entered twice, and Negro men were beaten and robbed. About 3:00 A.M. activities were transferred to Wabash Avenue. In the hunt for Negroes one restaurant was wrecked and the vandalism was continued in another restaurant where two Negroes were found. One was severely injured and the other was shot down. The gangsters rolled the body into the gutter and turned the pockets inside out; they stood on the corner of Wabash Avenue and Adams Street and divided the spoils, openly boasting later of having secured $52, a diamond ring, a watch, and a brooch.

Attacks in the "Loop" continued as late as ten o'clock Tuesday morning, Negroes being chased through the streets and beaten. Warned by the Pinkerton Detective Agency, business men with stores on Wabash Avenue came to protect their property. The rioting was reported to the police by the restaurant men. Policemen rescued two Negroes that morning, but so many policemen had been concentrated in and near the "Black Belt" that there were only a few patrolmen in the whole "Loop" district, and these did not actively endeavor to cope with the mob. In the meantime two Negroes were killed and others injured, while property was seriously damaged.

Tuesday's raids marked the peak of daring during the riot, and their subsidence was as gradual as their rise. For the next two days the gangs roamed the streets, intermittently attacking Negro homes. After Tuesday midnight their operations were not so open or so concerted. The riot gradually decreased in feeling and scope till the last event of a serious nature occurred, the incendiary fires back of the Stock Yards.

While there is general agreement that these fires were incendiary, no clue could be found to the perpetrators. Negroes were suspected, as all the houses burned belonged to whites. In spite of this fact, and the testimony of thirteen people who said they saw Negroes in the vicinity before or during the fires, a rumor persisted that the fires were set by white people with blackened faces. One of the men living in the burned district who testified to seeing a motor truck filled with Negroes said, when asked about the color of the men, "Sure, I know they were colored. Of course I don't know whether they were painted." An early milk-wagon driver said that he saw Negroes come out of a barn on Forty-third Street and Hermitage Avenue. Immediately afterward the barn burst into flames. He ran to a policeman and reported it. The policeman said he was "too busy" and "it is all right anyway." One of the colonels commanding a regiment of militia said he thought white people with blackened faces had set fire to the houses; he got this opinion from talking to the police in charge of that district.

Miss Mary McDowell, of the University of Chicago Settlement, which is located back of the Yards, said in testimony before the Commission:

> I don't think the Negroes did burn the houses. I think the white hoodlums burned them. The Negroes weren't back there, they stayed at home after that Monday. When we got hold of the firemen confidentially, they said no Negroes set fire to them at all, but the newspapers said so and the people were full of fear. All kinds of mythical stories were afloat for some time.

The general superintendent of Armour & Company was asked, when testifying before the Commission, if he knew of any substantial reason why Negroes were accused of setting fires back of the Yards. He answered:

> That statement was originated in the minds of a few individuals, radicals. It does not exist in the minds of the conservative and thinking people of the community, even those living in back of the Yards. They know better. I believe it goes without saying that there isn't a colored man, regardless of how little brains he'd have, who would attempt to go over into the Polish district and set fire to anybody's house over there. He wouldn't get that far.

The controlling superintendent of Swift & Company said he could not say it from his own experience, but he understood there was as much friction between the Poles and Lithuanians who worked together in the Yards as between the Negroes and the whites. The homes burned belonged to Lithuanians. The grand jury stated in its report: "The jury believes that these fires were started for the purpose of inciting race feeling by blaming same on the blacks."

---

[1] *Loop:* the business district in downtown Chicago (see Map 18.1, text p. 554).

The methods of attack used by Negroes and whites during the riot differed; the Negroes usually clung to individual attack and the whites to mob action. Negroes used chiefly firearms and knives, and the whites used their fists, bricks, stones, baseball bats, pieces of iron, hammers. Among the white men, 69 per cent were shot or stabbed and 31 per cent were beaten; among the Negroes almost the reverse was true, 35 per cent being shot and stabbed and 65 per cent beaten. A colonel in charge of a regiment of militia on riot duty says they found few whites but many Negroes armed.

Questions

1. In general, how were people attacked during the riot?
2. What role did the automobile play in the rioting?
3. Consider the impact of the riot on the participants, the city government, and the middle class. How might the incident have affected the city a decade or more later?

22-17 Returning Soldiers (1919)

W. E. B. Du Bois

Less than twelve months after Dr. W. E. B. Du Bois published two editorials endorsing African American support for the war, he expressed the postwar disillusionment of African Americans who had hoped that the war would make America, as well as the world, "safe for democracy."

Source: "Returning Soldiers," *The Crisis*, 18 (May 1919): 13–14.

We are returning from war! THE CRISIS and tens of thousands of black men were drafted into a great struggle. For bleeding France and what she means and has meant and will mean to us and humanity and against the threat of German race arrogance, we fought gladly and to the last drop of blood; for America and her highest ideals, we fought in far-off hope; for the dominant southern oligarchy entrenched in Washington, we fought in bitter resignation. For the America that represents and gloats in lynching, disfranchisement, caste, brutality and devilish insult—for this, in the hateful upturning and mixing of things, we were forced by vindictive fate to fight, also.

But today we return! We return from the slavery of uniform which the world's madness demanded us to don to the freedom of civil garb. We stand again to look America squarely in the face and call a spade a spade. We sing: This country of ours, despite all its better souls have done and dreamed, is yet a shameful land.

It *lynches*.

And lynching is barbarism of a degree of contemptible nastiness unparalleled in human history. Yet for fifty years we have lynched two Negroes a week, and we have kept this up right through the war.

It *disfranchises* its own citizens.

Disfranchisement is the deliberate theft and robbery of the only protection of poor against rich and black against white. The land that disfranchises its citizens and calls itself a democracy lies and knows it lies.

It encourages *ignorance*.

It has never really tried to educate the Negro. A dominant minority does not want Negroes educated. It wants servants, dogs, whores and monkeys. And when this land allows a reactionary group by its stolen political power to force as many black folk into these categories as it possibly can, it cries in contemptible hypocrisy: "They threaten us with degeneracy; they cannot be educated."

It *steals* from us.

It organizes industry to cheat us. It cheats us out of our land: it cheats us out of our labor. It confiscates our savings. It reduces our wages. It raises our rent. It steals our profit. It taxes us without representation. It keeps us consistently and universally poor, and then feeds us on charity and derides our poverty.

It *insults* us.

It has organized a nation-wide and latterly a world-wide propaganda of deliberate and continuous insult and defamation of black blood wherever found. It decrees that it shall not be possible in travel nor residence, work nor play, education nor instruction for a black man to exist without tacit or open acknowledgment of his inferiority to the dirtiest white dog. And it looks upon any attempt to question or even discuss this dogma as arrogance, unwarranted assumption and treason.

This is the country to which we Soldiers of Democracy return. This is the fatherland for which we fought! But it is *our* fatherland. It was right for us to fight. The faults of *our* country are *our* faults. Under similar circumstances, we would fight again. But by the God of Heaven, we are cowards and jackasses if now that that war is over, we do not marshal every ounce of our brain and brawn to fight a sterner, longer, more unbending battle against the forces of hell in our own land.

We *return.*
We *return from fighting.*
We *return fighting.*

Make way for Democracy! We saved it in France, and by the Great Jehovah, we will save it in the United States of America, or know the reason why.

Questions

1. Compare and contrast the content and tone of "Help Us to Help" (Document 22-11) and this selection.

2. Drawing on the text (Chapters 19, 20, and 22, as appropriate), flesh out the charges in W. E. B. Du Bois's indictment.

Questions for Further Thought

1. What do the text and documents on the wartime and postwar periods suggest about the relationship between foreign and domestic developments between 1917 and 1920?

2. Compare and contrast the gains—or lack thereof—of women and African Americans during and after World War I. How do you account for similarities and dissimilarities between the two groups?

CHAPTER TWENTY-THREE

Modern Times
1920–1932

The Business-Government Partnership of the 1920s

The White House of the 1920s seemed different from the White House of the Progressive Era. Gone were Theodore Roosevelt and Woodrow Wilson, succeeded there by Warren Harding and Calvin Coolidge. Government policy seemed different, too, stressing cooperation with, rather than regulation of, business. Still, such cooperation had been one aspect of progressivism and was central to the conduct of the Great War. Moreover, the most important figure in the Harding and Coolidge administrations was Secretary of Commerce Herbert Hoover, a progressive and an important wartime administrator. A few social justice concerns were addressed during the 1920s—Congress enacted the Sheppard-Towner Federal Maternity and Infancy Act (see text pp. 708–709) and proposed a constitutional amendment to prohibit child labor, and the Harding administration prevailed on the steel industry to shorten workers' hours—but in the main, business received a sympathetic hearing from the Harding and Coolidge administrations, and agriculture and labor did not.

The United States prospered during the 1920s. It had emerged from the war economically strengthened, not drained. Already the world's premier economic power, it was now the world's largest creditor as well. However, not all Americans shared fully in prosperity. Workers' standard of living rose, but insecurity—due to unemployment, illness or injury, or old age—remained their lot. Employers, not government or labor unions, bore responsibility for whatever worker benefits were provided. This was "welfare capitalism" before the birth of "the welfare state" and the revitalization of the labor movement during the 1930s (see text p. 710). Sectors of the agricultural economy—wheat, corn, and cotton farmers—also suffered economic declines during the 1920s (see text p. 710).

In Document 23-1, Herbert Hoover discusses the significance of American individualism in the new era of business-government partnership. Andrew W. Mellon elucidates his views on taxation (Document 23-2) in the postwar and post-progressive 1920s.

23-1 American Individualism (1922)

Herbert Hoover

Herbert Hoover (1874–1964) was the first U.S. president born west of the Mississippi River, in West Branch, Iowa. Hoover was raised on a ranch in Oregon and was educated at Stanford University in California. A mining consultant, he became a self-made millionaire and then turned his considerable energies and talents to government service. Under Woodrow Wilson, Hoover distinguished himself directing postwar relief efforts in Europe. He then worked to improve business-government relations as secretary of commerce in the Harding and Coolidge administrations before winning the U.S. presidency in 1928. In a world becoming crowded with competing ideologies, Hoover remained true to the values he grew up with and to a philosophy he called "American individualism."

Source: Herbert Hoover, "Introduction" from *American Individualism: The Challenge to Liberty* (West Branch, IA: Herbert Hoover Presidential Library Association, 1989), 31–36. Copyright © 1989 by the Herbert Hoover Presidential Library Association, Inc. Reprinted by permission.

We have witnessed in this last eight years the spread of revolution over one-third of the world. The causes of these explosions lie at far greater depths than the failure of governments in war. The war itself in its last stages was a conflict of social philosophies—but beyond this the causes of social explosion lay in the great inequities and injustices of centuries flogged beyond endurance by the conflict and greed from restraint by the destruction of war. The urgent forces which drive human society have been plunged into a terrible furnace. Great theories spun by dreamers to remedy the pressing human ills have come to the front of men's minds. Great formulas came into life that promise to dissolve all trouble. Great masses of people have flocked to their banners in hopes born of misery and suffering. Nor has this great social ferment been confined to those nations that have burned with revolutions.

Now, as the storm of war, of revolution and of emotion subsides there is left even with us of the United States much unrest, much discontent with the surer forces of human advancement. To all of us, out of this crucible of actual, poignant, individual experience has come a deal of new understanding, and it is for all of us to ponder these new currents if we are to shape our future with intelligence.

Even those parts of the world that suffered less from the war have been partly infected by these ideas. Beyond this, however, many have had high hopes of civilization suddenly purified and ennobled by the sacrifices and services of the war; they had thought the fine unity of purpose gained in war would be carried into great unity of action in remedy of the faults of civilization in peace. But from concentration of every spiritual and material energy upon the single purpose of war the scene changed to the immense complexity and the many purposes of peace.

Thus there loom up certain definite underlying forces in our national life that need to be stripped of the imaginary—the transitory—and a definition should be given to the actual permanent and persistent motivation of our civilization. In contemplation of these questions we must go far deeper than the superficials of our political and economic structure, for these are but the products of our social philosophy—the machinery of our social system.

Nor is it ever amiss to review the political, economic, and spiritual principles through which our country has steadily grown in usefulness and greatness, not only to preserve them from being fouled by false notions, but more importantly that we may guide ourselves in the road to progress.

Five or six great social philosophies are at struggle in the world for ascendency. There is the Individualism of America. There is the Individualism of the more democratic states of Europe with its careful reservations of castes and classes. There are Communism, Socialism, Syndicalism, Capitalism, and finally there is Autocracy—whether by birth, by possessions, militarism, or divine right of kings. Even the Divine Right still lingers on although our lifetime has seen fully two-thirds of the earth's population, including Germany, Austria, Russia, and China, arrive at a state of angry disgust with this type of social motive power and throw it on the scrap heap.

All these thoughts are in ferment today in every country of the world. They fluctuate in ascendency with times and places. They compromise with each other in daily reaction on governments and peoples. Some of these ideas are perhaps more adapted to one race than another. Some are false, some are true. What we are interested in is their challenge to the physical and spiritual forces of America.

The partisans of some of these other brands of social schemes challenge us to comparison; and some of their partisans even among our own people are increasing in their agitation that we adopt one or another or parts of their devices in place of our tried individualism. They insist that our social foundations are exhausted, that like feudalism and autocracy, America's plan has served its purpose—that it must be abandoned.

There are those who have been left in sober doubt of our institutions or are confounded by bewildering catchwords of vivid phrases. For in this welter of discussions there is much attempt to glorify or defame social and economic forces with phrases. Nor indeed should we disregard the potency of some of these phrases in their stir to action.—"The dictatorship of the Proletariat," "Capitalistic nations," "Germany over all," and a score of others. We need only to review those that have jumped to horseback during the last ten years in order that we may be properly awed by the great social and political havoc that can be worked where the bestial instincts of hate, murder, and destruction are clothed by the demagogue in the fine terms of political idealism.

For myself, let me say at the very outset that my faith in the essential truth, strength, and vitality of the developing creed by which we have hitherto lived in this country of ours has been confirmed and deepened by the searching experiences of seven years of service in the backwash and miseries of war. Seven years of contending with economic degeneration, with social disintegration, with incessant political dislocation, with all of its seething and ferment of individual and class conflict, could but impress me with the primary motivation of social forces, and the necessity for broader thought upon their great issue to humanity. And from it all I emerge a great individualist—an unashamed individualist. But let me say also that I am an American individualist. For America has been steadily developing the ideals that constitute progressive individualism.

No doubt, individualism run riot, with no tempering principle, would provide a long category of inequalities, of tyrannies, dominations, and injustices. America, however, has tempered the whole conception of individualism by the injection of a definite principle, and from this principle it follows that attempts at domination, whether in government or in the processes of industry and commerce, are under an insistent curb. If we would have the values of individualism, their stimulation to initiative, to the development of hand and intellect, to the high development of thought and spirituality, they must be tempered with that firm and fixed ideal of American individualism—*an equality of opportunity*. If we would have these values we must soften its hardness and stimulate progress through that sense of service that lies in our people.

Therefore, it is not the individualism of other countries for which I would speak, but the individualism of America. Our individualism differs from all others because it embraces these great ideals: *that while we build our society upon the attainment of the individual, we shall safeguard to every individual an equality of opportunity to take that position in the community to which his intelligence, character, ability, and ambition entitle him; that we keep the social solution free from frozen strata of classes; that we shall stimulate efforts of each individual to achievement; that through an enlarging sense of responsibility and understanding we shall assist him to this attainment; while he in turn must stand up to the emery wheel of competition.*

Individualism cannot be maintained as the foundation of a society if it looks to only legalistic justice based upon contracts, property, and political equality. Such legalistic safeguards are themselves not enough. In our individualism we have long since abandoned the *laissez faire* of the 18th Century—the notion that it is "every man for himself and the devil take the hindmost." We abandoned that when we adopted the ideal of equality of opportunity—the fair chance of Abraham Lincoln. We have confirmed its abandonment in terms of legislation, of social and economic justice,—in part because we have learned that the foremost are not always the best nor the hindmost the worst—and in part because we have learned that social injustice is the destruction of justice itself. We have learned that the impulse to production can only be maintained at high pitch if there is a fair division of the product. We have also learned that fair division can only be obtained by certain restrictions on the strong and the dominant. We have indeed gone even further in the 20th Century with the embracement of the necessity of a greater and broader sense of service and responsibility to others as a part of individualism.

Whatever may be the cause with regard to Old World individualism (and we have given more back to Europe than we received from her) the truth that is important for us to grasp today is that there is a world of difference between the principles and spirit of Old World individualism and that which we have developed in our own country.

We have, in fact, a special social system of our own. We have made it ourselves from materials brought in revolt from conditions in Europe. We have lived it; we constantly improve it; we have seldom tried to define it. It abhors autocracy and does not argue with it, but fights it. It is not capitalism, or socialism, or syndicalism, nor a cross breed of them. Like most Americans, I refuse to be damned by anybody's word-classification of it, such as "capitalism," "plutocracy," "proletariat" or "middle class," or any other, or to any kind of compartment that is based on the assumption of some group dominating somebody else.

The social force in which I am interested is far higher and far more precious a thing than all these. It springs from something infinitely more enduring; it springs from the one source of human progress—that each individual shall be given the chance and stimulation for development of the best with which he has been endowed in heart and mind; it is the sole source of progress; it is American individualism.

The rightfulness of our individualism can rest either on philosophic, political, economic, or spiritual grounds. It can rest on the ground of being the only safe avenue to further human progress.

Questions

1. How did Hoover describe the state of the world after the Great War?
2. In what respects did Hoover distinguish American individualism from earlier laissez-faire philosophies?
3. Compare and contrast the tone and ideas of Hoover's essay with William Graham Sumner's "The Forgotten Man" (Document 19-2).

23-2 Fundamental Principles of Taxation (1924)

Andrew W. Mellon

Andrew W. Mellon (1855–1937), a successful financier and businessman, served as secretary of the treasury in the Harding, Coolidge, and Hoover administrations. Mellon sharply reduced taxes on wealthy individuals and corporations to encourage investment, defending his controversial approach as the surest way to ensure general prosperity and sound fiscal health. Mellon's policies and views, presented in this excerpt, were discredited by the great stock market crash of 1929 and the Great Depression of the 1930s but enjoyed a revival in 1980 with the election of Ronald Reagan, who endorsed a similar tax philosophy.

Source: From *Taxation: The People's Business* (New York: Macmillan Company, 1924), 9–22. Copyright © 1952 by Nora McMullen Mellon. Reprinted with the permission of Scribner, an imprint of Simon & Schuster Adult Publishing Group. All rights reserved.

The problem of the Government is to fix rates which will bring in a maximum amount of revenue to the Treasury and at the same time bear not too heavily on the taxpayer or on business enterprises. A sound tax policy must take into consideration three factors. It must produce sufficient revenue for the Government; it must lessen, so far as possible, the burden of taxation on those least able to bear it; and it must also remove those influences which might retard the continued steady development of business and industry on which, in the last analysis, so much of our prosperity depends. Furthermore, a permanent tax system should be designed not merely for one or two years nor for the effect it may have on any given class of taxpayers, but should be worked out with regard to conditions over a long period and with a view to its ultimate effect on the prosperity of the country as a whole.

These are the principles on which the Treasury's tax policy is based, and any revision of taxes which ignores these fundamental principles will prove merely a makeshift and must eventually be replaced by a system based on economic, rather than political, considerations.

There is no reason why the question of taxation should not be approached from a non-partisan and business viewpoint. In recent years, in any discussion of tax revision, the question which has caused most controversy is the proposed reduction of the surtaxes. Yet recommendations for such reductions have not been confined to either Republican or Democratic administrations. My own recommendations on this subject were in line with similar ones made by Secretaries Houston and Glass, both of whom served under a Democratic President. Tax revision should never be made the football either of partisan or class politics but should be worked out by those who have made a careful study of the subject in its larger aspects and are prepared to recommend the course which, in the end, will prove for the country's best interest.

I have never viewed taxation as a means of rewarding one class of taxpayers or punishing another. If such a point of view ever controls our public policy, the traditions of freedom, justice and equality of opportunity, which are the distinguishing characteristics of our American civilization, will have disappeared and in their place we shall have class legislation with all its attendant evils. The man who seeks to perpetuate prejudice and class hatred is doing America an ill service. In attempting to promote or to defeat legislation by arraying one class of taxpayers against another, he shows a complete misconception of those principles of equality on which the country was founded. Any man of energy and initiative in this country can get what he wants out of life. But when that initiative is crippled by legislation or by a tax system which denies him the right to receive a reasonable share of his earnings, then he will no longer exert himself and the country will be deprived of the energy on which its continued greatness depends.

This condition has already begun to make itself felt as a result of the present unsound basis of taxation. The existing tax system is an inheritance from the war. During that time the highest taxes ever levied by any country were borne uncomplainingly by the American people for the purpose of defraying the unusual and ever-increasing expenses incident to the successful conduct of a great war. Normal tax rates were increased, and a system of surtaxes was evolved in order to make the man of large income pay more proportionately than the smaller taxpayer. If he had twice as much income, he paid not twice, but three or four times as much tax. For a short time the surtaxes yielded a large revenue. But since the close of the war people have come to look upon them as a business expense and have treated them accordingly by avoiding payment as much as possible. The history of taxation shows that taxes which are inherently excessive are not paid. The high rates inevitably put pressure upon the taxpayer to withdraw his capital from productive business and invest it in tax-exempt securities or to find other lawful methods of avoiding the realization of taxable income. The result is that the sources of taxation are drying up; wealth is failing to carry its share of the tax burden; and capital is being diverted into channels which yield neither revenue to the Government nor profit to the people.

Before the period of the war, taxes as high as those now in effect would have been thought fantastic and impossible of payment. As a result of the patriotic desire of the people to contribute to the limit to the successful prosecution of the war, high taxes were assessed and ungrudgingly paid. Upon the conclusion of peace and the gradual removal of war-time conditions of business, the opportunity is presented to Congress to make the tax structure of the United States conform more closely to normal conditions and to remove the inequalities in that structure which directly injure our prosperity and cause strains upon our economic fabric. There is no question of the fact that if the country is to go forward in the future as it has in the past, we must make sure that all retarding influences are removed.

Adam Smith, in his great work, "Wealth of Nations," laid down as the first maxim of taxation that "The subjects of every state ought to contribute toward the support of the Government, as nearly as possible, in proportion to their respective abilities," and in his fourth and last maxim, that "Every tax ought to be so contrived as both to take out and to keep out of the pockets of the people as little as possible over and above what it brings into the public treasury of the state," citing as one of the ways by which this last maxim is violated a tax which "may obstruct the industry of the people, and discourage them from applying to certain branches of business which might give maintenance and employment to great multitudes.... While it obliges the people to pay, it may thus diminish, or perhaps destroy, some of the funds, which might enable them more easily to do so."

The further experience of one hundred and fifty years since this was written has emphasized the truth of these maxims, but those who argue against a reduction of surtaxes to more nearly peace-time figures cite only the first maxim, and ignore the fourth. The principle that a man should pay taxes in accordance with his "ability to pay" is sound but, like all other general statements, has its practical limitations and qualifications, and when, as a result of an excessive or unsound basis of taxation, it becomes evident that the source of taxation is drying up and wealth is being diverted into unproductive channels, yielding neither revenue to the Government nor profit to the people, then it is time to readjust our basis of taxation upon sound principles.

It seems difficult for some to understand that high rates of taxation do not necessarily mean large revenue to the Government, and that more revenue may often be obtained by lower rates. There was an old saying that a railroad freight rate should be "what the traffic will bear"; that is, the highest rate at which the largest quantity of freight would move. The same rule applies to all private businesses. If a price is fixed too high, sales drop off and with them profits; if a price is fixed too low, sales may increase, but again profits decline. The most outstanding recent example of this principle is the sales policy of the Ford Motor Car Company. Does any one question that Mr. Ford has made more money by reducing the price of his car and increasing his sales than he would have made by maintaining a high price and a greater profit per car, but selling less cars? The Government is just a business, and can and should be run on business principles.

Experience has shown that the present high rates of surtax are bringing in each year progressively less revenue to the Government. This means that the price is too high to the large taxpayer and he is avoiding a taxable income by the many ways which are available to him. What rates will bring in the largest revenue to the Government experience has not yet developed, but it is estimated that by cutting the surtaxes in half, the Government, when the full effect of the reduction is felt, will receive more revenue from the owners of large incomes at the lower rates of tax than it would have received at the higher rates. This is simply an application of the same business principle referred to above, just as Mr. Ford makes more money out of pricing his cars at $380 than at $3,000.

Looking at the subject, therefore, solely from the standpoint of Government revenues, lower surtax rates are essential. If we consider, however, the far more important subject of the effect of the present high surtax rates on the development and prosperity of our country, then the necessity for a change is more apparent. The most noteworthy characteristic of the American people is their initiative. It is this spirit which has developed America, and it was the same spirit in our soldiers which made our armies successful abroad. If the spirit of business adventure is killed, this country will cease to hold the foremost position in the world. And yet it is this very spirit which excessive surtaxes are now destroying. Any one at all in touch with affairs knows of his own knowledge of buildings which have not been built, of businesses which have not been started, and of new projects which have been abandoned, all for the one reason—high surtaxes. If failure attends, the loss is borne exclusively by the adventurer, but if success ensues, the Government takes more than half of the profits. People argue the risk is not worth the return.

With the open invitation to all men who have wealth to be relieved from taxation by the simple expedient of investing in the more than $12,000,000,000 of tax-exempt securities now available, and which would be unaffected by any Constitutional amendment, the rich need not pay taxes. We violate Adam Smith's first maxim. Where these high surtaxes do bear, is not on the man who has acquired and holds available wealth, but on the man who, through his own initiative, is making wealth. The idle man is relieved; the producer is penalized. We violate the fourth maxim. We do not reach the people in proportion to their ability to pay and we destroy the initiative which produces the wealth in which the whole country should share, and which is the source of revenue to the Government.

In considering any reduction the Government must always be assured that taxes will not be so far reduced as to deprive the Treasury of sufficient revenue with which properly to run its business with the manifold activities now a part of the Federal Government and to take care of the public debt. Tax reduction must come out of surplus revenue. In determining the amount of surplus available these factors control: the revenue remaining the same, an increase in expenditures reduces the surplus, and expenditures remaining the same, anything which reduces the revenue reduces the surplus. The reaction, therefore, of the authorization of extraordinary or unsound expenditures is twofold—it serves, first, to raise the expenditures and so narrow the margin of available surplus; and, second, to decrease further or obliterate entirely this margin by a reduction of the Treasury's revenues through the disturbance of general business, which is promptly reflected in the country's income. On the other hand, a decrease of taxes causes an inspiration to trade and commerce which increases the prosperity of the country so that the revenues of the Government, even on a lower basis of tax, are increased. Taxation can be reduced to a point apparently in excess of the estimated surplus, because by the cumulative effect of such reduction, expenses remaining the same, a greater revenue is obtained.

High taxation, even if levied upon an economic basis, affects the prosperity of the country, because in its ultimate analysis the burden of all taxes rests only in part upon the individual or property taxed. It is largely borne by the ultimate consumer. High taxation means a high price level and high cost of living. A reduction in taxes, therefore, results not only in an immediate saving to the individual or property directly affected, but an ultimate saving to all people in the country. It can safely be said, that a reduction in the income tax reduces expenses not only of the income taxpayers but of the entire 110,000,000 people in the United States. It is for this basic reason that the present question of tax reform is not how much each individual taxpayer reduces his direct contribution, although this, of course, is a powerful influence upon the individual affected; the real problem to determine is what plan results in the least burden to the people and the most revenue to the Government.

Questions

1. How did Mellon use business principles to interpret the federal government's approach to taxation?
2. According to Mellon, why was the Great War an exception to the principles of taxation?
3. Taxation remains an important political issue today. How do modern politicians employ Mellon's principles in debating tax codes?

Questions for Further Thought

1. How do Herbert Hoover's philosophy of individualism (Document 23-1) and Andrew W. Mellon's views on taxation (Document 23-2) complement each other?
2. How do the "New Era" concerns of Hoover and Mellon differ from the older concerns of the Progressive Era reformers?

A New National Culture

During the 1920s, a national culture emerged, one that cut across (though it hardly obliterated) class, regional, racial, religious, and ethnic lines. To a considerable degree, this new mass culture was created by automobiles (and passable roads), radios, movies, mass-circulation magazines, and department and chain stores. Although large numbers of Americans did not share in the prosperity of the decade, living standards were rising in a society that stressed consumption and leisure. Advertising created wants, and various credit arrangements encouraged consumers to satisfy those wants. Sales of automobiles and electric household appliances boomed. Increasing numbers of Americans took to the road as tourists and attended movies and a range of athletic events, the stars of which became celebrities (see text pp. 713–718).

Document 23-3 provides the insight of Bruce Barton, who reveals "the Real Jesus" as the founder of modern business. Document 23-4 is an advertisement from the period. Document 23-5 analyzes the impact of the automobile on the people of "Middletown" (Muncie, Indiana).

23-3 *The Man Nobody Knows* (1925)

Bruce Barton

The advertising industry was not central to the "associative state" sought by Herbert Hoover, but it was essential to the consumer goods–based economy and the "new national culture" of the 1920s.

Bruce Barton (1886–1967) was among advertising's leaders. The son of a Protestant clergyman, and a Phi Beta Kappa graduate (voted "most likely to succeed") of Amherst College, Barton worked as an editor and magazine sales manager. During the First World War, he did volunteer work for the Salvation Army and served as publicity director of the United War Work Agencies. It was then that he met Roy Durstine and Alex Osborne, with whom he founded an advertising agency in 1919. With a merger in 1928, the firm became even more famous as Batten, Barton, Durstine, and Osborne (BBD&O).

Barton's *The Man Nobody Knows*, excerpted here, led the nonfiction best-seller list in 1925 and 1926. ("Jeffries," to whom he refers, was James Jeffries, a heavyweight boxing champion.)

Source: Bruce Barton, "How It Came to Be Written" from *The Man Nobody Knows.* Copyright © 1925 by The Bobbs-Merrill Company and renewed © 1953 by Bruce Barton. Reprinted with the permission of Scribner, a division of Simon & Schuster Adult Publishing Group. All rights reserved.

HOW IT CAME TO BE WRITTEN

The little boy's body sat bolt upright in the rough wooden chair, but his mind was very busy.

This was his weekly hour of revolt.

The kindly lady who could never seem to find her glasses would have been terribly shocked if she had known what was going on inside the little boy's mind.

"You must love Jesus," she said every Sunday, "and God."

The little boy did not say anything. He was afraid to say anything; he was almost afraid that something would happen to him because of the things he thought.

Love God! Who was always picking on people for having a good time, and sending little boys to hell because they couldn't do better in a world which he had made so hard! Why didn't God take on some one his own size?

Love Jesus! The little boy looked up at the picture which hung on the Sunday-school wall. It showed a pale young man with flabby forearms and a sad expression. The young man had red whiskers.

Then the little boy looked across to the other wall. There was Daniel, good old Daniel, standing off the lions. The little boy liked Daniel. He liked David, too, with the trusty sling that landed a stone square on the forehead of Goliath. And Moses, with his rod and his big brass snake. They were winners—those three. He wondered if David could whip Jeffries. Samson could! Say, that would have been a fight!

But Jesus! Jesus was the "lamb of God." The little boy did not know what that meant, but it sounded like Mary's little lamb. Something for girls—sissified. Jesus was also "meek and lowly," a "man of sorrows and acquainted with grief." He went around for three years telling people not to do things.

Sunday was Jesus' day; it was wrong to feel comfortable or laugh on Sunday.

The little boy was glad when the superintendent thumped the bell and announced: "We will now sing the closing hymn." One more bad hour was over. For one more week the little boy had got rid of Jesus.

Years went by and the boy grew up and became a business man.

He began to wonder about Jesus.

He said to himself: "Only strong magnetic men inspire great enthusiasm and build great organizations. Yet Jesus built the greatest organization of all. It is extraordinary."

The more sermons the man heard and the more books he read the more mystified he became.

One day he decided to wipe his mind clean of books and sermons.

He said, "I will read what the men who knew Jesus personally said about him. I will read about him as though he were a new historical character, about whom I had never heard anything at all."

The man was amazed.

A physical weakling! Where did they get that idea? Jesus pushed a plane and swung an adze; he was a successful carpenter. He slept outdoors and spent his days walking around his favorite lake. His muscles were so strong that when he drove the money-changers out, nobody dared to oppose him!

A kill-joy! He was the most popular dinner guest in Jerusalem! The criticism which proper people made was that he spent too much time with publicans and sinners (very good fellows, on the whole, the man thought) and enjoyed society too much. They called him a "wine bibber and a gluttonous man."

A failure! He picked up twelve men from the bottom ranks of business and forged them into an organization that conquered the world.

When the man had finished his reading he exclaimed, "This is a man nobody knows.

"Some day," said he, "some one will write a book about Jesus. Every business man will read it and send it to his partners and his salesmen. For it will tell the story of the founder of modern business."

So the man waited for some one to write the book, but no one did. Instead, more books were published about the "lamb of God" who was weak and unhappy and glad to die.

The man became impatient. One day he said, "I believe I will try to write that book, myself."

And he did.

Questions

1. Which view of Christ did Barton reject?
2. How did he portray Jesus instead?
3. How do you account for the popularity of Barton's best-selling book?

23-4 Advertisement for Listerine (1923)

During the 1920s, it has been noted, advertising copywriters increasingly emphasized the *consumers* to whom they hoped to sell products rather than the *products* themselves. Advertising for Listerine provided a classic and successful illustration of this strategy: the product's advertising budget rose by 5,000 percent, the producer's profits by 4,000 percent. Listerine was marketed as a treatment for colds, sore throats, and dandruff and as an astringent, aftershave, and deodorant as well as a mouthwash.

Source: Listerine ad by Lambert Pharmacal Company, St. Louis, in *Literary Digest*, November 17, 1923. Courtesy of Warner-Lambert Company, the copyright and trademark owner.

Questions

1. What is the role of the dentist in this ad?
2. What are the various reasons given for buying the product?
3. What kind of gender stereotyping is involved in both the artwork and the ad copy?

23-5 Remaking Leisure in Middletown (1929)

**Robert S. Lynd,
Helen Merrell Lynd**

Sociologists Robert S. Lynd (1892–1970) and Helen Merrell Lynd (1896–1982) wanted to study the effects of modernization on an urban community "in that common denominator of America, the Middle West." They chose Muncie, Indiana, which they referred to as Middletown (see text p. 714). The Lynds' work, first published in 1929, has become a classic in American sociology.

This selection considers the automobile a new but already troubling phenomenon in Middletown.

Source: Excerpt from *Middletown: A Study in American Culture,* 253–260. Copyright 1929 by Harcourt, Inc., and renewed 1957 by Robert S. and Helen M. Lynd. Reprinted by permission of the publisher.

In his discreet way he told her

It had never occurred to her before. But in his discreet, professional way he was able to tell her. And she was sensible enough to be grateful instead of resentful.

In fact, the suggestion he made came to mean a great deal to her.

It brought her greater poise—that feeling of self-assurance that adds to a woman's charm—and, moreover, a new sense of daintiness that she had never been quite so sure of in the past.

* * * * * * * *

Many people suffer in the same way. Halitosis (the scientific term for unpleasant breath) creeps upon you unawares. Usually you are not able to detect it yourself. And, naturally enough, even your best friends will not tell you.

Fortunately, however, halitosis is usually due to some local condition—often food fermentation in the mouth; something you have eaten; too much smoking. And it may be corrected by the systematic use of Listerine as a mouth wash and gargle.

Dentists know that this well-known antiseptic they have used for half a century, possesses these remarkable properties as a breath deodorant.

Your druggist will supply you. He sells lots of Listerine. It has dozens of other uses as a safe antiseptic. It is particularly valuable, too, at this time of year in combating sore throat. Read the circular that comes with each bottle.—*Lambert Pharmacal Company, Saint Louis, U. S. A.*

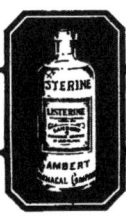

For **HALITOSIS** use **LISTERINE**

Advertisement for Listerine (1923). Listerine® is a registered trademark of Johnson & Johnson.

The first real automobile appeared in Middletown in 1900. About 1906 it was estimated that "there are probably 200 in the city and county." At the close of 1923 there were 6,221 passenger cars in the city, one for every 6.1 persons, or roughly two for every three families. Of these 6,221 cars, 41 per cent. were Fords; 54 per cent. of the total were cars of models of 1920 or later, and 17 per cent. models earlier than 1917. These cars average a bit over 5,000 miles a year. For some of the workers and some of the business class, use of the automobile is a seasonal matter, but the increase in surfaced roads and in closed cars is rapidly making the car a year-round tool for leisure-time as well as getting-a-living activities. As, at the turn of the century, business class people began to feel apologetic if they did not have a telephone, so ownership of an automobile has now reached the point of being an accepted essential of normal living.

Into the equilibrium of habits which constitutes for each individual some integration in living has come this new habit, upsetting old adjustments, and blasting its way through such accustomed and unquestioned dicta as "Rain or shine, I never miss a Sunday morning at church"; "A high school boy does not need much spending money"; "I don't need exercise, walking to the office keeps me fit"; "I wouldn't think of moving out of town and being so far from my friends"; "Parents ought always to know where their children are." The newcomer is most quickly and amicably incorporated into those regions of behavior in which men are engaged in doing impersonal, matter-of-fact things; much more contested is its advent where emotionally charged sanctions and taboos are concerned. No one questions the use of the auto for transporting groceries, getting to one's place of work or to the golf course, or in place of the porch for "cooling off after supper" on a hot summer evening; however much the activities concerned with getting a living may be altered by the fact that a factory can draw from workmen within a radius of forty-five miles, or however much old labor union men resent the intrusion of this new alternate way of spending an evening, these things are hardly major issues. But when auto riding tends to replace the traditional call in the family parlor as a way of approach between the unmarried, "the home is endangered," and all-day Sunday motor trips are a "threat against the church"; it is in the activities concerned with the home and religion that the automobile occasions the greatest emotional conflicts.

Group-sanctioned values are disturbed by the inroads of the automobile upon the family budget. A case in point is the not uncommon practice of mortgaging a home to buy an automobile. . . . That the automobile does represent a real choice in the minds of some at least is suggested by the acid retort of one citizen to the question about car ownership: "No, sir, we've *not* got a car. *That's* why we've got a home." According to an officer of a Middletown automobile financing company, 75 to 90 percent of the cars purchased locally are bought on time payment, and a working man earning $35.00 a week frequently plans to use one week's pay each month as payment for his car.

The automobile has apparently unsettled the habit of careful saving for some families. "Part of the money we spend on the car would go to the bank, I suppose," said more than one working class wife. A business man explained his recent inviting of social oblivion by selling his car by saying: "My car, counting depreciation and everything, was costing mighty nearly $100.00 a month, and my wife and I sat down together the other night and just figured that we're getting along, and if we're to have anything later on, we've just got to begin to save." The "moral" aspect of the competition between the automobile and certain accepted expenditures appears in the remark of another business man, "An automobile is a luxury, and no one has a right to one if he can't afford it. I haven't the slightest sympathy for any one who is out of work if he owns a car."

Men in the clothing industry are convinced that automobiles are bought at the expense of clothing, and the statements of a number of the working class wives bear this out:

"We'd rather do without clothes than give up the car," said one mother of nine children. "We used to go to his sister's to visit, but by the time we'd get the children shoed and dressed there wasn't any money left for carfare. Now no matter how they look, we just poke 'em in the car and take 'em along."

"We don't have no fancy clothes when we have the car to pay for," said another. "The car is the only pleasure we have."

Even food may suffer:

"I'll go without food before I'll see us give up the car," said one woman emphatically, and several who were out of work were apparently making precisely this adjustment. . . .

Many families feel that an automobile is justified as an agency holding the family group together. "I never feel as close to my family as when we are all together in the car," said one business class mother, and one or two spoke of giving up Country Club membership or other recreations to get a car for this reason. "We don't spend anything on recreation except for the car. We save every place we can and put the money into the car. It keeps the family together," was an opinion voiced more than once. Sixty-one per cent. of 337 boys and 60 per cent. of 423 girls in the three upper years of the high school say that they motor more often with their parents than without them.

But this centralizing tendency of the automobile may be only a passing phase; sets in the other direction are almost equally prominent. "Our daughters [eighteen and fifteen] don't use our car much because they are always with somebody else in their car when we go out motoring," lamented one business class mother. . . . "What on earth *do* you want me to do? Just sit around home all evening!" retorted a popular high school girl of today when her father discouraged her going out motoring for the evening with a young blade in a rakish car waiting at the curb. The fact that 348 boys and 382 girls in the three upper years of the high school placed "use of the automobile" fifth and fourth respectively in a list of twelve possible sources of disagreement between them and their parents suggests that this may be an increasing decentralizing agent.

An earnest teacher in a Sunday School class of working class boys and girls in their late teens was winding up the lesson on the temptations of Jesus: "These three temptations summarize all the temptations we encounter today: physical comfort, fame, and wealth. Can you think of any temptation we have today that Jesus didn't have?" "Speed!" rejoined one boy.... The boys who have cars "step on the gas," and those who haven't cars sometimes steal them: "The desire of youth to step on the gas when it has no machine of its own," said the local press, "is considered responsible for the theft of the greater part of the [154] automobiles stolen from [Middletown] during the past year."

The threat which the automobile presents to some anxious parents is suggested by the fact that of thirty girls brought before the juvenile court in the twelve months preceding September 1, 1924, charged with "sex crimes," for whom the place where the offense occurred was given in the records, nineteen were listed as having committed the offense in an automobile. Here again the automobile appears to some as an "enemy" of the home and society.

Sharp, also, is the resentment aroused by this elbowing new device when it interferes with old-established religious habits. The minister trying to change people's behavior in desired directions through the spoken word must compete against the strong pull of the open road strengthened by endless printed "copy" inciting to travel. Preaching to 200 people on a hot, sunny Sunday in midsummer on "The Supreme Need of Today," a leading Middletown minister denounced "automobilitis—the thing those people have who go off motoring on Sunday instead of going to church.". . .

"We had a fine day yesterday," exclaimed an elderly pillar of a prominent church, by way of Monday morning greeting. "We left home at five in the morning. By seven we swept into—. At eight we had breakfast at—, eighty miles from home. From there we went on to Lake—, the longest in the state. I had never seen it before, and I've lived here all my life, but I sure do want to go again. Then we went to—[the Y.M.C.A. camp] and had our chicken dinner. It's a fine thing for people to get out that way on Sundays. No question about it. They see different things and get a larger outlook."

"Did you miss church?" he was asked.

"Yes, I did, but you can't do both. I never missed church or Sunday school for thirteen years and I kind of feel as if I'd done my share. The ministers ought not to rail against people's driving on Sunday. They ought just to realize that they won't be there every Sunday during the summer, and make church interesting enough so they'll want to come."

But if the automobile touches the rest of Middletown's living at many points, it has revolutionized its leisure; more, perhaps, than the movies or any other intrusion new to Middletown since the nineties, it is making leisure-time enjoyment a regularly expected part of every day and week rather than an occasional event. The readily available leisure-time options of even the working class have been multiplied many-fold. As one working class housewife remarked, "We just go to lots of things we couldn't go to if we didn't have a car." Beefsteak and watermelon picnics in a park or a near-by wood can be a matter of a moment's decision on a hot afternoon.

Not only has walking for pleasure become practically extinct, but the occasional event such as a parade on a holiday attracts far less attention now.

Questions

1. Why did the people of Middletown worry about the automobile's effect on religious worship?
2. What habits did the car seem to alter?
3. How did adolescents adapt to the automobile culture?

Questions for Further Thought

1. How might Bruce Barton's portrayal of Jesus (Document 23-3) have strengthened the self-esteem of businessmen, including his own?
2. Is the ad reprinted in Document 23-4 different in degree or content from current advertising? In what ways?

3. Cars, movies, and advertising—were the residents of Middletown (Document 23-5) right to feel uneasy about the changes they saw occurring in their community? Why or why not?

Redefining American Identity

We often think of the 1920s in terms of its writers and other creative individuals, some of them disillusioned by the Great War and the materialism of the postwar decade, who contributed greatly and enduringly to American culture. Among them were Ernest Hemingway, F. Scott Fitzgerald, Gertrude Stein, Langston Hughes, John Dos Passos, Edith Wharton, Eugene O'Neill, Robert Frost, Marianne Moore, and William Faulkner. However, the decade was also noteworthy for the intensity of its cultural conflicts. Some of these were long-standing; others had originated in the Progressive Era or during and immediately after World War I. As Henry Louis Mencken, the "Sage from Baltimore," noted, the Great War had awakened all "the primitive racial fury of the Western nations." There were race riots and nativism flourished in the United States. The immigration-restriction movement, which before World War I had sought enactment of a literacy test requirement for immigrants, now secured passage of laws that for the first time numerically restricted and imposed national quotas on immigration from Europe and prohibited immigration from Japan (1924). However, in 1924, Congress also passed the Indian Citizenship Act, which granted citizenship to all Native Americans born in the United States who had not already acquired citizenship through other means. The second Ku Klux Klan, born in 1915, reached its short-lived peak during the mid-1920s. In Oregon, the Klan ("the most striking example of nativism in the 1920s") was instrumental in the 1922 passage of a popular initiative requiring children (ages eight to sixteen) to attend public schools, rather than permitting them to go to religious or private schools. Within private sectors of American life, religious and racial prejudice and discrimination were all too common. The Klan, one of the most vicious organizations this country has ever produced, was essentially about family values and faith. But its message was also one of racism, intolerance, bigotry, and xenophobia. The Klan also served as a social club for male and female members.

Meanwhile, the nationwide enforcement of Prohibition, now part of the Constitution (the Eighteenth Amendment, ratified in 1919, had gone into effect one year later), publicly and deeply divided "dry" supporters and "wet" opponents. Moreover, growing differences between modernists and fundamentalists within Protestant denominations spilled over into politics as a few states, most famously Tennessee, legislated against teaching evolution in public schools (see text pp. 721–722). Henry Louis Mencken (1880–1956) covered the Scopes Trial. Mencken was well known for his biting satire, social criticism, and secularism. He found much that was backward in American life, including, in his view, Christian fundamentalism. Many of the things he said, such as on race or ethnicity, clearly date him, but in the 1920s he was one of the leading spokesmen for the modern–traditional divide in America. Even as the country was becoming increasingly tribalized, however, Charles Lindbergh thrilled the world and united Americans in pride, at least, with his dramatic trans-atlantic flight. On the one hand, his courage and skill represented the older values of individualism and self-reliance. On the other, Lindbergh's pioneering flight marked the beginning of an entirely new transportation industry that would transform as well as shrink the world.

A number of the cultural conflicts of the 1920s deeply affected national politics, especially as they divided the Democrats, already in a minority position, between southerners and westerners (largely old-stock, Protestant, "dry," and rural) and northeasterners (largely of immigrant stock, Catholic or Jewish, "wet," and urban). In 1924 the party's polarized and deadlocked national convention was ultimately reduced to nominating a sacrificial presidential nominee, John W. Davis. Four years later, the Democrats nominated

Alfred E. Smith for president. The four-term governor of New York was Catholic, of immigrant stock, "wet, " and from New York City and Tammany Hall—in many ways the antithesis of Herbert Hoover, the Republican standard-bearer. After a bitter campaign, Smith went down to defeat—as any Democrat would have in 1928. The pattern of that defeat, however, revealed the potency of the cultural issues raised by Smith's candidacy.

Document 23-6 provides two examples of what motivated the Ku Klux Klan and reveal the nativisim that which fueled the debate over immigration restriction. In Document 23-7, William Jennings Bryan puts his faith on trial over the issue of teaching evolution in the schools. Document 23-8 is an excerpt from H. L. Mencken's introduction to his 1918 translation of Friedrich Nietzsche's *The Antichrist*. Document 23-9 is an excerpt from Charles Lindbergh's book about his memorable trans-atlantic flight. Document 23-10 is a political cartoon from the nasty presidential campaign of 1928. Document 23-11 provides an editorial by Marcus Garvey, who led the Universal Negro Improvement Association.

23-6 The Ku Klux Klan (1924)

The Klan used the print media to spread its message of white supremacy (see text pp. 718–721). State and local Klans reached followers through Klan publications; the piece excerpted here originally appeared in *The Good Citizen* (Zarephath, New Jersey). In 1926, Hiram W. Evans, imperial wizard of the Ku Klux Klan, explained "the Klan's fight for Americanism" to a cosmopolitan national audience through the prestigious *North American Review*.

"America for Americans" is an image of the statement of principles published by the Women of the Ku Klux Klan (WKKK), Little Rock, Arkansas.

Sources: "The Good Citizen" reprinted with permission of the Macmillan Publishing Company from *The Challenge of the Clan* (pp. 133–136) by Stanley Frost. Copyright 1924 by the Bobbs Merrill Company, Inc., renewed 1952 by Marion Y. Frost. Reprinted with permission of Scribner, an imprint of Simon & Schuster Adult Publishing Group. All rights reserved.

THE RISING OF THE KU KLUX KLAN— THE NEW REFORMATION

On account of the abuses of religion by the Roman Catholic hierarchy, civilization had reached a universal crisis in the sixteenth century; and Martin Luther, the chosen instrument of God, was placed in the breach to prevent the wheels of progress from being reversed and the world from being plunged into greater darkness than that of the Dark Ages.

The thousand years preceding the Reformation, known by religious historians as Satan's Millennium, was brought on by the Romish Church with her paganistic worship and practices, during which time millions of men and women poured out their blood as martyrs of the Christian religion. . . .

THE WHITE-ROBED ARMY

Now come the Knights of the Ku Klux Klan in this crucial hour of our American history to contend for the faith of our fathers who suffered and died in behalf of freedom. At the psychological moment they have arrived to encourage the hearts of those who have been battling heroically for the rights and privileges granted them under the Constitution of the United States.

How our hearts have been thrilled at the sight of this army! Words fail to express the emotions of the soul at the appearance of this mighty throng upon the battle-field, where a few faithful followers of the lowly Nazarene have been contending for the faith once delivered to the Saints, against Papal mobs who have torn down gospel tabernacles, wrecked buildings and imprisoned Protestant worshipers.

OUR NATIONAL PERIL

The World War was the signal for greater alarm than the average American has been willing to admit. Notwithstanding the sacrifices that had to be made at home and the thousands of our young men who crossed the sea and laid down their lives on the battlefields of the Old World, it has taken the

Ku Klux Klan to awaken even a portion of the population of the United States to our national peril. Our religious and political foes are not only within our gates, but are coming by the hundreds of thousands, bringing the chaos and ruin of old European and Asiatic countries to un-Americanize and destroy our nation, and to make it subserve the purposes of the Pope in his aspirations for world supremacy.

ROME WOULD OVERTHROW PUBLIC SCHOOLS

One of the great efforts of the Roman hierarchy toward this end is to get control of our public schools by placing Roman Catholics on school boards and in the schoolrooms and taking the Bible out of the schools. In the event of their success in their efforts to overthrow our present school system there would be a string of beads around every Protestant child's neck and a Roman Catholic catechism in his hand. 'Hail Mary, Mother of God,' would be on every child's lips, and the idolatrous worship of dead saints a part of the daily programme.

THE JEWISH AND CATHOLIC ALLIANCE

The money-grasping Jew, who has no use for the Christ of Calvary, does all in his power to bring discredit on Christianity, and would be pleased to see the whole structure broken down, and in this way get rid of his responsibility for crucifying the Christ on Calvary and bringing the curse on his race, which they have had to suffer since the beginning of the Christian era. The sons of Abraham have therefore become a

---

AMERICA
for
AMERICANS

✠

AS INTERPRETED BY THE
Women of the
KU KLUX KLAN

✠

CREED
OF
KLANSWOMEN

✠

Yesterday—Today and Forever
God and Government
Law and Liberty
peace and Prosperity

strong ally to the Papacy, not because they have anything in common with it in religion, but in their political propaganda against American institutions and principles.

While no true Christian has anything against the Jew, it must be admitted that this alliance with the Papacy is a dangerous menace to our flag and country. The Jew is insoluble and indigestible; and when he grows in numbers and power till he becomes a menace to Christianity and the whole moral fabric, drastic measures will have to be taken to counteract his destructive work, and more especially when he is in alliance with the old Papal religio-political machine.

Questions

1. Why, according to the Klan, was "this [a] crucial hour of our American history"?
2. How did the public schools figure in the Protestant-Catholic conflict?
3. How did the Klan explain the alleged Catholic-Jewish alliance?

23-7 Transcript of the Scopes Trial (1925)

William Jennings Bryan, Clarence Darrow

In 1925, the Tennessee legislature passed a statute banning the teaching of evolution in all public schools and universities. John T. Scopes challenged the ban, and the famous trial that followed epitomized the tensions of a society in transition, pitting the values of modernism and secularism against traditionalism and fundamentalism. This clash was embodied by the courtroom duel between Clarence Darrow, Scopes's defense lawyer, and William Jennings Bryan, assistant to A. T. Stewart, who led the prosecution. In the following excerpt, the defense team, which also included Arthur Hays and Dudley Malone, calls Bryan as a witness and questions him on his interpretation of the Bible.

Source: From Ray Ginger, ed., *William Jennings Bryan: Selections* (Indianapolis: Bobbs-Merrill, 1967), 234–246.

Q—You have given considerable study to the Bible, haven't you, Mr. Bryan?

A—Yes, sir, I have tried to.

Q—Well, we all know you have, we are not going to dispute that at all. But you have written and published articles almost weekly, and sometimes have made interpretations of various things.

A—I would not say interpretations, Mr. Darrow, but comments on the lesson.

Q—If you comment to any extent these comments have been interpretations.

A—I presume that my discussion might be to some extent interpretations, but they have not been primarily intended as interpretations.

Q—But you have studied that question, of course?

A—Of what?

Q—Interpretation of the Bible.

A—On this particular question?

Q—Yes, sir.

A—Yes, sir.

Q—Then you have made a general study of it.

A—Yes, I have; I have studied the Bible for about fifty years, or sometime more than that, but, of course, I have studied it more as I have become older than when I was but a boy.

Q—Do you claim that everything in the Bible should be literally interpreted?

A—I believe everything in the Bible should be accepted as it is given there; some of the Bible is given illustratively. For instance: "Ye are the salt of the earth." I would not insist that man was actually salt, or that he had flesh of salt, but it is used in the sense of salt as saving God's people. . . .

The Witness—These gentlemen have not had much chance—they did not come here to try this case. They came here to try revealed religion. I am here to defend it, and they can ask me any question they please.

The Court—All right.

(Applause from the court yard.)

Mr. Darrow—Great applause from the bleachers.

The Witness—From those whom you call "yokels."

Mr. Darrow—I have never called them yokels.

The Witness—That is the ignorance of Tennessee, the bigotry.

Mr. Darrow—You mean who are applauding you?

The Witness—Those are the people whom you insult.

Mr. Darrow—You insult every man of science and learning in the world because he does not believe in your fool religion.

The Court—I will not stand for that.

Mr. Darrow—For what he is doing?

The Court—I am talking to both of you.

Gen. Stewart—This has gone beyond the pale of a lawsuit, your honor. I have a public duty to perform, under my oath and I ask the court to stop it.

Mr. Darrow is making an effort to insult the gentleman on the witness stand, and I ask that it be stopped, for it has gone beyond the pale of a lawsuit. . . .

Q—But when you read that Jonah swallowed the whale—or that the whale swallowed Jonah—excuse me please—how do you literally interpret that?

A—When I read that a big fish swallowed Jonah—it does not say whale.

Q—Doesn't it? Are you sure?

A—That is my recollection of it. A big fish, and I believe it, and I believe in a God who can make a whale and can make a man and make both do what He pleases.

Q—Mr. Bryan, doesn't the New Testament say whale?

A—I am not sure. My impression is that it says fish; but it does not make so much difference; I merely called your attention to where it says fish—it does not say whale.

Q—But in the New Testament it says whale, doesn't it?

A—That may be true; I cannot remember in my own mind what I read about it.

Q—Now, you say, the big fish swallowed Jonah, and he there remained how long—three days—and then he spewed him upon the land. You believe that the big fish was made to swallow Jonah?

A—I am not prepared to say that; the Bible merely says it was done.

Q—You don't know whether it was the ordinary run of fish, or made for that purpose?

A—You may guess; you evolutionists guess.

Q—But when we do guess, we have a sense to guess right.

A—But do not do it often.

Q—You are not prepared to say whether that fish was made especially to swallow a man or not?

A—The Bible doesn't say, so I am not prepared to say.

Q—You don't know whether that was fixed up specially for the purpose.

A—No, the Bible doesn't say.

Q—But do you believe He made them—that He made such a fish and that it was big enough to swallow Jonah?

A—Yes, sir. Let me add: One miracle is just as easy to believe as another.

Q—It is for me.

A—It is for me.

Q—Just as hard?

A—It is hard to believe for you, but easy for me. A miracle is a thing performed beyond what man can perform. When you get beyond what man can do, you get within the realm of miracles; and it is just as easy to believe the miracle of Jonah as any other miracle in the Bible.

Q—Perfectly easy to believe that Jonah swallowed the whale?

A—If the Bible said so; the Bible doesn't make as extreme statements as evolutionists do.

Mr. Darrow—That may be a question, Mr. Bryan, about some of those you have known?

A—The only thing is, you have a definition of fact that includes imagination.

Q—And you have a definition that excludes everything but imagination, everything but imagination?

Gen. Stewart—I object to that as argumentative.

The Witness—You—

Mr. Darrow—The Witness must not argue with me, either.

Q—Do you consider the story of Jonah and the whale a miracle?

A—I think it is. . . .

Q—What do you think?

A—I do not think about things I don't think about.

Q—Do you think about things you do think about?

A—Well, sometimes.

(Laughter in the courtyard.)

The Policeman—Let us have order. . . .

Q—Do you think the earth was made in six days?

A—Not six days of twenty-four hours.

Q—Doesn't it say so?

Gen. Stewart—I want to interpose another objection. What is the purpose of this examination?

Mr. Bryan—The purpose is to cast ridicule on everybody who believes in the Bible, and I am perfectly willing that the world shall know that these gentlemen have no other purpose than ridiculing every Christian who believes in the Bible.

Mr. Darrow—We have the purpose of preventing bigots and ignoramuses from controlling the education of the United States and you know it, and that is all.

Mr. Bryan—I am glad to bring out that statement. I want the world to know that this evidence is not for the view Mr. Darrow and his associates have filed affidavits here stating, the purposes of which I understand it, is to show that the Bible story is not true.

Mr. Malone—Mr. Bryan seems anxious to get some evidence in the record that would tend to show that those affidavits are not true.

Mr. Bryan—I am not trying to get anything into the record. I am simply trying to protect the word of God against the greatest atheist or agnostic of the United States. (Prolonged applause.) I want the papers to know I am not afraid to get on the stand in front of him and let him do his worst. I want the world to know. (Prolonged applause.)

Mr. Darrow—I wish I could get a picture of these clackers.

Gen. Stewart—I am not afraid of Mr. Bryan being perfectly able to take care of himself, but this examination cannot be a legal examination and it cannot be worth a thing in the world, and, your honor, I respectfully except to it, and call on your honor, in the name of all that is legal, to stop this examination and stop it here.

Mr. Hays—I rather sympathize with the general, but Mr. Bryan is produced as a witness because he is a student of the Bible and he presumably understands what the Bible means. He is one of the foremost students in the United States, and we hope to show Mr. Bryan, who is a student of the Bible, what the Bible really means in connection with evolution. Mr. Bryan has already stated that the world is not merely 6,000 years old and that is very helpful to us, and where your evidence is coming from, this Bible, which goes to the jury, is that the world started in 4004 B.C.

Mr. Bryan—You think the Bible says that?

Mr. Hays—The one you have taken in evidence says that.

Mr. Bryan—I don't concede that it does.

Mr. Hays—You know that that chronology is made up by adding together all of the ages of the people in the Bible, counting their ages; and now then, let us show the next stage from a Bible student, that these things are not to be taken literally, but that each man is entitled to his own interpretation.

Gen. Stewart—The court makes the interpretation.

Mr. Hays—But the court is entitled to information on what is the interpretation of an expert Bible student.

Gen. Stewart—This is resulting in a harangue and nothing else.

Mr. Darrow—I didn't do any of the haranging: Mr. Bryan has been doing that.

Gen. Stewart—You know absolutely you have done it.

Mr. Darrow—Oh, all right.

Mr. Malone—Mr. Bryan doesn't need any support.

Gen. Stewart—Certainly he doesn't need any support, but I am doing what I conceive my duty to be, and I don't need any advice, if you please, sir. (Applause.)

The Court—That would be irrelevant testimony if it was going to the jury. Of course, it is excluded from the jury on the point it is not competent testimony, on the same ground as the affidaviting.

Mr. Hicks—Your honor, let me say a word right there. It is in the discretion of the court how long you will allow them to question witnesses for the purpose of taking testimony to the supreme court. Now, we as taxpayers of this county, feel that this has gone beyond reason.

The Court—Well, now, that taxpayers doesn't appeal to me so much, when it is only fifteen or twenty minutes time.

Mr. Darrow—I would have been through in a half-hour if Mr. Bryan had answered my questions.

Gen. Stewart—They want to put in affidavits as to what other witnesses would swear, why not let them put in affidavits as to what Mr. Bryan would swear?

Mr. Bryan—God forbid.

Mr. Malone—I will just make this suggestion—

Gen. Stewart—It is not worth anything to them, if your honor please, even for the record in the supreme court.

Mr. Hays—Is not it worth anything to us if Mr. Bryan will accept the story of creation in detail, and if Mr. Bryan, as a Bible student, states you cannot take the Bible necessarily as literally true?

Mr. Stewart—The Bible speaks for itself.

Mr. Hays—You mean to say the Bible itself tells whether these are parables? Does it?

Gen. Stewart—We have left all annals of procedure behind. This is a harangue between Col. Darrow and his witness. He makes so many statements that he is forced to defend himself.

Mr. Darrow—I do not do that.

Gen. Stewart—I except to that as not pertinent to this lawsuit.

The Court—Of course, it is not pertinent, or it would be before the jury.

Gen. Stewart—It is not worth anything before a jury.

The Court—Are you about through, Mr. Darrow?

Mr. Darrow—I want to ask a few more questions about the creation.

The Court—I know. We are going to adjourn when Mr. Bryan comes off the stand for the day. Be very brief, Mr. Darrow. Of course, I believe I will make myself clearer. Of course, it is incompetent testimony before the jury. The only reason I am allowing this to go in at all is that they may have it in the appellate courts, as showing what the affidavit would be.

Mr. Bryan—The reason I am answering is not for the benefit of the superior court. It is to keep these gentlemen from saying I was afraid to meet them and let them question me, and I want the Christian world to know that any atheist, agnostic, unbeliever, can question me any time as to my belief in God, and I will answer him.

Mr. Darrow—I want to take an exception to this conduct of this witness. He may be very popular down here in the hills. I do not need to have his explanation for his answer.

The Court—Yes.

Mr. Bryan—If I had not, I would not have answered the question.

Mr. Hays—May I be heard? I do not want your honor to think we are asking questions of Mr. Bryan with the expectation that the higher court will not say that those questions are proper testimony. The reason I state that is this, your law speaks for the Bible. Your law does not say the literal interpretation of the Bible. If Mr. Bryan, who is a student of the Bible, will state that everything in the Bible need not be interpreted literally, that each man must judge for himself; if he will state that, of course, then your honor would charge the jury. We are not bound by a literal interpretation of the Bible. If I have made my argument clear enough for the attorney-general to understand, I will retire.

Gen. Stewart—I will admit you have frequently been difficult of comprehension, and I think you are as much to blame as I am.

Mr. Hays—I know I am. . . .

Mr. Darrow:

Q—Mr. Bryan, do you believe that the first woman was Eve?
A—Yes.
Q—Do you believe she was literally made out of Adam's rib?
A—I do.
Q—Did you ever discover where Cain got his wife?
A—No sir; I leave the agnostics to hunt for her.
Q—You have never found out?
A—I have never tried to find.
Q—You have never tried to find?
A—No.
Q—The Bible says he got one, doesn't it? Were there other people on the earth at that time?
A—I cannot say.
Q—You cannot say. Did that ever enter your consideration?
A—Never bothered me.
Q—There were no others recorded, but Cain got a wife.
A—That is what the Bible says.
Q—Where she came from you do not know. All right. Does the statement, "The morning and the evening were the first day," and "The morning and the evening were the second day," mean anything to you?
A—I do not think it necessarily means a twenty-four-hour day.
Q—You do not?
A—No.
Q—What do you consider it to be?
A—I have not attempted to explain it. If you will take the second chapter—let me have the book. (Examining Bible.) The fourth verse of the second chapter says: "These are the generations of the heavens and of the earth, when they were created in the day that the Lord God made the earth and the heavens," the word "day" there in the very next chapter is used to describe a period. I do not see that there is any necessity for construing the words, "the evening and the morning," as meaning necessarily a twenty-four-hour day, "in the day when the Lord made the heaven and the earth."
Q—Then, when the Bible said, for instance, "and God called the firmament heaven. And the evening and the morning were the second day," that does not necessarily mean twenty-four hours?
A—I do not think it necessarily does.
Q—Do you think it does or does not?
A—I know a great many think so.
Q—What do you think?
A—I do not think it does.
Q—You think those were not literal days?
A—I do not think they were twenty-four-hour days.
Q—What do you think about it?
A—That is my opinion—I do not know that my opinion is better on that subject than those who think it does.
Q—You do not think that?

A—No. But I think it would be just as easy for the kind of God we believe in to make the earth in six days as in six years or in 6,000,000 years or in 600,000,000 years. I do not think it important whether we believe one or the other.
Q—Do you think those were literal days?
A—My impression is they were periods, but I would not attempt to argue as against anybody who wanted to believe in literal days.
Q—Have you any idea of the length of the periods?
A—No; I don't.
Q—Do you think the sun was made on the fourth day?
A—Yes.
Q—And they had evening and morning without the sun?
A—I am simply saying it is a period.
Q—They had evening and morning for four periods without the sun, do you think?
A—I believe in creation as there told, and if I am not able to explain it I will accept it. Then you can explain it to suit yourself.
Q—Mr. Bryan, what I want to know is, do you believe the sun was made on the fourth day?
A—I believe just as it says there.
Q—Do you believe the sun was made on the fourth day?
A—Read it.
Q—I am very sorry; you have read it so many times you would know, but I will read it again: "And God said, let there be lights in the firmament of the heaven, to divide the day from the night; and let them be for signs, and for seasons, and for days, and years?
"And let them be for lights in the firmament of the heaven, to give light upon the earth; and it was so.
"And God made two great lights; the greater light to rule the day, and the lesser light to rule the night; He made the stars also.
"And God set them in the firmament of the heaven, to give light upon the earth, and to rule over the day and over the night, and to divide the light from the darkness; and God saw that it was good. And the evening and the morning were the fourth day."
Do you believe, whether it was a literal day or a period, the sun and the moon were not made until the fourth day?
A—I believe they were made in the order in which they were given there, and I think in dispute with Gladstone and Huxley on that point—
Q—Cannot you answer my questions?
A— ——— I prefer to agree with Gladstone.
Q—I do not care about Gladstone.
A—Then prefer to agree with whoever you please.
Q—Can not you answer my question?
A—I have answered it. I believe that it was made on the fourth day, in the fourth day.
Q—And they had the evening and the morning before that time for three days or three periods. All right, that settles

it. Now, if you call those periods, they may have been a very long time.

A—They might have been.

Q—The creation might have been going on for a very long time?

A—It might have continued for millions of years.

Q—Yes. All right. Do you believe the story of the temptation of Eve by the serpent?

A—I do.

Q—Do you believe that after Eve ate the apple, or gave it to Adam, whichever way it was, that God cursed Eve, and that time decreed that all womankind thenceforth and forever should suffer the pains of childbirth in the reproduction of the earth?

A—I believe what it says, and I believe the fact as fully——

Q—That is what it says, doesn't it?

A—Yes.

Q—And for that reason, every woman born of woman, who has to carry on the race, the reason they have childbirth pains is because Eve tempted Adam in the Garden of Eden.

A—I will believe just what the Bible says. I ask to put that in the language of the Bible, for I prefer that to your language. Read the Bible and I will answer.

Q—All right, I will do that: "And I will put enmity between thee and the woman"—that is referring to the serpent?

A—The serpent.

Q—(Reading) "and between thy seed and her seed; it shall bruise thy head, and thou shalt bruise his heel. Unto the woman he said, I will greatly multiply thy sorrow and thy conception; in sorrow thou shalt bring forth children; and thy desire shall be to thy husband, and he shall rule over thee." That is right, is it?

A—I accept it as it is.

Q—And you believe that came about because Eve tempted Adam to eat the fruit?

A—Just as it says.

Q—And you believe that is the reason God made the serpent to go on his belly after he tempted Eve?

A—I believe the Bible as it is, and I do not permit you to put your language in the place of the language of the Almighty. You read that Bible and ask me questions, and I will answer them. I will not answer your questions in your language.

Q—I will read it to you from the Bible: "And the Lord God said unto the serpent, because thou hast done this, thou art cursed above all cattle, and above every beast of the field; upon thy belly shalt thou go and dust shalt thou eat all the days of thy life." Do you think that is why the serpent is compelled to crawl upon its belly?

A—I believe that.

Q—Have you any idea how the snake went before that time?

A—No, sir.

Q—Do you know whether he walked on his tail or not?

A—No, sir. I have no way to know. (Laughter in audience).

Q—Now, you refer to the cloud that was put in the heaven after the flood, the rainbow. Do you believe in that?

A—Read it.

Q—All right, Mr. Bryan, I will read it for you.

Mr. Bryan—Your honor, I think I can shorten this testimony. The only purpose Mr. Darrow has is to slur at the Bible, but I will answer his question. I will answer it all at once, and I have no objection in the world, I want the world to know that this man, who does not believe in a God, is trying to use a court in Tennessee—

Mr. Darrow—I object to that.

Mr. Bryan—(Continuing) to slur at it, and while it will require time, I am willing to take it.

Mr. Darrow—I object to your statement. I am exempting you on your fool ideas that no intelligent Christian on earth believes.

The Court—Court is adjourned until 9 o'clock tomorrow morning.

Questions

1. What was the defense trying to prove in this line of questioning?
2. What values appear to be in conflict? Explain.

23-8 Introduction to Friedrich W. Nietzsche's *The Antichrist* (1918)

H. L. Mencken

European ideas have influenced Americans since colonial times. In the early twentieth century, Albert Einstein, Sigmund Freud, Oswald Spengler, and Friedrich Nietzsche were but some of the European scientists, artists, and intellectuals whose ideas would profoundly influence American thought and culture. Here, H. L. Mencken explains for American readers Nietzsche's famous critique of Christianity and its relevance to postwar American democracy. Nietzsche (1844–1900) was a German philosopher who is probably best known for the provocation "God is dead." Nietzsche's influence was delayed but ultimately became pervasive in the western world.

Source: Excerpt of "Introduction," from *The Antichrist* by F. W. Nietzsche, translated and with an introduction by H. L. Mencken (1918; New York: Alfred A. Knopf, 1941), 13–26.

The late war, awakening all the primitive racial fury of the Western nations, and therewith all their ancient enthusiasm for religious taboos and sanctions, naturally focused attention upon Nietzsche, as upon the most daring and provocative of recent amateur theologians. The Germans, with their characteristic tendency to explain their every act in terms as realistic and unpleasant as possible, appear to have mauled him in a belated and unexpected embrace, to the horror, I daresay, of the Kaiser, and perhaps to the even greater horror of Nietzsche's own ghost. The folks of Anglo-Saxondom, with their equally characteristic tendency to explain all their enterprises romantically, simultaneously set him up as the Antichrist he no doubt secretly longed to be. The result was a great deal of misrepresentation and misunderstanding of him. From the pulpits of the allied countries, and particularly from those of England and the United States, a horde of patriotic ecclesiastics denounced him in extravagant terms as the author of all the horrors of the time, and in the newspapers, until the Kaiser was elected sole bugaboo, he shared the honors of that office with von Hindenburg, the Crown Prince, Capt. Boy-Ed, von Bernstorff and von Tirpitz. Most of this denunciation, of course, was frankly idiotic—the naïve prattle of suburban Methodists, notoriety-seeking college professors, almost illiterate editorial writers, and other such numskulls. In much of it, including not a few official hymns of hate, Nietzsche was gravely discovered to be the teacher of such spokesmen of the extremest sort of German nationalism as von Bernhardi and von Treitschke—which was just as intelligent as making George Bernard Shaw the mentor of Lloyd-George. In other solemn pronunciamentoes he was credited with being philosophically responsible for various imaginary crimes of the enemy—the wholesale slaughter or mutilation of prisoners of war, the deliberate burning down of Red Cross hospitals, the utilization of the corpses of the slain for soap-making. I amused myself, in those gaudy days, by collecting newspaper clippings to this general effect, and later on I shall probably publish a digest of them, as a contribution to the study of war hysteria. The thing went to unbelievable lengths. On the strength of the fact that I had published a book on Nietzsche in 1906, six years after his death, I was called upon by agents of the Department of Justice, elaborately outfitted with badges, to meet the charge that I was an intimate associate and agent of "the German monster, Nietzsky." I quote the official *procès verbal*, an indignant but often misspelled document. Alas, poor Nietzsche! After all his laborious efforts to prove that he was not a German, but a Pole—even after his heroic readiness, via anti-anti-Semitism, to meet the deduction that, if a Pole, then probably also a Jew!

But under all this alarmed and preposterous tosh there was at least a sound instinct, and that was the instinct which recognized Nietzsche as the most eloquent, pertinacious and effective of all the critics of the philosophy to which the Allies against Germany stood committed, and on the strength of which, at all events in theory, the United States had engaged itself in the war. He was not, in point of fact, involved with the visible enemy, save in remote and transient ways; the German, officially, remained the most ardent of Christians during the war and became a democrat at its close. But he was plainly a foe of democracy in all its forms, political, religious and epistemological, and what is worse, his opposition was set forth in terms that were not only extraordinarily penetrating and devastating, but also uncommonly offensive. It was thus quite natural that he should have aroused a degree of indignation verging upon the pathological in the two countries that had planted themselves upon the democratic platform most boldly, and that felt it most shaky, one may add, under their feet. I daresay that Nietzsche, had he been alive, would have got a lot of satisfaction out of the execration thus heaped upon him, not only because, being a vain fellow, he enjoyed execration as a tribute to his general singularity, and hence to his superiority, but also and more importantly because, being no mean psychologist, he would have recognized the disconcerting doubts underlying it. If Nietzsche's criticism of democracy were as ignorant and empty, say, as the average evangelical clergyman's criticism of Darwin's hypothesis of natural selection, then the advocates of democracy could afford to dismiss it as loftily as the Darwinians dismiss the blather of the holy clerks. And if his attack upon Christianity were mere sound and fury, signifying nothing, then there would be no call for anathemas from the sacred desk. But these onslaughts, in point of fact, have behind them a tremendous learning and a great deal of point and plausibility—there are, in brief, bullets in the gun, teeth in the tiger,—and so it is no wonder that they excite the ire of men who hold, as a primary article of belief, that their acceptance would destroy civilization, darken the sun, and bring Jahveh to sobs upon His Throne.

But in all this justifiable fear, of course, there remains a false assumption, and that is the assumption that Nietzsche proposed to destroy Christianity altogether, and so rob the plain people of the world of their virtue, their spiritual consolations, and their hope of heaven. Nothing could be more untrue. The fact is that Nietzsche had no interest whatever in the delusions of the plain people—that is, intrinsically. It seemed to him of small moment *what* they believed, so long as it was safely imbecile. What he stood against was not their beliefs, but the elevation of those beliefs, by any sort of democratic process, to the dignity of a state philosophy—what he feared most was the pollution and crippling of the superior minority by intellectual disease from below. His plain aim in "The Antichrist" was to combat that menace by completing the work begun, on the one hand, by Darwin and the other evolutionist philosophers, and, on the other hand, by German historians and philologists. The net effect of this earlier attack, in the eighties, had been the collapse of Christian theology as a serious concern of educated men. The mob, it must be obvious, was very little shaken; even to this day it has not put off its belief in the essential Christian doctrines. But the *intelligentsia*, by 1885, had been pretty well convinced. No man of sound information, at the time Nietzsche planned "The Antichrist," actually believed that the world was created in seven days, or that its fauna was once overwhelmed by a flood as a penalty for the sins of man, or that Noah saved the boa constrictor, the prairie dog and the *pediculus capitis* by taking a pair of each into the ark, or that Lot's wife was turned into a pillar of salt, or that a fragment of the True Cross could cure hydrophobia. Such notions, still almost universally prevalent in Christendom a century before, were now confined to the great body of ignorant and credulous men—that is, to ninety-five or ninety-six percent. of the race. For a man of the superior minority to subscribe to one of them publicly was already sufficient to set him off as one in imminent need of psychiatrical attention. Belief in them had become a mark of inferiority, like the allied belief in madstones, magic and apparitions.

But though the theology of Christianity had thus sunk to the lowly estate of a mere delusion of the rabble, propagated on that level by the ancient caste of sacerdotal parasites, the ethics of Christianity continued to enjoy the utmost acceptance, and perhaps even more acceptance than ever before. It seemed to be generally felt, in fact, that they simply *must* be saved from the wreck—that the world would vanish into chaos if they went the way of the revelations supporting them. In this fear a great many judicious men joined, and so there arose what was, in essence, an absolutely new Christian cult—a cult, to wit, purged of all the supernaturalism superimposed upon the older cult by generations of theologians, and harking back to what was conceived to be the pure ethical doctrine of Jesus. This cult still flourishes; Protestantism tends to become identical with it; it invades Catholicism as Modernism; it is supported by great numbers of men whose intelligence is manifest and whose sincerity is not open to question. Even Nietzsche himself yielded to it in weak moments, as you will discover on examining his somewhat laborious effort to make Paul the villain of Christian theology, and Jesus no more than an innocent bystander. But this sentimental yielding never went far enough to distract his attention for long from his main idea, which was this: that Christian ethics were quite as dubious, at bottom, as Christian theology—that they were founded, just as surely as such childish fables as the story of Jonah and the whale, upon the peculiar prejudices and credulities, the special desires and appetites, of inferior men—that they warred upon the best interests of men of a better sort quite as unmistakably as the most extravagant of objective superstitions. In belief, what he saw in Christian ethics, under all the poetry and all the fine show of altruism and all the theoretical benefits therein, was a democratic effort to curb the egoism of the strong—a conspiracy of the *chandala* against the free functioning of their superiors, nay, against the free progress of mankind. This theory is the thing he exposes in "The Antichrist," bringing to the business his amazingly chromatic and exigent eloquence at its finest flower. This is the "conspiracy" he sets forth in all the panoply of his characteristic italics, dashes, *sforzando* interjections and exclamation points.

Well, an idea is an idea. The present one may be right and it may be wrong. One thing is quite certain: that no progress will be made against it by denouncing it as merely immoral. If it is ever laid at all, it must be laid evidentially, logically. The notion to the contrary is thoroughly democratic; the mob is the most ruthless of tyrants; it is always in a democratic society that heresy and felony tend to be most constantly confused. One hears without surprise of a Bismarck philosophizing placidly (at least in his old age) upon the delusion of Socialism and of a Frederick the Great playing the host of his cynicism upon the absolutism that was almost identical with his own person, but men in the mass never brook the destructive discussion of their fundamental beliefs, and that impatience is naturally most evident in those societies in which men in the mass are most influential. Democracy and free speech are not facets of one gem; democracy and free speech are eternal enemies. But in any battle between an institution and an idea, the idea, in the long run, has the better of it. Here I do not venture into the absurdity of arguing that, as the world wags on, the truth always survives. I believe nothing of the sort. As a matter of fact, it seems to me that an idea that happens to be true—or, more exactly, as near to truth as any human idea can be, and yet remain generally intelligible—it seems to me that such an idea carries a special and often fatal handicap. The majority of men prefer delusion to truth. It soothes. It is easy to grasp. Above all, it fits more snugly than the truth into a universe of false appearances—of complex and irrational phenomena, defectively grasped. But though an idea that is true is thus not likely to prevail, an idea that is *attacked* enjoys a great advantage. The evidence behind it is now supported by sympathy, the sporting instinct, sentimentality—and sentimentality is as powerful as an army with banners. One never hears of a martyr in history whose notions are seriously disputed today. The forgotten ideas are those of the men who put them forward soberly and quietly, hoping fatuously that they would conquer by the force of their truth; these are the ideas that we now struggle to rediscover. Had Nietzsche lived to be burned at the stake by outraged Mississippi Methodists, it would have been a glorious day for his doctrines. As it is, they are helped on their way every time they are denounced as immoral and against God. The war brought down upon them the maledictions of vast herds of right-thinking men. And now "The Antichrist," after long neglect, is being reprinted and read again. . . .

One imagines the author, a sardonic wraith, snickering somewhat sadly over the fact. His shade, wherever it suffers, is favoured in these days by many such consolations, some of them of much greater horsepower. Think of the facts and arguments, even the underlying theories and attitudes, that have been borrowed from him, consciously and unconsciously, by the foes of Bolshevism during these last thrilling years! The face of democracy, suddenly seen hideously close, has scared the guardians of the reigning plutocracy half to death, and they have gone to the devil himself for aid. Southern Senators, almost illiterate men, have mixed his acids with well water and spouted them like affrighted geysers, not knowing what they did. Nor are they the first to borrow from him. Years ago I called attention to the debt incurred with characteristic forgetfulness of obligation by the late Theodore Roosevelt, in "The Strenuous Life" and elsewhere. Roosevelt, a typical apologist for the existing order, adeptly dragging a herring across the trail whenever it was menaced, yet managed to delude the native boobery, at least until toward the end, into accepting him as a fiery exponent of pure democracy. Perhaps he even fooled himself; charlatans usually do so soon or late. A study of Nietzsche reveals the sources of much that was honest in him, and exposes the hollowness of much that was sham. Nietzsche, an infinitely harder and more courageous intellect, was incapable of any such confusion of ideas; he seldom allowed sentimentality to turn him from the glaring fact. What is called Bolshevism today he saw clearly a generation ago and described for what it was and is—democracy in another aspect, the old *ressentiment* of the lower orders in free function once more. Socialism, Puritanism, Philistinism, Christianity—he saw them all as allotropic forms of democracy, as variations upon the endless struggle of quantity against quality, of the weak and timorous against the strong and enterprising, of the botched against the fit. The world needed a staggering exaggeration to make it see even half of the truth. It trembles today as it trembled during the French Revolution. Perhaps it would tremble less if it could combat the monster with a clearer conscience and less burden of compromising theory—if it could launch its forces frankly at the fundamental doctrine, and not merely employ them to police the transient orgy.

Questions

1. Mencken saw 1885 as a major turning point in American thought. Explain.
2. What connections did Mencken suggest here between Christianity and democracy or between Christianity and socialism—or even Bolshevism?
3. Mencken was very critical of America's "plutocrats." Why?

23-9 Preparing to Fly (1927)

Charles A. Lindbergh

Charles Lindbergh Jr. (1902–1974) was the first to pilot an aircraft, the *Spirit of St. Louis*, solo and nonstop across the Atlantic, in 1927. This impressive achievement made him a household name at home and abroad. In this document, Lindbergh recalls the preparations he made prior to his heroic and memorable flight.

Source: Excerpt from Charles A. Lindbergh, "San Diego—St. Louis—New York," in *"We": The Famous Flier's Own Story of His Life and His Transatlantic Flight, Together with His Views on the Future of Aviation*, 198–205; 209–212. Copyright 1927, renewed © 1955 by Charles Lindbergh. Used by permission of G. P. Putnam's Sons, a division of Penguin Group (USA) Inc.

The trans-Atlantic non-stop flight between New York and Paris was first brought into public consideration by Raymond Orteig who, in 1919, issued a challenge to the Aeronautical world by offering a prize of $25,000 to the first successful entrant. Details of the flight were placed in the hands of the National Aeronautic Association and a committee was appointed to form and administer the rules of the undertaking.

I first considered the possibility of the New York–Paris flight while flying the mail one night in the fall of 1926. Several facts soon became outstanding. The foremost was that with the modern radial air-cooled motor, high lift airfoils, and lightened construction, it would not only be possible to reach Paris but, under normal conditions, to land with a large reserve of fuel and have a high factor of safety throughout the entire trip as well.

I found that there were a number of public spirited men in St. Louis sufficiently interested in aviation to finance such a project, and in December 1926 I made a trip to New York to obtain information concerning planes, motors, and other details connected with the undertaking.

In connection with any important flight there are a number of questions which must be decided at the start, among the most important of which are the type of plane and the number of motors to be used. A monoplane, although just coming into general use in the United States, is much more efficient than a biplane for certain purposes due to the lack of interference between wings, and consequently can carry a greater load per square foot of surface at a higher speed. A single motored plane, while it is more liable to forced landings than one with three motors, has much less head resistance and consequently a greater cruising range. Also there is three times the chance of motor failure with a tri-motored ship, for the failure of one motor during the first part of the flight, although it would not cause a forced landing, would at least necessitate dropping part of the fuel and returning for another start.

The reliability of the modern air-cooled radial engine is so great that the chances of an immediate forced landing due to motor failure with a single motor, would in my opinion, be more than counterbalanced by the longer cruising range and consequent ability to reach the objective in the face of unfavorable conditions.

After careful investigation I decided that a single motored monoplane was, for my purpose, the type most suited to a long distance flight, and after two more trips to the east coast and several conferences in St. Louis, an order was placed with the Ryan Airlines of San Diego, California, on February 28, 1927, for a plane equipped with a Wright Whirlwind J. 5. C. 200-H.P. radial air-cooled motor and Pioneer navigating instruments including the Earth Inductor Compass.

I went to San Diego to place the order and remained in California during the entire construction of the plane.

The personnel of the Ryan Airlines at once caught the spirit of the undertaking, and during the two months of construction the organization labored as it never had before. Day and night, seven days a week, the structure grew from a few lengths of steel tubing to one of the most efficient planes that has ever taken the air. During this time it was not unusual for the men to work twenty-four hours without rest, and on one occasion Donald Hall, the Chief Engineer, was over his drafting table for thirty-six hours.

I spent the greater part of the construction period working out the details of navigation and plotting the course, with its headings and variations, on the maps and charts. After working out the track on the gnomonic and Mercators charts, I checked over the entire distance from New York to Paris with the nautical tables. The flight from San Diego to St. Louis and from St. Louis to New York was comparatively simple, and I took the courses directly from the state maps.

From New York to Paris I worked out a great circle, changing course every hundred miles or approximately every hour. I had decided to replace the weight of a navigator with extra fuel, and this gave me about three hundred miles additional range. Although the total distance was 3610 miles, the water gap between Newfoundland and Ireland was only about 1850 miles, and under normal conditions I could have arrived on the coast of Europe over three hundred miles off of my course and still have had enough fuel remaining to reach Paris; or I might have struck the coastline as far north as Northern Scandinavia, or as far south as Southern Spain and landed without danger to myself or the plane, even though I had not reached my destination. With these facts in view, I believed the additional reserve of fuel to be more important on this flight than the accuracy of celestial navigation.

For the flight from San Diego to St. Louis and New York I carried maps of the individual states and one of the United States with the course plotted on each. For the flight from New York to Paris I had two hydrographic charts of the North Atlantic Ocean containing the great circle course and its bearing at intervals of one hundred miles. In addition to these charts, I had a map of each state, territory and country passed over. This included maps of Connecticut, Rhode Island, Massachusetts, Nova Scotia, Newfoundland, Ireland, England and France. Also a map of Europe.

I expected to be able to locate my position approximately on the coast of Europe by the terrain. Ireland is somewhat mountainous; England rather hilly on the southern end; France is a lowland along the coast; Spain is mountainous. Therefore the coastline should indicate the country, and my accurate position could be obtained by the contours of that coastline and by the position of towns, rivers and railroads.

During the time of construction it was necessary to arrange for all equipment to be carried on the flight; including equipment for emergency use in a forced landing. After the first few hours there would be enough air in the fuel tanks to keep the ship afloat for some time. I also carried an air raft which could be inflated in several minutes and which could weather a fairly rough sea.

In addition to food for the actual flight, I carried five tins of concentrated Army rations each of which contained one day's food and which could be made to last much longer if necessary. I carried two canteens of water; one containing a quart for use during the actual flight and the other containing a gallon for emergency. In addition to this water, I had an Armburst cup which is a device for condensing the moisture from human breath into drinking water. The cup is cloth covered and contains a series of baffle plates through which the breath is blown. The cup is immersed in water and then removed and blown through. The evaporation of the water on the outside cools the cup walls and baffle plates on which the breath moisture collects and runs down to the bottom of the cup.

The following is a list of equipment carried on the flight:

2 Flashlights
1 Ball of string
1 Ball of cord
1 Hunting Knife
4 Red flares sealed in rubber tubes
1 Match safe with matches
1 larger needle
1 Canteen—4 qts.
1   "   —1 qt.
1 Armburst Cup
1 Air Raft with pump and repair kit
5 Cans of Army emergency rations
2 Air cushions
1 Hack saw blade

I was delayed four days at San Diego by a general storm area over the United States that would greatly jeopardize the success of an overnight non-stop flight to St. Louis. From this flight I expected to obtain some very important data for use on the final hop from New York.

On the afternoon of May 9th, Dean Blake, Chief of the San Diego Weather Bureau, predicted favorable flying conditions for the succeeding day. The next morning I took the plane to Rockwell Field and at 3:55 P.M. Pacific time, I took off from North Island with 250 gallons of gasoline for the flight to St. Louis, escorted by two Army observation planes and one of the Ryan monoplanes. We circled North Island and San Diego, then headed on a compass course for St. Louis.

The ship passed over the first ridge of mountains, about 4,000 feet, very easily with reduced throttle. The escorting planes turned back at the mountains and I passed on over the desert and the Salton Sea alone. And at sunset I was over the deserts and mountains of Western Arizona.

The moon was well above the horizon and with the exception of a short period before dawn I was able to distinguish the contour of the country the entire night. I flew a compass course, passing alternately over snow-capped ridges, deserts, and fertile valleys. One of the mountain ranges was over 12,000 feet high and completely snow covered. I cleared this range by about 500 feet and went on over the plains beyond.

The mountains passed quickly and long before daybreak I was flying over the prairies of Western Kansas. At dawn I located my position about twenty miles south of the course, just east of Wichita, Kansas. At 8:00 A.M. Central Standard time, I passed over Lambert Field and landed at 8:20 A.M., May 11th, fourteen hours and twenty-five minutes after leaving the Pacific Coast.

The weather during the entire distance had been exactly as Dean Blake had predicted.

At 8:13 the next morning (May 12th) I took off from Lambert Field for New York. The wind was west and the weather clear for the greater part of the distance. Over the Alleghanys, however, the sky was overcast and some of the mountain tops were in low hanging clouds and I followed the passes.

At 5:33 P.M. New York Daylight Saving time, I landed at Curtiss Field, Long Island.

Questions

1. Lindbergh was nicknamed "Lucky Lindy." What other adjectives would you use to describe this pilot?
2. What would you say was the "Spirit" of St. Louis? Of Lindbergh's undertaking?

23-10 Cabinet Meeting—If Al Were President (1928)

Alfred E. Smith (1873–1944) unsuccessfully contended for the Democratic presidential nomination in 1924 and then went on to his third and fourth gubernatorial election victories in New York State (1924, 1926). His presidential candidacy in 1928 touched off a national campaign unsurpassed in bitterness (see text pp. 726–727). This election-eve cartoon appeared in a publication of the Ku Klux Klan.

Source: The Fellowship Forum (Washington, DC), November 3, 1928, New York State Library, Albany, New York; reprinted in Edmund A. Moore, *A Catholic Runs for President: The Campaign of 1928* (New York: Ronald Press, 1956), 109.

> **Cabinet Meeting—If Al Were President**
>
> *This representation of Smith as the servant of the Catholic hierarchy appeared in* The Fellowship Forum, *November 3, 1928. It is typical of the extreme anti-Catholic Klan propaganda.* (*New York State Library, Albany*)

Ku Klux Klan, Cartoon Published during New York Governor Alfred E. Smith's Presidential Campaign (1928)

Questions

1. What are the central thrusts in this cartoon's attack on Al Smith?
2. How do the details fit into the broad pattern of this cartoon?

23-11 Editorial in *Negro World* (1924)

Marcus Garvey

Just as writers and artists of the Harlem Renaissance, based in New York City's premier African American community, "championed racial pride and cultural identity" in a white society, so the Universal Negro Improvement Association, based in northern cities receiving large numbers of black migrants, "sought to challenge white political and cultural hegemony" by preaching black separatism, rather than a continued quest for racial integration (see text pp. 723–726).

Source: Marcus Garvey, editorial in *Negro World* (New York), September 2, 1924; reprinted in *The Marcus Garvey and Universal Negro Improvement Association Papers*, ed. Robert A. Hill, 6:8–11. Copyright © 1989 by the Regents of the University of California. Reprinted by permission of the University of California Press and of the Marcus Garvey and UNIA Papers Project.

THE ENEMIES AT WORK

During the whole of the convention and a little prior thereto, the enemies of our cause tried to provoke and confuse our deliberation by the many unpleasant things they systematically published against the Universal Negro Improvement Association. Our enemies in America, especially the Negro Republican politicians of New York, used the general time fuse to explode on our tranquility and thereby destroy the purpose for which we were met, but as is customary, the Universal Negro Improvement Association is always ready for the enemy. They had arranged among themselves to get certain individuals of the Liberian government along with Ernest Lyons, the Liberian Consul-General, in Baltimore, himself a reactionary Negro politician of the old school, to circulate through the Negro press and other agencies such unpleasant news purported to be from Liberia as to create consternation in our ranks and bring about the demoralization that they hoped and calculated for, but as usual, the idiots counted without their hosts. The Universal Negro Improvement Association cannot be destroyed that way, in that it is not only an organization, but is the expression of the spiritual desires of the four hundred million black peoples of the world.

OUR COLONIZATION PROGRAM

As everybody knows, we are preparing to carry out our Liberian colonization program during this and succeeding months. Every arrangement was practically made toward this end.... Unfortunately, after all arrangements had been made in this direction, our steamship secured to carry the colonists and all plans laid, these enemies of progress worked in every way to block the carrying out of the plan. For the purpose of deceiving the public and carrying out their obstruction, they tried to make out by the protest that was filed by Ernest Lyons of Baltimore, with the government of Washington, that our Association was of an incendiary character and that it was the intention of the organization to disturb the good relationship that existed between Liberia and other friendly powers. A greater nonsense could not have been advanced by any idiot. What could an organization like the Universal Negro Improvement Association do to destroy the peace of countries that are already established and recognized? It is supposed that England and France are the countries referred to when, in fact, the authors of that statement know that England and France are only waiting an opportunity to seize more land in Liberia and to keep Liberia in a state of stagnation, so as to justify their argument that the blacks are not competent of self-government in Africa as well as elsewhere. If Edwin Barclay had any sense, he would know that the Universal Negro Improvement Association is more friendly to Liberia, because it is made up of Negroes, than England and France could be in a thousand years. Lyons' protest was camouflage.

NEGROES DOUBLE-CROSSING

Everybody knows that the hitch in the colonization plan of the Universal Negro Improvement Association in Liberia came about because of double-crossing. The Firestone Rubber and Tire Company, of Ohio, has been spending large sums of money among certain people. The offer, no doubt, was so attractive as to cause certain persons to found the argument to destroy the Universal Negro Improvement Association, so as to favor the Firestone Rubber and Tire Company who, subsequently, got one million acres of Liberian land for actually nothing, to be exploited for rubber and minerals, and in the face of the fact that Liberia is one of the richest rubber countries in the world, an asset that should have been retained for the Liberian people and members of the black race, but now wantonly given over to a white company to be exploited in the interest of white capital, and to create another international complication, as evidenced in the subsequent subjugation of Haiti and the Haitians, after the New York City Bank established itself in Haiti in a similar way as the Firestone Rubber and Tire Company will establish itself in Liberia. Why, every Negro who is doing a little thinking, knows that after the Firestone Rubber and Tire Company gets into Liberia to exploit the one million acres of land, it is only a question of time when the government will be taken out of the hands of the Negroes who rule it, and Liberia will become a white man's country in violation of the constitution of that government as guaranteeing its soil as a home for all Negroes of all climes and nationalities who desire to return to their native land. The thing is so disgraceful that we, ourselves, are ashamed to give full publicity to it, but we do hope that the people of Liberia, who control the government of Liberia, will be speedily informed so that they, through the Senate and House of Representatives, will repudiate the concessions granted to the Firestone Rubber and Tire Company, so as to save their country from eternal spoilation. If the Firestone Rubber and Tire Company should get the concessions in Liberia of one million acres of land, which should have been granted to the Universal Negro Improvement Association for development by Negroes for the good of Negroes, it simply means that in another short while thousands of white men will be sent away from America by the Firestone Rubber and Tire Company to exploit their concessions. These white men going out to colonize, as they generally regard tropical countries, will carry with them the spirit of all other white colonists, superiority over and subjugation of native peoples; hence it will only be a question of time when these gentlemen will change the black population of Liberia into a mongrel race, as they have done in America, [the] West Indies and other tropical countries, and there create another race problem such as is confusing us now in these United States of America. These white gentlemen are not going to allow black men to rule and govern them, so, like China and other places, there will be such complications as to ultimately lead to the abrogation of all native control and government and the setting up of new authority in a country that once belonged to the natives.

THE RAPE OF LIBERIA

It is the duty of every Negro in the world to protest against this rape of Liberia encouraged by those who are responsible for giving the concessions to the Firestone Rubber and Tire Company. Why, nearly one-half of the country has been given away and, when it is considered that out of the twelve million square miles of Africa, only Liberia is left as a free and independent black country, it becomes a shame and disgrace to see that men should be capable of giving away all this amount of land to the same people who have possession of over nine-tenths of the country's [continent's] area.

BRIGHT FUTURE FOR RACE

We beg to advise, however, the members and friends of the Universal Negro Improvement Association all over the world, that what has happened has not obstructed much the program of the Universal Negro Improvement Association as far as our colonization plans are concerned. All that we want is that everybody get behind the Black Cross Navigation and Trading Company and send us the necessary amount of money to pay for our first ship and secure other ships so as to carry out our trade contract with the Negroes of Africa, West Indies, South and Central America and these United States. The Association is devoting its time and energy now to building up an international commerce and trade so as to stabilize Negro industry. There is much for us to do. In taking the raw materials from our people in Africa to America, as well as materials [from] the West Indies, South and Central America to the United States[,] and taking back to them our finished and manufactured products in exchange, we have a whole world of industrial conquest to make and it can be done splendidly if each Negro will give us the support that is necessary. We want not only one, two or three ships, but we want dozens of ships, so that every week our ships can be going out of the ports of New York, Philadelphia, Boston, Baltimore, New Orleans, Savannah or Mobile for Liberia, Sierre [*sic*] Leone, Gold Coast, Lagos, Abyssinia, Brazil, Argentina, Costa Rica, Guatemala, Nicaragua, Honduras, Jamaica, Barbados, Trinidad, British Guiana and British Honduras. Let our ships be on the seven seas, taking our commerce to England, France, Germany, Italy, Japan, China and India. The chance of making good in commerce and trade is as much ours as it is other races and so we call upon you everywhere to get behind the industrial program of the Universal Negro Improvement Association. If we can control the field of industry we can control the sentiment of the world and that is what the Universal Negro Improvement Association seeks for the four hundred millions of our race.

MOVE THE LITTLE BARRIERS

So, the little barriers that have been placed in the way by the envious and wicked of our own race can easily be removed if we will get together and work together. Now that the convention has risen, let us redouble our energy everywhere to put the program over. Let us work with our hearts, soul and minds to see that everything is accomplished for the good of the race. We must have our ship in action by next month. At least, we are calculating to have our ship sail out of New York by the 29th of October, laden with the first cargo for the tropics, and to bring back to us tropical fruits and produce, and from thence to sail for Africa, the land of our fathers. Help us make this possible. . . .

With very best wishes for your success, I have the honor to be, Your obedient servant,

MARCUS GARVEY
President-General
Universal Negro Improvement Association

Questions

1. What did Garvey propose?
2. Why did he consider black Republicans to be the enemy? What was his purpose in attacking the Firestone Company?
3. How did Garvey's views differ from those of Booker T. Washington (see Document 19-8) and W. E. B. Du Bois (see Document 19-9)? Did Garvey echo any of the points made by the others?

Question for Further Thought

1. How do you account for the apparent explosion of cultural conflicts within the relatively brief period of the 1920s? Do any other periods of American history strike you as being marked by a number of such conflicts?

The Onset of the Great Depression, 1929–1932

The stock market crashed a little more than seven months into Herbert Hoover's presidency. During the final two years of his term, Hoover confronted a series of dilemmas posed by an ever-worsening economic crisis unprecedented in severity (see text pp. 727–733). That crisis, moreover, had major political and diplomatic implications. Only once before, during 1860 and 1861, had the nation and its chief executive faced a comparable crisis. Document 23-12 provides Herbert Hoover's plan for recovery. The Great Depression was recorded in statistics — unemployment, bank and business failures, mortgage foreclosures, and stock market averages. Graphed from 1929 to 1933, these figures resemble the vital signs on the medical chart of a seriously ill patient, data that disclose periodic upticks, but ominously, an overall worsening condition. For patient, family, and friends, hard times were experienced and felt as daily realities.

As more and more businesses and farms failed, construction continued to fall off and unemployment mounted. Increasingly fearful, those who were directly affected reached such numbers that their responses manifest themselves in falling marriage and birth rates. As the economy contracted, many whites were compelled to take jobs formerly held by blacks (such as office cleaning, laundry work, and domestic service); married women who worked were resented and discriminated against in government employment; high school attendance increased (especially among males) in the face of reduced job opportunities; and large numbers of young men and women, unable to contribute to meager family income, became tramps or hoboes.

Documents 23-13, 23-14, and 23-15 make painfully clear the impact of the Great Depression on individuals and families. For African Americans, farmers, Mexican Americans, and the elderly poor, the Great Depression meant that hard times became harder still. In Document 23-16, Richard Wright, who later became a novelist, offers testimony about his temporary attraction to Communism during this period.

23-12 Herbert Hoover's Plan (1931)

On June 15, 1931, President Hoover addressed the Indiana Editorial Association, presenting his solutions to the depression that was gripping the country.

Source: Herbert Hoover, "President Hoover's Plan" from *America Faces the Future*, ed. Charles A. Beard (Boston: Houghton Mifflin Company, 1932), 386–399. Copyright © 1932 and renewed 1960 by Houghton Mifflin Company. Reprinted by permission of Houghton Mifflin Company. All rights reserved.

The business depression is the dominant subject before the country and the world today. Its blight stretches from all quarters of the globe to every business place and every cottage door in our land. I propose to discuss it and the policies of the Government in respect to it.

Depressions are not new experiences, though none has hitherto been so widespread. We have passed through no less than fifteen major depressions in the last century. We have learned something as the result of each of these experiences. From this one we shall gain stiffening and economic discipline, a greater knowledge upon which we must build a better safeguarded system. We have come out of each previous depression into a period of prosperity greater than ever before. We shall do so this time.

As we look beyond the horizons of our own troubles and consider the events in other lands, we know that the main causes of the extreme violence and the long continuance of this depression came not from within but from outside the United States. Had our wild speculation; our stock promotion with its infinite losses and hardship to innocent people; our loose and extravagant business methods and our unprecedented drought, been our only disasters, we would have recovered months ago.

A large part of the forces which have swept our shores from abroad are the malign inheritances in Europe of the Great War — its huge taxes, its mounting armament, its political and social instability, its disruption of economic life by the new boundaries. Without the war we would have no such depression. Upon these war origins are superimposed the overrapid expansion of production and collapse in price of many foreign raw materials. The demonetization of silver in certain countries and a score of more remote causes have all contributed to dislocation.

Some particular calamity has happened to nearly every country in the world, and the difficulties of each have intensified the unemployment and financial difficulties of all the others. As either the cause or the effect, we have witnessed armed revolutions within the past two years in a score of nations, not to mention disturbed political life in many others. Political instability has affected three-fourths of the population of the world.

I do not at all minimize the economic interdependence of the world, but despite this, the potential and redeeming strength of the United States in the face of this situation is that we are economically more self-contained than any other great nation. This degree of independence gives assurance that with the passing of the temporary dislocations and shocks we can and will make a large measure of recovery irrespective of the rest of the world. We did so with even worse foreign conditions in 1921.

We can roughly indicate this high degree of self-containment. Our average annual production of movable goods before the depression was about fifty billion dollars. We exported yearly about five billions, or ten per cent. The world disruption has temporarily reduced our exports to about three and one half billions. In other words, the shrinkage of foreign trade by one and one half billions amounts to only two or three per cent of our total productivity.

Yet as a result of all the adverse forces our production has been reduced by, roughly, ten or twelve billions. This sharp contrast between a national shrinkage of, say, twelve billion dollars and a loss of one and one half billions from export trade is an indication of the disarrangement of our own internal production and consumption entirely apart from that resulting from decreased sales abroad.

Some of this enlarged dislocation is also due to the foreign effects upon prices of commodities and securities. Moreover, the repeated shocks from political disturbance and revolution in foreign countries stimulate fear and hesitation among our business men. These fears and apprehensions are unnecessarily increased by that minority of people who would make political capital out of the depression through magnifying our unemployment and losses. Other small groups in the business world make their contribution to distress by raids on our markets with purpose to profit from depreciation of securities and commodities. Both groups are within the law; they are equally condemned by our public and business opinion; they are by no means helpful to the nation.

Fear and apprehension, whether their origins are domestic or foreign, are very real, tangible, economic forces. Fear of loss of a job or uncertainty as to the future has caused millions of our people unnecessarily to reduce their purchases of goods, thereby decreasing our production and employment. These uncertainties lead our bankers and business men to extreme caution, and in consequence a mania for liquidation has reduced our stocks of goods and our credits far below any necessity. All these apprehensions and actions check enterprise and lessen our national activities. . . .

We must bear in mind at all times our marvelous resources in land, mines, mills, man power, brain power and courage. Over ninety-five per cent of our families have either an income or a bread winner employed. Our people are working harder and are resolutely engaged, individually and collectively, in overhauling and improving their methods and services. That is the fundamental method of repair to the wreckage from our boom of two years ago; it is the remedy for the impacts from abroad. It takes time, but it is going on.

Although fear has resulted in unnecessary reduction in spending, yet these very reductions are piling up savings in our savings banks until today they are the largest in our history. Surplus money does not remain idle for long. Ultimately it is the most insistent promoter of enterprise and of optimism. Consumption of retail goods in many lines is proceeding at a higher rate than last year. The harvest prospects indicate recovery from the drought and increased employment in handling the crop. Revolutions in many countries have spent themselves, and stability is on the ascendancy. The underlying forces of recovery are asserting themselves.

For the first time in history the Federal Government has taken an extensive and positive part in mitigating the effects of depression and expediting recovery. I have conceived that if we would preserve our democracy this leadership must take the part not of attempted dictatorship but of organizing coöperation in the constructive forces of the community and of stimulating every element of initiative and self-reliance in the country. There is no sudden stroke of either governmental or private action which can dissolve these world difficulties; patient, constructive action in a multitude of directions is the strategy of success. This battle is upon a thousand fronts.

I shall not detain you by a long exposition of these very extensive activities of our Government, for they are already well known. We have assured the country from panic and its hurricane of bankruptcy by coordinated action between the Treasury, the Federal Reserve System, the banks, the Farm Loan and Farm Board systems. We have steadily urged the maintenance of wages and salaries, preserving American standards of living, not alone for its contribution to consumption of goods, but with the far greater purpose of maintaining social goodwill through avoiding industrial conflict with its suffering and social disorder.

We are maintaining organized cooperation with industry systematically to distribute the available work so as to give income to as many families as possible.

We have reversed the traditional policy in depressions of reducing expenditures upon construction work. We are maintaining a steady expansion of ultimately needed construction work in cooperation with the states, municipalities, and industries.

Over two billions of dollars is being expended, and today a million men are being given direct and indirect employment through these enlarged activities. We have sustained the people in twenty-one states who faced dire disaster from the drought. We are giving aid and support to the farmers in marketing their crops, by which they have realized hundreds of millions more in prices than the farmers of any other country. Through the tariff we are saving our farmers and workmen from being overwhelmed with goods from foreign countries where, even since our tariff was revised, wages and prices have been reduced to much lower levels than before.

We are holding down taxation by exclusion of every possible governmental expenditure not absolutely essential or needed in increase of employment or assistance to the farmers. We are rigidly excluding immigration until our own people are employed. The departures and deportations today actually exceed arrivals.

We are maintaining and will maintain systematic voluntary organization in the community in aid of employment and care for distress. There are a score of other directions in which coöperation is organized and stimulation given. We propose to go forward with these major activities and policies. We will not be diverted from them.

By these and other measures which we shall develop as the occasion shall require we shall keep this ship steady in the storm. We will prevent any unnecessary distress in the United States, and by the activities and courage of the American people we will recover from the depression.

I would be remiss if I did not pay tribute to the business, industrial, labor, and agricultural leaders for their remarkable spirit of coöperation. Their action is magnificent proof of the fundamental progress of American institutions, of our growth in social and economic understanding, of our sense of responsibility, and of human brotherhood.

Leaders of industry have coöperated in an extraordinary degree to maintain employment and sustain our standards of living. There have been exceptions, but they represent a small per cent of the whole. Labor has coöperated in prevention of conflict in giving greater effort and consequently in reducing unit costs. We have had freedom from strikes, lockouts, and disorder unequaled even in prosperous times. We have made permanent gains in national solidarity....

While we are fostering the slow but positive processes of the healing of our economic wounds, our citizens are necessarily filled with anxiety, and in their anxiety there is the natural demand for more and more drastic action by the Federal Government. Many of their suggestions are sound and helpful. Every suggestion which comes within the proper authority and province of the Executive is given most earnest consideration. We are, of course, confronted with scores of theoretical panaceas which, however well intended, would inevitably delay recovery.

Some timid people, black with despair, have lost faith in our American system. They demand abrupt and positive change. Others have seized upon the opportunities of discontent to agitate for the adoption of economic patent medicines from foreign lands. Others have indomitable confidence that by some legerdemain we can legislate ourselves out of a world-wide depression. Such views are as accurate as the belief we can exorcise a Caribbean hurricane by statutory law.

For instance, nothing can be gained in recovery of employment by detouring capital away from industry and commerce into the Treasury of the United States, either by taxes or loans, on the assumption that the Government can create more employment by use of these funds than can industry and commerce itself. While I am a strong advocate of expansion of useful public works in hard times, and we have trebled our federal expenditure in aid to unemployment, yet there are limitations upon the application of this principle.

Not only must we refrain from robbing industry and commerce of its capital, and thereby increasing unemployment, but such works require long engineering and legal interludes before they produce actual employment. Above all, schemes of public works which have no reproductive value would result in sheer waste. The remedy to economic depression is not waste, but the creation and distribution of wealth.

It has been urged that the Federal Government should abandon its system of employment agencies and should appropriate large sums to subsidize their establishment in other hands. I have refused to accept such schemes, as they would in many places endow political organizations with the gigantic patronage of workmen's jobs. That would bring about the most vicious tyranny ever set up in the United States. We have instead expanded our Federal Government agencies which are on a non-political basis. They are of far greater service to labor.

We have had one proposal after another which amounts to a dole from the Federal Treasury. The largest is that of unemployment insurance. I have long advocated such insurance as an additional measure of safety against rainy days, but only through private enterprise or through coöperation of industry and labor itself. The moment the Government enters into this field it invariably degenerates into the dole. For nothing can withstand the political pressures which carry governments over this dangerous border.

The net results of governmental doles are to lower wages toward the bare subsistence level and to endow the slacker. It imposes the injustice of huge burdens upon farmers and other callings which receive no benefits. I am proud that so representative an organization as the American Federation of Labor has refused to approve such schemes....

With industry as well as agriculture we are concerned not merely in the immediate problems of the depression. From the experience of this depression will come not only a greatly sobered and more efficient economic system than we possessed two years ago, but a greater knowledge of its weaknesses as well as a greater intelligence in correcting them. When the time comes that we can look at this depression objectively, it will be our duty searchingly to examine every phase of it.

We can already observe some directions to which endeavor must be pointed. For instance, it is obvious that the Federal Reserve System was inadequate to prevent a large diversion of capital and bank deposits from commercial and industrial business into wasteful speculation and stock promotion. It is obvious our banking system must be organized to give greater protection to depositors against failures. It is equally obvious that we must determine whether the facilities of our security and commodity exchanges are not being used to create illegitimate speculation and intensify depressions.

It is obvious that our taxes upon capital gains viciously promote the booms and just as viciously intensify depressions. In order to avoid taxes, real estate and stocks are withheld from the market in times of rising prices, and for the same reason large quantities are dumped on the market in times of depression. The experiences of this depression indeed demand that the nation carefully and deliberately reconsider the whole national and local problem of the incidence of taxation.

The undue proportion of taxes which falls upon farmers, home-owners, and all real-property holders as compared to other forms of wealth and income, demands real relief. There are far wider questions of our social and economic life which this experience will illuminate. We shall know much more of the method of still further advance toward stability, security, and wider diffusion of the benefits of our economic system.

We have many citizens insisting that we produce an advance "plan" for the future development of the United States. They demand that we produce it right now. I presume the "plan" idea is an infection from the slogan of the "five-year plan" through which Russia is struggling to redeem herself from the ten years of starvation and misery.

I am able to propose an American plan to you. We plan to take care of twenty million increase in population in the next twenty years. We plan to build for them four million new and better homes, thousands of new and still more beautiful city buildings, thousands of factories; to increase the capacity of our railways; to add thousands of miles of highways and waterways; to install twenty-five million electrical horsepower; to grow twenty per cent more farm products. We plan to provide new parks, schools, colleges, and churches for this twenty million people. We plan more leisure for men and women and better opportunities for its enjoyment.

We not only plan to provide for all the new generation, but we shall, by scientific research and invention, lift the standard of living and security of life to the whole people. We plan to secure a greater diffusion of wealth, a decrease in poverty and a great reduction in crime. And this plan will be carried out if we just keep on giving the American people a chance. Its impulsive force is in the character and spirit of our people. They have already done a better job for one hundred and twenty million people than any other nation in all history.

Some groups believe this plan can only be carried out by a fundamental, a revolutionary, change of method. Other groups believe that any system must be the outgrowth of the character of our race, a natural outgrowth of our race, a natural outgrowth of our traditions; that we have established certain ideals, over one hundred and fifty years, upon which we must build rather than destroy. . . .

These ideas present themselves in practical questions which we have to meet. Shall we abandon the philosophy and creed of our people for one hundred and fifty years by turning to a creed foreign to our people? Shall we establish a dole from the Federal Treasury? Shall we undertake federal ownership and operation of public utilities instead of the rigorous regulation of them to prevent imposition? Shall we protect our people from the lower standards of living of foreign countries? Shall the Government, except in temporary national emergencies, enter upon business processes in competition with its citizens? Shall we regiment our people by an extension of the arm of bureaucracy into a multitude of affairs?

Our immediate and paramount task as a people is to rout the forces of economic disruption and pessimism that have swept upon us. . . .

If, as many believe, we have passed the worst of this storm, future months will not be difficult. If we shall be called upon to endure more of this period, we must gird ourselves to steadfast effort, to fail at no point where humanity calls or American ideals are in jeopardy. . . .

In conclusion, whatever the immediate difficulties may be, we know they are transitory in our lives and in the life of the nation. We should have full faith and confidence in those mighty resources, those intellectual and spiritual forces which have impelled this nation to a success never before known in the history of the world. Far from being impaired, these forces were never stronger than at this moment. Under the guidance of Divine Providence they will return to us a greater and more wholesome prosperity than we have ever known.

Questions

1. According to Hoover, what were the causes of the Great Depression?
2. What actions did Hoover take to help bring about the country's recovery?
3. What was the "American system"?

23-13 A Wise Economist Asks a Question (1931)

John T. McCutcheon

In a career that spanned forty-three years at the *Chicago Tribune*, John T. McCutcheon (1870–1949) demonstrated a sense of compassion that led him to be known as the "dean of American cartoonists" in the first half of the twentieth century. There is nothing obvious or partisan in this drawing, which may explain why it won a Pulitzer Prize in 1932.

Source: Copyright 1931, reprinted by permission: Tribune Media Services.

John T. McCutcheon, "A Victim of Bank Failure" (1931)

Questions

1. How did McCutcheon make the man a sympathetic character?
2. Why did he have a squirrel ask the question?
3. What was McCutcheon saying about the American belief in personal responsibility?

23-14 Mr. Patterson (1940)

Mirra Komarovsky

Barnard College sociologist Mirra Komarovsky measured the impact of hard times on men's self-esteem through case histories, such as that of "Mr. Patterson," in her 1940 book *The Unemployed Man and His Family*.

Source: From Mirra Komarovsky, *The Unemployed Man and His Family* (1940; New York: Octagon, 1973), 26–28. Reprinted with permission.

REACTION TO UNEMPLOYMENT AND RELIEF

Prior to the depression Mr. Patterson was an inventory clerk earning from $35 to $40 a week. He lost his job in 1931. At the present time he does not earn anything, while his 18-year-old girl gets $12.50 a week working in Woolworth's, and his wife has part-time work cleaning a doctor's office. Unemployment and depression have hit Mr. Patterson much more than the rest of the family.

The hardest thing about unemployment, Mr. Patterson says, is the humiliation within the family. It makes him feel very useless to have his wife and daughter bring in money to the family while he does not contribute a nickel. It is awful to him, because now "the tables are turned," that is, he has to ask his daughter for a little money for tobacco, etc. He would rather walk miles than ask for carfare money. His daughter would want him to have it, but he cannot bring himself to ask for it. He had often thought that it would make it easier if he could have 25 cents a week that he could depend upon. He feels more irritable and morose than he ever did in his life. He doesn't enjoy eating. He hasn't slept well in months. He lies awake and tosses and tosses, wondering what he will do and what will happen to them if he doesn't ever get work any more. He feels that there is nothing to wake up for in the morning and nothing to live for. He often wonders what would happen if he put himself out of the picture, or just got out of the way of his wife. Perhaps she and the girl would get along better without him. He blames himself for being unemployed. While he tries all day long to find work and would take anything, he feels that he would be successful if he had taken advantage of his opportunities in youth and had secured an education.

Mr. Patterson believes that his wife and daughter have adjusted themselves to the depression better than he has. In fact, sometimes they seem so cheerful in the evening that he cannot stand it any more. He grabs his hat and says he is going out for a while, and walks hard for an hour before he comes home again. That is one thing he never did before unemployment, but he is so nervous and jumpy now he has to do something like that to prevent himself from exploding.

Mrs. Patterson says that they have not felt the depression so terribly themselves, or changed their way of living so very much.

CHANGES IN HUSBAND-WIFE RELATIONS SINCE LOSS OF EMPLOYMENT

The wife thinks it is her husband's fault that he is unemployed. Not that he doesn't run around and try his very best to get a job, but he neglected his opportunities when he was young. If he had had a proper education and had a better personality, he would not be in his present state. Besides, he has changed for the worse. He has become irritable and very hard to get along with. He talks of nothing else, and isn't interested in anything else but his troubles. She and her daughter try to forget troubles and have a good time once in a while, but he just sits and broods. Of course that makes her impatient with him. She cannot sit at home and keep him company, so that during the past couple of years she and her daughter just go out together without him. It isn't that they leave him out—he just isn't interested and stays at home.

Mr. Patterson insists that his child is as sweet as ever and always tries to cheer him up, but the tenor of his conversation about his wife is different. She does go out more with the daughter, leaving him alone. He cannot stand it, worrying so and having them so lighthearted. "When you are not bringing in any money, you don't get as much attention. She doesn't nag all the time, the way some women do," but he knows she blames him for being unemployed. He intimates that they have fewer sex relations—"It's nothing that I do or don't do—no change in me—but when I tell her that I want more love, she just gets mad." It came about gradually, he said. He cannot point definitely to any time when he noticed the difference in her. But he knows that his advances are rebuffed now when they would not have been before the hard times.

The wife gives the impression that there might have been some decrease in sex relations, but declines to discuss them. She tells the following episode:

The day before the interview she was kissing and hugging the daughter. "I like to keep the girl sweet and young, and in the habit of kissing her mother good-night." The father walked in and said, "Don't you get enough of that?" Mrs. Patterson went on at great length as to how terribly that statement hurt her.

The interviewer also witnessed another episode. Towards the end of the interview with the wife, the husband walked into the living room and asked his wife if she thought the interviewer would be interested in talking to their neighbors. The woman said, "Don't bother us, we are talking about something else just now." He got up quietly and went into the kitchen. In a moment she called after him, "Oh, you can sit in here if you *want* to." Nevertheless, he stayed in the kitchen.

Questions

1. Judging from Mr. Patterson's experience, what was the impact of prolonged unemployment on American families?
2. Compare Mr. Patterson's reaction to the depression with the reactions of his wife and daughter.
3. Some contemporary observers suggested that the solution to the depression would be for married women to stay in the home and not "take jobs away from men." Judging from the Patterson family's experience, was this a realistic solution?

23-15 Women on the Breadlines (1932)

Meridel Le Sueur

Meridel Le Sueur (1900–1996), born in Iowa, was a writer who remained active in radical circles throughout her life. "Women on the Breadlines" was published in *New Masses* but drew fire from Communist editors for its defeatism and "nonrevolutionary spirit." After suffering through her "Dark Time" during the early Cold War, Le Sueur reemerged during the 1970s. Her writing continues to be of interest even today, some years after her death.

Source: From *Harvest: Collected Stories* by Meridel LeSueur. Reprinted with the permission of West End Press, Albuquerque, New Mexico. Originally published in the *New Masses*, January 1932. Reprinted in *Ripening: Selected Work*, 2nd edition, ed. Elaine Hedges, with a new afterward by Meridel LeSueur, 137–143. Copyright © 1990 by Meridel LeSueur.

I am sitting in the city free employment bureau. It's the women's section. We have been sitting here now for four hours. We sit here every day, waiting for a job. There are no jobs. Most of us have had no breakfast. Some have had scant rations for over a year. Hunger makes a human being lapse into a state of lethargy, especially city hunger. Is there any place else in the world where a human being is supposed to go hungry amidst plenty without an outcry, without protest, where only the boldest steal or kill for bread, and the timid crawl the streets, hunger like the beak of a terrible bird at the vitals?

We sit looking at the floor. No one dares think of the coming winter. There are only a few more days of summer. Everyone is anxious to get work to lay up something for that long siege of bitter cold. But there is no work. Sitting in the room we all know it. That is why we don't talk; much. We look at the floor dreading to see that knowledge in each other's eyes. There is a kind of humiliation in it. We look away from each other. We look at the floor. It's too terrible to see this animal terror in each other's eyes.

So we sit hour after hour, day after day, waiting for a job to come in. There are many women for a single job. A thin sharp woman sits inside a wire cage looking at a book. For four hours we have watched her looking at that book. She has a hard little eye. In the small bare room there are half a dozen women sitting on the benches waiting. Many come and go. Our faces are all familiar to each other, for we wait here every day.

This is a domestic employment bureau. Most of the women who come here are middle-aged, some have families, some have raised their families and are now alone, some have men who are out of work. Hard times and the man leaves to hunt for work. He doesn't find it. He drifts on. The woman probably doesn't hear from him for a long time. She expects it. She isn't surprised. She struggles alone to feed the many mouths. Sometimes she gets help from the charities. If she's clever she can get herself a good living from the charities, if she's naturally a lick spittle, naturally a little docile and cunning. If she's proud then she starves silently, leaving her children to find work, coming home after a day's searching to wrestle with her house, her children.

Some such story is written on the faces of all these women. There are young girls too, fresh from the country. Some are made brazen too soon by the city. There is a great exodus of girls from the farms into the city now. Thousands of farms have been vacated completely in Minnesota. The girls are trying to get work. The prettier ones can get jobs in the stores when there are any, or waiting on table, but these jobs are only for the attractive and the adroit. The others, the real peasants, have a more difficult time.

Bernice sits next to me. She is a Polish woman of thirty-five. She has been working in people's kitchens for fifteen years or more. She is large, her great body in mounds, her face brightly scrubbed. She has a peasant mind and finds it hard even yet to understand the maze of the city where trickery is worth more than brawn. Her blue eyes are not clever but slow and trusting. She suffers from loneliness and lack of talk. When you speak to her, her face lifts and brightens as if you had spoken through a great darkness, and she talks magically of little things as if the weather were magic, or tells some crazy tale of her adventures on the city streets, embellishing them in bright colors until they hang heavy and thick like embroidery. She loves the city anyhow. It's exciting to her, like a bazaar. She loves to go shopping and get a bargain, hunting out the places where stale bread and cakes can be had for a few cents. She likes walking the streets looking for men to take her to a picture show. Sometimes she goes to five picture shows in one day, or she sits through one the entire day until she knows all the dialog by heart....

She wants to get married but she sees what happens to her married friends, left with children to support, worn out before their time. So she stays single. She is virtuous. She is slightly deaf from hanging out clothes in winter. She had done people's washing and cooking for fifteen years and in that time saved thirty dollars. Now she hasn't worked steady for a year and she has spent the thirty dollars. She had dreamed of having a little house or a houseboat perhaps with a spot of ground for a few chickens. This dream she will never realize.

She has lost all her furniture now along with the dream. A married friend whose husband is gone gives her a bed for which she pays by doing a great deal of work for the woman. She comes here every day now sitting bewildered, her pudgy hands folded in her lap. She is hungry. Her great flesh has begun to hang in folds. She has been living on crackers. Sometimes a box of crackers lasts a week. She has a friend who's a baker and he sometimes steals the stale loaves and brings them to her.

A girl we have seen every day all summer went crazy yesterday at the YW. She went into hysterics, stamping her feet and screaming.

She hadn't had work for eight months. "You've got to give me something," she kept saying. The woman in charge flew into a rage that probably came from days and days of suffering on her part, because she is unable to give jobs, having none. She flew into a rage at the girl and there they were facing each other in a rage both helpless, helpless. This woman told me once that she could hardly bear the suffering she saw, hardly hear it, that she couldn't eat sometimes and had nightmares at night.

So they stood there, the two women, in a rage, the girl weeping and the woman shouting at her. In the eight months of unemployment she had gotten ragged, and the woman was shouting that she would not send her out like that. "Why don't you shine your shoes?" she kept scolding the girl, and the girl kept sobbing and sobbing because she was starving.

"We can't recommend you like that," the harassed YWCA woman said, knowing she was starving, unable to do anything. And the girls and the women sat docilely, their eyes on the ground, ashamed to look at each other, ashamed of something.

Sitting here waiting for a job, the women have been talking in low voices about the girl Ellen. They talk in low voices with not too much pity for her, unable to see through the mist of their own torment. "What happened to Ellen?" one of them asks. She knows the answer already. We all know it.

A young girl who went around with Ellen tells about seeing her last evening back of a cafe downtown, outside the kitchen door, kicking, showing her legs so that the cook came out and gave her some food and some men gathered in the alley and threw small coin on the ground for a look at her legs. And the girl says enviously that Ellen had a swell breakfast and treated her to one too, that cost two dollars.

A scrub woman whose hips are bent forward from stooping with hands gnarled like watersoaked branches clicks her tongue in disgust. No one saves their money, she says, a little money and these foolish young things buy a hat, a dollar for breakfast, a bright scarf. And they do. If you've ever been without money, or food, something very strange happens when you get a bit of money, a kind of madness. You don't care. You can't remember that you had no money before, that the money will be gone. You can remember nothing but that there is the money for which you have been suffering. Now here it is. A lust takes hold of you. You see food in the windows. In imagination you eat hugely; you taste a thousand meals. You look in windows. Colors are brighter; you buy something to dress up in. An excitement takes hold of you. You know it is suicide but you can't help it. You must have food, dainty, splendid food, and a bright hat so once again you feel blithe, rid of that ratty gnawing shame.

"I guess she'll go on the street now," a thin woman says faintly, and no one takes the trouble to comment further. Like every commodity now the body is difficult to sell and the girls say you're lucky if you get fifty cents.

It's very difficult and humiliating to sell one's body.

Perhaps it would make it clear if one were to imagine having to go out on the street to sell, say, one's overcoat. Suppose you have to sell your coat so you can have breakfast and a place to sleep, say, for fifty cents. You decide to sell your only coat. You take it off and put it on your arm. The street, that has before been just a street, now becomes a mart, something entirely different. You must approach someone now and admit you are destitute and are now selling your clothes, your most intimate possessions. Everyone will watch you talking to the stranger showing him your overcoat, what a good coat it is. People will stop and watch curiously. You will be quite naked on the street. It is even harder to try to sell one's self, more humiliating. It is even humiliating to try to sell one's labor. When there is no buyer.

The thin woman opens the wire cage. There's a job for a nursemaid, she says. The old gnarled women, like old horses, know that no one will have them walk the streets with the young so they don't move. Ellen's friend gets up and goes to the window. She is unbelievably jaunty. I know she hasn't had work since last January. But she has a flare of life in her that glows like a tiny red flame and some tenacious thing, perhaps only youth, keeps it burning bright. Her legs are thin but the runs in her old stockings are neatly mended clear down her flat shank. Two bright spots of rouge conceal her pallor. A narrow belt is drawn tightly around her thin waist, her long shoulders stoop and the blades show. She runs wild as a colt hunting pleasure, hunting sustenance.

It's one of the great mysteries of the city where women go when they are out of work and hungry. There are not many women in the bread line. There are no flop houses for women as there are for men, where a bed can be had for a quarter or less. You don't see women lying on the floor at the mission in the free flops. They obviously don't sleep in the jungle or under newspapers in the park. There is no law I suppose against their being in these places but the fact is they rarely are.

Yet there must be as many women out of jobs in cities and suffering extreme poverty as there are men. What happens to them? Where do they go? Try to get into the YW without any money or looking down at heel. Charities take care of very few and only those that are called "deserving." The lone girl is under suspicion by the virgin women who dispense charity.

I've lived in cities for many months broke, without help, too timid to get in bread lines. I've known many women to live like this until they simply faint on the street from privations, without saying a word to anyone. A woman will shut herself up in a room until it is taken away from her, and eat a cracker a day and be as quiet as a mouse so there are no social statistics concerning her.

I don't know why it is, but a woman will do this unless she has dependents, will go for weeks verging on starvation, crawling in some hole, going through the streets ashamed, sitting in libraries, parks, going for days without speaking to a living soul like some exiled beast, keeping the runs mended in her stockings, shut up in terror in her own misery, until she becomes too super-sensitive and timid to even ask for a job.

Bernice says even strange men she has met in the park have sometimes, that is in better days, given her a loan to pay her room rent. She has always paid them back.

In the afternoon the young girls, to forget the hunger and the deathly torture and fear of being jobless, try to pick up a man to take them to a ten-cent show. They never go to more expensive ones, but they can always find a man willing to spend a dime to have the company of a girl for the afternoon.

Sometimes a girl facing the night without shelter will approach a man for lodging. A woman always asks a man for help. Rarely another woman. I have known girls to sleep in men's rooms for the night on a pallet without molestation and be given breakfast in the morning.

It's no wonder these young girls refuse to marry, refuse to rear children. They are like certain savage tribes, who, when they have been conquered, refuse to breed.

Not one of them but looks forward to starvation for the coming winter. We are in a jungle and know it. We are beaten, entrapped. There is no way out. Even if there were a job, even if that thin acrid woman came and gave everyone in the room a job for a few days, a few hours, at thirty cents an hour, this would all be repeated tomorrow, the next day and the next.

Not one of these women but knows that despite years of labor there is only starvation, humiliation in front of them.

Mrs. Gray, sitting across from me, is a living spokesman for the futility of labor. She is a warning. Her hands are scarred with labor. Her body is a great puckered scar. She has given birth to six children, buried three, supported them all alive and dead, bearing them, burying them, feeding them. Bred in hunger they have been spare, susceptible to disease. For seven years she tried to save her boy's arm from amputation, diseased from tuberculosis of the bone. It is almost too suffocating to think of that long close horror of years of child-bearing, child-feeding, rearing, with the bare suffering of providing a meal and shelter.

Now she is fifty. Her children, economically insecure, are drifters. She never hears of them. She doesn't know if they are alive. She doesn't know if she is alive. Such subtleties of suffering are not for her. For her the brutality of hunger and cold. Not until these are done away with can those subtle feelings that make a human being be indulged.

She is lucky to have five dollars ahead of her. That is her security. She has a tumor that she will die of. She is thin as a worn dime with her tumor sticking out of her side. She is brittle and bitter. Her face is not the face of a human being. She has borne more than it is possible for a human being to bear. She is reduced to the least possible denominator of human feelings.

It is terrible to see her little bloodshot eyes like a beaten hound's, fearful in terror.

We cannot meet her eyes. When she looks at any of us we look away. She is like a woman drowning and we turn away. We must ignore those eyes that are surely the eyes of a person drowning, doomed. She doesn't cry out. She goes down decently. And we all look away.

The young ones know though. I don't want to marry. I don't want any children. So they all say. No children. No marriage. They arm themselves alone, keep up alone. The man is helpless now. He cannot provide. If he propagates he cannot take care of his young. The means are not in his hands. So they live alone. Get what fun they can. The life risk is too horrible now. Defeat is too clearly written on it.

So we sit in this room like cattle, waiting for a nonexistent job, willing to work to the farthest atom of energy, unable to work, unable to get food and lodging, unable to bear children—here we must sit in this shame looking at the floor, worse than beasts at a slaughter.

It is appalling to think that these women sitting so listless in the room may work as hard as it is possible for a human being to work, may labor night and day, like Mrs. Gray wash streetcars from midnight to dawn and offices in the early evening, scrub for fourteen and fifteen hours a day, sleep only five hours or so, do this their whole lives, and never earn one day of security, having always before them the pit of the future. The endless labor, the bending back, the water-soaked hands, earning never more than a week's wages, never having in their hands more life than that.

It's not the suffering of birth, death, love that the young reject, but the suffering of endless labor without dream, eating the spare bread in bitterness, being a slave without the security of a slave.

Questions

1. What aspects of "Women on the Breadlines" likely led to the criticism by editors of *New Masses*?
2. What aspects of Le Sueur's work, revealed in this piece, do you think have led to renewed interest in the writer and to the recent publication of many of her works?
3. What most strikes you about the women Le Sueur describes and their experiences? What of the men who figure in the piece?

23-16 Communism in the 1930s

Richard Wright

With the publication of *Native Son* in 1940, Richard Wright (1908–1960) became the best-known African American novelist of his generation. In the mid-1930s, Wright was attracted to the Communist Party. In this excerpt from his memoir, *American Hunger*, he suggests why Communism appealed to him for a time and why its appeal proved limited.

Source: Excerpt from Chapter IV in *American Hunger*. Copyright © 1944 by Richard Wright; copyright 1977 by Ellen Wright. Reprinted by permission of HarperCollins Publishers, Inc.

One Thursday night I received an invitation from a group of white boys I had known in the post office to meet in a South Side hotel and argue the state of the world. About ten of us gathered and ate salami sandwiches, drank beer, and talked. I was amazed to discover that many of them had joined the Communist party. I challenged them by reciting the antics of the Negro Communists I had seen in the parks, and I was told that those antics were "tactics" and were all right. I was dubious.

Then one Thursday night Sol, a Jewish chap, startled us by announcing that he had had a short story accepted by a little magazine called the *Anvil*, edited by Jack Conroy, and that he had joined a revolutionary artists' organization, the John Reed Club. Sol repeatedly begged me to attend the meetings of the club, but I always found an easy excuse for refusing.

"You'd like them," Sol said.

"I don't want to be organized," I said.

"They can help you to write," he said.

"Nobody can tell me how or what to write," I said.

"Come and see," he urged. "What have you to lose?"

I felt that Communists could not possibly have a sincere interest in Negroes. I was cynical and I would rather have heard a white man say that he hated Negroes, which I could have readily believed, then to have heard him say that he respected Negroes, which would have made me doubt him. I did not think that there existed many whites who, through intellectual effort, could lift themselves out of the traditions of their times and see the Negro objectively.

One Saturday night, sitting home idle, not caring to visit the girls I had met on my former insurance route, bored with reading, I decided to appear at the John Reed Club in the capacity of an amused spectator. I rode to the Loop and found the number. A dark stairway led upwards; it did not look welcoming. What on earth of importance could transpire in so dingy a place? Through the windows above me I saw vague murals along the walls. I mounted the stairs to a door that was lettered:

THE CHICAGO JOHN REED CLUB

I opened it and stepped into the strangest room I had ever seen. Paper and cigarette butts lay on the floor. A few benches ran along the walls, above which were vivid colors depicting colossal figures of workers carrying streaming banners. The mouths of the workers gaped in wild cries; their legs were sprawled over cities.

"Hello."

I turned and saw a white man smiling at me.

"A friend of mine, who's a member of this club, asked me to visit here. His name is Sol———," I told him.

"You're welcome here," the white man said. "We're not having an affair tonight. We're holding an editorial meeting. Do you paint?" He was slightly gray and he had a mustache.

"No," I said. "I try to write."

"Then sit in on the editorial meeting of our magazine, *Left Front*," he suggested.

"I know nothing of editing," I said.

"You can learn," he said.

I stared at him, doubting.

"I don't want to be in the way here," I said.

"My name's Grimm," he said.

I told him my name and we shook hands. He went to a closet and returned with an armful of magazines.

"Here are some back issues of the *Masses*," he said. "Have you ever read it?"

"No," I said.

"Some of the best writers in America publish in it," he explained. He also gave me copies of a magazine called *International Literature*. "There's stuff here from Gide, Gorky . . ."

I assured him that I would read them. He took me to an office and introduced me to a Jewish boy who was to become one of the nation's leading painters, to a chap who was to become one of the eminent composers of his day, to a writer who was to create some of the best novels of his generation, to a young Jewish boy who was destined to film the Nazi invasion of Czechoslovakia. I was meeting men and women whom I would know for decades to come, who were to form the first sustained relationships in my life.

I sat in a corner and listened while they discussed their magazine, *Left Front*. Were they treating me courteously because I was a Negro? I must let cold reason guide me with these people, I told myself. I was asked to contribute something to the magazine, and I said vaguely that I would consider it. After the meeting I met an Irish girl who worked for an advertising agency, a girl who did social work, a schoolteacher, and the wife of a prominent university professor. I had once worked as a servant for people like these and I was skeptical. I tried to fathom their motives, but I could detect no condescension in them.

I went home full of reflection, probing the sincerity of the strange white people I had met, wondering how they *really* regarded Negroes. I lay on my bed and read the magazines and was amazed to find that there did exist in the world an organized search for the truth of the lives of the oppressed and the isolated. When I had begged bread from the officials, I had wondered dimly if the outcasts could become united in action, thought, and feeling. Now I knew. It was being done in one-sixth of the earth already. The revolutionary words leaped from the printed page and struck me with tremendous force.

It was not the economics of Communism, nor the great power of trade unions, nor the excitement of underground politics that claimed me; my attention was caught by the similarity of the experiences of workers in other lands, by the possibility of uniting scattered but kindred peoples into a whole. My cynicism—which had been my protection against an America that had cast me out—slid from me and, timidly, I began to wonder if a solution of unity was possible. My life as a Negro in America had led me to feel—though my helplessness had made me try to hide it from myself—that the problem of human unity was more important than bread, more important than physical living itself; for I felt that without a common bond uniting men, without a continuous current of shared thought and feeling circulating through the social system, like blood coursing through the body, there could be no living worthy of being called human.

I hungered to share the dominant assumptions of my time and act upon them. I did not want to feel, like an animal in a jungle, that the whole world was alien and hostile. I did not want to make individual war or individual peace. So far I had managed to keep humanly alive through transfusions from books. In my concrete relations with others I had encountered nothing to encourage me to believe in my feelings. It had been by denying what I saw with my eyes, disputing what I felt with my body, that I had managed to keep my identity intact. But it seemed to me that here at least in the realm of revolutionary expression was where Negro experience could find a home, a functioning value and role. Out of the magazines I read came a passionate call for the experiences of the disinherited, and there were none of the same lispings of the missionary in it. It did not say: "Be like us and we will like you, maybe." It said: "If you possess enough courage to speak out what you are, you will find that you are not alone." It urged life to believe in life.

I read on into the night; then, toward dawn, I swung from bed and inserted paper into the typewriter. Feeling for the first time that I could speak to listening ears, I wrote a wild, crude poem in free verse, coining images of black hands playing, working, holding bayonets, stiffening finally in death . . . I read it and felt that in a clumsy way it linked white life with black, merged two streams of common experience.

I heard someone poking about the kitchen.

"Richard, are you ill?" my mother called.

"No. I'm reading."

My mother opened the door and stared curiously at the pile of magazines that lay upon my pillow.

"You're not throwing away money buying these magazines, are you?" she asked.

"No. They were given to me."

She hobbled to the bed on her crippled legs and picked up a copy of the *Masses* that carried a lurid May Day cartoon. She adjusted her glasses and peered at it for a long time.

"My God in heaven," she breathed in horror.

"What's the matter, mama?"

"What is this?" she asked, extending the magazine to me, pointing to the cover. "What's wrong with that man?"

With my mother standing at my side, lending me her eyes, I stared at a cartoon drawn by a Communist artist; it was the figure of a worker clad in ragged overalls and holding aloft a red banner. The man's eyes bulged; his mouth gaped as wide as his face; his teeth showed; the muscles of his neck were like ropes. Following the man was a horde of nondescript men, women, and children, waving clubs, stones, and pitchforks.

"What are those people going to do?" my mother asked.

"I don't know," I hedged.

"Are these Communist magazines?"

"Yes."

"And do they want people to act like this?"

"Well . . ." I hesitated.

My mother's face showed disgust and moral loathing. She was a gentle woman. Her ideal was Christ upon the cross. How could I tell her that the Communist party wanted her to march in the streets, chanting, singing?

"What do Communists think people are?" she asked.

"They don't quite mean what you see there," I said, fumbling with my words.

"Then what do they mean?"

"This is symbolic," I said.

"Then why don't they speak out what they mean?"

"Maybe they don't know how."

"Then why do they print this stuff?"

"They don't quite know how to appeal to people yet," I admitted, wondering whom I could convince of this if I could not convince my mother.

"That picture's enough to drive a body crazy," she said, dropping the magazine, turning to leave, then pausing at the door.

"You're not getting mixed up with those people?"

"I'm just reading, mama," I dodged.

Questions

1. Many Americans became dissatisfied with the status quo during the Great Depression. Which grievances shaped the response of African Americans to the social and economic hardships of that era?

2. Why did Communism appeal to Wright as a possible solution to the problems he faced?

3. Judging from Wright's account, what factors prevented Communism from becoming a more popular movement?

Questions for Further Thought

1. Based on your reading of the text and the selections in this chapter, how was Hoover's plan inadequate in the solutions it proposed for alleviating the suffering of the American people?

2. Drawing on these documents and the text, reflect on the position of men during hard times.

3. Doing likewise, reflect on the position of women during hard times.

4. Some historians argue that the only time that Communism ever had a chance to take hold in the United States was during the 1930s. Explain this argument in terms of Richard Wright's piece (Document 23-16) and the other selections in this section.

CHAPTER TWENTY-FOUR

Redefining Liberalism: The New Deal
1933–1939

The New Deal Takes Over, 1933–1935

From the beginning of his presidency, Franklin Delano Roosevelt demonstrated that his personality and voice would figure prominently in his administration. Indeed, even before his election, he had dramatically broken with precedent by flying to the Democratic National Convention and personally accepting the nomination. In his speech there, he had referred to a "new deal," a term that quickly gained currency. In his inaugural address (Document 24-1) the following March, President Roosevelt sought to rally a shaken nation at the very depths of the Great Depression. In late June, New Dealer Rexford G. Tugwell explained the significance of the president's dramatic and wide-ranging reforms to the Federation of Bar Associations of Western New York (Document 24-2). In 1933, there was a broad consensus that the federal government was going to have to play a much larger role in the economy, as indicated by an editorial from *Business Week* (Document 24-3). Broad public and congressional support did not mean that the New Deal lacked significant opposition. Indeed, the Supreme Court began to invalidate federal and state laws enacted by the Democrats. The Court's decision striking down the National Industrial Recovery Act drew fire from the frustrated president (Document 24-5). Even more ambitious than New Deal legislation were Louisiana senator Huey P. Long's populist schemes, which attracted national attention (Document 24-5).

24-1 First Inaugural Address (1933)

Franklin D. Roosevelt

With so many Americans suffering in poverty through the winter of 1932–1933, President Roosevelt (1882–1945) knew that he had to find a way to rekindle their spirits. Assisted by advisor Raymond Moley, Roosevelt crafted an inaugural address toward that end. The speech, given on March 4, 1933, was a resounding success.

Source: From Samuel I. Rosenman, ed., *The Public Papers and Addresses of Franklin D. Roosevelt*, 2 (New York: Random House, 1938).

President Hoover, Mr. Chief Justice, my friends:

This is a day of national consecration, and I am certain that my fellow Americans expect that on my induction into the Presidency I will address them with a candor and a decision which the present situation of our nation impels.

This is pre-eminently the time to speak the truth, the whole truth, frankly and boldly. Nor need we shrink from honestly facing conditions in our country today. This great nation will endure as it has endured, will revive and will prosper.

So first of all let me assert my firm belief that the only thing we have to fear is fear itself—nameless, unreasoning, unjustified terror which paralyzes needed efforts to convert retreat into advance.

In every dark hour of our national life a leadership of frankness and vigor has met with that understanding and support of the people themselves which is essential to victory. I am convinced that you will again give that support to leadership in these critical days.

In such a spirit on my part and on yours we face our common difficulties. They concern, thank God, only material things. Values have shrunken to fantastic levels; taxes have risen; our ability to pay has fallen, government of all kinds is faced by serious curtailment of income; the means of exchange are frozen in the currents of trade; the withered leaves of industrial enterprise lie on every side; farmers find no markets for their produce; the savings of many years in thousands of families are gone.

More important, a host of unemployed citizens face the grim problem of existence, and an equally great number toil with little return. Only a foolish optimist can deny the dark realities of the moment.

Yet our distress comes from no failure of substance. We are stricken by no plague of locusts. Compared with the perils which our forefathers conquered because they believed and were not afraid, we have still much to be thankful for. Nature still offers her bounty and human efforts have multiplied it. Plenty is at our doorstop, but a generous use of it languishes in the very sight of the supply.

Primarily, this is because the rulers of the exchange of mankind's goods have failed through their own stubbornness and their own incompetence, have admitted their failure and abdicated. Practices of the unscrupulous money changers stand indicted in the court of public opinion, rejected by the hearts and minds of men.

True, they have tried, but their efforts have been cast in the pattern of an outworn tradition. Faced by failure of credit, they have proposed only the lending of more money. Stripped of the lure of profit by which to induce our people to follow their false leadership, they have resorted to exhortations, pleading tearfully for restored confidence. They know only the rules of a generation of self-seekers. They have no vision, and when there is no vision the people perish.

The money changers have fled from their high seats in the temple of our civilization. We may now restore that temple to the ancient truths.

The measure of the restoration lies in the extent to which we apply social values more noble than mere monetary profit.

Happiness lies not in the mere possession of money; it lies in the joy of achievement, in the thrill of creative effort.

The joy and moral stimulation of work no longer must be forgotten in the mad chase of evanescent profits. These dark days will be worth all they cost us if they teach us that our true destiny is not to be ministered unto but to minister to ourselves and to our fellow men.

Recognition of the falsity of material wealth as the standard of success goes hand in hand with the abandonment of the false belief that public office and high political position are to be valued only by the standards of pride of place and personal profit; and there must be an end to a conduct in banking and in business which too often has given to a sacred trust the likeness of callous and selfish wrongdoing.

Small wonder that confidence languishes, for it thrives only on honesty, on honor, on the sacredness of obligations, on faithful protection, on unselfish performance. Without them it cannot live.

Restoration calls, however, not for changes in ethics alone. This nation asks for action, and action now.

Our greatest primary task is to put people to work. This is no unsolvable problem if we face it wisely and courageously.

It can be accomplished in part by direct recruiting by the government itself, treating the task as we would treat the emergency of a war, but at the same time, through this employment, accomplishing greatly needed projects to stimulate and reorganize the use of our natural resources.

Hand in hand with this, we must frankly recognize the overbalance of population in our industrial centers and, by engaging on a national scale in the redistribution, endeavor to provide a better use of the land for those best fitted for the land.

The task can be helped by definite efforts to raise the values of agricultural products and with this the power to purchase the output of our cities.

It can be helped by preventing realistically the tragedy of the growing loss, through foreclosure, of our small homes and our farms.

It can be helped by insistence that the Federal, State and local governments act forthwith on the demand that their cost be drastically reduced.

It can be helped by the unifying of relief activities which today are often scattered, uneconomical and unequal. It can be helped by national planning for and supervision of all forms of transportation and of communications and other utilities which have a definitely public character.

There are many ways in which it can be helped, but it can never be helped merely by talking about it. We must act, and act quickly.

Finally, in our progress toward a resumption of work we require two safeguards against a return of the evils of the old order; there must be a strict supervision of all banking and credits and investments; there must be an end to speculation with other people's money, and there must be provision for an adequate but sound currency.

There are the lines of attack. I shall presently urge upon a new Congress in special session detailed measures for their fulfillment, and I shall seek the immediate assistance of the several States.

Through this program of action we address ourselves to putting our own national house in order and making income balance outgo.

Our international trade relations, though vastly important, are, in point of time and necessity, secondary to the establishment of a sound national economy.

I favor as a practical policy the putting of first things first. I shall spare no effort to restore world trade by international economic readjustment, but the emergency at home cannot wait on that accomplishment.

The basic thought that guides these specific means of national recovery is not narrowly nationalistic.

It is the insistence, as a first consideration, upon the interdependence of the various elements in, and parts of, the United States—a recognition of the old and permanently important manifestation of the American spirit of the pioneer.

It is the way to recovery. It is the immediate way. It is the strongest assurance that the recovery will endure.

In the field of world policy I would dedicate this nation to the policy of the good neighbor—the neighbor who resolutely respects himself and, because he does so, respects the rights of others—the neighbor who respects his obligations and respects the sanctity of his agreements in and with a world of neighbors.

If I read the temper of our people correctly, we now realize as we have never before, our interdependence on each other; that we cannot merely take, but we must give as well; that if we are to go forward we must move as a trained and loyal army willing to sacrifice for the good of a common discipline, because, without such discipline, no progress is made, no leadership becomes effective.

We are, I know, ready and willing to submit our lives and property to such discipline because it makes possible a leadership which aims at a larger good.

This I propose to offer, pledging that the larger purposes will bind upon us all as a sacred obligation with a unity of duty hitherto evoked only in time of armed strife.

With this pledge taken, I assume unhesitatingly the leadership of this great army of our people, dedicated to a disciplined attack upon our common problems.

Action in this image and to this end is feasible under the form of government which we have inherited from our ancestors.

Our Constitution is so simple and practical that it is possible always to meet extraordinary needs by changes in emphasis and arrangement without loss of essential form.

That is why our constitutional system has proved itself the most superbly enduring political mechanism the modern world has produced. It has met every stress of vast expansion of territory, of foreign wars, of bitter internal strife, of world relations.

It is to be hoped that the normal balance of executive and legislative authority may be wholly adequate to meet the unprecedented task before us. But it may be that an unprecedented demand and need for undelayed action may call for temporary departure from that normal balance of public procedure.

I am prepared under my constitutional duty to recommend the measures that a stricken nation in the midst of a stricken world may require.

These measures, or such other measures as the Congress may build out of its experience and wisdom, I shall seek, within my constitutional authority, to bring to speedy adoption.

But in the event that the Congress shall fail to take one of these two courses, and in the event the national emergency is still critical, I shall not evade the clear course of duty that will then confront me.

I shall ask the Congress for the one remaining instrument to meet the crisis—broad executive power to wage a war against the emergency as great as the power that would be given me if we were in fact invaded by a foreign foe.

For the trust reposed in me I will return the courage and the devotion that befit the time, I can do no less.

We face the arduous days that lie before us in the warm courage of national unity; with the clear consciousness of seeking old and precious moral values; with the clean satisfaction that comes from the stern performance of duty by old and young alike.

We aim at the assurance of a rounded and permanent national life.

We do not distrust the future of essential democracy. The people of the United States have not failed. In their need they have registered a mandate that they want direct, vigorous action.

They have asked for discipline and direction under leadership. They have made me the present instrument of their wishes. In the spirit of the gift I take it.

In this dedication of a nation we humbly ask the blessing of God. May He protect each and every one of us! May He guide me in the days to come!

Questions

1. What did Roosevelt seek to achieve in this address?
2. What do you make of his analogy between wartime and depression circumstances?
3. How do you interpret Roosevelt's religious references?

24-2 Design for Government (1933)

Rexford G. Tugwell

Rexford G. Tugwell (1891–1979) was born in New York and became a professor of economics at Columbia University. Tugwell and other academics such as Raymond C. Moley and Adolf A. Berle Jr. served as advisors to President Roosevelt. The president relied so heavily on their input that they collectively came to be known as the "Brain Trust." In the following excerpt from his book *The Battle for Democracy*, Tugwell makes a case for an activist government.

Source: Excerpt from Rexford G. Tugwell, *The Battle for Democracy* (New York: Columbia University Press, 1935), 12–16. Copyright © 1935 by Columbia University Press. Reprinted with the permission of the publisher.

Let me say that it is my view that what we have done is to rediscover the Constitution, to revitalize the powers it was intended to create, many of which had been obscured in the interest of economic aims and purposes which have now become oppressively obsolete. Those who wrote that great state paper were wise and bold. The best of them, although they disagreed on details, were struggling to meet a crisis which, in some important respects, was not unlike that now confronting us. They were fighting economic disorganization fostered by inadequate centralization. The Constitution, as you recall, was, in effect, a coup d'état; it was adopted in contravention of the Articles of Confederation because the Government set up by those Articles was too weak, too decentralized, to meet contemporary economic necessities.

The governmental pattern set up by the founding fathers was adapted from the British pattern, but with notable modifications. Among them was the grant of wide powers to the Executive at a time when the powers of the Executive in England were declining. And that American set-up—a strong central government with a powerful executive—maintained itself for years, in spite of verbal protests from one political faction or another. Later, a variety of influences led to the rise of an opposed constitutional theory. And part of that new theory was an increased stress on the idea of checks and balances. That idea, in turn, was based on Montesquieu's false description of the workings of the English government. And Montesquieu's misdescription was, in the interest of this new theory, misdescribed and its errors magnified. It was as if an image in a defective mirror had been reflected in another defective mirror.

The resulting false image of a wise government became the controlling design for government in these United States. Governmental action was considered as, at best, a necessary evil. To check and balance government to a point just short of inaction was the desideratum. The prevailing constitutional theory, and therefore the constitutional law, of course corresponded to this prevailing economic outlook.

At the center of this constitutional law was the conception of government as policeman. Government was to stop flagrant abuses, but not, in any circumstances, to do more. It was to be negative and arresting, not positive and stimulating. Its rôle was minor and peripheral. It was important in this one sense: It was to prevent interferences with the competitive system. Behind that system (so it was said and thoroughly believed) was an invisible hand which beneficently guided warring business men to the promotion of the general welfare.

The jig is up. The cat is out of the bag. There is no invisible hand. There never was. If the depression has not taught us that, we are incapable of education. Time was when the anarchy of the competitive struggle was not too costly. Today it is tragically wasteful. It leads to disaster. We must now supply a real and visible guiding hand to do the task which that mythical, nonexistent, invisible agency was supposed to perform, but never did.

Men are, by impulse, predominantly coöperative. They have their competitive impulses, to be sure; but these are normally subordinate. Laissez faire exalted the competitive and maimed the coöperative impulses. It deluded men with the false notion that the sum of many petty struggles was aggregate coöperation. Men were taught to believe that they were, paradoxically, advancing coöperation when they were defying it. That was a viciously false paradox. Of that, today, most of us are convinced and, as a consequence, the coöperative impulse is asserting itself openly and forcibly, no longer content to achieve its ends obliquely and by stealth. We are openly and notoriously on the way to mutual endeavors.

And there is the importance of the rediscovery of the Constitution. We are turning our back on the policeman doctrine of government and recapturing the vision of a government equipped to fight and overcome the forces of economic disintegration. A strong government with an executive amply empowered by legislative delegation is the one way out of our dilemma, and on to the realization of our vast social and economic possibilities.

I have spoken of the resurgence of the coöperative impulse. It has long struggled for more active expression. That struggle might have been unsuccessful. But it is our great good fortune that at the moment when the failure of that struggle would almost surely have meant total collapse, there came into the presidency a man deeply moved by the coöperative impulse. And, above all, it is our good luck that that man was one whose integrity is beyond question.

That point cannot be overemphasized. The success of the new spirit demanded a restoration of power to the Executive. The executive branch of the Government is not a piece of mechanism, it is a body of men. If the new program is to succeed, those men must be wise, able, ingenious and honest. The shift to a new design for government would be a total failure if they were otherwise.

President Roosevelt is establishing, at this most critical period, an enduring pattern of administrative conduct. A lesser man, a self-aggrandizing, humorless one, a person less gifted with administrative talent and less eagerly hungry for wisdom, a dogmatizer without the experimental attitude, would merely have aroused false hopes which his accomplishments would have destroyed. The new design, with its unavoidable stress on vigorous governmental administration, possesses promise of endurance because it found precisely the right man. He is creating a lasting standard of administrative conduct below which none of his successors will dare to fall.

It is rather common to hear praise and criticism in one breath these days. The program is deplored because of its departures from tradition; the shaper and administrator of the program is praised because he embodies all those traits which we like to think of as American. But this is an antithesis which cannot be allowed. If praise is due for what he does, praise also is due for the program which permits the doing. The Executive is inseparable from his program—not any single part of it, but the total attempt to meet exigencies as, he has said, the football quarterback meets them, with power to do the expedient thing, to advance or to withdraw, creating strategy as the need for it appears.

There is nothing in all this which violates the spirit of our Constitution. As Mr. Justice Brandeis has said, "We do not need to amend the Constitution, we need to amend men's minds." And Mr. Justice Holmes, following in the footsteps of Marshall, has reminded us to remember always that it is a Constitution with which we are dealing and that "The Constitution was not designed to establish for all time any particular economic theory, whether of the organic relationship of the individual to the state or of laissez-faire." It is an experiment as all life is an experiment. We shall follow resolutely wherever the dictates of our minds propose. In the noble language of Mr. Justice Brandeis, "If we would guide by the light of reason, we must let our minds be bold."

Questions

1. What did Tugwell mean when he said that the New Deal rediscovered the Constitution?
2. According to Tugwell, what was the new spirit or new design for government? What was the old spirit?

24-3 *Business Week* Editorial (1933)

In 1933, the worldwide collapse of laissez-faire, or free-market, capitalism was spectacular and painfully evident. To many, the way out of this great slump was to turn to the federal government, or more accurately, the U.S. nation-state, which was potentially a very powerful organization, and use it in ways that had never before been tried in peacetime.

Source: Excerpt from David F. Burg, *The Great Depression: An Eyewitness History* (New York: Facts on File, 1996), 139. Reprinted with permission from Facts on File.

There is general agreement among the leading businessmen who have appeared before the congressional hearings that something must be done to regulate hours, pay, production, and prices. Even more convincing are the results of a questionnaire conducted by Cornell. Most of the leading businessmen questioned felt that the times demand drastic reorganization designed to reduce to a minimum the effects of the business cycle, to increase the stability of employment, and to insure adequate purchasing power. A minimum wage is necessary to prevent the unscrupulous from exploiting labor. Any plan devised to reach these ends must have in mind raising the standard of living of the country as a whole.

Question

1. The editorial called for a national recovery program instead of one based on individual initiative, assistance to a particular industry or sector, or help to a specific region. How was it national in scope?

24-4 Criticism of a U.S. Supreme Court Decision (1935)

Franklin D. Roosevelt

In a press conference on May 31, 1935, the president commented at length on a May 27 U.S. Supreme Court decision, *Schechter v. United States*, which completed the dismantling of the National Industrial Recovery Act (NIRA) begun in *Panama Refining Co. v. Ryan*. Key issues included the "delegation of legislative power to the executive," the distinction between interstate and intrastate commerce, and the extent of emergency government power. Chief Justice Charles Evans Hughes wrote the unanimous opinion.

This press conference was Roosevelt's 209th. Like his less frequent radio addresses and "fireside chats," these conferences were weapons in FDR's political arsenal. "Mr. Stephenson" is Francis Stephenson, a journalist, and "Mr. Early" is Stephen Early, Roosevelt's press secretary. The "old Knight case" to which FDR refers is *United States v. E. C. Knight*, decided in 1895, not 1885. (On the NIRA and *Schechter*, see text pp. 738–742, 744–745.)

Source: "The Two Hundred and Ninth Press Conference, May 31, 1935," in Samuel I. Rosenman, ed., *The Public Papers and Addresses of Franklin D. Roosevelt*, 4, *The Court Disapproves, 1935* (New York: Random House, 1938), 200–222.

... Now, coming down to the decision itself. What are the implications? For the benefit of those of you who haven't read it through I think I can put it this way: the implications of this decision are much more important than almost certainly any decision of my lifetime or yours, more important than any decision probably since the Dred Scott case, because they bring the country as a whole up against a very practical question. That is in spite of what one gentleman said in the paper this morning, that I resented the decision. Nobody resents a Supreme Court decision. You can deplore a Supreme Court decision, and you can point out the effect of it. You can call the attention of the country to what the implications are as to the future, what the results of that decision are if future decisions follow this decision. . . .

Now, they [the justices] have pointed out in regard to this particular Act that it was unconstitutional because it delegated certain powers which should have been written into the Act itself. And then there is this interesting language that bears that out. It is on page eight.

We are told that the provisions of the statute authorizing the adoption of the codes must be viewed in the light of the grave national crisis with which Congress was confronted. Undoubtedly, the conditions to which power is addressed are always to be considered when the exercise of power is challenged. Extraordinary conditions may call for extraordinary remedies. But the argument necessarily stops short of an attempt to justify action which lies outside the sphere of constitutional authority. Extraordinary conditions do not create or enlarge constitutional power.

Of course, that is a very interesting implication. Some of us are old enough to remember the war days—the legislation that was passed in April, May and June of 1917. Being a war, that legislation was never brought before the Supreme Court. Of course, as a matter of fact, a great deal of that legislation was far more violative of the strict interpretation of the Constitution than any legislation that was passed in 1933. All one has to do is to go back and read those war acts which conferred upon the Executive far greater power over human beings and over property than anything that was done in 1933. But the Supreme Court has finally ruled that extraordinary conditions do not create or enlarge constitutional power! It is a very interesting statement on the part of the Court.

However, the question of the delegation of legislative power is not so very important in this particular case because the Supreme Court has at least intimated that in so far as the delegation of power was concerned, the language of the Act could have been so improved as to give definite directions to administrative or quasi-judicial bodies and in that respect it refers to the methods already used in the case of the Federal Trade Commission and cites that with approval.

In other words, for the future the delegation of power is not an unsurmountable object, and undoubtedly an Act could be written which would in general conform to this opinion of the Supreme Court as to delegated powers—get that! So that is not the most serious implication yet.

However, you come down to something else which is the most important implication, and that relates to interstate commerce....

Let's put the decision in plain lay language in regard to at least the dictum of the Court and never mind this particular sick chicken or whatever they call it. That was a question of fact, but of course the Court in ruling on the question of fact about these particular chickens said they were killed in New York and sold and probably eaten in New York, and therefore it was probably intrastate commerce. But of course the Court does not stop there. In fact the Court in this decision, at least by dictum—and remember that dictum is not always followed in the future—has gone back to the old Knight case in 1885, which in fact limited any application of interstate commerce to goods in transit—nothing else!

Since 1885 the Court in various decisions has enlarged on the definition of interstate commerce—railroad cases, coal cases and so forth and so on. It was clearly the opinion of the Congress before this decision and the opinion of various attorneys-general, regardless of party, that the words "interstate commerce" applied not only to an actual shipment of goods but also to a great many other things that affected interstate commerce....

The whole tendency over these years has been to view the interstate commerce clause in the light of present-day civilization. The country was in the horse-and-buggy age when that clause was written and if you go back to the debates on the Federal Constitution you will find in 1787 that one of the impelling motives for putting in that clause was this: There wasn't much interstate commerce at all—probably 80 or 90 percent of the human beings in the thirteen original States were completely self-supporting within their own communities....

In other words, the whole picture was a different one when the interstate commerce clause was put into the Constitution from what it is now. Since that time, because of the improvement in transportation, because of the fact that, as we know, what happens in one State has a good deal of influence on the people in another State, we have developed an entirely different philosophy.

The prosperity of the farmer does have an effect today on the manufacturer in Pittsburgh. The prosperity of the clothing worker in the city of New York has an effect on the prosperity of the farmer in Wisconsin, and so it goes. We are interdependent—we are tied in together. And the hope has been that we could, through a period of years, interpret the interstate commerce clause of the Constitution in the light of these new things that have come to the country. It has been our hope that under the interstate commerce clause we could recognize by legislation and by judicial decision that a harmful practice in one section of the country could be prevented on the theory that it was doing harm to another section of the country. That was why the Congress for a good many years, and most lawyers, have had the thought that in drafting legislation we could depend on an interpretation that would enlarge the Constitutional meaning of interstate commerce to include not only those matters of direct interstate commerce, but also those matters which indirectly affect interstate commerce....

You see the implications of the decision. That is why I say it is one of the most important decisions ever rendered in this country. And the issue is not going to be a partisan issue for a minute. The issue is going to be whether we go one way or the other. Don't call it right or left; that is just first-year high-school language, just about. It is not right or left—it is a question for national decision on a very important problem of Government. We are the only Nation in the world that has not solved that problem. We thought we were solving it, and now it has been thrown right straight in our faces. We have been relegated to the horse-and-buggy definition of interstate commerce....

Q. (Mr. Stephenson) Can we use the direct quotation on that horse-and-buggy stage?

The President: I think so.

Mr. Early: Just the phrase.

Q. You referred to the Dred Scott decision. That was followed by the Civil War and by at least two amendments to the Constitution.

The President: Well, the reason for that, of course, was the fact that the generation of 1856 did not take action during the next four years.

Questions

1. How did Roosevelt criticize key arguments of the Supreme Court?
2. Why did he refer to the *Dred Scott* decision? to the "horse-and-buggy age" and the "horse-and-buggy definition of interstate commerce"? to laws passed during 1917?

24-5 The Long Plan (1933)

Huey P. Long

To his supporters, Senator Huey P. Long (1893–1935) of Louisiana (see text pp. 744–745) was a saint; to his enemies, he was Satan. Long referred to himself simply as "the Kingfish." Until an assassin murdered him, Long and his brand of populism seemed strong enough to pose a threat to FDR's winning a second term. Long titled his autobiography *Every Man a King*. Following is his plan to make that vision a reality.

Source: From Huey P. Long, *Every Man a King: The Autobiography of Huey P. Long* (1933; Chicago: Quadrangle Books, 1964), 338–340. Reprinted with permission.

THE MADDENED FORTUNE HOLDERS AND THEIR INFURIATED PUBLIC PRESS!

The increasing fury with which I have been, and am to be, assailed by reason of the fight and growth of support for limiting the size of fortunes can only be explained by the madness which human nature attaches to the holders of accumulated wealth.

What I have proposed is:—

THE LONG PLAN

1. A capital levy tax on the property owned by any one person of 1% of all over $1,000,000; 2% of all over $2,000,000 etc., until, when it reaches fortunes of over $100,000,000, the government takes all above that figure; which means a limit on the size of any one man's fortune to something like $50,000,000—the balance to go to the government to spread out in its work among all the people.

2. An inheritance tax which does not allow any one person to receive more than $5,000,000 in a lifetime without working for it, all over that amount to go to the government to be spread among the people for its work.

3. An income tax which does not allow any one man to make more than $1,000,000 in one year, exclusive of taxes, the balance to go to the United States for general work among the people.

The foregoing program means all taxes paid by the fortune holders at the top and none by the people at the bottom; the spreading of wealth among all the people and the breaking up of a system of Lords and Slaves in our economic life. It allows the millionaires to have, however, more than they can use for any luxury they can enjoy on earth. But, with such limits, all else can survive.

That the public press should regard my plan and effort as a calamity and me as a menace is no more than should be expected, gauged in the light of past events. . . .

In 1932, the vote for my resolution showed possibly a half dozen other Senators back of it. It grew in the last Congress to nearly twenty Senators. Such growth through one other year will mean the success of a venture, the completion of everything I have undertaken,—the time when I can and will retire from the stress and fury of my public life, maybe as my forties begin,—a contemplation so serene as to appear impossible.

That day will reflect credit on the States whose Senators took the early lead to spread the wealth of the land among all the people.

Then no tear dimmed eyes of a small child will be lifted into the saddened face of a father or mother unable to give it the necessities required by its soul and body for life; then the powerful will be rebuked in the sight of man for holding that which they cannot consume, but which is craved to sustain humanity; the food of the land will feed, the raiment clothe, and the houses shelter all the people; the powerful will be elated by the well being of all, rather than through their greed.

Then, those of us who have pursued that phantom of Jefferson, Jackson, Webster, Theodore Roosevelt and Bryan may hear wafted from their lips in Valhalla:

EVERY MAN A KING

Questions

1. What was Long proposing?
2. Who was most likely to support him? Why?
3. Was Long arguing for reform or revolution? In your answer, consider the status of the rich under the Long Plan.

Questions for Further Thought

1. Compare FDR's inaugural address (Document 24-1) with the *Business Week* magazine editorial (Document 24-3). To what extent do they make the same argument?
2. Compare and contrast Rexford G. Tugwell's "Design for Government" (Document 24-2) with Herbert Hoover's Plan (Document 23-12).

The Second New Deal, 1935–1938

The Second New Deal initially involved a leftward shift in Congress (the Democrats had gained additional House seats in 1934) and in the administration, which was under attack from the right for what it had done and under pressure from the left for what it had not done. In 1935, Congress took the lead in enacting the National Labor Relations Act to assist the labor movement, and the administration took the lead in passing the Social Security Act to provide old-age pensions, unemployment compensation, and assistance to the "deserving poor." These laws were to become part of the New Deal's legacy. In a landslide victory one year later, Roosevelt won reelection, while his party added to its congressional majority.

Roosevelt's second term proved to be less successful than his first. His early 1937 proposal to enlarge the Supreme Court aroused widespread opposition. A sharp economic downturn during 1937 and 1938, the so-called Roosevelt recession, damaged the president, his administration, and his party. The Democratic Party itself was increasingly divided between liberals (mostly northern and urban) and conservatives (mostly southern and rural). As a consequence, in 1937 and 1938, only a few New Deal measures passed Congress. During 1938, FDR failed to unseat conservative Democratic congressional opponents in party primary elections and the Republicans registered gains in midterm elections. Clearly, the New Deal tide that had flowed in 1935 and 1936 ebbed in 1937 and 1938, resulting in a lasting political stalemate (see text pp. 748–749).

Document 24-6 offers the dissenting opinion of Justice Harlan F. Stone in the 1936 decision of the Supreme Court that struck down the Agricultural Adjustment Act of 1933. Stone defended the constitutionality of this key piece of New Deal legislation. Document 24-7 provides portions of the 1936 Republican and Democratic national platforms, while Document 24-8 provides the Socialist Party's critique of the New Deal. Document 24-9 reveals the concern of southern Democrats over a proposed federal antilynching law early in 1938.

24-6 Dissenting Opinion, *United States v. Butler* (1936)

Harlan F. Stone

Unlike *Schechter*, a number of controversial cases before the Supreme Court during the mid-1930s were decided, one way or the other, by divided votes. (Before FDR's first appointment to the high court in 1937, it comprised four justices predictably opposed to the New Deal, two generally but not always opposed, and three sometimes though by no means always supportive of New Deal measures.) In *Butler*, a six-justice majority declared unconstitutional a tax on agricultural processors that was central to the Agricultural Adjustment Act of 1933 (see text pp. 739–742). Justice Harlan F. Stone (1872–1946) sharply dissented from that opinion.

Source: United States v. Butler, 297 U.S. 1 (1936), excerpted in Donald O. Dewey, ed., *Union and Liberty: A Documentary History of American Constitutionalism* (New York: McGraw-Hill, 1969), 236.

1. The power of courts to declare a statute unconstitutional is subject to two guiding principles of decision which ought never to be absent from judicial consciousness. One is that courts are concerned only with the power to enact statutes, not with their wisdom. The other is that while unconstitutional exercise of power by the executive and legislative branches of the government is subject to judicial restraint, the only check upon our own exercise of power is our own sense of self-restraint. For the removal of unwise laws from the statute books appeal lies not to the courts but to the ballot and to the processes of democratic government.

2. The constitutional power of Congress to levy an excise tax upon the processing of agricultural products is not questioned. The present levy is held invalid, not for any want of power in Congress to lay such a tax to defray public expenditures, including those for the general welfare, but because the use to which its proceeds are put is disapproved.

. . . "Let the end be legitimate," said the great Chief Justice, "let it be within the scope of the Constitution, and all means which are appropriate, which are plainly adapted to that end, which are not prohibited, but consistent with the letter and spirit of the Constitution, are constitutional." *McCulloch v. Maryland.* This cardinal guide to constitutional exposition must now be rephrased so far as the spending power of the federal government is concerned. Let the expenditure be to promote the general welfare, still, if it is needful in order to insure its use for the intended purpose to influence any action which Congress cannot command because within the sphere of state government, the expenditure is unconstitutional. And taxes otherwise lawfully levied are likewise unconstitutional if they are appropriated to the expenditure whose incident is condemned. . . .

. . . Courts are not the only agency of government that must be assumed to have capacity to govern. Congress and the courts both unhappily may falter or be mistaken in the performance of their constitutional duty. But interpretation of our great charter of government which proceeds on any assumption that the responsibility for the preservation of our institutions is the exclusive concern of any one of the three branches of government, or that it alone can save them from destruction is far more likely, in the long run, "to obliterate the constituent members" of "an indestructible union of indestructible states" than the frank recognition that language, even of a constitution, may mean what it says: that the power to tax and spend includes the power to relieve a nationwide economic maladjustment by conditional gifts of money.

Questions

1. What is the thrust of Stone's argument regarding judicial "self-restraint"?
2. In what ways, if any, does Stone's opinion resemble President Franklin D. Roosevelt's press conference remarks (Document 24-4)?

24-7 Republican and Democratic National Platforms (1936)

In 1936, the Republicans nominated Alfred M. Landon and Colonel Frank Knox for president and vice president, each on the first ballot. The Democrats renominated Franklin D. Roosevelt and John Nance Garner by acclamation. Before his nomination, Landon telegraphed the Republican convention to express agreement with the platform but advocated a constitutional amendment to safeguard women and children in the workplace and to establish wage and hour standards in case the courts struck down pending legislation. The Democratic platform chided the Republican document for proposing state action to cope with national problems and recommended a "clarifying amendment" if necessary to ensure that federal and state governments could constitutionally enact necessary legislation. The portions of the national platforms excerpted here reveal the depths of partisan differences over the New Deal.

Source: Donald Bruce Johnson, comp., *National Party Platforms*, rev. ed., 2 vols. (Urbana: University of Illinois Press, 1978), 1:360, 365–366.

REPUBLICAN

America is in peril. The welfare of American men and women and the future of our youth are at stake. We dedicate ourselves to the preservation of their political liberty, their individual opportunity and their character as free citizens, which today for the first time are threatened by Government itself.

For three long years the New Deal Administration has dishonored American traditions and flagrantly betrayed the pledges upon which the Democratic Party sought and received public support.

The powers of Congress have been usurped by the President.

The integrity and authority of the Supreme Court have been flouted.

The rights and liberties of American citizens have been violated.

Regulated monopoly has displaced free enterprise.

The New Deal Administration constantly seeks to usurp the rights reserved to the States and to the people.

It has insisted on the passage of laws contrary to the Constitution.

It has intimidated witnesses and interfered with the right of petition.

It has dishonored our country by repudiating its most sacred obligations.

It has been guilty of frightful waste and extravagance, using public funds for partisan political purposes.

It has promoted investigations to harass and intimidate American citizens, at the same time denying investigations into its own improper expenditures.

It has created a vast multitude of new offices, filled them with its favorites, set up a centralized bureaucracy, and sent out swarms of inspectors to harass our people.

It has bred fear and hesitation in commerce and industry, thus discouraging new enterprises, preventing employment and prolonging the depression.

It secretly has made tariff agreements with our foreign competitors, flooding our markets with foreign commodities.

It has coerced and intimidated voters by withholding relief to those opposing its tyrannical policies.

It has destroyed the morale of our people and made them dependent upon government.

Appeals to passion and class prejudice have replaced reason and tolerance.

To a free people, these actions are insufferable. This campaign cannot be waged on the traditional differences between the Republican and Democratic parties. The responsibility of this election transcends all previous political divisions. We invite all Americans, irrespective of party, to join us in defense of American institutions.

DEMOCRATIC

We hold this truth to be self-evident—that the test of a representative government is its ability to promote the safety and happiness of the people.

We hold this truth to be self-evident—that 12 years of Republican leadership left our Nation sorely stricken in body, mind, and spirit: and that three years of Democratic leadership have put it back on the road to restored health and prosperity.

We hold this truth to be self-evident—that 12 years of Republican surrender to the dictatorship of a privileged few have been supplanted by a Democratic leadership which has returned the people themselves to the places of authority, and has revived in them new faith and restored the hope which they had almost lost.

We hold this truth to be self-evident—that this three-year recovery in all the basic values of life and the reestablishment of the American way of living has been brought about by humanizing the policies of the Federal Government as they affect the personal, financial, industrial, and agricultural well-being of the American people.

We hold this truth to be self-evident—that government in a modern civilization has certain inescapable obligations to its citizens, among which are:

(1) Protection of the family and the home.

(2) Establishment of a democracy of opportunity for all the people.

(3) Aid to those overtaken by disaster.

These obligations, neglected through 12 years of the old leadership, have once more been recognized by American Government. Under the new leadership they will never be neglected.

Questions

1. What appeals to emotion do the platforms make?
2. Identify New Deal measures that were indicted by the Republicans.
3. Identify New Deal measures that fit into one or more of the three "inescapable obligations" of government enumerated by the Democrats.

24-8 What Was the New Deal? (1936)

Norman Thomas

Norman Thomas (1884–1968) was a Presbyterian pastor and pacifist who joined the Socialist Party in 1918. He became the party's leader in 1926, after the death of Eugene V. Debs (Document 17-10), four-time presidential candidate on the Socialist ticket. Thomas would receive his party's nomination for the presidency six times. Although he was handily defeated in each election, he represented a dissenting voice and helped to found what would become the American Civil Liberties Union. In the following excerpt, Thomas clearly distinguishes the New Deal from the Socialist Party's positions on the leading issues of the day.

Source: Excerpt from Norman Thomas, *After the New Deal, What?* (New York: Macmillan Company, 1936), 16–25. Copyright © 1936 by The Macmillan Company and renewed 1963 by Norman Thomas. Reprinted with the permission of the publisher.

It is a testimony to the economic illiteracy of America that the New Deal has been called almost everything from communism and socialism to fascism. Or, as one editor put it: "Socialism or Fascism—What's the difference? We don't like it." Actually the New Deal is, or rather was, an experimental attempt at reformed capitalism. Part of the time Mr. Roosevelt talked, and practiced very little, the gospel of the virtue of smallness. Little business was, he has said or implied, pretty good. His effort to break up big utility holding companies looked in that direction. He made gestures toward it in some of his tax proposals. His declaration of a war of liberation against "economic dynasties" in his acceptance speech can be interpreted as a modern renewal of the struggle of the individual against the growth of concentration of control in the hands of the masters of finance capital. But his main reliance has been state capitalism; that is a degree of government ownership and a much greater degree of government regulation of economic enterprises for the sake of bolstering up the profit system.

It was not socialism. The argument to the contrary was born partly from the American delusion that government ownership equals socialism and government regulation approaches it. That depends, of course, on who owns the government, and for what purpose the government owns industry: for war and militarism; for greater security of banking as a better instrument of the profit system, or for the sake of planned abundance for all.

There is, however, more definite reason why "Mr. John Q. Public" should think the New Deal and Mr. Roosevelt's present efforts are socialistic. He has been told so in various accounts by Mr. David Lawrence, Mr. Alfred Emanuel Smith and Mr. James P. Warburg, whose book *Hell Bent for Election* has been circulated as a campaign document. In Denver one of my Socialist friends was assured by a woman that it was entirely unnecessary for her to hear Mr. Thomas talk about socialism. She knew all about it. Mr. Warburg's book had told her that the New Deal was socialism and she knew all about the New Deal!

Now as everybody knows, or ought to know, the essence of socialism lies in the end of the class division of income; that is, in planned production for the general use rather than for the private profit of an owning class. Such planned production requires the social ownership of the great natural resources and the principal means of production and distribution. To this principle Mr. Roosevelt has not even professed allegiance; rather he has declared his support of a profit system that in one of his official addresses he inaccurately defined. Only in the Tennessee Valley Authority is there an approximation of a socialist approach to a great economic problem. For the rest Mr. Roosevelt put the banks in order and turned them back to the bankers; he set an able administrator or co-ordinator, Mr. Joseph B. Eastman, over the railroads, not to socialize them but to help to pull them out of depression primarily for the benefit of private stockholders whose railway holdings will thereby be made more expensive if and when the government takes them over.

That such a program should be confused with socialism by special pleaders like Mr. Warburg is perhaps in part the fault of European socialists who in office have so often been concerned only with reforms attainable within capitalism. It may be a little our fault in America that in our Socialist platform of 1932 we did not distinguish more plainly between immediate demands and our essential revolutionary purpose. But only a little. The Socialist platform of 1932 in its opening paragraphs gives the Socialist diagnosis of poverty and insecurity. It declares for socialization in more than one section. Mr. Warburg makes a plausible case that Mr. Roosevelt has carried out the Socialist platform by a highly selective choice of Socialist demands, and by a very superficial test of what it would mean to carry out effectively even those demands to which Mr. Roosevelt apparently paid some heed.

For example, during years of boondoggling and other forms of made work, public housing in the sense in which we Socialists developed our demand for it in 1932 and 1933 was grossly neglected. Only toward the end of the four-year term did Senator Wagner introduce his inadequate public housing bill which was not on the President's *must* list. Congress adjourned without passing it. The next Congress, even assuming Mr. Roosevelt's election, is likely to be less, not more, progressive in this matter. With a third of our people housed in shacks and slums fit only for destruction, the builders and the workers in materials were kept in unemployment on a miserable dole or some form of improvised or comparatively non-essential public work. And they call this socialism!

Or, to take an even more striking example: When the President finally got around to security legislation, long dear to the hearts of Socialists, he took the name rather than the substance of any Socialist proposal. Intelligent Socialists vigorously repudiate any responsibility for the President's so-called Security Bill. This omnibus measure neglects altogether the vital matter of health insurance or any equivalent for it. Its immediate allowance to the states for old age assistance is meager. The reserve to be set up for old age insurance is very large and the manner of its investment makes for a dangerous degree of political control over business in the future, without in the least changing the basic principles of that control from those appropriate to capitalism to those which would be necessary under a cooperative commonwealth.

Worst of all, however, is the treatment given to unemployment insurance. The federal government has set a certain tax on payrolls; ninety per cent of this tax to be rebated to employers who may come under state unemployment insurance schemes for the support of such schemes. Under the most favorable circumstances, the amount thus rebated cannot provide more than a fifteen-week period of insurance at a rate not to exceed $15 a week. The plan would work out somewhat as follows:

If you are now unemployed your chance of being helped by unemployment insurance depends upon your getting a job. You must hold a job while the reserve piles up in the Federal Treasury and while the state of which you are a citizen works out its own unemployment insurance plan. Then if you lose the job you may possibly get $15 a week for fifteen weeks provided the optimistic calculations of the amount to be received are correct, and provided your particular state takes advantage of the law and sets up its own machinery for insurance. There are forty-eight states. There will be forty-eight different systems—if all the states get around to providing unemployment insurance which is more than all of them have yet done in the case of workmen's compensation. There will be enormous confusion. The benefits to the unemployed will be kept down because of the fear of each state that adequate insurance measures will drive corporations into the borders of other states less generous in their treatment of the workers. The payroll tax itself will to a large extent be passed on to consumers; that is, the workers themselves, in an increase in prices. It will be added to the immense volume of indirect taxation or of sales taxes under which the American worker now struggles. Moreover the tax on employers as the sole support of unemployment insurance will inevitably spur them to reduce it by reducing the number of their employees. It will stimulate technological unemployment.

This is not socialism—not even what Mr. David Lawrence calls "unconscious socialism." The most that one can say is that in 1933 President Roosevelt had to act in a crisis. The principles to guide any effective action were not to be found in his own platform, and certainly not in the musty Republican document. Like many a politician before him, he had to turn to ideas advanced by Socialists. The trouble is not that he took some of them, but that he took so few and carried them out so unsatisfactorily. The moral of the tale is that if you want a child brought up right you better leave him with his parents, not turn him over to unsympathetic strangers.

But if what Mr. Roosevelt has given us is not socialism, neither is it fascism. The New Deal has gone a long way toward the economics of state capitalism which are the economics of fascism when it comes to power. A well-informed Italian journalist, a visitor in this country, told me that Roosevelt's achievements were not only in line with Mussolini's ideal of the corporative state, but that Mr. Roosevelt had gone so far in his first year that he had actually spurred Mussolini to action. He had good grounds for his argument. But fascism while it arises out of the economic distress of the middle class is not of itself primarily an economic program. It is an extra-legal revolutionary, or rather counter-revolutionary, effort of the middle class, led by a demagogue, to use the power of the state and the religion of nationalism to maintain its own status and, for a while longer, the grossly unequal division of the social income which the profit system has created and still maintains. In power the fascist demagogue as dictator does not satisfy the little men of the middle class by splitting things up. He operates, because he has to, under the forms of state capitalism, but his appeal is not to the excellencies of state capitalism as an economic device; it is to the national pride of his people. Mr. Roosevelt has not given or sought to give us the equivalent of a fascist dictatorship. This or that thing which has been done under or during his Administration can justly be called fascist in tendency. The President's economics are in action, if not in intention, more nearly the economics of fascism than of socialism. Yet he himself is less clearly a forerunner of fascism than was such a demagogue as Huey Long. Of this we shall have more to say in later chapters. Here we are absolving the New Deal of fascism.

Intelligent and sympathetic critics of the New Deal will agree with me that the New Deal is neither socialism nor fascism, but will vehemently deny that it is dead. Despite the Supreme Court they maintain that it still has some coherent shape of which N.R.A. and A.A.A. were not an essential part. Just what that shape is they are somewhat vague in describing. Of course, if all we are to understand by the New Deal is the President's willingness to sponsor more relief and social welfare legislation and to spend more on these causes than Mr. Hoover; his rather friendly attitude to organized labor; his occasionally resentful attitude toward the United States Chamber of Commerce; and his professed desire to befriend the "little man"—some of which he has incorporated into law and some of which, perhaps, he has impressed on his party—the New Deal is not dead. It is one more expression of an uncritical, moralizing progressivism like the first Roosevelt's Square Deal or Wilson's New Democracy. But for a time the New Deal seemed to have more definite outline and structure than that. Our criticism is that the New Deal if it is alive in this vaguely progressive sense has not been successful. Certainly it has solved no basic problem.

What it has done is to let in some of the farmers—by no means all—on the old game of subsidy; begin some excellent work in protecting the soil from erosion; give some recognition to organized labor and try to write into law its right to organize and bargain collectively; abate—at least while N.R.A. lasted—child labor, long hours, and sweatshop wages; lend money on fairly easy terms to home owners; give some protection to bank depositors and investors and speculators in the stock market; ease a little the money stringency and the burden of debt by devaluing the dollar; definitely assume some federal responsibility for social security and immediate unemployment relief through public work and outright doles; set up T.V.A. in the electric power field, and pass drastic legislation against holding companies. Incidentally it gave a genuine New Deal to the original Americans, the Indians.

How this has been done is a subject for criticism in this book. I believe that on the whole Mr. Roosevelt did more for such temporary capitalist "recovery" as we have than for reform. Nevertheless, for the liberal believer in a possible "good" capitalism the list records a notable effort at reform. To one who faces the American economic and political scene realistically, despite the program's serious theoretical and practical shortcomings, it was as much of an achievement along its own line and within capitalist limits as we could reasonably expect in a country where labor unions and other forces desiring change were so weak. It stands in sharp contrast to the Hoover record. That it is fundamentally a failure, is not primarily its fault as a New Deal of the old capitalist deck; it is the fault of the whole game. Neither the Old Deal nor the New Deal, nor any variant of them, can bring us plenty, peace, and freedom as long as our magnificent machinery is geared to the production of profit for private owners—most of them absentee owners. It is impossible to keep that system which depends upon relative scarcity and get the good society. This is the theme of our argument.

Questions

1. According to Thomas, the New Deal was neither socialism nor fascism. Explain.
2. Explain what Thomas meant by comparing the New Deal with Theodore Roosevelt's Square Deal and Woodrow Wilson's New Democracy or New Freedom.
3. What did Thomas criticize and praise about the New Deal?

24-9 The Federal Antilynching Bills (1938)

Changes in the national Democratic Party and the federal government during the New Deal cost the Democrats' southern wing a measure of influence. However, that wing remained potent, especially when, beginning in 1937, it worked with other conservative Democrats and the Republicans to thwart New Deal initiatives and even reverse programs. When Republicans and northern Democrats (*not* the administration) pushed a federal antilynching measure through the House of Representatives during 1937, southern Democrats blocked its enactment in the Senate the next year. In doing so, they revealed the importance of race to their wing of the party (see text pp. 752–754, 763).

This selection comprises *Time*'s coverage of the Wagner–Van Nuys Bill in the Senate and the *New York Times*'s report of the January 10, 1938, speech of Senator Pat Harrison, a Mississippi Democrat.

Source: Time (January 24, 1938): 7–8; "Anti-Lynch Bill Splits Leaders" from *The New York Times* (January 11, 1938), 18. Copyright © 1938 by The New York Times Co. Reprinted with permission from The New York Times Co.

(a) The Wagner–Van Nuys Bill

... Last spring under the spur of the two blow-torch lynchings at Duck Hill, Miss. (*Time*, April 26), the Gavagan Bill, a similar anti-lynching measure, passed the House. Passage by the Senate therefore meant that the bill would become law barring the unlikely event of a Presidential veto. So as predicted, Texas' Tom Connally promptly organized a filibuster. Not as predicted, that filibuster last week rounded out ten days and had gathered so much momentum that Tom Connally jubilantly announced he would keep it going if necessary until Christmas.

Filibuster. The actual contents of the Wagner-Van Nuys Bill, as simple as they were familiar, would scarcely keep the U.S. Senate busy for that period. Like its predecessors, it provided for Federal prosecution, and a $5,000 fine or up to five years' imprisonment, or both, for sheriffs & peace officers who did not afford criminals and suspected criminals reasonable protection from mobs (any gatherings of more than three persons). Its other principal provision, the payment of an indemnity up to $10,000 to the family of a victim of mob violence by the county whose officials are responsible, is already in the statute books of twelve States. ...

(b) The 1938 Speech of Senator Pat Harrison

ANTI-LYNCH BILL SPLITS LEADERS

Harrison, Using Bitter Irony, Says Some Back Measure for Political Gain

GIVES WARNING TO PARTY

Asks It Keep Faith With South — Assails Plan as Wedge for New Curbs on States

SPECIAL TO THE NEW YORK TIMES.

WASHINGTON, Jan. 10.—The racial issue over which the North and South have long differed drove today a deep cleavage in the Senate leadership when Senator Harrison assailed colleagues with whom he long had worked closely for sponsoring the Wagner Anti-lynching Bill. He spoke with blunt irony of members to whom he ascribed Presidential or Supreme Court ambitions and asked them if for the sake of votes they would "betray" the South.

"Is the faith of the South to be broken?" he asked. "Is its love for the Democratic party to be shattered and its devotion to those who have made that party great to be dissipated?"

But while he pleaded in this manner, the greater part of his speech, which consumed an hour, was scathing in its comment and as blunt as any he ever delivered in his attacks on former Republican Administrations.

"Let me say to all aspiring gentlemen in this body who may retain some hope of becoming the nominee of the Democratic party," he declared, "that they had best stop, look and listen. It is always better to put advocacy of a question upon better and higher grounds than that."

WARNS AMBITIOUS

"And those sweet, amiable gentlemen who every time a newspaper correspondent calls them go out with a fluttering of the heart because they think news has come from the White House that their nomination is going to be sent to the Senate to fill the vacancy on the Supreme Court caused by the resignation of Mr. Justice Sutherland, had better beware. They do not add to their standing as lawyers or their qualifications for places on the highest tribunal in this land by voting for such a legislative monstrosity as that now pending before the Senate, which destroys the dual form of government and robs the States of their sovereignty."

Senator Harrison maintained that "this bill will not appease anybody," and that, despite that, "we see the people of the South confronted with the terrible situation of a Democratic majority betraying the trust of the Southern people, destroying the things that they have idolized and in which they believe.

"The groups that form the Society for the Advancement of the Colored Race and others may be satisfied with it for a little while; those who are advocating the bill here may win favor with them for a little while, but paid lobbyists and representatives of these organized groups are never quiet; they must be active. They must be busy and when they have had this work performed, they must get to work upon another thing.

PICTURES POSIBILITIES [SIC.]

"I read the other day that the Negro Representative from Illinois had introduced a bill to abolish Jim Crow car laws in the States, to abolish those laws which provide for the segregation of the races. The next thing in all probability will be a bill to provide that miscegenation of the races cannot be prohibited, and when that has been accomplished they will come back here and seek the help of the majority party in power to take away from the States the right to say who shall vote in their elections, to say that every colored man in every Southern State should take part in the primaries in the State."

Questions

1. On what fears did Harrison play to gain support for opposition to the federal anti-lynching bill?
2. Harrison referred to "primaries" as well as "elections" in his speech. What was the importance of Democratic Party primary elections in the South during the 1930s?

Question for Further Thought

1. Compare Documents 24-6, 24-7, 24-8, and 24-9. Are there any similarities in the descriptions of the role of the federal government in regulating the American economy and society? How do the views presented differ?

The New Deal's Impact on Society

New Deal governmental policies would affect the nation for decades, even to the present. The federal government assumed a larger role in the economy, which continued to be based on the private sector, and with it a larger presence in the lives and minds of Americans. Agriculture and labor organizations received lasting recognition; for a time, the creative and performing arts were encouraged by government. A rudimentary welfare state came into existence, and the Democratic Party, which had come to national power during the Great Depression, remained the nation's majority party for more than two decades following the death of FDR (see text pp. 749–763).

A range of groups that contributed to and benefited from the New Deal merit attention in their own right. Women, ethnic and religious minorities, and African Americans came to play larger public roles; some in government, others in private organizations. With Eleanor Roosevelt (Document 24-10) in the White House; Francis Perkins in the cabinet; Mary McLeod Bethune, an African American, in the National Youth Administration; and Genora Johnson Dollinger in the labor movement, women figured significantly in the events of the period (see text pp. 750–755). Similarly, the government employed Jews and Catholics at a time when the private labor market was tight because of the Depression and jobs were frequently closed to them because of prejudice.

Document 24-11 deals with working men and women (Genora Johnson Dollinger among them) during the General Motors sit-down strike in Flint, Michigan, in 1936 and 1937. Document 24-12 is Lorena Hickok's 1934 report on conditions in Arizona to Harry L. Hopkins, administrator of the Federal Emergency Relief Administration. Document 25-13 is taken from Paul Sears's influential study on North American ecology, *Deserts on the March* (1935).

24-10 The State's Responsibility for Fair Working Conditions (1933)

Eleanor Roosevelt

Eleanor Roosevelt (1884–1962) brought to the White House her public and organizational experience in reform causes during the 1920s. As First Lady, she advised the president and advocated causes important to her (though not necessarily to him), including youth, women, and African Americans.

Source: From *Scribner's Magazine*, March 1933, 140. Copyright 1933 and renewed © 1961 by Charles Scribner's Sons. Reprinted with the permission of Scribner, an imprint of Simon & Schuster Adult Publishing Group.

No matter how fair employers wish to be, there are always some who will take advantage of times such as these to lower unnecessarily the standards of labor, thereby subjecting him to unfair competition. It is necessary to stress the regulation by law of these unhealthy conditions in industry. It is quite obvious that one cannot depend upon the worker in such times as these to take care of things in the usual way. Many women, particularly, are not unionized and even unions have temporarily lowered their standards in order to keep their people at work. If you face starvation, it is better to accept almost anything than to feel that you and your children are going to be evicted from the last and the cheapest rooms which you have been able to find and that there will be no food.

Cut after cut has been accepted by workers in their wages, they have shared their work by accepting fewer days a week in order that others might be kept on a few days also, until many of them have fallen far below what I would consider the normal and proper standard for healthful living. If the future of our country is to be safe and the next generation is to grow up to healthy and good citizens, it is absolutely necessary to protect the health of our workers now and at all times.

It has been found, for instance, in Germany, in spite of the depression and the difficulty in making wages cover good food, that sickness and mortality rates have been surprisingly low amongst the workers, probably because of the fact that they have not been obliged to work an unhealthy number of hours.

Limiting the number of working hours by law has a twofold result. It spreads the employment, thereby giving more people work, and it protects the health of the workers. Instead of keeping a few people working a great many hours and even asking them to share their work with others by working fewer days, it limits all work to a reasonable number of hours and makes it necessary to employ the number of people required to cover the work.

Refusing to allow people to be paid less than a living wage preserves to us our own market. There is absolutely no use in producing anything if you gradually reduce the number of people able to buy even the cheapest products. The only way to preserve our markets is to pay an adequate wage.

It seems to me that all fair-minded people will realize that it is self-preservation to treat the industrial worker with consideration and fairness at the present time and to uphold the fair employer in his efforts to treat his employees well by preventing unfair competition.

Questions

1. What group was Roosevelt attacking?
2. With whom was she aligning herself?
3. What kind of political fallout could such views have had for her husband? Should that have been a consideration for her? Why or why not?

24-11 The Sit-Down Strike at General Motors (1937)

Mary Heaton Vorse

The Flint, Michigan, sit-down strike against General Motors was among the most dramatic and significant episodes in American labor history (see text pp. 749–750). Defying court injunctions and police attacks, workers occupied the General Motors plant from December 31, 1936, to February 11, 1937. The strike led to the recognition of the United Automobile Workers by GM and Chrysler, though Ford continued to resist unionization for some time. Journalist Mary Heaton Vorse (1874–1966) here reports on the GM sit-down strike, the men and women involved in it, and labor's day of triumph.

Source: Excerpt from Mary Heaton Vorse, *Labor's New Millions* (1938; New York: Ayer, 1969), 76–77, 88–90. Reprinted with permission.

I went down to the Chevrolet plant with two members of the Emergency Brigade. The workers had now captured plant No. 4. The street was full of people—there were about twenty policemen between the bridge and the high gate of the plant. They were quiet and unprovocative, so the crowd of pickets was good-natured. The sound car was directing operations.

The use of the sound truck is new in strike procedure and it is hard to know how a strike was ever conducted without it. As we came down past the policemen a great voice, calm and benign, proclaimed that everything was in hand—the plant was under control.

Next the great disembodied voice, really the voice of auburn-haired young Roy Reuther [a young organizer of the United Automobile Workers], urged the men in the plant to barricade themselves from tear gas. Every now and then the voice boomed:

"Protection squad. Attention! Guard your sound car. Protection squad. Attention!"

Then the voice addressed the workers who crowded the windows of the lower levels. At the top of the steep flight of steps were the workers of the plant, lunch buckets under their arms, waving at the pickets in the street. A crowd of workers fringed the roof. The sound car inquired if they were union men. They shouted, "Yes." The crowd cheered.

The measured soothing voice of the sound car boomed:

"Word has come to us that there are men in the crowd anxious to join the union. Go to the last car, you will find the cards ready to sign. If you have no money for dues with you you can come to Pengally Hall later." The sound car struck up *Solidarity* and the men at the top of the steps, on top of the plant, in the street, all sang.

A woman's voice next—Genora Johnson [organizer of the Women's Emergency Brigade]. She told the crowd that the women had gone to the Hall to wipe their eyes clear of tear gas and would soon be back. "We don't want any violence; we don't want any trouble. We are going to do everything we can to keep from trouble, but we are going to protect our husbands."

Down the hill presently came a procession, preceded by an American flag. The women's bright red caps showed dramatically in the dark crowd. They were singing, *Hold the Fort*.

To all the crowd there was something moving about seeing the women return to the picket line after having been gassed in front of plant No. 9. A cheer went up; the crowd took up the song. The line of bright-capped women spread itself out in front of the high gate. Clasping hands, they struck up the song, *We Shall Not Be Moved*. Some of the men who had jumped over the gate went back, amid the cheers of the crowd.

I went to the top of the little hill and a file of men were coming out of the back of the building.

"Are you going home?"

"Home—Hell no! We're going back to picket the plant. Half of us are sitting down inside, and half of us are coming out to picket from the street."

"How many of you are for the sit-down?"

"Ninety per cent," a group of them chorused.

What happened that day [the day the workers left in victory—February 11, 1937] in Flint was something that no one who ever saw it could possibly forget. Never since Armistice Day has anything been seen comparable to its intensity. A mighty emotion shook the working people of that town. Joy and freedom dominated Flint's commonplace streets.

It was as if Flint had been under a spell for a long time, perhaps always. Fear and suspicion had walked through Flint's streets. People didn't dare to join unions. They'd get fired, they'd lose their jobs. Your next door neighbor might be a spy. No one knew who the stool pigeons were. The people who had got used to living that way didn't know how maimed they were.

General Motors had come into Flint and made a city out of a crossroads. General Motors had dominated the town. It had ruled its political life and it had set its face against unions. Men had organized on their peril. Unions were kept out by fear. And now that fear was over. No wonder that the people marching in the line stretched out their hands to their friends on the sidewalk and said:

"You can join now, you can join now, we are free!"

Freedom to join your own union seems a little thing. But one has to live in a town dominated by a great industry to see how far off a union can seem and how powerful the industry.

Now General Motors had bargained with the union officials. The long days of suspended violence were over. Here was the antithesis of a mob: the gathering together of people to express a great emotion. Such gathering together is at the very basis of civilization. It is the intensification of the individual, the raising of his power for good to a thousandth degree.

No one in that crowd remained isolated. People's small personalities were lost in this great Halleluiah.

When the men from Fisher No. 1 had accepted the agreement they marched in a parade to the plants at the other end of the town which were still guarded by the militia. The barrier of soldiers drew aside.

The crowd with flags marched cheering into the guarded zone.

The strikers were coming out of Chevrolet No. 4, flags preceding them. There were flags on the steps and flags on the street. Flares lighted up the scene. Cheers for Governor Murphy[1] filled the air. Strikers' wives were waving to husbands they had not seen for days. A woman held up a baby. The procession marched down the street. Another roar filled all space.

The Fisher No. 2 boys marched out. They marched out in military formation from the quiet of the empty, waiting plant, carrying neat bundles of their things. They became part of the crowd that was now bright with confetti. People carried toy balloons. The whole scene was lit up by the burst of glory of the photographers' flares. The big flags punctuated the crowd with color.

They shouted to the rhythm of "Freedom, Freedom, Freedom!"

Chevrolet Avenue was packed from bridge to bridge. People swarmed over the murky little Flint River with its new barbed wire fences. They came past Chevrolet No. 4 and they came up the street past Fisher No. 2. They came, flags at their head, singing. They marched from the plants back to union headquarters. The streets were lined all the way with cheering people. Men and women from the cars and marchers shouted to the groups of other working people who lined the streets, "Join the union! We are free!"

---

[1] *Governor Frank Murphy*, a Democrat, risked his political career by refusing to employ the National Guard to force the sit-down strikers to evacuate the plants.

The marchers arrived in front of Pengally Hall. They gathered in increasing thousands. The hall itself was jammed. They no longer let people into the building. Inside and outside, the loud speakers were going. Homer Martin, Wyndham Mortimer, Bob Travis and the other strike leaders addressed the roaring crowds.

The joy of victory tore through Flint. It was more than the joy of war ceasing, it was the joy of creation. The workers were creating a new life. The wind of Freedom had roared down Flint's streets. The strike had ended! The working people of Flint had begun to forge a new life out of their historic victory.

Questions

1. According to Vorse, why had Flint's workers remained nonunionized for so many years?
2. Which tactics brought victory to the union? What strikes you about the male and female participants?
3. Why did Vorse compare the emotions that were felt by workers after winning the strike to those felt on Armistice Day (the day on which the Great War ended)?

24-12 Field Report on Arizona to Harry L. Hopkins (1934)

Lorena Hickok

Lorena Hickok (1893–1968) was born in Wisconsin and became a reporter for the Associated Press in 1913. Sympathetic with the New Deal and a close friend to Eleanor Roosevelt, Hickok came to work as chief investigator for Harry L. Hopkins, the administrator of the Federal Emergency Relief Administration. Hickok wrote detailed field reports in 1933 and 1934 from all over the country, including this 1934 letter to Hopkins in which she documents the New Deal relief programs in the Southwest. Her reports—while certainly shaped by the blatant racial and ethnic prejudices of the times—raised serious concerns about both people's growing dependence on government-supplied relief payments and the underlying socioeconomic problems that the New Deal failed to address.

Source: Lorena Hickok, letter to Harry L. Hopkins from Phoenix, Arizona, May 4, 1934, from *One Third of a Nation: Lorena Hickok Reports on the Great Depression*, ed. Richard Lowitt and Maurine Beasley (Urbana: University of Illinois Press, 1981), 237–243. Reprinted with permission of the publisher.

Phoenix, Arizona, May 4, 1934
Dear Mr. Hopkins:
. . . I lost a day this week. On Sunday, driving across desert from Lordsburg, N.M., to Tucson, I turned over in loose gravel on a road which seems to be a sort of political football. The towns of Douglas and Bisbee, wishing to keep the road as bad as possible, have enough influence at the Statehouse to prevent its being repaired. The result is about one wreck a week, with a couple of fatalities every month or so. Douglas and Bisbee are interested because it diverts traffic away from them. . . . So, since I had apparently carried most of the weight of the car on the back of my neck during the split second while it was rolling over, the doctor seemed to think it might be a good idea for me to spend Monday in bed, which I did. Incidentally, sir, you have to have a darned good neck to get away with anything like that. I think mine had no doubt got toughened up these last five or six weeks from carrying the weight of the world on it. . . . Since Monday I've been moving fast, with little opportunity to write.

Anyway, I haven't felt much encouraged to write. Damn it, it's the same old story down here, wherever I go.

Two classes of people.

Whites, including white collar people, with white standards of living, for whom relief, as it is now, is anything but adequate. No jobs in sight. Growing restive.

Mexicans—or, East of the Mississippi, Negroes—with low standards of living, to whom relief is adequate and attractive. Perfectly contented. Willing to stay on relief the rest of their lives. Able, many of them, to get work, but at wages so low that they are better off on relief.

So many Mexicans and Negroes on relief that, with a limited amount of money, we are compelled to force the white man's standard of living down to that of the Mexicans and Negroes.

I believe that in the whole Southern half of the United States you will find this to be the big relief problem today. Certainly it is in every urban community. I've encountered it everywhere I've been on this trip: Alabama, Texas, Louisiana, New Mexico, although not so bad there, and Arizona.

Add to it newspaper publicity—carried out of Washington by the press associations, I am told—that has led the population to believe that everyone in the state on relief is going to get $21 a month cash, no more and no less, under the new program, and you have Arizona's problem. The Mexicans all want "the $21 a month the Government has promised us." The whites, who have actually been getting more than that on direct relief, don't see how they can get along on it and are worried stiff. It represents a "raise" for the Mexicans, from relief with which they were perfectly satisfied and which apparently was adequate, and a "cut" for the whites. . . .

I have been writing you right along that the only way I could see to clean up this Negro-Mexican business would be to reinvestigate thoroughly the Negro and Mexican case loads, closing the intakes to get them out of the habit of registering for relief for a few weeks and to turn the case workers loose for the reinvestigation, and to force every Negro or Mexican who could get any work at all, at WHATEVER wages, to take it and get off the relief rolls. . . . I must admit that there are people in the set-up who don't agree with me on this. They argue first of all that we are forcing these people into peonage. Employers, particularly farmers and housewives—the two worst classes of employers in the country, I believe—will take advantage of the situation. I've written you about housewives who think Negroes, Mexicans, or even white girls ought to be glad to work for their room and board. And last week in New Mexico I heard about sheep growers who want to hire herders at $7 a MONTH! It is also argued that, particularly in cities, thousands of the Mexicans and Negroes actually CAN'T get work—that, if there is any job, no matter how lowly and how poorly paid, a white man will take it, and that there would be Hell to pay if a Negro or a Mexican got it. I don't believe that, however, to the extent that some people do.

It's almost impossible to get to the bottom on this farm labor proposition. The farmers—sheep and cattle men, cotton growers, and so on—are all yelling that they can't get the Mexicans to work because they are all on relief. But when Mexicans and Spanish-Americans won't go out and herd sheep for $7 a month because they can get $8 or $10 on relief, it seems to me that the farmer ought to raise his wages a little. Oh, they don't admit trying to get herders for $7 a month. If you ask them what they are paying, they will say, "Anywhere from $15 a month up." But our relief people looked into the matter and found out what they actually were willing to pay.

A thing that complicates the whole situation right now is our hourly rate under the new program. In Arizona, for instance, the minimum is 50 cents an hour. We adopted it because it is the hourly rate on public works in the state of Arizona. But, don't you see, it's a "political" hourly rate? Jobs on highways on public works in Arizona are dealt out as political patronage. The ACTUAL prevailing wage in Arizona is nowhere nearly that high. Up to now there haven't been many people getting 50 cents an hour in Arizona—and damned few Mexicans. Now we come along and announce we are going to pay everybody on relief 50 cents an hour. You can imagine the furor.

You've got the Latin temperament to deal with down here, too. Latin and Indian. They don't "want" things. They haven't any ambition. A man who is half Spanish and half Indian has an entirely different slant on life from ours. To begin with, it's a semi-tropical country. The Spaniards came here generations ago. They are easy-going, pleasure loving. It isn't in their makeup to "get out and hustle." And the Indian in them certainly wouldn't make them ambitious. The Indian never was a hustler. He wanted just enough, no more. Your Mexican, or your Spanish-American, is a simple fellow, with simple needs, to be obtained with the least effort. And if he could work five days a week at 50 cents an hour or three days a week at 50 cents an hour, he'd work three days, even though it meant less income. His attitude is: "Why work any more after you've got enough?" And when it comes to working seven days a week, 10 hours a day, for no more than, or even less than, he'd be getting on relief—well, he just can't see that at all. . . . And so, this 50-cent hourly rate is just swell for a Mexican, even though the number of hours he can work and the amount of money he can get per month on it are limited. And $21 a month, earned at the rate of 50 cents an hour—why, that's just Heaven to him! He'd have a grand time on $10 or $12. And has been.

The Mexican or Spanish-American diet is so different from ours. Chili beans, red beans, a little grease, flour or cornmeal, a few vegetables and a little fruit in the fall. It's a cheap diet. But they've thrived—or would it be "thriven"?—on it for 500 years. We're silly to try to change it. As a matter of fact, doctors over in New Mexico have been making a study of that diet, observing the effect on the children. They've had the surprise of their lives. Those children are a darn sight better off physically, on that diet, than most of our white children are in families living on minimum subsistence rations.

In Tucson not long ago arrived a huge shipment of surplus commodity butter. They had no place to keep it. They had to ration it out to Mexicans and Indians as well as whites. The Mexicans and Indians had never tasted butter before. They didn't even like it. They tried to fry beans in it—and came back yelling for lard!

Now if these people can live on $10 or $12 a month and be reasonably healthy and so contented that they won't even take work when it is offered them, let alone go out and look for it, why, in the name of common sense, raise them above that? Especially when we have a limited amount of money. I'll grant that the work that is offered them pays darned little—that it's practically peonage—but it's all they've ever known, and I doubt if the Relief administration is financially in a position to battle low wage scales all over the South and Southwest.

There is a way of handling the problem, other than throwing the Mexicans and Negroes off relief—and the local relief administrations have been doing it. Discrimination. Two standards of relief. The idea will sound horrible in Washington, but—I'm beginning to wonder.

The only place where they've come right out and admitted to me that they've been doing it is in Tucson. They were doing it before Federal money came in, there, and during April, between CWA and the new program, which went into effect May 1, they went back to it. They said April had been the smoothest month they'd had for a long time.

In Tucson—without any publicity, but so quietly that people didn't even know they were being classified—they divided their case load into four groups, Classes A, B, C, and D. They have about 2,800 families on relief there: 1,200 Mexicans, American citizens, but with a low standard of living; 800 Yaqui Indian families, political refugees from old Mexico; 800 white families.

Into Class A went 60 families. Engineers, teachers, lawyers, contractors, a few former businessmen, architects, and some chemists who used to be connected with the mines. They and each of the other three groups had their own intakes. No mixing. They gave this group a $50 a month maximum, 50 per cent cash. It took care of them fairly adequately, rents, clothing, and everything. They set up projects for them, manning their auxiliary staff with them. Although they were required to work only a few hours a week for what they were getting, these people have been giving full time, voluntarily.

Into Class B went 250 families, on a maximum of $36 a month, from 33⅓ to 40 per cent cash. It consisted of some white collar people—clerks, stenographers, bookkeepers, and so on—and skilled labor. Many of these people were able to augment their incomes by a few days work now and then.

Into Class C went 1,000 families, on a $25 maximum, 30 per cent cash. It consisted of white unskilled labor and Mexican and Spanish-American unskilled labor with standards of living higher than those of most Mexicans.

And into Class D went 1,490 families, on a $10 maximum, all in kind. These were the low class Mexican, Spanish-American, and Indian families.

They have a commissary in Tucson—and I'm beginning to wonder, too, if a commissary IS such a bad thing where you've got a large crowd of people with low standards of living to feed. As a work project, they raise two-thirds of the vegetables distributed through the commissary. They buy milk wholesale, giving it out at 8 cents a quart instead of 15 as charged retail. Incidentally, from school districts where these low class Mexicans and Indians live and where distribution of milk to children has been going on for years there came a few weeks ago word that the health of the children had improved to such an extent that they no longer needed to distribute the milk!

"Now this all may seem pretty bad to you," the relief administrator told me, "but you're going to quit some day and leave us, here in these communities, to carry on. We'll never be able to carry on under the conditions Washington is imposing on us now."

And so—I'm wondering if perhaps we should try to set up a national standard and impose it on a state like Arizona, a town like Tucson. I'm wondering if we shouldn't give these state and local committees a little more latitude, a little more discretionary power.... Don't think I can't see the dangers in it. And I realize the terrific pressure brought to bear by the Labor crowd on those wage scales. But, dammit, man, our job is to feed people and clothe them and shelter them, with as little damage to their morale as possible. And that's all, as I see it. We haven't got the money to do any more. I can't see—I've never been able to see—that it was the job of the Federal Emergency Relief Administration to fight the battle of the American Federation of Labor. We ARE feeding people, clothing them, and providing shelter for them as best we can. But what are we doing to their morale? I've been on the road nearly a year now. More and more I've come to the conclusion that, the less we interfere with the normal lives of these families, the less damage we're going to do to their morale. If, by relief, we raise a family's income beyond whatever [it] has been before or beyond what it has any chance of becoming normally, we are damaging the morale of that family. And if we lower a family's standard of living too much, we are going to ruin its morale, too—or make a rebel out of the head of that family.

In Tucson, if we enforce that 50-cent hourly wage rate with the limit on hours, we're going to do both of those things, I'm afraid.

I was in Tucson May 1, the day the new program went in.

All the Mexicans who could read—and even more who couldn't—were over at their intake, demanding the $21 a month "the Government has promised us."

In the office of the administrator, I sat talking for an hour with half a dozen white collar clients. Among them were a landscape painter, a certified public accountant, a former businessman, an architect, a former bank cashier. All save the artist were men of 45 or thereabouts. All had been in the group of 60, Class A. We went over their budgets, to see if they could possibly get along on that $21 maximum.

Said the painter:

"I pay $6.50 a month rent. There are three of us, my wife, my 18-months-old baby, and myself. We have three rooms in a garage. No water. An outside toilet. The baby's food costs us $6.03 a month—$4.11 for milk, .46 for Cream of Wheat, .26 for prunes, $1.20 for vegetables. He should have more, but he can get by on that. Our lights and coal oil for fuel come to $4.30 a month. Add $6.50 for rent, $6.03 for the baby's food, and $4.30 for light and oil, and you get $16.83. Subtract that from $21, and you see my wife and I will have $4.17 a month for food for ourselves. Can't do it."

The certified public accountant was trying to hang onto his home. "If I lose that," he said, "it's the end—that's all." He has a Federal Home Loan, which requires that he pay $10 a month interest. That leaves him an $11 balance, and he has six in the family and a baby coming. In April he got $40 and managed to get by, although, of course, he had to keep one of the children out of school to help his wife because he couldn't hire any one. He wasn't kicking about that, however.

The former bank cashier also had six in the family—himself, his wife, his parents, his crippled sister, and her child. He wasn't paying rent. They had moved in with friends. But they were paying half of the electric, water and fuel bills.

"I'm afraid for my parents," he said. "Lord only knows how we'll get along. They are unhappy now and feel they are in the way. It's a bad situation."

The former businessman, who told me that, when the depression hit, he was worth $60,000—and other people told me he was telling me the truth—had only three in his family, his wife, himself, and a son, who had to leave college, but who has been unable to get steady work of any kind. He is paying $15 a month rent, having recently moved out of a $25 apartment. That leaves $6 a month for food for the three of them.

"All this—it breaks you down," he said quietly. "We men who have been the backbone of commerce, who have had ambitions and hopes, who have always taken care of our families—what is going to become of us? I've lost twelve and a half pounds this last month, just thinking. You can't sleep, you know. You wake up about 2 A.M., and then you lie and think.

"Why, I've sat across the tables from Jesse Jones and talked contracts with him, running up into many thousands of dollars! But I'd be afraid to face him now. You get so you feel so whipped!"

There was a moment's silence. Then the former bank cashier spoke.

"Yes," he said, "all those years of practical experience you and I have had don't count for anything now.

"When you're 45 and trying to get a job, they say to you, 'I'll get in touch with you later, Mr. So-and-So. Mighty glad you dropped in.'

"But you never hear from them."

In Albuquerque the other day, I was talking with a lawyer, a former judge, who is one of the big men in the town.

"The Government has got to take care of these people," he said, "if it takes your hat and mine. Why, we don't know the beginning of taxation in this country yet. And if society, as it is now organized, can't give a man a job, then the Government, representing all the people, must do it—a decent job, at a living wage."

Questions

1. What complications in the level of relief payments and local prevailing wages did Hickok describe? How does the question of race or ethnicity seem to complicate this situation further?
2. What comparisons did Hickok make between the South and the Southwest?
3. What political as well as other concerns did Hickok identify or foresee in administering a national relief program?

24-13 *Deserts on the March* (1937)

Paul B. Sears

In the 1930s, the federal government assumed many new responsibilities in terms of managing the economy and otherwise providing for the general welfare. The spirit of reform did not extend just to people, however. It also brought with it a new attitude toward the land. The massive dust storms on the Great Plains, which seemed to blow away everything but the farmer's mortgage, exposed agriculture as dangerously out of step with the environment. Many Americans left their farms in Oklahoma, Nebraska, and North Dakota and headed to the West Coast in search of a better, more stable way of life. The government started new conservation programs and responded in many other ways. The views of the country's scientists, such as those of ecologist Paul B. Sears (1891–1990), whose *Deserts on the March* provided a compelling narrative and explanation for the dust bowl, influenced government policymakers.

Source: Excerpt from Paul B. Sears, "The Great Pattern," in *Deserts on the March* (New York: Simon and Schuster, 1937), 87–92. Reprinted with permission. All rights reserved.

The picture, then, of the continent undisturbed by man is one of the most abundant life possible. Forests extend far inland and the grass extends beyond them to its utmost possible limits. Deserts are shrunken to their least possible compass under the existing climatic conditions. In the midst of this order there is, of course, no absolute uniformity. Hilltops are drier and more exposed than valleys and ravines, although if it were not for the constant shiftings of the earth's crust the hills would be cut down and the valleys slowly built up. Within each province the drier and more exposed situations tend to have those kinds of vegetation which would occur in valleys farther inland. For example, the bur oak, which grows in stream valleys in Nebraska and Oklahoma, grows on very dry hilltops in Indiana. The shorter grasses which are found in eastern Colorado are also found on the drier hilltops in central Kansas. But here again the course of nature has its effect and as time goes on the pattern of vegetation in any place tends to become more and more uniform and appropriate to the climate. Even on the hilltops there is some accumulation of humus which makes possible to a considerable extent the upward climb of valley plants. Just as the desert in the interior comes to occupy the least possible space, so do the drier types of vegetation within each area.

The picture we have drawn is a fair description of the continent of North America when the white man entered upon it. There were, of course, extensive Indian cultures and in Mexico genuine civilization, but the primitive tools which the Indian possessed did not enable him seriously to disturb the general balance. Like the other living creatures, he fitted into the picture rather than dominated it. His agriculture, while sound and skilful, was necessarily casual and restricted. The more systematic and extensive agriculture of the mound builders had long since passed into oblivion. He depended largely upon game and fish but he made moderate use of these and all other resources about him. There is in the whole story of Indian economy nothing to compare with the ruthless, methodical, and finally successful extermination of the wild buffalo, the passenger pigeon and the plains antelope. Even with the aid of the white man's railroad and high-powered firearms these great, enlightened, progressive and humane measures required some time for their completion.

Observe the changes inaugurated with white settlement. The first point of contact was with the forest and its denizens. All the resources of European mechanical invention were brought to bear against nature. The forest was speedily stripped by every means at the command of civilized man. Its removal was not governed by the need for lumber. The sweep was clean; trees of all ages and sizes were destroyed. Nor were the immediate needs of the actual population for agricultural land considered. Every effort was made to produce a surplus for export without regard to maintaining any balance between need and supply, removal and return. We have already described the details of this relentless and extravagant march towards the interior of the continent. The forest which had been so slowly developed wherever trees could grow was destroyed. On land unfit for agriculture it was replaced either by grassland or by a second growth of pioneer and hence inferior type of forest. Moving west into the grasslands, with certain honorable exceptions, plow, fire and overstocked herds of cattle did to the native grass what the ax and fire had done to the forests of the east. Here again there was considerable land not suitable to continuous agriculture. After the first wave of destruction, instead of returning to its original, bountiful crop of nutritious grass, it too was covered by inferior or pioneer types. The second-growth plants in the grassland area did not represent the best that the climate could produce in a state of nature. Instead they are akin to the drier, less desirable forms which composed the native vegetation still further inland. Actually the area of short grass, cactus and scrub shifted eastward into what had been lush prairie.

Thus was broken the magic girdle which had thrown its green expanse about the shrinking desert. As time went on the further destruction wrought by man released the forces of wind and water which had been held in check. No longer was the surface protected against their action by a continuous carpet of plant life. Quickly the mantle of tempering soil with its sponge-like humus was washed and blown away from the uplands, lodging in the valleys, choking them with its new burden and concealing their rich alluvium. Gullies grew at the margins of the hills. Between what clumps of green were left appeared the color of the bare soil—the sure mark of the desert. In places the wash of wind and water scoured away everything that was loose, leaving floors of bare rock and pebbles not to be distinguished in their practical significance from the so-called desert pavements which mark the most barren and hopeless spots on the earth's surface.

Thus the white man in a few centuries, mostly in one, reversed the slow work of nature that had been going on for millennia. Thus have come the deserts, so long checked and held in restraint, to break their bonds. At every step the girdle of green about the inland deserts has been forced to give way and the desert itself literally allowed to expand. On the coast where once was forest the trees are gone. In the grassland which once was unbroken is inferior growth and much bare soil. Just as we have seen that under extremely favorable conditions the vegetation can move inland beyond its usual climatic limits, so now we see the process reversed. With the restraining influence of soil and vegetation broken, the desert moves outward from its proper climatic confine, and because of cultural or artificial conditions comes to occupy the place that rightfully belongs to other provinces.

The laws which govern the development of soil and vegetation are as inescapable as the laws of the conservation of energy and of matter upon which they are based. No matter how complex or seemingly mysterious the operations of the organic world, they are still based upon cause and effect. It is as impossible to get something for nothing as it is to make water run uphill. Balance and equilibrium are demanded by nature. If man destroys the old order he must take the consequences. There is no magic which will undo the mischief he has wrought.

Questions

1. Compare this document with Document 16-6. On what points do John Wesley Powell and Paul Sears seem to have agreed, despite the sixty years that separates these two documents?
2. What role did Sears seem to imply the federal government should play in the agriculture of the Great Plains?

Questions for Further Thought

1. Drawing on the text and documents for Chapter 24, compare and contrast the roles of women, African Americans, Mexican Americans, and Native Americans in government and the private sector during the New Deal and the effects of government policies on these groups.
2. The supporters of the New Deal were a political coalition that included industrial workers, professionals, intellectuals, and scientists. Why did the New Deal appeal to so varied a group? What problems were likely to strain this coalition?

CHAPTER TWENTY-FIVE

The World at War
1939–1945

The Road to War

World War II began on September 3, 1939, when Germany invaded Poland; Great Britain and France declared war on Germany two days later. Japan, of course, had been at war with China since 1937. For the time being, Italy, the Soviet Union, and the United States remained out of the European war. The Roosevelt administration and the American public favored both the Allies and America's nonparticipation in the conflict.

Germany's smashing victory over France and accompanying developments during June 1940 dramatically changed the international situation. Germany was paramount in Europe; Italy had joined the war on Germany's side; and the Soviet Union continued to assist Germany, as it had since the August 1939 German-Soviet pact. Great Britain stood alone and on the defensive, and the Asian colonies of France, the Netherlands (also overrun by the Germans), and Great Britain were more vulnerable than ever to the Japanese, who continued their war against the Chinese.

Alarmed by the implications of the altered international equation following France's defeat, in 1940 and 1941 the Roosevelt administration moved to assist Great Britain by various means short of war—exchanging American destroyers for leases on British military bases in the Western Hemisphere (1940) and securing congressional passage of the Lend-Lease Act, which authorized shipment of war materiel to nations deemed vital to American security (1941). Administration policy touched off heated public debate in the United States. Meanwhile, during 1940, the president added two supportive Republicans to his cabinet: Secretary of War Henry Stimson, former secretary of war (under Taft) and secretary of state (under Hoover), and Secretary of the Navy Frank Knox, the GOP vice presidential candidate in 1936. In the same year, Congress authorized sharply increased spending to enlarge and modernize the American military and provided the first peacetime draft in the nation's history.

America's new stance and ambitions led Japan, Germany, and Italy to draw closer together. In June 1941, Germany and its European allies suddenly invaded the Soviet Union. They had three motivations—to secure *lebensraum* (territory deemed essential to the future well-being of Nazi Germany), to destroy a Communist state, and to deprive embattled Great Britain of its only possible future European ally. That August, Prime Minister Winston Churchill of Great Britain and President Franklin D. Roosevelt issued the Atlantic Charter. By autumn, the United States and Germany were waging an undeclared Atlantic war, which neither side moved to escalate. Meanwhile, Japan decided to seize the European colonial empires in the Far East, which were rich in vital natural resources, especially petroleum in the Dutch East Indies (now Indonesia). To do so without American interference, Japan attacked the U.S. Pacific fleet at Pearl Harbor early in the morning of December 7. The United States declared war on Japan, and when Germany and Italy declared war on the United States in response, America reciprocated. What had begun as wars in East Asia and Europe was now truly a world war (see text pp. 771–773).

Although the United States sought to increase foreign trade during the Great Depression, isolationism—an aversion to international involvements that risked war—ran deep in the nation and found expression in Congress (Documents 25-1 and 25-2). Two documents present the pro-involvement arguments of President Roosevelt: his fireside chat on the "Great Arsenal of Democracy" (Document 25-3) and his "Four Freedoms" speech (Document 25-4).

25-1 The Profits of War and Preparedness (1934)

Gerald P. Nye

Gerald P. Nye (1892–1971) was a U.S. senator from North Dakota. A Republican, he was best known for his role in the Senate investigations of profiteering by U.S. banks and businesses during the Great War. Nye's revelations helped contribute to the public support for the passage of the Neutrality Acts.

Source: "The Profits of War and Preparedness," radio address by Senator Gerald P. Nye, April 10, 1934, in *Congress Investigates: A Documented History, 1792–1974*, eds. Arthur M. Schlesinger Jr. and Roger Bruns (New York: Chelsea House Publishers, 1975), 4:2800–2804.

A restless mind exists throughout the world today. One naturally is concerned about our nation's preparedness for war. The cause of preparedness, however, has lent itself to abuses which amount to national scandal and in time will cause nations to bow their heads in shame of the frightful things done in its name.

To provide an adequate national defense is a positive duty of government. But what constitutes an *adequate* defense? Is it preparation to defend ourselves against aggressors? Or is it preparation to go to all quarters of the earth to carry on warfare? If the questions were left to the people there is not serious doubt as to what the answers would be. If the people, unhampered by interests with selfish purposes, had their way, *adequate* defense would involve alone preparation for war at home. Then, with no nation preparing to leave its own borders to make war there would quickly dawn a golden opportunity and invitation to further prune the expense of defensive preparation.

The sad facts are, though, that the people do not have their way upon matters involving ultimate war. Influences are constantly at work which disarm people of a feeling of security in what was once thought to be an adequate defense. These influences are by men who hold positions of great influence in our social and political order, men who have been highly successful in inducing others to accept as truth the baseless assertions of their false though profitable propaganda.

Americans left to their good sense and judgment will declare that never again will our country engage in war away from home. But never at any time is there let-up of that propaganda intended to convince us that other nations are more adequately prepared for war than are we. And the propaganda so effective with us is equally effective when used in other lands. The result is an increasing competition so insane in its accomplishment that the world finds itself completely forgetting what really is adequate in the way of national defense; a competition which witnesses nations launched upon preparation program on a scale never known to the world in peace times. Already the race is one which causes nations, including our own to spend two and three times more money now than before the late world war. And here we are, only fifteen years removed from that war with its painful and expensive economic and physical consequences, still upon us.

Under these circumstances it is fair to ask: where does preparedness and national defense end? Viewing the insane trend of competition between nations it is equally fair to answer: It ends in war, war more terrible than any yet known; war, no one knows just where, when or for what cause, but war nevertheless. And to whose profit and satisfaction, pray tell? Certainly not to that of the men and boys who will be called upon to carry on, not to that of their loved ones; certainly not to the profit of the nation, for now, while still bleeding from the last war, we see that war gives, not profit, but debt—burdensome, crushing debt.

Is our civilization helplessly insane and laboring under a complex utterly suicidal? Who profits, who gains any satisfaction from this mad race of so-called preparedness?

The answer is not difficult of finding for those who will face facts.

Many studies are being made resulting in published articles on the subject of War and Profit. One of the most notable of these is to be found in the current number of Fortune Magazine. Here we find a most sordid tale of the scheming of European manufacturers to create a market for their instruments of war, of their perfect will of these manufacturers to supply the material to be used by enemy governments against their own, perhaps against the very factory workers whose labor created the munitions. These patriots have no prejudice. They perfect new death-dealing instruments and sell to whichever or however many governments will buy. There has been recorded the fact that French soldiers were mowed down by French-made guns in the hands of the enemy. German soldiers moving westward were killed by German-made guns sold to Belgium while German-made machines sold to Russia visited death and destruction upon the men fighting for the Fatherland on the Eastern front. Mounted in monumental fashion in a small English community is a great gun captured from the Germans in an engagement which cost the lives of many of the young men of that British community. On one side of the gun are engraved the names of the sons of British who gave up their lives in that engagement before the machine was captured; on the other side is engraved the name of the British munitions maker who sold the instrument to Germany. The story of the commercialism of war and preparation for it is ugly, gruesome. It does no credit to European munition makers or to the countries which permitted these merchants to ply their trade.

But who are we to pity the poor souls with whom these European manufacturers play as with toys? Look at ourselves in America and the history of our own munitions makers who supply Uncle Sam's needs in "an adequate defense program" and rush their supersalesmen off to foreign lands to ply their trade of peace conferences!

Last Friday was Army Day, and past the Capitol and down the city's parade avenue there marched and rode five thousand of America's finest—America's defenders—strong splendidly uniformed men, beautiful, well-matched steeds, shining steel helmets, rifles and mounted guns. All this, with the proudly waving colors, is at once inspiring. Hats off to these well-trained men prepared at a moment's notice to rush to the defense of country and flag! Yet, even in that inspiring moment, I could not fully restrain myself and be blind to the fact that those glistening steel helmets, for example, were the profit-returning products of American manufacturers, a product intended to protect those fine heads under the helmets against the shrapnel and shells which the same manufacturers had sold to the military departments of other nations which might some day be our foe in war! What madness! What rotten commercialism! Name a more inhuman trade! Was ever a more insane racket conceived in depraved mind or tolerated by an enlightened people?

After the adequate defensive needs of the American government have been provided for by the annual appropriations, it is said, off to South America go these manufacturers, breeding there suspicion and fear between countries while American statesmen strive to accomplish understanding and maintain peace. Incidentally, order books are carried along to record the orders for military needs which always grow out of suspicion and fear. China and Japan likewise seem to offer a fine market for our American merchants of death and destruction.

Just before the Civil War a leading financial figure conceived the idea of buying at auction thousands of rifles which the American Army was casting aside. The purchase was at a price of just over $3.00 per gun. The following year, when the Union forces desperately needed guns, this financier sold these same guns to the government at $22.00 each, a 700% profit. When Fremont's soldiers tried to fire these guns they shot off their own thumbs. But Morgan finally got his money, through court action, the court holding the contract was sacred. Is there profit for anyone in war?

But look out for Japan!—we are cautioned.

If we should, by some unbelievable chance find ourselves at war with Japan, it is safe to wager that our soldiers and sailors will find their enemy armed with and mowed down by instruments produced by American manufacturers—at a profit, of course.

In the name of "adequate defense" our American costs of maintaining the Army and Navy are now more than $700,000,000 annually compared with $343,000,000 just before we entered the World War—the war that was going to end war. From 1913 to 1930 Great Britain's cost of national defense increased 42%; France 30%; Italy 44%; Japan 142%; Russia 30%; while your Uncle Sam rushed to a 200% increase in his "defense" costs.

When will we cease this mad game? But, let us remember that the surest way to maintain peace is to prepare for war, we are urged.

I deny that there is any foundation in fact or historical experience for the claim that preparation for war maintains peace. The claim is a myth, sponsored and nursed by those whose unclean profits would vanish if ever they permitted the world to know that preparation for war is marvelously profitable for a few.

Between the United States and Canada there stretches a boundary of thousands of miles. During the lifetime of these two neighbors there has never been stationed a soldier, a mounted gun, or any evidence of military defense. It is encouraging to know that today fine minds in both countries are conceiving the establishment of a monument to commemorate these years of peace without demonstration of armed strength.

This monument is to take most unusual form. On each side of the boundary, in the Turtle Mountains of my state of North Dakota and Canada, hundreds of acres are being set aside to be developed and made known as the International Peace Garden. These acres will be landscaped and made a beautiful spot in commemoration of the peaceful relationship that has existed through all of these years without that common demonstration of "adequate" defense.

Oh, that there could be more such monuments!

There is a book about to come from the press which would save our nation billions and our people much of suffering if it could be read by every American. It is the story of profits and methods of munition makers, written by Engelbrecht and Hanighan, published by Dodd, Mead & Company, and chosen by the Book of the Month Club for May. And, what a title this work has: "Merchants of Death" is its name. It is packed full of worth-while facts about our munition makers. To this book I must credit some of the information I have offered tonight, and to it I am indebted for a reminder of that advertisement once published by an American munitions manufacturer. This manufacturer had developed a death-dealing instrument which it was anxious to sell and it advertised its accomplishment to the world as follows:

> The material is high in tensile strength and very special. The timing of the fuse of this shell is similar to the shrapnel shell, but it differs in that two explosive acids are used to explode the shell in the large cavity. The combination of these two acids causes a terrific explosion, having more power than anything of its kind yet used. Fragments become coated with the acids in exploding and wounds caused by them mean death in terrible agony within four hours if not attended to immediately.

From what we are able to learn of conditions in the trenches, it is not possible to get medical assistance to anyone in time to prevent fatal results.

This is not a pleasant story with which to close my remarks. There ought to be something a little more cheering and I think that cheer is to be found in the prospect which is large that within the next few days the Senate will pass the resolution which has been offered by Senator Vandenberg and myself calling for a sweeping investigation of the activities and methods resorted to by our munitions makers to fatten thin bank accounts in the name of preparedness. I am sure that such an investigation will develop facts which will let people know how they are made monkeys of by profit-sundry, soulless madmen who are making lunatics of the people of the world by their incessant propaganda for ever-larger appropriations in the name of an "adequate defense." Truth always produces worth-while results. Truth concerning the methods and program of our munitions makers might fetch an awakening which would demand the removal of the element of profit from national defense and war. I am sure such action will not necessitate additional relief camps to accommodate those gentlemen who profit most largely when millions of men are giving their lives to the cause of flag and country. And it most assuredly will reduce the danger of more war and the terrific burdens of expense now required in the name of adequate defense.

Questions

1. How would Nye have defined an *adequate* defense?
2. Who were the "merchants of death"?

25-2 The Reluctance to Go to War (1936)

C. D. Batchelor

C. D. Batchelor's editorial cartoon earned him a Pulitzer Prize in 1937. The *New York Daily News*, for which Batchelor drew, was a highly successful tabloid newspaper during the period. The billboard on the wall reads "Follies of 1936" and lists European heads of state in the cast.

Source: *New York Daily News*, 1936, reprinted with permission in Walter LaFeber, *The American Age: United States Foreign Policy at Home and Abroad*, 2nd ed. (New York: W. W. Norton, 1994), 384.

C. D. Batchelor, "I Used to Know Your Daddy" (1936)

Questions

1. What significance do you attach to the depiction of war as a female and a prostitute?
2. To whom does the woman refer when she speaks of the youth's "daddy"?

25-3 Fireside Chat on the Great Arsenal of Democracy (1940)

Franklin D. Roosevelt

During late 1939, President Roosevelt (1882–1945) persuaded Congress to repeal the arms embargo of earlier neutrality legislation. Belligerents could now purchase weapons from American manufacturers on a strict cash-and-carry basis—as the Neutrality Act of 1937 had allowed for other goods. This step, which favored Britain and France, touched off debate in the United States (see text pp. 769–771).

By December 29, 1940, when the president delivered this fireside chat, France had long since fallen, Great Britain had survived the aerial Battle of Britain, and Greece was (as FDR notes) resisting an Italian invasion. Twelve days earlier, during a press conference, Roosevelt had strongly advocated the policy that would be embodied in the Lend-Lease Act (see text p. 771).

Source: From Samuel I. Rosenman, ed., *The Public Papers and Addresses of Franklin D. Roosevelt, 1940* (New York: Macmillan, 1941), 633–644.

Never before since Jamestown and Plymouth Rock has our American civilization been in such danger as now.

For, on September 27, 1940, by an agreement signed in Berlin, three powerful nations, two in Europe and one in Asia, joined themselves together in the threat that if the United States of America interfered with or blocked the expansion program of these three nations—a program aimed at world control—they would unite in ultimate action against the United States.

The Nazi masters of Germany have made it clear that they intend not only to dominate all life and thought in their own country, but also to enslave the whole of Europe, and then to use the resources of Europe to dominate the rest of the world. . . .

Some of our people like to believe that wars in Asia and in Europe are of no concern to us. But it is a matter of most vital concern to us that European and Asiatic war-makers should not gain control of the oceans which lead to this hemisphere. . . .

Does anyone seriously believe that we need to fear attack anywhere in the Americas while a free Britain remains our most powerful naval neighbor in the Atlantic? Does anyone seriously believe, on the other hand, that we could rest easy if the Axis powers were our neighbors there?

If Great Britain goes down, the Axis powers will control the continents of Europe, Asia, Africa, Australia, and the high seas—and they will be in a position to bring enormous military and naval resources against this hemisphere. It is no exaggeration to say that all of us, in all the Americas, would be living at the point of a gun—a gun loaded with explosive bullets, economic as well as military.

We should enter upon a new and terrible era in which the whole world, our hemisphere included, would be run by threats of brute force. To survive in such a world, we would have to convert ourselves permanently into a militaristic power on the basis of war economy.

Some of us like to believe that even if Great Britain falls, we are still safe, because of the broad expanse of the Atlantic and of the Pacific.

But the width of those oceans is not what it was in the days of clipper ships. At one point between Africa and Brazil the distance is less than from Washington to Denver, Colorado—five hours for the latest type of bomber. And at the North end of the Pacific Ocean America and Asia almost touch each other. . . .

There are those who say that the Axis powers would never have any desire to attack the Western Hemisphere. That is the same dangerous form of wishful thinking which has destroyed the powers of resistance of so many conquered peoples. The plain facts are that the Nazis have proclaimed, time and again, that all other races are their inferiors and therefore subject to their orders. And most important of all, the vast resources and wealth of this American Hemisphere constitute the most tempting loot in all the round world. . . .

The experience of the past two years has proven beyond doubt that no nation can appease the Nazis. . . . There can be no appeasement with ruthlessness. There can be no reasoning with an incendiary bomb. We know now that a nation can have peace with the Nazis only at the price of total surrender. . . .

The history of recent years proves that shootings and chains and concentration camps are not simply the transient tools but the very altars of modern dictatorships. They may talk of a "new order" in the world, but what they have in mind is only a revival of the oldest and the worst tyranny. In that there is no liberty, no religion, no hope.

The proposed "new order" is the very opposite of a United States of Europe or a United States of Asia. It is not a Government based upon the consent of the governed. It is not a union of ordinary, self-respecting men and women to protect themselves and their freedom and their dignity from oppression. It is an unholy alliance of power and pelf to dominate and enslave the human race.

The British people and their allies today are conducting an active war against this unholy alliance. Our own future security is greatly dependent on the outcome of that fight. Our ability to "keep out of war" is going to be affected by that outcome.

Thinking in terms of today and tomorrow, I make the direct statement to the American people that there is far less chance of the United States getting into war, if we do all we can now to support the nations defending themselves against attack by the Axis than if we acquiesce in their defeat, submit tamely to an Axis victory, and wait our turn to be the object of attack in another war later on.

If we are to be completely honest with ourselves, we must admit that there is risk in any course we may take. But I deeply believe that the great majority of our people agree that the course that I advocate involves the least risk now and the greatest hope for world peace in the future.

The people of Europe who are defending themselves do not ask us to do their fighting. They ask us for the implements of war . . . which will enable them to fight for their liberty and for our security. Emphatically we must get these weapons to them in sufficient volume and quickly enough, so that we and our children will be saved the agony and suffering of war which others have had to endure. . . .

We must be the great arsenal of democracy. For us this is an emergency as serious as war itself. We must apply ourselves to our task with the same resolution, the same sense of urgency, the same spirit of patriotism and sacrifice as we would show were we at war.

We have furnished the British great material support and we will furnish far more in the future.

There will be no "bottlenecks" in our determination to aid Great Britain. No dictator, no combination of dictators, will weaken that determination by threats of how they will construe that determination.

The British have received invaluable military support from the heroic Greek army, and from the forces of all the governments in exile. Their strength is growing. It is the strength of men and women who value their freedom more highly than they value their lives.

Questions

1. According to Roosevelt, how did events in Europe and Asia threaten American interests?
2. How did Roosevelt describe Great Britain's role in the international conflict?
3. What actions did Roosevelt propose?

25-4 Four Freedoms Speech (1941)

Franklin D. Roosevelt

President Roosevelt stated his opposition to isolationism more strongly than ever in his 1941 State of the Union message to Congress. In this speech, he tied lend-lease and other international initiatives to his agenda for domestic politics. His concluding paragraphs on the "four freedoms" soon became the most famous rationale for American participation in the war (see text p. 771).

Source: From Samuel I. Rosenman, ed., *The Public Papers and Addresses of Franklin D. Roosevelt, 1940* (New York: Macmillan, 1941), 663–672.

I address you, the Members of the Seventy-Seventh Congress, at a moment unprecedented in the history of the Union. I use the word "unprecedented," because at no previous time has American security been as seriously threatened from without as it is today. . . .

It is true that prior to 1914 the United States often had been disturbed by events in other Continents. We had even engaged in two wars with European nations and in a number of undeclared wars in the West Indies, in the Mediterranean and in the Pacific for the maintenance of American rights and for the principles of peaceful commerce. In no case, however, had a serious threat been raised against our national safety or our independence.

What I seek to convey is the historic truth that the United States as a nation has at all times maintained opposition to any attempt to lock us in behind an ancient Chinese wall while the procession of civilization went past. Today, thinking of our children and their children, we oppose enforced isolation for ourselves or for any part of the Americas.

Even when the World War broke out in 1914, it seemed to contain only small threat of danger to our own American future. But, as time went on, the American people began to visualize what the downfall of democratic nations might mean to our own democracy.

We need not over-emphasize imperfections in the Peace of Versailles. We need not harp on failure of the democracies to deal with problems of world deconstruction. We should remember that the Peace of 1919 was far less unjust than the kind of "pacification" which began even before Munich, and which is being carried on under the new order of tyranny that seeks to spread over every continent today. The American people have unalterably set their faces against that tyranny.

Every realist knows that the democratic way of life is at this moment being directly assailed in every part of the world—assailed either by arms, or by secret spreading of poisonous propaganda by those who seek to destroy unity and promote discord in nations still at peace. During sixteen months this assault has blotted out the whole pattern of democratic life in an appalling number of independent nations, great and small. The assailants are still on the march, threatening other nations, great and small.

Therefore, as your President, performing my constitutional duty to "give to the Congress information of the state of the Union," I find it necessary to report that the future and the safety of our country and of our democracy are overwhelmingly involved in events far beyond our borders.

Armed defense of democratic existence is now being gallantly waged in four continents. If that defense fails, all the population and all the resources of Europe, Asia, Africa and Australasia will be dominated by the conquerors. The total of those populations and their resources greatly exceeds the sum total of the population and resources of the whole of the Western Hemisphere—many times over.

In times like these it is immature—and incidentally untrue—for anybody to brag that an unprepared America, single-handed, and with one hand tied behind its back, can hold off the whole world. . . .

A free nation has the right to expect full cooperation from all groups. A free nation has the right to look to the leaders of business, of labor, and of agriculture to take the lead in stimulating effort, not among other groups but within their own groups. The best way of dealing with the few slackers or trouble makers in our midst is, first, to shame them by patriotic example, and, if that fails, to use the sovereignty of government to save government.

As men do not live by bread alone, they do not fight by armaments alone. Those who man our defenses, and those behind them who build our defenses, must have the stamina and courage which come from an unshakable belief in the manner of life which they are defending. The mighty action which we are calling for cannot be based on a disregard of all things worth fighting for.

The Nation takes great satisfaction and much strength from the things which have been done to make its people conscious of their individual stake in the preservation of democratic life in America. Those things have toughened the fibre of our people, have renewed their faith and strengthened their devotion to the institutions we make ready to protect. Certainly this is no time to stop thinking about the social and economic problems which are the root cause of the social revolution which is today a supreme factor in the world.

There is nothing mysterious about the foundations of a healthy and strong democracy. The basic things expected by our people of their political and economic systems are simple. They are: equality of opportunity for youth and for others; jobs for those who can work; security for those who need it; the ending of special privilege for the few; the preservation of civil liberties for all; the enjoyment of the fruits of scientific progress in a wider and constantly rising standard of living.

These are the simple and basic things that must never be lost sight of in the turmoil and unbelievable complexity of our modern world. The inner and abiding strength of our economic and political systems is dependent upon the degree to which they fulfill these expectations.

Many subjects connected with our social economy call for immediate improvement. As examples: We should bring more citizens under the coverage of old age pensions and unemployment insurance. We should widen the opportunities for adequate medical care. We should plan a better system by which persons deserving or needing gainful employment may obtain it.

I have called for personal sacrifice. I am assured of the willingness of almost all Americans to respond to that call. . . .

In the future days, which we seek to make secure, we look forward to a world founded upon four essential human freedoms.

The first is freedom of speech and expression—everywhere in the world.

The second is freedom of every person to worship God in his own way—everywhere in the world.

The third is freedom from want—which, translated into world terms, means economic understandings which will secure to every nation a healthy peace time life for its inhabitants—everywhere in the world.

The fourth is freedom from fear—which, translated into world terms, means a world-wide reduction of armaments to such a point and in such a thorough fashion that no nation will be in a position to commit an act of physical aggression against any neighbor—anywhere in the world.

That is no vision of a distant millennium. It is a definite basis for a kind of world attainable in our own time and generation. That kind of world is the very antithesis of the so-called new order of tyranny which the dictators seek to create with the crash of a bomb.

To that new order we oppose the greater conception—the moral order. A good society is able to face schemes of world domination and foreign revolutions alike without fear.

Since the beginning of our American history we have been engaged in change—in a perpetual peaceful revolution—a revolution which goes on steadily, quietly adjusting itself to changing conditions—without the concentration camp or the quick-lime in the ditch. The world order which we seek is the cooperation of free countries, working together in a friendly, civilized society.

This nation has placed its destiny in the hands and heads and hearts of its millions of free men and women; and its faith in freedom under the guidance of God. Freedom means the supremacy of human rights everywhere. Our support goes to those who struggle to gain those rights or keep them. Our strength is in our unity of purpose.

To that high concept there can be no end save victory.

Questions

1. What four freedoms did Roosevelt identify?
2. How did Roosevelt link domestic and foreign concerns in this speech? Why did he link them?
3. How did Roosevelt extend his argument against the principles of the Neutrality Acts and in favor of an internationalist foreign policy?

Question for Further Thought

1. Compare and contrast Nye's "Profits of War and Preparedness" radio address with Roosevelt's "Great Arsenal of Democracy" fireside chat. Is there any common ground between the two?

Organizing for Victory

Mobilizing the nation's human and material resources to win World War II required organization that involved the interaction of governmental agencies, some old, others newly created, and private organizations (business, labor, and agricultural). Under changing circumstances, adversarial relations between government and business largely gave way to cooperation. The government's role expanded, as well as changed, as it recruited, trained, and fielded large military forces; spent lavishly to equip and maintain our armed forces and assist our allies; and taxed and borrowed to finance the war. Wartime economics achieved the prosperity that had eluded the Hoover and Roosevelt administrations during peacetime and established precedents for the postwar era (see text pp. 774–775, 777, 780).

The war created opportunities for women, African Americans, and Mexican Americans, though all confronted obstacles even as they and the war cleared some away. Women served in all four military services; others filled positions vacated by men entering the armed forces or jobs newly created by wartime demands. Yet the government and employers did not provide women with equal job opportunities, necessary support (child care, flexible work schedules), or organizations to articulate their needs and press for policies to address them. African Americans and Mexican Americans served in large numbers in the armed forces. The former were largely segregated; the latter were not. Both groups experienced gains but also prejudice and discrimination in the wartime labor market. During the war, African Americans and Mexican Americans protested segregation and discrimination. Blacks led in this regard: the National Association for the Advancement of Colored People (NAACP) gained markedly in membership, and the Congress of Racial Equality (CORE) was founded. Both organizations would, of course, figure prominently in the later civil rights movement.

Wartime federal action on behalf of minorities was limited. Congress was unsupportive, and the president's 1941 executive order prohibiting discrimination in war industries and government (issued under blacks' threat to mount a "march on Washington") did break new ground but little more. Increasingly liberal, the Supreme Court took the most decisive action, striking down Texas's Democratic primary election in *Smith v. Allwright*, 1944 (see text pp. 780–781).

Document 25-5 is the *Time* magazine report on the wartime work of the Truman Committee. Document 25-6 reports the wartime experiences, on the job and at home, of one female worker. Document 25-7 indicates that the employment of women in war work was conceived as a temporary measure. Propaganda was deemed essential to motivating the armed forces and the civilian population, as Document 25-8 illustrates.

25-5 Billion-Dollar Watchdog (1943)

In light of the events of the Second World War, regarded as the "Good War," the Neutrality Acts have come to be seen as essentially negative and the result of a naïve isolationism. But there was a cynical side to isolationism as well, which translated into support for congressional scrutiny of the many relationships and contracts between business and government, in order to protect the U.S. taxpayer against the threat of war profiteering. The U.S. senator (and later President) from Missouri, Harry Truman (1884–1972), championed this cause and chaired a Senate investigative committee during the war, which saved the U.S. Treasury many billions of dollars.

Source: Time magazine article, "Billion-Dollar Watchdog" March 8, 1943, in *Congress Investigates: A Documented History 1792–1974*, eds. Arthur M. Schlesinger Jr. and Roger Bruns (New York: Chelsea House Publishers, 1975), 4:3223–3227. Reprinted with permission of Time, Inc. www.time.com.

Anywhere but in a democracy, the Senate's irreverent Truman Committee would be fair game for liquidation. In a perfect state, free from butterfingers and human frailty, it would be unnecessary. In the U.S., democratic but far from perfect, the Truman Committee this week celebrated its second successful birthday as one of the most useful Government agencies of World War II.

Had they had time, its ten members might have toasted their accomplishments all night. They had served as watchdog, spotlight, conscience and spark plug to the economic war-behind-the-lines. They had prodded Commerce Secretary Jesse Jones into building synthetic-rubber plants, bludgeoned the President into killing off doddering old SPAB and setting up WPB.

They had called the turn on raw-materials shortages, had laid down the facts of the rubber famine four months before the famed Baruch report. One single investigation, of graft and waste in Army camp building, had saved the U.S. $250,000,000 (according to the Army's own Lieut. General Brehon B. Somervell). Their total savings ran into billions, partly because of what their agents had ferreted out in the sprawling war program, partly because their hooting curiosity was a great deterrent to waste.

The Truman Committee was too busy to celebrate. In its 16th month of war, the U.S. had still not digested some of war's first readers. The first annual Truman report, with its shocking evidence of all-around bungling, had not spelled the end of bungling. This week the Committee worked on its second annual report, which would have to recite much the same story, chastise many of the same men, pose some of the same old problems. How big should the Army be? How could the manpower tangle be solved? Where would the nation get its food this year? What was wrong with WPB?

Over these basic questions, which the Truman Committee, on behalf of all American citizens, had hoped would be solved two years ago, the committee still sweated, glowed and tried to shed light.

The bigger the U.S. arsenal grew, the more important the Truman Committee became. As the arsenal turned into a modern-day Great Pyramid, most Washington officials still lugged just one stone, and many carried it in the wrong direction.

The closest thing yet to a domestic high command was the Truman Committee. Its members had no power to act or order. But, using Congress's old prerogative to look, criticize and recommend, they had focused the strength of public opinion on the men who had the power. They had a fund of only $200,000 (some still unspent) only twelve investigators, 18 clerks and stenographers. But it was an obscure war plant that had never been visited by the committee. Its members had heard hundreds of witnesses, taken 4,000,000 words of testimony. With battle-royal impartiality, they had given thick ears and red faces to Cabinet members, war agency heads, generals, admirals, big businessmen, little businessmen, labor leaders.

In wartime, even more than in peace, a democracy must keep an eye on itself. This eye the Truman Committee has kept unblinkingly and, by & large, well. It has made mistakes. Some of its data have been gathered too quickly, then reduced to generalities that glittered without illuminating. Its members, including Chairman Harry S. Truman, have sometimes failed to look before they leaped to conclusions. But it has never strayed too far off the beam, nor stayed there too long.

Said one Washingtonian last week: "There's only one thing that worries me more than the present state of the war effort. That's to think what it would be like by now without Truman." For a Congressional committee to be considered the first line of defense—especially in a nation which does not tend to admire its representatives, in Congress assembled—is encouraging to believers in democracy. So is the sudden emergence of Harry Truman, whose presence in the Senate is a queer accident of democracy, as the committee's energetic generalissimo.

Neat, grey Harry Shippe Truman was sworn in as Senator from Missouri in 1934. The only men seen to smile during the ceremony were two husky lieutenants of Boss Tom Pendergast's notorious Kansas City Democratic machine, who sat beaming in the gallery.

In a perfect democracy, free from bosses, string-pulling and finagling at the polls, Harry Truman would probably never have reached Washington. He was Tom Pendergast's hand-picked candidate, yanked out of obscurity so deep that few Missouri voters had ever heard of him. He was nominated, over two more deserving candidates, largely by a vast plurality rolled up in Boss Pendergast's Jackson County, whose registration lists were loaded with dead men and men who had never lived. Thanks to the Boss's great power and the New Deal's 1934 popularity, his election was then automatic.

No one yet knows exactly why Boss Pendergast picked Truman for the Senate. One theory: the Boss was in the whimsical mood of a socialite sneaking a pet Pekingese into the *Social Register*. A better theory: the Boss was impressed by the Midwestern adage that every manure pile should sprout one rose—he saw in Truman a personally honest, courageous man whose respectability would disguise the odors of the Pendergast mob. Certainly Truman was no statesman in 1934. Neither had he ever been touched by scandal.

Truman grew up on a Jackson County farm 15 miles from Kansas City. He tried for West Point, was rejected for one weak eye, gave up the thought of college and went to work instead. He dusted bottles in a drugstore, wrapped papers for the Kansas City *Star*, clerked in Kansas City banks. Five years out of high school he was droning along at $100 a month and ready to go back to his father's farm for good.

World War I pulled him off the farm again. He went to France a lieutenant, became captain of the 129th Field Artillery's rough-&-tumble Battery D. He was shy, reserved, wore big shell-rimmed glasses: to his pugnacious Irish privates he looked like something of a milquetoast. At the start he was perhaps the most unpopular captain in France. But he led his men doggedly through St. Mihiel and the Argonne, spiked a panic when German artillery once drew a bead on his battery, lost only one soldier killed and one wounded, was promoted to major. On the ship back from France his men took a cut out of all crap games, bought him a monstrous loving cup four feet high and big enough to hold ten gallons.

The war, brightest spot in Truman's pre-Senate record, was soon followed by the saddest. With a soldier buddy and $15,000 saved and borrowed, he opened a haberdashery on Kansas City's sporty Twelfth Street, roamed behind the counters selling socks, neckties and garters. In twelve months the store went broke, with debts it took years to pay off.

At 37, Harry Truman, bottle duster, bank clerk and would-be haberdasher, was bogged deep in failure. All he had to show for his career was an old army uniform and a loving cup too ostentatious to keep on the mantel.

Most U.S. political machines, however disreputable, have two saving graces to their credit: 1) they are close enough to the people to know basic human desires, tragedies and needs; 2) their bosses, earthy and disillusioned men, have sometimes found talent where more snobbish souls would never have thought to look. In 1921, with his haberdashery under the hammer and black days ahead, Truman looked up some old servicemen friends in the Pendergast organization. Truman was a veteran, a farmer, a Mason, a Democrat from three generations back; he had friends all over Jackson County. The machine made him road overseer, then country judge (an administrative post), finally U.S. Senator.

Truman was no ball of fire in his first term. He sat meekly in the freshman row, blinked when critics called him Pendergast's "errand boy," was second only to Pennsylvania's Joseph Guffey (whose vote for New Deal measures was pure automatic reflex) in unswerving support of Administration policies.

On Burt Wheeler's Interstate Commerce Committee, he showed unexpected talents as an investigator of railroad high shenanigans. (He and canny Burt Wheeler are still good friends, despite their schism on foreign policy.) But this was too esoteric an assignment to impress many voters back home. They saw him chiefly in another light.

A young U.S. attorney named Maurice M. Milligan was cleaning up Kansas City, sending one Pendergast henchman after another to jail for vote frauds, getting closer & closer to the Big Boss himself. When Milligan came up for reappointment, Truman did his best to ease him out, made one of the bitterest speeches ever heard on the Senate floor. Milligan got the reappointment anyway, promptly sent Pendergast to prison for evading income taxes on some of his slush money. Truman shouted: "Purely political. . . . I won't desert a ship in distress. . . .

In a perfect democracy, run without hitch, Truman would never have been returned to the Senate in 1940. A majority of Missouri Democrats, in full revolt against the machine, opposed him in the primary. But Attorney Milligan and ex-Governor Lloyd Crow Stark split the opposition vote, and Truman slipped in with an 8,000-vote plurality. For a nation whose Administration, army and war contractors are not perfect either, it has turned out to be a good thing.

The Senate Committee Investigating National Defense was Truman's own idea. As country judge he had awarded $60,000,000 in contracts; he knew how hard it had been to get honest performance. Up rose the Senator to demand that Congress keep an eye on war expenditures: he had never yet found a contractor who, left unwatched, "wouldn't leave the Government holding the bag."

At first nobody took the Truman Committee seriously. The Senate gave him $15,000 (about as much as the Dies Committee spends every seven weeks) and a group of colleagues chosen mostly from junior Senators, such as Minnesota's young Joseph Ball, Washington's first-terming Mon C. Wallgren, New York's busy James M. Mead. Also on the committee went cagey old Tom Connally of Texas, to see that the juniors kept their heads. For its first assignment, the Committee chose a modest chore: delving into the more flagrant charges of graft in camp and war-plant construction, plugging some of the more open sewers down which Government money drained.

But Truman had bigger ideas. In selecting the Committee's chief counsel, he rejected all political recommendations, went instead to Attorney General (now Justice) Robert H. Jackson for advice. Thus he got a top-flight investigator: rotund, brilliant, young Hugh Fulton, a Justice Department prosecutor who had sent Howard C. Hopson, head of Associated Gas & Electric Corp., to prison.

Truman's junior Senators, hungry for tough assignments, went to work with a will. Harry Truman, a shrewd politician, a maker of friends, a great man for shooting trouble, always kept his committee happy and on the ball. It got more money, branched out, found itself deep in every phase of the war. Today few committees, and few men, wield such power.

Harry Truman would rather be fighting the war than policing it. At 58, he still goes solemnly through his setting up exercises every morning, can still get into his World War I uniform. In 1939, like any old soldier, he dug out his old artillery maps, hung them on his office wall to help follow the fighting. He applied for active duty after Pearl Harbor, still likes to think the Army was wrong to say no. When Senate office building janitors began marking off air-raid shelters, he fetched his two rusty World War I helmets to his office, announced that he was ready to serve as warden. No planes came over Washington, so he finally stacked the helmets in his office fireplace and redoubled his efforts on the committee.

To a man once called errand boy, those efforts have produced gratifying results. The St. Louis *Post-Dispatch*, which once threw at him everything its angry editors thought fit to print, recently called him "one of the most useful and at the same time one of the most forthright and fearless" of today's

Senators. In Kansas City he was feted by the Chamber of Commerce, which once fought him tooth & nail. A naturally shy and self-effacing man, Harry Truman brushes off the praise: instead of speaking himself in Kansas City, he introduced the members of his committee, let them talk. But even a perfect democrat could not have helped being pleased.

Truman is still a politician, would be loyal to the Pendergast machine today if it still existed. "Tom Pendergast never asked me to do a dishonest deed," he says. "He knew I wouldn't do it if he had asked me. He was always my friend. He was always honest with me, and when he made a promise he kept it. I wouldn't kick a friend when he was down."

But Harry Truman has many another quality not usually associated with machine politicians. He is scrupulously honest: when a magazine paid him $750 for an article on his committee, he added the money to the committee's funds.

His only vices are small-stakes poker, an occasional drink of bourbon.

As committee chairman he is a man with a crusade: he says, "The goal of every man on the committee is to promote the war effort to the limit of efficiency and exertion. It doesn't do any good to go around digging up dead horses after the war is over, like the last time. The thing to do is dig this stuff up now, and correct it. If we run this war program efficiently, there won't be any opportunity for someone to stir up a lot of investigations after the war—and cause a wave of revulsion that will start the country on the downhill road to unpreparedness and put us in another war in 20 years. . . ."

In many ways Harry Truman and his committee, celebrating their anniversary this week by poring over another report, seemed the best living proof that democracy, even when imperfect, can be a success.

Questions

1. Describe the activities of the Truman Committee.
2. The *Time* article assumes a connection between a healthy democracy and vigorous congressional oversight. Explain.

25-6 Women Working at the Home Front (1944)

Norma Yerger Queen

Responding to a request from the U.S. Office of War Information for the observations of wartime female workers, Norma Yerger Queen—a Utahan married to a professional and employed in a military hospital—wrote about her work, community, and home life.

Source: Norma Yerger Queen to the Office of War Information, 1944.

The people of this community all respect women who work regardless of the type of work. Women from the best families & many officers' wives work at our hospital. It is not at all uncommon to meet at evening parties in town women who work in the kitchens or offices of our hospital (Army-Bushnell-large general). The city mayor's wife too works there.

The church disapproves of women working who have small children. The church has a strong influence in our county.

For the canning season in our county men's & women's clubs & the church all recruited vigorously for women for the canneries. . . .

I personally have encouraged officers' wives who have no children to get out and work. Those of us who have done so have been highly respected by the others and we have not lost social standing. In fact many of the social affairs are arranged at our convenience.

Some husbands do not approve of wives working & this has kept home some who do not have small children. Some of the women just do not wish to put forth the effort.

The financial incentive has been the strongest influence among most economic groups but especially among those families who were on relief for many years. Patriotic motivation is sometimes present but sometimes it really is a front for the financial one. A few women work to keep their minds from worrying about sons or husbands in the service.

In this county, the hospital is the chief employer of women. A few go to Ogden (20 miles away) to work in an arsenal, the depot, or the air field. When these Ogden plants first opened quite a few women started to work there, but the long commuting plus the labor at the plants plus their housework proved too much.

Many women thoroughly enjoy working & getting away from the home. They seem to get much more satisfaction out of it than out of housework or bringing up children.

Those who quit have done so because of lack of good care for their children, or of inability to do the housework & the job. . . .

I am convinced that if women could work 4 days a week instead of 5½ or 6 that more could take jobs. I found it impossible to work 5½ days & do my housework but when I arranged for 4 days I could manage both. These days one has to do everything—one cannot buy services as formerly. For instance—laundry. I'm lucky. I can send out much of our laundry to the hospital but even so there is a goodly amount that must be done at home—all the ironing of summer dresses is very tiring. I even have to press my husband's trousers—a thing I never did in all my married life. The weekly housecleaning—shoe shining—all things we formerly had done by others. Now we also do home canning. I never in the 14 yrs. of my married life canned 1 jar. Last summer I put up dozens of quarts per instructions of Uncle Sam. I'm only one among many who is now doing a lot of manual labor foreign to our usual custom. I just could not take on all that & an outside job too. It is no fun to eat out—you wait so long for service & the restaurants cannot be immaculately kept—therefore it is more pleasant & quicker to cook & eat at home even after a long day's work. I've talked with the personnel manager at the hospital & he agrees that fewer days a week would be better. The canneries finally took women for as little as 3 hrs. a day.

This is a farming area & many farm wives could not under any arrangements take a war job. They have too much to do at their farm jobs & many now have to go into the fields, run tractors & do other jobs formerly done by men. I marvel at all these women are able to do & feel very inadequate next to them. . . .

Here is the difference between a man working & a woman as seen in our home—while I prepare the evening meal, my husband reads the evening paper. We then do the dishes together after which he reads his medical journal or cogitates over some lecture he is to give or some problem at his lab. I have to make up grocery lists, mend, straighten up a drawer, clean out the ice box, press clothes, put away anything strewn about the house, wash bric a brac, or do several of hundreds of small "woman's work is never done" stuff. This consumes from 1 to 2 hrs. each evening after which I'm too weary to read any professional social work literature & think I'm lucky if I can keep up with the daily paper, Time Life or Reader's Digest. All this while my husband is relaxing & resting. When I worked full time, we tried doing the housecleaning together but it just didn't click. He is responsible for introducing penicillin into Bushnell & thus into the army & there were so many visiting brass hats & night conferences he couldn't give even one night a week to the house. Then came a mess of lectures of all kinds of medical meetings—he had to prepare those at home. I got so worn out it was either quit work or do it part time.

This has been a lot of personal experience but I'm sure we are no exception. I thought I was thro[ugh] working in 1938. My husband urged me to help out for the war effort—he's all out for getting the war work done & he agreed to do his share of the housework. He is not lazy but he found we could not do it. I hope this personal experience will help to give you an idea of some of the problems.

Questions

1. According to Queen, why did women take jobs during the war? Which reasons were especially important?

2. What practical factors limited women's participation in the labor force? How did practical factors affect women who came from different circumstances—farms, towns, the military base?

3. How did their outside jobs affect women's work at home? What problems and options did Queen mention?

25-7 Mother, When Will You Stay Home Again? (1944)

Wartime advertising encouraged married women with children to work in war industries, but increasingly such messages included references to the postwar lives of such women. This advertisement appeared a year before Germany's surrender, fifteen months before Japan's. (Far more American military casualties were suffered during this period than during the first twenty-nine months of America's involvement.)

Source: Advertisement, Adel Manufacturing Company, *Saturday Evening Post*, May 6, 1944. Courtesy Gaslight Advertising Archives, Inc.

War Industry Employment Advertisement (1944)

Questions

1. What role does the child play in the advertisement?
2. What purposes are served by placing the husband-father in military service?
3. How would the wartime experience of the wife-mother contribute to her postwar life, according to the ad?

25-8 Wartime Posters: The Japanese and Venereal Disease as Enemies (c. 1944)

World War II propaganda took many forms—radio broadcasts, films, and print media. As during World War I, posters played a role, whether directed against the United States' wartime enemies, especially the Japanese, or against the threat of venereal disease (see text pp. 775–776).

Sources: "This Is the Enemy," shown at the Museum of Modern Art (New York City), reprinted in *Life*, from John W. Dower, *War without Mercy: Race and Power in the Pacific War* (New York: Pantheon, 1986), 189; "V. D.: Worst of the Three," National Archives, Washington, DC, from Allan M. Brandt, *No Magic Bullet: A Social History of Venereal Disease in the United States*, exp. ed. (New York: Oxford University Press, 1987), following 164.

Posters of the Enemy (c. 1944)

Questions

1. Compare and contrast the depiction of a Japanese soldier of World War II (Document 25-8) with depictions of German soldiers during World War I (Document 22-9) and World War II (see text p. 776).

2. Compare and contrast the depiction of women in World War I posters (Document 22-6), a 1936 political cartoon (Document 25-2), and a World War II poster (Document 25-8).

Question for Further Thought

1. Compare Documents 25-6 and 25-7. What light do they shed on issues of gender, class, and status in wartime America?

Life on the Home Front

Life on the home front for Americans involved neither heavy civilian casualties nor widespread property destruction, as it did for citizens in other warring nations. For Americans with loved ones in the armed forces, there was fear; for those losing loved ones in the war, grief. But rationing and wartime shortages of consumer products were inconveniences, rarely hardships in a nation experiencing war-based prosperity. Publicized drives to secure blood, collect scrap metal, sell government bonds, and plant "victory gardens" contributed to the war effort and reminded those on the home front that American soldiers were fighting in a war (see text pp. 782–783). Document 25-9 offers the reminiscences of a woman on the home front during World War II.

In describing life in the United States during World War II, the text makes clear that Japanese Americans, most of them American-born citizens, suffered as no other group did during the war — or during World War I, for that matter, for all its intolerance and repression (see text pp. 784–787). Document 25-10 is President Roosevelt's executive order authorizing the prescribing of military areas.

25-9 Remembering the War Years on the Home Front (1984)

Decades after World War II, a retired music teacher in Los Angeles reminisced about her life during the war years for Studs Terkel's oral history of the war. After the war, she divorced her husband, with whom she had had two children.

Source: Studs Terkel, *"The Good War": An Oral History of World War Two* (New York: Pantheon, 1984), 117–122. Reprinted with permission.

While my conscience told me the war was a terrible thing, bloodshed and misery, there was excitement in the air. I had just left college and was working as a substitute teacher. Life was fairly dull. Suddenly, single women were of tremendous importance. It was hammered at us through the newspapers and magazines and on the radio. We were needed at USO, to dance with the soldiers.

A young woman had a chance to meet hundreds of men in the course of one or two weeks, more than she would in her entire lifetime, because of the war. Life became a series of weekend dates.

I became a nurse's aide, working in the hospital. Six or eight weeks of Red Cross training. The uniform made us special people.

I had a brother three years younger than I. He was a cadet at the Santa Ana Air Base. Your cadet got to wear these great hats, with the grommets taken out. Marvelous uniform.

I met my future husband. I really didn't care that much for him, but the pressure was so great. My brother said, "What do you mean you don't like Glenn? You're going to marry him, aren't you?" The first time it would occur to me that I would marry anybody. The pressure to marry a soldier was so great that after a while I didn't question it. I have to marry sometime and I might as well marry him.

That women married soldiers and sent them overseas happy was hammered at us. We had plays on the radio, short stories in magazines, and the movies, which were a tremendous influence in our lives. The central theme was the girl meets the soldier, and after a weekend of acquaintanceship they get married and overcome all difficulties. Then off to war he went. Remember Judy Garland and Robert Walker in *The Clock*?

I knew Glenn six weekends, not weeks. They began on Saturday afternoon. We'd go out in herds and stay up all night. There was very little sleeping around. We were still at the tail-end of a moral generation. Openly living together was not condoned. An illegitimate child was a horrendous handicap. It was almost the ruination of your life. I'm amazed and delighted the way it's accepted now, that a girl isn't a social outcast any more.

The OWI, Office of War Information, did a thorough job of convincing us our cause was unquestionably right. We were stopping Hitler, and you look back at it and you had to stop him. We were saving the world. We were allied with Russia, which was great at that time. Germany had started World War One and now it had started World War Two, and Germany would be wiped off the face of the map. A few years later, when we started to arm Germany, I was so shocked. I'd been sold a bill of goods—I couldn't believe it. I remember sitting on the back porch here, I picked up the paper, and I read that our sworn enemy was now our ally. The disillusionment was so great, that was the beginning of distrusting my own government.

Russia was the enemy from the time I was born right up to '40. Then Russia became our ally. It's funny nobody stopped to think that this was a complete turnabout. As soon as the war was over, we dropped Russia. During the war, I never heard any anti-Russian talk. . . .

I had one of those movie weddings, because he couldn't get off the base. My parents approved. My mother had a talk with the head of the army base. She wanted to know why the guy I was to marry was restricted to quarters. He said they were having nothing but trouble with this guy. The major advised her to think twice before permitting her daughter to marry a man like this: he was totally irresponsible. My mother told me this, and we both laughed about it. He was a soldier. He could not be anything but a marvelous, magnificent human being. I couldn't believe for one minute what this major had said. He was given a weekend pass and we were married.

Shortly after that he was thrown out of the air force. This was my first doubt that he was magnificent. So he became a sergeant, dusting off airplanes. He was sent to various parts of the country: Panama City, Florida; Ypsilanti, Michigan; Amarillo, Texas. I followed him.

That's how I got to see the misery of the war, not the excitement. Pregnant women who could barely balance in a rocking train, going to see their husbands for the last time before the guys were sent overseas. Women coming back from seeing their husbands, traveling with small children. Trying to feed their kids, diaper their kids. I felt sorriest for them. It suddenly occurred to me that this wasn't half as much fun as I'd been told it was going to be. I just thanked God I had no kids. . . .

I ran across a lot of women with husbands overseas. They were living on allotment. Fifty bucks a month wouldn't support you. Things were relatively cheap, but then we had very little money, too. It wasn't so much the cost of food as points. I suspected the ration system was a patriotic ploy to keep our enthusiasm at a fever pitch. If you wanted something you didn't have points for, it was the easiest thing in the world. . . . Almost everybody had a cynical feeling about what we were told was a food shortage.

When it started out, this was the greatest thing since the Crusades. The patriotic fervor was such at the beginning that if "The Star-Spangled Banner" came on the radio, everybody in the room would stand up at attention. As the war dragged on and on and on, we read of the selfish actions of guys in power. We read stories of the generals, like MacArthur taking food right out of the guys' mouths when he was in the Philippines, to feed his own family. Our enthusiasm waned and we became cynical and very tired and sick of the bloodshed and killing. It was a completely different thing than the way it started. At least, this is the way I felt. . . .

There were some movies we knew were sheer bullshit. There was a George Murphy movie where he gets his draft induction notice. He opens the telegram, and he's in his pajamas and bare feet, and he runs around the house and jumps over the couch and jumps over the chair, screaming and yelling. His landlady says, "What's going on?" "I've been drafted! I've been drafted." Well, the whole audience howled. 'Cause they know you can feed 'em only so much bullshit.

If a guy in a movie was a civilian, he always had to say— what was it? Gene Kelly in *Cover Girl*? I remember this line: "Well, Danny, why aren't you in the army?" "Hell, I was wounded in North Africa, and now all I can do is keep people happy by putting on these shows." They had to explain why the guy wasn't in uniform. Always. There was always a line in the movie: "Well, I was turned down." "Oh, tough luck." There were always soldiers in the audience, and they would scream. So we recognized a lot of the crap. . . .

The good war? That infuriates me. Yeah, the idea of World War Two being called a good war is a horrible thing. I think of all the atrocities. I think of a madman who had all this power. I think of the destruction of the Jews, the misery, the horrendous suffering in the concentration camps. In 1971, I visited Dachau. I could not believe what I saw. There's one barracks left, a model barracks. You can reconstruct the rest and see what the hell was going on. It doesn't take a visit to make you realize the extent of human misery.

I know it had to be stopped and we stopped it. But I don't feel proud, because the way we did it was so devious. How many years has it been? Forty years later? I feel I'm standing here with egg on my face. I was lied to. I was cheated. I was made a fool of. If they had said to me, Look, this has to be done and we'll go out and do the job . . . we'll all get our arms and legs blown off but it has to be done, I'd understand. If they didn't hand me all this shit with the uniforms and the girls in their pompadours dancing at the USO and all those songs—"There'll Be Bluebirds over the White Cliffs of Dover"—bullshit! . . .

My brother was killed. Not even overseas. He was killed in North Carolina on a fight exercise. It ruined my mother, because she just worshipped my brother. He was the only boy. I don't think she ever recovered from it.

There was *one* good thing came out of it. I had friends whose mothers went to work in factories. For the first time in their lives, they worked outside the home. They realized that they were capable of doing something more than cook a meal. I remember going to Sunday dinner one of the older women invited me to. She and her sister at the dinner table were talking about the best way to keep their drill sharp in the factory. I had never heard anything like this in my life. It was just marvelous. I was tickled.

But even here we were sold a bill of goods. They were hammering away that the woman who went to work did it temporarily to help her man, and when he came back, he took her job and she cheerfully leaped back to the home. . . .

I think a lot of women said, Screw that noise. 'Cause they had a taste of freedom, they had a taste of making their own money, making their own decisions. I think the beginning of the women's movement had its seeds right there in World War Two.

Question

1. What strikes you about this woman's memories of World War II, the home front, and herself during the war?

25-10 Executive Order 9066 to Prescribe Military Areas (1942)

After the surprise Japanese attack on Pearl Harbor, amid rumors of espionage and subversion in Hawaii, the American people grew fearful of enemy aliens. On February 19, 1942, President Roosevelt issued an executive order authorizing the secretary of war to identify areas of the country where movements of people could be controlled or restricted. Prescription was followed by executive and military orders that resulted in the internment of Japanese and Japanese Americans in relocation camps (see text pp. 784–787).

Source: Executive Order No. 9066, "Authorizing the Secretary of War to Prescribe Military Areas," *Federal Register* 7, no. 38 (February 25, 1942): 1407.

AUTHORIZING THE SECRETARY OF WAR TO PRESCRIBE MILITARY AREAS

WHEREAS the successful prosecution of the war requires every possible protection against espionage and against sabotage to national-defense material, national-defense premises, and national-defense utilities. . . .

NOW, THEREFORE, by virtue of the authority vested in me as President of the United States, and Commander in Chief of the Army and Navy, I hereby authorize and direct the Secretary of War, and the Military Commanders whom he may from time to time designate, whenever he or any designated Commander deems such actions necessary or desirable, to prescribe military areas in such places and of such extent as he or the appropriate Military Commanders may determine, from which any or all persons may be excluded, and with such respect to which, the right of any person to enter, remain in, or leave shall be subject to whatever restrictions the Secretary of War or the appropriate Military Commander may impose in his discretion. The Secretary of War is hereby authorized to provide for residents of any such area who are excluded therefrom, such transportation, food, shelter, and other accommodations as may be necessary, in the judgement of the Secretary of War or the said Military Commander, and until other arrangements are made, to accomplish the purpose of this order. The designation of military areas in any region or locality shall supersede designations of prohibited and restricted areas by the Attorney General under the Proclamations of December 7 and 8, 1941, and shall supersede the responsibility and authority of the Attorney General under the said Proclamations in respect of such prohibited and restricted areas.

I hereby further authorize and direct the Secretary of War and the said Military Commanders to take such other steps as he or the appropriate Military Commander may deem advisable to enforce compliance with the restrictions applicable to each Military area hereinabove authorized to be designated, including the use of Federal troops and other Federal Agencies, with authority to accept assistance of state and local agencies.

I hereby further authorize and direct all Executive Departments, independent establishments and other Federal Agencies, to assist the Secretary of War or the said Military Commanders in carrying out this Executive Order, including the furnishing of medical aid, hospitalization, food, clothing, transportation, use of land, shelter, and other supplies, equipment, utilities, facilities and services.

This order shall not be construed as modifying or limiting in any way the authority heretofore granted under Executive Order No. 8972, dated December 12, 1941, nor shall it be construed as limiting or modifying the duty and responsibility of the Federal Bureau of Investigation, with respect to the investigation of alleged acts of sabotage or the duty and responsibility of the Attorney General and the Department of Justice under the Proclamations of December 7 and 8, 1941, prescribing regulations for the conduct and control of alien enemies, except as such duty and responsibility is superseded by the designation of military areas hereunder.

FRANKLIN D. ROOSEVELT
The White House
February 19, 1942

Questions

1. What specific concerns about national security led to the issuance of Executive Order 9066?
2. Did the order restricting the actions of residents of prescribed military areas identify specific individuals or groups? In your opinion, why was it written this way?
3. What limitations did the order place on the secretary of war and others authorized to enforce its provisions?

Questions for Further Thought

1. How do you account for differences between the treatment of Japanese Americans during World War II and the treatment of German Americans and Italian Americans during that war?
2. Review Norma Yerger Queen's account (Document 25-6) and an anonymous music teacher's account (Document 25-9) of women's lives during World War II, and compare and contrast the two women's lives on the home front during the war.

Fighting and Winning the War

Fighting in World War II took place on many fronts. In Document 25-11, Pulitzer Prize–winning war correspondent Ernie Pyle offers a firsthand account of how ordinary men braved extraordinary conditions in wartime Europe, from "hedgerow to hedgerow . . . from street to street." Document 25-12 provides American eyewitness accounts of concentration camps. In Document 25-13, Albert Einstein warns President Roosevelt in 1939 that "it is conceivable . . . that extremely powerful bombs of a new type may be constructed." The dropping of two atomic bombs and the entry of the Soviet Union in the Pacific-Asian war brought about Japan's surrender in August 1945. In Document 25-14, Henry L. Stimson, then secretary of war, makes the case for employing the atomic bomb against Japan.

25-11 Street Fighting (1944)

Ernie Pyle

Ernie Pyle (1900–1945) was a popular war correspondent whose columns were based not on press conferences or official releases but on the combat experiences of the average enlisted man or "G.I. Joe," which Pyle witnessed firsthand in the field. Historian William L. O'Neill called Pyle the "master of this form" and noted that some thought that "Pyle's hold on public opinion made him more important than many generals." Pyle left the battlefields of Europe to report on the closing action in the Pacific, where he was killed in 1945. At the time of his death, Pyle had a worldwide readership and his columns, like the one excerpted below, appeared in over seven hundred newspapers.

Source: Excerpt from Ernie Pyle, *Brave Men* (New York: Henry Holt and Company, 1944), 398–407. Copyright © 1943, 1944 by Scripps-Howard Newspaper Alliance; copyright © 1944 by Henry Holt and Company, Inc. Reprinted by permission of the Scripps Howard Foundation.

War in the Normandy countryside was a war from hedgerow to hedgerow, and when we got into a town or city it was a war from street to street. One day I went along—quite accidentally, I assure you—with an infantry company that had been assigned to clean out a pocket in the suburbs of Cherbourg. Since the episode was typical of the way an infantry company advanced into a city held by the enemy, I would like to try to give you a picture of it.

As I say, I hadn't intended to do it. I started out in the normal fashion that afternoon to go up to a battalion command post and just look around. I was traveling with Correspondent Charles Wertenbaker and Photographer Bob Capa, both of *Time* and *Life* magazines.

Well, when we got to the CP we were practically at the front lines. The post was in a church that stood on a narrow street. In the courtyard across the street MP's were frisking freshly taken prisoners. I mingled with them for a while. They were still holding their hands high in the air, and it's pretty close to the front when prisoners do that. They were obviously frightened and eager to please their captors. A soldier standing beside me asked one German kid about the insigne on his cap, so the kid gave it to him. The prisoners had a rank odor about them, like silage. Some of them were Russians, and two of these had their wives with them. They had been living together right at the front. The women thought we were going to shoot their husbands and they were frantic. That's one way the Germans kept the conscripted Russians fighting—they had thoroughly sold them on the belief that we would shoot them as soon as they were captured.

Below us there were big fires in the city, and piles of black smoke. Explosions were going on all around us. Our own big shells would rustle over our heads and explode on beyond with a crash. German 20-millimeter shells would spray over our heads and hit somewhere in the town behind us. Single rifle shots and machine-pistol blurps were constant. The whole thing made me tense and jumpy. The nearest fighting Germans were only 200 yards away.

We were just hanging around absorbing all this stuff when a young lieutenant, in a trench coat and wearing sun glasses—although the day was miserably dark and chill—came over to us and said, "Our company is starting in a few minutes to go up this road and clean out a strong point. It's about half a mile from here. There are probably snipers in some of the houses along the way. Do you want to go with us?"

I certainly didn't. Going into battle with an infantry company is not the way to live to a ripe old age. But when I was invited, what could I do? So I said, "Sure." And so did Wertenbaker and Capa. Wert never seemed nervous, and Capa was notorious for his daring. Fine company for me to be keeping. We started walking. Soldiers of the company were already strung out on both sides of the road ahead of us, just lying and waiting till their officers came along and said go. We walked until we were at the head of the column. As we went the young officer introduced himself. He was Lieutenant Orion Shockley, of Jefferson City, Missouri. I asked him how he got the odd name Orion. He said he was named after Mark Twain's brother. Shockley was executive officer of the company. The company commander was Lieutenant Lawrence McLaughlin, from Boston. One of the company officers was a replacement who had arrived just three hours previously and had never been in battle before. I noticed that he ducked sometimes at our own shells, but he was trying his best to seem calm.

The soldiers around us had a two weeks' growth of beard. Their uniforms were worn slick and very dirty—the uncomfortable gas-impregnated clothes they had come ashore in. The boys were tired. They had been fighting and moving constantly forward on foot for nearly three weeks without rest—sleeping out on the ground, wet most of the time, always tense, eating cold rations, seeing their friends die. One of them came up to me and said, almost belligerently, "Why don't you tell the folks back home what this is like? All they hear about is victories and a lot of glory stuff. They don't know that for every hundred yards we advance somebody gets killed. Why don't you tell them how tough this life is?"

I told him that was what I tried to do all the time. This fellow was pretty fed up with it all. He said he didn't see why his outfit wasn't sent home; they had done all the fighting. That wasn't true at all, for there were other divisions that had fought more and taken heavier casualties. Exhaustion will make a man feel like that. A few days' rest usually has him smiling again.

As we waited to start our advance, the low black skies of Normandy let loose on us and we gradually became soaked to the skin. Lieutenant Shockley came over with a map and explained to us just what his company was going to do to wipe out the strong point of pillboxes and machine-gun nests. Our troops had made wedges into the city on both sides of us, but nobody had yet been up this street where we were heading. The street, they thought, was almost certainly under rifle fire.

"This is how we'll do it," the lieutenant said. "A rifle platoon goes first. Right behind them will go part of a heavy-weapons platoon, with machine guns to cover the first platoon. Then comes another rifle platoon. Then a small section with mortars, in case they run into something pretty heavy. Then another rifle platoon. And bringing up the rear, the rest of the heavy-weapons outfit to protect us from behind. We don't know what we'll run into, and I don't want to stick you right out in front, so why don't you come along with me? We'll go in the middle of the company."

I said, "Okay." By this time I wasn't scared. You seldom are once you're into something. Anticipation is the worst. Fortunately, this little foray came up so suddenly there wasn't time for much anticipation.

The rain kept coming down, and we could sense that it had set in for the afternoon. None of us had raincoats, and by evening there wasn't a dry thread on us. I could go back to a tent for the night, but the soldiers would have to sleep the way they were.

We were just ready to start when all of a sudden bullets came whipping savagely right above our heads. "It's those damn 20-millimeters again," the lieutenant said. "Better hold it up a minute." The soldiers all crouched lower behind the wall. The vicious little shells whanged into a grassy hillside just beyond us. A French suburban farmer was hitching up his horses in a barnyard on the hillside. He ran into the house. Shells struck all around it. Two dead Germans and a dead American still lay in his driveway. We could see them when we moved up a few feet.

The shells stopped, and finally the order to start was given. As we left the protection of the high wall we had to cross a little culvert right out in the open and then make a turn in the road. The men went forward one at a time. They crouched and ran, ape-like, across this dangerous space. Then, beyond the culvert, they filtered to either side of the road, stopping and squatting down every now and then to wait a few moments. The lieutenant kept yelling at them as they started, "Spread it out now. Do you want to draw fire on yourselves? Don't bunch up like that. Keep five yards apart. Spread it out, dammit."

There is an almost irresistible pull to get close to somebody when you are in danger. In spite of themselves, the men would run up close to the fellow ahead for company. The other lieutenant now called out, "You on the right, watch the left side of the street for snipers; you on the left, watch the right side. Cover each other that way."

And a first sergeant said to a passing soldier, "Get that grenade out of its case. It won't do you no good in the case. Throw the case away. That's right."

Some of the men carried grenades already fixed in the ends of their rifles. All of them had hand grenades. Some had big Browning automatic rifles. One carried a bazooka. Interspersed in the thin line of men every now and then was a medic, with his bags of bandages and a Red Cross armband on his left arm. The men didn't talk among themselves. They just went. They weren't heroic figures as they moved forward one at a time, a few seconds apart. You think of attackers as being savage and bold. These men were hesitant and cautious. They were really the hunters, but they looked like the hunted. There was a confused excitement and a grim anxiety in their faces.

They seemed terribly pathetic to me. They weren't warriors. They were American boys who by mere chance of fate had wound up with guns in their hands, sneaking up a death-laden street in a strange and shattered city in a faraway country in a driving rain. They were afraid, but it was beyond their power to quit. They had no choice. They were good boys. I talked with them all afternoon as we sneaked slowly forward along the mysterious and rubbled street, and I know they were good boys. And even though they weren't warriors born to the kill, they won their battles. That's the point.

It came time for me to go — out alone into that empty expanse of fifteen feet — as we began our move into the street that led to what we did not know. One of the soldiers asked if I didn't have a rifle. Every time I was really in the battle lines they would ask me that. I said no, correspondents weren't allowed to; it was against international law. The soldiers thought that didn't seem right. Finally the sergeant motioned — it was my turn. I ran with bent knees, shoulders hunched, out across the culvert and across the open space. Lord, but I felt lonely out there. I had to stop right in the middle of the open space, to keep my distance behind the man ahead. I got down behind a little bush, as though that would have stopped anything.

Just before starting I had got into conversation with a group of soldiers who were to go right behind me. I was just starting to put down the boys' names when my turn came to go. So it wasn't till an hour or more later, during one of our long waits as we crouched against some buildings, that I worked my way back along the line and got their names. It was pouring rain, and as we squatted down for me to write on my knee each soldier would have to hold my helmet over my notebook to keep it from getting soaked.

Here are the names of just a few of my "company mates" in that little escapade that afternoon: Sergeant Joseph Palajsa, of 187 I Street, Pittsburgh. Pfc. Arthur Greene, of 618 Oxford Street, Auburn, Massachusetts; his New England accent was so broad I had to have him spell out "Arthur" and "Auburn" before I could catch what he said. Pfc. Dick Medici, of 5231 Lemy Avenue, Detroit. Lieutenant James Giles, a platoon leader, from Athens, Tennessee; he was so wet, so worn, so soldier-looking that I was startled when he said "lieutenant," for I thought he was a GI. Pfc. Arthur Slageter, of 3915 Taylor Avenue, Cincinnati; he was an old reader of my column back home, and therefore obviously a fine fellow. Pfc. Robert Eddie, of New Philadelphia, Pennsylvania; Eddie was thirty, he was married, and he used to work in a brewery back home; he was a bazooka man, but his bazooka was broken that day so he was just carrying a rifle. Pfc. Ben Rienzi, of 430 East 115 Street, New York. Sergeant Robert Hamilton, of 2940 Robbins Avenue, Philadelphia, who was wounded in Africa. Sergeant Joe Netscavge, of Shenandoah, Pennsylvania, who sported two souvenirs of the Normandy campaign—a deep dent in his helmet where a sniper's bullet glanced off, and a leather cigarette case he got from a German prisoner. These boys were Ninth Division veterans, most of whom had fought in Tunisia and in Sicily too.

Gradually we moved on, a few feet at a time. The soldiers hugged the walls on both sides of the street, crouching all the time. The city around us was still full of sound and fury. We couldn't tell where anything was coming from or going to. The houses had not been blown down. But now and then a wall would have a round hole through it, and the windows had all been knocked out by concussion, and shattered glass littered the pavements. Gnarled telephone wire was lying everywhere. Most of the people had left the city. Shots, incidentally, always sound louder and distorted in the vacuumlike emptiness of a nearly deserted city. Lonely doors and shutters banged noisily back and forth. All of a sudden a bunch of dogs came yowling down the street, chasing each other. Apparently their owners had left without them, and they were running wild. They made such a noise that we shooed them on in the erroneous fear that they would attract the Germans' attention.

The street was a winding one and we couldn't see as far ahead as our forward platoon. But soon we could hear rifle shots not far ahead, and the rat-tat-tat of our machine guns, and the quick blurp-blurp of German machine pistols. For a long time we didn't move at all. While we were waiting the lieutenant decided to go into the house just behind us. A middle-aged Frenchman and his wife were in the kitchen. They were poor people. The woman was holding a terrier dog in her arms, belly up, the way you cuddle a baby, and soothing it by rubbing her cheek against its head. The dog was trembling with fear from the noise.

Pretty soon the word was passed back down the line that the street had been cleared as far as a German hospital about a quarter of a mile ahead. There were lots of our own wounded in that hospital and they were now being liberated. So Lieutenant Shockley and Wertenbaker and Capa and I went on up the street, still keeping close to the walls. I lost the others before I had gone far. For as I passed doorways soldiers would call out to me and I would duck in and talk for a moment and put down a name or two.

By now the boys along the line were feeling cheerier, for no word of casualties had been passed back. And up there the city was built up enough so that the waiting riflemen had the protection of doorways. It took me half an hour to work my way up to the hospital—and then the excitement began. The hospital was in our hands, but just barely. There seemed to be fighting in the next block. I say seemed to be, because actually it was hard to tell. Street fighting is just as confusing as field fighting. One side would bang away for a while, then the other side. Between the sallies there were long lulls, with only stray and isolated shots. Just an occasional soldier was sneaking about, and I didn't see anything of the enemy at all. I couldn't tell half the time just what the situation was, and neither could the soldiers.

About a block beyond the hospital entrance two American tanks were sitting in the middle of the street, one about fifty yards ahead of the other. I walked toward them. Our infantrymen were in doorways along the street. I got within about fifty feet of our front tank when it let go its 75-millimeter gun. The blast was terrific there in the narrow street. Glass came tinkling down from nearby windows, smoke puffed around the tank, and the empty street was shaking and trembling with the concussion. As the tank continued to shoot I ducked into a doorway, because I figured the Germans would shoot back. Inside the doorway was a sort of street-level cellar, dirt-floored. Apparently there was a wine shop above, for the cellar was stacked with wire crates for holding wine bottles on their sides. There were lots of bottles, but they were all empty.

I went back to the doorway and stood peeking out at the tank. It started backing up. Then suddenly a yellow flame pierced the bottom of the tank and there was a crash of such intensity that I automatically blinked my eyes. The tank, hardly fifty feet from where I was standing, had been hit by an enemy shell. A second shot ripped the pavement at the side of the tank. There was smoke all around, but the tank didn't catch fire. In a moment the crew came boiling out of the turret. Grim as it was, I almost had to laugh as they ran toward me. I have never seen men run so violently. They ran all over, with arms and heads going up and down and with marathon-race grimaces. They plunged into my doorway.

I spent the next excited hour with them. We changed to another doorway and sat on boxes in the empty hallway. The floor and steps were thick with blood where a soldier had been treated within the hour. What had happened to the tank was this: They had been firing away at a pillbox ahead when their 75 backfired, filling the tank with smoke and blinding them. They decided to back up in order to get their bearings, but after backing a few yards the driver was so blinded that he stopped. Unfortunately, he stopped exactly at the foot of a side street. More unfortunately, there was another German pillbox up the side street. All the Germans had to do was take easy aim and let go at the sitting duck. The first shot hit a tread, so the tank couldn't move. That was when the boys got out. I don't know why the Germans didn't fire at them as they poured out.

The escaped tankers naturally were excited, but they were as jubilant as June bugs and ready for more. They had never been in combat before the invasion of Normandy, yet in three weeks their tank had been shot up three times. Each time it was repaired and put back into action. And it could be repaired again. The name of their tank, appropriately, was "Be Back Soon."

The main worry of these boys was the fact that they had left the engine running. We could hear it chugging away. It's bad for a tank motor to idle very long. But they were afraid to go back and turn the motor off, for the tank was still right in line with the hidden German gun. Also, they had come out wearing their leather crash helmets. Their steel helmets were still inside the tank, and so were their rifles. "We'll be a lot of good without helmets or rifles!" one of them said.

The crew consisted of Corporal Martin Kennelly, of 8040 Langley Street, Chicago, the tank commander; Sergeant L. Wortham, Leeds, Alabama, driver; Private Ralph Ogren, of 3551 32nd Avenue South, Minneapolis, assistant driver; Corporal Albin Stoops, Marshalltown, Delaware, gunner, and Private Charles Rains, of 1317 Madison Street, Kansas City, the loader. Private Rains was the oldest of the bunch, and the only married one. He used to work as a guard at the Sears, Roebuck plant in Kansas City. "I was MP to fifteen hundred women," he said with a grin, "and how I'd like to be back doing that!" The other tankers all expressed loud approval of this sentiment.

Commander Kennelly wanted to show me just where his tank had been hit. As a matter of fact he hadn't seen it for himself yet, for he came running up the street the moment he jumped out of the tank. So when the firing died down a little we sneaked up the street until we were almost even with the disabled tank. But we were careful not to get our heads around the corner of the side street. The first shell had hit the heavy steel brace that the tread runs on, and then plunged on through the side of the tank, very low. "Say!" Kennelly said in amazement. "It went right through our lower ammunition storage box! I don't know what kept the ammunition from going off. We'd have been a mess if it had. Boy, it sure would have got hot in there in a hurry!"

The street was still empty. Beyond the tank about two blocks was a German truck, sitting all alone in the middle of the street. It had been blown up, and its tires had burned off. This truck was the only thing we could see. There wasn't a human being in sight anywhere. Then an American soldier came running up the street shouting for somebody to send a medic. He said a man was badly wounded just ahead. He was extremely excited, yelling, and getting madder because there was no medic in sight. Word was passed down the line, and pretty soon a medic came out of a doorway and started up the street. The excited soldier yelled at him and began cussing, and the medic broke into a run. They ran past the tanks together, and up the street a way they ducked into a doorway.

On the corner just across the street from where we were standing was a smashed pillbox. It was in a cut-away corner like the entrances to some of our corner drugstores at home, except that instead of there being a door there was a pillbox of reinforced concrete, with gun slits. The tank boys had shot it to pieces and then moved their tank up even with it to get the range of the next pillbox. That one was about a block ahead, set in a niche in the wall of a building. That's what the boys had been shooting at when their tank was hit. They had knocked it out, however, before being knocked out themselves.

For an hour there was a lull in the fighting. Nobody did anything about a third pillbox, around the corner. Our second tank pulled back a little and just waited. Infantrymen worked their way up to second-story windows and fired their rifles up the side street without actually seeing anything to shoot at. Now and then blasts from a 20-millimeter gun would splatter the buildings around us. Then our second tank would blast back in that general direction, over the low roofs, with its machine gun. There was a lot of dangerous-sounding noise, but I don't think anybody on either side got hit.

Then we saw coming up the street, past the wrecked German truck I spoke of, a group of German soldiers. An officer walked in front, carrying a Red Cross flag on a stick. Bob Capa braved the dangerous funnel at the end of the side street where the damaged tank stood, leapfrogging past it and on down the street to meet the Germans. First he snapped some pictures of them. Then, since he spoke German, he led them on back to our side of the invisible fence of battle. Eight of them were carrying two litters bearing two wounded German soldiers. The others walked behind with their hands up. They went on past us to the hospital. We assumed that they were from the second knocked-out pillbox. I didn't stay to see how the remaining pillbox was knocked out. But I suppose our second tank eventually pulled up to the corner, turned, and let the pillbox have it. After that the area would be clear of everything but snipers. The infantry, who up till then had been forced to keep in doorways, would then continue up the street and poke into the side streets and into the houses until everything was clear.

That's how a strong point in a city is taken. At least that's how ours was taken. There are not always tanks to help, and not always is it done with so little shedding of blood. But the city was already crumbling when we started in on this strong point, which was one of the last, and they didn't hold on too bitterly. But we didn't know that when we started.

Questions

1. Why do you think Pyle's columns appealed to readers back home?
2. What role did Pyle see the press playing in wartime?
3. It is often said that journalists write the first draft of history. Explain this in terms of Pyle's work.

25-12 Remembering the Holocaust (1945)

William McConahey, Dorothy Wahlstrom

During the winter of 1944–1945, the advancing Red Army seized German extermination, or death, camps, which had been built in Eastern Europe to slaughter Jews and others, from all areas of German-occupied Europe. The following spring, the advancing armies of the Western Allies liberated German concentration camps within the Reich itself (see text pp. 790–791). Originally built to terrorize "enemies" of the Nazi regime, these had increasingly become forced and slave-labor camps during the war. Large numbers of those imprisoned within them died—from overwork, malnutrition, disease, and brutal treatment—or were murdered. Here, two Americans recall the concentration camps that they helped free during the final weeks of the war in Europe.

Source: Recollections of Dr. William McConahey and Dorothy Wahlstrom, excerpted from *Witnesses to the Holocaust: An Oral History*, ed. Rhoda G. Lewin, 202–203, 214–215. Copyright © 1990 by Jewish Community Relations Council / Anti-Defamation League of Minnesota and the Dakotas. Reprinted with permission of the publisher.

(a) William McConahey, Medical Officer at Flossenburg with the 337th Infantry

. . . As we moved into Germany we started hearing about the concentration camps at army briefings. April 23 our division liberated Flossenburg, and I went in there next day.

Flossenburg held 15,000 prisoners but there were only about 1,500 left. The German guards had marched out about 13,000 toward Dachau, to get away from our advancing army. It was a very poignant, sad-looking road because they were marched out carrying blankets or maybe a jacket, but they were too weak to carry things, and they'd dropped them along the way.

A few very emaciated prisoners were wandering around in blue and white striped prison garb. My jeep driver spoke German, so he had conversations with many of the prisoners. They were from all over Europe—Poles, Russians, Czechs, French, Belgian, Spanish. They had a lot of Jewish people there, of course, but many were political prisoners, from the underground, or just people picked up by the Gestapo because they thought they were anti-Hitler. They all bore the scars of beatings and being knocked around.

The camp was laid out in very neat barracks style, with two big barbed wire fences around it. Running through it was a little railroad with a little pushcart like you see in coal mines, pushed by hand, to haul bodies to the crematory.

Three inmates, pretty much zombies, were still burning bodies in the crematory because prisoners were still dying left and right, and for sanitation you had to do something! About sixteen corpses were lined up to be burned. They were just skin and bone, each one weighing about forty pounds, I'd guess, because you could pick them up with one hand. One fellow opened the furnace door, and there were a couple of bodies in there, sizzling away.

We saw the beautiful houses where the S.S. guards lived with their women. Then I walked into the barracks, very drab and cold, with three tiers of bunks on each side. It was nothing but boards—no mattresses, no straw, nothing. Each bunk was big enough for one, but they said three slept there every night.

I visited the "hospital" where they brought prisoners to die. They'd put them on the bare wooden floor with straw on it, and they'd lie there in their own excrement and vomitus, until they died.

Some prisoners, their spirits were broken, they were just shells and they'd lost the will to live. Some were so close to death you couldn't feed them because they hadn't eaten for so long their stomachs were atrophied, and if they got food in, they vomited and bloated and obstructed. We tried to get them back on small feedings very slowly, over a period of weeks, but we couldn't save them. We felt terrible. They were dying under our eyes, and there was nothing we could do.

After the war ended, we drove to Dachau one day. Dachau was much bigger than Flossenburg. Again, we toured the barracks and saw the crematories, six big ovens. Outside were thousands of jars stacked up, the charred bones and ashes of people who had been burned there. I was told they used these for fertilizing the gardens, and that sometimes they would send a political prisoner's family a box of bones, anybody's bones. We saw the whipping posts, the torture chambers. It was obviously degradation and terror and horror and suffering, just like Flossenburg, only on a bigger scale.

It was those concentration camps that made us realize what we were fighting for. We really felt this was a holy crusade to wipe out this diabolical regime. We have sadistic bums and misfits and psychopaths in this country who could do what the S.S. did in Germany, but Hitler gave them a rank, a uniform, a purpose and a mission, and encouraged them.

The infantry medical corps was not like *M.A.S.H.* or the movies. Unless you're there, unless you're in combat, and fight the battle, and crawl on your belly under machine gun bullets, and dig a foxhole in the rain, and get shelled, you can't understand what it's like. We were with the infantry, having the same life as they were having, and the same death they were having, too.

The war marked me for life. I realized that making a lot of money or being a big shot, that wasn't as important as doing something worthwhile. To really be a person was what counted.

(b) Dorothy Wahlstrom, Captain with the 127th Evac Hospital, Whose Unit Entered Dachau on May 3, 1945

The dead and dying were all around us. Piles of naked dead were stacked beside the crematorium and inside. Dachau was certainly a calculated attempt by the Nazis to desecrate not only the body, but also the mind and spirit.

We set up ward units in the S.S. barracks. Dead dogs lay in the kennels nearby, killed by our military after survivors told us they were used to tear away parts of prisoners' bodies on command. Survivors told us infants were torn limb from limb as their mothers watched. They told us that prisoners who could no longer work were used as live targets for machine gun practice. They mentioned other unspeakable atrocities—medical experiments, torture chambers—horrors too terrible to think up without having experienced them.

Each of the two hospital units at Dachau, the 127th and the 116th, was equipped to care for 450 patients at one time, but each unit cared for 1,500 or more at peak times.

We felt we were dancing with death. We couldn't get away from it, and wondered if it would ever stop. We couldn't care for everyone, and often we could not admit a patient until another one died or was discharged from the hospital. It was truly heartbreaking for our medical officers to have to choose the people they thought might live and leave the sickest ones to die. Of those we thought would live, seven or eight stretchers were lined up in front of each ward in the morning—people who had died during the night.

The severely malnourished did not tolerate increased rations too well, and dysentery was out of control. We had double bunk beds for our patients, and the diarrhea was so severe it leaked from bed to bed. Many were so emaciated that even with the care we gave them, it was too late.

The diseases were those that go with filth and lack of sanitation. One and one-half tons of DDT powder were used in dusting the camp to get control of the infected lice that spread typhus. Perhaps 20 percent of the camp population had active tuberculosis.

I wish I could describe the smells and the silence of death. Even now, certain sights and sounds can remind me of that pain, that suffering, that sorrow and loss and anguish and degradation.

I find comfort in the sacred Scriptures that record that the Lord will vindicate His Israel, and that there will always be a House of David. I am truly grateful to the Lord for having allowed me to serve His people.

Questions

1. Which sights and smells affected McConahey and Wahlstrom the most as they toured the death camps?
2. Why did medical personnel feel so frustrated in their efforts to save the victims they found in the camps?
3. How did their experiences with the victims of the Holocaust change the lives of McConahey and Wahlstrom?

25-13 Letter to President Roosevelt (1939)

Albert Einstein

Albert Einstein (1879–1955), perhaps the most famous scientist of the twentieth century, left his native Germany when the Nazis took over the country and accepted a post at the Institute for Advanced Study in Princeton, New Jersey. A pacifist, Einstein nevertheless wrote a letter on August 2, 1939, to President Roosevelt informing him of the military implications of recent developments in atomic physics. President Roosevelt responded by appointing an advisory committee to investigate the matter, which led to the creation of the Manhattan Project, America's successful effort to build an atomic bomb.

Source: Albert Einstein, letter to President Roosevelt, August 2, 1939, from *Einstein on Peace*, ed. Otto Nathan and Heinz Norden (New York: Simon and Schuster, 1960), 294–296. Copyright © 1960 by the Estate of Albert Einstein. Reprinted by permission of the Roger Richman Agency.

Albert Einstein
Old Grove Road
Nassau Point
Peconic, Long Island
August 2, 1939

F. D. Roosevelt
President of the United States
White House
Washington, D.C.

Sir:

Some recent work by E. Fermi and L. Szilard, which has been communicated to me in manuscript, leads me to expect that the element uranium may be turned into a new and important source of energy in the immediate future. Certain aspects of the situation seem to call for watchfulness and, if necessary, quick action on the part of the Administration. I believe, therefore, that it is my duty to bring to your attention the following facts and recommendations.

In the course of the last four months it has been made probable—through the work of Joliot in France as well as Fermi and Szilard in America—that it may become possible to set up nuclear chain reactions in a large mass of uranium, by which vast amounts of power and large quantities of new radium-like elements would be generated. Now it appears almost certain that this could be achieved in the immediate future.

This new phenomenon would also lead to the construction of bombs, and it is conceivable—though much less certain—that extremely powerful bombs of a new type may thus be constructed. A single bomb of this type, carried by boat or exploded in a port, might very well destroy the whole port together with some of the surrounding territory. However, such bombs might very well prove to be too heavy for transportation by air.

The United States has only very poor ores of uranium in moderate quantities. There is some good ore in Canada and the former Czechoslovakia, while the most important source of uranium is the Belgian Congo.

In view of this situation you may think it desirable to have some permanent contact maintained between the Administration and the group of physicists working on chain reactions in America. One possible way of achieving this might be for you to entrust with this task a person who has your confidence and who could perhaps serve in an unofficial capacity. His task might comprise the following:

a) To approach Government Departments, keep them informed of the further developments, and put forward recommendations for Government action, giving particular attention to the problem of securing a supply of uranium ore for the United States.

b) To speed up the experimental work which is at present being carried on within the limits of the budgets of University laboratories, by providing funds, if such funds be required, through his contacts with private persons who are willing to make contributions for this cause, and perhaps also by obtaining the cooperation of industrial laboratories which have the necessary equipment.

I understand that Germany has actually stopped the sale of uranium from the Czechoslovakian mines which she has taken over. That she should have taken such early action might perhaps be understood on the ground that the son of the German Under-Secretary of State, von Weizsäcker, is attached to the Kaiser Wilhelm Institut in Berlin, where some of the American work on uranium is now being repeated.

Yours very truly,
A. Einstein

Questions

1. What were Einstein's recommendations to the president?
2. What evidence did Einstein provide to encourage the United States to act quickly?

25-14 The Decision to Use the Atomic Bomb (1945)

Henry L. Stimson

Given the increasing bloodiness and brutality of World War II and the massive scientific and engineering investment in developing the atomic bomb, it was nearly inevitable that, once built, the bomb would be used. Germany surrendered in May 1945 before the successful testing of the atomic bomb, so the first—and to date, only—atomic bombs employed in war were dropped on Japan that August (see text pp. 793–796). Secretary of War Henry L. Stimson (1867–1950) served Presidents Roosevelt and Truman throughout World War II. His postwar account of the decision to employ the bomb includes an assessment of the war written shortly before the testing of the atomic bomb.

Source: Henry L. Stimson, "The Decision to Use the Atomic Bomb" from *Harper's Magazine*, February 1947, 102–107. Copyright 1947 by *Harper's Magazine*. All rights reserved. Reproduced by special permission.

It was already clear in July that even before the invasion we should be able to inflict enormously severe damage on the Japanese homeland by the combined application of "conventional" sea and air power. The critical question was whether this kind of action would induce surrender. It therefore became necessary to consider very carefully the probable state of mind of the enemy, and to assess with accuracy the line of conduct which might end his will to resist.

With these considerations in mind, I wrote a memorandum for the President, on July 2, which I believe fairly represents the thinking of the American government as it finally took shape in action. This memorandum was prepared after discussion and general agreement with Joseph C. Grew, Acting Secretary of State, and Secretary of the Navy Forrestal, and when I discussed it with the President, he expressed his general approval.

JULY 2, 1945

MEMORANDUM FOR THE PRESIDENT:

PROPOSED PROGRAM FOR JAPAN

1. The plans of operation up to and including the first landing have been authorized and the preparation for the operation are now actually going on. This situation was accepted by all members of your conference on Monday, June 18.

2. There is reason to believe that the operation for the occupation of Japan following the landing may be a very long, costly, and arduous struggle on our part. The terrain, much of which I have visited several times, has left the impression on my memory of being one which would be susceptible to a last ditch defense such as has been made on Iwo Jima and Okinawa and which of course is very much larger than either of those two areas. According to my recollection it will be much more unfavorable with regard to tank maneuvering than either the Philippines or Germany.

3. If we once land on one of the main islands and begin a forceful occupation of Japan, we shall probably have cast the die of last ditch resistance. The Japanese are highly patriotic and certainly susceptible to calls for fanatical resistance to repel an invasion. Once started in actual invasion, we shall in my opinion have to go through with an even more bitter finish fight than in Germany. We shall incur the losses incident to such a war and we shall have to leave the Japanese islands even more thoroughly destroyed than was the case with Germany. This would be due both to the difference in the Japanese and German personal character and the differences in the size and character of the terrain through which the operations will take place.

4. A question then comes: Is there any alternative to such a forceful occupation of Japan which will secure for us the equivalent of an unconditional surrender of her forces and a permanent destruction of her power again to strike an aggressive blow at the "peace of the Pacific"? I am inclined to think that there is enough such chance to make it well worthwhile our giving them a warning of what is to come and a definite op-

portunity to capitulate. As above suggested, it should be tried before the actual forceful occupation of the homeland islands is begun and furthermore the warning should be given in ample time to permit a national reaction to set in.

We have the following enormously favorable factors on our side—factors much weightier than those we had against Germany:

- Japan has no allies.
- Her navy is nearly destroyed and she is vulnerable to a surface and underwater blockade which can deprive her of sufficient food and supplies for her population.
- She is terribly vulnerable to our concentrated air attack upon her crowded cities, industrial and food resources.
- She has against her not only the Anglo-American forces but the rising forces of China and the ominous threat of Russia.
- We have inexhaustible and untouched industrial resources to bring to bear against her diminishing potential.
- We have great moral superiority through being the victim of her first sneak attack.

The problem is to translate these advantages into prompt and economical achievement of our objectives. I believe Japan is susceptible to reason in such a crisis to a much greater extent than is indicated by our current press and other current comment. Japan is not a nation composed wholly of mad fanatics of an entirely different mentality from ours. On the contrary, she has within the past century shown herself to possess extremely intelligent people, capable in an unprecedentedly short time of adopting not only the complicated technique of Occidental civilization but to a substantial extent their culture and their political and social ideas. Her advance in all these respects during the short period of sixty or seventy years has been one of the most astounding feats of national progress in history—a leap from the isolated feudalism of centuries into the position of one of the six or seven great powers of the world. She has not only built up powerful armies and navies. She has maintained an honest and effective national finance and respected position in many of the sciences in which we pride ourselves. Prior to the forcible seizure of power over her government by the fanatical military group in 1931, she had for ten years lived a reasonably responsible and respectable international life.

My own opinion is in her favor on the two points involved in this question:

a. I think the Japanese nation has the mental intelligence and versatile capacity in such a crisis to recognize the folly of a fight to the finish and to accept the proffer of what will amount to an unconditional surrender; and

b. I think she has within her population enough liberal leaders (although now submerged by the terrorists) to be depended upon for her reconstruction as a responsible member of the family of nations. I think she is better in this last respect than Germany was. Her liberals yielded only at the point of pistol and, so far as I am aware, their liberal attitude has not been personally subverted in the way which was so general in Germany.

On the other hand, I think that the attempt to exterminate her armies and her population by gunfire or other means will tend to produce a fusion of race solidity and antipathy which has no analogy in the case of Germany. We have a national interest in creating, if possible, a condition wherein the Japanese nation may live as a peaceful and useful member of the future Pacific community.

5. It is therefore my conclusion that a carefully timed warning be given to Japan by the chief representatives of the United States, Great Britain, China, and, if then a belligerent, Russia by calling upon Japan to surrender and permit the occupation of her country in order to insure its complete demilitarization for the sake of the future peace.

This warning should contain the following elements:

The varied and overwhelming character of the force we are about to bring to bear on the islands.

The inevitability and completeness of the destruction which the full application of this force will entail.

The determination of the Allies to destroy permanently all authority and influence of those who have deceived and misled the country into embarking on world conquest.

The determination of the Allies to limit Japanese sovereignty to her main islands and to render them powerless to mount and support another war.

The disavowal of any attempt to extirpate the Japanese as a race or to destroy them as a nation.

A statement of our readiness, once her economy is purged of its militaristic influence, to permit the Japanese to maintain such industries, particularly of a light consumer character, as offer no threat of aggression against their neighbors, but which can produce a sustaining economy, and provide a reasonable standard of living. The statement should indicate our willingness, for this purpose, to give Japan trade access to external raw materials, but no longer any control over the sources of supply outside her main islands. It should also indicate our willingness, in accordance with our now established foreign trade policy, in due course to enter into mutually advantageous trade relations with her.

The withdrawal from their country as soon as the above objectives of the Allies are accomplished, and as soon as there has been established a peacefully inclined government, of a character representative of the masses of the Japanese people. I personally think that if in saying this we should add that we do not exclude a constitutional monarchy under her present dynasty, it would substantially add to the chances of acceptance.

6. Success of course will depend on the potency of the warning which we give her. She has an extremely sensitive national pride and, as we are now seeing every day, when actually locked with the enemy will fight to the very death. For that reason the warning must be tendered before the actual invasion has occurred and while the impending destruction, though clear beyond peradventure, has not yet reduced her to fanatical despair. If Russia is a part of the threat, the Russian attack, if actual, must not have progressed too far. Our own bombing should be confined to military objectives as far as possible.

It is important to emphasize the double character of the suggested warning. It was designed to promise destruction if Japan resisted, and hope, if she surrendered.

It will be noted that the atomic bomb is not mentioned in this memorandum. On grounds of secrecy the bomb was never mentioned except when absolutely necessary, and furthermore, it had not yet been tested. It was of course well forward in our minds, as the memorandum was written and discussed, that the bomb would be the best possible sanction if our warning were rejected.

THE USE OF THE BOMB

The adoption of the policy outlined in the memorandum of July 2 was a decision of high politics; once it was accepted by the President, the position of the atomic bomb in our planning became quite clear. I find that I stated in my diary, as early as June 19, that "the last chance warning . . . must be given before an actual landing of the ground forces in Japan, and fortunately the plans provide for enough time to bring in the sanctions to our warning in the shape of heavy ordinary bombing attack and an attack of S-1." S-1 was a code name for the atomic bomb.

There was much discussion in Washington about the timing of the warning to Japan. The controlling factor in the end was the date already set for the Potsdam meeting of the Big Three. It was President Truman's decision that such a warning should be solemnly issued by the U.S. and the U.K. from this meeting, with the concurrence of the head of the Chinese government, so that it would be plain that *all* of Japan's principal enemies were in entire unity. This was done, in the Potsdam ultimatum of July 26, which very closely followed the above memorandum of July 2, with the exception that it made no mention of the Japanese Emperor.

On July 28 the Premier of Japan, Suzuki, rejected the Potsdam ultimatum by announcing that it was "unworthy of public notice." In the face of this rejection we could only proceed to demonstrate that the ultimatum had meant exactly what it said when it stated that if the Japanese continued the war, "the full application of our military power, backed by our resolve, will mean the inevitable and complete destruction of the Japanese armed forces and just as inevitably the utter devastation of the Japanese homeland."

For such a purpose the atomic bomb was an eminently suitable weapon. The New Mexico test occurred while we were at Potsdam, on July 16. It was immediately clear that the power of the bomb measured up to our highest estimates. We had developed a weapon of such a revolutionary character that its use against the enemy might well be expected to produce exactly the kind of shock on the Japanese ruling oligarchy which we desired, strengthening the position of those who wished peace, and weakening that of the military party.

Because of the importance of the atomic mission against Japan, the detailed plans were brought to me by the military staff for approval. With President Truman's warm support I struck off the list of suggested targets the city of Kyoto. Although it was a target of considerable military importance, it had been the ancient capital of Japan and was a shrine of Japanese art and culture. We determined that it should be spared. I approved four other targets including the cities of Hiroshima and Nagasaki.

Hiroshima was bombed on August 6, and Nagasaki on August 9. These two cities were active working parts of the Japanese war effort. One was an army center; the other was naval and industrial. Hiroshima was the headquarters of the Japanese Army defending southern Japan and was a major military storage and assembly point. Nagasaki was a major seaport and it contained several large industrial plants of great wartime importance. We believed that our attacks had struck cities which must certainly be important to the Japanese military leaders, both Army and Navy, and we waited for a result. We waited one day.

Many accounts have been written about the Japanese surrender. After a prolonged Japanese cabinet session in which the deadlock was broken by the Emperor himself, the offer to surrender as made on August 10. It was based on the Potsdam terms, with a reservation concerning the sovereignty of the Emperor. While the Allied reply made no promises other than those already given, it implicitly recognized the Emperor's position by prescribing that his power must be subject to the orders of the Allied Supreme Commander. These terms were accepted on August 14 by the

Japanese, and the instrument of surrender was formally signed on September 2, in Tokyo Bay. Our great objective was thus achieved, and all the evidence I have seen indicates that the controlling factor in the final Japanese decision to accept our terms of surrender was the atomic bomb.*

The two atomic bombs which we had dropped were the only ones we had ready, and our rate of production at the time was very small. Had the war continued until the projected invasion on November 1, additional fire raids of B-29's would have been more destructive of life and property than the very limited number of atomic raids which we could have executed in the same period. But the atomic bomb was more than a weapon of terrible destruction; it was a psychological weapon. In March 1945 our Air Force had launched its first great incendiary raid on the Tokyo area. In this raid more damage was done and more casualties were inflicted than was the case at Hiroshima. Hundreds of bombers took part and hundreds of tons of incendiaries were dropped. Similar successive raids burned out a great part of the urban area of Japan, but the Japanese fought on. On August 6 one B-29 dropped a single atomic bomb on Hiroshima. Three days later a second bomb was dropped on Nagasaki and the war was over. So far as the Japanese could know, our ability to execute atomic attacks, if necessary by many planes at a time, was unlimited. As Dr. Karl Compton has said, "it was not one atomic bomb, or two, which brought surrender; it was the experience of what an atomic bomb will actually do to a community, *plus the dread of many more*, that was effective."

The bomb thus served exactly the purpose we intended. The peace party was able to take the path of surrender, and the whole weight of the Emperor's prestige was exerted in favor of peace. When the Emperor ordered surrender, and the small but dangerous group of fanatics who opposed him were brought under control, the Japanese became so subdued that the great undertaking of occupation and disarmament was completed with unprecedented ease.

A PERSONAL SUMMARY

In the foregoing pages I have tried to give an accurate account of my own personal observations of the circumstances which led up to the use of the atomic bomb and the reasons which underlay our use of it. To me they have always seemed compelling and clear, and I cannot see how any person vested with such responsibilities as mine could have taken any other course or given any other advice to his chiefs.

Two great nations were approaching contact in a fight to a finish which would begin on November 1, 1945. Our enemy, Japan, commanded forces of somewhat over 5,000,000 armed men. Men of these armies had already inflicted upon us, in our breakthrough of the outer perimeter of their defenses, over 300,000 battle casualties. Enemy armies still unbeaten had the strength to cost us a million more. *As long as the Japanese government refused to surrender*, we should be forced to take and hold the ground, and smash the Japanese ground armies, by close-in fighting of the same desperate and costly kind that we had faced in the Pacific islands for nearly four years.

In the light of the formidable problem which thus confronted us, I felt that every possible step should be taken to compel a surrender of the homelands, and a withdrawal of all Japanese troops from the Asiatic mainland and from other positions, before we had commenced an invasion. We held two cards to assist us in such an effort. One was the traditional veneration in which the Japanese Emperor was held by his subjects and the power which was thus vested in him over his loyal troops. It was for this reason that I suggested in my memorandum of July 2 that his dynasty should be continued. The second card was the use of the atomic bomb in the manner best calculated to persuade that Emperor and the counselors about him to submit to our demand for what was essentially unconditional surrender, placing his immense power over his people and his troops subject to our orders.

In order to end the war in the shortest possible time and to avoid the enormous losses of human life which otherwise confronted us, I felt that we must use the Emperor as our instrument to command and compel his people to cease fighting and subject themselves to our authority through him, and that to accomplish this we must give him and his controlling advisers a compelling reason to accede to our demands. This reason furthermore must be of such a nature that his people could understand his decision. The bomb seemed to me to furnish a unique instrument for that purpose.

My chief purpose was to end the war in victory with the least possible cost in the lives of the men in the armies which I had helped to raise. In the light of the alternatives which, on a fair estimate, were open to us I believe that no man, in our position and subject to our responsibilities, holding in his hands a weapon of such possibilities for accomplishing this purpose and saving those lives, could have failed to use it and afterwards looked his countrymen in the face.

As I read over what I have written, I am aware that much of it, in this year of peace, may have a harsh and unfeeling sound. It would perhaps be possible to say the same things and say them more gently. But I do not think it would be wise. As I look back over the five years of my service as Secretary of War, I see too many stern and heartrending decisions to be willing to pretend that war is anything else than what it is. The face of war is the face of death; death is an inevitable part of every order that a wartime leader gives. The decision to use the atomic bomb was a decision that brought death to over a hundred thousand Japanese. No explanation can change that fact and I do not wish to gloss it over. But this

---

*Report of United States Strategic Bombing Survey; "Japan's Struggle to End the War"; "If the Atomic Bomb Had Not Been Used," by K. T. Compton, *Atlantic Monthly*, December 1946; unpublished material of historical division, War Department Special Staff, June 1946.

deliberate, premeditated destruction was our least abhorrent choice. The destruction of Hiroshima and Nagasaki put an end to the Japanese war. It stopped the fire raids, and the strangling blockade; it ended the ghastly specter of a clash of great land armies.

In this last great action of the Second World War we were given final proof that war is death. War in the twentieth century has grown steadily more barbarous, more destructive, more debased in all its aspects. Now, with the release of atomic energy, man's ability to destroy himself is very nearly complete. The bombs dropped on Hiroshima and Nagasaki ended a war. They also made it wholly clear that we must never have another war. This is the lesson men and leaders everywhere must learn, and I believe that when they learn it they will find a way to lasting peace. There is no other choice.

Questions

1. What case did Stimson make for using the atomic bomb?
2. Were his postwar reflections consistent with his wartime assessment of the war against Japan, as revealed in the memorandum of July 2, 1945?
3. What were Stimson's views of the Japanese in 1945 and 1947?

Questions for Further Thought

1. Drawing on the text, reflect on Documents 25-12 and 25-14. How do they contribute to your understanding of World War II?
2. Historians estimate that twice as many civilians as soldiers were killed in World War II. Using Documents 25-12 and 25-14, explain why civilian deaths were so high.

PART SIX *The Age of Cold War Liberalism, 1945–1980*

CHAPTER TWENTY-SIX

Cold War America
1945–1960

The Cold War

With the defeat of Nazi tyranny and Japanese militarism, the new postwar world order was defined by the growing confrontation — military, economic, and ideological — between the two remaining superpowers: the United States and the Soviet Union. Soviet perceptions of U.S. intentions after the war are evident in the "Long Telegram" that was sent by Nikolai Novikov, the Soviet ambassador to the United States, to Viacheslav Molotov, the Soviet foreign minister (Document 26-1). Containment of the Soviet Union became central to American foreign policy, a doctrine articulated by George F. Kennan, a U.S. diplomat to Moscow, in 1946 and 1947 (Document 26-2). The United States used economic as well as military means to pursue this policy. The Marshall Plan was formulated to stimulate Europe's distressed postwar economy and promote an economic recovery that would benefit the United States as well as the European participants and also make Europe less susceptible to Communism (see text pp. 805–806, including "Voices from Abroad: Jean Monnet," text p. 807). To shield America's European allies from Soviet-bloc military threats, the United States and eleven other nations created the North Atlantic Treaty Organization (NATO), though not without debate in the U.S. Senate (Document 26-3). Finally, ominous developments during 1949 — the Communist Party's triumph over the nationalists in China's civil war and the Soviets' detonation of an atomic bomb — led the National Security Council (NSC) to prepare a sweeping strategic plan for waging the Cold War (see text pp. 809–810). Two months after President Truman received the report, known as NSC-68 (Document 26-4), the Cold War became a hot war in Asia, when Communist North Korea invaded South Korea (see text pp. 810–812).

26-1 Telegram: A Soviet View of U.S. Foreign Policy (1946)

Nikolai Novikov

The Novikov telegram became public in 1990, a year after the fall of the Berlin Wall and a year before the collapse of the Soviet Union. In this "Long Telegram," which was sent to Soviet Foreign Minister Viacheslav Molotov on September 27, 1946, Nikolai Novikov, the Soviet ambassador to the United States, attempts to interpret U.S. foreign policy for his superiors. This communication invites comparison with George F. Kennan's "Long Telegram" of February 22 of the same year (Document 26-2). In the following excerpt, the underline marks are Molotov's.

Source: From Kenneth M. Jensen, ed., *Origins of the Cold War: The Novikov, Kennan, and Roberts "Long Telegrams" of 1946*, rev. ed. (Washington, DC: United States Institute of Peace, 1993), 3–16. Reprinted with permission of The United States Institute of Peace.

U.S. FOREIGN POLICY IN THE POSTWAR PERIOD

The foreign policy of the United States, which reflects the imperialist tendencies of American monopolistic capital, is characterized in the postwar period by a striving <u>for world supremacy</u>. This is the real meaning of the many statements by President Truman and other representatives of American ruling circles: that the United States has the right to lead the world. All the forces of American diplomacy—the army, the air force, the navy, industry, and science—are enlisted in the service of this foreign policy. For this purpose broad plans for expansion have been developed and are being implemented through diplomacy and the establishment of a system of naval and air bases stretching far beyond the boundaries of the United States, through the arms race, and through the creation of ever newer types of weapons.

1. a) The foreign policy of the United States is conducted now <u>in a situation that differs greatly</u> from the one that existed in the prewar period. This situation does not fully conform to the calculations of those reactionary circles which hoped that during the Second World War they would succeed in avoiding, at least for a long time, the main battles in Europe and Asia. They calculated that the United States of America, if it was unsuccessful in completely avoiding direct participation in the war, would enter it only at the last minute, when it could easily affect the outcome of the war, completely ensuring its interests.

In this regard, it was thought that the main competitors of the United States would be crushed or greatly weakened in the war, and the United States by virtue of this circumstance would assume <u>the role of the most powerful factor</u> in resolving the fundamental questions of the postwar world. These calculations were also based on the assumption, which was very widespread in the United States in the initial stages of the war, that the Soviet Union, which had been subjected to the attack of German Fascism in June 1941, would also be exhausted or even completely destroyed as a result of the war.

Reality did not bear out the calculations of the American imperialists.

b) The two main aggressive powers, fascist Germany and militarist Japan, which were at the same time the main competitors of the United States in both the economic and foreign policy fields, were thoroughly defeated. The third great power, Great Britain, which had taken heavy blows during the war, now faces enormous economic and political difficulties. The political foundations of the British Empire were appreciably shaken, and crises arose, for example, in India, Palestine, and Egypt.

Europe has come out of the war with a completely dislocated economy, and the economic devastation that occurred in the course of the war cannot be overcome in a short time. All of the countries of Europe and Asia are experiencing a colossal need for consumer goods, industrial and transportation equipment, etc. Such a situation provides American monopolistic capital with <u>prospects for enormous shipments of goods and the importation of capital</u> into these countries—a circumstance that would permit it to infiltrate their national economies.

Such a development would mean a serious strengthening of the economic position of the United States in the whole world and would be a stage on the road to world domination by the United States.

c) On the other hand, we have seen a failure of calculations on the part of U.S. circles which assumed that the Soviet Union would be destroyed in the war or would come out of it so weakened that it would be forced to go begging to the United States for economic assistance. Had that happened, they would have been able to dictate conditions permitting the United States to carry out its expansion in Europe and Asia without hindrance from the USSR.

In actuality, despite all of the economic difficulties of the postwar period connected with the enormous losses inflicted by the war and the German fascist occupation, the Soviet Union continues to remain economically independent of the outside world and is rebuilding its national economy with its own forces.

At the same time <u>the USSR's international position is currently stronger than it was in the prewar period</u>. Thanks to the historical victories of Soviet weapons, the Soviet armed forces are located on the territory of Germany and other formerly hostile countries, thus guaranteeing that these countries will not be used again for an attack on the USSR. In formerly hostile countries, such as <u>Bulgaria, Finland, Hungary, and Romania</u>, democratic reconstruction has established regimes that have undertaken to strengthen and maintain friendly relations with the Soviet Union. In the Slavic countries that were liberated by the Red Army or with its assistance—<u>Poland, Czechoslovakia, and Yugoslavia</u>—democratic regimes have also been established that maintain relations with the Soviet Union on the basis of agreements on friendship and mutual assistance. . . .

Such a situation in Eastern and Southeastern Europe cannot help but be regarded by the American imperialists as an obstacle in the path of the expansionist policy of the United States.

2. a) The foreign policy of the United States is not determined at present by the circles in the Democratic party that (as was the case during Roosevelt's lifetime) strive to strengthen the cooperation of the three great powers that constituted the basis of the anti-Hitler coalition during the war. The ascendance to power of President Truman, a politically unstable person but with certain conservative tendencies, and the subsequent appointment of [James] Byrnes as Secretary of State meant <u>a strengthening of the influence on U.S. foreign policy of the most reactionary circles of the Democratic party</u>. . . .

b) At the same time, there has been <u>a decline in the influence on foreign policy of those who follow Roosevelt's course for cooperation among peace-loving countries</u>. Such persons in the government, in Congress, and in the leadership of the Democratic party are being pushed farther and farther into the background. . . .

3. Obvious indications of the U.S. effort to establish world dominance are also to be found in the increase in military potential in peacetime and in the establishment of a large number of naval and air bases both in the United States and beyond its borders.

In the summer of 1946, for the first time in the history of the country, Congress passed a law <u>on the establishment of a peacetime army, not on a volunteer basis but on the basis of universal military service</u>. The size of the army, which is supposed to amount to about one million persons as of July 1, 1947, was also increased significantly. The size of the navy at the conclusion of the war decreased quite insignificantly in comparison with wartime. At the present time, the American navy occupies first place in the world, leaving England's navy far behind, to say nothing of those of other countries.

<u>Expenditures on the army and navy have risen colossally</u>, amounting to 13 billion dollars according to the budget for 1946–47 (about 40 percent of the total budget of 36 billion dollars). This is more than ten times greater than corresponding expenditures in the budget for 1938, which did not amount to even one billion dollars.

Along with maintaining a large army, navy, and air force, the budget provides that these enormous amounts also will be spent on establishing a very extensive system of naval and air bases in the Atlantic and Pacific oceans. According to existing official plans, in the course of the next few years <u>228 bases</u>, points of support, and radio stations are to be constructed <u>in the Atlantic Ocean and 258 in the Pacific</u>. . . .

All of these facts show clearly that a decisive role in the realization of plans for world dominance by the United States is played by its armed forces.

4. a) One of the stages in the achievement of dominance over the world by the United States is its <u>understanding with England concerning the partial division of the world on the basis of mutual concessions</u>. The basic lines of the secret agreement between the United States and England regarding the division of the world consist, as shown by facts, in their agreement on the inclusion of Japan and China in the sphere of influence of the United States in the Far East, while the United States, for its part, has agreed not to hinder England either in resolving the Indian problem or in strengthening its influence in Siam and Indonesia.

b) In connection with this division, the United States at the present time is in control of China and Japan without any interference from England.

The American policy <u>in China</u> is striving for the complete economic and political submission of China to the control of American monopolistic capital. Following this policy, the American government does not shrink even from interference in the internal affairs of China. At the present time in China, there are more than 50,000 American soldiers. In a number of cases, American Marines participated directly in military operations against the people's liberation forces. The so-called "mediation" mission of General [George] Marshall is only a cover for interference in the internal affairs of China. . . .

. . . The measures carried out in northern China by the American army show that it intends to stay there for a long time.

<u>In Japan</u>, despite the presence there of only a small contingent of American troops, control is in the hands of the Americans. Although English capital has substantial interests in the Japanese economy, English foreign policy toward Japan is conducted in such a way as not to hinder the Americans from carrying out their penetration of the Japanese national economy and subordinating it to their influence. In the Far Eastern Commission in Washington and in the Allied Council in Tokyo, the English representatives as a rule make common cause with the U.S. representatives conducting this policy.

Measures taken by the American occupational authorities in the area of domestic policy and intended to support reactionary classes and groups, which the United States plans to use in the struggle against the Soviet Union, also meet with a sympathetic attitude on the part of England.

c) The United States follows a similar line with regard to the English sphere of influence in the Far East. Recently, the United States has ceased the attempts it has made over the past year to influence the resolution of <u>Indian</u> questions. Lately there have been frequent instances in which the reputable American press, more or less faithfully reflecting the official policy of the U.S. government, has made positive statements with regard to the English policy <u>in India</u>. American foreign policy also did not hinder British troops in joint action with the Dutch army from suppressing the national liberation movement <u>in Indonesia</u>. Moreover, there have even been instances in which the United States facilitated this British imperialist policy, handing over American weapons and equipment to the English and Dutch troops in Indonesia, sending Dutch naval personnel from the United States to Indonesia, etc.

5. a) If the division of the world in the Far East between the United States and England may be considered an accomplished fact, it cannot be said that an analogous situation exists in the basin of the Mediterranean Sea and in the countries adjacent to it. Rather, the facts indicate that an agreement of this sort has not yet been reached in the region of the Near East and the Mediterranean Sea. The difficulty experienced by the United States and England in reaching an agreement over this region derives from the fact that concessions on the part of England to the United States in the Mediterranean basin would be fraught with serious consequences for the whole future of the British Empire, for which the basin has exceptional strategic and economic significance. England would have nothing against using American armed forces and influence in this region, directing them northward against the Soviet Union. The United States, however, is not interested in providing assistance and support to the British Empire in this vulnerable point, but rather in its own more thorough penetration of the Mediterranean basin and Near East, to which the United States is attracted by the area's natural resources, primarily oil.

b) In recent years American capital has penetrated very intensively into the economy of the Near Eastern countries, in particular into the oil industry. At present there are American oil concessions in all of the Near Eastern countries that have oil deposits (Iraq, Bahrain, Kuwait, Egypt, and Saudi Arabia). American capital, which made its first appearance in the oil industry of the Near East only in 1927, now controls about 42 percent of all proven reserves in the Near East, excluding Iran. Of the total proven reserves of 26.8 billion barrels, over 11 billion barrels are owned by U.S. concessions. Striving to ensure further development of their concessions in different countries (which are often very large—Saudi Arabia, for example), the American oil companies plan to build a trans-Arabian pipeline to transport oil from the American concession in Saudi Arabia and in other countries on the southeastern shore of the Mediterranean Sea to ports in Palestine and Egypt.

In expanding in the Near East, American capital has English capital as its greatest and most stubborn competitor. The fierce competition between them is the chief factor preventing England and the United States from reaching an understanding on the division of spheres of influence in the Near East, a division that can occur only at the expense of direct British interests in this region. . . .

6. a) Relations between the United States and England are determined by two basic circumstances. On the one hand, the United States regards England as its greatest potential competitor; on the other hand, England constitutes a possible ally for the United States. Division of certain regions of the globe into spheres of influence of the United States and England would create the opportunity, if not for preventing competition between them, which is impossible, then at least of reducing it. At the same time, such a division facilitates the achievement of economic and political cooperation between them.

b) England needs American credits for reorganizing its economy, which was disrupted by the war. To obtain such credits England is compelled to make significant concessions. This is the significance of the loan that the United States recently granted England. With the aid of the loan, England can strengthen its economy. At the same time this loan opens the door for American capital to penetrate the British Empire. . . .

c) The political support that the United States provides for England is very often manifested in the international events of the postwar period. At recent international conferences the United States and England have closely coordinated their policies, especially in cases when they had to oppose the policy of the Soviet Union. The United States provided moral and political assistance to England in the latter's reactionary policy in Greece, India, and Indonesia. American and English policy is fully coordinated with regard to the Slavic and other countries adjoining the Soviet Union. The most important *démarches* of the United States and England in these countries after the end of the war were quite similar and parallel in nature. The policy of the United States and England in the Security Council of the United Nations (particularly in questions concerning Iran, Spain, Greece, the withdrawal of foreign troops from Syria and Lebanon, etc.) has the same features of coordination.

d) The ruling circles of the United States obviously have a sympathetic attitude toward the idea of a military alliance with England, but at the present time the matter has not yet culminated in an official alliance. Churchill's speech in Fulton calling for the conclusion of an Anglo-American military alliance for the purpose of establishing joint domination over the world was therefore not supported officially by Truman or Byrnes, although Truman by his presence [during the "Iron Curtain" speech] did indirectly sanction Churchill's appeal. . . .

e) The current relations between England and the United States, despite the temporary attainment of agreements on very important questions, are plagued with great internal contradictions and cannot be lasting.

The economic assistance from the United States conceals within itself a danger for England in many respects. First of all, in accepting the loan, England finds herself in a certain financial dependence on the United States from which it will not be easy to free herself. Second, it should be kept in mind that the conditions created by the loan for the penetration by American capital of the British Empire can entail serious political consequences. The countries included in the British Empire or dependent on it may—under economic pressure from powerful American capital—reorient themselves toward the United States, following in this respect the example of Canada, which more and more is moving away from the influence of England and orienting itself toward the United States. The strengthening of American positions in the Far East could stimulate a similar process in Australia and New Zealand. In the Arabic countries of the Near East, which are striving to emancipate themselves from the British Empire, there are groups within the ruling circles that would not be averse to working out a deal with the United States. It is quite possible that the Near East will become <u>a center of Anglo-American contradictions</u> that will explode the agreements now reached between the United States and England.

7. a) <u>The "hard-line" policy with regard to the USSR</u> announced by Byrnes after the rapprochement of the reactionary Democrats with the Republicans is at present the main obstacle on the road to cooperation of the Great Powers. It consists mainly of the fact that in the postwar period the United States no longer follows a policy of strengthening cooperation among the Big Three (or Four) but rather has striven to undermine the unity of these countries. The <u>objective</u> has been to <u>impose</u> the will of other countries on the Soviet Union. This is precisely the tenor of the policy of certain countries, which is being carried out with the blessing of the United States, to undermine or completely <u>abolish the principle of the veto</u> in the Security Council of the United Nations. This would give the United States opportunities to form among the Great Powers narrow groupings and blocs directed primarily against the Soviet Union, and thus to split the United Nations. Rejection of the veto by the Great Powers would transform the United Nations into an Anglo-Saxon domain in which the United States would play the leading role.

b) The present policy of the American government with regard to the USSR is also directed at limiting or dislodging the influence of the Soviet Union from neighboring countries. In implementing this policy in former enemy or Allied countries adjacent to the USSR, the United States attempts, at various international conferences or directly in these countries themselves, to support reactionary forces with <u>the purpose of creating obstacles to the process of democratization of these countries. In so doing, it also attempts to secure positions for the penetration of American capital into their economies</u>. Such a policy is intended to weaken and overthrow the democratic governments in power there, which are friendly toward the USSR, and replace them in the future with new governments that would obediently carry out a policy dictated from the United States. In this policy, the United States receives full support from English diplomacy.

c) One of the most important elements in the general policy of the United States, which is directed toward limiting the international role of the USSR in the postwar world, is the <u>policy with regard to Germany</u>. In Germany, the United States is taking measures to strengthen reactionary forces for the purpose of opposing democratic reconstruction. Furthermore, it displays special insistence on accompanying this policy with completely inadequate measures for the demilitarization of Germany.

The American occupation policy does not have the objective of eliminating the remnants of <u>German Fascism</u> and rebuilding German political life <u>on a democratic basis</u>, so that Germany might cease to exist as an aggressive force. The United States is not taking measures <u>to eliminate the monopolistic associations</u> of German industrialists on which German Fascism depended in preparing aggression and waging war. Neither is any <u>agrarian</u> reform being conducted to eliminate large landholders, who were also a reliable support for the Hitlerites. Instead, the United States is considering the possibility <u>of terminating the Allied occupation</u> of German territory before the main tasks of the occupation—the demilitarization and democratization of Germany—have been implemented. This would create the prerequisites for the revival of an imperialist Germany, which the United States plans to use in a future war on its side. One cannot help seeing that such a policy has a clearly outlined <u>anti-Soviet edge</u> and constitutes a serious danger to the cause of peace.

d) The numerous and extremely hostile statements by American government, political, and military figures with regard to the Soviet Union and its foreign policy are very characteristic of the current relationship between the ruling circles of the United States and the USSR. These statements are echoed in an even more unrestrained tone by the overwhelming majority of the American press organs. <u>Talk about a "third war,"</u> meaning a war against the Soviet Union, and even a direct call for this war—with the threat of using the atomic bomb—such is the content of the statements on relations with the Soviet Union by reactionaries at public meetings and in the press. At the present time, preaching war against the Soviet Union is not a monopoly of the far-right, yellow American press represented by the newspaper associations of Hearst and McCormick. This anti-Soviet campaign also has been joined by the "reputable" and "respectable" organs of the conservative press, such as the *New York Times* and *New York Herald Tribune*. Indicative in this respect are the numerous articles by Walter Lippmann in which he almost undisguisedly calls on the United States to launch a strike against the Soviet Union in the most vulnerable areas of the south and southeast of the USSR.

The basic goal of this anti-Soviet campaign of American "public opinion" is to exert political pressure on the Soviet Union and compel it to make concessions. Another, no less important goal of the campaign is the attempt <u>to create an atmosphere of war psychosis</u> among the masses, who are weary of war, thus making it easier for the U.S. government to carry out measures for the maintenance of high military potential. It was in this very atmosphere that the law on universal military service in peacetime was passed by Congress, that the huge military budget was adopted, and that plans are being worked out for the construction of an extensive system of naval and air bases.

e) Of course, all of these measures for maintaining a high military potential are not goals in themselves. They are only intended <u>to prepare the conditions for winning world supremacy</u> in a new war, the date for which, to be sure, cannot be determined now by anyone, but which is contemplated by the most bellicose circles of American imperialism.

Careful note should be taken of the fact that the preparation by the United States for a future war is being conducted with the prospect of <u>war against the Soviet Union</u>, which in the eyes of American imperialists is the main obstacle in the path of the United States to world domination. This is indicated by facts such as the tactical training of the American army for war with the Soviet Union as the future opponent, the siting of American strategic bases in regions from which it is possible to launch strikes on Soviet territory, intensified training and strengthening of Arctic regions as close approaches to the USSR, and attempts to prepare Germany and Japan to use those countries in a war against the USSR.

[signed]
N. NOVIKOV

Questions

1. How would you characterize Novikov's analysis of U.S. foreign policy?
2. Compare and contrast the Novikov telegram with George F. Kennan's analysis of Soviet conduct (Document 26-2).

26-2 Containment Policy (1947)

George F. Kennan

George F. Kennan (1904–2005), a career diplomat attached to the American embassy in Moscow, assessed the Soviet Union and its foreign policy in a "long telegram" to the U.S. government in 1946 and in an anonymous article the next year. In doing so, he helped to define America's policy of containment, which was to remain important throughout the Cold War. (On containment and Kennan, see text pp. 803–804).

Source: Excerpt from X [George Kennan], "The Sources of Soviet Conduct." Reprinted by permission of *Foreign Affairs* (July 1947):566–582. Copyright © 1947 by the Council on Foreign Relations, Inc.

The political personality of Soviet power as we know it today is the product of ideology and circumstances: ideology inherited by the present Soviet leaders from the movement in which they had their political origin, and circumstances of the power which they now have exercised for nearly three decades in Russia. . . .

It is difficult to summarize the set of ideological concepts with which the Soviet leaders came into power. Marxian ideology, in its Russian-Communist projection, has always been in process of subtle evolution. The materials on which it bases itself are extensive and complex. But the outstanding features of Communist thought as it existed in 1916 may perhaps be summarized as follows: (a) that the central factor in the life of man, the factor which determines the character of public life and the "physiognomy of society," is the system by which material goods are produced and exchanged; (b) that the capitalist system of production is a nefarious one which inevitably leads to the exploitation of the working class by the capital-owning class and is incapable of developing adequately the economic resources of society or of distributing fairly the material goods produced by human labor; (c) that capitalism contains the seeds of its own destruction and must, in view of the inability of the capital-owning class to adjust itself to economic change, result eventually and inescapably in a revolutionary transfer of power to the working class; and (d) that imperialism, the final phase of capitalism, leads directly to war and revolution.

The rest may be outlined in Lenin's own words: "Unevenness of economic and political development is the inflexible law of capitalism. It follows from this that the victory of Socialism may come originally in a few capitalist countries or even in a single capitalist country. The victorious proletariat of that country, having expropriated the capitalists and having organized Socialist production at home, would rise against the remaining capitalist world, drawing to itself in the process the oppressed classes of other countries." It must be noted that there was no assumption that capitalism would perish without proletarian revolution. A final push was needed from a revolutionary proletariat movement in order to tip over the tottering structure. But it was regarded as inevitable that sooner or later that push be given. . . .

The circumstances of the immediate post-revolution period—the existence in Russia of civil war and foreign intervention, together with the obvious fact that the Communists represented only a tiny minority of the Russian people—made the establishment of dictatorial power a necessity. The experiment with "war Communism" and the abrupt attempt to eliminate private production and trade had unfortunate economic consequences and caused further bitterness against the new revolutionary régime. While the temporary relaxation of the effort to communize Russia, represented by the New Economic Policy, alleviated some of this economic distress and thereby served its purpose, it also made evident that the "capitalist sector of society" was still prepared to profit at once from any relaxation of governmental pressure, and would, if permitted to continue to exist, always constitute a powerful opposing element to the Soviet régime and a serious rival for influence in the country. Somewhat the same situation prevailed with respect to the individual peasant who, in his own small way, was also a private producer....

Now the outstanding circumstance concerning the Soviet régime is that down to the present day this process of political consolidation has never been completed and the men in the Kremlin have continued to be predominantly absorbed with the struggle to secure and make absolute the power which they seized in November 1917. They have endeavored to secure it primarily against forces at home, within Soviet society itself. But they have also endeavored to secure it against the outside world. For ideology, as we have seen, taught them that the outside world was hostile and that it was their duty eventually to overthrow the political forces beyond their borders. The powerful hands of Russian history and tradition reached up to sustain them in this feeling. Finally, their own aggressive intransigence with respect to the outside world began to find its own reaction; and they were soon forced, to use another Gibbonesque phrase, "to chastise the contumacy" which they themselves had provoked. It is an undeniable privilege of every man to prove himself right in the thesis that the world is his enemy; for if he reiterates it frequently enough and makes it the background of his conduct he is bound eventually to be right....

Now the maintenance of this pattern of Soviet power, namely, the pursuit of unlimited authority domestically, accompanied by the cultivation of the semi-myth of implacable foreign hostility, has gone far to shape the actual machinery of Soviet power as we know it today. Internal organs of administration which did not serve this purpose withered on the vine. Organs which did serve this purpose became vastly swollen. The security of Soviet power came to rest on the iron discipline of the Party, on the severity and ubiquity of the secret police, and on the uncompromising economic monopolism of the state. The "organs of suppression," in which the Soviet leaders had sought security from rival forces, became in large measure the masters of those whom they were designed to serve. Today the major part of the structure of Soviet power is committed to the perfection of the dictatorship and to the maintenance of the concept of Russia as in a state of siege, with the enemy lowering beyond the walls. And the millions of human beings who form that part of the structure of power must defend at all costs this concept of Russia's position, for without it they are themselves superfluous.

As things stand today, the rulers can no longer dream of parting with these organs of suppression. The quest for absolute power, pursued now for nearly three decades with a ruthlessness unparalleled (in scope at least) in modern times, has again produced internally, as it did externally, its own reaction. The excesses of the police apparatus have fanned the potential opposition to the régime into something far greater and more dangerous than it could have been before those excesses began.

But least of all can the rulers dispense with the fiction by which the maintenance of dictatorial power has been defended. For this fiction has been canonized in Soviet philosophy by the excesses already committed in its name; and it is now anchored in the Soviet structure of thought by bonds far greater than those of mere ideology.

II

... Once a given party line has been laid down on a given issue of current policy, the whole Soviet governmental machine, including the mechanism of diplomacy, moves inexorably along the prescribed path, like a persistent toy automobile wound up and headed in a given direction, stopping only when it meets with some unanswerable force. The individuals who are the components of this machine are unamenable to argument or reason which comes to them from outside sources. Their whole training has taught them to mistrust and discount the glib persuasiveness of the outside world. Like the white dog before the phonograph, they hear only the "master's voice." And if they are to be called off from the purposes last dictated to them, it is the master who must call them off. Thus the foreign representative cannot hope that his words will make any impression on them. The most that he can hope is that they will be transmitted to those at the top, who are capable of changing the party line. But even those are not likely to be swayed by any normal logic in the words of the bourgeois representative. Since there can be no appeal to common purposes, there can be no appeal to common mental approaches. For this reason, facts speak louder than words to the ears of the Kremlin; and words carry the greatest weight when they have the ring of reflecting, or being backed up by, facts of unchallengeable validity.

But we have seen that the Kremlin is under no ideological compulsion to accomplish its purposes in a hurry. Like the Church, it is dealing in ideological concepts which are of long-term validity, and it can afford to be patient. It has no right to risk the existing achievements of the revolution for the sake of vain baubles of the future. The very teachings of Lenin himself require great caution and flexibility in the pursuit of Communist purposes. Again, these precepts are fortified by the lessons of Russian history: of centuries of obscure battles between nomadic forces over the stretches of a vast unfortified plain. Here caution, circumspection, flexibility and deception are the valuable qualities; and their value finds natural appreciation in the Russian or the oriental mind. Thus the Kremlin has no compunction about retreating in the face of superior force. And being under the compulsion of no timetable, it does not get panicky under the necessity for such retreat. Its political action is a fluid stream which moves constantly, wherever it is permitted to move, toward a given goal. Its main concern is to make sure that it has filled every nook and cranny available to it in the basin of world power. But if it finds unassailable barriers in its path, it accepts these philosophically and accommodates itself to them. The main thing is that there should always be pressure, unceasing constant pressure, toward the desired goal. . . .

In these circumstances it is clear that the main element of any United States policy toward the Soviet Union must be that of a long-term, patient but firm and vigilant containment of Russian expansive tendencies. It is important to note, however, that such a policy has nothing to do with outward histrionics: with threats or blustering or superfluous gestures of outward "toughness." . . .

III

In the light of the above, it will be clearly seen that the Soviet pressure against the free institutions of the western world is something that can be contained by the adroit and vigilant application of counter-force at a series of constantly shifting geographical and political points, corresponding to the shifts and manœuvres of Soviet policy, but which cannot be charmed or talked out of existence. . . .

Thus the future of Soviet power may not be by any means as secure as Russian capacity for self-delusion would make it appear to the men in the Kremlin. That they can keep power themselves, they have demonstrated. That they can quietly and easily turn it over to others remains to be proved. Meanwhile, the hardships of their rule and the vicissitudes of international life have taken a heavy toll of the strength and hopes of the great people on whom their power rests. . . . This cannot be proved. And it cannot be disproved: But the possibility remains (and in the opinion of this writer it is a strong one) that Soviet power, like the capitalist world of its conception, bears within it the seeds of its own decay, and that the sprouting of these seeds is well advanced.

IV

It is clear that the United States cannot expect in the foreseeable future to enjoy political intimacy with the Soviet régime. It must continue to regard the Soviet Union as a rival, not a partner, in the political arena. It must continue to expect that Soviet policies will reflect no abstract love of peace and stability, no real faith in the possibility of a permanent happy coexistence of the Socialist and capitalist worlds, but rather a cautious, persistent pressure toward the disruption and weakening of all rival influence and rival power.

Balanced against this are the facts that Russia, as opposed to the western world in general, is still by far the weaker party, that Soviet policy is highly flexible, and that Soviet society may well contain deficiencies which will eventually weaken its own total potential. This would of itself warrant the United States entering with reasonable confidence upon a policy of firm containment, designed to confront the Russians with unalterable counter-force at every point where they show signs of encroaching upon the interests of a peaceful and stable world.

But in actuality the possibilities for American policy are by no means limited to holding the line and hoping for the best. It is entirely possible for the United States to influence by its actions the internal developments, both within Russia and throughout the international Communist movement, by which Russian policy is largely determined. This is not only a question of the modest measure of informational activity which this government can conduct in the Soviet Union and elsewhere, although that, too, is important. It is rather a question of the degree to which the United States can create among the peoples of the world generally the impression of a country which knows what it wants, which is coping successfully with the problems of its internal life and with the responsibilities of a World Power, and which has a spiritual vitality capable of holding its own among the major ideological currents of the time. To the extent that such an impression can be created and maintained, the aims of Russian Communism must appear sterile and quixotic, the hopes and enthusiasm of Moscow's supporters must wane, and added strain must be imposed on the Kremlin's foreign policies. For the palsied decrepitude of the capitalist world is the keystone of Communist philosophy. Even the failure of the United States to experience the early economic depression which the ravens of the Red Square have been predicting with such complacent confidence since hostilities ceased would have deep and important repercussions throughout the Communist world. . . .

It would be an exaggeration to say that American behavior unassisted and alone could exercise a power of life and death over the Communist movement and bring about the early fall of Soviet power in Russia. But the United States has it in its power to increase enormously the strains under which Soviet policy must operate, to force upon the Kremlin a far greater degree of moderation and circumspection than it has had to observe in recent years, and in this way to promote tendencies which must eventually find their outlet in either the break-up or the gradual mellowing of Soviet power. For no mystical, Messianic movement—and particularly not that of the Kremlin—can face frustration indefinitely without eventually adjusting itself in one way or another to the logic of that state of affairs.

Thus the decision will really fall in large measure in this country itself. The issue of Soviet-American relations is in essence a test of the over-all worth of the United States as a nation among nations. To avoid destruction the United States need only measure up to its own best traditions and prove itself worthy of preservation as a great nation.

Surely, there was never a fairer test of national quality than this. In the light of these circumstances, the thoughtful observer of Russian-American relations will find no cause for complaint in the Kremlin's challenge to American society. He will rather experience a certain gratitude to a Providence which, by providing the American people with this implacable challenge, has made their entire security as a nation dependent on their pulling themselves together and accepting the responsibilities of moral and political leadership that history plainly intended them to bear.

Questions

1. How did Kennan explain "the sources of Soviet conduct"?
2. What strategies did he propose for implementing the policy of containment?
3. What did Kennan see as the outcome of containment?

26-3   On NATO (1949)

Arthur Vandenberg

Senator Arthur Vandenberg (1884–1951), a Michigan Republican and a prewar noninterventionist, shifted position during the postwar period to support containment. His championing of American involvement in the North Atlantic Treaty Organization helped make Senate ratification of the NATO treaty bipartisan. During the debate, he explained his position in correspondence with constituents and others.

Source: Excerpted from *The Private Papers of Senator Vandenberg*, ed. Arthur H. Vandenberg Jr. with the collaboration of Joe Alex Morris, 475, 477–480, 499–500. Copyright 1952 by Arthur Vandenberg Jr. and © renewed 1980. Reprinted by permission of Houghton Mifflin Company. All rights reserved.

January 27, 1949
There is no doubt about the fact that it is a "calculated risk" for us to even partially arm the countries of Western Europe. It is also very much of a "calculated risk" if we do *not*. One risk will have to be weighed against the other. You suggest that it will be a safe thing to do "when the economic stability of these countries shall have improved." The basic question we have to settle is whether "economic stability" can precede the creation of a greater sense of physical security. I am inclined to think that "physical security" is a prerequisite to the kind of long-range economic planning which Western Europe requires. The fact remains that the problem is fraught with many hazardous imponderables. I am withholding my own final judgment until I see the precise terms of the treaty under which this new cooperation will be proposed. I think we ought to have wit enough to write it on a basis which is relatively safe....

February 21, 1949
... In my opinion, when Mr. Hitler was contemplating World War Two, I believe he would have never launched it if he had had any serious reasons to believe that it might bring him into armed collision with the United States. I think he was sure it would not do so because of our then existing neutrality laws. If an appropriate North Atlantic Pact is written, I think it will exactly reverse this psychology so far as Mr. Stalin is concerned if, as and when he contemplates World War Three. Under such circumstances, I very much doubt whether World War Three happens....

February 22, 1949
I am one of its [the Pact's] authors. I heartily believe in it. I want to give it a maximum chance to help prevent World War Three before it starts. But this requires absolute candor as to what it does and does not promise. I can think of no greater tragedy than to permit our friends in Western Europe to interpret the Pact beyond its actual realities. One reality is that we cannot commit ourselves to automatic war in the future.... We are recognizing facts of life as established in the Constitution of the United States. I will go as far as I can within the Constitution. I will not go farther because it would be an imposition upon our own good faith and a false reliance for our friends abroad. I hasten to add that I think we can achieve every essential result for the North Atlantic Pact by staying strictly within the Constitution of the United States and within the Charter of the United Nations....

March 18, 1949
... I am glad to know your preliminary reaction to the North Atlantic Pact. I agree with you one thousand percent

that "this world cannot stand another war." Every effort of my remaining days will be dedicated to this truth. My greatest fear in this connection is that we will somehow drift into another war. . . . If Soviet Russia does start to march it would seem to be completely inevitable that the United States will be the ultimate target and that we shall inevitably be in that war—Pact or no Pact. So it seems to me that our best insurance is to make our position plan in advance. This includes above all else a clear demonstration that our objectives are totally defensive; that we have no goal except peace with honor and justice in a live-and-let-live world.

If you are right and this proposed North Atlantic Pact is "another provocation to another World War" then the Pact ought to be rejected. If I am right in believing that the Pact is our best protection against another World War then the Pact ought to be ratified. Therefore, our current problem is to fully and publicly explore every phase and every angle of the Pact. You may be very sure that I shall insist upon extensive public hearings which will clarify the issue. I want everything ventilated in this connection so that we may reach the wisest possible decision in a situation where we must take a "calculated risk" whichever way the decision goes. . . .

[*July 21, 1949*]

Well—as you know we won the big battle [over the North Atlantic Treaty] today by a vote of 82 to 13. . . . It's a great relief to have the battle over—yet I seem to feel a greater responsibility than ever tonight—how will it all work out? At best, it's a calculated risk. But I have a feeling that this day will go down in history as one of the big dates.

Questions

1. According to Vandenberg, what kinds of dangers did the United States face in the Cold War?
2. What risks did the United States run by aligning itself so closely with the states of Western Europe? What kinds of gains did NATO make possible?
3. What lessons did Vandenberg learn from the events preceding World War II? How did he put them to use in his support for NATO?

26-4 NSC-68 (1950)

The National Security Council had come into existence in 1947 as a result of the Cold War. In the wake of the victory of the Communist Party in China's civil war and the Soviet Union's detonation of an atomic device, the council prepared NSC-68, a paper that marked Communism as the enemy and suggested possible military strategies. Meanwhile, George Kennan, increasingly concerned over the implementation of containment and opposed to the development of the hydrogen bomb, had resigned as head of the Department of State's Policy Planning Staff (see text pp. 808–810).

Source: Foreign Relations of the United States, no. 1 (1950), 237–292.

Analysis

I. BACKGROUND OF THE PRESENT CRISIS

. . . During the span of one generation, the international distribution of power has been fundamentally altered. . . .

Two complex sets of factors have now basically altered this historical distribution of power. First, the defeat of Germany and Japan and the decline of the British and French Empires have interacted with the development of the United States and the Soviet Union in such a way that power has increasingly gravitated to these two centers. Second, the Soviet Union, unlike previous aspirants to hegemony, is animated by a new fanatic faith, antithetical to our own, and seeks to impose its absolute authority over the rest of the world. Conflict has, therefore, become endemic and is waged, on the part of the Soviet Union, by violent or nonviolent methods in accordance with the dictates of expediency. With the development of increasingly terrifying weapons of mass destruction, every individual faces the ever-present possibility of annihilation should the conflict enter the phase of total war.

On the one hand, the people of the world yearn for relief from the anxiety arising from the risk of atomic war. On the other hand, any substantial further extension of the area under the domination of the Kremlin would raise the possibility that no coalition adequate to confront the Kremlin with greater strength could be assembled. It is in this context that this Republic and its citizens in the ascendancy of their strength stand in their deepest peril. . . .

II. FUNDAMENTAL PURPOSE OF THE UNITED STATES

The fundamental purpose of the United States is laid down in the Preamble to the Constitution. . . . In essence, the fundamental purpose is to assure the integrity and vitality of our free society, which is founded upon the dignity and worth of the individual.

Three realities emerge as a consequence of this purpose: Our determination to maintain the essential elements of individual freedom, as set forth in the Constitution and Bill of Rights; our determination to create conditions under which our free and democratic system can live and prosper; and our determination to fight if necessary to defend our way of life. . . .

III. FUNDAMENTAL DESIGN OF THE KREMLIN

The fundamental design of those who control the Soviet Union and the international communist movement is to retain and solidify their absolute power, first in the Soviet Union and second in the areas now under their control. In the minds of the Soviet leaders, however, achievement of this design requires the dynamic extension of their authority and the ultimate elimination of any effective opposition to their authority.

The design, therefore, calls for the complete subversion or forcible destruction of the machinery of government and structure of society in the countries of the non-Soviet world and their replacement by an apparatus and structure subservient to and controlled from the Kremlin. To that end Soviet efforts are now directed toward the domination of the Eurasian land mass. The United States, as the principal center of power in the non-Soviet world and the bulwark of opposition to Soviet expansion, is the principal enemy whose integrity and vitality must be subverted or destroyed by one means or another if the Kremlin is to achieve its fundamental design.

IV. THE UNDERLYING CONFLICT IN THE REALM OF IDEAS AND VALUES BETWEEN THE U.S. PURPOSE AND THE KREMLIN DESIGN

A. Nature of Conflict

The Kremlin regards the United States as the only major threat to the achievement of its fundamental design. There is a basic conflict between the idea of freedom under a government of laws, and the idea of slavery under the grim oligarchy of the Kremlin, which has come to a crisis with the polarization of power described in Section I, and the exclusive possession of atomic weapons by the two protagonists. The idea of freedom, moreover, is peculiarly and intolerably subversive of the idea of slavery. But the converse is not true. The implacable purpose of the slave state to eliminate the challenge of freedom has placed the two great powers at opposite poles. It is this fact which gives the present polarization of power the quality of crisis. . . .

B. Objectives

In a shrinking world, which now faces the threat of atomic warfare, it is not an adequate objective merely to seek to check the Kremlin design, for the absence of order among nations is becoming less and less tolerable. This fact imposes on us, in our own interests, the responsibility of world leadership. It demands that we make the attempt, and accept the risks inherent in it, to bring about order and justice by means consistent with the principles of freedom and democracy. We should limit our requirement of the Soviet Union to its participation with other nations on the basis of equality and respect for the rights of others. Subject to this requirement, we must with our allies and the former subject peoples, seek to create a world society based on the principle of consent. Its framework cannot be inflexible. It will consist of many national communities of great and varying abilities and resources, and hence of war potential. The seeds of conflicts will inevitably exist or will come into being. To acknowledge this is only to acknowledge the impossibility of a final solution. Not to acknowledge it can be fatally dangerous in a world in which there are no final solutions. . . .

V. SOVIET INTENTIONS AND CAPABILITIES— ACTUAL AND POTENTIAL

A. Political and Psychological

. . . Soviet ideas and practices run counter to the best and potentially the strongest instincts of men, and deny their most fundamental aspirations. Against an adversary which effectively affirmed the constructive and hopeful instincts of men and was capable of fulfilling their fundamental aspirations, the Soviet system might prove to be fatally weak. . . .

C. Military

The Soviet Union is developing the military capacity to support its design for world domination. The Soviet Union actually possesses armed forces far in excess of those necessary to defend its national territory. These armed forces are probably not yet considered by the Soviet Union to be sufficient to initiate a war which would involve the United States. This excessive strength, coupled now with an atomic capability, provides the Soviet Union with great coercive power for use in time of peace in furtherance of its objectives and serves as a deterrent to the victims of its aggression from taking any action in opposition to its tactics which would risk war.

Should a major war occur in 1950 the Soviet Union and its satellites are considered by the Joint Chiefs of Staff to be in a sufficiently advanced state of preparation immediately to undertake and carry out the following campaigns.

  a. To overrun Western Europe, with the possible exception of the Iberian and Scandinavian Peninsulas; to drive toward the oil-bearing areas of the Near and Middle East; and to consolidate Communist gains in the Far East;

b. To launch air attacks against the British Isles and air and sea attacks against the lines of communications of the Western Powers in the Atlantic and the Pacific;
c. To attack selected targets with atomic weapons, now including the likelihood of such attacks against targets in Alaska, Canada, and the United States. Alternatively, this capability, coupled with other actions open to the Soviet Union, might deny the United Kingdom as an effective base of operations for allied forces. It also should be possible for the Soviet Union to prevent any allied "Normandy" type amphibious operations intended to force a reentry into the continent of Europe.

After the Soviet Union completed its initial campaigns and consolidated its positions in the Western European area, it could simultaneously conduct:

a. Full-scale air and limited sea operations against the British Isles;
b. Invasions of the Iberian and Scandinavian Peninsulas;
c. Further operations in the Near and Middle East, continued air operations against the North American continent, and air and sea operations against Atlantic and Pacific lines of communication; and
d. Diversionary attacks in other areas. . . .

For planning purposes, therefore, the date the Soviets possess an atomic stockpile of 200 bombs would be a critical date for the United States, for the delivery of 100 atomic bombs on targets in the United States would seriously damage this country.

At the time the Soviet Union has a substantial atomic stockpile and if it is assumed that it will strike a strong surprise blow and if it is assumed further that its atomic attacks will be met with no more effective defense opposition than the United States and its allies have programmed, results of those attacks could include:

a. Laying waste to the British Isles and thus depriving the Western Powers of their use as a base;
b. Destruction of the vital centers and of the communications of Western Europe, thus precluding effective defense by the Western Powers; and
c. Delivering devastating attacks on certain vital centers of the United States and Canada.

The possession by the Soviet Union of a thermonuclear capability in addition to this substantial atomic stockpile would result in tremendously increased damage.

During this decade, the defensive capabilities of the Soviet Union will probably be strengthened, particularly by the development and use of modern aircraft, aircraft warning and communications devices, and defensive guided missiles. . . .

VI. U.S. INTENTIONS AND CAPABILITIES—ACTUAL AND POTENTIAL

A. Political and Psychological

In a world of polarized power, policies designed to develop a healthy international community are more than ever necessary to our own strength.

As for the policy of "containment," it is one which seeks by all means short of war to (1) block further expansion of Soviet power, (2) expose the falsities of Soviet pretensions, (3) induce a retraction of the Kremlin's control and influence, and (4) in general, so foster the seeds of destruction within the Soviet system that the Kremlin is brought at least to the point of modifying its behavior to conform to generally accepted international standards.

It was and continues to be cardinal in this policy that we possess superior overall power in ourselves or in dependable combination with other like-minded nations. One of the most important ingredients of power is military strength. In the concept of "containment," the maintenance of a strong military posture is deemed to be essential for two reasons: (1) as an ultimate guarantee of our national security and (2) as an indispensable backdrop to the conduct of the policy of "containment." Without superior aggregate military strength, in being and readily mobilizable, a policy of "containment"—which is in effect a policy of calculated and gradual coercion—is no more than a policy of bluff. . . .

VII. PRESENT RISKS

B. Specific

It is quite clear from Soviet theory and practice that the Kremlin seeks to bring the free world under its dominion by the methods of the cold war. The preferred technique is to subvert by infiltration and intimidation. Every institution of our society is an instrument which it is sought to stultify and turn against our purposes. Those that touch most closely our material and moral strength are obviously the prime targets, labor unions, civic enterprises, schools, churches, and all media for influencing opinion. The effort is not so much to make them serve obvious Soviet ends as to prevent them from serving our ends, and thus to make them sources of confusion in our economy, our culture, and our body politic. The doubts and diversities that in terms of our values are part of the merit of a free system, the weaknesses and the problems that are peculiar to it, the rights and privileges that free men enjoy, and the disorganization and destruction left in the wake of the last attack on our freedoms, all are but opportunities for the Kremlin to do its evil work. Every advantage is taken of the fact that our means of prevention and retaliation are limited by those principles and scruples which are precisely the ones that give our freedom and democracy its meaning for us. None of our scruples deter those whose only code is "morality is that which serves the revolution."

Since everything that gives us or others respect for our institutions is a suitable object for attack, it also fits the Kremlin's design that where, with impunity, we can be insulted and made to suffer indignity the opportunity shall not be missed, particularly in any context which can be used to cast dishonor on our country, our system, our motives, or our methods. Thus the means by which we sought to restore our own economic health in the '30's, and now seek to restore that of the free world, come equally under attack. The military aid by which we sought to help the free world was frantically denounced by the Communists in the early days of the last war, and of course our present efforts to develop adequate military strength for ourselves and our allies are equally denounced.

At the same time the Soviet Union is seeking to create overwhelming military force, in order to back up infiltration with intimidation. In the only terms in which it understands strength, it is seeking to demonstrate to the free world that force and the will to use it are on the side of the Kremlin, that those who lack it are decadent and doomed. In local incidents it threatens and encroaches both for the sake of local gains and to increase anxiety and defeatism in all the free world....

VIII. ATOMIC ARMAMENTS

A. *Military Evaluation of U.S. and USSR Atomic Capabilities*

... As the atomic capability of the USSR increases, it will have an increased ability to hit at our atomic bases and installations and thus seriously hamper the ability of the United States to carry out an attack such as that outlined above. It is quite possible that in the near future the USSR will have a sufficient number of atomic bombs and a sufficient deliverability to raise a question whether Britain with its present inadequate air defense could be relied upon as an advance base from which a major portion of the U.S. attack could be launched.

It is estimated that, within the next four years, the USSR will attain the capability of seriously damaging vital centers of the United States, provided it strikes a surprise blow and provided further that the blow is opposed by no more effective opposition than we now have programmed. Such a blow could so seriously damage the United States as to greatly reduce its superiority in economic potential.

Effective opposition to this Soviet capability will require among other measures greatly increased air warning systems, air defenses, and vigorous development and implementation of a civilian defense program which has been thoroughly integrated with the military defense systems.

In time the atomic capability of the USSR can be expected to grow to a point where, given surprise and no more effective opposition than we now have programmed, the possibility of a decisive initial attack [by the USSR] cannot be excluded....

B. *Stockpiling and Use of Atomic Weapons*

In the event the USSR develops by 1954 the atomic capability which we now anticipate, it is hardly conceivable that, if war comes, the Soviet leaders would refrain from the use of atomic weapons unless they felt fully confident of attaining their objectives by other means.

In the event we use atomic weapons either in retaliation for their prior use by the USSR or because there is no alternative method by which we can attain our objectives, it is imperative that the strategic and tactical targets against which they are used be appropriate and the manner in which they are used be consistent with those objectives.

It appears to follow from the above that we should produce and stockpile thermonuclear weapons in the event they prove feasible and would add significantly to our net capability. Not enough is yet known of their potentialities to warrant a judgment at this time regarding their use in war to attain our objectives....

C. *International Control of Atomic Energy*

The principal immediate benefit of international control would be to make a surprise atomic attack impossible, assuming the elimination of large reactors and the effective disposal of stockpiles of fissionable materials. But it is almost certain that the Soviet Union would not agree to the elimination of large reactors, unless the impracticability of producing atomic power for peaceful purposes had been demonstrated beyond a doubt. By the same token, it would not now agree to elimination of its stockpile of fissionable materials....

[T]he absence of good faith on the part of the USSR must be assumed until there is concrete evidence that there has been a decisive change in Soviet policies. It is to be doubted whether such a change can take place without a change in the nature of the Soviet system itself....

IX. POSSIBLE COURSES OF ACTION

Introduction. Four possible courses of action by the United States in the present situation can be distinguished. They are:

a. Continuation of current policies, with current and currently projected programs for carrying out these policies;
b. Isolation;
c. War; and
d. A more rapid building up of the political, economic, and military strength of the free world than provided under a, with the purpose of reaching, if possible, a tolerable state of order among nations without war and of preparing to defend ourselves in the event that the free world is attacked....

The Kremlin will have three major objectives in negotiations with the United States. The first is to eliminate the atomic capabilities of the United States; the second is to prevent the effective mobilization of the superior potential of the free world in human and material resources; and the third is to secure a withdrawal of United States forces from, and commitments to, Europe and Japan. Depending on its evaluation of its own strengths and weaknesses as against the

West's (particularly the ability and will of the West to sustain its efforts), it will or will not be prepared to make important concessions to achieve these major objectives. It is unlikely that the Kremlin's evaluation is such that it would now be prepared to make significant concessions.

It must be presumed that for some time the Kremlin will accept agreements only if it is convinced that by acting in bad faith whenever and wherever there is an opportunity to do so with impunity, it can derive greater advantage from the agreements than the free world. For this reason, we must take care that any agreements are enforceable or that they are not susceptible of violation without detection and the possibility of effective counter-measures....

A. The First Course—Continuation of Current Policies, with Current and Currently Projected Programs for Carrying Out These Policies

1. Military aspects.... A review of Soviet policy shows that the military capabilities, actual and potential, of the United States and the rest of the free world, together with the apparent determination of the free world to resist further Soviet expansion, have not induced the Kremlin to relax its pressures generally or to give up the initiative in the cold war. On the contrary, the Soviet Union has consistently pursued a bold foreign policy, modified only when its probing revealed a determination and an ability of the free world to resist encroachment upon it. The relative military capabilities of the free world are declining, with the result that its determination to resist may also decline and that the security of the United States and the free world as a whole will be jeopardized.

From the military point of view, the actual and potential capabilities of the United States, given a continuation of current and projected programs, will become less and less effective as a war deterrent. Improvement of the state of readiness will become more and more important not only to inhibit the launching of war by the Soviet Union but also to support a national policy designed to reverse the present ominous trends in international relations. A building up of the military capabilities of the United States and the free world is a pre-condition to the achievement of the objectives outlined in this report and to the protection of the United States against disaster.

Fortunately, the United States military establishment has been developed into a unified and effective force as a result of the policies laid down by the Congress and the vigorous carrying out of these policies by the Administration in the fields of both organization and economy. It is, therefore, a base upon which increased strength can be rapidly built with maximum efficiency and economy.

2. Political aspects.... Politically, recognition of the military implications of a continuation of present trends will mean that the United States and especially other free countries will tend to shift to the defensive, or to follow a dangerous policy of bluff, because the maintenance of a firm initiative in the cold war is closely related to aggregate strength in being and readily available....

3. Economic and social aspects. As was pointed out in Chapter VI, the present foreign economic policies and programs of the United States will not produce a solution to the problem of international economic equilibrium, notably the problem of the dollar gap, and will not create an economic base conducive to political stability in many important free countries....

The Executive Branch is now undertaking a study of the problem of the United States balance of payments and of the measures which might be taken by the United States to assist in establishing international economic equilibrium. This is a very important project and work on it should have a high priority. However, unless such an economic program is matched and supplemented by an equally far-sighted and vigorous political and military program, we will not be successful in checking and rolling back the Kremlin's drive.

4. Negotiation. In short, by continuing along its present course the free world will not succeed in making effective use of its vastly superior political, economic, and military potential to build a tolerable state of order among nations. On the contrary, the political, economic, and military situation of the free world is already unsatisfactory and will become less favorable unless we act to reverse present trends....

The idea that Germany or Japan or other important areas can exist as islands of neutrality in a divided world is unreal, given the Kremlin design for world domination.

B. The Second Course—Isolation

[A policy of isolation] overlooks the relativity of capabilities. With the United States in an isolated position, we would have to face the probability that the Soviet Union would quickly dominate most of Eurasia, probably without meeting armed resistance. It would thus acquire a potential far superior to our own, and would promptly proceed to develop this potential with the purpose of eliminating our power, which would, even in isolation, remain as a challenge to it and as an obstacle to the imposition of its kind of order in the world. There is no way to make ourselves inoffensive to the Kremlin except by complete submission to its will. Therefore isolation would in the end condemn us to capitulate or to fight alone and on the defensive, with drastically limited offensive and retaliatory capabilities in comparison with the Soviet Union. (These are the only possibilities, unless we are prepared to risk the future on the hazard that the Soviet Empire, because of overextension or other reasons, will spontaneously destroy itself from within....)

C. The Third Course—War

... [A] surprise attack upon the Soviet Union, despite the provocativeness of recent Soviet behavior, would be repugnant to many Americans. Although the American people would probably rally in support of the war effort, the shock of responsibility for a surprise attack would be morally corrosive....

... If the argument of Chapter IV is accepted, it follows that there is no "easy" solution and that the only sure victory lies in the frustration of the Kremlin design by the steady development of the moral and material strength of the free world and its projection into the Soviet world in such a way as to bring about an internal change in the Soviet system.

D. The Remaining Course of Action—A Rapid Build-up of Political, Economic, and Military Strength in the Free World

A more rapid build-up of political, economic, and military strength and thereby of confidence in the free world than is now contemplated is the only course which is consistent with progress toward achieving our fundamental purpose....

The threat to the free world involved in the development of the Soviet Union's atomic and other capabilities will rise steadily and rather rapidly. For the time being, the United States possesses a marked atomic superiority over the Soviet Union which, together with the potential capabilities of the United States and other free countries in other forces and weapons, inhibits aggressive Soviet action. This provides an opportunity for the United States, in cooperation with other free countries, to launch a build-up of strength which will support a firm policy directed to the frustration of the Kremlin design. The immediate goal of our efforts to build a successfully functioning political and economic system in the free world backed by adequate military strength is to postpone and avert the disastrous situation which, in light of the Soviet Union's probable fission bomb capability and possible thermonuclear bomb capability, might arise in 1954 on a continuation of our present programs. By acting promptly and vigorously in such a way that this date is, so to speak, pushed into the future, we would permit time for the process of accommodation, withdrawal and frustration to produce the necessary changes in the Soviet system. Time is short, however, and the risks of war attendant upon a decision to build up strength will steadily increase the longer we defer it.

Conclusions

The foregoing analysis indicates that the probable fission bomb capability and possible thermonuclear bomb capability of the Soviet Union have greatly intensified the Soviet threat to the security of the United States. This threat is of the same character as that described in NSC 20/4 (approved by the President on November 24, 1948) but is more immediate than had previously been estimated. In particular, the United States now faces the contingency that within the next four or five years the Soviet Union will possess the military capability of delivering a surprise atomic attack of such weight that the United States must have substantially increased general air, ground, and sea strength, atomic capabilities, and air and civilian defenses to deter war and to provide reasonable assurance, in the event of war, that it could survive the initial blow and go on to the eventual attainment of its objectives. In return, this contingency requires the intensification of our efforts in the fields of intelligence and research and development....

Allowing for the immediacy of the danger, the following statement of Soviet threats contained in NSC 20/4, remains valid:

14. The gravest threat to the security of the United States within the foreseeable future stems from the hostile designs and formidable power of the USSR, and from the nature of the Soviet system.

15. The political, economic, and psychological warfare which the USSR is now waging has dangerous potentialities for weakening the relative world position of the United States and disrupting its traditional institutions by means short of war, unless sufficient resistance is encountered in the policies of this and other non-communist countries.

16. The risk of war with the USSR is sufficient to warrant, in common prudence, timely and adequate preparation by the United States.

   a. Even though present estimates indicate that the Soviet leaders do not intend deliberate armed action involving the United States at this time, the possibility of such deliberate resort to war cannot be ruled out.
   b. Now and for the foreseeable future there is a continuing danger that war will arise either through Soviet miscalculation of the determination of the United States to use all the means at its command to safeguard its security, through Soviet misinterpretation of our intentions, or through U.S. miscalculation of Soviet reactions to measures which we might take.

17. Soviet domination of the potential power of Eurasia, whether achieved by armed aggression or by political and subversive means, would be strategically and politically unacceptable to the United States.

18. The capability of the United States either in peace or in the event of war to cope with threats to its security or to gain its objectives would be severely weakened by internal development, important among which are:

   a. Serious espionage, subversion and sabotage, particularly by concerted and well-directed communist activity.
   b. Prolonged or exaggerated economic instability.
   c. Internal political and social disunity.
   d. Inadequate or excessive armament or foreign aid expenditures.
   e. An excessive or wasteful usage of our resources in time of peace.
   f. Lessening of U.S. prestige and influence through vacillation or appeasement or lack of skill and imagination in the conduct of its foreign policy or by shirking world responsibilities.

g. Development of a false sense of security through a deceptive change in Soviet tactics. . . .

19.

a. To reduce the power and influence of the USSR to limits which no longer constitute a threat to the peace, national independence, and stability of the world family of nations.
b. To bring about a basic change in the conduct of international relations by the government in power in Russia, to conform with the purposes and principles set forth in the UN Charter.

In pursuing these objectives, due care must be taken to avoid permanently impairing our economy and the fundamental values and institutions inherent in our way of life.

20. We should endeavor to achieve our general objectives by methods short of war through the pursuit of the following aims:

a. To encourage and promote the gradual retraction of undue Russian power and influence from the present perimeter areas around traditional Russian boundaries and the emergence of the satellite countries as entities independent of the USSR.
b. To encourage the development among the Russian peoples of attitudes which may help to modify current Soviet behavior and permit a revival of the national life of groups evidencing the ability and determination to achieve and maintain national independence.
c. To eradicate the myth by which people remote from Soviet military influence are held in a position of subservience to Moscow and to cause the world at large to see and understand the true nature of the USSR and the Soviet-directed world communist party, and to adopt a logical and realistic attitude toward them.
d. To create situations which will compel the Soviet Government to recognize the practical undesirability of acting on the basis of its present concepts and the necessity of behaving in accordance with precepts of international conduct, as set forth in the purposes and principles of the UN Charter.

21. Attainment of these aims requires that the United States:

a. Develop a level of military readiness which can be maintained as long as necessary as a deterrent to Soviet aggression, as indispensable support to our political attitude toward the USSR, as a source of encouragement to nations resisting Soviet political aggression, and as an adequate basis for immediate military commitments and for rapid mobilization should war prove unavoidable.
b. Assure the internal security of the United States against dangers of sabotage, subversion, and espionage.
c. Maximize our economic potential, including the strengthening of our peacetime economy and the establishment of essential reserves readily available in the event of war.
d. Strengthen the orientation toward the United States of the non-Soviet nations; and help such of those nations as are able and willing to make an important contribution to U.S. security, to increase their economic and political stability and their military capability.
e. Place the maximum strain on the Soviet structure of power and particularly on the relationship between Moscow and the satellite countries.
f. Keep the U.S. public fully informed and cognizant of the threats to our national security so that it will be prepared to support the measures which we must accordingly adopt.

In the light of present and prospective Soviet atomic capabilities, the action which can be taken under present programs and plans, however, becomes dangerously inadequate, in both timing and scope, to accomplish the rapid progress toward the attainment of the United States political, economic, and military objectives which is now imperative.

A continuation of present trends would result in a serious decline in the strength of the free world relative to the Soviet Union and its satellites. This unfavorable trend arises from the inadequacy of current programs and plans rather than from any error in our objectives and aims. These trends lead in the direction of isolation, not by deliberate decision but by lack of the necessary basis for a vigorous initiative in the conflict with the Soviet Union.

Our position as the center of power in the free world places a heavy responsibility upon the United States for leadership. We must organize and enlist the energies and resources of the free world in a positive program for peace which will frustrate the Kremlin design for world domination by creating a situation in the free world to which the Kremlin will be compelled to adjust. Without such a cooperative effort, led by the United States, we will have to make gradual withdrawals under pressure until we discover one day that we have sacrificed positions of vital interest.

It is imperative that this trend be reversed by a much more rapid and concerted build-up of the actual strength of both the United States and the other nations of the free world. The analysis shows that this will be costly and will involve significant domestic financial and economic adjustments.

The execution of such a build-up, however, requires that the United States have an affirmative program beyond the solely defensive one of countering the threat posed by the Soviet Union. This program must light the path of peace and order among nations in a system based on freedom and justice, as contemplated in the Charter of the United Nations. Further, it must envisage the political and economic measures with which and the military shield behind which the free world can work to frustrate the Kremlin design by the strategy of the cold war; for every consideration of devotion to our fundamental values and to our national security demands that we achieve our objectives by the strategy of the cold war, building up our military strength in order that it may not have to be used. The only sure victory lies in the frustration of the Kremlin design by the steady development of the moral and material strength of the free world and its projection into the Soviet world in such a way as to bring about an internal change in the Soviet system. Such a positive program—harmonious with our fundamental national purpose and our objectives—is necessary if we are to regain and retain the initiative and to win and hold the necessary popular support and cooperation in the United States and the rest of the free world.

This program should include a plan for negotiation with the Soviet Union, developed and agreed with our allies and which is consonant with our objectives. The United States and its allies, particularly the United Kingdom and France, should always be ready to negotiate with the Soviet Union on terms consistent with our objectives. The present world situation, however, is one which militates against successful negotiations with the Kremlin—for the terms of agreements on important pending issues would reflect present realities and would therefore be unacceptable, if not disastrous, to the United States and the rest of the free world. After a decision and a start on building up the strength of the free world has been made, it might then be desirable for the United States to take an initiative in seeking negotiations in the hope that it might facilitate the process of accommodation by the Kremlin to the new situation. Failing that, the unwillingness of the Kremlin to accept equitable terms or its bad faith in observing them would assist in consolidating popular opinion in the free world in support of the measures necessary to sustain the build-up.

In summary, we must, by means of a rapid and sustained build-up of the political, economic, and military strength of the free world, and by means of an affirmative program intended to wrest the initiative from the Soviet Union, confront it with convincing evidence of the determination and ability of the free world to frustrate the Kremlin design of a world dominated by its will. Such evidence is the only means short of war which eventually may force the Kremlin to abandon its present course of action and to negotiate acceptable agreements on issues of major importance.

The whole success of the proposed program hangs ultimately on recognition by this Government, the American people, and all free peoples, that the cold war is in fact a real war in which the survival of the free world is at stake. Essential prerequisites to success are consultations with Congressional leaders designed to make the program the object of non-partisan legislative support, and a presentation to the public of a full explanation of the facts and implications of the present international situation. The prosecution of the program will require of us all the ingenuity, sacrifice, and unity demanded by the vital importance of the issue and the tenacity to persevere until our national objectives have been attained. . . .

Questions

1. According to the authors of NSC-68, what were the fundamental sources of conflict between the Soviet Union and the United States?
2. Why did NSC-68 rule out, for the present, negotiations between the United States and its allies and the Soviet Union?
3. Given these circumstances, what policies did the authors of NSC-68 believe should be undertaken? What alternative policies did they reject?

Question for Further Thought

1. After reviewing Documents 26-2 through 26-4 and the relevant text, critically assess American foreign policy during the early Cold War (1945–1950). How do you judge Kennan's formulation of containment policy (Document 26-2) and NSC-68 (Document 26-4)? How do they resemble one another? How do they differ?

The Truman Era

Responding to the call in NSC-68 (1950) for a "rapid building-up of political, economic, and military strength in the free world" (Document 26-4), the U.S. government ensured that the country would wage the long and protracted Cold War—as it had World War II—as much within its borders as abroad. Indeed, with the Korean War, U.S. military spending had risen sharply and remained high afterward. The creation of a permanent military-industrial complex had important local, regional, and national implications as politicians such as Senator Lyndon B. Johnson (D-Texas) worked to ensure that defense dollars were spent in their home districts or states (Document 26-5). Defense spending on research and development, as well as on production, was an economic stimulus, but it also overspent in some sectors of the economy while shortchanging others. Other politicians such as Senator Joe McCarthy (R-Wisconsin) used "the Great Fear" of a world Communist conspiracy not to create jobs but to create a climate of fear (Document 26-6).

The civil rights movement emerged as perhaps the most important force for social change in postwar America. President Truman confronted difficulties in his efforts to achieve his Fair Deal—an expansion of the New Deal that would lead to the attainment of civil rights for African Americans—in a postwar period very different from the 1930s. Not only did the Republicans control Congress during the second half of Truman's first term, but both the left and right wings of his own party staged revolts in 1948, running national tickets of their own. The issue of civil rights was central to the growing anger of Deep South Democrats with the national Democratic Party. Still, Truman won reelection, and his party recaptured Congress. Document 26-7 offers the 1948 national party platform planks on the civil rights issue. The landmark Supreme Court decision in *Brown v. Board of Education of Topeka* (Document 26-8), which declared segregation to be unconstitutional, brought national attention to civil rights. Despite this victory, civil rights activists faced tremendous opposition from a broad base of whites who sought to protect the status quo. In response to the Brown decision, ninety-six U.S. congressmen and senators signed "The Southern Manifesto" (Document 26-9), a declaration condemning the decision and assuring southern constituents that their representatives would resist by any lawful means judges who made law from the bench—what was then called judicial "usurpation" or "encroachment." Despite tremendous resistance, blacks continued to organize and embrace nonviolent forms of protest, such as the Montgomery, Alabama, bus boycott of 1955 and 1956. Triggered by Rosa Parks, a black woman who was arrested after refusing to give up her bus seat to a white man (Document 26-10), the boycott demonstrated the potential of grassroots organization and brought the Reverend Martin Luther King Jr. into the national spotlight. In 1957, King and others founded the Southern Christian Leadership Conference (SCLC), which would play a major role in advancing the cause of civil rights.

26-5 The American West: America's Answer to Russia (1950)

Lyndon B. Johnson

In the opening months of the Korean War, Senator Lyndon B. Johnson (1908–1973) spoke before an audience of Texas college students in Lubbock on November 11, 1950. Johnson took this opportunity to articulate a new vision of the American West.

Source: Lyndon B. Johnson, Armistice Day Address at Texas Technological College, Lubbock, Texas, November 11, 1950, in *Statements of LBJ*, Lyndon B. Johnson Library and Museum.

Dr. Wiggins, Fellow Texans:
This is a genuine thrill to be in Lubbock and West Texas once again—and at Texas Tech in particular.
Out here, the air is good to breathe; it is not clogged with cynicism, or doubt and timidity. Out here on the South Plains, the enthusiasm is contagious, the vitality is inspiring, and the self-confidence of the people is everlastingly impressive....

On this day, we have come to observe an anniversary in the world's history.
November 11th, 1918, was a day when men rejoiced around the world; they believed a Century of Peace was dawning.
We know now; it was a false dawn.
Yet for all of us, November 11th has a deep significance. A spiritual significance. If the original cause of celebration

now seems a lost cause, we must look more deeply for the real meaning which all of us associate with Armistice Day.

Unless the past has a lesson for the present and the future, men have died in vain.

What is it that most Americans . . . most free men everywhere . . . want, more fervently than anything else?

It is, first of all, Peace. Peace, in which to live our lives; to love and be loved.

Although the peace of Armistice Day proved an illusion, its deeper significance is, I believe, that on this day we may rededicate ourselves to achieving peace.

That rededication cannot be done with words alone. It must be done with deeds. What are the deeds?

For the answer, we must look to the lessons of history.

The Kaiser was not crushed on the battlefields of Europe by sheer weight of superior manpower, nor superior military skill and experience. We arrived at this hour, 32 years ago, because of one decisive factor: the productive ability of America, translated into ships and weapons.

That productive might was the one thing the Kaiser feared above all else. He did not march until he was falsely convinced that America would never turn its productive capacities against him.

Two decades later, history repeated.

Hitler unleashed his armies of aggression only because he believed Americans would not again dedicate their great production strength to the defense of freedom.

And for a second time, the gigantic production of America's economy proved the decisive factor.

The Kaiser in 1916; and Hitler in the thirties, mistook the clamour of the isolationists for the voice of the American people. No error could have been more fatal.

Each time the sleeping giant angrily awoke, and turned its industrial might against the aggressor.

That is the supreme lesson we have learned: that our industrial might . . . our infinite productive capacity . . . is the greatest peace-making weapon in the history of the human race.

We have learned that if we want to keep the peace, we must be ready at all times to use this great weapon. We have learned that timidity draws aggression as the lightning rod draws the lightning from the skies.

And within the past 140 days, the lesson has been relearned, most convincingly.

On June 25th, not quite five months ago, the Communist Armies of North Korea started their march down that same long road of conquest which the Kaiser took in 1914 and Hitler took in 1939.

This time, America did not hesitate or vacillate. We used our strength.

And I believe our bold and prompt answer to aggression when the Communist Armies crossed the 38th parallel was the only answer free men could make.

Because we used our strength, the world took a long firm step toward Peace.

We have not reached the end of the road. No man can say what perils and heartbreak lie in store for us.

But this much of the future is clear: So long as Communist aggressors control great armies and great land masses, we in this country must be prepared, every hour and every day, to fight for Peace.

For ten years, for twenty years, perhaps even for so long as 30 years, the United States must be a preparedness state.

Our Armed Forces must be maintained in a constant state of readiness. Our civilian population must be prepared for whatever challenge we may encounter. And most important of all, our productive capacity must be in constant, full operation, arming this Nation and helping arm all free Nations, to withstand the onslaughts of aggression anywhere in the world.

All of us must understand this fact: Although we know who our enemy is, and where he is, it is entirely possible that we may never meet that enemy directly, on a field of battle.

Let me emphasize and reiterate that statement. The present struggle between the free nations and the Communist nations is—above all else—a struggle between two economies; two mighty production machines. Unlike the struggle with the Kaiser in 1918, unlike the struggle with the Axis in 1941, this is not a struggle in which two great armed forces will reach a final showdown on some well-defined battlefield. This is a struggle which may be decided by endurance; the economy with the greatest productive power and the greatest staying power will be triumphant.

What does this mean to you?

How do you, the people of the South Plains, fit into that picture? In a few moments, I hope to make that clear.

On June 25th, when the Communists crossed the 38th parallel in Korea, our economy was operating at nearly its full capacity. Our basic industries were turning out almost their top production capacity; and dozens of industries were setting all-time production records. We were approaching full employment.

But Korea makes it clear that we must produce still more goods—still more basic commodities—to defend ourselves and to help the other free nations defend themselves.

Korea compelled us to add heavy new burdens to an already near-peak production. Our economy was not geared to absorb this added burden with its present capacity to produce.

When our producing capacity is not adequate for the security of the nation, two courses are open to us.

One is to cut back production for civilian use. We can eliminate that part of our production which is deemed not essential to our defense. That is what we did during World War One, and to a greater extent during World War Two. But is that the right answer?

The cutback method involves questions of judgment, and men's judgment never is infallible. Let me give you an example. Suppose we eliminate the production of automobiles for civilian use. Yet our entire producing economy is geared to the worker who must get back and forth to his job. If he cannot travel in his own car, he must travel by public conveyance. So to offset the loss of private transportation facilities, we must divert production into public conveyance facilities—buses, train coaches, and the like.

What we have gained by elimination in one direction, we have partly lost in another.

Such examples could be multiplied. If freight cars to haul our farm products are diverted to hauling war supplies, trucks must be put on the road.

So it seems to me that the cutback method is, as a long-range answer, unsatisfactory. Cutbacks may become necessary as a stop-gap expedient; but in the long view, this method offers an illusion, not a solution.

Then there is the second approach. We can approach the problem directly: we can expand our productive facilities.

If steel is in short supply, we can expand our steel producing facilities. If aluminum is limited, we can enlarge the facilities for producing it.

Can we expand those facilities and still maintain a stable and prosperous economy?

The record says we can. The record says we have.

From 1939 to 1945, we increased our production 75 per cent.

At the start of the war, we had to curtail civilian production because our capacity was not increasing rapidly enough. But the fact remains that it was not the curtailment of civilian production which won the war. It was the overall expansion of our producing capacity by 75 per cent. If we had not done this, we could not have defeated the Axis, no matter what else we did.

If another all-out war were to come, I certainly would favor diverting present civilian production to war to the end that all possible production capacity be channeled into the manufacture of defense items.

Meanwhile, I believe we should start upon the second course with all dispatch: the course of expanding our production. America cannot hope to survive if it relies on half-measures to win this struggle against the economy of Russia.

Mark this: the Russians long ago realized that the war was one of production. The Communists have been feverishly expanding Russia's productive capacity ever since they came into power. They have been handicapped by a political system which stifles men's freedom and therefore their enterprise; nevertheless, they are gaining ground.

If we sit back on our records; if we for an instant think that we have reached the ultimate levels, if we refuse to expand, we may wake up five or ten years hence to find that Russia has outstripped us in the production race. That could only mean our destruction.

Therefore I say that America must now expand its productive capacity to that point where the capacity will serve our preparedness needs without throwing our civilian economy out of joint ... because that civilian economy is the basis of our production potential.

America's production machine must grow—and grow rapidly. We have proved that there is no top limit to our potential; we must translate that potential into actual capacity.

You, here in the West, can play a decisive role in this expanding production.

The expansion must be, and I believe it will be, in the great American West.

From the days of the colonies in New England, on down to the Twentieth Century, the West has been the hope and the future of this land. The West, from the beginning of our history, has been the great American challenge.

In the West, America found its early strength.

In the West, America found its power and its maturity as a Nation.

In the West today, America will find its salvation.

Here are the untapped resources—the resources to fuel and supply our expansion for the struggle with communism. Here is the space in which to grow. Here is the area in which a prudent nation can disperse its industrial machine with greatest hope for security. And here is the region where the Nation will find a people with the boldness, the self-assurance, the vitality and the imagination to create a new and greater empire of industrial production.

I tell you young people here especially—America's destiny is in your hands, and the hands of all of the youth of the West.

You have an opportunity—and a responsibility—that I and all men envy.

You need not look to New York or Detroit or Chicago for your future. The greatest future in America is right here before you. America and the entire free world must rely on you to meet the challenge of that future.

Your fathers and your grandfathers met and mastered a challenge in these lands. What a tremendous accomplishment this City of Lubbock is! Think how daring it was to found a city here, miles away from a river or any major body of water—and in a few short years of intensive and tireless labor, to build this city into a capital for a whole vast prospering region.

Think how bold and imaginative it was to found this institution, Texas Technological College, out here 25 years ago, and build it into an effective, universally-respected institution for the training of young minds.

What you have done here can be multiplied many fold all over the West.

People who built a city on this dry, vast plain certainly can also build an industrial empire here.

Out here, the men and women who started Lubbock and Amarillo and all the other cities of this region placed their faith in something more dynamic and vital than worship of the status quo.

The men and women who conquered the American West had no roadsigns to guide them; they charted their course by the stars. You who have inherited their empire must keep your eyes on the stars. The roadsigns along the path of status quo will lead you into dead end streets. The stars point the way to achievement, to hope ... and at the end of the road, to Peace.

The West can be America's answer—and the Free World's answer—to Russia's famed empire of production in the land beyond the Uraals.

Just as Russia saved herself during the German invasion through the production of her industrial machine beyond the Uraals so America can—and must—save herself by building a great new production strength here in the land West of the Mississippi.

We have barely scratched the surface of the West's great potential.

After V-J Day, many gloomy prophets shook their heads sadly and said the United States was running out of oil. All of the oil in the United States, they said, had been discovered.

What happened? Only a few short months ago, one of the great oil fields in the world was discovered over at Snyder, where the big oil companies, in their wisdom, had said there was no oil.

Nor was that discovery made by men who worshipped status quo.

The time has come for all of us—Americans here in the West and Americans in all regions—to face up to our future, and to our own manifest destiny. It is time for us to realize that we are capable of achievement far beyond our present capacity—and to glory in that realization. It is time for us to flex our muscles, and again display that vigor, daring, imagination and vitality which transformed this nation into the most productive nation on earth.

Our system of free men and free minds is superior to the Communist system. Our strength is superior to Communist strength. We will be a helpless prey only when we surrender and quit because we are afraid to change . . . afraid to expand . . . afraid to rise to the challenge of our times.

You young men and young women have the finest future of any generation in our future. War need not and will not be your destiny if you will it otherwise. Your destiny is peace . . . peace through achievement. Your destiny is to build a great new arsenal of freedom here in our native land.

Only fear can defeat us . . . more quickly and more completely than Communism. Fear and timidity: a lack of courage, a lack of vitality.

If our history means anything, it means we will never succumb to fear. Texans and Americans will look to the future unafraid—bold—determined.

Because our forefathers had that splendid daring we, their inheritors, are the best-fed, best-housed, best-clothed, best-educated, best-informed, best-cared-for people ever to live on this earth.

With such an inheritance, with such a shining example, free Americans shall never be intimidated by the sabre-rattling of the ill-fed, ill-housed, uneducated, uninformed, afflicted hordes and puppets of Communism.

We know what we must do, and what we can do, to answer the challenge to our way of life.

If we do those things, our children and their children may indeed celebrate November 11th as a Day of Peace.

Questions

1. What did Johnson believe would be the key to U.S. success in the Cold War?
2. What role did Johnson want Texas and the American West to play in the Cold War?

26-6 Communists in the U.S. Government (1950)

Joseph R. McCarthy

Joseph R. McCarthy (1908–1957), a freshman Republican senator from Wisconsin, joined the anti-Communist crusade during February 1950, in a speech delivered in Wheeling, West Virginia. He read the version of that speech excerpted here into the *Congressional Record* on February 20, 1950. The secretary of state whom he excoriated and caricatured was Dean Acheson; the individual whom Acheson had refused to disown was Alger Hiss. Hiss, accused as early as 1948 of having been a Communist spy while in government, had been convicted of perjury the previous month (see text pp. 815–818, 820–821).

Source: Congressional Record, 81st Cong., 2nd sess., vol. 96, part 2, 1954–1957.

Five years after a world war has been won, men's hearts should anticipate a long peace, and men's minds should be free from the heavy weight that comes with war. But this is not such a period—for this is not a period of peace. This is a time of the "cold war." This is a time when all the world is split into two vast, increasingly hostile armed camps—a time of a great armaments race.

Today we can almost physically hear the mutterings and rumblings of an invigorated god of war. You can see it, feel it, and hear it all the way from the hills of Indochina, from the shores of Formosa, right over into the very heart of Europe itself. . . .

[W]e are now engaged in a show-down fight — not the usual war between nations for land areas or other material gains, but a war between two diametrically opposed ideologies.

The great difference between our western Christian world and the atheistic Communist world is not political, ladies and gentlemen, it is moral. . . .

The real, basic difference, however, lies in the religion of immoralism — invented by Marx, preached feverishly by Lenin, and carried to unimaginable extremes by Stalin. This religion of immoralism, if the Red half of the world wins — and well it may — this religion of immoralism will more deeply wound and damage mankind than any conceivable economic or political system.

Karl Marx dismissed God as a hoax, and Lenin and Stalin have added in clear-cut, unmistakable language their resolve that no nation, no people who believe in a God, can exist side by side with their communistic state.

Karl Marx, for example, expelled people from his Communist Party for mentioning such things as justice, humanity, or morality. He called this soulful ravings and sloppy sentimentality.

While Lincoln was a relatively young man in his late thirties, Karl Marx boasted that the Communist specter was haunting Europe. Since that time, hundreds of millions of people and vast areas of the world have fallen under Communist domination. Today, less than 100 years after Lincoln's death, Stalin brags that this Communist specter is not only haunting the world, but is about to completely subjugate it.

Today we are engaged in a final, all-out battle between communistic atheism and Christianity. The modern champions of communism have selected this as the time. And, ladies and gentlemen, the chips are down — they are truly down. . . .

Ladies and gentlemen, can there be anyone here tonight who is so blind as to say that the war is not on? Can there be anyone who fails to realize that the Communist world has said, "The time is now" — and that this is the time for the show-down between the democratic Christian world and the Communist atheistic world?

Unless we face this fact, we shall pay the price that must be paid by those who wait too long.

Six years ago, at the time of the first conference to map out the peace — Dumbarton Oaks — there was within the Soviet orbit 180,000,000 people. Lined up on the antitotalitarian side there were in the world at that time roughly 1,625,000,000 people. Today only 6 years later, there are 800,000,000 people under the absolute domination of Soviet Russia — an increase of over 400 percent. On our side, the figure has shrunk to around 500,000,000. In other words, in less than 6 years the odds have changed from 9 to 1 in our favor to 8 to 5 against us. This indicates the swiftness of the tempo of Communist victories and American defeats in the cold war. As one of our outstanding historical figures once said, "When a great democracy is destroyed, it will not be because of enemies from without, but rather because of enemies from within."

The truth of this statement is becoming terrifyingly clear as we see this country each day losing on every front.

At war's end we were physically the strongest nation on earth and, at least potentially, the most powerful intellectually and morally. Ours could have been the honor of being a beacon in the desert of destruction, a shining living proof that civilization was not yet ready to destroy itself. Unfortunately, we have failed miserably and tragically to arise to the opportunity.

The reason why we find ourselves in a position of impotency is not because our only powerful potential enemy has sent men to invade our shores, but rather because of the traitorous actions of those who have been treated so well by this Nation. It has not been the less fortunate or members of minority groups who have been selling this Nation out, but rather those who have had all the benefits that the wealthiest nation on earth has had to offer — the finest homes, the finest college education, and the finest jobs in Government we can give.

This is glaringly true in the State Department. There the bright young men who are born with silver spoons in their mouths are the ones who have been worst. . . .

When Chiang Kai-shek [Jiang Jieshi] was fighting our war, the State Department had in China a young man named John S. Service. His task, obviously, was not to work for the communization of China. Strangely, however, he sent official reports back to the State Department urging that we torpedo our ally Chiang Kai-shek and stating, in effect, that communism was the best hope of China.

Later, this man — John Service — was picked up by the Federal Bureau of Investigation for turning over to the Communists secret State Department information. Strangely, however, he was never prosecuted. However, Joseph Grew, the Under Secretary of State, who insisted on his prosecution, was forced to resign. Two days after Grew's successor, Dean Acheson, took over as Under Secretary of State, this man — John Service — who had been picked up by the FBI and who had previously urged that communism was the best hope of China, was not only reinstated in the State Department but promoted. And finally, under Acheson, placed in charge of all placements and promotions.

Today, ladies and gentlemen, this man Service is on his way to represent the State Department and Acheson in Calcutta — by far and away the most important listening post in the Far East. . . .

This, ladies and gentlemen, gives you somewhat of a picture of the type of individuals who have been helping to shape our foreign policy. In my opinion the State Department, which is one of the most important government departments, is thoroughly infested with Communists.

I have in my hand 57 cases of individuals who would appear to be either card carrying members or certainly loyal to the Communist Party, but who nevertheless are still helping to shape our foreign policy.

One thing to remember in discussing the Communists in our Government is that we are not dealing with spies who get 30 pieces of silver to steal the blueprints of a new weapon. We are dealing with a far more sinister type of activity because it permits the enemy to guide and shape our policy. . . .

It is the result of an emotional hang-over and a temporary moral lapse which follows every war. It is the apathy to evil which people who have been subjected to the tremendous evils of war feel. As the people of the world see mass murder, the destruction of defenseless and innocent people, and all of the crime and lack of morals which go with war, they become numb and apathetic. It has always been thus after war.

However, the morals of our people have not been destroyed. They still exist. This cloak of numbness and apathy has only needed a spark to rekindle them. Happily, this spark has finally been supplied.

As you know, very recently the Secretary of State proclaimed his loyalty to a man guilty of what has always been considered as the most abominable of all crimes—of being a traitor to the people who gave him a position of great trust. The Secretary of State in attempting to justify his continued devotion to the man who sold out the Christian world to the atheistic world, referred to Christ's Sermon on the Mount as a justification and reason therefor, and the reaction of the American people to this would have made the heart of Abraham Lincoln happy.

When this pompous diplomat in striped pants, with a phony British accent, proclaimed to the American people that Christ on the Mount endorsed communism, high treason, and betrayal of a sacred trust, the blasphemy was so great that it awakened the dormant indignation of the American people.

He has lighted the spark which is resulting in a moral uprising and will end only when the whole sorry mess of twisted, warped thinkers are swept from the national scene so that we may have a new birth of national honesty and decency in Government.

Questions

1. How did McCarthy characterize the opposing sides in the Cold War?
2. How did he explain the successes of the Communists in the Cold War?
3. Who were the villains in his account?

26-7 Civil Rights and the National Party Platforms (1948)

A growing but still far from nationally dominant concern over civil rights figured in the 1948 presidential campaign (see text p. 814). The Democratic Party was particularly affected. Its national convention rejected southerners' efforts to weaken a general civil rights plank (largely based on the 1944 platform) and then strengthened that plank (in its two final paragraphs) by a vote of 651½–582½. This precipitated the creation of the States' Rights Democratic (Dixiecrat) Party. At that time, the Republican Party had no significant base in the South, and the Progressive Party of 1948 barely existed there.

Source: Kirk H. Porter and Donald Bruce Johnson, comps., *National Party Platforms, 1840–1968* (Urbana: University of Illinois Press, 1970), 435, 437, 441, 442, 447, 450, 452, 453, 468.

DEMOCRATS

. . . The Democratic Party is responsible for the great civil rights gains made in recent years in eliminating unfair and illegal discrimination based on race, creed or color.

The Democratic Party commits itself to continuing its efforts to eradicate all racial, religious and economic discrimination.

We again state our belief that racial and religious minorities must have the right to live, the right to work, the right to vote, the full and equal protection of the laws, on the basis of equality with all citizens as guaranteed by the Constitution.

We highly commend President Harry S. Truman for his courageous stand on the issue of civil rights.

We call upon the Congress to support our President in guaranteeing these basic and fundamental American Principles: (1) the right of full and equal political participation; (2) the right to equal opportunity of employment; (3) the right of security of person; (4) and the right of equal treatment in the service and defense of our nation.[1] . . .

PROGRESSIVES

. . . The American people cherish freedom.

But the old parties, acting for the forces of special privilege, conspire to destroy traditional American freedoms.

They deny the Negro people the rights of citizenship. They impose a universal policy of Jim Crow and enforce it with every weapon of terror. They refuse to outlaw its most bestial expression—the crime of lynching.

They refuse to abolish the poll tax, and year after year they deny the right to vote to Negroes and millions of white people in the South. . . .

The Progressive Party condemns segregation and discrimination in all its forms and in all places.

We demand full equality for the Negro people, the Jewish people, Spanish-speaking Americans, Italian Americans, Japanese Americans, and all other nationality groups.

We call for a Presidential proclamation ending segregation and all forms of discrimination in the armed services and Federal employment.

We demand Federal anti-lynch, anti-discrimination, and fair-employment-practices legislation, and legislation abolishing segregation in interstate travel.

We call for immediate passage of anti-poll tax legislation, enactment of a universal suffrage law to permit all citizens to vote in Federal elections, and the full use of Federal enforcement powers to assure free exercise of the right to franchise.

We call for a Civil Rights Act for the District of Columbia to eliminate racial segregation and discrimination in the nation's capital.

We demand the ending of segregation and discrimination in the Panama Canal Zone and all territories, possessions and trusteeships. . . .

We will develop special programs to raise the low standards of health, housing, and educational facilities for Negroes, Indians and nationality groups, and will deny Federal funds to any state or local authority which withholds opportunities or benefits for reasons of race, creed, color, sex or national origin.

We will initiate a Federal program of education, in co-operation with state, local, and private agencies to combat racial and religious prejudice.

We support the enactment of legislation making it a Federal crime to disseminate anti-Semitic, anti-Negro, and all racist propaganda by mail, radio, motion picture or other means of communication. . . .

. . . The Progressive Party demands abolition of Jim Crow in the armed forces. . . .

The Progressive Party proposes to guarantee, free from segregation and discrimination, the inalienable right to a good education to every man, woman, and child in America. Essential to good education are the recognized principles of academic freedom—in particular, the principle of free inquiry into and discussion of controversial issues by teachers and students.

We call for the establishment of an integrated Federal grant-in-aid program to build new schools, libraries, raise teachers' and librarians' salaries, improve primary and secondary schools, and assist municipalities and states to establish free colleges.

We call for a system of Federal scholarships, fellowships, and cost-of-living grants, free from limitations or quotas based on race, creed, color, sex or national origin, in order to enable all those with necessary qualifications but without adequate means of support to obtain higher education in institutions of their own choice.

We call for a national program of adult education in co-operation with state and local authorities.

We oppose segregation in education and support legal action on behalf of Negro students and other minorities aimed at securing their admission to state-supported graduate and professional schools which now exclude them by law.

REPUBLICANS

. . . Constant and effective insistence on the personal dignity of the individual, and his right to complete justice without regard to race, creed or color, is a fundamental American principle.

We aim always to unite and to strengthen; never to weaken or divide. In such a brotherhood will we Americans get results. Thus we will overcome all obstacles. . . .

. . . Lynching or any other form of mob violence anywhere is a disgrace to any civilized state, and we favor the prompt enactment of legislation to end this infamy.

One of the basic principles of this Republic is the equality of all individuals in their right to life, liberty, and the pursuit of happiness. This principle is enunciated in the Declaration of Independence and embodied in the Constitution of the United States; it was vindicated on the field of battle and became the cornerstone of this Republic. This right of equal opportunity to work and to advance in life should never be limited in any individual because of race, religion, color, or country of origin. We favor the enactment and just enforcement of such Federal legislation as may be necessary to maintain this right at all times in every part of this Republic.

We favor the abolition of the poll tax as a requisite to voting.

We are opposed to the idea of racial segregation in the armed services of the United States. . . .

STATES' RIGHTS DEMOCRATS

. . . 1. We believe that the Constitution of the United States is the greatest charter of human liberty ever conceived by the mind of man.

---

[1] When this platform was presented to the Convention, this section stated: "We again call upon the Congress to exert its full authority to the limit of its constitutional powers to assure and protect these rights." The last two paragraphs in the text above were inserted as an amendment to the platform by a vote of 651½ to 582½.

2. We oppose all efforts to invade or destroy the rights vouchsafed by it to every citizen of this republic.

3. We stand for social and economic justice, which we believe can be vouchsafed to all citizens only by a strict adherence to our Constitution and the avoidance of any invasion or destruction of the constitutional rights of the states and individuals. We oppose the totalitarian, centralized, bureaucratic government and the police state called for by the platforms adopted by the Democratic and Republican conventions.

4. We stand for the segregation of the races and the racial integrity of each race; the constitutional right to choose one's associates; to accept private employment without governmental interference, and to earn one's living in any lawful way. We oppose the elimination of segregation employment by Federal bureaucrats called for by the misnamed civil rights program. We favor home rule, local self-government and a minimum interference with individual rights.

5. We oppose and condemn the action of the Democratic convention in sponsoring a civil rights program calling for the elimination of segregation, social equality by Federal fiat, regulation of private employment practices, voting and local law enforcement.

6. We affirm that the effective enforcement of such a program would be utterly destructive of the social, economic and political life of the Southern people, and of other localities in which there may be differences in race, creed or national origin in appreciable numbers.

7. We stand for the checks and balances provided by the three departments of our Government. We oppose the usurpation of legislative functions by the executive and judicial departments. We unreservedly condemn the effort to establish nation-wide a police state in this republic that would destroy the last vestige of liberty enjoyed by a citizen.

8. We demand that there be returned to the people, to whom of right they belong, those powers needed for the preservation of human rights and the discharge of our responsibility as Democrats for human welfare. We oppose a denial of those rights by political parties, a barter or sale of those rights by a political convention, as well as any invasion or violation of those rights by the Federal Government.

We call upon all Democrats and upon all other loyal Americans who are opposed to totalitarianism at home and abroad to unite with us in ignominiously defeating Harry S. Truman and Thomas E. Dewey, and every other candidate for public office who would establish a police state in the United States of America.

Questions

1. What did the Democrats call for in the civil rights plank of their national platform? What demands of the civil rights movement of the 1950s and 1960s were not part of the 1948 Democratic platform?

2. In what respects did the Progressive Party platform go beyond the Democratic and Republican platforms in dealing with civil rights?

3. What did the States' Rights Democratic Party platform mean by "social equality"? Why did it term the Democratic and Republican platforms as favoring "totalitarian, centralized, bureaucratic government and the police state"?

26-8 *Brown v. Board of Education of Topeka* (1954)

In the *Brown* case, the U.S. Supreme Court considered whether segregation in the public schools deprived black students of equal protection under the law, which is guaranteed by the Fourteenth Amendment. The case challenged the "separate but equal" precedent set in the *Plessy v. Ferguson* decision (1896), in which the Court validated segregation by stating that separate facilities for blacks were legal so long as they were equal to those provided for whites. In deciding *Brown*, the Court bypassed comparing the equality of "physical facilities" and other "tangible factors" and instead focused on the psychology of segregation. In taking this approach, the Court overturned the "separate but equal" doctrine and found that segregation is unconstitutional.

Source: Brown v. Board of Education of Topeka, 347 U.S. 483 (1954).

BROWN ET AL. v. BOARD OF EDUCATION OF TOPEKA, SHAWNEE COUNTY, KAN., ET AL.

These cases come to us from the States of Kansas, South Carolina, Virginia, and Delaware. They are premised on different facts and different local conditions, but a common legal question justifies their consideration together in this consolidated opinion.

In each of the cases, minors of the Negro race, through their legal representatives, seek the aid of the courts in obtaining admission to the public schools of their community on a nonsegregated basis. In each instance, they have been denied admission to schools attended by white children under laws requiring or permitting segregation according to race. This segregation was alleged to deprive the plaintiffs of the equal protection of the laws under the Fourteenth Amendment. In each of the cases other than the Delaware case, a three-judge federal district court denied relief to the plaintiffs on the so-called "separate but equal" doctrine announced by this Court in *Plessy v. Ferguson*, 163 U.S. 537. Under that doctrine, equality of treatment is accorded when the races are provided substantially equal facilities, even though these facilities be separate. In the Delaware case, the Supreme Court of Delaware adhered to that doctrine, but ordered that the plaintiffs be admitted to the white schools because of their superiority to the Negro schools.

The plaintiffs contend that segregated public schools are not "equal" and cannot be made "equal," and that hence they are deprived of the equal protection of the laws. Because of the obvious importance of the question presented, the Court took jurisdiction. Argument was heard in the 1952 Term, and reargument was heard this Term on certain questions propounded by the Court.

Reargument was largely devoted to the circumstances surrounding the adoption of the Fourteenth Amendment in 1868. It covered exhaustively consideration of the Amendment in Congress, ratification by the states, then existing practices in racial segregation, and the views of proponents and opponents of the Amendment. This discussion and our own investigation convince us that, although these sources cast some light, it is not enough to resolve the problem with which we are faced. At best, they are inconclusive. The most avid proponents of the post-War Amendments undoubtedly intended them to remove all legal distinctions among "all persons born or naturalized in the United States." Their opponents, just as certainly, were antagonistic to both the letter and the spirit of the Amendments and wished them to have the most limited effect. What others in Congress and the state legislatures had in mind cannot be determined with any degree of certainty.

An additional reason for the inconclusive nature of the Amendment's history, with respect to segregated schools, is the status of public education at that time. In the South, the movement toward free common schools, supported by general taxation, had not yet taken hold. Education of white children was largely in the hands of private groups. Education of Negroes was almost nonexistent, and practically all of the race were illiterate. In fact, any education of Negroes was forbidden by law in some states. Today, in contrast, many Negroes have achieved outstanding success in the arts and sciences as well as in the business and professional world. It is true that public school education at the time of the Amendment had advanced further in the North, but the effect of the Amendment on Northern States was generally ignored in the congressional debates. Even in the North, the conditions of public education did not approximate those existing today. The curriculum was usually rudimentary; ungraded schools were common in rural areas; the school term was but three months a year in many states; and compulsory school attendance was virtually unknown. As a consequence, it is not surprising that there should be so little in the history of the Fourteenth Amendment relating to its intended effect on public education.

In the first cases in this Court construing the Fourteenth Amendment, decided shortly after its adoption, the Court interpreted it as proscribing all state-imposed discriminations against the Negro race. The doctrine of "separate but equal" did not make its appearance in this Court until 1896 in the case of *Plessy v. Ferguson*, supra, involving not education but transportation. American courts have since labored with the doctrine for over half a century. In this Court, there have been six cases involving the "separate but equal" doctrine in the field of public education. In *Cumming v. Board of Education of Richmond County*, 175 U.S. 528, and *Gong Lum v. Rice*, 275 U.S. 78, the validity of the doctrine itself was not challenged. In more recent cases, all on the graduate school level, inequality was found in that specific benefits enjoyed by white students were denied to Negro students of the same educational qualifications. *State of Missouri ex rel. Gaines v. Canada*, 305 U.S. 337; *Sipuel v. Board of Regents of University of Oklahoma*, 332 U.S. 631; *Sweatt v. Painter*, 339 U.S. 629; *McLaurin v. Oklahoma State Regents*, 339 U.S. 637. In none of these cases was it necessary to re-examine the doctrine to grant relief to the Negro plaintiff. And in *Sweatt v. Painter*, supra, the Court expressly reserved decision on the question whether *Plessy v. Ferguson* should be held inapplicable to public education.

In the instant cases, that question is directly presented. Here, unlike *Sweatt v. Painter*, there are findings below that the Negro and white schools involved have been equalized, or are being equalized, with respect to buildings, curricula, qualifications and salaries of teachers, and other "tangible" factors. Our decision, therefore, cannot turn on merely a comparison of these tangible factors in the Negro and white schools involved in each of the cases. We must look instead to the effect of segregation itself on public education.

In approaching this problem, we cannot turn the clock back to 1868 when the Amendment was adopted, or even to 1896 when *Plessy v. Ferguson* was written. We must consider public education in the light of its full development and its present place in American life throughout the Nation. Only in this way can it be determined if segregation in public schools deprives these plaintiffs of the equal protection of the laws.

Today, education is perhaps the most important function of state and local governments. Compulsory school attendance laws and the great expenditures for education both demonstrate our recognition of the importance of education to our democratic society. It is required in the performance of our most basic public responsibilities, even service in the armed forces. It is the very foundation of good citizenship. Today it is a principal instrument in awakening the child to cultural values, in preparing him for later professional training, and in helping him to adjust normally to his environment. In these days, it is doubtful that any child may reasonably be expected to succeed in life if he is denied the opportunity of an education. Such an opportunity, where the state has undertaken to provide it, is a right which must be made available to all on equal terms.

We come then to the question presented: Does segregation of children in public schools solely on the basis of race, even though the physical facilities and other "tangible" factors may be equal, deprive the children of the minority group of equal educational opportunities? We believe that it does.

In *Sweatt v. Painter*, supra [339 U.S. 629], in finding that a segregated law school for Negroes could not provide them equal educational opportunities, this Court relied in large part on "those qualities which are incapable of objective measurement but which make for greatness in a law school." In *McLaurin v. Oklahoma State Regents*, supra [339 U.S. 637], the Court, in requiring that a Negro admitted to a white graduate school be treated like all other students, again resorted to intangible considerations: ". . . his ability to study, to engage in discussions and exchange views with other students, and, in general, to learn his profession." Such considerations apply with added force to children in grade and high schools. To separate them from others of similar age and qualifications solely because of their race generates a feeling of inferiority as to their status in the community that may affect their hearts and minds in a way unlikely ever to be undone. The effect of this separation on their educational opportunities was well stated by a finding in the Kansas case by a court which nevertheless felt compelled to rule against the Negro plaintiffs:

Segregation of white and colored children in public schools has a detrimental effect upon the colored children. The impact is greater when it has the sanction of the law; for the policy of separating the races is usually interpreted as denoting the inferiority of the negro group. A sense of inferiority affects the motivation of a child to learn. Segregation with the sanction of law, therefore, has a tendency to [retard] the educational and mental development of Negro children and to deprive them of some of the benefits they would receive in a racial[ly] integrated school system.

Whatever may have been the extent of psychological knowledge at the time of *Plessy v. Ferguson*, this finding is amply supported by modern authority. Any language in *Plessy v. Ferguson* contrary to this finding is rejected.

We conclude that in the field of public education the doctrine of "separate but equal" has no place. Separate educational facilities are inherently unequal. Therefore, we hold that the plaintiffs and others similarly situated for whom the actions have been brought are, by reason of the segregation complained of, deprived of the equal protection of the laws guaranteed by the Fourteenth Amendment. This disposition makes unnecessary any discussion whether such segregation also violates the Due Process Clause of the Fourteenth Amendment.

Because these are class actions, because of the wide applicability of this decision, and because of the great variety of local conditions, the formulation of decrees in these cases presents problems of considerable complexity. On reargument, the consideration of appropriate relief was necessarily subordinated to the primary question—the constitutionality of segregation in public education. We have now announced that such segregation is a denial of the equal protection of the laws. In order that we may have the full assistance of the parties in formulating decrees, the cases will be restored to the docket, and the parties are requested to present further argument on Questions 4 and 5 previously propounded by the Court for the reargument this Term. The Attorney General of the United States is again invited to participate. The Attorneys General of the states requiring or permitting segregation in public education will also be permitted to appear as *amici curiae* upon request to do so by September 15, 1954, and submission of briefs by October 1, 1954.

Questions

1. How did the Court interpret the histories of public education and the Fourteenth Amendment?
2. According to the ruling in this case, what psychological damage does segregation perpetrate? Why are separate schools for blacks and whites inherently unequal?

26-9 The Southern Manifesto (1956)

Attacking the unanimous ruling in *Brown v. Board of Education of Topeka* (Document 26-8), a group of congressmen wrote the following "Southern Declaration on Integration," which was entered into the *Congressional Record* and appeared in the *New York Times* on March 12, 1956.

Source: "Southern Declaration on Integration" from *The New York Times*, March 12, 1956. Copyright © 1956 by The New York Times Co. Reprinted with permission.

SOUTHERN DECLARATION ON INTEGRATION

We regard the decision of the Supreme Court in the school cases as clear abuse of judicial power. It climaxes a trend in the Federal judiciary undertaking to legislate, in derogation of the authority of Congress, and to encroach upon the reserved rights of the states and the people.

The original Constitution does not mention education. Neither does the Fourteenth Amendment nor any other amendment. The debates preceding the submission of the Fourteenth Amendment clearly show that there was no intent that it should affect the systems of education maintained by the states.

The very Congress which proposed the amendment subsequently provided for segregated schools in the District of Columbia.

When the amendment was adopted in 1868, there were thirty-seven states of the Union. Every one of the twenty-six states that had any substantial racial differences among its people either approved the operation of segregated schools already in existence or subsequently established such schools by action of the same law-making body which considered the Fourteenth Amendment.

As admitted by the Supreme Court in the public school case (*Brown v. Board of Education*), the doctrine of separate but equal schools "apparently originated in *Roberts v. City of Boston* (1849), upholding school segregation against attack as being violative of a state constitutional guarantee of equality." This constitutional doctrine began in the North—not in the South—and it was followed not only in Massachusetts but in Connecticut, New York, Illinois, Indiana, Michigan, Minnesota, New Jersey, Ohio, Pennsylvania and other northern states until they, exercising their rights as states through the constitutional processes of local self-government, changed their school systems.

In the case of *Plessy v. Ferguson* in 1896 the Supreme Court expressly declared that under the Fourteenth Amendment no person was denied any of his rights if the states provided separate but equal public facilities. This decision has been followed in many other cases. It is notable that the Supreme Court, speaking through Chief Justice Taft, a former President of the United States, unanimously declared in 1927 in *Lum v. Rice* that the "separate but equal" principle is ". . . within the discretion of the state in regulating its public schools and does not conflict with the Fourteenth Amendment."

This interpretation, restated time and again, became a part of the life of the people of many of the states and confirmed their habits, customs, traditions and way of life. It is founded on elemental humanity and common sense, for parents should not be deprived by Government of the right to direct the lives and education of their own children.

Though there has been no constitutional amendment or act of Congress changing this established legal principle almost a century old, the Supreme Court of the United States, with no legal basis for such action, undertook to exercise their naked judicial power and substituted their personal political and social ideas for the established law of the land.

This unwarranted exercise of power by the court, contrary to the Constitution, is creating chaos and confusion in the states principally affected. It is destroying the amicable relations between the white and Negro races that have been created through ninety years of patient effort by the good people of both races. It has planted hatred and suspicion where there has been heretofore friendship and understanding.

Without regard to the consent of the governed, outside agitators are threatening immediate and revolutionary changes in our public school systems. If done, this is certain to destroy the system of public education in some of the states.

With the gravest concern for the explosive and dangerous condition created by this decision and inflamed by outside meddlers:

> We reaffirm our reliance on the Constitution as the fundamental law of the land.
>
> We decry the Supreme Court's encroachments on rights reserved to the states and to the people, contrary to established law and to the Constitution.
>
> We commend the motives of those states which have declared the intention to resist forced integration by any lawful means.
>
> We appeal to the states and people who are not directly affected by these decisions to consider the constitutional principles involved against the time when they too, on issues vital to them, may be the victims of judicial encroachment.

Even though we constitute a minority in the present Congress, we have full faith that a majority of the American people believe in the dual system of government which has enabled us to achieve our greatness and will in time demand that the reserved rights of the states and of the people be made secure against judicial usurpation.

We pledge ourselves to use all lawful means to bring about a reversal of this decision which is contrary to the Constitution and to prevent the use of force in its implementation.

In this trying period, as we all seek to right this wrong, we appeal to our people not to be provoked by the agitators and troublemakers invading our states and to scrupulously refrain from disorder and lawless acts.

Question

1. What principal objections did the Southern Manifesto raise with regard to the U.S. Supreme Court's rulings on ending segregation in public schools?

26-10 Describing My Arrest (1955)

Rosa Parks

By refusing to give up her seat on a segregated local bus in Montgomery, Alabama, Rosa Parks (1913–2005), a seamstress and a member of the National Association for the Advancement of Colored People, played a pioneering role in community-based, nonviolent resistance to Jim Crow. Nonviolent resistance became highly important to the emerging civil rights movement. E. D. Nixon, an African American, was active in the NAACP; Clifford and Virginia Durr were local whites who supported the civil rights cause. (See text pp. 852–858).

Source: From "Rosa L. Parks" in *My Soul Is Rested* by Howell Raines. Copyright © 1977 by Howell Raines. Used by permission of G. P. Putnam's Sons, a division of Penguin Group (USA) Inc.

I had left my work at the men's alteration shop . . . in the Montgomery Fair department store. . . . I came across the street and looked for a Cleveland Avenue bus that apparently had some seats on it. At that time it was a little hard to get a seat on the bus. . . .

As I got up on the bus and walked to the seat I saw there was only one vacancy that was just back of where it was considered the white section. So this was the seat that I took, next to the aisle, and a man was sitting next to me. Across the aisle there were two women, and there were a few seats at this point in the very front of the bus that was called the white section. . . . And on the third stop there were some people getting on, and at this point all of the front seats were taken. Now in the beginning, at the very first stop I had got on the bus, the back of the bus was filled up with people standing in the aisle and I don't know why this one vacancy that I took was left, because there were quite a few people already standing toward the back of the bus. The third stop is when all the front seats were taken, and this one man was standing and when the driver looked around and saw he was standing, he asked the four of us, the man in the seat with me and the two women across the aisle, to let him have those front seats.

At his first request, didn't any of us move. Then he spoke again and said, "You'd better make it light on yourselves and let me have those seats." At this point, of course, the passenger who would have taken the seat hadn't said anything. In fact, he never did speak to my knowledge. When the three people, the man who was in the seat with me and the two women, stood up and moved into the aisle, I remained where I was. When the driver saw that I was still sitting there, he asked if I was going to stand up. I told him, no, I wasn't. He said, "Well, if you don't stand up, I'm going to have you arrested." I told him to go on and have me arrested.

He got off the bus and came back shortly. A few minutes later, two policemen got on the bus, and they approached me and asked if the driver had asked me to stand up, and I said yes, and they wanted to know why I didn't. I told them I didn't think I should have to stand up. . . . They placed me under arrest then and had me get in the police car, and I was taken to jail and booked on suspicion. . . . They had to determine whether or not the driver wanted to press charges or swear out a warrant, which he did. Then they took me to jail and I was placed in a cell. In a little while I was taken from the cell, and my picture was made and fingerprints taken. I went back to the cell then, and a few minutes later I was called back again, and when this happened I found out that Mr. E. D. Nixon and Attorney and Mrs. Clifford Durr had come to make bond for me.

Questions

1. What elements of nonviolent protest are evident in Parks's recollection?
2. Do you think that the fact that Parks was a woman was an important element in this event? Why or why not?
3. What does Parks's story indicate about whites in Montgomery?

Questions for Further Thought

1. Compare the responses of Senators Johnson and McCarthy to the Cold War.
2. How would you compare and contrast the Red Scare following World War I with the Great Fear of the 1940s and 1950s?
3. What events and developments, both at home and abroad, contributed to the meteoric rise of Senator Joseph R. McCarthy?
4. What constitutional issues did the civil rights movement raise?
5. What issues did the movement raise with regard to the relationship between federal and state government?

Modern Republicanism

To support long-term and large-scale military commitments, the military draft was continued, and the salience of foreign relations and military policy increased the power of the executive branch of the federal government even more than the New Deal. The Cold War struggle—a clash of ideologies, subversion, and espionage—also placed a premium on conformity.

Committed to both containing and limiting military spending, Eisenhower's administration stressed a "New Look" foreign policy that emphasized the threat of massive retaliation with nuclear weapons; selective intervention, covert and overt, from Latin America to Asia; and additional bilateral and multilateral regional security pacts. In Document 26-11, Nikita Khrushchev charts Soviet international relations for the post-Stalinist era. In 26–12, John Foster Dulles discusses Cold War policy before a meeting of Baghdad Pact nations. In Document 26-13, President Eisenhower, about to leave office, expresses his concern about "the impact of the Cold War" on the United States.

26-11 Peaceful Coexistence (1956)

Nikita Khrushchev

Nikita Khrushchev (1894–1971) was a pipe fitter who rose up through party ranks to lead the Soviet Union following the death of Joseph Stalin in 1953. In 1956, after Khrushchev had consolidated his power, he signaled a relative break with Stalin's brutal and repressive methods at home, indicating that there could be a thaw in the Cold War with the United States and the West. In this speech, delivered on February 14 as part of the Report of the

Central Committee of the Communist Party of the Soviet Union to the 20th Party Congress, he outlines the international position of the Soviet Union and discusses peaceful coexistence between different social systems.

Source: From Nikita S. Khrushchev, "The International Position of the Soviet Union," in *Readings in American Foreign Policy*, eds. Robert A. Goldwin et al. (New York: Oxford University Press, 1959), 362–369. Reprinted with permission.

The steady consolidation of the forces of socialism, democracy and peace, and of the forces of the national-liberation movement is of decisive significance. The international position of the Soviet Union, the People's Republic of China, and the other socialist countries has been further strengthened during this period, and their prestige and international ties have grown immeasurably. The international camp of socialism is exerting ever-growing influence on the course of international events. (*Applause.*)

The forces of peace have been considerably augmented by the emergence in the world arena of a group of peace-loving European and Asian states which have proclaimed non-participation in blocs as a principle of their foreign policy. The leading political circles of these states rightly hold that to participate in restricted military imperialist alignments would merely increase the danger of their countries being involved in military gambles by the aggressive forces and draw them into the maelstrom of the arms drive.

As a result, a vast Zone of Peace including peace-loving states, both socialist and non-socialist, of Europe and Asia, has emerged in the world. This zone includes vast areas inhabited by nearly 1,500 million people, that is, the majority of the population of our planet. . . .

The October Socialist Revolution struck a most powerful blow at the imperialist colonial system. Under the influence of the Great October Revolution the national-liberation struggle of the colonial peoples developed with particular force, it continued throughout the subsequent years and has led to a deep-going crisis of the entire imperialist colonial system.

The defeat of fascist Germany and imperialist Japan in the Second World War was an important factor stimulating the liberation struggles in the colonies and dependent countries. The democratic forces' victory over fascism instilled faith in the possibility of liberation in the hearts of the oppressed peoples.

The victorious revolution in China struck the next staggering blow at the colonial system; it marked a grave defeat for imperialism.

India, the country with the world's second biggest population, has won political independence. Independence has been gained by Burma, Indonesia, Egypt, Syria, the Lebanon, the Sudan, and a number of other former colonial countries. More than 1,200 million people, or nearly half of the world's population, have freed themselves from colonial or semi-colonial dependence during the last ten years. (*Prolonged applause.*)

The disintegration of the imperialist colonial system now taking place is a post-war development of history-making significance. Peoples who for centuries were kept away by the colonialists from the high road of progress followed by human society are now going through a great process of regeneration. People's China and the independent Indian Republic have joined the ranks of the Great Powers. We are witnessing a political and economic upsurge of the peoples of South-East Asia and the Arab East. The awakening of the peoples of Africa has begun. The national-liberation movement has gained in strength in Brazil, Chile and other Latin-American countries. The outcome of the wars in Korea, Indo-China and Indonesia has demonstrated that the imperialists are unable, even with the help of armed intervention, to crush the peoples who are resolutely fighting for a life of freedom and independence. The complete abolition of the infamous system of colonialism has now been put on the agenda as one of the most acute and pressing problems. (*Applause.*)

The new period in world history which Lenin predicted has arrived, and the peoples of the East are playing an active part in deciding the destinies of the whole world, are becoming a new mighty factor in international relations. In contrast to the pre-war period, most Asian countries now act in the world arena as sovereign states or states which are resolutely upholding their right to an independent foreign policy. International relations have spread beyond the bounds of relations between the countries inhabited chiefly by peoples of the white race and are beginning to acquire the character of genuinely world-wide relations.

The winning of political freedom by the peoples of the former colonies and semi-colonies is the first and most important prerequisite of their full independence, that is, of the achievement of economic independence. The liberated Asian countries are pursuing a policy of building up their own industry, training their own technicians, raising the living standards of the people, and regenerating and developing their age-old national culture. History-making prospects for a better future are opening up before the countries which have embarked upon the path of independent development.

These countries, although they do not belong to the socialist world system, can draw on its achievements to build up an independent national economy and to raise the living standards of their peoples. Today they need not go begging for up-to-date equipment to their former oppressors. They can get it in the socialist countries, without assuming any political or military commitments.

The very fact that the Soviet Union and the other countries of the socialist camp exist, their readiness to help the underdeveloped countries in advancing their industries on terms of equality and mutual benefit are a major stumbling-block to colonial policy. The imperialists can no longer regard the underdeveloped countries solely as potential sources for making maximum profits. They are compelled to make concessions to them.

Not all the countries, however, have thrown off the colonial yoke. A big part of the African continent, some countries of Asia, Central and South America continue to remain in colonial or semi-colonial dependence. They are still retained as agrarian raw-material appendages of the imperialist countries. The living standard of the population in the dependent countries remains exceedingly low.

The contradictions and rivalry between the colonial powers for spheres of influence, sources of raw materials, and markets are growing. The United States is out to grab the colonial possessions of the European powers. South Viet-Nam is passing from France to the United States. The American monopolies are waging an offensive against the French, Belgian, and Portugese possessions in Africa. Once Iran's oil riches were fully controlled by the British, but now the British have been compelled to share them with the Americans; moreover, the American monopolists are fighting to oust the British entirely. American influence in Pakistan and Iraq is increasing under the guise of "free enterprise."

The American monopolies, utilizing their dominant position in the Central and South-American countries, have moulded the economies of many of them in a distorted, one-sided way, extremely disadvantageous for the population. They are hampering their industrial development and shackling them with the heavy chains of economic dependence.

To preserve, and in some places also to re-establish their former domination, the colonial powers are resorting to the suppression of the colonial peoples by the force of arms, a method which has been condemned by history. They also have recourse to new forms of colonial enslavement under the guise of so-called "aid" to underdeveloped countries, which brings colossal profits to the colonialists. Let us take the United States as an example. The United States renders such "aid" above all in the form of deliveries of American weapons to the underdeveloped countries. This enables the American monopolies to load up their industry with arms orders. Then the products of the arms industry, worth billions of dollars and paid for through the budget by the American taxpayers, are sent to the underdeveloped countries. States receiving such "aid" in the form of weapons, inevitably fall into dependence; they increase their armies, which leads to higher taxes and a decline in living standards.

The monopolists are interested in continuing the "positions of strength" policy; the ending of the "cold war" is to their disadvantage. Why? Because the fanning of war hysteria is used to justify imperialist expansion, to intimidate the masses and dope their minds in order to justify the higher taxes which then go to pay for war orders and flow into the safes of the millionaires. Thus, the "cold war" is a means for maintaining the war industry at a high level and for extracting colossal profits.

Naturally, "aid" to underdeveloped countries is granted on definite political terms, terms providing for their integration into aggressive military blocs, the conclusion of joint military pacts, and support for American foreign policy aimed at world domination, or "world leadership," as the American imperialists themselves call it. . . .

The peaceful co-existence of the two systems. The Leninist principle of peaceful co-existence of states with different social systems has always been and remains the general line of our country's foreign policy.

It has been alleged that the Soviet Union advances the principle of peaceful co-existence merely out of tactical considerations, considerations of expediency. Yet it is common knowledge that we have always, from the very first years of Soviet power, stood with equal firmness for peaceful co-existence. Hence, it is not a tactical move, but a fundamental principle of Soviet foreign policy.

This means that if there is indeed a threat to the peaceful co-existence of countries with differing social and political systems, it by no means comes from the Soviet Union or the rest of the socialist camp. Is there a single reason why a socialist state should want to unleash aggressive war? Do we have classes and groups that are interested in war as a means of enrichment? We do not. We abolished them long ago. Or, perhaps, we do not have enough territory or natural wealth, perhaps we lack sources of raw materials or markets for our goods? No, we have sufficient of all those and to spare. Why then should we want war? We do not want it, as a matter of principle we renounce any policy that might lead to millions of people being plunged into war for the sake of the selfish interests of a handful of multi-millionaires. Do those who shout about the "aggressive intentions" of the U.S.S.R. know all this? Of course they do. Why then do they keep up the old monotonous refrain about some imaginary "communist aggression"? Only to stir up mud, to conceal their plans for world domination, a "crusade" against peace, democracy, and socialism.

To this day the enemies of peace allege that the Soviet Union is out to overthrow capitalism in other countries by "exporting" revolution. It goes without saying that among us Communists there are no supporters of capitalism. But this does not mean that we have interfered or plan to interfere in the internal affairs of countries where capitalism still exists. Romain Rolland was right when he said that "freedom is not brought in from abroad in baggage trains like Bourbons." (*Animation.*) It is ridiculous to think that revolutions are made to order. We often hear representatives of bourgeois countries reasoning thus: "The Soviet leaders claim that they are for peaceful co-existence between the two systems. At the same time they declare that they are fighting for communism, and say that communism is bound to win in all countries. Now if the Soviet Union is fighting for communism, how can there be any peaceful co-existence with it?" This view is the result of bourgeois propaganda. The ideologists of the bourgeoisie distort the facts and deliberately confuse questions of ideological struggle with questions of relations between states in order to make the Communists of the Soviet Union look like advocates of aggression.

When we say that the socialist system will win in the competition between the two systems—the capitalist and the socialist—this by no means signifies that its victory will be achieved through armed interference by the socialist countries in the internal affairs of the capitalist countries. Our certainty of the victory of communism is based on the fact that the socialist mode of production possesses decisive advantages over the capitalist mode of production. Precisely because of this, the ideas of Marxism-Leninism are more and more capturing the minds of the broad masses of the working people in the capitalist countries, just as they have captured the minds of millions of men and women in our country and the People's Democracies. (*Prolonged applause.*) We believe that all working men in the world, once they have become convinced of the advantages communism brings, will sooner or later take the road of struggle for the construction of socialist society. (*Prolonged applause.*) Building communism in our country, we are resolutely against war. We have always held and continue to hold that the establishment of a new social system in one or another country is the internal affair of the peoples of the countries concerned. This is our attitude, based on the great Marxist-Leninist teaching. . . .

Questions

1. Describe the official Soviet worldview as outlined by Khrushchev. In what key respects did it contrast with the official U.S. position at the time?
2. What did Khrushchev mean by "peaceful co-existence"?

26-12 Cold War Foreign Policy (1958)

John Foster Dulles

In opening remarks before the fourth session of the Council of Ministers of the Baghdad Pact, a defensive alliance between Turkey, Iraq, Iran, Pakistan, and Great Britain, Secretary of State John Foster Dulles (1888–1959) stressed the importance of "defensive security" and "economic health" in "meeting the Communist threat." He spoke in Ankara, Turkey, on January 27, 1958. The United States had encouraged Turkey and Iraq to enter into a defensive alliance, which the other three nations later joined. Iraqi nationalists soon overthrew the regime that had supported the pact.

Source: Department of State Bulletin, (February 17, 1958), 38:251–254.

Gentlemen, the close of World War II raised mankind's hopes that a new era of peace and security for all might now prevail. Unfortunately, these hopes were soon dashed. Instead, free men and free nations found themselves faced with a struggle to preserve their independence from the predatory ambitions of Communist imperialism. Moscow and Peiping [Beijing] directly or through local Communist parties, have relentlessly sought to extend their control in every direction. Where they have succeeded, freedom of choice has become a sham, the dignity of the individual a hollow mockery. The list of once free and proud nations that must today wear the Communist yoke is painful to recall. They are nearly a score in number. Coercion alone keeps them in this state of bondage, as was demonstrated by the recent revolt of the Hungarian people against their alien masters. Yet the parties of international communism continue openly to proclaim their goal of world domination. They did so again, only last November, at Moscow.

Currently the use and threat of military power are supplemented by intensified and enlarged efforts at subversion and seduction. These efforts are insidious and deceptive. They seize upon mankind's yearning for economic and social betterment to undermine his vigilance to resist enslavement. . . .

Fortunately, there is, in general, a clear perception of the threat to independence posed by Communist imperialism. Around the world, the free nations have drawn together in collective regional associations as authorized and encouraged by the charter of the United Nations. These associations would, I believe, profit from exchange of information and of experience as between themselves. . . .

We are well aware of the fact that in this general area political independence, always an aspiration, has sometimes been lost and oftentimes been threatened, as indeed it is threatened today.

Also we recognize that it is not enough merely to want, or now have, independence. Reliable independence rests on two pillars: the pillar of defensive security and the pillar of economic health. The United States is prepared to cooperate, where desired, in assisting in these two ways any nation or group of nations in the general area of the Middle East to maintain national independence.

DEFENSIVE SECURITY

Let me speak first of security.

Security cannot be taken for granted. It must be won by positive efforts. It is not won by pacifism, by weakness, or by appeasement. That has been demonstrated time after time. Security is won by conditions which make it apparent that aggression does not pay. If a potential aggressor realizes that he will, by aggression, lose more than he could gain, it can be reliably assumed that he will not attempt aggression. That is where collective security plays its indispensable role. Few nations, by themselves, possess the resources needed to deter aggression. Collectively they can do so. Therefore, sometimes by treaty, sometimes by congressional resolution, the United States has associated itself with over 40 nations in defense of national independence and of peace. . . .

The Baghdad Pact group of countries can be confident that mobile power of great force would, as needed, be brought to bear against any Communist aggressor. And by the same token any such potential aggressor knows in advance that his losses from aggression would far exceed any possible gains. That is an effective deterrent to aggression and a guaranty of peace.

Also, it is vital that there be forces of national defense. These constitute indispensable, visible evidence of the will of people to fight and die, if need be, for their homes, their nation, and their faith. There is no "pushbutton" substitute for this. Furthermore, such forces, with the reinforcement where needed of mobile power, can save the people from the scourge of invasion if, perchance, deterrence fails. The United States has contributed, and will contribute, to this aspect of defense. . . .

I assure you that the United States strives earnestly both to end the nuclear menace and to limit conventional armaments. I recall that a decade ago the United States, possessing a monopoly of atomic weapons, offered to forgo that monopoly and to join in establishing a system to assure that atomic power would be used only for peaceful purposes. The Soviet Union alone blocked that peaceful and humanitarian measure.

And we act in the same spirit today. Outer space is becoming, for the first time, usable, and both the United States and the Soviet Union are experimentally using outer space for weapons purposes. So the United States has proposed to the Soviet Union that the nations forgo the use of outer space for war and dedicate it for all time to the peaceful purposes of mankind, to man's fuller life, not to his greater peril. So far that proposal remains without positive response.

The Soviet Union has, however, by a statement made last week, advanced the grotesque theory that only atheistic governments, as are the Communists, can properly possess modern weapons. The argument is that it would be a sacrilege for religious peoples, for defenders of the faith, to have such weapons; thus only the atheists, the Communists, can have them.

The United States ardently seeks limitation of armament on the basis of equality. But never will the United States accept the Soviet Communist thesis that men, because they are religious, must deny themselves the means to defend their religious freedom.

ECONOMIC HEALTH

Let me speak now of economic health. This is an equally indispensable pillar of independence. Without it no nation can maintain adequate and dependable security forces or be able surely to resist subversion.

Large military establishments are not easily reconciled with economic welfare. One of the merits of collective self-defense is that it reduces the requirements for individual self-defense. For under a collective system the mobile power that protects one can equally protect many. In this way, and only in this way, is it made possible for nations confronted by superior hostile power to avoid making the people fear an excessive nonproductive military burden and enable them to combine military security with economic health.

Military authorities can advise us about military security. But there is need also for a broad political judgment that comprehends both military and economic factors. Some economic sacrifices are needed for military security. We dare not give so absolute a priority to military requirements that economic health collapses. Indeed a sound and developing economy is the indispensable foundation for sustained military effort. Furthermore, given the deterrent military power that exists in the world today, there may be greater risk to independence in economic weakness than in local military weakness. It is not easy to strike the proper balance between military and economic effort. To achieve that is, however, the paramount duty of statesmanship. . . .

Social and economic progress is a universal desire. It is understandably most acute among those peoples who, for various historical reasons, do not yet fully share in the benefits of modern technology and science. These improve man's health, ease his labor, and afford him greater opportunities to develop his own talents and spiritual resources. . . .

MEETING THE COMMUNIST THREAT

Gentlemen, we live in difficult days. By great efforts over the centuries—efforts marked by successes and failures—men have reached a great appreciation of the dignity of the human individual and the need for an organization of the society of nations in accordance with the tested principles of collective security and friendly cooperation. Yet at the moment, when so much seems possible, all is endangered. A small group believes fanatically in a materialistic, atheistic society. It believes in mechanistic conformity, both in terms of human beings and of national groups. It would turn men into cogs in a materialistic machine, thinking and acting under central dictatorship. It boasts that it is "internationalist" in the sense of bringing all governments everywhere under the domination of a single power, that of international communism, acting under the guiding direction of the Communist Party of the Soviet Union.

This fanatical group, using every device without moral restraint—for they deny the existence of a moral law—by use of revolution, military conquest, and subversion have come to rule a great part of the world, and they exploit the human and material resources they now control to extend their domination over the rest of us.

That is a threat of immense proportions. We need not, however, be dismayed. The greatest danger is always the danger which comes from blindness to danger. Today we see the danger, and we are allied with forces that have repeatedly demonstrated their ability to prevail as against materialistic despotisms. There are, we know, God-given aspirations for freedom of mind and spirit and for opportunity. These are beyond the power of man to destroy. So long as we ally ourselves loyally and sacrificially with what is good, what is true, our cause surely will prevail.

Gentlemen, the United States observer delegation, animated by these sentiments, will endeavor to make a constructive contribution to your deliberations.

Thank you.

Questions

1. Dulles saw a significant difference between what had been anticipated at the end of World War II and what had actually occurred. How did he account for that difference?
2. How did Dulles explain that military strength and economic well-being are in opposition to each other? What economic benefits of collective security did he mention?

26-13   Farewell Address (1961)

Dwight D. Eisenhower   Speaking on national television on January 17, 1961, just three days before the inauguration of his youthful successor, John F. Kennedy, President Dwight D. Eisenhower (1890–1969) reflected on the Cold War and its impact on the United States (see text pp. 827–828).

Source: Public Papers of the Presidents of the United States: Dwight D. Eisenhower, 1960–1961 (Washington, DC: U.S. Government Printing Office, 1961), 1035–1040.

We now stand ten years past the midpoint of a century that has witnessed four major wars among great nations. Three of these involved our own country. Despite these holocausts America is today the strongest, the most influential and most productive nation in the world. Understandably proud of this preeminence, we yet realize that America's leadership and prestige depend, not merely upon our unmatched material progress, riches and military strength, but on how we use our power in the interests of world peace and human betterment.

Throughout America's adventure in free government, our basic purposes have been to keep the peace; to foster progress in human achievement; and to enhance liberty, dignity and integrity among people and among nations. To strive for less would be unworthy of a free and religious people. Any failure traceable to arrogance, or our lack of comprehension or readiness to sacrifice would inflict upon us grievous hurt both at home and abroad.

Progress toward these noble goals is persistently threatened by the conflict now engulfing the world. It commands our whole attention, absorbs our very beings. We face a hostile ideology—global in scope, atheistic in character, ruthless in purpose, and insidious in method. Unhappily the danger it poses promises to be of indefinite duration. To meet it successfully, there is called for, not so much the emotional and transitory sacrifices of crisis, but rather those which enable us to carry forward steadily, surely, and without complaint the burdens of a prolonged and complex struggle—with liberty the stake. Only thus shall we remain, despite every provocation, on our charted course toward permanent peace and human betterment. . . .

A vital element in keeping the peace is our military establishment. Our arms must be mighty, ready for instant action, so that no potential aggressor may be tempted to risk his own destruction.

Our military organization today bears little relation to that known by any of my predecessors in peacetime, or indeed by the fighting men of World War II or Korea.

Until the latest of our world conflicts, the United States had no armaments industry. American makers of plowshares could, with time and as required, make swords as well. But now we can no longer risk emergency improvisation of national defense; we have been compelled to create a permanent armaments industry of vast proportions. Added to this, three and a half million men and women are directly engaged in the defense establishment. We annually spend on military security more than the net income of all United States corporations.

This conjunction of an immense military establishment and a large arms industry is new in the American experience. The total influence—economic, political, even spiritual—is felt in every city, every State house, every office of the Federal government. We recognize the imperative need for this development. Yet we must not fail to comprehend its grave implications. Our toil, resources and livelihood are all involved; so is the very structure of our society.

In the councils of government, we must guard against the acquisition of unwarranted influence, whether sought or unsought, by the military-industrial complex. The potential for the disastrous rise of misplaced power exists and will persist.

We must never let the weight of this combination endanger our liberties or democratic processes. We should take nothing for granted. Only an alert and knowledgeable citizenry can compel the proper meshing of the huge industrial and military machinery of defense with our peaceful methods and goals, so that security and liberty may prosper together.

Akin to, and largely responsible for the sweeping changes in our industrial-military posture, has been the technological revolution during recent decades.

In this revolution, research has become central; it also becomes more formalized, complex, and costly. A steadily increasing share is conducted for, by, or at the direction of, the Federal government.

Today, the solitary inventor, tinkering in his shop, has been overshadowed by task forces of scientists in laboratories and testing fields. In the same fashion, the free university, historically the fountainhead of free ideas and scientific discovery, has experienced a revolution in the conduct of research. Partly because of the huge costs involved, a government contract becomes virtually a substitute for intellectual curiosity. For every old blackboard there are now hundreds of new electronic computers.

The prospect of domination of the nation's scholars by Federal employment, project allocations, and the power of money is ever present—and is gravely to be regarded.

Yet, in holding scientific research and discovery in respect, as we should, we must also be alert to the equal and opposite danger that public policy could itself become the captive of a scientific-technological elite.

It is the task of statesmanship to mold, to balance, and to integrate these and other forces, new and old, within the principles of our democratic system—ever aiming toward the supreme goals of our free society.

Another factor in maintaining balance involves the element of time. As we peer into society's future, we—you and I, and our government—must avoid the impulse to live only for today, plundering, for our own ease and convenience, the precious resources of tomorrow. We cannot mortgage the material assets of our grandchildren without risking the loss also of their political and spiritual heritage. We want democracy to survive for all generations to come, not to become the insolvent phantom of tomorrow.

Down the long lane of the history yet to be written America knows that this world of ours, ever growing smaller, must avoid becoming a community of dreadful fear and hate, and be, instead, a proud confederation of mutual trust and respect.

Such a confederation must be one of equals. The weakest must come to the conference table with the same confidence as do we, protected as we are by our moral, economic, and military strength. That table, though scarred by many past frustrations, cannot be abandoned for the certain agony of the battlefield.

Disarmament, with mutual honor and confidence, is a continuing imperative. Together we must learn how to compose differences, not with arms, but with intellect and decent purpose. Because this need is so sharp and apparent I confess that I lay down my official responsibilities in this field with a definite sense of disappointment. As one who has witnessed the horror and the lingering sadness of war—as one who knows that another war could utterly destroy this civilization which has been so slowly and painfully built over thousands of years—I wish I could say tonight that a lasting peace is in sight.

Happily, I can say that war has been avoided. Steady progress toward our ultimate goal has been made. But, so much remains to be done. As a private citizen, I shall never cease to do what little I can to help the world advance along that road....

You and I—my fellow citizens—need to be strong in our faith that all nations, under God, will reach the goal of peace with justice. May we be ever unswerving in devotion to principle, confident but humble with power, diligent in pursuit of the Nation's great goals.

To all the peoples of the world, I once more give expression to America's prayerful and continuing aspiration:

We pray that peoples of all faiths, all races, all nations, may have their great human needs satisfied; that those now denied opportunity shall come to enjoy it to the full; that all who yearn for freedom may experience its spiritual blessings; that those who have freedom will understand, also, its heavy responsibilities; that all who are insensitive to the needs of others will learn charity; that the scourges of poverty, disease and ignorance will be made to disappear from the earth, and that, in the goodness of time, all peoples will come to live together in a peace guaranteed by the binding force of mutual respect and love.

Questions

1. Eisenhower seems to have seen a threat to the independence of universities and the sciences as a result of governmental invasion of university laboratories. How did he describe changes in laboratories that would make them subject to such an invasion?
2. Eisenhower's use of the term *military-industrial complex* suggests the potential for a conspiracy against the public interest. How did he relate the military to public and governmental concerns? What role did government play in the development of industrial power?
3. Liberty, Eisenhower stated, was at stake. From his speech, which institutions seem to have been involved? Who was threatening liberty, and what could be done to protect it?

Questions for Further Thought

1. Analyze the Cold War from the U.S. and Soviet perspectives (Documents 26-1, 26-2, 26-11, and 26-12).
2. John Foster Dulles (Document 26-12) and President Eisenhower (Document 26-13) discerned both foreign and domestic threats to which they wanted to call attention. What were those threats, and what responses did they want their audiences to have?
3. Both Dulles and Eisenhower were concerned with the expansion of American military power and its effect on the national and international roles of the United States. How did each of these men define this new, post–World War II issue for Americans? Were they saying essentially the same things?
4. How do you judge the diplomatic and military policies of the Eisenhower administration in the light of the concerns expressed by President Eisenhower in his farewell address?

CHAPTER TWENTY-SEVEN

The Age of Affluence
1945–1960

Economic Powerhouse

The decades after World War II were marked not only by the Cold War but also by increasing prosperity for most, though not all, Americans. The war had strengthened, not damaged, the nation's economy. After experiencing want during the Depression and then rationing and shortages during the war years, Americans were now ready and able to go on a postwar buying spree—to purchase homes, automobiles, and household appliances (including newly available television sets). Government lent a hand: the GI Bill of Rights helped veterans purchase homes, start businesses, and acquire higher education or technical training. Highway construction, sponsored by the federal government (Document 27-1), helped open suburban areas where inexpensive, reliable, and abundant energy as well as lower land costs encouraged home ownership, and allowed Americans to move into the more sparsely settled Sun Belt states. The reforms of the New Deal survived largely intact, as did the partial socialization of the risks involved in living in a free-enterprise society. But Congress was much more conservative than it had been before the war. The anti-union Taft-Hartley bill, which Truman vetoed, calling it a "slave-labor bill," was passed in 1947. There was also a return of tax avoidance, as depicted in Document 27-2. In another important change, more women worked after World War II than before, though they were concentrated in some occupations and largely absent from others. Document 27-3 presents job ads for women in Chicago, twelve years into the postwar period. The powerful American economy both dominated and sustained the war-ravaged world, further contributing to domestic prosperity. Again, government played a role, with the Marshall Plan assisting European nations' recovery from the war and their purchase of U.S. exports.

27-1 The Interstate Highway System (1955)

George M. Humphrey

Federal construction of the interstate highway system made clear the interrelationships between interested businesses, the public, and the government (see text pp. 839–841). On May 16, 1955, testifying before the Subcommittee on Roads of the House Committee on

Public Works, Secretary of the Treasury George M. Humphrey (1890–1970) made the case for the proposal that became the National Interstate and Defense Highway Act of 1956.

Source: Treasury Secretary George M. Humphrey, testimony before a House Subcommittee, 1955. In Nathaniel Howard, ed., *The Basic Papers of George M. Humphrey* (Cleveland: Western Reserve Historical Society, 1965), 513–515.

In my view, the new highways will be earning assets, making possible a continuation of expansion in the case of motor transportation which would otherwise be seriously handicapped by the growing inadequacy of our highway network. You already know of the savings possible from improved safety, reduced time delays, greater vehicle efficiency, and lower repair and maintenance costs. . . .

There is probably . . . no thinking person in America who does not know that the nation needs better highways. We need them for the daily business and safety of everyone. And we need them to help our defense should this nation ever be attacked by a foreign power. This being the case, I believe that men of good will and good intentions must be able to get together on a plan for starting these better highways—not on a small scale, and not just a little amount a year—but on a major scale, and right now. Every year, every month lost in having these extra miles of better highways means loss to our economy and so less better living for our citizens. It means loss of lives through loss of the safety these better highways would bring. It means loss of the best possible transportation of our defense equipment and evacuation of our people in the event of an enemy attack.

Questions

1. According to Humphrey, why would the proposed highways become "earning assets"?
2. What role did Humphrey believe the highways would play in national defense? (How did the highways in the Gulf states fare in this role during Hurricane Katrina in 2005?)
3. What interests would be positively affected by the highways? What interests would be negatively affected?

27-2 "Let's See, Now—Where Can We Raise More Taxes?" (1953)

Herbert Block

Herbert Lawrence Block (1909–2001) was a noted liberal editorial cartoonist in a liberal era in American politics, which lasted from Franklin Roosevelt's election in 1932 to Lyndon Johnson's resignation in 1968. During this period, Eisenhower was elected to two terms but he made no effort to roll back New Deal programs such as Social Security. "Herblock" won three Pulitzer Prizes and other awards during his career at the *Washington Post*, which began in 1946. He was famous for his caricatures of Joseph McCarthy and Richard M. Nixon. With Dwight Eisenhower's election in 1952, the Republican Party returned to the White House after a twenty-year hiatus and two of the most eventful decades in U.S. history. The GOP quickly reasserted its traditional antitax and probusiness agenda, and Herblock worried about the implications in this 1953 cartoon.

Source: Cartoon, "Let's See, Now—Where Can We Raise More Taxes?" in *Herblock's Here and Now*, by Herbert Block (New York: Simon and Schuster, 1955), 241. Reprinted with permission of Herb Block Foundation, Washington, D.C.

"*Let's See, Now—Where Can We Raise More Taxes?*"

Question

1. Since the Eisenhower administration decided against cutting government programs, and actually expanded some of them, such as Social Security, whom did Herblock indicate would have to pay more for them if corporations that sold natural resources were given tax exemptions?

27-3 Help Wanted — Women (1957)

After the war, married women, especially mothers, confronted difficult questions over whether to work. All women who were considering work faced dilemmas relating to the job market. Examine these want ads in the light of text pages 846–847.

Source: Classified ads, *Chicago Sunday Tribune*, May 12, 1957, pt. 5, 36, 40. Copyright © 1957 Chicago Tribune. Reprinted with permission.

Executive Secretary $100 Week

$100 paid weekly to the PRESIDENT'S private secretary. Your own carpeted private office. Average skills nec. as you'll be handling most of your own correspondence. Ability to deal with people important, heavy public contact work involved. FREE at CHICAGO Personnel. 6 E. Randolph [Above Walgreens.] RAndolph 6–2355.

Arrange Social Functions

Famous college fraternity needs you to take over in their beautiful new national headquarters office. Make arrangements for social functions, send invitations to members, handle enrollments and all convention plans. $70 to start with raise in 30 days for this unusually different position. FREE at LAKE Personnel. 29 E. Madison.
RAndolph 6–4650.   11th Fl.

RECEPTION LITE TYPING

No exp. nec. for this front office reception position. Answer pushbutton phones, greet visitors in beautiful modern office from 9–5. Lt. typing. Sal. high. FREE at LAKE Personnel. 29 E. Madison. RAndolph 6–4650.

Reservation Secretary

Lite steno desired for unique position as secretary in charge of reservations for beautiful hotel. Handle accommodations for important people in the public eye. Poise and ability to deal with people important. Extremely high starting salary. FREE at LAKE Personnel. 29 E. Madison.
RAndolph 6–4650   11th Fl.

AIRLINE TICKET SALES GIRL

$305 mo. even during 10 day training period as ticket sales girl with high paying airline. All public contact—no office skills. Single girls receive travel passes for themselves and their families. Absolutely no exp. nec. For details see
BOULEVARD   22 W. Madison st.
5th Floor   FInancial 6–3780

RECEPTION WILL TEACH SWBD.

No experience or typing needed to be front office girl in well known commercial art studio. Your nice appearance, friendly manner, interest in public contact qualify. Salary open and high! Vacation this summer! Beginner qualifies. No fee at
BOULEVARD   22 W. Madison st.
5th Floor   FInancial 6–3780

SECRETARY

Permanent position available for girl to perform secretarial work of a varied nature. Requires person with pleasing personality, experience and ability. Modern air conditioned office located for convenient transportation.
GOSS
PRINTING PRESS CO.
5601 W. 31ST-ST.
BIshop 2–3300   Ext. 311

SECRETARY
PUBLIC RELATIONS DIR.

Must have good stenographic skills and like to do a variety of work. Age 22–30. Paid vacations, holidays, company cafeteria, and other employee benefits.
ILLINOIS TOOL WORKS
2501 N. Keeler [4200 W.]

SECRETARY

VACATION WITH PAY THIS SUMMER!

If you're not happy where you are, but don't want to lose your vacation this summer, here's your chance. We need a secretary for a vice president of this advertising agency, one who's neat, accurate taking and transcribing heavy copy dictation on electric typewriter, who can handle details herself, keep her boss on the beam, help out elsewhere in this six-girl office. We're in a spanking new office just a few steps from Van Buren I. C. station. A happy place to work in an expanding organization. Salary starts at $70 per week, but you must work 1 month before vacation starts. We'll test you before hiring—to start at once.

CALL MR. DEAN
WAbash 2–8056

Classified Ads for Women (1957)

SALES POSITIONS

HOUSEWIVES

NO EXPERIENCE NECESSARY

EARN EXTRA MONEY FOR VACATION

WORK FULL TIME

PART TIME

SALARY + COMMISSION

GOOD EARNINGS

IMMEDIATE MERCHANDISE DISCOUNT

APPLY NOW!

GOLDBLATTS

LOOP
STATE AND VAN BUREN

NORTH
4722 N. BROADWAY
3149 N. LINCOLN-AV.

SOUTH
250 PLAZA—PARK FOREST
7975 S. CICERO

Brides! Housewives!

Have You 2 or 3 days to Spare, Each Week?

This part-time job—in a pleasant, air conditioned Michigan avenue office—will take you away from home just enough each week, to sharpen up your interest in your household tasks.

Type of duties in this job? You will alternate chiefly between telephone work and general office work. You'll be working with nice people, and you'll find the days go quickly.

You have your choice of working either 2 or 3 full days [8 hours] each week, but one of the days must be Friday. Also, we have one opening for Sunday work, combined with 2–3 other weekdays.

No previous experience is necessary, but an alert, intelligent attitude and liking for people are important.

If you find this offer appealing—and you're between the ages of 22 and 45 with a high school education—apply Monday through Friday, 9 to 11 a.m. or 1 to 4 p.m.

ROOM 635
CHICAGO TRIBUNE
435 N. Michigan

APPAREL
STORE MANAGER or
DEPT. MGR.
EXPERIENCED for store
at GRAND AND HARLEM

REAL FUTURE FOR AGGRESSIVE LADIES. RTW. MGR. GOOD SALARY, COMMISSIONS. COMPANY BENEFITS AND FUTURE. WILL TRAIN. WRITE FULLY.

Write MDV 397, Tribune

GIRLS!

Now That Spring's Here
Why Not
Put Your
EXTRA ENERGY
into a Job
at

Motorola

where
YOU ARE NEEDED
IN
Work You'll Enjoy

WE HAVE OPENINGS FOR

Wirers and Solderers

TO WORK DAY SHIFT ON

TV.

HIGH WAGES
FREE INSURANCE
PROFIT SHARING

FOR THOSE
WHO CAN QUALIFY

EMPLOYMENT OFFICE
OPEN DAILY
8:30 A.M.-4 P.M.
APPLY AT

Motorola
4545 W. AUGUSTA-BLVD.
OR 1450 N. CICERO

Questions

1. What is the significance of separate want-ad sections for women and men?
2. What kinds of jobs for women predominated in these ads? What kinds were absent?
3. What strikes you about the language of the want ads (regarding prospective jobs, applicants, work environments, and so forth)?

Question for Further Thought

1. Historians have described the 1950s as a decade of consensus for the general agreement that existed between the parties on domestic and foreign policy issues, although there were some important differences. What were the areas of agreement?

The Affluent Society

Prosperity, like depression, shapes society as well as the economy. One manifestation of prosperity was the expansion of neighborhoods into suburbia. Innovative developers played an important role in the "suburban explosion," as Document 27-4 suggests. In Document 27-5, Neil Morgan declares the rise of the Sun Belt, the rapid growth of western and southern cities that was bolstered by the defense industry.

27-4 Green Acres (1950)

Suburbanization—the movement of people, institutions, and activities out of the city—was one of the central developments of the postwar period. The following newspaper ad carries the message of Long Island developers to potential home buyers in New York City (see text pp. 837–839).

Source: Advertisement, Green Acres, *New York Times*, June 25, 1950, sec. 8, 6.

Questions

1. What strikes you about the home described in the ad?
2. How does the ad try to sell the house?
3. What appears to be the relationship between the Green Acres development in Valley Stream, Long Island, and New York City, at least as of 1950?

A New Home by CHANIN

Six rooms, all on one floor, attached garage, full basement, 34x25, exclusive of laundry space, make this a complete home for all the family—comfortable to live in, easy to keep, interesting and inviting to your friends.

Chanin skill of design has given it graciousness and luxury. Rooms are well-proportioned. Friendly entrance vestibule with guest closet, picture windows, front and rear, venetian blinds, china closet with service bar between dining room and kitchen, combination linen closet and laundry hamper, color-harmonized bath with vanitory, medicine cabinet with 14 feet of shelf-room, ceramic tile wainscoting and floor add finish and charm.

The basement easily becomes a recreation or hobby room, a play place for the children.

Chanin precision construction—poured concrete foundation and basement walls, full insulation, weather stripping, copper piping—mean low-cost maintenance. Oil-fired hot water circulating heat provides winter comfort; keeps down fuel bills.

The Hotpoint all-electric kitchen lightens housework. Steel cabinets have 23 square feet of textolite work surfaces. Refrigerator, range, dishwasher, ventilating fan and washing machine (in the basement) all are included in the purchase price.

But more important than details are the experience and integrity of the designer and builder. The Chanin Organization has created more than 6,000 dwelling units. Chanin "know-how" means lasting charm, sturdy lifetime quality.

The purchase price is less than you may think—$14,790 for everything mentioned, plus your choice of several exteriors, 6,000-square foot landscaped plot, sewers, curb, paved street, sidewalk. Veterans pay nothing down. Their 30-year mortgages bear 4 percent interest. Terms to nonveterans are equally attractive.

Compare this house with anything you have seen anywhere near its price range. Compare its location, in a planned, established community, 5 minutes walk from the Valley Stream station, 29 minutes from Penn Station, 17 miles from midtown New York or Brooklyn, near main highways, parkways, schools, churches, stores.

Then walk around Green Acres a bit. Hundreds of other homes, now 8 to 14 years old themselves will tell you that "Chanin-built is well-built" and much more than a phrase. It is a hallmark, a guarantee of building perfection.

Hotpoint appliances used exclusively

BY TRAIN: *Long Island train from Penn Station or Brooklyn to Valley Stream; walk back through park to property.* BY CAR: *Sunrise Highway to Central Avenue; from Merrick Road or Southern State Parkway, turn on Central Avenue to Sunrise Highway.* BY SUBWAY AND BUS: *6th Avenue or 8th Avenue IND train to Parsons Boulevard, Queens. Change to Bee Line's Grant Park bus which passes entrance gates.*

• GREEN ACRES •

"The Planned Residential Community"

SUNRISE HIGHWAY AT CENTRAL AVE., VALLEY STREAM, L. I.

Advertisement for Green Acres, "The Planned Residential Community" (1950)

27-5 The Footloose Migration (1961)

Neil Morgan

Neil Morgan was born in North Carolina, but World War II took him to California as a navy ensign in 1944. Morgan remained out West after the war, like many servicemen, and he made a living as a newspaper columnist in San Diego. He wrote numerous books on California and the West and was particularly interested in postwar America's overall population shift to the West and South, which he called "the largest migration in the history of the world."

Source: Excerpt from Neil Morgan, *Westward Tilt: The American West Today*, foreword by James A. Michner, maps by Edward Malsberg (New York: Random House, 1963), 3–12. Copyright © 1961, 1962, 1963 by Neil Morgan. Used by permission of Random House, Inc.

Today an awesome hunk of America has come loose. The move to Western America is the largest migration in the history of the world. Since the birth of the nation, its geographical center of population has been moving inexorably westward across West Virginia, Ohio, Indiana and into Illinois. Now it is within fifty miles of crossing the Mississippi River. California is supplanting New York as the most populous state. Americans are moving to California in greater numbers than today's entire immigration to the United States. The five boroughs of New York City would have to be emptied of every man, woman and child to match the population increase of the past decade in the eleven states between the Rocky Mountains and the Pacific Ocean. . . .

Yet the move West is one of the least-understood wonders of our modern world. Less is written of it than is written about Disneyland. Most reportage is understandably haphazard, shallow, or distorted. Most journalists who try to interpret the contemporary West parrot that malignant stereotype of the West created by Eastern editors whose rare forays to the region are for a whiff of Hollywood saffron or a sojourn in San Francisco—which they assume to be an oasis of urbanity in an uncivilized desert. The Western past has been recorded with more charm and less bias than its present. Its stagecoaches are better understood than its freeways, its United States marshals than its city managers, its Gold Rush than the westward tilt of today. . . .

The truth is that this is a vastly misunderstood region, even by those who live in it, because it is exploding too fast in every direction. Interpreting its cities, in the words of one brilliant Westerner, Wallace Stegner, is "like trying to hold a stethoscope to the chest of an angry cat." Its subtleties and intricacies discourage those who prefer a tidy problem with only one answer. There is a startling absence of studies of Western mores and attitudes. The Westerner is easy prey for the quick-impression writer who knows he can buy his audience cheap through time-proven broadsides at seashore culture or freeway madness.

Americans have sought to interpret the twentieth-century move westward in historic terms, but this is a move without precedent. It does not fit traditional migratory patterns. This continental tilt has been born of a modern American phenomenon: a nation so prosperous and so mobile that its people are free to go in search of a more luxurious way of life. The Westerners of today are the first people in world history to attain that freedom in the mass.

They seek a wide spectrum of amenities: sunshine and warmth in California, Nevada, Arizona, and New Mexico, fishing in Oregon, boating in Washington, hunting in Wyoming, skiing in Colorado—and almost everywhere, the scenic extravagances of the rawboned West, escape from conventional urban crowding, the leisurely pace and more amiable human relationships which derive from that pace and which lead many toward concentration on the less tangible pursuits of the arts and the intellect. . . .

As the new Westerner has been set free from other regions to seek these amenities, industrial evolution has provided a new world of industry so footloose that it can move with him, oblivious to the traditional industrial requirements of location. The industries of the space age are less dependent on pivotal market areas and power resources than on an environment which will lure the scientist and skilled technician. Western factories are short on smokestacks and spur lines. Their products may be electronic components so small that they are flown away, or the actual aircraft itself. One of the most significant products of Western factories is ideas; the "think factory" and the laboratory are the epitome of the industrial move West.

Thus, sustained by footloose industry, the newcomer to the West develops a sense of having discovered the life of tomorrow. The selectivity that dominates this migration provides a unity among its diverse people. They are integrated by common bonds of supreme self-confidence and hope in the future. And it is this common spirit of the new breed dominating the westward tilt which has unified for the first time the vast area between the Rocky Mountains and the Pacific Ocean. Its vitality is obvious from the pulp mills of Montana to the electronics plants of Phoenix, from the missile producers of Denver to the aircraft and space industry of Seattle. It is obvious in the rapid urbanization of the cities of every Western state. . . .

Despite the regional unity of the new West, its surface pattern is a marvel of diversity. Party politics are unpredictable. Nine of the eleven Western states gave Richard Nixon pluralities over President Kennedy in the 1960 election. But after the 1962 elections, only eight of twenty-two Western United States senators were Republicans. Republican governors outnumbered Democrats by seven to four. Whatever his party, the Westerner is a political paradox. He has an almost emotional commitment to individualism, and a generally stronger abhorrence for federal intervention than the people of other regions. He is aggressively liberal in economic affairs, but distrustful of big debt. He is slow to move toward sociologic reform, lacking the cultural flexibility of older regions, and yet he bears the scars of some of the most extreme reform movements in American history. More recently, a voluble small group of extremists has unfairly stamped parts of the West as reactionary.

One characteristic shared by the states of the new West is the relative lack of social need. In this prospering land, the burning cause is the bizarre oddity. At Christmas, service clubs cast about frantically for targets for their charitable instincts. The migrant worker has the lowest net income in America, but often he is driving a late-model car; welfare systems, usually generous, give him a last-line bulwark against crisis. The slums of Western cities cannot be compared in misery with those of cities in older regions; no settlement house exists in the West. Racial conflicts are milder than in other regions; the few serious racial crises of the West have been related to the tensions of wartime. No strong voice of social consciousness has been heard in the West since World War II; social crisis has not reached a level to provoke reform. . . .

It is California which dominates the new West. Of every one hundred Westerners in the eleven states, fifty-eight are in California and twenty-five in metropolitan Los Angeles. Washington, the second most populous Western state, ranks twenty-third among the fifty states. There are four million more Californians than the combined population of the ten other Western states. In population, others rank as follows: Washington, Oregon, Colorado, Arizona, New Mexico, Utah, Idaho, Montana, Wyoming, and Nevada.

The casual student of maps (which only suggest the vast dimensions of the West) may need reminding of the contrasts in population density. There are so many more people in California than in the rest of the West that an almost colonial quality sometimes is detected in the relations between California and the other Western states. In 1961 I attended a conference of Western governors in Salt Lake City at which California's Governor Pat Brown arrived two days late. It was obvious that nothing much would be settled until Brown appeared. In those two days, resentments of other states toward California occasionally flared—most of them involved California's aggressive search for Western water and power, some were connected with California's tremendous market for raw products of the Western states which are less economically sophisticated. When Governor Brown finally arrived at this conference, there was a subtle closing of ranks among some other governors.

Although California leads the way, and certain tensions inevitably result from one state being so rich and so large, there is widespread economic strength among the Western states. With one-third of the land area of the fifty states, these eleven have fifteen percent of the national population, earn seventeen percent of personal income, produce nineteen percent of agricultural commodities, furnish fifty-four percent of its lumber, extract twenty-three percent of its minerals, and erect twenty-seven percent of its buildings.

Some of the notable misconceptions about the West are economic. The West is not agrarian. Agricultural employment represents a lower percentage of the labor force than the national average. More Westerners live in the cities than the national average. Industry dominates the job market—and so does the federal government. In New Mexico, Utah, and Wyoming, government employment by federal, state, and local agencies is the primary source of work. Only in Nevada, where tourism dominates, do services loom near the top as the source of jobs. Manufacturing is the leading source of employment in California, Oregon, and Washington, the three Pacific Coast states. In agriculture, crops are more important than livestock in the coastal states and in Idaho and Arizona; livestock dominates in the other six Western states.

The overriding factor in Western unity is growth. Between 1950 and 1960, the population increase of these eleven Western states was more than seven and two-thirds million. This accounted for more than one-fourth of the nation's growth. California's growth made up two-thirds of the growth of the West. The California increase of nearly five million persons was far more than the combined growth of Florida and Texas, the next ranking states in growth. California alone accounted for almost one-fifth of the nation's growth during that decade. Yet no Western state lost population rank in relation to other states between 1950 and 1960. Arizona and New Mexico each moved past three other states. Four states moved up one position: Colorado, Idaho, Montana, and Utah. The remaining five held their rank; among them, California is expected to pass New York by mid-1963 to become the most populous state. . . .

The West is the most dynamic region of America today. It is the most intense in its feelings, the most open to commitment to causes, good or bad, right or left. But newness and bigness are not adequate in themselves. Rapid growth and vigor are not goals but symptoms. In dedication and direction, the West flounders like America, only more so.

The westward tilt is wiping out most of the American frontier finally and forever. The driving urge of the American to move on and conquer new lands soon will have nowhere to spend itself but in space—and space will remain an arena for the few. The westward rush in America has a somber element of the climacteric. Soon there will be nowhere else to seek new resources, new values, new meaning, except within ourselves.

If the new West is indeed scouting ahead in the directions which the nation will take, its responsibilities are awesome, and its actions deeply involve the future of America.

Questions

1. Why did the postwar West appeal to Americans?
2. On what basis did Morgan assert that the West was America's "most dynamic" region?
3. Compare and contrast Morgan's piece with President Lyndon B. Johnson's "American West" speech (Document 26-5).

Questions for Further Thought

1. Using Neil Morgan's excerpt (Document 27-5) and the Chapter 27 text as your sources, explain several of the reasons for American optimism in the postwar era (1945–1965).
2. What were some of the major social and demographic changes brought on by postwar affluence?

The Other America

John Kenneth Galbraith did not celebrate the affluent society about which he wrote in 1958. Rather, he contrasted private affluence with public squalor and questioned the society that tolerated the discrepancy. Not everyone shared the widespread affluence of the 1950s and 1960s. Furthermore, both countless private decisions (such as those that led businesses and individuals to locate in suburbia) and important governmental policies (especially highway construction and urban renewal) worked to the disadvantage of urban groups that were part of "the other America" (see text pp. 849–858). In Document 27-6, Carey McWilliams draws attention to the contemporary significance of U.S. lands that were once a part of the Spanish empire. In Document 27-7, Herbert Gans writes sympathetically of "the urban villagers" who lived in Boston's West End before urban renewal began there. Document 27-8 offers Chicago city government's case for urban renewal. Early in the 1960s, Michael Harrington wrote powerfully about an America that contained within it "an affluent society" *and* "an underdeveloped nation, a culture of poverty" (Document 27-9).

27-6 *North from Mexico* (1949)

Carey McWilliams

Carey McWilliams (1905–1980) was born in Steamboat Springs, Colorado, but is known for his commitment to social issues in California and his leadership of the New York–based magazine of radical opinion *The Nation*. Like many U.S. intellectuals during the 1930s, McWilliams was drawn to socialism—ideas evident in his classic 1939 study, *Factories in the Field: The Story of Migratory Farm Labor*. In *North from Mexico: The Spanish-Speaking People of the United States*, published ten years later, McWilliams examined the history and importance of the Spanish-speaking people in what historian Herbert E. Bolton called "the Spanish Borderlands," that vast area within the United States which was once part of the Spanish empire. In this excerpt from the foreword to *North from Mexico*, McWilliams notes the unique problems and issues in discussing and framing the history and peoples of this region of the United States.

Source: Foreword from *North from Mexico: The Spanish-Speaking People of the United States*, by Carey McWilliams (Philadelphia: J.B. Lippincott Company, 1949), 7–11. Used by permission.

Titles have always bothered me and never more so than in selecting a title for this book. My assignment was to tell the story of Spanish-speaking people in the United States; or, as Louis Adamic put it, "the story of those who came from Spain and Mexico." But how is one to characterize, in a phrase, a people so diverse in origin? An ethnic group has been defined as a people living competitively in relationship of superordination or subordination with respect to some other people or peoples within one state, country, or economic area. In this sense there can be no doubt that the Spanish-speaking constitute a clearly delineated ethnic group. But one must also recognize that there is no more heterogeneous ethnic group in the United States than the Spanish-speaking. Hence it is quite impossible to hit upon a phrase that aptly characterizes all the people now living in this country who by national origin, appearance, speech, or background might be called, and probably are called, "Mexican" or "Mexican-American."

Any phrase selected to characterize the Spanish-speaking will necessarily prove to be misleading, inaccurate, or possibly libelous. If there is a generally accepted usage it is to be found in the phrase "Spanish-speaking," but many people speak Spanish who cannot be identified with the Spanish-speaking group. Besides, the people who are generically Spanish-speaking are more Indian in racial origin, and perhaps in culture, than they are Spanish. "Latin-American" is vague and euphemistic; "Spanish-American" detracts from the importance of the Mexican and Indian heritage; while "Mexican-American" implies a certain condescension.

I was told that "Americans From Mexico" would be an appropriate title. But, strictly speaking, the Spanish-language minority did not come from Spain and Mexico; they were already very much a part of the landscape when the Anglo-Americans came to the Southwest. Basically the difficulty in nomenclature arises from the fact that the Spanish-speaking represent a fusion of Spanish, Mexican, and Indian heritages, both racially and culturally, and in every possible combination and mixture. The Spanish strain, as Mary Austin once observed, has chiefly served "to mollify temperamentally the aboriginal strain" and is therefore perhaps the least significant element in the heritage of the people. In the Southwest, the Spanish-speaking stand midway between the Indians and the Anglo-Americans, a people whose culture represents a fusion of Indian and non-Indian elements. While it is possible, of course, to distinguish between Indian-Spanish and Anglo-American elements in the culture of the Spanish-speaking, it is well-nigh impossible to label any one trait "Indian" or "Spanish" or "Mexican."

Since two or more ethnic groups constitute an ethnic system, one ethnic always implies the existence of another. In most portions of the Southwest, the term "Anglo" is used as a catchall expression to designate all persons who are neither Mexican nor Indian, while the term "Hispano" is used to designate the Spanish-speaking. In essence, therefore, the terms "Anglo" and "Hispano" are the heads and the tails of a single coin, a single ethnic system; each term has meaning only as the other is implied. The terms do not define homogeneous entities; they define a relationship. For the term "Anglo" is essentially as meaningless as the term "Hispano": it embraces all the elements in the population that are *not* Spanish-speaking. Thus a Jew is an "Anglo" in the Southwest and so is a Japanese or a Chinese. Erna Fergusson even tells of a Negro in Albuquerque who, in conversation with an Anglo-American, referred to "us Anglos."

The dichotomy implied in the terms "Anglo" and "Hispano," however, is real enough, no matter how vague either term may be as descriptive of the heterogeneous elements making up the two categories. The reality of this cleavage is to be found in the social history of the Southwest (much of which has been forgotten); and in the nature of the region. No matter how sharply the Spanish-speaking may differ among themselves over the question of nomenclature, the sense of cleavage from or opposition to the Anglos has always been an important factor in their lives and it is this feeling which gives cohesion to the group. The sense of group identity also arises from the fact that the Spanish-speaking have had a similar history and experience and have been influenced by a similar relationship to a sharply differentiated environment. "The race is not to the swift," wrote D. H. Lawrence, "but to those who sit still and let the waves go over them." Waves and still more waves have passed over the Spanish-speaking people, but they are still as firmly rooted in the Southwest as a forest of Joshua trees. In part, therefore, the difference between "Anglo" and "Hispano" relates to a difference in the degree of attachment to, and identification with, a most compulsive environment. The Spanish-speaking have an identification with the Southwest which can never be broken. They are not interlopers or immigrants but an indigenous people. As a consequence, they resent, and will always resent, any designation which implies a hyphenated relationship to their native environment and particularly so when this designation is applied by Anglo-American interlopers and immigrants. This sense of identification with the environment is most complex for it relates back to a memory of things Spanish. Mary Austin once suggested the real basis for this feeling when she said that the area of Spanish exploration north of the Rio Grande was substantially coterminous, as the gypsy of the cactus family, the pricklypear, had travelled. Did they stop where they did because the environment had ceased to be familiar? Whatever the reason, it is important to remember that geographically the Southwest is one with Mexico.

Obviously a title should characterize its subject; but just what, I asked, is the subject of this book? The people that constitute its subject are a product of their history, of the struggles and conflicts which have taken place in the Southwest. "Man is not himself only," as Mrs. Austin wrote, "not solely a variation of his racial type in the pattern of his immediate experience. He is all that he sees; all that flows to him from a thousand sources, half noted, or noted not at all except by some sense that lies too deep for naming." Hence the Southwest, as a sharply delineated region, is very much a part of the story of Spanish-speaking people in America. And so are the relationships which have emerged out of conflicts between Anglos and Hispanos in the region. But to emphasize these relationships or the region itself in the title would be to shift attention from the people, their origins and ordeals, their struggles and experiences.

And so, in the end, I was driven to the conclusion that the title would have to refer to a process, a movement, a point on the compass. For it is the direction in which the people have moved that has given unity to their lives; it is the point on the compass that has remained fixed and constant. The Spanish-speaking in the United States, whatever their origin, have moved "North from Mexico" and this is still the lodestar in their horizon. Whether born in Spain or Mexico, the ancestors of the present-day Spanish-speaking people of the Southwest came "North from Mexico" along the same trails from similar points of origin to similar destinations. Furthermore the phrase implies the extension of a way of life rather than a crossing or a jumping of barriers which, in this case, are non-existent. It also suggests a oneness of experience if not of blood or language or ancestry; a similar movement within a similar environment.

Invited to visit Santa Fe in 1883, Walt Whitman wrote to "Messrs. Griffin Martínez and Prince and other gentlemen" that he must decline the invitation but would "say a few words off-hand." After first pointing out that the "states" showed too much of the British and German influence, he went on to say: "The seething materialistic and business vortices of the United States, in their present devouring relations, controlling and belittling everything else, are, in my opinion, but a vast and indispensable stage in the new world's development. . . . Character, literature, a society worthy the name, are yet to be establish'd. . . . To that composite American identity of the future," he concluded, "Spanish character will supply some of the most needed parts. No stock shows a grander historic retrospect—grander in religiousness and loyalty, or for patriotism, courage, decorum, gravity and honor." Three of these qualities are ineluctably apposite: "decorum" is one; "gravity" is another; "honor"—broadly construed—is the third. But, like so many of Whitman's catalogues, this one suggests rather than defines and to his roster of qualities one must add a belief in joy and happiness. As Haniel Long has said, "The Spaniard has known as little joy as anybody; but he bravely sees joy as an object of life, and speaks up for it." The charm of the Spanish-speaking people, in the borderlands, in Mexico, and in Spain, is that they have not been molded by modern industrialism; neither the want nor the caste bondage nor the deprivations which they have known has succeeded in destroying their sense of joyous living. They are a people, as Lorca said of the Spanish gypsies, "with their hearts in their heads—*gente con el corazón en la cabeza.*"

While that "composite American identity" is yet to be achieved in the Southwest, it is incontestably true that "Spanish character will supply some of the most needed parts." And it is also true that there is something about the Southwest, as Haniel Long has also said, that "gives to each type of human being more of its rightful chance to survive than is usual." Here identities change slowly; the spacing between peoples gives differences a chance to survive; and what survives has value for it has been severely tested. The naked earth shows through everything that grows in the Southwest and the desert light brings out, with distinctness, the unique character of plants and trees, of rocks and mountain ranges; things are seen sharply, distinctly, for what they are, as they were meant to be. Not only is the environment respectful of differences, but it preserves the unique qualities of the things, the institutions, the people that it permits to survive. The living qualities of "the Spanish character" that one can see in the region today have survived the test of time and can never be obliterated. Indelibly imprinted on the land, they are part of the cultural landscape of the Southwest.

Questions

1. How does the social history of the American Southwest, according to McWilliams, differ from other regions of the country?

2. McWilliams noted that one's ethnic identity in America is relative to other ethnic identities. Explain this in terms of the Southwest.

27-7 Boston's West Enders (1962)

Herbert Gans

Herbert Gans (b. 1927) wrote of the people whose neighborhood was Boston's West End. These "urban villagers" and "true urbanites," as he termed them, were predominantly working-class Italian Americans. Urban renewal razed the tenements of the West End, displacing those who had dwelled in them, in favor of high-rent apartment houses and those who could afford them (see text pp. 850–852).

Source: Excerpted and abridged from *The Urban Villagers*, Revised and Expanded Edition, 20–24. Copyright © 1982 by Herbert J. Gans. Abridged with the permission of The Free Press, a Division of Simon & Schuster Adult Publishing Group.

West Enders did not think of their area as a slum and resented the city's description of the area because it cast aspersions on them as slum dwellers. They were not pleased that the apartment buildings were not well kept up outside, but, as long as the landlord kept the building clean, maintained the mechanical system, and did not bother his tenants, they were not seriously disturbed about it. People kept their apartments up-to-date as they could afford to, and most of the ones I saw differed little from lower-middle-class ones in urban and suburban neighborhoods.

Housing is not the same kind of status symbol for the West Enders that it is for middle-class people. They are as concerned about making a good impression on others as anyone else, but the people to be impressed and the ways of impressing them do differ. The people who are entertained in the apartment are intimates. Moreover, they all live in similar circumstances. As a result they evaluate the host not on the basis of his housing, but on his friendliness, his moral qualities, and his ability as a host. Not only are acquaintances and strangers invited less freely to the home than in the middle class, but they are also less important to the West Enders' way of life, and therefore less significant judges of their status. Thus, West Enders, unlike the middle class, do not have to put on as impressive a front for such people. . . .

Whereas most West Enders have no objection to the older suburban towns that surround the Boston city limits, they have little use for the newer suburbs. They described these as too quiet for their tastes, lonely — that is, without street life — and occupied by people concerned only with trying to appear better than they are. West Enders avoid "the country." . . . They do not like its isolation. . . . I was told by one social worker of an experiment some years back to expose West End children to nature by taking them on a trip to Cape Cod. The experiment failed, for the young West Enders found no pleasure in the loneliness of natural surroundings and wanted to get back to the West End as quickly as possible. They were incredulous that anyone could live without people around them. . . .

Many West Enders impressed me as being true urbanites, with empathy for the pace, crowding, and excitement of city life. . . . They are not [cosmopolitan], however; the parts of the city that they use and enjoy are socially, culturally, and physically far different from those frequented by the upper-middle class.

Questions

1. What did Gans mean by "urban villagers"? Why, to him, were the West Enders "true urbanites"?
2. Why did West Enders feel uncomfortable in suburban and rural surroundings, according to Gans?
3. What institutions were likely to have played important roles in the West End? What might have happened to them following urban renewal?

27-8 What Does Chicago's Renewal Program Mean? (1963)

By the early 1960s, American cities were using urban renewal as a weapon of desperation in an attempt to hold on to their middle-class population (see text pp. 850–852). The city of Chicago printed this pamphlet in the hope that the upbeat tone would allay fears of urban decline.

Source: Pamphlet *What Does Chicago's Renewal Program Mean . . . to You . . . to Your Family . . . Your Neighbors . . . and Your Chicago?* (Chicago: City of Chicago, 1963). Courtesy of the Municipal Reference Collection, Chicago Public Library.

Pamphlet, Chicago's Urban Renewal Program (1963)

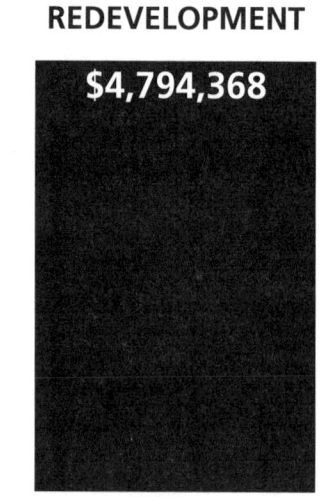

BEFORE REDEVELOPMENT
$2,321,442

AFTER REDEVELOPMENT
$4,794,368

Tax yields in clearance projects before and after redevelopment.

Questions

1. How is *urban renewal* defined here?
2. What did it promise?
3. Which consequences of urban renewal were ignored?

27-9 *The Other America* (1962)

Michael Harrington

Like Walter Rauschenbusch (Document 20-2), Michael Harrington (1928–1989) believed that religious conviction should lead to social action. As a member of the Catholic Worker Movement, he had come to see Christ even in "the pathetic, shambling, shivering creature who would wander in off the streets." Here, he focuses on the "millions who are poor in the United States [and who] tend to become increasingly invisible"—in urban slums, Appalachian backwaters, migrant labor camps, and Native American reservations (see text pp. 849–852).

Source: Excerpt from Michael Harrington, *The Other America: Poverty in the United States*, 158–162. Copyright © 1962, 1969, 1981 by Michael Harrington and renewed 1990 by Stephanie Harrington. Reprinted with the permission of Scribner, an imprint of Simon & Schuster Adult Publishing Group.

The United States in the sixties contains an affluent society within its borders. Millions and tens of millions enjoy the highest standard of life the world has ever known. This blessing is mixed. It is built upon a peculiarly distorted economy, one that often proliferates pseudo-needs rather than satisfying human needs. For some, it has resulted in a sense of spiritual emptiness, of alienation. Yet a man would be a fool to prefer hunger to satiety, and the material gains at least open up the possibility of a rich and full existence.

At the same time, the United States contains an underdeveloped nation, a culture of poverty. Its inhabitants do not suffer the extreme privation of the peasants of Asia or the tribesmen of Africa, yet the mechanism of the misery is similar. They are beyond history, beyond progress, sunk in a paralyzing, maiming routine.

The new nations, however, have one advantage: poverty is so general and so extreme that it is the passion of the entire society to obliterate it. Every resource, every policy, is measured by its effect on the lowest and most impoverished. There is a gigantic mobilization of the spirit of the society: aspiration becomes a national purpose that penetrates to every village and motivates a historical transformation.

But this country seems to be caught in a paradox. Because its poverty is not so deadly, because so many are enjoying a decent standard of life, there are indifference and blindness to the plight of the poor. There are even those who deny that the culture of poverty exists. It is as if Disraeli's famous remark about the two nations of the rich and the poor had come true in a fantastic fashion. At precisely the moment in history where for the first time a people have the material ability to end poverty, they lack the will to do so. They cannot see; they cannot act. The consciences of the well-off are the victims of affluence; the lives of the poor are the victims of a physical and spiritual misery.

The problem, then, is to a great extent one of vision. The nation of the well-off must be able to see through the wall of affluence and recognize the alien citizens on the other side. And there must be vision in the sense of purpose, of aspiration: if the word does not grate upon the ears of a gentile America, there must be a passion to end poverty, for nothing less than that will do.

In this summary chapter, I hope I can supply at least some of the material for such a vision. Let us try to understand the other America as a whole, to see its perspective for the future if it is left alone, to realize the responsibility and the potential for ending this nation in our midst.

But, when all is said and done, the decisive moment occurs after all the sociology and the description is in. There is really no such thing as "the material for a vision." After one reads the facts, either there are anger and shame, or there are not. And, as usual, the fate of the poor hangs upon the decision of the better-off. If this anger and shame are not forthcoming, someone can write a book about the other America a generation from now and it will be the same, or worse.

I

Perhaps the most important analytic point to have emerged in this description of the other America is the fact that poverty in America forms a culture, a way of life and feeling, that it makes a whole. It is crucial to generalize this idea, for it profoundly affects how one moves to destroy poverty.

The most obvious aspect of this interrelatedness is in the way in which the various subcultures of the other America feed into one another. This is clearest with the aged. There the poverty of the declining years is, for some millions of human beings, a function of the poverty of the earlier years. If there were adequate medical care for everyone in the United States, there would be less misery for old people. It is as simple as that. Or there is the relation between the poor farmers and the unskilled workers. When a man is driven off the land because of the impoverishment worked by technological progress, he leaves one part of the culture of poverty and joins another. If something were done about the low-income farmer, that would immediately tell in the statistics of urban unemployment and the economic underworld. The same is true of the Negroes. Any gain for America's minorities will immediately be translated into an advance for all the unskilled workers. One cannot raise the bottom of a society without benefiting everyone above.

Indeed, there is a curious advantage in the wholeness of poverty. Since the other America forms a distinct system within the United States, effective action at any one decisive point will have a "multiplier" effect; it will ramify through the entire culture of misery and ultimately through the entire society.

Then, poverty is a culture in the sense that the mechanism of impoverishment is fundamentally the same in every part of the system. The vicious circle is a basic pattern. It takes different forms for the unskilled workers, for the aged, for the Negroes, for the agricultural workers, but in each case the principle is the same. There are people in the affluent society who are poor because they are poor; and who stay poor because they are poor.

To realize this is to see that there are some tens of millions of Americans who are beyond the welfare state. Some of them are simply not covered by social legislation: they are omitted from Social Security and from minimum wage. Others are covered, but since they are so poor they do not know how to take advantage of the opportunities, or else their coverage is so inadequate as not to make a difference.

The welfare state was designed during that great burst of social creativity that took place in the 1930's. As previously noted its structure corresponds to the needs of those who played the most important role in building it: the middle third, the organized workers, the forces of urban liberalism, and so on. At the worst, there is "socialism for the rich and free enterprise for the poor," as when the huge corporation farms are the main beneficiaries of the farm program while the poor farmers get practically nothing; or when public funds are directed to aid in the construction of luxury housing while the slums are left to themselves (or become more dense as space is created for the well-off).

So there is the fundamental paradox of the welfare state: that it is not built for the desperate, but for those who are already capable of helping themselves. As long as the illusion persists that the poor are merrily freeloading on the public dole, so long will the other America continue unthreatened. The truth, it must be understood, is the exact opposite. The poor get less out of the welfare state than any group in America.

This is, of course, related to the most distinguishing mark of the other America: its common sense of hopelessness. For even when there are programs designed to help the other Americans, the poor are held back by their own pessimism.

On one level this fact has been described in this book as a matter of "aspiration." Like the Asian peasant, the impoverished American tends to see life as a fate, an endless cycle from which there is no deliverance. Lacking hope (and he is realistic to feel this way in many cases), that famous solution to all problems—let us educate the poor—becomes less and less meaningful. A person has to feel that education will do something for him if he is to gain from it. Placing a magnificent school with a fine faculty in the middle of a slum is, I suppose, better than having a run-down building staffed by incompetents. But it will not really make a difference so long as the environment of the tenement, the family, and the street counsels the children to leave as soon as they can and to disregard schooling.

On another level, the emotions of the other America are even more profoundly disturbed. Here it is not lack of aspiration and of hope; it is a matter of personal chaos. The drunkenness, the unstable marriages, the violence of the other America are not simply facts about individuals. They are the description of an entire group in the society who react this way because of the conditions under which they live.

In short, being poor is not one aspect of a person's life in this country; it is his life. Taken as a whole, poverty is a culture. Taken on the family level, it has the same quality. These are people who lack education and skill, who have bad health, poor housing, low levels of aspiration and high levels of mental distress. They are, in the language of sociology, "multiproblem" families. Each disability is the more intense because it exists within a web of disabilities. And if one problem is solved, and the others are left constant, there is little gain.

One might translate these facts into the moralistic language so dear to those who would condemn the poor for their faults. The other Americans are those who live at a level of life beneath moral choice, who are so submerged in their poverty that one cannot begin to talk about free choice. The point is not to make them wards of the state. Rather, society must help them before they can help themselves.

Questions

1. Why was Harrington critical of the welfare state?
2. What did he mean by saying that "poverty is a culture"?
3. What is the difference between helping the poor and making them wards of the state?

Questions for Further Thought

1. To what extent would Michael Harrington's treatment of poverty in his own time (Document 27-9) be relevant to understanding poverty in the 1930s? in the early twenty-first century?
2. According to Harrington's analysis, why might the poor "tend to become increasingly invisible"?
3. Do "the urban villagers" of Boston's West End (Document 27-7) fit Harrington's definition of those in *The Other America*?

CHAPTER TWENTY-EIGHT

The Liberal Consensus: Flaming Out
1960–1968

John F. Kennedy and the Politics of Expectation

The transfer of power from President Eisenhower to President Kennedy struck many Americans as it appeared to strike Kennedy himself in his inaugural address: "The torch has been passed to a new generation of Americans." (Not only was Kennedy twenty-seven years younger than his predecessor; he had been born later than four of the next five presidents to follow him.)

Television, which had grown remarkably in importance during the 1950s, was Kennedy's medium of choice. The first two documents in this chapter deal with important episodes in the public career of John F. Kennedy, both of which reached large television audiences. Senator Kennedy's four debates with Vice President Richard Nixon, his opponent for the presidency in 1960, were, of course, staged for television (Document 28-1). Kennedy's inaugural address the following January (Document 28-2) conveyed his hopes for the nation and his administration.

However, the 1960s would prove that traditional forms of communication still retained all of their power, as is evident in the statement issued by the founders of the Students for a Democratic Society (28–3).

28-1 The Television Debates (1960)

Theodore H. White

Journalist Theodore H. White (1915–1986) believed that "the central fact of politics has always been the quality of leadership under the pressure of great forces." White tested his hypothesis during the presidential campaign of 1960, when the television cameras created their own great pressure during a series of debates between John F. Kennedy and Richard M. Nixon (see text pp. 862–863).

Source: Excerpted from Theodore H. White, *The Making of the President, 1960* (New York: Atheneum, 1961), 279–287. Reprinted with permission of Simon & Schuster Adult Publishing Group. All rights reserved.

At 8:30 P.M., Chicago time, on the evening of September 26th, 1960, the voice and shadow of the previous show faded from the screen; in a few seconds it was followed by another voice and by a visual clip extolling the virtues of Liggett and Myers cigarettes; fifteen seconds were then devoted to Maybelline, the mascara "devoted exclusively to eye beauty, velvety soft and smooth." Then a deep voice regretfully announced that the viewers who turned to this channel would tonight be denied the privilege of viewing the Andy Griffith Show—and the screen dissolved to three men who were about to confirm a revolution in American Presidential politics.

This revolution had been made by no one of the three men on screen—John F. Kennedy, Richard M. Nixon or Howard K. Smith, the moderator. It was a revolution born of the ceaseless American genius in technology; its sole agent and organizer had been the common American television set. Tonight it was to permit the simultaneous gathering of all the tribes of America to ponder their choice between two chieftains in the largest political convocation in the history of man.

Again, it is the census that best describes this revolution. Ten years earlier (in 1950) of America's then 40,000,000 families only 11 percent (or 4,400,000) enjoyed the pleasures of a television set. By 1960 the number of American families had grown to 44,000,000, and of these *no less than 88 percent, or 40,000,000, possessed a television set.* The installation of this equipment had in some years of the previous decade partaken of the quality of stampede—and in the peak stampede years of 1954—1955—1956 no fewer than 10,000 American homes had each been installing a new television set for the first time *every single day of the year.* The change that came about with this stampede is almost immeasurable. By the summer of 1960 the average use of the television set in the American home was four or five hours out of the twenty-four in each day. The best judgment on what television had done to America comes from the research departments of the large television networks. According to them, it is now possible for the first time to answer an inquiring foreign visitor as to what Americans do in the evening. The answer is clear: *they watch television.* Within a single decade the medium has exploded to a dimension in shaping the American mind that rivals that of America's schools and churches. . . .

In 1960 this yearning of the television networks to show their best was particularly acute. For the men who direct television are sensitive to public criticism; they wince and weep in public like adolescents at the slightest touch of hostility in print—and in 1959 they had suffered the worst round of public criticism and contempt since their industry was founded. The shock of the "payola" scandals of 1959; the Congressional hearings on these scandals; the editorial indignation in the "Gutenberg" media not only at these scandals but at the drenching of the air by violence, vulgarity and horse opera—all these had not only given the masters of television an inferiority complex but also frightened them with the prospect that the franchise on the air given to them so freely in return for their legal obligation of "public service" might be withdrawn, curtailed or abolished. It was a time for the "upgrading" of television; and the Presidential campaign of 1960 seemed to offer a fine opportunity for public service—if only Congress would relax those regulations and laws that had manacled and *prevented* television from doing its best. . . .

It is important to understand why the debates of 1960 were to be different from previous political use of the medium.

Television had already demonstrated its primitive power in politics from, at least, the fall of 1952, when, in one broadcast, it had transformed Richard M. Nixon from a negative Vice-Presidential candidate, under attack, into a martyr and an asset to Dwight D. Eisenhower's Presidential campaign. But from 1952 until 1960 television could be used only as an expensive partisan instrument; its time had to be bought and paid for by political parties for their own candidates. The audiences such partisan broadcasts assembled, like the audiences at political rallies, were audiences of the convinced—of convinced Republicans for Republican candidates, of convinced Democrats for Democratic candidates. Generally, the most effective political broadcast could assemble hardly more than half the audience of the commercial show that it replaced. This was why so many candidates and their television advisers sought two-minute or five-minute spots tacked on to the major programs that engaged the nation's fancy; the general audience would not tune out a hostile candidate if he appeared for only two or three minutes, and thus a candidate, using TV "spots" had a much better chance of reaching the members of the opposition party and the "independents," whom he must lure to listen to and then vote for him. The 1960 idea of a "debate," in which both major candidates would appear simultaneously, thus promised to bring both Democrats and Republicans together in the same viewing audience for the first time. Some optimists thought the debates would at least double the exposure of both candidates. How much more they would do than "double" the exposure no one, in the summer of 1960, dreamed.

The future was thus still obscure when the representatives of the two candidates and the spokesmen for the broadcasting networks first met at the Waldorf-Astoria Hotel in New York in September to discuss the conditions and circumstances of the meetings. By this time each of the two major networks had offered eight hours of free time to the campaign, and the third had offered three hours, for a total of nineteen hours of nationwide broadcasting, worth about $2,000,000; they had also made it clear to the candidates that this was not "gift" time but time over which they, the networks, meant to exercise an editorial control to insure maximum viewing interest. Slowly, in discussion, the shape and form of the debates emerged—a controlled panel of four press interlocutors; no notes; dignity to be safeguarded; opening statements of eight minutes by each candidate in the first and last debates; two-and-one-half minute responses to questions. The Nixon negotiators fought to restrict the number of debates—their man, they felt, was the master of the form and one "sudden-death" debate could eliminate Kennedy with a roundhouse swing. They viewed the insistence of the Kennedy negotiators on the maximum possible number of debates as weakness. ("If they weren't scared," said one Nixon staffman, "why shouldn't they be willing to pin everything on one show?") The Kennedy negotiators insisted on at least five debates, then let themselves be whittled to four. ("Every time we get those two fellows on the screen side by side," said J. Leonard Reinsch, Kennedy's TV maestro, "we're going to gain and he's going to lose.")

By mid-September all had been arranged. There would be four debates—on September 26th, October 7th, October 13th and October 21st. The first would be produced by CBS out of Chicago, the second by NBC out of Washington, the third by ABC out of New York and Los Angeles and the fourth, again by ABC, out of New York.

In the event, when all was over, the audience exceeded the wildest fancies and claims of the television networks. Each individual broadcast averaged an audience set at a low of 65,000,000 and a high of 70,000,000. The greatest previous audience in television history had been for the climactic game of the 1959 World Series, when an estimated 90,000,000 Americans had tuned in to watch the White Sox play the Dodgers. When, finally, figures were assembled for all four debates, the total audience for the television debates on the Presidency exceeded even this figure.

All this, of course, was far in the future when, on Sunday, September 25th, 1960, John F. Kennedy arrived in Chicago from Cleveland, Ohio, to stay at the Ambassador East Hotel, and Richard M. Nixon came from Washington, D.C., to stop at the Pick-Congress Hotel, to prepare, each in his own way, for the confrontation.

Kennedy's preparation was marked by his typical attention to organization and his air of casual self-possession; the man behaves, in any crisis, as if it consisted only of a sequence of necessary things to be done that will become complicated if emotions intrude. His personal Brain Trust of three had arrived and assembled at the Knickerbocker Hotel in Chicago on Sunday, the day before. The chief of these three was, of course, Ted Sorensen; with Sorensen was Richard Goodwin, a twenty-eight-year-old lawyer, an elongated elfin man with a capacity for fact and reasoning that had made him Number One man only two years before at the Harvard Law School; and Mike Feldman, a burly and impressive man, a one-time instructor of law at the University of Pennsylvania, later a highly successful businessman, who had abandoned business to follow Kennedy's star as Chief of the Senator's Legislative Research. With them, they had brought the portable Kennedy campaign research library—a Sears Roebuck foot locker of documents—and now, for a twenty-four-hour session at the Knickerbocker Hotel, stretching around the clock, they operated like young men at college cramming for an exam. When they had finished, they had prepared fifteen pages of copy boiling down into twelve or thirteen subject areas the relevant facts and probable questions they thought the correspondents on the panel, or Mr. Nixon, might raise. All three had worked with Kennedy closely for years. They knew that as a member of the House and the Senate Committees on Labor he was fully familiar with all the issues that might arise on domestic policy (the subject of the first debate) and that it was necessary to fix in his mind, not the issues or understanding, but only the latest data.

Early on Monday they met the candidate in his suite for a morning session of questions and answers. The candidate read their suggestions for his opening eight-minute statement, disagreed, tossed their suggestions out, called his secretary, dictated another of his own; and then for four hours Kennedy and the Brain Trust considered together the Nixon position and the Kennedy position, with the accent constantly on fact: What was the latest rate of unemployment? What was steel production rate? What was the Nixon stand on this or that particular? The conversation, according to those present, was not only easy but rather comic and rambling, covering a vast number of issues entirely irrelevant to the debate. Shortly before one o'clock Goodwin and Feldman disappeared to a basement office in the Ambassador East to answer new questions the candidate had raised, and the candidate then had a gay lunch with Ted Sorensen, his brother Robert and public-opinion analyst Louis Harris. The candidate left shortly thereafter for a quick address to the United Brotherhood of Carpenters and Joiners of America (which Nixon had addressed in the morning) and came back to his hotel room for a nap. About five o'clock he rose from his nap, quite refreshed, and assembled brother Robert, Sorensen, Harris, Goodwin and Feldman for another Harvard tutorial skull session.

Several who were present remember the performance as vividly as those who were present at the Hyannisport meeting in October, 1959. The candidate lay on his bed in a white, open-necked T shirt and army suntan pants, and fired questions at his intimates. He held in his hand the fact cards that Goodwin and Feldman had prepared for him during the afternoon, and as he finished each, he sent it spinning off the bed to the floor. Finally, at about 6:30, he rose from his bed and decided to have dinner. He ate what is called "a splendid dinner" all by himself in his room, then emerged in a white shirt and dark-gray suit, called for a stop watch and proceeded to the old converted sports arena that is now CBS Station WBBM at McClurg Court in Chicago, to face his rival for the Presidency of the United States.

Richard M. Nixon had preceded him to the studio. Nixon had spent the day in solitude without companions in the loneliness of his room at the Pick-Congress. The

Vice-President was tired; the drive of campaigning in the previous two weeks had caused him to lose another five pounds since he had left the hospital; his TV advisers had urged that he arrive in Chicago on Saturday and have a full day of rest before he went on the air on Monday, but they had been unable to get through to him, and had not even been able to reach his press secretary, Herbert Klein. Mr. Nixon thus arrived in Chicago late on Sunday evening, unbriefed on the magnitude of the trial he was approaching; on Monday he spoke during the morning to the United Brotherhood of Carpenters and Joiners, an appearance his TV advisers considered a misfortune—the Brotherhood was a hostile union audience, whose negative reaction, they knew, would psychologically disturb their contender.

When Nixon returned to his hotel from the Brotherhood appearance at 12:30, he became incommunicado while his frantic TV technicians tried to reach him or brief him on the setting of the debate, the staging, the problems he might encounter. The Vice-President received one visitor for five minutes that afternoon in his suite, and he received one long telephone call—from Henry Cabot Lodge, who, reportedly, urged him to be careful to erase the "assassin image" when he went on the air. For the rest, the Vice-President was alone, in consultation with no one. Finally, as he emerged from the hotel to drive through Chicago traffic to the studio, one TV adviser was permitted to ride with him and hastily brief him in the ten-minute drive. The adviser urged that the Vice-President come out swinging—that this was a contest, a fight, and that Kennedy must be jolted at the first exchange. The Vice-President was of another mind, however—and wondered whether the suggestion had originated with his adviser or with someone else, like Frank Stanton, President of CBS, who, said the Vice-President, only wanted a good show. Thus they arrived at the studio; as Nixon got out, he struck his knee again—a nasty crack—on the edge of the automobile door, just as he had on his first accident to the knee at Greensboro, North Carolina. An observer reports that his face went all "white and pasty" but that he quickly recovered and entered the studio. . . .

Mr. Nixon's advisers and representatives, understandably nervous since they could not communicate with their principal, had made the best preparation they could. They had earlier requested that both candidates talk from a lectern, standing—and Kennedy had agreed. They had asked several days earlier that the two candidates be seated farther apart from each other than originally planned—and that had been agreed on too. Now, on the day of the debate, they paid meticulous attention to each detail. They were worried about the deep eye shadows in Nixon's face and they requested and adjusted two tiny spotlights ("inkies" in television parlance) to shine directly into his eye wells and illuminate the darkness there; they asked that a table be placed in front of the moderator, and this was agreed to also; they requested that no shots be taken of Nixon's left profile during the debate; and this was also agreed to.

The Kennedy advisers had no requests; they seemed as cocky and confident as their chief.

Nixon entered the studio about an hour before air time and inspected the setting, let himself be televised on an interior camera briefly for the inspection of his advisers, then paced moodily about in the back of the studio. He beckoned the producer to him at one point as he paced and asked as a personal favor that he not be on camera if he happened to be mopping sweat from his face. (That night, contrary to most reports, Nixon was wearing no theatrical make-up. In order to tone down his dark beard stubble on the screen, an adviser had applied only a light coating of "Lazy Shave," a pancake make-up with which a man who has heavy afternoon beard growth may powder his face to conceal the growth.)

Senator Kennedy arrived about fifteen minutes after the Vice-President; he inspected the set; sat for the camera; and his advisers inspected him, then declared they were satisfied. The producer made a remark about the glare of the Senator's white shirt, and Kennedy sent an aide back to his hotel to bring back a blue one, into which he changed just before air time. The men took their seats, the tally lights on the cameras blinked red to show they were live now.

"Good evening," said Howard K. Smith, the gray and handsome moderator. "The television and radio stations of the United States . . . are proud to provide for a discussion of issues in the current political campaign by the two major candidates for the Presidency. The candidates need no introduction. . . ."

And they were on air, before seventy million Americans.

Questions

1. By 1960, how important had television become in national politics?
2. What problems did Nixon experience going into the debate that might have affected viewers' perception of his performance?
3. Are televised debates a fair and accurate measure of a candidate's abilities? Why or why not?

28-2 Inaugural Address (1961)

John F. Kennedy

Standing coatless in the subfreezing cold of Inauguration Day, January 20, 1961, the youthful president delivered an inaugural address that historian Allen J. Matusow terms "the best campaign speech Kennedy ever gave" (see text p. 861). Kennedy subsequently became the first president to have his press conferences televised live.

Source: Excerpt from *Public Papers of the Presidents of the United States: John F. Kennedy, 1961* (Washington, DC: U.S. Government Printing Office, 1962), 1–3.

[W]e observe today not a victory of party but a celebration of freedom—symbolizing an end as well as a beginning—signifying renewal as well as change. For I have sworn before you and Almighty God the same solemn oath our forebears prescribed nearly a century and three quarters ago.

The world is very different now. For man holds in his mortal hands the power to abolish all forms of human poverty and all forms of human life. And yet the same revolutionary beliefs for which our forebears fought are still at issue around the globe—the belief that the rights of man come not from the generosity of the state but from the hand of God.

We dare not forget today that we are the heirs of that first revolution. Let the word go forth from this time and place, to friend and foe alike, that the torch has been passed to a new generation of Americans—born in this century, tempered by war, disciplined by a hard and bitter peace, proud of our ancient heritage—and unwilling to witness or permit the slow undoing of those human rights to which this nation has always been committed, and to which we are committed today at home and around the world.

Let every nation know, whether it wishes us well or ill, that we shall bear any burden, meet any hardship, support any friend, oppose any foe, to assure the survival and the success of liberty.

This we pledge and more.

To those allies whose cultural and spiritual origins we share, we pledge the loyalty of faithful friends. United, there is little we cannot do in a host of cooperative ventures. Divided, there is little we can do—for we do not meet a powerful challenge at odds and split asunder.

To those new states whom we welcome to the ranks of the free, we pledge our word that one form of colonial control shall not have passed away merely to be replaced by a far more iron tyranny. We shall not always expect to find them supporting our view. But we shall always hope to find them strongly supporting their own freedom—and to remember that in the past, those who foolishly sought power by riding the back of the tiger ended up inside.

To those peoples in the huts and villages of half the globe struggling to break the bonds of mass misery, we pledge our best efforts to help them help themselves . . . not because the Communists may be doing it, not because we seek their votes, but because it is right. If a free society cannot help the many who are poor, it cannot save the few who are rich. . . .

Finally, to those nations who would make themselves our adversary, we offer not a pledge but a request: that both sides begin anew the quest for peace, before the dark powers of destruction unleashed by science engulf all humanity in planned or accidental self-destruction.

We dare not tempt them with weakness. For only when our arms are sufficient beyond doubt can we be certain beyond doubt that they will never be employed. . . .

In the long history of the world, only a few generations have been granted the role of defending freedom in its hour of maximum danger. I do not shrink from this responsibility—I welcome it.

Questions

1. Kennedy began his speech with appeals to the "revolutionary beliefs for which our forebears fought." How could those beliefs have been used to fight the Cold War in the developing world?

2. What parts of the address were aimed at the Communist superpowers, and what was Kennedy's posture toward them?

28-3 The Port Huron Statement (1962)

Students for a Democratic Society

Youths figured prominently in liberal and radical movements and organizations during the 1960s, including the Students for a Democratic Society (SDS). The SDS was a "New Left" organization that challenged both liberalism, then dominant, and the "Old Left" of communism and socialism, and sought to reinvigorate American democracy. In 1962, well before the war in Vietnam became a major political issue, two University of Michigan activists, Al Haber and Tom Hayden, organized the founding meeting of SDS, held at a United Auto Workers center in Port Huron, Michigan. The students approved the manifesto excerpted here.

Source: Reprinted by permission of Senator Tom Hayden. A copy of the third printing is available in the Labadie Collection, Hatcher Graduate Library, University of Michigan.

INTRODUCTION: AGENDA FOR A GENERATION

We are people of this generation, bred in at least modest comfort, housed now in universities, looking uncomfortably to the world we inherit.

When we were kids the United States was the wealthiest and strongest country in the world; the only one with the atom bomb, the least scarred by modern war, an initiator of the United Nations that we thought would distribute Western influence throughout the world. Freedom and equality for each individual, government of, by, and for the people—these American values we found good, principles by which we could live as men. Many of us began maturing in complacency.

As we grew, however, our comfort was penetrated by events too troubling to dismiss. First, the permeating and victimizing fact of human degradation, symbolized by the Southern struggle against racial bigotry, compelled most of us from silence to activism. Second, the enclosing fact of the Cold War, symbolized by the presence of the Bomb, brought awareness that we ourselves, and our friends, and millions of abstract "others" we knew more directly because of our common peril, might die at any time. We might deliberately ignore, or avoid, or fail to feel all other human problems, but not these two, for these were too immediate and crushing in their impact, too challenging in the demand that we as individuals take the responsibility for encounter and resolution.

While these and other problems either directly oppressed us or rankled our consciences and became our own subjective concerns, we began to see complicated and disturbing paradoxes in our surrounding America. The declaration "all men are created equal . . ." rang hollow before the facts of Negro life in the South and the big cities of the North. The proclaimed peaceful intentions of the United States contradicted its economic and military investments in the Cold War status quo. . . .

Not only did tarnish appear on our image of American virtue, not only did disillusion occur when the hypocrisy of American ideals was discovered, but we began to sense that what we had originally seen as the American Golden Age was actually the decline of an era. The worldwide outbreak of revolution against colonialism and imperialism, the entrenchment of totalitarian states, the menace of war, overpopulation, international disorder, supertechnology—these trends were testing the tenacity of our own commitment to democracy and freedom and our abilities to visualize their application to a world in upheaval.

Our work is guided by the sense that we may be the last generation in the experiment with living. But we are a minority—the vast majority of our people regard the temporary equilibriums of our society and world as eternally-functional parts. In this is perhaps the outstanding paradox: we ourselves are imbued with urgency, yet the message of our society is that there is no viable alternative to the present. Beneath the reassuring tones of the politicians, beneath the common opinion that America will "muddle through," beneath the stagnation of those who have closed their minds to the future, is the pervading feeling that there simply are no alternatives, that our times have witnessed the exhaustion not only of Utopias, but of any new departures as well. Feeling the press of complexity upon the emptiness of life, people are fearful of the thought that at any moment things might be thrust out of control. They fear change itself, since change might smash whatever invisible framework seems to hold back chaos for them now. For most Americans, all crusades are suspect, threatening. The fact that each individual sees apathy in his fellows perpetuates the common reluctance to organize for change. The dominant institutions are complex enough to blunt the minds of their potential critics, and entrenched enough to swiftly dissipate or entirely repel the energies of protest and reform, thus limiting human expectancies. Then, too, we are a materially improved society, and by our own improvements we seem to have weakened the case for further change. . . .

The search for truly democratic alternatives to the present, and a commitment to social experimentation with them, is a worthy and fulfilling human enterprise, one which moves us and, we hope, others today. On such a basis do we offer this document of our convictions and analysis: as an effort in understanding and changing the conditions of humanity in the late twentieth century, an effort rooted in the ancient, still unfulfilled conception of man attaining determining influence over his circumstances of life.

VALUES

Making values explicit—an initial task in establishing alternatives—is an activity that has been devalued and corrupted. The conventional moral terms of the age, the politician moralities—"free world," "people's democracies"—reflect realities poorly, if at all, and seem to function more as ruling myths than as descriptive principles. But neither has our experience in the universities brought us moral enlightenment. Our professors and administrators sacrifice controversy to public relations; their curriculums change more slowly than the living events of the world; their skills and silence are purchased by investors in the arms race; passion is called unscholastic. The questions we might want raised—what is really important? can we live in a different and better way? if we wanted to change society, how would we do it?—are not thought to be questions of a "fruitful, empirical nature," and thus are brushed aside....

Men have unrealized potential for self-cultivation, self-direction, self-understanding, and creativity. It is this potential that we regard as crucial and to which we appeal, not to the human potentiality for violence, unreason, and submission to authority. The goal of man and society should be human independence: a concern not with image of popularity but with finding a meaning in life that is personally authentic; a quality of mind not compulsively driven by a sense of powerlessness, nor one which unthinkingly adopts status values, nor one which represses all threats to its habits, but one which has full, spontaneous access to present and past experiences, one which easily unites the fragmented parts of personal history, one which openly faces problems which are troubling and unresolved; one with an intuitive awareness of possibilities, an active sense of curiosity, an ability and willingness to learn.

This kind of independence does not mean egotistic individualism—the object is not to have one's way so much as it is to have a way that is one's own. Nor do we deify man—we merely have faith in his potential.

Human relationships should involve fraternity and honesty. Human interdependence is contemporary fact; human brotherhood must be willed, however, as a condition of future survival and as the most appropriate form of social relations. Personal links between man and man are needed, especially to go beyond the partial and fragmentary bonds of function that bind men only as worker to worker, employer to employee, teacher to student, American to Russian....

We would replace power rooted in possession, privilege, or circumstance by power and uniqueness rooted in love, reflectiveness, reason, and creativity. As a *social system* we seek the establishment of a democracy of individual participation, governed by two central aims: that the individual share in those social decisions determining the quality and direction of his life; that society be organized to encourage independence in men and provide the media for their common participation.

Questions

1. What indictments did the Port Huron Statement bring against mainstream American society?
2. How did the statement address generational differences?
3. What did the statement say about civil rights? What did it say about academia?

Questions for Further Thought

1. Compare and contrast President Dwight D. Eisenhower's farewell address (Document 26-13) and President John F. Kennedy's inaugural address (Document 28-2)—speeches delivered only days apart.
2. Contrast the sentiments expressed in Kennedy's inaugural address (Document 28-2), with the critique and vision contained in the Port Huron Statement (Document 28-3).

Lyndon B. Johnson and the Great Society

Before being elected vice president, Lyndon B. Johnson was a seasoned politician who had served nearly a quarter of a century in the U.S. House of Representatives and the U.S. Senate. With the assassination of John Kennedy in November 1963, Johnson was thrust into the presidency. By the time he won a landslide victory in the presidential election of 1964, Johnson had already begun to enact an ambitious liberal agenda, pushing through civil rights, social welfare, and environmental legislation (see text p. 874, Table 28.1). With Democratic congressional majorities, Johnson fostered an unprecedented liberal consensus to achieve his vision of the "Great Society" (see text pp. 872–877).

Of course, not everyone shared Johnson's vision. Document 28-4 is the nomination acceptance speech of Barry Goldwater, Johnson's presidential opponent, at the Republican National Convention in 1964. In Document 28-5, Johnson lays out his vision of a Great Society. Document 28-6 is an excerpt from the Wilderness Act of 1964, one part of Johnson's program to protect the natural environment.

28-4 Acceptance Speech at the Republican National Convention (1964)

Barry Goldwater

A variety of circumstances contributed to the easy victory of Senator Barry Goldwater (1909–1998) of Arizona at the divisive Republican National Convention of 1964. The party's platform promised "full implementation and faithful execution" of the 1964 civil rights law. In an effort to further strengthen the civil rights plank, northeastern convention delegates proposed the inclusion of an expression of pride in Republican support for the recent enactment of the law. The delegates failed, 409–897. Goldwater had been among only five (of thirty-three) Republican senators to oppose the original 1964 civil rights law. He delivered his acceptance speech as the Republican nominee on July 16.

Source: Excerpted with the express permission of the Republican National Committee from "Acceptance Speech by Senator Barry Goldwater, Republican National Convention, San Francisco, California," in Barry Goldwater, *Where I Stand* (New York: McGraw-Hill, 1964), 9–16.

From this moment, united and determined, we will go forward together—dedicated to the ultimate and undeniable greatness of the whole man.

I accept your nomination with a deep sense of humility. I accept the responsibility that goes with it. I seek your continued help and guidance.

Our cause is too great for any man to feel worthy of it.

Our task would be too great for any man, did he not have with him the hearts and hands of this great Republican Party.

I promise you that every fibre of my being is consecrated to our cause, that nothing shall be lacking from the struggle that can be brought to it by enthusiasm and devotion—and hard work!

In this world, no person—no party—can guarantee anything. What we *can* do, and what we *shall* do, is to *deserve* victory.

The good Lord raised up this mighty Republic to be a home for the brave and to flourish as the land of the free—*not* to stagnate in the swampland of collectivism—*not* to cringe before the bullying of Communism.

The tide has been running against freedom. Our people have followed false prophets. We must and we *shall* return to proven ways—*not* because they are old, but because they are *true*. We must and we shall set the tides running again in the cause of freedom.

This Party, with its every action, every word, every breath, and every heartbeat, has but a single resolve:

Freedom!

Freedom—made orderly for this nation by our Constitutional government.

Freedom—under a government limited by the laws of nature and of nature's God.

Freedom—balanced so that order, lacking liberty, will not become the slavery of the prison cell; balanced so that liberty, lacking order, will not become the license of the mob and the jungle.

We Americans understand freedom. We have earned it, lived for it, and died for it.

This nation and its people *are* freedom's model in a searching world. We *can be* freedom's missionaries in a doubting world. But first we *must renew* freedom's vision in our own hearts and in our own homes.

During four futile years, the Administration which we shall replace has distorted and lost that vision.

It has talked and talked and talked the *words* of freedom. But it has failed and failed and failed in the *works* of freedom.

Failures cement the wall of shame in Berlin. Failures blot the sands of shame at the Bay of Pigs. Failures mark the slow death of freedom in Laos. Failures infest the jungles of Vietnam. Failures haunt the houses of our once great alliances, and undermine the greatest bulwark ever erected by free nations—the NATO community.

Failures proclaim lost leadership, obscure purpose, weakening will, and the risk of inciting our sworn enemies to new aggressions and new excesses.

Because of this Administration, we are a world divided—we are a nation becalmed.

We have lost the brisk pace of diversity and the genius of individual creativity. We are plodding at a pace set by centralized planning, red tape, rules without responsibility, and regimentation without recourse.

Rather than useful jobs, our people have been offered bureaucratic make-work. Rather than moral leadership, they have been given bread and circuses, spectacle and even scandal.

There is violence in our streets, corruption in our highest offices, aimlessness among our youth, anxiety among our elders. There is virtual despair among the many who look beyond material success for the inner meaning of their lives.

Where examples of morality should be set, the opposite is seen. Small men, seeking great wealth or power, have too often and too long turned even the highest levels of public service into mere personal opportunity.

Certainly, simple honesty is not too much to demand of men in government. We find it in most. Republicans demand it from everyone—no matter how exalted or protected his position.

The growing menace to personal safety, to life, limb, and property, in homes, churches, playgrounds, and places of business, particularly in our great cities, is the mounting concern of every thoughtful citizen. Security from domestic violence, no less than from foreign aggression, is the most elementary and fundamental purpose of any government. A government that cannot fulfill this purpose is one that cannot long command the loyalty of its citizens. History demonstrates that nothing prepares the way for tyranny more than the failure of public officials to keep the streets safe from bullies and marauders.

We Republicans see all this as more, *much* more than the result of mere political differences, or mere political mistakes. We see this as the result of a fundamentally and absolutely wrong view of man, his nature, and his destiny.

Those who seek to live your lives for you, to take your liberties in return for relieving you of your responsibilities—those who elevate the state and downgrade the citizen—must see ultimately a world in which earthly power can be substituted for divine will. This nation was founded upon the rejection of that notion and upon the acceptance of God as the author of freedom.

Those who seek absolute power, even though they seek it to do what they regard as good, are simply demanding the right to enforce *their* version of heaven on earth. They are the very ones who always create the most hellish tyrannies.

Absolute power *does* corrupt. And those who seek it must be suspect and must be opposed.

Their mistaken course stems from false notions of equality.

Equality, rightly understood, as our Founding Fathers understood it, leads to liberty and to the emancipation of creative differences.

Wrongly understood, as it has been so tragically in our time, it leads first to conformity and then to despotism.

It is the cause of Republicanism to resist concentrations of power, *private* or *public*, which enforce such conformity and inflict such despotism.

It is the cause of Republicanism to ensure that power remains in the hands of the people. And, so help us God, that is exactly what a Republican President will do—with the help of a Republican Congress.

It is the cause of Republicanism to restore a clear understanding of the tyranny of man over man in the world at large. It is our cause to dispel the foggy thinking which avoids hard decisions in the delusion that a world of conflict will mysteriously resolve itself into a world of harmony—if we just don't rock the boat or irritate the forces of aggression.

It is the cause of Republicanism to remind ourselves and the world that only the strong *can* remain free—that only the strong *can* keep the peace!

Republicans have shouldered this hard responsibility and marched in this cause before. It was Republican leadership under Dwight David Eisenhower that kept the peace and passed along to this Administration the mightiest arsenal for defense the world has ever known.

It was the strength and believable will of the Eisenhower years that kept the peace by using our strength—by using it in the Formosa Straits and in Lebanon, and by showing it *courageously* at all times.

It was during those Republican years that the thrust of Communist imperialism was blunted. It was during those years of Republican leadership that this world moved closer to *peace* than at any other time in the last three decades.

It has been during *Democratic* years that our strength to deter war has stood still and even gone into a planned decline.

It has been during *Democratic* years that we have weakly stumbled into conflict—*timidly* refusing to draw our own lines against aggression—*deceitfully* refusing to tell even our own people of our full participation—and *tragically* letting our finest men die on battlefields unmarked by purpose, pride, or the prospect of victory.

Yesterday it was Korea. Today it is Vietnam.

We are at war in Vietnam—yet the President who is the Commander in Chief of our forces refuses to say whether or not the objective is victory. His Secretary of Defense continues to mislead and misinform the American people.

It has been during *Democratic* years that a billion persons were cast into Communist captivity and their fate cynically sealed. Today, we have an Administration which seems eager to deal with Communism in every coin known—from gold to wheat, from consulates to confidences, and even human freedom itself.

The Republican cause demands that we brand Communism as the principal disturber of peace in the world today—indeed, the only significant disturber of the peace. We must make clear that until its goals of conquest are absolutely renounced, and its relations with all nations tempered, Communism and the governments it now controls are enemies of every man on earth who is or wants to be free....

I can see, and I suggest that all thoughtful men must contemplate, the flowering of an Atlantic civilization: the *whole* of Europe reunified and freed, trading openly across its borders, communicating openly across the world.

This is a goal more meaningful than a moon shot—a truly inspiring goal for all free men to set for themselves during the latter half of the twentieth century.

I can see, and all free men must thrill to, the advance of this Atlantic civilization joined by its great ocean highway to the United States. What a destiny can be ours—to stand as a great central pillar linking Europe, the Americas, and the venerable and vital peoples and cultures of the Pacific.

I can see a day when all the Americas, North and South, will be linked in a mighty system, a system in which the errors and misunderstandings of the past will be submerged, one by one, in a rising tide of prosperity and interdependence. We know that the misunderstandings of centuries are not to be wiped away in a day or an hour. But we pledge that human sympathy—what our neighbors to the South call an attitude that is *simpatico*—no less than enlightened self-interest, will be our guide.

I can see this Atlantic civilization galvanizing and *guiding* emergent nations everywhere....

During Republican years this again will be a nation of men and women, of families proud of their roles, jealous of their responsibilities, unlimited in their aspirations—a nation where all who *can, will* be self-reliant....

We see, in private property and an economy based upon and fostering private property, the one way to make government a durable ally of the whole man, rather than his determined enemy. We see, in the sanctity of private property, the only durable foundation for Constitutional government in a free society.

And beyond that, we see and cherish diversity of ways, diversity of thoughts, of motives and accomplishments. We do not seek to live anyone's life for him—we seek only to secure his rights, guarantee him opportunity to strive, with government performing only those needed and Constitutionally-sanctioned tasks which cannot otherwise be performed.

We seek a government that attends to its inherent responsibilities of maintaining a stable monetary and fiscal climate—encouraging a free and competitive economy, and enforcing law and order.

Thus do we seek inventiveness, diversity, and creative difference within a stable order. For we Republicans define government's role, where needed, at *many* levels, preferably the one *closest* to the people involved.

Our towns and our cities, then our counties and states, then our regional compacts—and *only then* the national government! *That* is the ladder of liberty built by decentralized power. On it, also, we must have balance *between* branches of government at *every* level.

Balance, diversity, creative difference—*these* are the elements of the Republican equation. Republicans agree on these elements and they heartily agree to disagree on many, many of their applications.

This is a party for free men—*not* for blind followers and *not* for conformists....

Any who join us in all sincerity, we welcome. Those who do not care for our cause we do not expect to enter our ranks in any case.

And let our Republicanism, so focused and so dedicated, not be made fuzzy and futile by unthinking labels.

Extremism in the defense of liberty is no vice. Moderation in the pursuit of justice is no virtue.

Questions

1. What was Goldwater's definition of *freedom*?
2. Was his speech partisan or accurate in its treatment of the Democrats? Explain.
3. What were the enemies of freedom at home and abroad, according to Goldwater? Could they be fought with the same weapons?

28-5 Address at the University of Michigan (1964)

Lyndon B. Johnson

Very much a product of the New Deal and the liberal tradition, Lyndon B. Johnson had his own vision for bold reform—the Great Society. Unlike Franklin D. Roosevelt's New Deal, which was formulated in response to economic depression, Johnson's program aimed to harness the nation's unprecedented prosperity and extend its benefits to a larger number of Americans. He laid out his vision for the Great Society in a commencement address delivered to the University of Michigan on May 22, 1964.

Source: Lyndon B. Johnson, Remarks of the President at the University of Michigan, Ann Arbor, Michigan, May 22, 1964, in *Statements of LBJ*, Lyndon B. Johnson Library and Museum.

I have come today from the turmoil of your Capitol to the tranquility of your campus to speak about the future of our country. The purpose of protecting the life of our Nation and preserving the liberty of our citizens is to pursue the happiness of our people. Our success in that pursuit is the test of our success as a nation. For a century we labored to settle and to subdue a continent. For half a century, we called upon unbounded invention and untiring industry to create an order of plenty for all of our people. The challenge of the next half century is whether we have the wisdom to use that wealth to enrich and elevate our national life, and to advance the quality of our American civilization.

Your imagination, your initiative and your indignation will determine whether we build a society where progress is the servant of our needs, or a society where old values and new visions are buried under unbridled growth. For in your time we have the opportunity to move not only toward the rich society and the powerful society, but upward to the Great Society. The Great Society rests on abundance and liberty for all. It demands an end to poverty and racial injustice, to which we are totally committed in our time. But that is just the beginning. The Great Society is a place where every child can find knowledge to enrich his mind and to enlarge his talents. It is a place where leizure is a welcome chance to build and reflect, not a feared cause of boredom and restlessness. It is a place where the city of man serves not only the needs of the body and the demands of commerce, but the desire for beauty and the hunger for community.

It is a place where man can renew contact with nature. It is a place which honors creation for its own sake and for what it adds to the understanding of the race. It is a place where men are more concerned with the quality of their goals than the quantity of their goods. But most of all, the great society is not a safe harbor, a resting place, a final objective, a finished work. It is a challenge constantly renewed, beckoning us toward a destiny where the meaning of our lives matches the marvelous products of our labor.

So I want to talk to you today about three places where we begin to build the Great Society—in our cities, in our countryside, and in our classrooms. Many of you will live to see the day, perhaps 50 years from now, when there will be 400 million Americans; four-fifths of them in urban areas. In the remainder of this century urban population will double, city land will double, and we will have to build homes, highways and facilities equal to all those built since this country was first settled. So in the next 40 years we must rebuild the entire urban United States.

Aristotle said, "Men come together in cities in order to live, but they remain together in order to live the good life."

It is harder and harder to live the good life in American cities today. The catalogue of ills is long: There is the decay of the centers and the despoiling of the suburbs. There is not enough housing for our people or transportation for our traffic. Open land is vanishing and old landmarks are violated. Worst of all, expansion is eroding the precious and time honored values of community with neighbors and communion with nature. The loss of these values breeds loneliness and boredom and indifference. Our society will never be great until our cities are great. Today the frontier of imagination and innovation is inside those cities, and not beyond their borders. New experiments are already going on. It will be the task of your generation to make the American city a place where future generations will come, not only to live but to live the good life.

I understand that if I stay here tonight I would see that Michigan students are really doing their best to live the good life.

This is the place where the Peace Corps was started. It is inspiring to see how all of you, while you are in this country, are trying so hard to live at the level of the people.

A second place where we begin to build the Great Society is in our countryside. We have always prided ourselves on being not only America the strong and America the free, but America the beautiful. Today that beauty is in danger. The water we drink, the food we eat, the very air that we breathe, are threatened with pollution. Our parks are overcrowded. Our seashores overburdened. Green fields and dense forests are disappearing.

A few years ago we were greatly concerned about the Ugly American. Today we must act to prevent an Ugly America.

For once the battle is lost, once our natural splendor is destroyed, it can never be recaptured. And once man can no longer walk with beauty or wonder at nature, his spirit will wither and his sustenance be wasted.

A third place to build the Great Society is in the classrooms of America. There your childrens' lives will be shaped. Our society will not be great until every young mind is set free to scan the farthest reaches of thought and imagination. We are still far from that goal. Today, eight million adult Americans, more than the entire population of Michigan, have not finished five years of school. Nearly 20 million have not finished eight years of school. Nearly 54 million, more than one-quarter of all America, have not even finished high school.

Each year more than 100,000 high school graduates, with proved ability, do not enter college because they cannot afford it. And if we cannot educate today's youth, what will we do in 1970 when elementary school enrollment will be 5 million greater than 1960? And high school enrollment will rise by five million. College enrollment will increase by more than three million. In many places, classrooms are overcrowded and curricula are outdated. Most of our qualified teachers are underpaid, and many of our paid teachers are unqualified. So we must give every child a place to sit and a teacher to learn from. Poverty must not be a bar to learning, and learning must offer an escape from poverty.

But more classrooms and more teachers are not enough. We must seek an educational system which grows in excellence as it grows in size. This means better training for our teachers. It means preparing youth to enjoy their hours of leizure as well as their hours of labor. It means exploring new techniques of teaching, to find new ways to stimulate the love of learning and the capacity for creation.

These are three of the central issues of the Great Society. While our government has many programs directed at those issues, I do not pretend that we have the full answer to those problems. But I do promise this: We are going to assemble the best thought and the broadest knowledge from all over the world to find those answers for America. I intend to establish working groups to prepare a series of White House conferences and meetings on the cities, on natural beauty, on the quality of education, and on other emerging challenges.

And from these meetings and from this inspiration and from these studies we will begin to set our course toward the Great Society.

The solution to these problems does not rest on a massive program in Washington, nor can it rely solely on the strained resources of local authority. They require us to create new concepts of cooperation, a creative federalism, between the national capitol and the leaders of local communities.

Woodrow Wilson once wrote: "Every man sent out from his university should be a man of his Nation as well as a man of his time."

Within your lifetime powerful forces, already loosed, will take us toward a way of life beyond the realm of our experience, almost beyond the bounds of our imagination. For better or for worse, your generation has been appointed by history to deal with those problems and to lead America toward a new age. You have the chance never before afforded to any people in any age. You can help build a society where the demands of morality, and the needs of the spirit, can be realized in the life of the Nation. So will you join in the battle to give every citizen the full equality which God enjoins and the law requires, whatever his belief, or race, or the color of his skin? Will you join in the battle to give every citizen an escape from the crushing weight of poverty? Will you join in the battle to make it possible for all nations to live in enduring peace as neighbors and not as mortal enemies? Will you join in the battle to build the Great Society, to prove that our material progress is only the foundation on which we will build a richer life of mind and spirit?

There are those timid souls who say this battle cannot be won, that we are condemned to a soulless wealth. I do not agree. We have the power to shape the civilization that we want. But we need your will, your labor, your hearts, if we are to build that kind of society.

Those who came to this land sought to build more than just a new country. They sought a free world.

So I have come here today to your campus to say that you can make their vision our reality. Let us from this moment begin our work so that in the future men will look back and say: It was then, after a long and weary way, that man turned the exploits of his genius to the full enrichment of his life.

Questions

1. What three central issues did Johnson outline in his speech? What problems were posed by each of these?
2. In what ways was Johnson's vision liberal?
2. Johnson framed his vision of the Great Society as satisfying not just material needs but "the needs of the spirit." What was the significance of this approach?

28-6 The Wilderness Act (1964)

In President Lyndon B. Johnson's University of Michigan speech (Document 28-5), he named the natural environment as one of the three most important frontiers in building his Great Society. After signing the Wilderness Act, which created a national wilderness protection system, President Johnson declared, "If future generations are to remember us with gratitude rather than contempt, we must leave them more than the miracles of technology. We must leave them a glimpse of the world as it was in the beginning, not just after we got through with it."

Source: An Act to Establish a National Wilderness Preservation System for the Permanent Good of the Whole People, and for Other Purposes, 1964 (78 Stat. 890).

AN ACT TO ESTABLISH A NATIONAL WILDERNESS PRESERVATION SYSTEM FOR THE PERMANENT GOOD OF THE WHOLE PEOPLE, AND FOR OTHER PURPOSES,

1964 (78 Stat. 890)

SHORT TITLE

Section 1. This Act may be cited as the "Wilderness Act."

WILDERNESS SYSTEM ESTABLISHED: STATEMENT OF POLICY

Sec. 2. (a) In order to assure that an increasing population, accompanied by expanding settlement and growing mechanization, does not occupy and modify all areas within the United States and its possessions, leaving no lands designated for preservation and protection in their natural condition, it is hereby declared to be the policy of the Congress to secure for the American people of present and future generations the benefit of an enduring resource of wilderness. For this purpose there is hereby established a National Wilderness Preservation System to be composed of federally owned areas designated by Congress as "wilderness areas," and these shall be administered for the use and enjoyment of the American people in such manner as will leave them unimpaired for future use and enjoyment as wilderness, and so as to provide for the protection of these areas, the preservation of their wilderness character, and for the gathering and dissemination of information regarding their use and enjoyment as wilderness; and no Federal lands shall be designated as "wilderness areas" except as provided for in this Act or by a subsequent Act....

(c) A wilderness, in contrast with those areas where man and his own works dominate the landscape, is hereby recognized as an area where the earth and its community of life are untrammeled by man, where man himself is a visitor who does not remain. An area of wilderness is further defined to mean in this Act an area of undeveloped Federal land retaining its primeval character and influence, without permanent improvements or human habitation, which is protected and managed so as to preserve its natural conditions and which (1) generally appears to have been affected primarily by the forces of nature, with the imprint of man's work substantially unnoticeable; (2) has outstanding opportunities for solitude or a primitive and unconfined type of recreation; (3) has at least five thousand acres of land or is of sufficient size as to make practicable its preservation and use in an unimpaired condition; and (4) may also contain ecological, geological, or other features of scientific, educational, scenic, or historical value.

Questions

1. What was the rationale for establishing a national wilderness preservation system?
2. How did the Wilderness Act fit into President Lyndon B. Johnson's Great Society (see Document 28-5)?

Questions for Further Thought

1. Using Documents 28-4 and 28-5, describe the different political philosophies of Barry Goldwater and Lyndon B. Johnson.
2. In what ways did Johnson's "Great Society" perpetuate the optimism and energy of the Kennedy administration (Document 28-2)?

Into the Quagmire, 1960–1968

The Vietnam War was one of the most divisive and protracted conflicts in American history. U.S. involvement in the region began during the Truman administration, when the United States began funding France's efforts to fight Vietnam's Communist-led nationalist movement and to reclaim the French prewar empire in Indochina. Following the humiliating defeat of French forces in 1954, Vietnam was divided into a Communist North and a non-Communist South. The United States propped up the pro-American government of Ngo Dinh Diem in South Vietnam, which suppressed free elections that would have surely been swept by the Communists.

The situation was difficult but stable until 1959, when the North renewed its push for national reunification by supporting armed resistance to Diem's incompetent regime. Unsuccessful in fighting off the National Liberation Front (NLF, or Vietcong) and its North Vietnamese backers, Diem was deposed and murdered by the South Vietnamese army in a coup backed by the United States, just weeks before the assassination of President Kennedy. The change in leadership in Saigon, however, did little to change the military situation on the ground, and Vietnam's violent reunification under Communist rule looked increasingly likely as Lyndon B. Johnson took office.

Faced with the stark choice of presiding over the loss of South Vietnam to Communism or deepening military involvement in the region, President Johnson chose the latter. Document 28-7 excerpts the Gulf of Tonkin Resolution, which gave Johnson congressional authorization for future military action. Document 28-8 provides President Johnson's public justification of his escalation of the war. Document 28-9 is a selection from *A Rumor of War* (1977) by Philip Caputo, an infantry officer who was part of the first U.S. combat unit sent to Vietnam.

28-7 The Gulf of Tonkin Resolution (1964)

After two ambiguous naval skirmishes in the Gulf of Tonkin, President Johnson ordered retaliatory air strikes and sought congressional support for future actions if necessary. In doing so, Johnson sent a warning to North Vietnam and a message to Americans on the eve of the 1964 presidential campaign. On August 7, overwhelming bipartisan congressional majorities granted the president extraordinary authority in the Gulf of Tonkin Resolution (see text pp. 877–878).

Source: Department of State Bulletin (August 29, 1964), 268.

Whereas naval units of the Communist regime in Vietnam, in violation of the principles of the Charter of the United Nations and of international law, have deliberately and repeatedly attacked the United States naval vessels present in international waters, and have thereby created a serious threat to international peace;

Whereas these attacks are part of a deliberate and systematic campaign of aggression that the Communist regime in North Vietnam has been waging against its neighbors and the nations joined with them in the collective defense of their freedom;

Whereas the United States is assisting the peoples *of southeast Asia to protect their political freedom and has not territorial, military or political ambitions in that area, but desires only that these peoples should be left in peace to work out their own destinies in their own way: Now, therefore, be it*

Resolved by the Senate and House of Representatives of the United States of America in Congress assembled, That the Congress approves and supports the determination of the President, as Commander in Chief, to take all necessary measures to repel any armed attack against the forces of the United States and to prevent further aggression.

SEC. 2. The United States regards as vital to its national interests and to world peace the maintenance of international peace and security in southeast Asia.... The United States is, therefore, prepared, as the President determines, to take all necessary steps, including the use of armed force, to assist any member or protocol state of the Southeast Asia Collective Defense Treaty requesting assistance in defense of its freedom.

SEC. 3. This resolution shall expire when the President shall determine that the peace and security of the area is reasonably assured....

Questions

1. What were the North Vietnamese accused of in this resolution?
2. What were the American interests in the region, according to the resolution?
3. In what ways did the resolution grant a free hand to the president?

28-8 Peace Without Conquest (1965)

Lyndon B. Johnson

President Lyndon B. Johnson (1908–1973) spoke at Johns Hopkins University on April 7, 1965, shortly after American air and ground forces escalated the military effort in Vietnam. Support for administration policies was still widespread; the antiwar movement had not yet hit its stride (see text pp. 877–879).

Source: Public Papers of the Presidents of the United States: Lyndon Johnson, 1965 (Washington, DC: U.S. Government Printing Office, 1966), 394–397.

... Tonight Americans and Asians are dying for a world where each people may choose its own path to change.

This is the principle for which our ancestors fought in the valleys of Pennsylvania. It is the principle for which our sons fight tonight in the jungles of Viet-Nam.

Viet-Nam is far away from this quiet campus. We have no territory there, nor do we seek any. The war is dirty and brutal and difficult. And some 400 young men, born into an America that is bursting with opportunity and promise, have ended their lives on Viet-Nam's steaming soil.

Why must we take this painful road? ...

The first reality is that North Viet-Nam has attacked the independent nation of South Viet-Nam. Its object is total conquest.

Of course, some of the people of South Viet-Nam are participating in attack on their own government. But trained men and supplies, orders and arms, flow in a constant stream from north to south.

This support is the heartbeat of the war....

Over this war—and all Asia—is another reality: the deepening shadow of Communist China. The rulers in Hanoi are urged on by Peking. This is a regime which has destroyed freedom in Tibet, which has attacked India, and has been condemned by the United Nations for aggression in Korea. It is a nation which is helping the forces of violence in almost every continent. The contest in Viet-Nam is part of a wider pattern of aggressive purposes....

Why are these realities our concern? Why are we in South Viet-Nam?

We are there because we have a promise to keep. Since 1954 every American President has offered support to the people of South Viet-Nam. We have helped to build, and we have helped to defend. Thus, over many years, we have made a national pledge to help South Viet-Nam defend its independence.

And I intend to keep that promise.

To dishonor that pledge, to abandon this small and brave nation to its enemies, and to the terror that must follow, would be an unforgivable wrong.

We are also there to strengthen world order. Around the globe, from Berlin to Thailand, are people whose well-being rests, in part, on the belief that they can count on us if they are attacked. To leave Viet-Nam to its fate would shake the confidence of all these people in the value of an American commitment and in the value of America's word. The result would be increased unrest and instability, and even wider war.

We are also there because there are great stakes in the balance. Let no one think for a moment that retreat from Viet-Nam would bring an end to conflict. The battle would be renewed in one country and then another. The central lesson of our time is that the appetite of aggression is never satisfied. To withdraw from one battlefield means only to prepare for the next. We must say in southeast Asia—as we did in

Europe—in the words of the Bible: "Hitherto shalt thou come, but no further." . . .

Our objective is the independence of South Viet-Nam, and its freedom from attack. We want nothing for ourselves—only that the people of South Viet-Nam be allowed to guide their own country in their own way.

We will do everything necessary to reach that objective. And we will do only what is absolutely necessary.

In recent months attacks on South Viet-Nam were stepped up. Thus, it became necessary for us to increase our response and to make attacks by air. This is not a change of purpose. It is a change in what we believe that purpose requires.

We do this in order to slow down aggression.

We do this to increase the confidence of the brave people of South Viet-Nam who have bravely borne this brutal battle for so many years with so many casualties.

And we do this to convince the leaders of North Viet-Nam—and all who seek to share their conquest—of a very simple fact:

We will not be defeated.

We will not grow tired.

We will not withdraw, either openly or under the cloak of a meaningless agreement. . . .

Once this is clear, then it should also be clear that the only path for reasonable men is the path of peaceful settlement.

Such peace demands an independent South Viet-Nam—securely guaranteed and able to shape its own relationships to all others—free from outside interference—tied to no alliance—a military base for no other country.

These are the essentials of any final settlement.

We will never be second in the search for such a peaceful settlement in Viet-Nam.

There may be many ways to this kind of peace: in discussion or negotiation with the governments concerned; in large groups or in small ones; in the reaffirmation of old agreements or their strengthening with new ones. . . .

These countries of southeast Asia are homes for millions of impoverished people. . . .

Stability and peace do not come easily in such a land. Neither independence nor human dignity will ever be won, though, by arms alone. It also requires the work of peace. The American people have helped generously in times past in these works. Now there must be a much more massive effort to improve the life of man in that conflict-torn corner of our world.

The first step is for the countries of southeast Asia to associate themselves in a greatly expanded cooperative effort for development. We would hope that North Viet-Nam would take its place in the common effort just as soon as peaceful cooperation is possible.

The United Nations is already actively engaged in development in this area. . . .

For our part I will ask the Congress to join in a billion dollar American investment in this effort as soon as it is underway.

And I would hope that all other industrialized countries, including the Soviet Union, will join in this effort to replace despair with hope, and terror with progress.

The task is nothing less than to enrich the hopes and the existence of more than a hundred million people. And there is much to be done.

The vast Mekong River can provide food and water and power on a scale to dwarf even our own TVA.

The wonders of modern medicine can be spread through villages where thousands die every year from lack of care.

Schools can be established to train people in the skills that are needed to manage the process of development.

And these objectives, and more, are within the reach of a cooperative and determined effort.

I also intend to expand and speed up a program to make available our farm surpluses to assist in feeding and clothing the needy in Asia. We should not allow people to go hungry and wear rags while our own warehouses overflow with an abundance of wheat and corn, rice and cotton. . . .

In areas that are still ripped by conflict, of course development will not be easy. Peace will be necessary for final success. But we cannot and must not wait for peace to begin this job. . . .

This will be a disorderly planet for a long time. In Asia, as elsewhere, the forces of the modern world are shaking old ways and uprooting ancient civilizations. There will be turbulence and struggle and even violence. Great social change—as we see in our own country now—does not always come without conflict. . . .

Questions

1. What, according to Johnson, underlay the war in Vietnam?
2. What were America's objectives in Vietnam? Why did the United States need to persevere in seeking to attain them? Did any of Johnson's arguments draw on earlier American experience and policies?
3. Why do you think Johnson discussed "the work of peace" in his speech?

28-9 The Splendid Little War (1965)

Philip Caputo

Since the end of the Vietnam War, a growing number of participants, both American and Vietnamese, have written accounts of their wartime experiences. Philip Caputo, who served as a lieutenant in the U.S. Ninth Marine Expeditionary Brigade, wrote a particularly vivid account in his book *A Rumor of War*, which was published two years after the fall of Saigon in 1975. Caputo's account reveals firsthand the harrowing experiences of American soldiers in Vietnam and, in his words, "does not pretend to be history. It has nothing to do with politics, power, strategy, influence, national interests, or foreign policy. . . . [I]t is simply a story about war, about the things men do in war and the things war does to them."

Source: Excerpt from Philip Caputo, *A Rumor of War* (New York: Ballantine Books, 1977), 89–96. Copyright © 1977 by Philip Caputo. Reprinted by permission of Henry Holt and Company, LLC.

For the next few weeks, the rifle companies kept to a schedule almost as regular as that of office clerks or factory workers. In effect, we commuted to and from the war. We went into the bush for a day or two or three, returned for a brief rest, and went out again.

There was no pattern to these patrols and operations. Without a front, flanks, or rear, we fought a formless war against a formless enemy who evaporated like the morning jungle mists, only to materialize in some unexpected place. It was a haphazard, episodic sort of combat. Most of the time, nothing happened; but when something did, it happened instantaneously and without warning. Rifle or machine-gun fire would erupt with heart-stopping suddenness, as when quail or pheasant explode from cover with a loud beating of wings. Or mortar shells would come in from nowhere, their only preamble the cough of the tubes.

In those weeks we did not see heavy fighting; the battalion's casualties averaged no more than twenty a month, out of a total combat strength of about a thousand men. But we saw enough to learn those lessons that could not be taught in training camps: what fear feels like and what death looks like, and the smell of death, the experience of killing, of enduring pain and inflicting it, the loss of friends and the sight of wounds. We learned what war was about, "the cares of it, and the forms of it." We began to change, to lose the boyish awkwardness we had brought to Vietnam. We became more professional, leaner and tougher, and a callus began to grow around our hearts, a kind of emotional flak jacket that blunted the blows and stings of pity.

Because of the sporadic, confused nature of the fighting, it is impossible to give an orderly account of what we did. With one or two exceptions, I have only disjointed recollections of this period, the spring of 1965. The incidents I do remember, I remember vividly; but I can come up with no connecting thread to tie events neatly together.

The company is tramping down a dirt road past a Catholic church built long ago by French missionaries. Its gothic style looks out of place in this Asian landscape. Its walls are made of a dark, volcanic-looking rock. The courtyard is enclosed by a stone fence which bougainvillaea covers like bunting and there is a crucifix atop the arched gate. We are marching in a double file through a pall of dust raised by our boots. The dust drifts slowly away from the road and sifts down on the courtyard, dulling the brilliance of the bougainvillaea. It is an extremely hot day, hotter than any we have yet experienced. We have been told that the temperature is over one hundred and ten degrees, but the figure is meaningless. The cruelty of this sun cannot be measured by an instrument. Head bowed, a machine-gunner in front of me is walking with his weapon braced across the back of his shoulders, one hand hanging over the muzzle and the other over the butt, so that his shadow resembles the Christ figure on the cross atop the gate of the church. Farther on, the road runs past a stretch of low, grassy hills and flooded rice paddies. A deserted village lies ahead, a little more than halfway to our objective, an abandoned tea plantation.

Lemmon's platoon is at point, and I can see them through the dust, marching heavy-legged beneath a sky that is as bright as a plate of stainless steel. There is a sudden spattering of small-arms fire, the bullets raising geysers in the flooded paddies. The column stops while Lemmon's men deploy into a skirmish line and charge toward the hills. They splash across the fields, dodge the sudden eruptions of mud and water, then vanish into the elephant grass that covers the high ground. Passing through it, they enter the village. Two squads file back onto the road, a third remains behind to search the huts. We hear calls of "Fire in the hole!" and muffled explosions as grenades are thrown into bunkers and tunnels. But the enemy is not there. The squad returns to the column, and we are marching again, marching in the heat and choking dust.

My platoon is manning an outpost on a hill at the tip of a ridgeline a thousand yards forward of C Company's lines. We have been on the outpost for two days, though it seems more like two weeks. There is nothing to do during the day except sit in the sandbagged foxholes and gaze out at the rice paddies and the mountains beyond. The nights have been hours of nervous wakefulness broken by intervals of fitful sleep. Listening to things — men? snakes? animals? — crawling in the underbrush. Swatting mosquitoes. Trying to see in a blackness that is occasionally lighted by a distant flare.

It is now the afternoon of the third day. I am sitting in the platoon command post with Sergeant Gordon. We have rigged a lean-to over the foxhole to shield ourselves from the sun, but it is still hot. The rubber poncho billows and sags in the spasmodic breezes that blow through the tops of the trees. Gordon, a short, pink-faced career marine, is talking about fear and bravery. He says that bravery is the conquest of fear, which is not an entirely new idea. I am only half listening to him, anyway. I am trying to read the paperback Kipling which lies open in my lap, but I cannot concentrate because Gordon is talking and because an invincible weariness prevents me from reading more than a few lines at a time. Also, I keep thinking about a girl, a tall, blond girl with whom I spent my leave in San Francisco five months and a hundred years ago. I miss her a good deal, but when I think of her, I find it difficult to remember her face clearly. She and San Francisco are so far away that they seem not to exist. Sweat dips off my nose and onto the Kipling, smudging the print. Gordon chatters away.

I pick up my field glasses and scan the valley below. Dampness has smeared the lenses, so all I see is a blurred, light-dappled green. It is as though I were sitting with goggles on at the bottom of a green river. I wipe the lenses and my face, but in a few seconds a fresh flood of sweat cascades into my eyes. I wipe the lenses again, and sweep the glasses over the empty valley. I have done this dozens of times in the past forty-eight hours. That is my mission: "To keep the Song Tuy Loan river valley under observation and report on all enemy movement and activity sighted." There isn't any enemy movement or activity, of course. All I see are the sun-stricken paddies, a cone-shaped hill half a mile away, Hill 324, and the jagged wall of the Annamese range. It is interesting how the color green, which poets and songwriters always associate with youth and hope, can be so depressing when there is no other color to contrast with it. Green. It is embedded in my consciousness. My vision is filled with green rice paddies, green hills, green mountains, green uniforms; light green, medium green, dark green, olive green. It is as monotonous as Gordon's voice.

I interrupt him by reading aloud the stanza to a poem which has caught my eye:

And the end of the fight is a tombstone white
  with the name of the late deceased,
And the epitaph drear: "A Fool lies here
  who tried to hustle the East."

Gordon misses the irony, and launches into a discussion of his favorite poem, a ballad called "Rye Whiskey." He begins singing it in a nasal twang.

Rye whiskey, rye whiskey, rye whiskey I cry
If I don't get rye whiskey, I surely will die.

And I think, If you don't shut up, Gordon, you surely will and a lot sooner than you expected. That is what I think, but I don't say it. I recognize that I am in the second stage of the *cafard*, the stage in which you feel a hatred for everything and everyone around you. To get away from Gordon, I go check the perimeter. The marines are all in the same state of mind as I, "fed-up, fucked-up, and far from home." Their arms are tanned a deep brown, but the heat has bled the color from their faces, and their eyes have that blank expression known as the "thousand-yard stare."

It is night on the same outpost, and in at least one marine, PFC Buchanan, boredom has given way to terror. He has fired several shots at something he heard moving in front of his position. I am raging at him: "You goddamned amateur. You're supposed to throw a grenade if there's something there, not fire your weapon. The muzzle-flash could give your position away. You ought to know that." The lecture does not do any good. Buchanan stands in a tense crouch, his rifle resting on the sandbagged parapet, his finger on the trigger. He won't look at me, keeping his eyes fixed on the jungle straight ahead. The vegetation is gray-green in the moonlight. "Buchanan," I whisper, "take your finger off the trigger. Relax. It was probably one of those rock apes they've got up here." He does not move. Fear has overmastered him. Looking down the length of his rifle, he insists that the noise was made by a man. "All right. I'll stay here for a while. I don't want you firing unless you've got a target." I slide down into the foxhole, remove a grenade from my pocket, crimp the pin, and lay it aside.

A while later, Buchanan says in a low voice, "There he is, there he is." I hear a loud, dry rustling, as if someone were crumpling a sheet of crepe paper. Standing up, I look over the parapet and see some bushes moving twenty or twenty-five yards downhill. Whatever is in there is big, as big as a man; but I cannot believe an infiltrator would make so much noise. Unless he is trying to draw our fire. The rustling stops. There is a soft click as Buchanan eases the safety off. Again I tell him that it is probably a rock ape. I no longer completely believe this, and Buchanan does not believe it at all. "That ain't no fuckin' monkey, lieutenant." The rustling begins again. A bush quivers and grows still; the one next to it moves, then the one next to that. Something or someone is crawling along the hillside, parallel to the perimeter line. Before Buchanan can fire, I pull the pin on the grenade. Lobbing it with one hand, I pull Buchanan down with the other. The grenade explodes. A cloud of smoke drifts up through the gray-green underbrush, like dry-ice vapor, and the rustling has stopped. "If there really was a VC out there," I say, "that either killed him or scared the hell out of him." Buchanan at last takes the rifle from his shoulder; the grenade appears to have restored his confidence.

I return to the command post by way of a trail that leads through an avenue of trees with black, greasy trunks. It is dark in there, almost as dark as a vault, and I feel relieved when I am safely back in the CP. Widener is calling the hourly situation report to company HQ. "Charley Six, this is Charley Two. All secure, situation remains the same."

Later, I am startled awake by rifle fire. I seem to have developed an odd ability to sleep and not sleep at the same time. My head is instantly clear, and I know what has happened, just as if I had been awake all the time. There have been a couple of shots from a carbine and a burst from an M-14. The firing has come from my right rear, near Lance Corporal Marshall's position. I climb out of the foxhole and walk in that direction down the trail that leads through the dark avenue of trees. I stop when I see the silhouette of a man thirty or forty feet ahead. I think it is a man. The figure is not moving. He must have seen me at the same moment. We look at each other for what seems a long time. I cannot see if he is armed, although I know I heard a carbine. Or did I imagine it? Am I imagining now? Maybe I am looking at nothing more than a bush shaped like a man. As I have been trained to do, I look at the outline of the figure rather than directly at it. If you look straight at an object at night, your eyes play tricks on you. So I look at the edges of the form, the figure, the bush, whatever it is. Yes, it is a man, frozen in mid-stride, apparently because he is trying to figure out if I have seen him. I cannot see a weapon, but he could have one; or he could be carrying grenades. I want to challenge him, to shout "Dung lai" (halt), but the words catch in my throat and a weakness creeps into my legs. Transfixed, I am still watching him as he watches me. Time passes as in a nightmare that lasts only a few seconds but seems to go on and on. A marine yells something, something like "He's over there." The figure moves, and in one motion I unsnap the flap of my holster, draw the pistol, pull back the slide to chamber a round, and take aim. He is gone, crashing through the underbrush downhill. I aim at the sound but hold my fire, afraid of hitting one of my own men. Then I am aware that my heart is beating very fast and that the checkered grip of the pistol is slick with sweat.

Marshall comes up to me and tells me what happened. He had been off watch, lying in his hooch, when he heard movement a short distance away. There was a challenge from a sentry, followed by a few shots. Scrambling out of his hooch, Marshall saw a VC running past, toward the command post; but the infiltrator vanished into the darkness before anyone could get a clear shot at him.

After passing the word that there is to be a one-hundred-percent alert for the next hour, I walk back to the CP and take over radio watch from Widener. I am still not sure if the figure I saw and heard was a Viet Cong, an animal of some kind, or a chimera. The fear is real enough, though. We pass an uneventful but nervous night, and I feel like rejoicing when the sky begins to lighten and I call in the last situation report. "Charley Six, this is Charley Two. All secure, situation remains the same."

Questions

1. According to Caputo and your reading of the text (pp. 880–881), what were some of the unique challenges that American soldiers faced in Vietnam?
2. Using Caputo's account and Ernie Pyle's column on World War II (Document 25-11) as sources, what are some of the universal challenges that all soldiers face?

Questions for Further Thought

1. Compare the second page of President Lyndon B. Johnson's 1965 "Peace Without Conquest" speech (Document 28-8) to Johnson's 1964 address at the University of Michigan (Document 28-5).
2. How might the soldiers in Philip Caputo's firsthand account (Document 28-9) have reacted to Johnson's speech (Document 28-8)?

Coming Apart

During the mid- to late 1960s, the civil rights and antiwar movements grew and changed character as the war intensified, casualties mounted, and more young men were conscripted to fight against their will; at the same time, many of the nation's cities became centers of racial strife. To many, it seemed as if the country was being torn apart. A youth culture mobilized to challenge the status quo and Americans of all ages were forced to reassess their basic assumptions about their society and their government.

Document 28-10 offers the remarks of Malcolm X to Mississippi students visiting New York City and a poem by Yusef Iman. Increasing group awareness among Chicanos and Native Americans also marked the period. Although the two groups' histories differed, both had long-standing grievances and fought for their rights before the 1960s. Now, younger Chicanos and Native Americans were prominent in protests. See Document 28-11 for Inés Hernández's "Para Teresa." Document 28-12 presents testimony of Menominee Native American activists from Wisconsin regarding the adverse effects of the government's policy of termination on their tribe. Feminism revived in the 1960s, led by politically active older women but also influenced by younger women, many of them radicalized by their subordination in civil rights, student, and antiwar protest groups. Document 28-13 provides the National Organization for Women's statement of purpose.

28-10 Black Nationalism (1964)

Malcolm X and Yusef Iman

Black Muslim leader Malcolm X (1925–1965) became a major spokesperson for black nationalism, a viewpoint that appealed especially to young urban African Americans (see text pp. 885–886). Some elements of Malcolm X's views are expressed in a speech he gave to Mississippi students visiting New York in 1964. Malcolm X had a tremendous impact on Stokely Carmichael and others associated with black power. The ideas expressed in Yusef Iman's poem "Love Your Enemy" are clearly influenced by Malcolm X's philosophy.

Sources: Excerpts from Malcolm X "To Mississippi Youth," speech given at the Hotel Theresa, Harlem, January 1, 1965, from *Malcolm X Speaks: Selected Speeches and Statements*, ed. George Breitman, 137–146. Copyright © 1965, 1989 by Betty Shabazz and Pathfinder Press. Reprinted by permission of Pathfinder Press. Yusef Iman, "Love Your Enemy" from *Black Fire: An Anthology of Afro-American Writing*, comp. Amiri Baraka (New York: Morrow, 1968), 387–388. Copyright 1968 by Amiri Baraka. Reprinted by permission of Sterling Lord Literistic.

(a) To Mississippi Youth, by Malcolm X

One of the first things I think young people, especially nowadays, should learn is how to see for yourself and listen for yourself and think for yourself. Then you can come to an intelligent decision for yourself. If you form the habit of going by what you hear others say about someone, or going by what others think about someone, instead of searching that thing out for yourself and seeing for yourself, you will be walking west when you think you're going east, and you will be walking east when you think you're going west. This generation, especially of our people, has a burden, more so than any other time in history. The most important thing that we can learn to do today is think for ourselves. . . .

I myself would go for nonviolence if it was consistent, if everybody was going to be nonviolent all the time. I'd say, okay, let's get with it, we'll all be nonviolent. But I don't go along with any kind of nonviolence unless everybody's going to be nonviolent. If they make the Ku Klux Klan nonviolent, I'll be nonviolent. If they make the White Citizens Council nonviolent, I'll be nonviolent. But as long as you've got somebody else not being nonviolent, I don't want anybody coming to me talking any nonviolent talk. I don't think it is fair to tell our people to be nonviolent unless someone is out there making the Klan and the Citizens Council and these other groups also be nonviolent. . . .

If the leaders of the nonviolent movement can go into the white community and teach nonviolence, good. I'd go along with that. But as long as I see them teaching nonviolence only in the black community, we can't go along with that. We believe in equality, and equality means that you have to put the same thing over here that you put over there. And if black people alone are going to be the ones who are nonviolent, then it's not fair. We throw ourselves off guard. In fact, we disarm ourselves and make ourselves defenseless. . . .

[W]e of the Organization of Afro-American Unity realized that the only time the black man in this country is given any kind of recognition, or even listened to, is when America is afraid of outside pressure, or when she's afraid of her image abroad. So we saw that it was necessary to expand the problem and the struggle of the black man in this country until it went above and beyond the jurisdiction of the United States. . . .

And today you'll find in the United Nations, and it's not an accident, that every time the Congo question or anything on the African continent is being debated, they couple it with what is going on, or what is happening to you and me, in Mississippi and Alabama and these other places. In my opinion, the greatest accomplishment that was made in the struggle of the black man in America in 1964 toward some kind of real progress was the successful linking together of our problem with the African problem, or making our problem a world problem. Because now, whenever anything happens to you in Mississippi, it's not just a case of somebody in Alabama getting indignant, or somebody in New York getting indignant. The same repercussions that you see all over the world when an imperialist or foreign power interferes in some section of Africa—you see repercussions, you see the embassies being bombed and burned and overturned—nowadays, when something happens to black people in Mississippi, you'll see the same repercussions all over the world.

I wanted to point this out to you because it is important for you to know that when you're in Mississippi, you're not alone. As long as you think you're alone, then you take a stand as if you're a minority or as if you're outnumbered, and that kind of stand will never enable you to win a battle. You've got to know that you've got as much power on your side as that Ku Klux Klan has on its side. And when you know that you've got as much power on your side as the Klan has on its side, you'll talk the same kind of language with that Klan as the Klan is talking with you. . . .

I think in 1965, whether you like it, or I like it, or they like it, or not, you will see that there is a generation of black people becoming mature to the point where they feel that they have no more business being asked to take a peaceful approach than anybody else takes, unless everybody's going to take a peaceful approach.

So we here in the Organization of Afro-American Unity are with the struggle in Mississippi one thousand percent. We're with the efforts to register our people in Mississippi to vote one thousand percent. But we do not go along with anybody telling us to help nonviolently. We think that if the government says that Negroes have a right to vote, and then some Negroes come out to vote, and some kind of Ku Klux Klan is going to put them in the river, and the government doesn't do anything about it, it's time for us to organize and band together and equip ourselves and qualify ourselves to protect ourselves. And once you can protect yourself, you don't have to worry about being hurt. . . .

You get freedom by letting your enemy know that you'll do anything to get your freedom; then you'll get it. It's the only way you'll get it. When you get that kind of attitude, they'll label you as a "crazy Negro," or they'll call you a "crazy nigger"—they don't say Negro. Or they'll call you an extremist or a subversive, or seditious, or a red or a radical. But when you stay radical long enough, and get enough people to be like you, you'll get your freedom. . . .

(b) Love Your Enemy, by Yusef Iman

Brought here in slave ships and pitched over board.
Love your enemy.
Language taken away, culture taken away.
Love your enemy.
Work from sun up to sun down.
Love your enemy.
Work for no pay.
Love your enemy.
Last hired, first fired.
Love your enemy.
Rape your mother.
Love your enemy.
Lynch your father.
Love your enemy.
Bomb your churches.
Love your enemy.
Kill your children.
Love your enemy.
Forced to fight his wars.
Love your enemy.
Pay the highest rent.
Love your enemy.
Sell you rotten foods.
Love your enemy.
Sell dope to your children.
Love your enemy.
Forced to live in the slums.
Love your enemy.
Dilapidated schools.
Love your enemy.
Puts you in jail.
Love your enemy.
Bitten by dogs.
Love your enemy.
Water hose you down.
Love your enemy.
    Love.
    Love.
    Love.
    Love.
    Love.
    Love, for everybody else.
But when will we love ourselves?

Questions

1. What was Malcolm X's opinion of the philosophy of nonviolence?
2. What strategy did Iman use to convey his message, and what was that message? How was Malcolm X's advice reflected in the poem "Love Your Enemy"?
3. What emotions do you believe Malcolm X and Iman hoped to stir in their readers?

28-11 Para Teresa[1]

Inés Hernández

Like African Americans, Chicanos experienced feelings of being treated like outsiders and interlopers in American society. As was true for all minority groups, there were differences in the Hispanic community as to what strategy would best overcome this prejudice and discrimination. Inés Hernández's poem about a confrontation with a schoolmate illustrates some of those differences (see text pp. 886–888).

Source: From Inés Hernández, *Con Razon, Corazon: Poetry*, rev. ed. (San Antonio, TX: M & A Editions, n.d.). Inés Hernández-Avila is Chicana and Nez Perce; she is an Associate Professor of Native American Studies at the University of California, Davis. Used by permission.

A tí-Teresa
Te dedico las palabras estás
que explotan de mi corazón[2]

That day during lunch hour
at Alamo which-had-to-be-its-name
Elementary
my dear raza
That day in the bathroom
Door guarded
Myself cornered
I was accused by you, Teresa
Tú y las demás de tus amigas
Pachucas todos
Eran Uds. Cinco.[3]

Me gritaban que porque me creía tan grande[4]
What was I trying to do, you growled
Show you up?
Make the teachers like me, pet me,
Tell me what a credit to my people I was?
I was playing right into their hands, you challenged
And you would have none of it.
I was to stop.
I was to be like you

I was to play your game of deadly defiance
Arrogance, refusal to submit.
The game in which the winner takes nothing
Asks for nothing
Never lets his weakness show.

But I didn't understand.
My fear salted with confusion
Charged me to explain to you
I did nothing for the teachers.
I studied for my parents and for my grandparents
Who cut out honor roll lists
Whenever their nietos'[5] names appeared
For my shy mother who mastered her terror
to demand her place in mother's clubs
For my carpenter-father who helped me patiently with my math.
For my abuelos que me regalaron lápices en la Navidad[6]
And for myself.

Porque reconocí en aquel entonces
una verdad tremenda
que me hizo mi un rebelde
Aunque tú no te habías dado cuenta[7]
We were not inferior
You and I, y las demás de tus amigas

---

[1] For Teresa.
[2] To you, Teresa, I dedicate these words that explode from my heart.
[3] You and the rest of your friends, all Pachucas (female natives of Pachuca, capital of the Mexican state of Hidalgo), there were five of you.
[4] You were screaming at me, asking me why I thought I was so hot.
[5] Grandchildren's.
[6] Grandparents who gave me gifts of pencils at Christmas.
[7] Because I recognized a great truth then that made me a rebel, even though you didn't realize it.

Y los demás de nuestra gente[8]
I knew it the way I knew I was alive
We were good, honorable, brave
Genuine, loyal, strong

And smart.
Mine was a deadly game of defiance, also.
My contest was to prove
beyond any doubt
that we were not only equal but superior to them.
That was why I studied.
If I could do it, we all could.
You let me go then.
Your friends unblocked the way
I who-did-not-know-how-to-fight
was not made to engage with you-who-grew-up-fighting
Tu y yo, Teresa[9]
We went in different directions
Pero fuimos juntas.[10]

In sixth grade we did not understand
Uds. With the teased, dyed-black-but-reddening hair,
Full petticoats, red lipsticks
and sweaters with the sleeves
pushed up
Y yo conformándome con lo que deseaba mi mama.[11]
Certainly never allowed to dye, to tease, to paint myself
I did not accept your way of anger,
Your judgements
You did not accept mine.

But now in 1975, when I am twenty-eight
Teresa
I remember you.
Y sabes—
Te comprendo,
Es más, te respeto.
Y, si me permites,
Te nombro—"hermana."[12]

---

[8] And the rest of your friends / And the rest of our people.
[9] You and I.
[10] But we were together.

[11] And I conforming to my mother's wishes.
[12] And do you know what, I understand you. Even more, I respect you. And, if you permit me, I name you my sister.

Questions

1. What did the poem's speaker do to combat racism, and what did Teresa advocate?
2. How did the speaker's attitude toward Teresa change, and how do you account for this change?
3. Which position do you think was most effective—that of Teresa or the poem's speaker?

28-12 The Consequences of Termination for the Menominee of Wisconsin (1971)

DRUMS Committee of the Menominee

In the 1950s, Congress endorsed a new policy for Native Americans. It was called *termination* and was intended to end "the legal standing of native tribes and move their members off reservations" (see text p. 888). But what looked good in Washington did not necessarily work for people such as the Menominee of Wisconsin.

Source: Hearings on Senate Concurrent Resolution Number 26, Senate Committee on Interior and Insular Affairs, July 21, 1971, in Peter Nabokov, ed., *Native American Testimony: A Chronicle of Indian-White Relations from Prophecy to the Present, 1492–1992* (New York: Viking Penguin, 1991), 344–347. Reprinted with permission of Viking Penguin.

Early in 1953, we Menominee wanted a portion of our 1951 settlement—about $5,000,000—distributed among ourselves on a $1,500 per capita basis. Since Congressional approval was required for such disbursement of our assets, [then] Representative Melvin Laird and Senator Joseph McCarthy introduced in Congress on behalf of our Tribe a bill to authorize the payment of *our* money to us.

This bill passed the House, but in hearings before the Senate Committee on Interior and Insular Affairs, it ran up against an amendment sponsored by the late Senator Arthur

V. Watkins (R. Utah) calling for "termination" of federal supervision and assistance to the Menominee. Watkins and the Committee refused to report the bill favorably, calling upon us Menominee to submit a termination plan *before* we would be given *our* money! "Termination!" What did *that* mean? Certainly at that time, none of us Menominee realized what it meant!... In June, 1953, we Menominee invited Senator Watkins to visit the Reservation and explain "termination" to us.

Senator Watkins badly wanted our termination. He was firmly convinced that factors such as our status as Reservation Indians, our tribal ownership of land, and our tax exemption were blocking our initiative, our freedom, and our development of private enterprise. He wished to see us rapidly assimilated into the mainstream of American society—as tax paying, hard working, "emancipated" citizens....

On June 20, 1953, Senator Watkins spoke for 45 minutes to our General Council. He told us that Congress had already decided on terminating us, and that at most we could have three years before our "affairs would be turned over to us"—and that we would not receive our per capitas until *after* termination.

After he left, our Council had the opportunity to vote on the "principle of termination!" Some opportunity! What little understanding we had of what termination would mean! The vote was 169 to 5 in favor of the "principle of termination." A mere 5 percent of the 3,200 Menominee people participated in this vote. Most of our people chose to be absent from the meeting in order to express their negative reaction to termination. Many who did vote affirmatively that day believed that termination was coming from Congress whether the Menominee liked it or not. Others thought that they were voting *only* in favor of receiving their per capitas....

We then set about preparing a termination plan, which the BIA [Bureau of Indian Affairs] subsequently emasculated, and we received word that Senator Watkins was pressing ahead with his *own* termination bill. *Another* general council meeting was called, one which is seldom mentioned, but at which the Menominee voted 197 to 0 to *oppose and reject* termination. But our feelings did not matter—and although the Watkins bill met a temporary defeat on technical grounds in the House in late 1953, Senator Watkins reintroduced it in 1954.

We became convinced that there was *no* alternative to accepting termination. Therefore, all we pleaded for was adequate time to plan this sudden and revolutionary change in our lives! On June 17, 1954, the Menominee Termination Act was signed into law by President Eisenhower....

Termination represented a gigantic and revolutionary *forced* change in the traditional Menominee way of life. Congress expected us to replace our Indian way of life with a complicated corporate style of living. Congress expected immediate Menominee assimilation of non-Indian culture, values, and life styles....

The immediate effect of termination on our tribe was the loss of most of our hundred-year-old treaty rights, protections, and services. No amount of explanation or imagination prior to termination could have prepared us for the shock of what these losses meant.

Congress withdrew its trusteeship of our lands, transferring to MEI [Menominee Enterprises, Inc., the corporation which was to supervise Menominee holdings after termination] the responsibility for protecting these lands, our greatest assets. As we shall explain, far from being able to preserve our land, MEI has been forced to sell it. And because our land is now being sold to non-Menominee, termination is doing to us what allotment has done to other Indian tribes.

Congress also extinguished our ancient system of tribal "ownership" of land (under which no individual had separate title to his home) and transferred title to MEI. Consequently, we individual Menominee suddenly discovered that we would be forced to buy from MEI the land which had always been considered our own, and to pay title to our homesites. Thus began the tragic process of our corporation "feeding off" our people.

We Menominee lost our right to tax exemption. Both MEI and individual Menominee found themselves saddled with tax burdens particularly crushing to a small tribe struggling to develop economically.

BIA health, education and utility services ceased. We lost all medical and dental care within the Reservation. Both our reservation and hospital were closed because they failed to meet state standards. Individual Menominee were forced to pay for electricity and water that they previously received at no cost. Our county found it had to renovate at high cost its substandard sewerage system.

Finally, with termination and the closing of our tribal rolls, our children born since 1954 have been legally deprived of their birthright as Menominee Indians. Like all other Menominee, they have lost their entitlement to United States Government benefits and services to Indians.... The only major Menominee treaty right which the government has allowed us to retain has been our hunting and fishing right. Wisconsin had tried to deprive us of this right, but in 1968, after costly litigation, the United States Supreme Court ruled that this treaty right had "survived" termination....

We hope you can appreciate the magnitude of these treaty losses to us. Visualize a situation similar to ours happening in one of your home states. Imagine the outrage of the people in one of your own communities if Congress should attempt to terminate their basic property, inheritance, and civil rights....

Today Menominee County is the poorest county in Wisconsin. It has the highest birthrate in the state and ranks at or near the bottom of Wisconsin counties in income, housing, property value, education, employment, sanitation and health. The most recent figures available (1967) show that the annual income of nearly 80 percent of our families falls below the federal poverty level of $3,000. The per capita annual income of our wage earners in 1965 was estimated at $881, the lowest in the state....

This lack of employment opportunities, combined with our high birthrate, forced nearly 50 percent of our county residents to go on welfare in 1968. Welfare costs in the county for 1968 were over $766,000 and our per capita welfare payment was the highest in the state. The majority of Menominee who have left our county to seek work in the cities have become trapped in poverty there also.

With the closing of the BIA hospital, we lost most of our health services, and most Menominee continue to suffer from lack of medical care. There have been no full-time doctors or dentists in Menominee County since termination. Shortly before termination, our people were stricken by a TB epidemic which caused great suffering and hardship because of the lack of local medical facilities....

The loss of the BIA school required that our youth be sent to Shawano County for their high school training. The Shawano school system had assumed that Menominee children possess the same cultural and historical background as [children from the] middle-class white community.... Since 1961, our high school drop-out rates have increased substantially, absenteeism has soared, and our children apparently are suffering a downward trend in achievement....

We have told a story which is very tragic, yet it is a true story of the Menominee people since termination. We have told how termination has meant the loss of treaty benefits, has pushed our already poor community further into the depths of poverty, forced our sale of assets; and denied us a democratic community.

DRUMS COMMITTEE, *Menominee*

Questions

1. Who decided on termination?
2. What were the consequences of this policy?

28-13 Statement of Purpose (1966)

National Organization for Women

The National Organization for Women (NOW) was founded in 1966 by a small group of women. One of the founders, Betty Friedan, had gained widespread recognition with the publication of her book *The Feminine Mystique* three years earlier. The organizers of NOW hoped the group would serve women as the NAACP had long served African Americans (see text pp. 902–903).

Source: "Statement of Purpose, National Organization for Women," excerpted from Betty Friedan, *It Changed My Life: Writings on the Women's Movement* (New York: W. W. Norton, 1976), 87–91. Copyright, © 1963, 1964, 1966, 1970, 1971, 1972, 1973, 1974, 1975, 1976, 1985, 1991, 1998 by Betty Friedan. Originally published by Random House, Inc. Reprinted by permission of Curtis Brown, Ltd.

We, men and women who hereby constitute ourselves as the National Organization for Women, believe that the time has come for a new movement toward true equality for all women in America, and toward a fully equal partnership of the sexes, as part of the world-wide revolution of human rights now taking place within and beyond our national borders.

The purpose of NOW is to take action to bring women into full participation in the mainstream of American society now, exercising all the privileges and responsibilities thereof in truly equal partnership with men....

There is no civil rights movement to speak for women, as there has been for Negroes and other victims of discrimination. The National Organization for Women must therefore begin to speak.

WE BELIEVE that the power of American law, and the protection guaranteed by the U.S. Constitution to the civil rights of all individuals, must be effectively applied and enforced to isolate and remove patterns of sex discrimination, to ensure equality of opportunity in employment and education, and equality of civil and political rights and responsibilities on behalf of women, as well as for Negroes and other deprived groups....

WE DO NOT ACCEPT the token appointment of a few women to high-level positions in government and industry as a substitute for a serious continuing effort to recruit and advance women according to their individual abilities. To this end, we urge American government and industry to mobilize the same resources of ingenuity and command with which they have solved problems of far greater difficulty than those now impeding the progress of women.

WE BELIEVE that this nation has a capacity at least as great as other nations, to innovate new social institutions which will enable women to enjoy true equality of opportunity and responsibility in society, without conflict with their responsibilities as mothers and homemakers. In such innovations, America does not lead the Western world, but lags by decades behind many European countries. We do not accept the traditional assumption that a woman has to choose between marriage and motherhood, on the one hand, and serious participation in industry or the professions on the other. We question the present expectation that all normal women will retire from job or profession for ten or fifteen years, to devote their full time to raising children, only to reenter the job market at a relatively minor level. This in itself is a deterrent to the aspirations of women, to their acceptance into management or professional training courses, and to the very possibility of equality of opportunity or real choice, for all but a few women. Above all, we reject the assumption that these problems are the unique responsibility of each individual woman, rather than a basic social dilemma which society must solve. True equality of opportunity and freedom of choice for women requires such practical and possible innovations as a nationwide network of child-care centers, which will make it unnecessary for women to retire completely from society until their children are grown, and national programs to provide retraining for women who have chosen to care for their own children full time.

WE BELIEVE that it is as essential for every girl to be educated to her full potential of human ability as it is for every boy—with the knowledge that such education is the key to effective participation in today's economy and that, for a girl as for boy [sic], education can only be serious where there is expectation that it will be used in society. We believe that American educators are capable of devising means of imparting such expectations to girl students. Moreover, we consider the decline in the proportion of women receiving higher and professional education to be evidence of discrimination. This discrimination may take the form of quotas against the admission of women to colleges and professional schools; lack of encouragement by parents, counselors and educators; denial of loans or fellowships; or the traditional or arbitrary procedures in graduate and professional training geared in terms of men, which inadvertently discriminate against women. We believe that the same serious attention must be given to high school dropouts who are girls as to boys.

WE REJECT the current assumptions that a man must carry the sole burden of supporting himself, his wife, and family, and that a woman is automatically entitled to lifelong support by a man upon her marriage, or that marriage, home and family are primarily woman's world and responsibility—hers, to dominate, his to support. We believe that a true partnership between the sexes demands a different concept of marriage, an equitable sharing of the responsibilities of home and children and of the economic burdens of their support. We believe that proper recognition should be given to the economic and social value of homemaking and child care. To these ends, we will seek to open a reexamination of laws and mores governing marriage and divorce, for we believe that the current state of "half-equality" between the sexes discriminates against both men and women, and is the cause of much unnecessary hostility between the sexes.

WE BELIEVE that women must now exercise their political rights and responsibilities as American citizens. They must refuse to be segregated on the basis of sex into separate-and-not-equal ladies' auxiliaries in the political parties, and they must demand representation according to their numbers in the regularly constituted party committees—at local, state, and national levels—and in the informal power structure, participating fully in the selection of candidates and political decision-making, and running for office themselves.

IN THE INTERESTS OF THE HUMAN DIGNITY OF WOMEN, we will protest and endeavor to change the false image of women now prevalent in the mass media, and in the texts, ceremonies, laws, and practices of our major social institutions. Such images perpetuate contempt for women by society and by women for themselves. We are similarly opposed to all policies and practices—in church, state, college, factory, or office—which, in the guise of protectiveness, not only deny opportunities but also foster in women self-denigration, dependence, and evasion of responsibility, undermine their confidence in their own abilities and foster contempt for women. . . .

WE BELIEVE THAT women will do most to create a new image of women by *acting* now, and by speaking out in behalf of their own equality, freedom, and human dignity—not in pleas for special privilege, nor in enmity toward men, who are also victims of the current half-equality between the sexes—but in an active, self-respecting partnership with men. By so doing, women will develop confidence in their own ability to determine actively, in partnership with men, the conditions of their life, their choices, their future and their society.

Questions

1. What major issues did NOW identify in its statement of purpose?
2. How, according to NOW, should these issues be addressed?

Questions for Further Thought

1. Based on your reading of the text and Documents 28-3, and 28-10 through 28-13, what similarities and dissimilarities do you see among these activists?
2. Were these activists completely disillusioned with the government, or were they still committed to improving it? Explain.
3. Compare and contrast the feminist movement and the earlier woman suffrage movement.

1968: A Year of Shocks

The year 1968 was a remarkably eventful and troubled year in U.S. and world history. It started with the election in Czechoslovakia of Alexander Dubček, which began the hopeful but short-lived "Prague Spring" and ended with *Apollo 8*, a U.S. manned-spacecraft successfully orbiting the moon. In between this brief burst of political optimism in the midst of the Cold War and a spectacular technological achievement, there were student demonstrations from the streets of Paris to the Plaza of Three Cultures in Mexico City, as well as, of course, in many U.S. cities. The boldness of the Tet offensive in Vietnam shocked Americans, as did the assassinations of Martin Luther King Jr. and Robert F. Kennedy.

The most important political event of that important year was President Lyndon Johnson's surprise announcement that he would, in effect, quit the presidency by deciding not to seek reelection. This decision was a blow to mainstream liberalism from which the Democratic Party never fully recovered. The civil disorder that later marred the Democratic Party's National Convention in Chicago reflected this sea change in American politics. Richard Nixon would narrowly win the U.S. presidency in 1968, but this victory marked the beginning of the country's conservative reaction to problems at home and abroad. The environmental and civil rights movements, although they influenced each other, especially the latter on the former, were nevertheless entirely distinct, with their own unique histories. Document 28-14 is an excerpt from Edward Abbey's wilderness classic. Document 28-15 provides a position paper on African Americans sent to President Nixon by Daniel Patrick Moynihan, a domestic policy advisor.

28-14 *Desert Solitaire: A Season in the Wilderness* (1968)

Edward Abbey

The counterculture was a complicated mix of political and social elements and did not neatly fit into liberal or conservative categories. The growing environmental movement called on government to regulate industry, reduce pollution, and protect endangered species, even as it became ever more distrustful of the very sources that would enable government to do these things, namely science and technology. At the same time, the back to the land movement, which in certain ways complemented environmentalism, distrusted government and urban life in general and championed the more traditional virtues of self-reliance and hard work. Many artists and writers came to capture this ambiguity or contradiction in the American mind. Certainly Edward Abbey (1927–1989) was one of them. His *Desert Solitaire* was a defense of wilderness—specifically the slick rock country of southern Utah—a critique of industrial capitalism, a denunciation of the military-industrial complex, an indictment of big government, and much else.

Source: Excerpt from "Polemic: Industrial Tourism and the National Parks," in *Desert Solitaire: A Season in the Wilderness* by Edward Abbey (New York: Simon and Schuster, 1968), 47–52. Reprinted by permission Simon & Schuster Adult Publishing Group. All rights reserved.

There may be some among the readers of this book, like the earnest engineer, who believe without question that any and all forms of construction and development are intrinsic goods, in the national parks as well as anywhere else, who virtually identify quantity with quality and therefore assume that the greater the quantity of traffic, the higher the value received. There are some who frankly and boldly advocate the eradication of the last remnants of wilderness and the complete subjugation of nature to the requirements of—not man—but industry. This is a courageous view, admirable in its simplicity and power, and with the weight of all modern history behind it. It is also quite insane. I cannot attempt to deal with it here.

There will be other readers, I hope, who share my basic assumption that wilderness is a necessary part of civilization and that it is the primary responsibility of the national park system to preserve *intact and undiminished* what little still remains.

Most readers, while generally sympathetic to this latter point of view, will feel, as do the administrators of the National Park Service, that although wilderness is a fine thing, certain compromises and adjustments are necessary in order to meet the ever-expanding demand for outdoor recreation. It is precisely this question which I would like to examine now.

The Park Service, established by Congress in 1916, was directed not only to administer the parks but also to "provide for the enjoyment of same in such manner and by such means as will leave them unimpaired for the enjoyment of future generations." This appropriately ambiguous language, employed long before the onslaught of the automobile, has been understood in various and often opposing ways ever since. The Park Service, like any other big organization, includes factions and factions. The Developers, the dominant faction, place their emphasis on the words "*provide for the enjoyment.*" The Preservers, a minority but also strong, emphasize the words "*leave them unimpaired.*" It is apparent, then, that we cannot decide the question of development versus preservation by a simple referral to holy writ or an attempt to guess the intention of the founding fathers; we must make up our own minds and decide for ourselves what the national parks should be and what purpose they should serve.

The first issue that appears when we get into this matter, the most important issue and perhaps the only issue, is the one called *accessibility*. The Developers insist that the parks must be made fully accessible not only to people but also to their machines, that is, to automobiles, motorboats, etc. The Preservers argue, in principle at least, that wilderness and motors are incompatible and that the former can best be experienced, understood, and enjoyed when the machines are left behind where they belong—on the superhighways and in the parking lots, on the reservoirs and in the marinas.

What does accessibility mean? Is there any spot on earth that men have not proved accessible by the simplest means—feet and legs and heart? Even Mt. McKinley, even Everest, have been surmounted by men on foot. (Some of them, incidentally, rank amateurs, to the horror and indignation of the professional mountaineers.) The interior of the Grand Canyon, a fiercely hot and hostile abyss, is visited each summer by thousands and thousands of tourists of the most banal and unadventurous type, many of them on foot—self-propelled, so to speak—and the others on the backs of mules. Thousands climb each summer to the summit of Mt. Whitney, highest point in the forty-eight United States, while multitudes of others wander on foot or on horseback through the ranges of the Sierras, the Rockies, the Big Smokies, the Cascades and the mountains of New England. Still more hundreds and thousands float or paddle each year down the currents of the Salmon, the Snake, the Allagash, the Yampa, the Green, the Rio Grande, the Ozark, the St. Croix and those portions of the Colorado which have not yet been destroyed by the dam builders. And most significant, these hordes of nonmotorized tourists, hungry for a taste of the difficult, the original, the real, do not consist solely of people young and athletic but also of old folks, fat folks, pale-faced office clerks who don't know a rucksack from a haversack, and even children. The one thing they all have in common is the refusal to live always like sardines in a can—they are determined to get outside of their motorcars for at least a few weeks each year.

This being the case, why is the Park Service generally so anxious to accommodate that other crowd, the indolent millions born on wheels and suckled on gasoline, who expect and demand paved highways to lead them in comfort, ease and safety into every nook and corner of the national parks? For the answer to that we must consider the character of what I call Industrial Tourism and the quality of the mechanized tourists—the Wheelchair Explorers—who are at once the consumers, the raw material and the victims of Industrial Tourism.

Industrial Tourism is a big business. It means money. It includes the motel and restaurant owners, the gasoline retailers, the oil corporations, the road-building contractors, the heavy equipment manufacturers, the state and federal engineering agencies and the sovereign, all-powerful automotive industry. These various interests are well organized, command more wealth than most modern nations, and are represented in Congress with a strength far greater than is justified in any constitutional or democratic sense. (Modern politics is expensive—power follows money.) Through Congress the tourism industry can bring enormous pressure to bear upon such a slender reed in the executive branch as the poor old Park Service, a pressure which is also exerted on every other possible level—local, state, regional—and through advertising and the well-established habits of a wasteful nation.

When a new national park, national monument, national seashore, or whatever it may be called is set up, the various forces of Industrial Tourism, on all levels, immediately expect action—meaning specifically a road-building program. Where trails or primitive dirt roads already exist, the Industry expects—it hardly needs to ask—that these be developed into modern paved highways. On the local level, for example, the first thing that the superintendent of a new park can anticipate being asked, when he attends his first meeting of the area's Chamber of Commerce, is not "Will roads be built?" but rather "When does construction begin?" and "Why the delay?"

(The Natural Money-Mint. With supersensitive antennae these operatives from the C. of C. look into red canyons and see only green, stand among flowers snorting out the smell of money, and hear, while thunderstorms rumble over mountains, the fall of a dollar bill on motel carpeting.)

Accustomed to this sort of relentless pressure since its founding, it is little wonder that the Park Service, through a process of natural selection, has tended to evolve a type of administration which, far from resisting such pressure, has usually been more than willing to accommodate it, even to encourage it. Not from any peculiar moral weakness but simply because such well-adapted administrators are themselves believers in a policy of economic development. "Resource management" is the current term. Old foot trails may be neglected, back-country ranger stations left unmanned, and interpretive and protective services inadequately staffed, but the administrators know from long experience that millions for asphalt can always be found; Congress is always willing to appropriate money for more and bigger paved roads, anywhere—particularly if they form loops. Loop drives are extremely popular with the petroleum industry—they bring the motorist right back to the same gas station from which he started.

Great though it is, however, the power of the tourist business would not in itself be sufficient to shape Park Service policy. To all accusations of excessive development the administrators can reply, as they will if pressed hard enough, that they are giving the public what it wants, that their primary duty is to serve the public not preserve the wilds. "Parks are for people" is the public-relations slogan, which decoded means that the parks are for people-in-automobiles. Behind the slogan is the assumption that the majority of Americans, exactly like the managers of the tourist industry, expect and demand to see their national parks from the comfort, security, and convenience of their automobiles.

Is this assumption correct? Perhaps. Does that justify the continued and increasing erosion of the parks? It does not. Which brings me to the final aspect of the problem of Industrial Tourism: the Industrial Tourists themselves.

They work hard, these people. They roll up incredible mileages on their odometers, rack up state after state in two-week transcontinental motor marathons, knock off one national park after another, take millions of square yards of photographs, and endure patiently the most prolonged discomforts: the tedious traffic jams, the awful food of park cafeterias and roadside eateries, the nocturnal search for a place to sleep or camp, the dreary routine of One-Stop Service, the endless lines of creeping traffic, the smell of exhaust fumes, the ever-proliferating Rules & Regulations, the fees and the bills and the service charges, the boiling radiator and the flat tire and the vapor lock, the surly retorts of room clerks and traffic cops, the incessant jostling of the anxious crowds, the irritation and restlessness of their children, the worry of their wives, and the long drive home at night in a stream of racing cars against the lights of another stream racing in the opposite direction, passing now and then the obscure tangle, the shattered glass, the patrolman's lurid blinker light, of one more wreck.

Hard work. And risky. Too much for some, who have given up the struggle on the highways in exchange for an entirely different kind of vacation—out in the open, on their own feet, following the quiet trail through forest and mountains, bedding down at evening under the stars, when and where they feel like it, at a time when the Industrial Tourists are still hunting for a place to park their automobiles.

Industrial Tourism is a threat to the national parks. But the chief victims of the system are the motorized tourists. They are being robbed and robbing themselves. So long as they are unwilling to crawl out of their cars they will not discover the treasures of the national parks and will never escape the stress and turmoil of those urban-suburban complexes which they had hoped, presumably, to leave behind for a whole.

How to pry the tourists out of their automobiles, out of their back-breaking upholstered mechanized wheel-chairs and onto their feet, onto the strange warmth and solidity of Mother Earth again? This is the problem which the Park Service should confront directly, not evasively, and which it cannot resolve by simply submitting and conforming to the automobile habit. The automobile, which began as a transportation convenience, has become a bloody tyrant (50,000 lives a year), and it is the responsibility of the Park Service, as well as that of everyone else concerned with preserving both wilderness and civilization, to begin a campaign of resistance. The automotive combine has almost succeeded in strangling our cities; we need not let it also destroy our national parks.

It will be objected that a constantly increasing population makes resistance and conservation a hopeless battle. This is true. Unless a way is found to stabilize the nation's population, the parks cannot be saved. Or anything else worth a damn. Wilderness preservation, like a hundred other good causes, will be forgotten under the overwhelming pressure of a struggle for mere survival and sanity in a completely urbanized, completely industrialized, ever more crowded environment. For my own part I would rather take my chances in a thermonuclear war than live in such a world.

Assuming, however, that population growth will be halted at a tolerable level before catastrophe does it for us, it remains permissible to talk about such things as the national parks. Having indulged myself in a number of harsh judgments upon the Park Service, the tourist industry, and the motoring public, I now feel entitled to make some constructive, practical, sensible proposals for the salvation of both parks and people.

Question

1. Compare this document with Documents 28-4 and 28-5. In what respects does Abbey seem to have been more liberal? More conservative?

28-15 Memorandum on Benign Neglect (1970)

Daniel Patrick Moynihan   As a member of the Kennedy, Johnson, Nixon, and Ford administrations, Daniel Patrick Moynihan (1927–2003) served as a domestic policy advisor. In the Nixon administration, Moynihan drafted the following memorandum on the status of African Americans.

Source: Originally titled "Memorandum for the President" (1970), in "Text of the Moynihan Memorandum on the Status of Negroes," *New York Times*, March 1, 1970. Copyright © 1970 by The New York Times Company. Reprinted by permission.

As the new year begins, it occurs to me that you might find useful a general assessment of the position of Negroes at the end of the first year of your Administration, and of the decade in which their position has been the central domestic political issue.

In quantitative terms, which are reliable, the American Negro is making extraordinary progress. In political terms, somewhat less reliable, this would also appear to be true. In each case, however, there would seem to be countercurrents that pose a serious threat to the welfare of the blacks and the stability of the society, white and black.

1. EMPLOYMENT AND INCOME

The nineteen-sixties saw the great breakthrough for blacks. A third (32 per cent) of all families of Negro and other races earned $8,000 or more in 1968 compared, in constant dollars, with 15 per cent in 1960.

The South is still a problem. Slightly more than half (52 per cent) of the Negro population lived in the South in 1969. There, only 19 per cent of families of Negro and other races earned over $8,000.

Young Negro families are achieving income parity with young white families. Outside the South, young husband-wife Negro families have 99 per cent of the income of whites! For families headed by a male age 25 to 34 the proportion was 87 per cent. Thus, it may be this ancient gap is finally closing.

Income reflects employment, and this changed dramatically in the nineteen-sixties. Blacks continued to have twice the unemployment rates of whites, but these were down for both groups. In 1969, the rate for married men of Negro and other races was only 2.5 per cent. Teenagers, on the other hand, continued their appalling rates: 24.4 per cent in 1969.

Black occupations improved dramatically. The number of professional and technical employees doubled in the period 1960–68. This was two and a half times the increase for whites. In 1969, Negro and other races provided 10 per cent of the other-than-college teachers. This is roughly their proportion of the population (11 per cent).

2. EDUCATION

In 1968, 19 per cent of Negro children 3 and 4 years old were enrolled in school, compared to 15 per cent of white children. Forty-five per cent of Negroes 18 and 19 years old were in school, almost the equal of the white proportion of 51 per cent. Negro college enrollment rose 85 per cent between 1964 and 1968, by which time there were 434,000 Negro college students. (The total full-time university population of Great Britain is 200,000.)

Educational achievement should not be exaggerated. Only 16 per cent of Negro high school seniors have verbal test scores at or above grade level. But blacks are staying in school.

3. FEMALE-HEADED FAMILIES

This problem does not get better, it gets worse. In 1969, the proportion of husband-wife families of Negro and other races declined once again, this time to 68.7 per cent. The illegitimacy ratio rose once again, this time to 29.4 per cent of all live births. (The white ratio rose more sharply, but was still only 4.9 per cent.)

Increasingly, the problem of Negro poverty is the problem of the female-headed family. In 1968, 56 per cent of Negro families with income under $3,000 were female-headed. In 1968, for the first time, the number of poor Negro children in female-headed families (2,241,000) was greater than the number in male-headed families (1,947,000).

4. SOCIAL PATHOLOGY

The incidence of antisocial behavior among young black males continues to be extraordinarily high. Apart from white racial attitudes, this is the biggest problem black Americans face, and in part it helps shape white racial attitudes. Black Americans injure one another. Because blacks live in de facto segregated neighborhoods and go to de facto segregated schools, the socially stable elements of the black population cannot escape the socially pathological ones. Routinely, their children get caught up in the antisocial patterns of the others.

You are familiar with the problem of crime. Let me draw your attention to another phenomenon, exactly parallel, and originating in exactly the same social circumstances: Fire. Unless I mistake the trends, we are heading for a genuinely serious fire problem in American cities. . . .

Many of these fires are the result of population density. But a great many are more or less deliberately set. (Thus, on Monday, welfare protestors set two fires in the New York State Capitol.) Fires are in fact a "leading indicator" of social pathology for a neighborhood. They come first. Crime, and the rest, follows. The psychiatric interpretation of fire-setting is complex, but it relates to the types of personalities which slums produce. (A point of possible interest: Fires in the black slums peak in July and August. The urban riots of 1964–1968 could be thought of as epidemic conditions of an endemic situation.)

5. SOCIAL ALIENATION

With no real evidence, I would nonetheless suggest that a great deal of the crime, the fire-setting, the rampant school violence and other such phenomenon in the black community have become quasi-politicized. Hatred—revenge—against whites is now an acceptable excuse for doing what might have been done anyway. This is bad news for any society, especially when it takes forms which the Black Panthers seem to have adopted.

This social alienation among the black lower classes is matched and probably enhanced, by a virulent form of anti-white feeling among portions of the large and prosperous black middle class. It would be difficult to overestimate the degree to which young, well-educated blacks detest white America.

6. THE NIXON ADMINISTRATION

As you have candidly acknowledged, the relation of the Administration to the black population is a problem. I think it ought also to be acknowledged that we are a long way from solving it. During the past year, intense efforts have been made by the Administration to develop programs that will be of help to the blacks. I dare say, as much or more time and attention goes into this effort in this Administration than any in history. But little has come of it. There has been a great deal of political ineptness in some departments, and you have been the loser.

I don't know what you can do about this. Perhaps nothing. But I do have four suggestions.

First. Sometime early in the year, I would gather together the Administration officials who are most involved with these matters and talk out the subject a bit. There really is a need for a more coherent Administration approach to a number of issues. (Which I can list for you, if you like.)

Second. The time may have come when the issue of race could benefit from a period of "benign neglect." The subject has been too much talked about. The forum has been too much taken over to hysterics, paranoids and boodlers on all sides. We may need a period in which Negro progress continues and racial rhetoric fades. The Administration can help bring this about by paying close attention to such progress—as we are doing—while seeking to avoid situations in which extremists of either race are given opportunities for martyrdom, heroics, histrionics or whatever. Greater attention to Indians, Mexican-Americans and Puerto Ricans would be useful. A tendency to ignore provocations from groups such as the Black Panthers might also be useful. (The Panthers were apparently almost defunct until the Chicago police raided one of their headquarters and transformed them into culture heroes for the white—and black—middle class. You perhaps did not note on the society page of yesterday's Times that Mrs. Leonard Bernstein gave a cocktail party on Wednesday to raise money for the Panthers. Mrs. W. Vincent Astor was among the guests. Mrs. Peter Duchin, "the rich blonde wife of the orchestra leader," was thrilled. "I've never met a Panther," she said. "This is a first for me.")

Third. We really ought to be getting on with research on crime. We just don't know enough. It is a year now since the Administration came to office committed to doing something about crime in the streets. But frankly, in that year I don't see that we have advanced either our understanding of the problem, or that of the public at large. (This of course may only reveal my ignorance of what is going on.)

At the risk of indiscretion, may I put it that lawyers are not professionally well-equipped to do much to prevent crime. Lawyers are not managers, and they are not researchers. The logistics, the ecology, the strategy and tactics of reducing the incidence of certain types of behavior in large urban populations simply are not things lawyers think about often.

We are never going to "learn" about crime in a laboratory sense. But we almost certainly could profit from limited, carefully done studies. I don't think these will be done unless you express a personal interest.

Fourth. There is a silent black majority as well as a white one. It is mostly working class, as against lower middle class. It is politically moderate (on issues other than racial equality) and shares most of the concerns of its white counterpart. This group has been generally ignored by the Government and the media. The more recognition we can give to it, the better off we shall all be. (I would take it, for example, that Ambassador [Jerome H.] Holland is a natural leader of this segment of the black community. There are others like him.)

Questions

1. What advances for African Americans did Moynihan cite? What problems continued, in his view?
2. What was Moynihan's view of race relations?
3. Moynihan's memorandum generated controversy. Why? What did he mean by "benign neglect"? How might critics have read the phrase?

Question for Further Thought

1. In terms of the role of government, on what might Abbey and Moynihan have agreed?

CHAPTER TWENTY-NINE

The 1970s: Toward a Conservative America

The Nixon Years

The years of Richard Nixon's presidency, 1969 through 1974, were eventful abroad and at home and came to a painful climax with the first presidential resignation in the nation's history. Nixon involved himself deeply in foreign policy, which had been central to presidencies since Franklin Roosevelt's. Assisted by advisor Henry Kissinger and despite Johnson's bitter experience, Nixon decided to fight a second ground war in Vietnam. The result was that over 20,000 more Americans died in combat between 1969 and 1973, even as Nixon tried to turn the fighting over to South Vietnam through a process called "Vietnamization." To implement this strategy of U.S. disengagement and to achieve a peace with honor, Nixon intensified the aerial war in Southeast Asia to keep pressure on Hanoi, and widened the conflict in 1970 by attacking enemy bases in neighboring Cambodia.

At home, the invasion of Cambodia touched off campus antiwar demonstrations, which escalated beyond earlier protests when Ohio national guardsmen killed students at Kent State University and Mississippi state policemen did likewise at Jackson State University, a black school. Strikes, arson, and bombings closed numerous campuses.

U.S. military involvement in Southeast Asia finally drew to a close with the signing of the Paris Peace Accords on January 27, 1973. It was a paper settlement, however. Two years later, Eisenhower's and Dulles's fear of a united Vietnam under communist rule was finally realized, when the Saigon government collapsed in the face of a determined North Vietnamese offensive. The south's final and humiliating defeat was a significant but relatively minor Cold War reversal. It was a major tragedy, however, for the region, which had been left terribly scarred by years of conflict. Approximately 3.2 million Vietnamese had been killed in the war; over 58,000 Americans had lost their lives. With the north's victory over the south, all of Vietnam now found itself subject to a communist-controlled government determined to extend the collectivist experiment to the south, which, predictably, resulted in economic catastrophe and widespread suffering. In Cambodia, the Khmer Rouge, a communist party dedicated to an extremist Maoist agenda, seized control in 1975 and, in their brutal attempt to reengineer Cambodian society, succeeded in killing over a million of their countrymen and women.

If domestic policy did not engage President Nixon in quite the same way as foreign policy, his efforts at home were nevertheless important. To weaken the antiwar movement, Nixon divided young Americans by class. He did this by ending the draft, thus sparing the middle class the burden of military service, which, in turn, effectively depoliticized college campuses. This turning point in the life of the republic was made possible with the creation in 1973 of an all-volunteer military. To fill its ranks, the military now turned primarily to poorer Americans, appealing to their desires for social advancement and to their patriotism. Nixon also sought to scale down Great Society antipoverty programs and compiled a mixed record regarding race. However, he offered a welfare program of his own, the Family Assistance Plan, and supported, or at least accepted, entitlement and regulatory policies that enlarged, rather than reduced, the role of the federal government.

Richard Nixon and Spiro Agnew, who had won a narrow popular vote victory in 1968, were reelected in a landslide four years later. During 1973, however, Agnew was compelled to resign over kickbacks he had received while governor of Maryland and vice president. The next year Nixon resigned to avoid impeachment and conviction for offenses so serious that a substantial minority of Republicans on the Judiciary Committee of the House of Representatives joined Democrats in support of the three articles of impeachment after the release, ordered by the Supreme Court, of incriminating audiotapes. Neither Gerald Ford, who succeeded first Agnew and then Nixon, nor Nelson Rockefeller, whom President Ford selected as vice president, had been popularly elected to national office.

In Document 29-1 Columbia Broadcasting System (CBS) White House correspondent Dan Rather interviews President Richard Nixon. The live broadcast from the White House took place on January 2, 1972. Documents 29-2 and 29-3 provide war policy statements by Richard Nixon — the first on Vietnamization and the Nixon Doctrine, the second justifying the invasion of Cambodia. Document 29-4 offers portions of transcripts of secretly taped presidential conversations during the Watergate affair.

29-1 Dan Rather's Conversation with President Nixon (1972)

Richard Nixon was not the first president to have a troubled relationship with the press, but his difficulties in this regard were legendary, even before the Watergate scandal. Here, Nixon is interviewed by Dan Rather, a noted American journalist who later succeeded Walter Cronkite in 1981 as anchor and managing news editor of the *CBS Evening News*.

Source: Dan Rather, "Conversation with the President, January 2, 1972," in *Historic Documents 1972* (Washington, DC: Congressional Quarterly, 1973), 3–13. Reprinted with permission.

BOMBING RESUMPTION AND TROOP WITHDRAWALS

Mr. Rather. Mr. President, as you enter this election year, there are quite obviously two central themes that you have been emphasizing. You have stated them over again in the phrases "a generation of peace" and "a prosperity without war."

I would like to take advantage of this opportunity to examine in some detail and some depth the concepts beneath those phrases.

First, on a generation of peace. On everyone's mind is the resumption of the widespread bombing of North Vietnam. Other than what we already know from the authorities in Saigon and what Secretary Laird has said, could you assess the military benefits of that?

The President. With regard to the military benefits, let me say first why we did it. You were present in the White House Press Room, as you always are, when I was there making the last troop withdrawal announcement which will bring the troops down to 139,000 by the first of February. And, at that time, I said that in the event that the enemy stepped up its infiltration, or engaged in other activities which imperiled, in my opinion, our remaining forces as our forces were becoming less, that I would take action to deal with the situation.

Most of you reported it. And most of the reporters also wrote it. I meant exactly what I said. The enemy did step up its infiltration. They violated the understanding of 1968 when the bombing halt was agreed to, with regard to firing on our unarmed reconnaissance planes. They shelled Saigon on December 19.

Under those circumstances, I had no other choice but to bomb, in this case, selected military targets and supply build-up areas. Those were the only areas that were hit.

The results have been very, very effective and I think that their effectiveness will be demonstrated by the statement I am now going to make.

Before the first of February, well before the first of February, I will make another withdrawal announcement. Our withdrawal will continue on schedule, at least at the present rate, possibly at somewhat a larger rate. I will not make the decision with regard to the rate at this point, but the withdrawal can go forward on schedule and as far as our American casualties are concerned, which, as you know, as reported on Thursday of last week on CBS and other networks, were one—the lowest in 6 years.

Mr. Rather. That included a truce period for Christmas, did it not?

The President. It included a truce period, but as you know they have averaged less than 10 for 3 months, whereas they were averaging 300—up to 300 a week when we came into office. But our casualties as a result of these activities, I believe, can be kept at this very low level.

AMERICAN INVOLVEMENT IN VIETNAM

Mr. Rather. Mr. President, you were quoted in a Time magazine interview this past week, and I want to get the direct quotation, if I may, saying "The issue of Vietnam will not be an issue in the campaign as far as this administration is concerned, because we will have brought the American involvement to an end."

Now, may one properly assume from that that by election day there will be no Americans, land, sea, or air, no residual force, fighting in support of Laotians, Cambodians, or South Vietnamese?

The President. Mr. Rather, that depends on one circumstance, which is very much in my mind, and in the minds I know of all our listeners and viewers. That is the situation with regard to our POW's. First, as far as American involvement is concerned, we are still pursuing the negotiating track. There is a possibility, I know many believe there is no possibility, but I believe there is some, and we are continuing to pursue it with the meeting resuming next week, of ending the war through negotiation. We have offered, as you know, a cease-fire throughout Indochina, including Laos and Cambodia. We have offered a total withdrawal of all outside forces. We would offer an exchange of POW's, and under these circumstances, we believe that this is a time that those offers should seriously be considered.

In the event that no progress is made on the negotiating front, then we will have to continue on what we call the Vietnamization front. Now it is quite obvious, if you look at the numbers, if we are down to 139,000 by the first of February, if I make another announcement of approximately the same level or at an even somewhat higher level for a period in the future, that the number of Americans in Vietnam will be down to a very low level, well before the election.

Now the question arises then, can the President of the United States, sitting in this office, with the responsibility for 400 POW's and 1,500 missing in action throughout Southeast Asia, because they are also potential POW's, can he withdraw all of our forces as long as the enemy holds one American as a prisoner of war? The answer is no.

So I would have to say that with regard to the statement that I made to Time magazine, our goal is to end the American involvement in Vietnam before the end of this year, and before the election, not just because it is an election, but because these are the ways our plans are working out—our preference is to end it by negotiation. If that does not work we will do it by withdrawal through Vietnamization, but if POW's are still retained by North Vietnam, in order to have any bargaining position at all with the Vietnamese, North Vietnamese, we will have to continue to retain a residual force in Vietnam, and we will have to continue the possibility of air strikes on the North Vietnamese.

Mr. Rather. If you have to continue both of those, and the likelihood at the moment concerning the negotiating posture of both sides in Paris, is that that is very likely—if you have to maintain a residual force and keep open at least the threat of additional air strikes, then how can you campaign saying you have ended the American involvement?

The President. Well, the important thing is not how I can campaign with regard to the American involvement, but the important thing is whether the American people are convinced that the President of the United States has done everything that he can to bring this desperately difficult war to an end, and that he is doing everything that he can in view of dealing with international outlaws to protect American men and to get back Americans who are held, as are our Americans who are POW's at the present time.

Now, let's look at the situation when we came into office. I remember the first day I sat in this room. I looked at the number of Americans in Vietnam, 539,000. I looked at the casualty rates, averaging as high as 300 a week. I saw that there was no plan to bring any home. There was no negotiating plan on the table at Paris. And what has happened?

Well, we have brought 400,000 home. As we have already indicated the rate of withdrawal will continue throughout the next few months. We have reduced the casualties from 300 a month, last week to one, to an average of less than 10 over the past 3 months. Now, that is too many. One American dying in war any place in the world is too many as far as I am concerned. But that is a considerable achievement.

As far as the POW problem is concerned, that is one that we unfortunately are confronted with. But let me just give this much hope to our POW people. I believe that as the enemy looks at the alternatives that they may decide as they see the American involvement ending, that it would be well for them not to retain our POW's and run the risk that it would be necessary for the United States to stay in Vietnam.

I know sometimes you and some of your colleagues have pointed out, and with very good reason, that if when we had 540,000 in Vietnam that had no effect in getting the enemy to negotiate on POW's, why would having 25 or 35 thousand as a residual force have any effect. And the answer is: Does the enemy want the United States to withdraw from Vietnam, or doesn't it?

PRISON-OF-WAR NEGOTIATIONS

Mr. Rather. Mr. President, speaking of POW families, a lady from Florida called in this afternoon and asked that I ask you this question. She is Mrs. Gerald Gartley, from Florida, who is the mother of a 27-year-old Navy lieutenant who is a prisoner. Her question, which I take this opportunity to ask on her behalf is, have we ever asked the North Vietnamese and the Provisional Revolutionary Government if they will release the POW's and guarantee the safety of our withdrawing troops if we set a date for withdrawal of all U.S. forces from South Vietnam? Have we ever asked them that?

The President. Mr. Rather, that particular matter has been one that has been under discussion at various times in the Paris peace talks, but you yourself recall, because you reported it, or at least your Paris correspondent reported it on CBS, and I think even NBC and ABC had this as well, that when that was floated out this fall, the North Vietnamese totally rejected it.

In other words, that is the deal of saying that if we set a deadline, then they will give us back our POW's—

Mr. Rather. Excuse me, that was publicly done, Mr. President?

The President. That was publicly done, that is correct. You remember the United States senator had met, he said, with some of the people from North Vietnam. He was convinced that in the event that we set a deadline that that would mean that they would release the prisoners. The North Vietnamese said deadline for prisoners was no deal. That was publicly stated.

Under those circumstances, this, of course, is a very cruel action on their part, to reject out of hand even the possibility of that kind of discussion.

I would say this, looking to the future, that as I have just pointed out, that when we come down to the end, as far as our own involvement in Vietnam is concerned, the question of whether or not they will return our prisoners in exchange for a total American withdrawal is one that they will have a chance to answer, and I could also point out that we have participated in a great number of discussions other than those public discussions in Paris.

Sitting right here in this room—as a matter of fact, you are sitting in my chair, Mr. Gromyko[1] was sitting in this chair—I raised the subject of POW's with him. Dr. Kissinger raised the subject with Chou En-lai[2] on both of his visits to the People's Republic of China.

Mr. Rather. Excuse me, Mr. President. Did we do that before—

The President. In the event that at the time of the meetings that I will have in China and later on in the Soviet Union, we have not made progress in this area, the subjects will again be raised.

Now, I am not suggesting—because, believe me, it is a heartrending matter to read the letters from the POW wives and their next of kin in other ways, to read those letters and to realize how their hopes have been dashed year after year. But I can tell you that we have pursued every negotiating channel; that we have made a number of offers in various channels and that when the record, total record is published, and it will be published in due time, at an appropriate time, our lady from Florida and the others will realize that we have gone the extra mile as far as POW's are concerned. I do not want to disclose any further details because negotiations are under way. . . .

TIMING OF THE PRESIDENT'S ACTIONS

Mr. Rather. Mr. President, you have raised the subject of China, and I am sure it comes as no surprise to you that I would like to talk with you about that. Everyone is interested. You have also mentioned that you hope to reach your goals in the war this year, 1972; that everything seems to have been pointed in the direction of climaxing in this election year: besides your ultimate goals in the war, victory over inflation, driving down unemployment, agreement for the strategic arms limitations, trips to Peking and Moscow.

Is all of this coincidental, the timing, or is it, as some of even your friends say, some of the timing must be politically motivated?

The President. Well, that is a very legitimate question, and I understand why many would feel that it was politically motivated. After all, when you look at the bombing halt of 1968, I know many on our side felt that that was politically motivated, at least the timing of it. I, of course, never made such a charge, and would not, and I don't think you would, because I think President Johnson was interested in doing everything that he could while he was President, and before the election, to start some negotiations in Paris.

But I realize that anyone who sits in this office is one that is going to be charged with having a political motivation for everything that he does. But just let me point this out: Let me say that if I could have ended the war the day I came into office, in a way that would not have encouraged this kind of aggression in other parts of the world, that would not have resulted in what I would have thought—and I thought then and think now—would have been a disastrous blow to America's foreign policy leadership in the world, believe me, I would have done it.

Anyone who signs, as the President does, letters to the next of kin of men killed in war has, as his constant thought in his mind, the first time he wakes up in the morning and the last time as he goes to sleep at night, when he goes to bed, he has in mind what can he do to bring that war to an end in a way that isn't going to bring on other wars, or in a way that will discourage other wars.

---

[1] Andrei Gromyko was the Soviet Foreign Minister.
[2] Chou En-lai (Zhou Enlai) was Premier of the People's Republic of China.

So as far as the Peking visit and the Moscow visit are concerned, we could have had a Moscow summit when we first came into office. It would have been a failure, just as the Glassboro summit was a failure. When summits are not well planned, when they have for their purpose just cosmetics, they raise great hopes and then there is a great thud when they fall down.

In the case of the Soviet summit, both the Soviet leaders and I—and I have been in direct correspondence, as you know, with Mr. Brezhnev on this for some time, as well as discussions with Gromyko and Dobrynin[3]—were convinced that until we had items for an agenda which would lead to possible substantive agreements, we should not have a summit.

What broke the back as far as having the Moscow summit was concerned, and what brought this timing, was the Berlin agreement. That historic agreement indicated that the United States and the Soviet Union, agreeing on that critical area, might find a possibility of agreeing on other problems, where our interests might run in conflict—possibly the Mideast, possibly arms limitation, certainly trade and other areas. That is why the Moscow summit is timed at this point.

Now, the Chinese summit is one that I, as you may recall, wrote about in 1967. You may not recall it, because in 1967 there weren't many who thought I would be sitting here now, and certainly I wasn't sure.

Mr. Rather. Frankly, I didn't think that you would be.

Mr. President. And that makes you not a bad prophet, either. But looking at the situation in 1967, I wrote an article for Foreign Affairs. As you know, I traveled very extensively while I was out of office, and much more freely than I can travel now. But in that article, I raised the lid on what many think was the biggest surprise in history when I made the 90-second-announcement that we were going to go to China.

I said then that the United States, looking to the future, had to find a way to open communications with the leaders of 750 million people who lived in Mainland China, and so the long process began. If we could have had it in 1969 or 1970, if it could have been properly prepared, we would have done so; but I can assure you it wasn't delayed because I was thinking, "Well, if I could just have it before the New Hampshire primary, in the year 1972, what a coup."

And the other side of that is, you see, it takes two to work out this neat little conspiracy that someone set up. Does anybody suggest the Soviet Union is interested in my reelection; that the Chinese would set their summit so that I could do well at that time of year?

Mr. Rather. Well, I don't know—

The President. The answer, of course, is that I would doubt if that were the case. I don't mean that they would be against my reelection; but I am simply suggesting that those of us who make decisions in offices like this, certainly we think politically. We have that responsibility. We are leaders of our party; we are leaders of our country. But the country comes first.

I can assure you ending the war in Vietnam, building a lasting peace through opening to China, limiting tensions between the United States and the Soviet Union—those decisions have no political connotations whatever. If we could have done it earlier, we would have done it. And if this is not the right time to do it, we would have postponed it.

SUMMITRY

Mr. Rather. Well, that raises the question, Mr. President, that has always bothered me about summitry and I know from your writings before you became President, just before you came to this office, about the danger of summitry. Doesn't it give the Communists in both capitals, Peking and Moscow, a bargaining advantage to bargain with you at the summit in the middle of an American election year? Wouldn't it have been better to say we either have the summits in both cases before our election year starts or postpone them a few months until after the election so as not to give the Communists this bargaining advantage?

The President. Well, first, peace is too important to postpone, and I will elaborate on that for just a moment if I can, after I cover the second part of the question. The second part of the question deals with the whole problem of summitry and whether or not it is a good idea. You raised that point and I think I should respond to it. Summits which are held for the sake of having summits are a very bad idea, but when you are dealing with governments which have basically one-man rule—and that is true of the Soviet Union, it is true of the People's Republic of China—then for the major decisions summitry sometimes becomes a necessity. I became convinced that with regard to China and with regard to the Soviet Union that it would serve our interests and their interests in avoiding those confrontations that might lead to war, in building a world of peace, to meet, and the timing was such that it had to be now. To postpone it might have meant that something could have occurred in between so it would not be held at all. And as I have already pointed out, we could not arrange to have it earlier.

Now, second, with regard to the bargaining position, let me make one thing—It seems to me in that connection is very possibly a misunderstanding. Let me get the misunderstanding out of the way. When I go to meet with the leaders of the People's Republic of China, with Mr. Chou En-lai, Mr. Mao Tse-tung, and later on with Mr. Brezhnev and Mr. Kosygin,[4] I can assure you that there is not going to be any bargaining advantage due to my desire to affect our election

---

[3] Anatoly Dobrynin was the Soviet Ambassador to the United States.

[4] Alexey Kosygin was Premier of the Soviet Union.

campaign. And I say that not to be sanctimonious, not to be pious, but because I know what is riding. What is riding here is the future for generations to come, and the wrong kind of an agreement with the Soviet Union, one, for example, in the arms control field that would give them an advantage and make us the second strongest nation in the world, the wrong kind of an agreement with the Chinese, one that would discourage our friends in non-Communist Asia, that kind of an agreement, and so forth, would be one that simply would not be worth making.

Let me say, any President — it would not be just me, any President — would not want to win an election at that cost, and I certainly will not. I am going into these meetings, I can assure you, well prepared, and I will go well prepared and I will go there to defend the interest of the United States, to negotiate as well as I can, to reduce the differences, recognizing that there are basic philosophical differences between us and the two Communist powers. But unless we talk about those differences eventually we may end up fighting about them, and that will be the end of civilization as we know it. . . .

THE ECONOMY

Mr. Rather. Mr. President, a couple of questions on the economy, if I may. It occurs to me that your until recently Chairman of the Council of Economic Advisers, Dr. Paul McCracken, said a few days ago that government controls on the economy would be "necessary long past this year," I believe was his phrase. Is that true?

The President. Well, Chairman McCracken is reflecting the view that in some areas controls may be necessary. I would put it another way, without disagreeing with Chairman McCracken. We will keep controls on only as long as we need them, and we are going to decontrol just as fast as we can, as the inflation psychology runs its course.

I do not believe in a controlled economy. I believe that we had to have these controls in order to break an inflationary psychology which had been fueled by war, and which apparently was not going to be broken unless we took the very hard action that we did take. But having taken it, we are now going to see it through. We want to reach our goal, and we believe that we will achieve our goal of keeping inflation at the 2 to 3 percent level for the year 1972, which will be a major achievement. That is half of what it was last year.

Mr. Rather. I gather the answer to the question then is "perhaps." The question was whether controls may be necessary beyond this year.

The President. Perhaps, but I would emphasize very strongly, because I would not want to mislead you and all others who have to comment on this, and then to say that I have changed my mind, "perhaps," except that if the program of controls is successful, as successful as we would hope that it would be, the amount of controls that we have toward the end may be far less than the statement by Chairman McCracken implied.

I see the decontrol coming perhaps at a faster pace, but we will keep them on if they are necessary.

BLACKS IN AMERICA

Mr. Rather. Mr. President, you were quoted in a recent interview as saying, and again I quote, "Black people are different from white people." I don't understand what you mean by that. Exactly what did you mean by that? How are black people different from white people?

The President. Well, the main way to answer that question is to talk to black people, as I do, to black people on my staff, to black people that I have gone to school with. An individual who grows up in America as a black has, whenever he talks frankly with you, the inevitable memory of what has happened to his people through the years. He looks back to the days of slavery. He looks back to the days of prejudice. He knows that some of that prejudice is still there. He realizes therefore that when he is in school, when he is looking for a job, whatever the case might be, that he is different, he is different from the white person, and for that reason he therefore has problems that the white person does not have. And I think unless we recognize that fact, we are not going to do the right kind of job that we should in handling black-white relations.

AMNESTY FOR DRAFT EVADERS

Mr. Rather. Mr. President, recently you were asked a question about amnesty. You were asked if you foresaw any possibility of granting amnesty to those young men who have fled the country to avoid the draft, and you had a one-word answer, which was "No."

Since then some Congressmen, among others, have proposed allowing those young men who want to come back, who are willing to do it, to come back without punishment, if they will take alternative service, 2 years, 4 years. Is there no amount of alternative service under which you could foresee granting amnesty?

The President. No. The question that I was answering in that conference that you referred to, as you recall, followed one where I had talked about the withdrawal of our forces, and the question was prefaced with that, as I recall.

Mr. Rather. Correct. It was.

The President. In view of the withdrawal of forces, how about amnesty? And I said, "No." The answer is at this time "No." As long as there are Americans who chose to serve their country rather than desert their country — and it is a hard choice — are there in Vietnam, there will be no amnesty for those who deserted their country. As long as there are any POW's held by the North Vietnamese, there will be no amnesty for those who have deserted their country.

Just let me say, Mr. Rather, on that score, I don't say this because I am hardhearted. I say it because it is the only right thing to do. Two and a half million young Americans had to make the choice when they went to serve in Vietnam. Most of them, I am sure, did not want to go. It is not a very pleasant place. I have been there a number of times; nice people, but it is not a pleasant place for an American to serve, and particularly in uniform.

I imagine most of those young Americans when they went out there did so with some reluctance, but they chose to serve. Of those that chose to serve, thousands of them died for their choice, and until this war is over, and until we get the POW's back, those who chose to desert their country, a few hundred, they can live with their choice. That is my attitude.

Mr. Rather. But, at some future time, the door might be opened?

The President. We always, Mr. Rather, under our system, provide amnesty. You remember Abraham Lincoln in the last days of the Civil War, as a matter of fact just before his death, decided to give amnesty to anyone who had deserted if he would come back and rejoin his unit and serve out his period of time. Amnesty, of course, is always in the prerogative of the Chief Executive. I, for one, would be very liberal with regard to amnesty, but not while there are Americans in Vietnam fighting to serve their country and defend their country, and not while POW's are held by North Vietnam. After that we will consider it, but it would have to be on a basis of their paying the price, of course, that anyone should pay for violating the law.

Questions

1. What did Nixon and Rather spend the majority of the interview discussing?
2. How did Nixon connect the Vietnam War, relations with the Soviet Union, and diplomacy with China?

29-2 Vietnamization and the Nixon Doctrine (1969)

Richard Nixon

Addressing Americans on November 3, 1969, President Richard Nixon (1913–1994) made the case for his administration's policy in Vietnam (Vietnamization) and, more broadly, Asia (the Nixon Doctrine). (See text pp. 898–901.)

Source: Department of State Bulletin, November 24, 1969.

Let me briefly explain what has been described as the Nixon doctrine—a policy which not only will help end the war in Viet-Nam but which is an essential element of our program to prevent future Viet-Nams.

We Americans are a do-it-yourself people. We are an impatient people. Instead of teaching someone else to do a job, we like to do it ourselves. And this trait has been carried over into our foreign policy.

In Korea and again in Viet-Nam, the United States furnished most of the money, most of the arms, and most of the men to help the people of those countries defend their freedom against Communist aggression.

Before any American troops were committed to Viet-Nam, a leader of another Asian country expressed this opinion to me when I was traveling in Asia as a private citizen. He said: "When you are trying to assist another nation defend its freedom, U.S. policy should be to help them fight the war, but not to fight the war for them."

Well, in accordance with this wise counsel, I laid down in Guam three principles as guidelines for future American policy toward Asia:

—First, the United States will keep all of its treaty commitments.

—Second, we shall provide a shield if a nuclear power threatens the freedom of a nation allied with us or of a nation whose survival we consider vital to our security.

—Third, in cases involving other types of aggression, we shall furnish military and economic assistance when requested in accordance with our treaty commitments. But we shall look to the nation directly threatened to assume the primary responsibility of providing the manpower for its defense. . . .

The defense of freedom is everybody's business—not just America's business. And it is particularly the responsibility of the people whose freedom is threatened. In the previous administration we Americanized the war in Viet-Nam. In this administration we are Vietnamizing the search for peace.

The policy of the previous administration not only resulted in our assuming the primary responsibility for fighting the war but, even more significantly did not adequately stress the goal of strengthening the South Vietnamese so that they could defend themselves when we left.

The Vietnamization plan was launched following Secretary [of Defense Melvin R.] Laird's visit to Viet-Nam in March. Under the plan, I ordered first a substantial increase in the training and equipment of South Vietnamese forces.

In July, on my visit to Viet-Nam, I changed General Abrams' orders so that they were consistent with the objectives of our new policies. Under the new orders, the primary mission of our troops is to enable the South Vietnamese forces to assume the full responsibility for the security of South Viet-Nam. . . .

We have adopted a plan which we have worked out in cooperation with the South Vietnamese for the complete withdrawal of all U.S. combat ground forces and their replacement by South Vietnamese forces on an orderly scheduled timetable. This withdrawal will be made from strength and not from weakness. As South Vietnamese forces become stronger, the rate of American withdrawal can become greater. . . .

If the level of infiltration or our casualties increase while we are trying to scale down the fighting, it will be the result of a conscious decision by the enemy.

Hanoi could make no greater mistake than to assume that an increase in violence will be to its advantage. If I conclude that increased enemy action jeopardizes our remaining forces in Viet-Nam, I shall not hesitate to take strong and effective measures to deal with that situation.

This is not a threat. This is a statement of policy which as Commander in Chief of our Armed Forces I am making in meeting my responsibility for the protection of American fighting men wherever they may be.

My fellow Americans, I am sure you can recognize from what I have said that we really only have two choices open to us if we want to end this war:

—I can order an immediate, precipitate withdrawal of all Americans from Viet-Nam without regard to the effects of that action.

—Or we can persist in our search for a just peace, through a negotiated settlement if possible or through continued implementation of our plan for Vietnamization if necessary—a plan in which we will withdraw all of our forces from Viet-Nam on a schedule in accordance with our program, as the South Vietnamese become strong enough to defend their own freedom.

I have chosen this second course. It is not the easy way. It is the right way. It is a plan which will end the war and serve the cause of peace, not just in Viet-Nam but in the Pacific and in the world.

In speaking of the consequences of a precipitate withdrawal, I mentioned that our allies would lose confidence in America.

Far more dangerous, we would lose confidence in ourselves. Oh, the immediate reaction would be a sense of relief that our men were coming home. But as we saw the consequences of what we had done, inevitable remorse and divisive recrimination would scar our spirit as a people. . . .

If [the plan for peace] does succeed, what the critics say now won't matter. If it does not succeed, anything I say then won't matter.

I know it may not be fashionable to speak of patriotism or national destiny these days. But I feel it is appropriate to do so on this occasion.

Two hundred years ago this nation was weak and poor. But even then, America was the hope of millions in the world. Today we have become the strongest and richest nation in the world. The wheel of destiny has turned so that any hope the world has for the survival of peace and freedom will be determined by whether the American people have the moral stamina and the courage to meet the challenge of free-world leadership.

Let historians not record that when America was the most powerful nation in the world we passed on the other side of the road and allowed the last hopes for peace and freedom of millions of people to be suffocated by the forces of totalitarianism.

And so tonight—to you, the great silent majority of my fellow Americans—I ask for your support.

I pledged in my campaign for the Presidency to end the war in a way that we could win the peace. I have initiated a plan of action which will enable me to keep that pledge.

The more support I can have from the American people, the sooner that pledge can be redeemed; for the more divided we are at home, the less likely the enemy is to negotiate at Paris.

Let us be united for peace. Let us also be united against defeat. Because let us understand: North Viet-Nam cannot defeat or humiliate the United States. Only Americans can do that.

Questions

1. How did Nixon generalize his Vietnamization policy into the "Nixon doctrine"?
2. According to Nixon, how did his Vietnamization policy differ from the policy followed by President Johnson?
3. What arguments did Nixon use to persuade Americans to support Vietnamization?

29-3 The Invasion of Cambodia (1970)

Richard Nixon

On April 30, 1970, American and South Vietnamese forces invaded Cambodia. That very day, President Nixon justified the "incursion" to a nation divided over the war and antiwar dissent (see text pp. 898–899).

Source: Department of State Bulletin, May 18, 1970.

Ten days ago, in my report to the Nation on Viet-Nam, I announced a decision to withdraw an additional 150,000 Americans from Viet-Nam over the next year. I said then that I was making that decision despite our concern over increased enemy activity in Laos, in Cambodia, and in South Viet-Nam.

At that time, I warned that if I concluded that increased enemy activity in any of these areas endangered the lives of Americans remaining in Viet-Nam, I would not hesitate to take strong and effective measures to deal with that situation.

Despite that warning, North Viet-Nam has increased its military aggression in all these areas, and particularly in Cambodia.

After full consultation with the National Security Council . . . and my other advisers, I have concluded that the actions of the enemy in the last 10 days clearly endanger the lives of Americans who are in Viet-Nam now and would constitute an unacceptable risk to those who will be there after withdrawal of another 150,000.

To protect our men who are in Viet-Nam and to guarantee the continued success of our withdrawal and Vietnamization programs, I have concluded that the time has come for action. . . .

For the past 5 years . . . North Viet-Nam has occupied military sanctuaries all along the Cambodian frontier with South Viet-Nam. Some of these extend up to 20 miles into Cambodia. The sanctuaries . . . are on both sides of the border. They are used for hit-and-run attacks on American and South Vietnamese forces in South Viet-Nam.

These Communist-occupied territories contain major base camps, training sites, logistics facilities, weapons and ammunition factories, airstrips, and prisoner of war compounds. . . .

Tonight American and South Vietnamese units will attack the headquarters for the entire Communist military operation in South Viet-Nam. This key control center has been occupied by the North Vietnamese and Viet Cong for 5 years in blatant violation of Cambodia's neutrality.

This is not an invasion of Cambodia. The areas in which these attacks will be launched are completely occupied and controlled by North Vietnamese forces. Our purpose is not to occupy the areas. Once enemy forces are driven out of these sanctuaries and once their military supplies are destroyed, we will withdraw.

These actions are in no way directed at the security interests of any nation. Any government that chooses to use these actions as a pretext for harming relations with the United States will be doing so on its own responsibility and on its own initiative, and we will draw the appropriate conclusions.

Now, let me give you the reasons for my decision.

A majority of the American people, a majority of you listening to me, are for the withdrawal of our forces from Viet-Nam. The action I have taken tonight is indispensible for the continuing success of that withdrawal program.

A majority of the American people want to end this war rather than to have it drag on interminably. The action I have taken tonight will serve that purpose.

A majority of the American people want to keep the casualties of our brave men in Viet-Nam at an absolute minimum. The action I take tonight is essential if we are to accomplish that goal.

We take this action not for the purpose of expanding the war into Cambodia, but for the purpose of ending the war in Viet-Nam and winning the just peace we all desire. We have made and we will continue to make every possible effort to end this war through negotiation at the conference table rather than through more fighting on the battlefield. . . .

My fellow Americans, we live in an age of anarchy, both abroad and at home. We see mindless attacks on all the great institutions which have been created by free civilizations in the last 500 years. Even here in the United States, great universities are being systematically destroyed. Small nations all over the world find themselves under attack from within and from without.

If, when the chips are down, the world's most powerful nation, the United States of America, acts like a pitiful, helpless giant, the forces of totalitarianism and anarchy will threaten free nations and free institutions throughout the world.

It is not our power but our will and character that is being tested tonight. The question all Americans must ask and answer tonight is this: Does the richest and strongest nation in the history of the world have the character to meet a direct challenge by a group which rejects every effort to win a just peace, ignores our warning, tramples on solemn agreements, violates the neutrality of an unarmed people, and uses our prisoners as hostages?

If we fail to meet this challenge, all other nations will be on notice that despite its overwhelming power the United States, when a real crisis comes, will be found wanting.

During my campaign for the Presidency, I pledged to bring Americans home from Viet-Nam. They are coming home.

I promised to end this war. I shall keep that promise.
I promised to win a just peace. I shall keep that promise.
We shall avoid a wider war. But we are also determined to put an end to this war.

Questions

1. How did Nixon seek to persuade Americans that the attack was not "an invasion of Cambodia"?
2. How did he try to persuade his listeners that he was avoiding a "wider war"?
3. What did Nixon mean by his reference to "the forces of totalitarianism and anarchy"?

29-4 Watergate: Taped White House Conversations (1972)

Watergate, a "third-rate burglary attempt" that became a national crisis, ultimately forced Richard Nixon to resign the presidency to avoid certain impeachment and conviction (and possible criminal charges). It also resulted in criminal convictions of several of the president's advisors and in the enactment of a number of reforms (see text pp. 901–902).

Secretly taped White House conversations between President Nixon and various associates proved to be central to the exposure of Watergate. Two important conversations are excerpted here—the first involving H. R. Haldeman, the president's chief of staff, the second John Dean, White House counsel. Among those referred to but not fully identified in the following passages were John Mitchell, a former attorney general who headed the Committee to Re-Elect the President; Maurice Stans, finance chair of the committee; John Ehrlichman, domestic affairs assistant to the president; and E. Howard Hunt and G. Gordon Liddy, former operatives of the Central Intelligence Agency, who were security consultants to the Nixon White House.

Source: White House transcripts of conversations between H. R. Haldeman and Richard Nixon in the Oval Office of the President, June 23, 1972; and between John Dean and Richard Nixon, September 15, 1972. U.S. Congress, House, *Hearings before the Committee on the Judiciary*, 93rd Cong., 2nd sess., 1974.

JUNE 23, 1972

Haldeman. Now, on the investigation, you know the Democratic break-in thing, we're back in the problem area because the FBI is not under control, because [Director Patrick] Gray doesn't exactly know how to control it and they have—their investigation is now leading into some productive areas.... They've been able to trace the money—not through the money itself—but through the bank sources—the banker. And it goes in some directions we don't want it to go. Ah, also there have been some [other] things—like an informant came in off the street to the FBI in Miami who was a photographer or has a friend who is a photographer who developed some films through this guy [Bernard] Barker and the films had pictures of Democratic National Committee letterhead documents and things. So it's things like that that are filtering in.... [John] Mitchell came up with yesterday, and John Dean analyzed very carefully last night and concludes, concurs now with Mitchell's recommendation that the only way to solve this ... is for us to have [CIA Assistant Director Vernon] Walters call Pat Gray and just say, "Stay to hell out of this—this is ah, [our] business here. We don't want you to go any further on it." That's not an unusual development, and ah, that would take care of it.

President. What about Pat Gray—you mean Pat Gray doesn't want to?

Haldeman. Pat does want to. He doesn't know how to, and he doesn't have any basis for doing it. Given this, he will then have the basis. He'll call [FBI Assistant Director] Mark Felt[1] in, and the two of them—and Mark Felt wants to cooperate because he's ambitious—

President. Yeah.

Haldeman. He'll call him in and say, "We've got the signal from across the river to put the hold on this." And that will fit rather well because the FBI agents who are working the case, at this point, feel that's what it is.

President. This is CIA? They've traced the money? Who'd they trace it to? . . .

Haldeman. Ken Dahlberg.

President. Who the hell is Ken Dahlberg?

Haldeman. He gave $25,000 in Minnesota and, ah, the check went directly to this guy Barker.

President. It isn't from the Committee though, from [Maurice] Stans?

Haldeman. Yeah. It is. It's directly traceable and there's some more through some Texas people that went to the Mexican bank which can also be traced to the Mexican bank—they'll get their names today.

President. Well, I mean, there's no way—I'm just thinking if they don't cooperate, what do they say? That they were approached by the Cubans? That's what Dahlberg has to say, the Texans too.

Haldeman. Well, if they will. But then we're relying on more and more people all the time. That's the problem and they'll [the FBI] . . . stop if we could take this other route.

President. All right.

Haldeman. [Mitchell and Dean] say the only way to do that is from White House instructions. And it's got to be to [CIA Director Richard] Helms and to—ah, what's his name? . . . Walters. . . . And the proposal would be that . . . [John] Ehrlichman and I call them in, and say, ah—

President. All right, fine. How do you call him in—I mean you just—well, we protected Helms from one hell of a lot of things.

Haldeman. That's what Ehrlichman says.

President. Of course; this [Howard] Hunt [business.] That will uncover a lot of things. You open that scab there's a hell of a lot of things and we just feel that it would be very detrimental to have this thing go any further. This involves these Cubans, Hunt, and a lot of hanky-panky that we have nothing to do with ourselves. Well, what the hell, did Mitchell know about this?

Haldeman. I think so. I don't think he knew the details, but I think he knew.

President. He didn't know how it was going to be handled though—with Dahlberg and the Texans and so forth? Well who was the asshole that did? Is it [G. Gordon] Liddy? Is that the fellow? He must be a little nuts!

Haldeman. He is.

President. I mean he just isn't well screwed on, is he? Is that the problem?

Haldeman. No, but he was under pressure, apparently, to get more information, and as he got more pressure, he pushed the people harder.

President. Pressure from Mitchell?

Haldeman. Apparently. . . .

President. All right, fine, I understand it all. We won't second-guess Mitchell and the rest. Thank God it wasn't [special White House counsel Charles] Colson.

Haldeman. The FBI interviewed Colson yesterday. They determined that would be a good thing to do. To have him take an interrogation, which he did, and the FBI guys working the case concluded that there were one or two possibilities—one, that this was a White House (they don't think that there is anything at the Election Committee) they think it was either a White House operation and they had some obscure reasons for it—non-political, or it was a—Cuban [operation] and [involved] the CIA. And after the interrogation of Colson yesterday, they concluded it was not the White House, but are now convinced it is a CIA thing, so the CIA turnoff would—

President. Well, not sure of their analysis, I'm not going to get that involved. I'm (unintelligible).

Haldeman. No, sir, we don't want you to.

President. You call them in.

Haldeman. Good deal.

President. Play it tough. That's the way they play it and that's the way we are going to play it. . . .

President. O.K. . . . Just say (unintelligible) very bad to have this fellow Hunt, ah, he knows too damned much. . . . If it gets out that this is all involved, the Cuba thing, it would be a fiasco. It would make the CIA look bad, it's going to make Hunt look bad, and it is likely to blow the whole Bay of Pigs thing which we think would be very unfortunate—both for CIA, and for the country, at this time, and for American foreign policy. Just tell him to lay off. Don't you [think] so?

Haldeman. Yep. That's the basis to do it on. Just leave it at that. . . .

SEPTEMBER 15, 1972

President. We are all in it together. This is a war. We take a few shots and it will be over. We will give them a few shots and it will be over. Don't worry. I wouldn't want to be on the other side right now. Would you?

Dean. Along that line, one of the things I've tried to do, I have begun to keep notes on a lot of people who are emerging as less than our friends because this will be over some day and we shouldn't forget the way some of them have treated us.

President. I want the most comprehensive notes on all those who tried to do us in. They didn't have to do it. If we had had a very close election and they were playing the other side I would understand this. No—they were doing this quite deliberately and they are asking for it and they

---

[1] W. Mark Felt was the secret source know as "Deep Throat" who guided the *Washington Post's* breaking coverage of the Watergate Scandal.

are going to get it. We have not used the power in this first four years, as you know. . . . We have not used the Bureau, and we have not used the Justice Department, but things are going to change now. And they are either going to do it right or go.

Dean. What an exciting prospect.

President. Thanks. It has to be done. We have been (adjective deleted) fools for us to come into this election campaign, and not do anything with regard to the Democratic Senators who are running, et cetera. And who the hell are they after? They are after us. It is absolutely ridiculous. It is not going to be that way any more.

Questions

1. According to these transcripts, how much did President Nixon know about the financial and security operations of his reelection campaign?
2. According to the transcripts, what did Nixon know on June 23, 1972, about the Watergate break-in and related matters? What evidence do the transcripts provide that Nixon ordered the CIA and the FBI to participate in the cover-up?
3. Do the transcripts reveal other matters that Nixon might not have wished to have made public or that might have affected public respect for government?

Questions for Further Thought

1. Compare and contrast President Richard Nixon's rationale for continuing American involvement in Vietnam (Document 29-2) with President Lyndon B. Johnson's rationale (Document 28-8).
2. Based on your reading of the text and the documents in this and the preceding chapters, explain why the Vietnam War is often credited with creating for many Americans a deep disillusionment with and distrust of their government.
3. What was the Watergate scandal fundamentally about?

Battling for Civil Rights: The Second Stage

Reform often triggers reaction: just as the civil rights movement of the 1950s and 1960s generated opposition even as it mobilized support, so did social movements of the 1960s and 1970s. Diverse groups contested a broad range of issues during the period—and beyond. Controversies raged within communities and in political arenas from local to national. The courts, legislative bodies, executive departments and agencies, and the electorate (in referenda)—all were involved. The environmental and consumer movements met with significant successes, including federal laws enacted during the Nixon administration. Race-related issues, especially affirmative action and school busing, were fought out in the courts and, in the case of busing, in communities, most bitterly in Boston. The gay liberation movement and its foes fought over local measures, attacking discrimination on the basis of sexual orientation. Among the most public debates were those between feminists and antifeminists over the proposed Equal Rights Amendment (ERA) to the U.S. Constitution and over abortion rights, especially after the 7–2 decision of the Supreme Court in *Roe v. Wade* (1973), which declared that the constitutionally guaranteed right to privacy "is broad enough to encompass a woman's decision whether or not to terminate her pregnancy" (see text p. 910).

Document 29-5 provides Gloria Steinem's testimony in support of the ERA; Document 29-6 is an excerpt from Phyllis Schlafly's antifeminist *The Power of the Positive Woman.*

29-5 Statement in Support of the Equal Rights Amendment (1970)

Gloria Steinem

Gloria Steinem (b. 1934), a graduate of Smith College, became a journalist, gaining a measure of fame for an exposé based on her experiences as an undercover reporter posing as a Playboy Bunny. She edited *Ms.*, the most successful mass-circulation feminist publication (see text pp. 902–906, 908–909), which made her a major figure in the feminist movement. Even before this, however, she was prominent enough to testify before a Senate subcommittee on behalf of the ERA. Mentioned in her essay are Friedrich Engels (1820–1895), a German socialist and a collaborator of Karl Marx, and Gunnar Myrdal (1898–1987), the Swedish author of the classic *An American Dilemma: The Negro Problem and American Democracy* (1944). Myrdal was also the cowinner of the Nobel Prize for economics in 1974.

Source: The "Equal Rights" Amendment: Hearings before the Subcommittee on Constitutional Amendments of the Committee on the Judiciary, United States Senate, Ninety-First Congress, Second Session, on S. J. Res. 61, To Amend the Constitution so as to Provide Equal Rights for Men and Women, May 5, 6, and 7, 1970 (Washington, DC: U.S. Government Printing Office, 1970), 331–335 (May 6, 1970).

During 12 years of working for a living, I have experienced much of the legal and social discrimination reserved for women in this country. I have been refused service in public restaurants, ordered out of public gathering places, and turned away from apartment rentals; all for the clearly-stated, sole reason that I am a woman. And all without the legal remedies available to blacks and other minorities. I have been excluded from professional groups, writing assignments on so-called "unfeminine" subjects such as politics, full participation in the Democratic Party, jury duty, and even from such small male privileges as discounts on airline fares. Most important to me, I have been denied a society in which women are encouraged, or even allowed to think of themselves as first-class citizens and responsible human beings.

However, after 2 years of researching the status of American women, I have discovered that in reality, I am very, very lucky. Most women, both wage-earners and housewives, routinely suffer more humiliation and injustice than I do.

As a freelance writer, I don't work in the male-dominated hierarchy of an office. (Women, like blacks and other visibly different minorities, do better in individual professions such as the arts, sports, or domestic work; anything in which they don't have authority over white males.) I am not one of the millions of women who must support a family. Therefore, I haven't had to go on welfare because there are no day-care centers for my children while I work, and I haven't had to submit to the humiliating welfare inquiries about my private and sexual life, inquiries from which men are exempt. I haven't had to brave the sex bias of labor unions and employers, only to see my family subsist on a median salary 40 percent less than the male median salary.

I hope this committee will hear the personal, daily injustices suffered by many women—professionals and day laborers, women house-bound by welfare as well as by suburbia. We have all been silent for too long. But we won't be silent anymore.

The truth is that all our problems stem from the same sex based myths. We may appear before you as white radicals or the middle-aged middle class or black soul sisters, but we are all sisters in fighting against these outdated myths. Like racial myths, they have been reflected in our laws. Let me list a few.

That women are biologically inferior to men. In fact, an equally good case can be made for the reverse. Women live longer than men, even when the men are not subject to business pressures. Women survived Nazi concentration camps better, keep cooler heads in emergencies currently studied by disaster-researchers, are protected against heart attacks by their female sex hormones, and are so much more durable at every stage of life that nature must conceive 20 to 50 percent more males in order to keep the balance going.

Man's hunting activities are forever being pointed to as tribal proof of superiority. But while he was hunting, women built houses, tilled the fields, developed animal husbandry, and perfected language. Men, being all alone in the bush, often developed into a creature as strong as women, fleeter of foot, but not very bright.

However, I don't want to prove the superiority of one sex to another. That would only be repeating a male mistake. English scientists once definitively proved, after all, that the English were descended from the angels, while the Irish were descended from the apes; it was the rationale for England's domination of Ireland for more than a century. The point is that science is used to support current myth and economics almost as much as the church was.

What we do know is that the difference between two races or two sexes is much smaller than the differences to be found within each group. Therefore, in spite of the slide show on female inferiorities that I understand was shown to you yesterday, the law makes much more sense when it treats individuals, not groups bundled together by some condition of birth. . . .

Another myth, that women are already treated equally in this society. I am sure there has been ample testimony to prove that equal pay for equal work, equal chance for advancement, and equal training or encouragement is obscenely scarce in every field, even those—like food and fashion industries—that are supposedly "feminine."

A deeper result of social and legal injustice, however, is what sociologists refer to as "Internalized Aggression." Victims of aggression absorb the myth of their own inferiority, and come to believe that their group is in fact second class. Even when they themselves realize they are not second class, they may still think their group is, thus the tendency to be the only Jew in the club, the only black woman on the block, the only woman in the office.

Women suffer this second class treatment from the moment they are born. They are expected to be, rather than achieve, to function biologically rather than learn. A brother, whatever his intellect, is more likely to get the family's encouragement and education money, while girls are often pressured to conceal ambition and intelligence, to "Uncle Tom."

I interviewed a New York public school teacher who told me about a black teenager's desire to be a doctor. With all the barriers in mind, she suggested kindly that he be a veterinarian instead.

The same day, a high school teacher mentioned a girl who wanted to be a doctor. The teacher said, "How about a nurse?"

Teachers, parents, and the Supreme Court may exude a protective, well-meaning rationale, but limiting the individual's ambition is doing no one a favor. Certainly not this country; it needs all the talent it can get.

Another myth, that American women hold great economic power. Fifty-one percent of all shareholders in this country are women. That is a favorite male-chauvinist statistic. However, the number of shares they hold is so small that the total is only 18 percent of all the shares. Even those holdings are often controlled by men.

Similarly, only 5 percent of all the people in the country who receive $10,000 a year or more, earned or otherwise, are women. And that includes the famous rich widows.

The constantly repeated myth of our economic power seems less testimony to our real power than to the resentment of what little power we do have.

Another myth, that children must have full-time mothers. American mothers spend more time with their homes and children than those of any other society we know about. In the past, joint families, servants, a prevalent system in which grandparents raised the children, or family field work in the agrarian systems—all these factors contributed more to child care than the labor-saving devices of which we are so proud.

The truth is that most American children seem to be suffering from too much mother, and too little father. Part of the program of Women's Liberation is a return of fathers to their children. If laws permit women equal work and pay opportunities, men will then be relieved of their role as sole breadwinner. Fewer ulcers, fewer hours of meaningless work, equal responsibility for his own children: these are a few of the reasons that Women's Liberation is Men's Liberation too.

As for psychic health of the children, studies show that the quality of time spent by parents is more important than the quantity. The most damaged children were not those whose mothers worked, but those whose mothers preferred to work but stayed home out of the role-playing desire to be a "good mother."

Another myth, that the women's movement is not political, won't last, or is somehow not "serious."

When black people leave their 19th century roles, they are feared. When women dare to leave theirs, they are ridiculed. We understand this; we accept the burden of ridicule. It won't keep us quiet anymore.

Similarly, it shouldn't deceive male observers into thinking that this is somehow a joke. We are 51 percent of the population; we are essentially united on these issues across boundaries of class or race or age; and we may well end by changing this society more than the civil rights movement. That is an apt parallel. We, too, have our right wing and left wing, our separatists, gradualists, and Uncle Toms. But we are changing our own consciousness, and that of the country. Engels noted the relationship of the authoritarian, nuclear family to capitalism; the father as capitalist, the mother as means of production, and the children as labor. He said the family would change as the economic system did, and that seems to have happened, whether we want to admit it or not. Women's bodies will no longer be owned by the state for the production of workers and soldiers; birth control and abortion are facts of everyday life. The new family is an egalitarian family.

Gunnar Myrdal noted 30 years ago the parallel between women and Negroes in this country. Both suffered from such restricting social myths as: smaller brains, passive natures, inability to govern themselves (and certainly not white men), sex objects only, childlike natures, special skills, and the like. When evaluating a general statement about women, it might be valuable to substitute "black people" for "women"—just to test the prejudice at work.

And it might be valuable to do this constitutionally as well. Neither group is going to be content as a cheap labor pool anymore. And neither is going to be content without full constitutional rights.

Finally, I would like to say one thing about this time in which I am testifying.

I had deep misgivings about discussing this topic when National Guardsmen are occupying our campuses, the country is being turned against itself in a terrible polarization, and America is enlarging an already inhuman and unjustifiable war. But it seems to me that much of the trouble in this country has to do with the "masculine mystique"; with the myth that masculinity somehow depends on the subjugation of other people. It is a bipartisan problem; both our past and current Presidents seem to be victims of this myth, and to behave accordingly.

Women are not more moral than men. We are only uncorrupted by power. But we do not want to imitate men, to join this country as it is, and I think our very participation will change it. Perhaps women elected leaders—and there will be many of them—will not be so likely to dominate black people or yellow people or men; anybody who looks different from us.

After all, we won't have our masculinity to prove.

Questions

1. What comparisons did Steinem make between women and African Americans?
2. What arguments involving the family did Steinem indicate were used by ERA opponents? What was Steinem's response to those arguments?
3. According to Steinem, in what ways are women different from men? Why is this significant?

29-6 *The Power of the Positive Woman* (1977)

Phyllis Schlafly

Phyllis Schlafly (b. 1924) worked her way (at night, in a wartime munitions factory) through Washington University, earned an M.A. at Radcliffe College, married, and raised six children. Involved in the Republican Party for some years, she contributed a polemical book, *A Choice, Not an Echo*, to Barry Goldwater's drive for nomination in 1964. She regained prominence in the 1970s when she founded the National Committee to Stop ERA and played an important part in defeating the amendment (while simultaneously earning her J.D. from Washington University). An excerpt from her antifeminist book of this period follows (see text pp. 905–906).

Source: Excerpt from Phyllis Schlafly, *The Power of the Positive Woman* (New Rochelle, NY: Arlington House, 1977), 16–19. Reprinted by permission of Phyllis Schlafly.

The women's liberationists and their dupes who try to tell each other that the sexual drive of men and women is really the same, and that it is only societal restraints that inhibit women from an equal desire, an equal enjoyment, and an equal freedom from the consequences, are doomed to frustration forever. It just isn't so, and pretending cannot make it so. The differences are not a woman's weakness but her strength. . . .

The new generation can brag all it wants about the new liberation or the new morality, but it is still the woman who is hurt the most. The new morality isn't just a "fad"—it is a cheat and a thief. It robs the woman of her virtue, her youth, her beauty, and her love—for nothing, just nothing. It has produced a generation of young women searching for their identity, bored with sexual freedom, and despondent from the loneliness of living a life without commitment. They have abandoned the old commandments, but they can't find any new rules that work.

The Positive Woman recognizes the fact that, when it comes to sex, women are simply not the equal of men. The sexual drive of men is much stronger than that of women. That is how the human race was designed in order that it might perpetuate itself. The other side of the coin is that it is easier for women to control their sexual appetites. A Positive Woman cannot defeat a man in a wrestling or boxing match, but she can motivate him, inspire him, encourage him, teach him, restrain him, reward him, and have power over him that he can never achieve over her with all his muscle. How or whether a Positive Woman uses her power is determined solely by the way she alone defines her goals and develops her skills.

The differences between men and women are also emotional and psychological. Without woman's innate maternal instinct, the human race would have died out centuries ago. There is nothing so helpless in all earthly life as the newborn infant. It will die within hours if not cared for. Even in the most primitive, uneducated societies, women have always cared for their newborn babies. They didn't need any schooling to teach them how. They didn't need any welfare workers to tell them it is their social obligation. Even in societies to whom such concepts as "ought," "social responsibility," and "compassion for the helpless" were unknown, mothers cared for their new babies.

Why? Because caring for a baby serves the natural maternal need of a woman. Although not nearly so total as the baby's need, the woman's need is nonetheless real.

The overriding psychological need of a woman is to love something alive. A baby fulfills this need in the lives of most women. If a baby is not available to fill that need, women search for a baby-substitute. This is the reason why women have traditionally gone into teaching and nursing careers. They are doing what comes naturally to the female psyche. The schoolchild or the patient of any age provides an outlet for a woman to express her natural maternal need.

This maternal need in women is the reason why mothers whose children have grown up and flown from the nest are sometimes cut loose from their psychological moorings. The maternal need in women can show itself in love for grandchildren, nieces, nephews, or even neighbors' children. The maternal need in some women has even manifested itself in an extraordinary affection lavished on a dog, cat, or a parakeet.

This is not to say that every woman must have a baby in order to be fulfilled. But it is to say that fulfillment for most women involves expressing their natural maternal urge by loving and caring for someone.

The women's liberation movement complains that traditional stereotyped roles assume that women are "passive" and that men are "aggressive." The anomaly is that a woman's most fundamental emotional need is not passive at all, but active. A woman naturally seeks to love affirmatively and to show that love in an active way by caring for the object of her affections.

The Positive Woman finds somebody on whom she can lavish her maternal love so that it doesn't well up inside her and cause psychological frustrations. Surely no woman is so isolated by geography or insulated by spirit that she cannot find someone worthy of her maternal love. All persons, men and women, gain by sharing something of themselves with their fellow humans, but women profit most of all because it is part of their very nature. . . .

Most women's organizations, recognizing the preference of most women to avoid hard-driving competition, handle the matter of succession of officers by the device of a nominating committee. This eliminates the unpleasantness and the tension of a competitive confrontation every year or two. Many women's organizations customarily use a prayer attributed to Mary, Queen of Scots, which is an excellent analysis by a woman of women's faults:

> Keep us, O God, from pettiness; let us be large in thought, in word, in deed. Let us be done with fault-finding and leave off self-seeking. . . . Grant that we may realize it is the little things that create differences, that in the big things of life we are at one. . . .

Finally, women are different from men in dealing with the fundamentals of life itself. Men are philosophers, women are practical and 'twas ever thus. Men may philosophize about how life began and where we are heading; women are concerned about feeding the kids today. No woman would ever, as Karl Marx did, spend years reading political philosophy in the British Museum while her child starved to death. Women don't take naturally to a search for the intangible and the abstract. The Positive Woman knows who she is and where she is going, and she will reach her goal because the longest journey starts with a very practical first step.

Questions

1. Why did Schlafly refer to psychology in three instances?
2. How did Schlafly compare to reformers such as Frances E. Willard (Document 19-4) and Jane Addams (Document 20-4)?
3. Did Schlafly see men and women as true equals? Why or why not?

Questions for Further Thought

1. How do you account for the emergence during the 1960s and 1970s of controversies over issues relating to women?
2. How do Documents 29-5 and 29-6 fit into an overview of these controversies?

Lean Years

The national economy, which had flourished since the war years of the 1940s, began to reveal problems during the late 1960s. These intensified during the following decade, resulting in "stagflation," inflation, and unemployment. Many interacting factors contributed to the worsening economic situation. During the Johnson presidency, escalating expenditures on the war in Vietnam, combined with spending on domestic programs (from the space race to the Great Society), fueled budget deficits. In 1971, the nation experienced its first trade deficit of the century, and international confidence in the dollar waned. President Nixon twice devalued the dollar to spur American exports and imposed temporary wage-price controls. Long accustomed to cheap energy but increasingly dependent on imported petroleum, the United States proved to be vulnerable to an oil embargo (1973–1974) and to price increases imposed by the Organization of the Petroleum Exporting Countries (OPEC). The impact on economic developments was profound: overall economic growth slowed; workers' real income began to decline; "deindustrialization," the downsizing or closing of manufacturing plants and the laying off of workers, affected the nation's industrial heartland (the Northeast and Midwest); and optimism began to give way to pessimism.

At the same time, a new environmental awareness swept the country. In 1970, Earth Day was first celebrated and Richard Nixon established the Environmental Protection Agency. A raft of new environmental laws were passed by Congress, including the National Environmental Policy Act, the Clean Air Act, the Clean Water Act, the Ocean Dumping Act, the Endangered Species Act, the Resource Conservation and Recovery Act, and many more.

Noneconomic issues remained significant during the 1970s and beyond, of course, but the period cannot be understood without reference to America's changed economic fortunes. Document 29-7 provides periodic Gallup poll findings for 1950 to 1999. Document 29-8 is an excerpt from perhaps the single most important book in the literature of the modern environmental movement. Document 29-9 reports on Homestead, Pennsylvania, and its residents during the deindustrialization of the 1970s and 1980s.

29-7 National Problems, 1950–1999

Gallup Polls

Polls reveal respondents' thinking at particular points in time. A series of such polls sheds light on change and continuity in public opinion, albeit not annually in this case. The nationwide Gallup polls reported here asked interviewees, "What do you think is the most important problem facing the country today?"

Source: Gallup polls reported in the *New York Times*, August 1, 1999. Copyright © 1999 by The New York Times Company. Reprinted by permission.

Questions

1. What most strikes you about the 1975 Gallup poll responses? How do you explain the differences between the 1970 and 1975 poll responses?

2. What most strikes you about the 1980 Gallup poll responses? How do you explain the differences between 1975 and 1980?

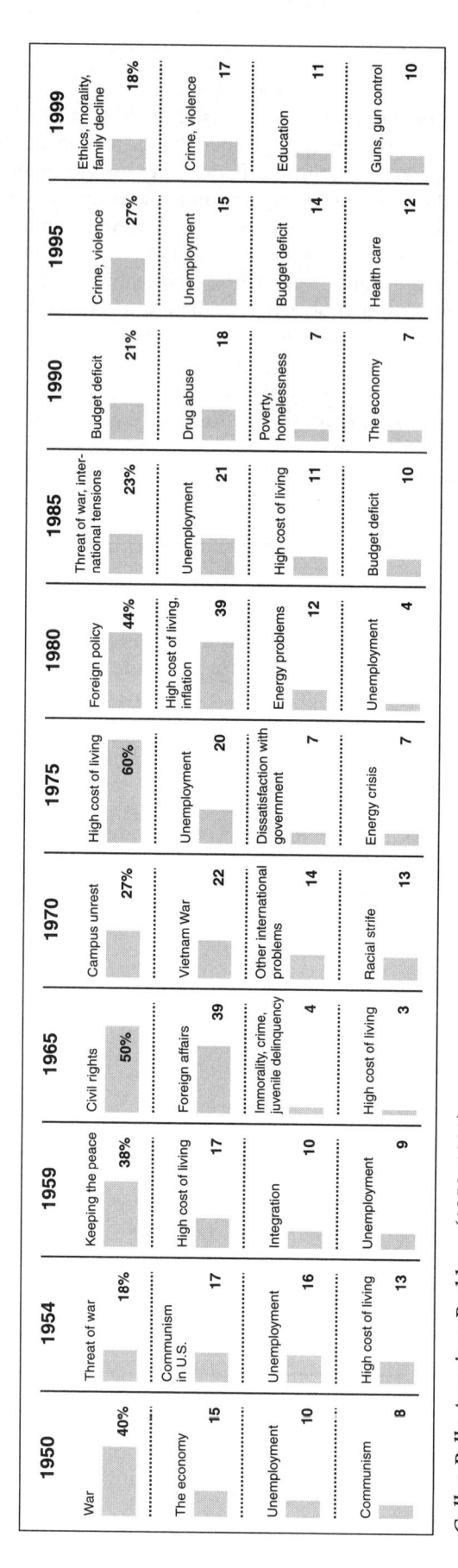

1950	1954	1959	1965	1970	1975	1980	1985	1990	1995	1999
War 40%	Threat of war 18%	Keeping the peace 38%	Civil rights 50%	Campus unrest 27%	High cost of living 60%	Foreign policy 44%	Threat of war, international tensions 23%	Budget deficit 21%	Crime, violence 27%	Ethics, morality, family decline 18%
The economy 15	Communism in U.S. 17	High cost of living 17	Foreign affairs 39	Vietnam War 22	Unemployment 20	High cost of living, inflation 39	Unemployment 21	Drug abuse 18	Unemployment 15	Crime, violence 17
Unemployment 10	Unemployment 16	Integration 10	Immorality, crime, juvenile delinquency 4	Other international problems 14	Dissatisfaction with government 7	Energy problems 12	High cost of living 11	Poverty, homelessness 7	Budget deficit 14	Education 11
Communism 8	High cost of living 13	Unemployment 9	High cost of living 3	Racial strife 13	Energy crisis 7	Unemployment 4	Budget deficit 10	The economy 7	Health care 12	Guns, gun control 10

Gallup Polls, American Problems (1950–1999)

29-8 And No Birds Sing (1962)

Rachel Carson

Like Aldo Leopold in *A Sand County Almanac* (1949), Rachel Carson's groundbreaking book *Silent Spring* effectively combined a scientist's training with a poet's sensibility. The result was a powerful work that quickly became one of the founding documents of the modern environmental movement. Carson challenged the nation's powerful chemical industry by questioning the use of pesticides and herbicides, particularly DDT; she challenged the world by questioning humans' impact on their natural environment.

Source: Excerpt from Rachel Carson, *Silent Spring* (1962; Boston: Houghton Mifflin, 1982), 103–109, 126–127. Copyright © 1962 by Rachel L. Carson and renewed 1990 by Roger Christie. Reprinted by permission of Houghton Mifflin Company. All rights reserved.

Over increasingly large areas of the United States, spring now comes unheralded by the return of the birds, and the early mornings are strangely silent where once they were filled with the beauty of bird song. This sudden silencing of the song of birds, this obliteration of the color and beauty and interest they lend to our world have come about swiftly, insidiously, and unnoticed by those whose communities are as yet unaffected.

From the town of Hinsdale, Illinois, a housewife wrote in despair to one of the world's leading ornithologists, Robert Cushman Murphy, Curator Emeritus of Birds at the American Museum of Natural History.

> Here in our village the elm trees have been sprayed for several years [she wrote in 1958]. When we moved here six years ago, there was a wealth of bird life; I put up a feeder and had a steady stream of cardinals, chickadees, downies and nuthatches all winter, and the cardinals and chickadees brought their young ones in the summer.
>
> After several years of DDT spray, the town is almost devoid of robins and starlings; chickadees have not been on my shelf for two years, and this year the cardinals are gone too; the nesting population in the neighborhood seems to consist of one dove pair and perhaps one catbird family.
>
> It is hard to explain to the children that the birds have been killed off, when they have learned in school that a Federal law protects the birds from killing or capture. "Will they ever come back?" they ask, and I do not have the answer. The elms are still dying, and so are the birds. *Is* anything being done? *Can* anything be done? Can *I* do anything?

A year after the federal government had launched a massive spraying program against the fire ant, an Alabama woman wrote: "Our place has been a veritable bird sanctuary for over half a century. Last July we all remarked, 'There are more birds than ever.' Then, suddenly, in the second week of August, they all disappeared. I was accustomed to rising early to care for my favorite mare that had a young filly. There was not a sound of the song of a bird. It was eerie, terrifying. What was man doing to our perfect and beautiful world? Finally, five months later a blue jay appeared and a wren."

The autumn months to which she referred brought other somber reports from the deep South, where in Mississippi, Louisiana and Alabama the *Field Notes* published quarterly by the National Audubon Society and the United States Fish and Wildlife Service noted the striking phenomenon of "blank spots weirdly empty of virtually *all* bird life." The *Field Notes* are a compilation of the reports of seasoned observers who have spent many years afield in their particular areas and have unparalleled knowledge of the normal bird life of the region. One such observer reported that in driving about southern Mississippi that fall she saw "no land birds at all for long distances." Another in Baton Rouge reported that the contents of her feeders had lain untouched "for weeks on end," while fruiting shrubs in her yard, that ordinarily would be stripped clean by that time, still were laden with berries. Still another reported that his picture window, "which often used to frame a scene splashed with the red of 40 or 50 cardinals and crowded with other species, seldom permitted a view of as many as a bird or two at a time." Professor Maurice Brooks of the University of West Virginia, an authority on the birds of the Appalachian region, reported that the West Virginia bird population had undergone "an incredible reduction."

One story might serve as the tragic symbol of the fate of the birds—a fate that has already overtaken some species, and that threatens all. It is the story of the robin, the bird known to everyone. To millions of Americans, the season's first robin means that the grip of winter is broken. Its coming is an event reported in newspapers and told eagerly at the breakfast table. And as the number of migrants grows and the first mists of green appear in the woodlands, thousands of people listen for the first dawn chorus of the robins throbbing in the early morning light. But now all is changed, and not even the return of the birds may be taken for granted.

The survival of the robin, and indeed of many other species as well, seems fatefully linked with the American elm, a tree that is part of the history of thousands of towns from the Atlantic to the Rockies, gracing their streets and their village squares and college campuses with majestic archways of green. Now the elms are stricken with a disease that afflicts them throughout their range, a disease so serious that many experts believe all efforts to save the elms will in the end be futile. It would be tragic to lose the elms, but it would be doubly tragic if, in vain efforts to save them, we plunge vast segments of our bird populations into the night of extinction. Yet this is precisely what is threatened.

The so-called Dutch elm disease entered the United States from Europe about 1930 in elm burl logs imported for the veneer industry. It is a fungus disease; the organism invades the water-conducting vessels of the tree, spreads by spores carried in the flow of sap, and by its poisonous secretions as well as by mechanical clogging causes the branches to wilt and the tree to die. The disease is spread from diseased to healthy trees by elm bark beetles. The galleries which the insects have tunneled out under the bark of dead trees become contaminated with spores of the invading fungus, and the spores adhere to the insect body and are carried wherever the beetle flies. Efforts to control the fungus disease of the elms have been directed largely toward control of the carrier insect. In community after community, especially throughout the strongholds of the American elm, the Midwest and New England, intensive spraying has become a routine procedure.

What this spraying could mean to bird life, and especially to the robin, was first made clear by the work of two ornithologists at Michigan State University, Professor George Wallace and one of his graduate students, John Mehner. When Mr. Mehner began work for the doctorate in 1954, he chose a research project that had to do with robin populations. This was quite by chance, for at that time no one suspected that the robins were in danger. But even as he undertook the work, events occurred that were to change its character and indeed to deprive him of his material.

Spraying for Dutch elm disease began in a small way on the university campus in 1954. The following year the city of East Lansing (where the university is located) joined in, spraying on the campus was expanded, and, with local programs for gypsy moth and mosquito control also under way, the rain of chemicals increased to a downpour.

During 1954, the year of the first light spraying, all seemed well. The following spring the migrating robins began to return to the campus as usual. Like the bluebells in Tomlinson's haunting essay "The Lost Wood," they were "expecting no evil" as they reoccupied their familiar territories. But soon it became evident that something was wrong. Dead and dying robins began to appear on the campus. Few birds were seen in their normal foraging activities or assembling in their usual roosts. Few nests were built; few young appeared. The pattern was repeated with monotonous regularity in succeeding springs. The sprayed area had become a lethal trap in which each wave of migrating robins would be eliminated in about a week. Then new arrivals would come in, only to add to the numbers of doomed birds seen on the campus in the agonized tremors that precede death.

"The campus is serving as a graveyard for most of the robins that attempt to take up residence in the spring," said Dr. Wallace. But why? At first he suspected some disease of the nervous system, but soon it became evident that "in spite of the assurances of the insecticide people that their sprays were 'harmless to birds' the robins were really dying of insecticidal poisoning; they exhibited the well-known symptoms of loss of balance, followed by tremors, convulsions, and death."

Several facts suggested that the robins were being poisoned, not so much by direct contact with the insecticides as indirectly, by eating earthworms. Campus earthworms had been fed inadvertently to crayfish in a research project and all the crayfish had promptly died. A snake kept in a laboratory cage had gone into violent tremors after being fed such worms. And earthworms are the principal food of robins in the spring.

A key piece in the jigsaw puzzle of the doomed robins was soon to be supplied by Dr. Roy Barker of the Illinois Natural History Survey at Urbana. Dr. Barker's work, published in 1958, traced the intricate cycle of events by which the robins' fate is linked to the elm trees by way of the earthworms. The trees are sprayed in the spring (usually at the rate of 2 to 5 pounds of DDT per 50-foot tree, which may be the equivalent of as much as *23 pounds per acre* where elms are numerous) and often again in July, at about half this concentration. Powerful sprayers direct a stream of poison to all parts of the tallest trees, killing directly not only the target organism, the bark beetle, but other insects, including pollinating species and predatory spiders and beetles. The poison forms a tenacious film over the leaves and bark. Rains do not wash it away. In the autumn the leaves fall to the ground, accumulate in sodden layers, and begin the slow process of becoming one with the soil. In this they are aided by the toil of the earthworms, who feed in the leaf litter, for elm leaves are among their favorite foods. In feeding on the leaves the worms also swallow the insecticide, accumulating and concentrating it in their bodies. Dr. Barker found deposits of DDT throughout the digestive tracts of the worms, their blood vessels, nerves, and body wall. Undoubtedly some of the earthworms themselves succumb, but others survive to become "biological magnifiers" of the poison. In the spring the robins return to provide another link in the cycle. As few as 11 large earthworms can transfer a lethal dose of DDT to a robin. And 11 worms form a small part of a day's rations to a bird that eats 10 to 12 earthworms in as many minutes.

Not all robins receive a lethal dose, but another consequence may lead to the extinction of their kind as surely as fatal poisoning. The shadow of sterility lies over all the bird studies and indeed lengthens to include all living things within its potential range. There are now only two or three dozen robins to be found each spring on the entire 185-acre campus of Michigan State University, compared with a conservatively estimated 370 adults in this area before spraying. In 1954 every robin nest under observation by Mehner produced young. Toward the end of June, 1957, when at least 370 young birds (the normal replacement of the adult population) would have been foraging over the campus in the years before spraying began, Mehner could find *only one young robin*. A year later Dr. Wallace was to report: "At no time during the spring or summer [of 1958] did I see a fledgling robin anywhere on the main campus, and so far I have failed to find anyone else who has seen one there."

Part of this failure to produce young is due, of course, to the fact that one or more of a pair of robins dies before the nesting cycle is completed. But Wallace has significant records which point to something more sinister—the actual destruction of the birds' capacity to reproduce. He has, for example, "records of robins and other birds building nests but laying no eggs, and others laying eggs and incubating them but not hatching them. We have one record of a robin that sat on its eggs faithfully for 21 days and they did not hatch. The normal incubation period is 13 days.... Our analyses are showing high concentrations of DDT in the testes and ovaries of breeding birds," he told a congressional committee in 1960. "Ten males had amounts ranging from 30 to 109 parts per million in the testes, and two females had 151 and 211 parts per million respectively in the egg follicles in their ovaries."

Soon studies in other areas began to develop findings equally dismal. Professor Joseph Hickey and his students at the University of Wisconsin, after careful comparative studies of sprayed and unsprayed areas, reported the robin mortality to be at least 86 to 88 per cent. The Cranbrook Institute of Science at Bloomfield Hills, Michigan, in an effort to assess the extent of bird loss caused by the spraying of the elms, asked in 1956 that all birds thought to be victims of DDT poisoning be turned in to the institute for examination. The request had a response beyond all expectations. Within a few weeks the deep-freeze facilities of the institute were taxed to capacity, so that other specimens had to be refused. By 1959 a thousand poisoned birds from this single community had been turned in or reported. Although the robin was the chief victim (one woman calling the institute reported 12 robins lying dead on her lawn as she spoke), 63 different species were included among the specimens examined at the institute.

The robins, then, are only one part of the chain of devastation linked to the spraying of the elms, even as the elm program is only one of the multitudinous spray programs that cover our land with poisons. Heavy mortality has occurred among about 90 species of birds, including those most familiar to suburbanites and amateur naturalists. The populations of nesting birds in general have declined as much as 90 per cent in some of the sprayed towns. As we shall see, all the various types of birds are affected—ground feeders, treetop feeders, bark feeders, predators....

As the habit of killing grows—the resort to "eradicating" any creature that may annoy or inconvenience us—birds are more and more finding themselves a direct target of poisons rather than an incidental one. There is a growing trend toward aerial applications of such deadly poisons as parathion to "control" concentrations of birds distasteful to farmers. The Fish and Wildlife Service has found it necessary to express serious concern over this trend, pointing out that "parathion treated areas constitute a potential hazard to humans, domestic animals, and wildlife." In southern Indiana, for example, a group of farmers went together in the summer of 1959 to engage a spray plane to treat an area of river bottomland with parathion. The area was a favored roosting site for thousands of blackbirds that were feeding in nearby cornfields. The problem could have been solved easily by a slight change in agricultural practice—a shift to a variety of corn with deep-set ears not accessible to the birds—but the farmers had been persuaded of the merits of killing by poison, and so they sent in the planes on their mission of death.

The results probably gratified the farmers, for the casualty list included some 65,000 red-winged blackbirds and starlings. What other wildlife deaths may have gone unnoticed and unrecorded is not known. Parathion is not a specific for blackbirds: it is a universal killer. But such rabbits or raccoons or opossums as may have roamed those bottomlands and perhaps never visited the farmers' cornfields were doomed by a judge and jury who neither knew of their existence nor cared.

And what of human beings? In California orchards sprayed with this same parathion, workers handling foliage that had been treated *a month* earlier collapsed and went into shock, and escaped death only through skilled medical attention. Does Indiana still raise any boys who roam through woods or fields and might even explore the margins of a river? If so, who guarded the poisoned area to keep out any who might wander in, in misguided search for unspoiled nature? Who kept vigilant watch to tell the innocent stroller that the fields he was about to enter were deadly—all their vegetation coated with a lethal film? Yet at so fearful a risk the farmers, with none to hinder them, waged their needless war on blackbirds.

In each of these situations, one turns away to ponder the question: Who has made the decision that sets in motion these chains of poisonings, this ever-widening wave of death that spreads out, like ripples when a pebble is dropped into a still pond? Who has placed in one pan of the scales the leaves that might have been eaten by the beetles and in the other the pitiful heaps of many-hued feathers, the lifeless remains of the birds that fell before the unselective bludgeon of insecticidal poisons? Who has decided—who has the *right* to decide—for the countless legions of people who were not consulted that the supreme value is a world without insects, even though it be also a sterile world ungraced by the curving wing of a bird in flight? The decision is that of the authoritarian temporarily entrusted with power; he has made it during a moment of inattention by millions to whom beauty and the ordered world of nature still have a meaning that is deep and imperative.

Questions

1. What evidence did Carson present to support her argument?
2. Focusing on the last paragraph of the excerpt, explain how Carson's book might have mobilized environmental activists.
3. Compare and contrast Carson's attitude toward nature with John Muir's in Document 16-12.

29-9 Homestead (1970s)

William Serrin

Homestead, Pennsylvania, was an industrial community dependent on the production of steel. It had been the scene of one of the most famous labor-management confrontations of the late nineteenth century (see text p. 543). The deindustrialization of the 1970s, which continued during the following decade, profoundly affected Homestead, its economic base, and its people (see text pp. 915–916). William Serrin left the *New York Times* to write about this story.

Source: Excerpt from William Serrin, *Homestead: The Glory and Tragedy of an American Steel Town* (New York: Times Books, 1992), 392–398. Copyright © 1992 by William Serrin. Reprinted by permission of the author.

Eighth Avenue continued to run down, and now the once-bustling street was a tatterdemalion thoroughfare made up of the few old stores that were hanging on and the Goodwill, Salvation Army, and Saint Vincent de Paul thrift shops. One of Chief Kelly's last fights had been to attempt to persuade the managers of the thrift shops to stop putting their collections of junk—worn-out toys, skates, sleds, books, kitchenware, clothes, shoes—on the sidewalk. He was not successful. But there was little market for such items. In the end, even Goodwill closed, and the windows were boarded up with plywood.

The borough building, constructed in 1909, the place where Mother Jones had been jailed and Frances Perkins had been refused permission by Burgess Cavanaugh to speak in Frick Park, was also closed. The building had not been maintained and was getting run-down. One day Chief Kelly was going down to the basement. A rotten step gave way, and he fell and wrenched his ankle. He was on crutches for several days. A half-dozen people who worked there came down with cancer, and it was thought that the building contained some carcinogen—asbestos perhaps—although this was never proven. Council meetings were moved to the old high school. The fire department was moved to a garage across the street, and the police department was moved into the old post office, which the country [*sic*] remodeled for the borough in exchange for the borough's agreeing to house a number of work-release prisoners in the building.

In June 1990, Saint Mary Magdalene's School closed. It was the last Roman Catholic school in Homestead. In the fall, it would have begun its one hundredth year. The students knew that they would miss their school enormously. "Everybody cares about you," Jackie Piskor said. "If you have a problem, you can go to any of the teachers, and they will help you, or to your friends, and they will help you." The students, even at their young age, knew that hard times had fastened on Homestead. They could not go across the street to play in Frick Park because they feared they would be bullied. There were often drugs being sold there, they said. Even Saint Mary Magdalene's Roman Catholic Church was locked, day and night.

Most of the students were enrolling in public schools. They said that they would especially miss their prayers. "How many times a day do you pray?" I asked. They counted the prayers, some using their fingers. "Seven," they said. The last day, the children came for half a day, and there was much crying in the halls and on the asphalt playground. A second-grade teacher, Nancy Stanich, tearfully embraced her students. Dave Lasos, a seventh grader, sat disconsolately in the hall, his head buried in his arms. Sister Marie Margaret, the principal, said "We have met our Waterloo."

The town government continued to face enormous problems. The borough's deficit increased from $30,000 in 1989 to $300,000 in 1990, and the population continued to fall. It was 4,179 in the 1990 census, down 17.9 percent from

5,092 in 1980. In 1988, the corporation sold the Homestead Works to the Park Corporation for $14 million — $2.5 million for the land and $11.5 million for the equipment and machinery. Soon, demolition crews arrived, and one by one the old mills came down. For a time, Mayor Simko continued to believe that the Valley Machine Shop would be purchased from Park and reopened, but the letter of intent that he had been expecting the day we had toured the works had not come through. The investors said that reopening the mill would not be feasible, in view of the depressed condition of the steel industry.

In 1990, Allegheny County reduced the assessed value of the mill site from $30 million to $14 million. In November, Homestead, Munhall, West Homestead, and the Steel Valley School District reached an agreement with Park to reduce the assessed value of the site from $14 million to $9.5 million. The agreement entitled Park to a refund on 1989 real estate taxes of $67,000 from the boroughs and $45,500 from the school district, which Park agreed to apply to future tax bills.

The town had become a place for small-time speculators. Wayne Laux, a man whom almost no one in Homestead knew anything about, began to buy buildings near the mill site — including the one that had housed Rufus "Sonnyman" Jackson's Skyrocket Lounge and Manhattan Music Club — and then sold them to Park. Many were demolished. Half a century after the demolition that had preceded the wartime expansion of the works, lower Homestead was again being razed.

The corporation and the union continued the missteps that had helped to bring about their downfall. In June 1990, the corporation agreed to pay $34 million in costs and penalties for the cleanup of waste water that had been illegally dumped into the Calumet River, in Indiana, by its Gary plant. In September 1990, a federal district court judge in Birmingham, Alabama, fined the corporation $4.1 million and gave prison terms to two union officials, Thermon Phillips and E. B. Rich, found guilty of conspiring with the corporation to obtain lucrative pensions for themselves in exchange for agreeing to concessions during contract negotiations in December 1983. This was the agreement that the corporation had used to persuade local unions across the country to grant similar concessions. In December 1990, the corporation agreed to pay a $3.2 million fine levied by the Occupational Safety and Health Administration for hundreds of violations the administration said had occurred at its Pennsylvania plants.

The corporation's interest in steel continued to shrink. In early 1991, its steel operations became an independent subsidiary. In May, its stock was split into two — one for energy, one for steel — and the steel stock was dropped from the Dow Jones Industrial Average and replaced by the stock of the Walt Disney Company.

By this time, the national union's membership had dropped to 490,000, one-third of the 1.4 million who had belonged in 1979. In 1991, a plan to organize white-collar workers was announced, and a woman organizer with substantial experience in the field was hired. But the effort failed.

The local union meetings continued until the summer of 1987, and the union hall remained open after that to assist laid-off workers. No dues had come in from Homestead since the mill had been closed, and the national union had been helping the local with its bills. But the bad blood between the national union leaders and Weisen had continued, and finally the union saw an opportunity to close the hall. In December, Weisen had gone to the Soviet Union with his wife and their son Bobby for an operation on the broken vertebra in Bobby's neck. A drive to raise money for the trip had been started by Weisen's old supporters, but everyone wanted Bobby to get well, and Lynn Williams, the new president of the national union, stopped by the Weisens' home to give them a thousand dollars.

In February 1988, while Weisen was still in the Soviet Union, the national union ordered the Homestead union hall closed. Mike Stout, the grievance man, was furious, and to keep him quiet the union reluctantly allowed him to set up a local headquarters in an empty, ramshackle orange building, once a restaurant, on McClure Street, at the top of the hill. He put a sign on the door of the old hall that said: "The international has shut our union hall down and moved us to a storefront on the corner of Seventeenth Street and McClure Street (orange building). We should have the same number, but if you have any problems with TRA or SUB [Training and Relocation Allowance and Supplemental Unemployment Benefits], call me at home."

The orange building was run-down and hot and stuffy. There was no longer much spirit among the men who sat there in front of fans at desks trucked up from the old union hall. The place smelled like old hamburgers and french fries. Occasionally, unemployed workers came by for assistance, but soon they stopped coming. Not even Weisen came by much anymore. He was unemployed, like most others, and was looking for work. In November 1988 the orange building was closed. There had been eight union lodges in Homestead at the time of the 1892 strike. An Amalgamated Association lodge, the Spirit of Ninety-two, had been established in Homestead with the passage of the National Industrial Recovery Act, in June 1933. The steelworkers' union had had a local in Homestead since 1936, for more than half a century. Now there was no union in Homestead.

Most of the men who lost their jobs when the mill went down accepted their fate and settled in, living on part-time work or on pensions. Many had trouble sleeping and finding things to do with the time on their hands. They dropped children or grandchildren off at school, helped around the house, worked on the lawn. After a time, their wives and children got used to having them around. Sometimes the men drove down by the works and watched the demolition crews taking it down. The men would have reunions at one of the firehouses or social clubs, but those were not much fun. One by one they stopped going, and soon no one planned reunions anymore.

"I still think about that damn place," Bob Krovocheck said. He had worked in the mill for thirty-eight years and was fifty-six years old when he lost his job. His highest pay was twenty-seven thousand dollars in 1985. He tried working as a janitor for four dollars an hour, but he was overweight and had bad knees, and the work was too demanding, so he had to quit. His wife had been seriously injured in an automobile accident on the Pennsylvania Turnpike in 1981, and he spent much of his time taking care of her. They lived on his pension of $1,100 a month, $876 after taxes and medical deductions.

Krovocheck missed the mill enormously. "I dream about it every once in a while," he said. "I miss going to work, being around the guys, the eight-hour turn, the routine. I miss the money, too. It was a good living. I wasn't living from payday to payday. It's funny. I remember that every once in a while one of us in the mill would say, 'Let's get our pension and get out of here.' But pensioneering ain't all that great, especially if you've got somebody sick you're taking care of.

"During the day, I take care of the wife, get the meals, keep the house halfway decent. It ain't like she would keep it. I do the cooking and laundry. I read quite a bit. I go up the street and have a couple of beers. I go to the store and get the groceries. I come home and make supper. I watch TV. I go to bed. I get rather depressed, especially when I drive up past where we worked, the structural mill. I'm okay, if you want to call me okay."

Richard Holoman, a craneman, had worked in the mill for thirty-two years and was fifty-one when he lost his job. His highest pay was $22,500 a year. After the mill went down, he had a job as a security guard for three months and worked for a short time cleaning an industrial garage, three and a half hours a night, for fourteen dollars a night. Then he got a job as a janitor at Saint Agnes's Roman Catholic Church, in West Mifflin. He changed light bulbs, mopped floors, cut the grass, fixed the sisters' car. It wasn't bad, as work goes. He could set his own hours, but mostly he worked 6:00 A.M. to 2:00 P.M., five days a week—good hours for an old steelworker, steady daylight.

Denny Wilcox, a roller, got a part-time job as a bank courier, twenty-five hours a week at $6.10 an hour. He received a pension of $1,100 a month. "We're not living high off the hog, but we're making it," he said. "It's hard. You start looking down on yourself. You'd think, if you put on an application that you have thirty five years of service, an employer would know that you are dedicated. You'd think they'd grab you in a minute. But they discriminate against you because of age. They all do. I think that's why I'm not full-time now, because they discriminate because of age. They know I get a pension."

Ray McGuire, a repairman, had worked in the mill for thirty-six years and had taken only two sick days. He got a pension of $1,000 a month and caught on as an electrician, going from one shop to another, wherever he was needed. Sometimes a temporary agency found him work, or else he would hear of something himself. He worked for a while at the machine company that now occupied part of the old Mesta Machine plant. One day he had to go to the Homestead Works to pick up some tools. "I went to the exact place where I worked, and I got so nauseated I thought I was going to throw up," he said. "I thought: 'I worked here. What are you people doing to this place? What are you doing to my cranes?' And then I thought: 'Wait a minute. This wasn't my place. These weren't my cranes.' But that's the way I thought—that it was my place." He lived in Pleasant Hills, not far from Homestead, but he no longer went to Homestead at night. He was afraid of crime there, and besides, he got despondent when he went to Homestead, even when he just drove through the town. "The place looks like a morgue," he said.

Bob Todd, a craneman and grievance man, was unemployed for a year. Then he was called to the Edgar Thomson Works, where he got a job as a safety man in the slab mill, making seventeen thousand dollars a year. It was not as much as he had been making at Homestead, but it was a job. About two hundred Homestead workers were given jobs there, and another few dozen were hired by the Irvin Works.

Bill Brennan, a millwright, had worked in the mill for thirty-nine years and was sixty-four when he retired on his pension of $775 a month after deductions. He also got Social Security, and his house was paid for. His father had worked at the Homestead Works, and so had his three brothers. In 1984, when he had a heart-bypass operation, he was on sick-leave for six months. His heart was now okay, though he had to take three pills a day. When he went back into the mill after his bypass, the other millwrights carried him, hid him out, for six months—they did the heavy work that he had done and did not tell the supervisors. He would pick up a sledgehammer or a big crescent wrench, and the others would take it from him and tell him to go somewhere, get lost, and they would do the job. "I miss guys like that, good working people," he said.

Bobby Schneider, a roller, got a part-time job tending bar at the Slovak Club in Munhall. He had worked in the mill for thirty-one years and had earned $35,000 in his best year. The bartender's job wasn't much, though it got him out of the house and gave him something to do. He lived on a pension check of $1,077 a month after deductions. His wife worked as a secretary in a real-estate company. His section of the last beam rolled at the Homestead Works was still in the trunk of his car, four years after the mill went down. He had intended to shine it up and put it in the house, but he never got around to it. His two pals, Red Hrabic and Jimmie Sherlock, both lived on pensions of about $900 a month and were doing okay. The three of them met at Hess's Bar in Hunkie Hollow almost every afternoon at about four, or maybe at the Slovak Club, in Munhall, if Schneider was tending bar there.

There was much crying in Homestead. Men and women often went to wakes and funerals, for there were many deaths among the men from the works. I knew or heard of three dozen men who died or committed suicide. That's a lot of men gone, and at an early age, too. I think that many of them died because the mill closed, though I can't prove it. But it's a lot of dead guys, isn't it?

There was one man I never got out of my mind—Rich Locher, the hooker from Number Two Structural who had denounced the government's retraining programs at the meeting with the two men in the pinstripe suits from Senator Heinz's staff. I had planned to meet with Locher, but time passed, and I was busy. One winter day, preparing for a trip to Homestead, I wrote down his telephone number, thinking I would go see him. When I got to Homestead, I ran into Mike Stout, the former grievance man. When I told him that I was going to call Locher, he said: "Don't bother. Locher is dead. He finished the retraining program but couldn't get a nursing job, so he took a gun and killed himself—shot half his head away, in his garage." Stout continued with his paperwork and did not look up. One more death was not much to him. He knew too many stories like this.

I liked Locher. He was a good man. He had a temper and often used profane language, but don't many of us? He was an excellent father and husband, and he probably deserved more out of life than to take two brief vacations at hot trailer parks in Virginia and go out to eat once a month at McDonald's or Long John Silver's, to lose his job as a craneman and not get a job as a nurse. One more thing. Locher was right about the training programs. They were bullshit.

Questions

1. How did the plant's closing affect community institutions?
2. Why did the mill exert such a strong influence on its former workers?
3. What program was supposed to help unemployed steelworkers get back into the economy? Why was Serrin so critical of it?

Questions for Further Thought

1. Reflecting on the 1950s and 1960s, what most strikes you about the Gallup polls of 1950 and 1970?
2. How did the polls of 1985 and 1999 compare and contrast with those of 1950 to 1970 and 1975 and 1980?
3. What democratic issue did Carson raise in the conflict she described between industry and nature (Document 29-8)?
4. After reviewing the text description of the Homestead strike of 1892 and reflecting on the text discussion of deindustrialization and Document 29-9, compare and contrast the two chapters in regard to the history of Homestead, its industry, and its people.

Politics in the Wake of Watergate

The presidencies of Gerald Ford and Jimmy Carter were embattled. President Ford beat off the challenge of Ronald Reagan for his party's nomination in 1976 but lost to Carter in that year's general election. Although Carter received 50 percent of the popular vote (the only Democrat from 1968 through 1996 to do so), he failed to be reelected four years later, losing to Ronald Reagan. The mood of the electorate also revealed itself in reduced voter turnout rates, from a mean of 62 percent during the 1960s to a mean of 54 percent from 1972 to 1980. The nationwide enfranchisement of eighteen-year-olds in 1972 contributed to the sharp decline that year—young adults typically have a low turnout rate—but long-term trends were also at work: the turnout rate declined in every presidential election from 1964 through 1988.

President Ford labored under heavy burdens. Undistinguished as a long-time congressman, he had not been elected to national office. Having pardoned Richard Nixon shortly after becoming president, he soon faced Democratic congressional majorities swollen in the 1974 elections held in the wake of Nixon's resignation and pardon. Economic problems, already discussed, beset the nation, whose chief executive was widely liked, but not necessarily respected.

President Carter likewise struggled in office. A former governor of Georgia, Carter had no national political experience. Being an outsider may have stood him in good stead as a post-Watergate presidential candidate, but it handicapped him as president. Carter did score successes in both diplomacy (brokering the Camp David accords between Israel and Egypt and securing, at political cost to himself, the Panama Canal Treaties) and domestic policy (beginning the deregulation of industries). However, he failed to articulate a politically persuasive vision of America's future as the United States struggled with stagflation, the energy crisis, and the humiliating hostage crisis in Iran.

It would fall to Ronald Reagan to formulate a vision of America. Reagan, a former governor of California and a presidential aspirant since 1968, was a better actor than Carter. He would also prove to be a more successful president.

Document 29-10 provides a key section from an address by President Carter during July 1979, and Document 29-11 excerpts Reagan's acceptance speech at the Republican National Convention one year later.

29-10 The National Crisis of Confidence (1979)

Jimmy Carter

During the first half of 1979, various indicators pointed to economic problems for the United States—including spiraling inflation and unemployment and, as a consequence, political problems for the Carter administration. Unpleasant shocks added to widespread uneasiness. In March, an accident at the nuclear power station at Three Mile Island, near Harrisburg, Pennsylvania, reminded Americans that atomic energy carried serious risks. An energy crisis originating overseas brought gasoline shortages and higher prices, angering many, especially motorists in long lines at service stations (see text pp. 913–915).

President Carter (b. 1924), who during April had proposed to Congress measures to deal with future energy needs, planned to address the nation regarding energy at the beginning of July. Instead, he retired to the Camp David presidential retreat, where for several days he consulted with public and private figures about problems confronting the nation. Carter then spoke to the nation on July 15. His address, "Energy and National Goals," dealt not only with America's energy crisis but also with its "crisis of confidence." For Carter, worse was still to come, of course, in Iran and Afghanistan (see text pp. 920–922).

Source: Public Papers of the Presidents of the United States: Jimmy Carter, 1979, Book 2, *June 23 to December 31, 1979* (Washington, DC: U.S. Government Printing Office, 1980), 1236–1241.

... I want to speak to you first tonight about a subject even more serious than energy or inflation. I want to talk to you right now about a fundamental threat to American democracy.

I do not mean our political and civil liberties. They will endure. And I do not refer to the outward strength of America, a nation that is at peace tonight everywhere in the world, with unmatched economic power and military might.

The threat is nearly invisible in ordinary ways. It is a crisis of confidence. It is a crisis that strikes at the very heart and soul and spirit of our national will. We can see this crisis in the growing doubt about the meaning of our own lives and in the loss of a unity of purpose of our Nation.

The erosion of our confidence in the future is threatening to destroy the social and the political fabric of America.

The confidence that we have always had as a people is not simply some romantic dream or a proverb in a dusty book that we read just on the Fourth of July. It is the idea which founded our Nation and has guided our development as a people. Confidence in the future has supported everything else—public institutions and private enterprise, our own families, and the very Constitution of the United States.

Confidence has defined our course and has served as a link between generations. We've always believed in something called progress. We've always had a faith that the days of our children would be better than our own.

Our people are losing that faith, not only in government itself but in the ability as citizens to serve as the ultimate rulers and shapers of our democracy. As a people we know our past and we are proud of it. Our progress has been part of the living history of America, even the world. We always believed that we were part of a great movement of humanity itself called democracy, involved in the search for freedom, and that belief has always strengthened us in our purpose. But just as we are losing our confidence in the future, we are also beginning to close the door on our past.

In a nation that was proud of hard work, strong families, close-knit communities, and our faith in God, too many of us now tend to worship self-indulgence and consumption. Human identity is no longer defined by what one does, but by what one owns. But we've discovered that owning things and consuming things does not satisfy our longing for meaning. We've learned that piling up material goods cannot fill the emptiness of lives which have no confidence or purpose.

The symptoms of this crisis of the American spirit are all around us. For the first time in the history of our country a majority of our people believe that the next 5 years will be worse than the past 5 years. Two-thirds of our people do not even vote. The productivity of American workers is actually dropping, and the willingness of Americans to save for the future has fallen below that of all other people in the Western world.

As you know, there is a growing disrespect for government and for churches and for schools, the news media, and other institutions. This is not a message of happiness or reassurance, but it is the truth and it is a warning.

These changes did not happen overnight. They've come upon us gradually over the last generation, years that were filled with shock and tragedy. We were sure that ours was a nation of the ballot not of the bullet, until the murders of John Kennedy and Robert Kennedy and Martin Luther King, Jr. We were taught that our armies were always invincible and our causes were always just only to suffer the agony of Vietnam. We respected the presidency as a place of honor until the shock of Watergate. . . .

Energy will be the immediate test of our ability to unite this Nation, and it can also be the standard around which we rally. On the battlefield of energy we can win for our Nation a new confidence, and we can seize control again of our common destiny.

In little more than two decades we've gone from a position of energy independence to one in which almost half the oil we use comes from foreign countries, at prices that are going through the roof. Our excessive dependence on OPEC has already taken a tremendous toll on our economy and our people. This is the direct cause of the long lines which have made millions of you spend aggravating hours waiting for gasoline. It's a cause of the increased inflation and unemployment that we now face. This intolerable dependence on foreign oil threatens our economic independence and the very security of our Nation.

The energy crisis is real. It is worldwide. It is a clear and present danger to our Nation. These are facts and we simply must face them. . . .

In closing, let me say this: I will do my best, but I will not do it alone. Let your voice be heard. Whenever you have a chance, say something good about our country. With God's help and for the sake of our Nation, it is time for us to join hands in America. Let us commit ourselves together to a rebirth of the American spirit. Working together with our common faith we cannot fail.

Questions

1. What evidence did Carter offer to support his argument that the American people were experiencing a "crisis of confidence"?
2. In his view, why was the crisis of confidence a much deeper problem than the shortage of energy, inflation, and the recession?
3. What did Carter propose to do to resolve the crisis of confidence? How do you think the American people—and American voters—responded to this speech?

29-11 Acceptance Speech, Republican National Convention (1980)

Ronald Reagan

Ronald Reagan (1911–2004), once a liberal Democratic supporter of Franklin D. Roosevelt and Harry S. Truman, moved into the conservative Republican camp during the 1950s. His support of Barry Goldwater in 1964 contributed to his own nomination for governor of California two years later. Elected, he won a second term in 1970. Twice unsuccessful in bids for the Republican presidential nomination (1968, 1976), Reagan triumphed in 1980 and went on to trounce Jimmy Carter in the election (see text pp. 929, 932).

Source: Ronald Reagan, Acceptance Address, Republican National Convention, Detroit, Michigan, July 17, 1980, from *Vital Speeches of the Day* 46 (August 15, 1980), 642–646.

. . . This convention has shown to all America a party united, with positive programs for solving the nation's problems; a party ready to build a new consensus with all those across the land who share a community of values embodied in these words: family, work, neighborhood, peace and freedom.

Now I know we've had a quarrel or two but only as to the method of attaining a goal. There was no argument here about the goal. As President, I will establish a liaison with the 50 Governors to encourage them to eliminate, wherever it exists, discrimination against women. I will monitor Federal laws to insure their implementation and to add statutes if they are needed.

More than anything else, I want my candidacy to unify our country; to renew the American spirit and sense of purpose. I want to carry our message to every American, regardless of party affiliation, who is a member of this community of shared values.

Never before in our history have Americans been called upon to face three grave threats to our very existence, any one of which could destroy us. We face a disintegrating economy, a weakened defense and an energy policy based on the sharing of scarcity.

The major issue of this campaign is the direct political, personal, and moral responsibility of Democratic Party leadership—in the White House and in the Congress—for this unprecedented calamity which has befallen us. They tell us they've done the most that humanly could be done. They say that the United States has had its day in the sun, that our nation has passed its zenith. They expect you to tell your children that the American people no longer have the will to cope with their problems; that the future will be one of sacrifice and few opportunities.

My fellow citizens, I utterly reject that view. The American people, the most generous on earth, who created the highest standard of living, are not going to accept the notion that we can only make a better world for others by moving backward ourselves. And those who believe we can have no business leading this nation. . . .

Isn't it once again time to renew our compact of freedom; to pledge to each other all that is best in our lives; all that gives meaning to them—for the sake of this, our beloved and blessed land?

Together, let us make this a new beginning. Let us make a commitment to care for the needy; to teach our children the virtues handed down to us by our families; to have the courage to defend those values and virtues and the willingness to sacrifice for them.

Let us pledge to restore, in our time, the American spirit of voluntary service, of cooperation, of private and community initiative; a spirit that flows like a deep and mighty river through the history of our nation.

As your nominee, I pledge to you to restore to the Federal Government the capacity to do the people's work without dominating their lives. I pledge to you a Government that will not only work well but wisely, its ability to act tempered by prudence, and its willingness to do good balanced by the knowledge that government is never more dangerous than when our desire to have it help us blinds us to its great power to harm us. . . .

The head of a Government which has utterly refused to live within its means and which has, in the last few days, told us that this coming year's deficit will be $60 billion, dares to point the finger of blame at business and labor, both of which have been engaged in a losing struggle just trying to stay even.

High taxes, we are told, are somehow good for us, as if, when government spends our money it isn't inflationary, but when we spend it, it is.

Those who preside over the worst energy shortage in our history tell us to use less, so that we will run out of oil, gasoline and natural gas a little more slowly. Well, now, conservation is desirable, of course. We must not waste energy. But conservation is not the sole answer to our energy needs.

America must get to work producing more energy. The Republican program for solving economic problems is based on growth and productivity.

Large amounts of oil and natural gas lay beneath our land and off our shores, untouched because the present Administration seems to believe the American people would rather see more regulation, more taxes and more controls than more energy.

Coal offers a great potential. So does nuclear energy produced under rigorous safety standards. It could supply electricity for thousands of industries and millions of jobs and homes. It must not be thwarted by a tiny minority opposed to economic growth which often finds friendly ears in regulatory agencies for its obstructionist campaigns.

Now make no mistake. We will not permit the safety of our people or our environmental heritage to be jeopardized, but we are going to reaffirm that the economic prosperity of our people is a fundamental part of our environment. . . .

It is essential that we maintain both the forward momentum of economic growth and the strength of the safety net between those in our society who need help. We also believe it is essential that the integrity of all aspects of Social Security be preserved.

Beyond these essentials, I believe it is clear our Federal Government is overgrown and overweight. Indeed, it is time our Government should go on a diet. Therefore, my first act as chief executive will be to impose an immediate and thorough freeze on Federal hiring. Then, we are going to enlist the very best minds from business, labor and whatever quarter to conduct a detailed review of every department, bureau and agency that lives by Federal appropriation....

Our instructions to the groups we enlist will be simple and direct. We will remind them that Government programs exist at the sufferance of the American taxpayer and are paid for with money earned by working men and women and programs that represent a waste of their money—a theft from their pocketbooks—must have that waste eliminated or that program must go....

Everything that can be run more effectively by state and local government we shall turn over to state and local government, along with the funding sources to pay for it. We are going to put an end to the money merry-go-round where our money becomes Washington's money, to be spent by states and cities exactly the way the Federal bureaucrats tell us it has to be spent.

I will not accept the excuse that the Federal Government has grown so big and powerful that it is beyond the control of any President, any administration or Congress. We are going to put an end to the notion that the American taxpayer exists to fund the Federal Government. The Federal Government exists to serve the American people and to be accountable to the American people. On January 20, we are going to reestablish that truth.

Also on that date we are going to initiate action to get substantial relief for our taxpaying citizens and action to put people back to work. None of this will be based on any new form of monetary tinkering or fiscal sleight-of-hand. We will simply apply to government the common sense that we all use in our daily lives.

Work and family are at the center of our lives, the foundation of our dignity as a free people. When we deprive people of what they have earned, or take away their jobs, we destroy their dignity and undermine their families. We can't support families unless there are jobs; and we can't have jobs unless the people have both money to invest and the faith to invest it....

The American people are carrying the heaviest peacetime tax burden in our nation's history—and it will grow even heavier, under present law, next January. We are taxing ourselves into economic exhaustion and stagnation, crushing our ability and incentive to save, invest and produce.

This must stop. We must halt this fiscal self-destruction and restore sanity to our economic system.

I've long advocated a 30 percent reduction in income tax rates over a period of three years. This phased tax reduction would begin with a 10 percent "down payment" tax cut in 1981, which the Republicans in Congress and I have already proposed.

A phased reduction of tax rates would go a long way toward easing the heavy burden on the American people. But we shouldn't stop there....

For those without skills, we'll find a way to help them get new skills.

For those without job opportunities we'll stimulate new opportunities, particularly in the inner cities where they live.

For those who've abandoned hope, we'll restore hope and we'll welcome them into a great national crusade to make America great again.

When we move from domestic affairs, and cast our eyes abroad, we see an equally sorry chapter in the record of the present Administration....

—A Soviet combat brigade trains in Cuba, just 90 miles from our shores.

—A Soviet army of invasion occupies Afghanistan, further threatening our vital interests in the Middle East.

—America's defense strength is at its lowest ebb in a generation, while the Soviet Union is vastly outspending us in both strategic and conventional arms.

—Our European allies, looking nervously at the growing menace from the East, turn to us for leadership and fail to find it.

—And incredibly, more than 50, as you've been told from this platform so eloquently already, more than 50 of our fellow Americans have been held captive [in Tehran] for over eight years—eight months—by a dictatorial foreign power that holds us up to ridicule before the world.... [In this sentence Reagan misspoke (8 years) and corrected himself (8 months).]

Who does not feel a growing sense of unease as our allies, facing repeated instances of an amateurish and confused Administration, reluctantly conclude that America is unwilling or unable to fulfill its obligations as leader of the free world?

Who does not feel rising alarm when the question in any discussion of foreign policy is no longer, "Should we do something?" but "Do we have the capacity to do anything?"

The Administration which has brought us to this state is seeking your endorsement for four more years of weakness, indecision, mediocrity and incompetence. No. No. No American should vote until he or she has asked: Is the United States stronger and more respected now than it was three-and-a-half years ago? Is the world safer, a safer place in which to live?

It is the responsibility of the President of the United States, in working for peace, to insure that the safety of our people cannot successfully be threatened by a hostile foreign power. As President, fulfilling that responsibility will be my No. 1 priority....

Of all the objectives we seek, first and foremost is the establishment of lasting world peace. We must always stand ready to negotiate in good faith, ready to pursue any reasonable avenue that holds forth the promise of lessening tensions and furthering the prospects of peace. But let our friends and those who may wish us ill take note: the United States has an obligation to its citizens and to the people of the world never to let those who would destroy freedom dictate our future course of life on this planet. I would regard my election as proof that we have renewed our resolve to preserve world peace and freedom. That this nation will once again be strong enough to do that. . . .

[A]n American President told the generation of the Great Depression that it had a "rendezvous with destiny." I believe this generation of Americans today also has a rendezvous with destiny.

Tonight, let us dedicate ourselves to renewing the American compact. I ask you not simply to "trust me," but to trust your values—our values—and to hold me responsible for living up to them. I ask you to trust that American spirit which knows no ethnic, religious, social, political, regional or economic boundaries; the spirit that burned with zeal in the hearts of millions of immigrants from every corner of the earth who came here in search of freedom. . . .

I have thought of something that's not a part of my speech and worried over whether I should do it. Can we doubt that only a Divine Providence placed this land, this island of freedom, here as a refuge for all those people in the world who yearn to breathe free? Jews and Christians enduring persecution behind the Iron Curtain; the boat people of Southeast Asia, Cuba and of Haiti; the victims of drought and famine in Africa, the freedom fighters in Afghanistan, and our own countrymen held in savage captivity.

I'll confess that I've been a little afraid to suggest what I'm going to suggest. I'm more afraid not to. Can we begin our crusade joined together in a moment of silent prayer?

God bless America.

Thank you.

Questions

1. As outlined in this speech, what was Ronald Reagan's view of the proper relationship between the federal government and the American people?

2. What was Reagan's prescription for curing the ills of the American economy?

3. Candidate Reagan charged the Democratic administration with "weakness, indecision, mediocrity and incompetence." He also spoke positively of the need for a revival of the "American spirit." Do you think that Reagan's appeal to the voters had more to do with the perceived failings of the Democrats or the Republican Party's conservative agenda?

Questions for Further Thought

1. Compare and contrast the speeches of President Jimmy Carter (Document 29-10) and Ronald Reagan (Document 29-11). What strikes you most about them? Do they shed light on the two speakers? How does the context influence different types of speeches (for example, campaign speeches, inaugural addresses, and presidential addresses—examples of all of which you have read)?

2. Compare and contrast the factors that contributed during the 1930s to the triumphs of the Democrats and liberalism with the factors that contributed during the 1960s and 1970s to the triumphs of the Republicans and conservatism.

PART SEVEN   *Entering a New Era: Conservatism, Globalism, Terrorism, 1980–2006*

CHAPTER THIRTY

The Reagan Revolution and the End of the Cold War
1980–2001

The Rise of Conservatism

In the presidential election of 1968, Richard Nixon (Republican) received 31,783,783 or 43.4 percent of the popular vote, George Wallace (American Independent) received 9,901,118 or 13.5 percent, while Hubert Humphrey (Democrat) garnered only 31,271,839 or 42.7 percent. In short, over half the country's voters sided against Humphrey and the Democratic Party. Nixon and the Republican Party clearly saw where the new votes were, namely, the Democratic Party's disaffected Southern voters, and accordingly worked hard, to win over Wallace's largely Southern, prosegregationist vote. This "Southern strategy" produced a landslide victory in 1972 over George McGovern, the Democratic standard-bearer. What this change meant was that the Republican Party, the party of small government, low taxes, and anti-Communism, now increasingly became a political party that also appealed to voters, especially Southern voters, on the basis of traditional cultural or "family" values. Since 1968, the new Republican Party has won the presidency six out of the last nine elections. No Republican politician more successfully appealed to this new coalition of voters than did Ronald Reagan who was easily elected in 1980 and even more decisively reelected four years later. Document 30-1 is from a 1983 Reagan speech; Document 30-2 contains excerpts from Justice William Brennan's opinion of the Supreme Court on the unconstitutionality of requiring that public school teachers add religious instruction to the science curriculum.

30-1   Remarks at the Annual Convention of the National Association of Evangelicals (1983)

Ronald Reagan

President Ronald Reagan (1911–2004) made it clear here that he shared the values of conservative Christians. Such speeches appealed to his base but were controversial to others. This speech, which was delivered on March 8, 1983, was dubbed the "evil empire" speech. In it, Reagan did discuss the Soviet Union and foreign policy, as well as a range of other issues.

Source: Ronald Reagan, "Remarks at the Annual Convention of the National Association of Evangelicals," in *Speaking My Mind: Selected Speeches* (New York: Simon and Schuster, 1989), 168–180.

This is the "evil empire" speech that was so often quoted as defining my attitude toward the Soviets. At the time it was portrayed as some kind of know-nothing, archconservative statement that could only drive the Soviets to further heights of paranoia and insecurity.

For too long our leaders were unable to describe the Soviet Union as it actually was. The keepers of our foreign-policy knowledge—in other words, most liberal foreign-affairs scholars, the State Department, and various columnists—found it illiberal and provocative to be so honest. I've always believed, however, that it's important to define differences, because there are choices and decisions to be made in life and history.

The Soviet system over the years has purposely starved, murdered, and brutalized its own people. Millions were killed; it's all right there in the history books. It put other citizens it disagreed with into psychiatric hospitals, sometimes drugging them into oblivion. Is the system that allowed this not evil? Then why shouldn't we say so? Even the Soviets themselves are now admitting to annihilating their own people during Stalin's era.

I could not in good conscience today call the Soviet Union an evil empire. As I write this, the Soviets have just conducted the most democratic elections since their revolution. Remarkable things are happening under Mikhail Gorbachev.

In addition to taking a hard line on the morality of the Soviet Union, this speech also outlines my opinions on a number of other moral issues.

Reverend clergy all, Senator Hawkins, distinguished members of the Florida congressional delegation, and all of you:

I can't tell you how you have warmed my heart with your welcome. I'm delighted to be here today.

Those of you in the National Association of Evangelicals are known for your spiritual and humanitarian work. And I would be especially remiss if I didn't discharge right now one personal debt of gratitude. Thank you for your prayers. Nancy and I have felt their presence many times in many ways. And believe me, for us they've made all the difference.

The other day in the East Room of the White House at a meeting there, someone asked me whether I was aware of all the people out there who were praying for the President. And I had to say, "Yes, I am. I've felt it. I believe in intercessionary prayer." But I couldn't help but say to that questioner after he'd asked the question that—or at least say to them that if sometimes when he was praying he got a busy signal, it was just me in there ahead of him. [*Laughter*] I think I understand how Abraham Lincoln felt when he said, "I have been driven many times to my knees by the overwhelming conviction that I had nowhere else to go."

From the joy and the good feeling of this conference, I go to a political reception. [*Laughter*] Now, I don't know why, but that bit of scheduling reminds me of a story— [*Laughter*]—which I'll share with you.

An evangelical minister and a politician arrived at Heaven's gate one day together. And St. Peter, after doing all the necessary formalities, took them in hand to show them where their quarters would be. And he took them to a small, single room with a bed, a chair, and a table and said this was for the clergyman. And the politician was a little worried about what might be in store for him. And he couldn't believe it then when St. Peter stopped in front of a beautiful mansion with lovely grounds, many servants, and told him that these would be his quarters.

And he couldn't help but ask, he said, "But wait, how—there's something wrong—how do I get this mansion while that good and holy man only gets a single room?" And St. Peter said, "You have to understand how things are up here. We've got thousands and thousands of clergy. You're the first politician who ever made it." [*Laughter*]

But I don't want to contribute to a stereotype. [*Laughter*] So I tell you there are a great many God-fearing, dedicated, noble men and women in public life, present company included. And yes, we need your help to keep us ever mindful of the ideas and the principles that brought us into the public arena in the first place. The basis of those ideals and principles is a commitment to freedom and personal liberty that, itself, is grounded in the much deeper realization that freedom prospers only where the blessings of God are avidly sought and humbly accepted.

The American experiment in democracy rests on this insight. Its discovery was the great triumph of our Founding Fathers, voiced by William Penn when he said: "If we will not be governed by God, we must be governed by tyrants." Explaining the inalienable rights of men, Jefferson said, "The God who gave us life, gave us liberty at the same time." And it was George Washington who said that "of all the dispositions and habits which lead to political prosperity, religion and morality are indispensable supports."

And finally, that shrewdest of all observers of American democracy, Alexis de Tocqueville, put it eloquently after he had gone on a search for the secret of America's greatness and genius—and he said: "Not until I went into the churches of America and heard her pulpits aflame with righteousness did I understand the greatness and the genius of America. . . . America is good. And if America ever ceases to be good, America will cease to be great."

Well, I'm pleased to be here today with you who are keeping America great by keeping her good. Only through your work and prayers and those of millions of others can we hope to survive this perilous century and keep alive this experiment in liberty, this last, best hope of man.

I want you to know that this administration is motivated by a political philosophy that sees the greatness of America in you, her people, and in your families, churches, neighborhoods, communities—the institutions that foster and nourish values like concern for others and respect for the rule of law under God.

Now, I don't have to tell you that this puts us in opposition to, or at least out of step with, a prevailing attitude of many who have turned to a modern-day secularism, discarding the tried and time-tested values upon which our very civilization is based. No matter how well intentioned, their value system is radically different from that of most Americans. And while they proclaim that they're freeing us from superstitions of the past, they've taken upon themselves the job of superintending us by government rule and regulation. Sometimes their voices are louder than ours, but they are not yet a majority.

An example of that vocal superiority is evident in a controversy now going on in Washington. And since I'm involved, I've been waiting to hear from the parents of young America. How far are they willing to go in giving to government their prerogatives as parents?

Let me state the case as briefly and simply as I can. An organization of citizens, sincerely motivated and deeply concerned about the increase in illegitimate births and abortions involving girls well below the age of consent, some time ago established a nationwide network of clinics to offer help to these girls and, hopefully, alleviate this situation. Now, again, let me say, I do not fault their intent. However, in their well-intentioned effort, these clinics have decided to provide advice and birth control drugs and devices to underage girls without the knowledge of their parents.

For some years now, the federal government has helped with funds to subsidize these clinics. In providing for this, the Congress decreed that every effort would be made to maximize parental participation. Nevertheless, the drugs and devices are prescribed without getting parental consent or giving notification after they've done so. Girls termed "sexually active"—and that has replaced the word "promiscuous"—are given this help in order to prevent illegitimate birth or abortion.

Well, we have ordered clinics receiving federal funds to notify the parents such help has been given. One of the nation's leading newspapers has created the term "squeal rule" in editorializing against us for doing this, and we're being criticized for violating the privacy of young people. A judge has recently granted an injunction against an enforcement of our rule. I've watched TV panel shows discuss this issue, seen columnists pontificating on our error, but no one seems to mention morality as playing a part in the subject of sex.

Is all of Judeo-Christian tradition wrong? Are we to believe that something so sacred can be looked upon as a purely physical thing with no potential for emotional and psychological harm? And isn't it the parents' right to give counsel and advice to keep their children from making mistakes that may affect their entire lives?

Many of us in government would like to know what parents think about this intrusion in their family by government. We're going to fight in the courts. The right of parents and the rights of family take precedence over those of Washington-based bureaucrats and social engineers.

But the fight against parental notification is really only one example of many attempts to water down traditional values and even abrogate the original terms of American democracy. Freedom prospers when religion is vibrant and the rule of law under God is acknowledged. When our Founding Fathers passed the First Amendment, they sought to protect churches from government interference. They never intended to construct a wall of hostility between government and the concept of religious belief itself.

The evidence of this permeates our history and our government. The Declaration of Independence mentions the Supreme Being no less than four times. "In God We Trust" is engraved on our coinage. The Supreme Court opens its proceedings with a religious invocation. And the members of Congress open their sessions with a prayer. I just happen to believe the schoolchildren of the United States are entitled to the same privileges as Supreme Court justices and congressmen.

Last year, I sent the Congress a constitutional amendment to restore prayer to public schools. Already this session, there's growing bipartisan support for the amendment, and I am calling on the Congress to act speedily to pass it and to let our children pray.

Perhaps some of you read recently about the Lubbock school case, where a judge actually ruled that it was unconstitutional for a school district to give equal treatment to religious and nonreligious student groups, even when the group meetings were being held during the students' own time. The First Amendment never intended to require government to discriminate against religious speech.

Senators Denton and Hatfield have proposed legislation in the Congress on the whole question of prohibiting discrimination against religious forms of student speech. Such legislation could go far to restore freedom of religious speech for public school students. And I hope the Congress considers these bills quickly. And with your help, I think it's possible we could also get the constitutional amendment through the Congress this year.

More than a decade ago, a Supreme Court decision literally wiped off the books of fifty states statutes protecting the rights of unborn children. Abortion on demand now takes the lives of up to one and a half million unborn children a year. Human life legislation ending this tragedy will someday pass the Congress, and you and I must never rest until it does. Unless and until it can be proven that the unborn child is not a living entity, then its right to life, liberty, and the pursuit of happiness must be protected.

You may remember that when abortion on demand began, many, and indeed, I'm sure many of you, warned that the practice would lead to a decline in respect for human life, that the philosophical premises used to justify abortion on demand would ultimately be used to justify other attacks on the sacredness of human life—infanticide or mercy killing. Tragically enough, those warnings proved all too true. Only last year a court permitted the death by starvation of a handicapped infant.

I have directed the Health and Human Services Department to make clear to every health care facility in the United States that the Rehabilitation Act of 1973 protects all handicapped persons against discrimination based on handicaps, including infants. And we have taken the further step of requiring that each and every recipient of federal funds who provides health care services to infants must post and keep posted in a conspicuous place a notice stating that "discriminatory failure to feed and care for handicapped infants in this facility is prohibited by federal law." It also lists a twenty-four-hour, toll-free number so that nurses and others may report violations in time to save the infant's life.

In addition, recent legislation introduced in the Congress by Representative Henry Hyde of Illinois not only increases restrictions on publicly financed abortions, it also addresses this whole problem of infanticide. I urge the Congress to begin hearings and to adopt legislation that will protect the right of life to all children, including the disabled or handicapped.

Now, I'm sure that you must get discouraged at times, but you've done better than you know, perhaps. There's a great spiritual awakening in America, a renewal of the traditional values that have been the bedrock of America's goodness and greatness.

One recent survey by a Washington-based research council concluded that Americans were far more religious than the people of other nations; 95 percent of those surveyed expressed a belief in God and a huge majority believed the Ten Commandments had real meaning in their lives. And another study has found that an overwhelming majority of Americans disapprove of adultery, teenage sex, pornography, abortion, and hard drugs. And this same study showed a deep reverence for the importance of family ties and religious belief.

I think the items that we've discussed here today must be a key part of the nation's political agenda. For the first time the Congress is openly and seriously debating and dealing with the prayer and abortion issues—and that's enormous progress right there. I repeat: America is in the midst of a spiritual awakening and a moral renewal. And with your biblical keynote, I say today, "Yes, let justice roll on like a river, righteousness like a never-failing stream."

Now, obviously, much of this new political and social consensus I've talked about is based on a positive view of American history, one that takes pride in our country's accomplishments and record. But we must never forget that no government schemes are going to perfect man. We know that living in this world means dealing with what philosophers would call the phenomenology of evil or, as theologians would put it, the doctrine of sin.

There is sin and evil in the world, and we're enjoined by Scripture and the Lord Jesus to oppose it with all our might. Our nation, too, has a legacy of evil with which it must deal. The glory of this land has been its capacity for transcending the moral evils of our past. For example, the long struggle of minority citizens for equal rights, once a source of disunity and civil war, is now a point of pride for all Americans. We must never go back. There is no room for racism, anti-Semitism, or other forms of ethnic and racial hatred in this country.

I know that you've been horrified, as have I, by the resurgence of some hate groups preaching bigotry and prejudice. Use the mighty voice of your pulpits and the powerful standing of your churches to denounce and isolate these hate groups in our midst. The commandment given us is clear and simple: "Thou shalt love they neighbor as thyself."

But whatever sad episodes exist in our past, any objective observer must hold a positive view of American history, a history that has been the story of hopes fulfilled and dreams made into reality. Especially in this century, America has kept alight the torch of freedom, but not just for ourselves but for millions of others around the world.

And this brings me to my final point today. During my first press conference as president, in answer to a direct question, I pointed out that, as good Marxist-Leninists, the Soviet leaders have openly and publicly declared that the only morality they recognize is that which will further their cause, which is world revolution. I think I should point out I was only quoting Lenin, their guiding spirit, who said in 1920 that they repudiate all morality that proceeds from supernatural ideas—that's their name for religion—or ideas that are outside class conceptions. Morality is entirely subordinate to the interests of class war. And everything is moral that is necessary for the annihilation of the old, exploiting social order and for uniting the proletariat.

Well, I think the refusal of many influential people to accept this elementary fact of Soviet doctrine illustrates a historical reluctance to see totalitarian powers for what they are. We saw this phenomenon in the 1930s. We see it too often today.

This doesn't mean we should isolate ourselves and refuse to seek an understanding with them. I intend to do everything I can to persuade them of our peaceful intent, to remind them that it was the West that refused to use its nuclear monopoly in the forties and fifties for territorial gain and which now proposes a 50-percent cut in strategic ballistic missiles and the elimination of an entire class of land-based, intermediate-range nuclear missiles.

At the same time, however, they must be made to understand we will never compromise our principles and standards. We will never give away our freedom. We will never abandon our belief in God. And we will never stop searching for a genuine peace. But we can assure none of these things America stands for through the so-called nuclear freeze solutions proposed by some.

The truth is that a freeze now would be a very dangerous fraud, for that is merely the illusion of peace. The reality is that we must find peace through strength.

I would agree to a freeze if only we could freeze the Soviets' global desires. A freeze at current levels of weapons would remove any incentive for the Soviets to negotiate seriously in Geneva and virtually end our chances to achieve the major arms reductions which we have proposed. Instead, they would achieve their objectives through the freeze.

A freeze would reward the Soviet Union for its enormous and unparalleled military buildup. It would prevent the essential and long overdue modernization of United States and allied defenses and would leave our aging forces increasingly vulnerable. And an honest freeze would require extensive prior negotiations on the systems and numbers to be limited and on the measures to ensure effective verification and compliance. And the kind of a freeze that has been suggested would be virtually impossible to verify. Such a major effort would divert us completely from our current negotiations on achieving substantial reductions.

A number of years ago, I heard a young father, a very prominent young man in the entertainment world, addressing a tremendous gathering in California. It was during the time of the cold war, and communism and our own way of life were very much on people's minds. And he was speaking to that subject. And suddenly, though, I heard him saying, "I love my little girls more than anything—" And I said to myself, "Oh, no, don't. You can't—don't say that." But I had underestimated him. He went on: "I would rather see my little girls die now, still believing in God, than have them grow up under communism and one day die no longer believing in God."

There were thousands of young people in that audience. They came to their feet with shouts of joy. They had instantly recognized the profound truth in what he had said, with regard to the physical and the soul and what was truly important.

Yes, let us pray for the salvation of all of those who live in that totalitarian darkness—pray they will discover the joy of knowing God. But until they do, let us be aware that while they preach the supremacy of the state, declare its omnipotence over individual man, and predict its eventual domination of all peoples on the earth, they are the focus of evil in the modern world.

It was C. S. Lewis who, in his unforgettable *Screwtape Letters*, wrote: "The greatest evil is not done now in those sordid 'dens of crime' that Dickens loved to paint. It is not even done in concentration camps and labor camps. In those we see its final result. But it is conceived and ordered (moved, seconded, carried and minuted) in clean, carpeted, warmed, and well-lighted offices, by quiet men with white collars and cut fingernails and smooth-shaven cheeks who do not need to raise their voice."

Well, because these "quiet men" do not "raise their voices," because they sometimes speak in soothing tones of brotherhood and peace, because, like other dictators before them, they're always making "their final territorial demand," some would have us accept them at their word and accommodate ourselves to their aggressive impulses. But if history teaches anything, it teaches that simpleminded appeasement or wishful thinking about our adversaries is folly. It means the betrayal of our past, the squandering of our freedom.

So, I urge you to speak out against those who would place the United States in a position of military and moral inferiority. You know, I've always believed that old Screwtape reserved his best efforts for those of you in the church. So, in your discussions of the nuclear freeze proposals, I urge you to beware the temptation of pride—the temptation of blithely declaring yourselves above it all and label both sides equally at fault, to ignore the facts of history and the aggressive impulses of an evil empire, to simply call the arms race a giant misunderstanding and thereby remove yourself from the struggle between right and wrong and good and evil.

I ask you to resist the attempts of those who would have you withhold your support for our efforts, this administration's efforts, to keep America strong and free, while we negotiate real and verifiable reductions in the world's nuclear arsenals and one day, with God's help, their total elimination.

While America's military strength is important, let me add here that I've always maintained that the struggle now going on for the world will never be decided by bombs or rockets, by armies or military might. The real crisis we face today is a spiritual one; at root, it is a test of moral will and faith.

Whittaker Chambers, the man whose own religious conversion made him a witness to one of the terrible traumas of our time, the Hiss-Chambers case, wrote that the crisis of the Western world exists to the degree in which the West is indifferent to God, the degree to which it collaborates in communism's attempt to make man stand alone without God. And then he said, for Marxism-Leninism is actually the second-oldest faith, first proclaimed in the Garden of Eden with the words of temptation, "Ye shall be as gods."

The Western world can answer this challenge, he wrote, "but only provided that its faith in God and the freedom He enjoins is as great as communism's faith in Man."

I believe we shall rise to the challenge. I believe that communism is another sad, bizarre chapter in human history whose last pages even now are being written. I believe this because the source of our strength in the quest for human freedom is not material, but spiritual. And because it knows no limitation, it must terrify and ultimately triumph over those who would enslave their fellow man. For in the words of Isaiah: "He giveth power to the faint; and to them that have no might He increased strength.... But they that wait upon the Lord shall renew their strength; they shall mount up with wings as eagles; they shall run, and not be weary...."

Yes, change your world. One of our Founding Fathers, Thomas Paine, said, "We have it within our power to begin the world over again." We can do it, doing together what no one church could do by itself.

God bless you, and thank you very much.

Questions

1. What was Reagan's cultural and religious agenda for the United States?
2. How did Ronald Reagan frame the Cold War in theological terms? How did other contemporaries see the Cold War?

30-2 Creationism, the Public Schools, and the First Amendment, *Edwards v. Aguillard* (1987)

With the rise of the New Right came renewed attacks on the theory of evolution, which serves as the foundation of the life sciences. The teaching of evolution in public schools has been a source of contention for Christian fundamentalists going back to the Scopes Trial in 1925 (Document 23-7), since the theory is seen as challenging their literal reading of the Bible and as devaluing life, especially human life, because, they believe, it calls into question life's special or divine origin. Christian fundamentalists have advocated passing laws at the state level requiring that their religious beliefs, that is, creationism (later called "intelligent design"), be included in the science curriculum. However, in *Edwards v. Aguillard*, the Supreme Court ruled (7–2) that requiring the teaching of religion is a violation of the First Amendment since "Congress shall make no law respecting an establishment of religion, or prohibiting the free exercise thereof." Justice Brennan delivered the opinion of the Court that struck down Louisiana's Creationism Act.

Source: "Court on Creation Science, June 19, 1987," *Historic Documents of 1987* (Washington, DC: Congressional Quarterly, 1987), 567–572. Reprinted by permission.

JUSTICE BRENNAN delivered the opinion of the Court.

The question for decision is whether Louisiana's "Balanced Treatment for Creation-Science and Evolution-Science in Public School Instruction" Act (Creationism Act) is facially invalid as violative of the Establishment Clause of the First Amendment.

I

The Creationism Act forbids the teaching of the theory of evolution in public schools unless accompanied by instruction in "creation science." No school is required to teach evolution or creation science. If either is taught, however, the other must also be taught. The theories of evolution and creation science are statutorily defined as "the scientific evidences for [creation or evolution] and inferences from those scientific evidences."

Appellees, who include parents of children attending Louisiana public schools, Louisiana teachers, and religious leaders, challenged the constitutionality of the Act in District Court, seeking an injunction and declaratory relief. Appellants, Louisiana officials charged with implementing the Act, defended on the ground that the purpose of the Act is to protect a legitimate secular interest, namely, academic freedom. Appellees attacked the Act as facially invalid because it violated the Establishment Clause and made a motion for summary judgment. The District Court granted the motion. . . . The court held that there can be no valid secular reason for prohibiting the teaching of evolution, a theory historically opposed by some religious denominations. The court further concluded that "the teaching of 'creation-science' and 'creationism,' as contemplated by the statute, involves teaching 'tailored to the principles' of a particular religious sect or group of sects." . . . The District Court therefore held that the Creationism Act violated the Establishment Clause either because it prohibited the teaching of evolution or because it required the teaching of creation science with the purpose of advancing a particular religious doctrine.

The Court of Appeals affirmed. The court observed that the statute's avowed purpose of protecting academic freedom was inconsistent with requiring, upon risk of sanction, the teaching of creation science whenever evolution is taught. The court found that the Louisiana legislature's actual intent was "to discredit evolution by counterbalancing its teaching at every turn with the teaching of creationism, a religious belief." Because the Creationism Act was thus a law furthering a particular religious belief, the Court of Appeals held that the Act violated the Establishment Clause. A suggestion for rehearing en banc was denied over a dissent. We noted probable jurisdiction and now affirm.

II

The Establishment Clause forbids the enactment of any law "respecting an establishment of religion." The Court has applied a three-pronged test to determine whether legislation comports with the Establishment Clause. First, the legislature must have adopted the law with a secular purpose. Second, the statute's principal or primary effect must be one that neither advances nor inhibits religion. Third, the statute must not result in an excessive entanglement of government with religion. *Lemon v. Kurtzman* (1971). State action violates the Establishment Clause if it fails to satisfy any of these prongs.

In this case, the Court must determine whether the Establishment Clause was violated in the special context of the public elementary and secondary school system. States and local school boards are generally afforded considerable discretion in operating public schools. . . . "At the same time . . . we have necessarily recognized that the discretion of the States and local school boards in matters of education must be exercised in a manner that comports with the transcendent imperatives of the First Amendment." *Board of Education v. Pico* (1982).

The Court has been particularly vigilant in monitoring compliance with the Establishment Clause in elementary and secondary schools. Families entrust public schools with the education of their children, but condition their trust on the understanding that the classroom will not purposely be used to advance religious views that may conflict with the private beliefs of the student and his or her family. Students in such institutions are impressionable and their attendance is involuntary.... The State exerts great authority and coercive power through mandatory attendance requirements, and because of the students' emulation of teachers as role models and the children's susceptibility to peer pressure.... Furthermore, "[t]he public school is at once the symbol of our democracy and the most pervasive means for promoting our common destiny. In no activity of the State is it more vital to keep out divisive forces than in its schools...." *Illinois ex rel. McCollum v. Board of Education* (1948)....

Consequently, the Court has been required often to invalidate statutes which advance religion in public elementary and secondary schools....

Therefore, in employing the three-pronged *Lemon* test, we must do so mindful of the particular concerns that arise in the context of public elementary and secondary schools. We now turn to the evaluation of the Act under the *Lemon* test.

III

Lemon's first prong focuses on the purpose that animated adoption of the Act. "The purpose prong of the *Lemon* test asks whether government's actual purpose is to endorse or disapprove of religion." *Lynch v. Donnelly* (1984).... In this case, the petitioners have identified no clear secular purpose for the Louisiana Act.

True, the Act's stated purpose is to protect academic freedom. This phrase might, in common parlance, be understood as referring to enhancing the freedom of teachers to teach what they will. The Court of Appeals, however, correctly concluded that the Act was not designed to further that goal. We find no merit in the State's argument that the "legislature may not [have] use[d] the terms 'academic freedom' in the correct legal sense. They might have [had] in mind, instead, a basic concept of fairness; teaching all of the evidence." Even if "academic freedom" is read to mean "teaching all of the evidence" with respect to the origin of human beings, the Act does not further this purpose. The goal of providing a more comprehensive science curriculum is not furthered either by outlawing the teaching of evolution or by requiring the teaching of creation science.

A

... It is clear from the legislative history that the purpose of the legislative sponsor, [state] Senator Bill Keith, was to narrow the science curriculum. During the legislative hearings, Senator Keith stated: "My preference would be that neither [creationism nor evolution] be taught." Such a ban on teaching does not promote — indeed, it undermines — the provision of a comprehensive scientific education.

It is equally clear that requiring schools to teach creation science with evolution does not advance academic freedom. The Act does not grant teachers a flexibility that they did not already possess to supplant the present science curriculum with the presentation of theories, besides evolution, about the origin of life. Indeed, the Court of Appeals found that no law prohibited Louisiana public schoolteachers from teaching any scientific theory.... The Act provides Louisiana schoolteachers with no new authority. Thus the stated purpose is not furthered by it.

The Alabama statute held unconstitutional in *Wallace v. Jaffree* [1985] is analogous. In *Wallace*, the State characterized its new law as one designed to provide a one-minute period for meditation. We rejected that stated purpose as insufficient, because a previously adopted Alabama law already provided for such a one-minute period. Thus, in this case, as in *Wallace*, "[a]ppellants have not identified any secular purpose that was not fully served by [existing state law] before the enactment of [the statute in question]."

Furthermore, the goal of basic "fairness" is hardly furthered by the Act's discriminatory preference for the teaching of creation science and against the teaching of evolution. While requiring that curriculum guides be developed for creation science, the Act says nothing of comparable guides for evolution. Similarly, research services are supplied for creation science but not for evolution. Only "creation scientists" can serve on the panel that supplies the resource services. The Act forbids school boards to discriminate against anyone who "chooses to be a creation-scientist" or to teach "creationism," but fails to protect those who choose to teach evolution or any other non-creation science theory, or who refuse to teach creation science.

If the Louisiana legislature's purpose was solely to maximize the comprehensiveness and effectiveness of science instruction, it would have encouraged the teaching of all scientific theories about the origins of humankind. But under the Act's requirements, teachers who were once free to teach any and all facets of this subject are now unable to do so. Moreover, the Act fails even to ensure that creation science will be taught, but instead requires the teaching of this theory only when the theory of evolution is taught. Thus we agree with the Court of Appeals' conclusion that the Act does not serve to protect academic freedom, but has the distinctly different purpose of discrediting "evolution by counterbalancing its teaching at every turn with the teaching of creation science...."

B

... [W]e need not be blind in this case to the legislature's preeminent religious purpose in enacting this statute. There is a historic and contemporaneous link between the teachings of certain religious denominations and the teaching of evolution. It was this link that concerned the Court in *Epperson v. Arkansas* (1968), which also involved a facial challenge to a statute regulating the teaching of evolution. In that case, the Court reviewed an Arkansas statute that made it unlawful for an instructor to teach evolution or to use a textbook that referred to this scientific theory. Although the ... law did not explicitly state its predominate religious purpose, the Court could not ignore that "[t]he statute was a product of the upsurge of 'fundamentalist' religious fervor" that has long viewed this particular scientific theory as contradicting the literal interpretation of the Bible. After reviewing the history of anti-evolution statutes, the Court determined that "there can be no doubt that the motivation for the [Arkansas] law was the same [as other anti-evolution statutes]: to suppress the teaching of a theory which, it was thought, 'denied' the divine creation of man." The Court found that there can be no legitimate state interest in protecting particular religions from scientific views "distasteful to them," and concluded "that the First Amendment does not permit the State to require that teaching and learning must be tailored to the principles or prohibitions of any religious sect or dogma."

These same historic and contemporaneous antagonisms between the teachings of certain religious denominations and the teaching of evolution are present in this case. The preeminent purpose of the Louisiana legislature was clearly to advance the religious viewpoint that a supernatural being created humankind. . . .

Furthermore, it is not happenstance that the legislature required the teaching of a theory that coincided with this religious view. The legislative history documents that the Act's primary purpose was to change the science curriculum of public schools in order to provide persuasive advantage to a particular religious doctrine that rejects the factual basis of evolution in its entirety. . . .

. . . [T]he Creationism Act is designed *either* to promote the theory of creation science which embodies a particular religious tenet by requiring that creation science be taught whenever evolution is taught *or* to prohibit the teaching of a scientific theory disfavored by certain religious sects by forbidding the teaching of evolution when creation science is not also taught. The Establishment Clause, however, "forbids *alike* the preference of a religious doctrine *or* the prohibition of theory which is deemed antagonistic to a particular dogma." Because the primary purpose of the Creationism Act is to advance a particular religious belief, the Act endorses religion in violation of the First Amendment.

We do not imply that a legislature could never require that scientific critiques of prevailing scientific theories be taught. . . . [T]eaching a variety of scientific theories about the origins of humankind to schoolchildren might be validly done with the clear secular intent of enhancing the effectiveness of science instruction. But because the primary purpose of the Creationism Act is to endorse a particular religious doctrine, the Act furthers religion in violation of the Establishment Clause. . . .

Questions

1. What is the *Lemon* test?
2. Compare and contrast Documents 23-7 and 30-2. What were the different legal issues and strategies in these two cases?

Question for Further Consideration

1. What was the New Right? How did it differ from the "old right"?

The Reagan Presidency, 1981–1989

Reagan's election victories and presidency (especially his first term) defined the 1980s much as Franklin D. Roosevelt's election victories and presidency had defined the 1930s. Each made effective use of his era's most direct and seemingly personal means of mass communication—radio in Roosevelt's case, television in Reagan's. Indeed, Reagan had been a Hollywood movie actor. Although the periods in which FDR and Reagan led the nation differed, as did the priorities of the two presidents, each sought to reorient government—to such an extent that the term *revolutionary* was applied to both administrations.

For his part, President Reagan sought to cut taxes, reduce spending, sharply increase military expenditures (beyond Carter's buildup), and (again outdoing Carter) curtail government's regulatory functions. In the end, tax cutting and spending priorities combined to produce budget deficits and a mounting national debt. Domestic spending restraints and reductions primarily affected smaller programs that benefited the poor rather than larger ones that benefited the broader public. Reagan, like Roosevelt, fell short of effecting revolutionary change in America, but both presidents achieved much and reoriented the national debate.

President Roosevelt died in office, to be succeeded by his vice president, Harry S. Truman, who went on to win a presidential term in his own right. Ronald Reagan, who left the presidency after two terms, was followed by George H. W. Bush, who by winning handily in 1988 over the Democratic Party's nominee, Michael Dukakis, became the first serving vice president since Martin Van Buren (1836) to become president. Bush failed to win reelection in 1992, however.

Reagan's presidency proved to be a difficult act to follow, in part, because Bush had to deal with the problems inherited from his predecessor, especially chronic budget deficits and the financial crisis of the nation's savings and loans associations (S&Ls). Bush addressed the budget crisis by negotiating a major tax increase and a freeze on discretionary spending with congressional Democrats. However, conservative Republicans were furious over this deal, since it was a violation of his politic but unwise 1988 pledge of "no new taxes." Bush's administration cleaned up the S&L situation, but doing so proved to be expensive. In the final analysis, however, a short-lived economic recession, not as serious as the one that had buffeted the nation during Reagan's first term, likely hurt Bush most of all. Unlike Reagan, Bush lacked the political skills and the public support to survive the rocky spell.

In Document 30-3, Donald T. Regan describes the Reagan administration from the inside.

30-3 For the Record (1988)

Donald T. Regan

Donald T. Regan (1918–2003) served President Reagan first as secretary of the treasury and then as chief of staff. Here, in a book written while Reagan was still in office, Regan discusses the president.

Source: Excerpted from Donald T. Regan, *For the Record: From Wall Street to Washington*, 246–250, 266–268. Copyright © 1988 by Donald T. Regan. Reprinted by permission of Harcourt, Inc.

Ronald Reagan seemed to be regarded by certain members of his inner circle not as the powerful and utterly original leader that he was, but as a sort of supreme anchorman whose public persona was the most important element of the Presidency. According to the rules of this school of political management, controversy was to be avoided at nearly any cost: every Presidential action must produce a positive public effect. In practice, this meant stimulating a positive effect in the media, with the result that the press, not the people, became the President's primary constituency. . . .

It was [deputy chief of staff Michael] Deaver's job to advise the President on image, and image was what he talked about nearly all the time. It was Deaver who identified the story of the day at the eight o'clock staff meeting and coordinated the plans for dealing with it, Deaver who created and approved photo opportunities, Deaver who alerted the President to the snares being laid by the press that day. Deaver was a master of his craft. He saw—designed—each Presidential action as a one-minute or two-minute spot on the evening network news, or a picture on page one of the *Washington Post* or the *New York Times*, and conceived every Presidential appearance in terms of camera angles. . . .

Every moment of every public appearance was scheduled, every word was scripted, every place where Reagan was expected to stand was chalked with toe marks. The President was always being prepared for a performance, and this had the inevitable effect of preserving him from confrontation and the genuine interplay of opinion, question, and argument that form the basis of decision. . . .

The President is possessed of a philosophical agenda based on a lifetime of experience and thought. He is a formidable reader and a talented conversationalist with a gift for listening. It was precisely this gift that led to many of his gaffes and misstatements in encounters with the press: Ronald Reagan remembered nearly everything that was said to him. If someone told him (to use a wholly fictitious example) that there had been 35,987 hairs in Stalin's mustache, this fact would go into the Presidential memory bank, possibly to emerge weeks or months later in the middle of a press conference. It never seemed to occur to him that anyone would give him incorrect information. His mind was a trove of facts and anecdotes, something like the morgue of one of his favorite magazines, *Reader's Digest*, and it was impossible to guess when or why he might access any one of these millions of bytes of data. . . .

Reagan shunned the abstract, the theoretical, the cold and impersonal approach to problems. His love of stories was connected to this same tendency to see everything in human terms. Although even some of his intimates scoffed (ever so discreetly) at his bottomless fund of anecdotes about it, Reagan's experience as governor of California constituted a unique body of executive and political experience. He had a formidable gift for debate when he was allowed to debate in a spontaneous way. His problems in these matters, as in the first debate with Walter Mondale in 1984, nearly always resulted from his being overprogrammed. His briefers, forgetting that a President has a cast of thousands to remember facts for him, had crammed his mind with so many bits of information that he tried to rely on data instead of explaining the issue and defending his policy. I had seen him defend his ideas and critique the proposals of other heads of state with the best of them at six international economic summits, and it was not uncommon for him to render courageous decisions on domestic economic questions in the face of nearly unanimous advice and pressure to do the opposite. . . .

[Regan describes giving the president a working paper in August 1985 outlining what he thought the White House's priorities should be for the following year.]

Ronald Reagan read the paper while he was at the ranch and handed it back to me on his return without spoken or written comment.

"What did you think of it?" I asked.

It's good, the President replied, nodding in approval. It's really good, Don.

I waited for him to say more. He did not. He had no questions to ask, no objections to raise, no instructions to issue. I realized that the policy that would determine the course of the world's most powerful nation for the next two years and deeply influence the fate of the Republican party in the 1986 midterm elections had been adopted without amendment. It seemed, also, that I had been authorized as Chief of Staff to make the necessary arrangements to carry out the policy. It was taken for granted that the President would do whatever was asked of him to make the effort a success. We went on to the next item on the agenda.

I confess that I was surprised that this weighty matter was decided so quickly and with so little ceremony. In a way, of course, it was flattering; it is always gratifying to anticipate the boss's wishes with acceptable accuracy. Still, I was uneasy. Did the President really want us to do all these things with no more discussion than this? I decided that this must be the case, since always in the past, if he did not say no, the answer was yes. By now I understood that the President did not share my love of detail and my enthusiasm for planning. I knew that he was not an aggressive manager. Perhaps I should have quizzed him on tax policy or Central America or our approach to trade negotiations; certainly my instincts and the practice of a lifetime nudged me in that direction. But I held my tongue. It is one thing brashly to speak your mind to an ordinary mortal and another to say, "Wait a minute!" to the President of the United States. The mystery of the office is a potent inhibitor. The President, you feel, has his reasons.

Another President would almost certainly have had his own ideas on the mechanics of policy, but Reagan did not trouble himself with such minutiae. His preoccupation was with what might be called "the outer Presidency." He was content to let others cope with the inner details of running the Administration. . . . Reagan chose his aides and then followed their advice almost without question. He trusted his lieutenants to act on his intentions, rather than on his spoken instructions, and though he sometimes asked what some of his less visible Cabinet officers were doing with their departments, he seldom spontaneously called for a detailed status report. The degree of trust involved in this method of leadership must be unprecedented in modern American history. Sometimes—as was inevitable given that many of his closest aides, including almost all of the Cabinet, were virtual strangers to him—this trust was betrayed in shocking fashion. When that happened Reagan seldom criticized, seldom complained, never scolded. Not even the Iran-Contra debacle could provoke him into harsh words, much less subordinates who had let him down.

Never—absolutely never in my experience—did President Reagan really lose his temper or utter a rude or unkind word. Never did he issue a direct order, although I, at least, sometimes devoutly wished that he would. He listened, acquiesced, played his role, and waited for the next act to be written. From the point of view of my own experience and nature, this was an altogether baffling way of doing things. But my own style was not the case in point. Reagan's method had worked well enough to make him President of the United States, and well enough for the nation under his leadership to transform its mood from pessimism to optimism, its economy from stagnation to steady growth, and its position in the world from weakness to strength. Common sense suggested that the President knew something that the rest of us did not know. It was my clear duty to do things his way.

Questions

1. What did Regan see as Ronald Reagan's strengths and weaknesses as president?
2. What relation, if any, do you see between the president's strengths and weaknesses, as viewed by Regan?

Questions for Further Thought

1. Compare Ronald Reagan's acceptance speech (Document 29-11) with Donald Regan's account of Reagan's presidency (Document 30-3).
2. Based on the Regan selection (Document 30-3), how would you account for Ronald Reagan's popularity?

Defeating Communism and Creating a New World Order

Ronald Reagan became president at a difficult juncture for American foreign policy. Relations with the Soviet Union soured following the invasion of Afghanistan late in 1979. The Carter administration had responded by curtailing key exports to the Soviet Union, boycotting the 1980 summer Olympic games in Moscow, and calling for increased military spending and registration for the draft. President Carter had also enunciated the Carter Doctrine, warning that any "outside" effort to dominate the Persian Gulf would be resisted, by "military force" if need be. Meanwhile, developments in Iran during 1979 and 1980—the ouster of the shah, the militants' later seizure of the American embassy and diplomatic personnel in Tehran, and the failure of an American military mission to rescue the hostages—created another crisis, this one both serious (especially in its effect on petroleum prices) and humiliating.

President Reagan's first term was marked by further escalation of the renewed Cold War. Reagan not only employed strident anti-Soviet rhetoric (see Document 30-1), he also accelerated the military buildup initiated by Carter and increased support for the Afghan mujahideen; these were men, including Osama bin Laden, who fiercely resisted the Soviet occupation. These "freedom fighters," as Ronald Reagan called them, succeeded in defeating the Soviets and forcing their withdrawal from Afghanistan. Elsewhere, Reagan ordered air strikes against Libya's leader, Muammar al-Qaddafi, to punish him for his sponsorship of terrorism (which he would renounce in 2003 after years of negotiation), and dispatched marines to Lebanon, which was reeling under Muslim-Christian civil strife and the presence of the Palestine Liberation Organization (PLO) and Syrian and Israeli forces. In 1983, Muslim terrorists blew up the American embassy in Beirut and later a military barracks, killing more than two hundred marines, more than had died on any single day during the war in Vietnam. In response to these deadly attacks, Reagan ordered the U.S. Marines to withdraw from Lebanon early the next year. In the Western Hemisphere, the United States took sides in the internal conflicts in Guatemala, El Salvador, and Nicaragua and militarily overthrew a Cuban-backed leftist government on the island of Grenada, in the Caribbean.

During Reagan's second term, his administration was bruised by the Iran-Contra affair, but it also played a role in defusing Soviet-American tensions. Iran-Contra, first exposed during 1986, involved clandestine dealings with the militant regime of Iran, then at war with Saddam Hussein's Iraq, including weapons sales, in the hope that Iran would persuade its allies in Lebanon to release American hostages there. Proceeds from the arms sales were channeled to the Contras, who were fighting Nicaragua's Sandinista government. The Sandinistas were a Marxist group that had overthrown the Somoza dictatorship in 1979, and they had allied themselves with Cuba and the Soviet Union. At the same time, Reagan established a working relationship with Mikhail Gorbachev, who came to power in 1985 and sought to modernize his nation's deteriorating economy. Arms control talks resumed, and the two leaders met at four summit conferences between 1985 and 1988.

President George H. W. Bush, who succeeded Reagan, was standing watch when most Communist regimes (including the Soviet Union) collapsed, the Warsaw Pact was terminated, and Germany reunified. Although Communist governments remained very much in power in North Korea, China, Vietnam, and Cuba, the Cold War was nevertheless declared over, with the United States and its allies victorious. Diplomatic-military crises still existed, however, leading to United Nations peacekeeping missions involving U.S. troops (as in Somalia, 1992–1993) or U.S. intervention in yet another Latin American country (Panama, 1989). Above all, large American and allied forces were deployed in the Persian Gulf area to pressure — and ultimately force — Saddam Hussein's Iraqis out of Kuwait (1990–1991). President Bush prudently refrained, however, from invading and occupying Iraq itself. In the process of compelling Hussein out of Kuwait, the United States built up a military presence in Saudi Arabia, a development which would become a major grievance for Al Qaeda, a group that had originally been created to help force the Soviet Union out of Afghanistan.

Document 30-4 is an excerpt from Francis Fukuyama's famous article "The End of History" (1989); Document 30-5 offers the address of President Bush to the United Nations General Assembly on the implications of the crisis in the Persian Gulf; Document 30-6 presents the reflections of university students who would not be called to serve in the military; and Document 30-7 is an excerpt from Samuel P. Huntington's often-cited article "The Clash of Civilizations?" (1993).

30-4 The End of History (1989)

Francis Fukuyama

With the fall of the Berlin Wall in 1989, it seemed to many contemporary observers that the twentieth century, which had been marked by intense ideological conflict, was finally over. Francis Fukuyama (b. 1952), an influential American philosopher and professor at Johns Hopkins University, put it this way: "the century that began full of self-confidence in the ultimate triumph of Western liberal democracy seems at its close to be returning full circle to where it started: not to 'an end of ideology' or a convergence between capitalism and socialism, as earlier predicted, but to an unabashed victory of economic and political liberalism." The following is an excerpt from his optimistic essay "The End of History," which was published in the foreign affairs journal *The National Interest*.

Source: Francis Fukuyama, "The End of History," *The National Interest* (Summer 1989) 16:3–18.

In watching the flow of events over the past decade or so, it is hard to avoid the feeling that something very fundamental has happened in world history. The past year has seen a flood of articles commemorating the end of the Cold War, and the fact that "peace" seems to be breaking out in many regions of the world. Most of these analyses lack any larger conceptual framework for distinguishing between what is essential and what is contingent or accidental in world history, and are predictably superficial. If Mr. Gorbachev were ousted from the Kremlin or a new Ayatollah proclaimed the millennium for a desolate Middle Eastern capital, these same commentators would scramble to announce the rebirth of a new era or conflict.

And yet, all of these people sense dimly that there is some larger process at work, a process that gives coherence and order to the daily headlines. The twentieth century saw the developed world descend into a paroxysm of ideological violence, as liberalism contended first with the remnants of absolutism, then bolshevism and fascism, and finally an updated Marxism that threatened to lead to the ultimate apocalypse of nuclear war. But the century that began full of self-confidence in the ultimate triumph of Western liberal democracy seems at its close to be returning full circle to where it started: not to an "end of ideology" or a convergence between capitalism and socialism, as earlier predicted, but to an unabashed victory of economic and political liberalism.

The triumph of the West, of the Western *idea*, is evident first of all in the total exhaustion of viable systematic alternatives to Western liberalism. In the past decade, there have been unmistakable changes in the intellectual climate of the world's two largest communist countries, and the beginnings of significant reform movements in both. But this phenomenon extends beyond high politics and it can be seen also in the ineluctable spread of consumerist Western culture in such diverse contexts as the peasants' markets and color television sets now omnipresent throughout China, the cooperative restaurants and clothing stores opened in the past year in Moscow, the Beethoven piped into Japanese department stores, and the rock music enjoyed alike in Prague, Rangoon, and Tehran.

What we may be witnessing is not just the end of the Cold War, or the passing of a particular period of postwar history, but the end of history as such: that is, the end point of mankind's ideological evolution and the universalization of Western liberal democracy as the final form of human government. This is not to say that there will no longer be events to fill the pages of *Foreign Affairs*'s yearly summaries of international relations, for the victory of liberalism has occurred primarily in the realm of ideas or consciousness and is as yet incomplete in the real or material world. But there are powerful reasons for believing that it is the ideal that will govern the material world *in the long run*. To understand how this is so, we must first consider some theoretical issues concerning the nature of historical change.

I

The notion of the end of history is not an original one. Its best known propagator was Karl Marx, who believed that the direction of historical development was a purposeful one determined by the interplay of material forces, and would come to an end only with the achievement of a communist utopia that would finally resolve all prior contradictions. But the concept of history as a dialectical process with a beginning, a middle, and an end was borrowed by Marx from his great German predecessor Georg Wilhelm Friedrich Hegel.

For better or worse, much of Hegel's historicism has become part of our contemporary intellectual baggage. The notion that mankind has progressed through a series of primitive stages of consciousness on his path to the present, and that these stages corresponded to concrete forms of social organization, such a tribal, slave owning, theocratic, and finally democratic egalitarian societies, has become inseparable from the modern understanding of man. Hegel was the first philosopher to speak the language of modern social science, insofar as man for him was the product of his concrete historical and social environment and not, as earlier natural right theorists would have it, a collection of more or less fixed "natural" attributes. The mastery and transformation of man's natural environment through the application of science and technology was originally not a Marxist concept, but a Hegelian one. Unlike later historicists whose historical relativism degenerated into relativism *tout court*, however, Hegel believed that history culminated in an absolute moment—a moment in which a final, rational form of society and state became victorious.

It is Hegel's misfortune to be known now primarily as Marx's precursor, and it is our misfortune that few of us are familiar with Hegel's work from direct study, but only as it has been filtered through the distorting lens of Marxism. In France, however, there has been an effort to save Hegel from his Marxist interpreters and to resurrect him as the philosopher who most correctly speaks to our time. Among those modern French interpreters of Hegel, the greatest was certainly Alexandre Kojève, a brilliant Russian emigre who taught a highly influential series of seminars in Paris in the 1930's at the *Ecole Practique des Hautes Etudes*. While largely unknown in the United States, Kojève had a major impact on the intellectual life of the continent. Among his students ranged such future luminaries as Jean-Paul Sartre on the Left and Raymond Aron on the Right; postwar existentialism borrowed many of its basic categories from Hegel via Kojève.

Kojève sought to resurrect the Hegel of the *Phenomenology of Mind*, the Hegel who proclaimed history to be at an end in 1806. For as early as this Hegel saw in Napoleon's defeat of the Prussian monarchy at the Battle of Jena the victory of the ideals of the French Revolution, and the imminent universalization of the state incorporating the principles of liberty and equality. Kojève, far from rejecting Hegel in light of the turbulent events of the next century and a half, insisted that the latter had been essentially correct. The Battle of Jena marked the end of history because it was at that point that the *vanguard* of humanity (a term quite familiar to Marxists) actualized the principles of the French Revolution. While there was considerable work to be done after 1806—abolishing slavery and the slave trade, extending the franchise to workers, women, blacks, and other racial minorities, etc.—the basic *principles* of the liberal democratic state could not be improved upon. The two world wars in this century and their attendant revolutions and upheavals simply had the effect of extending those principles spatially, such that the various provinces of human civilization were brought up to the level of its most advanced outposts, and of forcing those societies in Europe and North America at the vanguard of civilization to implement their liberalism more fully.

The state that emerges at the end of history is liberal insofar as it recognizes and protects through a system of law man's universal right to freedom, and democratic insofar as it exists only with the consent of the governed. For Kojève, this so-called "universal homogenous state" found real-life embodiment in the countries of postwar Western Europe—precisely those flabby, prosperous, self-satisfied, inward-looking, weak-willed states whose grandest project was nothing more heroic than the creation of the Common Market. But this was only to be expected. For human history and the conflict that characterized it was based on the existence of "contradictions": primitive man's quest for mutual recognition, the dialectic of the master and slave, the transformation and mastery of nature, the struggle for the universal recognition of rights, and the dichotomy between proletarian and capitalist. But in the universal homogenous state, all prior contradictions are resolved and all human needs are satisfied. There is no struggle or conflict over "large" issues, and consequently no need for generals or statesmen; what remains is primarily economic activity. And indeed, Kojève's life was consistent with his teaching. Believing that there was no more work for philosophers as well, since Hegel (correctly understood) had already achieved absolute knowledge, Kojève left teaching after the war and spent the remainder of his life working as a bureaucrat in the European Economic Community, until his death in 1968.

To his contemporaries at mid-century, Kojève's proclamation of the end of history must have seemed like the typical eccentric solipsism of a French intellectual, coming as it did on the heels of World War II and at the very height of the Cold War. To comprehend how Kojève could have been so audacious as to assert that history has ended, we must first of all understand their meaning of Hegelian idealism.

II

For Hegel, the contradictions that drive history exist first of all in the realm of human consciousness, i.e. on the level of ideas—not the trivial election year proposals of American politicians, but ideas in the sense of large unifying worldviews that might best be understood under the rubric of ideology. Ideology in this sense is not restricted to the secular and explicit political doctrines we usually associate with the term, but can include religion, culture, and the complex of moral values underlying any society as well.

Hegel's view of the relationship between the ideal and the real or material worlds was an extremely complicated one, beginning with the fact that for him the distinction between the two was only apparent. He did not believe that the real world conformed or could be made to conform to ideological preconceptions of philosophy professors in any simpleminded way, or that the "material" world could not impinge on the ideal. Indeed, Hegel the professor was temporarily thrown out of work as a result of a very material event, the Battle of Jena. But while Hegel's writing and thinking could be stopped by a bullet from the material world, the hand on the trigger of the gun was motivated in turn by the ideas of liberty and equality that had driven the French Revolution.

For Hegel, all human behavior in the material world, and hence all human history, is rooted in a prior state of consciousness—an idea similar to the new [idea] expressed by John Maynard Keynes when he said that the views of men of affairs were usually derived from defunct economists and academic scribblers of earlier generations. This consciousness may not be explicit and self-aware, as are modern political doctrines, but may rather take the form of religion or simple cultural or moral habits. And yet this realm of consciousness *in the long run* necessarily becomes manifest in the material world, indeed creates the material world in its own image. Consciousness is causes and not effect, and can develop autonomously from the material world, hence the real subtext underlying the apparent jumble of current events is the history of ideology.

Hegel's idealism has fared poorly at the hands of later thinkers. Marx revered the priority of the real and the ideal completely, relegating the entire realm of consciousness—religion, art, culture, philosophy itself—to a "superstructure" that was determined entirely by the prevailing material mode of production. Yet another unfortunate legacy of Marxism is our tendency to retreat into materialists or utilitarian explanations of political or historical phenomena, and our disinclination to believe in the autonomous power of ideas. A recent example of this is Paul Kennedy's hugely successful *The Rise and Fall of the Great Powers*, which ascribes the decline of great powers to simple economic overextension. Obviously, this is true on some level: an empire whose economy is barely above the level of subsistence cannot bankrupt its treasury indefinitely. But whether a highly productive modern industrial society chooses to spend 3 or 7 percent of its GNP on defense rather than consumption is entirely a matter of that society's political priorities, which are in turn determined in the realm of consciousness.

The materialist bias of modern thought is characteristic not only of people on the Left who may be sympathetic to Marxism, but of many passionate anti-Marxists as well. Indeed, there is on the right what one might label the *Wall Street Journal* school of deterministic materialism that discounts the importance of ideology and culture and sees man as essentially a rational, profit-maximizing individual. It is precisely this kind of individual and his pursuit of material incentives that is posited as the basis for economic life as such in economic textbooks. One small example will illustrate the problematic character of such materialist views.

Max Weber begins his famous book, *The Protestant Ethic and the Spirit of Capitalism*, by noting the different economic performance of Protestant and Catholic communities throughout Europe and America, summed up in the proverb that Protestants eat well while Catholics sleep well. Weber notes that according to any economic theory that posited man as a rational profit-maximizer, raising the piece-work rate should increase labor productivity. But in fact, in many traditional peasant communities, raising the piece-work rate actually had the opposite effect of *lowering* labor productivity: at the higher rate, a peasant accustomed to earning two and one-half marks per day found he could earn the same amount by working less, and did so because he valued leisure more than income. The choices of leisure over income, or of the militaristic life of the Spartan hoplite over the wealth of the Athenian trader, or even the ascetic life of the early capitalist entrepreneur over that of a traditional leisured aristocrat, cannot possibly be explained by the impersonal working of material forces, but come preeminently out of the sphere of consciousness—what we have labeled here broadly as ideology. And indeed, a central theme of Weber's work was to prove that contrary to Marx, the material mode of production, far from being the "base," was itself a "superstructure" with roots in religion and culture, and that to understand the emergence of modern capitalism and the profit motive one had to study their antecedents in the realm of the spirit.

As we look around the contemporary world, the poverty of materialist theories of economic development is all too apparent. The *Wall Street Journal* school of deterministic materialism habitually points to the stunning economic success of Asia in the past few decades as evidence of the viability of free market economics, with the implication that all societies would see similar development were they simply to allow their populations to pursue their material self-interest freely. Surely free markets and stable political systems are a necessary precondition to capitalist economic growth. But just as surely the cultural heritage of those Far Eastern societies, the ethic of work and saving and family, a religious heritage that does not, like Islam, place restrictions on certain forms of economic behavior, and other deeply ingrained moral qualities, are equally important in explaining their economic performance. And yet the intellectual weight of materialism is such that not a single respectable contemporary theory of economic development addresses consciousness and culture seriously as the matrix within which economic behavior is formed.

Failure to understand that the roots of economic behavior lie in the realm of consciousness and culture leads to the common mistake of attributing material causes to phenomena that are essentially ideal in nature. For example, it is commonplace in the West to interpret the reform movements first in China and most recently in the Soviet Union as the victory of the material over the ideal—that is, a recognition that ideological incentives could not replace material ones in stimulating a highly productive modern economy, and that if one wanted to prosper one had to appeal to baser forms of self-interest. But the deep defects of socialist economies were evident thirty or forty years ago to anyone who chose to look. Why was it that these countries moved away from central planning in the 1980's? The answer must be found in the consciousness of the elites and leaders ruling them, who decided to opt for the "Protestant" life of wealth and risk over the "Catholic" path of poverty and security. That change was in no way made inevitable by the material condition in which either country found itself on the eve of the reform, but instead came about as the result of the victory of one idea over another.

For Kojève, as for all good Hegelians, understanding the underlying processes of history requires understanding developments in the realm of consciousness or ideas, since consciousness will ultimately remake the material world in its own image. To say that history ended in 1806 meant that mankind's ideological evolution ended in the ideals of the French or American Revolutions: while particular regimens in the real world might not implement these ideals fully, their theoretical truth is absolute and could not be improved upon. Hence it did not matter to Kojève that the consciousness of the postwar generation of Europeans had not been universalized throughout the world; if ideological development had in fact ended, the homogenous state would eventually become victorious throughout the material world.

I have neither the space nor, frankly, the ability to defend in depth Hegel's radical idealist perspective. The issue is not whether Hegel's system was right, but whether his perspective might uncover the problematic nature of many materialist explanations we often take for granted. This is not to deny the role of material factors as such. To a literal minded idealist, human society can be built around any arbitrary set of principles regardless of their relationship to the material world. And in fact men have proven themselves able to endure the most extreme material hardships in the name of ideas that exist in the realm of the spirit alone, be it the divinity of cows or the nature of the Holy Trinity.

But while man's very perception of the material world is shaped by his historical consciousness of it, the material world can clearly affect in return the viability of a particular state of consciousness. In particular, the spectacular abundance of advanced liberal economies and the infinitely diverse consumer culture made possible by them seem to both foster and preserve liberalism in the political sphere. I want to avoid the materialist determinism that says that liberal economics inevitably produces liberal politics, because I believe that both economics and politics presuppose an autonomous prior state of consciousness that makes them possible. But that state of consciousness that permits the growth of liberalism seems to stabilize in the way one would expect at the end of history if it is underwritten by the abundance of a modern free market economy. We might summarize the content of the universal homogenous state as liberal democracy in the political sphere combined with easy access to VCRs and stereos in the economic.

Questions

1. In philosophical terms, what did Fukuyama mean by the "end of history"? What, according to the author, is the nature of historical change?
2. How are economic and political liberalism defined here?

30-5 Iraqi Aggression in Kuwait (1990)

George H. W. Bush

Speaking before the United Nations General Assembly as Communism was collapsing in Eastern Europe and the Soviet Union, President George H. W. Bush (b. 1924) spoke of the promise of "a new international order" and the threat posed to that new world order by Iraqi aggression.

Source: George Bush, "Aggression in the Gulf: A Partnership of Nations," October 1, 1990, in *Vital Speeches of the Day* 57 (October 15, 1990), 2–4. Reprinted by permission.

. . . The founding of the United Nations embodied our deepest hopes for a peaceful world. And during the past year, we've come closer than ever before to realizing those hopes. We've seen a century sundered by barbed threats and barbed wire, give way to a new era of peace and competition and freedom. . . .

Not since 1945 have we seen the real possibility of using the United Nations as it was designed, as a center for international collective security. . . .

. . . Can we work together in a new partnership of nations? Can the collective strength of the world community expressed by the United Nations unite to deter and defeat aggression? Because the cold war's battle of ideas is not the last epic battle of this century.

Two months ago, in the waning weeks of one of history's most hopeful summers, the vast, still beauty of the peaceful Kuwaiti desert was fouled by the stench of diesel and the roar of steel tanks. And once again, the sound of distant thunder echoed across a cloudless sky. And once again, the world awoke to face the guns of August.

But this time, the world was ready. The United Nations Security Council's resolute response to Iraq's unprovoked aggression has been without precedent. Since the invasion on August 2, the Council has passed eight major resolutions setting the terms for a solution to the crisis. The Iraqi regime has yet to face the facts. But as I said last month, the annexation of Kuwait will not be permitted to stand. And this is not simply the view of the United States. It is the view of every Kuwaiti, the Arab League, the United Nations. Iraq's leaders should listen. It is Iraq against the world.

Let me take this opportunity to make the policy of my Government clear. The United States supports the use of sanctions to compel Iraq's leaders to withdraw immediately and without condition from Kuwait. We also support the provision of medicine and food for humanitarian purposes, so long as distribution can be properly monitored. Our quarrel is not with the people of Iraq. We do not wish for them to suffer. The world's quarrel is with the dictator who ordered that invasion.

Along with others, we have dispatched military forces to the region to enforce sanctions, to deter and if need be defend against further aggression. And we seek no advantage for ourselves, nor do we seek to maintain our military forces in Saudi Arabia for one day longer than is necessary. U.S. forces were sent at the request of the Saudi Government.

The American people and this President want every single American soldier brought home as soon as this mission is completed.

Let me also emphasize that all of us here at the U.N. hope that military force will never be used. We seek a peaceful outcome, a diplomatic outcome. And one more thing: in the aftermath of Iraq's unconditional departure from Kuwait, I truly believe there may be opportunities for Iraq and Kuwait to settle their differences permanently, for the states of the gulf themselves to build new arrangements for stability and for all the states and the peoples of the region to settle the conflicts that divide the Arabs from Israel.

But the world's key task, now, first and always, must be to demonstrate that aggression will not be tolerated or rewarded. . . .

The United Nations can help bring about a new day—a day when these kinds of terrible weapons and the terrible despots who would use them, or both, were a thing of the past. It is in our hands to leave these dark machines behind, in the dark ages where they belong, and to press forward to cap a historic movement towards a new world order, and a long era of peace.

We have a vision of a new partnership of nations that transcends the cold war; a partnership based on consultation, cooperation and collective action, especially through international and regional organizations; a partnership united by principle and the rule of law and supported by an equitable sharing of both cost and commitment; a partnership whose goals are to increase democracy, increase prosperity, increase the peace and reduce arms. . . .

I see a world of open borders, open trade and, most importantly, open minds, a world that celebrates the common heritage that belongs to all the world's people, taking pride not just in hometown or homeland but in humanity itself. I see a world touched by a spirit like that of the Olympics, based not on competition that's driven by fear, but sought out of joy and exhilaration and a true quest for excellence.

And I see a world where democracy continues to win new friends and convert old foes, and where the Americas—North, Central and South—can provide a model for the future of all humankind, the world's first completely democratic hemisphere. And I see a world building on the emerging new model of European unity, not just Europe, but the whole world whole and free.

This is precisely why the present aggression in the gulf is a menace not only to . . . one region's security, but to the entire world's vision of our future. It threatens to turn the dream of a new international order into a grim nightmare of anarchy in which the law of the jungle supplants the law of nations. And that's why the United Nations reacted with such historic unity and resolve. And that's why this challenge is a test that we cannot afford to fail.

Questions

1. What role did Bush see the United Nations playing in the "new international order"?
2. Why, according to Bush, was Iraq's invasion of Kuwait a "menace" to "the dream of a new international order"?

30-6 University Students Reflect on the Gulf War (1991)

David Maraniss

The American military that fought and won the war against Iraq was an all-volunteer force. (Not since the 1970s had the United States resorted to the draft.) The students whose discussion is reported here by David Maraniss of the *Washington Post* talked during the aerial phase of Operation Desert Storm, before the mounting of the ground offensive against Iraq.

Source: David Maraniss, "It's Their War, Too" from *Washington Post*, February 11, 1991. Copyright © 1991 by The Washington Post. Reprinted with permission from the Washington Post Writers Group.

Seven buddies sit in the living room of their dormitory suite 12 floors above the classical orderliness of Vanderbilt University. They are the same age as many of the young men fighting in the Persian Gulf War: 20 and 21, on the cusp of adulthood. As privileged sons of professional America, their lives are not on the line, yet this is their war, too, and they sense that somehow it has changed them forever.

Perhaps the effect is not immediately obvious as they spend the day. They watch basketball at Memorial Gym. They eat pizza from Mazzio's and junk food from the Munchi Mart. They play baseball and racetrack Nintendo computer games. They retreat into their rooms to study English and political science. They listen to "Living Colour" and "Public Enemy" on their compact-disc players. They go to a dance or a movie.

But the change is occurring inside as they struggle with tough questions about who they are and what they are doing while so many of their chronological peers—so alike, yet different—sleep in trenches and drive light armored vehicles in the Saudi Arabian desert.

Here are the questions for these students: Should you fight in this war? Would you? Should there be a draft? Is it fair that you, white and middle class, are here while a disproportionate number of blacks and Hispanics are over there? Would you die if you went? Didn't your life seem so safe and comfortable for so many years? What happened? Does this war open up the possibility of one military conflict after another for the course of your life? Is that what you expected?

"No, this is not something we expected to face in our lives," said Mark Dusek, 20, a junior from Houston majoring in math and biology. On that point, all seven agreed. War was far from their minds as they entered college. They thought the world was becoming safer, especially as tension eased with the Soviet Union. Grenada and Panama did not seem like war to them. They could not remember Vietnam.

During the first semester, the television was used mostly to watch sports; now they tune in the war on CNN. From September to December, the only part of the newspaper read in their suite was the sports section, said Greg Anglum, 20, a junior economics major from Walt Whitman High School in Bethesda, Md. "Now we all read the front page."

This semester has been different from the day they returned in the second week of January. Mike Penn, 21, a senior communications major from Indianapolis, remembers driving back to school down Interstate 65 and seeing three big trucks hauling coffins from the Batesville Casket Co. "That's when it hit me that this was really happening and all our lives were changing," Penn said. "People were going to die."

Five of the seven agree with President Bush that the war is just or at least necessary. But not one wants to fight in it.

All are opposed to a draft, though a few said one might be necessary as a last resort. They said they would gladly serve in non-military public service jobs.

"This might sound selfish, but I think it would be a shame to put America's best young minds on the front line," said Jason Bell, 20, a junior English major from Elizabethtown, Ky. "If we have to go, we have to go, but I think it would be a shame."

In one sense, these young men seem superfluous when considered within the war's urgent context. Yet they loom as potentially key players if war drags on and a draft—despite Bush's pledge to the contrary—is suddenly resurrected. Fair or not, it is then that the nation's support of the war might face its stiffest test, when the educated sons of influential white professionals are part of the equation. These seven understand that.

"If we get to the point where we need a draft, we should pull out," said Matt Pender, 21, a junior political science major from Ayer, Mass. Pender, editor of the campus newspaper, opposes the war. He and Penn hold the minority view among those in the suite, but that might change.

"If the ground war starts and they need more troops, who knows how the tide could turn?" said Bill Pierros, 21, a junior English major from Elgin, Ill.

Anglum, who worked last summer in Vice President Quayle's office, said he hopes there will not be a draft but would totally support one if needed. While he said he considers the war necessary, largely to protect U.S. energy needs, this is not a war he wants to fight. "I guess if I was trained to fight maybe I'd have a little different attitude," he said. "But I can't see myself shooting a gun. . . . I don't feel I could be an effective soldier."

None of the seven has relatives in the war. Only two have close high school friends in the conflict—Pierros and Chad Sanchez, 20, a junior chemical engineering major from Gonzales, La., a working-class town west of New Orleans where the military is a routine part of life. "A lot of guys from home signed up with the Marine reserves or National Guard right out of high school," Sanchez said. "None of them, I don't think, ever thought about going to war, but that's where they are now. Back home at Christmas, a friend and I spent a whole night with another friend who was about to go. He was scared. He's a gunner on the front line."

If these seven were on the front line, would they come home alive? Sanchez said he has thought about that many times since war started. He has decided that he would get killed trying to help a buddy in trouble. Perhaps he will never know. The students also have pondered the question of color and fairness in the volunteer military. Yes, they said, blacks and Hispanics seem to be in the war disproportionately. But the only short-range way to even things out would be a draft, an unacceptable solution to them.

"What do they say? White man's war, black man's fight," Bell said.

"We're talking about the injustices of a whole system," Penn said.

As late afternoon shadows fell across their living room, the seven came to grips with how their insular lives had changed. Pender said the United States has started something that will be hard to stop. Anglum said he is afraid that there will be more conflicts. Sanchez said he has been thinking more about what it means to bring children into the world. Pierros said he fears for his relatives in Greece, scene of terrorist activity. Penn said he would not feel as safe flying from Nashville to Chicago.

They were safe, a world away. They did not want to fight. They would rather eat cold pizza or write a term paper on dictators. "War is something you played in the backyard," Penn said. "None of us knew what it really was." They still do not, but they are thinking about it for the first time.

Questions

1. With which student statements do you most agree? Most disagree?
2. What light does the conversation shed on class and race in the United States?

30-7 The Clash of Civilizations? (1993)

Samuel P. Huntington

In 1993, Samuel P. Huntington (b. 1927), an influential political scientist at Harvard University, wrote "The Clash of Civilizations?" which seemed perhaps a more sober and realistic description of the post–Cold War era than Francis Fukuyama's triumphal expounding of Western values. Huntington emphasized the enduring role of civilizations and the persistence of culture as major factors in determining the "next pattern of conflict." The ethnic and religious hatreds that exploded in the Balkans, Africa, and the Middle East in the 1990s seemed to more than justify this conservative, even pessimistic, view of the future of foreign affairs. The following are several excerpts from Huntington's "Clash of Civilizations?"

Source: Excerpts from Samuel P. Huntington, "The Clash of Civilizations?" *Foreign Affairs* 72 (Summer 1993), 22–29, 39–41, 48–49. Reprinted by permission of the publisher.

THE NEXT PATTERN OF CONFLICT

World politics is entering a new phase, and intellectuals have not hesitated to proliferate visions of what it will be—the end of history, the return of traditional rivalries between nation states, and the decline of the nation state from the conflicting pulls of tribalism and globalism, among others. Each of these visions catches aspects of the emerging reality. Yet they all miss a crucial, indeed a central, aspect of what global politics is likely to be in the coming years.

It is my hypothesis that the fundamental source of conflict in this new world will not be primarily ideological or primarily economic. The great divisions among humankind and the dominating source of conflict will be cultural. Nation states will remain the most powerful actors in world affairs, but the principal conflicts of global politics will occur between nations and groups of different civilizations. The clash of civilizations will dominate global politics. The fault lines between civilizations will be the battle lines of the future.

Conflict between civilizations will be the latest phase in the evolution of conflict in the modern world. For a century and a half after the emergence of the modern international system with the Peace of Westphalia, the conflicts of the Western world were largely among princes—emperors, absolute monarchs and constitutional monarchs attempting to expand their bureaucracies, their armies, their mercantilist economic strength and, most important, the territory they ruled. In the process they created nation states, and beginning with the French Revolution the principal lines of conflict were between nations rather than princes. In 1793, as R. R. Palmer put it, "The wars of kings were over; the wars of peoples had begun." This nineteenth-century pattern lasted until the end of World War I. Then, as a result of the Russian Revolution and the reaction against it, the conflict of nations yielded to the conflict of ideologies, first among communism, fascism-Nazism and liberal democracy, and then between communism and liberal democracy. During the Cold War, this latter conflict became embodied in the struggle between the two superpowers, neither of which was a nation state in the classical European sense and each of which defined its identity in terms of its ideology.

These conflicts between princes, nation states and ideologies were primarily conflicts within Western civilization, "Western civil wars," as William Lind has labeled them. This was as true of the Cold War as it was of the world wars and the earlier wars of the seventeenth, eighteenth and nineteenth centuries. With the end of the Cold War, international politics moves out of its Western phase, and its centerpiece becomes the interaction between the West and non-Western civilizations and among non-Western civilizations. In the politics of civilizations, the peoples and governments of non-Western civilizations no longer remain the objects of history as targets of Western colonialism but join the West as movers and shapers of history.

THE NATURE OF CIVILIZATIONS

During the Cold War the world was divided into the First, Second and Third Worlds. Those divisions are no longer relevant. It is far more meaningful now to group countries not in terms of their political or economic systems or in terms of their level of economic development but rather in terms of their culture and civilization.

What do we mean when we talk of a civilization? A civilization is a cultural entity. Villages, regions, ethnic groups, nationalities, religious groups, all have distinct cultures at different levels of cultural heterogeneity. The culture of a village in southern Italy may be different from that of a village in northern Italy, but both will share in a common Italian culture that distinguishes them from German villages. European communities, in turn, will share cultural features that distinguish them from Arab or Chinese communities. Arabs, Chinese and Westerners, however, are not part of any broader cultural entity. They constitute civilizations. A civilization is thus the highest cultural grouping of people and the broadest level of cultural identity people have short of that which distinguishes humans from other species. It is defined both by common objective elements, such as language, history, religion, customs, institutions, and by the subjective self-identification of people. People have levels of identity: a resident of Rome may define himself with varying degrees of intensity as a Roman, an Italian, a Catholic, a Christian, a European, a Westerner. The civilization to which he belongs is the broadest level of identification with which he intensely identifies. People can and do redefine their identities and, as a result, the composition and boundaries of civilizations change.

Civilizations may involve a large number of people, as with China ("a civilization pretending to be a state," as Lucian Pye put it), or a very small number of people, such as the Anglophone Caribbean. A civilization may include several nation states, as is the case with Western, Latin American and Arab civilizations, or only one, as is the case with Japanese civilization. Civilizations obviously blend and overlap, and may include subcivilizations. Western civilization has two major variants, European and North American, and Islam has its Arab, Turkic and Malay subdivisions. Civilizations are nonetheless meaningful entities, and while the lines between them are seldom sharp, they are real. Civilizations are dynamic; they rise and fall; they divide and merge. And, as any student of history knows, civilizations disappear and are buried in the sands of time.

Westerners tend to think of nation states as the principal actors in global affairs. They have been that, however, for only a few centuries. The broader reaches of human history have been the history of civilizations. In *A Study of History*, Arnold Toynbee identified 21 major civilizations; only six of them exist in the contemporary world.

WHY CIVILIZATIONS WILL CLASH

Civilization identity will be increasingly important in the future, and the world will be shaped in large measure by the interactions among seven or eight major civilizations. These include Western, Confucian, Japanese, Islamic, Hindu, Slavic-Orthodox, Latin American and possibly African civilization. The most important conflicts of the future will occur along the cultural fault lines separating these civilizations from one another.

Why will this be the case?

First, differences among civilizations are not only real; they are basic. Civilizations are differentiated from each other by history, language, culture, tradition and, most importantly, religion. The people of different civilizations have different views on the relations between God and man, the individual and the group, the citizen and the state, parents and children, husband and wife, as well as differing views of the relative importance of rights and responsibilities, liberty and authority, equality and hierarchy. These differences are the product of centuries. They will not soon disappear. They are far more fundamental than differences among political ideologies and political regimes. Differences do not necessarily mean conflict, and conflict does not necessarily mean violence. Over the centuries, however, differences among civilizations have generated the most prolonged and the most violent conflicts.

Second, the world is becoming a smaller place. The interactions between peoples of different civilizations are increasing; these increasing interactions intensify civilization consciousness and awareness of differences between civilizations and commonalities within civilizations. North African immigration to France generates hostility among Frenchmen and at the same time increased receptivity to immigration by "good" European Catholic Poles. Americans react far more negatively to Japanese investment than to larger investments from Canada and European countries. Similarly, as Donald Horowitz has pointed out, "An Ibo may be . . . an Owerri Ibo or an Onitsha Ibo in what was the Eastern region of Nigeria. In Lagos, he is simply an Ibo. In London, he is a Nigerian. In New York, he is an African." The interactions among peoples of different civilizations enhance the civilization-consciousness of people that, in turn, invigorates differences and animosities stretching or thought to stretch back deep into history.

Third, the processes of economic modernization and social change throughout the world are separating people from longstanding local identities. They also weaken the nation state as a source of identity. In much of the world religion has moved in to fill this gap, often in the form of movements that are labeled "fundamentalist." Such movements are found in Western Christianity, Judaism, Buddhism and Hinduism, as well as in Islam. In most countries and most religions the people active in fundamentalist movements are young, college-educated, middle-class technicians, professionals and business persons. The "unsecularization of the world," George Weigel has remarked, "is one of the dominant social facts of life in the late twentieth century." The revival of religion, "la revanche de Dieu," as Gilles Kepel labeled it, provides a basis for identity and commitment that transcends national boundaries and unites civilizations.

Fourth, the growth of civilization-consciousness is enhanced by the dual role of the West. On the one hand, the West is at a peak of power. At the same time, however, and perhaps as a result, a return to the roots phenomenon is occurring among non-Western civilizations. Increasingly one hears references to trends toward a turning inward and "Asianization" in Japan, the end of the Nehru legacy and the "Hinduization" of India, the failure of Western ideas of socialism and nationalism and hence "re-Islamization" of the Middle East, and now a debate over Westernization versus Russianization in Boris Yeltsin's country. A West at the peak of its power confronts non-Wests that increasingly have the desire, the will and the resources to shape the world in non-Western ways.

In the past, the elites of non-Western societies were usually the people who were most involved with the West, had been educated at Oxford, the Sorbonne or Sandhurst, and had absorbed Western attitudes and values. At the same time, the populace in non-Western countries often remained deeply imbued with the indigenous culture. Now, however, these relationships are being reversed. A de-Westernization and indigenization of elites is occurring in many non-Western countries at the same time that Western, usually American, cultures, styles and habits become more popular among the mass of the people.

Fifth, cultural characteristics and differences are less mutable and hence less easily compromised and resolved than political and economic ones. In the former Soviet Union, communists can become democrats, the rich can become poor and the poor rich, but Russians cannot become Estonians and Azeris cannot become Armenians. In class and ideological conflicts, the key question was "Which side are you on?" and people could and did choose sides and change sides. In conflicts between civilizations, the question is "What are you?" That is a given that cannot be changed. And as we know, from Bosnia to the Caucasus to the Sudan, the wrong answer to that question can mean a bullet in the head. Even more than ethnicity, religion discriminates sharply and exclusively among people. A person can be half-French and half-

Arab and simultaneously even a citizen of two countries. It is more difficult to be half-Catholic and half-Muslim.

Finally, economic regionalism is increasing. The proportions of total trade that were intraregional rose between 1980 and 1989 from 51 percent to 59 percent in Europe, 33 percent to 37 percent in East Asia, and 32 percent to 36 percent in North America. The importance of regional economic blocs is likely to continue to increase in the future. On the one hand, successful economic regionalism will reinforce civilization-consciousness. On the other hand, economic regionalism may succeed only when it is rooted in a common civilization. The European Community rests on the shared foundation of European culture and Western Christianity. The success of the North American Free Trade Area depends on the convergence now underway of Mexican, Canadian and American cultures. Japan, in contrast, faces difficulties in creating a comparable economic entity in East Asia because Japan is a society and civilization unique to itself. However strong the trade and investment links Japan may develop with other East Asian countries, its cultural differences with those countries inhibit and perhaps preclude its promoting regional economic integration like that in Europe and North America.

Common culture, in contrast, is clearly facilitating the rapid expansion of the economic relations between the People's Republic of China and Hong Kong, Taiwan, Singapore and the overseas Chinese communities in other Asian countries. With the Cold War over, cultural commonalities increasingly overcome ideological differences, and mainland China and Taiwan move closer together. If cultural commonality is a prerequisite for economic integration, the principal East Asian economic bloc of the future is likely to be centered on China. This bloc is, in fact, already coming into existence. As Murray Weidenbaum has observed,

> Despite the current Japanese dominance of the region, the Chinese-based economy of Asia is rapidly emerging as a new epicenter for industry, commerce and finance. This strategic area contains substantial amounts of technology and manufacturing capability (Taiwan), outstanding entrepreneurial, marketing and services acumen (Hong Kong), a fine communications network (Singapore), a tremendous pool of financial capital (all three), and very large endowments of land, resources and labor (mainland China).... From Guangzhou to Singapore, from Kuala Lumpur to Manila, this influential network—often based on extensions of the traditional clans—has been described as the backbone of the East Asian economy.[1]

Culture and religion also form the basis of the Economic Cooperation Organization, which brings together ten non-Arab Muslim countries: Iran, Pakistan, Turkey, Azerbaijan, Kazakhstan, Kyrgyzstan, Turkmenistan, Tadjikistan, Uzbekistan and Afghanistan. One impetus to the revival and expansion of this organization, founded originally in the 1960s by Turkey, Pakistan and Iran, is the realization by the leaders of several of these countries that they had no chance of admission to the European Community. Similarly, Caricom, the Central American Common Market and Mercosur rest on common cultural foundations. Efforts to build a broader Caribbean-Central American economic entity bridging the Anglo-Latin divide, however, have to date failed.

As people define their identity in ethnic and religious terms, they are likely to see an "us" versus "them" relation existing between themselves and people of different ethnicity or religion. The end of ideologically defined states in Eastern Europe and the former Soviet Union permits traditional ethnic identities and animosities to come to the fore. Differences in culture and religion create differences over policy issues, ranging from human rights to immigration to trade and commerce to the environment. Geographical propinquity gives rise to conflicting territorial claims from Bosnia to Mindanao. Most important, the efforts of the West to promote its values of democracy and liberalism as universal values, to maintain its military predominance and to advance its economic interests engender countering responses from other civilizations. Decreasingly able to mobilize support and form coalitions on the basis of ideology, governments and groups will increasingly attempt to mobilize support by appealing to common religion and civilization identity.

The clash of civilizations thus occurs at two levels. At the micro-level, adjacent groups along the fault lines between civilizations struggle, often violently, over the control of territory and each other. At the macro-level, states from different civilizations compete for relative military and economic power, struggle over the control of international institutions and third parties, and competitively promote their particular political and religious values....

THE WEST VERSUS THE REST

The West is now at an extraordinary peak of power in relation to other civilizations. Its superpower opponent has disappeared from the map. Military conflict among Western states is unthinkable, and Western military power is unrivaled. Apart from Japan, the West faces no economic challenge. It dominates international political and security institutions and with Japan international economic institutions. Global political and security issues are effectively settled by a directorate of the United States, Britain and France, world economic issues by a directorate of the United States, Germany and Japan, all of which maintain extraordinarily close relations with each other to the exclusion of lesser and largely non-Western countries. Decisions made at the U.N. Security Council or in the International Monetary Fund that reflect the interests of the West are presented to the world as

---

[1] Murray Weidenbaum, *Greater China: The Next Economic Superpower?*, St. Louis: Washington University Center for the Study of American Business, Contemporary Issues, Series 57, February 1993, pp. 2–3. [*Huntington's note.*]

reflecting the desires of the world community. The very phrase "the world community" has become the euphemistic collective noun (replacing "the Free World") to give global legitimacy to actions reflecting the interests of the United States and other Western powers.[2] Through the IMF and other international economic institutions, the West promotes its economic interests and imposes on other nations the economic policies it thinks appropriate. In any poll of non-Western peoples, the IMF undoubtedly would win the support of finance ministers and a few others, but get an overwhelmingly unfavorable rating from just about everyone else, who would agree with Georgy Arbatov's characterization of IMF officials as "neo-Bolsheviks who love expropriating other people's money, imposing undemocratic and alien rules of economic and political conduct and stifling economic freedom."

Western domination of the U.N. Security Council and its decisions, tempered only by occasional abstention by China, produced U.N. legitimation of the West's use of force to drive Iraq out of Kuwait and its elimination of Iraq's sophisticated weapons and capacity to produce such weapons. It also produced the quite unprecedented action by the United States, Britain and France in getting the Security Council to demand that Libya hand over the Pan Am 103 bombing suspects and then to impose sanctions when Libya refused. After defeating the largest Arab army, the West did not hesitate to throw its weight around in the Arab world. The West in effect is using international institutions, military power and economic resources to run the world in ways that will maintain Western predominance, protect Western interests and promote Western political and economic values.

That at least is the way in which non-Westerners see the new world, and there is a significant element of truth in their view. Differences in power and struggles for military, economic and institutional power are thus one source of conflict between the West and other civilizations. Differences in culture, that is basic values and beliefs, are a second source of conflict. V. S. Naipaul has argued that Western civilization is the "universal civilization" that "fits all men." At a superficial level much of Western culture has indeed permeated the rest of the world. At a more basic level, however, Western concepts differ fundamentally from those prevalent in other civilizations. Western ideas of individualism, liberalism, constitutionalism, human rights, equality, liberty, the rule of law, democracy, free markets, the separation of church and state, often have little resonance in Islamic, Confucian, Japanese, Hindu, Buddhist or Orthodox cultures. Western efforts to propagate such ideas produce instead a reaction against "human rights imperialism" and a reaffirmation of indigenous values, as can be seen in the support for religious fundamentalism by the younger generation in non-Western cultures. The very notion that there could be a "universal civilization" is a Western idea, directly at odds with the particularism of most Asian societies and their emphasis on what distinguishes one people from another. Indeed, the author of a review of 100 comparative studies of values in different societies concluded that "the values that are most important in the West are least important worldwide."[3] In the political realm, of course, these differences are most manifest in the efforts of the United States and other Western powers to induce other peoples to adopt Western ideas concerning democracy and human rights. Modern democratic government originated in the West. When it has developed in non-Western societies it has usually been the product of Western colonialism or imposition.

The central axis of world politics in the future is likely to be, in Kishore Mahbubani's phrase, the conflict between "the West and the Rest" and the responses of non-Western civilizations to Western power and values.[4] Those responses generally take one or a combination of three forms. At one extreme, non-Western states can, like Burma and North Korea, attempt to pursue a course of isolation, to insulate their societies from penetration or "corruption" by the West, and, in effect, to opt out of participation in the Western-dominated global community. The costs of this course, however, are high, and few states have pursued its exclusively. A second alternative, the equivalent of "band-wagoning" in international relations theory, is to attempt to join the West and accept its values and institutions. The third alternative is to attempt to "balance" the West by developing economic and military power and cooperating with other non-Western societies against the West, while preserving indigenous values and institutions; in short, to modernize but not to Westernize. . . .

IMPLICATIONS FOR THE WEST

This article does not argue that civilization identities will replace all other identities, that nation states will disappear, that each civilization will become a single coherent political entity, that groups within a civilization will not conflict with and even fight each other. This paper does set forth the hypotheses that differences between civilizations are real and important; civilization-consciousness is increasing; conflict between civilizations will supplant ideological and other

---

[2] Almost invariably Western leaders claim they are acting on behalf of "the world community." One minor lapse occurred during the run-up to the Gulf War. In an interview on "Good Morning America," Dec. 21, 1990, British Prime Minister John Major referred to the actions "the West" was taking against Saddam Hussein. He quickly corrected himself and subsequently referred to "the world community." He was, however, right when he erred. [*Huntington's note.*]

[3] Harry C. Triandis, *The New York Times*, Dec. 25, 1990, p. 41, and "Cross-Cultural Studies of Individualism and Collectivism," Nebraska Symposium on Motivation, vol. 37, 1989, pp. 41–133. [*Huntington's note.*]

[4] Kishore Mahbubani, "The West and the Rest," *The National Interest*, Summer 1992, pp. 3–13. [*Huntington's note.*]

forms of conflict as the dominant global form of conflict; international relations, historically a game played out within Western civilization, will increasingly be de-Westernized and become a game in which non-Western civilizations are actors and not simply objects; successful political, security and economic international institutions are more likely to develop within civilizations than across civilizations; conflicts between groups in different civilizations will be more frequent, more sustained and more violent than conflicts between groups in the same civilization; violent conflicts between groups in different civilizations are the most likely and most dangerous source of escalation that could lead to global wars; the paramount axis of world politics will be the relations between "the West and the Rest"; the elites in some torn non-Western countries will try to make their countries part of the West, but in most cases face major obstacles to accomplishing this; a central focus of conflict for the immediate future will be between the West and several Islamic-Confucian states.

This is not to advocate the desirability of conflicts between civilizations. It is to set forth descriptive hypotheses as to what the future may be like. If these are plausible hypotheses, however, it is necessary to consider their implications for Western policy. These implications should be divided between short-term advantage and long-term accommodation. In the short term it is clearly in the interest of the West to promote greater cooperation and unity within its own civilization, particularly between its European and North American components; to incorporate into the West societies in Eastern Europe and Latin America whose cultures are close to those of the West; to promote and maintain cooperative relations with Russia and Japan; to prevent escalation of local inter-civilization conflicts into major inter-civilization wars; to limit the expansion of the military strength of Confucian and Islamic states; to moderate the reduction of Western military capabilities and maintain military superiority in East and Southwest Asia; to exploit differences and conflicts among Confucian and Islamic states; to support in other civilizations groups sympathetic to Western values and interests; to strengthen international institutions that reflect and legitimate Western interests and values and to promote the involvement of non-Western states in those institutions.

In the longer term other measures would be called for. Western civilization is both Western and modern. Non-Western civilizations have attempted to become modern without becoming Western. To date only Japan has fully succeeded in this quest. Non-Western civilizations will continue to attempt to acquire the wealth, technology, skills, machines and weapons that are part of being modern. They will also attempt to reconcile this modernity with their traditional culture and values. Their economic and military strength relative to the West will increase. Hence the West will increasingly have to accommodate these non-Western modern civilizations whose power approaches that of the West but whose values and interests differ significantly from those of the West. This will require the West to maintain the economic and military power necessary to protect its interests in relation to these civilizations. It will also, however, require the West to develop a more profound understanding of the basic religious and philosophical assumptions underlying other civilizations and the ways in which people in those civilizations see their interests. It will require an effort to identify elements of commonality between Western and other civilizations. For the relevant future, there will be no universal civilization, but instead a world of different civilizations, each of which will have to learn to coexist with the others.

Questions

1. What are civilizations? Why are they, according to the author, destined to clash?
2. How do non-Westerners see the new world, according to Huntington?
3. On what grounds does Huntington see conflict between the "West and the Rest"?

Questions for Further Thought

1. Compare and contrast the crisis of the first Gulf War with the crises of the Cold War.
2. What implications, if any, do you see in the present reliance on all-volunteer armed forces in the United States? Which earlier wars were wholly or largely fought by volunteer forces? Which involved drafts?
3. Compare and contrast Fukuyama's thesis (Document 30-4) with Huntington's thesis (Document 30-7).

The Clinton Presidency, 1993–2001

President William Jefferson Clinton compiled a mixed record during his two terms in office. He achieved limited political victories at home and abroad, but the economy prospered, even boomed, under his stewardship. Toward the end of President Clinton's second term, the budget was in surplus for the first time in decades, and the government was paying down its multitrillion-dollar national debt. But although Clinton could point to prosperity at home and a successful foreign policy abroad, his administrations were marked by intense partisan rancor. In 1994, the Republican Party took control of both the House and Senate and effectively blocked many of the president's initiatives, while putting forth its own vision for America (Document 30-8). Clinton was reelected in 1996 and in Document 30-9 he provided an alternative vision to the Republican plan.

During his time in office, President Clinton, and his wife, Hillary Clinton, were subject to continuous investigations by Congress for alleged wrongdoings. In September 1998, Kenneth Starr, the special prosecutor who was investigating an Arkansas real estate development deal (known as Whitewater), reported that Clinton had lied to a federal grand jury when questioned about his sexual relationship with Monica Lewinsky, a White House intern. While this affair was not an abuse of executive power, the Republican-controlled House subsequently impeached him, but the Senate acquitted Clinton. His job approval ratings remained high, but many Americans were embarrassed and embittered by the scandal.

30-8 Contract with America (1994)

In 1994, the Republicans captured the House of Representatives (for the first time since 1952) and the Senate (control of which they had lost in 1986). The *Contract with America* had provided the Republicans with a single campaign tract for midterm House races across the nation. That representatives Newt Gingrich (Georgia) and Dick Armey (Texas) were prominent among the drafters of the contract reflected the southernization of the Republicans' congressional delegation. As late as 1960, Republicans held no Senate seats and only 7 of the 106 House seats from the eleven former Confederate states. In 1998, Republicans occupied 15 of the 22 seats in the Senate and 71 of the 125 in the House from these states (see text pp. 948–950).

Gingrich and Armey, already prominent in the House, rose to power following the GOP victory—Gingrich as Speaker, Armey as majority leader. Gingrich did not enjoy success for long. Early in 1999, he resigned from the House.

Source: Republican National Committee, *Contract with America: The Bold Plan by Representative Newt Gingrich, Representative Dick Armey, and the House Republicans to Change the Nation*, Ed Gillespie and Bob Schellhas, eds. (New York: Times Books, 1994), 1–11. Reprinted with the express permission of the Republican National Committee.

The Contract's Core Principles

The Contract with America is rooted in 3 core principles:

ACCOUNTABILITY

The government is too big and spends too much, and Congress and unelected bureaucrats have become so entrenched to be unresponsive to the public they are supposed to serve. The GOP contract restores accountability to government.

RESPONSIBILITY

Bigger government and more federal programs usurp personal responsibility from families and individuals. The GOP contract restores a proper balance between government and personal responsibility.

OPPORTUNITY

The American Dream is out of the reach of too many families because of burdensome government regulations and harsh tax laws. The GOP contract restores the American dream.

The Contract

As Republican Members of the House of Representatives and as citizens seeking to join that body we propose not just to change its policies, but even more important, to restore the bonds of trust between the people and their elected representatives.

That is why, in this era of official evasion and posturing, we offer instead a detailed agenda for national renewal, a written commitment with no fine print.

This year's election offers the chance, after four decades of one-party control, to bring to the House a new majority that will transform the way Congress works. That historic change would be the end of government that is too big, too intrusive, and too easy with the public's money. It can be the beginning of a Congress that respects the values and shares the faith of the American family.

Like Lincoln, our first Republican president, we intend to act "with firmness in the right, as God gives us to see the right." To restore accountability to Congress. To end its cycle of scandal and disgrace. To make us all proud again of the way free people govern themselves.

On the first day of the 104th Congress, the new Republican majority will immediately pass the following major reforms, aimed at restoring the faith and trust of the American people in their government:

- FIRST, require all laws that apply to the rest of the country also apply equally to the Congress;
- SECOND, select a major, independent auditing firm to conduct a comprehensive audit of Congress for waste, fraud or abuse;
- THIRD, cut the number of House committees, and cut committee staff by one-third;
- FOURTH, limit the terms of all committee chairs;
- FIFTH, ban the casting of proxy votes in committee;
- SIXTH, require committee meetings to be open to the public;
- SEVENTH, require a three-fifths majority vote to pass a tax increase;
- EIGHTH, guarantee an honest accounting of our Federal Budget by implementing zero base-line budgeting.

Thereafter, within the first 100 days of the 104th Congress, we shall bring to the House Floor the following bills, each to be given full and open debate, each to be given a clear and fair vote and each to be immediately available this day for public inspection and scrutiny.

1. THE FISCAL RESPONSIBILITY ACT

A balanced budget/tax limitation amendment and a legislative line-item veto to restore fiscal responsibility to an out-of-control Congress, requiring them to live under the same budget constraints as families and businesses.

2. THE TAKING BACK OUR STREETS ACT

An anti-crime package including stronger truth-in-sentencing, "good faith" exclusionary rule exemptions, effective death penalty provisions, and cuts in social spending from this summer's "crime" bill to fund prison construction and additional law enforcement to keep people secure in their neighborhoods and kids safe in their schools.

3. THE PERSONAL RESPONSIBILITY ACT

Discourage illegitimacy and teen pregnancy by prohibiting welfare to minor mothers and denying increased AFDC for additional children while on welfare, cut spending for welfare programs, and enact a tough two-years-and-out provision with work requirements to promote individual responsibility.

4. THE FAMILY REINFORCEMENT ACT

Child support enforcement, tax incentives for adoption, strengthening rights of parents in their children's education, stronger child pornography laws, and an elderly dependent care tax credit to reinforce the central role of families in American society.

5. THE AMERICAN DREAM RESTORATION ACT

A $500 per child tax credit, begin repeal of the marriage tax penalty, and creation of American Dream Savings Accounts to provide middle class tax relief.

6. THE NATIONAL SECURITY RESTORATION ACT

No U.S. troops under U.N. command and restoration of the essential parts of our national security funding to strengthen our national defense and maintain our credibility around the world.

7. THE SENIOR CITIZENS FAIRNESS ACT

Raise the Social Security earnings limit which currently forces seniors out of the work force, repeal the 1993 tax hikes on Social Security benefits and provide tax incentives for private long-term care insurance to let Older Americans keep more of what they have earned over the years.

8. THE JOB CREATION AND WAGE ENHANCEMENT ACT

Small business incentives, capital gains cut and indexation, neutral cost recovery, risk assessment/cost-benefit analysis, strengthening the Regulatory Flexibility Act and unfunded mandate reform to create jobs and raise worker wages.

9. THE COMMON SENSE LEGAL REFORM ACT

"Loser pays" laws, reasonable limits on punitive damages and reform of product liability laws to stem the endless tide of litigation.

10. THE CITIZEN LEGISLATURE ACT

A first-ever vote on term limits to replace career politicians with citizen legislators.

Further, we will instruct the House Budget Committee to report to the floor and we will work to enact additional budget savings, beyond the budget cuts specifically included in the legislation described above, to ensure that the Federal budget deficit will be less than it would have been without the enactment of these bills.

Respecting the judgment of our fellow citizens as we seek their mandate for reform, we hereby pledge our names to this Contract with America.

Questions

1. How does the *Contract with America* demonize government?
2. What public sentiments does the contract capitalize on? How did those sentiments arise?
3. What are the advantages and dangers of using this kind of election strategy?

30-9 State of the Union Address (1996)

Bill Clinton

Congressional Republicans, in the majority in 1995 and 1996, soon provided President Clinton (b. 1946) with opportunities to counterattack. The temporary shutting down of the federal government during an impasse over the federal budget was blamed on the GOP. Meanwhile, Clinton moved toward the center on issues like reducing budget deficits and the national debt and reforming welfare. In doing so, he at once frustrated congressional Republicans, who felt that he was stealing their thunder, and unsettled congressional Democrats, who felt that he was abandoning their party's traditional positions. Less than ten months after delivering the State of the Union Address excerpted here, Clinton won reelection over Bob Dole (Kansas), the Senate majority leader.

Source: Congressional Record: House of Representatives, 104th Congress, 2nd session, 142, no. 8 (January 23, 1996), H768–H769.

My duty tonight is to report on the State of the Union, not the state of our government but of our American community, and to set forth our responsibilities, in the words of our Founders, to "form a more perfect union."

The State of the Union is strong. Our economy is the healthiest it has been in three decades. We have the lowest combined rates of unemployment and inflation in 27 years. We have created nearly 8 million new jobs, over a million of them in basic industries like construction and automobiles. America is selling more cars than Japan for the first time since the 1970s, and for three years in a row we have had a record number of new businesses started in our country.

Our leadership in the world is also strong, bringing hope for new peace. And perhaps most important, we are gaining ground and restoring our fundamental values. The crime rate, the welfare and food stamp rolls, the poverty rate and the teen pregnancy rate are all down. And as they go down, prospects for America's future go up.

We must answer here three fundamental questions: First, how do we make the American dream of opportunity for all a reality for all Americans who are willing to work for it? Second, how do we preserve our old and enduring values as we move into the future? And third, how do we meet these challenges together as one America?

We know big government does not have all the answers. We know there's not a program for every problem. We know and we have worked to give the American people a smaller, less bureaucratic government in Washington. And we have to give the American people one that lives within its means. The era of big government is over. But we cannot go back to the time when our citizens were left to fend for themselves. Instead, we must go forward as one America, one nation, working together to meet the challenges we face together. Self-reliance and teamwork are not opposing virtues. We must have both.

I believe our new, smaller government must work in an old-fashioned American way, together with all of our citizens through State and local governments, in the workplace, in religious, charitable and civic associations. Our goal must be to enable all our people to make the most of their own lives, with stronger families, more educational opportunities, economic security, safer streets, a cleaner environment and a safer world.

To improve the state of our union, we must ask more of ourselves. We must expect more of each other and we must face our challenges together.

Here in this place our responsibility begins with balancing the budget in a way that is fair to all Americans. There is now broad bipartisan agreement that permanent deficit spending must come to an end.

I compliment the Republican leadership and their membership for the energy and determination you have brought to this task of balancing the budget. And I thank the Democrats for passing the largest deficit reduction plan in history in 1993, which has already cut the deficit nearly in half in three years.

Since 1993, we have all begun to see the benefits of deficit reduction. Lower interest rates have made it easier for businesses to borrow and to invest and to create new jobs. Lower interest rates have brought down the cost of home mortgages, car payments and credit card rates to ordinary citizens. Now it is time to finish the job and balance the budget.

Though differences remain among us which are significant, the combined total of the proposed savings that are common to both plans is more than enough, using the numbers from your Congressional Budget Office, to balance the budget in 7 years and to provide a modest tax cut. These cuts are real. They will require sacrifice from everyone. But these cuts do not undermine our fundamental obligations to our parents, our children and our future by endangering Medicare or Medicaid or education or the environment or by raising taxes on working families.

I have said before, and let me say again, many good ideas have come out of our negotiations. I have learned a lot about the way both Republicans and Democrats view the debate before us. I have learned a lot about the good ideas that each side has that we could all embrace. We ought to resolve our remaining differences.

I am willing to work to resolve them. I am ready to meet tomorrow. But I ask you to consider that we should at least enact the savings that both plans have in common and give the American people their balanced budget, a tax cut, lower interest rates, and a brighter future. We should do that now and make permanent deficits yesterday's legacy.

Now it is time for us to look also to the challenges of today and tomorrow, beyond the burdens of yesterday. The challenges are significant. But our Nation was built on challenges. America was built on challenges, not promises. And when we work together to meet them we never fail. That is the key to a more perfect union. Our individual dreams must be realized by our common efforts.

Questions

1. How did Clinton's rhetoric and proposals suggest that he was seeking the political center?
2. In what ways did Clinton seek to establish that there were differences between even moderate Democrats and Republicans?

Question for Further Thought

1. Compare and contrast the tone and proposals of congressional Republicans (Document 30-8) with those of President Bill Clinton (Document 30-9).

CHAPTER THIRTY-ONE

A Dynamic Economy, A Divided People
1980–2000

America in a Global Economy and Society

Americans faced a range of economic and social problems during the last two decades of the twentieth century, leaving them apprehensive about the future. Some of those problems have since diminished but not disappeared, and some have been replaced with graver concerns. The 1980s saw a drop-off in economic productivity, with many Americans "underemployed" or jobless and a growing disparity between the rich and the poor. Documents 31-1 and 31-2 explore these problems. As welcome as was the prosperity of the 1990s, many Americans felt ambivalent about the increasing interdependence of the American economy with the rest of the world. On the occasion of the World Trade Organization (WTO) conference in Seattle in 1999, which was met with large protests, President Clinton addressed the economic, social, and environmental concerns raised by the opponents of globalization.

Document 31-1 provides George Gilders's analysis of wealth and poverty in the early 1980s. Document 31-2 excerpts Jonathan Kozol's account of mothers and their children on welfare. In Document 31-3, President Clinton makes the case for expanding trade and strengthening the global economy.

31-1 *Wealth and Poverty* (1981)

George Gilder

In *Wealth and Poverty*, a book that strongly influenced the Reagan administration, conservative theorist George Gilder argued that it was the immoral and irresponsible behavior of the poor themselves rather than any structural defects in the economy that perpetuated poverty in the United States.

Source: Excerpt from George Gilder, *Wealth and Poverty* (New York: Basic Books, 1981), 68–71. Copyright © 1981, 1982, 1983 by George Gilder. Reprinted by permission of Georges Borchardt, Inc., on behalf of the author.

The only dependable route from poverty is always work, family, and faith. The first principle is that in order to move up, the poor must not only work, they must work harder than the classes above them. Every previous generation of the lower class has made such efforts. But the current poor, white even more than black, are refusing to work hard. Irwin Garfinkel and Robert Haveman, authors of the ingenious and sophisticated study of what they call *Earnings Capacity Utilization Rates*, have calculated the degree to which various income groups use their opportunities—how hard they work outside the home. This study shows that, for several understandable reasons, the current poor work substantially less, for fewer hours and weeks a year, and earn less in proportion to their age, education, and other credentials (even *after* correcting the figures for unemployment, disability, and presumed discrimination) than either their predecessors in American cities or those now above them on the income scale. (The study was made at the federally funded Institute for Research on Poverty at the University of Wisconsin and used data from the census and the Michigan longitudinal survey.) The findings lend important confirmation to the growing body of evidence that work effort is the crucial unmeasured variable in American productivity and income distribution, and that current welfare and other subsidy programs substantially reduce work. The poor choose leisure not because of moral weakness, but because they are paid to do so.

A program to lift by transfers and preferences the incomes of less diligent groups is politically divisive—and very unlikely—because it incurs the bitter resistance of the real working class. In addition, such an effort breaks the psychological link between effort and reward, which is crucial to long-run upward mobility. Because effective work consists not in merely fulfilling the requirements of labor contracts, but in "putting out" with alertness and emotional commitment, workers have to understand and feel deeply that what they are given depends on what they give—that they must supply work in order to demand goods. Parents and schools must inculcate this idea in their children both by instruction and example. Nothing is more deadly to achievement than the belief that effort will not be rewarded, that the world is a bleak and discriminatory place in which only the predatory and the specially preferred can get ahead. Such a view in the home discourages the work effort in school that shapes earnings capacity afterward. As with so many aspects of human performance, work effort begins in family experiences, and its sources can be best explored through an examination of family structure.

Indeed, after work the second principle of upward mobility is the maintenance of monogamous marriage and family. Adjusting for discrimination against women and for child-care responsibilities, the Wisconsin study indicates that married men work between two and one-third and four times harder than married women, and more than twice as hard as female family heads. The work effort of married men increases with their age, credentials, education, job experience, and birth of children, while the work effort of married women steadily declines. Most important in judging the impact of marriage, husbands work 50 percent harder than bachelors of comparable age, education, and skills.

The effect of marriage, thus, is to increase the work effort of men by about half. Since men have higher earnings capacity to begin with, and since the female capacity-utilization figures would be even lower without an adjustment for discrimination, it is manifest that the maintenance of families is the key factor in reducing poverty.

Once a family is headed by a woman, it is almost impossible for it to greatly raise its income even if the woman is highly educated and trained and she hires day-care or domestic help. Her family responsibilities and distractions tend to prevent her from the kind of all-out commitment that is necessary for the full use of earning power. Few women with children make earning money the top priority in their lives.

A married man, on the other hand, is spurred by the claims of family to channel his otherwise disruptive male aggressions into his performance as a provider for a wife and children. These sexual differences alone, which manifest themselves in all societies known to anthropology, dictate that the first priority of any serious program against poverty is to strengthen the male role in poor families.

These narrow measures of work effort touch on just part of the manifold interplay between family and poverty. Edward Banfield's *The Unheavenly City* defines the lower class largely by its lack of an orientation to the future. Living from day to day and from hand to mouth, lower class individuals are unable to plan or save or keep a job. Banfield gives the impression that short-time horizons are a deep-seated psychological defect afflicting hundreds of thousands of the poor.

There is no question that Banfield puts his finger on a crucial problem of the poor and that he develops and documents his theme in an unrivaled classic of disciplined social science. But he fails to show how millions of men, equally present oriented, equally buffeted by impulse and blind to the future, have managed to become far-seeing members of the middle classes. He also fails to explain how millions of apparently future-oriented men can become dissolute followers of the sensuous moment, neglecting their jobs, dissipating their income and wealth, pursuing a horizon no longer than the most time-bound of the poor.

What Banfield is in fact describing in his lower-class category is largely the temperament of single, divorced, and separated men. The key to lower-class life in contemporary America is that unrelated individuals, as the census calls them, are so numerous and conspicuous that they set the tone for the entire community. Their congregation in ghettos, moreover, magnifies greatly their impact on the black poor, male and female (though, as Banfield rightly observes, this style of instant gratification is chiefly a male trait).

The short-sighted outlook of poverty stems largely from the breakdown of family responsibilities among fathers. The lives of the poor, all too often, are governed by the rhythms of tension and release that characterize the sexual experience of young single men. Because female sexuality, as it evolved over the millennia, is psychologically rooted in the bearing and nurturing of children, women have long horizons within their very bodies, glimpses of eternity within their wombs. Civilized society is dependent upon the submission of the short-term sexuality of young men to the extended maternal horizons of women. This is what happens in monogamous marriage; the man disciplines his sexuality and extends it into the future through the womb of a woman. The woman gives him access to his children, otherwise forever denied him; and he gives her the product of his labor, otherwise dissipated on temporary pleasures. The woman gives him a unique link to the future and a vision of it; he gives her faithfulness and a commitment to a lifetime of hard work. If work effort is the first principle of overcoming poverty, marriage is the prime source of upwardly mobile work.

It is love that changes the short horizons of youth and poverty into the long horizons of marriage and career. When marriages fail, the man often returns to the more primitive rhythms of singleness. On the average, his income drops by one-third and he shows a far higher propensity for drink, drugs, and crime. But when marriages in general hold firm and men in general love and support their children, Banfield's lower-class style changes into middle-class futurity.

The key to the intractable poverty of the hardcore American poor is the dominance of single and separated men in poor communities. Black "unrelated individuals" are not much more likely to be in poverty than white ones. The problem is neither race nor matriarchy in any meaningful sense. It is familial anarchy among the concentrated poor of the inner city, in which flamboyant and impulsive youths rather than responsible men provide the themes of aspiration. The result is that male sexual rhythms tend to prevail, and boys are brought up without authoritative fathers in the home to instill in them the values of responsible paternity: the discipline and love of children and the dependable performance of the provider role. "If she wants me, *she*'ll pay," one young stud assured me in prison, and perhaps, in the welfare culture, she can and will. Thus the pattern is extended into future generations.

Questions

1. What did Gilder see as the major causes of poverty? What was his solution to poverty?
2. What was Gilder's analysis of the roles of women and men? What are the implications of this analysis?
3. Would Gilder's argument have appealed to President Reagan? Why or why not?

31-2 *Rachel and Her Children* (1988)

Jonathan Kozol

Social critic Jonathan Kozol described the world of the "welfare hotel" in his 1988 study *Rachel and Her Children*. Such institutions were the only shelter available for many homeless families in New York City in the 1980s.

Source: Excerpt from Jonathan Kozol, *Rachel and Her Children*, 51–55. Copyright © 1988 by Jonathan Kozol. Used by permission of Crown Publishers, a division of Random House, Inc.

There are families in this building whose existence, difficult though it may be, still represents an island of serenity and peace. Annie Harrington's family has a kind of pained serenity. Gwen and her children live with the peace of resignation. I think of these families like refugees who, in the midst of war, cling to each other and establish a small zone of safety. Most people here do not have resources to create a zone of safety. Terrorized already on arrival, they are quickly caught up in a vortex of accelerating threats and are tossed about like bits of wood and broken furniture and shattered houses in an Arkansas tornado. Chaos and disorder alternate with lethargy and nearly absolute bewilderment in face of regulations they cannot observe or do not understand.

Two women whom I meet in the same evening after Christmas, Wanda and Terry, frighten me by their entire inability to fathom or to govern what is going on inside and all around them.

Terry is pregnant, in her ninth month. She's afraid that, when she gives birth, she may not be able to bring home her baby from the hospital because she is not legally residing here.

Wanda, curled up like a newborn in a room no larger than a closet, is three months pregnant, planning an abortion.

Would doctors say these women are emotionally unwell? They might have no choice. Were these women sick before they came here? I don't see how we could possibly find out. What startles me is not that they have difficulty coping but that neither yet has given up entirely.

Terry: twenty-eight years old. She has three kids. She graduated from a school in Flushing and has worked for eight years as a lab assistant. Burnt out of her home, she stayed for two years with her sister's family: three adults, eight children, crowded into four unheated rooms. Evicted by her sister when the pressure on her sister's husband and their kids began to damage their own marriage, she had to take her children to the EAU at Church Street in Manhattan. Refusing to accept a placement at a barracks shelter, she's been sleeping here illegally for several nights in a small room rented to her cousin.

When we meet, she's in the corridor outside the crisis center, crying and perspiring heavily. She sits on a broken chair to talk to me. She's not on Medicaid and has been removed from AFDC. "My card's being reprocessed," she explains, although this explanation explains nothing. She's not on WIC. "I've got to file an application." Her back is aching. She is due to have her child any day.

This is the reason for her panic: "If I can't be placed before the baby's born, the hospital won't let me take the baby. They don't let you take a newborn if you haven't got a home." As we will see, this is not always so, but the possibility of this occurrence is quite real. Where are her kids? "They're here. I've got them hidden in the room."

She takes me to her cousin Wanda's room. I measure it: nine feet by twelve, a little smaller than the room in which I store my files on the homeless. Wanda's been here fifteen months, has four kids, no hot plate, and no food in the refrigerator. She's had no food stamps and no restaurant allowance for two months. I ask her why. (You ask these questions even though you know the answer will be vague, confused, because so many of these women have no possible idea of why they do or don't receive the benefits they do or don't deserve.) She's curled up in a tattered slip and a torn sweater on a mattress with no sheet. Her case was closed, she says. Faintly, I hear something about "an application." Her words are hard to understand. I ask her whether she was here for Christmas. The very few words she speaks come out in small reluctant phrases: "Where else would I go?" She says her children got some presents from the fire department. There's a painting of Jesus and Mary on the wall above the bed. "My mother gave it to me."

A week later I stop by to visit. She's in the same position: drowsy and withdrawn. I ask her if she celebrated New Year's Eve. "Stayed by my lonesome" is all that I understand. She rouses herself enough to ask me if I have a cigarette. In the vacuum of emotion I ask if she ever gets to do something for fun. "Go to a movie . . ." But when I ask the last time she's been to a movie she says: "1984." What was the movie? "*Dawn of the Living Dead*."

When she says she's pregnant and is planning an abortion I don't care to ask her why, but she sits up halfway, props herself against a pillow, looks at Terry, shrugs, and mumbles this: "What you want to bring another baby into this place for? There ain't nothin' waitin' for them here but dirty rooms and dyin'."

Her children, scattered like wilted weeds around her on the floor, don't talk or play or move around or interrupt. Outside in the corridor I ask her cousin if the kids are sick. Terry says: "They're okay. They just didn't have no food to eat today." So I ask: "Did you?" She shakes her head. I go down to Herald Square, buy french fries and chicken at a fast-food store, milk and cookies at a delicatessen, and return. The minute I walk in Wanda sits up, clearheaded and alert. Her kids wake from their stupor. Fifteen minutes later, every bit of chicken, all the french fries, cookies, milk have been consumed. There is a rush of energy and talking in the room. The kids are pestering the adults, as they ought to.

"I have a problem," Wanda says. "My blood sugar goes down. It is called [pronounced very precisely] hypoglycemia."

I meet Terry one year later by sheer chance outside Grand Central Station. She's in a food line for the sandwiches distributed by a charitable group at 10:00 P.M. Her kids are with her. She's holding a baby in her arms. She tells me she's in another hotel near the Martinique. "Don't have no refrigerators there . . ."

I lose her in the crowd of people waiting for a meal.

In the subway station under Herald Square a woman who has seen me coming from the Martinique follows me and stops me by the stairs. Her hair is disheveled. Words spill from her mouth. She says that she was thrown out of the Martinique. Her children were sick with diarrhea. Someone "reported" her; for what I do not ask. After the Martinique she says that she was in a place I've never heard of called the Brooklyn Arms. Her youngest child, one year old, became much sicker there. City workers finally persuaded her to give up all three kids to foster care. She's living now in a crowded women's shelter where, she says, there are twelve women in a room. She shrieks this information at me on the platform not far from the shrieking trains.

"There's no soap, no hygiene. You go to the desk and ask for toilet paper. You get a single sheet. If you need another sheet you go back down and ask them for some more. I sleep on an army cot. The bathroom's flooded."

Is she telling me the truth? Is she on drugs? Is she unwell? Why did she elect to tell me this? Why do the words come out so fast? I feel unkind to cut her off, but I am frightened by her desperation. I leave her there, pouring out her words into the night.

The nurse in the Martinique says this: "A mother gave birth last week to a baby that weighed just over a pound. She was in her seventh month. Her children rubbed her belly while she cried. I called an ambulance."

The nurse is kind, compassionate, and overwhelmed. "People are fractured by this system. I'm responsible for 500 families, here and in another building. Custody cases. Pregnant women. Newborn children. I can get them into WIC. I'm snowed . . ." She's on the telephone, buried in papers, talking with women, hearing their questions, trying to come up with answers. There are others like her in the crisis center who create a tiny zone of safety in the larger zone of fear. But twenty-five hardworking nurses like this woman would be scarcely equal to the miseries that flood across her desk out of this factory of pain and tears.

Questions

1. How did Kozol challenge the belief that a "safety net" is in place to protect the welfare of the neediest?
2. Why did Kozol, an opponent of then current governmental social welfare policies, focus on the experiences of families?
3. Why do the families depicted in Kozol's account seem incapable of improving their lot in life?

31-3 On World Trade Talks in Seattle (1999)

Bill Clinton

Throughout his two terms as president, Bill Clinton stressed the importance of free trade and, in 1994, signed the North American Free Trade Agreement (NAFTA) with Canada and Mexico. At the same time, an antiglobalization movement grew during the 1990s in the United States and Europe, focusing on the persistent divide between rich countries and poor, on the destruction of local communities and the economies upon which they were based, and on environmental problems, including global warming. These issues and concerns, which were defined largely in national terms as late as the 1980s were, by the 1990s, seen increasingly in global and "transnational" terms.

Source: "Remarks by the President in Telephone Interview with *Seattle Post-Intelligencer* Newspaper," from the White House Office of the Press Secretary, November 30, 1999. http://clinton4.nara.gov/textonly/WH/New/WTO-Conf-1999/remarks/19991130–1650.html

The President. How are you?

Q. I'm good, how are you doing?

The President. I'm great. I'm going to the San Francisco Airport, on my way to L.A. and then to Seattle.

Q. Excellent. So as far as you know, are there still talks taking place? We just heard on CNN, claiming that the talks are actually cancelled—which, we don't even know if that's true.

The President. Well, that's certainly news to me. I heard that the talks were still going on.

Q. Tell me—I'm sure you've heard it's been kind of a chaotic day here. Do you regret choosing Seattle as the location for this? Do you wish you were heading some place sunny, like Honolulu and San Diego?

The President. Well, I don't think the—I think certainly if we had had it any place in the continental United States we would have had the same thing; and even if we had gone to Honolulu there might have been thousands of people there.

What I regret is not that there are protestors there—I have supported the right of people whose interests represent labor unions, who represent environmental groups, people who represent the poorer countries of the world—coming and expressing their opinions. And I've repeatedly said I thought the WTO process was too closed, it ought to be opened up and labor and environmental interests ought to be represented and it ought to be fair for poor countries, as well as wealthy countries.

What I regret is that a small number of people have done non-peaceful things and have tried to block access and to prevent meetings. That's wrong. It's not only illegal, it's just wrong.

On the other hand, I think the larger number of people that are there for peaceful purposes are healthy. I think what they represent is that in the last five years you've seen a dramatic change—trade is now no longer the province of CEOs, organized interest groups that deal with the economy and political leaders. It's now—we not only live in a global economy, you've got a global information society and this whole process is being democratized. And we're going to have to build a new consensus that goes down deeper into every society about what kind of trade policy we want. And I think that is, on balance, a healthy thing.

Anyway, that's kind of where I am on it. I regret very much that a few people have given the protestors a bad name, because I think the fact that the protestors are there—were it not for those stopping meetings, stopping movements, not being peaceful—would be a positive.

Q. Right. What is your theory about why people are so upset here?

The President. Well, for one thing, I think that a lot of people feel threatened by all these changes that are going on in the global economy; and the process by which the decisions are made changing the rules of trade are made by people who generally have not been very accountable.

I mean, the whole WTO—I went to Geneva last year to tell them they ought to open their records.

Q. Right.

The President. I mean, they have secret proceedings and things of that kind. For another thing, a lot of times when decisions have been made they aren't honored. The United States won 22 out of 24 cases we filed, and in several cases the people say, well, so what?

And then I think, finally, there are people who question whether these trading rules are benefiting lower income countries, poor countries; and who question whether they're a damage to the environment from certain trading arrangements that wouldn't otherwise be there, and who question whether this is a race to the bottom or the top.

So that labor unions in wealthier countries want to have certain basic, core labor standards observed in poorer countries because they think it will be better for average people, so that the trading system actually benefits them. So I think that is bringing all those people out.

Q. What in your mind will make this week a success or a failure?

The President. Well, I think if we can continue to negotiate and can reach some accord on the terms under which to start a new trade round; and if I can persuade more of my colleagues that if you don't want people like the protestors outside of every trade meeting from now until the end of time, they're going to have to open the process so that the voices of labor, the environment and the developing countries can be heard; and so that the decisions are transparent, the records are open and the consequences are clear—we're going to continue to have problems.

And I think, on balance, the world is much better off because we've expanded trade over the last 50 years. And I bet you a lot of the protestors came to the protest wearing shoes that were made in other countries, using cell phones, and maybe a lot of them drove cars that were made—

Q. Right.

The President. —or forcign manufactured. We live in a global economy that, on balance, has been quite good for the United States, but also good for developing countries. But we've got to make a better case down deeper into society. It's not just trying to convince a few elites in every society that the system of integrated trade on fair and open terms is good for them.

Q. Let me ask you about labor, which, you know, is a big issue here. What is your position on allowing trade sanctions against countries that violate core labor standards?

The President. I think what we ought to do, first of all, is to adopt the United States' position on having a working group on labor within the WTO. And then that working group should develop these core labor standards and then they ought to be a part of every trade agreement. And, ultimately, I would favor a system in which sanctions would come for violating any provision of a trade agreement. But we've got to do this in steps.

I do think it is worth noting that the strongest opposition to this position, however, comes from the leaders of developing countries—including a lot of developing countries that have left-wing governments, not right-wing governments—who believe that this is a strategy by the American labor movement to keep them down and keep them poor and keep them from selling products that they would otherwise be highly competitive in, in the American market.

Q. Right. Are they right?

The President. Well, I don't think so. That is, it certainly could be used that way. But what the American labor movement has a right, it seems to me, to is to know that their brothers and sisters throughout the world are actually going to be benefiting from expanded trade.

When I ran for President there were some countries, small countries in the Caribbean where we had dramatically expanded trade in the years before I became President, where average hourly wages had fallen during the time trade had expanded and the incomes of the countries had gone up. That's not right.

So I wouldn't support labor's objectives if I thought they were just purely protectionist and they didn't want Americans to compete with people from other places, because we can compete quite well. And for every job we've lost in America, we've gained two or three more. That's why we've got 19.8 million jobs in the last seven years. We never had job growth like this before. And the trade related jobs pay higher wages.

So if I thought the labor agenda was purely protectionist, I wouldn't be for that. On the other hand, I think it is legitimate to say that if people are out there working and selling their products in the international arena and Americans are going to buy them, and Europeans are going to buy them, all of us who come from wealthy countries where most people have the basic necessities of life—we ought not to buy from countries that violate the child labor norms; we ought not to buy from countries that basically oppress their workers with labor conditions and lack of a living income. And there is a way to strike the right balance here so that we put a more human face on the global economy.

I feel the same way about environmental standards.

Q. That's the subject I want to ask you about next. As you know, critics are pointing at cases like the shrimp-turtle dispute and saying that corporate lawyers, meeting in secret, can invalidate U.S. laws. Are we yielding some of our sovereignty in being part of the WTO?

The President. Well, we yield the right to be unilateral and not bound by a system of rules every time we join any kind of organization. I mean, if you join any kind of organization in which there are going to be disputes, you can't say that, I'll only follow the rules when we win.

Q. Right.

The President. And you can't say that any organization made up of human beings will be error-free.

But I know there was a lot of concern about the way the turtle case was handled. There is also — earlier the Venezuelan oil —

Q. Right.

The President. — where we had a lot of concerns.

But I think the answer to that is to make sure that these environmental standards are properly integrated into the WTO deliberation and that we agree that countries ought to have more leeway on higher environmental standards than in other areas.

And, again, some people in the developing countries may say, well, that's a protectionist strategy. But from my point of view, it is not at all. I think that with climate change being the number one environmental problem in the world, it is a mistake not to take into account the environmental consequences to not only a particular nation, but to the climate as a whole, to anything that leads to accelerated deforestation or the increase in greenhouse gas emission.

But, see, I've got a whole different take on this than most people do. I believe that one of the biggest economic, as well as environmental, problems the world has today is that most decision makers — not only in the United States, but in all the developing countries — still believe the only way to get rich is the way the U.S. and Europe got rich in the Industrial Era, by burning more coal, burning more oil, putting more greenhouse gases into the atmosphere. And then countries say, when we get as rich as they are, then we'll turn around and clean it up.

But, as you know, with climate change, it doesn't work that way. If you warm the climate, you put all this stuff into the air, it takes between 50 and 100 years to turn a lot of this around. But we know now that it is technologically possible to grow the economy and reduce greenhouse gas emission, if you're a rich country — and stabilize them, if you're a poor country, by taking a totally different energy course into the future. The technologies are available right now.

And that's what I think we have to sell people on. And then we've got to really work hard to get these technologies widely disseminated into the developing economies, so that India, China, these other places, can use them to create jobs and raise income while they protect their environment. That's a sale we've got to make and it ought to be part of the decision-making process of the WTO to promote that policy.

Q. Let me ask you one last question. What is the U.S. willing to give up at these talks? I mean, these are negotiations and other countries would like to talk about our antidumping laws. What can we put on the table?

The President. Well, first of all, I think we ought to support the general rules that reduce tariffs and other trade barriers. And we ought to be for accelerating access to our market, for countries that follow responsible policies. That's at the heart of my Caribbean Basin Initiative and my Africa Trade bill. And I have reached out to those countries to try to do that. And we ought to do that.

But I would not be for giving up our dumping laws, and I'll tell you why. Because we already have the most open markets in the world. We have — when the Asian economy collapsed in '97, we could have closed our markets, and we didn't. And so it exploded our trade deficit. Our trade deficit is about 4 percent of our income now. I'm for open borders because we get more products at lower cost and it's a great pressure against inflation coming back into our economy — and we still have created almost 20 million jobs.

But I don't think it's right to allow a temporary economic emergency to lead to a surge of steel dumping, for example, like we went through, and then to throw a lot of Americans out of business in capital-intensive industries, who might not be able to get back into business, just because of an economic crisis somewhere else and because nobody else will take the products. I mean, for the Europeans to tell us we should stop dumping, when during the Asian crisis we bought literally ten times as much foreign steel as they did, is a little ludicrous — when they have absolute quotas on the number of foreign cars they will buy, that we don't have, is ludicrous.

So we can't give up our dumping laws as long as we have the most open markets in the world and we keep them open to help these countries keep going, and other countries don't do the same. They shouldn't be able to take advantage of temporary economic developments to do something that otherwise the free market economy wouldn't support.

If you look at what our steel industry did, they shed over half of their employment, they spent billions of dollars modernizing technology. They were, under normal circumstances, internationally competitive. They should not have been put out of business by people dumping from Japan, from Russia, from any other country during the period of crisis that we just went through.

Q. Okay. So as far as you know, the talks are still on, right? You haven't learned anything —

The President. Yes. While we've been talking, as far as I know, they're still on. And I think they ought to stay on. And I think, again, if we can just get by the few people that are being — that aren't being peaceful, and the people that are trying to stop people from meeting, I think the presence of others with legitimate questions about the WTO process, the environment and labor, and how poor countries are treated, I think this can be a net positive — because we're going to have to build a much deeper consensus for global trade to carry it forward.

Q. Okay. We'll see you tomorrow.

The President. Thank you.

Questions

1. What did Clinton mean by putting "a more human face on the global economy"?
2. What is the case for globalization? Against?

Questions for Further Thought

1. Compare and contrast the essays of George Gilder (Document 31-1) and Jonathan Kozol (Document 31-2).
2. What are seen as the benefits and problems of globalization?

The New Technology

As the millennium drew to a close, the economy, boosted by new technologies and a booming stock market, showed a remarkable capacity for growth, and both unemployment rates and inflation were low. Technology, in fact, did change the lives of Americans, and some predicted it would completely transform business as well (Document 31-4). However, the boom did not last: by the end of 2000, a number of technology companies folded, the stock market depreciated, and economic growth slowed dramatically. In Document 31-4, Bill Gates explains how the information revolution will transform the capitalist system.

31-4 Friction-Free Capitalism (1995)

Bill Gates

More than anything, the advent of the affordable personal computer and the World Wide Web changed the way people communicated and conducted business at the end of the twentieth century. This new technology fostered an "information revolution"—a dramatic change in the way people accessed and processed all kinds of information about the world around them. In his optimistic book *The Road Ahead*, Bill Gates, founder of the software company Microsoft (see text pp. 970–971), describes his company's role in fostering the information revolution. In the excerpt that follows, Gates waxes philosophical about how the "information highway" will fundamentally change the market economy and lead us all to a "shopper's heaven."

Source: Excerpts from Bill Gates, *The Road Ahead* (New York: Viking Penguin, 1995), 157–183. Copyright © 1995, 1996 by William H. Gates III. Used by permission of Viking Penguin, a division of Penguin Group (USA) Inc.

When Adam Smith described the concept of markets in *The Wealth of Nations* in 1776, he theorized that if every buyer knew every seller's price, and every seller knew what every buyer was willing to pay, everyone in the "market" would be able to make fully informed decisions and society's resources would be distributed efficiently. To date we haven't achieved Smith's ideal because would-be buyers and would-be sellers seldom have complete information about one another.

Not many consumers looking to buy a car stereo have the time or patience to canvass every dealer and thus are acting on imperfect and limited information. If you've bought a product for $500 and see it advertised in the paper for $300 a week or two later, you feel foolish for overpaying. But you feel a lot worse if you end up in the wrong job because you haven't done thorough enough research.

A few markets are already working fairly close to Smith's ideal. Investors buying and selling currency and certain other commodities participate in efficient electronic markets that provide nearly complete instantaneous information about worldwide supply, demand, and prices. Everyone gets pretty much the same deal because news about all offers, bids, and transactions speeds across wires to trading desks everywhere. However, most marketplaces are very inefficient. For instance, if you are trying to find a doctor, lawyer, accountant, or similar professional, or are buying a house, information is incomplete and comparisons are difficult to make.

The information highway will extend the electronic marketplace and make it the ultimate go-between, the universal middleman. Often the only humans involved in a transaction will be the actual buyer and seller. All the goods for sale in the world will be available for you to examine, compare, and, often, customize. When you want to buy something you'll be able to tell your computer to find it for you at the best price offered by any acceptable source or ask your computer to "haggle" with the computers of various sellers. Information about vendors and their products and services will be available to any computer connected to the highway. Servers distributed worldwide will accept bids, resolve offers into completed transactions, control authentication and security, and handle all other aspects of the marketplace, including the transfer of funds. This will carry us into a new world of low-friction, low-overhead capitalism, in which market information will be plentiful and transaction costs low. It will be a shopper's heaven.

Every market, from a bazaar to the highway, facilitates competitive pricing and allows goods to move from seller to buyer efficiently with modest friction. This is thanks to the market makers—those whose job it is to bring buyers and sellers together. As the information highway assumes the role of market maker in realm after realm, traditional middlemen will have to contribute real value to a transaction to justify a commission. For example, stores and services that until now have profited just because they are "there"—in a particular geographic location—may find they have lost that advantage. But those who provide added value will not only survive, they will thrive, because the information highway will let them make their services available to customers everywhere.

This idea will scare a lot of people. Most change feels a bit threatening, and I expect dramatic changes in the business of retailing as commerce flows across the highway. But, as with so many changes, I think once we get used to it we'll wonder how we did without it. The consumer will get not only competitive cost savings, but also a much wider variety of products and services to choose from. Although there may be fewer stores, if people continue to enjoy shopping in today's outlets, as many stores as their demand justifies will remain available. And because the highway will simplify and standardize shopping, it will also save time. If you are buying a gift for a loved one, you will be able to consider more choices and often you will find something more imaginative. You could use the time saved from shopping to think up a fun clue to put on the package, or create a personalized card. Or you could spend the time you save with the recipient.

We all recognize the value of a knowledgeable salesperson when we are shopping for insurance, clothes, investments, jewelry, a camera, a home appliance, or a home. We also know the salesperson's advice is sometimes biased because he or she is ultimately hoping to make a sale from a particular inventory.

On the information highway lots of product information will be available directly from manufacturers. As they do today, vendors will use a variety of entertaining and provocative techniques to attract us. Advertising will evolve into a hybrid, combining today's television commercials, magazine ads, and a detailed sales brochure. If an ad catches your attention, you'll be able to request additional information directly and very easily. Links will let you navigate through whatever information the advertiser has made available, which might be product manuals consisting of video, audio, and text. Vendors will make getting information about their products as simple as possible....

Industry after industry will be changed, and change is unsettling. Some middlemen who handle information or product distribution will find they no longer add value and change fields, whereas others will rise to the competitive challenge. There is a nearly infinite number of tasks left undone in services, education, and urban affairs, to say nothing of the workforce the highway itself will require. So this new efficiency will create all sorts of exciting employment opportunities. And the highway, which will put an immense amount of information at anyone's fingertips, will be an invaluable training tool. Someone who decides to change careers and go into computer consulting will have access to the best texts, the greatest lectures, and information about course requirements, exams, and accreditation. There will be dislocations. However, overall, society will benefit from these changes.

Capitalism, demonstrably the greatest of the constructed economic systems, has in the past decade clearly proved its advantages over the alternative systems. The information highway will magnify those advantages. It will allow those who produce goods to see, a lot more efficiently than ever before, what buyers want, and will allow potential consumers to buy those goods more efficiently. Adam Smith would be pleased. More important, consumers everywhere will enjoy the benefits.

Questions

1. According to Gates, how will the information highway change the marketplace?
2. Do you think Gates's vision is utopian or realistic?

Question for Further Thought

1. What are the connections between globalization (Document 31-3) and the computer revolution (Document 31-4)?

Culture Wars

America became an increasingly pluralistic society in the 1980s and 1990s. The immigrant population was larger than it had been since World War II, and a large-scale influx of immigrants from Latin America and Asia changed the composition of the nation's population. Although many recognized the positive contributions that immigrants made to the economy and the overall society, anti-immigrant sentiments flared in places like California, where voters enacted legislation to prevent undocumented aliens from receiving public aid (Document 31-6). This issue would take on new life after members of Al Qaeda attacked the World Trade Center in New York City and the Pentagon in Washington, D.C., in 2001. Abortion, new-wave feminism, the gay rights movement, the AIDS epidemic, and, early in the twenty-first century, same-sex marriage, also polarized Americans and forced them to reevaluate their society.

31-5 Don't Ask, Don't Tell (1993)

One of the first issues President Clinton faced after his election in 1992 was whether to lift the controversial ban on gays serving in the military. Clinton settled on a policy based on compromise, known as "don't ask, don't tell." The following is the "Policy Concerning Homosexuality in the Armed Forces." Despite the policy, from 1993 to 2000 the number of discharges for homosexuality in all the services sharply increased.

Source: "Policy Concerning Homosexuality in the Armed Forces" from *United States Code Title 10, Subtitle A, Part II, Chapter 37, Section 654.* http://www.law.cornell.edu/uscode/search/display.html?terms=654&url=/uscode/html/uscode10/usc_sec_10_00000654----000-.html

(a) **Findings.**—Congress makes the following findings:
   (1) Section 8 of article I of the Constitution of the United States commits exclusively to the Congress the powers to raise and support armies, provide and maintain a Navy, and make rules for the government and regulation of the land and naval forces.
   (2) There is no constitutional right to serve in the armed forces.
   (3) Pursuant to the powers conferred by section 8 of article I of the Constitution of the United States, it lies within the discretion of the Congress to establish qualifications for and conditions of service in the armed forces.
   (4) The primary purpose of the armed forces is to prepare for and to prevail in combat should the need arise.
   (5) The conduct of military operations requires members of the armed forces to make extraordinary sacrifices, including the ultimate sacrifice, in order to provide for the common defense.
   (6) Success in combat requires military units that are characterized by high morale, good order and discipline, and unit cohesion.
   (7) One of the most critical elements in combat capability is unit cohesion, that is, the bonds of trust among individual service members that make the combat effectiveness of a military unit greater than the sum of the combat effectiveness of the individual unit members.
   (8) Military life is fundamentally different from civilian life in that—
      (A) the extraordinary responsibilities of the armed forces, the unique conditions of military ser-

vice, and the critical role of unit cohesion, require that the military community, while subject to civilian control, exist as a specialized society; and
: (B) the military society is characterized by its own laws, rules, customs, and traditions, including numerous restrictions on personal behavior, that would not be acceptable in civilian society.
(9) The standards of conduct for members of the armed forces regulate a member's life for 24 hours each day beginning at the moment the member enters military status and not ending until that person is discharged or otherwise separated from the armed forces.
(10) Those standards of conduct, including the Uniform Code of Military Justice, apply to a member of the armed forces at all times that the member has a military status, whether the member is on base or off base, and whether the member is on duty or off duty.
(11) The pervasive application of the standards of conduct is necessary because members of the armed forces must be ready at all times for worldwide deployment to a combat environment.
(12) The worldwide deployment of United States military forces, the international responsibilities of the United States, and the potential for involvement of the armed forces in actual combat routinely make it necessary for members of the armed forces involuntarily to accept living conditions and working conditions that are often Spartan, primitive, and characterized by forced intimacy with little or no privacy.
(13) The prohibition against homosexual conduct is a longstanding element of military law that continues to be necessary in the unique circumstances of military service.
(14) The armed forces must maintain personnel policies that exclude persons whose presence in the armed forces would create an unacceptable risk to the armed forces' high standards of morale, good order and discipline, and unit cohesion that are the essence of military capability.
(15) The presence in the armed forces of persons who demonstrate a propensity or intent to engage in homosexual acts would create an unacceptable risk to the high standards of morale, good order and discipline, and unit cohesion that are the essence of military capability.

(b) **Policy.**—A member of the armed forces shall be separated from the armed forces under regulations prescribed by the Secretary of Defense if one or more of the following findings is made and approved in accordance with procedures set forth in such regulations:
: (1) That the member has engaged in, attempted to engage in, or solicited another to engage in a homosexual act or acts unless there are further findings, made and approved in accordance with procedures set forth in such regulations, that the member has demonstrated that—
  : (A) such conduct is a departure from the member's usual and customary behavior;
  : (B) such conduct, under all the circumstances, is unlikely to recur;
  : (C) such conduct was not accomplished by use of force, coercion, or intimidation;
  : (D) under the particular circumstances of the case, the member's continued presence in the armed forces is consistent with the interests of the armed forces in proper discipline, good order, and morale; and
  : (E) the member does not have a propensity or intent to engage in homosexual acts.
: (2) That the member has stated that he or she is a homosexual or bisexual, or words to that effect, unless there is a further finding, made and approved in accordance with procedures set forth in the regulations, that the member has demonstrated that he or she is not a person who engages in, attempts to engage in, has a propensity to engage in, or intends to engage in homosexual acts.
: (3) That the member has married or attempted to marry a person known to be the same biological sex.

(c) **Entry Standards and Documents.**—
: (1) The Secretary of Defense shall ensure that the standards for enlistment and appointment of members of the armed forces reflect the policies set forth in subsection (b).
: (2) The documents used to effectuate the enlistment or appointment of a person as a member of the armed forces shall set forth the provisions of subsection (b).

(d) **Required Briefings.**—The briefings that members of the armed forces receive upon entry into the armed forces and periodically thereafter under section 937 of this title (article 137 of the Uniform Code of Military Justice) shall include a detailed explanation of the applicable laws and regulations governing sexual conduct by members of the armed forces, including the policies prescribed under subsection (b).

(e) **Rule of Construction.**—Nothing in subsection (b) shall be construed to require that a member of the armed forces be processed for separation from the armed forces when a determination is made in accordance with regulations prescribed by the Secretary of Defense that—
: (1) the member engaged in conduct or made statements for the purpose of avoiding or terminating military service; and
: (2) separation of the member would not be in the best interest of the armed forces.

(f) **Definitions.**—In this section:
   (1) The term "homosexual" means a person, regardless of sex, who engages in, attempts to engage in, has a propensity to engage in, or intends to engage in homosexual acts, and includes the terms "gay" and "lesbian."
   (2) The term "bisexual" means a person who engages in, attempts to engage in, has a propensity to engage in, or intends to engage in homosexual and heterosexual acts.
   (3) The term "homosexual act" means—
      (A) any bodily contact, actively undertaken or passively permitted, between members of the same sex for the purpose of satisfying sexual desires; and
      (B) any bodily contact which a reasonable person would understand to demonstrate a propensity or intent to engage in an act described in subparagraph (A).

Questions

1. What distinctions does the military draw between military and civilian life?
2. According to the policy, what can Americans in the service do and not do? What can military officials do and not do?

31-6 Proposition 187 (1994)

Anxiety about immigration often occurs during periods of economic stress, and California in the mid-1990s was no exception. As a bulwark of the military-industrial complex, the state might have suffered more than any other from the end of the Cold War. The "peace dividend" seemed to be a combination of high unemployment and taxes. Such was the environment in 1994, when Californians passed Proposition 187. The referendum sought to deny government services to illegal immigrants.

Source: California Secretary of State's Office, *1994 California Voter Information: Proposition 187, Text of Proposed Law.*

SECTION 1. FINDINGS AND DECLARATION.

The People of California find and declare as follows:

That they have suffered and are suffering economic hardship caused by the presence of illegal aliens in this state.

That they have suffered and are suffering personal injury and damage caused by the criminal conduct of illegal aliens in this state.

That they have a right to the protection of their government from any person or persons entering this country unlawfully.

Therefore, the People of California declare their intention to provide for cooperation between their agencies of state and local government with the federal government, and to establish a system of required notification by and between such agencies to prevent illegal aliens in the United States from receiving benefits or public services in the State of California.

SECTION 2. MANUFACTURE, DISTRIBUTION OR SALE OF FALSE CITIZENSHIP OR RESIDENT ALIEN DOCUMENTS: CRIME AND PUNISHMENT.

Section 113 is added to the Penal Code, to read:

113. Any person who manufactures, distributes or sells false documents to conceal the true citizenship or resident alien status of another person is guilty of a felony, and shall be punished by imprisonment in the state prison for five years or by a fine of seventy-five thousand dollars ($75,000).

SECTION 3. USE OF FALSE CITIZENSHIP OR RESIDENT ALIEN DOCUMENTS: CRIME AND PUNISHMENT.

Section 114 is added to the Penal Code, to read:

114. Any person who uses false documents to conceal his or her true citizenship or resident alien status is guilty of a felony, and shall be punished by imprisonment in the state prison for five years or by a fine of twenty-five thousand dollars ($25,000).

SECTION 4. LAW ENFORCEMENT COOPERATION WITH INS.

Section 834b is added to the Penal Code, to read:

834b. (a) Every law enforcement agency in California shall fully cooperate with the United States Immigration and Naturalization Service regarding any person who is arrested if he or she is suspected of being present in the United States in violation of federal immigration laws. . . .

SECTION 5. EXCLUSION OF ILLEGAL ALIENS FROM PUBLIC SOCIAL SERVICES.

Section 10001.5 is added to the Welfare and Institutions Code, to read:

10001.5. (a) In order to carry out the intention of the People of California that only citizens of the United States and aliens lawfully admitted to the United States may receive the benefits of public social services and to ensure that all persons employed in the providing of those services shall diligently protect public funds from misuse, the provisions of this section are adopted.

(b) A Person shall not receive any public social services to which he or she may be otherwise entitled until the legal status of that person has been verified as one of the following:

(1) A citizen of the United States.

(2) An alien lawfully admitted as a permanent resident.

(3) An alien lawfully admitted for a temporary period of time.

(c) If any public entity in this state to whom a person has applied for public social services determines or reasonably suspects, based upon the information provided to it, that the person is an alien in the United States in violation of federal law, the following procedures shall be followed by the public entity:

(1) The entity shall not provide the person with benefits or services.

(2) The entity shall, in writing, notify the person of his or her apparent illegal immigration status, and that the person must either obtain legal status or leave the United States.

(3) The entity shall also notify the State Director of Social Services, the Attorney General of California, and the United States Immigration and Naturalization Service of the apparent illegal status, and shall provide any additional information that may be requested by any other public entity.

SECTION 6. EXCLUSION OF ILLEGAL ALIENS FROM PUBLICLY FUNDED HEALTH CARE.

Chapter 1.3 (commencing with Section 130) is added to Part 1 of Division 1 of the Health and Safety Code, to read:

Chapter 1.3. Publicly-Funded Health Care Services

130. (a) In order to carry out the intention of the People of California that, excepting emergency medical care as required by federal law, only citizens of the United States and aliens lawfully admitted to the United States may receive the benefits of publicly-funded health care, and to ensure that all persons employed in the providing of those services shall diligently protect public funds from misuse, the provisions of this section are adopted.

(b) A person shall not receive any health care services from a publicly-funded health care facility, to which he or she is otherwise entitled until the legal status of that person has been verified as one of the following:

(1) A citizen of the United States.

(2) An alien lawfully admitted as a permanent resident.

(3) An alien lawfully admitted for a temporary period of time.

(c) If any publicly-funded health care facility in this state from whom a person seeks health care services, other than emergency medical care as required by federal law, determines or reasonably suspects, based upon the information provided to it, that the person is an alien in the United States in violation of federal law, the following procedures shall be followed by the facility:

(1) The facility shall not provide the person with services.

(2) The facility shall, in writing, notify the person of his or her apparent illegal immigration status, and that the person must either obtain legal status or leave the United States.

(3) The facility shall also notify the State Director of Health Services, the Attorney General of California, and the United States Immigration and Naturalization Service of the apparent illegal status, and shall provide any additional information that may be requested by any other public entity. . . .

SECTION 7. EXCLUSION OF ILLEGAL ALIENS FROM PUBLIC ELEMENTARY AND SECONDARY SCHOOLS.

Section 48215 is added to the Education Code, to read:

48215. (a) No public elementary or secondary school shall admit, or permit the attendance of, any child who is not a citizen of the United States, an alien lawfully admitted as a permanent resident, or a person who is otherwise authorized under federal law to be present in the United States. . . .

SECTION 8. EXCLUSION OF ILLEGAL ALIENS FROM PUBLIC POSTSECONDARY EDUCATIONAL INSTITUTIONS.

Section 66010.8 is added to the Education Code, to read:

66010.8. (a) No public institution of postsecondary education shall admit, enroll, or permit the attendance of any person who is not a citizen of the United States, an alien lawfully admitted as a permanent resident in the United States, or a person who is otherwise authorized under federal law to be present in the United States. . . .

SECTION 9. ATTORNEY GENERAL COOPERATION WITH THE INS.

Section 53069.65 is added to the Government Code, to read:

53069.65. Whenever the state or a city, or a county, or any other legally authorized local governmental entity with jurisdictional boundaries reports the presence of a person who is suspected of being present in the United States in violation of federal immigration laws to the Attorney General of California, that report shall be transmitted to the United States Immigration and Naturalization Service. The Attorney General shall be responsible for maintaining ongoing and accurate records of such reports, and shall provide any additional information that may be requested by any other government entity.

Questions

1. To what extent are these findings and declarations convincing? What, if any, facts are missing?
2. Which provisions seem reasonable, and which seem unfair? Why?

31-7 On Women-Owned Businesses (1996)

U.S. Census Bureau

Women have always made a large contribution to the American economy, but not always in easily measurable ways. During the First and especially the Second World Wars, large numbers of women entered the workforce for the first time. In the second half of the twentieth century, growing numbers of women continued to enter the workforce, in part to maintain family income levels. By the end of the century, the role of women in the U.S. economy, both as employees and as employers, had become a significant, measurable force. In 1996, the U.S. Census Bureau reported that one-third of the nation's businesses were owned by women.

Source: "One-Third of Nation's Businesses Owned by Women, Census Bureau Says," *United States Department of Commerce News,* Economics and Statistics Administration, Census Bureau, Public Information, Press Release, January 29, 1996. http://www.census.gov/Press-Release/cb96–07.html

The number of women-owned businesses in the United States reached 6.4 million in 1992, representing one-third of all domestic firms and 40 percent of all retail and service firms. Businesses owned by women generated $1.6 trillion in business revenues and employed 13.2 million people. About 19 percent of these were businesses with paid employees, averaging 10.6 employees and $1.2 million in receipts per firm. This is according to a report from the Commerce Department's Census Bureau entitled, "1992 Women-Owned Businesses" (WB92-1), that will be published later this year.

Secretary of Commerce Ronald H. Brown said, "These findings confirm that women-owned businesses are substantial and growing contributors to the nation's economy, particularly in terms of job creation."

Nearly 520,000 of the businesses owned by women were "C" corporations which were covered in this survey for the first time in 1992. They include all types of corporations except subchapter S corporations, and tend to be larger business operations. In 1992, women-owned "C" corporations:

- Generated $932 billion in revenues, nearly 60 percent of all women-owned business revenues.
- Included over 426,000 employer firms, about 82 percent of the women-owned "C" corporations, with 7 million employees and payrolls of $154 billion.

Women-owned "C" corporations were active in all major kinds of businesses, ranging from 22 percent each in mining and manufacturing businesses, to 31 percent in retail trade.

Of the more than 2 million "C" corporations in the United States, women owned nearly 26 percent and their businesses contributed nearly 9 percent of all revenues for the year.

In addition to "C" corporations, women owned 5.9 million sole proprietorships, partnerships, and subchapter S corporations in 1992. Subchapter S corporations have no more than 35 shareholders and are not taxed as corporations. In 1992, these women-owned "non-C" businesses:

- Generated nearly $643 billion in revenues, over 40 percent of the total for all women-owned businesses.
- Included some 818,000 employer firms, 14 percent of all women-owned "non-C" businesses, with 6.3 million employees and payrolls of nearly $105 billion.
- Were predominantly retail and service businesses, accounting for over 72 percent of women-owned unincorporated businesses and subchapter S corporations.

Previous surveys have covered women-owned unincorporated businesses and subchapter S corporations, and in the past five years the number of women-owned "non-C" businesses has increased 43 percent (up from 4.1 million in 1987). In addition, between 1987 and 1992:

- Growth rates for women-owned firms were above average in several "nontraditional" business sectors, including construction (up over 50 percent) and wholesale trade (up over 85 percent).
- Receipts for women-owned "non-C" businesses more than doubled, from a total of $278 million in 1987.
- Firms with 100 or more employees increased nearly 130 percent, to more than 6,600 businesses in 1992.

Nationwide, of some 17 million sole proprietorships, partnerships and subchapter S corporations in 1992, more than one-third were women-owned and their businesses generated more than 19 percent of all "non-C" business revenues. In addition, over 40 percent of all U.S. "non-C" retail and service businesses were owned by women and showed strong rates of growth since the prior five-year survey. Between 1987 and 1992:

- The number of U.S. "non-C" businesses grew by 26 percent, while comparable women-owned businesses grew some 43 percent.
- Growth rates for U.S. "non-C" construction and wholesale businesses were about one-fourth those of comparable women-owned businesses.
- Total revenues for all U.S. "non-C" businesses grew by 67 percent, versus nearly twice that rate (131 percent) for women-owned businesses.

The report provides information on the number of women-owned firms, receipts, number of paid employees, and annual payroll. These data are presented by geographic area (the nation, states, and selected metropolitan areas, counties, and cities), industry, size of firm, and legal form of organization with comparative 1992 data for all U.S. firms.

The data in this report were collected as part of the 1992 Economic Census from a large sample of all non-farm businesses filing tax forms as sole proprietors, partnerships, or any type of corporations, and with receipts of $500 or more in 1992.

Since this was a sample survey, the data are subject to sampling variability as well as reporting and coverage errors. All comparisons made using only 1992 data are statistically significant at the 90 percent confidence level. However, comparisons between 1987 and 1992 should be made with extreme caution because changes in tax laws cause inconsistencies between the data and changes in survey methods may contribute to differences.

Question

1. What impact did the growing importance of women in the U.S. economy have on the women's rights movement in the last quarter of the twentieth century?

Question for Further Thought

1. Discuss and relate the impact of globalization, the computer revolution, and the increasing pluralization of American society on the U.S. economy.

CHAPTER THIRTY-TWO

Into the Twenty-First Century

The Advent of George W. Bush

Presidents are often judged by whether their terms are marked by peace abroad and prosperity at home. By these two measures, Bill Clinton's presidency was a success. However, the Clinton years were marked by political bitterness, which carried over into the 2000 presidential election. Al Gore of Tennessee, the Democratic nominee who was also vice president and a leading figure in the Clinton administration, won a majority of the popular vote, but George W. Bush of Texas, the Republican candidate and son of former president George Herbert Walker Bush, was ultimately awarded Florida's contested electoral votes (Document 32-1). This result made George W. Bush the forty-third president of the United States by the narrowest of margins.

Despite lacking a popular mandate, President Bush pushed his compassionate conservative agenda through Congress (Document 32-2). With the Republican Party in control of the House and the Senate (since 1994), Bush expected to win passage of most of his priorities. However, in May of the next year, moderate Republican James M. Jeffords of Vermont left the Republican Party to become an independent, which turned control of the Senate over to the Democrats. The Bush administration's legislative strategy was complicated but not derailed by this unexpected change in political fortunes. As it turned out, the loss of the upper house was temporary. The Republicans would win back the Senate in 2002 in the midterm elections. Moreover, Republicans could look forward to appointing conservative judges to the federal courts, over limited Democratic opposition, and thus moving the judiciary to the right as well.

The conservative trend in American politics, which had started in 1968, was largely realized in the early years of the twenty-first century, with the Republican Party's control of the executive, the legislative, and increasingly, the judicial branches of the federal government.

Yet, this remarkable monopoly on power was broken with the 2006 congressional elections. The Democratic Party made strong gains at both the state and federal levels, taking control of both houses of Congress. An unpopular war in Iraq, mounting national debt (President Bush refused to pay for the war on terrorism by raising taxes or cutting spending elsewhere in the budget), the inept response of the federal government to Hurricane Katrina, the politicization of medical and scientific research, and low approval ratings were some of the major issues that worked against George W. Bush as he prepared to govern in the final two years of his presidency.

32-1 *Bush v. Gore* (2000)

In the 2000 presidential election, George W. Bush, the Republican candidate, received fewer popular votes than his Democratic challenger, Al Gore. The returns in Florida, however, were initially too close to call. On November 26, Florida officials finally declared Bush the winner, by a razor-thin margin, of the state's popular vote, giving him the necessary electoral votes to carry the election. The Florida Supreme Court revived Gore's hopes for victory, however, when it mandated a recount of thousands of disputed ballots. Bush's lawyers contested this decision in the U.S. Supreme Court, arguing that a recount would cause their client "irreparable harm." On December 9, the U.S. Supreme Court stayed the recount, as the excerpt below shows. But in a subsequent ruling on December 13, five weeks after the election, the Court ruled in favor of Bush in a bitter 5–4 split decision and thus broke what was, in effect, a tie election (see text pp. 990–991).

Source: George W. Bush, et al., Petitioners v. Albert Gore Jr. et al., 00–949 U.S. 531 (2000).

GEORGE W. BUSH ET AL., PETITIONERS V. ALBERT GORE JR. ET AL.

ON APPLICATION FOR STAY

December 9, 2000

The application for stay presented to Justice Kennedy and by him referred to the Court is granted, and it is ordered that the mandate of the Florida Supreme Court, case No. SC00–2431, is hereby stayed pending further order of the Court. In addition, the application for stay is treated as a petition for a writ of certiorari, and the petition for a writ of certiorari is granted. [. . .] The case is set for oral argument on Monday, December 11, 2000 at 11 A.M., and a total of 1½ hours is allotted for oral argument.

JUSTICE SCALIA, CONCURRING

Though it is not customary for the Court to issue an opinion in connection with its grant of a stay, I believe a brief response is necessary to Justice Stevens' dissent. I will not address the merits of the case, since they will shortly be before us in the petition for certiorari that we have granted. It suffices to say that the issuance of the stay suggests that a majority of the Court, while not deciding the issues presented, believe that the petitioner has a substantial probability of success.

On the question of irreparable harm, however, a few words are appropriate. The issue is not, as the dissent puts it, whether "[c]ounting every legally cast vote ca[n] constitute irreparable harm." One of the principal issues in the appeal we have accepted is precisely whether that votes that have been ordered to be counted are, under a reasonable interpretation of Florida law, "legally cast vote[s]." The counting of votes that are of questionable legality does in my view threaten irreparable harm to petitioner, and to the country, by casting a cloud upon what he claims to be the legitimacy of his election. Count first, and rule upon legality afterwards, is not a recipe for producing election results that have the public acceptance democratic stability requires. Another issue in the case, moreover, is the propriety, indeed the constitutionality of letting the standard for determination of voters' intent — dimpled chads, hanging chads, etc. — vary from county to county, as the Florida Supreme Court opinion, as interpreted by the Circuit Court, permits. If petitioner is correct that counting in this fashion is unlawful, permitting the count to proceed on that erroneous basis will prevent an accurate record from being conducted on a proper basis later, since it is generally agreed that each manual recount produces a degradation of the ballots, which renders a subsequent count inaccurate.

For these reasons, I have joined the Court's issuance of stay, with a highly accelerated timetable for resolving this case on the merits.

JUSTICE STEVENS, WITH WHOM JUSTICE SOUTER, JUSTICE GINSBURG, AND JUSTICE BREYER JOIN, DISSENTING

To stop the counting of legal votes, the majority today departs from three venerable rules of judicial restraint that have guided the Court throughout its history. On questions of state law, we have consistently respected the opinions of the highest-courts of the States. On questions whose resolution is committed at least in large measure to another branch of the Federal Government, we have construed our own jurisdiction narrowly and exercised it cautiously. On federal constitutional questions that were not fairly presented to the court whose judgment is being reviewed, we have prudently declined to express an opinion. The majority has acted unwisely.

Time does not permit a full discussion of the merits. It is clear, however, that a stay should not be granted unless an applicant makes a substantial showing of a likelihood of irreparable harm. In this case, applicants have failed to carry that heavy burden. Counting every legally cast vote cannot constitute irreparable harm. On the other hand, there is a danger that a stay may cause irreparable harm to the respondents—and, more importantly, the public at large—because of the risk that "the entry of the stay would be tantamount to a decision on the merits in favor of the applicants." *National Socialist Party of America v. Skokie*, 434 U.S. 1327, 1328 (1977) (Stevens, J., in chambers). Preventing the recount from being completed will inevitably cast a cloud on the legitimacy of the election.

It is certainly not clear that the Florida decision violated federal law. The Florida Code provides elaborate procedures for ensuring that every eligible voter has a full and fair opportunity to case a ballot and that every ballot so cast is counted. See, e.g., Fla. Stat. §§ 101.5614(5), 102.166 (2000). In its opinion, the Florida Supreme Court gave weight to that legislative command. Its ruling was consistent with earlier Florida cases that have repeatedly described the interest in correctly ascertaining the will of the voters as paramount. See *State ex rel Chappell v. Martinez*, 563 So. 2d 1007 (1998); *Boardman v. Estreva*, 323 So. 2d 259 (1976); *McAlpin v. State ex rel. Avriett*, 19 So. 2d 420 (1944); *State ex rel. Peacock v. Latham*, 169 So. 597, 598; *State ex rel. Carpenter v. Barber*, 198 So. 49 (1940). Its ruling also appears to be consistent with the prevailing view in other states. See, e.g., *Pullen v. Milligan*, 561 N.E. 2d 585, 611 (Ill. 1990). As a more fundamental matter, the Florida court's ruling reflects the basic principle, inherent in our Constitution and our democracy, that every legal vote should be counted. See *Reynolds v. Sims*, 377 U.S. 533, 544–555 (1964); cf. *Hardke v. Roudebush*, 321 F. Supp. 1370, 1378–1379 (S.D. Ind. 1970) (Stevens, J., dissenting); accord *Roudebush v. Hartke*, 405 U.S. 15 (1972).

Accordingly, I respectfully dissent.

Questions

1. In Scalia's opinion, what is the argument for granting a stay?
2. What argument did Stevens make in his dissent to the stay?

32-2 What Compassionate Conservatism Is—and Is Not (2000)

Stephen Goldsmith

Stephen Goldsmith, former mayor of Indianapolis, Indiana, served as chief domestic policy advisor to the George W. Bush campaign. After the 2000 election, Goldsmith was named as George Bush's advisor on faith-based initiatives, in which public money was to be made available through federal grants to private churches and religious groups with the objective of furthering their proven work in social service.

Source: Adapted from a speech given at the Hoover Institution, April 30, 2000. Special to the *Hoover Digest*. Reprinted by permission.

This political year features the "compassionate conservatism" espoused by Republican presidential candidate George W. Bush. Some question whether it is a political slogan or a philosophy. I would submit that it is a coherent, principled philosophy that organizes and explains a superior approach to domestic policy. As a political philosophy, compassionate conservatism serves as a true bridge from the era of big government as a way to solve social problems to a new era in which we will have a full and healthy trust in the people of this nation to govern themselves.

Fundamentally, compassionate conservatism is a form of political conservatism. In other words, compassionate conservatives believe that government should have a limited role in people's lives and that competition in the marketplace is the most effective means of producing social and economic progress. Consequently, compassionate conservatives believe in low taxes, limited government regulation, and the vast power of the free enterprise system.

Like traditional conservatism, compassionate conservatism assumes that the marketplace is the best way to deliver value. But compassionate conservatives also recognize that the prosperity created by the marketplace has left many Americans behind and that government has a responsibility to reach out to those who are at the bottom rungs of the economic ladder. According to the principles of compassionate conservatism, government has a responsibility, not to redistribute the wealth of citizens but to provide the underprivileged with skills and opportunities to create their own wealth.

Indeed, compassionate conservatives believe that prosperity must have a moral purpose, that its economic fruits must be available to as many citizens as possible. To accomplish their goals, however, compassionate conservatives do not believe in a paternalistic form of governance in which decisions that affect all people—no matter what their personal beliefs, values, and outlooks—are made at the top by professional bureaucrats. Compassionate conservatives do not believe in big government programs that simply throw money at people, that discourage personal choice and responsibility, or that result in keeping people forever out of the mainstream of American life.

Consequently, compassionate conservatives believe that the best way to help people is to provide them with opportunities to maximize their own capabilities to gain a real stake in the continuing economic and social health of the nation.

Let's look then at three tenets of compassionate conservatism: first, that it is optimistic and confident about how all individuals can do better; second, its belief that the best way to help people is through the marketplace; and third, that prosperity must have a purpose—that is, that more than just the marketplace is necessary for America to be a successful country.

EMPOWERMENT, NOT ENTITLEMENT

Through its hopeful, optimistic belief in people's ability to overcome adversity, compassionate conservatism offers a stark contrast to the fundamentally pessimistic view of the liberal establishment that people can never really overcome their problems. For the most part, Democratic liberalism, instead of creating opportunities for people to enter the mainstream, has sought to "buy out" the less fortunate by creating a system of government that actually *disempowers* those most in need by giving them less control over their own lives. And by promoting the redistribution of income rather than the creation of new wealth and new opportunities for investment, liberals have consigned people in need to the sidelines, where they remain dependent for their survival on the largesse of the state and the distant decisions of bureaucrats.

Compassionate conservatism, on the other hand, believes in giving people the tools to help them overcome their adversity and join the economic mainstream. It does that through a combination of tax cuts—a policy that rests on the assumption that if people have more control over their own wealth, they will invest it in what they and their families need—and the creation of incentives to encourage such investment.

If we truly want a higher percentage of Americans to own part of this country and the hope that goes with it, compassionate conservatives say, then we should be encouraging the creation of wealth. For most people, wealth can most often be created in two key areas—retirement accounts and home ownership. In both those areas, the principles of compassionate conservatism lead to specific policy choices that show respect for both the marketplace and individuals.

The current debate over Social Security is a litmus test for compassionate conservatism. The suggestion that individuals should be allowed to invest a portion of their payroll taxes in equities is not only an issue that concerns the solvency of the Social Security fund but a fundamental matter of how we look at America and its people. Compassionate conservatives believe that by giving citizens the opportunity to own and control equities through their Social Security accounts, we can encourage people to invest in the country and to build wealth for the future—to bring into the mainstream people who may not otherwise have that opportunity. To pass up that opportunity for inclusion—or to add another bureaucratic government program to create such accounts, as some have proposed—is simply bad policy.

The same is true in the area of housing. Instead of giving people without much money the means to build personal wealth through home ownership, the Department of Housing and Urban Development has too often over the past three decades poured more money onto the problem, giving people a roof over their heads but no real stake in the future.

Compassionate conservatives recognize that those without economic means need assistance, but they believe that the way to do that is to create the conditions that allow more individuals to become homeowners. Rather than providing public housing, government can offer low-cost home loans or help people with down payments or even encourage the creation of independent development accounts so that citizens who don't have a lot of money receive tax incentives to encourage them to save and invest.

The Power of the Marketplace

Compassionate conservatism acknowledges the need to help those that prosperity has left behind but insists that the best way to deliver the help is by giving poor individuals the means to secure their help through the marketplace. Along with providing citizens the opportunity to build wealth comes the obligation for government to provide people with a wide variety of choices as to how they can best put government assistance to use. Big-government, one-size-fits-all solutions demean struggling individuals by treating them merely as members of aggrieved identity groups, passively awaiting government subsidies and restitution for crippling wounds inflicted by what is perceived to be an inherently unjust society.

Compassionate conservatism rejects the Washington-centric view that the way to help people is through the same rigid, bureaucratic programs or narrowly targeted tax incentives that, in the past, permitted very little true self-governance. That brand of liberalism, for all its talk of empathy and compassion, imposes its own values and decides what options will work best for individuals and their families.

According to compassionate conservatives, competition in the marketplace is the surest way to produce value. When governments gain a monopoly in a way that renders performance irrelevant in the provision of services, the results invariably tend to be bureaucratic, wasteful, and inefficient.

This can be seen most clearly in the public education system. Having been accorded monopoly status over the years, the public school system in this nation is deeply troubled, with many students not learning even basic reading and math skills by the time they graduate from high school. Although many factors contribute to this troubling state of affairs, one key truth remains: there is inadequate information about performance and insufficient parental choice—and, thus, inadequate impetus for improved quality.

In this country, a debate has been raging concerning the role of the federal government in education. Compassionate conservatives would argue that there *is* a role, which is primarily to make sure that students who are poor or disabled receive the resources they need but in a way that demands accountability and performance. Over the past 35 years, billions of dollars have been poured into Title I, which was created specifically to help poor children. Yet in that time, not a single Title I dollar has gone to a poor child or to that child's parents. Instead, it has all gone to various state and local bureaucracies to continue a system that clearly isn't working.

Although compassionate conservatives believe in the need to continue to provide funds for children who qualify under the Title I program, they reject the notion that such funds must continue to be wasted in the ineffective and bureaucratic public school system.

The first step, then, is to bring accountability to school districts through rigorous testing in both math and reading of every child in grades 3 through 8. The testing should be done at the state and local levels to ensure local control, and the scores should be posted on the Internet—by classroom and school—for every parent to see. If schools don't show measurable increases in performance for Title I children, then the parents should have control over those dollars and be allowed to make the decisions about the education of their children. In other words, such funds could be used to put poor parents on equal footing with more affluent parents in having a choice of where to send their children to school.

The same is true in the area of health care. Nobody disputes the fact that there are millions of uninsured individuals today in this country who need health care, and compassionate conservatives agree that government has a responsibility to provide funds to such individuals. But rather than create a new national health care system, compassionate conservatives believe that the best way to discharge that responsibility is to provide refundable tax credits that individuals can use to purchase policies in the insurance market. In that way both the marketplace and the individual are given the respect they are due, and customer competition is used to create innovations and efficiencies in the provision of services.

The same argument applies to Medicare and prescription drugs. Currently, Medicare provides few choices to seniors. It is a program with 130,000 pages of regulations that assumes that government has a right to—indeed, that it must—tell seniors what services they are allowed to receive and when. A better way to truly help seniors with pharmaceuticals, compassionate conservatives believe, would be to subsidize those who are in need, reform Medicare, and give individuals choices of a variety of insurance options.

PROSPERITY WITH A PURPOSE

Compassionate conservatism recognizes that we're not going to become a virtuous and robust community of neighborhoods in this country just by relying on the forces of the marketplace. Instead, prosperity needs to have a purpose as well.

Compassionate conservatives are keenly aware that individuals thrive when they are rooted in a strong value system that is imparted through the family, church, or some other institution of civil society. Indeed, compassionate conservatives believe that the great needs of this country are cultural and spiritual. They believe that our nation's great weaknesses—crime, drug abuse, out-of-wedlock births—arise out of weaknesses in our culture. That culture must be rebuilt, not from the top down but from the bottom up. To compassionate conservatives, families matter, religion matters, and the self-respect gained from the ability to control one's own life matters. And compassion involves recognizing that such values lie at the heart of what it means to be human.

Consequently, compassionate conservatives support the use of neighborhood and faith-based groups to provide essential services and to bring value to those individuals who need assistance, whether it be in finding a job, treating an addiction, dealing with mental health problems, or otherwise trying to get their lives in order. Unfortunately, the big-government systems of the Great Society supplanted the local, faith-based groups that often were highly effective in transforming individuals' lives, and America's value generating civic institutions were derided as oppressive, parochial backwaters of bigotry and ignorance.

Compassionate conservatives want to correct that misconception. Although they acknowledge the role of government in helping those who need assistance, they do not believe that government *itself* needs to deliver those services. Small, local civic associations and religious organizations have the detailed knowledge and flexibility necessary to administer the proper combination of loving compassion and rigorous discipline appropriate for each citizen.

To be sure, compassionate conservatives recognize the need to observe the strict separation of church and state, and no public money should be devoted to advancing any particular religion. But to deny that the American people hold religious beliefs, or that faith-based organizations can truly make a difference in people's lives, is foolish. If the Salvation Army or Catholic Relief Services or Jewish Social Services or

Muslim antidrug drives can provide social services to people in need, and dollars are available, then those organizations should be allowed to bid on the right to provide those services. Even better, government can, through the tax code, encourage charitable giving, which altogether removes the problems associated with government participation.

Such a system would allow people to receive the assistance they need in a voluntary way, meaning that no one would be forced through the front door of a faith-based organization. Secular options would also be available for those who prefer them. But including faith-based groups in a cooperative effort to find solutions to society's problems would allow those organizations to do what they've been proven to be good at: transforming individuals by teaching them the skills and providing them with the confidence and self-respect they need to succeed in the world at large.

Compassionate conservatives believe that most people, most of the time, have the capacity to run their own lives and affairs for themselves (i.e., to be self-governing citizens, not passive clients of government or helpless victims of external social forces). Their compassion is defined by their belief that, where citizens presently lack the means or the capacity for self-governance, they must indeed be helped. Insofar as possible, that means allowing citizens to select for themselves how they wish to be helped, to demonstrate faith that people can indeed run their own affairs.

Compassionate conservatism, then, refocuses government to respect both individuals and the market, providing opportunities that allow individuals to achieve their highest potential, which in and of itself is compassionate. In the words of Governor Bush:

> It is conservative to cut taxes, and compassionate to give people more money to spend. It is conservative to insist upon local control of schools and high standards and results; it is compassionate to make sure every child learns to read and no one is left behind. It is conservative to reform the welfare system by insisting on work; it's compassionate to free people from dependency on government. It is conservative to reform the juvenile justice code to insist on consequences for bad behavior; it is compassionate to recognize that discipline and love go hand in hand.

Compassionate conservatives strongly believe that if we respect both individuals and the marketplace, we can achieve great things. Only by fully empowering people to select freely among various options do we treat Americans as proud, dignified, self-governing citizens, able to make disciplined and responsible decisions about their own lives and those of their families and children. If we give individuals the education and other tools they need for success, allow them to control their own dollars, and help them enter the mainstream of American life through facilitating the ownership of stocks and homes, then we will succeed in producing a country that is even more prosperous, more civilized, and more prepared for the future.

Questions

1. What, according to Goldsmith, is conservatism? And how does "compassionate conservatism" differ from it?
2. In politics, what someone is for is often the flip side of what one is against. With this in mind, what, by implication and according to Goldsmith, is liberalism?

Questions for Further Thought

1. Explain, in general, how, under the U.S. Constitution, a president may lose the popular vote but still win the election. How, in particular, did events in Florida complicate the 2000 presidential election?
2. Compare and contrast the goals of the Reagan Revolution (see text in Chapter 30), with George Bush's "compassionate conservative" agenda (Document 32-2).

American Hegemony Challenged

On the morning of September 11, 2001, members of Al Qaeda commandeered four commercial airliners, three of which were flown into their intended targets—the Pentagon and World Trade Center (the two towers of the World Trade Center were also attacked in February 1993). The passengers of the fourth plane heroically prevented the terrorists from carrying out their mission, but were killed in doing so. As early as 1996, Osama bin Laden, the Al Qaeda leader, had declared war on the United States. In response to the 9/11 attacks, the following month the United States took the war directly to the Taliban government and Al Qaeda's bases in Afghanistan, an invasion on which there was bipartisan agreement and for which there was strong popular support. Moreover, the Bush administration's invasion had the strong backing of much of the world community, which saw the 9/11 attacks not aimed specifically at the United States but at civilization itself.

If the U.S. invasion of Afghanistan was marked by consensus at home and abroad, George Bush's decision to invade Iraq on March 20, 2003, and the subsequent occupation of the country, proved to be very divisive. This war was strikingly different from the war against Al Qaeda. Iraqi leader Saddam Hussein had not attacked the United States or, for that matter, any of his neighbors, since his army was forced to withdraw from Kuwait. In fact, because the government of Iraq was secular, it had been at odds with the religious extremists of the Islamic world, including Al Qaeda. The evidence that Iraq possessed or was stockpiling weapons of mass destruction (WMDs) was qualified but the Bush administration's case to the U.S. public and the world for going to war with Iraq was not (see Document 32-3). Moreover, the Bush administration asserted it had the right to wage a preemptive war against any country it deemed a threat or even a potential threat (Document 32-4), a radical position that generated controversy at home and concern abroad about U.S. intentions. In the meantime, Osama bin Laden remained at large and large-scale terrorist attacks continued to occur, such as the train bombings in Madrid (2004) and the transportation-related bombings in London (2005). The Bush administration's war in Iraq was not the only action that put the U.S. government at odds with the rest of the world community. The decision to abrogate the ABM Treaty with Russia, the refusal to sign the Kyoto Accords or cooperate on reducing gases that caused global warming, or to sign the treaty creating the International Criminal Court were other cases in point. The result was that as the new century progressed the United States found that its once high standing in the world as a leader and positive force in the international community had been significantly lowered.

32-3 Bush on Iraq (2002)

On October 7, 2002, President Bush addressed an audience at the Cincinnati Museum Center–Cincinnati Union Terminal in Cincinnati, Ohio. In this speech, he argued that Saddam Hussein's weapons of mass destruction (WMDs) posed a threat to U.S. security and that the time for diplomacy and pressure was almost at an end. After the U.S. invasion and occupation of Iraq, and an extensive search, U.S. officials concluded, however, that there were no WMD stockpiles in the country and that Saddam Hussein, therefore, had been much less of a threat than had originally been believed. By then, the United States was deeply committed to bringing democracy to Iraq, rebuilding Iraq's economy, and trying to maintain order there while preventing civil war between the country's different ethnic and religious groups.

Source: "President Bush Outlines Iraqi Threat," remarks made by the president on Iraq, from the White House Office of the Press Secretary, October 7, 2002. http://www.whitehouse.gov/news/releases/2002/10/20021007-8.html

The President. Thank you all. Thank you for that very gracious and warm Cincinnati welcome. I'm honored to be here tonight; I appreciate you all coming.

Tonight I want to take a few minutes to discuss a grave threat to peace, and America's determination to lead the world in confronting that threat.

The threat comes from Iraq. It arises directly from the Iraqi regime's own actions—its history of aggression, and its drive toward an arsenal of terror. Eleven years ago, as a condition for ending the Persian Gulf War, the Iraqi regime was required to destroy its weapons of mass destruction, to cease all development of such weapons, and to stop all support for terrorist groups. The Iraqi regime has violated all of those obligations. It possesses and produces chemical and biological weapons. It is seeking nuclear weapons. It has given shelter and support to terrorism, and practices terror against its own people. The entire world has witnessed Iraq's eleven-year history of defiance, deception and bad faith.

We also must never forget the most vivid events of recent history. On September the 11th, 2001, America felt its vulnerability—even to threats that gather on the other side of the earth. We resolved then, and we are resolved today, to confront every threat, from any source, that could bring sudden terror and suffering to America.

Members of the Congress of both political parties, and members of the United Nations Security Council, agree that Saddam Hussein is a threat to peace and must disarm. We agree that the Iraqi dictator must not be permitted to threaten America and the world with horrible poisons and diseases and gases and atomic weapons. Since we all agree on this goal, the issue is: how can we best achieve it?

Many Americans have raised legitimate questions: about the nature of the threat; about the urgency of action—why be concerned now; about the link between Iraq developing weapons of terror, and the wider war on terror. These are all issues we've discussed broadly and fully within my administration. And tonight, I want to share those discussions with you.

First, some ask why Iraq is different from other countries or regimes that also have terrible weapons. While there are many dangers in the world, the threat from Iraq stands alone—because it gathers the most serious dangers of our age in one place. Iraq's weapons of mass destruction are controlled by a murderous tyrant who has already used chemical weapons to kill thousands of people. This same tyrant has tried to dominate the Middle East, has invaded and brutally occupied a small neighbor, has struck other nations without warning, and holds an unrelenting hostility toward the United States.

By its past and present actions, by its technological capabilities, by the merciless nature of its regime, Iraq is unique. As a former chief weapons inspector of the U.N. has said, "The fundamental problem with Iraq remains the nature of the regime, itself. Saddam Hussein is a homicidal dictator who is addicted to weapons of mass destruction."

Some ask how urgent this danger is to America and the world. The danger is already significant, and it only grows worse with time. If we know Saddam Hussein has dangerous weapons today—and we do—does it make any sense for the world to wait to confront him as he grows even stronger and develops even more dangerous weapons?

In 1995, after several years of deceit by the Iraqi regime, the head of Iraq's military industries defected. It was then that the regime was forced to admit that it had produced more than 30,000 liters of anthrax and other deadly biological agents. The inspectors, however, concluded that Iraq had likely produced two to four times that amount. This is a massive stockpile of biological weapons that has never been accounted for, and capable of killing millions.

We know that the regime has produced thousands of tons of chemical agents, including mustard gas, sarin nerve gas, VX nerve gas. Saddam Hussein also has experience in using chemical weapons. He has ordered chemical attacks on Iran, and on more than forty villages in his own country. These actions killed or injured at least 20,000 people, more than six times the number of people who died in the attacks of September the 11th.

And surveillance photos reveal that the regime is rebuilding facilities that it had used to produce chemical and biological weapons. Every chemical and biological weapon that Iraq has or makes is a direct violation of the truce that ended the Persian Gulf War in 1991. Yet, Saddam Hussein has chosen to build and keep these weapons despite international sanctions, U.N. demands, and isolation from the civilized world.

Iraq possesses ballistic missiles with a likely range of hundreds of miles—far enough to strike Saudi Arabia, Israel, Turkey, and other nations—in a region where more than 135,000 American civilians and service members live and work. We've also discovered through intelligence that Iraq has a growing fleet of manned and unmanned aerial vehicles that could be used to disperse chemical or biological weapons across broad areas. We're concerned that Iraq is exploring ways of using these UAVS for missions targeting the United States. And, of course, sophisticated delivery systems aren't required for a chemical or biological attack; all that might be required are a small container and one terrorist or Iraqi intelligence operative to deliver it.

And that is the source of our urgent concern about Saddam Hussein's links to international terrorist groups. Over the years, Iraq has provided safe haven to terrorists such as Abu Nidal, whose terror organization carried out more than 90 terrorist attacks in 20 countries that killed or injured nearly 900 people, including 12 Americans. Iraq has also provided safe haven to Abu Abbas, who was responsible for seizing the *Achille Lauro* and killing an American passenger. And we know that Iraq is continuing to finance terror and gives assistance to groups that use terrorism to undermine Middle East peace.

We know that Iraq and the al Qaeda terrorist network share a common enemy—the United States of America. We know that Iraq and al Qaeda have had high-level contacts that go back a decade. Some al Qaeda leaders who fled Afghanistan went to Iraq. These include one very senior al Qaeda leader who received medical treatment in Baghdad this year, and who has been associated with planning for chemical and biological attacks. We've learned that Iraq has trained al Qaeda members in bomb-making and poisons and deadly gases. And we know that after September the 11th, Saddam Hussein's regime gleefully celebrated the terrorist attacks on America.

Iraq could decide on any given day to provide a biological or chemical weapon to a terrorist group or individual terrorists. Alliance with terrorists could allow the Iraqi regime to attack America without leaving any fingerprints.

Some have argued that confronting the threat from Iraq could detract from the war against terror. To the contrary; confronting the threat posed by Iraq is crucial to winning the war on terror. When I spoke to Congress more than a year ago, I said that those who harbor terrorists are as guilty as the terrorists themselves. Saddam Hussein is harboring terrorists and the instruments of terror, the instruments of mass death and destruction. And he cannot be trusted. The risk is simply too great that he will use them, or provide them to a terror network.

Terror cells and outlaw regimes building weapons of mass destruction are different faces of the same evil. Our security requires that we confront both. And the United States military is capable of confronting both.

Many people have asked how close Saddam Hussein is to developing a nuclear weapon. Well, we don't know exactly, and that's the problem. Before the Gulf War, the best intelligence indicated that Iraq was eight to ten years away from developing a nuclear weapon. After the war, international inspectors learned that the regime has been much closer—the regime in Iraq would likely have possessed a nuclear weapon no later than 1993. The inspectors discovered that Iraq had an advanced nuclear weapons development program, had a design for a workable nuclear weapon, and was pursuing several different methods of enriching uranium for a bomb.

Before being barred from Iraq in 1998, the International Atomic Energy Agency dismantled extensive nuclear weapons-related facilities, including three uranium enrichment sites. That same year, information from a high-ranking Iraqi nuclear engineer who had defected revealed that despite his public promises, Saddam Hussein had ordered his nuclear program to continue.

The evidence indicates that Iraq is reconstituting its nuclear weapons program. Saddam Hussein has held numerous meetings with Iraqi nuclear scientists, a group he calls his "nuclear mujahideen"—his nuclear holy warriors. Satellite photographs reveal that Iraq is rebuilding facilities at sites that have been part of its nuclear program in the past. Iraq has attempted to purchase high-strength aluminum tubes and other equipment needed for gas centrifuges, which are used to enrich uranium for nuclear weapons.

If the Iraqi regime is able to produce, buy, or steal an amount of highly enriched uranium a little larger than a single softball, it could have a nuclear weapon in less than a year. And if we allow that to happen, a terrible line would be crossed. Saddam Hussein would be in a position to blackmail anyone who opposes his aggression. He would be in a position to dominate the Middle East. He would be in a position to threaten America. And Saddam Hussein would be in a position to pass nuclear technology to terrorists.

Some citizens wonder, after 11 years of living with this problem, why do we need to confront it now? And there's a reason. We've experienced the horror of September the 11th. We have seen that those who hate America are willing to crash airplanes into buildings full of innocent people. Our enemies would be no less willing, in fact, they would be eager, to use biological or chemical, or a nuclear weapon.

Knowing these realities, America must not ignore the threat gathering against us. Facing clear evidence of peril, we cannot wait for the final proof—the smoking gun—that could come in the form of a mushroom cloud. As President Kennedy said in October of 1962, "Neither the United States of America, nor the world community of nations can tolerate deliberate deception and offensive threats on the part of any nation, large or small. We no longer live in a world," he said, "where only the actual firing of weapons represents a sufficient challenge to a nation's security to constitute maximum peril."

Understanding the threats of our time, knowing the designs and deceptions of the Iraqi regime, we have every reason to assume the worst, and we have an urgent duty to prevent the worst from occurring.

Some believe we can address this danger by simply resuming the old approach to inspections, and applying diplomatic and economic pressure. Yet this is precisely what the world has tried to do since 1991. The U.N. inspections program was met with systematic deception. The Iraqi regime bugged hotel rooms and offices of inspectors to find where they were going next; they forged documents, destroyed evidence, and developed mobile weapons facilities to keep a step ahead of inspectors. Eight so-called presidential palaces were declared off-limits to unfettered inspections. These sites actually encompass twelve square miles, with hundreds of structures, both above and below the ground, where sensitive materials could be hidden.

The world has also tried economic sanctions—and watched Iraq use billions of dollars in illegal oil revenues to fund more weapons purchases, rather than providing for the needs of the Iraqi people.

The world has tried limited military strikes to destroy Iraq's weapons of mass destruction capabilities—only to see them openly rebuilt, while the regime again denies they even exist.

The world has tried no-fly zones to keep Saddam from terrorizing his own people—and in the last year alone, the Iraqi military has fired upon American and British pilots more than 750 times.

After eleven years during which we have tried containment, sanctions, inspections, even selected military action, the end result is that Saddam Hussein still has chemical and biological weapons and is increasing his capabilities to make more. And he is moving ever closer to developing a nuclear weapon.

Clearly, to actually work, any new inspections, sanctions or enforcement mechanisms will have to be very different. America wants the U.N. to be an effective organization that helps keep the peace. And that is why we are urging the Security Council to adopt a new resolution setting out tough, immediate requirements. Among those requirements: the Iraqi regime must reveal and destroy, under U.N. supervision, all existing weapons of mass destruction. To ensure that we learn the truth, the regime must allow witnesses to its illegal activities to be interviewed outside the country—and these witnesses must be free to bring their families with them so they are all beyond the reach of Saddam Hussein's terror and murder. And inspectors must have access to any site, at any time, without pre-clearance, without delay, without exceptions.

The time for denying, deceiving, and delaying has come to an end. Saddam Hussein must disarm himself—or, for the sake of peace, we will lead a coalition to disarm him.

Many nations are joining us in insisting that Saddam Hussein's regime be held accountable. They are committed to defending the international security that protects the lives of both our citizens and theirs. And that's why America is challenging all nations to take the resolutions of the U.N. Security Council seriously.

And these resolutions are clear. In addition to declaring and destroying all of its weapons of mass destruction, Iraq must end its support for terrorism. It must cease the persecution of its civilian population. It must stop all illicit trade outside the Oil for Food program. It must release or account for all Gulf War personnel, including an American pilot, whose fate is still unknown.

By taking these steps, and by only taking these steps, the Iraqi regime has an opportunity to avoid conflict. Taking these steps would also change the nature of the Iraqi regime itself. America hopes the regime will make that choice. Unfortunately, at least so far, we have little reason to expect it. And that's why two administrations—mine and President Clinton's—have stated that regime change in Iraq is the only certain means of removing a great danger to our nation.

I hope this will not require military action, but it may. And military conflict could be difficult. An Iraqi regime faced with its own demise may attempt cruel and desperate measures. If Saddam Hussein orders such measures, his generals would be well advised to refuse those orders. If they do not refuse, they must understand that all war criminals will be pursued and punished. If we have to act, we will take every precaution that is possible. We will plan carefully; we will act with the full power of the United States military; we will act with allies at our side, and we will prevail. (Applause.)

There is no easy or risk-free course of action. Some have argued we should wait—and that's an option. In my view, it's the riskiest of all options, because the longer we wait, the stronger and bolder Saddam Hussein will become. We could wait and hope that Saddam does not give weapons to terrorists, or develop a nuclear weapon to blackmail the world. But I'm convinced that is a hope against all evidence. As Americans, we want peace—we work and sacrifice for peace. But there can be no peace if our security depends on the will and whims of a ruthless and aggressive dictator. I'm not willing to stake one American life on trusting Saddam Hussein.

Failure to act would embolden other tyrants, allow terrorists access to new weapons and new resources, and make blackmail a permanent feature of world events. The United Nations would betray the purpose of its founding, and prove irrelevant to the problems of our time. And through its inaction, the United States would resign itself to a future of fear.

That is not the America I know. That is not the America I serve. We refuse to live in fear. (Applause.) This nation, in world war and in Cold War, has never permitted the brutal and lawless to set history's course. Now, as before, we will secure our nation, protect our freedom, and help others to find freedom of their own.

Some worry that a change of leadership in Iraq could create instability and make the situation worse. The situation could hardly get worse, for world security and for the people of Iraq. The lives of Iraqi citizens would improve dramatically if Saddam Hussein were no longer in power, just as the lives of Afghanistan's citizens improved after the Taliban. The dictator of Iraq is a student of Stalin, using murder as a tool of terror and control, within his own cabinet, within his own army, and even within his own family.

On Saddam Hussein's orders, opponents have been decapitated, wives and mothers of political opponents have been systematically raped as a method of intimidation, and political prisoners have been forced to watch their own children being tortured.

America believes that all people are entitled to hope and human rights, to the non-negotiable demands of human dignity. People everywhere prefer freedom to slavery; prosperity to squalor; self-government to the rule of terror and torture. America is a friend to the people of Iraq. Our demands are directed only at the regime that enslaves them and threatens us. When these demands are met, the first and greatest benefit will come to Iraqi men, women and children. The oppression of Kurds, Assyrians, Turkomans, Shi'a, Sunnis and others will be lifted. The long captivity of Iraq will end, and an era of new hope will begin.

Iraq is a land rich in culture, resources, and talent. Freed from the weight of oppression, Iraq's people will be able to share in the progress and prosperity of our time. If military action is necessary, the United States and our allies will help the Iraqi people rebuild their economy, and create the institutions of liberty in a unified Iraq at peace with its neighbors.

Later this week, the United States Congress will vote on this matter. I have asked Congress to authorize the use of America's military, if it proves necessary, to enforce U.N. Security Council demands. Approving this resolution does not mean that military action is imminent or unavoidable. The resolution will tell the United Nations, and all nations, that America speaks with one voice and is determined to make the demands of the civilized world mean something. Congress will also be sending a message to the dictator in Iraq: that his only chance—his only choice is full compliance, and the time remaining for that choice is limited.

Members of Congress are nearing an historic vote. I'm confident they will fully consider the facts, and their duties.

The attacks of September the 11th showed our country that vast oceans no longer protect us from danger. Before that tragic date, we had only hints of al Qaeda's plans and designs. Today in Iraq, we see a threat whose outlines are far more clearly defined, and whose consequences could be far more deadly. Saddam Hussein's actions have put us on notice, and there is no refuge from our responsibilities.

We did not ask for this present challenge, but we accept it. Like other generations of Americans, we will meet the responsibility of defending human liberty against violence and aggression. By our resolve, we will give strength to others. By our courage, we will give hope to others. And by our actions, we will secure the peace, and lead the world to a better day.

May God bless America. (Applause.)

Questions

1. What are the threats from Iraq that President Bush identified?
2. What are the connections President Bush made between Al Qaeda and the regime of Saddam Hussein?

32-4 U.S. National Security Strategy (2002)

The National Security Strategy of the United States was a report published by the White House in September 2002, one year after the terrorist events in New York, Washington, D.C., and Pennsylvania. The language of the report was as striking as it was sweeping. George W. Bush boldly declared that there was only one "sustainable model for national success: freedom, democracy, and free enterprise" and that America would preempt or "act against . . . emerging threats before they are fully formed." This official policy of preemption was controversial; some celebrated it as taking a tough stance against terrorism, while others thought it was a thinly veiled justification for unilateral aggression, which could alienate American allies and provoke further terrorist acts. In a speech delivered on September 23 of that year, Al Gore warned that "if what America represents to the world is leadership in a commonwealth of equals, then our friends are legion. If what we represent to the world is empire, then it is our enemies who will be legion."

Source: George W. Bush, *The National Security Strategy of the United States* (The White House, September 2002), 29–31.

The major institutions of American national security were designed in a different era to meet different requirements. All of them must be transformed.

It is time to reaffirm the essential role of American military strength. We must build and maintain our defenses beyond challenge. Our military's highest priority is to defend the United States. To do so effectively, our military must:

- assure our allies and friends;
- dissuade future military competition;
- deter threats against U.S. interests, allies, and friends; and
- decisively defeat any adversary if deterrence fails.

The unparalleled strength of the United States armed forces, and their forward presence, have maintained the peace in some of the world's most strategically vital regions. However, the threats and enemies we must confront have changed, and so must our forces. A military structured to deter massive cold war-era armies must be transformed to focus more on how an adversary might fight rather than where and when a war might occur. We will channel our energies to overcome a host of operational challenges.

The presence of American forces overseas is one of the most profound symbols of the U.S. commitments to allies and friends. Through our willingness to use force in our own defense and in defense of others, the United States demonstrates its resolve to maintain a balance of power that favors freedom. To contend with uncertainty and to meet the many security challenges we face, the United States will require bases and stations within and beyond Western Europe and Northeast Asia, as well as temporary access arrangements for the long-distance deployment of U.S. forces.

Before the war in Afghanistan, that area was low on the list of major planning contingencies. Yet, in a very short time, we had to operate across the length and breadth of that remote nation, using every branch of the armed forces. We must prepare for more such deployments by developing assets such as advanced remote sensing, long-range precision strike capabilities, and transformed maneuver and expeditionary forces. This broad portfolio of military capabilities must also include the ability to defend the homeland, conduct information operations, ensure U.S. access to distant theaters, and protect critical U.S. infrastructure and assets in outer space.

Innovation within the armed forces will rest on experimentation with new approaches to warfare, strengthening joint operations, exploiting U.S. intelligence advantages, and taking full advantage of science and technology. We must also transform the way the Department of Defense is run, especially in financial management and recruitment and retention. Finally, while maintaining near-term readiness and the ability to fight the war on terrorism, the goal must be to provide the President with a wider range of military options to discourage aggression or any form of coercion against the United States, our allies, and our friends.

We know from history that deterrence can fail; and we know from experience that some enemies cannot be deterred. The United States must and will maintain the capability to defeat any attempt by an enemy—whether a state or non-state actor—to impose its will on the United States, our allies, or our friends. We will maintain the forces sufficient to support our obligations, and to defend freedom. Our forces will be strong enough to dissuade potential adversaries from pursuing a military build-up in hopes of surpassing, or equaling, the power of the United States.

Intelligence—and how we use it—is our first line of defense against terrorists and the threat posed by hostile states. Designed around the priority of gathering enormous information about a massive, fixed object—the Soviet bloc—the intelligence community is coping with the challenge of following a far more complex and elusive set of targets.

We must transform our intelligence capabilities and build new ones to keep pace with the nature of these threats. Intelligence must be appropriately integrated with our defense and law enforcement systems and coordinated with our allies and friends. We need to protect the capabilities we have so that we do not arm our enemies with the knowledge of how best to surprise us. Those who would harm us also seek the benefit of surprise to limit our prevention and response options and to maximize injury.

We must strengthen intelligence warning and analysis to provide integrated threat assessments for national and homeland security. Since the threats inspired by foreign governments and groups may be conducted inside the United States, we must also ensure the proper fusion of information between intelligence and law enforcement.

Initiatives in this area will include:

- strengthening the authority of the Director of Central Intelligence to lead the development and actions of the Nation's foreign intelligence capabilities;
- establishing a new framework for intelligence warning that provides seamless and integrated warning across the spectrum of threats facing the nation and our allies;
- continuing to develop new methods of collecting information to sustain our intelligence advantage;
- investing in future capabilities while working to protect them through a more vigorous effort to prevent the compromise of intelligence capabilities; and
- collecting intelligence against the terrorist danger across the government with all-source analysis.

As the United States Government relies on the armed forces to defend America's interests, it must rely on diplomacy to interact with other nations. We will ensure that the Department of State receives funding sufficient to ensure the success of American diplomacy. The State Department takes the lead in managing our bilateral relationships with other governments. And in this new era, its people and institutions must be able to interact equally adroitly with non-governmental organizations and international institutions. Officials trained mainly in international politics must also extend their reach to understand complex issues of domestic governance around the world, including public health, education, law enforcement, the judiciary, and public diplomacy.

Our diplomats serve at the front line of complex negotiations, civil wars, and other humanitarian catastrophes. As humanitarian relief requirements are better understood, we must also be able to help build police forces, court systems, and legal codes, local and provincial government institutions, and electoral systems. Effective international cooperation is needed to accomplish these goals, backed by American readiness to play our part.

Just as our diplomatic institutions must adapt so that we can reach out to others, we also need a different and more comprehensive approach to public information efforts that can help people around the world learn about and understand America. The war on terrorism is not a clash of civilizations. It does, however, reveal the clash inside a civilization, a battle for the future of the Muslim world. This is a struggle of ideas and this is an area where America must excel.

We will take the actions necessary to ensure that our efforts to meet our global security commitments and protect Americans are not impaired by the potential for investigations, inquiry, or prosecution by the International Criminal Court (ICC), whose jurisdiction does not extend to Americans and which we do not accept. We will work together with other nations to avoid complications in our military operations and cooperation, through such mechanisms as multilateral and bilateral agreements that will protect U.S. nationals from the ICC. We will implement fully the American Servicemembers Protection Act, whose provisions are intended to ensure and enhance the protection of U.S. personnel and officials.

We will make hard choices in the coming year and beyond to ensure the right level and allocation of government spending on national security. The United States Government must strengthen its defenses to win this war. At home, our most important priority is to protect the homeland for the American people.

Today, the distinction between domestic and foreign affairs is diminishing. In a globalized world, events beyond America's borders have a greater impact inside them. Our society must be open to people, ideas, and goods from across the globe. The characteristics we most cherish—our freedom, our cities, our systems of movement, and modern life—are vulnerable to terrorism. This vulnerability will persist long after we bring to justice those responsible for the September 11 attacks. As time passes, individuals may gain access to means of destruction that until now could be wielded only by armies, fleets, and squadrons. This is a new condition of life. We will adjust to it and thrive—in spite of it.

In exercising our leadership, we will respect the values, judgment, and interests of our friends and partners. Still, we will be prepared to act apart when our interests and unique responsibilities require. When we disagree on particulars, we will explain forthrightly the grounds for our concerns and strive to forge viable alternatives. We will not allow such disagreements to obscure our determination to secure together, with our allies and our friends, our shared fundamental interests and values.

Ultimately, the foundation of American strength is at home. It is in the skills of our people, the dynamism of our economy, and the resilience of our institutions. A diverse, modern society has inherent, ambitious, entrepreneurial energy. Our strength comes from what we do with that energy. That is where our national security begins.

Questions

1. What was the Cold War policy of deterrence? How does Bush's preemptive strategy represent a departure from this policy?
2. Bush's policy assumes that the United States will remain the sole superpower in the world. How might Bush's policy change if another superpower (China, for example) were to emerge?

Questions for Further Thought

1. In Document 32-4, do the authors of the report emphasize building up American arms at home or expanding democracy abroad? What is the significance of this?
2. Given that no WMDs were found in Iraq despite President Bush's case to the contrary (Document 32-3), what relation, if any, is there between this false alarm and the right to wage wars of preemption claimed in Document 32-4?

Unfinished Business

President Bush was reelected in 2004 and the Republican Party strengthened its control over the federal government, solidifying the conservative shift of the country. President Bush's initiatives included large tax cuts, even during wartime; education reform; Social Security reform; expansion of Medicare; government financing of churches or faith-based organizations; reduction of government funding for stem-cell research; filling court vacancies with conservative judges; emphasizing pro-business, pro-industry (especially energy), and pro-creditor policies; reducing environmental regulations; and working to strengthen and expand the power of the presidency in relation to the other branches of government. The Bush administration was remarkably successful in enacting much of its agenda (Document 32-2); a notable exception was President Bush's failed attempt to start phasing out Social Security, which remains a very popular program. Despite these achievements, President Bush's approval ratings remained low for much of his second term. Reasons for the president's unpopularity included the war in Iraq, which steadily lost public support; the unsteady and uneven economic recovery; large budget deficits (annual) and a sharply increasing national debt (cumulative); and the federal government's widely criticized response to Hurricane Katrina, a powerful storm that exposed a government unprepared to deal with crisis at home and a nation still deeply divided along lines of class and race.

32-5 Report on Catastrophic Hurricane Evacuation Plan Evaluation (2006)

In late August 2005, Hurricane Katrina (a Category 5 hurricane) caused catastrophic damage to the Gulf Coast region and led to the flooding of New Orleans. It was one of the most deadly storms in U.S. history, taking over 1,800 lives, with Louisiana suffering the highest death toll. Property worth billions of dollars was damaged or lost. The city of New Orleans was effectively closed, raising questions about its very future. Millions of people throughout the region were affected and many were temporarily displaced or else relocated. Recovery would be a long-term process. The government's response at all levels was inadequate, revealing poor leadership and mismanagement. What struck many Americans as unacceptable and disgraceful was that society's most vulnerable—the sick, the elderly, and the poor, many of whom were African American—were left by the storm and by their government to fend for themselves for extended periods of time in what were deplorable conditions (see text pp. 1006–1007). Document 32-5 is an evaluation of the government's evacuation plan and recommendations for how to improve the response to the next natural or man-made catastrophe requiring the mass movement of people.

Source: Excerpts from "Report on Catastrophic Hurricane Evacuation Plan Evaluation," U.S. Department of Transportation in cooperation with the U.S. Department of Homeland Security, June 1, 2006. http://www.fhwa.dot.gov/reports/hurricanevacuation/index.htm

A catastrophic incident is defined as "Any natural or manmade incident, including terrorism, that results in extraordinary levels of mass casualties, damage, or disruption severely affecting the population, infrastructure, environment, economy, national morale, and/or government functions. A catastrophic event could result in sustained national impacts over a prolonged period of time; almost immediately exceeds resources normally available to State, local, tribal, and private-sector authorities in the impacted area; and significantly interrupts governmental operations and emergency services to such an extent that national security could be threatened. All catastrophic events are Incidents of National Significance."

National Response Plan [1]

Executive Summary

The U.S. Congress requested the U.S. Department of Transportation (DOT), in cooperation with the U.S. Department of Homeland Security (DHS), to "review and assess Federal and State evacuation plans (including the costs of the plans) for catastrophic hurricanes and other catastrophic events impacting the Gulf Coast region and to report its findings and recommendations to Congress." In Section 10204 of the Safe, Accountable, Flexible, and Efficient Transportation Equity Act: A Legacy for Users (SAFETEA-LU) (P.L. 109-59) and Section 187 of the FY 2006 Department of Transportation Appropriations Act (P.L. 109-115), Congress specified that this assessment should include: (1) all safe and practical modes of transportation available for evacuations; (2) the extent to which evacuation plans are coordinated with neighboring States and adjoining jurisdictions; (3) methods of communicating evacuation plans and preparing citizens in advance of evacuations; (4) methods of coordinating communication with evacuees during plan execution; (5) the availability of food, water, restrooms, fueling stations, and shelter opportunities along the evacuation routes; (6) the time required to evacuate under the plan; and (7) the physical and mental strains associated with the evacuation. The assessment also includes issues and lessons learned from evacuations associated with Hurricanes Katrina and Rita and other recent hurricanes.

Summary of Major Findings

Table ES-1 summarizes the overall assessment of State and local evacuation plans with respect to the key elements of evacuation planning and implementation. The table shows that evacuation plans in the Gulf Coast States generally reflect current guidance contained in the Federal Emergency Management Agency's (FEMA's) 1996 *Guide for All-Hazard Emergency Operations Planning* commonly known as *State and Local Guide (SLG)* 101.

> "Catastrophic events are, by their nature, difficult to imagine and to adequately plan for, and the existing plans and training proved inadequate in Katrina."
>
> U.S. Senate Committee on Homeland Security and Governmental Affairs, April 2006.

DECISION MAKING AND MANAGEMENT

Most State and local evacuation plans have adequate decision making and management structures for evacuations associated with non-catastrophic incidents. However, many of these plans do not adequately address requirements for decision making and management of mass evacuations associated with catastrophic incidents. There are several reasons for this. First, existing guidance does not provide sufficient technical assistance on how to manage evacuations associated with catastrophic incidents. Second, few multi-State exercises have been conducted until recently to test the decision making and management structure against requirements for catastrophic incidents. State and local agencies have not had the benefits of these exercises to refine their decision making and management processes based on lessons learned from them.

PLANNING

Generally, the planning components of State and local evacuation plans were rated effective in terms of how well they met existing planning guidelines. As shown in Table ES-1, plans were strong in requiring the development of standard operating procedures for agencies involved in evacuations, and adequately covered general evacuation planning considerations including hazards that could require a large-scale evacuation, the communities that should be evacuated under different conditions, the number of people and vehicles to be evacuated, decision points for an evacuation, the estimated time needed to complete the evacuation, and the distance evacuees must travel to ensure their safety. Plans were weaker in terms of provisions for returning evacuees to their homes.

While many State and local plans include contingencies and are scalable to reflect evacuation requirements for different intensity hurricanes, plans generally do not assume evacuations on the scale of those required for Hurricane Katrina. The demands associated with a catastrophe such as Hurricane Katrina are simply beyond the scenarios upon which the

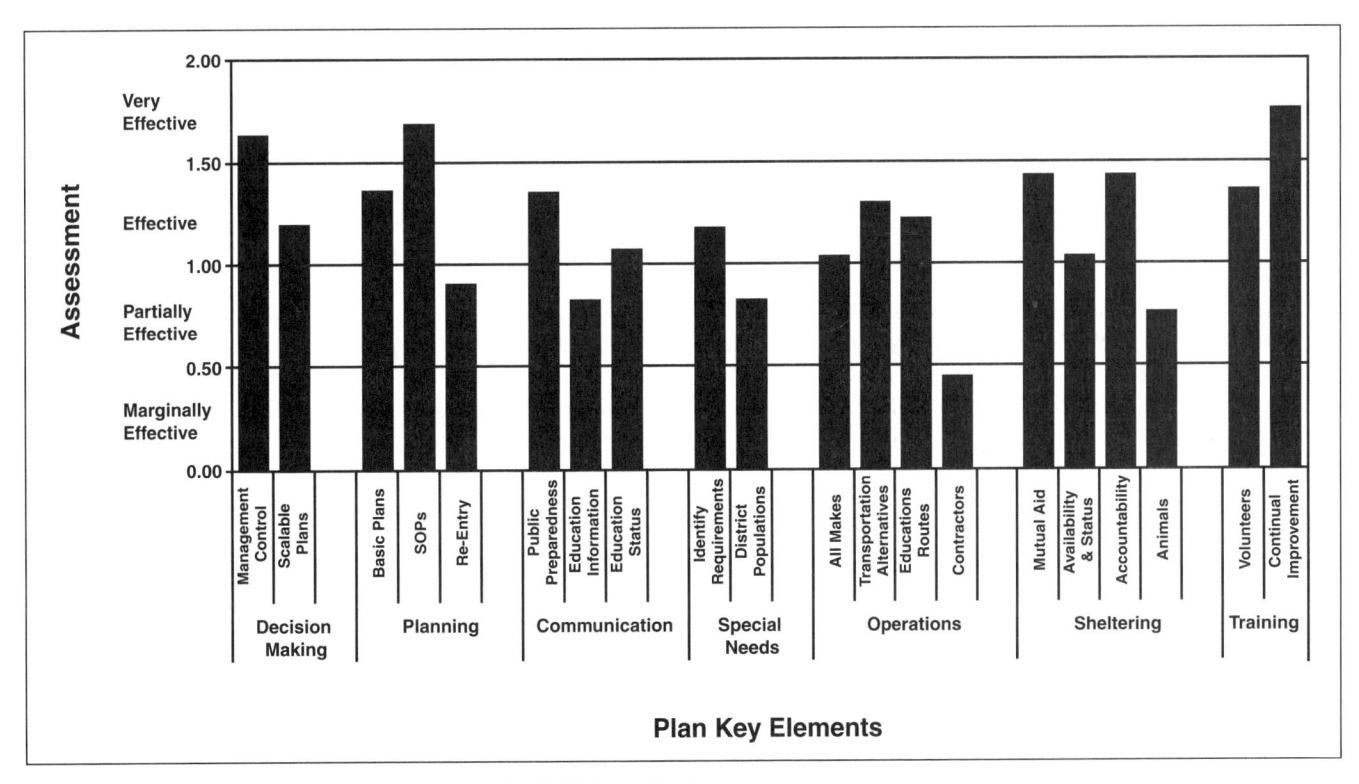

TABLE ES-1. *Status of Evacuation Plans in the Gulf Coast Region*

plans are based. Many States in the Gulf Coast region and elsewhere are in the process of updating their evacuation plans based on lessons learned from evacuations associated with Hurricanes Katrina and Rita and other recent hurricanes. In particular, State and local officials are reviewing provisions for obtaining outside transportation services to augment local resources and the coordination of plans with neighboring States and jurisdictions. They are also reviewing their existing mutual aid agreements which are formal agreements among emergency responders to lend assistance across jurisdictional boundaries when needed. These updates should improve State and local ability to manage mass evacuation needs related to catastrophic incidents.

Having a good plan, however is no guarantee that evacuations will be carried out smoothly, particularly mass evacuations that involve many different agencies at all levels of government. Joint exercises at the regional level in which plans are tested against different scenarios are important ways that officials from different agencies can become accustomed to working together and can assess how their plans address different contingencies. As noted, States seldom conduct the kind of regional exercise that would be required to test some of the requirements that were faced during Hurricane Katrina. The multi-State regional tabletop exercises that DHS is conducting to prepare for the 2006 hurricane season should help to strengthen the decision making and management elements of local, State, and Federal plans, as well as identify weaknesses in specific plan elements that can be corrected.

In the Gulf Coast region, there is some coordination of evacuation plans with adjoining jurisdictions, but the coordination is inadequate for catastrophes on the scale of Hurricane Katrina. Most States have multi-aid agreements and belong to the Emergency Management Assistance Compact (EMAC). EMAC is a legal agreement among member States that outlines the procedures, including reimbursement and liability issues, for providing assistance to other member States in the event of an emergency or disaster. However, mass evacuations place tremendous demands on transportation and sheltering systems that overwhelm the capacity of adjacent States. The Gulf Coast States have attempted to coordinate contraflow plans with neighboring States that may be affected, but exercises, traffic simulations, and other analyses to evaluate evacuation options for catastrophic incidents on the scale of Hurricane Katrina have not been conducted.

PUBLIC COMMUNICATION AND PREPAREDNESS

Good communications with the public is one of the most important elements of an evacuation. This includes both communicating information to prepare citizens to evacuate and communicating with evacuees during the course of an evacuation. As shown in Table ES-1, most State and local evacuation plans have adequate provisions for communicating basic information to residents about when they should evacuate, the designated evacuation routes, what they should take with them, the location of shelters, and other information needed before they evacuate.

State and local governments use a variety of methods of communications to inform residents before an evacuation begins. These methods include television, radio, the Internet, telephone, and a variety of other methods. Not everyone regularly listens to media outlets or has access to all of these means of communications. This situation is especially true for those with the greatest need for specialized information. Several Gulf Coast States provide evacuation-related information in Spanish for their Spanish-speaking residents and New Orleans provides information and conducts classes in Vietnamese. These programs are excellent for providing general evacuation-related information, but plans are not as well developed for providing real-time information to persons with limited English proficiency about who should evacuate, when they should evacuate, and any changes that may have been made in plans for evacuation by public transportation. Few States, counties, or parishes have special programs to provide information to people with visual or hearing impairments, the homeless, or other special needs groups that are difficult to reach through normal communications channels. One good practice is that all of the televised hurricane briefings in Florida from the State Emergency Operations Center also include a sign language interpreter as part of the briefings.

Methods for communicating evacuation options by modes other than personal vehicles are not well developed in most cases. A number of jurisdictions indicate locations where public transportation may be obtained, but many have no specific services identified to assist persons in getting to those designated locations. This situation is a particular problem for people with various disabilities.

Methods of communicating with evacuees during plan execution are not as well developed as are plans for communicating prior to an evacuation and need to be improved in most jurisdictions. Communications are essential to provide information on the availability of hotels, shelters, food, fuel, and medical and other essential services along evacuation routes; traffic conditions on alternative evacuation routes; the location of shelters that will accept pets and that are equipped to handle people with various special needs; the identities of those being evacuated on public transportation; and where those persons are being taken.

Methods of communicating information prior to an evacuation may not be available during an evacuation. Evacuees typically will not have access to the Internet or to television—two of the primary means of providing pre-evacuation information. Radio may be available to those in cars and those who have battery-operated radios. Many States position dynamic message signs along evacuation routes. State personnel staff rest areas, truck weigh stations, welcome centers, and service plazas to provide information to evacuees en route. Motorist information services such as the 511 telephone system Florida has deployed or highway advisory radio can provide route-specific information.

However, to get real-time traffic information on evacuation routes, traffic monitoring equipment is required. That equipment is not widely deployed in most rural areas along the Gulf Coast, except in Florida, which has an extensive statewide traffic monitoring system.

Effective communications before a catastrophic incident can play an important role in convincing residents that they should evacuate. During an evacuation, effective communications will enhance the efficiency of the system and also reduce the associated mental and physical strains. People must leave most of their possessions and the security of their homes, often with little knowledge of where they will stay or for how long. The more information that can be provided to residents about the availability of shelters, what they can take, provisions for accommodating pets and service animals, security that will be provided while they are away from their homes, and other factors of concern, the less stress there will be. Technical assistance and other information is available for some of these special requirements, but additional work is required to develop a comprehensive resource describing the special needs of different groups.

EVACUATION OF PEOPLE WITH SPECIAL NEEDS

Plans in the Gulf Coast region for evacuating persons with various special needs generally are not well developed. Hospitals, nursing homes, prisons, and other institutions generally are responsible for developing their own evacuation plans and deciding when to evacuate their residents. They face unique issues such as whether the risks of not evacuating outweigh the risks of moving seriously ill individuals. Widely reported stories about the breakdown of these plans during the 2005 hurricane season at certain institutions highlight the need to ensure responsible individuals have access to the latest information about a catastrophic incident and that institutions' evacuation plans will work in the event of a mass evacuation of the entire population of an area.

Evacuating those with special needs who are not in institutions also presents problems that are not well addressed in most State and local plans. Locating where these individuals live often is difficult, despite attempts by local agencies to maintain lists of persons with various special needs. New Orleans, for instance, is establishing a 311 information hotline to register residents with special needs for evacuations. Other areas in the region have similar registration programs, but those programs are only as good as the willingness of persons to register. Privacy interests and some individuals' reluctance to identify themselves as having special needs are considerations that must be addressed in establishing a comprehensive registry.

Persons who use wheelchairs, those who rely on special medical equipment, those with hearing or visual impairments, the elderly, and other groups all have unique communication, transportation, and sheltering needs that must be planned for in advance. This includes ensuring that all forms of temporary housing (e.g., shelters, trailers, etc.) meet Americans with Disabilities Act guidelines. Providing these specialized services in the course of a mass evacuation presents particular challenges. Provisions to meet transportation and sheltering requirements of these various special needs groups must be improved in most evacuation plans.

EVACUATION OPERATIONS

The actual operation of transportation systems throughout the course of catastrophic incidents is one of the most important parts of the evacuation process. For known or imminent incidents such as hurricanes, State and local operations plans in the Gulf Coast region are generally adequate for highway evacuations, although there are significant differences in the extent to which certain issues are covered. Almost all jurisdictions do a good job in terms of designating highway evacuation routes and directing evacuees in private vehicles to those routes. Plans are less robust for monitoring traffic on evacuation routes and providing real-time operational information to emergency managers, upon which they can make decisions concerning those routes.

Understanding the time required for evacuations is essential for all those who must evacuate to do so safely. A number of evacuation planning and operations models have been developed by Federal agencies and are available to State and local agencies. FEMA, the United States Army Corps of Engineers (USACE), and the National Oceanic & Atmospheric Administration (NOAA) conduct hurricane evacuation studies for the Gulf Coast and other States to help State and local emergency managers decide who should evacuate during a hurricane threat and when the evacuation order should be given based on the estimated time to evacuate a certain number of persons from a given location. Many emergency managers rely on the information in these studies, but some States reported that they sometimes forgo study updates because their 25-percent share of the cost of the study is a constraint. If outdated studies are used, the times required to evacuate may not take into account new development, highway improvements that have been made and other changes that have occurred. While hurricane evacuation studies do consider people with special needs, they often do not provide all of the information that would be desirable or the time needed to evacuate various special needs populations.

An important lesson learned in evacuations associated with Hurricanes Katrina and Rita was the necessity of having food, water, restrooms, fuel, and shelter opportunities along evacuation routes. State and local plans generally recognize the need to have these services prepositioned and available along evacuation routes. However, plans for providing real-time information on the availability and location of these services are not as well developed.

All States in the region have a plan for contraflow operations on certain limited access evacuation routes, but county plans often do not address those contraflow plans. This failure to integrate State and local activities in these contraflow plans is the primary reason why overall plans are rated low in terms of contraflow operations.

While State and local evacuation operations plans were generally rated as adequate, most need improvement with respect to the role of all safe and practical modes of transportation. In rural areas, the only alternative to the automobile that may be mentioned in evacuation plans is the school bus, but some State officials noted that their school buses are in poor condition and not capable of making long highway trips. Plans may provide information on who to contact to mobilize those buses, but few details typically are given on how those vehicles will be used, the availability of drivers to operate those vehicles, or the bus routes or staging areas to collect evacuees.

Even in urban areas where more modes are available, few plans recognize the potential role for intercity buses, trains, airplanes, and boats. These modes may be particularly important for persons who cannot evacuate in personal vehicles including persons with various disabilities, the elderly who cannot or prefer not to drive, low-income households that do not own automobiles, and those who are incarcerated or are in other institutions such as nursing homes or hospitals. Transportation needs associated with each of these groups may differ, but few plans address these specific needs.

With advanced planning, school buses and local transit buses can be mobilized by local jurisdictions with little advanced notice; commercial vehicles such as intercity buses, trains, airplanes, and boats require more advanced notice. Memoranda of Understanding (MOU) or other such formal agreements with owners and operators of these vehicles are the best way to be sure they will be available if needed. Several States, including Texas, have contracted for buses to be available for mass evacuations. The potential need to provide national or regional level coordination of the use of these other modes, especially aviation, must also be addressed. Amtrak has developed a generic MOU to provide evacuation services to jurisdictions. Care must be taken to ensure that agreements involving several jurisdictions and the same commercial carrier do not exceed the carrier's capacity.

Many other details must be considered when using commercial carriers from outside of the immediate area. These include ensuring that destinations where persons will be taken for each of these modes have been identified and confirmed; ensuring that interstate operating authority is in place or can quickly be obtained; and ensuring that everyone is aware of how to get to those modes, where they will be taken, limitations on what can be brought on board, and how they can return to their community once it is safe. Few State and local plans address these details.

Experiences in New Orleans in 2005 accentuated the need to include all modes of transportation in evacuation plans. New Orleans had a large segment of its population that could not evacuate in personal vehicles, and the City was unprepared to evacuate so many persons using other modes. Since Hurricane Katrina, however, the City has developed a plan for the use of multiple modes of transportation to evacuate those who cannot evacuate by private vehicle. This plan identifies target groups that will be evacuated by bus, railroad, and airplane, and how persons from each of these target groups will be transported to those modes. In addition, the City has enhanced their sheltering plan and will provide more information to citizens early in the season. One goal of the plan is to "create and maintain an environment where the decision to evacuate becomes more desirable than remaining behind."

SHELTERING

Sheltering is one of the most important considerations when planning evacuations. Table ES-1 shows that, in general, State and local plans adequately address sheltering. However, while Gulf Coast evacuation plans generally do a good job of identifying shelter locations in their State, most do not mention specific provisions for monitoring the status of those shelters and providing real-time information on the availability of space. The plans generally do not contain information on shelters in other States. Neither do they have plans for providing information on the availability of rooms at hotels, motels, and other private facilities where evacuees may want to stay. The availability of such information would significantly improve the efficiency of evacuations and reduce evacuees' stress.

All States along the Gulf Coast are members of the EMAC and have mutual-aid agreements with other member States, including agreements to accommodate evacuees. They recognize that if any sizeable number of persons must be evacuated, their own shelter capacity may be insufficient and they will have to rely on shelters in adjacent jurisdictions. Many State and local governments rely on local chapters of the American Red Cross and other volunteer organizations to set up, staff, and operate shelters. The American Red Cross and DHS/FEMA are the lead agencies for Emergency Support Function (ESF) 6, Mass Care, which covers sheltering activities. Other States, such as Alabama, are assuming more of the responsibility themselves, although they continue to work with the American Red Cross.

Accommodating pets at shelters is a significant issue. The American Red Cross indicates that it generally cannot accept pets in shelters because of State health and safety regulations, although they do accept service animals. Many States are in the process of reevaluating these regulations and more latitude in accommodating pets can be expected in the future. Guidelines will have to be developed to ensure that public health and safety are not compromised when accommodating pets at public shelters.

TRAINING AND EXERCISES

Most State and local evacuation plans contain provisions for training and conducting exercises to test their plans that are generally adequate for most evacuations. Few, however, contain provisions for conducting multi-State exercises involving officials from other States, the Federal government, and other organizations with evacuation responsibilities to test the adequacy of plans for catastrophic incidents. This lack of regional exercises prior to Hurricanes Katrina and Rita contributed to some of the problems encountered during those evacuations. There now is a much greater recognition of the importance of regional exercises, and as noted above, the DHS is sponsoring a series of regional exercises that will provide an opportunity for officials from different States to work together with Federal agencies to evaluate their plans, identify weaknesses, and develop strategies for meeting the needs of future catastrophic incidents.

Costs to Develop and Update Plans

The costs to develop and update plans varies based on the population, the geography and surge areas, the number of potential evacuation routes to be analyzed, the demographics of the area (e.g., large populations of people with low income or large numbers of people with special needs), the number of neighboring jurisdictions to coordinate with, and other factors. In addition to costs to develop and update plans, State and local agencies incur costs to exercise those plans on a regular basis.

Very little data is available on the costs of evacuation plans and the limited cost information received for this study is incomplete. State officials noted that determining the amount of funding allocated and spent for evacuation planning would be difficult since funding comes from many sources at the Federal, State, and local level, and many agencies within the various levels of government have agencies involved in evacuation planning.

The States do not appear to budget specific amounts for evacuation planning, but include these costs within broader emergency management programs. While State officials reported evacuation plans are executed with current funding, they felt that funding was constrained. The officials did not identify what activities were constrained, and constraints were not discernible from the data as there is no accounting of budgeted versus actual costs for evacuation plans.

Activities to Prepare for the 2006 Hurricane Season

As noted above, Federal, State, and local officials recognize the need to be better prepared for the 2006 hurricane season than they were for the 2005 season. All of the States and some of the local jurisdictions in the Gulf Coast region have reviewed their evacuation and overall emergency operations plans and many made changes to address lessons learned last year. For example, on March 21, Governor Perry of Texas signed an Executive Order that, among other things, calls for development of a statewide hurricane evacuation and shelter plan, a separate evacuation and shelter plan for people with special needs, contraflow plans for all major evacuation routes, a plan to ensure fuel availability along all evacuation routes, and a public awareness initiative. In addition to the regional tabletop exercises being conducted by DHS, States and several urban areas in the Gulf Coast region are conducting exercises to improve their preparedness for hurricanes.

The U.S. DOT has undertaken a number of initiatives to prepare for the 2006 hurricane season including: (1) improving coordination among those with transportation responsibilities associated with a catastrophic incident, (2) coordinating with the United States Army Corp of Engineers (USACE) and FEMA to improve communications capabilities, (3) examining current regulations that may affect the transportation industry's ability to respond to catastrophic incidents and developing procedures to remove or dramatically reduce impediments, (4) coordinating with transportation industry representatives, the American Red Cross, the Humane Society, and other stakeholders to improve evacuation capabilities based on lessons learned in 2005, and (5) conducting training and process improvements based on after-action reviews.

Federal, State, and local agencies, transportation and shelter providers, and others involved in evacuations are now better prepared to handle the demands of a catastrophic hurricane or other catastrophic incident. The challenges of responding to an incident like Hurricane Katrina and the flooding that followed remain daunting, however, and many additional steps need to be taken before we can be confident that we are fully prepared to respond to another incident of similar proportions.

Recommendations

Throughout the assessment of State and local evacuation plans, actions that could be taken to improve various aspects of evacuation planning and implementation are identified in the main report. Based on lessons learned from recent mass evacuations, State and local governments already are beginning to incorporate some of those improvements into their plans. Federal agencies also are in the process of examining how they can improve their response to catastrophic incidents that overwhelm State and local resources. Near-term actions that will improve overall capabilities to respond to hurricanes during the 2006 hurricane season include the regional exercises that DHS recently conducted in the Gulf Coast States, the U.S. DOT activities noted above, the many State and local actions that have been taken based on lessons learned during Hurricanes Katrina and Rita, and actions that transportation and shelter providers have already taken to enhance their capabilities.

The following are recommendations for ways to further improve mass evacuation planning and implementation capabilities that extend beyond what Federal, State, and local governments are already doing.

1. Develop regional plans for mass evacuations in connection with catastrophic incidents on the scale of Hurricane Katrina. These plans should be developed jointly by

State and local officials within the region in cooperation with officials from appropriate Federal agencies; providers of all safe and practical modes of transportation and providers of shelters, food, fuel, and other necessities; managers of hospitals, nursing homes, emergency medical services (air, ground, etc.) jails, and other institutions with their own evacuation plans; and representatives of various special needs populations.

This recommendation goes beyond the recommendation in the Homeland Security Council Report, *The Federal Response to Hurricane Katrina: Lessons Learned*. This report, which is the result of a comprehensive review of the Federal response to Hurricane Katrina directed by the President to identify changes needed to improve the Nation's preparedness to respond to natural and manmade disasters, recommends that individual State and local agencies should be required to have evacuation plans as a condition of receiving Homeland Security grants.

2. Regional exercises to test plans and decision making structures for different mass evacuation scenarios should be conducted on a regular basis to ensure that Federal, State, and local agencies are prepared to respond to different types of catastrophic incidents.

3. Responsible Federal agencies should review the National Response Plan, FEMA's State and Local Guide 101, concepts of operations for the various Emergency Service Functions, and other appropriate planning guidance related to evacuations and update as needed to cover the special requirements of mass evacuations from incidents of Hurricane Katrina's magnitude.

In particular, these guidance documents should be refined to more specifically recognize needs and challenges associated with coordinating the activities of multiple agencies representing different levels of government across a multi-State region of the country.

4. Transportation agencies and operators should be more directly involved in key aspects of evacuation planning and implementation.

Transportation by all safe and practical modes is a key element of evacuations. Failure to include transportation agencies in the evacuation planning and operations can lead to inefficiencies and delays in evacuating citizens, especially those most in need of assistance. Including highway, rail, air, and other appropriate modes in planning and operations helps to ensure that required resources are identified, including those needed for mass evacuations, and that transportation is available to meet the unique needs of various special needs groups. It also helps to ensure that critical details such as the need for agreements on the destinations to which various modes will transport evacuees are considered.

5. Responsible State and local agencies should develop and deploy systems to provide information to evacuees and emergency managers during the course of evacuations on the status of traffic, shelters, fuel, and other services along evacuation routes.

Systems should be based on existing communications network and intelligent transportation systems (ITS) architecture and to the maximum extent possible should be incorporated into general purpose motorist information and traffic monitoring services used during normal traffic operations.

6. State and local agencies should work with the special needs communities to develop systems whereby those requiring specialized transportation or sheltering services during evacuations can make those needs known to emergency managers and operators of transportation and sheltering services before evacuations.

This information should be maintained in a way that can easily be updated and that recognizes privacy and other concerns of various special needs groups.

7. Sheltering requirements for all segments of the population and evacuees by all modes of transportation should be more directly integrated into the evacuation planning process.

Sheltering needs vary considerably for different groups of people and must be explicitly recognized in evacuation plans. There are significant issues regarding accommodation of pets at shelters that need to be resolved.

DHS is conducting a series of hurricane preparedness exercises in the Gulf Coast region to prepare for the 2006 hurricane season. The U.S. DOT and other Federal agencies are participating in these exercises. The Federal government should continue to organize and facilitate these types of regional exercises in high-priority areas to bring together local, State, and Federal agencies to integrate and test their plans and procedures.

The Homeland Security Council, the House of Representatives, the Senate, and the Government Accountability Office have all issued reports looking at various aspects of the Federal response to the catastrophic hurricanes that struck in 2005. These reports contain numerous recommendations on actions that could allow the Federal Government to work more effectively with State and local government in responding to future catastrophic incidents. Many of these recommendations touch on aspects of mass evacuations. The U.S. DOT, DHS, and other Federal agencies are reviewing these recommendations along with other internal and external assessments of responses to recent catastrophic incidents. In the meantime, special federal assistance will be provided this year in areas that are still recovering from the 2005 hurricane season and which are at enhanced risk due to the damage experienced last year. The U.S. DOT, in coordination with DHS, stands ready to quickly make evacuation experts available to local and state governments that want to better understand their strengths and vulnerabilities in preparing for and implementing successful evacuations.

While many short-term actions have already been taken, other changes could require legislative changes. Potential longer-term changes are being carefully considered before any legislative proposals are sent forward. The U.S. DOT is examining a number of specific options that will enhance its ability to respond to evacuation needs associated with catastrophic incidents. In addition to activities noted above that have already been done to prepare for the 2006 hurricane season, the U.S. DOT is examining a range of potential longer-term options including ways to strengthen internal resources and processes to better respond to catastrophic incidents and ways to enhance the contribution of various U.S. DOT programs to improve State and local evacuation capabilities. Once decisions have been made on changes that would enhance the U.S. DOT's contribution to a coordinated Federal, State, and local response effort, as well as changes to improve State and local planning and operations capabilities, any required legislative proposals will be developed and sent to Congress.

Questions

1. According to the report, what were the principal reasons for the failed response to Katrina and the storm's aftermath?
2. What were the recommendations for addressing groups with special needs?

Question for Further Thought

1. What connections, if any, were there between the U.S. war on terrorism and its slow and inadequate response to Hurricane Katrina?